AN INTRODUCTION TO THE NEW TESTAMENT

Zondervan Books by D. A. Carson

Becoming Conversant with the Emerging Church
The Gagging of God
An Introduction to the New Testament (coauthor)
Matthew in the Expositor's Bible Commentary
Telling the Truth (general editor)
Worship by the Book (editor)

Zondervan Books by Douglas J. Moo

2 Peter, Jude in the NIV Application Commentary Series
Romans in the NIV Application Commentary Series
Romans, James, 2 Peter, Jude in the Zondervan Illustrated
Bible Background Commentary

SECOND EDITION

AN INTRODUCTION TO THE NEW TESTAMENT

D. A. CARSON & DOUGLAS J. MOO

ZONDERVAN™

GRAND RAPIDS, MICHIGAN 49530 USA

ZONDERVAN™

An Introduction to the New Testament—Second Edition
Copyright © 1992, 2005 by D. A. Carson and Douglas J. Moo

Requests for information should be addressed to:

Zondervan, *Grand Rapids, Michigan 49530*

Library of Congress Cataloging-in-Publication Data

Carson, D. A.
   An introduction to the New Testament / D.A. Carson and Douglas J. Moo.–2nd ed.
        p. cm.
   Includes bibliographical references and index.
   ISBN-10: 0-310-23859-5
   ISBN-13: 978-0-310-23859-1
   1. Bible. N.T.—Introductions. I. Moo, Douglas J. II. Title.
   BS2330.3.C37 2005
   225.6'1—dc22   2005005186

This edition printed on acid-free paper.

The website addresses recommended throughout this book are offered as a resource to you. These websites are not intended in any way to be or imply an endorsement on the part of Zondervan, nor do we vouch for their content for the life of this book.

Interior design by Nancy Wilson

Printed in the United States of America

05 06 07 08 09 10 11 12 / ❖ DCI/ 15 14 13 12 11 10 9 8 7 6 5 4

This book is gratefully dedicated to Joy and Jenny

CONTENTS

PREFACE

The primary focus of this book is "special introduction"—that is, it treats historical questions dealing with authorship, date, sources, purpose, destination, and the like. Many recent books devote more space than we do to literary form, rhetorical criticism, and historical parallels. We do not minimize the importance of such topics, and we have introduced them where they directly bear on the subject at hand. However, in our experience, they are better given extended treatment in courses on exegesis, especially the exegesis of particular books. Moreover, we fear that too much focus on these topics at the expense of traditional questions of introduction tends to divorce the New Testament books from their historical settings and students from some important debates in the first centuries of the Christian church. This also means that we have often referred to primary sources. In debates over such questions as what Papias means by "John the elder," we have tended to cite the passage and work through it, so that students may see for themselves what the turning points in the debate are (or should be!).

Although the emphasis of this book is on "special introduction," we have included a brief outline or résumé of each New Testament document, sometimes providing a rationale for the choices we have made. In each case we have provided a brief account of current studies on the book and have indicated something of the theological contribution that each New Testament document makes to the canon. Our ultimate concern is that new generations of theological students will gain a better grasp of the Word of God.

We have tried to write with the first- and second-year student of seminaries and theological colleges in mind. Doubtless in most instances the material will be supplemented by lectures. Some teachers will want to use the material in some order other than that presented here (e.g., by assigning chapters on Matthew, Mark, and Luke before assigning the chapter on the Synoptic Gospels). Bibliographies are primarily in English, but a small number of works in German, French, and other modern languages appear. These bibliographies are meant to be brief enough not to be daunting, and comprehensive enough not to be reductionistic. Lecturers may provide guidance as to what in these lists is especially useful in particular contexts.

Not least important, we have restricted the length of this New Testament introduction so that it can be used as a textbook. One or two well-known introductions are so long that only relatively short parts of them are assigned to students. This means that it is possible to graduate from a seminary without ever having read a single New Testament introduction right through. Although the brevity of this volume precludes detailed discussion of many topics we would have liked to pursue, we hope the constraints we have chosen will enhance its value for classroom use.

Confessionally, the two authors are evangelicals. Doubtless that heritage biases our readings somewhat, but (we hope) no more than other New Testament scholars are influenced by their heritage. If we have tried to eschew obscurantism, we have nevertheless sometimes raised possibilities and questions that are too quickly turned aside in some introductions. We have tried to engage a representative sampling of the vast amount of current literature, sometimes following traditional paths and at other times suggesting a fresh way of looking at an issue. Where the evidence seems entirely inconclusive to us, we have left questions open.

Some readers will want to know how this book relates to the earlier one (1992) with the same title but written by three of us—Carson, Moo, and Leon Morris. In many ways this is an update of that earlier volume. Nevertheless, several important changes have been introduced: (1) Because advancing years have meant that Leon Morris was unable to contribute to this volume, we decided, with his concurrence, that it would be simpler if the two of us divided his chapters between us. As a result, each of us has written about half of this volume. We have updated and revised our own work and have largely revised or rewritten the chapters we inherited from Leon Morris. (2) The chapter on Paul has been expanded to include a brief analysis of the current debates on the "new perspective." (3) A preliminary chapter has been added to provide a brief history to explain how Christians have moved from the reading of the first hand-written documents that make up the New Testament to contemporary study of the New Testament. That kind of survey is rather daunting, but our aim has been to help the student locate current trends within a stream of historical discussion and debate. (4) The section on "pseudonymity" in the chapter on the Pastoral Epistles has been removed from that chapter and significantly expanded. It has been added to an expanded section on Paul's letters to constitute a new chapter, "New Testament Letters." (5) We have included in each chapter a more substantial summary of the content of the biblical books and brief interaction, where relevant, with some of the more recent literary and social-science approaches to New Testament interpretation.

These changes have added length to this volume, but we hope that the work has retained enough compactness that it will still be useful—indeed, more useful—to new generations of students.

Each of us has offered suggestions and critiques of the work of the other. We have also tried to reduce stylistic and other differences to a minimum. Although in a few instances, references in the text betray the identity of the author, the work has been very much a team effort. Readers who love to compare editions will discover where, in a few instances, we have changed our minds on some matters.

We are profoundly grateful to Jonathan Davis and Michael Thate for compiling the indexes.

Soli Deo gloria.

D. A. Carson and Douglas J. Moo

ABBREVIATIONS

AB	Anchor Bible
ABD	*Anchor Bible Dictionary*
Achtemeier/Green/Thompson	
	Paul J. Achtemeier, Joel B. Green, and Marianne Meye Thompson, *Introducing the New Testament: Its Literature and Theology* (Grand Rapids: Eerdmans, 2001)
AGJU	Arbeiten zur Geschichte des antiken Judentums und des Urchristentums
AGSU	Arbeiten zur Geschichte des Spätjudentums und Urchristentums
AJT	*American Journal of Theology*
ALGHJ	Arbeiten zur Literatur und Geschichte des hellenistischen Judentums
AnBib	Analecta Biblica
ANRW	*Aufstieg und Niedergang der römischen Welt*
Ant	Josephus, *Antiquities of the Jews*
ANTC	Abingdon New Testament Commentaries
ASNU	Acta Seminarii Neotestamentici Upsaliensis
ATR	*Anglican Theological Review*
AusBibRev	*Australian Biblical Review*
AUSS	*Andrews University Seminary Studies*
BAGD	Walter Bauer, William F. Arndt, F. Wilbur Gingrich, and Frederick W. Danker, *A Greek-English Lexicon of the New Testament and Other Early Christian Literature*, 2nd ed. (Chicago: University of Chicago Press, 1979)
Barker/Lane/Michaels	
	Glenn W. Barker, William L. Lane, and J. Ramsey Michaels, *The New Testament Speaks* (San Francisco: Harper & Row, 1969)

BBR	*Bulletin for Biblical Research*
BCBC	Believers Church Bible Commentary
BDAG	Walter Bauer, Frederick W. Danker, William F. Arndt, and F. Wilbur Gingrich, *A Greek-English Lexicon of the New Testament and Other Early Christian Literature*, 3rd ed. (Chicago: University of Chicago Press, 2000)
BECNT	Baker Exegetical Commentary on the New Testament
BETL	Bibliotheca Ephemeridum Theologicarum Lovaniensium
BFCT	Beiträge zur Förderung christlicher Theologie
BGBE	Beiträge zur Geschichte der biblischen Exegese
BI	*Biblical Interpretation*
Bib	*Biblica*
BIP	Biblical Institute Press
BIS	Biblical Interpretation Series
BJRL	*Bulletin of the John Rylands University Library of Manchester*
BL	Bampton Lectures
BNTC	Black's New Testament Commentaries (= HNTC)
Bornkamm	Günther Bornkamm, *The New Testament: A Guide to Its Writings* (London: SPCK, 1974)
Brown	Raymond E. Brown, *An Introduction to the New Testament* (New York: Doubleday, 1997)
BR	*Biblical Research*
BS	*Bibliotheca Sacra*
BTB	*Biblical Theology Bulletin*
BU	Biblische Untersuchungen
BWANT	Beiträge zur Wissenschaft vom Alten und Neuen Testament
BZ	*Biblische Zeitschrift*
BZNW	Beihefte zur Zeitschrift für die neutestamentliche Wissenschaft
c.	circa
CAH	Cambridge Ancient History
CBET	Contributions to Biblical Exegesis and Theology
CBQ	*Catholic Biblical Quarterly*
CBQMS	Catholic Biblical Quarterly Monograph Series
CEB	Commentaire Évangélique de la Bible
CGSTJ	*China Graduate School of Theology Journal*
CGTC	Cambridge Greek Testament Commentary
Childs	Brevard S. Childs, *The New Testament as Canon: An Introduction* (Philadelphia: Fortress, 1984)
CIL	*Corpus Inscriptionum Latinarum*

CJT	*Canadian Journal of Theology*
Clogg	Frank Bertram Clogg, *An Introduction to the New Testament* (London: University Press and Hodder & Stoughton, 1940)
CNT	Commentaire du Nouveau Testament
ConBNT	Coniectanea neotestamentica or Coniectanea biblica: New Testament Series
Contra Ap.	Josephus, *Contra Apion* (Against Apion)
d.	died
Davies	W. D. Davies, *Invitation to the New Testament* (London: DLT, 1957)
De Vita Contemp.	Philo, *De Vita Contemplativa* (The Contemplative Life)
DBI	*A Dictionary of Biblical Interpretation*
Dibelius	Martin Dibelius, *A Fresh Approach to the New Testament and Early Christian Literature* (London: Ivor Nicholson & Watson, 1936)
DJG	*Dictionary of Jesus and the Gospels*
DLNT	*Dictionary of the Later New Testament and Its Developments*
DLT	Darton, Longman and Todd
DPL	*Dictionary of Paul and His Letters*
EBC	*The Expositor's Bible Commentary*
EBib	*Etudes bibliques*
ECC	Eerdmans Critical Commentary
EFN	Estudios de Filología Neotestamentaria
EGGNT	Exegetical Guide to the Greek New Testament
EGT	*The Expositor's Greek Testament*
Ehrman	Bart D. Ehrman, *The New Testament: A Historical Introduction to the Early Christian Writings,* 3rd ed. (New York: Oxford University Press, 2004)
EKKNT	Evangelisch-katholischer Kommentar zum Neuen Testament
Ellis	E. Earle Ellis, *History and Interpretation in New Testament Perspective,* BIS 54 (Leiden: Brill, 2001)
Enslin	Morton Scott Enslin, *Christian Beginnings* (New York: Harper, 1936)
EphThLov	*Ephemerides Theologicae Lovanienses*
EQ	*Evangelical Quarterly*
ERT	*Evangelical Review of Theology*
EstBib	*Estudios bíblicos*
ET	English translation
EuroJTh	*European Journal of Theology*
Exp	*The Expositor*

ExpTim	*Expository Times*
FRLANT	Forschungen zur Religion und Literatur des Alten und Neuen Testaments
Fs.	*Festschrift*
GBS	Guides to Biblical Scholarship
GNC	Good News Commentaries
Goodspeed	Edgar J. Goodspeed, *An Introduction to the New Testament* (Chicago: University of Chicago Press, 1937)
GP	*Gospel Perspectives: Studies of History and Tradition in the Four Gospels*, 6 vols., ed. R. T. France, David Wenham, and Craig Blomberg (Sheffield: JSOT, 1980–86)
Grant	Robert M. Grant, *A Historical Introduction to the New Testament* (London: Collins, 1963)
Guthrie	Donald Guthrie, *New Testament Introduction*, 4th ed. (Downers Grove, Ill.: IVP, 1990)
Harrison	Everett F. Harrison, *Introduction to the New Testament*, rev. ed. (Grand Rapids: Eerdmans, 1971)
Hennecke	E. Hennecke, ed., *New Testament Apocrypha*, 2 vols. (ET London: Lutterworth, 1963–65)
Hermeneia	Hermeneia—A Critical and Historical Commentary on the Bible
HNT	Handbuch zum Neuen Testament
HNTC	Harper's New Testament Commentaries (= BNTC)
HTKNT	Herders theologischer Kommentar zum Neuen Testament
HTR	*Harvard Theological Review*
HTS	Harvard Theological Studies
Hunter	A. M. Hunter, *Introducing the New Testament* (London: SCM, 1945)
HUT	Hermeneutische Untersuchungen zur Theologie
IB	*Interpreter's Bible*
IBS	*Irish Biblical Studies*
IBT	Interpreting Biblical Texts
ICC	International Critical Commentary
ICE	Institute for Christian Economics
IDB	*Interpreter's Dictionary of the Bible*
IDBSup	*Interpreter's Dictionary of the Bible Supplement*
Int	*Interpretation*
ISBE	*International Standard Bible Encyclopedia*
ISCAST Bulletin	*Bulletin of the Institute for the Study of Christianity in an Age of Science and Technology*
IVP	InterVarsity Press
IVPNTC	IVP New Testament Commentary

JASA	*Journal of the American Scientific Affiliation*
JB	Jerusalem Bible
JBL	*Journal of Biblical Literature*
JBR	*Journal of Bible and Religion*
JCE	*Journal of Christian Education*
JETS	*Journal of the Evangelical Theological Society*
JNES	*Journal of Near Eastern Studies*
Johnson	Luke T. Johnson, *The Writings of the New Testament*, rev. ed. (Minneapolis: Fortress, 1999)
JPTSS	Journal of Pentecostal Theology Supplement Series
JSHJ	*Journal for the Study of the Historical Jesus*
JSNT	*Journal for the Study of the New Testament*
JSNTSup	Journal for the Study of the New Testament: Supplement Series
JSOT	*Journal for the Study of the Old Testament*
JTC	*Journal for Theology and the Church*
JTS	*Journal of Theological Studies*
Jülicher	Adolf Jülicher, *An Introduction to the New Testament* (London: Smith, Elder, 1904)
KBW	Katholisches Bibelwerk
KEK	Meyers Kritish-exegetischer Kommentar über das Neue Testament
KJV	King James Version
Klijn	A. F. J. Klijn, *An Introduction to the New Testament* (Leiden: Brill, 1967)
Kümmel	Werner Georg Kümmel, *Introduction to the New Testament*, rev. ed. (Nashville: Abingdon, 1975)
Lake	Kirsopp Lake and Silva Lake, *An Introduction to the New Testament* (London: Christophus, 1938)
LCL	Loeb Classical Library
LEC	Library of Early Christianity
LLC	*Literary and Linguistic Computing*
LouvStud	*Louvain Studies*
LSJ	Henry George Liddell, Robert Scott, and Henry Stuart Jones, *A Greek-English Lexicon*, 9th ed. (Oxford: Clarendon, 1940)
LW	*Luther's Works*
LXX	Septuagint
McDonald/Porter	Lee Martin McDonald and Stanley E. Porter, *Early Christianity and its Sacred Literature* (Peabody: Hendrickson, 2000).

McNeile	A. H. McNeile, *An Introduction to the Study of the New Testament*, 2nd ed., revised by C. S. C. Williams (Oxford: Clarendon, 1953)
Martin	Ralph P. Martin, *New Testament Foundations: A Guide for Christian Students*, 2 vols. (Grand Rapids: Eerdmans, 1975–78)
Marxsen	Willi Marxsen, *Introduction to the New Testament* (Philadelphia: Fortress, 1968)
Metzger	Bruce M. Metzger, *A Textual Commentary on the Greek New Testament* (London: UBS, 1971)
MNTC	Moffatt New Testament Commentary
Moffatt	James Moffatt, *An Introduction to the Literature of the New Testament*, rev. ed. (Edinburgh: T. & T. Clark, 1918)
Moule	C. F. D. Moule, *The Birth of the New Testament*, 3rd ed. (San Francisco: Harper & Row, 1981)
MS(S)	manuscript(s)
NA26	Nestle-Aland Greek New Testament, 26th ed.
NA27	Nestle-Aland Greek New Testament, 27th ed.
NABPRDS	The National Association of Baptist Professors of Religion Dissertation Series
NAC	New American Commentary
NAG	*Nachrichten der Akademie der Wissenschaften in Göttingen, philologisch-historische Klasse*
NCB	New Century Bible
NCBC	New Cambridge Bible Commentaries
NClarB	New Clarendon Bible
NEB	New English Bible
Neot	*Neotestamentica*
NewDocs	*New Documents Illustrating Early Christianity*
NIBC	New International Bible Commentary
NICNT	New International Commentary on the New Testament
NIGTC	New International Greek Testament Commentary
NIV	New International Version
NIVAC	New International Version Application Commentary
NovT	*Novum Testamentum*
NovTSup	Supplements to Novum Testamentum
NPNF2	*The Nicene and Post-Nicene Fathers*, ed. Philip Schaff and Henry Wace, 2nd ser., 14 vols. (reprint, Grand Rapids: Eerdmans, 1975)
NRSV	New Revised Standard Version
NRT	*La Nouvelle Revue Théologique*
NSBT	New Studies in Biblical Theology

NTAbh	Neutestamentliche Abhandlungen
NTC	New Testament Commentary
NTD	Das Neue Testament Deutsch
NTG	New Testament Guides
NTL	The New Testament Library
NTS	*New Testament Studies*
NTT	New Testament Theology (series from Cambridge University Press)
ÖstK	*Östkirchliche Studien*
Penguin	Penguin New Testament Commentaries
Perrin/Duling	Norman Perrin and Dennis C. Duling, *The New Testament: An Introduction,* 2nd ed.; ed. Robert Ferm (San Diego: Harcourt Brace Jovanovich, 1982)
PL	*Patrologia Latina* (Migne)
PNTC	Pillar New Testament Commentaries
Readings	Readings: A New Biblical Commentary
RevBib	*Revue biblique*
RevQ	*Revue de Qumran*
RHPR	*Revue d'histoire et de philosophie religieuses*
RNT	Regensburger Neues Testament
Robert/Feuillet	A. Robert and A. Feuillet, eds., *Introduction to the New Testament* (New York: Desclée, 1965)
RSV	Revised Standard Version
RTR	*Reformed Theological Review*
RVV	Religionsversuche und Vorarbeiten
SacPag	Sacra Pagina
SBET	*Scottish Bulletin of Evangelical Theology*
SBG	Studies in Biblical Greek
SBL	Society of Biblical Literature
SBLDS	Society of Biblical Literature Dissertation Series
SBLMS	Society of Biblical Literature Monograph Series
SBS	Stuttgarter Bibelstudien
SBT	Studies in Biblical Theology
Schürer	E. Schürer, *The History of the Jewish People in the Age of Jesus Christ,* 3 vols., new ed. (Edinburgh: T. & T. Clark, 1973–87)
SD	Studies and Documents
SE	*Studia Evangelica*
SIL	Summer Institute of Linguistics
SJLA	Studies in Judaism in Late Antiquity
SJT	*Scottish Journal of Theology*
SN	Studia Neotestamentica

SNT	Studien zum Neuen Testament
SNTSMS	Society of New Testament Studies Monograph Series
SNTU	*Studien zum Neuen Testament und seiner Umwelt*
SNTW	Studies of the New Testament and Its World
SP	Scholars Press
SPB	Studia Postbiblica
SR	*Studies in Religion = Sciences religieuses*
ST	*Studia Theologica*
SUNT	Studien zur Umwelt des Neuen Testaments
SWJT	*Southwest Journal of Theology*
TDNT	*Theological Dictionary of the New Testament*
Theol	*Theology*
THNT	Theologischer Handkommentar zum Neuen Testament
ThR	*Theologische Rundschau*
TLZ	*Theologische Literaturzeitung*
TNIV	Today's New International Version
TNTC	Tyndale New Testament Commentary
TOTC	Tyndale Old Testament Commentary
TrinJ	*Trinity Journal*
TSAJ	Texte und Studien zum antiken Judentum
TSK	*Theologische Studien und Kritiken*
TU	Texte und Untersuchungen
TynB	*Tyndale Bulletin*
UBS	United Bible Societies
UBSMS	United Bible Societies Monograph Series
UPA	University Press of America
van Unnik	W. C. van Unnik, *The New Testament* (London: Collins, 1964)
Wars	Josephus, *History of the Jewish War*
WBC	Word Biblical Commentary
WC	Westminster Commentaries
WdF	Wege der Forschung
WEC	Wycliffe Exegetical Commentary
Weiss	Bernhard Weiss, *A Manual of Introduction to the New Testament*, 2 vols. (New York: Funk & Wagnalls, n.d.)
WH	B. F. Westcott and F. J. A. Hort, *The New Testament in the Original Greek* (London: Macmillan, 1881)
Wikenhauser	Alfred Wikenhauser and Josef Schmid, *Einleitung in das Neue Testament*, 6th ed. (Freiburg: Herder, 1973)
WMANT	Wissenschaftliche Monographien zum Alten und Neuen Testament
WTJ	*Westminster Theological Journal*

WUNT	Wissenschaftliche Untersuchungen zum Neuen Testament
Zahn	Theodore B. Zahn, *Introduction to the New Testament*, 3 vols. (Edinburgh: T. & T. Clark, 1909)
ZNW	*Zeitschrift für die neutestamentliche Wissenschaft*
ZTK	*Zeitschrift für Theologie und Kirche*

ABBREVIATIONS AND TRANSLATIONS OF WORKS OF THE CHURCH FATHERS

Chrysostom

Hom. in Matt.	*Homilies in St. Matthew*

Clement of Alexandria

Quis div.	*Quis dives salvetur (Who Is the Rich Man That Shall Be Saved?)*
Strom.	*Stromateis (Miscellanies)*

Epiphanius

Haer.	*Panarion Haereses (Medicine Box of Heresies)*

Eusebius

H.E.	*Historia Ecclesiastica (History of the Church)*

Ignatius of Antioch

Eph.	*Pros Ephesious (Letter to Ephesus)*
Magn.	*Magnesieusin (Letter to Magnesia)*
Phil.	*Philadelpheusin (Letter to Philadelphia)*
Rom.	*Pros Romaious (Letter to Rome)*
Smyr.	*Smyrnaiois (Letter to Smyrna)*
Trall.	*Trallianois (Letter to Tralles)*

Irenaeus

Adv. Haer.	*Adversus Haereses (Against Heresies)*

Jerome

De vir. ill.	*De viris illustribus (On Illustrious Men)*

Justin Martyr

Apol.	*Apologia*
Dial.	*Dialogue with Trypho*

Origen

    Comm. on Matt.   *Commentary on Matthew*
    Comm. on John   *Commentary on John*

Papias

                             Logion Kyriakon Exegesis (Greek)
                             Exegesis of the Dominical Logia (Latin)
                             (Exposition of the Oracle of the Lord)

Polycarp

    Phil.   *Epistle to the Philippians*

Tertullian

    Adv. Marc.   *Adversus Marcion (Against Marcion)*

Victorinus

    Apoc.   *Commentary on the Apocalypse*

CHAPTER ONE

THINKING ABOUT THE STUDY OF THE NEW TESTAMENT

People have been reading and studying the New Testament for as long as its documents have been in existence. Even before all twenty-seven canonical New Testament books were written, some found the interpretation of the available documents more than a little challenging (see the comment of 2 Pet. 3:15–16 regarding Paul). A distance of two millennia, not to mention changes of language, culture, and history, have not made the task any easier. The torrential outpouring of commentaries, studies, and essays across the centuries, all designed to explain—or in some cases, explain away—the New Testament documents, makes the task both easier and harder. It is easier because there are many good and stimulating guides; it is harder because the sheer volume of the material, not to mention its thoroughly mixed nature and, frequently, its mutually contradictory content, is profoundly daunting to the student just beginning New Testament study.

This chapter provides little more than a surface history of a selection of the people, movements, issues, and approaches that have shaped the study of the New Testament. The student setting out to come to terms with contemporary study of the New Testament must suddenly confront a bewildering array of new disciplines (e.g., text criticism, historical criticism, hermeneutics), the terminology of new tools (e.g., form criticism, redaction criticism, discourse analysis, postmodern readings), and key figures (e.g., F. C. Baur, J. B. Lightfoot, E. P. Sanders). Students with imagination will instantly grasp that they do not pick up New Testament scrolls as they were dropped from an apostolic hand; they pick up a bound sheaf of documents, printed, and probably in translation. Moreover, the text itself is something that believers and unbelievers alike have been studying and explaining for two millennia.

The aim here, then, is to provide enough of a framework to make the rest of this textbook, and a lot of other books on the New Testament, a little easier to understand.

PASSING ON THE TEXT

At the beginning of his gospel, Luke comments that "many others" had already undertaken to write accounts of Jesus (Luke 1:1–4). Although some scholars have argued that there was a long period of oral tradition before anything substantial about Jesus or the early church was written down, the evidence is against such a stance: the world into which Jesus was born was highly literate.[1] From such a perspective, the existence of the documents that make up the New Testament canon is scarcely surprising.

These documents were originally hand-written on separate scrolls. There is very good evidence that the writing was in capital letters, without spaces, and with very little punctuation. Printing was still almost a millennium and a half away, so additional copies were made by hand. In theory, this could be done by professional copiers: in a scriptorium, one man would read at dictation speed, several scribes would take down his dictation, and another would check each copy against the original, often using ink of a different color to make the corrections. This kind of professional multiplying of copies was labor-intensive and therefore expensive. Most early Christian copies of the New Testament were doubtless done by laypeople eager to obtain another letter by Paul or a written account of the life, ministry, death, and resurrection of Jesus. That brought the price down: Christians were investing their own time to make their own copies, and they were not having to pay large sums to professional scribes. On the other hand, the private copy made by an eager and well-meaning layperson was likely to include more transcriptional errors than copies made and checked in a scriptorium.

How the New Testament canon came together is briefly discussed in the final chapter of this book. For the moment it is sufficient to observe that as the numbers of copies of New Testament documents multiplied, three formal changes were soon introduced. First, the scroll gave way to the codex, that is, to a book bound more or less like a modern book, which enabled readers to look up passages very quickly without having to roll down many feet of scroll. Second, increasingly (though certainly not exclusively) the capital letters (scholars call them "uncials") gave way to cursive scripts that were messier but much more quickly written. And third, because the early church, even within the Roman Empire, was made up of highly diverse groups, it was not long before the New Testament, and in fact the whole Bible, was translated into other languages. These "versions" of the Bible (as translations are called) varied widely in quality.[2] There were no copyright laws and no central publishing houses, so there were

---

[1]See especially Alan Millard, *Reading and Writing in the Time of Jesus* (Sheffield: Sheffield Academic Press, 2000).

[2]The best survey is Bruce M. Metzger, *The Early Versions of the New Testament: Their Origin, Transmission and Limitations* (Oxford: Clarendon Press, 1977).

soon numerous Latin versions, Syriac versions, and so forth, as individuals or local churches produced what seemed necessary for their own congregations.

Today the printing press churns out thousands of *identical* copies. When each copy is written by hand, however, if the work is of substantial length, each copy will be a little different than all others because the accidental mistakes introduced by successive copying will not all congregate in the same place. The challenge of producing a copy that is perfectly true to the original soon multiplies. A slightly later Christian, making a copy of a copy, spots what he judges to be mistakes in the manuscript before him and corrects them in his fresh copy. Unfortunately, however, it is possible that some things he *thought* were mistakes were actually in the original. For instance, it is well known that there are many grammatical anomalies in the book of Revelation. The reason for this is disputed; there are three major theories and several minor ones. But a later copyist might well have thought that errors had been introduced by intervening copyists and "corrected" them to "proper" grammar—thereby introducing new errors.

Two further "accidents" of history and geography have helped to determine just what material has come down to us. First, just as the Roman Empire divided between East and West (stemming from the decision of Emperor Constantine to establish an eastern capital in what came to be called Constantinople), so also did the church. In the West, because it was not only the official language of Rome but also tended in time to squeeze out Greek as the *lingua franca,* Latin soon predominated in the church. Initially, there were many Latin versions, but toward the end of the fourth century, Damasus, Bishop of Rome, commissioned Jerome to prepare an official Latin version that would be widely distributed and sometimes imposed throughout the churches of the West. This Latin version, revised several times, became the Vulgate, which held sway in the West for a millennium. By contrast, Greek dominated in the East, in what eventually became the Byzantine Empire. Inevitably, Greek manuscripts were used and copied much more often under this linguistic heritage than in the West, until Constantinople fell to the Muslim Turks in 1453. Many Eastern scholars then fled West, bringing their Greek manuscripts with them—a development that helped to fuel both the Reformation and the Renaissance.

Second, the material on which ancient books were written (i.e., their equivalent of paper) decomposed more readily in some climates than in others. The most expensive books were made of *parchment,* treated animal skin. Higher quality parchment was called *vellum.* More commonly, books were made of *papyrus,* a plant that grew plentifully in the Nile Delta. Papyrus has the constituency of celery or rhubarb. Long strips could be peeled off, pounded, and glued together to make sheets. Although parchment is tougher than papyrus, both materials are organic and thus readily decompose, especially when there is moisture in the atmosphere. So it is not surprising that the best caches of really ancient manuscripts come from the hot, dry sands of Egypt.

So just what textual evidence has come down to us? There are about five thousand manuscripts or parts of manuscripts (some of them mere fragments) of all or part of the Greek New Testament, and about eight thousand manuscripts or parts of manuscripts of versions. All of this evidence can be classified in various ways. For example, one can break it down according to writing material (parchment or papyrus). More importantly, *uncial* manuscripts of the Greek New Testament (i.e., those written in capital letters) number under three hundred, whereas there are almost three thousand *miniscules* (manuscripts not written in capitals). In addition, there are over two thousand *lectionaries*—church reading books that contain selections of the biblical text to be read on many days of the ecclesiastical year. Other sources include quotations of the Bible found in the early church fathers, and short portions of New Testament writings on *ostraca* (pieces of pottery often used by poor people as writing material) and amulets,[3] ranging from the fourth to the thirteenth century. Similar breakdowns can be put forward for all the versional evidence. Although most of this material springs from the thousand-year period between A.D. 500 and 1500, the earliest fragments come from the first half of the second century.

> There are about five thousand manuscripts or parts of manuscripts (some of them mere fragments) of all or part of the Greek New Testament.

It is useful to observe that of all the works that have come down to us from the ancient world, the New Testament is the most amply attested in textual evidence. For example, for the first six books of the *Annals,* written by the famous Roman historian Tacitus, there is but a single manuscript, dating from the ninth century. The extant works of Euripides, the best-attested of the Greek tragedians, are preserved in 54 papyri and 276 parchment manuscripts, almost all of the latter deriving from the Byzantine period. The history of Rome by Velleius Paterculus came down to us in one incomplete manuscript, which was lost in the seventeenth century after a copy had been made. By comparison, the wealth and range of material supporting the Greek New Testament is staggering.

The printing press made the hand-copying of manuscripts forever obsolete. The first printed edition of the Greek New Testament appeared on 10 January 1514. It was volume 5 of a polyglot Bible commissioned by the cardinal primate of Spain, Francisco Ximenes de Cisneros (1437–1517). Printed in the town of Alcalá, called Complutum in Latin, the work came to be known as the Complutensian Polyglot Bible. Volume 5 also contained the first printed Greek glossary, the progenitor of countless lexicons that have been published since then.[4]

---

[3]Amulets are charms, often worn around the neck to ward off assorted evils. Some amulets were simply "magic" stones or the like, but others were sayings or cherished quotations written on papyrus, vellum, potsherd, or wood. Where superstition overlaid Christian faith, inevitably some of these quotations were biblical. Obviously, neither ostraca nor amulets can provide evidence for extensive passages.

[4]For further reading, see John A. L. Lee, *A History of New Testament Lexicography*, SBG 8 (New York: Peter Lang, 2003).

But although the Complutensian Bible contained the first Greek New Testament ever *printed,* it was not the first one to be *published* (i.e., both printed and put on the market). That honor belongs to the edition prepared by Desiderius Erasmus (1469–1536), a Dutch scholar from Rotterdam. Erasmus managed to complete the edition and have it out by 1516. The volume contains hundreds of typographical errors and was based primarily on two inferior twelfth-century manuscripts kept in a monastery in Basle.

Erasmus continued to prepare fresh editions that corrected many of the earlier typos, editions that were based on a few more Greek manuscripts. The best of these was a tenth-century miniscule. It was better than his other manuscripts, being a copy of an early uncial, but because it was rather different from the other manuscripts he had at hand, Erasmus did not rely on it very much. His definitive fourth edition (1527) was prepared after Erasmus had consulted the Complutensian. It boasts three columns: the Greek, the Vulgate, and Erasmus's own Latin translation. His fifth edition (1535) abandoned the Vulgate, but so far as the Greek text is concerned, it was largely indistinguishable from his fourth edition.

All the early editions of the Greek New Testament were copies or adaptations of the work of Erasmus. Robert Estienne (whose last name often appears in the Latinized form, Stephanus) published four such editions of the Greek New Testament, three in Paris (1546, 1549, and 1550) and the last one in Geneva (1551), where as a Protestant he spent his last years. His first two editions were a mix of the Erasmian and Complutensian editions; his third (1550) was much more like the fourth and fifth editions of Erasmus and included, for the first time, a *critical apparatus,* variant readings, printed on inner margins, of the fourteen Greek manuscripts that were his base, plus readings from the Complutensian Polyglot.[5] This third edition was destined to exercise an astonishing influence. In 1553 it was reprinted by Jean Crispin in Geneva, who introduced only a half-dozen changes to the Greek text. Théodore de Bèze (Beza), successor to Calvin in Geneva, published nine editions of the Greek New Testament. These editions contain some new textual evidence collated by Beza himself, but they are very similar to the third and fourth editions of Stephanus. The King James translators (1611) depended heavily on Beza's editions of 1588–89 and 1598.

Then, in 1624, the brothers Bonaventure and Abraham Elzevir published in Leiden a compact edition of the Greek New Testament largely taken from Beza's 1565 edition. The Elzevir brothers' second edition, dated 1633, boasts (in what would today be called an advertising blurb) that the reader now has "the *text* which is now *received* by all, in which we give nothing changed or corrupted": the words we have italicized reflect the Latin *textus receptus,* referring

---

[5]One of the fourteen was Codex Bezae, now recognized as the chief witness to the Western Text.

to a commonly received text, and thus a standard text. This is the "received text" which, more or less, stands behind all English translations of the Bible until 1881. This textual tradition is grounded in what was at the time a mere handful of mostly late miniscule manuscripts.

The following centuries uncovered the vast amount of textual evidence already briefly summarized. The work of the textual critic is to sift this evidence and look for patterns in the attempt to uncover what reading is closest to the original, which of course we do not have.[6] Textual critics have organized this vast manuscript evidence into *text types*: patterns of readings thought to reflect the textual tradition of a particular locale. Inevitably, if a manuscript was transported to another locale and a further copy was made using both this transported manuscript and manuscripts from the local region, it was possible to generate a copy with "mixed types." A small group of manuscripts with even stronger affinities, usually some evidence of direct borrowing, is sometimes called a *family*.

As a discipline, textual criticism begins with the work of Richard Simon, a French priest studying and writing at the end of the seventeenth century. Then, in 1707, John Mill, an Anglican theologian, produced, two weeks before his death, a beautiful edition of the Greek Testament, the product of decades of work (the latter part of which was enriched by the writing of Richard Simon). It reproduced the "received text" unaltered, but the apparatus, which took up more space on each page than the text itself, included not only parallel passages but the readings of all available manuscripts, versions, and printed editions. This edition also included succinct summaries of all the known data regarding the origin and textual descent of each book of the New Testament canon, plus descriptions of all New Testament manuscripts then known to be extant, plus comments on all translations.

In some ways, however, the crucial figure at the head of textual criticism is Johann Albrecht Bengel, a Swabian pietist. His edition of the Greek New Testament, published in 1734, offered not only a text that differs in countless passages from the "received text" (though most of the changes were unimportant), but also a substantial "critical apparatus." Here Bengel presented the most important of the textual variants in five groups, depending on their importance

---

[6]A small minority of textual critics argue that the pursuit of the original is a vain exercise: e.g., D. C. Parker, *The Living Text of the Gospels* (Cambridge: Cambridge University Press, 1997). The manuscript tradition is so fluid, they say, that the attempt to uncover the original reading is pointless. Worse, it diverts attention from the study of what the diverse textual traditions tell us of what the church thought at various times and places. However, not only does Parker overemphasize the freedom of the textual tradition, but he also fails to reflect on the significance of the fact that for every book there *was* an original. That we cannot reproduce it with perfect certainty with respect to every word does not vitiate the fact that the pursuit is valuable and that its goal is, in no small measure, attainable.

(a practice not unlike that followed in some editions of the Greek Testament today). His evaluation of what was most likely original corresponds to a high degree with similar judgments made today. Bengel formulated rules or principles on which he based his decisions, and in large measure these have stood the test of time.

For example, Bengel recognized that the number of manuscripts with a particular reading was a matter of little importance. After all, the many manuscripts might be largely late, or belong exclusively to one textual tradition. It is important to weigh *when* manuscripts were written, and how many text types support a reading (usually representing textual traditions in different parts of the world). Bengel understood that the most important question a text-critic can ask is this: Which reading is most likely to have generated all the others? Moreover, because on the whole scribes tended to eliminate perceived difficulties, Bengel formulated the rule, "The more difficult reading is to be preferred over the easier" *(Proclivi scriptioni praestat ardua).*

Of course, none of these rules is absolute. For a start, one must try to distinguish between unintentional errors that copyists made, and intentional changes. Intentional changes were often motivated by the desire to "improve" the text, under the assumption that some earlier scribe had made a mistake. Under such an assumption, Bengel's rule works very well: the more difficult reading is likely to be more original. But where there is an unintentional error—for instance, where a scribe became sloppy and accidentally inserted three words from a previous line and then carried on—then clearly the same rule does not work. The "more difficult reading" is the one with the unaccountable insertion, but even though it is more difficult, it is certainly not more original. The complexity of the text-critical task can be met only by scholars who spend an extraordinary amount of time in the manuscripts themselves, becoming deeply familiar with the writing, scribal corrections, and tendencies of individual manuscripts. The discipline is never merely mechanical. It calls for both vast knowledge and sound judgment.[7]

Intrinsic to these arguments, and progressively worked out during the next century, are two pairs of distinctions. First, one must distinguish between external evidence (i.e., what readings are supported by what manuscripts) and internal

---

[7]The best introductions to the subject are still those of Bruce Metzger, *The Text of the New Testament: Its Transmission, Corruption, and Restoration,* 3rd ed. (Oxford: Oxford University Press, 1992), and Kurt Aland and Barbara Aland, *The Text of the New Testament: An Introduction to the Critical Editions and to the Theory and Practice of Modern Textual Criticism,* trans. Erroll F. Rhodes (Leiden: Brill; Grand Rapids: Eerdmans, 1987). Students have long relied on the reasoning displayed in entry after entry of Bruce Metzger, *A Textual Commentary on the Greek New Testament,* 2nd ed. (London/New York: United Bible Societies, 1994).

evidence (i.e., what arguments from the text itself can be advanced in defense of this or that reading). Second, with respect to the internal evidence, textual critics came to distinguish between intrinsic probability (i.e., what the author is likely to have written, as judged by his observed proclivities) and transcriptional probability (i.e., what copyists were likely to have put down, whether in an intentional or an unintentional change).

This brief account of the rise of textual criticism does not begin to do justice to the countless scholars who toiled diligently on specific texts, still less to a handful of luminaries—for example, Brian Walton (1600–61), Richard Bentley (1662–1742), Johann Jakob Wettstein (1693–1754), Edward Harwood (1729–94), Johann Jakob Griesbach (1745–1812), Lobegott Friedrich Constantin von Tischendorf (1815–74), and the combined work of Brooke Foss Westcott (1825–1901) and Fenton John Anthony Hort (1828–92). Today the most important center for textual criticism of the New Testament, both for the comprehensiveness of its holdings and for the astonishingly high percentage of texts now digitized, is the Institut für Textforschung in Münster.

> *The overwhelming majority of the text of the Greek New Testament is firmly established. Where uncertainties remain, in no case is any doctrinal matter at issue.*

The overwhelming majority of contemporary textual critics adopt a position labeled *eclecticism*. That simply means that they *choose* (the Greek for the verb "to choose" is *eklegomai*) the reading on the basis of what they perceive to be the best fit once all the evidence, internal and external, is carefully evaluated. But there are two minority groups. One continues to support the "received text," if not in the form published by the Elzevir brothers, then at least the "majority text," that is, readings that are supported by the greatest number of manuscripts.[8] The other minority group promotes *thoroughgoing eclecticism*. Its members discount the external evidence (i.e., they do not think that any consideration should be given to arguments regarding which manuscripts or groups of manuscripts support any reading); all of their focus is on the internal evidence.[9]

---

[8]Perhaps the best defense of this view is Wilbur N. Pickering, *The Identity of the New Testament Text II*, 3rd ed. (Eugene: Wipf and Stock, 2003). The best succinct treatment of this position from the stance of mainstream eclecticism is probably that of Kurt Aland, "The Text of the Church?" *TrinJ* 8 (1987): 131–44. For popular treatments, see D. A. Carson, *The King James Version Debate: A Plea for Realism* (Grand Rapids: Baker, 1979); James R. White, *The King James Only Controversy* (Minneapolis: Bethany House, 1995); Doug Kutilek, *J. Frank Norris and His Heirs: The Bible Translation Controversy* (Pasadena: Pilgrim, 1999).

[9]In some ways this movement is rather a sustained critique of the weak spots in eclecticism. It is best represented by the work of J. K. Elliott and his best students (and earlier by the text-critical essays of G. D. Kilpatrick). See, for instance, J. K. Elliott, ed., *The Principles and Practice of New Testament Textual Criticism: Collected Essays of G. D. Kilpatrick*, BETL 96 (Leuven: Leuven University Press, 1990); idem, *Essays and Studies in New Testament Textual Criticism*, EFN 3 (Córdoba: Ediciones el Almendro, 1992); Kent D. Clarke, *Textual Optimism: A Critique of the United Bible Societies' Greek*

Whatever the ongoing scholarly disputes, serious Christian readers today are equipped with astonishingly accurate and detailed information in their printed Greek New Testaments. The overwhelming majority of the text of the Greek New Testament is firmly established. Where uncertainties remain, it is important to recognize that in no case is any doctrinal matter at issue. Of course, textual variants may raise the question as to whether a particular doctrinal stance or historical datum is or is not supported in this or that passage, but inevitably one can appeal to parallel passages where the text is secure to address the larger doctrinal or historical issues. In terms of the availability and range of textual evidence, owing to the large number of manuscript discoveries in the nineteenth and twentieth centuries, we are incomparably better off than Christians have been for almost nineteen hundred years.[10] Perhaps too, it is worth speculating that, in God's providence, we are better off without the originals, for we would almost certainly have treated them with idolatrous reverence focused more on the mere artifact than on what the manuscript actually said.

LONGSTANDING INTERPRETIVE TRADITIONS

A perennial danger among contemporary students of the New Testament is to overlook the two-thousand-year history of debate and interpretation generated by these twenty-seven books. The pressure to be up-to-date with the voluminous contemporary literature, combined with the penchant endemic to twenty-first-century Western culture to revere the innovative, even the faddish, and be suspicious of the traditional, conspires to blind us to our connections with twenty centuries of Christian readers. Moreover, both conservative and liberal scholars are inclined, for different reasons, to focus on the most recent centuries. On the conservative side, many (not least evangelicals) are sometimes tempted to think that serious theological reflection began with the Reformation and that, provided one does careful exegesis, there is not much to be learned from historical theology anyway. On the liberal side, many treat the period before the Enlightenment as a swamp of superstitious and unscientific interpretation now safely abandoned by our much greater learning.[11]

New Testament, JSNTSup 138 (Sheffield: Sheffield Academic Press, 1997). The best response to thoroughgoing eclecticism as a movement (though not necessarily to each particular criticism the movement offers) is the description of the goals and methods of mainstream textual criticism offered in the sort of standard texts listed in n. 7 above.

[10]The stance of Parker, *The Living Text of the Gospels*—that textual criticism is not concerned with getting as close as possible to the original text but is simply an exercise in hermeneutics—is frankly baffling. See the penetrating review by Moisés Silva in *WTJ* 62 (2000): 295–302.

[11]E.g., W. G. Kümmel, *The New Testament: The History of the Investigation of Its Problems* (Nashville: Abingdon, 1972), 13: "It is impossible to speak of a scientific view

Obviously, one short section of one chapter of a book cannot pretend to do justice to this long tradition. What follows is not a comprehensive catalog of interpretive developments across a millennium and a half, but a highly selective summary of a handful of important people and movements that proved influential in the interpretation of the New Testament and some small indication of the impact of the New Testament documents in history.

1. One of the most important developments was the collection of the New Testament documents into groups (Did the Pauline writings, or some of them, ever circulate together? Cf. 2 Pet. 3:15–16) and into the canon of the New Testament itself. Some of the steps in that process are sketched in the last chapter of this book and need not be probed here. But it is worth mentioning that debates during the first centuries of the church as to what should be included in the canon dealt with issues that are still addressed in any competent contemporary introduction to the New Testament. For instance, the church fathers refused to admit to the canon any book they judged *pseudonymous* (i.e., ostensibly written by someone such as Paul, when in fact it was not), and that refusal embroiled them in issues of authorship. In short, not only interpretive issues but also technical matters of "introduction" occupied the interest of the church from the beginning.

2. From its inception, Christianity inevitably defined itself, at least in part, against the background of the various forms of Judaism prevalent in the first century. Just as the worldwide movement we refer to today as "Christianity" has a wide diversity of forms and commitments, many of which would be considered only marginally Christian by some others in the movement, so also first-century Judaism was highly diverse, and some of its forms were zealously condemned by other branches as apostate. Full discussion of the relations between the early Christians and Judaism is therefore necessarily complex.

Most of the first Christians, of course, were themselves Jews. As rising numbers of Gentiles were added to the church, and as the earliest Christians reflected on what God had accomplished by the death and resurrection of Jesus Christ, various tensions inevitably developed among those who grappled with such issues (see Acts 15 and Gal. 2:11–14). The New Testament documents chronicle some of the early developments, as Christians came to recognize that if Jesus is the exclusively sufficient ground of salvation, then certain features

---

of the New Testament until the New Testament became the object of investigation as an independent body of literature with historical interest, as a collection of writings that could be considered apart from the Old Testament and without dogmatic or creedal bias. Since such a view began to prevail only during the course of the eighteenth century, earlier discussion of the New Testament can only be referred to as the prehistory of New Testament scholarship." It is doubtful if anyone informed by postmodern awareness of the unavoidable fact that *all* interpreters bring their biases to the text could make quite the same remark today.

intrinsic to Judaism, such as circumcision, or features widely observed in Judaism, such as kosher food restrictions, could not be mandated of all believers. Moreover, if Jesus' sacrifice dealt with our sin, then the role of the temple sacrifices could not go unchallenged. Christians were thus driven to think through their own relationship with the Mosaic covenant. If the Lord Jesus had inaugurated a new covenant in his blood (Luke 22:20; 1 Cor. 11:25; cf. 2 Cor. 3:6; Jer. 31:31–34), then the Mosaic covenant must be thought of as the old covenant (cf. 2 Cor. 3:6; Heb. 8:13).

Such reflections as these, already glimpsed in the pages of the New Testament, bred ongoing discussions between Jews and Christians in the second century. The most eloquent of these discussions comes from the pen of Justin Martyr (c. 100–165) in the book *Dialogue with Trypho*. It tells of Justin's conversation with a learned Jew, Trypho, and some of his friends. It not only shows Justin's desire to win Jews as well as Gentiles to Christ but also how a second-century Christian apologist interpreted the Old Testament in the light of the New to construct a whole-Bible theology.[12]

3. At the same time, the first Christians were soon winning Gentiles to Christ. The book of Acts reports the expansion, identifying Antioch as the city with the first strong church of mixed race of which we know anything substantial (Acts 11:19–30; 13:1–3; 15:1–35). Paul understood his role to be apostle to the Gentiles (Gal. 2:7–10). He was capable of evangelizing Jews and others who attended local synagogues (see especially the report of his evangelism in the synagogue in Pisidian Antioch, Acts 13:16–43), but he was called primarily to evangelize Gentile pagans, whether ordinary folk in small towns (Acts 14:8–18), sophisticated urbanites (Acts 19), or intellectuals (Acts 17:16–34). In such contexts he inevitably confronted various "philosophies": the Epicureans and the Stoics are mentioned in Acts 17:18, but there were many others. At the time, the word *philosophy* did not call to mind an esoteric discipline in which students are taught substantial doses of skepticism and not much constructive content. In the ancient world, philosophy meant something like what we mean by "worldview." Various teachers taught competing worldviews, and Christians earnestly sought to evangelize men and women who held these diverse pagan worldviews.

---

[12]*Dialogue with Trypho* almost certainly represents a later report of actual discussions Justin Martyr had with Jews. Its level and tone are remarkably elevated and fair-minded, unlike some later treatises. Almost every major Christian writer of the first five centuries either wrote a treatise against Judaism or incorporated substantial arguments of that sort within other works, but most scholars conclude that this became a literary conceit usefully deployed to defend the uniqueness of Christ and of Christianity. See especially Jaroslav Pelikan, *The Christian Tradition, The Emergence of the Catholic Tradition (100–600)* (Chicago: University of Chicago Press, 1971), 1:15–16.

In one sense, the Roman world of the first three centuries of the Christian era was highly pluralistic. To keep the peace, the Romans made it a capital offense to desecrate a temple—any temple. But the plurality of religions and worldviews was monolithic in at least one regard: these diverse religions agreed that there was no one way to god. On this there was strong agreement, for it was "an axiom of Greek culture that the cosmos was total (including the gods), perfect and changeless. Its harmony was endlessly repeated. Human error could be corrected by education."[13] In consequence, most Greeks thought that Christianity was notoriously bigoted and narrow. Thus, the pagan Celsus insisted on the equal validity of diverse ancient customs and beliefs, over against Origen's insistence on the unique superiority of Christianity. Porphyry argued, "No teaching has yet been established which offers a universal way for the liberation of the soul."[14] One scholar puts it this way:

> All the ancient critics of Christianity were united in affirming that there is no one way to the divine. . . . It was not the kaleidoscope of religious practices and feelings that was the occasion for the discussion of religious pluralism in ancient Rome; it was the success of Christianity, as well as its assertions about Christ and about Israel. . . . By appealing to a particular history as the source of knowledge of God, Christian thinkers transgressed the conventions that governed civilized theological discourse in antiquity.[15]

Thus, from the beginning Christians worked out their theology and interpreted their most sacred and authoritative documents within the context of disagreement, mission, cross-cultural communication, and competing claims.

4. Moreover, even within the fledgling movement itself, various aberrant positions soon arose, forcing Christian leaders to decide which were minor variations and which had to be condemned as thoroughly outside the Christian camp, regardless of what their proponents claimed. Thus, in one of the earliest of the New Testament documents, Paul warns about "a different gospel" that is really no gospel at all and pronounces his "anathema" on all who teach it (Gal. 1:6–9); while in one of the latest of the New Testament documents, John can describe the departure of a certain group that had once belonged to the church but that had departed over certain doctrinal and ethical issues as proving, by their departure, that they had never really belonged to Christ's people—for if they had, they would not have left (1 John 2:19). The early church was prepared to excommunicate not only those who refused to turn from gross moral turpitude (1 Cor. 5:1–13), but also those judged to be blasphemers (1 Tim. 1:20).

---

[13]E. A. Judge, "Ancient Contradictions in the Australian Soul," *ISCAST Bulletin* 33 (Winter 2001): 8.

[14]Cited by Augustine, *City of God* 10.32.

[15]R. L. Wilken, "Religious Pluralism and Early Christian Thought," in *Remembering the Christian Past* (Grand Rapids: Eerdmans, 1995), 42–43.

But although doctrinal and ethical disputes helped the church clarify its thinking from the beginning, it was soon beset by Gnosticism, a movement that was so large and so culturally supported that it proved to be a serious threat. Early voices of the movement (some scholars label them "proto-gnostic") constitute part of the background to some of the later New Testament documents,[16] but the movement crested in the second and third centuries. The most substantial cache of gnostic documents conveniently available in English translation is from Nag Hammadi.[17] An hour or two of quiet reading of these works discloses a very different world from that of the New Testament. The gnostic documents display ideas about human origins far removed from those in the New Testament or in the entire Bible. Usually matter is seen to be intrinsically bad; salvation is secured, not by the substitutionary death of a sacrifice, but by knowledge of one's true identity; and secret rites abound.

In all these domains, then, Christian apologists in the second and third centuries were called upon to understand their times and to use the Christian Scriptures to refute what were, from an orthodox perspective, insupportable and dangerous heresies. Perhaps the best known of the apologists is Irenaeus, bishop of Lyons, who devoted five volumes to the detection and overthrow of various forms of gnosticism. Though he wrote toward the end of the second century, in his youth he had listened to Polycarp, who had in turn been a disciple of John.

But for our purposes, the importance of the subject is found not only in its intrinsic interest but in two related matters. The first is that, under the influence of Walter Bauer,[18] a substantial body of contemporary opinion argues that in the earliest church there was no real distinction between orthodoxy and heresy. Fledgling Christianity was sufficiently robust and inclusive to avoid such distinctions, which were later and rather nasty developments, owing more to the fact that "orthodoxy" gained the ear of the Emperor Constantine than to any intrinsic superiority in its arguments. This argument has been refuted many times. Bauer himself examined only the texts from the second century on. Not only was he mistaken with respect to the second century, but he displayed more than a little cheek by referring to the second century as *earliest* Christianity[19]—

---

[16]See chapter 23 on the Johannine Epistles.

[17]James A. Robinson, ed., *The Nag Hammadi Library in English*, 3rd ed. (San Francisco: Harper, 1990).

[18]Walter Bauer, *Orthodoxy and Heresy in Earliest Christianity* (Philadelphia: Fortress Press, 1971 [orig. 1934]).

[19]So I. Howard Marshall, whose title amusingly draws attention to the point: "Orthodoxy and Heresy in Earlier Christianity," *Themelios* 2/1 (1976): 5–14. Other useful works on this subject include Daniel J. Harrington, "The Reception of Walter Bauer's *Orthodoxy and Heresy in Earliest Christianity* During the Last Decade," *HTR* 77 (1980): 289–99; Harold O. J. Brown, *Heresies: The Image of Christ in the Mirror of Heresy and Orthodoxy from the Apostles to the Present* (Garden City: Doubleday, 1984);

and the evidence already briefly scanned demonstrates that even in the earliest books of the New Testament, Christians were willing and able to distinguish between true and false teaching.

The second matter of some importance is the influence of The Jesus Seminar, whose work, discussed elsewhere in this book (see especially the next chapter), has been disseminated in the mass media. Most of the scholars connected with The Jesus Seminar not only accept the Bauer thesis but go farther and argue that the earliest strata of Christian teaching actually support gnosticism and often present Jesus as rather more akin to a traveling Cynic preacher than anything else. The historian Philip Jenkins has it right:

> The problem with these reconstructions is the suggestion that both orthodoxy and Gnosticism are equally ancient and valid statements of the earliest Christianity, which they are not. What became the orthodox view has very clear roots in the first century, and indeed in the earliest discernible strands of the Jesus movement; in contrast, all the available sources for the Gnostic view are much later, and that movement emerges as a deliberate reaction to that orthodoxy.[20]

5. Sometimes contemporary scholars give the impression that genuinely "critical" thought on the New Testament is of relatively recent provenance. It would be truer to say that the framework out of which "critical" thought has been undertaken has shifted again and again during the last twenty centuries, largely depending on the epistemological and cultural givens of the time. Christians did not have to wait until the eighteenth century, for example, before pondering the relationships among the gospels. Already in the second century Tatian (c. 110–72) produced his *Diatessaron*, essentially a harmony of the four canonical gospels. His work was used in the Syrian church as a guide for its liturgy until the fifth century.

6. It would be tedious to chart the interpretation of the New Testament espoused by every important patristic theologian or movement. This is not, after all, a volume of church history. Nevertheless, it is important for today's students of the New Testament to have some awareness of others who have studied the New Testament before them, to feel a part of an ongoing stream of New Testament interpretation and to know something of its continuities, its disputes, and its connections with certain events and interpretive approaches.

Graham N. Stanton and Guy G. Strousma, eds., *Tolerance and Intolerance in Early Judaism and Christianity* (Cambridge: Cambridge University Press, 1998); Craig L. Blomberg, "The New Testament Definition of Heresy (or When Do Jesus and the Apostles Really Get Mad?)," *JETS* 45 (2002): 59–72, which, despite the racy title, is penetrating.

[20]Philip Jenkins, *Hidden Gospels: How the Search for Jesus Lost Its Way* (Oxford: Oxford University Press, 2001), 115–16.

By the end of the third century, the two most influential approaches to the study of the Bible were centered on Alexandria and Antioch respectively. The *Alexandrian school* warmly embraced philosophy as a weapon in the arsenal of Christian apologetics, especially philosophy descended from Plato. Often resorting to allegorical method in their exegesis, the Alexandrians sometimes flirted with a view of the Trinity that bordered on tri-theism (belief in three Gods). By contrast, the *Antiochene school* favored a more literal, rational, and historical exegesis. As a result, they insisted that some parts of Scripture have more doctrinal and spiritual value than others and felt no need to extract such value from the less fecund parts by resorting to allegory. In general, they approached the subject of Christology by beginning with Christ's true humanity. The more radical fringe of the Antiochenes tended to see Christ, not as the God-man, but as a man indwelt by God.

The patristic period cast up more than its share of theologians and other Christian thinkers who took their primary cue from their reading of the Bible. Some of the contributions of Justin Martyr, Irenaeus, and Jerome have already been mentioned. The most stalwart defender of orthodox Christology was *Athanasius* (c. 296–373), an Egyptian by birth but Greek by education. He produced both theological apologetics, not least in defense of the full deity of Christ, and many commentaries on biblical books. The *Council of Nicea* (325) gave us the Nicene Creed, which stood against the teaching of Arius to the effect that the Logos ("Word" in John 1:1) was "made," insisting rather that Christ is of the same "being" as his Father. *John Chrysostom* (c. 344–407), bishop of Constantinople, was renowned for his expository preaching, which then multiplied his influence in published form—hundreds of his sermons have been preserved, along with practical and devotional writings and 236 letters. We are not so fortunate with the literary remains of *Origen* (c. 185–254), Alexandrian theologian extraordinaire. Most of his works have not come down to us, but we are aware of major commentaries from his pen, plus apologetic works, text-critical work (some have called him, not Bengel, the father of New Testament text criticism), and one of the first systematic theologies. Though elements of his theology were later condemned by some synods (e.g., the Synod of Constantinople of 543), and certainly his Alexandrian deployment of allegory seems forced by Antiochene standards (let alone by later standards), there is a fresh vitality in his writing that still bears pondering.[21] *Eusebius of Caesarea* (c. 265–339) has been

---

[21]Although relatively little of his enormous *oeuvre* survives, some of his extant work is accessible to those who read only modern English translations. Origen's massive commentary on Romans, written in Greek, is lost, but it was translated into Latin and somewhat condensed by Rufinus (345–410), and has only recently been translated from the Latin into English by Thomas P. Scheck: *Commentary on the Epistle to the Romans,* 2 vols. (Washington: Catholic Biblical Association of America, 2001–2).

called "The Father of Church History." Owing to his extensive quotations of sources, sometimes the only access we have to important earlier documents is his *Historia Ecclesiastica*. In addition to his history, he wrote numerous apologetic books.

And what shall we make of *Augustine of Hippo* in North Africa (354–430), the single most influential figure of the first four centuries after the apostles? His expositions of the Psalms and of John's Gospel can still be read with profit, and his *Confessions*—simultaneously a highly personal document and a mature theology—is still among the classic Christian works of all time. When the Roman Empire began to fall apart after the sack of Rome in A.D. 410, Augustine's *The City of God* was simultaneously a refutation of the pagan accusations that Christians were ultimately responsible for the disaster and an interpretation of Roman and Christian history to show that there are two "cities," an earthly, human city with all of its own loves and aims, and the city of God, which alone endures forever. This eschatological reading of both Testaments and of the contemporary history proved a hugely stabilizing factor for Christians as the foundations of order were progressively swept away.

The point of this summary is to drive home the fact that Christians were a profoundly textual people from the beginning: their access to the unique history and unique Person by whom they were saved was above all textual. The Old Testament pointed to Christ; the New Testament told of him. Christian teachers and pastors therefore gave themselves to the study of these documents, wrote commentaries on them, and sought to commend them and defend them. This does not always mean that these church fathers were in perfect agreement; still less does it mean that each one was always right. But this is the early part of the heritage that any student of the New Testament assumes when he or she begins the task of studying, interpreting, and teaching these twenty-seven documents.

7. One historical "hinge" that must be noted is the role played by Constantine, the first (nominally) Christian Roman emperor.

During its first three centuries, the church multiplied by the power of the Spirit, manifested in its preaching and in the quality of the life of its members. The church enjoyed no governmental advantages or support; frequently it suffered grievously under imperial persecution. For the Christians, this marked not defeat but victory, for they were the followers of One who died an ignominious death on a cross and yet was vindicated in the resurrection. Moreover, they remembered that he himself had taught, "Give back to Caesar what is Caesar's and to God what is God's" (Mark 12:17; cf. Matt. 22:21; Luke 20:25). Before that time, the authority of religion and the authority of the state were more tightly linked, often identified. Ancient Israel was, at least in theory, a theocracy. But Jesus established a kingdom which, when fully consummated, would embrace everything in heaven and earth, but which, until then, would be contested. His people on earth would be called forth from every language and tribe and nation

> *Christians were a profoundly textual people from the beginning: their access to the unique history and unique Person by whom they were saved was above all textual.*

but would not constitute a nation with geographical borders here on earth. Christians would find themselves living as citizens of two kingdoms, and they would owe allegiance to both: to Caesar, they should give what is his due; and to God, what is his due. Of course, if Caesar overstepped the mark and claimed more allegiance than was his due, Christians would be called to obey God rather than any human being. Nevertheless, the principle was put in place by the Master himself: we are citizens of two realms, we live in two cities, and the tensions are to be borne, even unto death, until the kingdom of God is consummated.

But shortly after he emerged victorious by defeating Maxentius in 312 at the battle of Milvian Bridge north of Rome, Constantine decreed full legal toleration for Christians. The church began to enjoy imperial favor. Previously confiscated property was restored, there were various exemptions for the clergy, financial aid flowed to Christians, and some bishops began to enjoy civil jurisdiction. The bishop of Rome, already preeminent among the bishops, could only gain in authority by these arrangements.

The tension between the civil and the ecclesiastical authority never disappeared, of course, and it kept changing its shape for more than a millennium, as individual monarchs and popes proved peculiarly able or influential. Nevertheless, the fundamental tension between the claims of Caesar and the claims of God, developed by Paul to help Roman Christians see that the authority of the state is God-ordained (especially Rom. 13:1–7) and by John to help Christians see that the state can wrongly claim idolatrous allegiance (so Revelation), remained in place and led, in due course, to a variety of theories of the distinction between church and state.[22] These developments have materially shaped, in various ways, not only the religious but also the political heritage of many countries that have long enjoyed a substantial number of Christians. The political and religious realities in which we work out our discipleship can often be traced back, in convoluted ways, to distinctions made in the New Testament itself.

8. One of the crucial developments that took place during the first few centuries was the rise of "monarchical bishops." Within the period when the New Testament documents were written, the labels "pastor" (which simply means

---

[22]We say "variety of theories" because how church and state relate to each other varies widely. Separation of church and state does not mean the same thing in, say, France, the United Kingdom, and the United States. But all Christian experience and heritage on this subject, as complex and as variegated as it is, remains profoundly different from, for example, the Muslim heritage. Once Muhammad gained power at Medina, the religious and civil authorities were one. The first three centuries of Islam witnessed rapid growth by military conquest. There is nothing in Islam quite like the seminal utterance found on the lips of Jesus, "Give back to Caesar the things that are Caesar's and to God the things that are God's." By the same token, Islam has never conceived of the nation-state quite the way the West has, nor has it ever had a "clergy" closely analogous to Christian clergy.

"shepherd"), "elder," and "bishop" (sometimes "overseer" in modern English versions) all referred to the same people, that is, those primarily responsible for the leadership of local congregations. As early as the beginning of the second century, however (and there are hints of this trend even earlier), some bishops or pastors came to have a measure of authority over *other* local congregations. Those who gained such oversight came to be called bishops, while those who did not retained the labels elder and pastor only. The reasons for the rise of monarchical bishops are doubtless complex, but some of them sprang from good motives, even if the result was rather more dubious. The number of Christians was growing so rapidly, and churches were being planted so frequently, that the level of training of many local Christian leaders was not very high. Partly to accommodate the need for teaching, a class of traveling Christian preachers arose who went from church to church.[23] But who was to authorize such travelers? Inevitably, some shysters arose, fluent in God-talk, who found this was an agreeable way to earn a living, even though they were woefully unqualified. Others were doubtless sincere and thought they were helping churches, but their vision of their own competence outstripped the reality. Some were frankly heretical. And worse, in many instances local church leaders were insufficiently knowledgeable and mature to distinguish those who could genuinely help from those who were incompetent or even dangerous. So it is not surprising that a second-century document gives instructions as to which traveling preachers or "prophets" were to be accepted as genuine and which were to be dismissed. The genuine ones did not stay too long, did not ask for money, and taught faithful Christian doctrine (cf. *Didache* xi).

Inevitably, under these circumstances some local pastors turned on occasion to the most knowledgeable bishop/elder/pastor in the vicinity, who then began to have a veto power over who was licensed to teach and preach in an entire area instead of in his congregation alone. Although they provided a valuable safeguard, eventually such bishops gained distinctive roles and authority unknown in the New Testament.

The reason why this is important for our purposes is that it is difficult to understand how the early church came in time to settle its disputes over what the apostles actually taught, without grasping the rising roles of bishops and occasionally of other noted teachers. The most serious disputes called together bishops from every region of the Empire in crucial "ecumenical councils" made up primarily of bishops from the whole (Roman) world, the *oikoumenē*. The seven

---

[23]Doubtless this system developed in part because traveling preachers/lecturers were common in the Roman world. The best of them could make a good living. They gained disciples who would pay for the privilege of attaching themselves to the teacher. Occasionally one of these traveling preachers would stop traveling and settle somewhere, opening a small academy. There were no institutions akin to modern universities.

councils that most Christians recognize to be truly "ecumenical," with their dates and the subjects with which they primarily wrestled are: Nicea I (325), Arianism; Constantinople (381), Apollinarianism; Ephesus (431), Nestorianism; Chalcedon (451), Eutychianism; Constantinople II (553), Three Chapters Controversy; Constantinople III (680–81), Monothelitism; and Nicea II (787), Iconoclasm.[24]

9. These councils on doctrinal issues understood themselves to be deciding what the truth of some issue really was. When the Council of Nicea (325) decided on appropriate terms to talk about the deity of Christ, or the Council of Chalcedon (451) deployed certain terms that have become standard in discussion of the Trinity, the participants did not think of themselves as inventing new theology or even as discovering new truth in the Bible that no one had ever seen before. Rather, they were adjudicating conflicting interpretations of the Christian message and trying to formulate biblical truth in a way that made ambiguity or outright error in that domain much more difficult.

Similarly, when in the sixteenth century the Reformers worked hard to articulate a doctrine of justification that they felt was rigorously in line with Paul and with the rest of the Bible, it is not that no one had believed in justification before or had failed to see how important it was. The theme constantly recurs during the patristic period.[25] But it took the disputes at the time of the Reformation to call forth a lot of detailed work. The reasons that generate doctrinal controversy may be ugly and painful, but God not infrequently uses such controversies to bring renewed theological strength and clarity of vision and understanding to his people. Such controversies therefore become part of the web of the history of the interpretation of the New Testament, indeed, of the whole Bible.

10. After the Roman Empire fell, standards of literacy declined sharply in the West. Latin, long dominant, virtually snuffed out remaining vestiges of what was once a deep knowledge of Greek and Hebrew. As the Middle Ages progressed, many local clergy were abysmally trained; countless rulers, even powerful ones, were illiterate or semi-literate. Perhaps the greatest centers of learning were the monasteries, although the quality of the work done in them varied a great deal. Nevertheless, for hundreds of years these were the centers where manuscripts were copied (even when they were poorly understood), where hymns were created, where commentaries and theological treatises were written.[26]

---

[24]The nature of these controversies can be quickly discovered in any good dictionary of church history, e.g., F. L. Cross and E. A. Livingstone, *The Oxford Dictionary of the Christian Church,* 3rd ed. (Oxford: Oxford University Press, 1997).

[25]See Thomas C. Oden, *The Justification Reader* (Grand Rapids: Eerdmans, 2002).

[26]For an interesting if overstated description of the role of monasteries, see Thomas Cahill, *How the Irish Saved Civilization* (New York: Doubleday, 1995).

Across the centuries, the church changed structurally and modified its teaching in many important ways, and inevitably these changes and modifications fed back into the way people handled the New Testament. Organizationally, the first really great schism was between the Western (or Latin) church, and the Eastern (or Orthodox) church. It is impossible to assign a beginning date to the division, but the date assigned to the final separation is usually 1054. Located primarily in the countries of Eastern Europe, the Orthodox church tends to organize itself nationally (hence the Greek Orthodox Church, the Serbian Orthodox Church, the Russian Orthodox Church, etc.) while recognizing the honorary primacy of the patriarch of Constantinople. Its distinctive doctrines and features need not be traced here.[27] In the West, primacy was gradually assigned to the bishop of Rome. What became the Roman Catholic Church soon embraced considerable diversity and faced the challenges of both failures and various renewal movements, the most powerful of which produced fresh schisms at the time of the Reformation.

Nevertheless, it is crucially important to understand that what became the Roman Catholic Church as we think of it today did not happen overnight. For instance, prayers for the dead began about 300. The title "Mother of God" was first applied to Mary by the Council of Ephesus (initially in order to defend the deity of Christ), but prayers directed to Mary, to dead saints, and to angels rose in popularity around 600, while the dogma of the assumption of Mary—that she ascended bodily into heaven—was not promulgated as a dogma (a teaching orthodox Catholics must believe) until 1950. The practice of sprinkling holy water with a pinch of salt in it and blessed by a priest, arose around 850. The College of Cardinals was established in 927. Canonization of dead saints was first undertaken in 995 by Pope John XV.[28] The doctrine of transubstantiation was proclaimed as dogma by Pope Innocent III in 1215 (though its roots stretch back much farther). The Bible was forbidden to laypeople and was actually placed on the Index of Forbidden Books by the Council of Valencia in 1229. Purgatory, which was taught by Gregory I in 593, was promulgated as dogma by the Council of Florence in 1439. The immaculate conception of Mary was pro-

---

[27]For easy access to the issues, see Daniel B. Clendenin, *Eastern Orthodox Theology: A Contemporary Reader* (Grand Rapids: Baker, 1995); idem, *Eastern Orthodox Christianity: A Western Perspective* (Grand Rapids: Baker, 1994); and especially Theodore G. Stylianopoulos, *The New Testament: An Orthodox Perspective*, Vol. 1: *Scripture, Tradition, Hermeneutics* (Brookline: Holy Cross Orthodox Press, 1997). Cf. also Bradley Nassif, "Eastern Orthodoxy and Evangelicalism: The Status of an Emerging Global Dialogue," *SBET* 18 (2000): 21–55.

[28]Intriguingly, during his reign, Pope John Paul II canonized sixty-four saints, which is more than all the canonizations by popes during the last four hundred years. This does not include several currently in process.

claimed by Pope Pius IX in 1854, and the infallibility of the pope in his teaching office on matters of faith and morals at the first Vatican Council in 1870.[29]

Some of these items will strike many contemporary readers as far removed
from the New Testament. But that is just the point. Once such items have
become entrenched as established orthodoxy, such orthodoxy is likely to be the
framework in which one reads the New Testament unless one rigorously
attempts to distance oneself from one's theological heritage, self-consciously
attempting, so far as it is possible, to read oneself into the frames of reference of
the biblical writers. That is one of the things that takes place during any reforming movement.

11. As a rubric, "the Middle Ages" covers countries and centuries so diverse
and complex that generalizations regularly call forth a "Yes, but" from scholars
familiar with the period. On the one hand, the Middle Ages gave us the Cru-
sades and a broader conflict with Islam, some of the most immoral popes, the
first rounds of the "Black Death" (bubonic plague), institutionalized illiteracy
among the masses, and rising superstition of the most appalling sort (one thinks
of the hungry search for magic-endowed Christian relics and the rising traffic in
indulgences). On the other hand, the Middle Ages gave us some glorious hymns,
some soaring conceptions of God (reflected not least in the design and construction of cathedrals), some theologians of immense gift and erudition, and,
toward the end of the period, some reformers of perception and courage who
urged a whole-hearted return to the Bible (e.g., Jan Hus [1373–1415] in Czecho-
slovakia, John Wycliffe [c. 1329–1384] in England), not a few of whom were
martyred.

At the risk of generalization, the theological contribution of the Middle
Ages was not so much in the domain of penetrating commentaries as in two
other fields. First, this extended period produced a stream of mystics (e.g.,
Bernard of Clairvaux [1090–1153], Julian of Norwich [c. 1342 to after 1413]).
Some of this mysticism succumbed to barely controlled subjectivism, but at its
best it gave us a corpus of hymns still being sung, in translation, today. Bernard,
for instance, wrote "O Sacred Head Now Wounded," "Jesus, the Very Thought
of Thee," and "Jesus, Thou Joy of Loving Hearts."

Second, and still more important for our purposes, was the stream of theo-
logians, including Anselm of Canterbury, Peter Abelard, William of Ockham,
Thomas Aquinas, and Duns Scotus.[30] The most influential of these by far was
Thomas Aquinas (1224–74), and the best known of his works is his *Summa*

---

[29]See further M. Fiedler and L. Rabben, eds., *Rome Has Spoken: A Guide to Forgotten Papal Statements, and How They Have Changed through the Centuries* (New York:
Crossroad, 1998).

[30]For further reading, see G. R. Evans, ed., *The Medieval Theologians: An Introduction to Theology in the Medieval Period* (Blackwell: Oxford, 2001).

Theologiae, which is simultaneously a systematic compendium of the data of Christian revelation as he understood them, a revision of Augustinian epistemology along Aristotelian lines, and an evangelistic work aimed at Muslims. Despite the enormous influence his work has wielded, especially but by no means exclusively within Catholicism, his categories belong rather more to the domains of philosophy and systematics than to rigorous exegesis. To take one small example: Although earlier Christian theologians, stretching back to the patristic period, had sometimes distinguished moral, civil, and ceremonial law, it was Aquinas who developed this tripartite division of Old Testament law to establish the patterns of continuity and discontinuity between the Old and New Testaments. This tripartite division, which was subsequently picked up and developed by John Calvin and others, offers many helpful insights, but it is not demonstrably the set of categories with which the New Testament writers themselves are operating when they work out the patterns of continuity and discontinuity between the old covenant and the new. Questions about how to conceive the relationships between the two Testaments are of course perennial, and the influence of Aquinas in this area as in numerous others is with us still as we read our New Testaments.

> *One must distinguish four levels of biblical interpretation during the Middle Ages: the literal sense, the allegorical sense, the moral sense, and the analogical sense.*

We have already mentioned that during the first few centuries of the church a remarkable debate arose between the Alexandrian and the Antiochene schools of interpretation—the former a champion of allegory in exegesis (though what was meant by "allegory" in those days was more flexible and less defined than in many contemporary treatments), and the latter insisting on a more direct or literal exegesis. During the Middle Ages a more systematic classification of different methods of biblical interpretation was codified. One must distinguish four levels of biblical interpretation (and different authors put them in different order): the literal sense, which teaches us what happened; the allegorical (sometimes called the tropological) sense, which teaches us what to believe; the moral sense, which tells us what to do; and the analogical (occasionally called the eschatological) sense, which tells us where we are going. Not infrequently such distinctions were tied to a mystical spirituality.[31] Inevitably they also had the effect of making the Bible a closed book, reserved for experts, rightly interpreted only by the authorities of the church, and closed to most laypeople (after all, the printing press had not yet been invented).

12. The Renaissance, a period of European history that historians customarily attach to the fourteenth, fifteenth, and sixteenth centuries, witnessed a "rebirth" (which is what *renaissance* means) of classical culture. The printing press was invented, the influence of which cannot easily be overstated. Constantinople fell to the Muslim Turks in 1453, which sent not a few scholars scur-

---

[31]See the important work of Henri de Lubac, *Medieval Exegesis*, 2 vols. (Grand Rapids: Eerdmans, 1998–2000).

rying to the West, bringing their Greek manuscripts with them. The rise of learning and the founding of several European universities trumpeted the call, *Ad fontes*—"to the sources." The study of Greek and Hebrew became commonplace; the authority of Latin was increasingly displaced. The renewal of interest in both Christian and pagan foundational documents produced a growing number of informed and highly literate "humanists" who were more than willing to criticize the clerical abuse then rampant at almost every level of the Catholic Church. By and large, the humanists in northern Europe became more interested in the classical Christian texts (the New Testament and the patristics) than in the classical pagan texts, and they have thus sometimes been labeled "Christian humanists." The most influential of these was Erasmus of Rotterdam, whom we have already met.

Those influenced by the Renaissance also became increasingly suspicious of the four interpretive levels that had been justified by the theologians of the Middle Ages. They wanted to read the primary sources for themselves, and they tried to read them more "literally" or more "naturally."[32]

13. Scholars still dispute the nature of the relationships between the Renaissance and the Reformation (sixteenth century). Certainly the demand for reform increasingly voiced by Christian humanists contributed to the growing unrest in Western Christendom. That fact generated the old saw that "Erasmus laid the egg that Luther hatched." Moreover, many younger humanists converted to Protestantism, including such leaders as Ulrich Zwingli (d. 1531), Philipp Melanchthon (d. 1560), John Calvin (d. 1564), and Theodore Beza (d. 1605).

The Reformation emphasis on *sola scriptura* ("Scripture alone") embraced in practice several emphases. Over against the Catholic view that revelation is a deposit entrusted to the church, a deposit of which Scripture is only a part, the Reformers insisted that while there is much to learn from Christian tradition, much indeed that holds us to account, only the Bible has final authority.

---

[32]In recent years it has been pointed out, not least by Thomas C. Oden ("A Patristic Perspective on European Christianity in World Perspective," *ERT* 27 [2003]: 318–36), that the Christianity of the first few centuries was not primarily a European phenomenon. The gospel spread out from Jerusalem into what is now called Turkey (which was for a millennium the heart of Byzantium), the North African coast, Egypt, Ethiopia, Arabia, Syria, northern Mesopotamia, and probably as far east as the Indus Valley, with some evidence of extension to China, not to mention extension to Rome, and then to what are now France and Spain. Thus, for either the friends or foes of Christianity to see the Christian religion, in its origins and initial expansion, as primarily a European phenomenon, is simply mistaken. On the other hand, one should also point out that, owing in substantial part to the expansionist pressures from Islam, Europe became the dominant voice preserving, articulating, defending, and expounding Christianity, especially after the fall of Constantinople. These roles, of course, contemporary Europe seems determined to shed.

The Bible must not be domesticated by the tradition. This emphasis had two complementary effects: (1) Ideally, the Scriptures should be studied in the languages in which they were written; and (2) the Scriptures should be disseminated as widely as possible, which meant that vernacular translations should be prepared. The aim of the Bible translator William Tyndale (strangled and burned in 1536) was to make the ploughboy as knowledgeable in the Bible as the high prelates of the church. Moreover, insistence on "Scripture alone" prompted the Reformers to study once again what constitutes Scripture, and this led to the rejection of the Apocrypha as part of the canon. The fact that the Catholic Church adjudged these books (the exact number of them is somewhat disputed) to be canonical or "deuterocanonical"—that is, canonical in a secondary sense—was not a sufficient reason for hanging onto them. Indeed, at one stage in his life Martin Luther questioned the authority of the canonical James ("a right strawy epistle," in his famous phrase).[33]

Partly under the influence of Renaissance learning, the Reformers learned to be suspicious of the fourfold hermeneutic they had inherited. This does not mean they became crass literalists. They could recognize (as all good readers can) metaphors and other figures of speech. They wrestled with what would today be called typology. The fact that the Bible is often talking of eternal things in the categories of everyday temporal things prompted Luther to think of Scripture as a *litera spiritualis*. One may doubt that this is the most helpful analysis, yet it is vital to recognize that although the Reformers dismissed as artificial the fourfold interpretive approach defended in the Middle Ages, they were not unaware that the "natural" reading was not always straightforward. Moreover, the efforts of both Luther and Calvin (to go no farther) to write both commentaries on books of the Bible *and* expositions of Christian doctrine had the effect of tying doctrine to the Bible itself. Indeed, Calvin's enormously influential *Institutes of the Christian Religion* was meant to be a kind of accurate introduction to what the Bible teaches. This work wrestles endlessly with Scripture yet works out its doctrinal formulations in interaction not only with issues of importance when Calvin was writing but also in interaction with eminent Christian thinkers throughout history. In conjunction with Calvin's commentaries, the *Institutes* taught many generations of believers what to believe and how to think. Inevitably, works such as these constituted models for the interpretation and the teaching of Scripture. It became impossible to try to understand the New Testament, let alone the entire Bible, without reflecting on such work.[34]

---

[33]For an introduction to the rise and definition of the canon, see the final chapter of this book.

[34]This is no less true of the Catholic Counter-Reformation, of course, than of, say, the Puritans, even though, transparently, the two parties emerged with radically different conclusions. Both felt the massive impact of the Reformation.

THE RISE OF BIBLICAL THEOLOGY[35]

The changing shape of biblical study, and New Testament study in particular, during the last four centuries is a story far too complex to be compressed into a few pages. So in this section and the next we will attempt brief probes into two areas that we hope will serve as useful test cases of the broader developments.

If theology is disciplined discourse about God, one might think that biblical theology is disciplined discourse about God that is based on the Bible. In that sense, of course, there has been biblical theology as long as there has been a Bible or any part of it. But the actual expression "biblical theology" was first coined, so far as we know, in a book by W. J. Christmann published in 1607 and no longer extant. The title was *Teutsche biblische Theologie* ("German Biblical Theology"). Apparently, it was a rather brief volume of proof-texts drawn from the Bible to support Protestant systematic theology. This use of "biblical theology" continued in some circles for another century and a half.

It was not long before other uses appeared. In his *Pia Desideria* (1675), P. J. Spener, and later the Pietists he influenced, distinguished *theologia biblica* (his own theology) from *theologia scholastica*, the prevailing Protestant (Lutheran) orthodoxy that had returned to the Aristotelianism Luther had rejected. Thus, "biblical theology" took on an overtone of protest, of being "more biblical" than the prevailing dogmatics. In the second half of the eighteenth century, under the influence of English Deism and the German *Aufklärung* (Enlightenment), a handful of theologians once again protested against the prevailing dogmatics—now, however, not in favor of Pietism but in favor of rationalism. Several of these works aimed to extract from the Bible timeless truths in accord with reason, while framing them in a way that was still largely, if sometimes uneasily, acceptable to the ecclesiastical establishment. By far the most influential of these theologians was Johann P. Gabler, whose inaugural lecture at the University of Altdorf, *An Oration on the Proper Distinction Between Biblical and Dogmatic Theology and the Specific Objectives of Each* (1787), captured the rising mood and precipitated the next step. Gabler charged that dogmatic theology, constantly changing and perpetually disputed, is too far removed from Scripture. The biblical theology that he himself was recommending would be a largely inductive study of the biblical text. Such study, he contended, would be much more likely to gain widespread assent among learned and godly scholars, and it

---

[35]See D. A. Carson, "New Testament Theology," in *Dictionary of the Later New Testament and Its Developments* (Downers Grove: IVP, 1997), 796–814, some of which has been adapted for use here, and the opening pages of Charles H. H. Scobie, *The Ways of Our God: An Approach to Biblical Theology* (Grand Rapids: Eerdmans, 2003). For an earlier survey, see Gerhard F. Hasel, *New Testament Theology: Basic Issues in the Current Debate* (Grand Rapids: Eerdmans, 1978); idem, "The Nature of Biblical Theology: Recent Trends and Issues," *AUSS* 32 (1994): 203–15.

could in turn become the foundation on which fresh systematic theology would be constructed. Thus, Gabler's primary appeal was not that the Bible must first be read historically or that the documents must be set out in historical sequence (though a little of this is implicit in what he said) but that biblical theologians may properly go about their task without being directly bound by doctrinal considerations[36]—an epoch-making suggestion at the time and one that has earned him the sobriquet "father of biblical theology."

The first part of Gabler's proposal, the invitation to inductive study of the biblical documents in a manner removed from dogmatic control, was rapidly taken up in many European universities; the second part, that fresh dogmatics be built on this new foundation, was largely ignored. Indeed, the more that scholars worked at a merely descriptive level without reflection on the importance of the *analogia fidei* (the "analogy of the faith")—the longstanding commitment to read the Bible within the framework of historic confessionalism—the more the diversities *within* the Bible achieved prominence. The differences between the two Testaments, for example, became so obvious under such a régime that in 1796 G. L. Bauer produced, not a *biblical* theology, but an Old Testament theology, followed in 1800–1802 by a two-volume New Testament theology. Although *biblical* theologies (i.e., whole-Bible biblical theologies) continued to be written for another half-century and even into the twentieth century, the move was away from them.

The tendency toward atomism in biblical theology has continued in certain strands of the discipline to the present day. Thus, by "New Testament theology" many writers mean the distinctive theologies found in the various New Testament writings: the theology of Paul, the theology of Matthew, the theology of Luke-Acts, and so forth. The atomism becomes yet more pronounced when three further tendencies are taken into account. (1) Many scholars who defend the atomism are persuaded that some of the New Testament documents are pseudonymous. The result is that "the theology of Paul," for instance, is based on an ostensibly authentic four or seven of the thirteen letters in the New Testament that bear Paul's name, while there are distinguishable theologies of, say, Ephesians, 2 Thessalonians, and the Pastoral Epistles, all judged to be pseudonymous. (2) Many scholars are convinced that they can isolate a source used by both Matthew and Luke, often designated "Q." This in turn leads to attempts to write a theology of Q (see chapter 2 of this book). (3) A variation of the second tendency occurs where scholars are convinced that some part of a New Testament document reflects an unassimilated or even contradictory source or editorial accretion (for example, see the chapters on 2 Thessalonians and Romans in this book). Similar source criticism is applied to other New Testament documents.

---

[36]See J. Sandys-Wunsch and L. Eldredge, "J. P. Gabler and the Distinction Between Biblical and Dogmatic Theology," *SJT* 33 (1980): 133–58.

Atomism triumphs, and it becomes harder to see the big picture and how the various New Testament (not to say biblical) documents might relate to one another.

Inevitably, then, biblical theology felt the impact of historical criticism. We shall reflect a little more on the nature of historical criticism in the next section and repeatedly in later chapters of this book. In some ways, however, we have already stumbled into the subject, and some of its further effects on biblical theology may be usefully probed here. Perhaps the most important intersection took place around the middle of the nineteenth century. In Tübingen, the great German scholar F. C. Baur undertook a fresh examination of how the Pauline Epistles, Acts, and the Gospels came to be written. To this task he brought more than a little philosophical naturalism (i.e., he was averse to admitting any appeal to the supernatural in any historical questions), and he advanced reasons for dating the various New Testament books on the assumption that his re-creation of early church history was correct. This early history, he claimed, saw the church emerge as a minor Jewish sect, then a major Jewish sect, then a peculiar Jewish sect in that it was admitting Gentiles under a variety of conditions; eventually it broke from Judaism to take on a life of its own. The New Testament documents, he argued, fit somewhere along the axis of this trajectory. The debates between the church and Judaism gradually rose in intensity and were soon hot and furious, but once the division took place, the debate died down until eventually it is attested only in barely remembered historical strands. On this basis, for instance, Baur dated Acts well into the second century (by which time the fight was over, so the tone is very different from, say, Galatians). The bearing of all this work on biblical theology was most clearly seen in 1864, when Baur's own New Testament theology was published posthumously. The combination of a rigidly developmental reconstruction of early church history and a fairly radical naturalism meant that the New Testament documents could not be thought of as revelatory in any proper sense. They could not be judged to reflect a coherent theological system; rather, they give evidence not only of historical and theological development but of something more: the various layers prove historically interesting but in some ways mutually incompatible. For the same reason, they could not be viewed as theologically binding.[37]

This historicist impulse came to a head in what came to be called "the history-of-religions school" (*die religionsgeschichtliche Schule*). Here valiant efforts were made to show that all religious movements and the documents they generate are themselves shaped by other religious movements and documents, whether the new ones merely take over antecedent material, or modify it, or react against it. All of this was judged to be responsible *historical* criticism, that is, a

---

[37]See Horton Harris, *The Tübingen School* (Grand Rapids: Baker, repr. 1990 [1975]); or, in shorter compass, Stephen Neill and N. T. Wright, *The Interpretation of the New Testament 1861–1986*, 2nd ed. (Oxford: Oxford University Press, 1988), 20–34.

deployment of critical reason that refuses to appeal to supernatural causes to account for the documents that make up the Christian Bible. We may study what first-century people *thought* were supernatural events and revelations, but critical study will show these first-century judgments to be primitive and naive. The bearing of these developments on New Testament theology came to a head, perhaps, in the blistering and influential little book of W. Wrede, *Über Aufgabe und Methode der sogenannten neutestamentliche Theologie* ("Concerning the Task and Method of So-Called New Testament Theology").[38] Wrede argued that to treat each book of the New Testament separately was absurd, because each book provides too little information to enable an interpreter to reconstruct the entire "theology" of its author. The only responsible way forward is to construct, as best we can, the *history* of early Christian religion and theology. Any unified New Testament theology, let alone biblical theology, is a chimera.

One must not think that these voices at the leading edge of the most skeptical criticism (not to say of dogmatic unbelief) were the only voices. In the nineteenth century, the most penetrating attempt at New Testament theology that sought to build on the Old Testament was probably that of J. C. K. von Hofmann.[39] In the first decades of the twentieth century, the most influential figure in the same heritage was doubtless Adolf Schlatter.[40] No less than their more skeptical opponents, these scholars recognized the historical nature of the New Testament documents, but they insisted that *God* had acted *in history* and therefore that a commitment to philosophical naturalism could not deal fairly with the evidence. They judged their works to be "critical" in that their conclusions were not naive leaps but extensively justified positions authorized by the texts.

Other voices soon assumed greater prominence. First, Karl Barth found the works traceable to the historical and naturalist impulse utterly arid and pastorally useless. He diminished the importance of historical research for the understanding of the Bible and focused on theological interpretation, remaining more interested in systematic theology than in biblical theology.

Second, Rudolf Bultmann tried another path to bridge the gap between historical understanding and theological usefulness. He adopted the naturalism

---

[38]Göttingen: Vandenhoeck & Ruprecht, 1897. The work was translated into English by Robert Morgan as "The Task and Methods of 'New Testament Theology,'" in Robert Morgan, *The Nature of New Testament Theology* (London: SCM, 1973), 68–116.

[39]*Biblische Theologie des Neuen Testaments* (Nördlingen: Beck, 1886).

[40]Of his many books, the most important to this discussion was his *Die Theologie des Neuen Testaments*, 2 vols. (Stuttgart: Verlag der Vereinsbuchhandlung, 1909–10)—though Schlatter revised his work significantly in a later edition. The 1923 edition has now been translated into English by Andreas Köstenberger in two volumes with the respective titles *The History of the Christ: The Foundations of New Testament Theology* and *The Theology of the Apostles: The Development of New Testament Theology* (Grand Rapids: Baker, 1997, 1999).

and historicist approach of Wrede, but instead of concluding, with Wrede, that theological synthesis was thereby ruled out of court, he "demythologized" the texts of everything he judged that "modern man" could no longer believe (essentially everything supernatural) in order to uncover what he held to be the real and essential kernel of the New Testament—a certain form of existentialism. The result is that God, faith, revelation, and much else besides become redefined. The language is the language of orthodoxy, but the substance is the substance of Heidegger. Astonishingly influential in the middle of the twentieth century,[41] Bultmann's work is now largely read out of historical interest, not because he is widely followed.

The third development was the rise of the "biblical theology movement." Eager to be theologically relevant, influenced in part by Barth and in part by von Hofmann, shattered by World War I and by the Great Depression and eventually by World War II, the exponents of the movement exerted increasing influence from the 1930s to the 1950s. Perhaps the most influential of these scholars was Oscar Cullmann, whose insistence on "salvation history" (*Heilsgeschichte*) attempted to bring together two components, salvation and history, that had been flying apart. Writing in a style calculated to be edifying, his delineation of development across time allowed for a historical reading of the canon while still preserving central canonical unity and therefore authority.[42] But the biblical theology movement was remarkably diverse. It included those who held that revelation was borne along on the great *events* of redemptive history to which Scripture bears witness,[43] and those who produced the magisterial *Theological Dictionary of the New Testament* with its peculiar theologically loaded word studies.[44] Nevertheless, by the 1960s the movement was largely dead, cut down by critics who dismissed the linguistic naiveté of many of its exponents or who argued that the unity they found in the canon was not really there.[45]

> *The last fifty years or so have been characterized by astonishing diversity in biblical theology.*

---

[41]See especially his *Theology of the New Testament*, 2 vols. (ET London: SCM, 1952–55 [1948–53]). For additional insight into his approach, see his important essay, "The Problem of a Theological Exegesis of the New Testament," available in ET in *The Beginnings of Dialectical Theology*, ed. J. M. Robinson (Richmond: John Knox, 1968), 47–72 (the original appeared in 1941).

[42]See especially his *Salvation in History* (New York: Harper & Row, 1967).

[43]See especially G. Ernest Wright, *God Who Acts: Biblical Theology as Recital*, SBT 8 (London: SCM, 1962).

[44]Gerhard Kittel and Gerhard Friedrich, eds., *Theologisches Wörterbuch zum Neuen Testament* (Stuttgart: Kohlhammer, 1933–74; ET: Grand Rapids: Eerdmans, 1964–1974).

[45]See especially Brevard Childs, *Biblical Theology in Crisis* (Philadelphia: Fortress Press, 1970). No less influential was James Barr, *The Semantics of Biblical Language* (Oxford: Oxford University Press, 1961); and most recently his magisterial *The Concept of Biblical Theology: An Old Testament Perspective* (London: SCM, 1999).

The last fifty years or so have been characterized by astonishing diversity. On the confessional flank, the biblical theology of Geerhardus Vos,[46] though it focused more on the Old Testament than the New, taught many Christians how to read the Bible as a single book. The contribution of George Eldon Ladd,[47] seminal at the time, in some ways adopted a more conservative line in a common form: a New Testament theology that devoted separate chapters to the theology of the Synoptic Gospels, the theology of Paul, the theology of Hebrews, and so forth, with little attempt at integration. Still in the confessional heritage, Donald Guthrie attempted to address the problem of integration by writing a New Testament theology that traced scores of themes (e.g., "Son of Man," "God," "the Cross") *through* the different New Testament corpora.[48] What was lost, of course, was the feel for how these and other themes hung together *within* any one particular corpus and then how the corpora related to one another.

Space does not permit discussion of the many works that marked out positions across the theological spectrum—from the centrist New Testament theologies of Werner Kümmel,[49] Joachim Jeremias,[50] Joachim Gnilka,[51] and Georg Strecker,[52] who all follow the more-or-less-standard critical orthodoxies, to the contribution of Hans Conzelmann, who does not think it necessary or helpful to include the historical Jesus as a presupposition to his work,[53] to the canonical theology of Brevard Childs,[54] to the imaginative work of George B. Caird, who mentally sits the authors of the New Testament around a table and gets them to "discuss" their respective contributions,[55] and to the large, provocative work of Klaus Berger, who, under the image of a tree with many branches, develops fairly speculative theologies of the many branches according to his radical and

---

[46]*Biblical Theology: Old and New Testaments* (Grand Rapids: Eerdmans, 1948).

[47]*A Theology of the New Testament* (Grand Rapids: Eerdmans, 1974 [rev. ed. 1993]).

[48]*New Testament Theology* (Downers Grove: IVP, 1981).

[49]*The Theology of the New Testament According to Its Major Witnesses* (London: SCM, 1974 [1969]).

[50]*New Testament Theology: The Proclamation of Jesus* (New York: Scribner's, 1971). This was the only volume to be published of what was supposed to be a multivolume series tracing the theology of the different sources and corpora.

[51]*Neutestamentliche Theologie: Ein Überblick* (Würzburg: Echter Verlag, 1989); idem, *Theologie des Neuen Testaments* (Freiburg: Herder, 1994).

[52]*Theology of the New Testament* (Louisville: Westminster John Knox, 2000).

[53]*An Outline of the Theology of the New Testament* (New York: Harper and Row, 1967).

[54]*Biblical Theology of the Old and New Testaments: Theological Reflection on the Christian Bible* (Minneapolis: Fortress Press, 1992).

[55]*New Testament Theology*, ed. Lincoln D. Hurst (Oxford: Clarendon Press, 1994).

detailed reconstruction of how the church developed into mutually exclusive theological communities within the first century.[56]

As a label, then, "biblical theology" refers to several different things, interacting with one another in different ways in the hands of various scholars. It may refer to the theology of groups *behind* the biblical texts, as attested by the biblical texts themselves, insofar as we can reconstruct those groups using a variety of historical-critical and literary-critical tools. Or it may refer to the theology of the biblical texts or corpora themselves and perhaps also to how those theologies fit together (if the biblical theologian thinks they *can* be fit together!) along a temporal trajectory. Moreover, this study of the biblical documents may be primarily a self-distanced description of what the texts *meant* (an attempt at historical description) or a self-conscious wrestling with what the texts *mean* (a more hermeneutically reflective endeavor). This and similar analyses are common in contemporary discussion of what biblical theology and, in particular, New Testament theology, truly is.[57]

The last fifty years have also seen works devoted to the theology of Paul, the theology of John, and so forth, and an even longer list of monographs and articles that purport to work out the shape of some individual theological theme *within* an individual corpus.[58] Some of these, of course, are described in the chapters that follow. During the last three decades, a renewed interest in how the New Testament writers use the Old Testament has generated a raft of monographs which are in some respects the building blocks of future works on New Testament and biblical theology. Add to these the many scores of commentaries on New Testament books published each year[59] and the countless specialist articles, and one begins to glimpse the spread of New Testament scholarship.

The purpose of this admittedly sketchy survey is to stake out the terrain in which contemporary students of the New Testament necessarily work. Perhaps it will be helpful to include one final survey of a slightly different kind.

---

[56]*Theologiegeschichte des Urchristentums* (Tübingen: Francke, 1994).

[57]See especially Peter Balla, *Challenges to New Testament Theology: An Attempt to Justify the Enterprise*, WUNT 95 (Tübingen: Mohr-Siebeck, 1997); Dan O. Via, *What Is New Testament Theology?* GBS (Minneapolis: Fortress Press, 2002); D. A. Carson, "Current Issues in Biblical Theology: A New Testament Perspective," *BBR* 5 (1995): 17–41; and many of the essays in T. D. Alexander and Brian S. Rosner, eds., *New Dictionary of Biblical Theology* (Downers Grove: IVP, 2000).

[58]E.g., Brian S. Rosner, *Paul, Scripture and Ethics: A Study of 1 Corinthians 1–7*, AGJU 12 (Leiden: Brill, 1994); Dorothy Lee, *Flesh and Glory: Symbol, Gender, and Theology in the Gospel of John* (New York: Crossroad, 2003).

[59]Cf. D. A. Carson, *New Testament Commentary Survey*, 5th ed. (Grand Rapids: Baker, 2001).

HISTORICAL CRITICISM, LITERARY TOOLS, AND THE IMPACT OF POSTMODERNISM

We have already seen how, under the impact of certain kinds of historical criticism, biblical theology as a discipline has divided, during the last 150 years, into several mutually polarized camps. The same could be said for debates over one's entire approach to the New Testament—whether over technical matters of "introduction" (such as date, authorship, historical setting, sources, authenticity), or over the relationship between history and revelation, or developments in literary theory or epistemology, or the impact of world Christianity on the study of Scripture. In these and other domains, those who devote their lives to the study of the New Testament occupy an ever-expanding circle of positions and options. These can be charted in the treatment of an individual book or corpus of the New Testament;[60] however, when it comes to the entire New Testament, the diversity and complexity of the stances adopted can be bewildering to the student beginning to plunge into the literature. What follows, therefore, is a sketchy outline of the literary tools, approaches, and stances that have shaped New Testament study, for better and for worse, during the last century or so.[61]

Historical Criticism

The historical reconstruction deployed by F. C. Baur to realign the dating of the New Testament documents discussed above led to the historicist reductionism of Wrede. Part of this movement coagulated around the development of various critical "tools." We briefly noted the source criticism of Rudolf Bultmann. Source criticism itself, of course, should never be demonized. After all, some reflection on source criticism is transparently called up by the nature of some of the New Testament documents themselves. On almost any accounting, either 2 Peter made use of Jude, or Jude made use of 2 Peter; on almost any accounting, some kind of borrowing, of literary dependence, and thus of the use of sources, lies behind the Synoptic Gospels: they are sufficiently close that complete independence is almost impossible to maintain, yet sufficiently independent that the precise nature of the relationship among them is hotly disputed (as will be discussed in the next chapter). Luke clearly had access to written sources before he put quill to papyrus (Luke 1:1–4). But Bultmann's immensely detailed source criticism of the Synoptic Gospels, frequently extending down to assign-

---

[60]See, for example, the important work of W. Ward Gasque, *A History of the Criticism of the Acts of the Apostles*, BGBE 17 (Tübingen: Mohr-Siebeck, 1975), though it is now somewhat dated.

[61]Although most of the ways of breaking down and ordering the following literary tools and approaches to the New Testament text are not remarkable, some scholars adopt slightly different classifications.

ing half-verses and even individual words to a particular source or layer,[62] turns out, on close inspection, to be frankly unbelievable, in part because of its detail; it is almost impossible to imagine how anyone could have put together any book the way his source theories demand that the gospels were composed. More importantly, such source criticism was little interested in the ostensible sources as *atemporal* documents that were somehow brought together. Rather, each source, real or imagined, was thought to reflect the theology and outlook of different communities, or different writers, or of the same community at a different time. Doubtless his most creative resort to source criticism lay in Bultmann's handling, not of the Synoptics, but of the Gospel of John.[63]

Of course, his was not the only complex source theory, whether of the Synoptics or of the fourth gospel. Whatever the ownership or popularity of a particular theory, however, because the sources were thought to reflect various layers of tradition, these could be laid out in trajectories that would explain the *development* of doctrine. Hence, "source criticism" gave rise to "form criticism" and to "tradition criticism." Form criticism focused on the formal shape or characteristics of various gospel units—miracle stories, for instance, or certain kinds of parables—in order to infer the characteristics and even the history of the Christian communities that either shaped such material or even called it into being.[64] Tradition criticism sought to construct trajectories that were judged to unpack the development of the tradition. This in turn led to charges that such theories reduced the final authors of our gospels to mere "scissors and paste" people who cut snippets out of other documents and pasted them into the pastiche that constitutes our canonical Gospels. Partly as a reaction against this objection, "redaction criticism" came into its own. It was argued that, whatever sources the evangelists had, they did not simply cut and paste, but "edited" or "redacted" them (hence "redaction criticism") to produce gospels that would have the distinctive voice and emphases of each evangelist. Thus, the evangelists were real theologians in their own right. These and other assorted historical-critical "tools" were, on the whole, more interested, at least initially, in drawing inferences about the Christian communities that called such material into being than in the historical Jesus such materials were ostensibly describing. As a result,

---

[62]See especially his *History of the Synoptic Tradition* (New York: Harper and Row, 1963).

[63]See his *The Gospel of John* (Oxford: Blackwell, 1971).

[64]For example, by comparing the forms of the parables recorded in different gospels, Joachim Jeremias (*The Parables of Jesus* [New York: Scribner's, 1963], 113–14) developed what he called ten "laws of [parable] transmission." At one time widely influential, this work is now almost entirely eclipsed. For a useful treatment of the history of parable research, see Craig Blomberg, *Interpreting the Parables* (Downers Grove: IVP, 1990).

these tools constitute a large part of the methodological heart of the three principal "quests for the historical Jesus" detailed in the next chapter. Somewhat different but not unrelated source- and form-critical work was also carried out on the rest of the New Testament.[65]

There are still a few voices as radical as that of Bultmann, but not many,[66] and some of them have become politically polarized.[67] At the same time, even mainstream historical-critical reconstruction of the historical Jesus is remarkably minimalistic in its conclusions.[68] Inevitably, other voices, less skeptical, usefully challenge the prevailing criteria of authenticity,[69] or point out the

---

[65]By and large, source and form critics have not been as adventuresome in the NT letters as in the gospels. Even so, there are many variations. Perhaps the most extreme source critic in recent memory is J. C. O'Neill, who argues, for instance, that Paul wrote no more than about two-thirds of Galatians: see his *The Recovery of Paul's Letter to the Galatians* (London: SPCK, 1972).

[66]See, for instance, Gerd Theissen and Dagmar Winter, *The Question of Criteria: The Quest for the Plausible Jesus* (Louisville: Westminster John Knox, 2002), and the biting review by R. T. France in *Theol* 106 (2003): 272–73.

[67]One thinks, for instance, of the work of The Jesus Seminar, with its color-coded gospels measuring out the historical probability of this or that snippet. Of the several books that reflect the work of the Seminar, perhaps easiest access is found in Robert W. Funk, *A Credible Jesus: Fragments of a Vision* (Santa Rosa: Polebridge, 2002). See the negative assessments by the classical historian Philip Jenkins, *Hidden Gospels;* Michael J. Wilkins and J. P. Moreland, eds., *Jesus Under Fire: Modern Scholarship Reinvents the Historical Jesus* (Grand Rapids: Zondervan, 1995).

[68]For instance, the multivolume work of John P. Meier, *A Marginal Jew* (New York: Doubleday: 1991–). The net results of the first three massive volumes (a fourth volume, on John, is still promised) conclude that Jesus was a prophetic figure emerging from the diversity of first-century Judaism; that he was linked in some way with John the Baptist, expected God's rule, and had some ill-defined group of followers (of whom only Judas and Peter are at all known); that he performed healings and associated with outcasts; and that he interacted with other Jewish religious groups. In the Bultmannian heritage, Meier wants to protect the Christ of faith—the Christ in whom Christians believe, if they are Christians at all—from the results of his own historical probings, that is, from what he calls the Jesus of history. Implicitly, of course, this denies the incarnation—the revelation of God himself in real history.

[69]E.g., Stanley E. Porter, *The Criteria for Authenticity in Historical-Jesus Research: Previous Discussion and New Proposals*, JSNTSup 191 (Sheffield: Sheffield Academic Press, 2000). There are also countless essays and books on particular historical-critical tools: e.g., on redaction criticism, see D. A. Carson, "Redaction Criticism: On the Legitimacy and Illegitimacy of a Literary Tool," in *Scripture and Truth,* ed. D. A. Carson and John D. Woodbridge (Grand Rapids: Zondervan, 1983), 115–42; Randall K. J. Tan, "Recent Developments in Redaction Criticism: From Investigation of Textual Prehistory Back to Historical-Grammatical Exegesis?" *JETS* 44 (2001): 599–614.

importance of well-preserved oral instruction amongst Jesus' followers[70] or the role of eyewitnesses in the formation of the gospel tradition.[71] Another small but articulate group of scholars have accumulated much useful evidence that the canonical gospels were never designed for individual communities (a Matthean community, a Markan community, and so on) but were designed from the beginning to be read by all Christians,[72] which of course calls into question the common practice of identifying a particular source or stratum or form or even a gospel with a well-defined "layer" of tradition that can be tied to an equally well-defined community.

All of this work has produced a few gains. For instance, we are far more aware of the complexities of synoptic relationships than we were in the past. For the most part, we are more sensitive to the individual emphases and nuances of each canonical gospel, refusing to read them and preach them as if they came to us in a tight "Harmony of the Gospels" instead of what they are: individual books, each with distinctive accents.[73] But what strikes the contemporary reader most powerfully, as he or she first breaks into all this discussion, is its immense disarray, the extraordinary smallness of the common ground shared by today's scholars.

Literary Criticism

One of the perennial dangers of much of the historical-critical work is its atomism: it keeps focusing on tinier and tinier details in the text, and reconstructing with great erudition what some scholar thinks lies behind the text, but it does not devote much attention to the actual reading of the text *as text*.

Interest in literary devices is scarcely new. Under categories such as "metaphor" and "type," Christians have dealt with literary aspects of the text for centuries. The last few decades have produced a stream of essays and monographs on such things as irony in the fourth gospel. But perhaps more important

---

[70]See especially Birger Gerhardsson, *Memory and Manuscript: Oral Tradition and Written Transmission in Rabbinic Judaism and Early Christianity* (Grand Rapids: Eerdmans, 1998).

[71]E.g., Samuel Byrskog, *Jesus the Only Teacher: Didactic Authority and Transmission in Ancient Israel, Ancient Judaism, and the Matthean Community* (Uppsala: Almqvist & Wiksell, 1994); idem, *Story as History—History as Story: The Gospel Tradition in the Context of Ancient Oral History*, WUNT 123 (Tübingen: Mohr-Siebeck, 2000). See the useful evaluation in the review article by Peter M. Head, "The Role of Eyewitnesses in the Formation of the Gospel Tradition," *TynB* 52 (2001): 275–94.

[72]See especially Richard Bauckham, ed., *The Gospels for All Christians: Rethinking the Gospel Audiences* (Grand Rapids: Eerdmans, 1998).

[73]Even here, however, we would be remiss not to notice that Ned B. Stonehouse was advocating precisely such sensitive reading of the canonical gospels before "redaction criticism" had become a household word. See esp. his *The Witness of the Synoptic Gospels to Christ* (Grand Rapids: Baker, repr. 1979 [1944]).

are the works that deal with larger units of text. They ask what a "gospel" is, and how it is to be related to other forms of biography in the first century. They examine the narrative structure of this or that account, working through such matters as the development of the plot, what characters are being "foregrounded" and "backgrounded," where the climax of the story is, who the implied readers are. A veritable industry has arisen around the different kinds of letters that were written around the time of Paul, and the extent to which his letters fit into recognizable patterns. A book like Revelation is carefully compared with Jewish apocalyptic works written during the previous two or three centuries. The shape of one of Paul's sustained arguments is compared with the rhetoric that was taught in Greek circles from at least the time of Aristotle on.

Most of these matters are introduced a little more fully, along with appropriate bibliography, in the pages ahead. One or two examples may help. In 1983, R. Alan Culpepper published a book that proved to be a seminal treatment of the Gospel of John. Its title, *Anatomy of the Fourth Gospel: A Study in Literary Design*,[74] nicely captures the kind of literary approach being discussed here. Culpepper was not interested in source-critical or historical questions. He acknowledged that such questions have their place, but he insisted that his focus was on the literary design of the final product. Most remarkable was his choice of literary model, the nineteenth-century English novel. His book was replete with suggestive insights, but the thoughtful reader cannot help but reflect on three things: (1) The choice of controlling model is remarkably anachronistic, not least when applied to a document like the fourth gospel, which purports to bear witness to events that happened *in history*. (2) The entire effort, stimulating as it is, studiously avoids asking any historical questions or drawing any historical conclusions. The text is being studied *as a text* in the narrowest sense, without raising questions of extratextual referentiality, that is, of things or events or people outside the text to which the text may be claiming to refer. (3) At least some of the textual features that Culpepper integrates into one literary whole were being used by the source critics and historical-critical scholars to justify the existence of "seams" that suggest an awkward melding of sources. But if certain literary features are suitably explained by the way they fit into a literary narrative, how can they also serve as evidence of sources deriving from distinguishable theological communities? Or, conversely, if certain literary features in the text justify the conclusion that the fourth gospel is made of disparate sources somewhat awkwardly joined together and reflecting rather disparate theologies, how can the same evidence be read as belonging to a seamless and ahistorical narrative? In other words, although it is rarely acknowledged, some approaches to historical criticism and some approaches to literary criticism use the textual evidence in contradictory ways.

---

[74]Philadelphia: Fortress Press.

Or consider the voluminous treatments of rhetoric, especially (but certainly not exclusively) with application to the writings of Paul. In addition to numerous surveys and several magisterial volumes, hundreds of essays have been written during the past decade on the rhetoric of this or that passage. Most of them presuppose at least a nodding acquaintance with the categories of Aristotle, modified and developed by educators and orators such as Quintilian and Cicero.[75] More recently, however, it has been pointed out rather strongly that the ancient handbooks on rhetoric were designed to help *orators,* those whose material was prepared for oral delivery, not for letter writers.[76] The ancient sources do not apply the categories of rhetoric to letter writing, which is what Paul was doing. In reply, those who defend the rigorous use of the categories of rhetoric point out that ancient tractate letters were meant to be read in public, and therefore the principles of orality are sustained. The debate continues, exacerbated by the fact that although Paul was recognized as a speaker (Acts 14:11–12), he himself was suspicious of rhetoric when it became manipulative or was in danger of masking the substance of the gospel, "Jesus Christ and him crucified" (1 Cor. 2:1–5).

Both of these literary approaches to the text of the New Testament can yield suggestive insights into its meaning, the shape of its arguments, its literary coherence, and the like. On the other hand, abstracted from questions of history and truth, such approaches sometimes project a remarkable feeling of unreality. Scholars from across the widest theological spectrum deploy these approaches in various ways or qualify their deployment in various ways; these literary approaches are not independent and neutral tools but part of the interpretive matrix in which contemporary interpreters do their work.

The New Literary Criticism and the Turn to Postmodern Readings

In some ways it is difficult to draw a hard line between "literary criticism" and the "new literary criticism." Inevitably, there are points of overlap and various confusions of labeling. Yet in the main, the distinction is clear enough.

---

[75]For a comprehensive introduction to the study of rhetoric, see Heinrich Lausberg, *Handbook of Literary Rhetoric: A Foundation for Literary Study* (Leiden: Brill, 1998). For a focus on classical rhetoric and an introduction to most of the categories used by NT scholars in this regard, see Stanley E. Porter, *Handbook of Classical Rhetoric in the Hellenistic Period 330 BC–AD 400* (Leiden: Brill, 1998). For a much briefer introduction, see A. J. Hauser and D. F. Watson, *Rhetorical Criticism of the Bible*, BIS 6 (Leiden: Brill, 1994); and, with special reference to Pauline studies, R. D. Anderson, *Ancient Rhetorical Theory and Paul*, CBET 18, 2nd ed. (Leuven: Peeters, 1999).

[76]See the essays collected by Stanley E. Porter and Dennis E. Stamps, eds., *The Rhetorical Interpretation of Scripture*, JSNTSup 180 (Sheffield: Sheffield Academic Press, 1999).

It may be useful to begin with an influential book by Hans W. Frei.[77] Frei argues that as liberal historical criticism grew stronger in the eighteenth and nineteenth centuries, scholars became less interested in what the Bible actually *says* and more interested in that which (they argued) lay *behind* the text—that is, what *really* happened. Conservative rebuttals fell into the same trap: everyone was arguing about the alleged history (real or imagined) *behind* the text and were no longer thinking in the categories of the text itself. Without wanting to deny that such historical questions are important, Frei argues that what the church must do is immerse itself in the text. After all, Christians before the rise of historical criticism believed that God himself was encountering them in the text. Similarly, today's Christians will find their imagination and understanding illumined by the text; they will worry less about historical re-creations, will encounter God, and will link themselves with believers before the eighteenth century.

Clearly Frei's approach is strongly *text-centered*. But what he fails to mention is that Christians before the rise of the more skeptical forms of historical criticism not only immersed themselves in the text (in this sense he is right: they were text-centered, believing that God was encountered there), but they also believed *that the text told them the truth*. Thus, the charge that conservatives and liberals alike at the end of the eighteenth century and throughout the nineteenth century focused too much attention on arguments over the ostensible reality *behind* the text and *not on the text itself* is slightly manipulative. At their best, the conservatives were not so much trying to draw attention *away* from the text to what lay *behind* it, as they were attempting to justify the view that the text was telling the truth about extratextual reality. However weighty this criticism, it has been largely ignored. As a result, this particular brand of text-centered reading, sometimes identified as "the Yale School," finds many able exponents, the most influential of whom is George Lindbeck.[78]

This is not the only kind of text-centered study that rightly belongs to the "new" literary criticism. One kind, popular three or four decades ago but now largely in eclipse, is *structuralism,* which "is distinguished by its rejection of those traditional notions according to which literature 'expresses' an author's meaning or 'reflects' reality. Instead, the 'text' is seen as an objective structure activating various codes and conventions which are independent of author, reader, and external reality." Indeed, structural criticism "is less interested in interpreting what literary works mean than in explaining *how* they can mean

---

[77]*The Eclipse of Biblical Narrative: A Study in Eighteenth and Nineteenth Century Hermeneutics* (New Haven: Yale University Press, 1974).

[78]Perhaps Lindbeck's most seminal work is *The Nature of Doctrine: Religion and Theology in a Post-liberal Age* (Philadelphia: Westminster, 1984)—though he has written a string of important essays and books since then.

what they mean; that is, in showing what implicit rules and conventions are operating in a given work."[79]

This movement led in turn to *deconstruction*. Deconstructionists are no less text-centered, but they add to the brew a radical skepticism. Convinced that no text is stable or coherent, deconstructionists argue that all texts are indeterminate in meaning and inevitably contain inherent contradictions. That leaves the thoughtful reader with only two alternatives: abandon any search for meaning in texts, which is tantamount to abandoning reading itself, or find meaning in the interplay between the reader and contradictory (though frequently evocative) ideas sparked by a text. Small wonder that Vanhoozer writes, "Deconstruction is not a method of interpretation but a method for undoing interpretations, for exposing readings as functions of various ideological forces."[80] In practice, this means that many readings of texts undertaken by deconstructionists have served the interests of overthrowing perceived injustices and inequities, based as they are on particular ideologies that must themselves be overthrown. But strictly speaking, this end is not achieved by finding such reforming pressures taught *by* the texts, but by finding them generated by the firm resolve to expose the alleged inconsistencies in the text, and in the interplay between such textual phenomena and the deconstructionist interpreters. In France, where it was born, deconstruction has now largely been eclipsed, but it still commands widespread allegiance in certain circles in North America. In any case, deconstruction locates more and more of the "meaning," not in the text itself, but in the readers, or in the readers' interaction with the text, and thus in some gray space between text and reader. If historical criticism tried to get at the historical reality *behind* the text, and various literary criticisms tried so to focus on the text that increasingly the text was cut off from all history, the end result of deconstruction is to locate shifting meanings *in front of* the text, in the direction of the readers themselves.

Thus, deconstruction has been one of the inspirations behind *reader-response theory*. This approach is neither author-centered (like most classical literary and historical criticism) nor text-centered, but reader-centered. In fact, there are several competing reader-response theories. One theory locates virtually all the meaning in the individual interpreter; the text is no more than some kind of stimulus. Another theory demands that more attention be paid to the social context of readers: readers interpret things out of the shared literary and cultural traditions of a particular social group, a group whose shared outlook generates a socially constructed competence. Thus, texts come to have shared meanings for people in a specified social group, but no other independent claim.

> *Deconstructionists are no less text-centered than structuralists, but they add to the brew a radical skepticism.*

---

[79]C. Baldick, ed., *Concise Dictionary of Literary Terms* (Oxford: Oxford University Press, 1991).

[80]Kevin J. Vanhoozer, "The Reader in New Testament Interpretation," in *Hearing the New Testament*, ed. Joel B. Green (Grand Rapids: Eerdmans, 1995), 313–14.

Another sort of reader-response theory focuses on the tensions between the individual and the group from which he or she springs or on the interactions between the readers and the text.

These and other approaches are often cumulatively labeled "postmodern readings." The term *postmodern* is notoriously slippery, of course, but it is useful nevertheless. If it is applied first and foremost to the domain of epistemology—the study of how we come to know anything, or think we know anything—then the term is useful. Unlike earlier *modernism,* which by and large was convinced that human beings could learn the utter and objective truth about reality and thus gain certainty and clarity of thought and that all of this enterprise was a good thing, postmodernism takes quite a different tack. Postmoderns are convinced that because we human beings are so small, our knowledge so microscopic, and our social frame of reference so limited, our putative knowledge can at best be never more than provisional. In the strongest forms of postmodernism, all human knowledge is in some sense a social construct and therefore provides no clear or objective knowledge of the objective world at all. Claims to certainty must be dismissed as arrogant bigotry. Indeed, in postmodern perspective, the univocal meaning cherished by modernists is narrow and confining. Surely it is far better to encourage a multiplicity of interpretations and approaches, none of them necessarily "right" or "wrong," "true" or "false," but all of them productive, thoughtful, fruitful, a reflection of a (legitimate) interaction between some reader or other and the text. Postmodern readers (we are told) are less interested in the hard lines drawn by truth and error, and more interested in the soft lines drawn by fuzziness and interpretive possibilities. They dislike exclusion, especially any view that says another view is wrong, and they admire inclusion, even of mutually incompatible ideas. They like possibilities and vistas and are suspicious of boundaries and of any insistence that there is such a thing as heresy, just as there is such a thing as orthodoxy.

In the last decade of the twentieth century, these sorts of approaches to the study of the New Testament produced books with titles like: *Reading Sacred Texts Through American Eyes,*[81] *Deconstructing the New Testament,*[82] *Mark and Luke in Poststructuralist Perspectives,*[83] *Poststructuralism and the New Testament: Derrida and Foucault at the Foot of the Cross,*[84] and *Liberating Exegesis.*[85] Schol-

---

[81]Charles Mabee, *Reading Sacred Texts Through American Eyes: Biblical Interpretation as Cultural Critique* (Macon: Mercer University Press, 1991).

[82]David Seeley, *Deconstructing the New Testament,* BIS 5 (Leiden: Brill, 1994).

[83]Stephen D. Moore, *Mark and Luke in Poststructuralist Perspectives: Jesus Begins to Write* (New Haven: Yale University Press, 1992).

[84]Stephen D. Moore, *Poststructuralism and the New Testament: Derrida and Foucault at the Foot of the Cross* (Minneapolis: Fortress Press, 1994).

[85]Christopher Rowland and Mark Corner, *Liberating Exegesis: The Challenge of Liberation Theology to Biblical Studies* (Louisville: Westminster John Knox, 1989).

arly conferences encourage participants to interpret biblical texts out of their own experience, without regard for whether any particular reading is "right" or "wrong"; indeed, such categories, it is argued, betray an old-fashioned modernist approach. A certain reading may be "right" or "wrong" for one particular group, but certainly not for everyone. Among the interesting stances that this creativity has generated is a flurry of books and essays on reading texts from a "postcolonial" perspective,[86] and a now voluminous literature on feminist readings.[87]

A brief introduction cannot properly evaluate these multiplying approaches to reading the New Testament. Some of the developments described here will turn out to be passing fancies without enduring relevance. For instance, one writer comments, "Structuralism may turn out to be for literary criticism what James Joyce's *Finnegans Wake* was for the novel—an experimental dead end. While the structure of Biblical books and narratives is clearly of crucial importance for their interpretation, we have yet to be convinced that structuralism is a useful heuristic tool for identifying such structures."[88] On the other hand, there is an obvious and important element in postmodern epistemology that must not be denied. None of us interprets anything from an entirely neutral stance. One would have to enjoy the attribute of omniscience to be *entirely* objective. Insofar as it reminds us that we are finite, and that our findings, at some level, must always be qualified by our limitations, postmodernism has been a salutary advance. It has been especially useful in checking the arrogance of modernist claims. The problem is that in the hands of many interpreters, postmodernism demands a nasty antithesis: *either* we claim we can know objective truth exhaustively, *or* we insist that our finitude means we cannot know objective truth and therefore cannot truly "know" reality. Since finite human beings can never know anything omnisciently, only the second alternative is defensible. In that case, all our "knowledge" is a social or a personal construct; the only "reality" we can know is the one we construct.

There is a sense, of course, in which this latter claim is transparently obvious: the only "reality" we can know is the one we construct. But the crucial issue

---

[86]E.g., Fernando F. Segovia, *Decolonizing Biblical Studies: A View from the Margins* (Maryknoll: Orbis, 2000); Heikki Räisänen, Elisabeth Schüssler Fiorenza, R. S. Sugirtharajah, Krister Stendahl, and James Barr, *Reading the Bible in the Global Village: Helsinki* (Atlanta: SBL, 2000); R. S. Sugirtharajah, *Postcolonial Reconfigurations: An Alternative Way of Reading the Bible and Doing Theology* (St. Louis: Chalice, 2003).

[87]As a mere sample from a very wide range, see the multivolume and growing series, The Feminist Companion to the Bible (Sheffield: Sheffield Academic Press, 1993–).

[88]Gordon J. Thomas, "Telling a Hawk from a Handsaw? An Evangelical Response to the New Literary Criticism," *EQ* 71 (1999): 48. Cf. similarly, Peter Cotterell and Max Turner, *Linguistics and Biblical Interpretation* (London: SPCK, 1989), 30.

is this: Can this "reality" that we ourselves "know" be tightly aligned with objective reality? In other words, even though we finite human beings can never enjoy omniscient knowledge, can we not legitimately claim to know some objective things truly, even if we do not know them perfectly, exhaustively? After all, this accords with our experience: in almost any field we can get to know some things better than we did before, and this suggests that our knowledge is improving. In principle, it can improve to the point that we may legitimately claim that we know (even if it is not omniscient knowledge) some things truly. And if more or different evidence arrives later and prompts us to change our minds, that too is part of the improvement, the approach to true knowledge.[89] We are most definitely not squeezed into the absolute antithesis: either we have perfect knowledge, or else none of our "knowledge" has any more significance than any other social construct.

This preliminary response deserves six brief further observations. *First,* as has often been noted, those who insist most vociferously on the relativity of all human knowledge without recognizing how our constructions can and do approach knowledge of the objective, place themselves in a terrible dilemma. For when they insist that all knowledge is a *mere* social construct, then they admit that their knowledge that all knowledge is a mere social construct is also a mere social construct—so why should we give the claim any more credence than the contrary claim? *Second,* there is more than a little irony in the fact that many interpreters of the New Testament who claim the independence of their own interpretive grid as their epistemological right, then attempt to influence others that they are right and even denigrate alternative views. To cite but one example, Neil Elliott insists on the rightness of his reading of Paul's letters, which, he thinks, should be used as a manifesto for political action—and part of Elliott's rhetoric is to inveigh against various theological understandings of Paul.[90] *Third,* Scripture itself speaks of the knowledge of Christians in a straightforward way. John says that he writes his first letter so that his readers may *know* that they have eternal life (1 John 5:13). Luke tells Theophilus that he is writing so that the latter "may *know* the certainty of the things [he has] been taught" (Luke 1:3–4). Sometimes the knowledge in view is personal (e.g., Phil. 3:10, "I want to know Christ"); sometimes it is experiential (e.g., Phil. 3:10, "I want to know . . . the power of his resurrection and participation in his sufferings"); and sometimes it is propositional (e.g., John 8:32, "you will know the truth"; John 20:31, the fourth gospel is written so that its readers may believe *that* certain

---

[89]Elsewhere, borrowing language from Karl Popper, this has been called the "asymptotic approach." See D. A. Carson, *The Gagging of God: Christianity Confronts Pluralism* (Grand Rapids: Zondervan, 1996), 121–22.

[90]Neil Elliott, *Liberating Paul: The Justice of God and the Politics of the Apostle* (Maryknoll: Orbis, 1994), 73 and passim.

things are true). The Christian gospel, the good news, has propositional content that is to be passed on from one believer to another. That is why it can be referred to as "the faith that the Lord has once for all entrusted to us, his people" (Jude 3). Though "truth" in Scripture can refer to more than propositional truth, propositional truth certainly lies within its embrace. So too strong an insistence that we cannot know the truth may assuage postmodern sensibilities, but it is a long step removed from Scripture itself. *Fourth,* for the same reason, the strongest voices in the Yale School, to which reference has already been made, are vaguely troubling. For it is not enough to fill our minds with biblical ideas, vocabulary, and images, unless we think that by so doing we are being led to think true thoughts about what is actually *there*—that the Bible actually refers to people, events, and even to God himself, as living outside the Bible, and that the Bible bears *true* witness to them (even though, transparently, it cannot bear exhaustive witness to them, or produce omniscient knowledge of these extra-biblical realities among those who read about them in the Bible's pages). We are not saved by biblical *ideas:* that is a narrowly intellectualist approach. We are saved by the God and the biblical events to which the Bible *refers,* bearing true witness. *Fifth,* these reflections suggest that postmodernism has swung the pendulum much too far. In the words of Brenda Watson,

> [Where a postmodern] sees the need for articulating the partiality and provisional nature of any knowledge we claim, I see the equal need for articulating what are strongly persuasive grounds for regarding as a secure basis for Christian faith—provided the enterprise is shorn of non-essential and unjustified notions of dogmatism or of rigidity.
>
> We live not by our doubts but by our certainties, however much later experience and fresh evidence may require them to be modified. And even then it is new certainties which act as the trigger in replacing the old ones.
>
> Released from being obliged to accept the tyranny of the naturalist presupposition and its progeny, a more confident yet appropriately flexible approach to certainty may be forthcoming. It will then be easier to accept that balance between complete ignorance and complete knowledge which each person has to reach for themselves and constantly monitor and modify according to their life experience.[91]

Failure to get this right means that either we will domesticate the Bible by our rigid and often merely traditional categories, or we will domesticate the Bible by insisting that every interpretive stance has as much merit as every other interpretive stance. In neither case will the Bible do its truly transforming work. And *sixth,* these reflections suggest that a responsible approach to the New Testament,

---

[91]Brenda Watson, "To Know, Or Not To Know? Re-assessing Historical Skepticism," *Theol* 103 (2000): 195–96.

and indeed to the whole Bible, will not only try to come to grips with the fact that this is a *text* and therefore all its textual characteristics must be understood, but that it conveys a grand story, and that although it can include parables like those of Jesus and a fable like that of Jotham, it purports to tell us some true things about God, his people, his enemies, our origins, and our destiny, and that this story line demands that, among other approaches, we remain sensitive to the *salvation-historical*[92] unfolding of this drama.

Approaches Based on the Selection of Background Material

Even while a substantial number of contemporary New Testament scholars operate out of the reader-response and postmodern matrices just described, several other groups are more interested in what happened *in history*. Many of these attempt to understand the New Testament documents by reading them against the background of particular first-century movements. Ideally, this sort of study is salutary: we are far more likely to avoid introducing hopeless anachronisms into our study of the New Testament if we are well informed about how words were used in the first century and what movements and thought patterns competed with Christian claims or fed into them. Moreover, when such study is done well, it avoids the feeling of unreality and disconnectedness that permeates some of the more subjective approaches. Nevertheless, here too there are several minefields through which one must carefully navigate.

First, the first century saw Israel at a confluence of huge cultural streams. Rooted in the Hebrew canon and Aramaic paraphrases (the Targums), and knowing itself to belong to streams of Judaism that stretched back for centuries, Israel was also part of a minor province in the mighty Roman Empire, whose official and military language was Latin and whose lingua franca was primarily Greek. Doubtless the New Testament writers most commonly cite what we call the Old Testament, but Paul can also quote minor pagan poets; and in any case, once the gospel was being preached in a predominantly Gentile world, inevitably the questions raised and the challenges to be faced ensured that the good news about Jesus the Messiah would be shaped to prove coherent and convincing in such environments. Thus, both streams can lay claim to being part of the legitimate "background" to the New Testament. Because of the enormous range of such background material, however, inevitably some scholars become experts in the Greco-Roman sources, and others in the Jewish sources. Very few have equal standing in both streams, and many books focus on one stream at the

---

[92]The term is notoriously slippery but cannot be unpacked here. One of the most informed treatments is that of Robert W. Yarbrough, "The 'heilsgeschichtliche' Perspective in Modern New Testament Theology" (Ph.D. dissertation, University of Aberdeen, 1985). A revised form of the dissertation is *The Salvation-Historical Fallacy? Re-assessing the History of New Testament Theology* (Leiderdorp: Deo, 2004).

expense of the other.[93] Moreover, even within one of these streams, some scholars focus on the textual material but know relatively little about the allied archaeology; others may know a good deal about the archaeology but have a more rudimentary grasp of the textual sources. To make matters still more complicated, some parts of the first-century populace, not least in Galilee, were at home in both worlds, and each of the two streams penetrated the other. Martin Hengel made this point most tellingly three decades ago.[94]

Second, even within these three bodies of opinion—that trace, respectively, a Jewish, Greco-Roman, or somehow merged stream—there are many shades of opinion. On the Greco-Roman side, for instance, some argue that the closest background to Jesus' sayings lies in Cynic thought. A generation or two ago, many scholars insisted that Gnosticism is older than Christianity and is, in fact, the religious movement out of which Christianity, as we know it, grew. Other scholars have focused on Stoic or Sophist elements to explain 1 and 2 Corinthians. All sides wrestle with the extent to which Paul self-consciously used the rhetorical categories that were common in the educated Greco-Roman world. Meanwhile, on the Jewish side, some scholars establish links between the New Testament documents and the Old Testament, while others focus on one part or another of the literature of Second Temple Judaism: the Dead Sea Scrolls, perhaps, or apocalyptic literature, or the writings of Philo, or some part of the vast corpus of rabbinic Judaism. In some instances complex issues of dating and provenance generate disparate schools of scholars with highly diverse opinions as to the extent to which a particular corpus may legitimately be used as background (e.g., the rabbinic literature).

The *third* minefield to be negotiated is the manner in which such studies of background sources may or may not be legitimately used to shed light on what the New Testament is saying. In other words, it is possible that by forcing a New Testament document onto the Procrustean bed of some particular ostensible background, a kind of interpretive rape takes place. This is what Samuel Sandmel rather

---

[93]E.g., compare F. Gerald Downing, *Making Sense in (and of) the First Christian Century,* JSNTSup 197 (Sheffield: Sheffield Academic Press, 2000), and Peter J. Tomson, *'If this be from Heaven . . .': Jesus and the New Testament Authors in their Relationship to Judaism* (Sheffield: Sheffield Academic Press, 2001).

[94]*Judaism and Hellenism: Studies in Their Encounter in Palestine During the Early Hellenistic Period,* 2 vols. (London: SCM, 1974). More recently, a collection of essays edited by Troels Engberg-Pedersen, *Paul Beyond the Judaism/Hellenism Divide* (Louisville: Westminster John Knox, 2001), despite its many seminal suggestions, goes too far in the attempt to obliterate distinctions between the two heritages, as if there were no distinction to be made whatsoever. Some of the argumentation in the book is in transparent and visceral reaction against any claim that the Old Testament and Judaism constitute the fundamental soil from which Christianity springs.

shrewdly labeled "parallelomania" several decades ago:[95] apparent parallels to New Testament texts may so domesticate those texts that the meaning of the "parallel" is read back into the New Testament, making it impossible to hear what the New Testament is actually saying. For instance, the major commentary on Galatians by Hans Dieter Betz[96] interprets the letter almost entirely from the matrix of Greco-Roman "parallels" of disputed relevance: by and large their thought-forms and assumptions succeed only in distorting Paul's thought.[97] The recent New Testament theology by Georg Strecker,[98] rather amazingly, reads Pauline Christology against the background of a pre-Christian gnostic-redeemer myth, a category that has been repeatedly shown to be post-Christian.[99] The so-called "new perspective on Paul" (discussed later in this volume), though it has earlier roots, was precipitated in large part when E. P. Sanders argued that the various Judaisms in Palestine of the first century all adopted a pattern of religion that he labeled "covenantal nomism."[100] No one disputes that Sanders identified certain important elements in first-century Judaism and that he corrected some important misjudgments of earlier scholars. But because he placed *all* of the relevant Palestinian Jewish background into one conceptual bucket, his theory exercised hegemonic control over the exegesis of Paul, especially in Anglo-American circles. That hegemonic control is now losing its grip, precisely because several have shown that there are important elements in first-century Palestinian Jewish thought that do not fit into Sanders's grid—and this is again freeing up the exegesis of Paul from a rather narrow and stifling paradigm that did not always listen very attentively to Paul himself.[101] Sometimes the nature of the ostensible background is itself disputed, and in any case, it should not be allowed to control the exegesis of the New

---

[95]"Parallelomania," *JBL* 81 (1962): 2–13.

[96]*Galatians: A Commentary on Paul's Letter to the Churches in Galatia,* Hermeneia (Philadelphia: Fortress Press, 1979).

[97]See esp. Philip H. Kern, *Rhetoric and Galatians: Assessing an Approach to Paul's Epistle to the Galatians,* SNTSMS 101 (Cambridge: Cambridge University Press, 1998).

[98]*Theology of the New Testament.* See also the review article by Simon Gathercole, *Themelios* 28/3 (2003): 40–48.

[99]Of the many books on this subject, one of the clearest is that of Edwin A. Yamauchi, *Pre-Christian Gnosticism: A Survey of the Proposed Evidences,* 2nd ed. (Grand Rapids: Baker, 1983). Half a century ago, there was somewhat more of an excuse for C. H. Dodd, *The Interpretation of the Fourth Gospel* (Cambridge: Cambridge University Press, 1953), when he mistakenly read John against the background of the Hermetica (a subset of the second-century gnostic movement). But there is very little excuse today.

[100]*Paul and Palestinian Judaism* (Philadelphia: Fortress Press, 1977).

[101]From the voluminous literature, see Seyoon Kim, *Paul and the New Perspective: Second Thoughts on the Origin of Paul's Gospel* (Grand Rapids: Eerdmans, 2002); D. A. Carson, Peter T. O'Brien, and Mark Seifrid, eds., *Justification and Variegated Nomism,* 2 vols. (Tübingen: Mohr-Siebeck/Grand Rapids: Baker, 2001–4).

Testament.[102] The first obligation of the interpreter of the New Testament is to try to understand the thoughts of these documents on their own terms.

But none of these warnings means we can dispense with the study of backgrounds. One should be as wary of "parallelophobia" as of parallelomania, since in the providence of God the New Testament documents were written in concrete historical circumstances in which they are embedded. One need only reflect, for instance, on the considerable light shed on Revelation 2–3 by the archaeological and textual probing of backgrounds undertaken by gifted scholars,[103] or the remarkable volumes in the series The Book of Acts in Its First-Century Setting,[104] or the comprehensive survey of background thought on resurrection, life after death, and immortality in N. T. Wright's recent and thorough examination of the resurrection of Jesus Christ,[105] to discern how impoverished we would be if there were no such research.

Social-Scientific Approaches

Social-scientific criticism is deeply indebted both to sociology and to cultural anthropology. Apart from isolated studies, its rise as a burgeoning field with a multiplying literature goes back only thirty or forty years. For the first decade and a half, it tended to apply specific sociological theories to the dynamics of the movements found in the New Testament. For instance, John Gager applied contemporary theories of millenarian movements, functions of social conflict, and cognitive dissonance to Paul's conversion and the experiences of the Pauline churches in the New Testament.[106] In his approach to the New Testament, Gerd Theissen leaned heavily not only on the sociological approaches of Weber but on Freudian psychology.[107] In other words, these sorts of

---

[102]E.g., see the dispute between Bruce Winter (*Seek the Welfare of the City* [Grand Rapids: Eerdmans, 1995]; idem, *Philo and Paul Among the Sophists*, SNTSMS 96 [Cambridge: Cambridge University Press, 1997]), who argues that much of 1 and 2 Corinthians should be interpreted against the background of a rather early Sophist movement in Corinth, and his most articulate critic, Jerome Murphy-O'Connor, in his review article in *RevBib* 110 (2003): 428–33.

[103]See, for instance, Colin J. Hemer, *The Letters to The Seven Churches in Their Local Settings*, JSNTSup 11 (Sheffield: JSOT Press, 1986 [repr. Grand Rapids: Eerdmans, 2001]).

[104]Grand Rapids: Eerdmans, 1993–.

[105]N. T. Wright, *The Resurrection of the Son of God* (Minneapolis: Fortress Press, 2003).

[106]John G. Gager, *Kingdom and Community: The Social World of Early Christianity* (Englewood Cliffs, N.J.: Prentice-Hall, 1975).

[107]Gerd Theissen, *The Sociology of Early Palestinian Christianity* (Philadelphia: Fortress Press, 1978); idem, *Social Reality and the Early Christians* (Edinburgh: T. & T. Clark, 1993); idem, *Psychological Aspects of Pauline Theology* (Edinburgh: T. & T. Clark, 1987).

approaches depended on adopting the kinds of global categories advanced by (largely) European sociology (the grand theories of Max Weber, Emile Durkheim, Clifford Geertz, and Mary Douglas, among others). Perhaps the most careful of the books in this line is Wayne Meeks's *The First Urban Christians,*[108] where he avoids careless transfer of contemporary social categories such as "middle class" to the first-century setting but attempts instead to isolate the social dynamics applicable at the time, including categories of status, honor, benefaction, and the like.

In some ways, Meeks's book anticipates the slight transition in focus and terminology that took place around 1986.[109] After that date, "social-scientific criticism" came increasingly to be used of a network of approaches that owed more to cultural anthropology than to European sociology. Now there is much more emphasis on personal and group relationships within a particular historical and social setting. Such an approach wants to know, for instance, how a father or mother would view his or her role in a first-century family in Ephesus, why first-century itinerant preachers could expect hospitality, what the obligations were between employers and employees, how the patronage system worked, what ingredients were tied to the honor/shame culture of the day, how a local assembly, a local church, would view itself, and be viewed, within the larger social matrix, and much more of the same.[110] Clearly such questions are, broadly speaking, historical, but only recently have they received the attention they deserve. At least they are avoiding the solipsism of text-based studies that entirely ignore the extratextual history.

---

[108]New Haven: Yale University Press, 1983.

[109]Effected, it appears, by the essay of J. H. Elliott, "Social-Scientific Criticism of the New Testament: More on Methods and Models," *Semeia* 35 (1986): 1–33.

[110]Among the more useful surveys are David G. Horrell, *Social-Scientific Approaches to New Testament Interpretation* (Edinburgh: T. & T. Clark, 1999) and Anthony J. Blasi, Jean Duhaime, and Paul-André Turcotte, eds., *Handbook of Early Christianity: Social Science Approaches* (Walnut Creek/Lanham: Altamira Press, 2003). Representative works include Bruce J. Malina, *The New Testament World: Insights from Cultural Anthropology* (Atlanta: John Knox, 1991); idem, *The Social World of Jesus and the Gospels* (London: Routledge, 1996); Jerome H. Neyrey, ed., *The Social World of Luke-Acts: Models for Interpretation* (Peabody: Hendrickson, 1991); idem, *Honor and Shame in the Gospel of Matthew* (Louisville: Westminster John Knox, 1998); Richard L. Rohrbaugh, "'Social Location of Thought' as a Heuristic Construct in New Testament Study," *JSNT* 30 (1987): 103–9; idem, ed., *The Social Sciences and New Testament Interpretation* (Peabody: Hendrickson, 1996); Vernon K. Robbins, *Exploring the Texture of Texts: A Guide to Socio-Rhetorical Interpretation* (Valley Forge: Trinity Press International, 1996)—which integrates some of the strengths of social-science criticism with some of the strengths of rhetorical analysis. Several of the commentaries by Ben Witherington III run down the same avenue.

As helpful as these approaches are, to some extent they have achieved, in the hands of some interpreters, their own regrettable hegemonic authority. By and large, scholars who focus on the social dynamics of the individuals and groups represented in the New Testament are at their best when they help us understand some of the givens and presuppositions of first-century life and outlook in this or that Roman province. Such study sheds useful light that helps us interpret the New Testament in its own historical (and therefore social) setting. They are at their worst when they give the impression that the horizontal axis of social dynamics is a sufficient explanation of New Testament texts, when the supernatural and revelatory dimensions are either systematically ignored or specifically disowned, when specific social theory is treated as a transcultural control that may not itself be questioned, when the values of today's Mediterranean or Palestinian world are read back into the first century without rigorous questioning—and above all, when the text of the New Testament, far from being illuminated by such study, is ignored or controverted or domesticated on the grounds of the external model.[111]

Language and Linguistic Approaches

Although the last century witnessed a decline in the number of people with a working knowledge of the primary languages important to New Testament study (Greek, of course, but also Hebrew, Aramaic, and Latin, followed by the other languages into which the New Testament was first translated), there have nevertheless been some remarkable advances. At the end of the nineteenth century and the beginning of the twentieth, the discovery of many colloquial Greek papyri helped to explain the differences in Greek syntax and vocabulary that anyone could discern between the New Testament documents and the works of Homer (eighth century B.C.) or the works of the "classical" period (fifth and fourth centuries B.C.). Of the numerous books that flowed out of these findings, the one by C. F. D. Moule probably still circulates most widely.[112] Similar finds have more recently enriched the study of Aramaic.

But what attracts attention here is a handful of linguistic and linguistic-philosophical advances. The three mentioned below are far from exhaustive; they merely represent a plethora of developments.

First, continual advance is being achieved in the study of words—words as they are found in lexica ("lexical semantics"), and words as they are actually used in concrete contexts (a branch of "pragmatics"). A recent volume by John

---

[111]See especially the essay by Kenneth Berding, "The Hermeneutical Framework of Social-Scientific Criticism: How Much Can Evangelicals Get Involved?" *EQ* 75 (2003): 3–22.

[112]*An Idiom-Book of New Testament Greek* (Cambridge: Cambridge University Press, 1953).

Lee has provided us with a highly competent history of New Testament lexicography.[113] In particular, Lee demonstrates how linguistic awareness is increasingly, and rightly, taking us away from thinking of the meaning of words in the categories of English "glosses" (i.e., quick translation equivalents). The latest English edition of the Bauer lexicon[114] is certainly an improvement on its predecessor in this regard, though doubtless there is more to be learned. An ongoing project in Australia is making available to a wider readership the scattered publication of papyrological finds that may have some bearing on our understanding of New Testament words.[115] And an innovative lexicon prepared by Johannes P. Louw and Eugene A. Nida organizes the Greek words to be studied, not in mere alphabetical order, but in "semantic fields"; that is, it groups words together that have similar or overlapping domains of meaning.[116]

Second, although linguistic theory falls into several disparate camps, one of the more productive of these camps has carefully distinguished *Aktionsart* (well known to every seminary student who has taken even the first year of Greek) from "aspect" in the verbal system (not the *kind* of action, but the author's choice of how to envisage the action).[117] The results challenge not a little of what traditionalists think that each tense of the Greek system actually grammaticalizes. With only occasional exceptions, this work, though some of it has been around for decades, has not yet broken into the general run of New Testament scholarship, though breaks are appearing in the dikes of partition commonly erected between disciplines.

---

[113]John A. L. Lee, *A History of New Testament Lexicography*, SBG 8 (New York: Peter Lang, 2003).

[114]Walter Bauer, Frederick W. Danker, W. F. Arndt, and F. W. Gingrich, *A Greek-English Lexicon of the New Testament and other Early Christian Literature*, 3rd ed. (Chicago: University of Chicago Press, 2000), now commonly abbreviated BDAG.

[115]This is the series of volumes titled *New Documents Illustrating Early Christianity*, edited by various people. The series began in 1983, and so far has reached volume 9. It is published by Macquarie University in Australia (more recently by Eerdmans in the United States).

[116]Johannes P. Louw and Eugene A. Nida, eds., *Greek-English Lexicon of the New Testament Based on Semantic Domains*, 2 vols. (New York: UBS, 1988).

[117]See especially Stanley E. Porter, *Verbal Aspect in the Greek of the New Testament with Reference to Tense and Mood*, SBG 1 (New York: Peter Lang, 1989); idem, *Idioms of the Greek New Testament* (Sheffield: JSOT Press, 1992); Buist M. Fanning, *Verbal Aspect in New Testament Greek* (Oxford: Oxford University Press, 1990); K. L. McKay, *A New Syntax of the Verb in New Testament Greek: An Aspectual Approach*, SBG 5 (New York: Peter Lang, 1994). These theoretical treatments are increasingly being tested on contiguous texts: e.g., Rodney J. Decker, *Temporal Deixis of the Greek Verb in the Gospel of Mark with Reference to Verbal Aspect*, SBG 10 (New York: Peter Lang, 2001).

Third, "speech act theory" has brought major advances to how words in text work. Words in contexts do not simply *mean* something, they may *do* something. Speech act theory springs from the seminal work of J. L. Austin,[118] but it has been developed in a large body of erudite literature,[119] and has now become part of the arsenal of every New Testament scholar.[120] This certainly does not mean that every subtheory or interpretive grid erected by speech act theorists is unquestioningly adopted—far from it. What it means is that every informed reader of the New Testament is a little more sensitive to the exigencies of thinking through how words function, what they actually perform, as well as what they mean. When Jesus cries to the storm, "Cease! Be still!" we may be misled if we think that the words themselves are primarily meant to convey some deep theological truth. We need to think through Jesus' intention in uttering the words and to mark their effect. Words *do* things as well as *teach* things. And that fact itself requires the reader to discern a new level of meaning as well as, vicariously in imagination, to grasp what the people described in the narrative experienced.

CONCLUDING REFLECTIONS

As long as it is, this chapter, which ventures to cover the distance from the first writing of the New Testament documents to contemporary study of them, cannot be more than a sketch. Several overwhelming impressions are conveyed by developments during the last century or so. *First,* an extraordinary diversity of approaches, methods, presuppositions, and conclusions now attends the study of the New Testament.[121] *Second,* the presentation here has been

---

[118]Especially in his work *How To Do Things with Words,* 2nd ed. (Oxford: Oxford University Press, 1975 [1962]). Austin distinguishes the *locutionary act* of an utterance (i.e., what it means, made up of sense and reference) from its *illocutionary act* (i.e., "the performance of an act *in* saying something as opposed to performance of an act *of* saying something") and its *perlocutionary act* (i.e., the consequential effects on the feelings, thoughts, or actions, whether intentional or otherwise, of the speaker or the audience).

[119]See esp. Richard S. Briggs, *Words in Action: Speech Act Theory and Biblical Interpretation* (Edinburgh: T. & T. Clark, 2001), and Kevin J. Vanhoozer, *Is There a Meaning in This Text? The Bible, the Reader, and the Morality of Literary Knowledge* (Grand Rapids: Zondervan, 1998).

[120]See, for instance, the use to which it is put in the important commentary by Anthony C. Thiselton, *The First Epistle to the Corinthians,* NIGTC (Grand Rapids: Eerdmans, 2000).

[121]One may usefully scan the four volumes that have appeared in the Renewing Biblical Interpretation series: vol. 1, Craig Bartholomew, Colin Greene, and Karl Möller, eds., *Renewing Biblical Interpretation* (Grand Rapids: Zondervan, 2000); vol. 2, idem, *After Pentecost: Language and Biblical Interpretation* (Grand Rapids: Zondervan, 2001);

somewhat schematized. In order to attain some degree of clarity, we have described some methods and movements piecemeal. In reality, many scholars mingle their approaches to produce hybrids that are both interesting and fruitful. For instance, there are social-science approaches and there are linguistic approaches, but there are also now sociolinguistic approaches.[122] *Third,* with only limited exceptions, this chapter has focused on Western study of the New Testament. But of course the New Testament, not to say the earliest centuries of the Christian church, was not characteristically Western.[123] Today there is a rapidly multiplying church in many parts of the world, and although the depth of scholarship in these fast-growing arenas is still a bit thin, new journals are being published every year, usually in languages that most Westerners cannot read. Insofar as it is possible to probe this literature, one is struck both by the commonality of historic, confessional Christianity, even if it has local flavor, and by the fresh questions that are sometimes asked by people with limited exposure to the Western heritage. And *fourth,* most of the approaches and historical developments surveyed in this chapter have had some value, but almost all of them have sometimes been deployed irresponsibly, primarily by claiming some kind of near-exclusive methodological control, or by being married to deep-seated rationalism or even philosophical naturalism, both of which find it difficult to read the New Testament sympathetically on its own terms.

One of the entailments of this burgeoning diversity of approaches is that the "introductions" to the New Testament written in the last decade or two have themselves taken on highly diverse emphases. It used to be that introductions to the New Testament primarily dealt with matters of date, authorship, background, authenticity, and perhaps a brief history of the discipline. These were written from various stances, of course, but the matters covered were rather similar. But today, although such matters remain the focus of some introductions,[124] others introduce

---

vol. 3, Craig Bartholomew, Jonathan Chaplin, Robert Song, Al Wolters, eds., *A Royal Priesthood? The Use of the Bible Ethically and Politically: A Dialogue with Oliver O'Donovan* (Grand Rapids: Zondervan, 2002); and vol. 4, Craig Bartholomew, C. Stephen Evans, Mary Healy, and Murray Rae, eds., *"Behind" the Text: History and Biblical Interpretation* (Grand Rapids: Zondervan, 2003).

[122]One of the seminal books in this area is Johannes P. Louw, *Sociolinguistics and Communication,* UBSMS 1 (London: UBS, 1986).

[123]See especially n. 33, above.

[124]See esp. the magisterial work of Raymond E. Brown, *An Introduction to the New Testament* (New York: Doubleday, 1997).

[125]E.g., Arthur G. Patzia, *The Emergence of the Church: Context, Growth, Leadership & Worship* (Downers Grove: IVP, 2001).

the New Testament by focusing on the growth and context of the church,[125] on its history and literature,[126] or on its history and theology[127] (not necessarily quite the same thing!); by attempting a fairly comprehensive and integrated interpretation of the whole (though inevitably that means that certain elements are *less* discussed than in other works);[128] by relatively brief surveys of the material written from a dogmatic and usually reductionistic stance that scarcely acknowledges there are other judgments;[129] or by providing a brief survey and a representative smattering of primary sources relevant to the origins of Christianity (though of course the selection itself says a great deal and can prove limiting).[130] The volume you are reading devotes most attention to the historical questions of traditional introductions but also introduces a range of hermeneutical and theological issues.

To project the future of the study of the New Testament demands a courage the authors of this volume lack. Some are convinced that it lies with postmodern approaches.[131] Rather amusingly, Bockmuehl lists "possible futures" to New Testament scholarship as he extrapolates what would happen if any of the current emphases now on offer had its way and became hegemonic. The effect, of course, is to expose the rather painful reductionism of so much of the current enterprise. He concludes by observing,

> At the end of the day it may turn out that the implied reader is in a better position to understand the text than the aloof or the distrusting interpreter.

---

[126]E.g., Lee Martin McDonald and Stanley E. Porter, *Early Christianity and Its Sacred Literature* (Peabody: Hendrickson, 2000).

[127]Achtemeier/Green/Thompson.

[128]E.g., Johnson.

[129]E.g., Gerd Theissen, *Fortress Introduction to the New Testament* (Minneapolis: Fortress Press, 2003); Bart D. Ehrman, *The New Testament: A Historical Introduction to the Early Christian Writings,* 3rd ed. (New York: Oxford University Press, 2004). One of the interesting features of Ehrman's *Introduction* is that it includes treatment of some noncanonical early Christian writings. This is historically useful, of course, but it also reflects the author's conviction that there is no difference in authority or revelation between the canonical books of the New Testament (which are "canonical" only for reasons of historical accident) and other first- and second-century Christian literature. In this regard Ehrman's work is a more user-friendly version of the older work by Helmut Koester, *Introduction to the New Testament,* 2 vols. (Philadelphia: Fortress Press, 1982).

[130]E.g., Delbert Burkett, *An Introduction to the New Testament and the Origins of Christianity* (Cambridge: Cambridge University Press, 2002).

[131]E.g., Robert F. Shedinger, "Kuhnian Paradigms and Biblical Scholarship: Is Biblical Studies a Science?" *JBL* 119 (2000): 453–71—and of course he offers a resounding "No" to his question.

Adolf Schlatter (1969) was perhaps right after all to criticize atheistic methods of theological study for their inadequate perception of what is in the text . . . : there are limits to how much you can usefully say about the stained glass windows of King's College Chapel without going inside.[132]

But perhaps the most perceptive advice is offered by Craig Blomberg: those with a confessional stance toward the New Testament must engage both with the text of holy Scripture and with the way it is discussed in their own generation, bearing in mind some of the long heritage that has gone before.[133]

---

[132]Markus Bockmuehl, "'To Be or Not To Be': The Possible Futures of New Testament Scholarship," *SJT* 51 (1998): 271–306, quote on 302.

[133]Craig L. Blomberg, "Where Should Twenty-first Century Evangelical Biblical Scholarship Be Heading?" *BBR* 11 (2001): 161–72

CHAPTER TWO

THE SYNOPTIC GOSPELS

INTRODUCTION

The first three gospels were first labeled the Synoptic Gospels by J. J. Griesbach, a German biblical scholar, at the end of the eighteenth century. The English adjective *synoptic* comes from the Greek συνόψις *(synopsis),* which means "seeing together," and Griesbach chose the word because of the high degree of similarity found among Matthew, Mark, and Luke in their presentations of the ministry of Jesus. These similarities, which involve structure, content, and tone, are evident even to the casual reader. They serve not only to bind the first three gospels together but also to separate them from the Gospel of John.

Matthew, Mark, and Luke structure the ministry of Jesus according to a general geographic sequence: ministry in Galilee, withdrawal to the north (with Peter's confession as a climax and point of transition), ministry in Judea and Perea while Jesus is on his way to Jerusalem (less clear in Luke), and final ministry in Jerusalem. Very little of this sequence is found in John, where the focus is on Jesus' ministry in Jerusalem during his periodic visits to the city. In content, the first three evangelists narrate many of the same events, focusing on Jesus' healings, exorcisms, and teaching in parables. John, while narrating several significant healings, has no exorcisms and no parables (at least of the type found in Matthew, Mark, and Luke). Also, many of the events we think of as characteristic of the first three gospels, such as the sending out of the Twelve, the transfiguration, the Olivet Discourse, and the Last Supper narrative, are absent from John. By having Jesus constantly on the move and by juxtaposing actions—miracles, especially—with (usually) brief teachings, the first three evangelists convey a tone of intense, rapid-fire action. This is quite in contrast to the more meditative tone of John, who narrates far fewer events than do the synoptic evangelists and who prefers to present Jesus as speaking in long discourses rather than in brief parables or pithy sayings.

Over the last two centuries, scholars have scrutinized the Synoptic Gospels from many angles and with many different results. This is inevitable, given the vital importance of these books for Christian belief and life. In these books is narrated the life of the One in whom God has chosen especially to make himself known to human beings. They depict the events on which the significance of history and the destiny of every single individual depend: the death and resurrection of Jesus the Messiah. Issues pertaining to these books individually will be treated in the chapters devoted to each; here we address significant issues that embrace all three accounts. Specifically, we examine three questions: How did the Synoptic Gospels come into being? How should we understand the gospels as works of literature? And what do the gospels tell us about Jesus?

THE EVOLUTION OF THE SYNOPTIC GOSPELS

How did the Synoptic Gospels come to be written? A simple and in some ways adequate answer would be to identify the people who, under inspiration of God's Spirit, wrote these books, and to note the circumstances in which they were written. These issues are addressed in the introductions devoted to each of the four gospels. But simply identifying the authors of the Synoptic Gospels leaves some questions unanswered. How did the authors get the material about Jesus that they have used? Why are the three accounts so similar at so many places and so different at others? What was the role of the evangelists themselves? Recorders of tradition? Authors with a viewpoint of their own? And, to raise the larger question that lurks behind all of these, why *four* gospels? These and similar questions have occupied thoughtful Christians since the beginning of the church. A second-century Christian, Tatian, combined all four gospels together in his *Diatessaron.* Augustine wrote a treatise entitled *The Harmony of the Gospels.*[1] But scholars have pursued these questions especially vigorously since the rise of modern biblical criticism at the end of the eighteenth century.

While we may dismiss as inconsequential some of the questions raised during this time, and even more of the answers as simply wrong, the issue of synoptic origins and relations is one that cannot be avoided. The number and nature of the gospels raise such literary and historical questions. Moreover, one of the evangelists refers to the process by which the gospel material has come to him:

> Many have undertaken to draw up an account of the things that have been fulfilled among us, just as they were handed down to us by those who from the first were eyewitnesses and servants of the word. With this in mind, since I myself have carefully investigated everything from the beginning, I too decided to write an orderly account for you, most excellent

---

[1] It can be found in *NPNF2* 6.77–236.

Theophilus, so that you may know the certainty of the things you have been taught. (Luke 1:1–4)

In this introduction to his two-volume "history of Christian origins," Luke acknowledges three stages in the genesis of his work: the "eyewitnesses and servants of the word" who "handed down" the truth of Jesus; those "many" who have already drawn up accounts of Jesus and the early church; and Luke himself, who, having "carefully investigated" these sources, now composes his own "orderly" account. Investigation of the process to which Luke refers appears to be quite in order. We look first, then, at the earliest stage of transmission, during which eyewitnesses and others handed down the tradition about Jesus, much of it orally; then at the stage when written sources began to grow and become more important; and last, at the stage of final authorship.[2]

The Stage of Oral Traditions: Form Criticism

In the course of investigation into the origins of the gospels over the last two centuries, several distinct approaches have emerged, each of them emphasizing different aspects or stages. Three approaches in particular have made distinct and significant contributions to the problem of gospel origins and development: form criticism (*Formgeschichte*), which focuses on the period of oral transmission; source criticism, which focuses on the way different literary units were put together to make up the gospels; and redaction criticism (*Redaktionsgeschichte*), which focuses on the literary and theological contributions of the authors of the gospels. These methods correspond generally to the three stages mentioned by Luke in his introduction. Yet they are not mutually exclusive; most contemporary gospel critics employ all three simultaneously in what is called traditions analysis or tradition criticism (*Traditionsgeschichte*). Nevertheless, these three approaches are both historically and methodologically distinct, and we examine each in turn.

We begin with form criticism because, though arising only after the heyday of source criticism, it concentrates on the earliest stage in the process by which the gospels came into being: the oral stage. Form critics claim that the early Christians transmitted the words and actions of Jesus by word of mouth for a considerable length of time. Only after two decades or so did the material begin to be put into written sources, with the gospels themselves coming shortly afterward.

Description. Form criticism was first applied to the Old Testament by scholars such as Hermann Gunkel and was then brought into New Testament studies in the second and third decades of the twentieth century by a trio of men who had come to recognize that the source-critical approach, pursued rigorously for

Form critics claim that the early Christians transmitted the words and actions of Jesus by word of mouth, and only after two decades or so did the material begin to be put into written sources.

---

[2]Martin uses Luke 1:1–4 in a similar way in his introduction (1.119–21).

several decades, had exhausted its potential. These men were Karl Ludwig Schmidt, Martin Dibelius, and Rudolf Bultmann.[3] Though differing at several important points, these pioneers of form criticism had in common at least six assumptions and beliefs that came to be the basis for form criticism.

1. The stories and sayings of Jesus circulated in small independent units. The early form critics argued that an exception to this rule was the passion narrative, which they thought was a self-contained literary unit from a very early period.[4] Even this exception is not admitted by many contemporary form critics.

2. The transmission of the gospel material can be compared to the transmission of other folk and religious traditions. Responsibility for this transmission rests not with individuals but with the community within which the material takes shape and is handed down. Certain laws of transmission generally observable in such instances of oral transmission can be applied to the transmission of the gospels.

3. The stories and sayings of Jesus took on certain standard forms (hence "form" criticism, or "the history of forms") that are for the most part still readily visible in the gospels. Form critics have not agreed on the number and exact nature of these forms. Table 1 presents three influential schemes.[5]

4. The form of a specific story or saying makes it possible to determine its *Sitz im Leben* ("setting in life"), or function in the life of the early church. According to Bultmann, "The proper understanding of form-criticism rests upon the judgement that the literature in which the life of a given community, even the primitive Christian community, has taken shape, springs out of quite definite conditions and wants of life from which grows up a quite definite style and quite specific forms and categories. Thus, every literary category has its 'life situation.'"[6]

5. As it passed down the sayings and stories of Jesus, the early Christian community not only put the material into certain forms, but it also modified it under the impetus of its own needs and situations. With this point we move from what may be called form criticism proper (a literary enterprise) into a broader

---

[3]Schmidt's *Der Rahmen der Geschichte Jesu: Literarkritische Untersuchungen zur ältesten Jesusüberlieferung* was published in 1919 by Trowitzsch & Son in Berlin and has never been translated. Also appearing in 1919 in its original German edition was Martin Dibelius's *From Tradition to Gospel* (ET New York: Charles Scribner's Sons, n.d.); *The History of the Synoptic Tradition* by Rudolf Bultmann was published in 1921 (ET New York: Harper & Row, 1963).

[4]E.g., Dibelius, *From Tradition to Gospel*, 178–79.

[5]In addition to the Dibelius and Bultmann works mentioned, see Vincent Taylor, *The Formation of the Gospel Tradition*, 2nd ed. (London: Macmillan, 1935). Taylor uses form criticism with less historical skepticism than does either Dibelius or Bultmann.

[6]Bultmann, *Synoptic Tradition*, 4.

Table 1
Terminology of Form Criticism

Form	Dibelius	Bultmann	Taylor
Brief Sayings of Jesus set in a context (e.g., Mark 12:13–17, which climaxes in Jesus' saying "Give to Caesar what is Caesar's and to God what is God's")	Paradigms	Apophthegms	Pronouncement Stories
Stories about Jesus' miraculous deeds (e.g., the feeding of the 5,000)	Tales	Miracle Stories	Miracle Stories
Stories that magnify Jesus as a "hero" (e.g., Luke's story about Jesus in the temple at twelve years of age [2:41–52])	Legends	Historical Stories and Legends	Stories about Jesus
Teaching of Jesus that does not climax in a single saying (e.g., the Lord's Prayer)	Paranesis	Dominical Sayings	Sayings and Parables

conception of the discipline in which historical judgments are being rendered that by and large do not grow out of the discipline as such.

Form critics differ widely over the degree to which the early church modified and created gospel material. Bultmann, for instance, thinks the influence was huge, attributing most of the gospel material to the early church and finding relatively little that can be reliably considered to have come from the earthly ministry of Jesus. He does so because he, with many other form critics, believes that the early church was not concerned to distinguish between things Jesus said while on earth and things that he was continuing to say through prophets in the life of the church. As Norman Perrin puts it, "The modern distinction between historical Jesus and risen Lord is quite foreign to the early church."[7]

Radical historical judgments such as these are not intrinsic to form criticism, and many form critics are much more conservative in their historical assessments. Vincent Taylor is one, and there are others still more conservative who confine the influence of the early church mainly to the arrangement of

[7]Norman Perrin, *Rediscovering the Teaching of Jesus* (London: SCM, 1967), 27; cf. Bultmann, *Synoptic Tradition,* 127–28.

material (e.g., the series of controversy stories in Mark 2:1–3:6 and parallels). But these are exceptions to the rule, and it must be said that the great majority of form critics have pursued their enterprise with a good measure of historical skepticism.

6. Classic form critics have typically used various criteria to enable them to determine the age and historical trustworthiness of particular pericopes. These criteria are based on certain laws of transmission that are thought to hold good for any orally transmitted material. According to these so-called laws, people tend to (1) lengthen their stories, (2) add details to them, (3) conform them more and more to their own language, and (4) generally preserve and create only what fits their own needs and beliefs. On the basis of these laws, many form critics have declared that gospel material that is shorter, lacks details, contains Semitisms, and does not fit with the interests of the early church or first-century Judaism is earlier and thus more likely to be historical. The last criterion, usually called the criterion of *dissimilarity,* is especially important for the more radical form critics. By eliminating anything that was likely to have been introduced by the early church or that could have been picked up from the Jewish milieu, advocates of this criterion claim to be able to secure a "critically assured" minimum number of sayings and activities on which a supposedly historical understanding of Jesus can be based. The criterion of dissimilarity, for instance, suggests that Mark 13:32—"But about that day or hour no one knows, not even the angels in heaven, nor the Son, but only the Father"—may well be original with Jesus, since it uses language not typical of Judaism ("the Son") and contains a premise (Jesus' ignorance) that runs counter to a view in the early church. A fifth criterion is a by-product of this one, holding material to be authentic that agrees with material isolated by the criterion of dissimilarity. A sixth criterion, *multiple attestation,* gives preference to material found in more than one stream of tradition (e.g., Mark and "Q"—about which more below).

Evaluation.　The historical skepticism that characterizes many of the most prominent form critics has given form criticism itself the reputation of attacking the historicity of the gospels. But as we have suggested above, this need not be the case. As a literary discipline, form criticism entails no a priori judgment about the historicity of the material it analyzes. Moreover, many of the assumptions on which form criticism is based appear to be valid: there was indeed a period of mainly oral transmission of the gospel material, much of it likely in small units; there probably was a tendency for this material to take on certain standard forms; and the early church undoubtedly influenced the way this material was handed down. Defined narrowly in this way, there is certainly a place for form criticism in the study of the gospels.

Nevertheless, we must register certain cautions even about this narrow application of the discipline. First, it is probable that more of the gospel material than many form critics allow existed from very early periods in written form and that much of the rest of it may already have been connected together into larger literary units.[8] Alan Millard, for example, has demonstrated that writing was quite common in Herodian Palestine and that there were many precedents for the recording in writing of a religious teacher's sayings.[9] Second, we must be careful not to impose a straitjacket of specified, clearly delineated forms on the material. The existence of so-called mixed forms suggests that any classification must be viewed as provisional and general at best. Third, the claims of form critics to be able to identify the setting in the life of the church that gave rise to specific forms must be treated with healthy skepticism. Often—perhaps usually—we lack sufficient data for any such identification. Finally, and perhaps most damaging, the assumptions of many of the form critics about the nature of the transmission process are suspect. Several authors have argued that most form critics have not sufficiently appreciated the dynamics and nature of oral transmission and that far too little attention has been given to the role of individuals—including eyewitnesses[10]—in shaping and handing down the material.[11]

More serious criticisms must be directed against the antihistorical application of form criticism typified by Bultmann, Dibelius, and many of their heirs. First, the claim that the early church did not distinguish the earthly Jesus from the risen Lord and thus felt free to place on the lips of the earthly Jesus sayings uttered by early Christian prophets is unjustified. Bultmann claimed that verses such as 2 Corinthians 5:16b—"if, indeed, we have known Christ according to the flesh, we now no longer will know him in this way" (authors' translation)—demonstrated that Paul and others in the early church had no interest in the earthly Jesus as such. But Paul is saying in this text, not that he would no longer have any interest in a "fleshly" (i.e., earthly) Jesus, but that he was determined no longer to regard Jesus "from a fleshly point of view." In fact, nothing in the New Testament substantiates the notion that early Christians did not distinguish the earthly Jesus and the risen Lord, and the radical form critics have never come near to explaining how the utterance of a Christian prophet in, say, Antioch in

---

[8]C. H. Dodd, for instance, proposes that from the beginning, the pattern of early Christian preaching had imposed a certain pattern in the gospel material ("The Framework of the Gospel Narrative," *ExpTim* 43 [1932]: 396–400).

[9]Alan Millard, *Reading and Writing in the Time of Jesus* (Washington Square: New York University Press, 2000).

[10]See Richard Bauckham, "The Eyewitnesses and the Gospel Traditions," *JSHJ* 1 (2003): 28–60.

[11]See esp. Erhardt Güttgemanns, *Candid Questions Concerning Gospel Form Criticism: A Methodological Sketch of the Fundamental Problematics of Form and Redaction Criticism* (ET Pittsburgh: Pickwick, 1979), and Werner H. Kelber, *The Oral and the Written Gospel* (Philadelphia: Fortress Press, 1983).

A.D. 42 would have been put on the lips of Jesus as he taught in a specific locale in Galilee thirteen or so years earlier. That Christian prophecy actually functioned in this way is being questioned more and more.[12]

Second, we must question whether the transmission of the gospel material over a period of twenty or so years can appropriately be compared with some of the other material that form critics use to draw conclusions about the gospels. The rabbinic literature, for instance, with which both Bultmann and Dibelius compare the gospels, was a very undefined body of material gathered over the course of centuries. And the rabbis never produced anything remotely resembling a gospel.

Third, and related to this last point, are doubts about the validity of the so-called laws of transmission. E. P. Sanders and others have shown that oral transmission by no means always tends to lengthen material.[13] The use of such laws, then, to attribute stories and sayings to the church rather than to Jesus is not valid.[14] Particularly to be criticized is the criterion of dissimilarity. To be sure, the application of this criterion is often misunderstood: most who use it do not claim that *only* those sayings that it can isolate are authentic, but rather that these are the only ones we can be sure about. Nevertheless, its use has the tendency to focus attention on what was peculiar to Jesus over against both his Jewish environment and the early church. Its use thus tends to skew our view of Jesus.[15] More conservative form critics insist that the criterion must not be used in isolation and must be used only with the positive purpose of providing evidence of historicity rather than the negative purpose of disproving historicity.[16] Even so, the use of the criterion assumes a discontinuity in the process of transmission that needs to be questioned.

A fourth problem with radical form criticism is its failure to come to grips with the presence of eyewitnesses, some of them hostile, who were in a position

---

[12]E.g., David Hill, *New Testament Prophecy* (Richmond: John Knox, 1979), 160–85; J. D. G. Dunn, "Prophetic 'I'-Sayings and the Jesus Tradition: The Importance of Testing Prophetic Utterances Within Early Christianity," *NTS* 24 (1978): 175–98; David Aune, *Prophecy in Early Christianity and the Ancient Mediterranean World* (Grand Rapids: Eerdmans, 1983), 245.

[13]E. P. Sanders, *The Tendencies of the Synoptic Tradition*, SNTSMS 11 (Cambridge: Cambridge University Press, 1969).

[14]Stanley Porter argues that, despite much criticism, little real progress has been made in updating the criteria. He proposes that new criteria focusing on the Greek language might help to move the discussion forward (*The Criteria for Authenticity in Historical-Jesus Research: Previous Discussion and New Proposals*, JSNTSup 191 [Sheffield: Sheffield Academic Press, 2000]).

[15]See, e.g., M. D. Hooker, "On Using the Wrong Tool," *Theol* 75 (1972): 570–81.

[16]See esp. Robert Stein, "The 'Criteria' of Authenticity," in *GP* 1.225–63; Ben F. Meyer, *The Aims of Jesus* (Philadelphia: Fortress Press, 1979), 85–87.

to contest any wholesale creation of gospel incidents and sayings. As McNeile puts it, "Form-critics write as though the original eye-witnesses were all caught up to heaven at the Ascension and the Christian Church was put to live on a desert island."[17]

Fifth, many form critics are guilty of underestimating the degree to which first-century Jews would have been able to remember and transmit accurately by word of mouth what Jesus had said and done. The so-called Scandinavian School, represented particularly in the work of Birger Gerhardsson,[18] looked to key authoritative figures in the early church as the transmitters of the gospel tradition and argued that the process would have been akin to the transmission of the rabbinic traditions, in which both written materials and careful memorization would have played key roles. Criticism that this particular approach assumes a similarity between the scholastic setting of the rabbis and the more popular setting of early Christianity is warranted. But the importance of memorization in first-century Jewish society is undeniable, and we are justified in thinking that this provides a sufficient basis for the careful and accurate oral transmission of gospel material.[19] Recent study of eyewitness testimony in the Greco-Roman world at large also generally confirms the value and accuracy of such testimony.[20] And when we add to these points the very real possibility that the words and actions of Jesus were being written down from the beginning, we have every reason to think that the early Christians were both able and willing to hand down accurately the deeds and words of Jesus.

The Stage of Written Sources: Source Criticism (the Synoptic Problem)

Introduction. The oral stage of the development of the Synoptic Gospels, which we examined in the last section, probably also included some written traditions about Jesus' life and teachings. Some of the apostles may have taken notes on Jesus' teachings and activities during the ministry itself, and they and other eyewitnesses probably accelerated that process after the resurrection. At the same time, of course, much of the material was being passed on orally. But as time moved on, we can suspect that these early written fragments were combined with oral testimony to produce lengthier written sources and, finally, the

Source criticism asks and seeks to answer this question: What written sources, if any, did the evangelists use in compiling their gospels?

---

[17]McNeile, 53.

[18]Birger Gerhardsson, *Memory and Manuscript: Oral Tradition and Written Transmission in Rabbinic Judaism and Early Christianity*, ASNU 22 (Lund: Gleerup, 1964). For a review of this proposal, see Peter Davids, "The Gospels and Jewish Tradition: Twenty Years after Gerhardsson," in *GP* 1.75–99.

[19]Rainer Riesner, *Jesus als Lehrer*, WUNT 7 (Tübingen: Mohr-Siebeck, 1981); idem, "Jüdische Elementarbildung und Evangelienüberlieferung," in *GP* 1.209–23.

[20]See S. Byrskog, *Story as History—History as Story: The Gospel Tradition in the Context of Ancient Oral History*, WUNT 123 (Tübingen: Mohr-Siebeck, 2000); Bauckham, "Eyewitnesses."

canonical gospels. Source criticism is devoted to the investigation of this written stage in the production of the gospels. It asks and seeks to answer this question: What written sources, if any, did the evangelists use in compiling their gospels?

The question is of particular interest to the historian of the early Christian movement and one that any student of the Synoptic Gospels is bound to ask. For there are startling similarities, both in general outline and in particular wording, among the Synoptic Gospels. Consider the italicized words in the example in table 2, the account of the healing of a paralytic.

Table 2
Synoptic Parallels: The Healing of a Paralytic

Matthew 9:1–8	Mark 2:1–12	Luke 5:17–26
Jesus stepped into a boat, crossed over and came to his own town. Some men brought to him a paralyzed man, lying on a mat. When Jesus saw their faith, he said to the man, "Take heart, son; your sins are forgiven." At this, some of the teachers of the law said to themselves, "This fellow is blaspheming!" Knowing their thoughts, Jesus said, "Why do you entertain evil thoughts in your hearts? Which is easier: to say, 'Your sins are forgiven,' or to say, 'Get up and walk'? *But I want you to know that the Son of Man has authority on earth to forgive sins." So he said to the paralyzed man, "Get up, take your mat and go home."* Then the man got up and went home. When the crowd saw this, they were filled with awe; and they praised God, who had	A few days later, when Jesus again entered Capernaum, the people heard that he had come home. They gathered in such large numbers that there was no room left, not even outside the door, and he preached the word to them. Some men came, bringing to him a paralyzed man, carried by four of them. Since they could not get him to Jesus because of the crowd, they made an opening in the roof above Jesus by digging through it and then lowered the mat the man was lying on. When Jesus saw their faith, he said to the paralyzed man, "Son, your sins are forgiven." Now some teachers of the law were sitting there, thinking to themselves, "Why does this fellow talk like that? He's blaspheming! Who can forgive sins but God alone?" Immediately Jesus knew in his spirit that this was what they were thinking in their	One day Jesus was teaching, and Pharisees and teachers of the law were sitting there. They had come from every village of Galilee and from Judea and Jerusalem. And the power of the Lord was with Jesus to heal the sick. Some men came carrying a paralyzed man on a mat and tried to take him into the house to lay him before Jesus. When they could not find a way to do this because of the crowd, they went up on the roof and lowered him on his mat through the tiles into the middle of the crowd, right in front of Jesus. When Jesus saw their faith, he said, "Friend, your sins are forgiven." The Pharisees and the teachers of the law began thinking to themselves, "Who is this fellow who speaks blasphemy? Who can forgive sins but God alone?" Jesus knew what they were thinking and asked, "Why are

Matthew 9:1–8 (cont.)	Mark 2:1–12 (cont.)	Luke 5:17–26 (cont.)
given such authority to human beings.	hearts, and he said to them, "Why are you thinking these things? Which is easier: to say to this paralyzed man, 'Your sins are forgiven,' or to say, 'Get up, take your mat and walk'? *But I want you to know that the Son of Man has authority on earth to forgive sins." So he said to the man, "I tell you, get up, take your mat and go home."* He got up, took his mat and walked out in full view of them all. This amazed everyone and they praised God, saying, "We have never seen anything like this!"	you thinking these things in your hearts? Which is easier: to say, 'Your sins are forgiven,' or to say, 'Get up and walk'? *But I want you to know that the Son of Man has authority on earth to forgive sins." So he said to the paralyzed man, "I tell you, get up, take your mat and go home."* Immediately he stood up in front of them, took what he had been lying on and went home praising God. Everyone was amazed and gave praise to God. They were filled with awe and said, "We have seen remarkable things today."

Not only is the wording almost exact (as is true in the Greek original), but each of the three evangelists inserts an abrupt break in Jesus' words at the same point. (This break, an awkward syntactical shift from a second person plural address—"I want you to know"—to the third singular—"he said to the man"—in Matthew 9:6/Mark 2:10/Luke 5:24, is smoothed out in the TNIV quoted above.) Such duplication of unusual or awkward constructions occurs at other places, along with passages in which two or three of the evangelists use precisely the same words, in the same order, over several lines of text. In table 3, for instance, note how Matthew and Luke use almost exactly the same words to record Jesus' lament over Jerusalem.[21] The student of the gospels naturally wants to know how we can account for so exact a similarity in wording.

But what makes the synoptic problem particularly knotty is the fact that, alongside such exact agreements, there are so many puzzling differences. Take the passage cited in table 2, for example. While the three accounts agree closely in the portion we have put in italics, Matthew omits the "I tell you" found in both Mark and Luke. And when we consider the passage as a whole, other potentially more significant differences appear. Matthew, for instance, does not

---

[21]The agreement in the Greek text is almost as close, with variations only in the tense of an infinitive, the inclusion of a nonessential verb in Luke, and the choice of a particle at the beginning of the last sentence. (Notice the "for" in Matthew, with nothing comparable in Luke (the Greek text has δέ [*de*], "and," "but").

Table 3
Synoptic Parallels: Jesus' Lament over Jerusalem

Matthew 23:37–39	Luke 13:34–35
"Jerusalem, Jerusalem, you who kill the prophets and stone those sent to you, how often I have longed to gather your children together, as a hen gathers her chicks under her wings, and you were not willing. Look, your house is left to you desolate. For I tell you, you will not see me again until you say, 'Blessed is he who comes in the name of the Lord.'"	"Jerusalem, Jerusalem, you who kill the prophets and stone those sent to you, how often I have longed to gather your children together, as a hen gathers her chicks under her wings, and you were not willing. Look, your house is left to you desolate. I tell you, you will not see me again until you say, 'Blessed is he who comes in the name of the Lord.'"

include the part about the paralyzed man's friends opening a hole in the roof to let his mat down in front of Jesus.

This combination of agreement and disagreement extends to the larger structure of the gospels as well. Consider the list of events in table 4, which follows Mark's order. (Any place where one gospel has deviated from the other two in order of events is indicated with bold type.) We find here, though not perhaps in the same proportion, the kinds of agreements and disagreements that recur throughout the Synoptic Gospels. All three roughly follow the same order of events, even when there is no clear chronological or historical reason to do so. Each evangelist, however, omits material found in the other two, each contains unique incidents, and some of the events that are found in one or both of the others are put in a different order.

The question behind the synoptic problem, then, may be reformulated in light of these data: What hypothesis best accounts for the combination of exact agreement and wide divergence that characterizes the first three gospels?

The Main Solutions. While the number of solutions to the synoptic problem is proportionate to the amazing amount of research and imaginative thinking that has been devoted to the matter,[22] we may single out four main options.

---

[22]Full accounts of the history of the investigation may be found in Werner Georg Kümmel, *The New Testament: The History of the Investigation of Its Problems* (New York: Abingdon, 1970), 74–88, 144–61; Stephen Neill and Tom Wright, *The Interpretation of the New Testament, 1861–1986* (Oxford: Oxford University Press, 1988), 112–36; William Baird, *History of New Testament Research*, vol. 1: *From Deism to Tübingen* (Minneapolis: Fortress Press, 1992), 295–310. The best account of recent study is Craig Blomberg, "The Synoptic Problem: Where We Stand at the Beginning of a New Century," in *Rethinking the Synoptic Problem*, ed. David Alan Black and David R. Beck (Grand Rapids: Baker, 2001), 17–40.

Table 4
Order of Events in the Synoptics

(**Note:** Bold type indicates places where Matthew and Luke deviate from the order of events followed in Mark. A dash indicates that the incident does not appear in the gospel.)

Pericope	Matthew	Mark	Luke
Jesus and Beelzebul	12:22–27	3:20–30	**11:14–28**
The Sign of Jonah	12:38–45	———	11:29–32
Jesus' Mother and Brothers	12:46–50	3:31–35	**8:19–21**
Parable of the Sower	13:1–9	4:1–9	8:4–8
The Reason for Parables	13:10–17	4:10–12	8:9–10
Interpretation of the Parable of the Sower	13:18–23	4:13–20	8:11–15
Parable of the Weeds	13:24–30	———	———
A Lamp on a Stand	———	4:21–25	8:16–18
Parable of the Seed Growing Secretly	———	4:26–29	———
Parable of the Mustard Seed	13:31–32	4:30–34	———
Parable of the Yeast	13:33	———	———
Jesus' Speaking in Parables	13:34–35	———	———
Interpretation of the Parable of the Weeds	13:36–43	———	———
Parable of the Hidden Treasure	13:44	———	———
Parable of the Pearl	13:45–46	———	———
Parable of the Net	13:47–50	———	———
The Householder	13:51–52	———	———
The Stilling of the Storm	**8:18, 23–27**	4:35–41	8:22–25
Healing of the Gerasene Demoniac	**8:28–34**	5:1–20	8:26–39
Raising of Jairus's Daughter/Healing of a Woman	**9:18–26**	5:21–43	8:40–56
Rejection at Nazareth	13:53–58	6:1–6a	**4:16–30**
Sending Out of the Twelve	**10:1–15**	6:6b–13	9:1–6
Beheading of John the Baptist	14:1–12	6:14–29	[9:7–9]
Feeding of the Five Thousand	14:13–21	6:30–44	9:10–17
Walking on the Water	14:22–36	6:45–56	———

Common dependence on one original gospel. In 1771 the German writer and literary critic G. E. Lessing argued that the relationships among the Synoptic Gospels could be explained if they had independently used one original gospel written in Hebrew or Aramaic.[23] This proposal was adopted by others and

---

[23]G. E. Lessing, *Neue Hypothese über die Evangelisten als blos menschichliche Geschichtschreiber betrachtet,* nos. 24–49 (1784).

received modification at the hands of J. G. Eichhorn, who postulated the existence of several lost gospels as the sources for the Synoptic Gospels.[24] The proposal has not met with much favor in the last one hundred years, although C. C. Torrey argued a form of it in 1933.[25]

Common dependence on oral sources. Shortly after Lessing had proposed an "Ur-gospel" as the solution to the synoptic problem, the German critic J. G. Herder argued that dependence of the Synoptic Gospels on a relatively fixed oral summary of the life of Christ explained the data better.[26] This approach was expanded and defended at length by J. K. L. Gieseler in 1818.[27] The view was more popular in the nineteenth century than it is today,[28] but it continues to be argued by a few scholars.[29]

Common dependence on gradually developing written fragments. The important and controversial theologian F. Schleiermacher suggested that several fragments of gospel tradition existed in the early church and that these gradually grew until they became incorporated into the Synoptic Gospels. This thesis is no longer argued in this form, but Schleiermacher was apparently the first to argue

---

[24]J. G. Eichhorn, *Einleitung in das Neue Testament* (1804).

[25]C. C. Torrey, *The Four Gospels* (New York: Harper, 1933). See also X. Léon-Dufour, "The Synoptic Gospels," in Robert/Feuillet, 252–86. Léon-Dufour argues that the synoptic evangelists are independent on the literary level, all the similarities arising through dependence on an Aramaic Matthew and oral tradition.

[26]J. G. Herder, *Von der Regel der Zusammenstimmung unserer Evangelien* (1797).

[27]J. K. L. Gieseler, *Historisch-kritischer Versuch über die Entstehung und die frühesten Schicksale der schriftlichen Evangelien* (1818).

[28]B. F. Westcott was one of the better-known defenders of the view. See his *Introduction to the Study of the Gospels,* 8th ed. (London: Macmillan, 1895), 165–212.

[29]John M. Rist has argued that the agreements between Matthew and Mark can be explained by common use of oral tradition without having to bring in written sources or to have one depend on the other (*On the Independence of Matthew and Mark,* SNTSMS 32 [Cambridge: Cambridge University Press, 1978]). Bo Reicke attributes the similarities among the Synoptic Gospels to a combination of shared (mainly) oral tradition and personal contacts among the authors (*The Roots of the Synoptic Gospels* [Philadelphia: Fortress Press, 1986]). And Eta Linnemann thinks that the similarities among the Synoptic Gospels can be explained by vivid and accurate memory of the actual events and sayings (*Is There a Synoptic Problem? Rethinking the Literary Dependence of the First Three Gospels* [Grand Rapids: Baker, 1992]). See also Robert L. Thomas and F. David Farnell, eds., *The Jesus Crisis: The Inroads of Historical Criticism into Evangelical Scholarship* (Grand Rapids: Kregel, 1998), esp. chap. 1, "The Synoptic Gospels in the Ancient Church," by Thomas and Farnell; chap. 3, "Source Criticism: The Two-Source Theory," by Thomas R. Edgar; and chap. 6, "Redaction Criticism," by Thomas.

that Papias's "logia"[30] refers to one of these fragments—a collection of the sayings of Jesus.[31]

Interdependence. The last basic solution to the synoptic problem maintains that two of the evangelists used one or more of the other gospels in constructing their own. Without necessarily denying the use of other sources now lost, advocates of this view argue that only borrowing at the final literary level can explain the degree of similarity among the Synoptic Gospels. This solution to the synoptic problem has been urged from early in the history of the church (e.g., Augustine; see below) and commands almost universal assent among contemporary New Testament scholars—with good reason. While the ability of first-century Jews to transmit traditions with a remarkable degree of accuracy must not be minimized (see the discussion of form criticism above), it is unlikely that the degree of agreement *in the Greek text* such as is illustrated above can be explained by recourse to oral tradition alone.[32] Robert Stein draws attention to Mark 13:14 = Matthew 24:15 in this regard, where each of the evangelists directs a parenthetical remark to the *reader*.[33] Moreover, as quoted above, Luke makes clear that he, at least, used written sources in writing his gospel (1:1–4).

The hypothesis of a Semitic-language Ur-gospel encounters the same difficulty in explaining the remarkable agreement in the Greek text of the gospels. What is the likelihood that independent translators would come up with exactly the same wording in so many places? To be sure, we could propose a large *Greek* Ur-gospel as the source for all three gospels. But this hypothesis has three serious drawbacks. First, we would have expected so major a literary product in Greek to have been mentioned somewhere in early Christian literature—but it is not. Second, it is harder to explain the genesis of the three Synoptic Gospels if so significant a text already existed. And third, viewed as a comprehensive hypothesis, this theory has difficulty explaining the differences among the Synoptic Gospels.

Interdependence as the solution to the synoptic problem has been urged from early in the history of the church and commands almost universal assent among contemporary New Testament scholars — with good reason.

---

[30]See Eusebius, *H.E.* 3.39.16, and the discussion below and in chapter 3.

[31]See esp. F. Schleiermacher, "Über die Zeugnisse des Papias von unseren ersten beiden Evangelien," *TSK* 5 (1832): 335–68.

[32]F. Gerald Downing notes that Josephus rarely quoted his sources word-for-word. If this tendency can be assumed for the synoptic evangelists, it is the similarities, not the differences, that require explanation ("Redaction Criticism: Josephus' *Antiquities* and the Synoptic Gospels," *JSNT* 8 [1980]: 33).

[33]Robert H. Stein, *Studying the Synoptic Gospels: Origin and Interpretation*, 2nd ed. (Grand Rapids: Baker, 2001), 46. Stein's entire discussion of this matter, replete with many examples, gives a detailed defense of synoptic interdependence (29–47).

Theories of Interdependence. Only a theory that includes as a major component literary interdependence among the Synoptic Gospels is capable of explaining the data. One aspect of these data stands out as particularly determinative for the viability of proposed theories: the relationship among the gospels in the order of their recording of the events of the ministry. A study of the sequential parallelism of the Synoptic Gospels at this point reveals a significant fact: while Matthew and Mark frequently agree against Luke in the order of events, and Luke and Mark frequently agree against Matthew, Matthew and Luke almost never agree against Mark. This can be seen from the data in table 4 above. Note that Matthew and Mark agree, against Luke, in placing the accusation that Jesus casts out demons in the name of Beelzebul just before the so-called parables of the kingdom; and Luke and Mark agree, against Matthew, in putting the stilling of the storm and the healing of Gerasene demoniac just after these parables. At no point, however, do Matthew and Luke agree against Mark. To put it another way, at no point does Mark follow an order that disagrees with the other two (hence the lack of any bold type in the Mark column). This phenomenon has given rise to one of the most important arguments for the nature of synoptic relationships: the argument from order. It appears to require that Mark be the "middle term" in any scheme of relationships among Mark, Matthew, and Luke. In other words, Mark must have a relationship to *both* Matthew and Luke, whether he is earlier than both, comes between both, or is later than both. Figure 1 shows the four possibilities.

Each of these schemes can explain the phenomenon of order. Moreover, we cannot exclude the possibility that there is a relationship between Matthew and Luke independent of their use of Mark. The argument from order, in and of itself, does not exclude dependence of Matthew and Luke on one another, although it requires that the evangelist who wrote last would have deliberately chosen to follow the order of the other two gospels, whenever they agreed. We thus have the six additional possibilities shown in figure 2.

Figure 1
Synoptic Relations: Mark as Middle Term

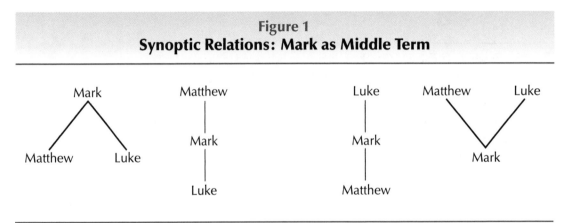

Figure 2
Synoptic Relations: Interdependence of Matthew and Luke

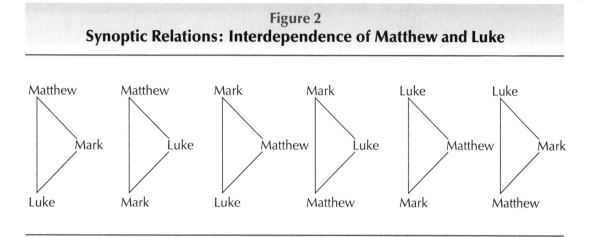

Of the ten schemes, only three have received significant support in the history of the study of the question.

The Augustinian Proposal. Taking its name from the famous North African theologian who first advocated it, this proposal holds that Matthew was the first gospel written. Mark then borrowed from Matthew, with Luke, finally, borrowing from both Matthew and Mark.[34] Until the nineteenth century this was the standard view of those who saw a literary relationship among the Synoptic Gospels. At that time, however, many began to prefer alternative proposals. Augustine's proposal has not won many modern advocates, with a few exceptions.[35]

The "Two-Gospel" Hypothesis. As part of his ground-breaking critical approach to the Synoptic Gospels, J. J. Griesbach, while agreeing that Matthew was the first gospel written, maintained that Luke was second and that Mark was dependent on both Matthew and Luke.[36] His proposal, dubbed the two-

---

[34]Augustine, *The Harmony of the Gospels* 1.2, in *NPNF2* Vol. 6.

[35]B. C. Butler, *The Originality of St. Matthew: A Critique of the Two-Document Hypothesis* (Cambridge: Cambridge University Press, 1951); see also D. J. Chapman, *Matthew, Mark, and Luke: A Study in the Order and Interrelation of the Synoptic Gospels,* ed. John M. T. Barton (London: Longmans, Green, 1937). The proposal of John Wenham is similar, though he puts more stress on independence (*Redating Matthew, Mark, and Luke: A Fresh Assault on the Synoptic Problem* [Downers Grove: IVP, 1992]).

[36]J. J. Griesbach, *Commentatio qua Marci evangelium totum e Matthaei et Lucae commentariis decerptum esse monstratur* ("Treatise in which is demonstrated that the gospel of Mark has been wholly derived from the commentaries of Matthew and Luke") (1789). Griesbach was anticipated in this proposal by H. P. Owen in 1764 (*Observations of the Four Gospels*).

gospel hypothesis to contrast it with the two-source hypothesis, has enjoyed a considerable resurgence in popularity in the last thirty years.[37]

The "Two-Source" Hypothesis. While the two-gospel hypothesis views Matthew and Luke as the building blocks of Mark, the two-source hypothesis holds that Mark and "Q," a lost collection of Jesus' sayings, have been used independently by Matthew and Luke. Markan priority was first proposed in the 1830s, apparently independently, by Karl Lachmann and C. G. Wilke, while the full two-source hypothesis was advanced by C. H. Weisse in 1838.[38] It was given its classic expression in an 1863 monograph by H. J. Holtzmann.[39] Finally, in a work that stands as the high-water mark in source criticism, *The Four Gospels: A Study of Origins* (1924),[40] B. H. Streeter posited the existence of two other sources in addition to Mark and Q: "M," the material peculiar to Matthew's gospel, and "L," the material peculiar to Luke's gospel. This "four-source" hypothesis was an attempt to provide a comprehensive explanation of the origin of the gospels through source criticism. Streeter even suggested dates and provenances for his sources. His resultant scheme may be diagramed as in figure 3.

Streeter took source criticism as far it could be taken (some would say beyond), and his was the last major work in the discipline to appear for some time. Not everyone agreed with the details of his scheme, and most contemporary gospel critics are skeptical about the existence of M and L as written documents and about the chronological and geographic conclusions he reached. (Some scholars use M and L simply to denote, respectively, material peculiar to Matthew and Luke.) But most scholars thought that Streeter and his predecessors had clearly proven the two-source hypothesis in general, and this explanation of gospel origins was generally assumed by those, such as the redaction critics, who were working on other aspects of the gospels.

---

[37]See esp. William Farmer, *The Synoptic Problem: A Critical Analysis* (New York: Macmillan, 1964); Hans-Herbert Stoldt, *History and Criticism of the Marcan Hypothesis* (Macon: Mercer University Press, 1980); William Farmer, ed., *New Synoptic Studies: The Cambridge Gospel Conference and Beyond* (Macon: Mercer University Press, 1983). A collection of significant essays for and against the hypothesis is found in Arthur J. Bellinzoni Jr., ed., *The Two-Source Hypothesis: A Critical Appraisal* (Macon: Mercer University Press, 1985). In his book *A History of the Synoptic Problem* (New York: Doubleday, 1999), David Dungan argues that the two-source hypothesis was adopted more for philosophical and political reasons than for scholarly ones.

[38]Karl Lachmann, "De Ordine narrationum im evangeliis synopticis," *TSK* 8 (1835): 570–90; C. G. Wilke, *Der Urevangelist oder exegetisch-kritische Untersuchungen über das Verwandtschaftsverhältniss der drei ersten Evangelien* (1838); C. H. Weisse, *Die evangelische Geschichte kritisch und philosophisch bearbeitet* (1838).

[39]H. J. Holtzmann, *Die synoptische Evangelien: Ihr Ursprung und ihr geschichtlicher Charakter* (1863).

[40]B. H. Streeter, *The Four Gospels: A Study of Origins* (London: Macmillan, 1924).

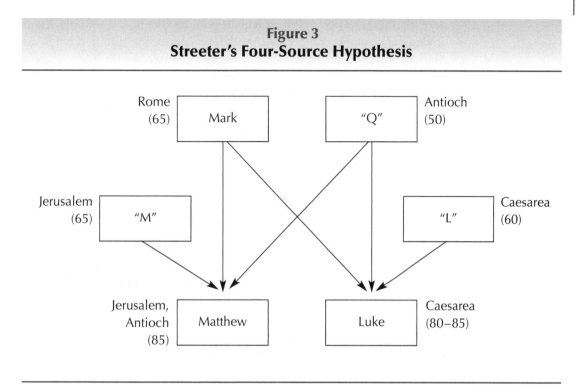

Figure 3
Streeter's Four-Source Hypothesis

As noted above, however, this is no longer true. The two-source hypothesis has been subjected over the last thirty years to serious criticism, most notably by advocates of the two-gospel, or Griesbach proposal, but also by others, some of whom maintain Markan priority while questioning the existence or nature of Q. To the extent that these challenges have introduced some caution into what was often an overly dogmatic and simplistic reconstruction of gospel origins, they have had a salutary effect. The two-source theory has been appropriately dethroned from the status of being an "assured result of scholarship." Nevertheless, properly nuanced, it remains the best general explanation of the data. In the sections that follow, we will examine the evidence for and against each of the two sources of the two-source hypothesis.

Markan Priority. Until the nineteenth century, most Christians assumed that Matthew was the first gospel to be written.[41] This tradition, which became the official position of the Roman Catholic Church, must be respected, particularly since it appears to be bolstered by the second-century testimony of Papias, as cited by Eusebius (see below). Nevertheless, it does not settle the issue. Many

---

[41]See the surveys in Zahn 2.392–96 and William Farmer, *Jesus and the Gospel* (Philadelphia: Fortress Press, 1982), 13–110.

gave Matthew priority on the inadequate grounds that he was the only apostle among the synoptic evangelists. Another equally strong tradition holds that Mark wrote his gospel based on the preaching of Peter (see the introduction to Mark), and this makes Markan dependence on Matthew difficult. Since Lukan priority is rarely argued,[42] the main alternative to Matthean priority is Markan priority. Why have so many scholars been convinced that Mark is the gospel that lies at the basis of both Matthew and Luke? The following are the most important arguments.[43]

The brevity of Mark. Mark is considerably shorter than both Matthew and Luke: 11,025 words as against 18,293 and 19,376, respectively. It is not Mark's relative brevity per se that provides evidence for Mark's priority (it cannot be demonstrated that the shorter is necessarily the earlier), but its brevity taken in conjunction with its close relationship to Luke, and especially to Matthew. Over 97 percent of Mark's words have a parallel in Matthew; over 88 percent in Luke.[44] It therefore makes more sense to think that Matthew and Luke have taken over much of Mark, expanding it with their own material, than that Mark has abbreviated Matthew and/or Luke with the omission of so much material. To be sure, it is possible to argue that Mark is a deliberate condensation of Matthew and Luke—as proponents of the two-gospel theory maintain.[45] But it would be a strange condensation that generally lengthens the narratives taken from these other gospels while omitting things like the Sermon on the Mount, the birth narratives, and the appearances of the risen Lord. Put simply, this argument runs: "Given Mark, it is easy to see why Matthew was written; given Matthew, it is hard to see why Mark was needed."[46]

The verbal agreements among the gospels. As we illustrated earlier, at many places the three Synoptic Gospels manifest a remarkable degree of verbal parallelism. But careful study reveals that while all three accounts sometimes agree

---

[42]See, however, R. L. Lindsey, "A Modified Two-Document Theory of the Synoptic Dependence and Interdependence," *NovT* 6 (1963): 239.

[43]For further details and other arguments, see esp. Kümmel, *The New Testament,* 56–63; Stein, *Studying the Synoptic Gospels,* 49–96; Joseph A. Fitzmyer, "The Priority of Mark and the 'Q' Source in Luke," in *Jesus and Man's Hope,* ed. Donald G. Miller (Pittsburgh: Pittsburgh Theological Seminary, 1970), 1:131–70; Scot McKnight, "Source Criticism," in *Interpreting the New Testament,* ed. David Black and David Dockery (Nashville: Broadman and Holman, 2001), 74–105.

[44]The statistics are from Stein, *Studying the Synoptic Gospels,* 48, who is citing Joseph B. Tyson and Thomas R. W. Longstaff, *Synoptic Abstract,* The Computer Bible 15 (Wooster, Ohio: College of Wooster, 1978), 169–71.

[45]E.g., David L. Dungan, "The Purpose and Provenance of the Gospel of Mark According to the Two-Gospel (Owen-Griesbach) Hypothesis," in *New Synoptic Studies,* 411–40.

[46]G. M. Styler, "The Priority of Mark," in Moule, 231.

(as in table 2), Matthew and Mark frequently agree, as do Mark and Luke, but Matthew and Luke agree less often. As with the argument from order, this phenomenon can be explained as long as Mark is the middle term of the three. It is much more difficult to explain if Mark is not the first, however, because on any other hypothesis, recourse must be had to the supposition of a deliberate and unlikely method of composition.[47] With the Augustinian hypothesis, we would have to think that Luke almost always chose to use Mark's wording rather than Matthew's; with the two-gospel hypothesis, we would have to assume that Mark almost never introduced any wording of his own. While possible, both procedures are less likely than the alternative. (The minor agreements between Matthew and Luke are discussed below.)

The order of events. We noted above that a comparison of the order of events in the Synoptic Gospels reveals a situation similar to what is observed about the verbal agreements: Matthew and Luke do not agree against Mark. This phenomenon was noted by Lachmann, who argued, furthermore, that this situation was best explained if Mark was the prior gospel. As with the verbal agreements, the phenomenon of order *can* be explained by other hypotheses. For example, Luke might have determined to follow Mark's order when he diverged from Matthew (on the Augustinian explanation), or Mark might have decided never to deviate from Matthew and Luke when they agreed. Again, the virtue of Markan priority is that it provides a natural explanation for this phenomenon rather than having to postulate an unlikely compositional procedure on the part of one of the evangelists.

Mark's awkward and more primitive style. It is generally agreed that Mark has more grammatical irregularities and awkward constructions than do Matthew and Luke. This, it is argued, favors Markan priority, because the natural tendency would have been for later authors to smooth out such irregularities (a similar criterion is used in textual criticism). Similarly, Mark preserves more Aramaic expressions than does either Matthew or Luke in their parallels with Mark. It is easier to see, it is argued, why Matthew and Luke would eliminate or translate Aramaic expressions that would be unintelligible to their Greek-speaking readers than why Mark would have added such Aramaic expressions without a basis in his sources.

Mark's more primitive theology. Many scholars find many more theologically difficult statements in Mark than in Matthew and Luke, and this suggests (again, paralleling textual-critical principles) that Mark is the earliest. An example is Mark 6:5, where the evangelist claims that, because of the unbelief of the

---

[47]See, however, David J. Neville (*Mark's Gospel: Prior or Posterior? A Reappraisal of the Phenomenon of Order*, JSNTSup 222 [Sheffield: Sheffield Academic Press, 2002]), who argues that the argument from order must be pursued with greater methodological precision and that it does not necessarily favor the priority of Mark.

people in Nazareth, Jesus *"could not do any miracles there."* In the parallel verse, Matthew says that Jesus *"did not do many miracles there"* (13:58). It is argued that it is more likely that Matthew has removed the potentially troublesome implication that Jesus was incapable of working a miracle than that Mark has added it. This argument has some weight, but it is not as decisive as the ones above. Not only could one argue about which evangelist has the more difficult statements, but one also must take into account the effect of each evangelist's compositional purposes and theology. This makes it much harder to be sure about the direction of borrowing. The same objection applies to the related argument that redaction critics have found it more plausible to explain Matthew on the basis of Mark than vice versa. At least in some pericopes, there would be disagreement about this,[48] and the sparsity of redactional studies assuming Matthean priority means that most of the data will be on one side in any case.

While not all of equal weight, these arguments taken together make a strong case for thinking that Matthew and Luke have independently used Mark's gospel in writing their own.

"Q". As we noted above, Schleiermacher was the first to posit the existence of a collection of Jesus' sayings as a source for the gospels. His suggestion was taken up by Weisse as the second main source of the two-source hypothesis. Like Schleiermacher, some critics think that Papias refers to this document in his famous statement about the logia (see the discussion in the introduction to Matthew), but this is doubtful. At some point toward the end of the nineteenth century, the source became known as "Q"; just how and where is a matter of debate.[49] Most proponents of Markan priority think that a sayings source such as Q must have been used by both Matthew and Luke.

The reason for positing the existence of such a written collection of Jesus' teaching is that there are approximately 250 verses common to Matthew and Luke that are not found in Mark. Most, though not all of this material, consists of teachings of Jesus. Many of these verses exhibit a degree of verbal parallelism that favors the existence of a common written source in Greek (see the example in table 3 above). The simplest explanation for this phenomenon would be dependence of one gospel on the other. Against this, however, is the lack of agreement between Matthew and Luke in their ordering of events and the general lack of verbal agreements between them. These factors strongly suggest that Matthew and Luke did not use one another; hence, the need to posit an additional source. Considerable effort has been expended in seeking to reconstruct this hypotheti-

---

[48]See, e.g., David Wenham, "The Synoptic Problem Revisited: Some New Suggestions About the Composition of Mark 4:1–34," *TynB* 23 (1972): 3–38.

[49]The designation is often thought to be the first letter of the German word *Quelle*, "source." See the discussion in John J. Schmitt, "In Search of the Origin of the Siglum Q," *JBL* 100 (1981): 609–11.

cal source,[50] and the degree of certainty with which the hypothesis is entertained by some may be gauged from the fact that a book has even been written entitled *A Theology of Q*.[51] Others go so far as to claim that Q was the first "gospel" and provides us with the earliest and most authentic picture of Jesus.[52] But despite these claims, there is considerable debate about Q, and we must consider below some of the main arguments for and against the hypothesis.

In addition to the argument from verbal agreement in non-Markan material, there are three main arguments for the existence of the Q source.

The agreement in order. A number of scholars have discerned in the non-Markan material common to Matthew and Luke (sometimes called the double tradition) a similar order.[53] Such a similar order would argue for a single written source. But the agreement in order is not all that clear, and this argument has limited force at best.[54]

Doublets in Matthew and Luke. "Doublets" are accounts that appear more than once in a single gospel. It is argued that these occur because the evangelist in question is following Mark at one point and Q at the other. An example is Luke 8:17 and 12:2, in both of which Jesus says "there is nothing hidden [concealed] that will not be disclosed, and [or] nothing concealed [hidden] that will not be known." The first is paralleled only in Mark 4:22 and the second in Matthew 10:26. The assumption is that Luke has taken the first from Mark and the second from Q.[55] Such doublets suggest the existence of a common source in addition to Mark; they are insufficient to show, however, that Q must have been a single written source.

Different placement of Q material. The non-Markan material shared by Luke and Matthew is put in different contexts, Matthew grouping much of it in his five

---

[50]See esp. James M. Robinson, Paul Hoffmann, and John Kloppenborg, *The Critical Edition of Q* (Minneapolis: Fortress Press, 2000). See also A. Polag, *Fragmenta Q: Texthelf zur Logienquelle,* 2nd ed. (Neukirchen-Vluyn: Neukirchener, 1982); Brown, 118–19, provides a helpful outline.

[51]Richard A. Edwards, *A Theology of Q* (Philadelphia: Fortress Press, 1976).

[52]See, e.g., Burton L. Mack, *The Lost Gospel: The Book of Q and Christian Origins* (San Francisco: Harper, 1993).

[53]See, e.g., Kümmel, *The New Testament,* 65–66; Joseph A. Fitzmyer, *The Gospel According to Luke I–IX*, AB (Garden City: Doubleday, 1981), 76–81. See the discussion of this matter, along with the issue of the relationship between the wording of Q and of Matthew and Luke in, respectively, Michael Goulder, "Self-Contradiction in the IQP," *JBL* 118 (1999): 506–17; Robert A. Derrenbacher Jr., and John S. Kloppenborg Verbin, "Self-Contradiction in the IQP? A Reply to Michael Goulder," *JBL* 120 (2001): 57–76; Michael Goulder, "The Derrenbacher-Kloppenborg Defense," *JBL* 121 (2002): 33–36.

[54]Stein, *Studying the Synoptic Gospels,* 111.

[55]See, on this point, John C. Hawkins, *Horae Synopticae* (Oxford: Clarendon Press, 1909), 80–107.

great discourses, Luke generally leaving it scattered throughout the gospel (mainly in 6:20–8:3 and 9:51–18:14). This phenomenon is easier to explain if both were making independent use of a common source than if Luke was using Matthew.

These arguments have convinced most scholars that Matthew and Luke have access to a common non-Markan tradition. Probably most of these think that Q was a single written document.[56] But other scholars disagree. They prefer to think of Q as a series of written fragments or as a combination of written and oral traditions.[57] But other scholars are not convinced that we need to posit the existence of any such tradition, arguing that it is far simpler to think that Luke has used Matthew. Since Luke's knowledge of Matthew would seriously undermine the evidence for Markan priority, most of those who deny the existence of Q also deny Markan priority.[58] But some maintain both Markan priority and the use of Matthew by Luke.[59]

The strongest argument in favor of Luke's use of Matthew, and therefore against the two-source theory as a whole, is the existence of what have been called minor agreements between Matthew and Luke and against Mark. These consist both of agreements in the order of particular verses or sayings, and of wording.[60] How can these be explained if Luke and Matthew have not used one

---

[56]See, for instance, David Catchpole, *The Quest for Q* (Edinburgh: T. & T. Clark, 1993); C. M. Tuckett, *Q and the History of Early Christianity* (Peabody: Hendrickson, 1996).

[57]Maurice Casey, for instance, posits multiple written sources, many, at least, in Aramaic (*An Aramaic Approach to Q: Sources for the Gospels of Matthew and Luke*, SNTSMS 122 [Cambridge: Cambridge University Press, 2002]). For a critical review, see Peter M. Head and P. J. Williams, "Q Review," *TynB* 54 (2003): 131–44.

[58]See esp. John Drury, *Tradition and Design in Luke's Gospel: A Study in Early Christian Historiography* (Atlanta: John Knox, 1976), 120–73; Allan J. McNicol, David L. Dungan, and David B. Peabody, *Beyond the Q Impasse: Luke's Use of Matthew* (Valley Forge: Trinity Press International, 1996).

[59]See especially Mark Goodacre, *The Case Against Q: Studies in Markan Priority and the Synoptic Problem* (Harrisburg: Trinity Press International, 2002); idem, *The Synoptic Problem: A Way through the Maze* (New York: Sheffield Academic Press, 2001). In response to Goodacre, see esp. Paul Foster, "Is It Possible to Dispense with Q?" *NovT* 45 (2003): 313–37. See also Michael D. Goulder, *Luke: A New Paradigm*, 2 vols.; JSNTSup 20 (Sheffield: JSOT Press, 1989); Austin Farrer, "On Dispensing with Q," in *Studies in the Gospels: Essays in Memory of R. H. Lightfoot*, ed. D. E. Nineham (Oxford: Blackwell, 1955), 55–88. A few scholars have even suggested that Matthew might have depended on Luke: e.g., R. V. Huggins, "Matthean Posteriority: A Preliminary Proposal," *NovT* 34 (1992): 1–22; cf. also Martin Hengel, *The Four Gospels and the One Gospel of Jesus Christ* (Harrisburg: Trinity Press International, 2000), 169–207.

[60]The number of these agreements is debated; see the tabulation and discussion in Franz Neirynck, *The Minor Agreements of Matthew and Luke Against Mark, with a Cumulative List*, BETL 37 (Louvain: Louvain University Press, 1974); Georg Strecker, ed.,

another? Whether we even attempt such an explanation will depend on how convinced we are by the arguments above that Luke did not know Matthew. If we concede the strength of these earlier arguments, then several such explanations are possible: (1) overlap of Mark and Q, with the agreement of Matthew and Luke being the result of their common use of Q; (2) coincidental redaction of Mark in the same way; (3) textual corruption, based on the known tendency of scribes to harmonize gospel accounts; and (4) common use of oral traditions that may have overlapped with Mark.[61]

These minor agreements demonstrate that the history of gospel origins was probably more complex than any single-source hypothesis can explain.[62] But they do not overthrow the strength of the case in favor of the two-source hypothesis. A source like Q remains the best explanation for the agreements between Matthew and Luke in non-Markan material. Almost certainly some, if not a substantial portion, of Q was in written form. But we must probably allow for more than one written source and for some mixture of oral traditions as well.[63]

A source like Q remains the best explanation for the agreements between Matthew and Luke in non-Markan material.

Proto-Gospel Theories. Partly in order to fill in some of the gaps left with the two-source hypothesis, partly because of early Christian testimony, and partly because of internal indications, various scholars have posited the existence of an earlier edition of each of the Synoptic Gospels. Lachmann, one of the first proponents of the two-source theory, worked from the assumption of an original gospel, arguing that Mark was the closest to that original. Some modern scholars, noting the problem of the minor agreements and some elements in Matthew and Luke that are difficult to explain if these evangelists were using the canonical Mark, have suggested that one or both may have used an earlier edition of Mark.[64] This hypothesis must remain doubtful. The minor agreements are not all of the same kind; many cannot be explained by positing dependence on an "Ur-Mark."[65] More basically, we must question the assumption that dependence on a different source must be used to explain all the changes Matthew and Luke have made in their Markan source. Source criticism takes too much on

---

Minor Agreements: Symposium Göttingen 1991 (Göttingen: Vandenhoeck & Ruprecht, 1993); Andreas Ennulat, Die "Minor Agreements": Untersuchungen zu einer offenen Frage des synoptischen Problems, WUNT 62 (Tübingen: Mohr-Siebeck, 1994).

[61]For these suggestions, see Streeter, Four Gospels, 293–331; Stein, Studying the Synoptic Gospels, 123–27; F. Neirynck, "Synoptic Problem," in IDBSup, 845.

[62]As R. E. Brown comments, "The process was probably more complex than the most complex modern reconstruction" (115).

[63]See Hengel, The Four Gospels, 169–86.

[64]E.g., Günther Bornkamm, Jesus of Nazareth (London: Hodder & Stoughton, 1960), 217; Vincent Taylor makes such a suggestion, but very cautiously in The Gospel According to St. Mark, 2nd ed. (London: Macmillan, 1966), 67–77.

[65]Kümmel, 62.

itself when it presumes to explain every line in Matthew and Luke with reference to a written source. The influence of eyewitness accounts, various oral traditions, and the evangelists' own theological purposes must be allowed. When these factors are taken into account, the need for an Ur-Mark disappears.

Much more popular has been the thesis that Matthew wrote an earlier edition of his gospel. In this case, however, the motivation is only partly a more satisfactory explanation of synoptic relations; more important is the apparent reference to such an earlier edition in the second-century remark of Papias (quoted by Eusebius, *H.E.* 3.39.16): "Matthew collected the oracles [τὰ λόγια *(ta logia)*] in the Hebrew language [Ἑβραΐδι διαλέκτῳ *(Hebraidi dialektō)*], and each interpreted [ἡρμήνευσεν *(hērmēneusen)*] them as best he could."[66] If Papias is referring to a gospel written in Aramaic or Hebrew, he must be referring to an earlier Semitic edition of our Greek Matthew, since later church fathers appealed to Papias to prove the priority of canonical Matthew. It has been popular, then, to suppose that a Semitic Matthew was the first gospel written; that Peter, or Peter and Mark together, used that edition in composing Greek Mark; and that Greek Matthew then made use of Mark.[67] The stubborn tradition that Matthew was first written in Aramaic or Hebrew, along with the widespread belief in the early church that Matthew was the first gospel, renders the hypothesis of a Semitic "first edition" of Matthew attractive.

Clearly, however, if such an edition existed, the canonical Matthew is not simply a translation of this Semitic original. Matthew does not read like "translation Greek"; more important, Matthew has probably, as we have seen, used Greek Mark in composing his gospel. And there are other problems for the supposition that Mark has used a Semitic-language Matthew. Strong early tradition views Mark as composing his gospel on the basis of Peter's preaching (see the introduction to Mark's gospel). But then it is hard to imagine how Mark could also be using an earlier edition of Matthew. Moreover, Papias may not be referring to a gospel at all (see the discussion in the introduction to Matthew). All in all, the hypothesis of an earlier, Semitic-language edition of Matthew cannot certainly be either proven or disproven.

The evidence for a proto-Luke comes from within Luke itself and rests on three considerations: (1) the greater amount of special material in Luke in comparison with Matthew and Mark; (2) Luke's tendency to "go his own way," even

---

[66]The translation is by Kirsopp Lake, from *Eusebius: Ecclesiastical History,* vol. 1, LCL (Cambridge: Harvard University Press, 1926). See further discussion of this passage in chap. 3 below under "Author."

[67]E.g., Zahn 2.601–17. Others who maintain the existence of an Aramaic or Hebrew Matthew lying behind the Synoptic Gospels are Westcott, *Introduction to the Study of the Gospels,* 188–89; Chapman, *Matthew, Mark, and Luke,* 90–92; X. Léon-Dufour, "Synoptic Problem," 283–86; and J. A. T. Robinson, *Redating the New Testament* (Philadelphia: Westminster, 1976), 97.

in material shared with Matthew and Mark (especially in the passion narrative); and (3) the fact that Luke includes material from Mark in blocks rather than scattered evenly throughout the gospel. These phenomena have suggested to many scholars that Luke had composed a first edition of this gospel with the use of Q and L (his special material) and then later integrated Mark into this initial work.[68] While the case remains unproven,[69] the hypothesis is an attractive one (see discussion in chap. 5).

Conclusion. The two-source hypothesis provides the best overall explanation for the relationships among the Synoptic Gospels, but two caveats must be introduced in conclusion. First, the process through which the gospels came into being was a complex one, so complex that *no* source-critical hypothesis, however detailed,[70] can hope to provide a complete explanation of the situation. Granted that at least one of the evangelists was an eyewitness, that various oral and written traditions unrecoverable to us were undoubtedly circulating, and that the evangelists may even have talked together about their work, the "scissors-and-paste" assumptions of some source critics are quite unfounded.[71] Indeed, some source critics assume processes of collection and editing quite unlike anything we know of from the ancient world.[72] Recognizing this complexity, along with the stubborn persistence of phenomena that the two-source hypothesis cannot satisfactorily explain, we should treat this hypothesis more as a working theory than as a conclusion set in concrete. Especially important is the need to be open to the possibility that, in a given pericope, an explanation based on the two-source hypothesis may not fit the data. For a given text, we thus may conclude that Matthew is more primitive than Mark, or that Luke has followed a special eyewitness source rather than Mark, or that Matthew has relied on his own remembrance or written notes rather than on Q.

The Stage of Final Composition: Redaction Criticism

In our account of gospel origins thus far, we have paid but scant attention to the evangelists themselves. We have looked at the earliest, mainly oral stage of transmission, where the apostles and other unknown Christian preachers and teachers preserved Jesus' teachings and the stories about him. And we have

---

[68]See esp. Streeter, *Four Gospels*, 199–221; Vincent Taylor, *The Passion Narrative of St. Luke: A Critical and Historical Investigation*, ed. Owen E. Evans, SNTSMS 19 (Cambridge: Cambridge University Press, 1972); Friedrich Rehkopf, *Der lukanische Sonderquelle*, WUNT 5 (Tübingen: Mohr-Siebeck, 1959).

[69]See Fitzmyer, *Luke I–IX*, 90–91, for criticisms.

[70]See, e.g., the complicated source-critical proposal of L. Vaganay, *Le problème synoptique: Une hypothèse de travail* (Paris: Desclée, 1954); note his summary on p. 444.

[71]Correctly emphasized by Robinson, *Redating*, 93–94.

[72]Sharon Lee Mattila, "A Question Too Often Neglected," *NTS* 41 (1995): 199–217.

examined the written sources, known and unknown, that the evangelists used in composing their gospels. The evangelist Mark, we have argued, is the author of one of those basic sources. But our interest in Mark from a source-critical standpoint is not in his work as an author but in his gospel as a source for Matthew and Luke. So in both form criticism and source criticism, interest in the evangelists themselves recedes into the background. It is redaction criticism that brings the evangelists back onto center stage.

Description. Redaction criticism seeks to describe the theological purposes of the evangelists by analyzing the way they use their sources. Without denying the need for form critics to study the oral traditions or for source critics to scrutinize written sources, redaction critics insist that the evangelists must be given their rightful place as *authors:* people who, however dependent on sources and traditions, have creatively and purposefully molded that tradition into a literary whole with a theology of its own. The evangelists have not simply collected traditions and sources and pasted them together. They have added their own modifications to those traditions, and in doing so, they have brought their own particular emphases to the story of Jesus.[73] Redaction criticism is therefore one method of gospel study, and it includes five basic elements.

1. Redaction criticism distinguishes between tradition and redaction. "Tradition," in this sense, is everything—from long written sources to brief orally transmitted stories and sayings—that the evangelist had before him as he wrote his gospel. "Redaction" refers to the process of modifying that tradition as the gospel was actually written. Because redaction criticism depends on our ability to identify the traditions on which the evangelist worked (so we can know what changes he made), it is accomplished most successfully on Matthew and Luke. We can compare their final edition with two extensive sources they have used: Mark and Q (albeit, a Q reconstructed from Matthew and Luke). For the same reason, redaction criticism of Mark is a much more difficult procedure, since we do not possess any sources that he has used.[74]

---

[73]Good descriptions of redaction criticism are found in Norman Perrin, *What is Redaction Criticism?* (Philadelphia: Fortress Press, 1969); R. H. Stein, "What Is Redaktionsgeschichte?" *JBL* 88 (1969): 45–56; idem, *Studying the Synoptic Gospels*, 262–72; Joachim Rohde, *Rediscovering the Teaching of the Evangelists* (London: SCM, 1968). R. T. France provides an illuminating example of redaction criticism at work in his "Exegesis in Practice: Two Samples," in *New Testament Interpretation: Essays on Principles and Methods*, ed. I. Howard Marshall (Grand Rapids: Eerdmans, 1977), 253–64.

[74]For the methodology of redaction criticism as applied to Mark, see E. J. Pryke, *Redactional Style in the Marcan Gospel: A Study of Syntax and Vocabulary as Guides to Redaction in Mark*, SNTSMS 33 (Cambridge: Cambridge University Press, 1978); Stein, *Synoptic Problem*, 251–63. Skeptical of the whole enterprise of redaction criticism as applied to Mark is C. Clifton Black, *The Disciples in Mark: Markan Redaction in Current Debate*, JSNTSup 27 (Sheffield: JSOT Press, 1989).

2. The redactional, or editorial activity of the evangelists can be seen in several areas:

The material they have chosen to include and exclude. For instance, it is generally agreed that the roughly parallel sermons recorded by Matthew in chapters 5–7 and Luke in 6:20–49 are taken from Q. Luke's, however, is less than one-third the length of Matthew's, and it is evident that Luke has omitted almost all reference to the Old Testament and the law (e.g., Matt. 5:17–19, and the antitheses of Matt. 5:21–48). This suggests that Matthew has a serious interest in teaching the church in his day about Jesus' relationship to the law, while Luke does not.

The arrangement of the material. It can be seen from table 4 above that Matthew differs from Mark and Luke in the placement of three significant miracle stories: the stilling of the storm (8:18, 23–27), the healing of the Gerasene demoniac(s) (8:28–34), and the intertwined accounts of the raising of Jairus's daughter and the healing of the woman with a flow of blood (9:18–26). Since Mark is probably Matthew's main source for these stories, it is evident that Matthew has chosen to put them in a different order. When we find him doing the same thing with other miracle stories that end up in Matthew 8–9, we are justified in concluding that Matthew is deliberately arranging the material to make a point about Jesus as miracle worker. Such rearrangement takes place within pericopes also: Does the change in order of the temptations (Matt. 4:1–11 = Luke 4:1–12) reveal different emphases of the respective evangelists?

The "seams" that the evangelist uses to stitch his tradition together. In order to fashion a continuous narrative from diverse sources, an evangelist has to supply transitions. These transitions, or seams, often reveal important concerns of the author. Matthew, for instance, alternates teaching and narrative in a very effective manner, signaling the transition at the end of discourses with a repeated formula: "when Jesus had finished saying these things" (7:28; 19:1; see also 11:1; 13:53; 26:1).

Additions to the material. In Luke's account of Jesus' healing ministry and call of the Twelve (6:12–19), which appears to depend on Mark 3:7–18, he mentions the fact, not found in Mark, that "Jesus went out to a mountainside to pray, and spent the night praying to God" (Luke 6:12). Here, perhaps, we find evidence of a Lukan concern.

Omission of material. Where the redaction critic can be pretty sure that an evangelist has had access to a tradition that he does not include, it is important to ask whether the omission serves a theological interest. For instance, it is frequently argued that Luke has omitted the reference to Jesus "coming on the clouds of heaven" (found in both Mark and Matthew) in his reply to the high priest (22:69) because he wants to avoid the idea of an imminent parousia.

Change of wording. In a well-known beatitude, Jesus, according to Matthew, pronounces a blessing on "the poor in spirit" (5:3); according to Luke, on the "poor" (6:20). The redaction critic would note this difference as perhaps indicating Luke's relatively greater interest in socioeconomic issues.

3. Redaction critics look for patterns in these kinds of changes within a gospel. Where such a pattern emerges, we may conclude that we are dealing with a theological concern of the author. For instance, the addition of reference to Jesus praying (noted above) is of a piece with similar additions about prayer that Luke makes throughout his gospel. Prayer, we can surmise, was a theological concern of Luke. Following this procedure, a general picture of the theological stance of a particular gospel is eventually built up.

4. On the basis of this general theological picture, the redaction critic then seeks to establish a setting for the production of the gospel. Luke's alleged omission of references to an imminent parousia, for instance, is said to show that he was writing in a setting where the delay of the parousia had become a problem. To "the setting in the life of Jesus" and "the setting in the life of the church" (the form-critical concern) is added "the setting in the life of the evangelist and his community."

5. Some include within redaction criticism not only the study of the evangelists' modification of tradition but the literary and theological characteristics of the gospels, however discerned—that is, what is sometimes called *composition criticism*. To some extent, this is a fruitless semantic quarrel, but it is perhaps better to maintain the narrower definition of redaction criticism so as to differentiate it from the composition criticism that good exegetes have always done.

Origins. William Wrede, though not a redaction critic in the sense defined above, was something of a precursor of the emphasis typical of redaction criticism. Wrede wrote at a time when the "Markan hypothesis" reigned in scholarly study of the gospels. This hypothesis was so named, not just because it maintained Markan priority, but because it also claimed that Mark gave a generally untheological, historically reliable portrait of Jesus. Wrede destroyed this assumption by demonstrating that Mark was as thoroughly theological as the other gospels. Specifically, Wrede argued that Mark had added the many references where Jesus urged silence about his messiahship. This "messianic secret" was designed to explain how it came about that so few people recognized Jesus to be the Messiah during his lifetime.[75] While Wrede's specific thesis is now generally discredited, his contention that Mark is as much theologian as historian (or theologian *instead of* historian) has been widely accepted.

The implications of Wrede's understanding of the evangelists as creative theologians were not immediately appropriated. Redaction criticism as an identifiable discipline did not develop until the 1950s. Three German critics were

---

[75]William Wrede, *Das Messiasgeheimnis in den Evangelien* (Göttingen: Vandenhoeck & Ruprecht, 1901 [ET *The Messianic Secret in Mark*]).

the pioneers in the field.[76] Günther Bornkamm's essay on the stilling of the storm, in which he sought to uncover Matthew's theological point by comparing his account with Mark's, was the earliest redaction-critical work.[77] More significant were two monographs that appeared later in the decade. Hans Conzelmann, in *The Theology of St. Luke,*[78] analyzed the theological standpoint of Luke, arguing that the evangelist imposed a threefold periodization of salvation history on the gospel material: the time of Israel, the time of Jesus, and the time of the church. In doing so, according to Conzelmann, Luke provided a basis for a continuing role of the Christian community in history, thereby defusing early Christian disappointment about the delay of the parousia, namely, the failure of Jesus to return as soon as expected. Willi Marxsen did for Mark what Conzelmann did for Luke. Mark, according to Marxsen, was also motivated by concern about the parousia, but Mark believed that the parousia was imminent and wrote his gospel with the overarching purpose of gathering together Christians in Galilee to await the Lord.[79]

Hardly any serious study of the gospels proceeds without considerable utilization of redaction criticism.

It would be impossible to select even the most outstanding redaction-critical works since these initial studies. The conclusions reached by Bornkamm, Marxsen, and Conzelmann are not widely held anymore, but the methodology they pioneered has won a secure place in the field of gospel studies.[80] Countless monographs, dissertations, and articles using redaction criticism analyze themes within a gospel or the gospel as a whole, or they compare and contrast the

---

[76]R. H. Lightfoot's 1934 Bampton Lectures, published as *History and Interpretation in the Gospels* (London: Hodder & Stoughton, 1935), anticipate many of the emphases of redaction criticism, as do Ned B. Stonehouse's *The Witness of Matthew and Mark to Christ* (1944) and *The Witness of Luke to Christ* (1951) (the two can be found in a one-volume edition from Baker Book House [1979]). On Stonehouse's work, see Moisés Silva, "Ned B. Stonehouse and Redaction Criticism. Part I: The Witness of the Synoptic Evangelists to Christ; Part II: The Historicity of the Synoptic Tradition," *WTJ* 40 (1977–78): 77–88, 281–303.

[77]It can be found in English translation in G. Bornkamm, G. Barth, and H. J. Held, *Tradition and Interpretation in Matthew* (Philadelphia: Westminster, 1974).

[78]Hans Conzelmann, *The Theology of St. Luke* (New York: Harper & Row, 1960). The German original, more revealingly titled *Die Mitte der Zeit* ("The Center of Time"), was published in 1954.

[79]Willi Marxsen, *Mark the Evangelist: Studies on the Redaction History of the Gospel* (Nashville: Abingdon, 1969); the German original appeared in 1956.

[80]Note particularly three monographs from conservative scholars that employ redaction-critical methods and that dissent from the conclusions of Marxsen, Conzelmann, and Bornkamm: Ralph Martin, *Mark: Evangelist and Theologian* (Grand Rapids: Zondervan, 1972); I. Howard Marshall, *Luke: Historian and Theologian,* new, enlarged ed. (Grand Rapids: Zondervan, 1989); R. T. France, *Matthew: Evangelist and Theologian* (Grand Rapids: Zondervan, 1989). See also Grant R. Osborne, "History and Theology in the Synoptic Gospels," *TrinJ* 24 (2003): 5–22.

contribution of two or more evangelists to a theme. Hardly any serious study of the gospels proceeds without considerable utilization of redaction criticism. This is not to say that redaction criticism has ousted form criticism or source criticism; contemporary scholars employ all three together as they seek to understand the final product, the gospels (the redactional stage), in terms of the raw material that has gone into them (the stage of tradition).

Evaluation. Popularity does not make anything right. As with any other method, we must take a critical look at redaction criticism before we endorse it as a method of gospel study. We begin with five criticisms of the discipline.[81]

1. Redaction criticism depends for its validity on our ability to distinguish tradition and redaction. We must have a rather clear idea about the sources that a given evangelist has used before we can begin speaking about his modifications to those sources. Almost all redaction critics have assumed the validity of the two-source hypothesis in their research—that is, that Matthew and Luke both used Mark and another source, Q, in writing their gospels. Those who question the accuracy of that hypothesis will also, of course, have to establish a different basis on which to do redaction criticism. Advocates of the two-gospel hypothesis, for instance, will have to speak about Mark's modifications of Matthew and Luke rather than Matthew's modifications of Mark, and they will be able to do redaction criticism of Matthew only with great difficulty. But even if we assume the general reliability of the two-source hypothesis, our difficulties for redaction criticism are not eliminated.

First, as we have argued, in some places the direction of dependence hypothesized with the two-source theory may be reversed. Some places in Mark, let us say, may depend on a version of a story that found its way eventually almost intact into Matthew's gospel. In such a situation we would have to speak of Mark's changes of "Matthew" rather than Matthew's changes of Mark. Second, Matthew or Luke may sometimes depend on a version of a story independent of, but parallel to, Mark. Again, then, what a redaction critic would label "Matthean redaction" (of Mark) may be a tradition that Matthew is simply passing on. Third, since we do not possess a copy of Q, arguments about whether Matthew or Luke has redacted Q are necessarily uncertain. Scholars generally think that they can identify, by various factors, what the original of Q probably was, and they base their redactional judgments on that supposition. But the process is necessarily subjective and leaves room for much disagreement. For instance, with respect to the difference between "poor" (Luke) and "poor in spirit" (Matthew) already mentioned, can we be sure that Luke has social-

---

[81]For more detail on these points and others, see D. A. Carson, "Redaction Criticism: On the Legitimacy and Illegitimacy of a Literary Tool," in *Scripture and Truth*, ed. D. A. Carson and John D. Woodbridge (Grand Rapids: Zondervan, 1983), 119–42, 376–81.

ized Q, rather than Matthew spiritualizing it? In this case, perhaps we can suspect that Luke is the one responsible, since his change conforms to an obvious emphasis in his gospel. But the decision is often much more difficult and is fraught with possibilities for error. All this goes to say that redaction critics often need to be much more cautious about claiming that an evangelist has changed his source. We may not be able to identify redactional elements as often as, or as certainly as, we might like.[82]

2. Redaction critics too often assume that all the changes an evangelist makes to his tradition are theologically motivated. Many no doubt are; but many others, and particularly minor changes affecting one or two words, are stylistic in nature. In other cases, even major additions may be due not to theological concerns but to historical interest. We cannot omit simple historical purposes from the intentions of the evangelists.[83]

3. Redaction critics have sometimes equated "redactional emphases" with the evangelist's theology. What is determined to be redaction shows us what is distinct about a particular gospel in comparison with the others or with its sources. We may often legitimately conclude that what is redactional, since it is what an evangelist has deliberately changed, is particularly significant to that evangelist. But it is certainly not the whole of, or perhaps even representative of, his theology. To assume so would be to assume that the tradition an evangelist takes over is *not* of interest to him or part of his theology. This is manifestly absurd. It would be as if, in comparing the writings of Calvin and Beza, the theologies of each of these men were determined only on the basis of what was unique in each one. The common emphases of Matthew, Mark, and Luke far outweigh their distinctives, and a holistic picture of what each teaches must take both into account.

4. The identification of the setting of a particular gospel on the basis of the author's theology is often far more specific than the data allow. That the additions of Matthew to both Mark and Q involving the Mosaic law and Old Testament quotations demonstrate that Matthew was writing in a setting and to an audience that needed teaching on this matter is evident. And that the tenor of these additions may even allow us to make some guesses about the particular problems of the community in which Matthew was writing is also clear. But the details of setting that some redaction critics hypothesize are often castles built on sand. They usually depend on only part of the evidence (hence, different

---

[82]The difficulty of isolating "redaction" has led some to suggest a more cautious approach that focuses on thematic studies within a gospel (e.g., "composition criticism"); see Randall K. T. Tan, "Recent Developments in Redaction Criticism: From Investigation of Textual Prehistory Back to Historical-Grammatical Exegesis?" *JETS* 44 (2001): 599–614.

[83]See Graham N. Stanton, *Jesus of Nazareth in New Testament Preaching,* SNTSMS 27 (Cambridge: Cambridge University Press, 1974).

critics working on the same gospel come up with conflicting settings) and draw conclusions far more specific than the evidence allows. Even the tendency of redaction critics to draw inferences about the nature of the communities to which the evangelists were writing may have to be given up if the argument of Richard Bauckham—that the gospels were written to the general Christian public and not to specific communities—is accepted.[84]

5. Redaction criticism is often pursued in such a way that the historical trustworthiness of the gospel material is called into question. It is not so much that redaction criticism seeks to prove the unhistorical nature of the changes introduced by the evangelists. Rather, many redaction critics assume that the evangelists would have little concern about it. Thus, as Marxsen puts it, "Within this approach, the question as to what really happened is excluded from the outset."[85] In this sense, redaction criticism is a true descendent of radical form criticism. Mark, Matthew, and Luke, according to many redaction critics, had no more interest in historical accuracy than did the early Christian community as reconstructed by Bultmann and Dibelius. So typical is the antihistorical bias of many of the best-known redaction critics that redaction criticism, like form criticism, has earned for itself the reputation of being a method that attacks the historical reliability of the gospels.

But it is unfair to generalize from the way many pursue redaction criticism to the method itself. Nothing about redaction criticism per se is antihistorical. Indeed, as we will argue below, redaction criticism has some very positive contributions to make to our interpretation of the Synoptic Gospels. Why, then, do so many redaction critics come to conclusions that question the historical credibility of the gospels?

One major reason is an assumption among many redaction critics that an evangelist cannot be both theologically motivated and historically accurate. We are often presented, explicitly or implicitly, with the choice between history and theology. Yet there is no reason why an evangelist cannot have both concerns. That Matthew, Mark, and Luke have redacted the gospel traditions that came to them is beyond doubt. And for some redaction critics, it appears, this is enough to justify the conclusion that, in tampering with the tradition, the evangelists have tampered with history. But this is not necessary. Rearranging, adding, omitting, and rewording need not detract from the historicity of the event or teaching concerned. For instance, newspapers will frequently rewrite for their own readers news-service reports that they receive, but their rewrites

---

[84]Richard Bauckham, "For Whom were the Gospels Written?" in *The Gospels for All Christians* (Grand Rapids: Eerdmans, 1998), 9–48. See also Hengel, *The Four Gospels*, 106–11. For criticism of Bauckham's hypothesis, see Joel Marcus, *Mark 1–8: A New Translation with Introduction and Commentary*, AB 27 (New York: Doubleday, 2000), 25–27.

[85]Marxsen, *Mark the Evangelist*, 23.

need not affect the accuracy of the report. Major speeches will sometimes be summarized in a few words, or excerpts will be taken from them. In doing so, different newspapers may focus on different emphases in the same speech. We do not accuse these newspapers of inaccuracy in doing this, nor should we accuse the evangelists of historical inaccuracies if they summarize, excerpt, or reword Jesus' own sayings. That they have done so seems clear, as a comparison among the evangelists at almost any page in a synopsis shows. But their failure to preserve the *ipsissima verba Jesu* (the authentic *words* of Jesus) does not mean that they have tampered with the *ipsissima vox Jesu* (the authentic *voice* of Jesus). As long as the evangelists' redactional modifications are consistent with what actually happened or with what Jesus actually said—even if they select, summarize, and reword—historical integrity is maintained.[86]

The question, then, boils down to the intentions of the evangelists as these can be determined from their express statements and their actual redactional work. Did they intend to write their gospels with a concern for historical accuracy? Or did they theologize the message of Jesus with little interest in whether it really happened that way or not? Redaction criticism, in itself, cannot answer these questions. And redaction critics themselves come to radically different conclusions about this matter. Some are convinced that a careful study of the modifications introduced by the evangelists shows no tampering with historicity. They separate redaction from tradition in order to understand the message of the gospels better, without supposing that the redaction has any less historical foundation than the tradition.[87] Thus, for instance, they may conclude that Luke has redacted Jesus' beatitude "Blessed are the poor" to include an economic focus by pairing it with his "Woe to you rich," while Matthew has redacted the same saying as "Blessed are the poor in spirit" to emphasize the spiritual dimension. But as long as Jesus intended both—and it is quite likely that he did, given the Old Testament concept of "poor"—then it would be unfair to accuse either evangelist of an unhistorical tampering with the words of Jesus. Many instances are of course more difficult, and only a text-by-text scrutiny of the data is finally adequate to demonstrate the case one way or the other. Our point here is simply that redaction criticism need not be destructive to the historical accuracy of the gospels and that redaction critics who assume that the evangelists had no concern for history in their redactional activity have not proven their point.

---

[86]The issue raised in this paragraph is very broad and important. For these points and others, see esp. R. T. France, "The Authenticity of the Sayings of Jesus," in *History, Criticism, and Faith,* ed. Colin Brown (Downers Grove: IVP, 1976), 101–41; Craig Blomberg, *The Historical Reliability of the Gospels* (Downers Grove: IVP, 1987), esp. 35–43, 113–52; I. Howard Marshall, *I Believe in the Historical Jesus* (Grand Rapids: Eerdmans, 1977).

[87]See, e.g., Grant R. Osborne, "The Evangelical and Redaction Criticism: Critique and Methodology," *JETS* 22 (1979): 305–22.

The problems of redaction criticism, then, are problems of exaggerated claims, false assumptions, and inappropriate applications. Pursued properly, redaction criticism offers the promise of real help in interpreting the gospels. Specifically, the discipline of redaction criticism has several positive elements.

1. By focusing on the final, authorial stage in the production of the gospels, it offers immediate help to the interpreter and theologian. In this respect it contrasts favorably with both form and source criticism, which, in their concern with the prehistory of the gospel tradition, are important for the historian of early Christianity but of only minimal help to the interpreter. Redaction criticism looks at the level that deserves most of our attention: the final literary product, the gospel.

2. Redaction criticism reminds us that the evangelists wrote with more than (though not less than) historical interest. They were preachers and teachers, concerned to apply the truths of Jesus' life and teaching to specific communities in their own day. This theological purpose of the evangelists has sometimes been missed, with a consequent loss of appreciation for the significance and application of the history that the evangelists narrate.

3. Redaction criticism recognizes, and increases our appreciation of, the multiplicity of the gospels. The story of Jesus has come to us, not in one supergospel, but in four gospels, each with its own distinct and important contribution to make to our understanding of Jesus. While creating occasional problems at the historical level, this fourfold gospel should be appreciated for the richness of perspective it brings. "Jesus is such a gigantic figure that we need all four portraits to discern him,"[88] and redaction criticism helps us to appreciate the artistry and meaning of each of those portraits.

THE GOSPELS AS WORKS OF LITERATURE

We have sketched the process by which the gospels have come into being. We now turn our attention to the final products, considered on their own as works of literature. Two matters call for specific consideration: the question of the gospel genre, and the new literary criticism.

The Genre of the Gospels

Nowhere in the New Testament is any of the four accounts of Jesus' ministry called a gospel (εὐαγγέλιον [*euangelion*]; on Mark 1:1, see the introduction to Mark). "Gospel" and the cognate verb "preach the gospel" (εὐαγγελίζομαι [*euangelizomai*]) are used in the New Testament, and especially frequently in Paul, to denote the message of God's saving act in his Son (e.g., in Mark 1:14–

---

[88]Leon Morris, *Studies in the Fourth Gospel* (Grand Rapids: Eerdmans, 1969), 107.

15; Rom. 1:16; 1 Cor. 15:1; Gal. 1:6–7).[89] Probably at some time toward the end of the first century or early in the second, titles were added to the church's authoritative accounts of Jesus' ministry. Certainly this was when "gospel" was first used to denote a work of literature.[90] These titles preserve the stress on the singleness of *the* gospel by the way they are phrased: not "the gospel *by* Mark," but "the [one] gospel, according to [the version of] Mark" (and Matthew and Luke and John). Justin, in the middle of the second century, is the first author to use the word *gospel* of the canonical accounts of Jesus' ministry (*Apol.* 1.66; *Dial.* 10.2). It was probably Mark's use of the word in prominent places in his gospel (e.g., 1:1, 14) that led to its use as a literary designation.[91] No books before our gospels had ever been given this designation. What implications does this hold for the literary genre of the gospels?

The question is an important one for the reader of the gospels because accurate interpretation depends to some extent on accurate decisions about genre. The phrase "red rose" will signify something quite different in a botanical treatise than it does in Robert Burns's line "O, my luve is like a red, red rose." Similarly, Jesus' walking on the water will mean one thing for the reader who takes the gospels to be straightforward history and a very different thing for the reader who is convinced that he or she is reading a myth or a midrash.

Modern study of the genre of the gospels began with K. L. Schmidt's decision to classify them as "popular literature" (*Kleinliteratur*) rather than "literary works" (*Hochliteratur*).[92] As popular literature, they could be expected to follow the rules of transmission typical of such literature—an important point for Schmidt, who was one of the pioneers of form criticism. This classification also meant that the gospels were to be viewed as distinct from the more literary biographies of various types prevalent in the ancient Greco-Roman world. From a slightly different perspective, C. H. Dodd viewed the gospels (and especially Mark) as mirroring the early Christian preaching (kerygma) about Christ. As expansions of this kerygma, the gospels were viewed more as the last stage in a

Accurate interpretation depends to some extent on accurate decisions about genre.

---

[89]The New Testament use of εὐαγγέλιον (*euangelion*, "gospel") and εὐαγγελίζομαι (*euangelizomai*, "to preach good news") is taken from the Old Testament. These Greek words translate Hebrew words (from the root בשׂר, "bear good tidings"]) that refer to the deliverance that God has promised his people (see esp. Isa. 40:9; 42:7; 52:7; 61:1; Ps. 95:1).

[90]See, e.g., G. Friedrich, "εὐαγγέλιον," in *TDNT* 2.721–35.

[91]E.g., Martin Hengel, "The Titles of the Gospels and the Gospel of Mark," in *Studies in the Gospel of Mark* (Philadelphia: Fortress Press, 1985), 64–84.

[92]K. L. Schmidt, "Die Stellung der Evangelien in der allgemeinen Literaturgeschichte," in ΕΥΧΑΡΙΣΤΗΡΙΟΝ: *Studien zur Religion und Literatur des Alten und Neuen Testaments, Fs.* Hermann Gunkel, ed. K. L. Schmidt, FRLANT 19.2 (Göttingen: Vandenhoeck & Ruprecht, 1923), 59–60.

continuous oral tradition than as self-conscious literary creations.[93] These approaches to the gospels led to the view that they could be fitted into no ancient literary genre but were unique. Without necessarily subscribing to either Schmidt's or Dodd's view of gospel origins, many (perhaps even a majority of) contemporary scholars think that the gospels do not fit into any established literary category.[94]

But others are convinced that, while possessing some unique features, the gospels share enough features with other works of the ancient world to be placed in the genre of these works. A number of specific genre identifications have been proposed, from Greek aretalogy (stories of the miraculous deeds of a godlike hero) to Jewish midrash. But the most popular suggestion, as well as the most defensible, is that the gospels are biographies. True, they are quite different from the standard modern biography: they lack accounts of Jesus' childhood development and education, his character and motivations, and chronological precision. But ancient Greco-Roman biographies did not always contain such features either. Indeed, the genre of biography was a very broad one in antiquity, encompassing works of considerable diversity. It was certainly broad enough, it is argued, to include the Synoptic Gospels.[95]

Our decision about how to classify the gospels will depend considerably on how much flexibility we give to the concept of genre. Most modern literary critics emphasize that genre does not impose a rigid set of requirements but creates

---

[93]See Robert Guelich, "The Gospel Genre," in *Das Evangelium und die Evangelien,* ed. Peter Stuhlmacher (Tübingen: Mohr-Siebeck, 1983), 183–219.

[94]See, e.g., Kümmel, 37; Guthrie, 16–19; Martin, 1:20; Robert H. Gundry, "Recent Investigations into the Literary Genre 'Gospel,'" in *New Dimensions in New Testament Study,* ed. Richard N. Longenecker and Merrill C. Tenney (Grand Rapids: Zondervan, 1974), 101–13.

[95]The most thorough defense is R. A. Burridge, *What are the Gospels? A Comparison with Greco-Roman Biography,* SNTSMS 70 (Cambridge: Cambridge University Press, 1992). See also C. W. Votaw, "The Gospels and Contemporary Biographies," *AJT* 19 (1915): 45–71; Charles H. Talbert, *What Is a Gospel? The Genre of the Canonical Gospels* (Philadelphia: Fortress Press, 1977); Philip L. Shuler, *A Genre for the Gospels: The Biographical Character of Matthew* (Philadelphia: Fortress Press, 1982); Detlev Dormeyer and Hubert Frankemölle, "Evangelium als literarische Gattung und als theologisches Begriff: Tendenzen und Aufgaben der Evangelienforschung im 20. Jahrhundert, mit einer Untersuchung des Markusevangeliums in seinem Verhältnis zur antiken Biographie," in *ANRW* 25.2, pp.1545–81; Albrecht Dihle, "Die Evangelien und die griechische Biographie," in *Das Evangelium und die Evangelien,* 383–411; David E. Aune, *The New Testament in Its Literary Environment,* LEC 8 (Philadelphia: Westminster, 1987), 17–76; Graham N. Stanton, *The Gospels and Jesus,* 2nd ed. (Oxford: Oxford University Press, 2002), 14–18 (a change from the earlier edition, in which the uniqueness of the gospel genre was emphasized).

the presumption of "a flexible set of expectations."[96] Moreover, they argue that there can really be no such thing as a "unique" book. To be understood at all, a book would have to conform to certain generic conventions. We should probably, therefore, place the gospels into the category of the ancient Greco-Roman *bios,* the biography. Even the Gospel of Luke, which might be classified as historiography because of its ties to the Acts of the Apostles, can be accomodated within the boundaries of the ancient biography.

But we should at the same time recognize the genuinely unique features of the gospels. Unlike most other ancient biographies, the gospels are anonymous; they lack the literary pretensions characteristic of most biographies; and, most of all, they combine teaching and action in a preaching-oriented work that stands apart from anything else in the ancient world.[97] This latter point is especially important in view of the tendency among some scholars to expand the concept of "gospel" to include such documents as Q, *The Gospel of Thomas,* and *The Gospel of Truth.*[98] As Philip Jenkins has shown, this tendency owes more to contemporary ideological trends than it does to serious scholarship.[99] In any case, these documents lack the narrative and kerygmatic mixture that seems to be intrinsic to the canonical gospel genre.

Literary Criticism

Description. We are using "Literary Criticism" as a catchall designation for contemporary approaches to the gospels that focus on careful study of the way the gospels function as pieces of literature. Of course, both scholars and laypeople have pursued this kind of study of the gospels for centuries. But what distinguishes modern literary criticism is a self-conscious turn from the preoccupation with the prehistory of the gospels that dominated gospel studies from 1800–1970 to a concentration on the text "as it is." Investigations of the prehistory of the Synoptic Gospels such as dominate form and source criticism, it is claimed, have resulted in a "critical distancing of the text" that "has transformed biblical writings into museum pieces without contemporary

---

[96]Burridge, *What are the Gospels?* 62.

[97]Patricia Cox makes the important point that ancient biographies recounted the "deeds" (πράξεις [*praxeis*]) of its subject only as a means of illuminating his or her "essence," or "manner of life" (ἔθος [*ethos*]) (*Biography in Late Antiquity* [Berkeley: University of California, 1983], 65). This does not match the intention of the evangelists.

[98]See, e.g., Helmut Koester, *Ancient Christian Gospels: Their History and Development* (Philadelphia: Trinity Press International, 1990), 1–48. And note the title of the important study of Q by John Kloppenborg: *Excavating Q: The History and Setting of the Sayings Gospel* (Minneapolis: Fortress Press, 2000).

[99]Philip Jenkins, *Hidden Gospels: How the Search for Jesus Lost its Way* (Oxford: Oxford University Press, 2001).

relevance."[100] Even redaction criticism falls under criticism, because it is built on traditions analysis and tends to be preoccupied with distilling theology from the narrative. Thus, many gospel scholars no longer bother themselves with the question of sources and forms, or even of author and circumstance of writing. They simply want to discover how the gospels function as autonomous literary texts. Applying insights from the wider world of literary studies, these scholars analyze the narratives of the gospels, seeking to discover how the plot unfolds and how the characters develop. The real meaning of the narrative, indeed, is often seen to lie behind the words of the text, in the "deep structures" that the narrative reveals. "Structuralism," appropriately, is the name given to the specific methodology that seeks to discover and classify these basic components of human thought and expression.[101] Various other related methods and viewpoints, such as deconstruction, rhetorical criticism, discourse analysis, social-science criticism, and ideological criticism are often added to the mix.[102]

It should be emphasized that specific approaches within this very broad movement vary widely. As we suggest above, many literary critics are clearly working from a radical postmodern agenda, questioning our ability to discover the "original" meaning of the text and the utility of doing so even if we could. For such critics, the text takes on a life of its own. The meaning it conveys is not tied to its historical origin—whether we think of that origin as located in a community or an author—but to the way it functions as it is read by the modern interpreter. For many literary critics, then, we cannot speak of a true or false meaning of any given gospel text or of the gospel as a whole but only of *my* meaning and *your* meaning. Meaning is located, not in an author's intention, but in the encounter of text and reader. Literary critics studying the gospels in this way

---

[100]Edgar V. McKnight, *Post-Modern Use of the Bible: The Emergence of Reader-Oriented Criticism* (Nashville: Abingdon, 1988), 14.

[101]A fine brief survey of the movement generally, with competent critique, is Tremper Longman III, *Literary Approaches to Biblical Interpretation* (Grand Rapids: Zondervan, 1987). Some important studies that consider various approaches within this general movement are Norman R. Peterson, *Literary Criticism for New Testament Critics* (Philadelphia: Fortress Press, 1978); Edgar V. McKnight, *Meaning in Texts* (Philadelphia: Fortress Press, 1974); idem, *Post-Modern Use of the Bible;* Daniel Patte, *What Is Structural Exegesis?* (Philadelphia: Fortress Press, 1976); idem, *Structural Exegesis for New Testament Critics* (Philadelphia: Fortress Press, 1990); Robert W. Funk, *The Poetics of Biblical Narrative* (Sonoma: Polebridge, 1989); S. D. Moore, *Poststructuralism and the New Testament* (Minneapolis: Fortress Press, 1994). See also Jack Dean Kingsbury, *Matthew as Story* (Philadelphia: Fortress Press, 1986).

[102]An excellent sample of these various approaches, applied to the Gospel of Mark, is found in *Mark and Method: New Approaches in Biblical Studies*, ed. Janice Capel Anderson and Stephen D. Moore (Minneapolis: Fortress Press, 1992).

mirror the movement in interpretation theory generally from an author-based hermeneutic to a text- or reader-based hermeneutic.

But not all literary critics have turned their backs entirely on author and history. Many use modern literary methods as a basic tool to uncover the meaning intended by the authors of the gospels. They share with the more radical literary critics a conviction that tradition criticism is of minimal help in illuminating the meaning of the text. But they view various forms of literary criticism as tools to illuminate the meaning that the evangelists intended their texts to have.

Evaluation. Literary criticism is rooted in a valid concern: study of the gospels has too often focused on the history of the tradition behind them to the extent that the gospels themselves become lost to sight. Focus on the text as we now have it is a welcome corrective to this tendency. Literary critics have also shed new light on the way different parts of the gospels function within the larger literary unit. And exegetes can profit from the taxonomies of narrative structures that literary critics use in their interpretations. But we must also point out some severe problems with the way many literary critics pursue their discipline.

First, there exists among many literary critics a reaction not only against excessive historical analysis but against history itself. It appears that literary criticism has sought to turn the problem of historical skepticism and uncertainty into a virtue. True, they say, we can know little for certain about Jesus, but by insisting that the truth of the gospels lies within their own "narrative world," the literary critic can ignore the problem. Yet the problem will not go away so easily, for the evangelists are demonstrably *referring* to events in the real world. The failure of literary criticism to deal with this means that it can never get to the real heart of the gospels.[103]

Second, the casting of the text loose from the author means—as many literary critics teach—that there can be no such thing as a correct meaning of the text. But the evangelists were individuals writing in specific circumstances and to specific audiences; this historical setting, not the individual reader, must set the context for interpretation.[104]

Third, the general tendency to derive categories of interpretation from modern literature, such as the novel, is a questionable procedure. Quite apart from the issue of the validity of modern theories of novel interpretation (and there is reason for skepticism), it is doubtful whether the gospels should be compared to the modern novel.

Fourth, there are questions about the structuralism used in much literary criticism. These questions have to do with both the existence of the alleged deep

---

[103]See, for this point, Kevin Vanhoozer, "A Lamp in the Labyrinth: The Hermeneutics of 'Aesthetic' Theology," *TrinJ* 8 (1987): 25–56.

[104]See, e.g., E. D. Hirsch Jr., *Validity in Interpretation* (New Haven: Yale University Press, 1967).

structures as well as their usefulness for interpretation. Are we attributing to ancient writers modern structures of thinking and writing? Must all writing fall into such structures? These questions do not apply to all forms of structuralism, but they should make us very cautious about the usefulness of some of the more popular and far-reaching wings of the movement.

Again, we want to emphasize that these criticisms apply only to certain kinds of literary criticism. As we mentioned above, many scholars pursue their literary studies of the gospels in combination with careful historical and philological study and with the aim of illuminating more clearly their original meaning. Such a melding of traditional exegesis and literary criticism holds great promise in discerning the message of the narratives through which God has chosen to communicate to us his good news.

JESUS AND THE SYNOPTIC GOSPELS

The two previous questions we have examined—How did the gospels come into being? How are they to be understood as literary works?—are important in their own right, but they become especially significant when we understand their ramifications for the historical issue. Do the gospels tell us a great deal about the early church but almost nothing about Jesus (Bultmann)? Do they tell us mainly about different forms of early Christianity, with Jesus but a shadowy and uncertain figure at its inception (some redaction critics)? Do they introduce us into a narrative world in which Jesus becomes little more than a protagonist in a story (some literary critics)? What do the gospels tell us of Jesus? This is a fundamental question for New Testament studies, and here we answer it only briefly by surveying some of the main approaches and indicating briefly our own position.

The Question of the "Historical" Jesus

Christians before the eighteenth century entertained few doubts that the gospels were to be read as historically reliable accounts of the life of Jesus. The main problem to be faced was that of harmonization: explaining how the four gospels could be combined together to produce a smooth and coherent account of Jesus' life. Such attempts date from the earliest days of the church (e.g., Tatian in the second century) and continue to be popular in our own day. But this generally unquestioned confidence in the historical accuracy of the gospels' portrait of Jesus changed in the eighteenth century under the onslaught of the Enlightenment. A new, critically oriented historiography was less disposed to accept ancient accounts at face value. This attitude applied especially to miracles, which did not fit well into the deistic view of a mechanical and reliable universe. The most famous early attack on the historicity of the gospels was that of Samuel Reimarus. His "Fragments," published by Lessing in 1774–78 after his death, raised serious doubts about the gospel accounts. Among other things, Reimarus suggested that the resurrection did not occur; instead, the disciples stole the body.[105]

Reimarus's attack on the gospels initiated what has been called the "first quest for the historical Jesus." Nineteenth-century scholars who pursued this quest often shared the skepticism of Reimarus about the miraculous element in the gospels. H. E. G. Paulus, for example, explained away the resurrection as a revival from a coma in the cold tomb and argued that Jesus' walking on the water was in reality his walking on a barely submerged sandbar. But a major break with this rationalistic approach came in the groundbreaking *Life of Jesus* by D. F. Strauss (1835–36). Strauss, while no more accepting of the historicity of the gospels than his rationalistic predecessors, insisted that they taught truth, but truth of a religious and philosophical nature. Much of the gospel material consisted of myths (stories with religious value) that were important witnesses to the "absolute spirit," a concept taken from the then-popular philosophy of Hegel. Reaction against Strauss and other such extreme skeptics took many forms. One was the Markan hypothesis, which viewed Mark as relatively untheological and therefore a generally reliable basis for a historical Jesus. Such a view fed into the many lives of Jesus, told from a liberal perspective, in which the theological and dogmatic layers of the Greek-influenced early church (and particularly Paul) were stripped off in order to get at the real Jesus: the humble teacher of Nazareth.

Three influential works ended the first quest. The most famous was Albert Schweitzer's *Quest for the Historical Jesus,* a chronicle of "lives of Jesus" from Reimarus to his own time (1906).[106] Schweitzer showed how each successive "historical" Jesus was little more than the projection of the writer's own cultural and philosophical outlook back into the plane of history. Building on the work of Johannes Weiss,[107] Schweitzer saw eschatology as the key to understanding Jesus. Jesus proclaimed the impending world-ending entrance of the kingdom of God and died disappointed when it had not come. Two other books written a bit earlier called into question the possibility of a nontheological, untendentious picture of Jesus: Martin Kähler's *The So-Called Historical Jesus and the Historic, Biblical Christ*[108] and William Wrede's *The Messianic Secret in*

> *Christians before the eighteenth century entertained few doubts that the gospels were to be read as historically reliable accounts of the life of Jesus. The main problem to be faced was that of harmonization.*

---

[105]On Reimarus and other key figures in the debate about the "historical Jesus" through the middle of the nineteenth century, see esp. Colin Brown, *Jesus in European Protestant Thought*, 1778–1860 (Grand Rapids: Baker, 1988). A broader survey is found in Charles C. Anderson, *Critical Quests of Jesus* (Grand Rapids: Eerdmans, 1969).

[106]Albert Schweitzer, *The Quest for the Historical Jesus* (New York: Macmillan, 1961). The German title is *Von Reimarus zu Wrede (From Reimarus to Wrede)*.

[107]Johannes Weiss, *Jesus' Proclamation of the Kingdom of God* (Philadelphia: Fortress Press, 1971); the German original was published in 1892.

[108]Martin Kähler, *The So-Called Historical Jesus and the Historic, Biblical Christ* (Philadelphia: Fortress Press, 1964); the German original was published in 1896.

Mark.[109] Thus, as E. E. Ellis puts it, "The Quest began with the supposition that history could be extracted from the Gospels like a kernel from the husk; it ended with the growing recognition that the process was more like peeling an onion with history and interpretation intermixed at every layer."[110]

Rudolf Bultmann kept peeling until there was almost nothing left. His form-critical studies of the gospels convinced him that we could know very little for sure about Jesus himself: the accounts have simply been reinterpreted too thoroughly by the early church. But this did not concern Bultmann, for it is not what we can uncover about Jesus in history that matters for us but what we can experience of Jesus in personal encounter with him here and now. Historical facts cannot prove articles of faith: "Rather, the acknowledgment of Jesus as the one in whom God's word decisively encounters man, whatever title be given him . . . is a pure act of faith independent of the answer to the historical question. . . . Faith, being personal decision, cannot be dependent on a historian's labor."[111] Bultmann, using existentialist philosophy as a guide, pursues a program of "demythologization" in which the modern reader penetrates through the myths of the gospels to find real truth.

A concern among Bultmann's own pupils that he had gone too far in casting loose the Christian faith from historical moorings led to the "second quest" for the historical Jesus. These scholars were concerned that Bultmann's lack of interest in history would leave the church adrift and helpless to make any claims for itself at all. Ernst Käsemann opened this new quest in 1953, and he was followed by several other influential German theologians.[112] Nevertheless, what even the "new questers" decided can be reliably known about Jesus was so small a residue of the whole that little was gained.

Study of the historical Jesus has not waned over the years, and the number and variety of approaches defy simple classification. But two rather contrasting movements deserve mention. The first, the Jesus Seminar, continues the generally negative historical judgments that typified both the first and the second "quest." Members of the Jesus Seminar, which has been in existence since 1985,

---

[109]The German original, *Das Messiasgeheimnis in den Evangelien*, was first published in 1901.

[110]E. E. Ellis, "Gospels Criticism: A Perspective on the State of the Art," in *Das Evangelium und die Evangelien*, 30.

[111]Rudolf Bultmann, *Theology of the New Testament* (New York: Charles Scribner's Sons, 1951–55), 1.26.

[112]Ernst Käsemann, "The Problem of the Historical Jesus," in *Essays on New Testament Themes* (Philadelphia: Fortress Press, 1964), 15–47; Bornkamm, *Jesus of Nazareth*, esp. 13–26; and note James M. Robinson, *A New Quest of the Historical Jesus*, SBT 25 (London: SCM, 1959). For a conservative appraisal, see Ralph P. Martin, "The New Quest of the Historical Jesus," in *Jesus of Nazareth: Savior and Lord*, ed. Carl F. H. Henry (Grand Rapids: Eerdmans, 1966), 31–45.

meet periodically to vote on the authenticity of gospel material. The vote has usually gone against the gospels; only 20 percent of the sayings of Jesus, for instance, have been accepted as possibly authentic.[113] The seminar, by means of an adroit media campaign, has attracted a great deal of attention—far more than its work merits. As several scholars have pointed out, the seminar is not representative of biblical scholarship generally, and its conclusions are driven by unwarranted presuppositions.[114] Two of its members have published significant "lives" of Jesus, revealing the general tendency of the Seminar as a whole. While the two differ in many important respects, they agree in presenting a portrait of Jesus, built mainly on Q and the noncanonical *Gospel of Thomas*, that emphasizes his antiestablishment preaching and ignores or plays down his miracles, atoning death, and resurrection.[115]

The second movement we wish to mention has been dubbed the "third quest for the historical Jesus." Scholars who might be placed under this rubric represent a wide spectrum of specific viewpoints. But they are generally characterized by a serious attempt to place Jesus squarely within the matrix of first-century Judaism and by a relatively positive approach to the historicity of the gospels.[116]

It would be impossible to catalog here the variety of interpretations of the life of Jesus that are current in scholarship in our own day;[117] nor have we done more than scratch the historical surface. Indeed, the picture we come away with from so cursory a survey can be seriously misleading, since it focuses on the new and the unusual at the expense of the many fine restatements of a more conservative approach. But at least it enables us to see the extent to which the gospels have come to be considered exceedingly weak reeds for the historian's labors.

---

[113]The results of the Seminar's work are collected in *The Five Gospels*, ed. R. W. Funk and R. W. Hoover (Sonoma: Polebridge, 1993).

[114]See especially L. T. Johnson, *The Real Jesus* (San Francisco: Harper, 1996).

[115]J. D. Crossan, *The Historical Jesus: The Life of a Mediterranean Jewish Peasant* (San Francisco: Harper, 1991); M. Borg, *Jesus: A New Vision* (San Francisco: Harper, 1987).

[116]See, e.g., E. P. Sanders, *Jesus and Judaism* (Philadelphia: Fortress Press, 1985); J. P. Meier, *A Marginal Jew: Rethinking the Historical Jesus*, 4 vols. (New York: Doubleday, 1991–); N. T. Wright, *Jesus and the Victory of God* (Minneapolis: Fortress Press, 1996).

[117]A helpful survey is Ben Witherington III, *The Jesus Quest* (Downers Grove: IVP, 1995); see also N. T. Wright, *Who Was Jesus?* (Grand Rapids: Eerdmans, 1993). Two books documenting the historical issues in some detail are Markus Bockmuehl, ed., *The Cambridge Companion to Jesus* (Cambridge: Cambridge University Press, 2001) and Gerd Theissen and Annette Merz, *The Historical Jesus: A Comprehensive Guide* (Minneapolis: Fortress Press, 1998 [1996]). And see the general survey of all four gospels in Darrell L. Bock, *Jesus According to Scripture: Restoring the Portrait from the Gospels* (Grand Rapids: Baker, 2002).

Yet such skepticism is not warranted. The evangelists certainly claim to be writing history. True, they write as passionate exponents of a certain interpretation of that history, and they select and arrange their facts accordingly. But as we have seen when discussing redaction criticism, there is no reason to think a person must be a bad historian because he or she is a strong partisan. As Martin Hengel points out, scholars have erred in thinking they had to choose between preaching and historical narration: "In reality the 'theological' contribution of the evangelist lies in the fact that he combines both these things inseparably: he preaches by narrating; he writes history and in so doing proclaims."[118] A truly open-minded approach is to listen sympathetically to the case the evangelists are arguing, trying to enter into their own world to see if it makes sense. We might find that it makes more sense than the worlds we have constructed for ourselves.[119]

The Possibility of a Historical Outline

We have made no attempt here to prove a position with respect to the historicity of the gospels. But if we may grant that others have provided, not a proven position (there is no such thing as proof, in an absolute sense, in such matters), but nonetheless solid grounds for accepting the gospels as historically reliable,[120] what kind of information about Jesus can we expect to find in them? Is it possible to reconstruct a historically coherent "life of Jesus"? Some deny the validity of any such attempt. Brevard Childs, for instance, insists that the "canonical shape" of the fourfold gospel should be respected. He faults traditional harmonies for seeking the meaning of the gospels in a historical construct that disregards this canonical shape.[121] While Childs is right to insist that meaning is to be found in the texts as we have them rather than in some necessarily hypothetical pasting together of all four accounts, he is wrong to deny all significance to harmonies. For the truth of what the evangelists are saying is inevitably tied to the historical reality of what they narrate. The attempt to put together that historical reality—the life and ministry of Jesus of Nazareth—is both necessary and significant.

But is it really possible? A major barrier to the enterprise has always been the many places in which the gospels appear to contradict themselves over historical details. The most troublesome texts have been the subject of many harmonizing interpretations, ranging from the ridiculous to the convincing. Our whole

---

[118]Martin Hengel, "Literary, Theological, and Historical Problems in the Gospel of Mark," in *Studies in the Gospel of Mark* (Philadelphia: Fortress Press, 1985), 41.

[119]Note, e.g., the approach advocated by Royce Gordon Gruenler, *New Approaches to Jesus and the Gospels: A Phenomenological and Exegetical Study of Synoptic Christology* (Grand Rapids: Baker, 1982).

[120]See, e.g., Marshall, *I Believe in the Historical Jesus;* Blomberg, *Historical Reliability of the Gospels.*

[121]Childs, 154–56.

approach to this matter will depend greatly on what we think of the evangelists' accuracy generally. The more we are impressed by their accuracy—as the authors of this volume are—the further we will search for satisfactory explanations. Nevertheless, there are some places where fully satisfactory answers simply are not available. In such cases, it is better, as Luther put it, just to let it alone than to force unlikely meanings on the text.[122]

These difficulties must not obscure the fact that the Synoptic Gospels exhibit a high degree of coherence about the general course of Jesus' ministry as well as about many of the incidents within that ministry. Some of the greatest divergences do not suggest contradictions so much as accounts that have little in common with one another (such as the infancy narratives in Matthew and Luke). Coherence at the historical level in such situations is relatively easy to attain. Nevertheless, a fully satisfactory historical harmony of Jesus' life is impossible. It was simply not the evangelists' intention to provide us with the kind of data we would need for such an enterprise. They give few exact chronological indicators, and those we do have (general phrases such as "after these things," "when," and Mark's "immediately") are often too general to be of real use to the historian. The evangelists narrate historical facts, but they so select, arrange, and present these facts that little information of the kind needed to piece together a detailed life of Jesus is available.

The generally similar chronological sequence in the Synoptic Gospels is not always matched by agreement on individual episodes. In such cases, it is not a matter of chronological error, but of chronological indifference. The evangelists, and sometimes the sources they use, arrange their material topically at times, often making it impossible for us to know when in the ministry of Jesus a particular incident occurred. An example is the series of controversy stories that Mark narrates in 2:1–3:6. That Mark or his source has grouped these stories together because of their similarity in subject matter (Jesus in controversy with Jews) seems likely, particularly when we note that none of the episodes is given a specific chronological relation to any other. When, then, did Jesus heal the man's hand in the synagogue on the Sabbath (Mark 3:1–6)? Early in the ministry, as we might conclude if Mark's placement was chronological? Or later on, as the placement of the incident in Matthew might suggest (see 12:9–14)? We might venture some guesses, but we cannot know for sure: the evangelists simply have not given us enough information. The fact, then, that a detailed life of Jesus cannot be reconstructed on the basis of the Synoptic Gospels in no way discredits the gospels as accurate historical sources. They should be judged for what they do tell us, not for what they do not tell us.

---

[122]On harmonizing, see esp. Craig L. Blomberg, "The Legitimacy and Limits of Harmonization," in *Hermeneutics, Authority, and Canon,* ed. D. A. Carson and John D. Woodbridge (Grand Rapids: Zondervan, 1986), 135–74, 388–97.

Gospel Chronology

The task of setting the events of the gospels against the background of secular history is made easy by the references to well-known historical personages such as Herod the Great (Matt. 2), Caesar Augustus (Luke 2:1), Herod Antipas (Luke 23:6–12), and Pontius Pilate (Matt. 27). With such indicators, we can situate the gospels generally within the history of first-century Palestine and the wider Roman Empire. But can we be any more exact? Several key incidents may yield more exact chronological data.

Jesus' Birth. Three data have been used to date Jesus' birth: the involvement of Herod the Great (Matt. 2); the decree of Caesar Augustus, issued when "Quirinius was governor of Syria" (Luke 2:1–2); and the appearance of the "star of Bethlehem" (Matt. 2:1–12). Herod the Great is undoubtedly the "king" of Matthew 2. It is almost certain that Herod died in late March or early April of 4 B.C.[123] Jesus must therefore have been born before 4 B.C.—but probably not much before, since Herod slays children only two years old and younger (2:16). Augustus ruled the Roman Empire from 31 B.C. to A.D. 14. Unfortunately, the census to which Luke refers cannot be identified from secular sources. Josephus refers to a local census that took place in A.D. 6, and some think that Luke has confused the census that brought Joseph and Mary to Bethlehem with this one. Adding fuel to the fire is the fact that the only reference to Quirinius in ancient sources places him in office in the years A.D. 6–8. But it is unlikely that Luke, proven so accurate in historical and geographic details in Acts, would have made so serious a blunder. We may surmise that Quirinius had held an earlier post in Syria,[124] or that Luke 2:2 should not be translated "this was the first census that took place while Quirinius was governor of Syria" (TNIV), but "this census was before the census taken when Quirinius was governor of Syria."[125] In any case, the census does not help us date the birth of Jesus. Nor does the appearance of the star give us much help. Several identifications of the star with known astronomical phenomena have been proposed—a comet reported in 5 B.C. or a conjunction of Jupiter, Saturn, and Mars in 7–6 B.C.—but none is certain. Moreover, in light of Matthew's statement that the star "went ahead of [the magi] until it stopped over the place where the child was" (2:9), it is perhaps unlikely that the star can be identified with any natural astronomical phenomenon.

All things considered, then, we can only estimate that Jesus must have been born sometime during 6–4 B.C.

---

[123] See esp. Harold Hoehner, *Chronological Aspects of the Life of Christ* (Grand Rapids: Zondervan, 1977), 12–13.

[124] E.g., William Ramsay, *The Bearing of Recent Discovery on the Trustworthiness of the New Testament,* reprint ed. (Grand Rapids: Baker, 1953), 238–300.

[125] E.g., Nigel Turner, *Grammatical Insights into the New Testament* (Edinburgh: T. & T. Clark, 1965), 23–24.

The Beginning of Jesus' Ministry. According to Luke 3:1, Jesus began his public ministry "in the fifteenth year of the reign of Tiberius Caesar." Here, we might think, is an indication that should yield an exact date. But the matter is not so simple. Tiberius became emperor after the death of Augustus in August of A.D. 14. If this is when Luke begins his fifteen years, then the date of the beginning of Jesus' ministry would be either 28 or 29.[126] But Tiberius began a coregency with Augustus in A.D. 11/12. Counting from this date would place the beginning of Jesus' ministry in 25/26 or 26/27.[127] However, while we cannot be certain, the former way of reckoning the beginning of Tiberius's reign is the most natural, and it is therefore likely that Luke dates the beginning of Jesus' ministry in either 28 or 29. With any of these dates, justice is done to Luke's approximation that Jesus was "about thirty years old" at the beginning of his ministry (3:23).

The Length of Jesus' Ministry. The synoptic evangelists provide little information that can be used to determine the length of the ministry. It has been proposed that the events in the Synoptics could be packed into less than a year, but this compresses events too much. Moreover, Mark indicates that at the time of the feeding of the five thousand, the grass was green (6:39), which points to the Palestinian springtime. Yet since Jesus was crucified in the spring, Mark's gospel suggests a ministry of at least a year's duration.

John supplies us with more information. He mentions the Passover three times in his narration of Jesus' ministry: at the time of the cleansing of the temple (2:13), at the time of the feeding of the five thousand (6:4), and at the time of Jesus' crucifixion (11:55). He also mentions a "feast" in 5:1 that may have been, although probably was not, a Passover. If the three Passovers that John mentions were distinct in time,[128] then John's gospel requires a ministry of at least two years.[129]

> *The synoptic evangelists provide little information that can be used to determine the length of Jesus' ministry.*

---

[126]E.g., Paul Barnett, *Jesus and the Rise of Early Christianity: A History of New Testament Times* (Downers Grove: IVP, 1999), 21. Within this general span, there are several possibilities for the exact month and date, depending on which calendar may have been used. See, e.g., George Ogg, *The Chronology of the Public Ministry of Jesus* (Cambridge: Cambridge University Press, 1940), 174–83.

[127]E.g., F. Godet, *A Commentary on the Gospel of St. Luke* (Edinburgh: T. & T. Clark, n.d.), 1:166–67.

[128]Most evangelical scholars argue that John's cleansing of the temple is a different cleansing than the one narrated in the Synoptic Gospels. If, however, they are one and the same event, then John would refer to only two separate Passovers.

[129]Hoehner's claim that John's gospel, as it now stands, requires a ministry of at least three years, appears to depend on taking Jesus' reference in 4:35 as an indication that it was January or February (*Chronological Aspects*, 56–63). But this is unlikely (see Leon Morris, *The Gospel According to John*, NICNT [Grand Rapids: Eerdmans, 1971], 278–80); nor does Hoehner seriously consider the possibility that John's cleansing is the

The Death of Jesus. On the basis of the previous two considerations, Jesus' death must have occurred in A.D. 30 or later. Two lines of evidence have been used to determine the precise year: astronomical/calendrical and historical. We know that Jesus was crucified on Friday ("the Preparation Day" [Mark 15:42 par.]) in the Jewish month of Nisan. The beginning of that month was fixed at the time when the new moon was sighted. Thus, if we knew the date of the crucifixion, we could use astronomical calculations to determine the years during which that date would have fallen on a Friday. Unfortunately, the date of Jesus' death continues to be a matter of considerable debate, Nisan 14 and 15 being the main possibilities. The uncertainty arises from apparently conflicting data from the Synoptic Gospels and from John. The Synoptics appear to make the Last Supper a Passover meal (see, e.g., Mark 14:12), making Friday Nisan 15. But on one reading of the fourth gospel, John implies that the Passover meal had not yet been eaten at the time of Jesus' trial (18:28), which suggests that the day of Jesus' death was Nisan 14. Numerous harmonization attempts have been offered, the two most likely being that the synoptic evangelists and John were utilizing different calendars in use in first-century Palestine,[130] or that John in 18:28 does not really intend to suggest that the official Passover meal was still to be eaten.[131] In any case, we must remain uncertain about the day of the month on which Jesus died. Nisan 14 probably occurred on a Friday in A.D. 30,[132] and almost certainly did in 33; Nisan 15 may have occurred on a Friday in A.D. 30, and possibly also in 31.[133] However, since the calculation of the beginning of Nisan depended on human observation, with many possibilities for uncertainty, we must not depend too strongly on the results. Nevertheless, the two most likely candidates are Nisan 14 (= April 3), A.D. 33, and Nisan 14 or 15 (= April 6 or 7), A.D. 30.

The historical argument estimates the time at which it was most likely that Pilate, the Roman governor in Palestine, would have caved in to the pressure

---

same as the one narrated in the Synoptics. See particularly the discussion in C. H. Turner, "Chronology of the New Testament," in *A Dictionary of the Bible,* ed. James Hastings (Edinburgh: T. & T. Clark, 1898–1904), 1.407–9; and Karl P. Donfried, "Chronology, New Testament," in *ABD* 1:1014–15.

[130]Morris, *John,* 774–86.

[131]D. A. Carson, "Matthew," in *EBC* 8 (Grand Rapids: Zondervan, 1984), 528–32.

[132]For this conclusion, which differs from the claims of some other scholars, see Rainer Riesner, *Paul's Early Period: Chronology, Mission Strategy, Theology* (Grand Rapids: Eerdmans, 1998), 57–58.

[133]The most recent calculations are found in Colin J. Humphreys and W. Graeme Waddington, "The Date of the Crucifixion," *JASA* 37 (1985): 2–10; see also J. K. Fotheringham, "The Evidence of Astronomy and Technical Chronology for the Date of the Crucifixion," *JTS* 35 (1934): 146–62; Joachim Jeremias, *The Eucharistic Words of Jesus* (London: SCM, 1966), 36–41.

exerted on him by the Jewish leaders at the time of Jesus' trial. Hoehner, for instance, has argued that Pilate's desire to accommodate the Jewish leaders is credible only after A.D. 31, in October of which year the anti-Semitic Sejanus, ruler of the empire in fact under Tiberius, was executed.[134] Combined with the astronomical argument, this narrows the possibilities down to one year: A.D. 33.

But it may be doubted whether this set of circumstances is needed to explain Pilate's behavior, for the Roman administration, whoever was in charge, was concerned to maintain stability in the provinces, and Pilate had already given some indication of failure at this point. Quite apart from this argument, however, some scholars think that the astronomical data are more favorable to the A.D. 33 date. In contrast, the year 33 is virtually ruled out if Jesus was crucified on Nisan 15, as the synoptic evangelists appear to suggest. Moreover, a crucifixion as late as A.D. 33 might fail to leave enough time between the death of Jesus and Paul's conversion (see chap. 7).

The various data do not, then, allow us at this time to decide the matter with certainty. But the A.D. 30 date is slightly preferable.

BIBLIOGRAPHY

Charles C. **Anderson**, *Critical Quests of Jesus* (Grand Rapids: Eerdmans, 1969) ▥Janice Capel **Anderson** and Stephen D. **Moore**, eds., *Mark and Method: New Approaches to Biblical Studies* (Minneapolis: Fortress Press, 1992) ▥David E. **Aune**, *The New Testament in Its Literary Environment*, LEC 8 (Philadelphia: Westminster, 1987) ▥idem, *Prophecy in Early Christianity and the Ancient Mediterranean World* (Grand Rapids: Eerdmans, 1983) ▥Paul **Barnett**, *Jesus and the Rise of Early Christianity: A History of New Testament Times* (Downers Grove: IVP, 1999) ▥Richard **Bauckham**, "For Whom were the Gospels Written?" in *The Gospels for All Christians* (Grand Rapids: Eerdmans, 1998), 9–48 ▥idem, "The Eyewitnesses and the Gospel Traditions," *JSHJ* 1 (2003): 28–60 ▥Arthur J. **Bellinzoni** Jr., ed., *The Two-Source Hypothesis: A Critical Appraisal* (Macon: Mercer University Press, 1985) ▥C. Clifton **Black**, *The Disciples in Mark: Markan Redaction in Current Debate*, JSNTSup 27 (Sheffield: JSOT Press, 1989) ▥Craig **Blomberg**, *The Historical Reliability of the Gospels* (Downers Grove: IVP, 1987) ▥idem, "The Legitimacy and Limits of Harmonization," in *Hermeneutics, Authority, and Canon*, ed. D. A. Carson and John D. Woodbridge (Grand Rapids: Zondervan, 1986), 135–74, 388–97 ▥idem, "The Synoptic Problem: Where We Stand at the Beginning of a New Century," in *Rethinking the Synoptic Problem*, ed. David Alan Black and David R. Beck (Grand Rapids: Baker, 2001), 17–40 ▥Darrell L. **Bock**, *Jesus According to Scripture: Restoring the Portrait from the Gospels* (Grand Rapids: Baker, 2002) ▥Markus **Bockmuehl**, ed. *The Cambridge Companion to Jesus* (Cambridge:

---

[134]Hoehner, *Chronological Aspects*, 105–11

Cambridge University Press, 2001) ▥M. **Borg**, *Jesus: A New Vision* (San Francisco: Harper, 1987) ▥Günther **Bornkamm**, *Jesus of Nazareth* (London: Hodder & Stoughton, 1960) ▥G. **Bornkamm**, G. **Barth**, and H. J. **Held**, *Tradition and Interpretation in Matthew* (Philadelphia: Westminster, 1974) ▥Colin **Brown**, *Jesus in European Protestant Thought, 1778–1860* (Grand Rapids: Baker, 1988) ▥Rudolf **Bultmann**, *The History of the Synoptic Tradition* (New York: Harper & Row, 1963) ▥idem, *Theology of the New Testament*, 2 vols. (New York: Charles Scribner's Sons, 1951–55) ▥R. A. **Burridge**, *What are the Gospels? A Comparison with Greco-Roman Biography*, SNTSMS 70 (Cambridge: Cambridge University Press, 1992) ▥B. C. **Butler**, *The Originality of St. Matthew: A Critique of the Two-Document Hypothesis* (Cambridge: Cambridge University Press, 1951) ▥S. **Byrskog**, *Story as History—History as Story: The Gospel Tradition in the Context of Ancient Oral History*, WUNT 123 (Tübingen: Mohr-Siebeck, 2000) ▥G. B. **Caird**, "Chronology of the New Testament," in *IDB* 1.599–607 ▥D. A. **Carson**, "Matthew," in *EBC* 8 (Grand Rapids: Zondervan, 1984) ▥idem, "Redaction Criticism: On the Legitimacy and Illegitimacy of a Literary Tool," in *Scripture and Truth*, ed. D. A. Carson and John D. Woodbridge (Grand Rapids: Zondervan, 1983), 119–42, 376–81 ▥Maurice **Casey**, *An Aramaic Approach to Q: Sources for the Gospels of Matthew and Luke*, SNTSMS 122 (Cambridge: Cambridge University Press, 2002) ▥David **Catchpole**, *The Quest for Q* (Edinburgh: T. & T. Clark, 1993) ▥D. J. **Chapman**, *Matthew, Mark, and Luke: A Study in the Order and Interrelation of the Synoptic Gospels*, ed. John M. T. Barton (London: Longmans, Green, 1937) ▥Hans **Conzelmann**, *The Theology of St. Luke* (New York: Harper & Row, 1960) ▥Patricia **Cox**, *Biography in Late Antiquity* (Berkeley: University of California Press, 1983) ▥J. D. **Crossan**, *The Historical Jesus: The Life of a Mediterranean Jewish Peasant* (San Francisco: Harper, 1991) ▥Peter **Davids**, "The Gospels and Jewish Tradition: Twenty Years After Gerhardsson," in *GP* 1:75–79 ▥Robert A. **Derrenbacher** Jr., and John S. **Kloppenborg Verbin**, "Self-Contradiction in the IQP? A Reply to Michael Goulder," *JBL* 120 (2001): 57–76 ▥Martin **Dibelius**, *From Tradition to Gospel* (ET: New York: Charles Scribner's Sons, n.d.) ▥Albrecht **Dihle**, "Die Evangelien und die griechische Biographie," in *Das Evangelium und die Evangelien*, ed. Peter Stuhlmacher, WUNT 28 (Tübingen: Mohr-Siebeck, 1983), 383–411 ▥C. H. **Dodd**, "The Framework of the Gospel Narrative," *ExpTim* 43 (1932): 396–400 ▥Karl P. **Donfried**, "Chronology, New Testament," in *ABD* 1.1011–22 ▥Detlev **Dormeyer** and Hubert **Frankemölle**, "Evangelium als literarische Gattung und als theologisches Begriff: Tendenzen und Aufgaben der Evangelienforschung im 20. Jahrhundert, mit einer Untersuchung des Markusevangeliums in seinem Verhältnis zur antiken Biographie," in *ANRW* 25.2, pp. 1545–81 ▥F. Gerald **Downing**, "Redaction Criticism: Josephus' *Antiquities* and the Synoptic Gospels," *JSNT* 8 (1980): 29–48; 9 (1980): 46–65 ▥David L. **Dungan**, *A History of the Synoptic Problem* (New York: Doubleday, 1999) ▥idem, "The Purpose and Provenance of the Gospel of Mark According to the Two-Gospel (Owen-Griesbach) Hypothesis," in *New Synoptic Studies: The Cambridge Gospel Conference and Beyond*, ed. William Farmer (Macon: Mercer University Press, 1983), 411–40 ▪J. D. G. **Dunn**, "Prophetic 'I'-Sayings and the Jesus Tradition: The Importance of Testing Prophetic Utterances Within Early Christianity," *NTS* 24 (1978): 175–98 ▪idem, *Jesus Remembered, Christianity in the Making*, vol. 1 (Grand Rapids: Eerdmans, 2003) ▪Richard A. **Edwards**, *A Theology of Q* (Philadelphia: Fortress Press, 1976) ▪J. G. **Eichhorn**, *Einleitung in das Neue Testament* (1804) ▪E. E. **Ellis**, "Gospels Criticism: A Perspective on the State of the Art," in *Das Evangelium und die Evangelien*, 27–54 ▪Andreas **Ennulat**, *Die "Minor Agreements": Untersuchungen zu einer offenen Frage des synoptischen Problems*, WUNT 62 (Tübingen: Mohr-Siebeck, 1994) ▪William **Farmer**, *Jesus and the Gospel* (Philadelphia: Fortress Press, 1982) ▪idem, *The Synoptic Problem: A Critical Analysis* (New York: Macmillan, 1964) ▪Austin **Farrer**, "On Dispensing with Q," in *Studies in the Gospels: Essays in Memory of R. H. Lightfoot*, ed. D. E. Nineham (Oxford: Blackwell, 1955) ▪Joseph A. **Fitzmyer,** *The Gospel According to Luke I-IX*, AB (Garden City: Doubleday, 1981) ▪idem, "The Priority of Mark and the 'Q' Source in Luke," in *Jesus and Man's Hope*, ed. Donald G. Miller (Pittsburgh: Pittsburgh Theological Seminary, 1970), 1:131–70 (reprinted in Bellinzoni, *The Two-Source Hypothesis*) ▪J. K. **Fotheringham**, "The Evidence of Astronomy and Technical Chronology for the Date of the Crucifixion," *JTS* 35 (1934): 146–62 ▪R. T. **France**, "The Authenticity of the Sayings of Jesus," in *History, Criticism, and Faith*, ed. Colin Brown (Downers Grove: IVP, 1976), 101–41 ▪idem, "Exegesis in Practice: Two Samples," in *New Testament Interpretation: Essays on Principles and Methods*, ed. I. Howard Marshall (Grand Rapids: Eerdmans, 1977), 253–64 ▪idem, *Matthew: Evangelist and Theologian* (Grand Rapids: Zondervan, 1989) ▪G. **Friedrich**, "εὐαγγέλιον," in *TDNT* 2.721–35 ▪Robert W. **Funk**, *The Poetics of Biblical Narrative* (Sonoma: Polebridge, 1989) ▪Robert W. **Funk** and Roy W. **Hoover**, *The Five Gospels* (Sonoma: Polebridge, 1993) ▪Birger **Gerhardsson**, *Memory and Manuscript: Oral Tradition and Written Transmission in Rabbinic Judaism and Early Christianity*, ASNU 22 (Lund: Gleerup, 1964) ▪J. K. L. **Gieseler**, *Historisch-kritischer Versuch über die Entstehung und die frühesten Schicksale der schriftlichen Evangelien* (1818) ▪F. **Godet**, *A Commentary on the Gospel of St. Luke,* 2 vols. (Edinburgh: T. & T. Clark, n.d.) ▪Mark **Goodacre**, *The Case Against Q: Studies in Markan Priority and the Synoptic Problem* (Harrisburg: Trinity Press International, 2002) ▪idem, *the Synoptic Problem: A Way through the Maze* (New York: Sheffield Academic Press, 2001) ▪Michael D. **Goulder**, *Luke: A New Paradigm*, 2 vols., JSNTSup 20 (Sheffield: JSOT Press, 1989) ▪idem, "Self-Contradiction in the IQP," *JBL* 118 (1999): 506–17 ▪idem, "The Derrenbacher-Kloppenborg Defense," *JBL* 121 (2002): 33–36 ▪J. J. **Griesbach,** *Commentatio qua Marci evangelium totum e Matthaei et Lucae commentariis decerptum esse monstratur* (Treatise in which is demonstrated that the gospel of Mark has been wholly derived from the commentaries of Matthew and Luke) (1789) ▪Royce Gordon **Gruenler**, *New Approaches to*

Jesus and the Gospels: A Phenomenological and Exegetical Study of Synoptic Christology (Grand Rapids: Baker, 1982) ▪Robert **Guelich**, "The Gospel Genre," in *Das Evangelium und die Evangelien*, 183–219 ▪Robert H. **Gundry**, "Recent Investigations into the Literary Genre 'Gospel,'" in *New Dimensions in New Testament Study*, ed. Richard N. Longenecker and Merrill C. Tenney (Grand Rapids: Zondervan, 1974), 101–13 ▪Erhardt **Güttgemanns**, *Candid Questions Concerning Gospel Form Criticism: A Methodological Sketch of the Fundamental Problematics of Form and Redaction Criticism* (ET Pittsburgh: Pickwick, 1979) ▪John C. **Hawkins**, *Horae Synopticae* (Oxford: Clarendon Press, 1909) ▪Peter M. **Head**, *Christology and the Synoptic Problem: An Argument for Markan Priority*, SNTSMS 94 (Cambridge: Cambridge University Press, 1997) ▪Peter M. **Head** and P. J. **Williams**, "Q Review," *TynB* 54 (2003): 119–44 ▪Martin **Hengel**, "Literary, Theological, and Historical Problems in the Gospel of Mark," in *Studies in the Gospel of Mark* (Philadelphia: Fortress Press, 1985), 221–65 ▪idem, "The Titles of the Gospels and the Gospel of Mark," in ibid., 64–84 ▪idem, *The Four Gospels and the One Gospel of Jesus Christ* (Harrisburg: Trinity Press International, 2000) ▪J. G. **Herder**, *Von der Regel der Zusammenstimmung unserer Evangelien* (1797) ▪David **Hill**, *New Testament Prophecy* (Richmond: John Knox, 1979) ▪E. D. **Hirsch** Jr., *Validity in Interpretation* (New Haven, Conn.: Yale University Press, 1967) ▪Harold **Hoehner**, *Chronological Aspects of the Life of Christ* (Grand Rapids: Zondervan, 1977) ▪H. J. **Holtzmann**, *Die synoptische Evangelien: Ihr Ursprung und ihr geschichtlicher Charakter* (Leipzig: W. Engelmann, 1863) ▪M. D. **Hooker**, "On Using the Wrong Tool," *Theol* 75 (1972): 570–81 ▪Colin J. **Humphreys** and W. Graeme **Waddington**, "The Date of the Crucifixion," *JASA* 37 (1985): 2–10 ▪Philip **Jenkins**, *Hidden Gospels: How the Search for Jesus Lost its Way* (Oxford: Oxford University Press, 2001) ▪Joachim **Jeremias,** *The Eucharistic Words of Jesus* (London: SCM, 1966) ▪Luke T. **Johnson**, *The Real Jesus* (San Francisco: Harper, 1996) ▪Martin **Kähler**, *The So-Called Historical Jesus and the Historic, Biblical Christ* (Philadelphia: Fortress Press, 1964) ▪Ernst **Käsemann**, "The Problem of the Historical Jesus," in *Essays on New Testament Themes* (Philadelphia: Fortress Press, 1964), 15–47 ▪Werner H. **Kelber**, *The Oral and the Written Gospel* (Philadelphia: Fortress Press, 1983) ▪Jack Dean **Kingsbury**, *Matthew as Story* (Philadelphia: Fortress Press, 1986) ▪John **Kloppenborg**, *Excavating Q: The History and Setting of the Sayings Gospel* (Minneapolis: Fortress Press, 2000) ▪W. L. **Knox**, *The Sources of the Synoptic Gospels*, 2 vols. (Cambridge: Cambridge University Press, 1957) ▪Helmut **Koester**, *Ancient Christian Gospels: Their History and Development* (Philadelphia: Trinity Press International, 1990) ▪Werner Georg **Kümmel**, *The New Testament: The History of the Investigation of Its Problems* (New York: Abingdon, 1970) ▪Karl **Lachmann**, "De Ordine narrationum im evangeliis synopticis," *TSK* 8 (1835): 570–90 ▪G. E. **Lessing**, *Neue Hypothese über die Evangelisten als bloss menschliche Geschichtschreiber betrachtet* (1784) ▪R. H. **Lightfoot**, *History and Interpretation in the Gospels* (London: Hodder & Stoughton, 1935) ▪R.

L. **Lindsey**, "A Modified Two-Document Theory of the Synoptic Dependence and Interdependence," *NovT* 6 (1963): 239–63 ▪Eta **Linnemann**, *Is There a Synoptic Problem? Rethinking the Literary Dependence of the First Three Gospels* (Grand Rapids: Baker, 1992) ▪Tremper **Longman** III, *Literary Approaches to Biblical Interpretation* (Grand Rapids: Zondervan, 1987) ▪Harvey K. **McArthur**, ed., *In Search of the Historical Jesus* (New York: Charles Scribner's Sons, 1969) ▪Edgar V. **McKnight**, *Meaning in Texts* (Philadelphia: Fortress Press, 1974) ▪idem, *Post-Modern Use of the Bible: The Emergence of Reader-Oriented Criticism* (Nashville: Abingdon, 1988) ▪Scot **McKnight**, *Interpreting the Synoptic Gospels* (Grand Rapids: Baker, 1988) ▪idem, "Source Criticism," in *Interpreting the New Testament,* ed. David Black and David Dockery (Nashville: Broadman and Holman, 2001), 74–105 ▪Allan J. **McNicol**, David L. **Dungan**, and David B. **Peabody**, *Beyond the Q Impasse: Luke's Use of Matthew* (Valley Forge: Trinity Press International, 1996) ▪Burton L. **Mack**, *The Lost Gospel: The Book of Q and Christian Origins* (San Francisco: Harper, 1993) ▪Joel **Marcus**, *Mark 1–8: A New Translation with Introduction and Commentary,* AB 27 (New York: Doubleday, 2000) ▪I. Howard **Marshall**, *I Believe in the Historical Jesus* (Grand Rapids: Eerdmans, 1977) ▪idem, *Luke: Historian and Theologian,* new, enlarged ed. (Grand Rapids: Zondervan, 1989) ▪Ralph **Martin**, *Mark: Evangelist and Theologian* (Grand Rapids: Zondervan, 1972) ▪idem, "The New Quest of the Historical Jesus," in *Jesus of Nazareth: Savior and Lord,* ed. Carl F. H. Henry (Grand Rapids: Eerdmans, 1966), 31–45 ▪Willi **Marxsen**, *Mark the Evangelist: Studies on the Redaction History of the Gospel* (Nashville: Abingdon, 1969) ▪Sharon Lee **Mattila**, "A Question Too Often Neglected," *NTS* 41 (1995): 199–217 ▪J. P. **Meier**, *A Marginal Jew: Rethinking the Historical Jesus,* 4 vols. (New York: Doubleday, 1991–) ▪Ben F. **Meyer**, *The Aims of Jesus* (Philadelphia: Fortress Press, 1979) ▪Alan **Millard**, *Reading and Writing in the Time of Jesus* (Washington Square: New York University Press, 2000) ▪S. D. **Moore**, *Poststructuralism and the New Testament* (Minneapolis: Fortress Press, 1994) ▪Leon **Morris**, *The Gospel According to John,* NICNT (Grand Rapids: Eerdmans, 1971) ▪idem, *Studies in the Fourth Gospel* (Grand Rapids: Eerdmans, 1969) ▪Stephen **Neill** and Tom **Wright**, *The Interpretation of the New Testament, 1861–1986* (Oxford: Oxford University Press, 1988) ▪Franz **Neirynck**, *The Minor Agreements of Matthew and Luke Against Mark, with a Cumulative List,* BETL 37 (Louvain: Louvain University Press, 1974) ▪David J. **Neville**, *Mark's Gospel: Prior or Posterior? A Reappraisal of the Phenomenon of Order,* JSNTSup 222 (Sheffield: Sheffield Academic Press, 2002) ▪George **Ogg**, *The Chronology of the Public Ministry of Jesus* (Cambridge: Cambridge University Press, 1940) ▪Grant R. **Osborne**, "The Evangelical and Redaction Criticism: Critique and Methodology," *JETS* 22 (1979): 305–22 ▪idem, "History and Theology in the Synoptic Gospels," *TrinJ* 24 (2003): 5–22 ▪H. P. **Owen**, *Observations of the Four Gospels* (1764) ▪Daniel **Patte**, *Structural Exegesis for New Testament Critics* (Philadelphia: Fortress Press, 1990) ▪idem, *What Is Structural Exegesis?* (Philadelphia: Fortress Press, 1976) ▪Norman

Perrin, *Rediscovering the Teaching of Jesus* (London: SCM, 1967) ▉idem, *What Is Redaction Criticism?* (Philadelphia: Fortress Press, 1969) ▉Norman R. **Peterson**, *Literary Criticism for New Testament Critics* (Philadelphia: Fortress Press, 1978) ▉A. **Polag**, *Fragmenta Q: Texthelf zur Logienquelle*, 2nd ed. (Neukirchen-Vluyn: Neukirchener Verlag, 1982) ▉Stanley E. **Porter**, *The Criteria for Authenticity in Historical-Jesus Research: Previous Discussion and New Proposals*, JSNTSup 191 (Sheffield: Sheffield Academic Press, 2000) ▉E. J. **Pryke**, *Redactional Style in the Marcan Gospel: A Study of Syntax and Vocabulary as Guides to Redaction in Mark*, SNTSMS 33 (Cambridge: Cambridge University Press, 1978) ▉William **Ramsay**, *The Bearing of Recent Discovery on the Trustworthiness of the New Testament* (repr., Grand Rapids: Baker, 1953) ▉Friedrich **Rehkopf**, *Der lukanische Sonderquelle*, WUNT 5 (Tübingen: Mohr-Siebeck, 1959) ▉Bo **Reicke**, *The Roots of the Synoptic Gospels* (Philadelphia: Fortress Press, 1986) ▉Rainer **Riesner,** *Jesus als Lehrer*, WUNT 7 (Tübingen: Mohr-Siebeck, 1981) ▉idem, "Jüdische Elementarbildung und Evangelienüberlieferung," in *GP* 1.209–23 ▉John M. **Rist**, *On the Independence of Matthew and Mark*, SNTSMS 32 (Cambridge: Cambridge University Press, 1978) ▉J. A. T. **Robinson**, *Redating the New Testament* (Philadelphia: Westminster, 1976) ▉James M. **Robinson**, *A New Quest of the Historical Jesus*, SBT 25 (London: SCM, 1959) ▉Joachim **Rohde**, *Rediscovering the Teaching of the Evangelists* (London: SCM, 1968) ▉E. P. **Sanders**, *Jesus and Judaism* (Philadelphia: Fortress Press, 1985) ▉F. **Schleiermacher**, "Über die Zeugnisse des Papias von unseren ersten beiden Evangelien," *TSK* 5 (1832): 335–68 ▉Karl Ludwig **Schmidt**, *Der Rahmen der Geschichte Jesu: Literarkritische Untersuchungen zur ältesten Jesusüberlieferung* (Berlin: Trowitzsch & Son, 1919) ▉idem, "Die Stellung der Evangelien in der allgemeinen Literaturgeschichte," in ΕΥΧΑΡΙΣΤΗΡΙΟΝ: *Studien zur Religion und Literatur des Alten und Neuen Testaments, Fs.* Hermann Gunkel, ed. K. L. Schmidt, FRLANT 19.2 (Göttingen: Vandenhoeck & Ruprecht, 1923) ▉John J. **Schmitt**, "In Search of the Origin of the Siglum Q," *JBL* 100 (1981): 609–11 ▉Albert **Schweitzer**, *The Quest for the Historical Jesus* (New York: Macmillan, 1961) ▉Philip L. **Shuler**, *A Genre for the Gospels: The Biographical Character of Matthew* (Philadelphia: Fortress Press, 1982) ▉Moisés **Silva**, "Ned B. Stonehouse and Redaction Criticism. Part I: The Witness of the Synoptic Evangelists to Christ; Part II: The Historicity of the Synoptic Tradition," *WTJ* 40 (1977–78): 77–88, 281–303 ▉Graham N. **Stanton**, *Gospel Truth? New Light on Jesus and the Gospels* (Valley Forge: Trinity Press International, 1995) ▉idem, *The Gospels and Jesus*, 2nd ed. (Oxford: Oxford University Press, 2002) ▉idem, *Jesus of Nazareth in New Testament Preaching*, SNTSMS 27 (Cambridge: Cambridge University Press, 1974) ▉Robert **Stein**, "The 'Criteria' of Authenticity," in *GP* 1.225–63 ▉idem, *Studying the Synoptic Gospels: Origin and Interpretation*, 2nd ed. (Grand Rapids: Baker, 2001) ▉idem, "What Is Redaktionsgeschichte?" in *JBL* 88 (1969): 45–56 ▉Hans-Herbert **Stoldt**, *History and Criticism of the Marcan Hypothesis* (Macon: Mercer University Press, 1980) ▉Ned B. **Stonehouse**, *The Witness of the Synoptic Gospels* to Christ (Grand Rapids: Baker, 1979) ▮Georg **Strecker**, ed., *Minor Agreements: Symposium Göttingen 1991* (Göttingen: Vandenhoeck & Ruprecht, 1993) ▮B. H. **Streeter**, *The Four Gospels: A Study of Origins* (London: Macmillan, 1924) ▮G. M. **Styler**, "The Priority of Mark," in *The Birth of the New Testament*, ed. C. F. D. Moule, 3rd ed. (San Francisco: Harper & Row, 1982), 285–316 ▮Charles H. **Talbert**, *What Is a Gospel? The Genre of the Canonical Gospels* (Philadelphia: Fortress Press, 1977) ▮Randall K. T. **Tan**, "Recent Developments in Redaction Criticism: From Investigation of Textual Prehistory Back to Historical-Grammatical Exegesis?" *JETS* 44 (2001): 599–614 ▮Vincent **Taylor**, *The Formation of the Gospel Tradition*, 2nd ed. (London: Macmillan, 1935) ▮idem, *The Gospel According to St. Mark*, 2nd ed. (London: Macmillan, 1966) ▮idem, *The Passion Narrative of St. Luke: A Critical and Historical Investigation*, ed. Owen E. Evans, SNTSMS 19 (Cambridge: Cambridge University Press, 1972) ▮Gerd **Theissen** and Annette **Merz**, *The Historical Jesus: A Comprehensive Guide* (Minneapolis: Fortress Press, 1998 [1996]) ▮Robert L. **Thomas** and F. David **Farnell**, eds., *The Jesus Crisis: The Inroads of Historical Criticism into Evangelical Scholarship* (Grand Rapids: Kregel, 1998) ▮C. C. **Torrey**, *The Four Gospels* (New York: Harper, 1933) ▮C. M. **Tuckett**, *Q and the History of Early Christianity* (Peabody: Hendrickson, 1996) ▮C. H. **Turner**, "Chronology of the New Testament," in *A Dictionary of the Bible*, ed. James Hastings, 5 vols. (Edinburgh: T. & T. Clark, 1898–1904), 1.403–25 ▮Nigel **Turner**, *Grammatical Insights into the New Testament* (Edinburgh: T. & T. Clark, 1965) ▮Joseph B. **Tyson** and Thomas R. W. **Longstaff**, *Synoptic Abstract*, The Computer Bible 15 (Wooster: College of Wooster, 1978) ▮L. **Vaganay**, *Le problème synoptique: Une hypothèse de travail* (Paris: Desclée, 1954) ▮Kevin **Vanhoozer**, "A Lamp in the Labyrinth: The Hermeneutics of 'Aesthetic' Theology," *TrinJ* 8 (1987): 25–56 ▮C. W. **Votaw**, "The Gospels and Contemporary Biographies," *AJT* 19 (1915): 45–71 ▮Johannes **Weiss,** *Jesus' Proclamation of the Kingdom of God* (Philadelphia: Fortress Press, 1971) ▮C. H. **Weisse**, *Die evangelische Geschichte kritisch und philosophisch bearbeitet* (1838) ▮David **Wenham**, "The Synoptic Problem Revisited: Some New Suggestions About the Composition of Mark 4:1–34," *TynB* 23 (1972): 3–38 ▮John **Wenham**, *Redating Matthew, Mark, and Luke: A Fresh Assault on the Synoptic Problem* (Downers Grove: IVP, 1992) ▮B. F. **Westcott**, *Introduction to the Study of the Gospels*, 8th ed. (London: Macmillan, 1895) ▮C. G. **Wilke**, *Der Urevangelist oder exegetisch-kritische Untersuchungen über das Verwandtschaftsverhältniss der drei ersten Evangelien* (1838) ▮William **Wrede**, *Das Messiasgeheimnis in den Evangelien* (Göttingen: Vandenhoeck & Ruprecht, 1901) ▮N. T. **Wright**, *Jesus and the Victory of God* (Minneapolis: Fortress Press, 1996).

CHAPTER THREE

MATTHEW

CONTENTS

That Matthew was a skilled literary craftsman no one denies. Disagreements over the structure of this gospel arise because there are so many overlapping and competing structural pointers that it appears impossible to establish a consensus on their relative importance.

If we consider the structure of the book as a whole, then, apart from several idiosyncratic proposals,[1] there are three dominant theories.

1. Some have detected a geographic framework that is related to Mark's gospel (see chap. 2 on the synoptic problem).[2] Matthew 1:1–2:23 is the prologue, and it is tied to 3:1–4:11 (Jesus' preparation for ministry) to constitute an introduction parallel to Mark 1:1–13. Matthew 4:12–13:58 finds Jesus ministering in Galilee (cf. Mark 1:14–6:13). This ministry extends to other locales in the north (Matt. 14:1–16:12; Mark 6:14–8:26) before Jesus begins to move toward Jerusalem (Matt. 16:13–20:34; Mark 8:27–10:52). The confrontation in Jerusalem (Matt. 21:1–25:46; Mark 11:1–13:37) issues in his passion and resurrection (Matt. 26:1–28:20; Mark 14:1–16:8).

This sort of analysis rightly reflects the broad chronological development of Jesus' ministry and preserves some geographic distinctions. But it is based

---

[1] E.g., C. H. Lohr proposes a giant chiasm ("Oral Techniques in the Gospel of Matthew," *CBQ* 23 [1961]: 403–35), but there are too many tenuous pairings to convince many scholars that Matthew had this in mind. M. D. Goulder attempts to tie the structure of this gospel to a lectionary cycle (*Midrash and Lection in Matthew* [London: SPCK, 1974]). So little is known about first-century lectionary cycles, however, that the proposal is long on speculation (cf. L. Morris, "The Gospels and the Jewish Lectionaries," in *GP* 1.129–56), quite apart from the extraordinary diversity of lection lengths that Goulder proposes.

[2] E.g., A. H. McNeile, *The Gospel According to St. Matthew* (London: Macmillan, 1915).

entirely on a selection of thematic considerations and does not reflect on the *literary* markers that Matthew has left us. Precisely because, with minor alterations, this sort of analysis could be applied to any of the Synoptic Gospels, it tells us very little of the purposes that are uniquely Matthew's.

2. Following suggestions made by Stonehouse, Lohmeyer, and Krentz,[3] Kingsbury has argued for three large sections, tightly tied to christological development.[4] The first he titles "The Person of Jesus Messiah" (1:1–4:16); the second, "The Proclamation of Jesus Messiah" (4:17–16:20); and the third, "The Suffering, Death, and Resurrection of Jesus Messiah" (16:21–28:20). Immediately after the two breaks come the decisive words ἀπὸ τότε (*apo tote*, "from that time on"), signaling progress in the plot. The last two of the three sections each contains three summary passages (4:23–25; 9:35; 11:1; and 16:21; 17:22–23; 20:17–19).

Though this outline has gained adherents (e.g., Kümmel), it suffers from several weaknesses. It is not at all clear that ἀπὸ τότε (*apo tote*) is so redactionally important for Matthew that his entire structure turns on it: after all, Matthew uses it at 26:16 without any break in the flow of the narrative. One could argue that there are four passion summaries in the third section, not three (add 26:2). At both structural transitions, Matthew may have been more influenced by his following of Mark than by other considerations. In any case, the outline breaks up the important Peter passage in Matthew 16 in an unacceptable way. Even the christological development is not as clear as Kingsbury alleges: the person of Jesus (section 1) is still a focal point in sections 2 and 3 (e.g., 16:13–16; 22:41–46); the proclamation of Jesus can scarcely be restricted to section 2, for two of the discourses (chaps. 18 and 24–25) and several important exchanges (chaps. 21–23) are reserved for the third section.

3. The most frequently proposed structures turn on the observation that Matthew presents five discourses, each of which begins in a specific context and ends with a formula found nowhere else (lit. "And it happened, when Jesus had finished saying these things, that . . ." [Matt. 7:28–29; 11:1; 13:53; 19:1; 26:1]). It becomes attractive to link narrative with discourse in five pairs. Bacon proposed just such a scheme, calling the five sections "books."[5] Book 1 deals with discipleship (narrative, chaps. 3–4; discourse, chaps. 5–7); book 2 with

---

[3]Ned B. Stonehouse, *The Witness of Matthew and Mark to Christ* (Grand Rapids: Eerdmans, 1944), 129–31; Ernst Lohmeyer, *Das Evangelium des Matthäus*, ed. W. Schmauck (Göttingen: Vandenhoeck & Ruprecht, 1956); E. Krentz, "The Extent of Matthew's Prologue," *JBL* 83 (1964): 409–14.

[4]J. D. Kingsbury, *Matthew: Structure, Christology, Kingdom* (Philadelphia: Fortress Press, 1975).

[5]B. W. Bacon, "The 'Five Books' of Moses Against the Jews," *Exp* 15 (1918): 56–66. The idea is then worked out in detail in Bacon's *Studies in Matthew* (London: Constable, 1930).

apostleship (narrative, 8–9; discourse, 10); book 3 with the hiding of the revelation (narrative, 11–12; discourse, 13); book 4 with church administration (narrative, 14–17; discourse, 18); and book 5 with the judgment (narrative, 19–22; discourse, 23–25). This leaves Matthew 1–2 as a preamble and 26–28 as an epilogue. Bacon himself thought that this was Matthew's self-conscious response to, and fulfillment of, the five books of Moses.

Few today think that Matthew intended any link between these five sections and the five books of Moses: proposed connections are just too tenuous. The ties between each narrative and discourse pair are not always very strong, and any outline that relegates the entire passion and resurrection narrative to the status of an epilogue must be seriously questioned.

But something of the scheme can be salvaged. That Matthew reports extensive teaching of Jesus outside the five discourses is no criticism of the outline: the fivefold sequence of narrative and discourse does not assume that Jesus is not portrayed as speaking in the narrative sections. He may do so, even extensively (e.g., chaps. 11, 21). The point, rather, is that the five discourses are so clearly marked, from a literary point of view, that it is well-nigh impossible to believe that Matthew did not plan them. Chapters 1–2 do constitute a preamble or prologue: all four canonical gospels preserve some kind of independent opening before turning to the first step taken in common, namely, the ministry of John the Baptist (in Matthew, beginning at 3:1). Certainly Matthew 26–28 must not be taken as a mere epilogue. But it is just possible that Matthew thinks of these chapters as the climactic, sixth narrative section, with the corresponding "teaching" section laid on the shoulders of the disciples (28:18–20) and therefore open-ended.

Superimposing on these literary markers the transparent development of the plot, we arrive at a seven-part outline:

The prologue (1:1–2:23). This is divisible into six sections, treating the genealogy of Jesus (1:1–17), his birth (1:18–25), the visit of the Magi (2:1–12), the escape to Egypt (2:13–15), the massacre at Bethlehem (2:16–18), and the return to Nazareth (2:19–23). A quotation from the Old Testament, introduced by an appropriate fulfillment formula, dominates the last five of these sections.

The gospel of the kingdom (3:1–7:29). The narrative (3:1–4:25) includes the foundational steps (3:1–4:11)—including the ministry of John the Baptist (3:1–12), the baptism of Jesus (3:13–17), and the temptation of Jesus (4:1–11)—and Jesus' early Galilean ministry (4:12–25). The first discourse (5:1–7:29) is the Sermon on the Mount. After the setting is established (5:1–2), the kingdom of heaven is introduced, with its norms (5:3–12) and its witness (5:13–16). The great body of the sermon runs from 5:17 to 7:12, beginning and ending with the way in which the kingdom is related to the Old Testament scriptures, "the Law and the Prophets." This is particularly the theme of 5:17–48, with its initial explanation (5:17–20) and dependent antitheses ("You have heard . . . but I tell you" [5:21–

48]). The demand for perfection (5:48) introduces correlative warnings against rank hypocrisy (6:1–18), with particular attention devoted to the proper way to go about the three traditional manifestations of Jewish piety: alms (6:2–4), prayer (6:5–15), and fasting (6:16–18). To maintain such a stance it is necessary to pursue kingdom perspectives (6:19–34), including unswerving loyalty to kingdom values (6:19–24) and uncompromised trust in God (6:25–34). The demand for balance and perfection, fulfilling Old Testament expectations (7:1–12), is followed by a conclusion that sets forth two ways (7:13–14), two trees (7:15–20), two claims (7:21–23), and two builders (7:24–27); every reader must choose. The closing verses (7:28–29) not only offer the first instance of the formula that terminates the five discourses but reaffirm Jesus' authority, thus preparing for the series of authoritative miracles that dominate the next two chapters.

The kingdom extended under Jesus' authority (8:1–11:1). The narrative (8:1–10:4) includes not only a number of miracles, each symbol-laden to portray some facet of the kingdom and its king, but the calling of Matthew (9:9) and Jesus' insistence on eating with public sinners (9:10–13) while announcing that the dawning kingdom, manifest in his own presence, was a time for joy (9:14–17). The miracles and Jesus' audacity are pushing back the frontiers of darkness, but the narrative ends with the demand for prayer for more workers (9:35–38) and the commissioning of the Twelve (10:1–4). This naturally leads to the second discourse, on mission and martyrdom (10:5–11:1), which moves from the immediate project (10:5b–16) to warnings of future sufferings (10:17–25), a prohibition of fear in the light of the Father's providence (10:26–31), and a more general description of authentic discipleship (10:32–39). Response to such disciples, for good or ill, is equivalent to response to Jesus himself (10:40–42). The transitional conclusion (11:1) points to Jesus' expanding ministry.

Teaching and preaching the gospel of the kingdom: rising opposition (11:2–13:53). The narrative (11:2–12:50) not only establishes the relative roles of John the Baptist and of Jesus in the stream of redemptive history (11:2–19) but reverses public expectations by reporting Jesus' strong condemnation of the "good," Jewish, religious towns of Galilee (which are aligned in his mind with pagan cities such as Tyre and Sidon, or a proverbially wicked center such as Sodom), and by announcing relief and rest to the weary and broken—provided they find it in the context of the "yoke" of the Son (11:20–30). Tension mounts as Sabbath conflicts erupt (12:1–14), as Jesus proves to be rather more a meek and suffering servant than a visibly conquering king (12:15–21), and as confrontation develops not only between Jesus and the Pharisees (12:22–45) but between Jesus and his own family (12:46–50). The reversal of expectations is a major theme of the discourse that follows, which is a series of parables (13:1–53; see outline below).

The glory and the shadow: progressive polarization (13:54–19:2). The narrative (13:54–17:27) is a series of vignettes that reflect the rising polarization (e.g., rejection at Nazareth, 13:54–58; Herod and Jesus, 14:1–12; demands for a sign, 16:1–4) or, where they display the power of Jesus' ministry, nevertheless betray the profound misunderstanding of its nature and focus (e.g., the feeding of the five thousand, 14:13–21; the walk on the water, 14:22–33; Jesus and the tradition of the elders, 15:1–20; the transfiguration, 17:1–13; the healing of the epileptic boy, 17:14–20[21]). The high point of the narrative is the confession of Jesus by Peter (16:13–20), but the aftermath—the first passion prediction (16:21–23; cf. the second in 17:22–23)—shows how little even he has understood. The fourth discourse (18:1–19:2) describes life under kingdom authority. Greatness is irrefragably tied to humility (18:3–4); few sins are more odious than causing believers, Jesus' "little ones," to sin (18:5–9); the saving of lost sheep is judged more important than the mere nurture of safe sheep (18:10–14); the priority of forgiveness and the importance of discipline in the messianic community are set forth (18:15–35). The transitional conclusion (19:1–2) serves as an introduction to the Judean ministry.

Opposition and eschatology: the triumph of grace (19:3–26:5). The narrative (19:3–23:39) leads through a number of exchanges and parables that stress the surprising conduct expected of those who would follow Jesus (19:3–20:34), leading up to the events of passion week (21:1–23:39). The triumphal entry (21:1–11), Jesus' cleansing of the temple (21:12–17), and his cursing of the fig tree (21:18–22) are preludes to a string of controversies in the temple court (21:23–22:46), increasingly pointed and focused on Jesus' messianic claims. Exasperated, Jesus pronounces his woes on the teachers of the law and the Pharisees (23:1–36) and utters his lament over Jerusalem (23:37–39). The Olivet (or eschatological) Discourse that follows (24:1–25:46), notoriously difficult to interpret, begins with the setting overlooking the temple (24:1–3), and describes the birth pains of the interadvent period (24:4–28) and the coming of the Son of Man (24:29–31), before reflecting on the significance of the birth pains (24:32–35) and urging the need to be prepared, since the day and hour of the coming of the Son are unknown (24:36–41). A series of parables presents variations on the theme of watchfulness (24:42–25:46). The transitional conclusion (26:1–5) includes this gospel's fourth major passion prediction and some details of the plot against Jesus, which prepares for the final section of the book.

The passion and resurrection of Jesus (26:6–28:20). The pace is now rapid. The anointing at Bethany (26:6–13) and Judas's betrayal agreement (26:14–16) are rapidly followed by the Last Supper (26:17–30), including the words of institution in vv. 26–30), a prediction of abandonment and denial (26:31–35), Gethsemane (26:36–46), the arrest (26:47–56), Jesus before the Sanhedrin (26:57–68), Peter's denial of Jesus (26:69–75), the formal decision of the Sanhedrin (27:1–2) and the death of Judas Iscariot (27:3–10), Jesus before Pilate (27:11–26), the soldiers' treatment of Jesus (27:27–31), the crucifixion and mocking (27:32–44), Jesus' death (27:45–50) and its immediate impact (27:51–56), the burial of Jesus (27:57–61), and the guard at the tomb (27:62–66). The resurrection narratives (28:1–17) climax in the Great Commission, placing the job of spreading the gospel and the content of Jesus' teaching squarely on the shoulders of the small enclave of witnesses, who are assured of Jesus' presence with them to the end of the age (28:18–20).

No outline can do justice to the numerous mini-structures that the text displays (cf. Kümmel, 106–7).[6] Nevertheless there are many that leap from the page. In particular, this gospel is full of triadic structures—not only in the Sermon on the Mount,[7] but throughout the work.[8] For instance, in the parables discourse (Matt. 13), Matthew largely agrees with Mark as far as 13:23, but from 13:24 on he goes his own way and starts producing triads. There are three parables of growth: 13:24–30; 13:31–32; 13:33. Each is introduced by Ἄλλην παραβολὴν + αὐτοῖς (allēn parabolēn + autois, "another parable" + "to them"). After a small interpretive explanation, another triad follows (13:44; 13:45–46; 13:47–50).

In fact, the challenge of sorting out Matthew's mini-structures is even more daunting, partly because by taking into account longer or shorter sections, it is possible to uncover multiple structures. Perhaps this should not be too surprising in a culture that loved various forms of parallelism, but the effect is sometimes striking. To take but one example: the third discourse, the parables of the kingdom, can be read as a large chiasm:

To the crowds (13:3b–33)
  1. the parable of the soils (13:3b–9)
    2. interlude (13:10–23)
    (a) on understanding parables (13:10–17)
    (b) interpretation of the parable of the soils (13:18–23)
        3. the parable of the weeds (13:24–30)
            4. the parable of the mustard seed (13:31–32)
                5. the parable of the yeast (13:33)
  Pause (13:34–35)
        —parables as fulfillment of prophecy (13:34–35)
        —interpretation of the parable of the weeds (13:36–43)

To the disciples (13:44–52)
                5'.the parable of the hidden treasure (13:44)

---

[6]Cf. Kümmel, 106–7. Doubtless that is why Robert H. Gundry prefers to assert that Matthew has no clear structure, but follows an indefinite plan (*Matthew: A Commentary on His Literary and Theological Art* [Grand Rapids: Eerdmans, 1982], 30).

[7]See D. C. Allison Jr., "The Structure of the Sermon on the Mount," *JBL* 106 (1987): 423–45.

[8]See esp., W. D. Davies and Dale C. Allison Jr., *The Gospel According to Saint Matthew*, ICC (Edinburgh: T. & T. Clark, 1988–97), 1.62–68.

> **4'.**the parable of the expensive pearl (13:45–46)
>   **3'.** the parable of the net (13:47–48)
> **2'.** interlude (13:49–51)
>   **(a')** interpretation of the parable of the net (13:49–50)
>   **(b')** on understanding parables (13:51)
> **1'.** the parable of the teacher of the law (13:52)[9]

AUTHOR

It is frequently asserted that the gospel commonly designated as Matthew's, like the other three canonical gospels, is anonymous. That is formally correct if the standard of comparison is, say, Paul's epistle to the Romans, where the opening lines of the agreed text designate both the author and the initial readers. There is nothing comparable in Matthew, Mark, Luke, or John. Nevertheless, we have no evidence that these gospels ever circulated without an appropriate designation, κατὰ μαθθαῖον (*kata Matthaion,* "according to Matthew") or the like. How early are these titles?

Until recently, most scholars tacitly assumed that the four gospels first circulated anonymously and that the present titles were first attached to them about A.D. 125. There is little evidence to support this date as the decisive turning point; it is little more than an educated guess, based only on the presupposition that the gospels were originally entirely anonymous and on the fact that by about 140, and perhaps earlier, the traditional attributions were widely known, without significant variation. Now, however, this consensus has been vigorously challenged by Martin Hengel.[10] Hengel examines the practice of book distribution in the ancient world, where titles were necessary to identify a work to which any reference was made. In this context he studies the manner in which second-century authors refer to the gospels, calling to mind, among other things, Tertullian's criticism of Marcion for publishing his own gospel (a highly truncated version of Luke) without the author's name. Tertullian contends that "a work ought not to be recognized, which holds not its head erect . . . which gives no promise of credibility from the fulness of its title and the just profession of its author."[11] Hengel argues that as soon as two or more gospels were publicly read in any one church—a phenomenon that certainly occurred, he thinks, not later than A.D. 100—it would have been necessary to distinguish between

---

[9]See D. A. Carson, "Matthew," *EBC* 8 (Grand Rapids: Zondervan, 1984), 303–4, 331–33, and sources cited there.

[10]Martin Hengel, *Studies in the Gospel of Mark* (Philadelphia: Fortress Press, 1985), 64–84. Cf. the admirable discussion in R. T. France, *Matthew—Evangelist and Teacher* (Grand Rapids: Zondervan, 1989), 50–80.

[11]Tertullian, *Against Marcion,* 4.2.

them by some such device as a title.[12] The unanimity of the attributions in the second century cannot be explained by anything other than the assumption that the titles were part of the works from the beginning. It is inconceivable, he argues, that the gospels could circulate anonymously for up to sixty years, and then in the second century suddenly display unanimous attribution to certain authors. If they had originally been anonymous, then surely there would have been some variation in second-century attributions (as was the case with some of the second-century apocryphal gospels). Hengel concludes that the four canonical gospels were never even formally anonymous.

Objections have been raised against this proposal in four areas.

1. Some of Hengel's arguments are of the "what must have been the case" variety. That is a fair charge. Even so, what must have been the case in the church's reference to the gospels that were circulating is based on demonstrable second-century practices. Certainly Hengel's reconstruction makes more sense than any other theory that seeks to explain the unanimity of second-century attribution.

2. Hengel's arguments are no defense against pseudonymity. Again, that is correct. But most scholars think of the four canonical gospels as anonymous, not pseudonymous. In any case, not only was pseudonymity in the first century largely restricted to apocalyptic works, but as soon as the church began to discuss the issue, there was unanimity in rejecting the authority of any work that fell under the suspicion of being a pseudonymous composition.

3. Anonymity was surely less threatening than Hengel intimates. Was not the epistle to the Hebrews, for example, written anonymously? Certainly Tertullian overstates the argument. Nevertheless, the epistle to the Hebrews is distinguished from other epistles by a title, namely, its (assumed) addressees; and its adoption by the church into the canon was constrained in part by doubts as to the identity of its author. It is not an accident that it was first accepted in the East, where tradition associated it with the apostle Paul. Hengel himself has discussed this question at length.[13]

4. Hengel's interpretation assumes that κατα` μαθθαῖον (*kata Matthaion,* "according to Matthew") is an attribution of authorship, whereas parallels show that the phrase "according to" serves other purposes. For example, in the titles "Gospel According to the Hebrews" and "Gospel According to the Egyptians," the prepositional expression does not indicate authorship. Plummer says it "implies *conformity to a type,* and need not mean more than 'drawn up according

---

[12]The argument has not been taken up and evaluated by many writers—e.g., Donald A. Hagner, *Matthew,* WBC (Dallas: Word Books, 1993–95), 1.lxxvi, simply asserts that the title κατὰ μαθθαῖον "was affixed to the Gospel sometime in the second century."

[13]Hengel, *Mark,* 170–72 n. 57.

to the teaching of.'"[14] Plummer and others acknowledge that by the time of Papias, κατά (*kata*, "according to") is understood to indicate authorship, but they insist that the expression does not necessarily bear that weight. Hengel agrees that κατά plus the accusative is not *itself* a necessary indication of authorship and indeed is only rarely used in that way in contemporary Greek literature. But he draws attention to a telling analogy. In the Greek fathers, the *one* Old Testament is referred to as "according to the Seventy" or "according to Aquila" or "according to Symmachus," where the prepositional expression is used to introduce the person or group thought to be responsible for producing the version concerned. In the same way, the *one* gospel early circulated in four distinct forms, "according to Matthew," "according to Mark," and so forth, where the prepositional expression introduces the person understood to be the originator of the particular form.

In short, the argument that Matthew was understood to be the author of the first gospel long before Papias wrote his difficult words affirming such a connection seems very strong, even if not unassailable.

Before considering Papias's disputed words, it is important to recognize that the credibility of Papias himself is widely questioned. Although Irenaeus, writing in the second half of the second century, insists that both Papias and Polycarp knew the apostle John personally, the fourth-century church historian Eusebius disputes the claim in the case of Papias (Eusebius, *H.E.* 3.39). Largely on this ground, modern scholarship tends to date Papias to A.D. 140 or later; but if Irenaeus is right and Eusebius is wrong, then there is no reason Papias could not have written twenty or more years earlier, and with excellent access to accurate information. In recent years it has been repeatedly shown that Eusebius misunderstood Papias on several points and tried his best to reduce his importance because he could not stand his millenarian views. (The evidence and arguments are summarized in chap. 6 below.)[15] It is far more likely that Irenaeus is correct in his assessment of Papias than that Eusebius is.

Whatever the date and knowledge of Papias, what he actually wrote is available to us only in quotations preserved by Eusebius. The five exegetical books of Papias, *Logion Kyriakon Exegesis* (Exegesis of the Dominical Logia), survived into the Middle Ages in some libraries in Europe, but they are no longer extant. It is from this work that Eusebius (*H.E.* 3.39.14–16) quotes Papias's two

---

[14]Alfred Plummer, *An Exegetical Commentary on the Gospel According to St. Matthew* (London: Robert Scott, 1909), vii.

[15]In addition to the literature cited in connection with John, see the following discussions that focus on the Matthean connections, all of them arguing against Eusebius: C. Stewart Petrie, "The Authorship of 'The Gospel According to Matthew': A Reconsideration of the External Evidence," *NTS* 14 (1967–68): 15–32; France, *Matthew— Evangelist and Teacher*, 53–56; Gundry, *Matthew*, 609ff. Gundry points out, among other things, that Eusebius had earlier (*H.E.* 3.36.1–2) associated Papias with Ignatius, who died not later than A.D. 110.

surviving comments on the authorship of the gospels. The one that bears on the fourth gospel is discussed later in this volume; the one that bears directly on Matthew is notoriously difficult to translate, as indicated here. "Matthew συνε-τάξετο (*synetaxeto,* 'composed'? 'compiled'? 'arranged [in an orderly form]'?) τὰ λόγια (*ta logia,* 'the sayings'? 'the gospel'?) in Ἑβραΐδι διαλέκτῳ (*Hebraïdi dialek-tō,* 'the Hebrew [Aramaic] language'? 'Hebrew [Aramaic] style'?), and each ἡρμήνευσεν (*hērmēneusen,* 'interpreted'? 'translated' 'transmitted'?) them as best he could."[16]

There is no doubt that the early church understood this to mean that Matthew first wrote his gospel in Hebrew or Aramaic (the same Greek word was used to refer to both cognate languages) and that it was then translated by others. But there are serious problems with this view. Although a few modern scholars argue that Matthew's entire gospel was first written in Aramaic,[17] substantial linguistic evidence is against them. In the first place, the many quotations from the Old Testament do not reflect a single text form. Some are unambiguously Septuagintal; others are apparently translations from a Semitic original; still others are so eccentric as to defy easy classification.[18] Had the gospel first been written in Aramaic, one might have expected that the Old Testament quotations would be either the translator's own rendering of the Aramaic or standard quotations from the accepted Bible of the early church, the LXX. The mix of text forms suggests an author writing in Greek but knowledgeable in Semitic languages and therefore able to vary his form.

Second, assuming that Matthew depends on Mark (see chap. 2 on the synoptic problem), the detailed verbal connections between Matthew and Mark make it extremely unlikely that Matthew was first written in Aramaic. Of course, those who do not accept the priority of Mark, or who propose that an Aramaic edition of Matthew preceded the publication of Mark, which then served as the heart of our Greek Matthew, will perceive no problem here.

Finally, the Greek text of Matthew does not read like translation Greek. True, there are Semitisms and, more frequently, Semitic enhancements,[19] but

---

[16]For the bearing of this Papias passage on the synoptic problem, see chap. 2 above.

[17]E.g., C. F. Burney, *The Poetry of Our Lord* (Oxford: Oxford University Press, 1925); C. C. Torrey, *Our Translated Gospels* (London: Hodder & Stoughton, n.d.); A. Schlatter, *Der Evangelist Matthäus: Seine Sprache, sein Ziel, seine Selbständigkeit,* 6th ed. (Stuttgart: Calwer, 1963); P. Gaechter, *Die literarische Kunst im Matthäusevangelium* (Stuttgart: Katholisches Bibelwerk, 1966); J. W. Wenham, "Gospel Origins," *TrinJ* 7 (1978): 112–34. In very recent times, a small number have argued that Hebrew (not Aramaic) underlies the canonical gospels, but this proposal has been rightly dismissed by the overwhelming majority of those who have looked into the matter.

[18]See the excellent charts in Davies and Allison, *Matthew,* 1.34-57.

[19]In modern linguistic theory, the term "Semitism" is rightly applied only to phenomena in the Greek New Testament where sense can be made of an expression only

these are largely restricted to the sayings of Jesus, and (arguably) they are introduced for effect by an author who is demonstrably capable of writing idiomatic Hellenistic Greek.[20] One could argue that a very good translator could have produced the same effect, but he would have had to be a very good translator indeed.

How, then, should the statement of Papias be taken? Among the dominant proposals are these (see also Guthrie, 44–49):

1. Some identify the λόγια (logia, "sayings") with some independent collection of Jesus' sayings, perhaps Q (on which see chap. 2 on the synoptic problem).[21] That would make Matthew the author of a sayings source (if Q, about 250 verses common to Matthew and Luke). Papias confused this source with the canonical Matthew. But it is not at all clear how an apostolic source as important as this could have fallen so completely out of use as to be lost to posterity. Indeed, the entire Q-hypothesis, however reasonable, is still merely a hypothesis. However much one may speak of material common to Matthew and Luke, it is far from clear that such material was all drawn from one common source. Besides, as we shall see, Papias does not normally use λόγια to refer only to sayings.

2. Some of the same criticisms can be raised against the view that λόγια (logia) refers to Old Testament "testimonia" books, that is, it was a book of Old Testament proof texts compiled by Matthew from the Hebrew canon, used in Christian apologetics and now incorporated in canonical Matthew.[22] It is not certain that such books ever existed independently. In any case, it does not explain the diversity of text forms in Old Testament quotations in Matthew, still less the fact that Matthew most closely follows the LXX where he is parallel to Mark.

3. J. Kürzinger,[23] followed by Gundry,[24] thinks that τὰ λόγια (ta logia) refers to canonical Matthew but that Ἑβραΐδι διαλέκτῳ (Hebraïdi dialektō) refers, not to the Hebrew or Aramaic language, but to Semitic style or literary form: Matthew arranged or composed (συνετάξετο [synetaxeto]) his gospel in Semitic (i.e., Jewish-Christian) literary form, dominated by Semitic themes and devices. This is an unlikely rendering, but certainly possible (see LSJ 1.401). In this view,

---

by appealing to a Semitic underlay. "Semitic enhancement" refers to literary phenomena that do occur elsewhere in purely Greek texts but whose *frequency* of occurrence in some New Testament book is most easily explained by observing that the construction or expression is common in one or more of the Semitic languages.

[20]See Moule, 276–80.

[21]This view was made popular by T. W. Manson, *The Sayings of Jesus* (London: SCM, 1949), 18ff.

[22]J. R. Harris, *Testimonies*, 2 vols. (Cambridge: Cambridge University Press, 1920); F. C. Grant, *The Gospels: Their Origin and Their Growth* (New York: Harper, 1957), 65, 144.

[23]J. Kürzinger. "Das Papiaszeugnis und die Erstgestalt des Matthäusevangeliums," *BZ* 4 (1960): 19–38; idem, "Irenäus und sein Zeugnis zur Sprache des Matthäusevangeliums," *NTS* 10 (1963): 108–15.

[24]Gundry, *Matthew*, 619–20.

the last clause of Papias's statement cannot refer to translation, since Semitic *language* is no longer in view: everyone simply *interpreted* the text to the world as he was able. Kürzinger points out that immediately preceding this passage, Papias describes Mark as the ἑρμηνευτής (*hermēneutēs*) of Peter; this, Kürzinger says, cannot mean that Mark was Peter's "translator," but that Mark "interpreted" Peter and thus "transmitted" his message to the world. If the same reasoning is applied to the cognate verb in Papias's statement about Matthew, Kürzinger's interpretation becomes possible.

But however possible, it is not the natural way to read the passage, and it is certainly not what later church fathers understood. Without exception, they held that the apostle Matthew wrote canonical Matthew and that it was first written in Semitic. That is true, for instance, of Irenaeus (*Adv. Haer.* 3.1.1, quoted in Eusebius, *H.E.* 5.8.2), Tertullian (*Adv. Marc.*, 4.2), Origen (quoted by Eusebius, *H.E.* 6.25.3–6), Eusebius himself (*H.E.* 3.24.5–6), and Jerome (*De vir. ill.* 3).[25]

There seems to be increasing agreement as to what τὰ λόγια (*ta logia*) means. Although at this period it would be most natural to use this expression to refer either to Old Testament oracles of God, and thus derivatively to the entire Old Testament, or else to the sayings of Jesus, two bits of evidence suggest that Papias used the term to refer to the words *and deeds* of Jesus—in short, to the substance of what became our gospels. First, although the title of his five-volume work is *Exegesis of the Dominical Logia,* enough is known of this work to conclude that it was not restricted in scope to an exposition of Jesus' *words* but included exposition also of *deeds* alleged to have been performed by Jesus. Moreover, in the sequence preserved in Eusebius, just before Papias tells us of how Matthew wrote, he tells us that Mark recorded from Peter's teaching "the things said or done by the Lord." This teaching, however, was given as the occasion demanded; Peter was not speaking "as if he were making an ordered collection (σύνταξις [*syntaxis*]) of the Lord's oracles (τὰ κυριακὰ λόγια [*ta kyriaka logia*])." Clearly, what Mark was writing was the gospel that bears his name, with its collection of "things either said or done by the Lord"; and the parallelism between this clause and τὰ λόγια (*ta logia*) shows that the latter expression can include deeds as well as words. When a few lines later we read that Matthew τὰ λόγια συνετάξετο (*ta logia synetaxeto,* "composed the *logia,*" or "put the *logia* in order"), it is most natural to conclude that what he was doing, at least in Papias's mind, was composing the gospel that bears his name. It is thus highly unlikely that τὰ λόγια should be understood to refer to Q or to a book of "testimonies."

---

[25]These and other passages are conveniently summarized in France, *Matthew—Evangelist and Teacher,* 60–62. For the fullest account of the use of Matthew in the early church, see Edouard Massaux, *Influence de l'évangile de Saint Matthieu sur la littérature chrétienne avant Saint Irénée,* BETL 75 (Louvain: Louvain University Press, 1986).

In short, the evidence leads to a difficult conclusion. Unless we adopt the solution of Kürzinger, we are gently nudged to the conclusion that Papias was wrong when he claimed that Matthew was first written in Aramaic. And if he was wrong on this point, what prevents us from supposing that he was likely wrong in his ascription of authorship to the apostle Matthew?

Such skepticism, superficially plausible, seems a trifle extreme. The two issues are not integrally connected. Authors have been known to err on one point without erring on all points! Moreover, plausible reasons have been advanced to suggest why Papias may have been led astray on the question of a Semitic original. It may have been an intelligent, albeit erroneous, guess. The early church fathers assumed that Matthew was the first gospel to be written. Since Jesus and his apostles lived and served among the Hebrews, it may well have been a natural conclusion that the first gospel to be written was produced "in the Hebrew [Aramaic] dialect"—the more so if Papias, living in the Hellenistic world, had no real knowledge of just how much Greek was spoken in first-century Palestine, especially in Galilee. Moreover, Papias may have confused canonical Matthew with another gospel, written in Aramaic or Hebrew, that was well known in the second century. Reports have come down to us of a "gospel according to the Hebrews," a "gospel of the Nazareans," and a "gospel of the Ebionites." It is uncertain whether these titles refer to three separate books or two or more of them refer to one book.[26] Epiphanius claims that the Ebionites, a group he regards as heretical, based their beliefs on a gospel of Matthew that they called "According to the Hebrews," written in Hebrew, but (as far as Epiphanius was concerned) falsified and mutilated; for a start, it eliminated the genealogy of Jesus and began with the ministry of John the Baptist. Similarly, Irenaeus says that the Ebionites used only the gospel of Matthew but denied the virgin birth—which again suggests that their Matthew did not include Matthew 1–2. The great translator Jerome claims that he translated the "gospel according to the Hebrews" into both Greek and Latin. This book he associates with the Nazareans, who, he insists, gave him permission to copy the Hebrew original of the gospel according to Matthew. Yet as far as we can tell from his frequent references, the actual content is far removed from canonical Matthew. All this suggests that there was ample opportunity for confusion to arise between some "gospel according to the Hebrews" and Matthew, engendering the theory that the latter was originally written in Hebrew or Aramaic.

We note several other factors in the contemporary debate over the authorship of Matthew:

1. Only this gospel refers to "Matthew the tax collector" (10:3). On the assumption of apostolic authorship, this is best seen as gentle self-deprecation, an allusive expression of gratitude for the freedom of grace (see 9:9–13). Those

---

[26]For a competent treatment of the sources, see P. Vielhauer in Hennecke 1.118–39.

who deny apostolic authorship of this book are inclined to interpret the same evidence as the reason why the unknown author(s) chose to associate the book with Matthew as opposed to some other apostle.

2. In Mark 2:14 and Luke 5:27, the man whom Jesus calls from his role as tax collector is identified as Levi. In what is transparently the same story, Matthew 9:9–13 identifies the man as Matthew. All three Synoptic Gospels, in their respective lists of the apostles (Matt. 10:2–4; Mark 3:16–18; Luke 6:13–16; cf. Acts 1:13), name a "Matthew," and Matthew 10:3 identifies this Matthew as the tax collector. The reasonable assumption is that Matthew and Levi are one and the same person. But other suggestions are not lacking. Pesch,[27] followed by Beare,[28] has argued that the calling of the tax collector concerned one Levi, but that the unknown first evangelist, choosing to identify this otherwise unknown disciple with an apostle, substituted the name of a relatively obscure apostle, Matthew, whom he then dubbed a tax collector. Albright and Mann suggest that "Matthew" is the personal name and that "Levi" refers to his tribe (i.e., that the original designation was "Matthew the Levite" but that at some early point in the tradition the designation was confused and became the common personal name Levi).[29] The theory has its attractions. It would explain why the author has such a detailed command of the Old Testament. As for the likelihood that a Levite would find employment as a disreputable tax collector, Albright and Mann argue that there were far more Levites than were needed to run the temple complex and that many therefore had to seek employment elsewhere. By taking on this task, Matthew the Levite forfeited the esteem of his tribe and his race, the most strict of whom viewed tax collectors not only as traitors (since they were indirectly serving the despised Herods; see Schürer 1.372–76) but as immoral and rapacious (since the tax-farming system ensured that a fair bit of corruption was bound up with the job). But the linguistic transformation of "Levite" to "Levi" is not very plausible, and no text preserves the designation "Matthew the Levite." On the whole, the most economical explanation still seems the best: "Matthew" and "Levi" are alternative Semitic names for one person—a phenomenon found not only in Simon/Cephas (= Peter) but also in inscriptional evidence.[30]

3. The assumption that Matthew was a tax collector (essentially a minor customs official collecting tariff on goods in transit) and was the author of this

---

[27]R. Pesch, "Levi-Matthäus (Mc 2¹⁴/Mt 9⁹ 10³): Ein Beitrag zur Lösing eines alten Problems," *ZNW* 59 (1968): 40–56.

[28]F. W. Beare, *The Gospel According to Matthew* (Oxford: Blackwell, 1981), 224–25.

[29]W. F. Albright and C. S. Mann, *Matthew*, AB 26 (Garden City: Doubleday, 1981), clxxvii–viii, clxxxiii–iv.

[30]See W. L. Lane, *The Gospel According to Mark*, NICNT (Grand Rapids: Eerdmans, 1974), 100–101 n. 29.

gospel makes sense of a number of details.[31] Not all the evidence cited is equally convincing. A number of peculiarly Matthean pericopes do depict financial transactions (17:24–27; 18:23–35; 20:1–16; 26:15; 27:3–10; 28:11–15), but none of them betrays an insider's knowledge of the customs system. Certainly a customs official in Matthew's position would have had to be fluent in both Aramaic and Greek, and such fluency must have been important when the gospel was first crossing racial barriers: indeed, it squares with the notion of a gospel written in Greek that nevertheless could draw on Semitic sources. C. F. D. Moule suggests that 13:52 is a subtle self-reference by the author: the "scribe" (γραμματεύς [*grammateus*], TNIV "teacher of the law") who becomes a disciple should not be understood as a reference to a rabbinic scribe but to a "scribe in the secular sense," that is, a well-educated writer.[32] Goodspeed goes further yet; after compiling impressive evidence that shorthand was widely practiced in the Roman world, he suggests that Matthew's training and occupation would have equipped him to be a kind of note taker or secretary for the group of disciples, even during Jesus' ministry.[33] The theory is plausible enough, but completely without hard evidence.

4. On the assumption of Markan priority, some think it unlikely that an apostle would so freely use the work of a secondary witness such as Mark and believe that this tells against any theory of apostolic authorship. But plagiarism in the modern sense, and the shame associated with it, developed in the wake of the invention of the printing press and the financial gain that could be associated with the mass production of some writing. The wholesale takeover, without acknowledgment, of someone else's literary work, with or without changes, was a common practice in the ancient world, and no opprobrium was connected with it. In that case, it is hard to think of a reason why an apostle might not also find the practice congenial, the more so if he knew that behind Mark's gospel was the witness of Peter.

5. Among the reasons Kümmel (p. 121) advances for holding that apostolic authorship is "completely impossible" is the insistence that this gospel is "systematic and therefore nonbiographical." This is a double non sequitur because (1) a topically ordered ("systematic") account can yield biographical information as easily as a strictly chronological account,[34] and (2) it is surely a false step to

---

[31]See Gundry, *Matthew*, 620–21.

[32]C. F. D. Moule, "St. Matthew's Gospel: Some Neglected Features," *SE* 2 (1964): 90–99; Moule, 94–95.

[33]E. J. Goodspeed, *Matthew: Apostle and Evangelist* (Philadelphia: J. C. Winston, 1959).

[34]Even contemporary biographies commonly treat certain parts of their subject's life in topical arrangements; see, e.g., Antonia Fraser, *Cromwell: Our Chief of Men* (St. Albans: Panther, 1975), 455ff.

assume that apostles would for some reason prove incapable of choosing anything other than a chronological form.

6. The most powerful reason today for denying even the possibility of apostolic authorship is bound up with an entire array of antecedent judgments about the development of the gospel tradition, about the shape of the history of the church in the first century, about the evidence of redactional changes, and much more. The conclusion drawn from these prior judgments is that Matthew is too late and too theologically developed to be assigned to any of the first witnesses.

It is impossible here to address all of these issues. Some of them have been briefly discussed in chapter 2. We must recognize that these interlocking theories not only discount the external evidence, such as it is, but in fact rest on far less tangible support than is often thought. For instance, how far the theology reflected in this gospel has developed is often judged on the basis of Matthew's Christology. But a high Christology developed very early, as the so-called Christ-hymns in the Pauline corpus (e.g., Phil. 2:5–11; Col. 1:15–20) testify, and it has been shown that Matthew is quite careful to distinguish, at point after point, what the first disciples understood during the time of Jesus' ministry and what he himself knows to be the case some decades later.[35] Such evidence might almost better be taken to *support* apostolic authorship; that is, only those present at the beginning would be likely to preserve such distinctions and point out with such sharpness how much the first disciples did *not* understand at the beginning (e.g., Matt. 16:21–23). Other factors alleged to demonstrate the lateness of Matthew's gospel are briefly mentioned in the next section.

7. Several scholars have argued that the author could not have been a Jew, let alone an apostle, on one of two grounds: (1) it is alleged that there are too many signs of a profound ignorance of Jewish customs and culture; (2) some have argued that the work is too anti-Jewish (some prefer the more emotionally laden term "anti-Semitic") to have been written by a Jew.[36] But the alleged ignorance of Jewish culture is sharply disputed. For example, it is alleged that Matthew lumps together the teaching of the Pharisees and the teaching of the Sadducees as if there were no difference between the two (16:12). But Matthew himself elsewhere highlights some of the differences (22:23–33). All that Matthew 16:12 requires us to hold is that in certain respects, allied with their joint failure to recognize the Messiah when he came, the Pharisees and the

---

[35]D. A. Carson, "Christological Ambiguities in the Gospel of Matthew," in *Christ the Lord, Fs.* Donald Guthrie, ed. Harold Rowdon (Leicester: IVP, 1982), 97–114.

[36]E.g., John P. Meier, *The Vision of Matthew: Christ, Church, and Morality in the First Gospel* (New York: Paulist, 1979), 17–23; G. Strecker, *Der Weg der Gerechtigkeit* (Göttingen: Vandenhoeck & Ruprecht, 1962), 34; Sjef van Tilborg, *The Jewish Leaders in Matthew* (Leiden: Brill, 1972), 17. This subject is admirably treated in Davies and Allison, *Matthew,* vol. 1, passim.

Sadducees were at one. Groups that differ do not have to differ on everything; compared with some other group—in this case, the group of nascent Christians—they may hold more in common than they themselves at first suspect. Common enemies make strange bedfellows. Many alleged errors (e.g., the use of Zech. 9:9 in Matt. 21:4–5, where Matthew has two animals) are better treated in the commentaries.[37]

As for the anti-Jewishness of Matthew, it must be remembered that this book depicts Jesus as being sent only to Israel (15:24) and recalls Jesus forbidding his disciples from extending their ministry beyond Israel (10:5–6), while at the same time it reports a commission to spread the gospel to all nations (28:18–20) and looks forward to people from every point on the compass participating in the Jewish messianic banquet (8:11–12). Arguably, the tension in presentation stems from two factors: (1) Matthew attempts to distinguish what happened "back then," during Jesus' ministry, from what is happening in his own day; (2) Matthew's ambivalent treatment of the Jews may well be shaped in part by the confusing cross-currents between Christianity and Judaism at the time of writing. Some Jews were still being converted, and Matthew wants to woo them and stabilize the faith of new Jewish converts; others, especially more conservative leaders, were appalled by this upstart faith and opposed it, ensuring that Matthew would warn his readers against their views, and especially against their rejection of Jesus the Messiah.[38]

It must be said that at one level very little hangs on the question of the authorship of this gospel. By and large, neither its meaning nor its authority is greatly changed if one decides that its author was not an apostle. What changes, however, is the matrix of thought in which these and related questions are evaluated. Strong commitments to the view that this gospel reflects late traditions that cannot possibly be tied directly to any apostle inevitably casts a hermeneutical shadow on how the evidence, including the external evidence, will be evaluated. Conversely, the judgment that in all probability the apostle Matthew was responsible for the work casts a hermeneutical shadow on the reconstruction of early church history. The web of interlocking judgments soon affects how one weighs evidence in other parts of the New Testament. Such problems can be addressed both as large-scale theoretical challenges and at the level of their constituent details. All that can be attempted in this short *Introduction* is a rather perfunctory statement of how we read the evidence and of why we weight things as we do.

> By and large, neither its meaning nor its authority is greatly changed if one decides that the author of Matthew was not an apostle. What changes, however, is the matrix of thought in which these and related questions are evaluated.

---

[37]On this particular passage, see Barnabas Lindars, *New Testament Apologetic* (London: SCM, 1961), 114; Carson, "Matthew," 436–40.

[38]See France, *Matthew—Evangelist and Teacher*, 70–73.

PROVENANCE

From the time of the influential work of Kilpatrick,[39] many have held that this book is not the work of an individual author but the product of a Christian community. Whoever wrote it was simply putting down the materials, liturgical and otherwise, that were circulating in his church. Doubtless this unknown writer ordered the material in various ways, but the book as a whole is best seen as the product of community thought and catechesis, rather than the theological and literary contribution of a single author. Indeed, Kilpatrick argues that the community deliberately and pseudonymously assigned the work to Matthew in order to ensure its wider acceptance in the Christian church.

On the basis of form criticism (see chap. 2 above), Stendahl argues that the conception of individual authorship must be relegated to an entirely subsidiary role. Unlike Kilpatrick, however, he thinks the group that produced Matthew is not some church as a whole but a school, a group within the community devoted to study and instruction, and particularly interested in the way the ancient Hebrew Scriptures are to be related to Christian life and thought.[40]

These proposals no longer have the influence they once did. In part, this owes something to redaction criticism (see chaps. 1 and 2), with its insistence that the evangelists, even if they took over traditional material, so presented it and shaped it that they gave it a distinctive theological cast. Reasons for a more traditional ascription of authorship were outlined in the last section. But whether this gospel is understood to be the product of a single author or a community of thought, one must try to hazard a guess as to its *geographic* provenance.[41]

Because the Fathers held the work to have been written first in Aramaic, quite naturally they also presupposed that it was written in Palestine. Indeed, Jerome specifically ties it to Judea (*De vir. ill.* 3). Certainly, a Palestinian origin makes sense of many features: the inclusion of Aramaic words without translation (see 5:22; 6:24; 27:46), the assumption of some Jewish customs, the bilingual character of the text forms when the Old Testament is cited, and the adoption for literary purpose of forms of speech that are more typically Semitic than Greek.

Most scholars today, however, opt for Syria as the place of origin. This choice depends primarily on two factors: (1) the adoption of a date after A.D. 70, by which time most of Palestine was destroyed; (2) the influence of Streeter,[42] who

---

[39]G. D. Kilpatrick, *The Origins of the Gospel According to St. Matthew* (Oxford: Clarendon Press, 1946).

[40] K. Stendahl, *The School of St. Matthew*, 2nd ed. (Philadelphia: Fortress Press, 1968).

[41] For an excellent survey, see Davies and Allison, *Matthew*, 1.138–47.

[42]B. H. Streeter, *The Four Gospels* (London: Macmillan, 1930), 500–23.

argued for Antioch as the provenance of this gospel. The first factor, we shall argue, is too subjective; the second is far more important. Not all of Streeter's arguments are weighty. But Antioch did boast a very large Jewish population yet was the first center for outreach to the Gentile world; these two realities come together rather forcefully in Matthew, "which breathes a Jewish atmosphere and yet looks upon the Gentile mission in a most favorable light."[43] Moreover, the Gospel of Matthew has its first convincing external attestation in the writings of Ignatius, bishop of Antioch in the early years of the second century (see *Eph.* 19:1–3 and Matt. 2; *Smyr.* 1:1 and Matt. 3:15; *Polyc.* 2:2 and Matt. 10:16). Neither argument is conclusive, still less so others that have been adduced, but Syria, if not necessarily Antioch, is an entirely plausible suggestion.

Other centers have been suggested: Alexandria, Caesarea Maritima, Edessa, and Phoenicia all have their champions. The most plausible alternative to Syria is the Transjordan, defended by Slingerland,[44] who notes that both 4:25 and 19:1 seem to view Jesus' presence in Palestine from the east side of the Jordan. That is possible, though Davies and Allison cautiously argue against such a reading of the text.[45]

In short, we cannot be certain of the geographic provenance of this gospel. Syria is perhaps the most likely suggestion, but nothing of importance hangs on the decision.

DATE

The quotations of Matthew in Ignatius (referred to above) put an upper limit on the date that can be assigned to the publication of this gospel. The modern consensus approaches that limit: most hold that Matthew was written during the period A.D. 80–100. Yet most of the reasons advanced in defense of this date depend on a network of disputed judgments.

1. Most scholars today hold that Matthew borrowed from Mark. Dates for Mark commonly vary from about A.D. 55 to 70, with opinion generally favoring the high end. Hence, a date of Matthew before 80 seems impracticable. There are several disputed points in this chain of reasoning. Some scholars continue to uphold the unanimous or virtually unanimous opinion of the early church that Matthew was written first.[46] Although we have argued that Markan priority is

---

[43]Davies and Allison, *Matthew,* 1.144.

[44]H. D. Slingerland, "The Transjordanian Origin of St. Matthew's Gospel," *JSNT* 3 (1979): 18–29.

[45]Davies and Allison, *Matthew,* 1.142, 420.

[46]"Virtually unanimous" because some have suggested that the fact that Papias treats Mark before he treats Matthew (at least as Eusebius represents Papias) indicates that Papias thought Mark was written first.

more likely, a theory of straightforward dependence is probably too simplistic, and in any case we recognize that the arguments are sufficiently fragile that we are reluctant to let too much rest on them. Moreover, even if Markan priority prevails and if Mark is dated to, say, A.D. 60, there is plenty of time for Matthew to be published before 70, when Jerusalem and its temple were destroyed.

2. Many aver that anachronisms in Matthew point to a date of writing after A.D. 70. The two most commonly cited are the reference to the destruction of a city and the references to the church. In the parable of the wedding feast, we are told that the king "sent his army and destroyed those murderers and burned their city" (22:7). This, it is argued, must be seen as an oblique reference to the destruction of Jerusalem at the end of the Jewish War (A.D. 66–70), and the mention of the burning suggests knowledge of what had already happened at the time of writing. The utterance is cast as a prophecy but depends on historical knowledge. This judgment, it is thought, is confirmed by the fact that such sweeping destruction of an entire city seems wildly disproportionate to the offense—namely, lame excuses for turning down a wedding invitation. But quite apart from the question as to whether Jesus *could* predict the future, most scholars who think that Mark was written before A.D. 70 concede that he predicts the fall of Jerusalem (Mark 13:14; cf. Matt. 24:15). They argue that if Mark wrote about 65, he was so close to the events that he could see how political circumstances were shaping up. But on this reasoning, Matthew, even if he borrowed from Mark, could have done the same thing in 66. More to the point, the language of Matthew 22:7, including the reference to the burning of the city, is the standard language of both the Old Testament and the Roman world describing punitive military expeditions against rebellious cities. Granted that Jesus foresaw the destruction of Jerusalem (as did many prophets before him), the language he used does not in any detail depend on specific knowledge as to how things actually turned out in A.D. 70.[47] In fact, Robinson goes so far as to argue that the synoptic prophecies about the fall of Jerusalem, including Matthew 22:7, are so restrained that they *must* have been written before 70.[48] Otherwise, he insists, we should expect to see some indication that the prophecies had actually been fulfilled. True, the punishment in this particular parable seems extravagant if the offense was nothing more than the social gaffe of turning down the wedding invitation of a petty monarch. But there is reason to think this offense

---

[47]See K. H. Rengstorf, "Die Stadt der Mörder (Mt 22⁷)," in *Judentum Urchristentum, Kirche, Fs.* J. Jeremias, ed. Walther Eltester (Berlin: Töpelmann, 1960), 106–29; B. Reicke, "Synoptic Prophecies on the Destruction of Jerusalem," in *Studies in New Testament and Early Christian Literature, Fs.* A. P. Wikgren, ed. D. E. Aune (Leiden: Brill, 1972), 121–34.

[48]J. A. T. Robinson, *Redating the New Testament* (Philadelphia: Westminster, 1976), chap. 2.

is more serious: in the first-century world, it smacks of rebellion against one's lord. More important, many of Jesus' parables begin with the commonplace and then introduce elements that destroy the listeners' world of expectations. The monarch represented by the king in this parable is God himself; the wedding is the wedding of God's own Son. To refuse *his* invitation—indeed, his command—is dangerous rebellion that invites catastrophic retribution.

Explicit references to "church" (ἐκκλησία [*ekklēsia*], Matt. 16:18; 18:17–18) are often taken to betray an interest in church order that developed only later. But these texts say nothing about church order. Bishops and deacons are not mentioned (though Phil. 1:1, written *before* A.D. 70, does!). The church envisaged is simply the messianic community. The discipline pictured in Matthew 18 is cast in broad principles applicable even in the earliest stages of Christianity. And Meyer has mounted an admirable defense of the authenticity of Matthew 16:18.[49]

3. The references in Matthew to the effect that something or other has continued "to this [very] day" (Matt. 27:8; 28:15)[50] are frequently taken as evidence that there was a long interval between the events of Jesus' day and the time of writing. But how long is a long interval? Would not three decades suffice? If we were to say that the effects of President Nixon's resignation continue "to this day," would that be thought an inappropriate judgment on the ground that the resignation took place some thirty years ago?

4. Tensions between Jews and Christians must have been high when this book was written, and the most plausible date for such tensions, it is argued, is either just before or just after the Council of Jamnia (c. 85), which allegedly introduced the so-called *Birkath ha-Minim* into the Jewish synagogue liturgy. This was a clause in the Eighteen Benedictions that were supposed to be recited three times a day by all pious Jews. In the version found in the Cairo Geniza,[51] it reads, "Let Nazarenes [= Christians] and *minim* [= heretics] perish in a moment; let them be blotted out of the book of the living, and let them not be written with the righteous." This had the effect (it is argued) of expelling Christians from the synagogues and was the climax of mutual antipathy between Jews and Christians in the first century. But mutual suspicions between Jews and Christians have much longer roots, as both Acts and the epistles of Paul testify. It is far from clear

---

[49]Ben F. Meyer, *The Aims of Jesus* (Philadelphia: Fortress Press, 1979), 189–91. See also France, *Matthew—Evangelist and Teacher*, 242ff.; Craig L. Blomberg, *Matthew*, NAC 22 (Nashville: Broadman, 1992), 252–53.

[50]Some add Matt. 11:12, but that passage is relevant only if an anachronism is read into the text; see Carson, "Matthew," 265–68.

[51]Probably this version was in use in Palestine at the end of the first century. For discussion of the various versions, including the Babylonian version still in use today (in which the "doers of wickedness" are not identified), see Schürer, 2.455–63.

that such antipathy followed a straight line of development, enabling us to plot its apex; it must have varied enormously from place to place and from time to time. Moreover, there is now very strong evidence that the circumstantial reconstruction that locates the *Birkath ha-Minim* at the time of Jamnia is to be questioned at every level (see discussion in chap. 6, the section "Date").

It appears, then, that arguments for a relatively late date of Matthew depend on a network of antecedent judgments, each of which can be questioned in turn. Theological developments that many scholars think must have taken at least two generations of believers may well have occurred more rapidly (after all, Romans was written within thirty years of the resurrection).[52] And some of the arguments, such as the contention that the prophecy of Matthew 22:7 is in reality a prophecy after the fact, can be turned on their heads to argue for a date *before* A.D. 70. Indeed, five other arguments point in the same direction.

1. The question of date is marginally bound up with the question of authorship. If the apostle Matthew is judged, on balance, to be the evangelist, a date before A.D. 70 is more plausible (though certainly not necessary—there is excellent evidence that the apostle John was active for at least two decades after 70).

2. The early church fathers are unanimous in assigning Matthew an early date. Because this is tied to Matthean priority, a view discounted by most scholars today, the relevant patristic evidence is given little weight in the contemporary debate. But the two issues do not have to be tied together. Whether Mark was written shortly after Peter's death, in the mid-sixties, as Irenaeus claims (see *H.E.* 3.1.1),[53] or while Peter was still alive, as Clement of Alexandria assumes (*H.E.* 2.15.1–2; 6.14.6–7), there is time for Matthew to write before A.D. 70. More can be said for Clement's dating than is sometimes thought.[54]

3. Some sayings of Jesus might be taken to indicate that the temple was still standing when Matthew wrote (Matt. 5:23–24; 12:5–7; 23:16–22; cf. 26:60–61). It might be objected that Matthew is simply being historically accurate: these things were said during Jesus' days, regardless of whether the temple was still standing when Matthew wrote. But one must at least inquire why Matthew would include so many utterances cast in terms no longer relevant to his readers. The story about the payment of the temple tax (17:24–27) is stronger evidence yet. Before A.D. 70, the episode, whatever else it meant, would be taken as a gesture reinforcing solidarity with Israel. After 70, when the tax still had to be paid by Jews but was collected on behalf of the temple of Jupiter in Rome,[55]

---

[52]See Moule, who argues that the period before A.D. 70 is "the most plausible dating" of Matthew's gospel (p. 242).

[53]Taking the ἔξοδος (*exodos*) of Peter and Paul to refer to their death.

[54] See Robinson, *Redating*, 107–15; contra Hengel, *Mark*, 2–6.

[55]Josephus, *Wars* 7.218; Dio Cassius, 65.7.2; Suetonius, *Domitian Hist. Rom.* 12. Cf. E. M. Smallwood, *The Jews Under Roman Rule* (Leiden: Brill, 1976), 371–76.

the same episode might suggest solidarity with idolatry. Even if for other reasons Matthew had wanted to preserve this pericope, it is hard to see how, if he was writing after 70, he could have permitted such an implication without comment.

4. While many assign Matthew to the period A.D. 70–100, we actually have few primary sources from that period, so it is difficult to check the claims. By contrast, Gundry has compiled a list of passages in Matthew that he thinks, on the basis of features known to have existed during that period, suggest a date before 70.[56] Not all of his suggestions are equally convincing, but many carry considerable weight (e.g., insertion of the Sabbath day alongside winter as an undesirable time to flee from Jerusalem [24:20]; baptism before teaching [28:19; cf. *Didache* 7:1 and other later sources]).

5. Arguing for a date earlier than A.D. 90, Kilpatrick draws attention to the fact that, although the apostolic fathers demonstrate their knowledge of many epistles from the Pauline corpus, in Matthew there is no undisputed instance of dependence on Paul.[57] Indeed, Kilpatrick argues that some passages in Matthew would not have been written as they are if certain passages in Paul were known (e.g., Matt. 28, with respect to the list of resurrection appearances in 1 Cor. 15). Kilpatrick concludes that a church unaffected by Paulinism and apparently unacquainted with Paul's epistles cannot possibly be dated after 90. We are inclined to agree, but wonder why this *terminus ad quem* must be so late. If Matthew was written before 70, this complete independence from Paul would be still easier to understand.

None of the arguments presented is conclusive. Other arguments tend to be even less decisive, owing to additional imponderables. For example, Gundry specifies a date not later than A.D. 63, but this depends on his view that Luke borrowed from Matthew and that Luke-Acts was published while Paul was still alive. Few agree with the latter (see the discussion in chap. 7), and fewer yet agree with the former.

On balance, then, the preponderance of evidence suggests that Matthew was published before 70, but not long before.

> On balance, the preponderance of evidence suggests that Matthew was published before 70, but not long before.

DESTINATION

The usual assumption is that the evangelist wrote this gospel to meet the needs of believers in his own area. There is a prima facie realism to this assumption if we hold that Matthew was working in centers of large Jewish population, whether in Palestine or Syria (see "Provenance" above). Since the book betrays so many Jewish features, it is not easy to imagine that the author had a *predominantly* Gentile audience in mind. But it is not implausible to suggest that

---

[56]Gundry, *Matthew*, 602–6.
[57]Kilpatrick, *Origins*, 129–30.

Matthew wrote his gospel with certain *kinds* of readers in mind, rather than readers in a particular location. Moreover, the strong arguments of Bauckham and others, to the effect that the gospels were first written to be read by *all* Christians, should not be lightly set aside.[58]

PURPOSE

Because Matthew includes no direct statement of his purpose in writing, all attempts at delineating it are inferences drawn from his themes and from the way he treats certain topics as compared with the way the other gospels treat similar topics. This forces us to recognize several limitations that must be imposed on quests to uncover his purpose. Matthew's dominant themes are several, complex, and to some extent disputed. Attempts to delineate a single narrow purpose are therefore doomed to failure. It is always possible for other scholars to emphasize complementary themes and correspondingly to shift the purpose to another area. Students of the New Testament are well aware how difficult it is to achieve consensus on the purpose of some of Paul's letters, even though most of them were written with occasional purposes in mind that may actually be articulated in the text. How much more difficult is it to isolate the distinguishing purpose of a gospel!

The challenge increases when we recognize that Matthew, like any gospel writer but unlike the writer of an epistle, is committed to describing what happened during the ministry and passion of the historical Jesus, while nevertheless addressing issues that are contemporary to his own ministry. This leads some commentators to try to infer what kind of situation might prompt Matthew to include this or that pericope (e.g., the transfiguration) and to present it as he does. But it is always possible that he sees no direct connection between what happened formerly and what is happening currently in his own congregation(s). For instance, he may at times be interested in explaining the basis in Jesus' ministry for beliefs and practices that are accepted (or disputed) in the evangelist's time. That means inferences must be more remote and therefore more speculative.

Because Matthew devotes so much space to Old Testament quotations, some have suggested that he wrote his gospel to teach Christians how to read their Bibles—what we refer to as the Old Testament. Others appeal to the same evidence to infer that he was trying to evangelize Jews. Or perhaps he wrote to train Christians to sharpen their apologetics as they wrestled with the Pharisaic Judaism of their own day. Because Matthew devotes many passages to Jesus' teaching on the law, some have thought he was aiming to confute incipient antinomianism, or

---

[58]Richard Bauckham, ed., *The Gospels for All Christians: Rethinking the Gospel Audiences* (Grand Rapids: Eerdmans, 1998). See the discussion in Craig S. Keener, *A Commentary on the Gospel of Matthew* (Grand Rapids: Eerdmans, 1999), 45–51.

even Paulinism. Others have appealed to the same evidence to argue that Matthew was a master churchman, struggling to develop a distinctively Christian ethical structure and to do so in a way that retains the unique place assigned to Jesus without offending too many Jewish sensitivities over the law. Conversely, others suppose that Matthew was trying to head off too rapid an institutionalization of the church, returning to an earlier, more charismatic emphasis while retaining some of the gains that a few decades of church experience had brought. Or did he write his work to train leaders, or as a catechesis for new converts?

These and many more suggestions have been put forward as *the* purpose of Matthew's gospel. Still others find contradictory strands in Matthew—for example, between Jewish exclusivism and worldwide mission, or between recognition of the place of law and the assumption that the law has been fulfilled in Christ—and conclude that *no* unitary purpose is possible: the conflicting emphases reflect different strands of tradition that have been brought together by incompetent redactors.

These diverse opinions do not prevent us from saying anything about Matthew's purpose. If we restrict ourselves to widely recognized themes, it is surely fair to infer that Matthew wishes to demonstrate, among other things: (1) that Jesus is the promised Messiah, the Son of David, the Son of God, the Son of Man, Immanuel, the one to whom the Old Testament points; (2) that many Jews, especially Jewish leaders, sinfully failed to recognize Jesus during his ministry (and, by implication, are in great danger if they continue in that stance after the resurrection); (3) that the promised eschatological kingdom has already dawned, inaugurated by the life, death, resurrection, and exaltation of Jesus; (4) that this messianic reign is continuing in the world as believers, both Jews and Gentiles, submit to Jesus' authority, overcome temptation, endure persecution, wholeheartedly embrace Jesus' teaching, and thus demonstrate that they constitute the true locus of the people of God and the true witness to the world of the "gospel of the kingdom"; and (5) that this messianic reign is not only the fulfillment of Old Testament hopes but the foretaste of the consummated kingdom that will dawn when Jesus the Messiah personally returns.

Doubtless this complex array of themes (and more could be enumerated) was designed to meet diverse needs. Such themes would effectively instruct and perhaps catechize the church (the latter facilitated by the carefully crafted, topical arrangement of many sections). They would also be effective in equipping Christians in the task of Jewish evangelism and might prove to be an effective evangelistic tool in their own right.

TEXT

Compared with Acts, for example, the text of Matthew is relatively stable. But as with all the Synoptic Gospels, Matthew's text is afflicted with many variants that are tied to the synoptic problem. This provides many opportunities for harmonizing or disharmonizing alterations in the transmission (e.g., variants at 12:47; 16:2–3; 18:10–11). But not every instance of possible harmonization should be taken as such and assumed to be secondary (12:4, 47; 13:35 may well be examples where caution is required). Davies and Allison provide an excellent bibliography on these textual matters.[59]

ADOPTION INTO THE CANON

The gospel of Matthew was universally received as soon as it was published and continued to be the most frequently cited gospel for centuries. The refusal of Marcion to accept it carries no weight, since his antipathy to all things Jewish is well known. So far as our sources go, the book never divided the Eastern and Western wings of the church as did, say, the epistle to the Hebrews.

MATTHEW IN RECENT STUDIES

Until a quarter of a century ago, English-language commentators ignored Matthew more than any other of the canonical gospels. This has been redressed by the publication of numerous major commentaries.[60] Two of these six, however, are mildly eccentric. The bibliography and discussion in Beare (1981) was fifteen years out of date the day it was published. Gundry's work (1982) is a detailed redaction-critical study of the Greek text but comes to so many conclusions that scholars of all stripes find implausible that it has not been well received. In particular, several of his contentions—(1) that Q (see chap. 2 above) embraces far more than the 250 or so verses normally assigned to it; (2) that the changes and additions Matthew makes in his sources are entirely motivated by theological concerns and are without historical referent (including, e.g., the birth narratives in Matt. 1–2); and (3) that the genre of literature he was writing (which Gundry labels "midrash") would have been recognized as a mixture of history and ahistorical reflection by the first readers—have all come in for considerable criticism. On the third point, it has repeatedly been observed that in the first century, "midrash" could refer to many different kinds of commentary: it was not a well-defined genre that readers would instantly recognize, thereby

---

[59]Davies and Allison, *Matthew*, 1.147–48 n. 127, to which must be added C. M. Martini, "La problématique générale du texte de Matthieu," in *L'évangile selon Matthieu: Rédaction et Théologie*, BETL 29, ed. M. Didier (Gembloux: Duculot, 1972), 21–36.

[60]See the commentaries by Albright and Mann (1981), Beare (1981), Gundry (1982), Carson (1984), France (1985), Davies and Allison (1988–97), Harrington (1991), Blomberg (1992), and Keener (2003).

enabling them to draw conclusions about its nonreferential nature.[61] Extending well beyond the commentaries, excellent surveys in English of recent Matthean studies are provided by Stanton[62] and France.[63]

Until fairly recently, much scholarly energy during the past half-century was devoted to redaction-critical studies of Matthew. Beginning with the groundbreaking work of Bornkamm, Barth, and Held,[64] many scholars focused on differences between Matthew and Mark, and between Matthew and what can be retrieved of Q, in order to determine what is distinctive in Matthew's gospel. Although many of these proved suggestive, not a few were so narrowly based as to be somewhat eccentric. Rolf Walker thinks that Matthew was written to show that Israel has been entirely rejected: the Great Commission authorizes that the gospel be preached exclusively to Gentiles.[65] Only rarely is Walker exegetically convincing. His treatment of πάντα τὰ ἔθνη (*panta ta ethnē*, "all nations") in 28:19 has persuaded almost no one; nowhere does he adequately struggle with the fact that all the disciples and early converts were Jews. Hubert Frankemölle argues that Matthew is so unlike Mark that it cannot meaningfully be called a gospel at all;[66] rather, like Deuteronomy and Chronicles, it is a book of history—the history, not of Jesus, but of the community, since in this "literary fiction," Jesus is an idealized figure intentionally fused with Matthew the theologian. But Frankemölle overemphasizes formal differences between Mark and Matthew and neglects substantial differences between Matthew and Deuteronomy or Chronicles. Although he is right to read Matthew as a unified book, he does not adequately reflect on the fact that for most of his gospel, Matthew heavily depends on Mark and Q (however Q is understood).

Some studies have been widely accepted, not least the work of Bornkamm.[67] He holds that whereas in Mark the disciples do not understand what Jesus says until he explains things to them in secret, Matthew attributes large and instant

---

[61]The most extended refutation, however—that of Charles L. Quarles, *Midrash Criticism: Introduction and Appraisal* (Lanham: University Press of America, 1998)— is itself sufficiently eccentric (though it makes a number of telling observations) that it cannot be entirely relied upon. See the review by Peter Enns in *WTJ* 62 (2000): 303-6.

[62]Stanton, "The Origin and Purpose of Matthew's Gospel: Matthean Scholarship from 1945 to 1980," in H. Temporini and W. Haase, eds., *ANRW* 2.25.3, pp. 1889–1951.

[63]France, *Matthew—Evangelist and Teacher.*

[64]G. Bornkamm, G. Barth, and H. J. Held, *Tradition and Interpretation in Matthew* (ET London: SCM, 1963).

[65]R. Walker, *Die Heilsgeschichte im ersten Evangelium* (Göttingen: Vandenhoeck & Ruprecht, 1967).

[66]Hubert Frankemölle, *Jahwebund und Kirche Christi: Studien zur Form- und Traditionsgeschichte des "Evangeliums" nach Matthäus* (Münster: Aschendorff, 1974).

[67]Bornkamm, Barth, and Held, *Tradition and Interpretation,* 105–16.

understanding to the disciples. In fact, this is what sets the disciples off from the crowds: the disciples understand. The faltering of the disciples at various points stems from their lack of faith, not from any lack of understanding. Yet one is tempted to qualify this thesis. Apart from the fact that he relies rather too heavily on the so-called Messianic secret in Mark, Bornkamm does not adequately deal with the disciples' request for private instruction (13:36), their failure to understand Jesus' teaching about his passion even after his explanations (e.g., 16:21–26; 17:23; 26:51–56), or the passages that deal with "stumbling" and "falling away." This is not a peripheral failure; at bottom, Bornkamm does not wrestle with the degree to which the failure of the disciples turns on their location in the stream of redemptive history. They were unprepared before the passion and resurrection to conceive of a messiah who could be defeated, who could die the ignominious and odious death of the scum of Roman society. To this extent, the disciples' coming to deeper understanding *and* faith was unique: it was in part a function of their place in salvation history, a place rendered forever obsolete by the triumph of Jesus' resurrection. Our coming to faith and understanding today, or even in Matthew's day, therefore, cannot be exactly like the coming to faith and understanding of the first disciples. In numerous ways Matthew makes this clear, but Bornkamm is so interested in reading Matthew's church into Matthew's description of the first disciples that the exegesis becomes skewed.[68]

Although a handful of scholars have argued that the author or final redactor of Matthew's gospel was a Gentile,[69] one of the most conspicuous recent trends in the study of the New Testament in general and of Matthew in particular has been the tendency to stress the essential Jewishness of many of its documents. In the case of Matthew, however, this trend has sometimes gone over the top. Several scholars have argued that Matthew's gospel is so Jewish that it is scarcely Christian at all, but a kind of Judaism. In such a reading, the evangelist may variously be considered an apostate, a reformer, or a revolutionary, but his document cannot really be judged to be genuinely Christian.[70] But Donald Hagner

---

[68]See esp. Andrew H. Trotter, "Understanding and Stumbling: A Study of the Disciples' Understanding of Jesus and His Teaching in the Gospel of Matthew" (Ph.D. diss., Cambridge University, 1987).

[69]One thinks of the works of Wolfgang Trilling, Georg Strecker, and others; see the review of such literature in Boris Repschinski, *The Controversy Stories in the Gospel of Matthew: Their Redaction, Form and Relevance for the Relationship between the Matthean Community and Formative Judaism*, FRLANT 189 (Göttingen: Vandenhoeck & Ruprecht, 2000), 13–61.

[70]See Andrew Overman, *Matthew's Gospel and Formative Judaism: The Social World of the Matthean Community* (Minneapolis: Fortress, 1990); idem, *Church and Community in Crisis: The Gospel According to Matthew*, The New Testament in Context (Valley Forge: Trinity Press International, 1996); Anthony Saldarini, *Matthew's*

has shown that the weight such authors rest on a singular reading of Matthew 5:17ff. and a few other texts is unjustified.[71] Moreover, the interest in evangelizing all the nations is not restricted to the Great Commission (28:18–20) but is embedded as well in utterances about how Gentiles will sit down with Abraham, Isaac, and Jacob in the kingdom (8:11–12) and in parables with a similar purpose (esp. 21:28–22:14),[72] while atonement language to describe Jesus' death is unswervingly taken over from Mark (Mark 10:45; Matt. 20:28).

Some recent studies, however, have manifested an increasing concern to read Matthew holistically—that is, to read Matthew in his own right, even while keeping an eye cocked on the synoptic (and other) parallels. Where the first gospel is studied as a book on its own and not simply as a modified Mark, its themes, unity, and essential power more easily come into focus. This is not to deny the validity of other approaches; it is to insist that the traditional historical-critical method be complemented by greater literary sensitivity. To take up again the theme of the disciples' understanding in Matthew: one recent work strenuously argues for a closer dialog between those engaged in narrative criticism and those committed to such historical-critical approaches as redaction criticism. Such dialog results in the conclusion that the disciples in Matthew, while at one level comprehending Jesus to be the Messiah, consistently misunderstand the kind of Messiah Jesus is.[73]

THE CONTRIBUTION OF MATTHEW

> *Because of the tight relationships among the Synoptic Gospels, the contribution made by any one of them must be evaluated in light of the contribution made by all three.*

Because of the tight relationships among the Synoptic Gospels, the contribution made by any one of them must be evaluated in light of the contribution made by all three. If Matthew suddenly disappeared, much of its material would still be found, more or less intact, in Mark and Luke. In that sense, Matthew cannot be said to make the same sort of independent contribution that Hebrews or the Apocalypse does, for example.

But the Synoptic Gospels as a whole make an irreplaceable contribution. Alongside John, they constitute the foundational witness to the person, min-

---

Christian-Jewish Community (Chicago: University of Chicago Press, 1994); David Sim, *The Gospel of Matthew and Christian Judaism: The History and Social Setting of the Matthean Community* (Edinburgh: T. & T. Clark, 1998).

[71]Donald A. Hagner, "Matthew: Apostate, Reformer, Revolutionary?" *NTS* 49 (2003): 193-209.

[72]See especially Wesley G. Olmstead, *Matthew's Trilogy of Parables: The Nation, the Nations and the Reader in Matthew 21.28–22.14,* SNTSMS 127 (Cambridge: Cambridge University Press, 2003).

[73]Jeannine K. Brown, *The Disciples in Narrative Perspective: The Portrayal and Function of the Matthean Disciples* (Atlanta: SBL, 2002).

istry, teaching, passion, and resurrection of Jesus the Messiah. Nor are the three Synoptic Gospels to be seen as merely redundant testimony. Each provides its own slant, together providing a kind of stereoscopic depth that would otherwise be almost entirely missing. And at a secondary level, each provides a window onto the life of the church at the time each was written. But this window, it must be insisted, is never transparent: it is at best translucent, and the shadows one sees through it have to be interpreted with some care.

Within this framework, we may highlight some of Matthew's emphases, and therefore some of the peculiar contributions this gospel makes to the canon.

1. Matthew preserves large blocks of Jesus' teaching in the discourses already enumerated. Doubtless that was one of the major reasons this gospel was so popular in the early church.[74] However they came to be preserved in this form, there can be no doubt that the church would be greatly impoverished without the Sermon on the Mount, Matthew's list of parables, his version of the eschatological discourse, and so forth.

2. Matthew complements the other gospels, Luke in particular, by giving an alternative account of Jesus' virginal conception, cast in Joseph's perspective. Quite apart from other stories in the birth narrative of which there is no other record (e.g., the visit of the Magi, the flight into Egypt), the whole account is strongly tied to the antecedent revelation in what we now call the Old Testament.[75]

3. More generally, Matthew's use of the Old Testament is particularly rich and complex. The most noticeable peculiarity is the number of Old Testament quotations (variously estimated between ten and fourteen) found only in Matthew and introduced by a fulfillment formula characterized by a passive form of πληρόω (*plēroō*, "to fulfill"). These "formula quotations" are all asides by the evangelist, his own reflections (hence, the widely used German word for them, *Reflexionszitate*). Characteristically, they adopt a text form rather more Semitic and rather less like the LXX than most of the other Old Testament quotations in Matthew. The precise significance of these features is disputed.[76] What is clear is that Matthew's appreciation for the links between the old covenant and the new is characterized by extraordinarily evocative nuances. For instance, his notion of prophecy and fulfillment cannot be reduced to mere verbal prediction and historical fulfillment in raw events (though it sometimes includes such a notion). He employs various forms of typology and a fortiori

---

[74]See especially Massaux, *Saint Matthieu*.

[75]The most detailed study is that of Raymond E. Brown, *The Birth of the Messiah: A Commentary on the Infancy Narratives* (Garden City: Doubleday, 1977).

[76]See, among other studies, the bibliographical entries under Doeve, France (*Jesus and the Old Testament*), Gundry, McConnell, Moo, Rothfuchs, Soarés-Prabhu, Stanton ("Matthew"), Stendahl, Westerholm, Knowles, and Beaton.

arguments and adopts a fundamentally christological reading of the Old Testament. Thus, Jesus' temptations (Matt. 4:1–11), for instance, are in some sense a reenactment of the temptations confronted in the wilderness by the Israelites, God's "son" (Exod. 4:22–23)—except that Jesus the Son of God is entirely victorious in them because he is determined by God's Word. Allison has shown how much of a role exodus typology plays in the book.[77]

4. In the same way, Matthew's treatment of the law is especially suggestive. Although many think Matthew internalizes the law, radicalizes it, subsumes it under the love command, absolutizes only its moral dimensions, or treats it as a schoolmaster that conducts people to Christ, it is better to use Matthew's own category: Jesus comes to "fulfill" the law (5:17). In Matthew's usage, that verb presupposes that even the law itself enjoys a teleological, prophetic function.[78]

5. Matthew's gospel is foundational not only as one looks backward to the scriptures of the old covenant but also as one looks forward to what the church became. The later debates on the relation between Israel and the church find much of their genesis in Matthew, John, Romans, and Hebrews. Not a little of this debate, as far as Matthew is concerned, has focused on his treatment of the Jewish leaders.[79]

6. Finally, there are shadings to Matthew's portrait of Jesus—surely the heart of his gospel—that are unique. It is important to say, again, that much of what is central in Matthew's thought in this regard is *not* unique;[80] it is not just in Matthew that Jesus is the Christ, the Son of David, the Son of God, the Son of Man, the Servant of the Lord, and so forth. Whatever special coloring these titles take on in Matthew, their semantic overlap with their usage in other gospels is even more striking. Nor is it justifiable to try to isolate one christological title as that which explains or hermeneutically controls all the others in this gospel.[81] But having entered these caveats, Matthew's shadings are important. He may achieve such shading by associating a particular title with some theme, as when he repeatedly links "Son of David" with Jesus' healing ministry (and he is not

---

[77]Dale C. Allison Jr., *The New Moses: A Matthean Typology* (Minneapolis: Fortress Press, 1993).

[78]See esp. the bibliographical entries under Meier (*Law*), Banks, and Carson (*Matthew*, 140ff.).

[79]See discussion of the options in D. A. Carson, "Jewish Leaders in Matthew's Gospel: A Reappraisal," *JETS* 25 (1982): 161–74.

[80]A point perhaps not sufficiently observed in the important article by G. M. Styler, "Stages in Christology in the Synoptic Gospels," *NTS* 10 (1963–64): 398–409.

[81]The best-known instance is the argument of Kingsbury (*Matthew*) that "Son of God" is for Matthew the controlling title under which all others must be subsumed. See the important response by David Hill, "Son and Servant: An Essay on Matthean Christology," *JSNT* 6 (1980): 2–16.

alone in this association).[82] He may also do it by introducing titles of which the other evangelists make no mention, as when he insists that Jesus is Immanuel, "God with us" (1:23).

BIBLIOGRAPHY

W. F. **Albright** and C. S. **Mann**, *Matthew*, AB 26 (Garden City: Doubleday, 1981) ▮Willoughby C. **Allen**, *A Critical and Exegetical Commentary on the Gospel According to S. Matthew*, ICC (Edinburgh: T. & T. Clark, 1912) ▮Dale C. **Allison** Jr., *The New Moses: A Matthean Typology* (Minneapolis: Fortress Press, 1993) ▮idem, "The Structure of the Sermon on the Mount," *JBL* 106 (1987): 423–45 ▮B. W. **Bacon**, "The 'Five Books' of Moses Against the Jews," *Exp* 15 (1918): 56–66 ▮idem, *Studies in Matthew* (London: Constable, 1930) ▮Robert **Banks**, *Jesus and the Law in the Synoptic Tradition* (Cambridge: Cambridge University Press, 1975) ▮F. W. **Beare**, *The Gospel According to Matthew* (Oxford: Blackwell, 1981) ▮Richard **Beaton**, *Isaiah's Christ in Matthew's Gospel*, SNTSMS 123 (Cambridge: Cambridge University Press, 2003) ▮Craig L. **Blomberg**, *Matthew*, NAC 22 (Nashville: Broadman, 1992) ▮Pierre **Bonnard**, *L'evangile selon Saint Matthieu* (Neuchâtel: Delachaux et Niestlé, 1970) ▮G. **Bornkamm**, G. **Barth**, and H. J. **Held**, *Tradition and Interpretation in Matthew* (ET London: SCM, 1963) ▮Jeannine K. **Brown**, *The Disciples in Narrative Perspective: The Portrayal and Function of the Matthean Disciples* (Atlanta: SBL, 2002) ▮Raymond E. **Brown**, *The Birth of the Messiah: A Commentary on the Infancy Narratives* (Garden City: Doubleday, 1977) ▮Steven M. **Bryan**, *Jesus and Israel's Traditions of Judgement and Restoration*, SNTSMS 117 (Cambridge: Cambridge University Press, 2002) ▮C. F. **Burney**, *The Poetry of Our Lord* (Oxford: Oxford University Press, 1925) ▮D. A. **Carson**, "Christological Ambiguities in the Gospel of Matthew," in *Christ the Lord, Fs.* Donald Guthrie, ed. Harold Rowdon (Leicester: IVP, 1982), 97–114 ▮idem, "Jewish Leaders in Matthew's Gospel: A Reappraisal," *JETS* 25 (1982): 161–74 ▮idem, "Matthew," in *EBC* 8 (Grand Rapids: Zondervan, 1984) ▮W. D. **Davies** and Dale C. **Allison** Jr., *The Gospel According to Saint Matthew*, ICC, 3 vols. (Edinburgh: T. & T. Clark, 1988–97) ▮J. W. **Doeve**, *Jewish Hermeneutics in the Synoptic Gospels and Acts* (Assen: Van Gorcum, 1954) ▮David **Duling**, "The Therapeutic Son of David: An Element in Matthew's Christological Apologetic," *NTS* 24 (1978): 392–410 ▮R. T. **France**, *Jesus and the Old Testament: His Application of Old Testament Passages to Himself and His Mission* (London: Tyndale, 1971) ▮idem, *Matthew*, TNTC (Grand Rapids: Eerdmans, 1985) ▮idem, *Matthew—Evangelist and Teacher* (Grand Rapids: Zondervan, 1989) ▮Hubert **Frankemölle**, *Jahwebund und Kirche Christi: Studien zur Form- und Traditionsgeschichte des*

---

[82]See David Duling, "The Therapeutic Son of David: An Element in Matthew's Christological Apologetic," *NTS* 24 (1978): 392–410

"*Evangeliums*" nach Matthäus (Münster: Aschendorff, 1974) ▮P. **Gaechter**, *Die literarische Kunst im Matthäusevangelium* (Stuttgart: Katholisches Bibelwerk, 1966) ▮E. J. **Goodspeed**, *Matthew: Apostle and Evangelist* (Philadelphia: J. C. Winston, 1959) ▮M. D. **Goulder**, *Midrash and Lection in Matthew* (London: SPCK, 1974) ▮F. C. **Grant**, *The Gospels: Their Origin and Their Growth* (New York: Harper, 1957) ▮Robert H. **Gundry**, *Matthew: A Commentary on His Literary and Theological Art* (Grand Rapids: Eerdmans, 1982) ▮idem, *The Use of the Old Testament in St. Matthew's Gospel* (Leiden: Brill, 1967) ▮Donald A. **Hagner**, *Matthew*, WBC 33, 2 vols. (Dallas: Word Books, 1993–95) ▮idem, "Matthew: Apostate, Reformer, Revolutionary?" *NTS* 49 (2003): 193–209 ▮Daniel J. **Harrington**, *The Gospel of Matthew*, SacPag 1 (Collegeville: Liturgical Press, 1991) ▮J. R. **Harris**, *Testimonies*, 2 vols. (Cambridge: Cambridge University Press, 1920) ▮Martin **Hengel**, *Studies in the Gospel of Mark* (Philadelphia: Fortress Press, 1985) ▮David **Hill**, *The Gospel of Matthew*, NCB (Grand Rapids: Eerdmans, 1972) ▮idem, "Son and Servant: An Essay on Matthean Christology," *JSNT* 6 (1980): 2–16 ▮Craig S. **Keener**, *A Commentary on the Gospel of Matthew* (Grand Rapids: Eerdmans, 1999) ▮G. D. **Kilpatrick**, *The Origins of the Gospel According to St. Matthew* (Oxford: Clarendon Press, 1946) ▮J. D. **Kingsbury**, *Matthew: Structure, Christology, Kingdom* (Philadelphia: Fortress, 1975) ▮Michael **Knowles**, *Jeremiah in Matthew's Gospel: The Rejected Profit Motif in Matthean Redaction*, JSNTSup 68 (Sheffield: Sheffield Academic Press, 1993) ▮E. **Krentz**, "The Extent of Matthew's Prologue," *JBL* 83 (1964): 409–14 ▮J. **Kürzinger**, "Irenäus und sein Zeugnis zur Sprache des Matthäusevangeliums," *NTS* 10 (1963): 108–15 ▮idem, "Das Papiaszeugnis und die Erstgestalt des Matthäusevangeliums," *BZ* 4 (1960): 19–38 ▮M.-J. **Lagrange**, *Evangile selon Saint Matthieu* (Paris: Lecoffre, 1948) ▮W. L. **Lane**, *The Gospel According to Mark*, NICNT (Grand Rapids: Eerdmans, 1974) ▮B. **Lindars**, *New Testament Apologetic* (London: SCM, 1961) ▮Ernst **Lohmeyer**, *Das Evangelium des Matthäus*, ed. W. Schmauck (Göttingen: Vandenhoeck & Ruprecht, 1956) ▮C. H. **Lohr**, "Oral Techniques in the Gospel of Matthew," *CBQ* 23 (1961): 403–35 ▮Ulrich **Luz**, *Matthew: A Commentary*, 3 vols. (Minneapolis: Augsburg/Fortress Press, 1989–) ▮Richard S. **McConnell**, *Law and Prophecy in Matthew's Gospel* (Basel: Friedrich Reinhardt, 1969) ▮A. H. **McNeile**, *The Gospel According to St. Matthew* (London: Macmillan, 1915) ▮T. W. **Manson**, *The Sayings of Jesus* (London: SCM, 1949) ▮C. M. **Martini**, "La problématique générale du texte de Matthieu," in *L'évangile selon Matthieu: Rédaction et Théologie*, BETL 29, ed. M. Didier (Gembloux: Duculot, 1972) ▮Edouard **Massaux**, *Influence de l'évangile de Saint Matthieu sur la littérature chrétienne avant Saint Irénée*, BETL 75 (Leuven: Leuven University Press, 1986) ▮John P. **Meier**, *Law and History in Matthew's Gospel: A Redactional Study of Mt. 5:17–48* (Rome: BIP, 1976) ▮idem, *Matthew* (Wilmington: Glazier, 1980) ▮idem, *The Vision of Matthew: Christ, Church, and Morality in the First Gospel* (New York: Paulist, 1979) ▮Ben F. **Meyer**, *The Aims of Jesus* (Philadelphia: Fortress, 1979) ▮Douglas J. **Moo**, *The Old Testament in the*

Gospel Passion Narratives (Sheffield: Almond Press, 1983) ▮L. **Morris**, "The Gospels and the Jewish Lectionaries," in *GP* 1.129–56 ▮C. F. D. **Moule**, "St. Matthew's Gospel: Some Neglected Features," *SE* 2 (1964): 90–99 ▮Wesley G. **Olmstead**, *Matthew's Trilogy of Parables: The Nation, the Nations and the Reader in Matthew 21.28–22.14*, SNTSMS 127 (Cambridge: Cambridge University Press, 2003) ▮Andrew **Overman**, *Matthew's Gospel and Formative Judaism: The Social World of the Matthean Community* (Minneapolis: Fortress Press, 1990) ▮idem, *Church and Community in Crisis: The Gospel According to Matthew*, The New Testament in Context (Valley Forge: Trinity Press International, 1996) ▮Daniel **Patte**, *The Gospel According to Matthew* (Philadelphia: Fortress Press) ▮R. **Pesch**, "Levi-Matthäus (Mc 2^{14} /Mt 9^{9}10^3): Ein Beitrag zur Lösing eines alten Problems," *ZNW* 59 (1968): 40–56 ▮Alfred **Plummer**, *An Exegetical Commentary on the Gospel According to S. Matthew* (London: Robert Scott, 1909) ▮B. **Reicke**, "Synoptic Prophecies on the Destruction of Jerusalem," in *Studies in New Testament and Early Christian Literature*, Fs. A. P. Wikgren, ed. D. E. Aune (Leiden: Brill, 1972) ▮K. H. **Rengstorf**, "Die Stadt der Mörder (Mt 22^7)," in *Judentum, Urchristentum, Kirche*, Fs. J. Jeremias, ed. Walther Eltester (Berlin: Töpelmann, 1960), 106–29 ▮Boris **Repschinski**, *The Controversy Stories in the Gospel of Matthew: Their Redaction, Form and Relevance for the Relationship between the Matthean Community and Formative Judaism*, FRLANT 189 (Göttingen: Vandenhoeck & Ruprecht, 2000) ▮H. N. **Ridderbos**, *Matthew* (Grand Rapids: Zondervan, 1987) ▮J. A. T. **Robinson**, *Redating the New Testament* (Philadelphia: Westminster, 1976) ▮Wilhelm **Rothfuchs**, *Die Erfüllungszitate des Matthäus-Evangeliums* (Stuttgart: Kohlhammer, 1969) ▮Anthony **Saldarini**, *Matthew's Christian-Jewish Community* (Chicago: University of Chicago Press, 1994) ▮Alexander **Sand**, *Das Gesetz und die Propheten: Untersuchungen zur Theologie des Evangeliums nach Matthäus* (Regensburg: Friedrich Pustet, 1976) ▮A. **Schlatter**, *Der Evangelist Matthäus: Seine Sprache, sein Ziel, seine Selbständigkeit*, 6th ed. (Stuttgart: Calwer, 1963) ▮Eduard **Schweizer**, *The Good News According to Matthew* (Atlanta: John Knox, 1975) ▮David **Sim**, *The Gospel of Matthew and Christian Judaism: The History and Social Setting of the Matthean Community* (Edinburgh: T. & T. Clark, 1998) ▮H. D. **Slingerland**, "The Transjordanian Origin of St. Matthew's Gospel," *JSNT* 3 (1979): 18–29 ▮E. M. **Smallwood**, *The Jews Under Roman Rule* (Leiden: Brill, 1976) ▮George M. **Soarès-Prabhu**, *The Formula Quotations in the Infancy Narrative of Matthew* (Rome: BIP, 1976) ▮G. N. **Stanton**, "Matthew," in *It Is Written: Scripture Citing Scripture*, Fs. Barnabas Lindars, ed. D. A. Carson and H. G. M. Williamson (Cambridge: Cambridge University Press, 1988), 205–19 ▮idem, "The Origin and Purpose of Matthew's Gospel: Matthean Scholarship from 1945 to 1980," in H. Temporini and W. Haase, eds., *ANRW* 2.25.3, pp. 1889–1951 ▮idem, *A Gospel for a New People: Studies in Matthew* (Edinburgh: T. & T. Clark, 1992) ▮K. **Stendahl**, *The School of St. Matthew*, 2nd ed. (Philadelphia: Fortress Press, 1968) ▮Ned B. **Stonehouse**, *The Witness of Matthew and Mark to Christ* (Grand

Rapids: Eerdmans, 1944) ▥G. **Strecker**, *Der Weg der Gerechtigkeit* (Göttingen: Vandenhoeck & Ruprecht, 1962) ▥B. H. **Streeter**, *The Four Gospels* (London: Macmillan, 1930) ▥G. M. **Styler**, "Stages in Christology in the Synoptic Gospels," *NTS* 10 (1963–64): 398–409 ▥C. C. **Torrey**, *Our Translated Gospels* (London: Hodder & Stoughton, n.d.) ▥Wolfgang **Trilling**, *Das wahre Israel: Studien zur Theologie des Matthäus-Evangeliums* (Munich: Kösel, 1964) ▥Sjef **van Tilborg**, *The Jewish Leaders in Matthew* (Leiden: Brill, 1972) ▥R. **Walker**, *Die Heilsgeschichte im ersten Evangelium* (Göttingen: Vandenhoeck & Ruprecht, 1967) ▥J. W. **Wenham**, "Gospel Origins," *TrinJ* 7 (1978): 112–34 ▥Stephen **Westerholm**, *Jesus and Scribal Authority* (Lund: Gleerup, 1978).

CHAPTER FOUR

MARK

CONTENTS

Mark's story of Jesus' ministry is action oriented. Recounting little extended teaching of Jesus, Mark shifts scenes rapidly (εὐθύς [*euthys*], "immediately," is almost a standard linking word in Mark). Jesus is constantly on the move, healing, exorcising demons, confronting opponents, and instructing the disciples. This fast-paced narrative is punctuated by six transitional paragraphs or statements, which divide Mark's account into seven basic sections.

Preliminaries to the ministry (1:1–13). While it could be the title of the entire gospel, Mark 1:1 is probably the heading for 1:1–13, the preliminaries to the ministry. The "beginning" (ἀρχή [*archē*]) of the "good news" about Jesus Christ consists in the ministry of John the Baptist, the eschatological forerunner (1:2–8), Jesus' baptism by John (1:9–11), and Jesus' temptation by Satan in the wilderness (1:12–13).[1]

First part of the Galilean ministry (1:16–3:6). The important summary in 1:14–15—Jesus' entrance into Galilee, proclaiming the good news that the time of fulfillment had come and that the kingdom was near—is the first of the six transitional sections. It introduces Jesus' ministry in Galilee (1:16–8:26) and, more immediately, the opening events in that period of ministry (1:16–3:6). After Jesus' call of four disciples (1:16–20), Mark gives us a glimpse of a typical day in Jesus' ministry, including teaching in the synagogue, exorcisms, and healings (1:21–34). The extraordinary nature of these events attracts great crowds of people, but Jesus insists on moving from Capernaum, on the Sea of Galilee (where these events took place), to other towns in Galilee (1:35–39). After another healing story (1:40–45), Mark narrates five events that focus on Jesus'

---

[1]For this view of Mark 1:1, along with nine others, see C. E. B. Cranfield, *The Gospel According to Saint Mark*, CGTC (Cambridge: Cambridge University Press, 1966), 34–35.

controversy with Jewish leaders: there are disputes over his claim to be able to forgive sins (2:1–12), over his fellowship with "tax collectors and 'sinners'" (2:13–17), over his disciples' failure to fast regularly (2:18–22), and over the Sabbath (2:23–28 and 3:1–6). The section climaxes with the plot of the Herodians to take Jesus' life.

Second part of the Galilean ministry (3:13–5:43). Mark's second transitional passage focuses on Jesus' immense popularity and emphasizes Jesus' ministry of healing and exorcism (3:7–12). It introduces the third major section of the gospel, in which Jesus continues the Galilean ministry. Mark here focuses especially on the kingdom (3:13–5:43). Like the second section, this one also begins with a narrative about the disciples—in this case, Jesus' appointment of twelve of them to be "apostles" (3:13–19). There follow further stories about the growing opposition to Jesus on the part of both Jesus' family (3:20–21, 31–34) and "the teachers of the law" (3:22–30). Jesus uses parables to explain this opposition as part of "the secret of the kingdom of God" (4:1–34). The section comes to a climax with four miracles, each of them representing one of the characteristic types of Jesus' miracles: the calming of the storm (a nature miracle, 4:35–41); the casting out of a "legion" of demons from a man in the region of the Gerasenes (an exorcism, 5:1–20); the healing of a woman with a flow of blood (a healing, 5:25–34); and the raising of the daughter of Jairus from the dead (a resurrection, 5:21–24, 35–43).

The concluding phase of the Galilean ministry (6:7–8:26). The story of Jesus' movement away from the region of the Sea of Galilee, where so much of the action of 1:16–5:43 takes place, to his hometown of Nazareth in the hill country of Galilee (6:1–6) is Mark's third transitional text. In the ensuing fourth section of his gospel (6:7–8:26), Mark amplifies notes that he has sounded in the two previous sections—Jesus' amazing feats of power, his criticism of certain Jewish customs, and the growing opposition to him. He also initiates what will become an important theme in the gospel: the disciples' lack of understanding. The disciples are again featured at the beginning of this section, as Jesus sends the Twelve out on a mission (6:7–13). The rumor that Jesus is John the Baptist returned from the dead, mentioned along with other popular estimates of his person, leads Mark to include here a flashback explanation of John's death at the hands of Herod Antipas (6:14–29). After the return of the Twelve, the press of the crowds forces Jesus and his disciples into the wilderness, where the five thousand are fed (6:30–44). This is followed by Jesus' miraculous walking on the water, as he meets the disciples crossing the Sea of Galilee (6:45–52). At Gennesaret, on the western shore of the sea, Jesus heals many people (6:53–56), and shortly afterward he explains the real nature of impurity in response to Jewish criticism (7:1–23). Jesus then leaves Galilee (and Israel) for the regions of Tyre and Sidon to the North, where he commends the faith of a Gentile woman (7:24–30). Very quickly, however, we find him back in the regions around the Sea of Galilee, healing (7:31–37), feeding the four thousand (8:1–13), teaching without much success the "blinded" disciples (8:14–21), and, with considerably greater success, healing a physically blinded man (8:22–26).

The way of glory and suffering (8:27–10:52). Mark's gospel reaches its climax with Peter's recognition of Jesus' messiahship (8:27–30). It forms the fourth major transition in the gospel, as the emphasis shifts from the crowds and the power of Jesus displayed in miracles to the disciples and the cross. The ensuing fifth section of the gospel (8:27–10:52) has at its heart a thrice-repeated sequence that embodies a central purpose of Mark at this point in his narrative:

Jesus predicts his death	8:31	9:30–31	10:32–34
The disciples misunderstand	8:32–33	9:32 (33–34)	10:35–40
Jesus teaches about the cost of discipleship	8:34–38	9:35–37	10:41–45

Followers of Jesus, Mark suggests, must imitate their master by humbling themselves and serving others. In addition, we have in this section the transfiguration (9:1–13), the driving of a demon out of a young lad (9:14–29), and teaching about putting others first (9:38–50), divorce (10:1–12), humility (10:13–16), and the difficulty of combining wealth with discipleship (10:17–31). The section concludes, as Jesus nears Jerusalem, with his giving sight to Bartimaeus in Jericho (10:46–52).

Final ministry in Jerusalem (11:1–13:37). Jesus' entrance into Jerusalem marks the beginning of the next major stage in the gospel: the days of confrontation with various Jewish groups and authorities preceding the passion (11:1–13:37). Jesus' public entry into the city, with its messianic overtones (11:1–11), sets the stage for the confrontation; and the cleansing of the temple (11:12–19), a strike at the heart of Judaism, forces the issue. The withering of the fig tree, in addition to being a lesson in faith, is also an acted parable of judgment upon Israel (11:20–25). It is thus no surprise that we find "the chief priests, the teachers of the law and the elders" challenging Jesus' authority (11:27–33), or Jesus telling a parable in which the Jewish leaders' rebelliousness to God is a prominent theme (12:1–12). Jesus is further questioned about the appropriateness of paying taxes to a Gentile ruler by "the Pharisees and Herodians" (12:13–17), about implications of the doctrine of resurrection by the Sadducees (12:18–27), and about the greatest commandment in the law by a teacher of the law (12:28–34). Finally, Jesus takes the initiative, asking about the interpretation of Psalm 110:1 in an effort to force the Jews to consider his claims to be Messiah (12:35–40). After Jesus' commending of a widow's sacrificial giving (12:41–44) comes the Olivet Discourse, in which Jesus encourages the disciples to be faithful in light of coming suffering and as they look toward his triumphant return in glory (13:1–37).

The passion and empty-tomb narratives (15:1–16:8). The last section of Mark's gospel has two parts: the passion narrative (chaps. 14–15) and the story of the empty tomb (chap. 16). Mark leads into the passion narrative with his only mention of a definite date: it is two days before the Passover when the chief priests and teachers of the law plot Jesus' death (14:1–2). The narrative of Jesus' anointing in Bethany is found here for topical reasons (for it took place "six days before the Passover"; see John 12:1–8): the anointing of Jesus' head points to his royal dignity (14:3–9). As Judas provides a means of arresting Jesus quietly, Jesus arranges for himself and the disciples to celebrate Passover together (14:12–26). After this meal, during which he uses elements of the Passover ritual to refer to his death, Jesus and the disciples leave the city for Gethsemane on the Mount of Olives, where Jesus agonizingly prays and is then arrested (14:27–52). There follows the series of judicial proceedings and trials: a nighttime hearing before the supreme Jewish council, the Sanhedrin (14:53–65), during which Peter denies the Lord (14:66–72), a quick morning trial before the Sanhedrin (15:1), and the decisive trial before the Roman procurator, Pontius Pilate (15:2–15). Pilate sentences Jesus to death by crucifixion; he is mocked by the soldiers and executed at Golgotha (15:16–41). The burial takes place that same day (15:42–47). But the despair of the women who saw him buried gives way to awe at the empty tomb and the angel's announcement of the resurrection (16:1–8).

AUTHOR

Like the other three gospels, Mark is anonymous. The title, "According to Mark" (κατὰ Μάρκον [*kata Markon*]),[2] was probably added when the canonical gospels were collected and there was need to distinguish Mark's version of the gospel from the others. The gospel titles are generally thought to have been added in the second century but may have been added much earlier.[3] Certainly we may say that the title indicates that by A.D. 125 or so an important segment of the early church thought that a person named Mark wrote the second gospel.

Mark's connection with the second gospel is asserted or assumed by many early Christian writers. Perhaps the earliest (and certainly the most important) of the testimonies is that of Papias, who was bishop of Hierapolis in Phrygia of Asia Minor until about A.D. 130. His statement about the second gospel is recorded in Eusebius's *Historia Ecclesiastica* (*History of the Church*), written in 325.

---

[2] Or "The Gospel According to Mark"—the manuscript tradition makes it hard to be sure whether the longer or shorter form is the original. NA27 prints the shorter, but Hengel argues for the longer ("The Titles of the Gospels and the Gospel of Mark," in *Studies in the Gospel of Mark* [Philadelphia: Fortress Press, 1985], 66–67).

[3] Ibid., 64–84; for a contrary view, see Helmut Koester, *Ancient Christian Gospels: Their History and Development* (Philadelphia: Trinity Press International, 1992), 26–27.

And the presbyter used to say this, "Mark became Peter's interpreter [*hermēneutēs*] and wrote accurately all that he remembered, not indeed, in order, of the things said or done by the Lord. For he had not heard the Lord, nor had he followed him, but later on, as I said, followed Peter, who used to give teaching as necessity demanded but not making, as it were, an arrangement of the Lord's oracles, so that Mark did nothing wrong in writing down single points as he remembered them. For to one thing he gave attention, to leave out nothing of what he had heard and to make no false statements in them. (*H.E.* 3.39.15)[4]

Three important claims about the second gospel emerge from this statement:

1. Mark wrote the gospel that, in Eusebius's day, was identified with this name.

2. Mark was not an eyewitness but obtained his information from Peter.[5]

3. Mark's gospel lacks "order," reflecting the occasional nature of Peter's preaching.[6]

The importance of these claims is magnified when we realize that the presbyter Papias is quoting is the presbyter John, probably the apostle John himself. If Papias is to be trusted, the identification of Mark as the author of the second gospel goes back to the first generation of Christians.

Christian writers of the second and third centuries confirm that Mark was the author of the second gospel and that he depended on Peter for his information: Justin Martyr, *Dialogue with Trypho* 106; Irenaeus, *Adversus Haereses* 3.1.2; Tertullian, *Adversus Marcion* 4:5; Clement of Alexandria, *Hypotyposeis* (according to Eusebius, *H.E.* 6.14.5–7); Origen, *Commentary on Matthew* (again according to Eusebius, *H.E.* 6.25.5); and, probably, the Muratorian Canon. [7] Some scholars dismiss these testimonies as secondhand evidence going back to

---

[4]The quotation is taken from the translation by Kirsopp Lake in *Eusebius: Ecclesiastical History,* vol. 1, LCL (Cambridge: Harvard University Press, 1926).

[5]In identifying Mark as Peter's *hermēneutēs,* Papias may mean that he was Peter's "translator" (from Aramaic into Greek) (see H. E. W. Turner, "The Tradition of Mark's Dependence upon Peter," *ExpTim* 71 [1959–60]: 260–63) or, more probably, his "interpreter," one who repeated and transmitted Peter's preaching (Zahn 2.442–44).

[6]This may mean that Mark, in the judgment of the presbyter, lacked chronological order (Martin Hengel, "Literary, Theological, and Historical Problems in the Gospel of Mark," in *Studies in the Gospel of Mark,* 48) or, more probably, that it lacked rhetorical/artistic order (Robert A. Guelich, *Mark 1–8:26,* WBC [Waco: Word, 1989], xxvii).

[7]This canon is a list of New Testament books found in a fragment named "Muratorian" because the sole manuscript to preserve the list, an incomplete Latin manuscript of the seventh or eighth century, was discovered and published by Cardinal L. A. Muratori in 1740. The fragment has traditionally been dated in the late second century, but that has been challenged recently, it being argued that a fourth-century date is more likely (see A. C. Sundberg Jr., "Canon Muratori: A Fourth Century List," *HTR* 66

Papias, believing that Papias invents his claim about Mark's connection with Peter in order to defend the gospel against its detractors.[8] But Papias does not appear to be defending Mark's authorship or his connection with Peter but only the reliability of the gospel, against the charge that it lacked "order." Moreover, no dissenting voice from the early church regarding the authorship of the second gospel is found. This is surprising, since the tendency in the early church was to associate apostles with the writing of the New Testament books. While we must not uncritically accept everything that early Christian writers say about the origins of the New Testament, we should not reject what they say without good reason. The early and uncontested claim that Mark wrote the second gospel based on Peter's teaching can be overturned only by rather clear indications to the contrary from the gospel itself.[9]

> *While we must not uncritically accept everything that early Christian writers say about the origins of the New Testament, we should not reject what they say without good reason.*

To assess this internal evidence, we must first identify the "Mark" intended by Papias and the other early Christian writers. That they refer to the (John) Mark mentioned in Acts (12:12, 25; 13:5, 13; 15:37) and in four New Testament epistles (Col. 4:10; Philem. 24; 2 Tim. 4:11; 1 Peter 5:13) is almost certain.[10] No other early Christian Mark would have been so well known as to be mentioned without further description.[11] Son of a woman prominent in the early Jerusalem church (Christians had gathered at her home during Peter's imprisonment [Acts 12:12]) and cousin of Barnabas (Col. 4:10), "John, also called Mark," accompanied Paul and Barnabas as far as Pamphylia, in Asia Minor, on the first missionary journey (Acts 13:5, 13). For whatever reason (and speculation has been rampant), Mark left Paul and Barnabas before the first journey ended, and Paul therefore refused to take him along on his second extended preaching trip. Barn-

---

[1973]: 1–41; G. M. Hahneman, *The Muratorian Fragment and the Development of the Canon* [Oxford: Clarendon, 1992]). But a second-century date may still be defended (e.g., Everett Ferguson, "Canon Muratori: Date and Provenance," *Studia Patristica* 18 [1982]: 677–83; C. E. Hill, "The Debate Over the Muratorian Fragment and the Development of the Canon," *WTJ* 57 [1995]: 437–52).

[8]E.g., Kümmel, 95; Rudolf Pesch, *Das Markusevangelium*, HTKNT (Freiburg: Herder, 1976–80), 1:4–7.

[9]In favor of Papias' early date and reliability, see esp. Robert W. Yarbrough, "The Date of Papias: A Reassessment," *JETS* 26 [1983]: 181–91; Robert H. Gundry, *Mark: A Commentary on His Apology for the Cross* (Grand Rapids: Eerdmans, 1993), 1026–34; on the need to respect the early traditions, see also Richard T. France, *The Gospel of Mark: A Commentary on the Greek Text*, NIGTC (Grand Rapids: Eerdmans, 2002), 37–41. Brown (159–61) thinks that "Peter" might be a kind of shorthand for the apostolic tradition in general.

[10]A few scholars think that an unknown Mark wrote the gospel (see, e.g., Pesch, *Markusevangelium*, 1.9–11).

[11]Jerome is the first to explicitly identify the Mark of the second gospel with the John Mark mentioned in the New Testament.

abas disagreed with Paul's decision and separated himself from Paul, taking Mark along with him (Acts 15:36–40). Yet Paul and Mark were eventually reconciled: Paul mentions Mark's presence with him during his Roman imprisonment (Philem. 24; Col. 4:10). Peter, writing from Rome, also mentions that Mark was with him, calling him his son (1 Pet. 5:13), perhaps implying that Mark had been converted through his ministry.[12] Mark has also been identified as the "young man" who "fled naked" from Gethsemane when Jesus was arrested (Mark 14:51–52). It has been argued that this enigmatic reference, peculiar to Mark's gospel, is an autobiographical reminiscence.[13] This may be the case, but the identification may call into question Papias's claim that Mark was not an eyewitness.[14]

Does the little we know of John Mark from the New Testament present any difficulty to identifying him as the author of the second gospel? Some scholars think so, pointing to Mark's alleged ignorance of Jewish customs and errors about Palestinian geography.[15] But neither difficulty stands up to scrutiny; careful and sympathetic interpretation of the alleged problem passages reveals no errors in such matters. In contrast, two features of Mark and his career as they are presented in the New Testament fit the author of the second gospel. The Greek style of Mark's gospel is simple and straightforward and full of the kind of Semitisms that one would expect of a Jerusalem-bred Christian.[16] And Mark's connection with Paul may help explain what many scholars have found to be a Pauline theological influence in the second gospel. Both features are far too general to offer any positive evidence toward an identification. But the important point is that nothing in the second gospel stands in the way of accepting the earliest tradition that identifies John Mark as its author. Our decision, then, will rest almost entirely on external evidence, and especially on the tradition handed down through Papias and Eusebius from the unnamed presbyter. Those who are skeptical of the reliability of Papias conclude that the author of the gospel is unknown.[17] Yet as we have seen, there is nothing in the New Testament that is

---

[12]See Zahn 2.427.

[13]E.g., A. B. Bruce, "The Synoptic Gospels," in *EGT* 1.441–42. Early tradition also identified the home of Mark and his mother as the location of the Last Supper.

[14]Kümmel calls the identification "a strange and wholly improbable conjecture" (p. 95), but he gives no better explanation for the inclusion of these verses in Mark's gospel.

[15]E.g., ibid., 96–97.

[16]Note Martin Hengel's judgment: "I do not know any other work in Greek which has so many Aramaic or Hebrew words and formulae in so narrow a space as does the second gospel" ("Literary, Theological, and Historical Problems," 46).

[17]E.g., Kümmel, 95–97; Joachim Gnilka, *Das Evangelium nach Markus,* EKKNT (Neukirchen-Vluyn: Neukirchener, 1978; Zürich: Benziger, 1979), 1.32–33; W. R. Telford, *The Theology of the Gospel of Mark* (Cambridge: Cambridge University Press, 1999), 10–12.

inconsistent with Papias's claim that Mark wrote the second gospel. And since we have no indication that anyone in the early church contested Papias's claim, we see no reason not to accept it.

But can we also accept the tradition that Mark is dependent on the preaching of Peter? Here again, skepticism is rampant. Modern approaches to the gospels consider the gospel material to be the product of a long and complex process of traditions-history, a view that has difficulty accommodating the direct connection between Mark and Peter suggested by Papias.[18] While recognizing this as something of a problem, two factors may mitigate its force. *First,* we must question whether the assuredness with which critics identify the origins and growth of traditions is always justified. In many cases the basis for such judgments does not appear to be strong, and we may well think that the derivation of a given pericope from Peter himself may satisfy the evidence equally well. Only a doctrinaire form critic would insist that all the gospel tradition must have been transmitted through the faceless "community."[19] *Second,* we must probably allow for Mark to have used sources other than Peter. As long as the apostle was a central source for the gospel, Papias's claim stands.

On the other side of the ledger are factors that could be taken to point to Peter's connection with this gospel. The vividness and detail of the second gospel are said to point to an eyewitness. Only Mark, for instance, mentions that the grass on which the five thousand sat was green (6:39). But even if valid (and some scholars insist that there was a tendency to *add* such detail to the tradition), this feature would do no more than show that there was some eyewitness testimony behind Mark's gospel.

This focus may be narrowed by another feature of the gospel: the especially critical light in which the Twelve are displayed. While found in all four gospels, the picture of the disciples as cowardly, spiritually blind, and hard of heart is particularly vivid in Mark. This, it is held, points to an apostolic viewpoint, for only an apostle would have been able to criticize the Twelve so harshly. Two other factors suggest that this apostolic witness may be Peter's. First, Peter figures prominently in Mark, and some of the references are most naturally explained as coming from Peter himself (e.g., the references to Peter "remembering" [11:21; 14:72]).[20] Second, C. H. Dodd has pointed out that Mark's gospel follows a pattern very similar to that found in Peter's rehearsal of the basic kerygma, the evangelistically oriented recitation of key events in Jesus' life found

---

[18]Thus, for instance, Guelich concludes that Papias is right in identifying Mark as the author but wrong in thinking that the gospel is based on the preaching of Peter (*Mark 1–8:26,* xxvi–xxix); cf. also Joel Marcus, *Mark 1–8: A New Translation with Introduction and Commentary,* AB 27 (New York: Doubleday, 2000), 17–24.

[19]Martin, 1.204–5.

[20]Ibid., 1.204.

in such texts as Acts 10:36–41.[21] We might add, finally, that Peter's reference to Mark as "my son" in his first letter fits nicely with the relationship between Peter and Mark mentioned by Papias; it discourages one from thinking Papias simply invented such a relationship.

Each of these factors is commensurate with the tradition that Mark is based on Peter's preaching, and one or two of them may even point slightly in that direction. But none of them, nor all of them together, is sufficient to establish the connection. Again, however, there seems to be no compelling reason to reject the common opinion of the early church on this matter.

PROVENANCE

Early tradition is not unanimous about the place where Mark wrote his gospel, but it favors Rome. The anti-Marcionite prologue to Mark (late second century?) claims that Mark wrote the gospel "in the regions of Italy." Both Irenaeus (*Adv. Haer.* 3.1.2) and Clement of Alexandria (according to Eusebius, *H.E.* 6.14.6–7) suggest the same thing. Several considerations are said to confirm a Roman provenance: (1) the large number of Latinisms in the gospel;[22] (2) the incidental mention of Simon of Cyrene's sons, Alexander and Rufus, at least one of whom may have been known to Mark in Rome (when writing to the Roman church, Paul greets a Rufus [16:13]); (3) the apparently Gentile audience of the gospel; (4) the many allusions to suffering, which would be appropriate if the gospel was written under the shadow of persecutions of the church in Rome; (5) the fact that 1 Peter 5:13 locates Mark in Rome with Peter in the early sixties; and (6) the connection with an important early center of Christianity, which would have explained the gospel's quick acceptance.

Some of these points are very weak: numbers one and three could fit a provenance anywhere that boasted Gentiles and Latin influence; number two assumes that there was only one Rufus in the early church; and number six is of questionable validity and, even if accepted, could point to several possible locations (Jerusalem, Antioch, Ephesus). The other two points, however, do carry some weight. The date of Mark's gospel is not certain (see below); but if it was written in the middle 60s, the Neronian persecution in Rome might explain the focus on suffering (point number four). The presence of Peter and Mark in Rome at

---

[21]C. H. Dodd, "The Framework of the Gospel Narrative," *ExpTim* 43 (1932): 396–400.

[22]See esp. Mark's explanation of the widow's two copper coins as equaling a κοδράν-της (*kodrantēs*), a Roman coin (12:42), and of the "courtyard" (αὐλή [*aulē*]) as being a πραιτώριον (*praitōrion*), another distinctively Roman/Latin name (15:16). Readers in the eastern part of the Roman Empire would almost certainly have known these Greek terms. For a complete list of Mark's Latinisms, see Kümmel, 97–98.

about the time the gospel was probably written (point number six) is certainly significant. Moreover, there is nothing in the gospel that is incompatible with a Roman provenance.

The only other provenance that finds support in early tradition is Egypt (Chrysostom, *Hom. Matt.* 1.3 [c. 400]). If Morton Smith is right, Clement of Alexandria may also have connected Mark with the church in Alexandria. According to Smith, a letter he discovered in the monastery of Mar-Saba in Egypt is an authentic letter of Clement, in which he says that Mark, after writing his gospel in Rome with Peter, came to Alexandria, where he composed a "deeper," gnostic-oriented gospel.[23] But the authenticity of the letter is disputed, and in any case, it simply corroborates a Roman provenance for the canonical Mark. Chrysostom's identification of Egypt as the place of Mark's composition may even be a mistaken inference from Eusebius.[24]

Three other specific provenances have gained support from modern scholars. Syria, or more specifically, Antioch, has been proposed by scholars who note, among other things, its proximity to Palestine (which explains why Mark assumes his readers will know Palestinian place-names), its large Roman colony, Peter's connection with Antioch, and the fact that the presbyter whom Papias quotes comes from the East.[25] Other scholars, while less specific, are inclined to think that Mark was written somewhere in the East.[26] In his groundbreaking redactional study of Mark, Willi Marxsen argues for a Galilean provenance. Noting the positive significance accorded to Galilee in Mark, Marxsen theorizes that for Mark, Galilee was the place of revelation and that the references to

> *While certainty is impossible, a Roman provenance is the best alternative for Mark, granted the strength of the early tradition and the lack of any evidence from within the New Testament to the contrary.*

---

[23]Morton Smith, *The Secret Gospel: The Discovery and Interpretation of the Secret Gospel According to Mark* (New York: Harper & Row, 1973). Despite the dispute over the authenticity of this letter, a handful of more radical scholars have not only affirmed its authenticity but have argued that Clement got the sequence wrong: our canonical Mark, they say, is actually an abbreviation of this long gnostic-oriented gospel (which, of course, we do not have). Even on the supposition that the ostensible letter of Clement is authentic, however, the overwhelming majority of scholars agree that Clement has the sequence right: the gnostic document is a later expansion of canonical Mark. See especially Scott G. Brown, "On the Composition History of the Longer ('Secret') Gospel of Mark," *JBL* 122 (2003): 89–110.

[24]*H.E.* 2.16.1: "Mark is said to have been the first man to set out for Egypt and preach there the gospel which he had himself written down." See, e.g., Vincent Taylor, *The Gospel According to St. Mark,* 2nd ed. (London: Macmillan, 1966), 32; Martin 1.215.

[25]J. Vernon Bartlet, *St. Mark* (London: Thomas Nelson & Sons, n.d.), 5–6; Marcus, *Mark 1–8,* 33–37.

[26]E.g., Kümmel, 98. Bo Reicke suggests Caesarea, its Palestinian location fitting his theory of gospel origins, and its Roman flavor (it was the Roman administrative center) explaining the large number of Latinisms (*The Roots of the Synoptic Gospels* [Philadelphia: Fortress Press, 1986], 165–66).

Jesus "going before" the disciples into Galilee (14:28; 16:7) were a summons to Christians to gather in Galilee and await the return of Christ.[27] Marxsen's theory is fraught with problems, however, and there is no convincing reason to locate Mark in Galilee. While certainty is impossible, a Roman provenance is the best alternative, granted the strength of the early tradition and the lack of any evidence from within the New Testament to the contrary.

DATE

Mark has been dated in four different decades: the 40s, the 50s, the 60s, and the 70s.

A Date in the 40s

A date in the 40s has been proposed on the basis of historical and papyrological considerations. C. C. Torrey argues that Mark's "abomination that causes desolation" (13:14) is a reference to the attempt in A.D. 40 of the Emperor Caligula to have his image set up in the Jerusalem temple, and he contends that the gospel was written shortly after this.[28] But the identification is unlikely. José O'Callaghan bases his early dating of Mark on three papyrus fragments found at Qumran (7Q5; 7Q6,1; 7Q7), dated c. 50, which he claims contain, respectively, Mark 6:52–53, 4:28, and 12:17.[29] But most scholars have contested the identification.[30] Even if it were valid, it would prove only the existence at this date of tradition that came to be incorporated into Mark.[31] Another theory holds that Peter may have journeyed to Rome in the 40s after being freed from prison (see Acts 12:17) and that Mark may have written the gospel at that

[27]Willi Marxsen, *Mark the Evangelist* (Nashville: Abingdon, 1969).

[28]C. C. Torrey, *The Four Gospels,* 2nd ed. (New York: Harper, 1947), 261–62. Moreover, Torrey's theory assumes an early Aramaic gospel of Mark. A similar proposal has recently been defended by Günther Zuntz ("Wann wurde das Evangelium Marci geschrieben?" in *Markus-Philologie: Historische, literargeschichtliche, und stilistische Untersuchungen zum zweiten Evangelium,* ed. Herbert Cancik, WUNT 33 [Tübingen: Mohr-Siebeck, 1984], 47–71).

[29]José O'Callaghan, "Papiros neotestamentarios en la cuere 7 de Qumran," *Bib* 53 (1972): 91–100. See William Lane, *The Gospel According to Mark,* NICNT (Grand Rapids: Eerdmans, 1974), 18–21, for a summary and discussion; see also, on 7Q5, C. P. Thiede, *The Earliest Gospel Manuscript? The Qumran Fragment 7Q5 and Its Significance for New Testament Studies* (Guernsey: Paternoster, 1992).

[30]See, e.g., Pierre Benoit, "Note sur les fragments grecs de la Grotte 7 de Qumran," *RevBib* 79 (1972): 321–24; Lane, *Mark,* 19–21.

[31]In a similar vein, Maurice Casey reconstructs Aramaic sources in Mark from the Dead Sea Scrolls, concluding that the gospel might have been written c. 40 (*Aramaic Sources of Mark's Gospel,* SNTSMS 102 [Cambridge: Cambridge University Press, 1998].

time.[32] But so early a date for Mark's gospel makes it hard to explain the silence of Paul and other New Testament writers about it, and it does not perhaps allow sufficient time for the development of the tradition behind Mark.

A Date in the 50s

Another problem in the way of dating Mark as early as the 40s arises if we give credence to the traditions that the gospel was written in Rome on the basis of the preaching of Peter. Although possible, it is not likely that Peter came to Rome in the early 40s.[33] But there is evidence that Peter was in Rome in the mid–50s, making it possible to date Mark in the later 50s without contradicting the well-established tradition of the origin of the gospel.[34] The strongest case for this dating comes not from Mark directly but from the relationship of Mark to Luke-Acts. The argument assumes that Acts ends where it does, with Paul languishing in a Roman prison, because Luke published the book of Acts at that time (about A.D. 62). This would require that the gospel of Luke, the first volume of Luke's literary effort, be dated at about the same time or slightly earlier. If we then accept the prevailing scholarly opinion that Luke used the canonical Mark as one of his key sources, Mark must have been written at the latest in the late 50s (to allow time for the gospel to circulate).[35] This argument is based on two key assumptions: that Acts is to be dated in about A.D. 62, and that Luke has used canonical Mark.[36] The latter may be granted; but the former is not so clear. The ending of Acts need not reflect its actual date of publication; Luke might have had other reasons for ending Acts where he does (see chap. 7).

---

[32]J. W. Wenham, "Did Peter Go to Rome in A.D. 42?" *TynB* 23 (1972): 97–102; idem, *Redating Matthew, Mark and Luke: A Fresh Assault on the Synoptic Problem* (Downers Grove: IVP, 1992), 146–82.

[33]Wenham is representative of those who think that Peter may have come to Rome after his miraculous release from prison, recorded in Acts 12 ("Did Peter Go to Rome?" 97–99). Yet Peter is back in Palestine by the time of the Jerusalem Council in A.D. 48 or 49 (Acts 15), and it is difficult to think that Paul and Barnabas would have taken along on the first missionary journey one who had worked closely with Peter in Rome for some years. For a discussion of Peter's movements, see Oscar Cullmann, *Peter: Disciple, Apostle, Martyr,* 2nd ed. (Philadelphia: Westminster, 1962), 38–39.

[34]Peter was probably in Corinth before A.D. 55 when Paul wrote 1 Corinthians (see 1:12; 2:22), and in Rome in about 63 (the probable date of 1 Peter). Eusebius implies that Peter was in Rome during the reign of Claudius, who died in 54 (*H.E.* 2.14.6). The absence of any reference to Peter in Romans suggests that Peter was not in Rome in 57.

[35]See esp. Adolf von Harnack, *The Date of Acts and of the Synoptic Gospels* (New York: Putnam's, 1911). Reicke's argument is similar, although he thinks Mark was written at about the same time as Luke (*Roots of the Synoptic Gospels*, 177–80). C. S. Mann thinks that Mark composed a first draft of his gospel in A.D. 55 (*Mark*, AB [Garden City: Doubleday, 1986], 72–83).

[36]See Gundry, *Mark*, 1026–45.

A Date in the 60s

The majority of contemporary scholars date Mark in the middle to late 60s for three reasons. First, the earliest traditions favor a date for Mark after the death of Peter.[37] Second, and perhaps more important for most, the internal evidence of Mark is said to favor a date during, or shortly after, the onset of persecution in Rome. Mark has much to say about the importance of disciples' following the "road to the cross" walked by our Lord. This emphasis best fits a situation when Christians were facing the grim prospect of martyrdom, a setting that would have obtained in Rome at the time of, or after, Nero's famous persecution of Christians in A.D. 65.[38] Third, Mark 13 is said to reflect the situation in Palestine during the Jewish revolt and just before the Roman entrance into the city, and thus it must be dated between 67 and 69.[39] None of these points is decisive. The tradition about the date of Mark is neither especially early nor widespread, and other traditions place the writing of Mark during Peter's lifetime.[40] Christians faced suffering on many occasions other than Rome in the

[37]The anti-Marcionite prologue (late second century?), Irenaeus (A.D. 185; see *Adv. Haer.* 3.1.2), and perhaps Papias's citation of the presbyter (note the tense: "Mark, who *had been* Peter's interpreter").

[38]For this case, see esp. Cranfield, *Mark,* 8; Hugh Anderson, *The Gospel of Mark,* NCB (London: Marshall, Morgan & Scott, 1976), 26; Brown, 163–64; Martin, 1.213; James R. Edwards, *The Gospel According to Mark,* PNTC (Grand Rapids: Eerdmans, 2002), 7–8. Martin Hengel cites other arguments in support of a late date: (1) the clarity of Mark's writing; (2) Mark's lateness in comparison with Q; (3) the assumption in Mark of the existence of a worldwide mission (see 13:10; 14:9); and (4) the prophecy of the martyrdom of James and John ("The Gospel of Mark: Time of Origin and Situation," in *Studies in the Gospel of Mark,* 12–28).

[39]Hengel, "Time of Origin," 2–28; Augustine Stock, *The Method and Message of Mark* (Wilmington: Glazier, 1989), 6–8; Guelich, *Mark 1–8:26,* xxi–xxxii.

[40]Clement of Alexandria says: "When Peter had preached the word publicly in Rome and announced the gospel by the Spirit, those present, of whom there were many, besought Mark, since for a long time he had followed him and remembered what had been said, to record his words. Mark did this, and communicated the gospel to those who made request of him. When Peter knew of it, he neither actively prevented nor encouraged the undertaking" (recorded by Eusebius in *H.E.* 6.14.6–7; the translation is from Taylor, *Mark,* 5–6). Tertullian may also witness to this tradition (see *Adv. Marc.* 4.5.3). It has even been argued that the key early traditions can be reconciled by understanding the word ἔξοδος (*exodos*) in Irenaeus (e.g., "after the 'exodos' of these [Peter and Paul]") to refer not to their death but to their departure from Rome (so T. W. Manson, *Studies in the Gospels and Epistles,* ed. Matthew Black [Philadelphia: Westminster, 1962], 34–40; France, *Gospel of Mark,* 37). Others reconcile the conflicting traditions by assuming that Mark began his gospel during Peter's lifetime but published it after his death (Zahn 2.433–34; Guthrie is favorable to the suggestion [p. 86]). This tradition about the date of Mark is neither especially early nor widespread, and other traditions place the writing of Mark during Peter's lifetime.

mid–60s, and as Joel Marcus has pointed out, Mark's treatment of suffering omits some of the features we might have expected had the Neronian persecution been in the background.[41] A similar point can be made with respect to Mark 13: the details of the discourse are not specific enough to suggest a particular historical situation.

A Date in the 70s

The main argument for dating Mark as late as the 70s rests on the assumption that Mark 13 reflects the actual experience of the sacking of Jerusalem by the Romans.[42] But the argument is seriously flawed. As several scholars have shown, Mark 13 shows very little evidence of being influenced by the course of events in A.D. 70. Jesus' predictions reflect stock Old Testament and Jewish imagery having to do with the besieging of cities rather than the specific circumstances of the siege of Jerusalem.[43] Even more damaging to this argument is the assumption on the part of these critics that Jesus could not accurately have predicted the course of events in 70. As long as we grant Jesus the ability to do so, Mark 13 will offer no help in dating the gospel.

Conclusion

A decision between a date in the 50s and one in the 60s is impossible to make. We must be content with dating Mark sometime in the late 50s or the 60s.

AUDIENCE AND PURPOSE

Mark is a self-effacing narrator. He tells his story with a minimum of editorial comments and says nothing about his purpose or his intended audience. We must depend, then, on the early testimonies about Mark and on the character of the gospel itself for information about his readers and his purpose.

Audience

The extrabiblical sources point to a Gentile Christian audience, probably in Rome. The Roman destination of Mark's gospel is simply an inference from its Roman provenance. If Mark wrote in Rome, he probably wrote to Romans. This is either stated or implied in the early traditions about the gospel, which

---

[41]Joel Marcus, *Mark 1–8*, 32–33.

[42]See Kümmel, 68; Pesch, *Markusevangelium* 1.14; Gnilka, *Das Evangelium nach Markus* 1.34.

[43]See esp. Bo Reicke, "Synoptic Prophecies of the Destruction of Jerusalem," in *Studies in New Testament and Early Christian Literature*, ed. David E. Aune, NovTSup 33 (Leiden: Brill, 1972), 121–33; John A. T. Robinson, *Redating the New Testament* (Philadelphia: Westminster, 1976), 13–30.

have Mark recording the preaching of Peter for those who had heard the great apostle in Rome. As we have noted above, the many Latinisms of the gospel are compatible with, if not conclusive for, a Roman audience. That Mark writes to Gentiles seems clear from his translation of Aramaic expressions, his explanation of Jewish customs such as the washing of hands before eating (7:3–4), and, in the few texts he includes on the subject, his interest in the cessation of the ritual elements in the Mosaic law (see 7:1–23, esp. v. 19; 12:32–34). It is also worth reminding ourselves that Mark's "audience" was almost certainly just that: Christians listening to Mark's gospel being read aloud to them.[44]

Purpose

Mark's purpose is much harder to determine. Interest in this question was stimulated by redaction criticism, which sought to discover the overall thrust of the gospels from the author/redactor's handling of tradition. Redaction critics typically stress theological purposes in the writing of the gospels, and this has certainly been the case with respect to Mark. However, the dominant view that Mark was the first gospel to be written always made redaction-critical study of Mark something of an uncertain enterprise. Setting aside questions of possible sources, therefore, recent scholarship has attacked the problem of Mark's purpose with an array of literary tools. The large number of specific proposals emerging from these redactional and literary studies forbids our giving anything close to a complete survey. We mention here four representative interpretations, the first focusing on eschatology, the second on Christology, the third on apologetics, and the fourth on politics.

Willi Marxsen, who initiated the modern redactional study of Mark, thought that Mark wanted to prepare Christians for Jesus' imminent parousia in Galilee.[45] He argued that Mark focuses on Galilee as the place where Jesus meets with his disciples at the expense of Jerusalem, where Jesus is rejected and killed. Jesus' command to his disciples to meet him in Galilee (14:28; cf. 16:7) was taken by Marxsen as a prediction to Mark's community of Jesus' glorious return to them. But the meeting with Jesus to which these verses refer is clearly a post-resurrection meeting, not the parousia.[46] Moreover, the geographic contrast that Marxsen (and some before him) discerns is much better explained as a reflection of the actual course of Jesus' ministry than as a theologically motivated invention of Mark's.

> *Redaction critics typically stress theological purposes in the writing of the gospels, and this has certainly been the case with respect to Mark.*

---

[44]See, e.g., Robert H. Stein, "Is Our Reading the Bible the Same as the Original Audience's Hearing It? A Case Study in the Gospel of Mark," *JETS* 46 (2003): 63–78. He notes that this oral context renders dubious some of the more complicated and esoteric proposals about Mark's text and intention.

[45]Marxsen, *Mark the Evangelist.*

[46]See, e.g., Robert H. Stein, "A Short Note on Mark XIV.28 and XVI.7," *NTS* 20 (1974): 445–52.

Theodore Weeden found in Mark a polemic against a "divine man" (*theios anēr*) Christology, a way of viewing Jesus that saw him as a wonder-working hero but denied or neglected his suffering and death.[47] To counter this tendency, Mark wrote a gospel that emphasized the humanity and suffering of Jesus. Weeden is correct to see in Mark a focus on Jesus' suffering, but he goes too far in identifying Mark's opponents as people who held to a divine-man Christology. For one thing, evidence for a polemical stance in Mark is not at all clear—he probably does not have any opponents in view at all.[48] For another, the very existence of a Hellenistic divine-man concept as a category into which early Christians would have put Jesus is open to question.[49]

A specific kind of apologetic was discerned in Mark by S. G. F. Brandon. He thought that Mark had attempted to mask the political implications of Jesus' life—and especially his death. According to Brandon, Jesus was a sympathizer with the Jewish revolutionaries, the Zealots. For this reason he was crucified by the Romans, a method of execution generally reserved for political criminals. By branding Jesus as a rebel against Rome, his crucifixion made it very difficult for Christians to win a hearing from the Roman public—particularly in the aftermath of the Jewish revolt in Palestine, when, according to Brandon, Mark wrote his gospel. To overcome this difficulty, Mark transferred as much of the blame for Jesus' death from the Romans to the Jews as he could, a process revealed by the many manifestly unhistorical features in the Sanhedrin and Roman trials.[50] But there is no need to follow Brandon in finding these trials to contain unhistorical fabrications.[51] In general, Brandon's theory can be sustained only by arguing, without any evidence, that Mark (and all other writers who

---

[47]Theodore Weeden, *Mark: Traditions in Conflict* (Philadelphia: Fortress Press, 1971).

[48]See Jack Dean Kingsbury, *The Christology of Mark's Gospel* (Philadelphia: Fortress Press, 1983).

[49]See, e.g., David Tiede, *The Charismatic Figure as Miracle Worker* (Missoula: SP, 1972).

[50]S. G. F. Brandon, *Jesus and the Zealots* (Manchester: Manchester University Press, 1967).

[51]For studies of Jesus' trials that generally vindicate the historicity of the gospel accounts, see David R. Catchpole, *The Trial of Jesus: A Study in the Gospels and Jewish Historiography from 1770 to the Present Day* (Leiden: Brill, 1971); Josef Blinzler, *Der Prozess Jesu,* 2nd ed. (Regensburg: Pustet, 1955); Darrell L. Bock, *Blasphemy and Exaltation in Judaism and the Final Examination of Jesus,* WUNT 110 (Tübingen: Mohr-Siebeck, 1998); James P. Sweeney, "The Death of Jesus in Contemporary Life-of-Jesus Historical Research," *TrinJ* 24 (2003): 221–41. See further, Raymond E. Brown, *The Death of the Messiah. From Gethsemane to the Grave: A Commentary on the Passion Narrative in the Four Gospels* (New York: Doubleday, 1994).

have come after him) has eliminated the political element from Jesus' teaching and ministry.

Another hypothesis about Mark's purpose also focuses on politics. Castigating interpreters for too often bringing their inherited Christian theological categories and concerns into the Gospel of Mark, Richard Horsley argues that the major purpose of Mark is to present Jesus as arguing for a particular social/political program. Opposition between Jesus and Jewish leaders in the gospel has to do with competing visions of Israel's restoration and kingdom programs, not religious issues per se.[52] Horsley may be justified in his claim that Christian interpreters have too often ignored the political dimension of the gospel.[53] But his political categories appear to be imposed on a gospel that self-evidently speaks in religious categories. Moreover, his criticism of interpreters for reading into the gospel a Christian theological agenda sounds a bit ironic in light of the similarity between his understanding of Mark and contemporary "liberation" theologies.

These four specific suggestions about Mark's purpose represent only a sampling of recent proposals, but they share with many others the fault of being overly specific and based on only a selection of the data. Any attempt to determine Mark's purpose must take into account the gospel as a whole and refrain from arguing beyond the evidence.

Certain features of Mark's gospel are especially relevant to an investigation into its purpose: its focus on the activity of Jesus, especially his working of miracles;[54] its interest in the passion of Jesus (Mark, claimed Martin Kähler in a famous aphorism, is "a passion narrative with an extended introduction"); its repeated correlation of Jesus' predicted sufferings and the "cost of discipleship" in 8:26–10:52. As Ralph Martin has shown, two general concerns emerge from these characteristics: Christology and discipleship.[55] Mark presents a balanced Christology in which Jesus' miracle-working power (the focus in 1:16–8:26) is set beside his suffering and death (the focus in 8:27–16:8). The one who is identified as the Son of God in the opening verse of the gospel[56] is confessed to be the

---

[52]Richard A. Horsley, *Hearing the Whole Story: The Politics of Plot in Mark's Gospel* (Louisville: Westminster John Knox Press, 2001).

[53]The neglect of political issues is also a theme in N. T. Wright, *Jesus and the Victory of God*, vol. 2 of *Christian Origins and the Question of God* (Minneapolis: Fortress Press, 1996).

[54]Peter Bolt argues, for instance, that Mark invites his readers to identify with those who are the recipients of Jesus' healing miracles and exorcisms as a means of convincing them that in Jesus they can overcome death (*Jesus' Defeat of Death: Persuading Mark's Early Readers*, SNTSMS 125 [Cambridge: Cambridge University Press, 2003]).

[55]Martin, *Mark*, esp. 156–62.

[56]For the textual problem, see the section "Text" below.

Son of God by the Roman centurion as Jesus dies, humiliated and in agony, on the cross (15:39). Mark wants his readers to understand that Jesus is the Son of God, but especially the *suffering* Son of God. Moreover, believers are to be *followers* of Jesus. Mark also shows that Christians must walk the same road as Jesus—the way of humility, of suffering, and even, should it be necessary, of death. Mark wants to impress on his readers the famous words of the Lord: "Whoever wants to be my disciple must deny themselves and take up their cross and follow me" (8:34).

Mark thus wants to help his readers understand who Jesus is and what real discipleship involves. But we must recognize that Mark has many other things to say that cannot easily be placed into these categories. Recent study has stressed the theological purposes behind the writing of the gospels, and we may agree that the evangelists were writing with some specific points to make to the Christian communities in their day. But we should not ignore two other more general purposes that were probably at work in the production of Mark: historical interest, and evangelism. In addition to encouraging certain beliefs and actions in his Christian readers, Mark was providing them with a record of Jesus' deeds and words. This was becoming a great need in Mark's day as the original eyewitnesses such as Peter were beginning to pass from the scene. While it is unlikely that Mark was written for non-Christians directly, the focus in the gospel on Jesus' actions, the similarity between the gospel's structure and the early Christian evangelistic preaching, and Mark's announced intention to write a book about "the gospel" (1:1 NIV) all suggest that Mark wanted to arm his Christian readers with a knowledge of the "good news of salvation."[57]

> *Our ability to identify the sources Mark has used in composing his gospel depends on our solution to the synoptic problem.*

SOURCES

Our ability to identify the sources Mark has used in composing his gospel depends on our solution to the synoptic problem. If the Griesbach, or two-gospel, solution is correct, then both Matthew and Luke are sources for Mark, and we could seek to identify the ways in which he has "epitomized" these two major sources. If, however, the two-source solution is correct, then both Matthew and Luke have depended on Mark, and we would possess no written source that Mark has used. As we argue in chapter 1, the two-source theory is much more likely to be correct. Any knowledge of Mark's sources, then, will be based on extrapolations from his gospel itself. And this, as the many conflicting reconstructions demonstrate, is a highly dubious procedure.[58]

---

[57]See Guthrie, 57–58; Cranfield, *Mark,* 14–15; Moule, 122.

[58]Kümmel, 84–85, lists a number of suggestions.

The most persistent theory is that there existed a written pre-Markan passion narrative,[59] but even this idea now meets with less favor than it used to.[60] We must admit that we have no certain knowledge of the written sources, if any, that Mark used in putting his gospel together. His material may have come to him in small pieces of tradition, as the classic form critics thought, in both small pieces of tradition and longer oral summaries, or in a combination of these along with some written sources. In any case, if, as we have argued, the traditions about the Petrine origin of Mark are correct, then Peter himself is the immediate source of much of Mark's material.

TEXT

The two most important textual problems in Mark's gospel concern its beginning and its end. The words "Son of God" (υἱοῦ θεοῦ [*huiou theou*]) in 1:1 are omitted in a few important early manuscripts (the original hand of the uncial ℵ, the uncial Θ, and a few minuscules). The words could have been accidentally omitted;[61] they are found in the majority of early and significant manuscripts (the uncials A, B, D, L, W), as well as in the mass of later manuscripts; and the inclusion of the phrase fits well with Mark's Christology. On the other hand, the phrase is the kind that later scribes were prone to insert in the narrative.[62] A decision is therefore difficult; but perhaps the evidence for including the words is slightly stronger.[63]

The ending of Mark's gospel poses quite a different, and more severe, problem.[64] The majority of manuscripts include the so-called long ending, in which

---

[59]See, e.g., Martin Dibelius, *From Tradition to Gospel* (New York: Charles Scribner's Sons, n.d.), 178–217.

[60]See esp. Eta Linnemann, *Studien zur Passionsgeschichte,* FRLANT 102 (Göttingen: Vandenhoeck & Ruprecht, 1970). A convenient summary of the discussion in English is found in John R. Donahue, "Introduction: From Passion Traditions to Passion Narrative," in *The Passion in Mark: Studies on Mark 14–16,* ed. Werner H. Kelber (Philadelphia: Fortress Press, 1976), 8–16. See also the survey of approaches and methods to the question in Marion L. Soards, "Appendix IX: The Question of a Premarcan Passion Narrative," in Brown, *The Death of the Messiah,* 2.1492–1524.

[61]The eye of a scribe may have passed from ου (*ou*) at the end of Χριστοῦ (*Christou,* lit. "of Christ") to the same letters at the end of θεοῦ (*theou,* lit. "of God"), omitting what is between, thereby effectively dropping out υἱοῦ θεοῦ (*huiou theou,* "of the Son of God").

[62]See, e.g., Marcus, *Mark,* 141.

[63]J. K. Elliott, on the other hand, has argued that 1:1–3 has been added by a scribe to compensate for a lost first sheet ("Mark 1.1–3—A Later Addition to the Gospel?" *NTS* 46 [2000]: 584–88).

[64]For a history of interpretation, see Stephen Lynn Cox, *A History and Critique of Scholarship Concerning the Markan Endings* (Lewiston: Edwin Mellen, 1993).

are narrated several resurrection appearances of Jesus, Jesus' commissioning of
the disciples, and his ascension. This long ending is printed as verses 9–20 in
the KJV; in modern English versions, it usually appears in the margin or with a
notation. Since it is found in the bulk of the manuscripts and can be traced to
the first half of the second century, this long ending can lay some claim to be
considered as the original ending of Mark's gospel.[65]

[65]William R. Farmer has recently argued that Mark composed vv. 9–20 before writing his gospel and then added it at the end of this gospel as he finished (*The Last Twelve
Verses of Mark,* SNTSMS 25 [Cambridge: Cambridge University Press, 1974]).

But the arguments against this ending being original are very strong. *First,* it is missing from what are generally considered the two most important manuscripts (the uncials ℵ and B), as well as several others. *Second,* Jerome and Eusebius both state that the best manuscripts available to them did not contain this longer ending. *Third,* two other endings to the gospel exist: a shorter ending (attested in the uncials L, Ψ, C, 099, 0112, and some other witnesses), and the longer ending combined with an interpolation (attested in the uncial W and mentioned by Jerome). The presence of these alternative endings suggests that there was uncertainty about the ending of Mark for some time. *Fourth,* the longer ending contains several non-Markan words and expressions. *Fifth,* the longer ending does not flow naturally after 16:8: Jesus is presumed to be the subject in verse 9 (the Greek does not have an expressed subject), although "the women" is the subject in verse 8; Mary is introduced in verse 9 as if she has not been mentioned in verse 1; and "when Jesus rose early on the first day of the week" (v. 9) sounds strange after "very early on the first day of the week" (v. 2). With the great majority of contemporary commentators and textual critics, then, we do not think that verses 9–20 were written by Mark as the ending for his gospel. The resemblances between what is narrated in these verses and the narrative of Jesus' resurrection appearances in the other gospels suggest that this longer ending was composed on the basis of these other narratives to supplement what was felt to be an inadequate ending to the gospel.[66]

If verses 9–20 were not the original ending to Mark's gospel, what was? Three main possibilities exist. *First,* Mark may have intended to write more but been prevented from doing so (by his death or arrest?).[67] *Second,* Mark may have written a longer ending to his gospel, including one or more resurrection appearances, and this ending may have been lost in the course of transmission. It has been suggested, for instance, that the last leaf of Mark's gospel—presuming the gospel was in the form not of a scroll but of a codex, or many-paged book—may have been accidentally torn off.[68] *Third,* Mark may have intended to end his gospel with verse 8. This third possibility is becoming more popular and is the most likely. Mark refrains from making very many editorial comments about the significance of the history he narrates. He lets his story speak for itself, forcing his readers to discover the ultimate significance of much of the story of Jesus. A somewhat enigmatic ending to the gospel suits this strategy perfectly. The reader knows that Jesus has been raised (v. 6). But the confusion and astonishment of the

---

[66]The secondary character of the longer ending has been argued in the monograph by Joseph Hug, *La finale de l'évangile de Marc,* EBib (Paris: Gabalda, 1978).

[67]E.g., Zahn, 2.479–80.

[68]C. F. D. Moule speculates that the loss of the bottom sheet could have resulted in both the ending and the beginning of the gospel being lost, and that 1:1, as 16:9–20, is a later attempt to fill in the resulting gaps (131–32n.).

women (v. 8) leaves us wondering about just what it all means. And that is just the question Mark wants us to ask—and find answers to.[69]

MARK IN RECENT STUDY

For many centuries, little attention was paid to Mark's gospel.[70] The early church quickly saw Matthew come to pride of place among the gospels, with Mark considered to be a rather inferior and inconsequential extract from Matthew. It was only in the nineteenth century that Mark came into a position of prominence. The liberal school of interpretation, pioneered by scholars such as H. J. Holtzmann, found in Mark's simplicity of style and relative paucity of theological embellishment evidence of an earlier and more factual account of the life of Jesus than was presented in the other gospels. This isolation of Mark was destroyed by the work of W. Wrede. Specifically, Wrede argued that Mark had imposed on the tradition the notion of the messianic secret. Jesus' many commands for silence about his status in the gospel, argued Wrede, were invented by Mark in order to explain how it was that Jesus was not recognized to be the Messiah during his lifetime.[71] Today few hold to this notion of the messianic secret.[72] The motif itself is more likely to reflect the actual situation in the life of Jesus than it does a later invention.[73] But at the time, Wrede's work was taken to indicate that Mark wrote with just as much theological interest and bias as did the other evangelists.

The dominance of the form-critical approach during most of the first half of the twentieth century resulted in little interest in Mark as a gospel as such—

---

[69]Joel F. Williams suggests, "Mark ends his Gospel by juxtaposing a promise for restoration in 16:7 with an example of failure in 16:8" ("Literary Approaches to the End of Mark's Gospel," *JETS* 42 [1999]: 21–35 [33]). See also, for this general approach, Donald H. Juel, *A Master of Surprise: Mark Interpreted* (Minneapolis: Fortress Press, 1994), 107–21; Andrew T. Lincoln, "The Promise and the Failure: Mark 16:7, 8," *JBL* 108 (1989): 283–300; cf. also Ned B. Stonehouse, *The Witness of Matthew and Mark to Christ*, reprint ed., with *The Witness of Luke to Christ* (Grand Rapids: Baker, 1979), 86–118; Kümmel, 100–101; Lane, *Mark,* 590–92; Pesch, *Markusevangelium,* 1.40–47.

[70]For a history of interpretation of Mark's gospel, see Sean Kealy, *Mark's Gospel: A History of Its Interpretation from the Beginning Until 1979* (New York: Paulist, 1982); Martin, *Mark,* 29–50.

[71]William Wrede, *The Messianic Secret* (London: J. Clarke, 1971); the German original was published in 1901.

[72]See David E. Aune, "The Problem of the Messianic Secret," *NovT* 11 (1969): 1–31. See also on the general topic, Neil Elliot, "The Silence of the Messiah: The Function of 'Messianic Secret' Motifs Across the Synoptics," *SBL 1993 Seminar Papers,* ed. Eugene H. Lovering Jr. (Atlanta: SP, 1993), 604–22; Paul Danove, "The Narrative Rhetoric of Mark's Ambiguous Characterization of the Disciples," *JSNT* 70 (1993): 21–38.

[73]See, e.g., Hengel, "Literary, Historical, and Theological Problems," 41–45.

attention was focused on the tradition before Mark. With the advent of redaction criticism in the 1950s, this changed, and an avalanche of studies on Mark's theology, purposes, and community flowed from the presses. The contributions of Willi Marxsen, Theodore Weeden, S. G. F. Brandon, and Ralph Martin have been described above. To these could be added numerous other studies, devoted either to the gospel as a whole or to specific themes within the gospel. Two themes received considerable attention in these studies and deserve special mention here: Mark's Christology[74] and his portrait of the disciples.[75]

The methodology of interpreting the gospels, and Mark in particular, has also been the subject of debate. Scholars have attempted to refine the technique of redaction criticism as it may be applied to Mark,[76] while at least one study questioned the fruitfulness of the whole approach for the study of Mark.[77] In this respect, we might mention two other methods that are being used in recent study of Mark. The first is sociological analysis, exhibited in Howard Clark Kee's *Community of the New Age*.[78] Kee analyzes Mark's community, suggesting that it was molded by an apocalyptic perspective and that Mark was seeking to redefine and encourage the community in light of God's purposes in history. Another direction is determined by the recent interest in the application of modern literary techniques to the gospels. These studies have dominated Markan scholarship in recent years. They focus on the way in which Mark, as a narrative, is put together and how it may be understood by the contemporary reader.[79] Some of these studies, by looking for the "deeper structures" below the surface of Mark's narrative, or by adopting a reader-response hermeneutic, or by explicitly pursuing an ideological approach, are of limited value in understanding the text of Mark's gospel. But

---

[74]E.g., Kingsbury, *Christology*.

[75]E.g., Ernest Best, *Following Jesus: Discipleship in the Gospel of Mark*, JSNTSup 4 (Sheffield: JSOT Press, 1981).

[76]E.g., E. J. Pryke, *Redactional Style in the Marcan Gospel: A Study of Syntax and Vocabulary as Guides to Redaction in Mark*, SNTSMS 33 (Cambridge: Cambridge University Press, 1978).

[77]C. Clifton Black, *The Disciples According to Mark: Markan Redaction in Current Debate*, JSNTSup 27 (Sheffield: JSOT Press, 1989).

[78]Howard Clark Kee, *Community of the New Age* (Philadelphia: Westminster, 1977).

[79]An excellent sample of these approaches to Mark can be found in Janice Capel Anderson and Stephen D. Moore, eds., *Mark and Method: New Approaches to Biblical Studies* (Minneapolis: Fortress Press, 1992). See also Elizabeth Struthers Malbon, *Narrative Space and Mythic Meaning in Mark* (San Francisco: Harper & Row, 1986); B. L. Mack, *A Myth of Innocence: Mark and Christian Origins* (Philadelphia: Fortress Press, 1988); Mary Ann Tolbert, *Sowing the Gospel: Mark's World in Literary-Historical Perspective* (Minneapolis: Augsburg/Fortress, 1989); Juel, *A Master of Surprise*; Horsley, *Hearing the Whole Story*.

other studies, taking seriously the text of Mark as we have it and applying useful literary tools, contribute significantly to our appreciation of Mark's structure and purposes. Of course, we should not give the impression that newer methods have displaced older approaches. Traditional critical, exegetical, and theological studies continue to enrich our understanding of Mark. Notable in this respect is the series of articles by Martin Hengel, which show that Mark must be taken seriously as a historian of early Christianity and that his obvious theological interests do not force us to abandon his material as historically worthless.[80]

THE CONTRIBUTION OF MARK

> *Mark is the creator of the gospel in its literary form — an interweaving of biographical and kerygmatic themes that perfectly conveys the sense of meaning of that unique figure in human history, Jesus of Nazareth, the Son of God.*

One might be tempted to mimic the early church and wonder why one should bother with Mark at all. Those who do not consider the gospel an inferior extract of Matthew and/or Luke may well find Mark's significance to lie almost entirely in his supplying to these more verbose evangelists the basic raw material of their own gospels. On this view, Mark's significance could be considered mainly historical: he was the first to compose a gospel, the first to set forth an account of the ministry of Jesus in this peculiar modification of the Greco-Roman biography genre.

But that accomplishment in itself should not be underrated. Mark is the creator of the gospel in its literary form—an interweaving of biographical and kerygmatic themes that perfectly conveys the sense of meaning of that unique figure in human history, Jesus of Nazareth, the Son of God. The newer approaches to Mark as literature have revealed the artistry and power of Mark's narrative. Furthermore, by tying the significance of Jesus for the church so tightly to a specific series of historical occurrences in Palestine in the third decade of the first century, Mark has ensured that the church, if it is to be true to its canonical documents, never abandons the real humanity of the Christ whom it worships. By reminding Christians that their salvation depends on the death and resurrection of Christ, Mark has inextricably tied Christian faith to the reality of historical events.

Mark's very organization of this history makes a point in this regard. The structure of the gospel has been understood in various ways. Philip Carrington suggested that a synagogue lectionary sequence lies at the basis of its structure,[81] but this is most unlikely.[82] Equally improbable is the complicated series of Old

---

[80]Hengel's essays have been collected in *Studies in the Gospel of Mark* (Philadelphia: Fortress Press, 1985).

[81]Philip Carrington, *The Primitive Christian Calendar* (Cambridge: Cambridge University Press, 1952).

[82]On the issue of Jewish lectionaries and the gospels, see Leon Morris, *The New Testament and the Jewish Lectionaries* (London: Tyndale, 1964).

Table 5
Parallels between Peter's Preaching and Mark

Acts 10	Mark
"good news" (v. 36)	"the beginning of the good news" (1:1)
"God anointed Jesus of Nazareth with the Holy Spirit" (v. 38)	the coming of the Spirit on Jesus (1:10)
"beginning in Galilee" (v. 37)	the Galilean ministry (1:16–8:26)
"He went around doing good and healing all who were under the power of the devil" (v. 38)	Jesus' ministry focuses on healings and exorcisms
"We are witnesses of everything he did . . . in Jerusalem" (v. 39)	the ministry in Jerusalem (chaps. 11–14)
"They killed him by hanging him on a cross" (v. 39)	focus on the death of Christ (chap. 15)
"God raised him from the dead on the third day" (v. 40)	"He has risen! He is not here" (16:6)

Testament correspondences discerned by Austin Farrer.[83] Most think that geography plays a significant role in the gospel's structure, and there is truth to this. But the significance of the geography lies, not in some particular theological scheme of Mark, but in the actual sequence of the ministry of Jesus. As C. H. Dodd has noted, the sequence of Mark's gospel follows the same sequence revealed in the early church's preaching.[84] Note the parallels between the preaching of Peter in Acts 10:36–40 and the structure of Mark in table 5.

While the sequence in table 5 is to a considerable extent dictated by the actual course of events, Mark's straightforward, action-oriented account preserves the sequence more clearly than do the other gospels. The kerygmatic structure of Mark helps the readers of the gospel understand the basic salvation events and prepares them to recite those events in their own evangelism.

This same bare-bones narrative sequence also throws into prominence the structural divide of Caesarea Philippi. Though often differing on the structure of Mark, commentators find in this incident the hinge on which the gospel turns.

---

[83]Austin Farrer, *A Study in St. Mark* (Westminster: Dacre, 1951).

[84]Dodd, "Framework of the Gospel Narrative." Dodd's scheme was criticized by D. E. Nineham (*Studies in the Gospels* [Oxford: Blackwell, 1955], 223–39) but has been accepted by others (e.g., Lane, *Mark*, 10–12).

The material in 1:1–8:26, with its stress on Jesus' miracles, leads up to Peter's divinely given insight into the true nature of the man Jesus of Nazareth. But immediately after the confession, and dominating the remainder of the gospel, is the focus on the suffering and death of Jesus. As we have noted, this combination of emphases reveals a major christological purpose of Mark's: Jesus is the *suffering* Son of God and can truly be understood only in terms of this suffering.

As we also noted above when discussing the purpose of the gospel, another central theme in Mark is discipleship. The Twelve figure very prominently in Mark and serve in general as a pattern for the disciples whom Mark addresses in his gospel. To be sure, the Twelve are not always presented as models to be emulated: their conspicuous failure, though present to some degree in the other gospels, is especially prominent in Mark. Mark portrays the disciples as hard of heart (e.g., 6:52), spiritually weak (e.g., 14:32–42), and incredibly dim-witted (e.g., 8:14–21). As Guelich puts it, Mark presents the disciples as both "privileged and perplexed."[85] Perhaps in both these ways they are models for the disciples of Mark's day and of ours: privileged to belong to the kingdom, yet perplexed about the apparent reverses suffered by that kingdom when Christians suffer. In another way, Mark perhaps wants implicitly to contrast the situation of the Twelve, seeking to follow Jesus before the cross and the resurrection, with that of Christian disciples at his time of writing: the latter, however, follow Jesus with the help of the powers of the new age of salvation that has dawned.

BIBLIOGRAPHY

Hugh **Anderson**, *The Gospel of Mark*, NCB (London: Marshall, Morgan & Scott, 1976) ▥Janet Capel **Anderson** and Stephen D. **Moore**, eds., *Mark and Method: New Approaches to Biblical Studies* (Minneapolis: Fortress Press, 1992) ▥David E. **Aune**, "The Problem of the Messianic Secret," *NovT* 11 (1969): 1–31 ▥J. Vernon **Bartlet**, *St. Mark* (London: Thomas Nelson & Sons, n.d.) ▥Pierre **Benoit**, "Note sur les fragments grecs de la Grotte 7 de Qumran," *RevBib* 79 (1972): 321–24 ▥Ernest **Best**, *Following Jesus: Discipleship in the Gospel of Mark*, JSNTSup 4 (Sheffield: JSOT Press, 1981) ▥idem, "Mark's Narrative Technique," *JSNT* 37 (1989): 4358 ▥Gilbert **Bilezikian**, *The Liberated Gospel: A Comparison of the Gospel of Mark and Greek Tragedy* (Grand Rapids: Baker, 1977) ▥C. Clifton **Black**, *The Disciples According to Mark: Markan Redaction in Current Debate*, JSNTSup 27 (Sheffield: JSOT Press, 1989) ▥Josef **Blinzler**, *Der Prozess Jesu*, 2nd ed. (Regensburg: Pustet, 1955) ▥Darrell L. **Bock**, *Blasphemy and Exaltation in Judaism and the Final Examination of Jesus*, WUNT 110 (Tübingen: Mohr-Siebeck, 1998) ▥Peter **Bolt**, *Jesus' Defeat of Death: Persuading Mark's Early Readers*, SNTSMS 125 (Cam-

---

[85]Guelich, *Mark 1–8:26*, p. xlii.

bridge: Cambridge University Press, 2003) ▥Raymond E. **Brown**, *The Death of the Messiah, from Gethsemane to the Grave: A Commentary on the Passion Narratives in the Four Gospels*, 2 vols. (New York: Doubleday, 1994) ▥Scott G. **Brown**, "On the Composition History of the Longer ('Secret') Gospel of Mark," *JBL* 122 (2003): 89–110 ▥A. B. **Bruce**, "The Synoptic Gospels," in *EGT* 1 ▥T. A. **Burkill**, *Mysterious Revelation: An Examination of the Philosophy of St. Mark's Gospel* (Ithaca: Cornell University Press, 1963) ▥Herbert **Cancik**, "Die Gattung Evangelium: Das Evangelium des Markus in Rahmen der antiken Historiographie," in *Markus-Philologie*, ed. H. Cancik, WUNT 33 (Tübingen: Mohr-Siebeck, 1984) ▥Philip **Carrington**, *The Primitive Christian Calendar: A Study in the Making of the Marcan Gospel* (Cambridge: Cambridge University Press, 1952) ▥Maurice **Casey**, *Aramaic Sources of Mark's Gospel*, SNTSMS 102 (Cambridge: Cambridge University Press, 1998) ▥David R. **Catchpole**, *The Trial of Jesus: A Study in the Gospels and Jewish Historiography from 1770 to the Present Day* (Leiden: Brill, 1971) ▥Stephen Lynn **Cox**, *A History and Critique of Scholarship Concerning the Markan Endings* (Lewiston: Edwin Mellen, 1993) ▥C. E. B. **Cranfield**, *The Gospel According to St. Mark*, CGTC (Cambridge: Cambridge University Press, 1966) ▥Oscar **Cullmann**, *Peter: Disciple, Apostle, Martyr*, 2nd ed. (Philadelphia: Westminster, 1962) ▥Paul **Danove**, "The Narrative Rhetoric of Mark's Ambiguous Characterization of the Disciples," *JSNT* 70 (1993): 21–38 ▥Martin **Dibelius**, *From Tradition to Gospel* (New York: Charles Scribner's Sons, n.d.) ▥C. H. **Dodd**, "The Framework of the Gospel Narrative," *ExpTim* 43 (1932): 396–400 ▥James R. **Edwards**, *The Gospel According to Mark*, PNTC (Grand Rapids: Eerdmans, 2002) ▥Neil **Elliot**, "The Silence of the Messiah: The Function of 'Messianic Secret' Motifs Across the Synoptics," *SBL 1993 Seminar Papers*, ed. Eugene H. Lovering Jr. (Atlanta: SP, 1993), 604–22 ▥William **Farmer**, *The Last Twelve Verses of Mark's Gospel*, SNTSMS 25 (Cambridge: Cambridge University Press, 1974) ▥Austin **Farrer**, *A Study in St. Mark* (Westminster: Dacre, 1951) ▥Everett **Ferguson**, "Canon Muratori: Date and Provenance," *Studia Patristica* 18 (1982): 677–83 ▥Richard T. **France**, *The Gospel of Mark: A Commentary on the Greek Text*, NIGTC (Grand Rapids: Eerdmans, 2002) ▥Joachim **Gnilka**, *Das Evangelium nach Markus*, 2 vols., EKKNT (Neukirchen-Vluyn: Neukirchener, 1978; Zürich: Benziger, 1979) ▥Robert A. **Guelich**, *Mark 1–8:26*, WBC (Waco: Word, 1989) ▥Robert H. **Gundry**, *Mark: A Commentary on His Apology for the Cross* (Grand Rapids: Eerdmans, 1993) ▥Ernst **Haenchen**, *Der Weg Jesu: Eine Erklarung des Markusevangelium und der kanonischen Parallelen* (Berlin: Töpelmann, 1966) ▥G. M. **Hahneman**, *The Muratorian Fragment and the Development of the Canon* (Oxford: Clarendon Press, 1992) ▥Adolf von **Harnack**, *The Date of Acts and of the Synoptic Gospels* (New York: Putnam, 1911) ▥Martin **Hengel**, *Studies in the Gospel of Mark* (Philadelphia: Fortress Press, 1985) ▥C. E. **Hill**, "The Debate Over the Muratorian Fragment and the Development of the Canon," *WTJ* 57 (1995): 437–52 ▥Morna **Hooker**, *The Gospel According to Saint Mark* (Peabody: Hendrickson,

1991) ▮Richard A. **Horsley**, *Hearing the Whole Story: The Politics of Plot in Mark's Gospel* (Louisville: Westminster John Knox, 2001) ▮Joseph **Hug**, *La finale de l'évangile de Marc*, EBib (Paris: Gabalda, 1978) ▮Donald H. **Juel**, *A Master of Surprise: Mark Interpreted* (Minneapolis: Fortress Press, 1994) ▮Sean **Kealy**, *Mark's Gospel: A History of Its Interpretation from the Beginning Until 1979* (New York: Paulist, 1982) ▮Howard Clark **Kee**, *Community of the New Age: Studies in Mark's Gospel* (Philadelphia: Westminster, 1977) ▮Werner H. **Kelber**, *Mark's Story of Jesus* (Philadelphia: Fortress Press, 1979) ▮idem, ed., *The Passion in Mark: Studies in Mark 14–16* (Philadelphia: Fortress Press, 1976) ▮Jack Dean **Kingsbury**, *The Christology of Mark's Gospel* (Philadelphia: Fortress Press, 1983) ▮Helmut **Koester**, *Ancient Christian Gospels: Their History and Development* (Philadelphia: Trinity Press International, 1992) ▮William L. **Lane**, *The Gospel According to Mark*, NICNT (Grand Rapids: Eerdmans, 1974) ▮Andrew T. **Lincoln**, "The Promise and the Failure: Mark 16:7, 8," *JBL* 108 (1989): 283–300 ▮Eta **Linnemann**, *Studien zur Passionsgeschichte*, FRLANT 102 (Göttingen: Vandenhoeck & Ruprecht, 1970) ▮Ernst **Loymeyer**, *Galiläa und Jerusalem*, FRLANT 34 (Göttingen: Vandenhoeck & Ruprecht, 1936) ▮B. L. **Mack**, *A Myth of Innocence: Mark and Christian Origins* (Philadelphia: Fortress Press, 1988) ▮Elizabeth Struthers **Malbon**, *Narrative Space and Mythic Meaning in Mark* (San Francisco: Harper & Row, 1986) ▮C. S. **Mann**, *Mark,* AB (Garden City: Doubleday, 1986) ▮T. W. **Manson**, *Studies in the Gospels and the Epistles*, ed. Matthew Black (Philadelphia: Westminster, 1962) ▮Joel **Marcus**, *Mark 1–8: A New Translation with Introduction and Commentary*, AB 27 (New York: Doubleday, 2000) ▮Ralph P. **Martin**, *Mark: Evangelist and Theologian* (Grand Rapids: Eerdmans, 1972) ▮Willi **Marxsen**, *Mark the Evangelist* (Nashville: Abingdon, 1969) ▮Frank J. **Matera**, *What Are They Saying About Mark?* (New York: Paulist, 1987) ▮G. **Minette de Tillesse**, *Le secret messianique dans l'évangile de Marc* (Paris: Cerf, 1968) ▮Francis J. **Moloney**, *The Gospel of Mark: A Commentary* (Peabody: Hendrickson, 2002) ▮Leon **Morris**, *The New Testament and the Jewish Lectionaries* (London: Tyndale, 1964) ▮D. E. **Nineham**, *Studies in the Gospels* (Oxford: Blackwell, 1955) ▮José **O'Callaghan**, "Papiros neotestamentarios en la cuere 7 de Qumran," *Bib* 53 (1972): 91–100 ▮David Barrett **Peabody**, *Mark as Composer* (Macon: Mercer University Press, 1987) ▮Rudolf **Pesch**, *Das Markusevangelium*, 2 vols., HTKNT (Freiburg: Herder, 1976–80) ▮E. J. **Pryke**, *Redactional Style in the Marcan Gospel*, SNTSMS 33 (Cambridge: Cambridge University Press, 1978) ▮Quentin **Quesnell**, *The Mind of Mark: Interpretation and Method Through the Exegesis of Mark 6,52*, AnBib 38 (Rome: Pontifical Biblical Institute, 1969) ▮Gottfried **Rau**, "Das Markusevangelium: Komposition und Intention der ersten Darstellung christliches Mission," *ANRW* 25.3 (1985): 2036–257 ▮Bo **Reicke**, *The Roots of the Synoptic Gospels* (Philadelphia: Fortress Press, 1986) ▮idem, "Synoptic Prophecies of the Destruction of Jerusalem," in *Studies in New Testament and Early Christian Literature*, ed. David E. Aune, NovTSup 33 (Leiden: Brill, 1972), 121–33 ▮J. A. T. **Robinson**,

Redating the New Testament (Philadelphia: Westminster, 1976) ▥Eduard **Schweizer**, *The Good News According to Mark* (Richmond: John Knox, 1970) ▥Morton **Smith**, *The Secret Gospel* (New York: Harper & Row, 1973) ▥Robert H. **Stein**, "A Short Note on Mark XIV.28 and XVI.8," NTS 20 (1974): 445–52 ▥idem, "Is Our Reading the Bible the Same as the Original Audience's Hearing It? A Case Study in the Gospel of Mark," *JETS* 46 (2003): 63–78 ▥Augustine **Stock**, *The Method and Message of Mark* (Wilmington: Glazier, 1989) ▥Ned B. **Stonehouse**, *The Witness of Matthew and Mark to Christ*, reprint ed., with *The Witness of Luke to Christ* (Grand Rapids: Baker, 1979) ▥A. C. **Sundberg** Jr., "Canon Muratori: A Fourth Century List," *HTR* 66 (1973): 1–41 ▥James P. **Sweeney**, "The Death of Jesus in Contemporary Life-of-Jesus Historical Research," *TrinJ* 24 (2003): 221–41 ▥Vincent **Taylor**, *The Gospel According to St. Mark*, 2nd ed. (London: Macmillan, 1966) ▥C. P. **Thiede**, *The Earliest Gospel Manuscript? The Qumran Fragment 7Q5 and Its Significance for New Testament Studies* (Guernsey: Paternoster, 1992) ▥David **Tiede**, *The Charismatic Figure as Miracle Worker* (Missoula: SP, 1972) ▥Mary Ann **Tolbert**, *Sowing the Gospel: Mark's World in Literary-Historical Perspective* (Minneapolis: Augsburg/Fortress, 1989) ▥C. C. **Torrey**, *The Four Gospels* (New York: Harper, 1947) ▥Etienne **Trocmé**, *The Formation of the Gospel According to Mark* (London: SPCK, 1975) ▥H. E. W. **Turner**, "The Tradition of Mark's Dependence upon Peter," *ExpTim* 71 (1959–60): 260–63 ▥Theodore J. **Weeden**, *Mark: Traditions in Conflict* (Philadelphia: Fortress Press, 1971) ▥J. W. **Wenham**, "Did Peter Go to Rome in A.D. 42?" *TynB* 23 (1972): 97–102 ▥Joel F. **Williams**, "Literary Approaches to the End of Mark's Gospel," *JETS* 42 (1999): 21–35 ▥William **Wrede**, *The Messianic Secret* (London: J. Clarke, 1971) ▥N. T. **Wright**, *Jesus and the Victory of God*, vol. 2 of *Christian Origins and the Question of God* (Minneapolis: Fortress Press, 1996) ▥Günther **Zuntz**, "Wann wurde das Evangelium Marci geschrieben?" in *Markus-Philologie*, ed. H. Cancik, WUNT 33 (Tübingen: Mohr-Siebeck, 1984).

CHAPTER FIVE

LUKE

CONTENTS

Luke's gospel is the longest book in the New Testament. Like Matthew, Luke follows the basic outline of Jesus' ministry established by Mark: preparation for the ministry, ministry in Galilee, movement to Jerusalem, passion and resurrection. But Luke introduces many more modifications to this basic sequence than does Matthew. Especially striking is the amount of space he devotes to Jesus' movement to Jerusalem. Occupying one chapter in Mark (10) and two in Matthew (19–20), this section accounts for almost ten chapters in Luke (9:51–19:27). And in order to make room for this expansion, Luke has abbreviated the Galilean phase of the ministry (Luke 4:14–9:17, compared to Mark 1:14–8:26; Matthew 4:12–16:12). But not only does Luke go his own way in terms of the basic structure of the ministry; he also introduces quite a bit of new material not found in any other gospel. Famous parables, such as the Good Samaritan (10:25–37), the Prodigal Son (15:11–32), and the Shrewd Manager (16:1–9) occur only in Luke. Only Luke records Jesus' encounter with Zacchaeus (19:1–10), his raising of a widow's son at Nain (7:11–17), and his words on the cross asking God to forgive his executioners (23:34) and assuring the dying thief of entrance into Paradise (23:43). Just why Luke differs in these ways from Mark and Matthew will be a matter to explore later when we consider the composition of Luke's gospel. For now we will content ourselves with a general overview of Luke's story of Jesus.

The Prologue (1:1–4). Alone among the evangelists, Luke introduces his gospel with a formal prologue modeled along the lines of those found in Hellenistic literature.

The Births of John the Baptist and Jesus (1:5–2:52). Luke's "infancy narrative" focuses especially on the parallel miraculous births of John the Baptist, Jesus' forerunner, and Jesus himself. Angels foretell the births of both John (1:5–25) and Jesus (1:26–38). The expectant mothers, Elizabeth and Mary, who are kinswomen, meet (1:39–45). Mary's song of praise (1:46–56) is matched by that of the father of John the Baptist, Zechariah, in response to the birth of the child (1:57–79). Luke concludes the story of John's birth by saying that he "grew and became strong in spirit" (1:80); just as he claims at the end of chapter 2 that Jesus "grew in wisdom and stature" (2:52 NIV). In chapter 2, Luke records the birth of Jesus in Bethlehem (2:1–7), the visit of the shepherds (2:8–20), the presentation of the baby Jesus in the temple (2:21–40), and the one story we have of the boy Jesus (2:41–52).

Preparation for the Ministry (3:1–4:13). Following the pattern set by Mark, but like Matthew going into considerably more detail, Luke narrates the ministry of John the Baptist (3:1–20), the baptism of Jesus (3:21–22), and Jesus' temptations (4:1–13). Like Matthew, Luke includes Jesus' genealogy, although the differences in the two suggest that different lines of descent are traced (3:23–38).

The Ministry of Jesus in Galilee (4:14–9:50). For thematic reasons, Luke opens his narrative of Jesus' public ministry with Jesus' sermon and rejection in Nazareth (4:16–30). By doing so, Luke forefronts Jesus' claim to be the anointed one (the Messiah) predicted in Isaiah. He then records typical activity of Jesus: an exorcism, a healing, and the proclamation of the kingdom of God (4:31–44). There follows a section contrasting the gathering of disciples with the opposition of Jewish authorities. Jesus brings about a miraculous catch of fish, ending in a call of Simon to catch men (5:1–11), and then heals a leper (5:12–16) and a paralytic (5:17–26). Controversies arise over Jesus' association with sinners (5:27–32), the failure of Jesus' disciples to follow Pharisaic guidelines for fasting (5:33–39), and the Sabbath (6:1–11). This unit ends with the appointing of the Twelve (6:12–16). As a fitting follow-up to the call of the Twelve, Luke then presents Jesus' teaching about discipleship (6:17–49). Chapter 7 includes miracles—the healing of the centurion's servant (1–10) and the raising of the widow's son in Nain (11–17)—as well as Jesus' teaching about John the Baptist (7:18–35) and the anointing of Jesus by a sinful woman (7:36–50). After a transitional interlude about women who followed Jesus (8:1–3), Luke goes on to highlight the importance of responding to the word of God by narrating the parable of the sower (8:4–15), which he follows with Jesus' teaching about the lamp and about the need to listen (8:16–18), and Jesus' re-definition of his "family" in terms of hearing and doing the word of God (8:19–21).

The next unit features four examples of Jesus' characteristic miracles: a "nature" miracle, the stilling of the storm (8:22–25); an exorcism, the healing of the Gerasene demoniac (8:26–39); and the twin story of the healing of the woman with the hemorrhage and the raising of the daughter of Jairus (8:40–56). Luke concludes his story of Jesus' ministry in Galilee with a section focusing on Jesus' identity and the nature of discipleship. Jesus sends out the Twelve (9:1–9), feeds the five thousand (9:10–17), and is recognized by Peter as the "Messiah of God" (9:18–27). Then comes the transfiguration (9:28–36), the healing of the boy with an evil spirit (9:37–45), and teaching about discipleship (9:46–50).

Jesus' journey to Jerusalem (9:51–19:44). In this long section about Jesus' journey from Galilee to Jerusalem, it is not easy to follow the course of the journey or to determine at most points of the narrative just where on the journey Jesus is. Luke seems more intent on stressing the journey motif than in giving precise locations. He is making the point that Jesus moved consistently forward on his way to Jerusalem for the consummation of the work he came to earth to accomplish.[1] Teaching of Jesus dominates this section of the gospel. Luke begins with a section (9:51–11:13) that continues his focus on discipleship. After being rejected by some Samaritans, Jesus warns about the cost of following him (9:51–62). He then sends out seventy-two preachers and rejoices at their report of success (10:1–24). In debate with a teacher of the law, Jesus uses the parable of the Good Samaritan to teach about true love for the neighbor. A dispute between two sisters is the occasion for Jesus to emphasize again the importance of listening to him (10:38–42). The unit concludes with teaching about the pattern and priority of prayer (11:1–13).

As Luke has done earlier, he turns at this point from Jesus' followers to his opponents. In 11:14–54, Jesus rebukes his opponents for accusing him of exorcising demons in Satan's name (11:14–28), condemns his generation for failing to repent (11:29–32), warns about the darkness of unbelief (11:33–36), and pronounces woes on his opponents (11:37–54). Chapters 12–14 blend further rebukes of Jesus' opponents with teaching of the disciples. Jesus warns that opposition to him is opposition to God himself (12:1–12). The right use of money then becomes the topic, with Jesus using a parable to rebuke the arrogant rich (12:13–21) and comforting his followers with the reminder of God's providential care (12:22–34). Jesus goes on to emphasize the need to discern the times and to take appropriate action in light of the situation (12:35–13:9). Jesus' healings on the Sabbath create further controversy (13:10–17; 14:1–6) and he teaches about the eventual spread of the kingdom (13:18–21) and how it is to be entered (13:22–30). Jesus' lament over Jerusalem underscores the failure of so many Jews to respond to him (13:31–35), a point reiterated in his warning about those who seek places of honor (14:7–14) and the parable of the great banquet (14:15–24). This section ends with another warning about the cost of discipleship (14:25–35; cf. 9:57–62).

God's grace is the theme of the three parables about "lost" things in chapter 15: the sheep (15:1–7), the coin (15:8–10), and the son (15:11–32). The right use of money is again the theme of chapter 16, in the parables of the dishonest manager, and the rich man and Lazarus. After teaching about faithful service (17:1–10), Luke includes varied teaching of Jesus, most of it centered on the kingdom of God and the proper response to it (17:11–19:27). Included is com-

---

[1]"He de-emphasizes all topographical data except those relating to Jerusalem, and the result is striking" (Robert/Feuillet, 230).

mendation for a Samaritan's faith (17:11–19), teaching about the nature of the kingdom and its final establishment (17:20–37), a call for persistent faith (18:1–8) and humility (18:9–17), a warning about the dangers of wealth (18:18–30), a prediction of the passion (18:31–34), and the healing of a blind man (18:35–43). The section climaxes with the story of Jesus' encounter with Zacchaeus (19:1–10), a tax collector who embodies Luke's call to disciples to manifest the sincerity of their repentance in the way they use their wealth. A parable about the need to use the resources Christ puts at our disposal concludes this unit (19:11–27). And concluding Luke's major section on the journey of Jesus to Jerusalem is the triumphal entry into Jerusalem (19:28–44).

Jesus in Jerusalem (19:45–21:38). This section is devoted to what Jesus did and taught in Jerusalem in the days before his passion. Luke reports the cleansing of the temple (19:45–46) and Jesus' teaching (19:47–48), including teaching about his authority (20:1–8). The parable of the wicked tenants (20:9–18) is followed by a series of attempts to trap Jesus (20:19–44) and by a warning about the teachers of the law (20:45–47). Luke tells us of the widow's gift (21:1–4) and describes Jesus' teaching about his coming again in glory (21:5–36). The section ends with further teaching in the temple (21:37–38).

Jesus' crucifixion and resurrection (22:1–24:53). In 9:51–19:44, Luke departs quite radically from the narrative pattern of Jesus' ministry established by Mark and followed largely by Matthew. But in chapters 22–23, the passion narrative proper, Luke, though still adding his distinctive touches, follows his predecessors quite closely. Luke sets up the action to follow by relating how Judas agreed to betray Jesus into the hands of the Jewish authorities (22:1–6). He then narrates the Last Supper and related teaching (22:7–38) and the arrest of Jesus in Gethsemane (22:39–54). Jesus is denied by his "chief" disciple, Peter, and mocked by the soldiers (22:55–65). There follow a series of trials: before the Jewish Sanhedrin (22:66–71), before Pilate (23:1–5), before Herod Antipas (23:6–12), and again before Pilate (23:13–25). Luke then narrates Jesus' crucifixion and burial (23:26–56). In his story of the resurrection, Luke again goes his own way. After the empty tomb account (24:1–12), he focuses on Jesus' conversation with a pair of disciples on the road to Emmaus (24:13–35). Another appearance of Jesus before his disciples follows (24:36–49), and Luke concludes his gospel with a brief account of the ascension (24:50–53).

LUKE–ACTS

No analysis of Luke's gospel can proceed without a preliminary decision about the nature of the relationship between the gospel and the book of Acts. The prologues to the books leave no doubt that a relationship exists. The same man— Theophilus—is addressed in each, and the "former book" mentioned in Acts 1:1 is undoubtedly the Gospel of Luke. While scholars have always recognized the relationship between these books, the implications of that relationship for the books' genre, purpose, and theology became a focus of attention only with the publication of H. J. Cadbury's *The Making of Luke-Acts* in 1927. Since then, the tendency has been to insist that Luke and Acts form one book, divided for logistical reasons (the limits of what a single papyrus scroll could hold) into two volumes. In the process of forming the canon, the two books were separated, giving rise to the unfortunate tendency to consider them separately. So today one generally finds the names linked by a hyphen as a way of marking their close relationship.

Nevertheless, the nature and extent of the unity of Luke-Acts must still be explored.[2] Virtually all scholars today agree that the same person wrote both books,[3] and most also find a considerable degree of thematic unity. Luke-Acts together shows how God has acted in history to fulfill his promises to Israel and to create a world-wide body of believers drawn from both Jews and Gentiles. The focus on Jerusalem in both Luke and Acts conveys this movement. As Luke in the gospel emphasizes (more than the other gospels) the movement *toward* Jerusalem (e.g., 9:51; 13:33; 17:11), the book of Acts describes a movement *away* from Jerusalem.[4] Luke thereby shows how Jesus fulfills God's plan for Israel as the basis for a movement out from Israel to embrace the entire world. Other specific themes, such as salvation, the activity of the Holy Spirit, and the power of the Word of God, run through both books.

But disagreement begins to set in when one turns to the issues of genre, purpose, and narrative development. If the Gospel of Luke, with the other gospels, belongs to the general category of Hellenistic biography (as we argued in chapter 2), then what can we say of Luke-Acts? For biography, however generally we define it, does not describe the book of Acts.[5] Most scholars would place Acts in the category of "history" (see chap. 7); and it is possible that Luke's gospel could also be considered a historical treatise.[6] But Luke is much more

> *Virtually all scholars today agree that the same person wrote Luke and Acts, and most also find a considerable degree of thematic unity.*

---

[2]See especially the thorough survey in J. Verheyden, "The Unity of Luke-Acts: What Are We Up To?" in *The Unity of Luke-Acts*, ed. J. Verheyden, BETL 142 (Leuven: Leuven University Press, 1999), 3–56.

[3]Although this is contested by Albert C. Clark, *The Acts of the Apostles: A Critical Edition with Introduction and Notes on Selected Passages* (Oxford: Clarendon Press, 1933), 393–408.

[4]See, e.g., Johnson, 220.

[5]Despite the attempt of Charles H. Talbert to argue otherwise (*Literary Patterns, Theological Themes, and the Genre of Luke-Acts*, SBLMS 20 [Missoula: SP, 1974]).

[6]See, e.g., Daryl D. Schmidt, "Rhetorical Influences and Genre: Luke's Preface and the Rhetoric of Hellenistic Historiography," in *Jesus and the Heritage of Israel*, ed. David P. Moessner (Harrisburg: Trinity Press International, 1999), 27–60; Gregory E. Sterling, *Historiography and Self-Definition: Josephus, Luke-Acts, and Apologetic Historiography*, NovTSup 44 (Leiden: Brill, 1992); David Aune, *The New Testament in its Literary*

like Matthew and Mark than like Acts; we would expect to classify it in the same category as the other gospels. The lack of generic unity between Luke and Acts at least raises questions about how closely the two books are related. The same point can be made with respect to the books' narrative unity. The popularity of narrative criticism in recent years has fostered the publication of a number of works dedicated to revealing the overall narrative scheme of Luke-Acts.[7] Most evident is the rough parallelism between the two books. Both open with a descent of the Holy Spirit, go on to narrate miracles and preaching, emphasize traveling, and feature trial scenes toward their close. But more detailed suggestions for narrative unity are generally unconvincing and, indeed, tend to be self-defeating by the very number of contradictory proposals.[8]

The upshot is that we should probably consider Luke and Acts to be two separate books that stand in close relationship to each other.[9] Luke almost certainly had both books in mind when he began to write, and certain common themes and purposes bind them together. But we should probably respect the canonical status of the two and consider each on its own when it comes to the question of genre, structure, purpose, and, to some extent, theology.

AUTHOR

As we noted above, scholars agree that Luke and Acts were written by the same individual. Not only do the prologues connect the two books, but language, style, and theology also point to common authorship. Internal and external evidence combine to point strongly to Luke, the doctor, Paul's "dear friend" (see Col. 4:14), as the author.

Environment (Philadelphia: Westminster, 1987), 77; Ben Witherington III, *The Acts of the Apostles: A Socio-Rhetorical Commentary* (Grand Rapids: Eerdmans, 1998), 12–24; François Bovon, *Luke 1: A Commentary on the Gospel of Luke 1:1–9:50*, Hermeneia (Minneapolis: Augsburg/Fortress, 2002), 8.

[7]See, for instance, Robert C. Tannehill, *The Narrative Unity of Luke-Acts: A Literary Interpretation*, 2 vols. (Minneapolis: Fortress Press, 1990); and the commentaries on Luke (*The Gospel of Luke*, NICNT [Grand Rapids: Eerdmans, 1997], 6–10) and Acts (forthcoming) by Joel B. Green.

[8]See especially, Mikeal C. Parsons and Richard I. Pervo, *Rethinking the Unity of Luke and Acts* (Minneapolis: Fortress Press, 1993). Wikenhauser thinks that Luke wrote Acts so long after the gospel that they can be considered separately (pp. 352–54).

[9]See, e.g., John Nolland, *Luke 1–9:20*, WBC (Dallas: Word, 1989), xxxiii–xxxiv; Joseph A. Fitzmyer, *The Acts of the Apostles: A New Translation with Introduction and Commentary*, AB 31 (New York: Doubleday, 1998), 49; Loveday Alexander, *The Preface to Luke's Gospel: Literary Convention and Social Context in Luke 1:1–4 and Acts 1:1*, SNTSMS 78 (Cambridge: Cambridge University Press, 1993), 145–46. Note also the discussion in *The Unity of Luke-Acts*, ed. J. Verheyden.

The prologue to the gospel (Luke 1:1–4) makes clear that the author was not an eyewitness to the ministry of Jesus.[10] He claims that the "things that have been fulfilled among us" "were handed down to us by those who from the first were eyewitnesses and servants of the word" (1:1, 2). The third gospel betrays considerable interest in Gentiles and may point to a Gentile author. He was quite clearly an educated man, and he writes very good Greek (note his reference to "their language" in Acts 1:19; Aramaic was not Luke's language). The opening paragraph, as we have noted, is written in good classical style (1:1–4). The rest of the first two chapters has a strong Semitic cast,[11] while the remainder of the book is in a good Hellenistic Greek that constantly reminds the reader of the Septuagint. This versatility points to a very competent writer.[12]

But the most important internal evidence comes from the book of Acts. The latter half of Acts contains several passages written in the first-person plural. These "we" passages seem to identify the author of Acts as a companion of Paul at these points in his travels. Comparison with references in Paul's letters to his companions narrows the field of candidates down to a handful—including Luke. (We develop the case for this identification and respond to objections that have been raised to it in chap. 7.) Analysis of the Greek of Luke and Acts has been used to bolster this identification, the argument being that the books use a great deal of medical language.[13] But H. J. Cadbury has called this argument into question, noting that most of the alleged medical vocabulary appears in everyday Greek writings of the period.[14] Nevertheless, if the language falls short

---

[10]There has been considerable debate over the meaning of the word παρηκολουθηκότι (parēkolouthēkoti) in v. 3 of the prologue. Cadbury insists that it must mean "having kept in touch with" and implies the author's personal involvement in at least some of the events narrated ("The Tradition," in *The Beginnings of Christianity*, Part 1: *The Acts of the Apostles*, by F. J. Foakes Jackson and Kirsopp Lake [London: Macmillan, 1920–33], 2.501–3). Others, probably correctly, argue that the word means simply "having investigated," with no implication of personal involvement (e.g., Joseph A. Fitzmyer, *The Gospel According to Luke I–IX*, 2nd ed. [New York: Doubleday, 1983], 297–98).

[11]On the significance of the Semitic flavor of the language in chaps. 1–2, esp. in the so-called hymns, see Stephen Farris, *The Hymns of Luke's Infancy Narratives: Their Origin, Meaning, and Significance*, JSNTSup 9 (Sheffield: JSOT Press, 1985).

[12]"He composed his narrative (*diegesis*) not merely as an ancient historian of the Hellenistic mode, nor merely as a theologian of the early church writing in a biblical mold, but also as a conscious littérateur of the Roman period" (Fitzmyer, *Luke I–IX*, 92). X. Léon-Dufour thinks that Luke "to a Greek ear was at once refined and often vulgar" (Robert/Feuillet, 223).

[13]See especially W. K. Hobart, *The Medical Language of St. Luke* (Dublin: Hodges, Figgis, 1882), and note also Adolf von Harnack, *Luke the Physician* (New York: Putnam, 1907).

[14]H. J. Cadbury, *The Style and Literary Method of Luke*, HTS 6 (Cambridge: Harvard University Press, 1919).

of proving that the author was a doctor, it certainly is compatible with the hypothesis. And some passages may indicate the particular outlook of a doctor, as, for example, when Luke speaks of a "high" fever, where Matthew and Mark speak only of a fever (Luke 4:38; Matt. 8:14; Mark 1:30).[15]

Yet the main reason for singling out Luke as the author of Luke-Acts comes from the external evidence. The heretic Marcion identified Luke as the author of these books in the middle of the second century. At about the same time, Justin Martyr speaks of Luke writing a "memoir of Jesus," noting that the author was a companion of Paul (*Dialogue with Trypho* 103.19). The same identification is made just slightly later in the Muratorian Canon (c. 180–200?[16]). In *Adversus Haereses*, Irenaeus claims that Luke, a doctor, Paul's companion, wrote the gospel (3.1.1, 3.14.1). The so-called "Anti-Marcionite" Prologue to Luke assumes that Luke is the author, claiming he was a native of Antioch and a doctor.[17] In the beginning of the second century, Tertullian characterizes the third gospel as a summary of Paul's gospel (*Against Marcion* 4.2.2 and 4.5.3). The oldest manuscript of Luke, Bodmer Papyrus XIV, cited as P[75] and dated A.D. 175–225, ascribes the book to Luke.[18] Some have claimed that these identifications are simply the product of a careful scrutiny of the internal evidence. But this is unlikely.[19] The tradition deserves to be taken seriously for three reasons. *First,* although both Luke and Acts are anonymous—there is no explicit claim to authorship—it is unlikely that the books ever circulated without a name

---

[15]Alfred Wikenhauser agrees that the language does not prove a medical author, but then adds, "Nevertheless the tradition need not be abandoned, and it may still be sustained, for the author displays familiarity with medical terminology (cf. e.g., Lk. 4,38; 5,12; 8,44; Acts 5,5 10; 9,40), and he indisputably describes maladies and cures from the point of view of a medical man (e.g., Lk. 4,35; 13,11; Acts 3,7; 9,18)" (*New Testament Introduction* [ET New York: Herder, 1963], 209); his conclusion is only slightly softened in the latest (German) edition (Wikenhauser, 254–55). Loveday Alexander has argued that Luke's preface finds its closest parallels in the technical prose or "scientific treatises" of the Hellenistic world—just the kind of book for a doctor to write (*The Preface to Luke's Gospel,* 176–77).

[16]On the date of the Muratorian fragment, see chap. 4, n. 7.

[17]Both the Greek and the Latin forms of the prologue are printed in Kurt Aland, *Synopsis Quattuor Evangeliorum* (Stuttgart: Württembergische Bibelanstalt, 1964), 533. R. G. Heard cites the Greek text and an English translation ("The Old Gospel Prologues," *JTS* 6 [1955]: 7).

[18]Fitzmyer, *Luke–IX,* 35–36. Note the comment of Kirsopp Lake about the titles of the gospels, "Why should this testimony not be accepted? No reason has ever been shown, for the view that antiquity tended to anonymous books is contrary to evidence" (p. 4).

[19]E. Earle Ellis calls the view that before the middle of the second century someone used "shrewd detective work" to discover a previously unknown author of this gospel "an exercise in improbabilities" (*The Gospel of Luke,* 2nd ed. [London: Marshall, Morgan & Scott, 1974], 42).

attached to them in some way. As Martin Dibelius notes, a book bearing the name of the person to whom it was dedicated is unlikely to have lacked the author's name (it would have been on an attached tag).[20] *Second,* no one in the early church disputes the identification of Luke as the author. Both Irenaeus and Tertullian write as though there was no doubt about the Lukan authorship of these books. And *third,* it is hard to understand why Luke's name would have been attached to the gospel if it had not been there from the beginning. The manifest tendency in the early church was to associate apostles with the books of the New Testament. The universal identification of a non-apostle as the author of almost one-quarter of the New Testament speaks strongly for the authenticity of the tradition.

On the basis of Colossians 4:10–14, Luke is usually thought to have been a Gentile Christian. In verses 10–11a of this passage, Paul transmits greetings from three men and then says, "These are the only Jews [literally, "those of the circumcision"] among my co-workers for the kingdom of God." He then goes on to extend greetings from Epaphras and Luke. The natural implication of the text is that Luke is not one of those fellow workers who is "of the circumcision," that is, a Jew. A few scholars have contested this conclusion and argued for various reasons that Luke was a Jew.[21] But the case is not a persuasive one. A suggestion that has greater merit is that Luke was a god-fearer—a Gentile who had strong sympathies for Judaism without becoming a convert.[22] Such a hypothesis explains, on the one hand, Colossians 4:10–14 and the Gentile focus of Luke's writings, and, on the other hand, the author's intimate knowledge of the Old Testament (in Greek) and Judaism.

PROVENANCE

Early tradition (the Anti-Marcionite prologue, c. 175, is the earliest) claims that Luke was from Antioch;[23] but we possess too little evidence to know for sure. The same tradition, along with at least one other (the Monarchian prologue) asserts that Luke wrote his gospel in the region of Achaia. Some scholars are

---

[20]M. Dibelius, *Studies in the Acts of the Apostles* (ET: London: SCM, 1956), 148. Note his claim: "Both writings, Gospel and Acts, were offered to the literary reading public from the very beginning under the name of Luke as author" (p. 89).

[21]E.g., Ellis, *The Gospel of Luke,* 52–53. Fitzmyer argues that Luke was a non-Jewish Semite (*Luke I–IX,* 41–47). John Wenham's suggestion that Luke is to be identified with Lucius of Cyrene, a kinsman of Paul's and one of the Seventy ("The Identification of Luke," *EQ* 63 [1991]: 3–44) is imaginative but has too much data against it.

[22]See, e.g., Darrell Bock, *Luke 1: 1:1–9:50,* vol. 1, BECNT (Grand Rapids: Baker, 1994), 5–7.

[23]Another small bit of evidence favoring Antioch is the fact that D and a few other authorities make Acts 11:28, locating events at Antioch, a "we" passage.

inclined to agree with this tradition,[24] and it would fit in with what we know if Luke remained in Rome until Paul was released from prison, then went to Greece and wrote his gospel. But the evidence is very slim. Still other traditions (e.g., some late manuscripts of Luke) give Rome as the place of composition, but it is not known on what basis. In the end we must say that there is not sufficient evidence to link the gospel definitely with any particular area. Achaia is a reasonable conjecture, but we cannot say more.

DATE

The date of Luke's gospel is closely intertwined with the dates of Mark and Acts. Luke must have been written a bit later than Mark if, as we have argued in chapter 2, Luke used Mark as a primary source for his gospel. And Luke must, of course, be earlier than Acts, since Acts presupposes the existence of Luke (see Acts 1:1). Two main options for the dating of Luke are extant in scholarly literature: the 60s and 75–85.[25] We will consider first some of the reasons to date Luke in the 60s.

The date of Luke's gospel is closely intertwined with the dates of Mark and Acts.

1. Acts makes no mention of several key events from the period 65–70 that we might have expected it to mention: the Neronian persecution, the deaths of Peter and Paul, and the destruction of Jerusalem at the hands of the Romans. No event later than 62 is mentioned.

2. Luke spends much of the last part of Acts describing Paul's arrest, trials, and journey to Rome. We would have expected him to have completed the story by telling us what happened to Paul in the end. But he ends Acts with Paul imprisoned in Rome. This may point to the date at which Luke published Acts (about A.D. 62).

3. Luke tells us how the prophecy of Agabus about a world-wide famine was fulfilled (Acts 11:28); we might have expected him all the more to show how Jesus' prophecy of the fall of Jerusalem (Luke 21:20) took place. The inference is that it had not yet taken place.

4. The most probable reading of the Pastoral Epistles is that Paul was released from his Roman custody described at the end of Acts and returned to the Eastern Mediterranean for further ministry—including ministry in Ephesus. But in Acts 20:25, 38 Paul claims that he would not see the Ephesians

---

[24]E.g., Brown, 270–71.

[25]A few scholars advocate dates beyond this range at either end. John Wenham, for instance, puts Luke in the period A.D. 57–59 (*Redating Matthew, Mark, and Luke*, 230–38); while J. C. O'Neil (*The Theology of Acts in Its Historical Setting* [London: SPCK, 1961], 1–53) and John Drury put it early in the second century (*Tradition and Design in Luke's Gospel: A Study in Early Christian Historiography* [Atlanta: John Knox, 1976], 15–25).

again. If the later visit to Ephesus had taken place, we might have expected Luke to have reflected the fact in some way.

5. The Pauline Epistles were evidently treasured in the early church, but they are ignored in Acts. The later we put Acts, the more difficult it is to account for this.

6. It is questioned whether a Christian writer would give as friendly a picture of Rome as we find in Luke-Acts after the Neronian persecution.

Not all these points, of course, are equally strong. But their cumulative weight is enough to give a date in the 60s considerable plausibility. Especially important is the lack of mention in either Luke or Acts of the fall of Jerusalem. So cataclysmic an event in the history of the Jewish people is unlikely to have gone completely unmentioned in books that focus so much on the nature and theological continuity of Israel and the people of God.[26] Along with many other scholars, therefore, we prefer to date Luke in the 60s.[27] Nevertheless, there are problems with so early a date—problems that lead many other scholars to date Luke after 70, usually in the period 75–85.[28] We next consider and respond to these arguments.

1. Luke's version of Jesus' prediction of the fall of Jerusalem reflects the actual events. In Mark (Luke's presumed source), Jesus refers to an "abomination that causes desolation" in the temple (Mark 13:14). But Luke has changed this to "Jerusalem . . . surrounded by armies" (Luke 21:20), more accurately depicting the actual circumstances of Jerusalem's envelopment by the Roman legions. Similar Lukan redactions are said to reflect the same "after-the-event" stance (Luke 13:35a; 19:43–44).[29] Two responses to this argument can be made. First, the argument to some extent reflects an anti-supernatural bias, denying, in effect, that Jesus could have accurately predicted the circumstances of Jerusalem's fall before the event. Once we truly come to grips with the nature of Jesus' person as presented in the gospels, we can hardly doubt his predictive powers. Second, Jesus' predictions about the fall of Jerusalem in Luke are, in fact, remarkably vague, employing standard first-century language for siege techniques.[30] To be sure, Philip Esler has challenged this argument, claiming

---

[26]This point is key to the early dating of almost all the New Testament documents by J. A. T. Robinson (*Redating the New Testament* [Philadelphia: Westminster, 1976]).

[27]See especially Leon Morris, *The Gospel According to St. Luke: An Introduction and Commentary,* TNTC (Grand Rapids: Eerdmans, 1974), 22–26. See also I. Howard Marshall, *The Gospel of Luke: A Commentary on the Greek Text,* NIGTC (Grand Rapids: Eerdmans, 1978), 33–35; Bock, *Luke 1:1–9:50,* 16–18.

[28]This is the dominant view in critical scholarship. See, e.g., Brown, 273–74; Fitzmyer, *Luke I–IX,* 53–57.

[29]See, for a brief presentation, Fitzmyer, *Luke I–IX,* 54.

[30]Bo Reicke characterizes the claim that this is a prophecy after the event as "an amazing example of uncritical dogmatism in New Testament studies" and points out

that Luke includes details not normally associated with a siege.[31] But many of these details reflect Old Testament language describing God's judgment for covenant unfaithfulness.[32] Nothing in Luke's predictions of the fall of Jerusalem need reflect detailed knowledge after the event.

2. A broad consensus of scholars holds that Luke used Mark in writing his gospel. But if we date Mark in the mid–60s or later, then Luke could not have been written before 70 at the earliest. For this argument to work, of course, Luke would have had to use Mark in its final form, and a good number of scholars question whether this was the case. Nevertheless, most scholars are convinced that Luke did use Mark, and we have argued for this position ourselves in chapter 2. But the issue of Mark's date still remains. While most scholars prefer a date for Mark in the mid–60s or later, we have argued in chapter 4 that it might be as early as the late 50s. And since both Mark and Luke were in the group associated with Paul, Luke might have obtained a copy of Mark very shortly after it was written.

3. Luke claims in his prologue that "many" people had drawn up accounts of the life and significance of Jesus (1:1). Considerable time would have had to elapse to allow for the writing of these accounts and their circulation to the extent that Luke would be able to know and evaluate them. But how much time? If we date the latest gospel event in about A.D. 30, and Luke writes in the 60s, then these predecessors of Luke's would have had over thirty years to produce their accounts. Surely this is enough time.

4. A broader and more subjective argument concerns some of the peculiar emphases of Luke's theology. A popular interpretation of the development of early Christianity holds that the church moved from a fervent belief in the imminent return of Jesus in glory to a resignation that his return would be postponed indefinitely. And with the early Christians' modified eschatological timetable went considerable theological revisions and developments. Specifically, for our immediate purposes, the problem of "the delay of the parousia" led to a theological movement dubbed "early Catholicism." The name reflects the fact that Christians who began to have to reckon with a long period of time on earth were led to replace the earliest charismatic-oriented church with an institutional church. And Luke, it is claimed, reflects the movement toward early Catholicism. He downplays references to Jesus' return in the gospel and refers often in

---

that in none of the synoptics does the prophecy conform exactly to what we know about the destruction of Jerusalem ("Synoptic Prophecies of the Destruction of Jerusalem," in *Studies in New Testament and Early Christian Literature*, ed. D. E. Aune [Leiden: Brill, 1972], 121).

[31]Philip F. Esler, *Community and Gospel in Luke-Acts*, SNTSMS 57 (Cambridge: Cambridge University Press, 1987), 27–30.

[32]See, e.g., Darrell Bock, "Gospel of Luke," in *DJG*, 499.

the book of Acts to the church and its leadership. We deal with Luke's eschatology below, and we cannot explore the whole matter of "early Catholicism" here. Suffice to say that the neat developmental scheme that is the foundation for "early Catholicism" is most improbable and that the "delay of the parousia" was not nearly the issue that some want to make it. Luke certainly betrays a different theological outlook than does Mark and Matthew; and a tendency to give less attention to the return of Christ is undoubtedly present in his gospel. But we have no reason for thinking that this de-emphasis must be a late development. Nor does Acts betray any real interest in an "institutional" church.[33] Many critics are far too prone to attribute different theological emphases in the books of the New Testament to long developments in time when in reality they reflect simply different circumstances and different purposes.

The only really significant argument for dating Luke after A.D. 70 is the argument that Mark must be dated in the mid-60s at the earliest. But we have seen reason to question the necessity of dating Mark as late as that. And if Mark is dated in the early 60s, then Luke could well have been written in the mid- or late-60s.

ADDRESSEE(S)

Following the convention of Hellenistic literature, Luke opens his gospel with a prologue in which he acknowledges his predecessors, states his purpose, and recognizes his addressee—Theophilus. Since "Theophilus" is the transliteration of a Greek word that means "lover of God," some scholars have suggested that the address is generic. Luke writes to any person who might fit into the category of a lover of God. But the more natural interpretation is that Luke has a definite individual in view.[34] This person's name might have been Theophilus; or Luke might be using an alias to guard the person's true identity.[35] By calling him "most excellent" (κράτιστε [kratiste]), Luke may also imply that Theophilus was a person of rank, perhaps a Roman aristocrat (compare Acts 24:3 and 26:25).[36] Theophilus may, in fact, have been Luke's patron, the person who incurred the costs of Luke's writing. Since Luke writes to convince Theophilus of the "certainty of the things you have been taught" (Luke 1:4), he was probably a recent convert to the faith.

However, while addressed to a single individual, it is almost certain that Luke had a wider reading public in view. Theophilus, though probably a real

---

[33]See on this especially I. Howard Marshall, *Luke: Historian and Theologian*, 2nd ed. (Grand Rapids: Zondervan, 1988), 81–83, 212–15.

[34]See, e.g., Alexander, *The Preface to Luke's Gospel*, 188.

[35]See, e.g., Martin Hengel, *The Four Gospels and the One Gospel of Jesus Christ* (Harrisburg: Trinity Press International, 2000), 102.

[36]Ibid.; contrast Alexander, *The Preface to Luke's Gospel*, 188–93.

person, stands as representative of a class of people whom Luke addresses in his two books.[37] Though not necessarily having the same social rank as Theophilus, the wider public Luke addresses probably shared with him a Gentile background.[38] Luke implies such an audience in many ways: his concern to situate the gospel events in the context of secular history (e.g., Luke 2:1; 3:1–2); his emphasis on the universal implications of the gospel (e.g., his genealogy begins with Adam in contrast to Matthew's, which begins with Abraham); his omission of material that focuses on the Jewish law (e.g., the antitheses of Matthew 5; the controversy about "uncleanness" [Mark 7:1–23]); his tendency to substitute Greek equivalents for Jewish titles (e.g., "Lord" or "Teacher" for "Rabbi"); his focus on Gentile converts in the book of Acts.[39] Some scholars have gone further, suggesting that the combination of a Gentile focus and a presumption that the readers know the Old Testament and Judaism point to an audience of god-fearers, Gentiles who, before their conversion, had strong sympathies with Judaism.[40] This is possible but not provable. Equally uncertain is the locale to which Luke is directed. Some scholars agree with the tradition that identifies Greece as the destination,[41] but the tradition is neither early nor widespread. And in any case, we should perhaps recognize the possibility that Luke, like the other gospels, was not so much written to a specific location as to a specific kind of reader.[42]

Luke clearly intends that his gospel and Acts be read in relationship to each other but not as a single narrative broken in two only by space considerations.

PURPOSE

Any assessment of Luke's purpose in writing his gospel must again touch base with the question of the relationship between the gospel and the book of Acts. We suggested above somewhat of a mediating view. Luke clearly intends the

[37]"The formal dedication of this work to Theophilus, whose title ('Your Excellency') shows that he held high office in the Roman government, strongly suggests that it was intended for publication and was therefore directed primarily to the outside world" (G. B. Caird, *The Gospel of St Luke* [Harmondsworth: Penguin, 1963], 14). It is even possible that Luke mentions Theophilus only because he is his patron and not because he represents the intended audience (see Achtemeier/Green/Thompson, 155).

[38]There have been only a few dissenters from this conclusion, as for instance, Jacob Jervell, who thinks the focus on Jewish-Christian relationships suggests a Jewish-Christian audience for Luke-Acts (*The People of God: A New Look at Luke-Acts* [Minneapolis: Augsburg, 1972], esp. 173–77).

[39]For these points, and others, see, e.g., Fitzmyer, *Luke I–IX*, 58–59.

[40]E.g., Walter L. Liefeld, "Luke," in EBC 8.802; Nolland, *Luke 1–9:20*, pp. xxxii-iii; Bock, *Luke 1:1–9:50*, 14–15.

[41]Brown, 270–71.

[42]See the argument of Richard Bauckham, "For Whom Were the Gospels Written?" in *The Gospels for All Christians* (Grand Rapids: Eerdmans, 1998), 9–48.

two books to be read in relationship to each other but not as a single narrative broken in two only by space considerations. The reader should be sensitive to commonalities between the two books even as he or she allows each book to stand on its own. This posture is certainly appropriate in considering Luke's purpose.

We begin with Luke's own claim about his purpose in writing, found in the prologue. He writes so that Theophilus "may know the certainty of the things you have been taught." The word "certainty" (ἀσφάλεια [asphaleia]) has the notion of assurance. Luke wants Theophilus, and other converts like him, to be certain in their own minds and hearts about the ultimate significance of what God has done in Christ. By the time Luke wrote his gospel, the early church had separated from Judaism and was, indeed, experiencing hostility from many Jews. At the same time, the new and tiny Christian movement was competing with a welter of religious and philosophical alternatives in the Greco-Roman world. Why should Theophilus think that Christianity is the one "right" religion out of all these alternatives? Why should he think that Christians and not Jews constitute the true people of God, those who are the true heirs of God's Old Testament promises? Why, to put the matter at its most foundational level, should Theophilus continue to believe that God has revealed himself decisively in Jesus of Nazareth? Luke's gospel, along with the book of Acts, is intended to answer these questions and to give new converts to the faith a "reason for the hope that is within them."[43]

COMPOSITION

As we noted in chapter 2 and above, Luke stands in a complex relationship to Mark and to Matthew. Verbal similarities among the three evangelists have convinced most scholars that a literary relationship exists among them; and most also conclude that Mark is the middle term among the three. We will not rehearse here the arguments that lead us to agree with the general consensus that Mark is not only the middle term between Matthew and Luke but that Mark also precedes Matthew and Luke and is the primary source for both (see chap. 2). But Matthew is more dependent on Mark than is Luke. Matthew takes over (though he often abbreviates) 90 percent of the material in Mark; Luke takes over only 55 percent.[44] Markan material accounts for about 40 percent of Luke's gospel. So over half of Luke's gospel must have originated from a source other than Mark. About 20 percent of this non-Markan material has parallels with Matthew.

---

[43]Most recent commentators on Luke agree in general about this central purpose. See, e.g., Bock, *Luke 1:1–9:50*, 14–15; Green, *The Gospel of Luke*, 21–25.

[44]The figures are from B. H. Streeter, *The Four Gospels: A Study of Origins* (London: Macmillan, 1924), 160.

As we noted in chapter 2, some scholars think that the simplest explanation for this similarity is that Luke has used Matthew.[45] But the problems with this view are so intractable that most scholars are persuaded that Luke and Matthew have independently used a lost source, called "Q." We think this hypothesis is likely, though the exact nature of Q (written? oral? one document or many?) must be left open (see again chap. 2). But this still leaves us with about 40 percent of Luke's gospel for which we must account. This material, traditionally labeled "L," was assigned to a single source in the heyday of source criticism. But most scholars today are inclined to think of a series of sources, ranging from personal interviews to brief written documents. The Semitic-flavored infancy narrative, for instance, may originate from a source; as may some of the parables in Luke's central section.[46] We must recall at this point that Luke would have had ample opportunity to gather material for the writing of his gospel. From the "we" passages of Acts, we know that Luke spent two years in Palestine while Paul languished in prison (see Acts 21:8; 24:27; 27:1). We can imagine him not only collecting written evidence but listening carefully for authentic oral teaching handed down in the Christian communities and interviewing eyewitnesses to the ministry.

Yet a further question pertaining to Luke's sources is the hypothesis of a "Proto-Luke." As we have seen in our survey of the gospel above, Luke not only takes over less of Mark than does Matthew, but his central section, featuring the movement of Jesus from Galilee to Jerusalem, has no real parallel in either Matthew or Mark. Luke's passion narrative, while sticking closely to the basic outline of events found in Matthew and Mark, has many distinctive features. And, perhaps most striking is the way Luke tends to put his Markan material into blocks. All these considerations suggest that Luke may have written an earlier edition of his gospel, using Q and "L," and only later added the material from Mark.[47] One can even suggest a plausible historical scenario: on the basis

---

[45]See esp. Mark Goodacre, *The Case Against Q: Studies in Markan Priority and the Synoptic Problem* (Harrisburg: Trinity Press International, 2002); idem, *The Synoptic Problem: A Way through the Maze* (New York: Sheffield Academic Press, 2001); Michael D. Goulder, *Luke: A New Paradigm*, 2 vols.; JSNTSup 20 (Sheffield: JSOT Press, 1989); Allan J. McNicol, David L. Dungan, and David B. Peabody, *Beyond the Q Impasse: Luke's Use of Matthew* (Valley Forge: Trinity Press International, 1996). See also, A. Farrer, "On Dispensing with Q," in *Studies in the Gospels,* ed. D. E. Nineham (Oxford: Oxford University Press, 1955), 55–58; Drury, *Tradition and Interpretation,* 120–73.

[46]See, for the former, Farris, *The Hymns of Luke's Infancy Narrative;* and, for the latter, Craig Blomberg, "Midrash, Chiasmus, and the Outline of Luke's Central Section," in *Gospel Perspectives,* vol. 3, ed. R. T. France and David Wenham (Sheffield: JSOT Press, 1983), 217–61.

[47]See esp. Streeter, *Four Gospels,* 199–221; Vincent Taylor, *The Passion Narrative of St. Luke: A Critical and Historical Investigation,* ed. Owen E. Evans, SNTSMS 19

of his researches in Palestine, Luke put together a first edition of his gospel ("Proto-Luke"); then, after arriving in Rome and finding a copy of Mark (written recently in Rome), he integrated material from it into his final edition.[48] The hypothesis of a Proto-Luke has, of course, met with considerable criticism, it being argued that none of the reasons for positing Proto-Luke really demands the hypothesis.[49] And we should certainly not think of Proto-Luke as a gospel in its own right, but more as a first draft of what became the gospel of Luke. Still, while it must remain in the realm of unproven hypothesis, we think the proposal retains some merit.

Luke, of course, does not slavishly take over the sources that he uses. Some of his alterations involve an improvement in style relative to Mark. We may note one example among many. Mark, perhaps from Semitic influence, uses parataxis (constructions linked with a simple "and") a great deal; Luke tends to replace parataxis with genitive absolutes or other subordinate clauses. We may surmise that he treated his Q source the same way.[50] Luke also abbreviates what Mark has written by omitting details that are not essential for his purpose. For example, in the parable of the sower Luke has 90 words where Mark has 151 (Luke 8:4–8; Mark 4:1–9). Luke's omissions often involve incidents he has included elsewhere, apparently derived from one of his other sources. But the situation is complex, because Luke sometimes includes material from two stories, creating "doublets." Thus, Jesus' words about taking up the cross and following him in 9:23–24 seem to come from Mark 8:34–35; but the very similar 14:27 and 17:33 resemble Matthew 10:38–39 and may well have come from Q.

Luke also shares more material with John than does either Matthew or Mark. For example, both Luke and John mention Martha and Mary, Annas, and a disciple named Judas in addition to Judas Iscariot. Both have an interest in Jerusalem generally and in the temple. Both attribute Jesus' betrayal to the activity of Satan (Luke 22:3; John 13:27). Both include the detail that the ear of the high priest's servant that Peter cut off in Gethsemane was the *right* ear (Luke 22:50; John 18:10). And both tell us that Pilate three times declared that Jesus was innocent (Luke 23:4, 14, 22; John 18:38; 19:4, 6). The relationship between John and the Synoptics is a complicated subject. Most scholars doubt that John has used Luke. But it is possible that John has at least read Luke and that some of the similarities we noted above are due to that knowledge (see the discussion in chap. 6).

(Cambridge: Cambridge University Press, 1972); Friedrich Rehkopf, *Der lukanische Sonderquelle*, WUNT 5 (Tübingen: Mohr-Siebeck, 1959).

[48]But would the MS have survived the "shipwreck voyage"?

[49]See, e.g., Guthrie, 203–7; Fitzmyer, *Luke I–IX*, 90–91.

[50]On Luke's style vis-à-vis Mark, see esp. Fitzmyer, *Luke I–IX*, 107–8.

TEXT

In most New Testament books textual variation is comparatively minor, but in Luke and Acts the so-called "Western" text presents a more complex situation. This text, whose principal representatives are Codex Bezae (D) and the Old Latin manuscripts, includes quite a lot of material not found in the other textual traditions. In Luke, for example, D includes, after the story of the man working on the Sabbath (6:4), the words "And he said, 'You do not know what kind of spirit you are of, for the Son of Man did not come to destroy men's lives, but to save them'" (9:55); additional clauses in the Lord's Prayer (11:2–4); Jesus' agony in the garden (22:43); the languages used in the inscription on the cross (23:38); and the information that the stone before Jesus' tomb was one "which twenty men could scarcely roll" (23:53). The Western text is certainly old, for it was used by Justin and Tatian and others in the second century. Although it sometimes omits passages found in other text types, it more often adds material (as we have just seen in the case in Luke). The changes and additions clarify passages that the scribe apparently considered unclear. It tends to harmonize passages and remove other kinds of "difficulties."[51] Few of the Western text's additions are likely to represent the original; but they must be taken seriously (see chap. 7 for discussion of the Western text and Acts).

More significant for the gospel is a series of passages in which the Western text omits readings that are well attested elsewhere. Westcott and Hort labeled these passages "Western non-interpolations," a cumbersome expression designed to avoid casting any doubt on their cherished "neutral" text. They considered these passages to be rare occasions when the Western text preserved the better reading. They reasoned that since the Western text so consistently includes additional material and longer readings, special attention must be given to it when it omits passages. Some of these Western omissions are: the words to Martha, "You are worried and upset about many things, but few things are needed—or indeed only one" (10:41–42); the command to repeat the Lord's Supper together with the words about the cup following those about the bread (22:19b–20); the prayer for forgiveness of those who crucified Jesus (23:34); the words "he is not here; he has risen" (24:6); Peter's visit to the tomb (24:12); Jesus' showing his hands and feet (24:40); and the ascension (24:51).

Each of these texts must, of course, be considered on its own. But the general tendency of modern textual criticism is to look more favorably on the possible authenticity of these passages than did Westcott and Hort.[52] Papyri such

---

[51]See J. F. J. Klijn, *A Survey of the Researches into the Western Text of the Gospels and Acts,* part 1 (Utrecht: Kemink & Zoon, 1949); part 2, NovTSup 21 (Leiden: Brill, 1969).

[52]See Klyne Snodgrass, "Western Non-Interpolations," *JBL* 91 (1972): 369–79; Metzger, 191–93.

as P[75] (the oldest manuscript of this gospel, which dates from the end of the second century or the beginning of the third) and P[45] (about much the same date), as well as careful study of the text of the fathers has tended to show that Westcott and Hort's "neutral" text—what is today called the Alexandrian—goes back to the second century. And the preservation of this basic text type in uncials such as Codex Vaticanus (B) shows that it was copied faithfully through the years. It is an austere form of text, avoiding the picturesque elaborations that we find in the Western text. Most textual critics still consider it the best form of the text, although they do not accord it the kind of pure status that Westcott and Hort did. Certainly, readings preserved by the Western text must be given serious consideration, but without other support they will generally not be considered to represent the original text. Especially is this the case where D is the only Greek manuscript to support a reading (which happens with quite a few Western readings; the strength of supporting evidence is with the Old Latin). In any case, the wealth of textual evidence for Luke's gospel gives us assurance that we possess the text substantially as he wrote it.

The wealth of textual evidence for Luke's gospel gives us assurance that we possess the text substantially as he wrote it.

ADOPTION INTO THE CANON

Pinning down the date when Luke is first clearly referred to in the early church is difficult. The church fathers often used language from a source without giving any explicit reference. So whether language that is similar to that now found in Luke's gospel comes from that gospel, from a source used by Luke, or from some other tradition is often not easy to say. This kind of uncertainty confronts us as we face a number of passages in Clement of Rome (*1 Clem.* 13:2; 48:4), Polycarp (*Phil.* 2:3), and Ignatius (*Magn.* 10). These resemble passages in Luke, but we cannot be sure that they are quotations from the gospel itself. It is more likely that the *Didache* (late first or second century) and the *Gospel of Peter* (perhaps middle of the second century) used Luke. Justin Martyr certainly used Luke (or a harmony based on it), and *2 Clement* seems to have done the same. Marcion, of course, had an expurgated Luke as the one gospel in his canon. Some have argued that it was not our Luke that Marcion used, but an earlier source that both he and Luke employed, but evidence for this is lacking, and there seems no real doubt that it was the third gospel that formed the basis of Marcion's work. In any case, from this time onward there is no real doubt: Luke is universally accepted in the church as authoritative and part of the canon of sacred books.

LUKE'S GOSPEL IN RECENT STUDY

As the author of two volumes that trace the history of the Christian movement from its inception in Judea to its arrival in the capital of the Empire, Luke as a historian has naturally enough been a central topic of scholarly discussion.[53] Interest in Luke's abilities and success as a historian has not disappeared, especially in conjunction with Acts (see chap. 7). But attention has shifted in the last forty years to Luke's work as a theologian and as a narrator.

The onset of redaction criticism in the late 1950s focused attention on the evangelists as authors and on their theological motivations for writing as they did. The first significant redaction-critical work on Luke was Hans Conzelmann's *The Theology of Saint Luke,* and his monograph set the agenda for much recent discussion of Luke's theology. The original German title, *Die Mitte der Zeit,* "The Middle of Time," captures one of the book's central thrusts. Citing Luke 16:16, Conzelmann thought that Luke had introduced the idea of a three-stage salvation history: the period of Israel; the period of Jesus' ministry; the period of the church. Luke's gospel, of course, focuses on the second of those stages: the "middle of time." In itself, this scheme is neither problematic nor particularly noteworthy. But what made Conzelmann's proposal significant was his explanation of the origin of this salvation history and its consequences. Luke, Conzelmann suggests, was the first to draw up such a conception of history. And he does so in response to the problem created by the delay of the parousia. Jesus and the earliest Christians expected Jesus to return in glory at any time. As time went by and the parousia did not take place, doubts about the faith began to spring up. In response to this difficulty, Luke re-interprets eschatology to focus on the present experience of the kingdom and develops a conception of history that helps Christians find their place in the world. Jesus' ministry is transformed from the basis for proclamation into a history with meaning in its own right. And to give that history meaning, it is anchored in a previous history, the period of Israel. The period of Jesus' ministry, in turn, gives rise to the period of the church, the time in which Luke's readers must find their place. To help them discover meaning and security for the indefinitely prolonged period before the delayed return of Christ, Luke attributes new power and significance to the church. It becomes, in the book of Acts, an institution dispensing salvation through the sacraments. This way of viewing the period of the church has become known as "early Catholicism" (*Frühkatholismus*).

More will be said about "early Catholicism" in the chapters on Acts, the Pastoral Epistles, and 2 Peter. Suffice to say here that the basic premise of the scheme—that the early church was shaken when Jesus did not return immediately—is questionable. Certainly Luke's gospel focuses more on the presence of the kingdom and less on its future manifestation than do Mark and Matthew.

---

[53]"Broadly speaking it may be said that in the period before 1950 Luke was almost exclusively viewed as a historian" (W. C. van Unnik, "Luke-Acts, a Storm Center in Contemporary Scholarship," in *Studies in Luke-Acts,* ed. Leander Keck and J. Louis Martyn [Philadelphia: Fortress Press, 1966], 19).

But Luke has by no means abandoned future eschatology, and his approach falls well within the parameters of the typical New Testament eschatology tension between "now" and "not yet."[54]

Conzelmann's redaction-critical approach to Luke spurred many other studies of a similar nature. Indeed, Conzelmann's monograph was one of the key factors in turning Luke-Acts into what W. C. van Unnik called "a storm center in contemporary scholarship" during the 1960s and 70s.[55] Many of these studies followed Conzelmann's lead in almost entirely displacing Luke the historian with Luke the theologian.[56] Other redaction-critical approaches to Luke, however, used redaction-critical methods to analyze Luke's theological contribution without dismissing Luke's historical interests.

If the onset of redaction-critical techniques turned Luke-Acts into a "storm center" in scholarship, the more recent popularity of narrative analysis has created a "sea change" in approach.[57] Redaction critics compared Luke's gospel to sources and traditions and to the other gospels. Narrative critics generally ignore the issue of sources and tradition and study Luke in close conjunction with the book of Acts. Their concern is to use narrative analysis to uncover the teaching and theology of the two-volume literary work Luke-Acts. Key themes and words are traced through the two books; larger structural components are analyzed; comparisons are made with other similar works of literature from the ancient world.[58] The turn to narrative analysis is a welcome recognition that the Gospel of Luke must be interpreted as a careful and well-thought out literary production. And while we have registered some reservations about tying the gospel too closely to Acts, there is no doubt that the two books must be interpreted in relationship to each another. The danger in narrative criticism is that it is sometimes practiced in isolation from other approaches that must also factor into any finally determinative interpretation of Luke's gospel. Luke's use of sources does not tell us the whole story; but analysis of his use of Mark and comparison with Matthew can still help us understand what Luke is about. Nor can serious historical study of the time of Jesus be abandoned. Luke is not creating a work of literature from whole cloth as a novelist might go about his or her work.

---

[54]See especially E. Earle Ellis, *Eschatology in Luke* (Philadelphia: Fortress Press, 1972).

[55]"Luke-Acts, a Storm Center in Contemporary Scholarship," is the title of van Unnik's contribution to the volume *Studies in Luke-Acts*, published in 1966.

[56]The valuable book by I. Howard Marshall, *Luke: Historian and Theologian*, analyzes and critiques this movement.

[57]The phrase is from David P. Moessner and David L. Tiede, "Introduction: Two Books but One Story?" in *Jesus and the Heritage of Israel: Luke's Narrative Claim upon Israel's Legacy* (Harrisburg: Trinity Press International, 2000), 1–3.

[58]Some representative works are Tannehill, *The Narrative Unity of Luke-Acts;* Green, *The Gospel of Luke.*

He is narrating events that transpired in a particular time and place; and these "historical constraints" must be recognized.

THE CONTRIBUTION OF LUKE

Pride of place in Luke's contribution to our understanding of the faith must be given to his sweeping historical survey of the life of Christ. Only Luke takes us from the very beginning of the "Jesus story," the birth of John the Baptist, to its end, the ascension of Jesus. Along the way, Luke includes many stories of Jesus and teachings of Jesus not found in the other gospels. What does Luke teach us by adding this material to the tradition he takes over from Mark and Q? Four contributions deserve particular mention.

First, as several scholars have emphasized, is the central importance of God's plan in Luke-Acts.[59] The hymns in the infancy narrative set the whole story of Jesus in the context of God's promises in the Old Testament to his people Israel (see esp. 1:54–55, 68–79; 2:29–32). The same theme is taken up by Jesus himself in the programmatic declaration in the synagogue at Nazareth (4:18–19). What happens in the ministry of Jesus happens because God is working out a program that he had set in place long ago. Luke's frequent use of the word δεῖ (*dei,* "it is necessary") underscores this point. "It is necessary" that Jesus be in his Father's house (2:49), that he preach the good news of the kingdom in many cities (4:43), that, as a prophet, he perish in Jerusalem (13:33), that he stay in Zacchaeus's house (19:5), and, especially, that he die on the cross (9:22; 17:25; 22:37; 24:7). As Jesus summarizes in a climactic assertion at the end of the gospel: "Everything must [*dei*] be fulfilled that is written about me in the Law of Moses, the Prophets and the Psalms" (24:44). In the events of Jesus' birth, life, death, and resurrection, God is pursuing a plan, a plan revealed in the Old Testament, brought to its decisive point in Jesus' death and resurrection, but only finally fulfilled in the proclamation of the gospel to all nations. The theme of God's plan thus binds together the gospel and Acts.[60]

The fulfillment of God's plan provides the overarching structure for Luke's gospel. That plan aims at the provision of salvation for the world, and this focus on salvation constitutes Luke's *second* main contribution. Often singled out as the key thematic verse in the Gospel of Luke is 19:10, Jesus' closing comment

---

[59]E.g., Joel Green, *The Theology of the Gospel of Luke* (Cambridge: Cambridge University Press, 1995), 47; Robert C. Tannehill, "The Story of Israel within the Lukan Narrative," in *Jesus and the Heritage of Israel,* ed. David P. Moessner (Harrisburg: Trinity Press International, 1999), 325–39; D. L. Bock, "Gospel of Luke," *DJG,* 502–3; John Squires, "The Plan of God in the Acts of the Apostles," in *Witness to the Gospel: The Theology of Acts,* ed. I. Howard Marshall and David Peterson (Grand Rapids: Eerdmans, 1997), 20.

[60]See especially Tannehill, "Story of Israel."

on the Zacchaeus episode: "For the Son of Man came to seek and to save what was lost." Luke is the only synoptic evangelist to use the noun "salvation" (*sōtē-ria* four times [1:69, 71, 77; 19:9]; *sōtērion* twice [2:30; 3:6]) and "savior" (*sōtēr* [1:47; 2:11]), and he uses the verb "save" (*sōdzō*) more than any other book in the New Testament (although this is mainly because of Luke's greater length). Salvation is the thematic center of Luke's gospel.[61] It will be noted from the references cited above that many come in the birth narrative. Luke again uses the hymns of these chapters to set the tone for the ministry of Jesus to follow. In Jesus God is coming to his people as their savior. Luke emphasizes that this salvation is available in the present time through Jesus with frequent references to "today" (eleven times) and "now" (fourteen times). Salvation in Luke focuses especially on role-reversal, programmatically summarized in Mary's song of praise: "He [God] has performed mighty deeds with his arm; he has scattered those who are proud in their inmost thoughts. He has brought down rulers from their thrones but has lifted up the humble. He has filled the hungry with good things but has sent the rich away empty" (1:51–53). Mary's reference to rulers, the hungry, and the rich touches on a key facet of Luke's presentation of salvation: the coming of the kingdom reverses worldly status. But Luke's story of salvation is ultimately concerned with spiritual, not social or economic, status: Jesus has come to rescue the lost and those who are "far away" by providing for the forgiveness of sins (e.g., 1:77; 5:17–26; 7:48–50; 19:1–10; 24:46–47). As we would expect, the hymns of Luke 1–2 initially cast this salvation in terms of the deliverance of Israel in fulfillment of God's promises (cf. 1:68–75). But before we leave these chapters, we find also the announcement that this salvation will not only mean "the glory of your people Israel" but also "a light for revelation to the Gentiles" (2:29–32). The same point is made even more emphatically in 3:6, where Luke (alone among the evangelists) climaxes the quotation from Isaiah 40:3–5 with the promise that "all people will see God's salvation."

With this reference we introduce the *third* of Luke's noteworthy contributions: his emphasis on Gentiles as ultimate recipients of God's salvation. Luke by no means ignores Jews; the initial focus on the fulfillment of God's promises to Israel is not lost. But the notion of what that fulfillment will mean for both Israel and the Gentiles changes as the gospel unfolds. Jesus' universal significance is hinted at in Luke's genealogy, which traces Jesus' ancestry back to Adam, not to Abraham (as in Matthew). In his teaching in the Nazareth synagogue, Jesus rebukes the townspeople and reminds them of God's grace to the widow of Zarephath and Naaman the Syrian (4:25–27). Jesus commends a Gentile centurion for his faith (7:1–10) and makes a Samaritan the hero of one of his

---

[61]See esp. Marshall, who says, "It is our thesis that the idea of salvation supplies the key to the theology of Luke" (*Luke: Historian and Theologian*, 92; cf. also 116–18).

most famous parables (10:30–37; 17:16). These hints of the extension of God's grace to Gentiles in the gospel prepare the way, of course, for the inclusion of Gentiles in God's people that Luke is so concerned to emphasize in the book of Acts.

A *fourth* theme in Luke's gospel is the concern of Jesus for the outcasts of society. Jesus is constantly seen interacting with those on the margins of Jewish society: the poor (e.g., 1:46–55; 4:18; 6:20–23; 7:22; 10:21–22; 14:13, 21–24; 16:19–31; 21:1–4), "sinners" (e.g., those who did not abide by all the pharisaic rituals—5:27–32; 7:28, 30, 34, 36–50; 15:1–2; 19:7), and women (7:36–50; 8:1–3, 48; 10:38–42; 13:10–17; 24:1–12). Luke often pictures these outcasts as particularly responsive to the message of Jesus. He warns both explicitly and implicitly about the importance of putting aside the entanglements of this world in order to embrace freely and wholeheartedly the message of the kingdom.[62] This message has been seized on by certain theologians, especially liberation theologians, to argue that the poor and the oppressed are specially favored by God, while the rich and powerful are rejected. Passages such as Jesus' blessing on the poor and his corresponding "woe" on the rich (6:20, 24) could suggest just such a view. But we must recall that Jesus uses the language of "poor" and "rich" against the background of the Old Testament, where these terms held not only economic but social and spiritual significance. The "poor" are those who not only do not have much money but who also depend on God, and the "rich" are those who not only have money, but who use their wealth and power to oppress the poor. Translation of Luke's categories of "poor" and "rich" into our cultural categories must take account of these nuances.[63]

Another facet of Luke's interest in socioeconomic issues is his strong teaching about the need for disciples to reveal their sincerity in following Jesus by the way they handle their money. Several of Luke's additions to the gospel tradition focus on the matter of stewardship: John's admonition (3:10–14), the parable of the "rich fool" (12:13–21), the parable of the shrewd manager (16:1–13), the parable of the rich man and Lazarus (16:19–31), Jesus' encounter with Zacchaeus (19:1–10). What special factors in Luke's situation or audience led him to say so much on this matter cannot be known. But the present state of the church in the developed nations eloquently attests to the continuing need for such teaching.

---

[62]See especially Craig L. Blomberg, *Neither Poverty Nor Riches: A Biblical Theology of Material Possessions*, NSBT (Grand Rapids: Eerdmans, 1999), 111–46, 160–74.

[63]See, e.g., Charles H. Talbert, *Reading Luke* (New York: Crossroad, 1984), p. 70; Green, *Theology*, 79–94

BIBLIOGRAPHY

Loveday **Alexander**, *The Preface to Luke's Gospel: Literary Convention and Social Context in Luke 1:1–4 and Acts 1:1*, SNTSMS 78 (Cambridge: Cambridge University Press, 1993) ▮C. K. **Barrett**, *Luke the Historian in Recent Study* (London: Epworth, 1961) ▮Richard **Bauckham**, "For Whom Were the Gospels Written?" in *The Gospels for All Christians* (Grand Rapids: Eerdmans, 1998) ▮O. **Betz**, "The Kerygma of Luke," *Int* 22 (1968): 131–46 ▮Craig **Blomberg**, "Midrash, Chiasmus, and the Outline of Luke's Central Section," in *Gospel Perspectives*, vol. 3, ed. R. T. France and David Wenham (Sheffield: JSOT Press, 1983), 217–61 ▮idem, *Neither Poverty Nor Riches: A Biblical Theology of Material Possessions*, NSBT (Grand Rapids: Eerdmans, 1999) ▮Darrell L. **Bock**, "Gospel of Luke," in *DJG* ▮idem, *Luke 1:1–9:50*, BECNT (Grand Rapids: Baker, 1994) ▮idem, *Proclamation from Prophecy and Pattern: Lucan Old Testament Christology*, JSNTSup 12 (Sheffield: Sheffield Academic Press, 1987) ▮F. **Bovon**, *Luc le théologien: Vingt-cinq ans de recherches (1950–75)* (Neuchâtel: Delachaux & Niestlé, 1978) ▮idem, *Luke 1: A Commentary on the Gospel of Luke 1:1–9:50*, Hermeneia (Minneapolis: Augsburg/Fortress, 2002) ▮Schuyler **Brown**, *Apostasy and Perseverance in the Theology of Luke*, AnBib 36 (Rome: Pontifical Biblical Institute, 1969) ▮F. F. **Bruce**, *The Acts of the Apostles* (London: Tyndale, 1951) ▮Henry J. **Cadbury**, *The Making of Luke-Acts* (London: Macmillan, 1927) ▮idem, *The Style and Literary Method of Luke*, HTS 6 (Cambridge: Harvard University Press, 1919) ▮G. B. **Caird**, *The Gospel of St Luke* (Harmondsworth: Penguin, 1963) ▮J. Bradley **Chance**, *Jerusalem, the Temple, and the New Age in Luke-Acts* (Macon: Mercer University Press, 1988) ▮Hans **Conzelmann**, "Luke's Place in the Development of Early Christianity," in *Studies in Luke-Acts*, ed. Leander E. Keck and J. Louis Martyn (Nashville: Abingdon, 1966), 298–316 ▮idem, *The Theology of St Luke* (London: Faber & Faber, 1961) ▮J. M. **Creed**, *The Gospel According to St. Luke* (London: Macmillan, 1950) ▮M. **Dibelius**, *Studies in the Acts of the Apostles* (ET London: SCM, 1956) ▮J. **Drury**, *Tradition and Design in Luke's Gospel* (London: Darton, Longman & Todd, 1976) ▮E. Earle **Ellis**, *Eschatology in Luke* (Philadelphia: Fortress Press, 1972) ▮idem, *The Gospel of Luke*, 2nd. ed. (London: Marshall, Morgan & Scott, 1974) ▮Philip F. **Esler**, *Community and Gospel in Luke-Acts*, SNTSMS 57 (Cambridge: Cambridge University Press, 1987) ▮A. **Farrer**, "On Dispensing with Q," in *Studies in the Gospels*, ed. D. E. Nineham (Oxford: Oxford University Press, 1955), 55–58 ▮Stephen **Farris**, *The Hymns of Luke's Infancy Narratives: Their Origin, Meaning, and Significance*, JSNTSup 9 (Sheffield: JSOT Press, 1985) ▮Joseph A. **Fitzmyer**, *The Gospel According to Luke*, 2 vols. (New York: Doubleday, 1983–85) ▮Helmut **Flender**, *St Luke, Theologian of Redemptive History* (London: SPCK, 1967) ▮E. **Franklin**, *Christ the Lord: A Study in the Purpose and Theology of Luke-Acts* (London: SPCK, 1975) ▮David **Gooding**, *According to Luke: A New Exposition of the Third Gospel* (Grand Rapids: Eerdmans, 1987) ▮Michael D. **Goulder**,

Luke: A New Paradigm, 2 vols., JSNTSup 20 (Sheffield: JSOT Press, 1989) ∎Joel
B. **Green**, *The Gospel of Luke*, NICNT (Grand Rapids: Eerdmans, 1997) ∎idem,
The Theology of the Gospel of Luke (Cambridge: Cambridge University Press, 1995)
∎Adolf von **Harnack**, *Luke the Physician* (New York: Putnam, 1907) ∎R. G.
Heard, "The Old Gospel Prologues," *JTS* 6 (1955): 1–16 ∎Martin **Hengel**, *The
Four Gospels and the One Gospel of Jesus Christ* (Harrisburg: Trinity Press Interna-
tional, 2000) ∎W. K. **Hobart**, *The Medical Language of St. Luke* (Dublin: Hodges,
Figgis, 1982) ∎J. **Jervell**, *The People of God: A New Look at Luke-Acts* (Min-
neapolis: Augsburg, 1973) ∎Luke T. **Johnson**, *The Literary Function of Possessions
in Luke-Acts*, SBLDS 39 (Missoula: SP, 1977) ∎Donald **Juel**, *Luke-Acts: The
Promise of History* (Atlanta: John Knox, 1985) ∎Robert J. **Karris**, *Luke: Artist and
Theologian. Luke's Passion Account as Literature* (New York: Paulist, 1985) ∎E.
Käsemann, *Essays on New Testament Themes* (London: SCM, 1964) ∎Leander E.
Keck and J. Louis **Martyn**, *Studies in Luke-Acts* (Nashville: Abingdon, 1966) ∎J.
F. J. **Klijn**, , *A Survey of the Researches in the Western Text of the Gospels and Acts:
Part One* (Utrecht: Kemink & Zoon, 1949), and *Part Two* (1949–1969), NovTSup
21 (Leiden: Brill, 1969) ∎William L. **Lane**, *The Gospel According to Mark*, NICNT
(Grand Rapids: Eerdmans, 1974) ∎A. R. C. **Leaney**, *The Gospel According to St
Luke*, BNTC, 2nd ed. (London: Black, 1966) ∎Walter L. **Liefeld**, "Luke," in *EBC*
∎J. B. **Lightfoot**, *Notes on Epistles of St Paul* (London: Macmillan, 1904) ∎Allan
J. **McNicol**, David L. **Dungan**, and David B. **Peabody**, *Beyond the Q Impasse:
Luke's Use of Matthew* (Valley Forge: Trinity Press International, 1996) ∎R. **Mad-
dox**, *The Purpose of Luke-Acts* (Edinburgh: T. & T. Clark, 1982) ∎I. Howard **Mar-
shall**, *The Gospel of Luke: A Commentary on the Greek Text*, NIGTC (Grand
Rapids: Eerdmans, 1978) ∎idem, *Luke: Historian and Theologian*, 2nd ed. (Grand
Rapids: Zondervan, 1988) ∎Donald G. **Miller**, ed., *Jesus and Man's Hope*, vol. 1
(Pittsburgh: Pittsburgh Theological Seminary, 1970) ∎David P. **Moessner**, ed.,
Jesus and the Heritage of Israel: Luke's Narrative Claim upon Israel's Legacy (Har-
risburg: Trinity Press International, 2000) ∎Leon **Morris**, "Luke and Early
Catholicism," in *Studying the New Testament Today*, I, ed. John H. Skilton (Nut-
ley: Presbyterian & Reformed, 1974), 60–75 ∎idem, *Luke: An Introduction and
Commentary*, 2nd ed., TNTC (Leicester: IVP/Grand Rapids: Eerdmans, 1988)
∎John **Nolland**, *Luke 1–9:20*, WBC (Dallas: Word, 1989) ∎Mikeal C. **Parsons**
and Richard I. **Pervo**, *Rethinking the Unity of Luke and Acts* (Minneapolis: Fortress
Press, 1993) ∎Alfred **Plummer**, *A Critical and Exegetical Commentary on the
Gospel According to S. Luke* (Edinburgh: T. & T. Clark, 1928) ∎Friedrich
Rehkopf, *Der lukanische Sonderquelle*, WUNT 5 (Tübingen: Mohr-Siebeck, 1959)
∎Bo **Reicke**, "Synoptic Prophecies of the Destruction of Jerusalem," in *Studies in
New Testament and Early Christian Literature*, ed. D. E. Aune (Leiden: Brill, 1972),
121–33 ∎M. **Rese**, *Alttestamentliche Motive in der Christologie des Lukas* (Güter-
sloh: Gerd Mohn, 1969) ∎J. A. T. **Robinson**, *Redating the New Testament*
(Philadelphia: Westminster, 1976) ∎Leopold **Sabourin**, *The Gospel According to*

St Luke: Introduction and Commentary (Bombay: St. Paul, 1984) ▮Daryl D. **Schmidt**, "Rhetorical Influences and Genre: Luke's Preface and the Rhetoric of Hellenistic Historiography," in *Jesus and the Heritage of Israel*, ed. David P. Moessner (Harrisburg: Trinity Press International, 1999), 27–60 ▮David Peter **Seccombe**, *Possessions and the Poor in Luke-Acts* (Linz: SNTU, 1982) ▮Robert B. **Sloan** Jr., *The Favorable Year of the Lord: A Study of Jubilary Theology in the Gospel of Luke* (Austin: SP, 1977) ▮Klyne **Snodgrass**, "Western Non-Interpolations," *JBL* 91 (1972): 369–79 ▮Gregory E. **Sterling**, *Historiography and Self-Definition: Josephus, Luke-Acts, and Apologetic Historiography*, NovTSup 44 (Leiden: Brill, 1992) ▮B. H. **Streeter**, *The Four Gospels* (London: Macmillan, 1930) ▮Charles H. **Talbert**, *Literary Patterns, Theological Themes, and the Genre of Luke-Acts*, SBLMS 20 (Missoula: SP, 1974) ▮idem, *Reading Luke* (New York: Crossroad, 1984) ▮idem, ed., *Perspectives on Luke-Acts* (Edinburgh: T. & T. Clark, 1978) ▮Robert C. **Tannehill**, *The Narrative Unity of Luke-Acts: A Literary Interpretation*, 2 vols. (Minneapolis: Fortress Press, 1990) ▮idem, "The Story of Israel within the Lukan Narrative," in *Jesus and the Heritage of Israel*, ed. David P. Moessner (Harrisburg: Trinity Press International, 1999), 325–39 ▮V. **Taylor**, *Behind the Third Gospel* (Oxford: Clarendon Press, 1926) ▮idem, *The Passion Narrative of St. Luke: A Critical and Historical Investigation*, ed. Owen E. Evans, SNTSMS 19 (Cambridge: Cambridge University Press, 1972) ▮M. M. B. **Turner**, "The Sabbath, Sunday, and the Law in Luke/Acts," in *From Sabbath to Lord's Day*, ed. D. A. Carson (Grand Rapids: Zondervan, 1982), 99–157 ▮W. C. **van Unnik**, "Luke-Acts, a Storm Center in Contemporary Scholarship," in *Studies in Luke-Acts*, ed. Leander Keck and J. Louis Martyn (Philadelphia: Fortress Press, 1966), 15–32 ▮J. **Verheyden**, "The Unity of Luke-Acts: What Are We Up To?" in *The Unity of Luke-Acts*, ed. J. Verheyden, BETL 142 (Leuven: Leuven University Press, 1999), 3–56 ▮John **Wenham**, *Redating Matthew, Mark, and Luke: A Fresh Assault on the Synoptic Problem* (Downers Grove: IVP, 1992) ▮Michael **Wilcock**, *Savior of the World: The Message of Luke's Gospel* (Leicester: IVP, 1979) ▮Ben **Witherington** III, *The Acts of the Apostles: A Socio-Rhetorical Commentary* (Grand Rapids: Eerdmans, 1998).

CHAPTER SIX

JOHN

CONTENTS

Like the other canonical gospels, John's gospel sets out to tell the story of Jesus' origins, ministry, death, and resurrection. Like them, it does not purport to be neutral. The evangelist intends to engender faith (20:30–31), and to that end he shapes his witness with the needs of his readers in mind.[1]

Like many other facets of the Gospel of John, its basic structure seems fairly simple until one starts to think more deeply about it. Doubtless this complexity wrapped in simplicity is the reason why scores of studies on John's structure have been published during the last few decades.

On the face of it, the fourth gospel offers a prologue (1:1–18) and an epilogue, or appendix (21:1–25), between which are the two central sections, 1:19–12:50 and 13:1–20:31. Under the influence of two or three influential scholars, these are now frequently designated, respectively, the Book of Signs and the Book of Glory,[2] or the Book of Signs and the Book of the Passion.[3]

Nevertheless, the designation "Book of Signs" makes it sound as if the signs are restricted to 1:19–12:50, whereas 20:30–31 makes it clear that from the evangelist's perspective the *entire* gospel is a book of signs: the passion and resurrection of Jesus is the greatest sign of all. Moreover, although Jesus' passion is related in chapters 13–20, the passion narrative itself does not begin until chapter 18. If chapters 13–17 can be included on the ground that they are thematically tied to

---

[1]At several points this chapter has used, with permission, material from D. A. Carson, *The Gospel According to John,* PNTC (Grand Rapids: Eerdmans, 1990)—sometimes verbatim, more frequently in condensed form.

[2]R. E. Brown, *The Gospel According to John* (Garden City: Doubleday, 1966–70), cxxxviii–cxxxix.

[3]C. H. Dodd, *The Interpretation of the Fourth Gospel* (Cambridge: Cambridge University Press, 1953), 289.

the passion, so also are many passages in chapters 1–12 (e.g., 1:29, 36; 6:35ff.; 11:49–52).

Others have advocated a quite different structure. Wyller,[4] for example, holds that 10:22–29 is the "structural summit" of the work, the "change of fate" of the hero, around which the rest of the material is organized. Despite the superficial plausibility of his argument, it is difficult to believe, on thematic grounds, that these verses have quite the structural importance Wyller assigns to them, and almost impossible to believe that Plato's simile of the cave is the most plausible model for the structure of a gospel. Another scholar has detected a massive concentric structure patterned after the concentric structure of the prologue.[5] However, structures that are so complex and disputed as not to be intuitively obvious should not be assigned much credibility.

Trying to account for all the complexity in John, one recent and important discussion of the structure of John's gospel finds major chiasms and what the author, George Mlakushyil, calls bridge-pericopes and bridge-sections—sections that fit into two or more structured units and that tie them together.[6] For instance, he suggests that 2:1–12:50 might be called the Book of Jesus' Signs, that 11:1–20:29 is the Book of Jesus' Hour, and that the overlapping chapters, 11–12, constitute a bridge section. Although this or that detail may be disputed, he does succeed in showing how unified and tightly organized the fourth gospel is. Many have pointed out, for instance, that individual sections of various length are neatly brought to a close (e.g., 1:18; 4:42; 4:53–54; 10:40–42; 12:44–50; 20:30–31; 21:25).

One of the reasons that critics find so many mutually exclusive structures in John is that his repeated handling of only a few themes makes it possible to postulate all kinds of parallels and chiasms. Another is that various structures seem to serve as overlays to other structures. For instance, it has often been noted that the section 2:1–4:54 reflects a geographic *inclusio* (i.e., a literary device that both introduces and concludes a passage by the same literary feature): the action moves from Cana to Cana. But although that device helps us see the boundaries of this unit, it is less than clear that Cana per se is so important in Johannine thought that it should be accorded paramount *theological* significance, beyond its minor role in helping readers to follow the movement of the text.[7]

---

[4]Egil A. Wyller, "In Solomon's Porch: A Henological Analysis of the Architectonic of the Fourth Gospel," *ST* 42 (1988): 151–67.

[5]Jeffrey Lloyd Staley, *The Print's First Kiss: A Rhetorical Investigation of the Implied Reader in the Fourth Gospel*, SBLDS 82 (Atlanta: SP, 1985).

[6]George Mlakushyil, *The Christocentric Literary Structure of the Fourth Gospel*, AnBib 117 (Rome: Pontifical Biblical Institute, 1987).

[7]See further Raymond E. Brown, *An Introduction to the Gospel of John*, ed. Francis J. Moloney (New York: Doubleday, 2003), 298–316.

Following the prologue (1:1–18), Jesus discloses himself in word and deed (1:19–10:42). This large unit begins with a prelude to Jesus' public ministry (1:19–51). As in the synoptic tradition, John the Baptist is first introduced: his relation to Jesus is articulated (1:19–28), as is his public witness concerning Jesus (1:29–34). The prelude ends with reports as to how Jesus gains his first disciples (1:35–51).

The rest of this first large unit (1:19–10:42) may be divided into three sections. The first reports Jesus' early ministry: his signs, works, and words (2:1–4:54). This includes the first sign, namely, the changing of the water into wine (2:1–11), the clearing of the temple (2:12–17), and the utterance about Jesus' replacing the temple (2:18–22). The inadequate faith of many who trust him at this juncture (2:23–25) sets the stage for the exchange between Jesus and Nicodemus (3:1–15), the dialogue rapidly turning to monologue. Twice in this chapter the evangelist himself apparently offers his own extended comment, the first at this point (3:16–21), and the second after his description of John the Baptist's continuing witness concerning Jesus (3:22–30, followed by 3:31–36). On his way to Galilee, Jesus stops in Samaria and leads both a Samaritan woman and many of her countrymen to faith in himself (4:1–42). The section is capped by the second sign, the healing of the official's son (4:43–54).

In the next section (5:1–7:53), there are more signs, works, and words, but now in the context of rising opposition. The healing of the paralytic at the pool of Bethesda (5:1–15), which connects sin and illness, is performed on the Sabbath, and this triggers some opposition, which Jesus quickly transforms into a *christological* question, especially regarding the nature of his sonship to the Father (5:16–30). These central christological claims give rise to treatment of the witnesses concerning Jesus (5:31–47). The feeding of the five thousand (6:1–15) and the walking on the water (6:16–21) serve to introduce the bread of life discourse (6:22–58), where Jesus' claims that he is himself the true manna (esp. 6:27–34), the bread of life (6:35–48) that must be eaten. This gives rise to more hesitations: opinion is divided over him, and even some of his disciples turn against him, while he himself retains the initiative in determining who truly are his followers (6:59–71). Skepticism and uncertainty regarding him continue, even among members of his own family (7:1–13). This means that the first round of exchanges at the Feast of Tabernacles (7:14–44), climaxing in his promise to pour out the eschatological Spirit consequent on his own glorification (7:37–44), is frankly confrontational and leads to the first organized opposition from the Jewish authorities (7:45–52).

After the pericope of the woman caught in adultery (7:53–8:11), which we believe was not part of the original text (see discussion below in the section "Text"), the last section (8:12–10:42) reports climactic signs, works, and words in the context of radical confrontation. The second round of exchanges at the Feast of Tabernacles (8:12–59) ends with Jesus telling the authorities they are children of the devil, while he himself is none less than the "I am"—and this sparks off a futile attempt to stone him to death. The healing of the man born blind (9:1–41), in which no connection between sin and the man's condition is allowed, comes to its climax with the denunciation of those who think they see. In chapter 10, Jesus presents himself as the good shepherd of the sheep. The effect is to make his own messianic flock the one locus of the people of God, with predictable reactions from the Jews (10:1–21). At the Feast of Dedication, Jesus' claims to be both Messiah and Son of God engender open opposition (10:22–39), prompting Jesus to make a strategic retreat to the area where John the Baptist had earlier baptized—a retreat that prompts the reader to recall John's true witness and that is nevertheless accompanied by growing numbers of people who are placing their faith in Jesus (10:40–42).

Although many include the next unit, 11:1–12:50, as part of the Book of Signs, there appear to be good reasons for treating these chapters as something of a transition. The account of the death and resurrection of Lazarus (11:1–44) is both a foil and an anticipation of Jesus' death and resurrection and directly leads to the judicial decision to kill Jesus (11:45–54). In the next section (11:55–12:36), set during the "Jewish Passover" (11:55–57) in anticipation of the death of the true Passover lamb, Mary anoints Jesus in anticipation of his death, thereby displaying sacrificial love for him—the only kind of any value (12:1–11); the triumphal entry announces Jesus' kingship, but the ominous signs are already present that this kingship will be unlike any other (12:12–19); and the arrival of the Gentiles triggers Jesus' announcement of the dawning "hour" of his death and exaltation (12:20–36). This transitional unit concludes with a theology of unbelief, that is, theological reflections that reveal the nature and inevitability of unbelief (12:37–50).

The final major unit of the book depicts Jesus' self-disclosure in his cross and exaltation (13:1–20:31). It opens with the Last Supper (13:1–30), but instead of preserving any report of the institution of the Lord's Supper, John recalls how Jesus washed his disciples' feet (13:1–17), an act that simultaneously anticipated the unique cleansing effected by his impending death and left an example for his disciples to emulate. Jesus' prediction of the betrayal (13:18–30) leaves no doubt that he remains in charge of his own destiny, in submission to his Father's will. The so-called farewell discourse that follows—partly dialogue and partly monologue—is conveniently broken up into two parts (13:31–14:31 and 15:1–16:33). In some ways this farewell discourse explains the significance of the last sign—Jesus' own death and exaltation—*before* the sign itself takes place and thus becomes a theology of the place of Jesus and his death and glorification in the stream of redemptive history, including the role and function of the promised Paraclete, the Holy Spirit whom Jesus bestows on believers in consequence of his exaltation. There follows the prayer of Jesus (17:1–26), in which Jesus prays for his own glorification (17:1–5), for his disciples (17:6–19), for those who will later believe (17:20–23), and, climactically, for the perfection of all believers so as to see Jesus' glory (17:24–26). The trial and passion of Jesus follow (18:1–19:42), with particular emphasis on the nature of Jesus' kingship. The resurrection of Jesus (20:1–31) includes not only several resurrection appearances but the remarkable saying regarding the gift of the Spirit and the forgiveness of sins (20:19–23) and the equally remarkable confession of Thomas, "My Lord and my God!" (20:28). This large unit ends with a concise statement of the fourth gospel's purpose (20:30–31).

The epilogue (21:1–25) not only ties up several loose ends (e.g., Peter's restoration to service) but, in symbolic ways, it points to the growth of the church and the diversity of gifts and callings within the church. Appropriately, it ends with the greatness of Jesus (21:25).

AUTHOR

The fourth gospel does not explicitly assert its author's name: like the Synoptics, it is formally anonymous. As far as we can prove, the title "According to John" was attached to it as soon as the four canonical gospels began to circulate together as "the fourfold gospel." In part, no doubt, this was to distinguish it from the rest of the collection; but it may have served as the title from the beginning (see chap. 3 above, on Matthew). But even if the attribution "According to John" was added two or three decades after the book was published, the observation of Bruce is suggestive: "It is noteworthy that, while the four canonical gospels could afford to be published anonymously, the apocryphal gospels which began to appear from the mid-second century onwards claimed (falsely) to be written by apostles or other persons associated with the Lord."[8]

External Evidence

Although there are several earlier documents, both within the orthodox stream and within Gnosticism, that allude to the fourth gospel or quote it (see the discussion below), the first writer to quote unambiguously from the fourth gospel and to ascribe the work to John was Theophilus of Antioch (c. A.D. 181). Before this date, however, several writers, including Tatian (a student of Justin Martyr), Claudius Apollinaris (bishop of Hierapolis), and Athenagoras, unambiguously quote from the fourth gospel as from an authoritative source. This pushes us back to Polycarp and Papias, information about whom derives primarily from Irenaeus (end of the second century) and Eusebius, the historian of the early church (fourth century). Polycarp was martyred in 156 at the age of eighty-six. There is no reason therefore to deny the truth of the claims that he associated with the apostles in Asia (John, Andrew, Philip) and was "entrusted

---

[8]F. F. Bruce, *The Gospel of John* (Basingstoke: Pickering & Inglis, 1983), 1.

with the oversight of the Church in Smyrna by those who were eye-witnesses and ministers of the Lord" (*H.E.* 3.36).

Irenaeus knew Polycarp personally, and it is Polycarp who mediates to us the most important information about the fourth gospel. Writing to Florinus, Irenaeus recalls:

> I remember the events of those days more clearly than those which have happened recently, for what we learn as children grows up with the soul and becomes united to it, so I can speak even of the place in which the blessed Polycarp sat and disputed, how he came in and went out, the character of his life, the appearance of his body, the discourse which he made to the people, how he reported his converse with John and with the others who had seen the Lord, how he remembered their words, and what were the things concerning the Lord which he had heard from them, including his miracles and his teaching,[9] and how Polycarp had received them from the eyewitnesses of the word of life, and reported all things in agreement with the Scriptures. (*H.E.* 5.20.5–6)

Most scholars recognize that this "John," certainly a reference to John the apostle, the son of Zebedee, is (so far as Irenaeus is concerned) none other than the John whom he emphatically insists is the fourth evangelist. For Irenaeus, that the gospel should be fourfold (in the sense already described) was as natural as that there should be four winds. As for the fourth gospel itself, he wrote, "John the disciple of the Lord, who leaned back on his breast, published the gospel while he was resident at Ephesus in Asia" (*Adv. Haer.* 2.1.2). In other words, the name of the fourth evangelist is John and is to be identified with the beloved disciple of John 13:23.

The evidence of Papias similarly depends on secondary sources. Papias was a contemporary of Polycarp and may himself have been a student of John (Irenaeus, *Adv. Haer.* 5.33.4, affirms it; Eusebius, *H.E.* 3.39.2, denies it). That Eusebius does not mention that Papias cited the fourth gospel is irrelevant: Eusebius's stated purpose was to discuss the disputed parts of the New Testament as well as some of those people who linked the first century with what follows, rather than to provide a list of citations regarding "acknowledged" books.[10]

Another piece of evidence regarding Papias is harder to evaluate. About A.D. 140 an eccentric follower of the writings of Paul, Marcion, who had become convinced that only this apostle had truly followed the teachings of Jesus

---

[9]The translation is from the Loeb edition of Eusebius, except for this clause, where the Loeb edition clearly errs.

[10]In this connection, however, it is rather remarkable that 1 John should be mentioned, since it *was* universally accepted. Perhaps, as some have suggested, it is because it belongs to the so-called General, or Catholic, Epistles, which constituted a rather exceptional group of writings.

while all the others had relapsed into Judaism, went to Rome to try to convince the church there of his views. He argued, unsuccessfully, that ten letters of Paul and one gospel, a mutilated version of Luke, comprised the proper New Testament canon. Marcion was so dangerous that he succeeded in arousing responses. In particular, the so-called anti-Marcionite prologues to the gospels have been viewed as part of these responses (though it must be admitted that some scholars think they emerged at a later period). The anti-Marcionite prologue to John has come down to us in a rather corrupt Latin version. It tells us that the Gospel of John was published while John was still alive and was written down at John's dictation by Papias, a man from Hierapolis and one of John's near disciples. As for Marcion, he had been expelled by John himself. This information, the prologue argues, derives from the five exegetical books of Papias himself: the reference is to his *Exegesis of the Dominical Logia,* which survived into the Middle Ages in some libraries in Europe but which is regrettably no longer extant.

Some of the information provided by the anti-Marcionite prologue is clearly mistaken. It is extremely doubtful that John excommunicated Marcion: the chronology is stretched too thin. Moreover, it has been suggested that Papias, for his part, may have said that the churches or certain disciples "wrote down" what John said and was subsequently misquoted as meaning "I wrote down," since in Greek the latter may be formally indistinguishable from "they wrote down."[11] Even so, there is no doubt in this document that John himself was responsible for the fourth gospel.

Not only Irenaeus but Clement of Alexandria and Tertullian provide firm second-century evidence for the belief that the apostle John wrote this gospel. According to Eusebius (*H.E.* 6.14.7), Clement wrote, "But that John, last of all, conscious that the outward facts had been set forth in the Gospels, was urged on by his disciples, and, divinely moved by the Spirit, composed a spiritual Gospel." A more enigmatic and, in its details, less believable version of the same development is preserved in the Muratorian Canon, the earliest orthodox list of New Testament books to come down to us, probably from A.D. 170–80. It tells us not only that John's fellow disciples and bishops urged him to write but that by a dream or prophecy it was revealed to Andrew that John should in fact take up the task, writing in his own name, but that the others should review his work and contribute to it. Most scholars take this to be someone's deduction from John 21:24.

Some indirect evidence is in certain respects much more impressive. Tatian, a student of Justin Martyr, composed the first harmony of the fourfold

---

[11]In the imperfect tense, ἀπέγραφον (*apegraphon*) means either "I wrote down" or "they wrote down"; in the aorist tense, there is normally a formal distinction: "I wrote down" is ἀπέγραψα (*apegrapsa*), while "they wrote down" is ἀπέγραψαν (*apegrapsan*). But even this distinction could be blurred; see J. B. Lightfoot, *Essays on the Work Entitled "Supernatural Religion"* (London: Macmillan, 1889), 214.

gospel: he took the books apart and wove them together into one continuous narrative known as the *Diatessaron*. First prepared in Greek, this harmony exerted an enormous influence in its Syriac translation. But the crucial point to observe is that it is the Gospel of John that provides the framework into which the other three gospels are fitted. This could not have been the case had there been questions about the authenticity of the book.

Indeed, by the end of the second century the only people who denied Johannine authorship to the fourth gospel were the so-called *Alogoi*—a substantivized adjective meaning "witless ones," used by the orthodox as a pun to refer to those who rejected the *Logos* (the "Word" of John 1:1) doctrine expounded in the fourth gospel, and therefore the fourth gospel itself. (Epiphanius gave them this name in *Haer.* 51.3; they are probably the same group mentioned by Irenaeus in *Adv. Haer.* 3.11.9.) Even here, there were sometimes competing forces at work. For instance, Gaius, an elder in the Roman church who was one of the *Alogoi*, maintained orthodoxy at every point except in his rejection of John's gospel and the Apocalypse. At least part of his motivation, however, was his virulent opposition to Montanism, an uncontrolled charismatic movement arising in the middle of the second century that claimed that its leader, Montanus, was the mouthpiece of the promised Paraclete. Since all of the Paraclete sayings that refer to the Spirit are found in John's gospel (14:16, 26; 15:26; 16:7–15), Gaius did not need much persuading to side with the *Alogoi* on this point.

> *From the end of the second century on, there is virtual agreement in the church as to the authority, canonicity, and authorship of the Gospel of John. An argument from silence in this case proves impressive.*

Certainly from the end of the second century on, there is virtual agreement in the church as to the authority, canonicity, and authorship of the Gospel of John. An argument from silence in this case proves impressive: "It is significant that Eusebius, who had access to many works that are now lost, speaks without reserve of the fourth gospel as the unquestioned work of St. John."[12] The silence is most significant precisely because it was Eusebius's concern to discuss the doubtful cases.

The external evidence that maintains that the fourth evangelist was none other than the apostle John, then, is virtually unanimous, though not impressively early. But even if we must turn to Irenaeus, toward the end of the second century, to find one of the first totally unambiguous witnesses, his personal connection with Polycarp, who knew John, means the distance in terms of personal memories is not very great. Even Dodd, who discounts the view that the apostle John wrote the fourth gospel, considers the external evidence formidable, adding, "Of any external evidence to the contrary that could be called cogent I am not aware."[13]

---

[12]B. F. Westcott, *The Gospel According to St John: The Greek Text with Introduction and Notes* (London: John Murray, 1908), 1:lix.

[13]C. H. Dodd, *Historical Tradition in the Fourth Gospel* (Cambridge: Cambridge University Press, 1963), 12; cf. J. A. T. Robinson, *The Priority of John* (London: SCM, 1985), 99–104.

The fact remains that, despite support for Johannine authorship by a few front-rank scholars in this century and by many popular writers, a large majority of contemporary scholars reject this view. As we shall see, much of their argumentation turns on their reading of the *internal* evidence. Nevertheless, it requires their virtual dismissal of the external evidence. This is particularly regrettable. Most historians of antiquity, other than New Testament scholars, could not so easily set aside evidence as plentiful and as uniform.

One way of circumventing the force of the external evidence is by appealing to the words of Papias, as reported and interpreted by Eusebius, in support of the hypothesis that there were two Johns. Papias writes (according to Eusebius): "And if anyone chanced to come who had actually been a follower of the elders, I would enquire as to the discourses of the elders, what Andrew or what Peter said, or what Philip, or what Thomas or James, or what John or Matthew or any other of the Lord's disciples; and things which Aristion and John the elder, disciples of the Lord, say." Eusebius then comments: "Here it is worth noting that twice in his enumeration he mentions the name of John: the former of these Johns he puts in the same list with Peter and James and Matthew and the other apostles, clearly indicating the evangelist; but the latter he places with the others, in a separate clause, outside the number of the apostles, placing Aristion before him; and he clearly calls him 'elder'" (*H.E.* 3.39.4–5).[14] From this passage, many have inferred that it was this second John, a disciple of John the son of Zebedee, who wrote the fourth gospel. Perhaps, indeed, Irenaeus and Theophilus and other early Fathers confused their Johns.[15]

But recent study has shown that this appeal to Papias is precarious, for four reasons.

1. It is now widely recognized that whereas Eusebius makes a distinction between apostles and elders, understanding that the latter are disciples of the former and therefore second-generation Christians, Papias himself makes no such distinction. In the terms of Papias, "the discourses of the elders" means the teaching of Andrew, Peter, and the other apostles. It is Eusebius who elsewhere writes, "Papias, of whom we are now speaking, acknowledges that he

---

[14]In this instance we have followed the translation of H. J. Lawlor and J. E. L. Oulton, *Eusebius: The Ecclesiastical History and the Martyrs of Palestine* (1927; reprint, London: SPCK, 1954), 1.89, since it observes distinctions in the Greek text overlooked by the more popular Loeb edition.

[15]To mention but three who follow this line with varying degrees of confidence, see Ben Witherington III, *John's Wisdom: A Commentary on the Fourth Gospel* (Louisville: Westminster John Knox Press, 1995), 16; Francis J. Moloney, *The Gospel of John*, SacPag 4 (Collegeville: Liturgical Press, 1998), 8; D. Moody Smith, *John,* ANTC (Nashville: Abingdon, 1999), 26–27.

received the discourses of the apostles from those who had been their followers" (*H.E.* 3.39.7). Transparently, that is not what Papias said.[16]

2. In the Papias quotation, John is designated "the elder" precisely because he is being grouped with the elders just mentioned, that is, with the apostles. It is worth noting that "apostle" and "elder" come together with a common referent in 1 Peter 5:1. Indeed, the Greek syntax Papias employs favors the view that "Aristion and John the elder" means something like "Aristion and the aforementioned elder John."[17] Not only here but in *H.E.* 3.39.14, it is John and not Aristion who is designated "the elder." In choosing to refer to the apostles as elders, Papias may well be echoing the language of 3 John (on the assumption that Papias thought that epistle was written by the apostle John).[18]

3. It appears that the distinction Papias is making in his two lists is not between apostles and elders of the next generation but between first-generation witnesses who have died (what they *said*) and first-generation witnesses who are still alive (what they *say*). Aristion, then, can be linked with John, not because neither is an apostle, but because both are first-generation disciples of the Lord. And this supports the witness of Irenaeus, who says that Papias, not less than Polycarp, was "a hearer of John."

4. In any case, Eusebius had his own agenda. He so disliked the apocalyptic language of Revelation that he was only too glad to find it possible to assign its authorship to a John other than the apostle, and he seizes on "John the elder" as he has retrieved him from Papias.[19]

Martin Hengel has recently devoted an entire monograph to the thesis that it was John the elder, not John the apostle, who was the author of the penultimate draft of the fourth gospel (which then, after his death, was lightly edited, with 21:24–25 also being added).[20] But Hengel's "elder" is not the second-century disciple of the aged apostle that many modern scholars have reconstructed. Hengel argues that "John the elder" is none other than the "beloved disciple" (13:23; 19:26–27; 20:2–9; 21:24), a Palestinian Jew who was a contemporary of Jesus and an eyewitness of at least some events in Jesus' life, but not John the son of Zebedee. Even Hengel admits his "hypothesis may sound fantastic."[21] He is

---

[16]See J. B. Lightfoot, *Essays* (London: Macmillan, 1893), 58ff.

[17]So C. S. Petrie, "The Authorship of 'The Gospel According to Matthew': A Reconstruction of the External Evidence," *NTS* 14 (1967–68): 21.

[18]Those who instead preserve a distinction between the apostles and the elders in Papias's words must introduce a couple of rather clumsy ellipses: see, inter alios, Richard Bauckham, "The Eyewitnesses and the Gospel Traditions," *JSHJ* 1 (2003): 31–32.

[19]Cf. G. M. Lee, *SE* 6.311–20.

[20]Martin Hengel, *The Johannine Question* (ET Philadelphia: Trinity Press International, 1989).

[21]Ibid., 130.

forced to concede that "the figures of John son of Zebedee and the teacher of the school [i.e. his hypothesized 'John the elder'] . . . are deliberately superimposed in a veiled way" and therefore admits that "it would be conceivable that with the 'beloved disciple' 'John the elder' wanted to point more to the son of Zebedee, who for him was an ideal, even *the* ideal disciple, in contrast to Peter, whereas in the end the pupils impress on this enigmatic figure the face of *their* teacher by identifying him with the author in order to bring the Gospel as near to Jesus as possible."[22] It is hard to imagine how one could get closer than this to affirming apostolic authorship while still denying it![23]

Why Hengel prefers his hypothesis of an otherwise unknown first-century Palestinian Jew by the name of John, who was a contemporary of the apostle John, to the apostle himself, is far from clear. He thinks, for instance, that the Judean focus of the fourth gospel argues for an author who was not a Galilean, as John the apostle was. He judges that the verbal link between "elder" (sometimes rendered "presbyter") in Papias and the same expression in 2 John 1 and 3 John 1 is very significant (though in fact apostles were known to refer to themselves as elders on occasion; see 1 Peter 5:1).[24] He hypothesizes that there may have been unambiguous evidence in Papias to the effect that this "John the elder" wrote the fourth gospel and holds that one must "reckon with the possibility that Eusebius sometimes concealed information which seemed disagreeable to him or omitted it through carelessness";[25] on this view the early church simply repeated the error.

All of this is exceedingly weak. From the evidence of Eusebius, it is far from certain that there ever was an "elder John" independent of the apostle; and if there was, it is still less certain that he wrote anything.[26] If against the evidence we accept Eusebius's interpretation of Papias, we will assign the fourth gospel to the apostle John and the Apocalypse to the elder John—while mainstream biblical scholarship assigns neither book to the apostle. Meanwhile, Hengel's objections to identifying the beloved disciple with the apostle John are not at all weighty. Because they turn on an evaluation of the internal evidence, to that we must turn.

---

[22]Ibid., 131–32.

[23]For detailed interaction with the somewhat similar views of Richard Bauckham (e.g., see his "The Beloved Disciple as Ideal Author," *JSNT* 49 [1993]: 21–44), see D. A. Carson, *The Letters of John*, NIGTC (Grand Rapids: Eerdmans, forthcoming).

[24]Hengel, *The Johannine Question*, 132.

[25]Ibid., 21.

[26]Most of the more recent introductions to John simply do not discuss the patristic evidence: e.g., Achtemeier/Green/Thompson; Johnson; Brown, *An Introduction to the Gospel of John*. By contrast, see Craig L. Blomberg, *The Historical Reliability of John's Gospel: Issues and Commentary* (Leicester: IVP, 2001), 23–26.

Internal Evidence

The classic approach of Westcott, updated by Morris[27] and Blomberg,[28] was to establish five points: the author of the fourth gospel was (1) a Jew, (2) of Palestine, (3) an eyewitness, (4) an apostle (i.e., one of the Twelve), and (5) the apostle John. The first two points are today rarely disputed and need not detain us here, except to make three observations.

1. The discovery of the Dead Sea Scrolls compels us to recognize that it is unnecessary to resort to a period of expansion into the Hellenistic world to account for John's characteristic expressions. See further discussion below in the section "Provenance." Moreover, the evangelist's detailed knowledge of Palestinian topography and of features in conservative Jewish debate probably reflects personal acquaintance, not mere dependence on reliable Jewish sources.

2. To this we must add the widely accepted fact, already appealed to by Lightfoot in the last century,[29] that at least in some instances John's quotations are closer in form to the Hebrew or Aramaic than to the Greek (esp. 12:40; 13:18; 19:37).

3. The attempt of Margaret Pamment to argue that the beloved disciple is a Gentile believer turns on her argument that 21:1ff. is concerned with the Gentile mission (in this she is partly right), which, she says, "suggests the beloved disciple [who appears in this chapter] is a gentile."[30] This is a classic non sequitur. Granted that all the first believers were Jews, at least *some* of the first witnesses to Gentiles had to be Jews!

The other three points, however, are all disputed and turn in large part on the identity of the "beloved disciple," the now-standard way of referring to the one whom the TNIV more prosaically describes as "the disciple whom Jesus loved" (e.g., 13:23). The raw information is quickly canvassed. The beloved disciple first appears as such at the Last Supper, where he is reclining next to Jesus and mediating Peter's question to the Master (13:23). He is found at the cross, where he receives a special commission having to do with Jesus' mother (19:26–27), and at the empty tomb, where he outstrips Peter in speed but not in boldness (20:2–9). In the epilogue (chap. 21), he is said to be the one who wrote "these things." If "wrote" means that he wrote the material himself (and did not simply cause the material to be written, as some have suggested) and "these things" refers to the entire book and not just to chapter 21, then the beloved disciple is the evangelist. If that is correct, then it is natural to identify the eyewitness who

---

[27]Leon Morris, *Studies in the Fourth Gospel* (Grand Rapids: Eerdmans, 1969), 218–92.

[28]Blomberg, *Historical Reliability,* 27–30.

[29]Lightfoot, *Essays,* 20–21.

[30]Margaret Pamment, "The Fourth Gospel's Beloved Disciple," *ExpTim* 94 (1983): 367.

saw the blood and water flow from Jesus' side as the beloved disciple, even though he is not so described.

But who is the beloved disciple? The traditional view, that he is John the son of Zebedee, has been advanced for reasons of quite different weight. That the beloved disciple was at the Last Supper is not disputed (13:23). The Synoptics insist that only the apostles joined Jesus for this meal (Mark 14:17 par.), which places the beloved disciple within the band of the Twelve (and coincidentally speaks against Hengel's hypothesis, described above). He is repeatedly distinguished from Peter (John 13:23–24; 20:2–9; 21:20), and by the same token should not be confused with any of the other apostles named in John 13–16. That he is one of the seven who go fishing in chapter 21 and, by implication, is not Peter, Thomas, or Nathanael, suggests he is one of the sons of Zebedee or one of the other two unnamed disciples (21:2). Of the sons of Zebedee, he cannot be James, since James was the first of the apostolic band to be martyred (probably toward the end of the reign of Herod Agrippa I, A.D. 41–44; see Acts 12:1–2), while the beloved disciple lived long enough to give weight to the rumor that he would not die (21:23). The fact that neither John nor James is mentioned by name in the fourth gospel, which nevertheless has place not only for prominent apostles such as Peter and Andrew but also for relatively obscure members of the apostolic band such as Philip and "Judas (not Judas Iscariot)" (14:22) is exceedingly strange, unless there is some reason for it. The traditional reason seems most plausible: the beloved disciple is none other than John, and he deliberately avoids using his personal name. This becomes more likely when we remember that the beloved disciple is constantly in the company of Peter, while the Synoptics (Mark 5:37; 9:2; 14:33; par.) and Acts (3:1–4:23; 8:15–25), not to mention Paul (Gal. 2:9), link Peter and John in friendship and shared experience. It has also been noted that in this gospel most of the important characters are designated with rather full expressions: Simon Peter; Thomas Didymus; Judas son of Simon Iscariot; Caiaphas, the high priest that year. Strangely, however, John the Baptist is simply called John, even when he is first introduced (1:6; cf. Mark 1:4 par.). The simplest explanation is that John the son of Zebedee is the one person who would *not* feel it necessary to distinguish the other John from himself.

The evidence is not entirely conclusive. For instance, it is just possible that the beloved disciple is one of the unnamed pair of disciples in John 21:2. But once the logical possibility has been duly noted, it seems to be a rather desperate expedient that stands against the force of the cumulative internal evidence and the substantial external evidence.

Other identifications have been advanced. Some, for instance, have suggested Lazarus, on the grounds that "beloved disciple" would be an appropriate form of self-reference for one of whom it is said that Jesus loved him (11:5, 36). One or two have suggested the rich young man of Mark 10:21, on much the same ground. Still others argue for the owner of the upper room, supposing that the reason he could lay his head on Jesus' breast was that, as the host, he was placed in a position of honor next to Jesus; perhaps he was John Mark.

None of this is convincing, and all of it is notoriously speculative. According to the synoptic evidence, only the Twelve were present at the Last Supper: that alone rules out all three suggestions. There is nothing to be said for the first two, other than that Jesus loved them; but that is surely an insufficient ground for identifying the beloved disciple, presupposing as it does that the circle of those whom Jesus loved was extremely limited. As for the second suggestion, to appeal to the Gospel of Mark to sort out the identity of the beloved disciple in John seems to be a dubious procedure. And if the owner of the upper room was present as host in any sense, why is it that all four gospels present Jesus taking the initiative at the meal, serving, in fact, as the host? Moreover, there is no patristic evidence that John the son of Zebedee and John Mark were ever confused.

In his commentary, Brown strongly argues that the beloved disciple is John the son of Zebedee (though he does not identify him with the evangelist), largely along the lines just taken. By the time of his more popular book, outlining his understanding of the history of the Johannine community, however, to say nothing of his final book, published posthumously,[31] Brown has changed his mind[32] without answering his own evidence. He now thinks the beloved disciple is an outsider, not one of the Twelve, but a Judean with access to the high priest's court (18:15–16), possibly the unnamed disciple in 1:35–40. Others have advanced extensive lists of reasons why the beloved disciple could not be John the son of Zebedee.[33] These vary considerably in quality, but they include such entries as these: John the son of Zebedee was a Galilean, yet much of the narrative of the fourth gospel takes place in Judea; John and Peter are elsewhere described as "unschooled, ordinary men" (Acts 4:13), so John could not be expected to write a book of subtlety and depth; John and James are elsewhere described as "Sons of Thunder" (Mark 3:17), presumably suggesting impetuosity, intemperance, and anger—yet this book is the most placid, even mystical, of the canonical gospels; John was vengeful against the Samaritans (Luke 9:54), so it is hard to imagine him writing a book that treats them so kindly (John 4).

None of these arguments seems to carry much weight against the mass on the other side.

---

[31]Brown, *An Introduction to the Gospel of John*, 192–99.

[32]R. E. Brown, *The Community of the Beloved Disciple* (New York: Paulist, 1979), 33–34.

[33]E.g., Pierson Parker, "John the Son of Zebedee and the Fourth Gospel," *JBL* 81 (1962): 35–43; see also Domingo León ("¿Es el apóstol Juan el discípulo amado?" *EstBib* 45 [1987]: 403–92), who raises the objections in order to rebut them.

1. Although John the son of Zebedee was a Galilean, by the time he wrote, he had not only lived for years in Judea (during the earliest period of the church) but (in any traditional view) in the great metropolitan center of Ephesus. To restrict John's focus of interest to the place of his origin, when at the time of writing he had not lived there for decades, seems rather unrealistic.[34]

2. It has long been pointed out that the expression in Acts 4:13 does not mean that Peter and John were illiterate or profoundly ignorant but, from the point of view of contemporary theological proficiency, "untrained laymen" (NEB), not unlike Jesus himself (John 7:15). The astonishment of the authorities was in any case occasioned by the competence of Peter and John when they should have been (relatively) ignorant, not by their ignorance when they should have been more competent. Jewish boys learned to read.[35] Since John sprang from a family that was certainly not poor (they owned at least one boat [Luke 5:3, 10] and employed others [Mark 1:20]), he may well have enjoyed an education that was better than average. And surely it would not be surprising if some of the leaders of the church, decades after its founding, had devoted themselves to some serious study.

3. The suggestion that a "son of thunder" could not have become the apostle of love, or that a man steeped in racial bias against the Samaritans could not have written John 4, is an implicit denial of the power of the gospel and the mellowing effect of years of Christian leadership in an age when the Spirit's transforming might was so largely displayed. The argument is as convincing as the view that Saul the persecutor of the church could not have become the apostle to the Gentiles.

4. Although the "other disciple" who arranges for Peter to be admitted to the high priest's courtyard (18:15–16) is not explicitly said to be the beloved disciple and may be someone else, the connection with John has more to be said for it than some think. It appears that this "other disciple" was in the band of those who were with Jesus when he was arrested and therefore one of the Eleven who had emerged from the upper room and had accompanied Jesus up the slopes of the Mount of Olives. His close association with Peter supports (though

---

[34]There is more than a little irony in this observation. Maurice Casey (*Is John's Gospel True?* [New York: Routledge, 1996], 172–74), as usual with more than a little scorn, dismisses those who point to the accurate knowledge of customs and places in Israel as evidence for the Palestinian Jewish nature of the author of the fourth gospel. But as Craig Blomberg (*The Historical Reliability of John's Gospel* [Leicester: IVP, 2001], 34 n. 25) points out, "To the extent that Casey's argument has any force, it boomerangs to undercut the critical consensus that precisely this same information demonstrates a Judean rather than Galilean home for the author."

[35]See especially Alan Millard, *Reading and Writing in the Time of Jesus,* The Biblical Seminar 49 (Sheffield: Sheffield Academic Press, 2000), esp. 146, 157–58.

it does not prove) the view that he is none other than John. That a Galilean fisherman could have access to the high priest's court is frequently dismissed on the ground that a fishmonger could not enter unquestioned into the waiting room of the prime minister. In fact, the social model is all wrong. We have already seen that John's family enjoyed some substance; it may have been rich, and in many societies money breaks down social barriers. The relevant social barriers of first-century Palestine may not have been that strong in any case; rabbis were expected to gain a skilled trade apart from their study (thus Paul was a leatherworker), so that the stratification that divided teacher from manual laborer in Stoic and other circles of the Hellenistic world was not a significant factor in much of Palestine. Galilee supplied the fish for all of the country except for the coast and was brought into Jerusalem through the Fish Gate (see Neh. 3:3; Zeph. 1:10). As Robinson comments, the tradition that says that John's acquaintance with the girl at the gate and with the high priest's household stemmed from familiarity with the tradesman's entrance may not be entirely fanciful.[36] He may have had a place in the city (19:27) and served on occasion as his father's agent (a role that crops up in the saying of 13:16). It has been pointed out that the peculiar term for cooked fish (ὀψάριον [opsarion]), the form in which much of the trade would be conducted, occurs five times in the fourth gospel (6:9, 11; 21:9, 10, 13) and not elsewhere in the New Testament.

5. Although in the past it has been argued that a Palestinian could not write such fluent Greek, the argument no longer stands. There is now a powerful consensus that at least in Galilee, and perhaps elsewhere in first-century Palestine, the populace was at least bilingual, and in some cases trilingual. Aramaic was used for everyday speech, at least in the villages. (Hebrew may have been used for some formal and cultic occasions, but how many people could *speak* it is uncertain.) And judging by the number of Greek coins and the amount of Greek inscriptional evidence uncovered, Greek was common enough as an alternative language that linked the Jews not only to the Mediterranean world in general but to the Jewish Diaspora and (in Galilee) to the Decapolis in particular. Some whose work brought them into close relationship with the army may also have attained a working knowledge of Latin. In any case, if John lived abroad for years before writing, he had ample time to practice his Greek. Moreover, although the Greek of John's gospel is reasonably competent, it is not elegant, and it betrays a fair number of Semitizing "enhancements."[37] It is, "with little exception, the language of the Septuagint."[38] This sort of evidence is per-

---

[36]Robinson, *Priority*, 117.

[37]On the difference between Semitisms and Semitic enhancements, see n. 19 in chap. 3 above. John's gospel undoubtedly betrays both Aramaic and Hebraic enhancements; whether it betrays any Aramaisms or Hebraisms is disputed.

[38]G. D. Kilpatrick, "The Religious Background of the Fourth Gospel," in *Studies in the Fourth Gospel*, ed. F. L. Cross (London: Mowbray, 1957), 43.

fectly consonant with what little we know of the background of John the son of Zebedee.

In short, the internal evidence is very strong, though not beyond dispute, that the beloved disciple is John the apostle, the son of Zebedee. What, then, is the relationship between the beloved disciple and the fourth evangelist?

The traditional answer is that they are one and the same. Today this is commonly denied. Some think that John the son of Zebedee probably in some way stands behind the tradition in the fourth gospel but that the material went through lengthy adaptations. It finally wound up in the hands of the evangelist (whose identity is unknown—unless he is the "elder" John), whose work was subsequently touched up by a redactor, whose hand is perhaps betrayed in 21:24–25. Others think that the influence of John the son of Zebedee is more immediate and pervasive: he did not actually write the book but caused it to be written, perhaps through an amanuensis who enjoyed certain liberties of expression and who might appropriately be called the evangelist. Important factors to be assessed are these:

1. Perhaps the most frequently advanced reason for denying that the beloved disciple is the evangelist lies in the expression "beloved disciple" itself. It is argued that no Christian would call him- or herself "the disciple whom Jesus loved": the expression smacks of exclusivism and is better thought of as something someone else would say *about* another disciple. Similarly, it is argued, the person who wrote that Jesus was in the bosom of the Father (εἰς τὸν κόλπον τοῦ πατρός [*eis ton kolpon tou patros*], 1:18) would be loath to say *of himself* that he reclined in the bosom of Jesus (ἐν τῷ κόλπῳ τοῦ Ἰησοῦ [*en tō kolpō tou Iēsou*], 13:23).

But these arguments, often repeated, should be abandoned. When a New Testament writer thinks of himself as someone whom Jesus loves, it is *never* to suggest that other believers are *not* loved or are somehow loved less. Thus Paul, in describing the saving work of the Son of God, can suddenly make that work personal: he "loved me and gave himself for me" (Gal. 2:20). In no way does this imply that Paul thinks the Galatians are loved less. The suggestion betrays a profound ignorance of the psychological dynamics of Christian experience: those who are most profoundly aware of their own sin and need, and who in consequence most deeply feel the wonders of the grace of God that has reached out and saved them, *even them,* are those who are most likely to talk about themselves as the objects of God's love in Christ Jesus. Those who do not think of themselves in such terms ought to (Eph. 3:14–21). If a "son of thunder" has become the apostle of love, small wonder he thinks of himself as the peculiar object of the love of Jesus. But that is scarcely the mark of arrogance; it is rather the mark of brokenness. This experience is the common coinage of Christians, so that even if the form of their words seems to single out the individual, it says little about any alleged narrowness of Christ's love, since such language is so common among Christians *as they speak of themselves.*

> *What is the relationship between the beloved disciple and the fourth evangelist? The traditional answer is that they are one and the same. Today this is commonly, but wrongfully, denied.*

Thus, if we are to hear overtones of 1:18 in the description of John lying on Jesus' bosom (13:23), it is no more than a suggestive example of a pattern that is constantly *prescribed* in the fourth gospel: Jesus is the mediator of his Father's love, his Father's judgment, his Father's redemption, his Father's knowledge, his Father's covenant, his Father's presence.

2. The same sort of reasoning probably explains why the evangelist does not name himself. He prefers to refer to himself obliquely, the better to focus on the One he serves; to achieve his purposes in writing, he does not need to stand explicitly on his apostolic dignity. He is already well known by his intended readership (21:24–25) and, like Paul when he is writing without strong polemical intent, does not need to call himself an apostle (Phil. 1:1; cf. Gal.1:1). As most scholars agree, the beloved disciple is no mere idealization but a historical figure; yet even so, in certain respects he serves as a model for his readers to follow. They too are to serve as witnesses to the truth and to make much of the love of Jesus in their lives.

Even if someone protested that this sort of reasoning does not seem to provide an adequate reason for the refusal of the beloved disciple to identify himself, it must surely be admitted that if the evangelist is someone other than John the son of Zebedee, his failure to mention the apostle John by name, when he mentions so many others, is even more difficult to explain.[39] The point may be pressed a little further. The suggestion that the expression "the disciple whom Jesus loved" is something one is more likely to say about someone else than about oneself is not only without merit, but it is self-defeating. It implies that the evangelist (someone other than the beloved disciple, on this view) thought Jesus loved certain disciples and not others. Whatever the reason that Jesus nurtured an inner three (Peter, James, and John) according to the synoptic witness, it is very doubtful that Jesus conveyed the impression that he did *not* love the other nine.

3. Some think the "these things" that the beloved disciple is said to have written (21:24) refers only to the contents of chapter 21, not to the book as a whole. Quite apart from the fact that this view depends on a certain reading of chapter 21, it results in an anomaly: the beloved disciple, apparently the apostle John, wrote only this chapter, but someone else wrote the rest—even though "beloved disciple" occurs much earlier than chapter 21.

4. It is frequently argued that wherever John appears with Peter, the superiority of his insight is stressed. In John 13, for instance, Peter merely signals to the beloved disciple, who in turn actually asks Jesus the fateful question; in John 20, not only does the beloved disciple reach the tomb before Peter, but only he is said to believe. Would John have said such things about himself?

---

[39]See Herman Ridderbos, *The Gospel of John: A Theological Commentary* (Grand Rapids: Eerdmans, 1997), 675–76.

But more careful expositors have argued, rightly, that there is no question of inferiority or superiority in these descriptions, but of different gifts and characters. Barrett, for instance, quite convincingly argues that 21:24 must be read with the verses that precede it: it is given to Peter to feed the flock of God and to glorify God by his death, while it is given to the beloved disciple to live a long time and, as the one who writes this book, to serve as witness to the truth.[40] If the beloved disciple arrives at the tomb first, Peter enters first. If the beloved disciple is said to believe, it is not said that Peter fails to believe; the statement is part of the description that is moving toward his authentication as the author of this book.

5. Some think that 21:22–23 must be taken to mean that the beloved disciple has died by the time the fourth gospel was published and that one of the reasons for publication was to alleviate the crisis that had consequently arisen. But it is just as easy to suppose that the widely circulating rumor had come to the ears of the aging apostle, who consequently feared what might happen to the faith of some after he died, since their faith was resting on a false implication of something Jesus had actually said.

6. The suggestion that the beloved disciple merely caused these things to be written, apparently through a disciple who served as an amanuensis of sorts (Tertius is commonly cited; see Rom. 16:22), receives minor support from John 19:19–22. Pilate himself probably did not write the *titulus* on the cross but simply caused it to be written. Certainly it is far from clear just how much freedom an amanuensis in the ancient world might be permitted.[41] Nevertheless, the example of Pilate suggests that what he caused to be written was *exactly* what he wanted written, and the verb "testifies" in 21:24 suggests that the influence of the beloved disciple is not remote.[42] This is not to argue that John could not have used an amanuensis; nor is it to argue that only authorship by the apostle John can be squared with the internal and external evidence. It is to say, however, that this rather traditional view squares most easily with the evidence and offers least tortuous explanations of difficulties that all of the relevant hypotheses must face.

---

[40]C. K. Barrett, *The Gospel According to St John* (London: SPCK, 1978), 118–19, 587–88.

[41]R. N. Longenecker, "On the Form, Function, and Authority of the New Testament Letters," in *Scripture and Truth,* ed. D. A. Carson and John D. Woodbridge (Grand Rapids: Zondervan, 1983), 101–14.

[42]Indeed, Andreas Köstenberger argues that οἶμαι (*oimai*, "I suppose") is a literary expression frequently used by ancient historians to reflect personal authorial modesty in stating a claim or opinion, and is commonly used at the beginning or end of a literary unit. There is no instance in such literature where the verb is used by later editors to authenticate the message of an original witness. See Köstenberger, "'I Suppose' [οἶμαι]: The Conclusion of John's Gospel in Its Literary and Historical Context," in *The New Testament in Its First Century Setting: Essays on Context and Background, Fs.* Bruce W. Winter, ed. P. J. Williams et al. (Grand Rapids: Eerdmans, 2004), 72–88.

Over against Brown, then, who (at least in his commentary) sees the beloved disciple as the apostle John but not as the evangelist, and Cullmann,[43] who sees the beloved disciple as the evangelist but not the apostle John, the evidence seems to favor Robinson, who writes, "I believe that both men are right in what they assert and wrong in what they deny."[44] Moreover, it is probably true to say that during the last couple of decades a majority of commentators have judged it not unlikely that the apostle John stands behind the Gospel of John in some way. The issue then becomes how far behind it he stands! For some scholars the distance is so great that questions of eyewitness authority and the like have little or no force in understanding the text. For them the acknowledgment that the apostle John is back there somewhere is merely a matter of marginalizing the considerable external and internal evidence. For others, the apostle John is not all that far behind the text, whether he actually wrote it or not; for still others, John is the author of this gospel, more or less as we have it.[45]

The fact remains that Kümmel[46] insists that Johannine authorship is "out of the question," while Barrett insists it is a "moral certainty" that John the son of Zebedee did not write the fourth gospel.[47] They represent many contemporary voices. One is frankly puzzled by their degree of dogmatism. Barrett writes:

> Apostolic authorship has been defended at length and with learning by L. Morris . . . and his arguments should be carefully considered. It must be allowed to be not impossible that John the apostle wrote the gospel; this is why I use the term "moral certainty." The apostle may have lived to a very great age; he may have seen fit to draw on other sources in addition to his own memory; he may have learnt to write Greek correctly; he may have learnt not only the language but the thought-forms of his new environment (in Ephesus, Antioch, or Alexandria); he may have pondered the words of Jesus so long that they took shape in a new idiom; he may have become such an obscure figure that for some time orthodox Christians took little or no notice of his work. These are all possible, but the balance of probability is against their having all actually happened.[48]

This is a mixed list. Apart from the acquisition of Greek language skills, already discussed, the other challenges do not seem insuperable.

---

[43]O. Cullmann, *The Johannine Circle* (London: SCM, 1976), 74–85.

[44]J. A. T. Robinson, *Redating the New Testament* (Philadelphia: Westminster, 1976), 310.

[45]Of these three positions, the commentaries by Brown and Smith might be taken to represent the first position (see chapter bibliography for the details); those by Keener, Ridderbos, and Schnackenburg, the second; and those by Carson and Morris, the third.

[46]Kümmel, 245.

[47]Barrett, *St John*, 132.

[48]Ibid., 132 n. 2.

1. Assessment of the "very great age" turns on one's dating of the book. If one opts for about A.D. 80 (see discussion below in the section "Date"), John need only have been, perhaps, seventy-five. Dodd published *Historical Tradition in the Fourth Gospel* when he was in his eighties; Goodspeed wrote his work on Matthew when he was ninety; John Stott is still writing books in his eighties. And in any case, it is not impossible that the fourth gospel was written before A.D. 70.

2. Why it should be thought at all improbable that an apostle should "draw on other sources in addition to his own memory" is hard to imagine. In any case, the question of the identification of sources in John's gospel is extremely problematic (see the section, "Stylistic Unity and the Johannine 'Community'").

3. As for making Jesus' words come home in his own idiom, that is the preacher's métier, especially if involved in cross-cultural ministry. One of the strengths of the commentary by Lindars is his suggestion that various parts of the fourth gospel are simply the skeletons of sermons polished and preached on various occasions over years of Christian ministry.[49] We need not adopt all of his detailed suggestions to appreciate the plausibility of the basic thesis.

4. The suggestion that the author of the fourth gospel was obscure or unknown in the sub-apostolic church is badly overstated. Scholars differ as to whether John is alluded to in the *Epistle of Barnabas,* the *Didache,* and the *Shepherd of Hermas* (all early second century). Probably a majority find echoes of the fourth gospel in Ignatius (c. A.D. 110). Justin Martyr wrote: "Christ indeed said, 'Unless you are born again you shall not enter into the kingdom of heaven.' It is evident to all that those who have once been born cannot re-enter their mothers' wombs" (*Apol.* 1.61.4–5). This is almost certainly a reference to John 3:3–5; it seems unduly skeptical to think that Justin simply found this as an independent saying in the oral tradition, the more so in the light of the reference to the mothers' wombs. The pattern of recognition is not too surprising if the Gospel of John was published toward the end of the first century. We should not then expect to find traces of it in, say, Clement of Rome (c. 95). There is more of a problem if the fourth gospel was published before 70 (as Morris and Robinson think). Even so, especially if the evidence of Irenaeus regarding Papias and Polycarp is read sympathetically, it is hard to credit the view that "orthodox Christians took little or no notice" of this gospel.

Moreover, Christians then as now had their favorite books. Many have argued that Matthew was an early favorite; John was not. In John's case, it is argued, this may have had a little to do with the fact that the fourth gospel was early used (and abused) by the gnostics. The gnostic Basilides (c. A.D. 130) cites John 1:9 (though this information depends on Hippolytus's *Refutation of Heresies* 7.22.4); the first commentary on a gospel that we know about is the treatment

---

[49]Barnabas Lindars, *The Gospel of John* (London: Oliphants, 1972).

of John by the gnostic Heracleon. But this line of thought has now been decisively overthrown by Charles Hill, who, against current scholarly opinion, shows how widely known and used John's gospel was in the second century. On this point, Barrett is simply wrong.

But perhaps the largest stumbling blocks to acceptance of Johannine authorship are (1) the amorphous assumption that the gospel was composed by a Johannine school or circle or community, to which we now turn; and (2) the disputed relationship that this gospel has with the Synoptics, which we will evaluate in due course.

Stylistic Unity and the Johannine "Community"

Although Bultmann,[50] Fortna,[51] and others have in the past attempted detailed source-critical analyses of the fourth gospel, it has increasingly been recognized that the retrieval of sources from this gospel is an extremely problematic endeavor.[52] There is no reason to doubt that John used sources: his fellow evangelist Luke certainly did (Luke 1:1–4), and there is no need to think that the fourth evangelist followed some different course. Even here, however, caution is needed: Luke does not purport to be the result of eyewitness testimony, while John does. But regardless of who wrote the fourth gospel, the presumption that the evangelist used written sources is quite different from the assumption that we can retrieve them.

One of the features of John's gospel on which virtually all sides now agree is that stylistically it is cut from one cloth.

One of the features of John's gospel on which virtually all sides now agree is that stylistically it is cut from one cloth. There are differences between, say, the vocabulary of Jesus' speech and the vocabulary of the rest of the fourth gospel, but they are so minor that they present us with a quite different problem: How accurate is John's presentation of Jesus if Jesus sounds so much like John? We shall address that problem in a moment; meanwhile, the fact that it is a problem should also serve as a warning against those who think they can distinguish separate sources buried in the text. The stylistic unity of the book has been demonstrated again and again as concrete evidence against this or that source theory.[53]

---

[50]R. Bultmann, *The Gospel of John* (ET Oxford: Blackwell, 1971).

[51]R. T. Fortna, *The Gospel of Signs*, SNTSMS 11 (Cambridge: Cambridge University Press, 1970).

[52]For a useful survey of the application of source criticism to the fourth gospel, see D. Moody Smith, *Johannine Christianity: Essays on Its Setting, Sources, and Theology* (Columbia: University of South Carolina Press, 1984), 39–93; and the penetrating analysis of Gilbert van Belle, *The Signs Source in the Fourth Gospel: Historical Survey and Critical Evaluation of the Semeia Hypothesis* (Leuven: Leuven University Press, 1994).

[53]E.g., E. Schweizer, *Ego Eimi: Die religionsgeschichtliche Bedeutung der johanneischen Bildreden, zugleich ein Beitrag zur Quellenfrage des vierten Evangeliums* (Göttingen: Vandenhoeck & Ruprecht, 1939); E. Ruckstuhl, *Die literarische Einheit des Johannesevangeliums* (Freiburg: Paulus, 1951; slightly enlarged ed., Freiburg: Universitätsverlag,

Even the prologue (1:1–18) and the epilogue (chap. 21) exhibit a style remarkably attuned to the rest of the book.[54]

Even the delineation of the so-called signs source has fallen on hard times.[55] Several scholars have postulated the existence of such a source of signs stories, suggested, it is argued, by the enumeration of the first two (2:11; 4:54), and climaxed by 20:30–31. But the enumeration ("first," "second") has been plausibly accounted for as a rhetorical feature within the text as it stands. Even if there were documents relating signs stories circulating in the early church, it is very doubtful that any of them was regarded as a "gospel of signs,"[56] since in the first century the gospel form, so far as we know, was rapidly associated with a balanced account of Jesus' ministry, including some of his teaching, and climaxing in his death and resurrection. Hengel rightly questions the likelihood that the evangelist took over something like the alleged signs source, which all sides admit (if it ever existed) boasted a theology radically different from that of the evangelist, and incorporated it so mechanically that it can be retrieved by contemporary scholarship.[57] In recent years, several scholars who long maintained not only the existence and retrievability of a signs source but also the relevance of that source for re-creating the history of the Johannine community, have publicly given up on the project.[58]

1987); idem, "Johannine Language and Style," in *L'évangile de Jean: Sources, rédaction, théologie,* ed. M. de Jonge (Louvain: Louvain University Press, 1977), 125–47; G. van Belle, *De semeia-bron in het vierde evangilie: Ontstaan en groei van een hypothese* (Louvain: Louvain University Press, 1975); D. A. Carson, "Current Source Criticism of the Fourth Gospel: Some Methodological Questions," *JBL* 97 (1978): 411–29; Hans-Peter Heekerens, *Die Zeichen-Quelle der johanneischen Redaktion* (Stuttgart: KBW, 1984).

[54]On the former, see Jeff Staley, "The Structure of John's Prologue: Its Implications for the Gospel's Narrative Structure," *CBQ* 48 (1986): 241–63; on the latter, see Paul S. Minear, "The Original Functions of John 21," *JBL* 102 (1983): 85–98.

[55]It is perhaps surprising that in a book published only a decade and a half ago, Robert T. Fortna simply assumes the validity of his postulated source, scarcely interacting with the numerous criticisms that have been raised against it; see his *Fourth Gospel and Its Predecessor* (Philadelphia: Fortress Press, 1988).

[56]Cf. Fortna, *The Gospel of Signs.*

[57]Martin Hengel, "The Wine Miracle at Cana," in *The Glory of Christ in the New Testament, Fs.* G. B. Caird, ed. L. D. Hurst and N. T. Wright (Oxford: Clarendon, 1987), 92.

[58]See especially the paper by Robert Kysar, "The De-Historicizing of the Gospel of John," presented as a paper in the "Jesus, John, and History Consultation" of SBL 2002. Conceivably the abandonment of a detailed source-critical approach to John might lead a critic in a more conservative assessment of the historical value of the document, but in Kysar's case, these conclusions lead him to conclude that we can know next to nothing about the historical Jesus from the Gospel of John.

One fairly recent and creative attempt to use stylistic features to probe the unity of the fourth gospel is the statistically informed and understated study by Poythress of the Greek conjunctions δέ (*de*), καί (*kai*), and οὖν (*oun*), along with the syntactic phenomenon of asyndeton.[59] The frequency of the conjunctions is abnormally low in John; the frequency of asyndeton, unusually high. He demonstrates, as far as such evidence will take him (and he is aware of the pitfalls of small samples and the like), that this test argues for unified authorship of the fourth gospel and common authorship between the fourth gospel and the Johannine Epistles.

It is this sort of evidence that has convinced commentators such as Brown, Lindars, Haenchen, and Keener that the pursuit of separable sources in the fourth gospel is a lost cause.[60] That is why Brown prefers his pursuit of separable *traditions* that have allegedly evolved over the length of a certain trajectory of theological development, and Lindars prefers to think of a series of homilies that were collected, published, edited, and added to over a period of time. But as influential as is, for example, the five-step theory of Brown,[61] it is important to see that it too is a kind of source theory, compounded with speculation about the "setting in life" *(Sitz im Leben)* of each source—only in his case the sources are much fuzzier around the edges than the source postulated by Fortna. Brown prefers to talk about the development of traditions rather than the delineation of sources. Still, someone has to enter John's text with a literary scalpel and retrieve those traditions. Some of these lie on the surface and are tied to certain words and expressions (which make them very similar indeed to literary sources), while

---

[59]Vern Poythress, "The Use of the Intersentence Conjunctions *De, Oun, Kai,* and Asyndeton in the Gospel of John," *NovT* 26 (1984): 312–40; idem, "Testing for Johannine Authorship by Examining the Use of Conjunctions," *WTJ* 46 (1984): 350–69.

[60]The commentaries by Brown and Lindars have already been mentioned; see E. Haenchen, A *Commentary on the Gospel of John,* 2 vols. (ET Philadelphia: Fortress Press, 1984); Craig S. Keener, *The Gospel of John: A Commentary* (Peabody: Hendrickson, 2003), esp. 1.79–80.

[61]In his posthumously published volume, *An Introduction to the Gospel of John,* Brown claims he has reduced these five stages to three. As far as we can see, however, he has merely changed some labels. In his new first stage, he has pulled in both the activity of Jesus and the witness of the disciple, originally designated two stages; in his new third stage, he has two figures operating: the evangelist and the redactor. We have thus returned to five stages. Francis J. Moloney, the editor of this posthumous volume, astutely observes in a separately published essay that if Brown's work, the work of a single author working on one subject and spanning three decades, can reflect these and many other tensions without invoking a string of distinguishable authors and redactors, what warrant is there for invoking such a complex composition theory for the Gospel of John? See Moloney's "Raymond Brown's New *Introduction to the Gospel of John*: A Presentation—And Some Questions," *CBQ* 65 (2003): 15.

others are the reconstructions Brown offers to explain what he thinks must have generated this or that bit of text.

In other words, the source criticism of Bultmann and Fortna has fallen on hard times because their hard evidence turns out to be patient of far simpler explanations, while the tradition probing of Brown (for example), which is far more speculative and much less controlled than Fortna's work, has exerted wide influence—presumably, one has to say, because it is self-coherent and therefore satisfying, but also utterly untestable. It must be remembered that the six groups Brown thinks the Gospel of John is confronting are mere inferences from the gospel's text, the fruit of imaginative mirror-reading. Again and again, other inferences are possible. And all of Brown's six groups, inferences as they are, are based on a prior inference, namely, that it is relatively easy to read off from a text that purports to be about *Jesus* the life and circumstances and opponents of the *group* that produces the document. Small wonder that Kysar concludes, "If the gospel evolved in a manner comparable to that offered by Brown and Lindars, it is totally beyond the grasp of the Johannine scholar and historian to produce even tentative proof that such was the case."[62]

It is this stack of inferences heaped on inferences that has bedeviled, until recent years, most discussions of Johannine authorship. A consensus arose that the history of the Johannine community can largely be delineated by the careful analysis of differentiable Johannine "traditions," each of which has its easily inferred setting-in-life. In the dominant view—a view that largely still pertains—these culminate in a situation toward the end of the first century when the church is locked in debate with the synagogue, and John's gospel, as we have it, more or less reflects that debate. We discuss this view further in the next section. For the moment it is sufficient to say that if this reconstruction is adopted, it is hard to see how the reader can take seriously the claims of this book to be the *witness* of the beloved disciple, most plausibly of the apostle John himself, to Jesus Christ. Thus, the harder literary and historical evidence is displaced by the softer inferential evidence of interlocking reconstructions. One should not object to historical reconstructions; one worries, however, when they are used to set aside large swaths of the actual literary and historical evidence.

For at least some contemporary scholars, this matrix of inherited beliefs, judgments, and commitments about the provenance of the fourth gospel makes it difficult to postulate apostolic authorship without abandoning the inherited web. As we have seen, this matrix turns on the existence of a Johannine circle or school,[63] the core of a Johannine community whose existence and history can to

---

[62]R. Kysar, *The Fourth Evangelist and His Gospel* (Minneapolis: Augsburg, 1975), 53.

[63]Cullmann, *Johannine Circle*; Alan R. Culpepper, *The Johannine School* (Missoula: SP, 1975).

some extent be delineated by inferences drawn from layers of tradition that are peeled back. But attempts to place this chain of inferences on a secure footing by positing ostensible parallels are not reassuring. For example, Culpepper attempts to delineate various schools in the ancient world: the Pythagorean school, the Greek academy, the lyceum, the school at Qumran, the house of Hillel, Philo's school, and so forth. But Culpepper's understanding of "school" is undifferentiable from that of "sect," except that a school has the additional characteristic of being preoccupied with studying, learning, teaching, and writing.[64] Even here, of course, his model runs into difficulty. Culpepper is forced to admit, for instance: "Nothing is known of the history of the synagogue-school in which Philo worked, and none of the names of his students has survived. The inference that his writings continued to be studied arises from the use made of them by the later Christian school in Alexandria and the evident popularity of allegorical exegesis there. . . . Perhaps the reason for the complete silence of our sources on the history of Philo's school is that he actually exerted little influence on his community."[65]

Here, then, is speculation on the reason for the silence of the sources regarding a school the existence of which is an inference drawn from the later use of an earlier Jewish writer! Out of this model emerges the construct of a Johannine school, with the beloved disciple serving as its head, functioning for the community as the Paraclete does in the Gospel of John.[66] But Culpepper offers no criteria whatsoever to distinguish how this school could be distinguished from a group of Christians who simply cherish the evangelist's writings and commend them to others. The history of the Johannine community (he now flips back and forth between "community" and "school") will, he assures us, be traced when there is greater consensus on the "composition-history" of the fourth gospel.[67] Judging by the fractious history of Johannine scholarship, the assumption is more than a little optimistic. He adds that the Johannine Epistles constitute evidence for the existence of "more than one community of believers which shared the same traditions, vocabulary, doctrines, and ethical principles"—though on the face of it this too invokes a major assumption about community participation in the writing, for the simpler inference is that the Johannine Epistles constitute evidence that their author wrote several pieces to several communities that were known to him. They *may* have constituted a collegial grouping of churches around one authority figure; it is entirely plausible to suppose that they did. But that is still a long way from delineating a school of writers and students who were responsible for *the composition* of the fourth gospel. Even the "we" in

---

[64]Culpepper, *Johannine School,* 213.

[65]Ibid.

[66]Ibid., 261–90.

[67]Ibid., 279.

John 21:24, a difficult pronoun on any view,[68] does not unambiguously argue for a school of writers. It could as easily refer to a group of attesting elders.

This is not to argue that there is no self-conscious recognition of development *within the fourth gospel itself*. From the perspective of the evangelist, there was a remarkable development in the disciples' *understanding* of who Jesus was, and much of this took place after the resurrection and exaltation of their Lord. But it is a development of understanding (e.g., 2:22; 12:16; 20:9), not a fresh theological invention. By constantly drawing attention to the *mis*understandings of observers and disciples alike during the days of Jesus' ministry, John shows he is able to distinguish what he and others understood originally and what he came to understand only later. Indeed, he *insists* on the distinction,[69] and this fact constitutes a remarkably strong piece of evidence that the evangelist was self-consciously aware of the possibility of anachronism and, for his own reasons, studiously avoided it. It flies in the face of such evidence to suppose that the evangelist happily cast the circumstances of his own church and situation back into the third decade, projecting them onto Jesus and his teaching, whether wittingly or unwittingly ignoring the anachronisms this generated.

None of this is meant to suggest that all problems in the fourth gospel are purely in the eye of the beholder. It is merely to suggest that comprehensive source and tradition theories are unacceptably speculative and too frequently end up contradicting the only textual evidence we actually have. Some of the most prominent theories of textual dislocation (such as the view that chaps. 5 and 6 have somehow become inverted) solve some problems—in this case, quick geographic movement—only to introduce others. All things considered, it seems least difficult to believe that the evangelist, himself a Christian preacher, proclaimed the gospel for years. Doubtless he made notes; doubtless he learned from others and incorporated the work of others. But whatever he took from other sources, he made his own. Eventually he put the material together and published it as a book. It is quite conceivable that he produced the work in stages; it is unlikely that the work was released in stages, at least in stages with long delays between them, since there is no textual evidence of a distinction between earlier and later editions. There is in any case a sureness of touch, a simplicity of diction, and a unity of theme and development that rhetorical criticism rightly applauds and that testifies to a mature Christian witness and theologian.

There is, of course, a converse problem. Why should the evangelist impose so uniform a stamp on his work that there is so *little* distinction between what

---

[68]See discussion of this passage in Carson, *John,* and especially Howard M. Jackson, "Ancient Self-Referential Conventions and Their Implications for the Authorship and Integrity of the Gospel of John," *JTS* 50 (1999): 1–34.

[69]See D. A. Carson, "Understanding Misunderstandings in the Fourth Gospel," *TynB* 33 (1982): 59–89.

he writes and what he ascribes to Jesus during the days of his flesh? Several observations may be helpful.

1. Although the style of the fourth gospel is remarkably uniform, the point must not be overstated. Reynolds lists about 150 words that are placed on Jesus' lips in John but are never used elsewhere by the evangelist.[70] Not a few of these are sufficiently general that they would have been as appropriate in the evangelist's narrative as in Jesus' discourse.

2. Many have argued, rightly, that fair reporting can be accomplished with other than verbatim quotations. A many-sided writer who is also an advocate will wisely choose the form of the reportage, especially if the communication is cross-cultural. If we also suppose that much of this material was first of all sermonic, the general point is strengthened. A number of features are probably best explained by supposing we are listening to a preacher's revised sermons. The doubled "Amen!" on Jesus' lips, for instance, found only in John, is just such a homiletic device and causes no umbrage unless for some strange reason we suppose that preachers in the ancient world could appeal only to verbatim quotations. Some of what is included in or excluded from John's gospel is much better accounted for by reflecting on the evangelist's situation *as a Christian preacher*, so far as we can reconstruct it from both internal and external evidence, than by supposing that the evangelist is including all he knows, or is attempting to correct some other gospel, or is simply ignorant of some vital fact preserved elsewhere. The absence of narrative parables, especially parables about the kingdom, suggests this preacher's audience is not steeped in apocalyptic and not linguistically Semitic. The prevalence of so much terminology that has almost *universal* religious appeal (see comments below) suggests the evangelist is trying to use language that will present the fewest barriers.

This does not mean that John is uninterested in, say, the kingdom of God. Quite apart from the few crucial places where he does use the expression (3:3, 5; cf. 18:36), the *theme* of the kingdom is very powerfully presented in certain passages (e.g., it dominates the plot line of chaps. 18–19). Moreover, the kingdom in the Synoptic Gospels is often a "tensive symbol" that can bear an extraordinary number of overtones.[71] This ensures that in some passages, for instance, "entering the kingdom" is indistinguishable from "entering into life" (e.g., Matt 7:14, 21)—and John certainly has a great deal to say about life. In short, the

---

[70]H. R. Reynolds, *The Gospel of St. John* (London: Funk & Wagnalls, 1906), 1.cxxiii–cxxv.

[71]See J. Jeremias, *New Testament Theology I: The Proclamation of Jesus* (London: SCM, 1971), 32–34; Norman Perrin, *Jesus and the Language of the Kingdom* (Philadelphia: Fortress Press, 1976), esp. 29–34; R. T. France, "The Church and the Kingdom of God: Some Hermeneutical Issues," in *Biblical Interpretation and the Church: Text and Context,* ed. D. A. Carson (Exeter: Paternoster, 1984), 30–44.

fourth evangelist is interested in presenting certain truths to certain people, and he exercises the preacher's prerogative of shaping his message accordingly.

It has often been remarked that John's gospel, however profound it may be, is narrower in focus than the Synoptics. When this narrowness of focus fills the entire page, certain things come to light that would not otherwise be seen, but a certain sense of dislocation in the reader is understandable. Once what the preacher (i.e., the evangelist) is doing becomes clear—that is, when the *scale* of his vision is clarified—the sense of dislocation largely evaporates.

3. Of course, this preacher is not *just* a preacher. He presents himself as an eyewitness, a reliable intermediary between the events themselves and the people who now need to hear them. Nor is he alone: he is conscious of the continuity of Christian truth (1:14–18) and especially of the Spirit's role in equipping him for this task (15:26–27; 16:12–15). So far as John's understanding of his task goes, we may speak of the liberty he felt to use his own language, of the principles of selection that governed his choices of material, of the nature of the audience that he envisioned, of the focus of his interests, of his remarkable habit of getting to the heart of an issue. But we may not glibly suppose that one who felt so strongly about the importance of fidelity in witnesses (10:40–42) could simply invent narrative and dialogue and pass them off as history.

4. Several of the discourses have been shown, with some degree of plausibility, to be modeled on midrashim, or the rabbinic commentaries of the day. These discourses are so tightly knit that it is very difficult to believe they are nothing more than a pastiche of isolated (and retrievable!) sayings of Jesus onto which Johannine commentary has been patched. This leads to one of two conclusions. Borgen, who has demonstrated the finely wrought nature of the bread of life discourse (6:26–59) as in part an exposition of Exodus 16, argues for the unity of the discourse but does not attribute it to Jesus.[72] Hunter likewise recognizes the unity but thinks there is no evidence to prevent us from concluding the discourse is authentic.[73] What must be added is that, granted its essential authenticity, the discourse has been cast into its shape and placed in the gospel by the evangelist, whose style so largely stamps the whole. Similar things could be said about the midrashic nature of parts of John 12, the chiastic structure of 5:19–30, the cohesiveness of the dialogue with Nicodemus, and much more.

The most straightforward reading of the evidence is still the traditional one: it is highly probable that John the son of Zebedee wrote the fourth gospel.

In short, the most straightforward reading of the evidence is still the traditional one: it is highly probable that John the son of Zebedee wrote the fourth gospel. In itself, this makes no difference whatsoever to the authority of the book (after all, Luke's gospel does not purport to be by an eyewitness; the epistle to the Hebrews is anonymous). It does, however, make a considerable difference

---

[72]P. Borgen, *Bread from Heaven,* NovTSup 10 (Leiden: Brill, 1965).
[73]A. M. Hunter, *According to John* (London: SCM, 1968), 39–40.

to how we think the book came to be written and therefore to the situation to which it was addressed, the purpose of the writing.

PROVENANCE

Discussion of the provenance of the fourth gospel can usefully be divided into two spheres: geographic provenance and conceptual provenance.

Geographic Provenance

Four places are commonly proposed.

1. *Alexandria* is championed by some on the ground that John has certain affinities to Philo. These are considerably overstated (see, e.g., the major commentaries on 1:1), and in any case one must assume that Philo was read outside Alexandria.

2. *Antioch* has been put forward on the ground that the fourth gospel has some affinities with the Syriac *Odes of Solomon,* presumed to come from this region, and with Ignatius, who served Antioch as its bishop. Again, however, the assumption that literary influence is possible only in the place of literary origin is seen to be unconvincing as soon as it is stated.

3. The view that the fourth gospel must have been written in *Palestine* because of its close familiarity with cultural and topographical details peculiar to the region entails the view, strange on its very surface, that any book about the historical Jesus must have been written in Palestine. Both then and now, authors have been known to move around.

4. The traditional view is that the fourth gospel was written in *Ephesus.* In large part this view depends on the weight given to the uniform but sometimes difficult patristic evidence. Eusebius (*H.E.* 3.1.1) says that Asia (i.e., Asia Minor, approximately the western third of modern Turkey) was allotted to John when the apostles were dispersed at the outbreak of the Jewish War (A.D. 66–70). Some of the allotments or assignments that Eusebius lists are likely legendary, but perhaps this one is reliable, since it agrees with other sources, for example, Irenaeus (*Adv. Haer.* 3.1.2), who says that "John, the disciple of the Lord . . . published the gospel while living at Ephesus in Asia." Some hold, however, that Irenaeus confuses John the apostle with another John, the John who writes the Apocalypse (see discussion in chap. 25, below). The fact that the Montanists, who were largely based on Phrygia, not too far from Ephesus, used John is often taken to support the case for Ephesian provenance; but again, John's gospel could have been circulating in Phrygia half a century and more after it was written, regardless of where it was first published. What must be acknowledged is that no other location has the support of the church fathers: rightly or wrongly, they point to Ephesus.

Conceptual Provenance

John's Religious World. The wealth of suggestions that various scholars have offered as to the background of the fourth gospel has an important bearing on how we view John's ostensible setting, the Palestine of Jesus' day, and how we understand his message. From the end of the nineteenth century until about the 1960s, the history-of-religions movement tied John's gospel to the Hellenistic world. As the gospel stretched outward from Jerusalem through the Jewish Diaspora and into the broader streams of Hellenistic culture, it was progressively transformed both in vocabulary and in substance. Typically, this Hellenistic culture was judged to be some combination of four influences.

Philo. Scholars have seen an influence from Philo, especially with respect to John's use of λόγος (*logos,* "word") in 1:1. Philo borrows the Stoic concept of the word as the principle of reality, the medium of creation and governance. Numerous other parallels can be observed.

The Hermetic writings. Alleged to be the instruction of Hermes Trismegistus (= the Egyptian god Thoth), these writings in the gnostic tradition display some distinctive features by mitigating the dualism of Gnosticism. The cosmos is related to God and may be called the son of God. Regeneration is an important theme in some Hermetic tractates: a person is born again when he or she gains the proper knowledge of God and thereby becomes divine. Dodd was the greatest defender of the pervasive influence of the Hermetic literature on John.[74]

Gnosticism. Sometimes (and rightly) described as an amorphous "theosophical hotchpotch," Gnosticism sprang out of neoplatonic dualism that tied what is good to the ideal, to the spiritual, and what is bad to the material. In full-blown Gnosticism, the gnostic redeemer comes to earth to inform those with ears to hear of their true origins. This "knowledge" (γνῶσις [*gnōsis*]) brings release and salvation to those who accept it.

Mandaism. This is a peculiar form of Gnosticism whose origins are much disputed. Probably it originated in one of the Jewish baptizing sects, but the form in which it has come down to us, in which the rite of baptism, oft repeated, is the key step by which the myth of the descent of the "knowledge of life" (*Manda d'Hayye*) is reenacted and release from the demonic powers secured, is exceedingly late.[75]

---

[74]See especially Walter Scott, ed., *Hermetica: The Ancient Greek and Latin Writings Which Contain Religious or Philosophic Teachings Ascribed to Hermes Trismegistus,* Vol. 1: *Introduction; Texts and Translation;* Vol. 2: *Notes on the Corpus Hermeticum;* Vol. 3: *Notes on the Latin Asclepius and the Hermetic Excerpts of Stobaeu;* Vol. 4: *Testimonia* (Oxford: Clarendon, 1924–63).

[75]For useful coverage of these and other movements, see G. R. Beasley-Murray, *John,* WBC 36; 2nd ed. (Waco: Word, 1999), liiiff. One of the best assessments of Gnosticism in general and Mandaism in particular is still that of Edwin A. Yamauchi, *Pre-Christian Gnosticism: A Survey of the Proposed Evidence,* 2nd ed. (Grand Rapids: Baker, 1983).

Quite apart from considerations of dating (all but the first of these are attested by sources that come from the second or third century or later), the conceptual differences between John and these documents are very substantial. Moreover, the discovery of the Dead Sea Scrolls in 1947 and their subsequent publication have shown that the closest religious movement to the fourth gospel, in terms of vocabulary at least, was an extremely conservative hermitic *Jewish* community. This is not to say that John springs from the Essenes, thought to be represented by the Dead Sea Scrolls, but that the appeal to strongly Hellenistic sources is now much less convincing than it was six decades ago. Thus, another stream of scholarship has attempted to plot the connections between John and various Palestinian movements, including rabbinic thought, Samaritan religion, the Essenes, and various apocalyptic movements. Whatever parallels can be drawn, it is now virtually undisputed that both John and these movements drew their primary inspiration from what we today call the Old Testament Scriptures.

John's indebtedness to this primary wellspring is profound, much more profound than the mere number of Old Testament quotations might suggest. The countless allusions to the Old Testament (e.g., references to the tabernacle, Jacob's ladder, Jacob's well, manna, the serpent in the wilderness, Sabbath, and various feasts) presuppose both a writer and readers who are steeped in the Scriptures.[76]

Even so, many scholars would be comfortable with the approaches displayed in the commentaries of, say, Barrett and Schnackenburg, who argue that a rich diversity of non-Christian influences was incorporated into the very substance of this gospel, providing it with its peculiar emphases and form. This is surely partly right, yet it is potentially misleading. One reason why interpreters are able to find parallels to John in so diverse an array of literature lies in John's vocabulary and pithy sayings. Words such as light, darkness, life, death, spirit, word, love, believing, water, bread, clean, birth, and children of God can be found in almost any religion. Frequently they have very different referents as one moves from religion to religion, but the vocabulary is as popular as religion itself.[77] Nowhere, perhaps, has the importance of this phenomenon been more clearly set forth than in a little-known essay by Kysar.[78] He compares the stud-

---

[76]See D. A. Carson, "The Use of the Old Testament in John and the Johannine Epistles," in *It Is Written: Scripture Citing Scripture, Fs.* Barnabas Lindars, ed. D. A. Carson and H. G. M. Williamson (Cambridge: Cambridge University Press, 1988), 245–64. Of the many specialist studies in this area, see esp. Andrew C. Brunson, *Psalm 118 in the Gospel of John: An Intertextual Study on the New Exodus Pattern in the Theology of John,* WUNT 158 (Tübingen: Mohr-Siebeck, 2003).

[77]See the important discussion in Keener, *The Gospel of John: A Commentary,* 1.324–30, passim.

[78]Robert Kysar, "The Background of the Prologue of the Fourth Gospel: A Critique of Historical Methods," *CJT* 16 (1970): 250–55.

ies of Dodd and Bultmann on the prologue (John 1:1–18), noting in particular the list of possible parallels each of the two scholars draws up to every conceivable phrase in those verses. Dodd and Bultmann each advance over three hundred parallels, but the overlap in their lists is only 7 percent. The dangers of what Sandmel calls parallelomania become depressingly obvious.[79]

This does not mean that there is no influence at all on the fourth gospel from other religious forms. The early Christians were certainly aware that they were expanding outward into a frequently hostile set of worldviews. The evangelist's efforts to communicate the truth of the gospel to men and women far removed from Palestine ensured that, if he was at all thoughtful in his task, he would not simply parrot the received traditions but would try to cast them in ways that would make them most easily understood. The question to be asked, then, is whether his attempt has succumbed, wittingly or unwittingly, to a syncretism that has admitted strands of thought essentially alien to the historic gospel or, better, has simply transposed the good news, as it were, to another key. It is surely here that John has proved to be not only a faithful witness but a gifted preacher.

John's Relation to the Synoptics. One cannot long speak of the conceptual provenance of the fourth gospel without weighing the relations between this gospel and the Synoptics. How much does John owe to the synoptists?

The differences between John and the Synoptics have often been detailed. John omits many things that are characteristic of the Synoptics: narrative parables, the account of the transfiguration, the record of the institution of the Lord's Supper, and many of Jesus' pithy sayings. Themes central to the Synoptics have all but disappeared (especially the theme of the kingdom of God/heaven). Conversely, John includes a fair bit of material of which the synoptists make no mention: virtually all the material in John 1–5, Jesus' frequent visits to Jerusalem and what takes place there, the resurrection of Lazarus, extended dialogues and discourses, and much more.

Doubtless some of this can be accounted for by the different geographic focus: John reports far more of Jesus' ministry in the south, in Judea and Samaria, than in Galilee, while the focus of the synoptists is the opposite. But one cannot legitimately reduce all distinctions to questions of geography. In John, Jesus is *explicitly* identified with God (1:1, 18; 20:28). Here too is a series of important "I am" statements, sometimes with predicates (e.g., 6:35; 8:12; 15:1–5), sometimes absolute (e.g., 8:28, 58). There are passages not superficially easy to integrate with other New Testament texts, such as John the Baptist's denial that he is Elijah (1:21; cf. Mark 9:11–13 par.) and the apparent bestowal of the Spirit (John 20:22; cf. Acts 2). John 1 begins with the disciples confessing Jesus as Son of God, Son of Man, Messiah, Rabbi, and King of Israel

---

[79]Samuel Sandmel, "Parallelomania," *JBL* 81 (1962): 2–13.

(all in chapter 1); in the Synoptics, the confession of Jesus as the Messiah is a great turning point at Caesarea Philippi, about halfway through Jesus' ministry (Mark 8:27–30 par.). Nor have we yet considered the chronological difficulties that the fourth gospel introduces: its date for the passion, for instance, is not easily squared with that of the Synoptics. The last line of 14:31 strikes many as the evidence of an awkward edit; the threat of synagogue excommunication (9:22) strikes others as desperately anachronistic, reflecting a situation in the late 80s, not in the ministry of the historical Jesus.

On the other hand, there are many notable points of comparison.[80] Parallel incidents include the Spirit's anointing of Jesus as testified by John the Baptist (Mark 1:10 par. and John 1:32), the contrast between the Baptist's baptism with water and the Messiah's anticipated baptism with the Spirit (Mark 1:7–8 par. and John 1:23), the feeding of the five thousand (Mark 6:32–44 par. and John 6:1–15), and the walking on the water (Mark 6:45–52 par. and John 6:16–21). Many sayings are at least partially parallel, though not decisively attesting literary dependence (Matt. 9:37–38 par. and John 4:35; Mark 6:4 par. and John 4:44; Matt. 25:46 par. and John 5:29; Matt. 11:25–27 par. and John 10:14–15; Mark 4:12 par. and John 12:39–40; and many more). More significant yet are the subtle parallels: both John and the synoptists describe a Jesus given to colorful metaphors and proverbs, many drawn from the world of nature (e.g., 4:37; 5:19–20a; 8:35; 9:4; 11:9–10; 10:1ff.; 12:24; 15:1–16; 16:21). All four gospels depict Jesus with a unique sense of sonship to his heavenly Father; all of them note the distinctive authority Jesus displays in his teaching; all of them show Jesus referring to himself as the Son of Man, with no one else using that title to refer to him or to anyone else (John 12:34 is no real exception).

More impressive yet are the many places where John and the Synoptics represent an *interlocking* tradition, that is, where they mutually reinforce or explain each other, without betraying overt literary dependence.[81] A very incomplete list includes the following items: John's report of an extensive Judean ministry helps to explain the assumption in Mark 14:49 that Jesus had constantly taught in the temple precincts (NEB "day after day"), the trepidation with which the final trip southward was viewed (Mark 10:32), and Jesus' ability to round up a colt (Mark 11:1–7) and secure a furnished upper room (Mark 14:12–16). The charge reported in the Synoptics that Jesus had threatened the destruction of the temple (Mark 14:58 par.; 15:29 par.) finds its only adequate explanation in John 2:19. Mark gives no reason as to why the Jewish authorities should bother bringing Jesus to Pilate; John provides the reason (18:31). Only John provides the reason (18:15–18) why

> *Very impressive are the many places where John and the Synoptics represent an interlocking tradition, that is, where they mutually reinforce or explain each other, without betraying overt literary dependence.*

---

[80] See Craig Blomberg, *The Historical Reliability of the Gospels* (Leicester: IVP, 1987), 156–57.

[81] See esp. Morris, *Studies*, 40–63; Robinson, *John*, chaps. 4–6; Carson, *John*, "Introduction," III(3).

Peter can be placed within the high priest's courtyard (Mark 14:54, 66–72 par.). Even the call of the disciples in the Synoptics is made easier to understand (Matt. 4:18–22 par.) if we presuppose, with John 1, that Jesus had already had contact with them and that their fundamental shift in allegiance had already occurred.

Conversely, numerous features in John are explained by details reported only by the synoptists. For instance, in John 18–19 the trial plunges so quickly into the Roman court that it is difficult to see just what judicial action the Jews have taken, if any, to precipitate this trial; the Synoptics provide the answer. It is quite possible that the reason Philip apparently hesitates to bring the Gentiles to Jesus in John 12:21–22, consulting with Andrew before actually approaching Jesus, is that Jesus had earlier issued his prohibition against going among the Gentiles (Matt. 10:5)—a point not reported by John.

We summarize here the complex scholarly debates on the relation between John and the Synoptics and offer some tentative conclusions.

1. Although the majority of contemporary scholars side with the magisterial work of Dodd,[82] who argues that there is no good evidence for any literary dependence of John on any of the Synoptic Gospels, a number of scholars[83] and at least two major commentators[84] argue that John had read at least Mark, perhaps Luke, and (one or two have argued) perhaps also Matthew—or, at the very least, substantial synoptic tradition. All agree that if John made use of any of the Synoptics, the dependency is quite unlike that between, say, Mark and Matthew, or Jude and 2 Peter. The fourth evangelist chose to write his own book.

2. The question of the relationship between John and the Synoptics is inextricably tied to complex debates about the authorship and dates of composition of all four gospels. For example, if, as is commonly the case, scholars think of the gospels as the products of anonymous faces in Christian communities that

---

[82]Dodd, *Historical Tradition*.

[83]E.g., F. Neirynck in M. de Jonge, *L'évangile de Jean*, 73–106; idem, in collaboration with Joël Delobel, Thierry Snoy, Gilbert van Belle, and Frans van Segbroeck, *Jean et les synoptiques: Examen critique de l'exégèse de M.-E. Boismard* (Louvain: Louvain University Press, 1979); Mgr. de Solages, *Jean et les synoptiques* (Leiden: Brill, 1979); J. Blinzler, *Johannes und die Synoptiker* (Stuttgart: KBW, 1965); E. F. Seigman, "St. John's Use of the Synoptic Material," *CBQ* 30 (1968): 182–98; M. E. Glasswell, "The Relationship Between John and Mark," *JSNT* 23 (1985): 99–115; Gerhard Maier, "Johannes und Matthäus—Zweispalt oder Viergestalt des Evangeliums?" in *GP* 2:267–91; Thomas M. Dowell, "Jews and Christians in Conflict: Why the Fourth Gospel Changed the Synoptic Tradition," *LouvStud* 15 (1990): 19–37; Thomas L. Brodie: *The Quest for the Origin of John's Gospel: A Source-Oriented Approach* (New York: Oxford University Press, 1993). For a summary of the earlier literature, see Smith, *Essays;* Blomberg, *Historical Reliability,* 159.

[84]Barrett, *John;* Thomas L. Brodie, *The Gospel According to John: A Literary and Theological Commentary* (New York: Oxford University Press, 1993).

are more or less independent of other Christian communities—indeed, as the products of long streams of tradition largely free from the constraints of eyewitnesses—then the only means of weighing whether the author(s) of one gospel (in this case John) had read any of the other gospels would be by testing for direct literary dependence. If that is the case, most scholars think the evidence is not strong enough to prove dependence, and one must either assume independence or leave the question open. A minority of scholars, as we have seen, think that a case for dependence can be made out.

But if, on the sorts of grounds that have already been canvassed here, we come to think that John the son of Zebedee wrote the fourth gospel and that Mark wrote the gospel that bears his name, with Peter behind him, then additional factors must be considered. Granted the close friendship that Peter and John enjoyed, would it be very likely that either of them would long remain ignorant of a publication for which the other was responsible? Considerations of date then become important. For instance, if Mark was written about A.D. 64, and John within a year or two of that date, then the likelihood of mutual independence is enhanced. But if Mark was written sometime between 50 and 64, and the fourth gospel not until about 80, it is very difficult to believe that John would not have read it. The idea of hermetically sealed communities is implausible in the Roman Empire anyway, where communications were as good as at any time in the history of the world until the nineteenth century.[85] It becomes doubly implausible while the apostles were still alive, living with friendships and the memory of friendships. In this case, tests for direct, literary dependence are too narrow if they are meant to answer the question whether or not John had read Mark. On balance, it appears likely that John had read Mark, Luke, and possibly even Matthew, but that in any case he chose to write his own book, so the burden of proving direct literary dependence remains overwhelmingly difficult.

3. The incidental nature of the interlocking patterns between John and one or more of the Synoptics cannot be used to prove dependency, but for the same reason it turns out to be of inestimable value to the historian. It is not that the theological thrusts connected with John's passion narrative, for example, cannot be appreciated without reading the Synoptics, or that the theological points the individual synoptists make when they describe the call of the disciples cannot be grasped without referring to what John has to say on the matter. Rather, the implication of the interlocking patterns is that *at the historical level* what actually took place was much bigger and more complex than any one gospel intimates. Something of that complexity can be sketched in by sympathetically examining the interlocking nature of the diverse gospel presentations. The result

---

[85]See further Richard Bauckham, ed., *The Gospels for All Christians: Rethinking the Gospel Audiences* (Grand Rapids: Eerdmans, 1998).

makes good historical sense of many passages that have too quickly been written off by those prone to disjunctive thinking.

4. This has considerable practical bearing on the evaluation of some of the differences between John and the Synoptics. For example, the lengthy list of christological confessions in John 1 is, as we have seen, often set against the rising christological awareness pictured in the Synoptic Gospels, which reaches its climax at Caesarea Philippi. It has been argued that the reason for this difference is that John, writing at the end of the first century, *presupposes* the appropriateness of the christological titles he introduces in his first chapter but is now concerned to move the church to adopt one further confession: Jesus is God. This interpretation of the evidence simultaneously assumes that the ascription of deity to Jesus is exceedingly late and that the ostensible setting in John 1 is entirely fictional.

Yet if we listen to John and to the Synoptics with *both* theological *and* historical sympathy, a simpler resolution presents itself. On its own, John's account makes good historical sense. For disciples of the Baptist to dissociate themselves from him while he is at the height of his power and influence and to transfer their allegiance to someone from Galilee, still unknown and unsought, is most readily explained as the evangelist explains it: John the Baptist himself pointed out who Jesus was, insisting that he came as Jesus' precursor, or forerunner. Those most in tune with the Baptist and most sympathetic to his message would then prove most likely to become the followers of Jesus, and for the reason given: they believed him to be the promised Messiah, the king of Israel, the Son of God (a category that our sources show could serve as a designation of the messiah). None of this means that Jesus' fledgling followers enjoyed a full, Christian understanding of these titles: of all four evangelists, it is John who most persistently catalogues how much the early disciples did *not* understand, how much they actively *mis*understood. All of this makes good intrinsic sense.

But so does the Synoptic presentation. It is only to be expected that Jesus' disciples grew in their understanding of who he was. Constantly astonished by the kind of Messiah he was turning out to be, they nevertheless came with time to settled conviction: he was no less than the Messiah, the hope of Israel. Even this was less than full Christian belief. Peter's next step (Mark 8:31–34 par.) was to tell Jesus that predictions about his imminent death were inappropriate to the Messiah they were following. Thus, the Synoptics portray rising understanding but still expose the massive *mis*understanding that stood at the core of all belief in Jesus that was exercised before his death and resurrection.

Superimposing both views of reality also makes good intrinsic sense. The evangelist who most quickly introduces the christological titles most heavily stresses the lack of understanding and the sheer misunderstanding of Jesus' followers; the evangelists who track their rising comprehension say less about the disciples' initial false steps but soon point out the profundity of their lingering misapprehensions. John's presentation no longer appears unhistorical; it is merely part of the undergirding historical realities.

5. But this does not mean we must constantly refer to the Synoptics to make sense of John. Superimposing the two visions gives us access to certain *historical* realities. Rightly handled, it may also enable us to discern what is peculiarly Johannine and thus to understand with greater sensitivity just what the evangelist is saying. His decision to structure his presentation this way, with the evangelist himself constantly drawing attention to the misunderstanding of the disciples and of others and explaining what was understood only later (e.g., 2:19–22; 3:3–5, 10; 6:32–35, 41, 42; 7:33–36; 8:18–20, 27–28; 10:1–6; 11:21–44, 49–53; 12:12–17; 13:6–10, 27–30; 16:1–4, 12–15; 18:10–11; 19:14; 20:3–9), enables him to operate at two levels, using irony to make his readers see, again and again, that the disciples believed better than they knew, that Caiaphas prophesied better than he thought, that Pilate gave verdicts more just than he could have imagined. The narrative unfolds like a Greek tragedy, every step followed by the reader even when the participants cannot possibly understand what they rightly confess. And then, unlike the Greek tragedy, there is triumph and glorification: the supreme irony is that in the ignominy and defeat of the cross, the plan of God achieved its greatest conquest, a conquest planned before the world began.

6. More generally, though the christological distinctiveness of John's gospel should not be denied, it should not be exaggerated. True, only this gospel explicitly designates Jesus as "God" (1:18; 20:28); but this gospel also insists not only on Jesus' humanity but also on his profound subordination to the Father (see esp. 5:16–30).[86] Conversely, the synoptists, for all their portrayal of Jesus as a man, portray him as the one who has the right to forgive sins (Mark 2:1–12 par.—and who can forgive sins but God alone?) and relate parables in which Jesus transparently takes on the metaphoric role most commonly assigned to God in the Old Testament. The Synoptic Gospels present in seed form the full flowering of the incarnational understanding that would develop only later; but the seed is there, the entire genetic coding for the growth that later takes place.[87] If

---

[86]On the humanity of Jesus in John's gospel, see D. A. Carson, *Divine Sovereignty and Human Responsibility* (Atlanta: John Knox, 1981), 146–60; Marianne M. Thompson, *The Humanity of Jesus in the Fourth Gospel* (Philadelphia: Fortress Press, 1986); Leon Morris, *Jesus Is the Christ: Studies in the Theology of John* (Grand Rapids: Eerdmans, 1989), 43–67; cf. E. Käsemann, *The Testament of Jesus* (ET London: SCM, 1968), who argues that the evidence for Jesus' humanity in John is nothing more than the trappings necessary to secure a docetic Christology.

[87]For a responsible treatment of this organic growth of Christology, see I. Howard Marshall, *The Origins of New Testament Christology* (Leicester: IVP, 1976); C. F. D. Moule, *The Origin of Christology* (Cambridge: Cambridge University Press, 1977); and many of the essays in H. H. Rowdon, ed., *Christ the Lord, Fs.* Donald Guthrie (Leicester: IVP, 1982).

John lets us see a little more of the opening flower, it is in part because he indulges in more explanatory asides that clarify for the reader what is really going on.

Even the "I am" statements constitute less of a historical problem than at first meets the eye. The statements themselves are quite varied.[88] Jesus' plain affirmation of his messianic status in 4:26 ("I, the one speaking to you—I am he"), contrasting sharply with the circumlocutions and symbol-laden language of so many Synoptic sayings, may turn on the identity of his interlocutor: she is a Samaritan woman and unlikely to harbor exactly the same political expectations bound up with ideas of messiahship in many strands of first-century Judaism. After all, John reports that Jesus resorts to circumspect language when he is in Judea (e.g., 7:28–44; 10:24–29). The majority of the "I am" statements in John have some sort of completion: bread of life, good shepherd, vine, or the like (6:35; 10:11; 15:1). They are plainly metaphoric, and although they are reasonably transparent to later readers, they were confusing and difficult for the first hearers (e.g., 6:60; 10:19; 16:30–32): religious leaders did not customarily say that sort of thing.[89] As for the occurrences of an absolute form of "I am," which can ultimately be traced back to Isaiah's use of the same expression as a reference for God (e.g., Isa. 43:10; 47:8, 10, esp. LXX), they are mixed in their clarity and are in any case partly paralleled by Mark 6:50; 13:6.[90] And if the most dramatic of the sayings in John, "Before Abraham was born, I am" (8:58), is without explicit synoptic parallel, it is hard to see how it makes a claim fundamentally superior to the synoptic portrayal of a Jesus who not only can adjudicate Jewish interpretations of the law but can radically abrogate parts of it (Mark 7:15–19) while claiming that all of it is fulfilled by him (Matt. 5:17ff.), who forgives sin (Matt. 9:1ff.) and insists that an individual's eternal destiny turns on obedience to him (Matt. 7:21–23), who demands loyalty that outstrips the sanctity of family ties (Matt. 10:37–39; Mark 10:29–30) and insists that no one knows the Father except those to whom the Son discloses him (Luke 10:22), who offers rest for the weary (Matt.11:28–30) and salvation for the lost (Luke 15), who muzzles nature (Mark 4:39) and raises the dead (Matt. 9:18–26). Individual deeds from such a list may in some cases find parallels in the

---

[88] See Philip B. Harner, *The "I Am" of the Fourth Gospel* (Philadelphia: Fortress Press, 1970).

[89] Most of the alleged parallels are from second- and third-century (or even later) Gnostic and Hermetic sources. Those closest in time to John, drawn from the first half of the first century, are claims of the mythical Egyptian goddess Isis, who was popular in the Greek-speaking world: "I am the one who discovered fruit for men"; "I am the one who is called the goddess among women" (see *NewDocs* 1.2). These are, however, remarkably *un*metaphorical and do not, in any case, bear the Old Testament resonances of the utterances in John.

[90] See further Catrin H. Williams, *I am He: The Interpretation of 'Anî Hû' in Jewish and Early Christian Literature*, WUNT 113 (Tübingen: Mohr-Siebeck, 2000).

prophets or in the apostles; the combination finds its only adequate parallel in God alone.[91]

Limitations of space preclude detailed treatment of other well-known difficulties in John and their relation to the synoptic tradition. They are in any case sympathetically treated in the stream of commentaries that seeks to keep history and theology together (e.g., Westcott, Morris, Carson) and in the longer New Testament introductions.[92]

DATE

During the past 150 years, suggestions as to the date of the fourth gospel have varied from before A.D. 70 to the final quarter of the second century. Dates in the second century are now pretty well ruled out by manuscript discoveries (see discussion below in the section "Text"). But apart from this limitation, none of the arguments is entirely convincing, and almost any date between about 55 and 95 is possible. John 21:23 "suggests it was probably nearer the end of that period than the beginning."[93]

Some dates seem implausibly early. Probably the inference to be drawn from 21:19 is that Peter had by his death glorified God when chapter 21 was composed. Peter died in A.D. 64 or 65; dates earlier than that for the composition of the fourth gospel seem unlikely. Those who hold to a date before 70 (but after 65) point to details of Palestine presented as if Jerusalem and its temple complex were still standing; for example, the evangelist writes: "Now there is in Jerusalem near the Sheep Gate a pool" (John 5:2). The argument would be conclusive except that John frequently uses the Greek present tense to refer to something in the past. The silence of the fourth gospel on the destruction of the temple is considered powerful evidence for a pre–70 date by some authors. Arguments from silence, however, are tricky things. At first glance there is some force to this one, since the theme of the evangelist in 2:19–22, for example, could have been strengthened if the overthrow of the temple had been mentioned. But the evidence is far from compelling. How prominent the temple was in the thinking of Jews in the Diaspora varied a great deal.[94] If some time had elapsed, perhaps a decade, between the destruction of the temple and the publication of this gospel, so that the initial shock of the reports had passed, there is no reason to think that the evangelist should have brought it up. Indeed, John is a writer

---

[91]For a useful defense of the authenticity of the "I am" sayings in John, see E. Stauffer, *Jesus and His Story* (London: SCM, 1960), 142–59.

[92]E.g., Guthrie, 248ff.

[93]J. Ramsey Michaels, *John* (San Francisco: Harper & Row, 1983), xxix.

[94]This is one of the major planks of Jörg Frey, *Die johanneische Eschatologie*, 3 vols., WUNT 96, 110, 117 (Tübingen: Mohr-Siebeck, 1997–2000).

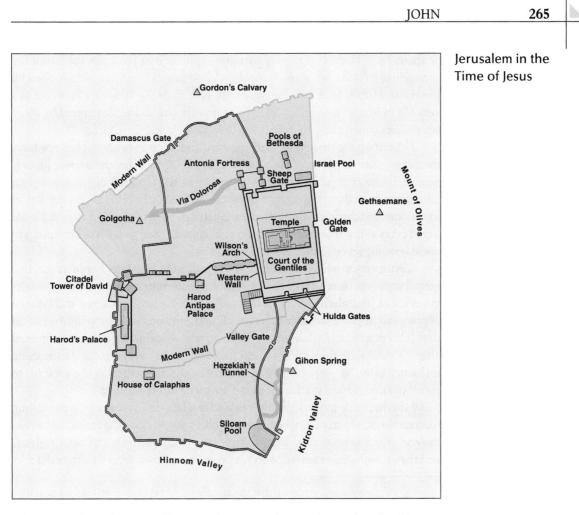

Jerusalem in the
Time of Jesus

who loves subtle allusions. If he wrote in, say, 80, he may have taken the destruction of the temple as a given and let this fact make its own contribution to his theological argument. Other arguments for a date before 70 do not seem any more convincing.

Those who defend a date toward the end of the first century, say between A.D. 85 and 95, commonly resort to four arguments:

1. Many theologians appeal to the tradition that the fourth gospel was written under the reign of Emperor Domitian (ruled A.D. 81–96). But Robinson has shown that this tradition rests on very little.[95] There is good, early tradition that the apostle John lived to a great age, surviving even into the reign of Emperor Trajan (98–117; see Irenaeus, *Adv. Haer.* 2.22.5; 3.3.4; quoted by Eusebius, *H.E.* 3.23.3–4). Jerome, admittedly in the fourth century, places John's death in the sixty-eighth year "after our Lord's passion" (*De vir. ill.* 9),

---

[95]Robinson, *Redating,* 256–58.

or about 98.[96] There is also good patristic evidence that John was the last of the evangelists to write his book (Irenaeus, *Adv. Haer.* 3.1.1; Clement, as cited by Eusebius, *H.E.* 6.14.7; Eusebius himself, *H.E.* 3.24.7). "But that he wrote as a very old man is an inference which only appears late and accompanied by other statements which show that it is clearly secondary and unreliable."[97]

2. A strong contingent of scholars argue that both the concept and the term meaning "put out of the synagogue" (9:22; 12:42; 16:2; ἀποσυνάγωγος [*aposynagōgos*]) betray a period after the decision of the Council of Jamnia to ban Christians from the synagogue.[98] In other words, they find in this expression an irreducible anachronism that dates the Gospel of John to a period after A.D. 85. Yet at every point this thesis has been challenged,[99] and today it is beginning to wield less influence than it did some years ago.

3. Numerous details are often taken to indicate a late date. For instance, this gospel makes no mention of the Sadducees, who contributed much to the religious life of Jerusalem and Judea before A.D. 70 but who withered and became of marginal importance after that date. The argument would be weighty, except that John is similarly silent on the scribes, whose influence actually increased after 70. And John does make it clear that the priests, with rapidly diminishing influence after 70, were largely in control of the Sanhedrin in the time up to Jesus' passion. Other matters of detail are no more convincing.

4. Perhaps the most pervasive reason for a late date is that in the prevailing reconstruction of early Christian history, John's gospel best fits into a date toward the end of the first century. For example, the ready ascription of deity to Jesus and the unapologetic insistence on his preexistence are said to fit a later date.

---

[96]On the very slight evidence that the apostle John was early martyred, almost universally dismissed, see Guthrie, 272–75. Surprisingly, Martin Hengel (*Johannine Question*, 21, 158–59) gives this tradition more credence than it deserves—doubtless because it makes coherent his proposal of the existence of another John who (Hengel argues) was also an eyewitness.

[97]Robinson, *Redating*, 257.

[98]Dominated by J. Louis Martyn, *History and Tradition in the Fourth Gospel* (Nashville: Abingdon, 1979).

[99]See R. Kimelman, "*Birkat ha-Minim* and the Lack of Evidence for an anti-Christian Jewish Prayer in Late Antiquity," in *Jewish and Christian Self-Definition*, vol. 2 of *Aspects of Judaism in the Greco-Roman Period*, ed. E. P. Sanders (Philadelphia: Fortress Press, 1981), 226–44, 391–403; W. Horbury, "The Benediction of the *Minim* and Early Jewish-Christian Controversy," *JTS* 33 (1982): 19–61; Robinson, *John*, 72ff.; Beasley-Murray, *John*, lxxvi–lxxviii; Ridderbos, *The Gospel of John: A Theological Commentary*, 341–44; and discussion in Carson, *John*. See also David E. Aune, "On the Origins of the 'Council of Javneh' Myth," *JBL* 110 (1991): 491–93. Furthermore, David Wenham, "The Enigma of the Fourth Gospel: Another Look," *TynB* 48 (1997): 149–78, points out in detail how all the controversies represented in the fourth gospel can be shown to exist much earlier than A.D. 85.

The issue turns in part on countless exegetical and historical details that cannot be canvassed here. Nevertheless, it must be noted that the New Testament passages closest in theology to John 1:1–18 are probably the so-called Christ-hymns (e.g., Phil. 2:5–11; Col. 1:15—20; see Rom. 9:5), which were doubtless already circulating in the mid-50s. Moreover, no gospel stresses the functional subordination of Jesus to his Father more strongly than does John. In other words, the emphasis in the fourth gospel on the deity of Christ must not be allowed to eclipse complementary emphases. Attempts to date the fourth gospel by charting christological trajectories do not appear very convincing.

If a date for the publication of the fourth gospel must be suggested, we may very tentatively advance A.D. 80–85, for these reasons:

1. There is no convincing pressure to place the Gospel of John as early on the spectrum as possible, but there is a little pressure to place John rather later on it, namely, the relatively late date at which it is cited with certainty by the Fathers.

2. Although the arguments from theological trajectories are, as we have seen, rather weak, yet if any weight is to be given to them at all, at several points John's gospel uses language that is on its way toward the less restrained language of Ignatius—in particular the ease and frequency with which Ignatius refers to Jesus as God, his sacramental language (where in our view he has misunderstood John rather badly), and his sharp antitheses.

3. Although the fall of the temple may not have had as much impact in the Diaspora as in Palestinian Judaism, yet it is hard to believe that, if the fourth gospel was written after A.D. 70, the date was *immediately* after 70, when the reverberations around the empire, in both Jewish and Christian circles, were still being felt.

4. If, as is argued later in this book, the Johannine Epistles are concerned in part to combat an incipient form of Gnosticism, predicated in part on a gnostic misunderstanding of the fourth gospel, then some time must be allowed between the publication of the gospel and the publication of the epistles of John. That tends to rule out a date in the nineties.

DESTINATION

No destination is specified by the fourth gospel itself. Inferences are largely controlled by conclusions drawn in the areas of authorship and purpose. If John the son of Zebedee wrote this book while residing in Ephesus, then it might be inferred that he prepared the book for readers in this general part of the empire. But he may have hoped for the widest possible circulation; in any case, the inference cannot be more certain than the assumption of authorship. Some general things may be inferred from the purposes John displays in the writing of his gospel. However, since these purposes are disputed, we must turn to them.

PURPOSE

Much of the discussion on this topic during the twentieth century turned on questionable assumptions or procedures, of which four are particularly common.

1. Many treatments at the beginning of the twentieth century depended on the assumption that John is parasitic on the Synoptic Gospels.[100] That means the governing purpose of John should be uncovered by contrasting what John does with what the synoptists do. He wrote a "spiritual" gospel, it is argued; or he wrote to supplement the earlier efforts, or even to supersede or to correct them. These theories refuse to let John be John; he must be John-compared-with-Mark, or with another synoptist. This approach has faded in recent decades, largely owing to the revised estimate of John's relation to the Synoptics.

2. Many modern proposals have sprung from a reconstruction of the Johannine community that is alleged to have called this book forth. Inevitably a degree of circularity is set up: the community is reconstructed by drawing inferences from the fourth gospel; once this background is sufficiently widely accepted, the next generation of scholars tends to build on it, or to modify it slightly by showing how the fourth gospel achieves its purpose by addressing that situation so tellingly. The circularity is not necessarily vicious, but the final picture is not as well substantiated as is often assumed, owing to the very high number of merely possible but by no means compelling inferences that are invoked to delineate the community in the first place.

Meeks, for instance, argues that the Johannine community is sectarian, an isolated conventicle struggling in opposition against a powerful synagogue.[101] The fourth gospel, then, is a summary of these polemics, possibly even a handbook for new converts, certainly something to strengthen the community in its continuing conflict. Martyn's reconstruction is a modification of this: the church is aggressively evangelizing the Jews, and this book not only reports the conflict but helps the church in its task.[102] But at least some components of these reconstructions may be called into question.[103] To think of the Johannine community as isolated and sectarian is to miss the grand vision of John 17, not to mention the fact that John's Christology finds its closest parallels in the New Testament

---

[100]In one form, the theory is as old as Clement of Alexandria (Eusebius, *H.E.* 6.14.7). In this century it was made famous by Hans Windisch, *Johannes und die Synoptiker* (Leipzig: J. C. Hinrichs'sche Buchhandlung, 1926).

[101]Wayne A. Meeks, *The Prophet-King: Moses Traditions and the Johannine Christology*, NovTSup 14 (Leiden: Brill, 1967).

[102]Martyn, *History and Theology*.

[103]See Tobias Hägerland, "John's Gospel: A Two-Level Drama?" *JSNT* 25 (2003): 309–22.

in the so-called hymns (e.g., Phil. 2:5–11; Col. 1:15–20), which suggests that the evangelist is thoroughly in touch with the wider church.

3. Many statements of John's purpose depend rather narrowly on a single theme, feature, or even literary tool. Mussner, for instance, examines all expressions dealing with knowledge, hearing the word of Jesus, and the like, and suggests that the evangelist is effecting a transfer of reference from the time of Jesus to his own time.[104] In this merged vision, the past is not annulled, but the angle of vision is from the present. This merging of visions, however, is so strong, in Mussner's view, that the distinctive word of the historical Jesus cannot be distinguished at all.

Whence, then, the evangelist's constant distinction between what Jesus' disciples understood at the time and what they understood only later? What starts off as a suggestive entry point for considering the purpose of the fourth gospel ends up disowning too many features integral to the book.

In the same way, Freed wonders if John 4 does not constitute evidence that the fourth gospel was written, at least in part, to win Samaritan converts.[105] One may well ask what methodological steps warrant the leap from circumstances ostensibly set in Jesus' day to identical circumstances set in the evangelist's day. Again, Malina attempts to locate the Johannine community by reading the fourth gospel in the framework of two models provided by sociolinguistics.[106] However, as subsequent debate demonstrated, not only the adequacy of the sociolinguistic models may be questioned, but also the extent to which data on the Johannine community are obtained to feed into the models by "mirror-reading" the text and seeing only what is being projected onto it. In David Rensberger's reading, the fourth evangelist is a kind of prototypical liberation theologian.[107] At some point, the text of the gospel is swamped by the rush of inferences.[108]

---

[104]F. Mussner, *The Historical Jesus and the Gospel of St. John* (ET London: Burns & Oates, 1967).

[105]E. D. Freed, "Did John Write His Gospel Partly to Win Samaritan Converts?" *NovT* 12 (1970): 241–56.

[106]Bruce J. Malina et al., *The Gospel of John in Sociolinguistic Perspective*, ed. Herman C. Waetjen, Protocol of the Forty-eighth Colloquy (Claremont: Center for Hermeneutical Studies in Hellenistic and Modern Culture, 1984).

[107]David Rensberger, *Overcoming the World: Politics and Community in the Gospel of John* (London: SPCK, 1988).

[108]For a summary and critique of Rensberger, see the review in *Themelios* 17/1 (1992): 27–28. On the general point, see the astute conclusion of Marinus de Jonge, "Christology, Controversy and Community in John," in *Christology, Controversy and Community*, ed. David G. Horrell and Christopher M. Tuckett, NovTSup 99 (Leiden: Brill, 2000): 229: "I have argued that it remains difficult to determine the situation directly envisaged in the Gospel or the earlier history of the community. After repeated consideration of the difficulties involved, I have (reluctantly) come to the conclusion

4. Finally, several commentators adopt what might be called a synthetic, or additive approach. What appear to be the best suggestions of others are blended together, so that the purpose of John's gospel is to evangelize Jews, to evangelize Hellenists, to strengthen the church, to catechize new converts, to provide materials for the evangelization of Jews, and so forth.[109] Part of the problem is the confusion between purpose and plausible effect. Just because John's gospel can be used to offer comfort to the bereaved in the twenty-first century does not mean that is why the evangelist wrote it. In the same way, just because this gospel could help Jewish Christians witnessing to unconverted Jews and proselytes in the nearby synagogue does not itself mean that is why the evangelist wrote it. Thinking through all the plausibly good effects various parts of this book could have does not provide adequate reasons for thinking that any one of them, or all of them together, was the purpose the evangelist had in mind when he put pen to paper.

Other purposes have been suggested. The proper place to begin, however, is with John's own statement of his purpose: "Jesus performed many other signs in the presence of his disciples, which are not recorded in this book. But these are written that you may believe that Jesus is the Messiah, the Son of God, and that by believing you may have life in his name" (20:30–31). The words rendered "that you may believe" hide a textual variant: either ἵνα πιστεύητε (*hina pisteuēte*, present subjunctive) or ἵνα πιστεύσητε (*hina pisteusēte*, aorist subjunctive). Some have argued that the latter expression supports an evangelistic purpose: that you may come to faith, come to believe. The former, then, supports an edificatory purpose: that you may continue in faith, continue to believe. In fact, it can easily be shown that both tenses are used in John for both initial faith and continuing in faith, so that nothing can be resolved by the appeal to one textual variant or the other.

It is worth comparing these verses with the stated purpose of 1 John: "I write these things to you who believe in the name of the Son of God so that you may know that you have eternal life" (1 John 5:13). This verse was clearly written to encourage Christians; by the contrasting form of its expression, John 20:30–31 sounds evangelistic.

This impression is confirmed by the firm syntactic evidence that the first purpose clause in 20:31 should be rendered "that you may believe that the Christ, the Son of God, is Jesus." Thus, the fundamental question the fourth gospel addresses is not "Who is Jesus?" but "Who is the Messiah, the Christ,

---

that we have to be content with the general observation that it is highly likely that controversies with others, Jews and Christians, played an important role." Nevertheless, de Jonge thinks this book was written for "the clarification of relevant Christological issues for the Johannine community itself."

[109]Beasley-Murray, *John*, lxxxvii–lxxxc, comes close to this range.

the Son of God?"[110] In its context, the latter is a question of identity, not of kind: that is, the question "Who is the Christ?" should not here be taken to mean "What kind of Christ are you talking about?" but "So you claim to know who the Christ is. Prove it, then: Who is he?"

Christians would not ask that kind of question, because they already knew the answer. The most likely people to ask that sort of question would be Jews and Jewish proselytes who know what "the Christ" means, have some sort of messianic expectation, and are perhaps in dialogue with Christians and want to know more. In short, John's gospel not only is evangelistic in its purpose (a dominant view until this century, when relatively few have defended it)[111] but aims in particular to evangelize Diaspora Jews and Jewish proselytes. This view is only a minority report,[112] yet much can be said for it. It may even receive indirect

> *John's gospel not only is evangelistic in its purpose, but aims in particular to evangelize Diaspora Jews and Jewish proselytes.*

---

[110]See D. A. Carson, "The Purpose of the Fourth Gospel: John 20:30–31 Reconsidered," *JBL* 108 (1987): 639–51. The argument is complex and has been called into question by Gordon D. Fee, who appeals to his earlier careful study of the anomalous use of the article with proper names in the Gospel of John ("The Use of the Definite Article with Personal Names in the Gospel of John," *NTS* 17 [1970–71]: 168–83) to conclude that John 20:30–31 must be translated " . . . that Jesus is the Christ, the Son of God," and therefore that the fourth gospel is best thought of as written for Christians (see his "On the Text and Meaning of John 20,30–31," in *The Four Gospels, Fs.* Frans Neirynck, ed. F. van Segbroeck, C. M. Tuckett, G. van Belle, and J. Verheyden; Vol. 3 [=BETL 100] [Leuven: Leuven University Press, 1992], 2193–205). But although Fee has successfully shown that, owing to John's anomalous use of the article with names, the syntax of 20:31 does not *require* the rendering we have suggested above, that rendering still remains the most plausible. The only close syntactical parallel is John 5:15, where, strictly speaking, the healed man attests that the person who made him well was Jesus—i.e., once again we are dealing with an identity question. The matter is discussed at length in D. A. Carson, "Syntactical and Text-Critical Observations on John 20:30–31: One More Round on the Purpose of the Fourth Gospel" (forthcoming).

[111]E.g., W. Oehler, *Das Johannesevangelium, eine Missionsschrift für die Welt* (Gütersloh: Bertelsmann, 1936); idem, *Zum Missionscharackter des Johannesevangeliums* (Gütersloh: Bertelsmann, 1941); Dodd, *Interpretation,* 9; Moule, 136–37; Morris, *John,* 855–57; Andreas Köstenberger, *The Missions of Jesus and the Disciples According to the Fourth Gospel: With Implications for the Fourth Gospel's Purpose and the Mission of the Contemporary Church* (Grand Rapids: Eerdmans, 1998). See the discussion in Guthrie, 283ff.

[112]But see K. Bornhäuser, *Das Johannesevangelium: Eine Missionsschrift für Israel* (Gütersloh: Bertelsmann, 1928); W. C. van Unnik, "The Purpose of St. John's Gospel," in *SE* 1:382–411; J. A. T. Robinson, *Twelve New Testament Studies* (London: SCM, 1962), 107–25; David D. C. Braine, "The Inner Jewishness of St. John's Gospel as the Clue to the Inner Jewishness of Jesus," *SNTU* 13 (1988): 101–55, esp. 105–11; George J. Brooke, "Christ and the Law in John 7–10," in *Law and Religion: Essays in the Place of the Law in Israel and Early Christianity,* ed. Barnabas Lindars (London: SPCK, 1988), 102–12; Carson, *John.*

support from some recent studies that try to interpret the fourth gospel as a piece of mission literature. Some of these[113] display generally excellent exegesis but give no attention to the fact that with very little adaptation the same exegesis could justify the thesis that the Gospel of John was not written to believers *about* mission but to outsiders to *perform* mission.

It goes beyond the limits of a brief introduction to show how this stated purpose of the evangelist sheds a great deal of light on the rest of his gospel: that is the work of an entire commentary. The constant allusions to the Old Testament show that John's intended readership is biblically literate; his translation of Semitic expressions (e.g., 1:38, 42; 4:25; 19:13, 17) shows he is writing to those whose linguistic competence is in Greek. His strong denunciation of "the Jews" cannot be taken as a mark against this thesis: John may well have an interest in driving a wedge between ordinary Jews and (at least) some of their leaders. The fourth gospel is not as anti-Jewish as some people think anyway: salvation is still said to be "from the Jews" (4:22), and often the referent of "the Jews" is "the Jews in Judea" or "the Jewish leaders" or the like. "Anti-Semitic" is simply the wrong category to apply to the fourth gospel: whatever hostilities are present turn on theological issues related to the acceptance or rejection of revelation, not on race.[114] How could it be otherwise, when all of the first Christians were Jews and when, on this reading, both the fourth evangelist and his primary readers were Jews and Jewish proselytes? Those who respond to Jesus, whether Jews, Samaritans, or "other sheep" (10:16) to be added to Jesus' fold, are blessed; those who ignore him or reject him do so out of unbelief, disobedience (3:36), and culpable blindness (9:29–41).

Within some such a framework as this, further inferences can usefully be drawn from the content of his gospel about the people to whom John was writ-

---

[113]See esp. Teresa Okure, *The Johannine Approach to Mission*, WUNT 31 (Tübingen: Mohr-Siebeck), 1988). Something similar could be said for Miguel Rodrigues Ruiz, *Das Missionsgedanke des Johannesevangeliums: Ein Beitrag zur johanneischen Soteriologie und Ekklesiologie* (Würzburg: Echter Verlag, 1987). Cf. also Köstenberger, *The Missions of Jesus and the Disciples*. For a survey of at least the earlier studies of John along this vein, see R. Schnackenburg, *Das Johannesevangelium* (Freiburg: Herder, 1965–84), 4.58–72.

[114]Many have argued that the fourth gospel is anti-Semitic, or at least anti-Judaism, but probably none with more heat than Maurice Casey, who argues that this gospel is so anti-Jewish and demonstrably untrue that it should be removed from the canon (*Is John's Gospel True?* esp. 229). More careful analysis is found in Ridderbos, *The Gospel of John: A Theological Commentary*, 324–30; Reimund Bieringer, Didier Pollefeyt, and Frederique Vandecasteele-Vanneuville, eds., *Anti-Judaism and the Fourth Gospel: Papers of the Leuven Colloquium, 2000* (Louisville: Westminster John Knox Press, 2001); and esp Stephen Motyer, *Your Father the Devil? A New Approach to John and "the Jews"* (Carlisle: Paternoster, 1997).

ing and the topics that interested them. But these inferences are secondary, always in principle to be challenged by other (and possibly competing) inferences and never capable of more than confirming John's purpose, which we must establish on other grounds.

TEXT

The earliest New Testament fragment known to us is a fragment of John, P[52], dating from about A.D. 130 and containing a few words from John 18. Two other papyrus witnesses, both codices, spring from the end of the second century: P[66] includes most of John 1–14 and parts of the remaining chapters, while P[75] contains most of Luke, followed by John 1–11 and parts of chapters 12–15. From the beginning of the third century comes P[45], which contains parts of all four gospels plus Acts, though the mutilated state of the manuscript ensures that no book is complete. Thereafter the manuscript evidence becomes richer, capped by the great fourth-century uncials (manuscripts written in capital letters) and followed by the many minuscules in succeeding centuries.

There is an excellent list of the most important textual witnesses, including versional and patristic evidence, along with a summary of scholarly discussion, in Schnackenburg.[115] On the whole, the text is in good shape, but there are a few passages where notorious difficulties are still disputed. Perhaps the most famous of these is 1:18. It appears likely that the original reading was μονογενὴς θεός (*monogenēs theos*), the second word probably understood appositionally: "[the] unique one, [himself] God," rather than "the only begotten God."

Despite the best efforts of Zane Hodges to prove that the narrative of the woman caught in adultery (John 7:53–8:11) was originally part of John's gospel,[116] the evidence is against him, and modern English versions are right to rule it off from the rest of the text (TNIV) or to relegate it to a footnote (RSV). These verses are present in most of the medieval Greek minuscule manuscripts, but they are absent from virtually all early Greek manuscripts that have come down to us, representing great diversity of textual traditions. The most notable exception is the Western uncial D, known for its independence in numerous other places. They are also missing from the earliest forms of the Syriac and Coptic Gospels, and from many Old Latin, Old Georgian, and Armenian manuscripts. All the early church fathers omit this narrative; in commenting on John, they pass immediately from 7:52 to 8:12. No Eastern Father cites the passage before the tenth century. Didymus the Blind (a fourth-century exegete from

---

[115]R. Schnackenburg, *The Gospel according to St John* (London: Burns & Oates, 1968–82), 1:173–91.

[116]Zane Hodges, "The Woman Taken in Adultery (John 7:53–8:11)," *BS* 136 (1979): 318–72; 137 (1980): 41–53.

Alexandria) reports a variation on this narrative,[117] not the narrative as we have it here. Moreover, a number of (later) manuscripts that include the narrative mark it off with asterisks or obeli, indicating hesitation as to its authenticity, while those that do include it display a rather high frequency of textual variants. Although most of the manuscripts that include the story place it at 7:53–8:11, some place it instead after Luke 21:38, and others variously after John 7:44, John 7:36, or John 21:25.[118] The diversity of placement confirms (though it cannot establish) the inauthenticity of the verses. Finally, even if someone should decide that the substance of the narrative is authentic—a position plausible enough— it would be very difficult to justify the view that the material is authentically Johannine: it includes numerous expressions and constructions that are found nowhere in John but that are characteristic of the Synoptic Gospels, Luke in particular.

ADOPTION INTO THE CANON

By the end of the second century, all four canonical gospels were accepted not only as authentic but as Scripture on a par with Old Testament Scripture. Even earlier, the fact that Tatian's *Diatessaron* (see discussion above) could use John as the chronological framework for the other three testifies to the authority that it enjoyed. Outside of Marcion and the *Alogoi*, the early church nowhere questioned either the authenticity or, once it began to address the subject, the canonicity of the fourth gospel.

JOHN IN RECENT STUDY

Until about a decade and a half ago, the overwhelming majority of scholarly energy on John during the previous two or three decades was devoted to some theme in the fourth gospel as a means of access to the ostensible Johannine community.[119] Enough has been said on this approach.

A second (and perennial) focus has been the examination, from fresh standpoints, of particular themes in John's gospel. For instance, the role of the Para-

---

[117]See Bart D. Ehrman, "Jesus and the Adulteress," *NTS* 34 (1988): 24–44.

[118]See Metzger, 219–22, for a summary of the evidence.

[119]For surveys of literature on John for that period, one might usefully consult R. Schnackenburg, "Entwicklung und Stand des johanneischen Forschung seit 1955," in *L'évangile*, 19–44; H. Thyen, "Aus der Literatur des Johannesevangeliums," *ThR* 39 (1974): 1–69, 222–52, 289–330; 42 (1977): 211–70; 44 (1979): 97–134; Jürgen Becker, "Aus der Literatur des Johannesevangeliums," *ThR* 47 (1982): 279–347; James McPolin, "Studies in the Fourth Gospel—Some Contemporary Trends," *IBS* 2 (1980): 3–26; D. A. Carson, "Recent Literature on the Fourth Gospel: Some Reflections," *Themelios* 9 (1983): 8–18; 14 (1989): 57–64.

clete, the Holy Spirit, in the fourth gospel continues to call forth books and articles.[120] There are similar treatments of many Johannine themes. Occasionally one encounters ongoing studies of a variety of historical matters—the trial of Jesus, the relation between John and the Synoptics, or this or that topographical detail.[121]

But by far the most important development in recent studies on the fourth gospel is the application of various forms of literary criticism, social-scientific analysis, and postmodern readings. At first these reflected the early stages of the so-called "new criticism." Thus, we were given a structuralist approach to certain chapters,[122] an examination of the asides in John,[123] or a consideration of some such literary device as irony.[124] The tendency in all of these approaches is to treat the text synchronically, that is, to treat the text as a finished product and to ask virtually no questions about its historical development or its referents. Nowhere was this better seen than in the magisterial and provocative work of Culpepper,[125] which analyzes the Gospel of John in the categories reserved for modern novels.

There were both gains and losses in these studies. Some of them did not say much more than the obvious, with the heavy weight of the formal categories of structuralism or the new literary criticism to drag them down. The most creative have in their favor that they treat the Gospel of John as a single text, a unified piece of work. This is both refreshing and something of a relief from older approaches whose primary goal was to detach sources or traditions from the text as we have it.

Yet there was a loss as well. These studies often ignore the rootedness of the gospels, including this gospel, in history—their passionate concern to bear witness, not simply to pass on abstract ideas. The genuine insights of these studies are sometimes offset by an air of unreality, of merely esoteric textual formality.

---

[120]See the books by Johnston, Franck, Burge, and Bennema in the Bibliography.

[121]Here it must be said, with regret, that apart from the work of Blomberg, few recent scholars have interacted in any detail with such valuable and detailed earlier works as J. Armitage Robinson, *The Historical Character of the Fourth Gospel* (London: Longmans-Green, 1908); E. H. Askwith, *The Historical Value of the Fourth Gospel* (London: Hodder & Stoughton, 1910); H. Scott Holland, *The Fourth Gospel* (London: John Murray, 1923); or A. C. Headlam, *The Fourth Gospel as History* (Oxford: Blackwell, 1948).

[122]B. Olsson, *Structure and Meaning of the Fourth Gospel* (Lund: Gleerup, 1974), on John 2–4; Hendrikus Boers, *Neither on This Mountain nor in Jerusalem*, SBLMS 35 (Atlanta: SP, 1988), on John 4.

[123]G. van Belle, *Les parenthèses dans l'évangile de Jean: Aperçu historique et classification* (Louvain: Louvain University Press, 1985).

[124]P. Duke, *Irony in the Fourth Gospel* (Atlanta: John Knox, 1985).

[125]R. A. Culpepper, *Anatomy of the Fourth Gospel: A Study in Literary Design* (Philadelphia: Fortress Press, 1983).

But the most innovative recent studies are those that focus on the social dynamics of the Johannine community (as re-created by earlier work),[126] or on its theology (rather than on the historical Jesus to which the fourth gospel ostensibly bears witness),[127] on evocative but sometimes speculative examinations of the symbolism of this gospel[128] (sometimes tied to gender issues[129]), and on candidly postmodern readings which insist that since all "history" is social-textual creation the issues of "what happened" are moot anyway.[130] As stimulating and helpful as many of these works are, one worries at times if they focus on all the things that John is *not* particularly interested in, while what he actually emphasizes, that to which he bears witness, is substantially ignored.

THE CONTRIBUTION OF JOHN

John's thought is so wonderfully integrated that attempts to compartmentalize it by itemizing its components are destined in some measure to misrepresent it. Excellent theological summaries are provided by Barrett, Schnackenburg, and Keener.[131] Among John's more important contributions are the following:

1. John adds stereoscopic depth to the picture we might gain of Jesus and his ministry, death, and resurrection from the synoptic accounts alone. By telling the same story from another angle, with many things omitted that they include and with many emphases that they scarcely treat, the total portrait is vastly richer than what would otherwise have been achieved.

2. John's presentation of who Jesus is lies at the heart of all that is distinctive in this gospel. It is not just a question of the shading assigned to certain

---

[126]E.g., Bruce J. Malina and Richard L. Rohrbaugh, *Social-Science Commentary on the Gospel of John* (Minneapolis: Fortress Press, 1998).

[127]John Painter, R. Alan Culpepper, and Fernando F. Segovia, eds., *Word, Theology, and Community in John* (St. Louis: Chalice, 2002).

[128]See esp. Craig R. Koester, *Symbolism in the Fourth Gospel: Meaning, Mystery, Community*, 2nd ed. (Minneapolis: Fortress Press, 2003).

[129]E.g., Dorothy Lee, *Flesh and Glory: Symbolism, Gender and Theology in the Gospel of John* (New York: Crossroad, 2002).

[130]See, for instance, Colleen M. Conway, "The Production of the Johannine Community: A New Historicist Perspective," *JBL* 121 (2002): 479–95. When Conway speaks, within the "new historicist" perspective, of the "historical Jesus," she does not refer to the Jesus of space-time history to which individuals via texts bear ongoing witness, but to the historical reconstruction within the texts: we cannot say anything about any extra-textual Jesus. At one level, of course, she is right: the only access we have to Jesus is through the texts. But to infer, on postmodern premises, that such texts provide no extra-textual referentiality, is to betray the texts themselves.

[131]Barrett, *John*, 67–99; Schnackenburg, *John*, esp. in the many excursuses; Keener, vol. 1.

christological titles—whether those found only in the fourth gospel (e.g., Lamb of God, Word, I Am), or those found in all four (e.g., Son of Man, Christ, King). Rather, fundamental to all else that is said of him, Jesus is peculiarly the Son of God, or simply the Son. Although "Son of God" can serve as a rough synonym for "Messiah," it is enriched by the unique manner in which Jesus as God's Son relates to his Father: he is functionally subordinate to him and does and says only those things the Father gives him to do and say, but he does *everything* that the Father does, since the Father shows him everything that he himself does (5:19ff.). The perfection of Jesus' obedience and the unqualified nature of his dependence thereby become the loci in which Jesus discloses nothing less than the words and deeds of God.

3. Despite the heavy emphasis on Jesus as the one who reveals his Father, salvation does not come (as in Gnosticism) merely by revelation. John's work is a gospel: all the movement of the plot is toward the cross and the resurrection. The cross is not merely a revelatory moment:[132] it is the death of the shepherd for his sheep (John 10), the sacrifice of one man for his nation (John 11), the life that is given for the world (John 6), the victory of the Lamb of God (John 1), the triumph of the obedient Son, who in consequence bequeaths his life, his peace, his joy, his Spirit (John 14–16).

4. John's distinctive emphasis on eschatology is bound up with his use of the "hour" theme (often rendered "time" in the NIV: e.g., 2:4; 7:6; the TNIV uses "hour" in 2:4). All the major New Testament corpora display the tension of trying simultaneously (1) to express the wonderful truth that in the ministry, death, resurrection, and exaltation of Jesus, God's promised "last days" have already arrived, and (2) to insist that the fullness of hope is still to come. Different authors set out the tension in different ways. In John, the hour "is coming and has now come" (4:23; 5:25); Jesus has bequeathed his peace, but in this world we will have trouble (16:33). Above all, in the wake of Jesus' exaltation and his gift of the Spirit, we can possess eternal life even now: that is characteristic of John, who tilts his emphasis to the *present* enjoyment of eschatological blessings. But this is never at the expense of all future hope: the time is coming when those who are in the graves will come out to face the judgment of the One to whom all judgment has been entrusted by the Father (5:28–30). If John asserts that Jesus even now makes himself present among his followers in the person of his Spirit (14:23), he also insists that Jesus himself is coming back to gather his own to the dwelling he has prepared for them (14:1–3).

5. Although John's teaching on the Holy Spirit has important similarities to synoptic emphases (e.g., cf. John 3:34 and Luke 4:14–21), there are numerous strands that are unique. Jesus not only bears and bestows the Spirit, but by

---

[132]Contra J. T. Forestell, *The Word of the Cross: Salvation as Revelation in the Fourth Gospel*, AnBib (Rome: BIP, 1974)

bequeathing the eschatological Spirit, he discharges his role as the one who introduces what is characteristic under the new covenant (3:5; 7:37–39). In the farewell discourse (John 14–16), the Spirit, the Counselor, is clearly given in consequence of Jesus' death and exaltation. The elements of what came to be called the doctrine of the Trinity find their clearest articulation, within the New Testament, in the Gospel of John.

6. Although John does not cite the Old Testament as frequently as does Matthew, for example, his use of the Old Testament is characterized by an extraordinary number of allusions, and above all by his insistence that Jesus in certain respects replaces revered figures and institutions from the old covenant (e.g., temple, vine, tabernacle, serpent, Passover). The underlying hermeneutic assumed deserves close study.

7. No gospel better preserves the ways in which Jesus was misunderstood by his contemporaries, including his own followers. This feature not only provides an entrance into various historical questions, as we have seen, but is itself a reflection on the relation between the old covenant and the new. For the same gospel that insists that Jesus fulfills and in certain respects replaces many Old Testament features equally insists that most of these points were not grasped by Jesus' disciples until after his exaltation.

8. Not a little attention is devoted to what it means to belong to the people of God. Although there is nothing on church order per se, there is much on the election, life, origin, nature, witness, suffering, fruit-bearing, prayer, love, and unity of the people of God.

9. We have seen that John in certain respects provides greater depth than do the Synoptic Gospels, but on relatively restricted topics. That is a major reason why his vocabulary is relatively small, with certain words and expressions occurring again and again. This repetition becomes an index of some of the things that are important to him. For instance, he uses the verb πιστεύω (*pisteuō*, "to believe") 98 times; the "love" words 57 times; κόσμος (*kosmos*, "world") 78 times, the "to send" verbs (πέμπω [*pempō*] and ἀποστέλλω [*apostellō*]) 60 times, "Father" 137 times (mostly with reference to God). However tricky it is to approach an author's theology through word studies, in John's case such studies constitute an important entrée.

10. The complexities that bind together election, faith, and the function of signs are repeatedly explored. If faith bursts forth in consequence of what is revealed in the signs, well and good: signs legitimately serve as a basis for faith (e.g., 10:38). In contrast, people are excoriated for their dependence on signs (4:48). It is a better faith that hears and believes rather than sees and believes (20:29). But in the last analysis, faith turns on sovereign election by the Son (15:16), on being part of the gift from the Father to the Son (6:37–44). This truth is at the heart of a book that is persistently evangelistic.

BIBLIOGRAPHY

Mark L. **Appold**, *The Oneness Motif in the Fourth Gospel*, WUNT 1 (Tübingen: J. C. B. Mohr [Paul Siebeck], 1976) ▪John **Ashton**, ed., *The Interpretation of John*, Studies in New Testament Interpretation, 2nd ed. (Edinburgh: T. & T. Clark, 1997) ▪E. H. **Askwith**, *The Historical Value of the Fourth Gospel* (London: Hodder & Stoughton, 1910) ▪David E. **Aune**, "On the Origins of the 'Council of Javneh' Myth," *JBL* 110 (1991): 491–93 ▪C. K. **Barrett**, *The Gospel According to St John* (London: SPCK / Philadelphia: Westminster, 1978) ▪Richard **Bauckham**, "The Eyewitnesses and the Gospel Traditions," *JSHJ* 1 (2003): 28–60 ▪idem, ed., *The Gospels for All Christians: Rethinking the Gospel Audiences* (Grand Rapids: Eerdmans, 1998) ▪G. R. **Beasley-Murray**, *John*, WBC 36, 2nd ed. (Waco: Word, 1999) ▪J. **Becker**, "Aus der Literatur des Johannesevangeliums," *ThR* 47 (1982): 279–347 ▪idem, *Das Evangelium des Johannes*, 2 vols. (Gütersloh: G. Mohn, 1979–81) ▪Cornelis **Bennema**, "The Power of Saving Wisdom: An Investigation of Spirit and Wisdom in Relation to the Soteriology of the Fourth Gospel" (Ph.D. diss., London Bible College, 2001) ▪J. H. **Bernard**, *The Gospel According to St John*, 2 vols., ICC (Edinburgh: T. & T. Clark, 1928) ▪Reimund **Bieringer**, Didier **Pollefeyt**, and Frederique **Vandecasteele-Vanneuville**, eds., *Anti-Judaism and the Fourth Gospel: Papers of the Leuven Colloquium, 2000* (Louisville: Westminster John Knox Press, 2001) ▪Josef **Blank**, *Krisis: Untersuchungen zur johanneischen Christologie und Eschatologie* (Freiburg: Lambertus, 1964) ▪J. **Blinzler**, *Johannes und die Synoptiker* (Stuttgart: KBW, 1965) ▪Craig L. **Blomberg**, *The Historical Reliability of the Gospels* (Leicester: IVP, 1987) ▪Hendrikus **Boers**, *Neither on This Mountain nor in Jerusalem*, SBLMS 35 (Atlanta: SP, 1988) ▪P. **Borgen**, *Bread from Heaven*, NovTSup 10 (Leiden: Brill, 1965) ▪K. **Bornhäuser**, *Das Johannesevangelium: Eine Missionsschrift für Israel* (Gütersloh: C. Bertelsmann, 1928) ▪David D. C. **Braine**, "The Inner Jewishness of St. John's Gospel as the Clue to the Inner Jewishness of Jesus," *SNTU* 13 (1989): 101–55 ▪Thomas L. **Brodie**, *The Quest for the Origin of John's Gospel: A Source-Oriented Approach* (New York: Oxford University Press, 1993) ▪idem, *The Gospel According to John: A Literary and Theological Commentary* (New York: Oxford University Press, 1993) ▪George J. **Brooke**, "Christ and the Law in John 7–10," in *Law and Religion: Essays in the Place of the Law in Israel and Early Christianity*, ed. Barnabas Lindars (London: SPCK, 1988), 34–43 ▪Raymond E. **Brown**, *The Community of the Beloved Disciple* (New York: Paulist, 1978) ▪idem, *The Gospel According to John*, 2 vols. (Garden City: Doubleday, 1966–70) ▪idem, *An Introduction to the Gospel of John*, ed. Francis J. Moloney (New York: Doubleday, 2003) ▪F. F. **Bruce**, *The Gospel of John* (Basingstoke: Pickering & Inglis, 1983) ▪Andrew C. **Brunson**, *Psalm 118 in the Gospel of John: An Intertextual Study on the New Exodus Pattern in the Theology of John*, WUNT 158 (Tübingen: Mohr-Siebeck, 2003) ▪R. **Bultmann**, *The Gospel of John: A Commentary* (ET Oxford: Blackwell, 1971) ▪Gary M. **Burge**, *The Anointed Community: The*

Holy Spirit in the Johannine Tradition (Grand Rapids: Eerdmans, 1987) ▪D. A. **Carson**, "Current Source Criticism of the Fourth Gospel: Some Methodological Questions," *JBL* 97 (1978): 411–29 ▪idem, *Divine Sovereignty and Human Responsibility* (Atlanta: John Knox, 1981) ▪idem, *The Gospel According to John,* PNTC (Grand Rapids: Eerdmans, 1990) ▪idem, "The Purpose of the Fourth Gospel: John 20:30–31 Reconsidered," *JBL* 108 (1987): 639–51 ▪idem, "Recent Literature on the Fourth Gospel: Some Reflections," *Themelios* 9 (1983): 8–18 ▪14 (1989): 57–64 ▪idem, "Understanding Misunderstandings in the Fourth Gospel," *TynB* 33 (1982): 59–89 ▪idem, "The Use of the Old Testament in John and the Johannine Epistles," in *It Is Written: Scripture Citing Scripture,* Fs. Barnabas Lindars, ed. D. A. Carson and H. G. M. Williamson SSF (Cambridge: Cambridge University Press, 1988), 245–64 ▪D. A. **Carson** and John D. **Woodbridge**, eds., *Scripture and Truth* (Grand Rapids: Zondervan, 1983) ▪Maurice **Casey**, *Is John's Gospel True?* (New York: Routledge, 1996) ▪Colleen M. **Conway**, "The Production of the Johannine Community: A New Historicist Perspective," *JBL* 121 (2002): 479–95 ▪O. **Cullmann**, *The Johannine Circle* (ET London: SCM, 1976) ▪R. Alan **Culpepper**, *Anatomy of the Fourth Gospel: A Study in Literary Design* (Philadelphia: Fortress Press, 1983) ▪idem, *The Johannine School* (Missoula: SP, 1975) ▪R. Alan **Culpepper** and C. Clifton **Black**, eds., *Exploring the Gospel of John,* Fs. D. Moody Smith (Louisville: Westminster John Knox Press, 1996) ▪M. **de Jonge**, "The Beloved Disciple and the Date of the Gospel of John," in *Text and Interpretation,* Fs. Matthew Black, ed. E. Best and R. M. Wilson (Cambridge: Cambridge University Press, 1979), 99–114 ▪Ignace **de la Potterie**, *La vérité dans Saint Jean,* 2 vols. (Rome: BIP, 1977) ▪Mgr. **de Solages**, *Jean et les synoptiques* (Leiden: Brill, 1979) ▪C. H. **Dodd**, *Historical Tradition in the Fourth Gospel* (Cambridge: Cambridge University Press, 1963) ▪idem, *The Interpretation of the Fourth Gospel* (Cambridge: Cambridge University Press, 1953) ▪Thomas **Dowell**, "Jews and Christians in Conflict: Why the Fourth Gospel Changed the Synoptic Tradition," *LouvStud* 15 (1990): 19–37 ▪P. **Duke**, *Irony in the Fourth Gospel* (Atlanta: John Knox, 1985) ▪Bart D. **Ehrman**, "Jesus and the Adulteress," *NTS* 34 (1988): 24–44 ▪Gordon D. **Fee**, "The Use of the Definite Article with Personal Names in the Gospel of John," *NTS* 17 (1970–71): 168–83 ▪idem, "On the Text and Meaning of John 20,30–31," in *The Four Gospels,* Fs. Frans Neirynck, ed. F. van Segbroeck, C. M. Tuckett, G. van Belle, and J. Verheyden, Vol. 3 [=BETL 100] (Leuven: Leuven University Press, 1992), 2193–2205 ▪J. T. **Forestell**, *The Word of the Cross: Salvation as Revelation in the Fourth Gospel,* AnBib 57 (Rome: BIP, 1974) ▪R. **Fortna**, *The Fourth Gospel and Its Predecessor* (Philadelphia: Fortress Press, 1988) ▪idem, *The Gospel of Signs,* SNTSMS 11 (Cambridge: Cambridge University Press, 1970) ▪Robert T. **Fortna** and Tom **Thatcher**, ed., *Jesus in Johannine Tradition* (Louisville: Westminster John Knox Press, 2001) ▪R. T. **France**, "The Church and the Kingdom of God: Some Hermeneutical Issues," in *Biblical Interpretation and the Church: Text and Context,* ed. D. A. Carson (Exeter: Paternoster,

1984), 30–44 ∎E. **Franck**, *Revelation Taught: The Paraclete in the Gospel of John* (Lund: Gleerup, 1985) ∎Edwin D. **Freed**, "Did John Write His Gospel Partly to Win Samaritan Converts?" *NovT* 12 (1970): 241–56 ∎Jörg **Frey**, *Die johanneische Eschatologie*, 3 vols., WUNT 96, 110, 117 (Tübingen: Mohr-Siebeck, 1997–2000) ∎M. E. **Glasswell**, "The Relationship Between John and Mark," *JSNT* 23 (1983): 99–115 ∎Ernst **Haenchen**, *A Commentary on the Gospel of John*, 2 vols. (ET Philadelphia: Fortress Press, 1984) ∎Tobias **Hägerland**, "John's Gospel: A Two-Level Drama?" *JSNT* 25 (2003): 309–322 ∎Philip B. **Harner**, *The "I Am" of the Fourth Gospel* (Philadelphia: Fortress Press, 1970) ∎A. E. **Harvey**, *Jesus on Trial: A Study in the Fourth Gospel* (London: SPCK, 1976) ∎A. C. **Headlam**, *The Fourth Gospel as History* (Oxford: Blackwell, 1948) ∎Hans-Peter **Heekerens**, *Die Zeichen-Quelle der johanneischen Redaktion* (Stuttgart: KBW, 1984) ∎William **Hendriksen**, *Exposition of the Gospel According to John*, 2 vols. (Grand Rapids: Baker, 1953–54) ∎Martin **Hengel**, *The Johannine Question* (Philadelphia: Trinity Press International, 1989) ∎Charles E. **Hill**, *The Johannine Corpus in the Early Church* (Oxford: Oxford University Press, 2004) ∎Zane **Hodges**, "The Woman Taken in Adultery (John 7:53–8:11)," *BS* 136 (1979): 318–72 ∎137 (1980): 41–53 ∎H. Scott **Holland**, *The Fourth Gospel* (London: John Murray, 1923) ∎W. **Horbury**, "The Benediction of the *Minim* and Early Jewish-Christian Controversy," *JTS* 33 (1982): 19–61 ∎David G. **Horrell** and Christopher M. **Tuckett**, *Christology, Controversy and Community*, NovTSup 99 (Leiden: Brill, 2000) ∎E. C. **Hoskyns**, *The Fourth Gospel*, ed. F. N. Davey (London: Faber & Faber, 1954) ∎A. M. **Hunter**, *According to John* (London: SCM, 1968) ∎Howard M. **Jackson**, "Ancient Self-Referential Conventions and Their Implications for the Authorship and Integrity of the Gospel of John," *JTS* 50 (1999): 1–34 ∎Joachim **Jeremias**, *New Testament Theology I: The Proclamation of Jesus* (London: SCM, 1971) ∎George **Johnston**, *The Spirit-Paraclete in the Gospel of John*, SNTSMS 12 (Cambridge: Cambridge University Press, 1970) ∎Ernst **Käsemann**, *The Testament of Jesus: A Study of the Gospel of John in the Light of Chapter 17* (ET London: SCM, 1968) ∎Craig S. **Keener**, *The Gospel of John: A Commentary*, 2 vols. (Peabody: Hendrickson, 2003) ∎G. D. **Kilpatrick**, "The Religious Background of the Fourth Gospel," in *Studies in the Fourth Gospel*, ed. F. L. Cross (London: Mowbray, 1957), 36–44 ∎R. **Kimelman**, "*Birkat ha-Minim* and the Lack of Evidence for an anti-Christian Jewish Prayer in Late Antiquity," in *Jewish and Christian Self-Definition*, vol. 2 of *Aspects of Judaism in the Greco-Roman Period*, ed. E. P. Sanders (Philadelphia: Fortress Press, 1981), 226–44, 391–403 ∎Craig R. **Koester**, *Symbolism in the Fourth Gospel: Meaning, Mystery, Community*, 2nd ed. (Minneapolis: Fortress Press, 2003) ∎Andreas **Köstenberger**, *The Missions of Jesus and the Disciples According to the Fourth Gospel: With Implications for the Fourth Gospel's Purpose and the Mission of the Contemporary Church* (Grand Rapids: Eerdmans, 1998) ∎idem, "'I Suppose' [οἶμαι]: The Conclusion of John's Gospel in Its Literary and Historical Context," in *The New Testament in Its First Century Setting: Essays on Context and Background,*

Fs. Bruce W. Winter, ed. P. J. Williams et al. (Grand Rapids: Eerdmans, 2004), 72–88 ▮Joachim **Kügler**, *Der Jünger, dem Jesus liebte* (Stuttgart: KBW, 1988) ▮Robert **Kysar**, "The Background of the Prologue of the Fourth Gospel: A Critique of Historical Methods," *CJT* 16 (1970): 250–55 ▮idem, *The Fourth Evangelist and His Gospel: An Examination of Contemporary Scholarship* (Minneapolis: Augsburg, 1975) ▮M.-J. **Lagrange**, *Evangile selon Saint Jean* (Paris: Gabalda, 1925) ▮Dorothy **Lee**, *Flesh and Glory: Symbolism, Gender and Theology in the Gospel of John* (New York: Crossroad, 2002) ▮Domingo **León**, "¿Es el apóstol Juan el discípulo amado?" *EstBib* 45 (1987): 403–92 ▮J. B. **Lightfoot**, *Essays on the Work Entitled "Supernatural Religion"* (London: Macmillan, 1893) ▮B. **Lindars**, *The Gospel of John*, NCB (London: Oliphants, 1972) ▮R. N. **Longenecker**, "On the Form, Function, and Authority of the New Testament Letters," in *Scripture and Truth*, ed. D. A. Carson and John D. Woodbridge (Grand Rapids: Zondervan, 1983), 101–14 ▮James **McPolin**, "Studies in the Fourth Gospel—Some Contemporary Trends," *IBS* 2 (1980): 3–26 ▮Gerhard **Maier**, "Johannes und Matthäus—Zweispalt oder Viergestalt des Evangeliums?" in *GP* 2.267–97 ▮Bruce J. **Malina** and Richard L. **Rohrbaugh**, *Social-Science Commentary on the Gospel of John* (Minneapolis: Fortress Press, 1998) ▮I. Howard **Marshall**, *The Origins of New Testament Christology* (Leicester: IVP, 1976) ▮J. L. **Martyn**, *History and Theology in the Fourth Gospel* (Nashville: Abingdon, 1979) ▮Wayne A. **Meeks**, *The Prophet-King: Moses Traditions and the Johannine Christology*, NovTSup 14 (Leiden: Brill, 1967) ▮J. Ramsey **Michaels**, *John* (San Francisco: Harper & Row, 1983) ▮Paul S. **Minear**, "The Original Functions of John 21," *JBL* 102 (1983): 85–98 ▮George **Mlakushyil**, *The Christocentric Literary Structure of the Fourth Gospel*, AnBib 117 (Rome: Pontifical Biblical Institute, 1987) ▮Francis J. **Moloney**, *The Gospel of John*, SacPag 4 (Collegeville: Liturgical Press, 1998) ▮Leon **Morris**, *The Gospel According to John* (Grand Rapids: Eerdmans, 1971) ▮idem, *Jesus Is the Christ: Studies in the Theology of John* (Grand Rapids: Eerdmans, 1979) ▮idem, *Studies in the Fourth Gospel* (Grand Rapids: Eerdmans, 1969) ▮Stephen **Motyer**, *Your Father the Devil? A New Approach to John and "the Jews"* (Carlisle: Paternoster, 1997) ▮C. F. D. **Moule**, *The Birth of the New Testament* (London: Black, 1982) ▮idem, *The Origin of Christology* (Cambridge: Cambridge University Press, 1977) ▮F. **Mussner**, *The Historical Jesus in the Gospel of St John* (ET London: Burns & Oates, 1967) ▮F. **Neirynck** et al., *Jean et les synoptiques* (Louvain: Louvain University Press, 1979) ▮W. **Oehler**, *Das Johannesevangelium, eine Missionsschrift für die Welt* (Gütersloh: Bertelsmann, 1936) ▮idem, *Zum Missionscharackter des Johannesevangeliums* (Gütersloh: Bertelsmann, 1941) ▮Teresa **Okure**, *The Johannine Approach to Mission*, WUNT 31 (Tübingen: J. C. B. Mohr [Paul Siebeck], 1988) ▮B. **Olsson**, *Structure and Meaning of the Fourth Gospel* (Lund: Gleerup, 1974) ▮John **Painter**, R. Alan **Culpepper** and Fernando F. **Segovia**, eds., *Word, Theology, and Community in John* (St. Louis: Chalice, 2002) ▮Margaret **Pamment**, "The Fourth Gospel's Beloved Disciple," *ExpTim* 94 (1983): 363–67 ▮Pierson **Parker**, "John the Son of Zebedee and the Fourth Gospel," *JBL* 81 (1962): 35–43 ▮Norman **Perrin**, *Jesus and the Language of the Kingdom* (Philadelphia: Fortress Press, 1976) ▮C. S. **Petrie**, "The Authorship of 'The Gospel According to Matthew': A Reconsideration of the External Evidence," *NTS* 14 (1967–68): 15–32 ▮David **Rensberger**, *Overcoming the World: Politics and Community in the Gospel of John* (London: SPCK, 1988) ▮H. R. **Reynolds**, *The Gospel of St. John*, 2 vols. (London: Funk & Wagnalls, 1906) ▮H. **Ridderbos**, *Het evangelie naar Johannes*, 2 vols. (Kampen: J. H. Kok, 1987–) ▮J. A. T. **Robinson**, *The Priority of John* (London: SCM, 1985) ▮idem, *Redating the New Testament* (Philadelphia: Westminster, 1976) ▮idem, *Twelve New Testament Studies* (London: SCM, 1962) ▮J. Armitage **Robinson**, *The Historical Character of the Fourth Gospel* (London: Longmans-Green, 1948) ▮H. H. **Rowdon**, ed., *Christ the Lord*, Fs. Donald Guthrie (Leicester: IVP, 1982) ▮Samuel **Sandmel**, "Parallelomania," *JBL* 81 (1962): 2–13 ▮R. **Schnackenburg**, *Das Johannesevangelium*, 4 vols. (Freiburg: Herder, 1965–84), vol. 4 only in German, subtitled *Ergänzende Auslegungen und Exkurse* (Freiburg: Herder, 1984) ▮idem, *The Gospel According to St John*, 3 vols. (ET London: Burns & Oates, 1968–82) ▮Walter **Scott**, ed., *Hermetica: The Ancient Greek and Latin Writings Which Contain Religious or Philosophic Teachings Ascribed to Hermes Trismegistus*: Vol. 1, *Introduction: Texts and Translation*; Vol. 2, *Notes on the Corpus Hermeticum*; Vol. 3, *Notes on the Latin Asclepius and the Hermetic Excerpts of Stobaeus*; Vol. 4, *Testimonia* (Oxford: Clarendon Press, 1924–36) ▮E. F. **Seigman**, "St. John's Use of the Synoptic Material," *CBQ* 30 (1968): 182–98 ▮S. S. **Smalley**, *John: Evangelist and Interpreter* (Exeter: Paternoster, 1978) ▮D. M. **Smith**, *Johannine Christianity: Essays on Its Setting, Sources, and Theology* (Columbia: University of South Carolina Press, 1984) ▮idem, *John*, ANTC (Nashville: Abingdon, 1999) ▮Jeffrey Lloyd **Staley**, *The Print's First Kiss: A Rhetorical Investigation of the Implied Reader in the Fourth Gospel*, SBLDS 82 (Atlanta: SP, 1988) ▮idem, "The Structure of John's Prologue: Its Implications for the Gospel's Narrative Structure," *CBQ* 48 (1986): 241–63 ▮E. **Stauffer**, *Jesus and His Story* (London: SCM, 1960) ▮Marianne M. **Thompson**, *The Humanity of Jesus in the Fourth Gospel* (Philadelphia: Fortress Press, 1988) ▮H. **Thyen**, "Aus der Literatur des Johannesevangeliums," *ThR* 39 (1974): 1–69, 222–52, 289–330; 42 (1977): 211–70; 44 (1979): 97–134 ▮G. **van Belle**, *Johannine Bibliography, 1966–1985*, BETL 82 (Louvain: Louvain University Press, 1988) ▮idem, *Les parenthèses dans l'évangile de Jean: Aperçu historique et classification* (Louvain: Louvain University Press, 1985) ▮idem, *The Signs Source in the Fourth Gospel: Historical Survey and Critical Evaluation of the Semeia Hypothesis* (Leuven: Leuven University Press, 1994) ▮W. C. **van Unnik**, "The Purpose of St. John's Gospel," in *SE* 1:382–411 ▮Herman C. **Waetjen**, ed., *The Gospel of John in Sociolinguistic Perspective*, Protocol of the Forty-eighth Colloquy (Claremont: Center for Hermeneutical Studies in Hellenistic and Modern Culture, 1984) ▮David **Wenham**, "The Enigma of the Fourth Gospel: Another Look," *TynB* 48 (1997): 149–78 ▮B. F. **Westcott**, *The Gospel According to St John: The Greek Text* *with Introduction and Notes,* 2 vols. (London: John Murray, 1908) ▮Catrin H. **Williams**, *I am He: The Interpretation of 'Anî Hû' in Jewish and Early Christian Literature,* WUNT 113 (Tübingen: Mohr-Siebeck, 2000) ▮Hans **Windisch**, *Johannes und die Synoptiker* (Leipzig: J. C. Hinrichs'sche Buchhandlung, 1926) ▮Ben **Witherington** III, *John's Wisdom: A Commentary on the Fourth Gospel* (Lousiville: Westminster John Knox Press, 1995) ▮Egil A. **Wyller**, "In Solomon's Porch: A Henological Analysis of the Architectonic of the Fourth Gospel," *ST* 42 (1988): 151–67 ▮Edwin A. **Yamauchi**, *Pre-Christian Gnosticism: A Survey of the Proposed Evidences,* 2nd ed. (Grand Rapids: Baker, 1983).

CHAPTER SEVEN

ACTS

CONTENTS

The book we know as the Acts of the Apostles belongs with the Gospel of Luke as the second volume in a history of Christian beginnings. Luke probably did not give this second book a title of its own; only when his gospel was separated from its companion volume and placed with the other gospels was there need to give the second part of his story a title. Second- and third-century authors made various suggestions, such as "The Memorandum of Luke" (Tertullian) and "The Acts of All the Apostles" (Muratorian Canon). The name that would eventually stick, "The Acts of the Apostles," is first used in the anti-Marcionite prologue to Luke (late second century?)[1] and in Irenaeus (*Adv. Haer.* 3.13.3).[2] The word "Acts" (πράξεις [*praxeis*]) denoted a recognized genre or subgenre in the ancient world, characterizing books that described the great deeds of people or of cities. In that Acts narrates the founding events of the church and ascribes most of them to apostles, the title is not inappropriate. Yet, judging from Luke's own emphases, he may have preferred a title such as "The Acts of the Holy Spirit" or "What Jesus Continued to Do and to Teach" (see 1:1).

In Acts, Luke conducts the reader on a whirlwind tour of three decades of church history. We visit Jerusalem, Judea, Samaria, Syria, Cyprus, many cities in Asia Minor, Macedonia, Greece, and, finally, Rome. We witness everything from preaching and miracles to jailbreaks and shipwrecks. And, while many

---

[1] For the date of this prologue to the third gospel, traditionally thought to be directed against Marcion (hence its name), see F. F. Bruce, *The Book of Acts,* rev. ed., NICNT (Grand Rapids: Eerdmans, 1988), 5 n. 6. For a summary of current scholarly views about these prologues, see esp. Joseph A. Fitzmyer, *The Gospel According to Luke I–IX,* AB 28 (New York: Doubleday, 1982), 39.

[2] See Frederick Fyvie Bruce, "The Acts of the Apostles: Historical Record or Theological Reconstruction?" *ANRW* 25.3 (1985): 2571.

individuals accompany us on our tour, two are rather constant companions: Peter, who is often with us in Jerusalem, Judea, and Samaria; and Paul, who is our almost constant companion from Syria to Rome. We can, in fact, divide our tour into two major parts based on the prominence of these two individuals: chapters 1–12 and chapters 13–28. Each of these major sections can be subdivided further into three parts, which are marked off by key summary statements. In these brief notes, Luke sums up a series of events by telling us that they have led to the growth of the Word of God or of the church (6:7; 9:31; 12:24; 16:5; 19:20). Each section carries us to a new geographic and/or cultural stage in the itinerary of the gospel, as Luke portrays the fulfillment of Jesus' command to the apostles that they be his witnesses "in Jerusalem, and in all Judea and Samaria, and to the ends of the earth" (1:8).[3]

Prologue: Foundations for the church and its mission (1:1–2:41). Luke begins by rooting the church and its mission in Jesus' acts and words. It is the risen Jesus who prepares the apostles for the coming of the Spirit (1:4–5) and charges them with their worldwide missionary mandate (1:8). Jesus' earthly ministry is then brought to a close with Luke's second narrative of his ascension into heaven (1:9–11; cf. also Luke 24:50–51), a narrative that serves as a hinge between the gospel and Acts. Luke then describes the choosing of Matthias to replace Judas (1:12–26), the coming of the Spirit on the Day of Pentecost (2:1–13), and the first missionary sermon (2:14–41).

The church in Jerusalem (2:42–6:7). Luke begins this section with a summary of the characteristics of the early church in Jerusalem (2:42–47). He then describes Peter's healing of a crippled man in the temple precincts (3:1–10), a notable and public miracle that gains Peter a hearing for another missionary sermon (3:13–26). Opposition arises from the Sanhedrin, but Peter and John boldly resist its request that they cease speaking "in the name of Jesus" (4:1–22). The church as a whole, infused with the power of the Spirit, follows the lead of the apostles, preaching the Word of God boldly after having prayed that God would grant them such opportunity (4:23–31). But all is not perfect, even in these early and exciting days in the life of the church. The lie of a married couple, Ananias and Sapphira, about their participation in the early community's voluntary sharing program (4:32–37) brings swift judgment upon them (5:1–11). The popular healing and preaching ministry of the apostles (5:12–16) again sparks opposition from the Jewish leaders, and again the apostles are arrested and brought before the Sanhedrin. Gamaliel, an important rabbi of his day, counsels moderation,

---

[3]The division of Acts into six sections based on these summary statements was proposed by C. H. Turner, "The Chronology of the New Testament," in *A Dictionary of the Bible,* ed. James Hastings (Edinburgh: T. & T. Clark, 1898–1904), 1.421, and is adopted by, among others, McNeile, 97–98, and Richard N. Longenecker, "The Acts of the Apostles," in *EBC* 9.234.

and the apostles are released (5:17–42). In order to give themselves fully to the preaching of the Word, the apostles appoint seven men to regulate the distribution of food among the community (6:1–6). In his first summary statement, Luke concludes that in this way "the word of God spread" (6:7).

Wider horizons for the church: Stephen, Samaria, and Saul (6:8–9:31). To this point in his narrative, Luke has portrayed the early believers as loyal, if somewhat unusual, Jews. The stories in this next section show how the church began to strain the bounds of traditional Judaism. Stephen is a pivotal figure in this respect. A charismatic figure who attracted a considerable following, Stephen was falsely accused of speaking against the temple and the law (6:8–15). When brought before the Sanhedrin to answer charges about his teaching, Stephen uses a sketch of Israel's history to suggest that God's revelation cannot be confined to one place and to charge the Sandedrin members themselves with resisting the Holy Spirit (7:1–53). So bold a charge does not go unanswered: Stephen is condemned to be stoned (7:54–60).

Stephen's radical stance sparks opposition to the young Christian movement, and "all except the apostles" are forced to leave Jerusalem (8:1–3). One of those who leaves, Philip, brings the gospel to Samaria, a territory to the north of Judea inhabited by people considered by most Jews to be renegade Jews at best. The Samaritans believe the message of Philip, and Peter and John are sent to confirm that the Samaritans had indeed been accepted into the kingdom of God (8:4–25). Philip, directed by an angel, travels south, where he meets and converts a court official of the queen of Ethiopia (8:26–40). Finally, Luke tells us of the conversion and early ministry of the one chosen by God to be the pioneer in the mission to the Gentiles—Saul of Tarsus (9:1–30). Again Luke summarizes: "The church . . . enjoyed a time of peace and was strengthened. Living in the fear of the Lord and encouraged by the Holy Spirit, it increased in numbers." (9:31).

Peter and the first Gentile convert (9:32–12:24). This section focuses on Peter, and especially on Peter's role in opening the way for Gentiles to become Christians. Peter performs miracles in Lydda and Joppa, cities in Judea to the northwest of Jerusalem (9:32–43). He is then used by God to bring Cornelius, a Gentile Roman soldier, into the church. Through visions and the direct command of the Spirit, God brings Cornelius and Peter together (10:1–23). At Cornelius's house, Peter's preaching of the gospel is interrupted by the sovereign action of God, bestowing the Spirit upon Cornelius in so evident a manner that Peter has to recognize that God had truly accepted a Gentile into his church (10:24–48).

The importance of so clear a witness is revealed in the next narrative, in which Peter is able to reassure Jewish-Christian skeptics in Jerusalem about the reality of Cornelius's conversion (11:1–18). It is surely significant that here Luke tells us of the church at Antioch, where the mixture of Jews and Gentiles required that believers in Jesus be given a new name: Christian (11:19–30). The section concludes with the story of Peter's miraculous escape from prison (12:1–19) and the death of Herod Agrippa I, who had initiated the persecution that led to Peter's arrest (12:20–23). Here again occurs Luke's transitional summary: "The word of God continued to increase and spread" (12:24).

Paul turns to the Gentiles (12:25–16:5). From Peter, Luke turns now to Paul, who dominates the remainder of the book. Paul's significance for Luke lies in his being used by God to pioneer an extensive ministry to Gentiles, to carry the gospel to the ends of the earth, and to show that the gospel was no direct threat to the Roman government. The vibrant Christian community at Antioch, to which Paul had been brought by Barnabas, is led by the Spirit to send Paul, along with Barnabas and John Mark, on the first missionary journey (12:25–13:3). The journey takes them first to Barnabas's home, Cyprus, where a Roman official is converted (13:4–12). The band then sails to the south coast of Asia Minor, where they quickly head inland to the important city of Pisidian Antioch. Paul delivers an evangelistic sermon in the synagogue there, a sermon that Luke summarizes, giving us a sample of the way Paul preached to a Jewish audience (13:13–43). Here also what becomes a typical pattern is first enacted: general Jewish rejection of the gospel, leading Paul and his companions to turn directly to the Gentiles, followed by Jewish persecution that forces them to move on (13:44–52).

Paul and his companions travel to Iconium (14:1–7), to Lystra, where Paul is stoned (14:8–20), and to Derbe, planting churches in each city and strengthening the new believers as they retrace their steps again to the coast (14:21–28). Upon arriving back in Antioch, the missionaries are confronted with a serious dispute about their outreach to the Gentiles. A council convened in Jerusalem to discuss the matter endorses the law-free offer of the gospel to the Gentiles, a decision that was of vital importance in establishing the character of the church and enabling its further growth (15:1–29). Paul and Barnabas bring the good news back to Antioch and begin planning a new missionary trip. But their inability to agree about taking along John Mark, who had turned for home before the first journey was complete, leads them to split, Barnabas taking Mark with him back to Cyprus and Paul taking Silas with him overland to Syria, Cilicia, and on to the churches established on the first journey (15:30–41). Here Paul also recruits Timothy for the cause (16:1–4). And thus, Luke again concludes, "the churches were strengthened in the faith and grew daily in numbers" (16:5).

Further Penetration into the Gentile world (16:6–19:20). It seems a bit odd that we should divide Luke's story at this point. Yet by the care with which he shows how Paul was directed by God's Spirit step-by-step to take the gospel into Macedonia (16:6–10), Luke implies that we have reached a decisive stage. (This is also the beginning of the first "we" passage—see v. 10.) The first stop is Philippi, a Roman colony in Macedonia, where an exorcism lands Paul and

Silas in jail. They (like Peter before them—one of the many parallels Luke draws between Peter and Paul) are miraculously rescued, and Paul turns his Roman citizenship to good account to secure his release (16:16–40). Paul and Silas move on to Thessalonica, but persecution forces them to flee by night to the relatively insignificant town of Berea (17:1–9). Trouble follows them even here, so Paul is sent away to Athens (17:10–15).

Here we are treated to a second sample of Paul's preaching, this time to a sophisticated, skeptical, Gentile audience on so-called Mars Hill in Athens (17:16–34). The results in Athens seem to be meager, however, so Paul travels across the narrow isthmus to Corinth, the chief city in the Peloponnese. Here Paul spends a year and a half, preaching, defending himself before the Roman official Gallio, and enlisting the Roman Jewish couple Priscilla and Aquila in the work of the gospel (18:1–17). The three leave Corinth for Ephesus, where Paul leaves the other two as he proceeds on to Caesarea, Antioch, and the churches of southern Asia Minor (18:18–23). In Ephesus, meanwhile, Priscilla and Aquila establish more firmly in the faith a gifted young man from Alexandria, Apollos (18:24–28). Paul himself arrives in Ephesus for a stay of two and a half years. We are given glimpses of Paul converting some disciples of John the Baptist (19:1–7), preaching in the synagogue and in his own hired hall (19:8–10), working miracles (19:11–12), and confronting the strong current of demonism for which the city was known (19:13–19). "In this way," Luke informs us, "the word of the Lord spread widely and grew in power" (19:20).

On to Rome (19:21–28:31). Again we may feel that it is rather artificial to insert a major break in the midst of Paul's stay in Ephesus. But Luke again suggests such a break with his first indication that Paul was determined to go to Rome (19:21–22). This determination drives Luke's narrative from this point on, but it takes Paul some time to get there. He leaves Ephesus only after a serious public uprising forces him to go (19:23–41). He revisits the churches in Macedonia and Greece and decides to return to Judea by the same route because of a plot against his life (20:1–6). On his way back, Paul stops to preach in Troas and stops again in Miletus to meet with the elders of the church of Ephesus (20:7–38). He arrives in Jerusalem via Tyre and Caesarea, with warnings about his impending arrest in Jerusalem ringing in his ears (21:1–16). The warning quickly becomes reality.

Paul's willingness to "fly his Jewish flag" for the sake of the Jewish Christians in Jerusalem by paying for, and joining in, some purification rites in the temple backfires (21:17–26). Certain Jews think that Paul has brought Gentiles into the temple with him, and the ensuing riot forces the Romans to intervene (21:27–36). Paul is arrested but is allowed to address the crowd before being taken away (21:37–22:22). Paul's Roman citizenship again stands him in good stead, and he is allowed to state his case before the Jewish Sanhedrin (22:30–23:10). The Lord assures Paul that he will live to testify about him in Rome

(23:11), despite a plot of the Jews to kill him (23:12–15). Paul is moved to Caesarea because of this threat, where he again defends himself, this time before the Roman governor, Felix (23:16–24:27). After Paul has languished in prison in Caesarea for two years, Festus replaces Felix, and Paul forces the issue by appealing to Caesar to hear his case (25:1–12). Before leaving, however, Paul again defends himself before Festus and his guests, King Agrippa II and his sister Bernice (25:13–26:32). Paul is then sent on to Rome. The trip, however, is interrupted by a severe storm, stranding Paul and his sailing companions for three months on the island of Malta (27:1–28:10). Paul finally arrives in Rome, where he is able to live in his own house, under guard, and preach the gospel freely (28:11–31). Here, with Paul in Rome for two years under house arrest, Luke's tour of the expansion of the gospel comes to an end.

AUTHOR

The Traditional Case

Both Luke and Acts are, strictly speaking, anonymous. From the preface to Luke, which is probably intended to introduce both the gospel and Acts, we can conclude that the author was well educated (the Greek of Luke 1:1–4 is good, literary Greek), not an original apostle or disciple of Christ (he writes about those things "handed down to us by those who from the first were eyewitnesses and servants of the word"), yet one who may have been a participant in some of the events he narrates ("fulfilled *among us* ").[4] He knows his Old Testament in the Greek Septuagint version, has an excellent knowledge of political and social conditions in the middle of the first century, and thinks a great deal of the apostle Paul.

Further inferences about the author come from the "we" passages in Acts. There are four passages in which the author shifts from his usual third-person narration to a first person plural narration. Note the beginning of the first such passage: "So *they* [Paul, Silas, and Timothy] passed by Mysia and went down to Troas. During the night Paul had a vision of a man of Macedonia standing and begging him, 'Come over to Macedonia and help us.' After Paul had seen the vision, *we* got ready at once to leave for Macedonia, concluding that God had called *us* to preach the gospel to them" (16:8–10). The author continues with his first person plural style through 16:17, and then uses it again in 20:5–15; 21:1–18; and 27:1–28:16. The natural reading of these passages is that the author of Acts was present during the events he narrates in these passages and that he kept a diary or itinerary report that he incorporates into the Book of Acts. If this is so, then the author was with Paul on the trip from Troas to Philippi and during the initial evangelization of Philippi on the first missionary journey

---

[4]See the section on "author" in chap. 5 for more detail on the prologue.

(16:10–17). Joining Paul again as the apostle came through Philippi at the end of the third missionary journey, he then accompanied him to Miletus, and from Miletus to Jerusalem (20:5–15; 21:1–18). Finally, he was with Paul on his voyage to Rome (27:1–28:16).

The author could not have been any of the companions of Paul who are mentioned in these passages. Furthermore, since the author accompanied Paul to Rome and was probably with him during Paul's two-year house arrest in Rome, we might expect Paul to mention him in the letters he wrote during that period of time: Colossians, Philemon, Ephesians, and, perhaps, Philippians.[5] Those companions who are named in these letters are Mark, Jesus Justus, Epaphras, Demas, Luke, Tychicus, Timothy, Aristarchus, and Epaphroditus. This line of reasoning is certainly not foolproof: the author of Acts may have left Paul after their arrival in Rome, or Paul may not have mentioned him in his letters, but it is suggestive. At least, this is as far as the internal evidence of Luke and Acts can take us.[6]

External evidence takes over at this point and singles out Luke from the list of possible candidates. The tradition that Luke, a companion of Paul, was the author of the third gospel and of Acts is early and unchallenged: the Muratorian Canon (c. A.D. 180–200?),[7] Irenaeus (*Adv. Haer.* 3.1; 3.14.1–4), the anti-Marcionite prologue (end of second century), Clement of Alexandria (*Strom.* 5.12), Tertullian (*Adv. Marc.* 4.2), and Eusebius (*H.E.* 3.4; 3.24.15).[8] Luke's authorship of these two books went virtually unchallenged until the onset of critical approaches to the New Testament at the end of the eighteenth century. Since then, doubt about the tradition has been widespread. We now examine the reasons for these doubts.

The Case against the Tradition

The external evidence. Critics of the tradition question the value of the testimony of the early church. Early Christians, it is said, produced many fanciful theories about the origin of New Testament books. Moreover, in an argument

> *Luke's authorship of the third gospel and the book of Acts went virtually unchallenged until the onset of critical approaches to the New Testament at the end of the eighteenth century.*

---

[5]We assume here, as is argued in the relevant chapters, that Colossians, Philemon, Ephesians, and (less certainly) Philippians were written during Paul's Roman imprisonment.

[6]Although Rendel Harris developed an argument that the original Western text of Acts 20:13 read, "But I Luke, and those who were with me, went on board." If this were so, we would have testimony to Lukan authorship from about A.D. 120 (cf. F. F. Bruce, *The Acts of the Apostles: The Greek Text with Introduction and Commentary*, 2nd ed. [Grand Rapids: Eerdmans, 1952], 5).

[7]On the date of the Muratorian Canon, see chap. 4, n. 7.

[8]See the very full and detailed analysis of the tradition in C. K. Barrett, *A Critical and Exegetical Commentary on the Acts of the Apostles*, 2 vols., ICC (Edinburgh: T. & T. Clark, 1994, 1998), 1.30–48.

echoed again and again in the literature, it is said that the tradition itself is probably no more than an inference from the text of the New Testament itself and has no independent historical value.[9] But as we saw above in our examination of the internal evidence, the New Testament does not furnish enough data to single out Luke as the author of Acts. Fitzmyer's criticism of the idea that the external evidence can be dismissed because it depends on the reasoning of early Christians is fair. "That an individual in the second century—or even several individuals—might have so reasoned is certainly possible; but that such inferences from the NT text are the sole basis of an otherwise uncontested or unambiguous tradition . . . is difficult to accept."[10] We must, then, attach importance to the testimony of the early church—particularly since this testimony runs against form in singling out a nonapostle as the author.

The "we" passages. The traditional argument (given above) is that the "we" passages reveal the presence of the author of Acts. Some think that the author depends on an itinerary or diary that he himself wrote in the first person plural at the time of the events and that he incorporates into his literary product; others, that the author has lapsed into the first person plural at these points as he writes. In either case, however, the "we" passages are thought to point to the author of the book.

But two other explanations for the phenomenon are advanced that would remove the value of this datum for the question of authorship. One is that the author has incorporated into his history a source written by another person in the first person plural.[11] But why would the author leave his source in that form? As critics never tire of pointing out, Luke has consistently reworded his sources, putting the stamp of his own style on everything he writes. And Harnack has shown that the style of the "we" passages is no different than the style of the text around these passages.[12] Why, then, would the author have left these several sections in this first person plural style, especially since it could hardly escape being misunderstood?

A second alternative explanation is that the use of the first person plural is a stylistic device, intended to make a rhetorical rather than a historical point.[13] But the evidence for such a rhetorical use of "we" is not strong, nor is it clear

---

[9]See, e.g., Gerhard Schneider, *Die Apostelgeschichte,* HTKNT (Freiburg: Herder, 1980–82), 1.108–10.

[10]Fitzmyer, *Luke I–IX,* 41.

[11]E.g., Barrett, *The Acts of the Apostles,* 2.xxv–xxx; Stanley E. Porter, *The Paul of Acts,* WUNT 115 (Tübingen: Mohr-Siebeck, 1999), 10–42; Kümmel, 184.

[12]Adolf von Harnack, *The Date of the Acts and of the Synoptic Gospels* (New York: Putnam, 1911), 1–89.

[13]Vernon K. Robbins, "The We-Passages in Acts and Ancient Sea Voyages," *BR* 20 (1975): 5–18.

why the author would have used such a device at the points where he does.[14] The attempts to explain the use of "we" in these four texts as anything other than an indication of the presence of the author are failures.

Acts and Paul. These first two points are not so much arguments against the traditional view of authorship as they are attempts to make the data conform to the view that Luke did not write Acts. The reason why so many scholars now conclude that Luke could not have written Acts lies in the picture the book gives us of the apostle Paul. This picture, it is alleged, distorts the "historical Paul" at a number of key points; so serious is this distortion that they find it impossible to think that a companion of Paul could have produced the picture. The alleged distortions are of two kinds: historical and theological.

One of the most frequently cited historical discrepancies is the disagreement between Acts and Paul about the number of trips the apostle made to Jerusalem. But this matter has a plausible solution, which we consider briefly toward the end of this chapter. Other historical discrepancies, such as the claim of Paul in Acts that he had been educated in Jerusalem (22:3), in contrast with Paul's own silence on the matter in his letters, can be resolved through a recognition of the different purposes of Acts and the letters of Paul. Paul tells us very little about his background in his letters, and his failure to mention items that Luke includes should not surprise us.

More serious are the alleged theological discrepancies. Philipp Vielhauer, whose essay on the subject is something of a classic,[15] points out four key areas of contrast between the Paul of Acts and the Paul of the epistles.

1. In the Areopagus speech of Acts 17, the Paul of Acts liberally uses Stoic notions about God, the world, and the relationship of human beings to God to make a case for natural theology. Nature and the world are so constituted, Paul here argues, that they serve as a preparation for the gospel. The Paul of the epistles, on the other hand, as Romans 1 reveals, viewed natural revelation as having only a negative purpose: to confirm the responsibility of people for their sins.

2. The Paul of Acts is utterly loyal to the law: he agrees to impose ritual requirements on Gentile Christians (15:22–35); he circumcises Timothy, who had a Gentile father (16:3); he claims to be a loyal Pharisee (23:6); he even goes so far as to participate in Jewish purification rites in the temple in Jerusalem (21:17–26). Contrast this picture with the Paul of the letters, the Paul who claimed that Christians should not impose ritual restrictions on one another (1 Cor. 8–10; Col. 2), who told the Galatians that their circumcision would

---

[14]Porter finds no clear affinities to the "we" passages in ancient literature (*The Paul of Acts*, 10–42); cf. also Colin J. Hemer, *The Book of Acts in the Setting of Hellenistic History*, WUNT 49 (Tübingen: Mohr-Siebeck, 1989), 316–21.

[15]Philipp Vielhauer, "On the 'Paulinism' of Acts," in *Studies in Luke-Acts*, ed. Leander E. Keck and J. Louis Martyn (Nashville: Abingdon, 1966), 33–50.

mean their being severed from Christ (Gal. 5:2–4), who viewed his Pharisaic background as so much refuse to be discarded (Phil. 3:5–8), and who proclaimed loudly and often that Christians were no longer "under the law."

3. The Paul of Acts lacks the emphasis on union with Christ and the expiatory benefits of Christ's death that is so central in the Paul of the letters.

4. The preaching of the Paul of Acts is uneschatological. Missing is the focus on fulfillment in Christ with the sense of imminence that is so typical of the "authentic Paul." Related to this lessening of eschatological intensity is the concern for orderly church government manifested by the Paul of Acts (e.g., on the first missionary journey he and Barnabas very quickly appoint elders in the newly founded churches [14:23]). Contrast the Paul of the Epistles, who insists that the Spirit should have sovereign freedom in ruling the churches (1 Cor. 12).

To answer these objections fully would require monographs on both Paul's theology and the theology of Acts. We will content ourselves with a few remarks on each of these points, along with some general comment.

The attitude toward natural revelation that emerges from Acts 17 and Romans 1 is certainly different, but the question is whether they are contradictory. Could not the Paul who wrote Romans 1, when arguing with sophisticated pagans in Athens, have used as many contacts with their culture as possible in order to establish some common ground as preparation for the gospel? Nothing in the theology of Romans 1 suggests that he could not. True, in Romans 1 Paul teaches that the ultimate effect of natural revelation *by itself* is wholly negative: people cannot be saved by it, only judged by it. But Paul never suggests in Acts 17 that knowledge of "an unknown god" could be saving—it is only by repentance and belief in God as now revealed in the resurrection of Jesus Christ that salvation can come (see v. 30). Moreover, we should probably view Paul's speech in Acts 17 more as a preparation for the gospel than his preaching of the gospel as such. The text suggests that Paul's mention of the resurrection led to a premature conclusion to his sermon.[16]

Two things must be said about the issue of the law. First, Paul's view of the law as found in his epistles has frequently been caricatured as being far more negative than it really is. Serious revision in the teaching of Paul on the law is now underway. While much of that revision is going too far in the other direction, it does serve to caution us about assuming a certain view of the law in Paul's letters that is at least unbalanced. Second, and more important, the practices of Paul in Acts are by no means incompatible with the standard interpretation of his teaching on the law. Paul's agreement with the decree of the apostolic council, which probably applied to mixed Jewish-Gentile Christian communities, is in keeping

---

[16]A treatment of the speech that is more sympathetic to the possibility that it stems from Paul himself is Bertil Gärtner, *The Areopagus Speech and Natural Revelation,* ASNU 21 (Uppsala: Gleerup, 1955).

with his principle that a Christian should not be a stumbling block to others (see 1 Cor. 8–10 and Rom. 14:1–15:13). Timothy, whose Jewish mother gave him rights as a Jew, is circumcised, not to enable him to be part of God's people (the issue in Galatia), but to enable him to carry out his mission more effectively. This is quite in keeping with Paul's claim that circumcision is a thing indifferent (Gal. 6:15). Paul's claim to be a Pharisee must be understood in its context to be a claim to adhere to the Pharisaic doctrine of resurrection, as over against the Sadducean rejection of the doctrine. And Paul's willingness to participate in a Jewish purification rite is in keeping with his expressed willingness to be all things to all people (1 Cor. 9:19–22). Nothing in Paul's letters suggests that he was opposed to participating in Jewish rites—as long as they were neither being imposed as necessary to salvation nor causing a stumbling block to other believers.[17]

Some of the distinctive Pauline christological and eschatological motifs are indeed missing in Acts. But this may be because the preaching of Paul that we have in Acts is almost entirely evangelistic, and we would not expect to see some of these motifs in such a context. Moreover, the picture of the Paul of the letters that Vielhauer and others set in contrast to the Paul of Acts is itself distorted and lacking in balance. In denying (in our opinion, wrongly) the Pauline authorship of Ephesians and the Pastoral Epistles, they eliminate a significant and distinctive part of Paul's own teaching—teaching that, if integrated into our total picture of Paul, would bring the Paul of the epistles much closer to the Paul of Acts.

Distortion of the Paul of the epistles takes place in another way as well. As Ulrich Wilckens has pointed out, many of those who find a great gulf between the Paul of the epistles and the Paul of Acts do so because they are committed to an existential interpretation of Paul.[18] It is this narrow and distorted understanding of Paul that creates a significant amount of the distance with the Paul of Acts.

The great distance between the Paul of Acts and the Paul of the epistles that so many find is, in reality, a distance between a caricature of the supposedly authentic Paul and a one-sided interpretation of the Paul of Acts. To be sure, some distance between the two remains, but no more than we might find between one's self-portrait and a portrait drawn by a sympathetic friend for a specific purpose.[19]

The great distance between the Paul of Acts and the Paul of the epistles that so many find is, in reality, a distance between a caricature of the supposedly authentic Paul and a one-sided interpretation of the Paul of Acts.

---

[17]On the subject of this paragraph, see esp. Richard N. Longenecker, *Paul, Apostle of Liberty,* reprint ed. (Grand Rapids: Baker, 1976), 245–63.

[18]Ulrich Wilckens, "Interpreting Luke-Acts in a Period of Existentialist Theology," in *Studies in Luke-Acts,* 60–83.

[19]To use the analogy employed by F. F. Bruce, *Paul: Apostle of the Heart Set Free* (Grand Rapids: Eerdmans, 1977), 17. See further Bruce's article "Is the Paul of Acts the Real Paul?" *BJRL* 58 (1975–76): 282–305 and especially, Porter, *The Paul of Acts* (summary on pp. 205–206).

Conclusion

We have shown that there is no convincing reason to deny that the author of Acts was a companion of Paul. That he was his companion is the natural implication of the "we" passages. That this companion was none other than Luke "the beloved physician" is the unanimous opinion of the early church. We have good reason, then, to conclude that Luke was the author of Acts.

We know almost nothing about Luke's background. That he was a Gentile seems clear from Colossians 4:10–14, where Luke is not included among Paul's Jewish fellow workers. Several scholars have speculated that Luke might have been a "God-fearer," a Gentile who had attached himself to Judaism without becoming a Jew as such.[20] That he had not been a follower of Christ from the beginning is clear from the prologue to the gospel. William Ramsay speculated that Luke may have been the "man of Macedonia" who appeared to Paul in a vision (Acts 16:9).[21] On the basis of theological parallels between Acts and Roman documents, others have suggested that Luke was from Rome.[22] But the oldest and most respected tradition associates Luke with Syrian Antioch,[23] and several scholars are inclined to accept the tradition as probably authentic.[24] But the evidence is far from conclusive, and we would perhaps do better simply to admit that we do not know very much about Luke's background.

DATE

Suggested dates for the book of Acts range across almost a century, from A.D. 62, the date at which the last event of the book takes place, to the middle of the second century, when the first clear reference to Acts occurs.[25] Most scholars locate Acts in one of three periods of time within this range: 62–70, 80–95, or 115–130.

---

[20]E.g., Darrell Bock, *Luke, vol. 1: 1:1–9:50*, BECNT (Grand Rapids: Baker, 1994), 5–7; Jacob Jervell, *Die Apostelgeschichte*, KEK (Göttingen: Vandenhoeck & Ruprecht, 1998), 79–84.

[21]William Ramsay, *St. Paul, the Traveller and the Roman Citizen* (London: Hodder & Stoughton, 1897), 200–205.

[22]F. J. Foakes Jackson and Kirsopp Lake, eds., *The Beginnings of Christianity*, 5 vols. (London: Macmillan, 1920–33), in "The Internal Evidence of Acts," 2.200–204.

[23]The anti-Marcionite prologue to the gospel of Luke (late second century); Eusebius, *H.E.* 3.4; Jerome, *De vir. ill.* 7. The Western text of Acts may indirectly suggest the same tradition by making Acts 11:28, which mentions an incident that takes place in Antioch, the first "we" passage in Acts.

[24]E.g., Zahn 3.2–3; Fitzmyer, *Luke I–IX*, 45–47.

[25]In Justin's *Apology* 1.50.12 (see Ernst Haenchen, *The Acts of the Apostles: A Commentary* [Philadelphia: Westminster, 1971], 3–8).

A Second-Century Date

A second-century date for the Acts is associated especially with the Tübingen School, a number of like-thinking scholars from the famous German university, whose best-known member was F. C. Baur. These scholars attributed to Acts a definite theological tendency—a desire to reconcile the opposing early Christian factions of Jewish Christianity, whose representative was Peter, and Gentile Christianity, whose representative was Paul. The author of Acts plays down the differences between these factions, making Peter more Gentile and Paul more Jewish than they really were. He thus prepares the way for a middle-of-the-road position, the position of the "old catholic church." This attempt at reconciliation could have been made only after sufficient time had elapsed for these factions to have mellowed, so the Tübingen School dated Acts in the middle of the second century.[26]

While remnants of its approach remain, the Tübingen interpretation of early Christian history and the place of the book of Acts within this history are no longer defended. Scholars such as J. B. Lightfoot demonstrated that the apostolic fathers of the late first century reveal none of the factionalism and polemics that Baur and his disciples attributed to this period in the history of the church. An impressive ideological synthesis, the Tübingen approach was without historical underpinnings. But there are still some who date Acts in the second century. One reason for doing so has been the belief that the author of Acts depended on Josephus's *Antiquities* (written c. A.D. 94).[27] But dependence of Acts on Josephus is most unlikely.[28] J. C. O'Neill argues on the basis of theological parallels to *1 Clement,* the Pastoral Epistles, and especially Justin that Acts must be dated in the period 115–30.[29] But the parallels O'Neill finds are both questionable and susceptible of a different interpretation. Few scholars now think that Acts is a second-century document.

A Date of 80–95

Most scholars now date Acts in the 80s, or a bit later.[30] Acts cannot be dated any earlier than this, it is argued, because it shows signs of having been written

---

[26]On this approach to the book of Acts, see W. Ward Gasque, *A History of the Criticism of the Acts of the Apostles,* BGBE 17 (Tübingen: Mohr-Siebeck, 1975), 21–54.

[27]E.g., F. C. Burkitt, *The Gospel History and Its Transmission,* 3rd ed. (Edinburgh: T. & T. Clark, 1911), 105–10.

[28]This has been argued convincingly in Zahn 3.94–100; Bruce, *The Acts of the Apostles: The Greek Text,* 24–25.

[29]J. C. O'Neill, *The Theology of Acts in Its Historical Setting* (London: SPCK, 1961).

[30]E.g., Kümmel, 185–87; Schneider, *Apostelgeschichte,* 1.118–21; Joseph A. Fitzmyer, *The Acts of the Apostles: A New Translation with Introduction and Commentary,* AB 31 (New York: Doubleday, 1998), 51–55.

some years after the first volume of Luke's work, the gospel,[31] which cannot be dated before A.D. 70. Furthermore, Acts cannot be dated much later than 95 or so because of its optimistic attitude toward the Roman government—an attitude that would have been inconceivable after the persecution of Domitian in the middle 90s—and because the author of Acts does not know about the letters of Paul, which were collected and made generally available at the end of the first century.

None of these reasons is convincing. A date after A.D. 70 for Luke's gospel is based on two assumptions: that the gospel reflects the actual circumstances of the Roman sack of Jerusalem in 70, and that the Gospel of Mark, which Luke has probably used, must be dated in the middle or late 60s. But neither of these assumptions is valid (see above, respectively, the section "Date" in chap. 5 and in chap. 9). Acts does not mention the letters of Paul, and the author probably has not used them in writing the book. But this may be because Acts is early, rather than late, or because it was simply not Luke's purpose to refer to the letters. Acts is indeed generally optimistic about Rome's attitude toward the church. Yet one could argue on this basis that Acts must be dated before the infamous persecution of Christians by the Emperor Nero in Rome in 64–65. So while the arguments for dating Acts after 80 are not persuasive, the arguments for dating Acts before 100 suggest, in fact, a date long before the turn of the century—indeed, a date in the early or middle 60s.

A Date Before 70

Arriving at a firm date for books within the New Testament is not easy—there are few solid data to go by, and many of the arguments cancel each other or are so subjective that they can only confirm a conclusion reached on other grounds. But a significant number of scholars have thought that the book of Acts furnishes one piece of evidence that determines a relatively firm and exact date for the book: its abrupt ending.

Acts ends with Paul languishing for two years under house arrest in Rome. This conclusion seems to be rather lame and unfulfilling. Is not the best explanation for this ending that Luke had decided it was necessary at this point to publish his work? After all, Luke has spent eight chapters detailing the course of Paul's judicial proceedings. Is it likely that he would have left us in suspense about the outcome of these proceedings? It is almost certain that Paul was not executed at the end of this two-year period. Why, if Luke knew this, did he not tell us that Paul was released from prison, as a final, climactic indication of the innocence of the Christian movement in the eyes of the Romans? Alternatively, if Luke was writing late enough to know of Paul's execution in A.D. 64 or 65,

---

[31]A few scholars have suggested that Acts was written only after the first edition of Luke's gospel—what they claim to be a proto-Luke—but there is little to commend the suggestion.

why did he keep this from the reader? Would not Paul's execution have made a fitting parallel to the execution of James earlier in Acts (12:2) and brought Acts to a similar climax as the gospel of Luke, with its narrative of Jesus' death? And would Luke have left as it is Paul's solemn assurance to the elders of Ephesus that he would never see them again (20:25, 38) if he had known that Paul had returned and ministered in Ephesus (as 1 Timothy assumes that he did, probably in the years 63–64)? Our difficulty in answering these questions satisfactorily suggests that the simplest and most natural explanation for the abrupt ending of Acts is that Luke finished writing the book when Paul had been in Rome for two years—in 62, according to the most probable chronology.[32]

This line of argument appears to be objective, simple, and persuasive. But there are other possible explanations for the ending of Acts that might invalidate this argument. One explanation is that Luke may have intended to write a third volume and that Acts ends where it does to keep the reader in suspense until he or she can begin that third volume.[33] Indication that Luke intended a third volume has been found in his use of the word πρῶτος (prōtos, "first") in Acts 1:1 to describe the gospel of Luke. This word is technically a superlative adjective and would thus refer to the first of three or more books rather than to the former of two. But Hellenistic Greek tended to confuse the degrees of comparison in adjectives, and little can be built on the use of this word here. We have no other indication that Luke intended another volume, and this explanation for the ending must be considered purely speculative.

The explanation of the ending of Acts that is most popular today is that Paul's arrival in Rome and his unhindered preaching of the gospel in the capital of the empire bring the book to its intended conclusion.[34] Luke's focus is not biographical but theological—he is not interested in a life of Paul but in the expansion of the gospel. To have the gospel being preached in Rome "without hindrance" (Acts 28:31) brings Luke's epic account of the growth and expansion of the Christian movement to its natural terminus. To argue, then, that Acts is strangely incomplete because it does not tell us the outcome of Paul's appeal to

---

[32]The most important defenders of this line of argument are Harnack, *Date of Acts,* esp. 90–116; Richard Belward Rackham, *The Acts of the Apostles,* WC (London: Methuen, 1901), l-lv (and see the updating of Rackham's arguments by A. J. Mattill Jr., "The Date and Purpose of Luke-Acts: Rackham Reconsidered," *CBQ* 40 [1978]: 335–50); and J. A. T. Robinson, *Redating the New Testament* (Philadelphia: Westminster, 1976), 88–92. See also John Wenham, *Redating Matthew, Mark, and Luke: A Fresh Assault on the Synoptic Problem* (Downers Grove: IVP, 1992), 223–30.

[33]Zahn 3.57–61; Ramsay, *St. Paul,* 23, 27–28.

[34]See, e.g., Bruce, *Book of Acts,* 11; Longenecker, "Acts," 234–35; Floyd V. Filson, "The Journey Motif in Luke-Acts," in *Apostolic History and the Gospel, Fs.* F. F. Bruce, ed. W. Ward Gasque and Ralph P. Martin (Grand Rapids: Eerdmans, 1970), 68–77; Fitzmyer, *Acts,* 52.

the emperor or the ultimate fate of the apostle is to assume that Luke was more interested in Paul per se than he really was. Perhaps, indeed, Luke knew that the outcome of Paul's trial in Rome was a negative one or that Paul had been executed by the Romans, but he deliberately refrained from giving us this information because it would have spoiled his upbeat conclusion. Perhaps Luke knew that Paul had been freed after this first Roman trial and did not want to get Paul in trouble by publishing the details of his further ministry.[35] Or perhaps—and this is the most probable explanation—Luke knew that Paul was continuing to minister in the churches of the East but did not include this information because it did not make as neat a climax as did Paul's preaching in Rome. In any case, it is argued, the ending of Acts, being the natural climax of the narrative, gives no help at all in dating the book.

This argument carries considerable weight. Further substantiating it is Luke's mention of a specific period of time—"two whole years"—during which Paul preached in Rome. This suggests that Luke knew that Paul's circumstances changed after this two-year period. While it is difficult to be certain, then, we are inclined to think that the ending of Acts does not point conclusively to the date of its writing or publication.

But other considerations suggest a date not long after A.D. 62: (1) Luke's apparent ignorance of the letters of Paul; (2) Luke's portrayal of Judaism as a legal religion, a situation that would have changed abruptly with the outbreak of the Jewish rebellion against Rome in 66; (3) Luke's omission of any reference to the Neronian persecution, which, if it had occurred when Luke was writing, would surely have affected his narrative in some way; (4) the vivid detail of the shipwreck voyage narrative (27:1–28:16), which suggests very recent experience. For these reasons, Acts should be dated in the mid–60s.[36]

GENRE, ADDRESSEES, AND PURPOSE

Genre

The earliest identification of the genre of Acts may be reflected in the second-century authors who began calling Luke's second volume the Acts. As noted above, several ancient historians used the word "acts" to describe the narratives in which they recounted the heroic deeds of individuals or cities (e.g., Polybius, 1.1.1; Diodorus Siculus, 1.1.1), and the early church may then have

---

[35]Hemer, *Book of Acts*, 406–8.

[36]See esp. ibid., 376–90; Longenecker, "Acts," 236–38; McDonald and Porter, 296. E. Earle Ellis further suggests that "the ends of the earth" in Acts 1:8 refers to Spain and that Paul did, indeed, eventually preach the gospel there. Luke's failure to mention this preaching implies that he had not yet done so and so requires an early date for Acts ('The Ends of the Earth'(Acts 1:8)," *BBR* 1 [1991]: 123–32).

thought that this was the category into which Luke's narrative fit. But "acts" was not the name of a technical genre as such,[37] so the title does not help much in establishing a well-defined literary classification for the book of Acts. Most scholars agree that Acts should be put into the category "history."[38] This identification has recently been challenged by some who find the differences between Acts and other ancient works of history too great to admit of their common categorization. C. H. Talbert has styled Acts a "succession narrative,"[39] while Richard Pervo suggests that Acts be read as a historical novel.[40] Both these scholars remind us of important features in Acts—Talbert the relationship of Acts to Luke's gospel, Pervo the element of storytelling in Acts—but neither of their proposed genre identifications has much to be said for it.[41] Others, noting these same differences, argue that Acts is unique and cannot be fit into any known genre.[42] However, while the features unique to Acts (e.g., its theological perspective and its relationship to the gospel of Luke) should not be minimized, we doubt that they are sufficient to take Acts out of the category of ancient history. Ancient historical works differ a great deal among themselves, with most—perhaps all of them—possessing some features unique to themselves.[43]

Addressees and Purpose

Acts, like the gospel of Luke, is addressed to Theophilus (1:1), who was probably Luke's patron, the person who was putting up the money for the publication of Luke's literary effort. But we learn, and can infer, almost nothing more about him from either book. Moreover, it is almost certain that Luke had a broader audience than one individual in mind. Just who made up Luke's intended audience can be determined only after we have identified his purpose in writing.

> *The earliest identification of the genre of Acts may be reflected in the second-century authors who began calling Luke's second volume the Acts.*

---

[37]See David E. Aune, *The New Testament in Its Literary Environment*, LEC 8 (Philadelphia: Westminster, 1987), 78.

[38]E.g., Martin Hengel, *Acts and the History of Earliest Christianity* (Philadelphia: Fortress Press, 1979), 36–37; W. Ward Gasque, "A Fruitful Field: Recent Study of the Acts of the Apostles," *Int* 42 (1988): 129; Fitzmyer, *Acts,* 47–49; Darryl W. Palmer, "Acts and the Ancient Historical Monograph," in *The Book of Acts in its First Century Setting,* vol. 1, *The Book in its Ancient Literary Setting,* ed. Bruce W. Winter and Andrew D. Clarke (Grand Rapids: Eerdmans, 1993), 1–29; Ben Witherington III, *The Acts of the Apostles: A Socio-Rhetorical Commentary* (Grand Rapids: Eerdmans, 1998), 12–24; Jervell, *Apostelgeschichte,* 76–79.

[39]Charles H. Talbert, *Literary Patterns, Theological Themes, and the Genre of Luke-Acts,* SBLMS 20 (Missoula: SP, 1974).

[40]Richard I. Pervo, *Profit with Delight: The Literary Genre of the Acts of the Apostles* (Philadelphia: Fortress Press, 1987).

[41]See Aune, *The New Testament in Its Literary Environment,* 78–80.

[42]Wikenhauser, 351–52; Kümmel, 165; Schneider, *Apostelgeschichte* 1.73–76.

[43]Aune, *The New Testament in its Literary Environment,* 80.

Identifying Luke's purpose in writing Acts is complicated by the relationship between Acts and the Gospel of Luke. Most scholars stress that these books form a literary unity—"Luke-Acts." Most also think that Luke intends the prologue of the first of these books (Luke 1:1–4) to cover his second volume as well.[44] Ancient writers were severely limited in their verbosity by the need to compress their work into the space of a papyrus scroll. The Gospel of Luke and Acts each would have occupied a full-sized papyrus roll. The division of Luke's work into two volumes was therefore dictated by physical limitations, and like other ancient writers, he has used the opening of this second volume to tie it to the first and to the prologue of that first volume.[45] But recognizing the applicability of the prologue to the matter in hand does not solve all our problems. It is not certain, for instance, how much of the prologue applies to Acts. At least some of its statements—such as Luke's reference to the many who had written before him—seem to apply only to the gospel. Nevertheless, we are safe in concluding that the purpose stated in Luke 1:4, namely, to communicate the "certainty of the things you have been taught," applies equally to the gospel and to Acts. This, the author's own statement, must be considered basic to any discussion of the purpose of Acts. But instilling certainty in his readers is a very broad aim and may not cover all the purposes that Luke had. Moreover, Luke may well pursue some purposes in Acts distinct from what he has done in the gospel. We have argued that some modern scholars have perhaps gone too far in their insistence on the unity of Luke and Acts (see chap. 5). "Since Luke clearly distinguishes the second volume from the first, there is no reason why he could not have accomplished his purpose mainly in the first volume and then continued the story of 'all that Jesus began to do and teach' in the second one to accomplish yet further objectives."[46] Nevertheless, any finally satisfactory estimation of Luke's purpose in Acts must at least consider the gospel. We need, then, to examine some of the suggested purposes for Acts and test them against Luke's own claim and against the data of the text.

Conciliation. As we noted above, the Tübingen School viewed the book of Acts as a second-century attempt to create a synthesis out of the supposed antitheses of Jewish Christianity and Gentile Christianity. The author of Acts

---

[44]E.g., Fitzmyer, *Luke I–IX,* 9; I. Howard Marshall, "Luke and His 'Gospel,'" in *Das Evangelium und die Evangelien,* ed. Peter Stuhlmacher, WUNT 28 (Tübingen: Mohr-Siebeck, 1983), 289–308. For the contrary view, see Loveday Alexander, *The Preface to Luke's Gospel: Literary Convention and Social Context in Luke 1:1–4 and Acts 1:1,* SNTSMS 78 (Cambridge: Cambridge University Press, 1993), 146; Witherington, *Acts of the Apostles,* 5–8.

[45]A. J. B. Higgins, "The Prologue to Luke and the Kerygma in Acts," in *Apostolic History and the Gospel,* 78–83.

[46]Liefeld, "Luke," in *EBC* 8.801.

seeks to accomplish this particularly through his portrayals of the two key figures in Acts, Peter and Paul. Texts such as 1 Corinthians 1:10–17 and Galatians 2:11–14 show that there was a sharp division between Peter and Paul, a division between a conservative Jewish theological outlook and a liberal Gentile-oriented outlook that was perpetuated in warring church factions into the late first and early second centuries. But the antagonism between Peter and Paul disappears in Acts. The author of Acts "Gentilizes" Peter, turning him into the initiator (chap. 10) and defender (11:1–18; 15:6–11) of the outreach to the Gentiles. Paul, on the other hand, is "Judaized": he accepts the council decree (15:22–35), circumcises Timothy (16:3), takes Jewish vows (18:18; 21:17–26), and claims to be a loyal Pharisee (23:6). By thus rewriting the history of the early church, the author of Acts hopes to conciliate the factions in his second-century context.

The Tübingen approach to the book of Acts did not survive the criticisms of scholars such as J. B. Lightfoot and Albrecht Ritschl. The assumption that the late-first-century and early-second-century church was torn by factions was shown to be unfounded. More important, the Tübingen critics were guilty of seriously overemphasizing the differences between Peter and Paul. That they differed occasionally is clear (e.g., Gal. 2:11–14). But that they were leaders of opposing theological tendencies in the early church is an idea that finds no basis in the New Testament text. We therefore have no grounds on which to accuse the author of Acts of creating an unhistorical and tendentious scenario, and as little reason to think that the second-century church was in need of conciliation. We may still, however, think that conciliation was Luke's subsidiary purpose; perhaps he knew of continuing tensions between Jewish Christians and Gentile Christians and wanted to show that Peter and Paul were in essential agreement over the basics of the faith.

Evangelism/Apologetics. Luke's inclusion of a number of evangelistic speeches and his emphasis on the miraculous accrediting of the early preachers suggest that he may have written in order to awaken faith. Many scholars think that evangelism was, then, at least a subsidiary purpose of (Luke-) Acts. Particularly influential is the notion that Acts is intended to create an apologetic for Christianity in the eyes of Romans.

One of the puzzling features of Acts is the amount of time Luke spends describing in detail the trials and defenses of Paul. Almost one-fourth of the whole book of Acts (chaps. 22–28) is occupied with this topic. Why is this, when undoubtedly Luke could have told us much else about evangelistic outreaches in various parts of the world or about Paul's missionary work? The traditional answer has been that Luke wanted to prove to Roman citizens that Christianity was a religion to be tolerated—a *religio licita* in the official terminology. Rome had become quite skeptical about Oriental religions, even fearful of their harmful effects on the population. For Christian missionaries to work effectively with Roman citizens, it was necessary to stifle these fears and to make Christianity a religion that Romans could embrace without being considered traitors to their country. This Luke does by showing how Roman official after Roman official refuses to stand in the way of the new movement. The city officers in Philippi apologize to Paul for imprisoning him (16:38–39); Gallio, the Roman official in charge of the province of Achaia, declines to forbid Christian preaching in Corinth (18:12–17); King Agrippa II and Festus, the Roman procurator of Judea, agree that Paul had done nothing wrong and could have been released had he not appealed to Caesar (26:31–32).

Most scholars think that this kind of apologetic plays some role in Acts, but a few elevate this to the central concern of the book.[47] As mentioned, some have suggested that Luke intended Acts to be used as a brief for Paul at his trial in Rome, a document that Paul could submit to a Roman magistrate (Theophilus?) or even to the emperor himself as part of his defense. This last suggestion, at least, is most unlikely. Luke would hardly have written as much as he did, had this been his purpose. A few scholars go further and question whether apologetic to Romans plays any role at all in Luke's purpose. They argue that Luke-Acts must be considered as a whole and that apologetic to a Roman audience is not very clear in the gospel. Moreover, Luke gives many indications that he is writing to a Christian rather than to a non-Christian audience.[48] One writer, in fact, reverses the traditional understanding, arguing that Luke was not trying to legitimize the church before Rome, but Rome before the church.[49] These scholars make some good points: Luke-Acts is primarily directed to Christians, and it is easy to overemphasize the theme of Roman apologetic at the expense of other themes. Nevertheless, the way in which Luke goes out of his way to bring out Roman acceptance of the church, seen particularly in the latter chapters of Acts, strongly suggests that apologetic to Romans is one of Luke's purposes. Perhaps, while writing mainly for Christians, Luke knew that Acts would also be read by non-Christian Romans and so included this material. Or perhaps Luke wanted to help new converts from a Roman background understand better the relationship between their new faith and their Roman political and social identity.

A rather different apologetic purpose is discerned in the book of Acts by A. J. Mattill Jr. Reviving the thesis of Matthias Schneckenburger, he argues that Acts is directed to Jewish Christians in Rome and has as its central purpose an apology for the apostle Paul. By emphasizing the parallels between Peter and

---

[47] E.g., Johannes Weiss, *Absicht und literarischer Charakter der Apostelgeschichte* (Marburg: Vandenhoeck & Ruprecht, 1897); O'Neill, *Theology of Acts,* 166–77; cf. Bruce, *Book of Acts,* 8–13.

[48] See Schneider, *Apostelgeschichte* 1.139–45.

[49] Paul W. Walaskay, *"And So We Came to Rome": The Political Perspective of St. Luke,* SNTSMS 49 (Cambridge: Cambridge University Press, 1983).

Paul and by selecting incidents that revealed Paul's continuing allegiance to his own people, Luke wanted to scotch rumors to the effect that Paul was an apostate Jew.[50] There is much to be said for this proposal, for there is no doubt that Paul is Luke's hero and that his emphasis on Paul's Jewishness would be most appropriate for a Jewish Christian audience. In contrast, many other features of Luke-Acts imply a Gentile Christian audience. Apologetic to Jewish Christians may, then, be one of Luke's purposes, but it is not his main purpose.

Theological Polemics. No one today doubts that Luke writes with theological purposes. But some scholars think that he has a definite theological ax to grind and that this theological polemic is his central purpose. Charles Talbert, for instance, suggests that Luke is writing to oppose Gnosticism.[51] But it is unlikely that Gnosticism existed as a movement requiring refutation at this stage in history, and there is far too much in both Luke and Acts that would be immaterial for this purpose. Hans Conzelmann and others think that Luke is propagating a new conception of salvation history in response to the problem of the delay of the parousia.[52] More will be said about this theological issue below; here we note simply that while Luke indeed has much to contribute to our understanding of salvation history, there is little evidence that he was the initiator of such a view or that his writing was occasioned by the delay of the parousia. In general, then, we may conclude that Luke was writing with theological purposes and that he has many specific theological points to make but that the evidence for a particular theological polemic as central to his purpose is lacking. Such proposals are reductionistic: they oversimplify Luke's complex and many-faceted work.

Edification. We agree with a growing number of scholars who think that Luke wrote with a variety of specific purposes and that these purposes are part of a larger, general purpose—the edification of Christians.[53] Luke tells us in the prologue to his gospel that confirmation of the gospel is his overriding purpose[54] and implies by using the word κατηχέω (katēcheō ["to teach"]) that this confirmation is directed to a Christian, perhaps a recent convert. Perhaps, indeed, we should

---

[50]A. J. Mattill Jr., "The Purpose of Acts: Schneckenburger Reconsidered," in *Apostolic History and the Gospel*, 108–122.

[51]Charles H. Talbert, *Luke and the Gnostics: An Examination of the Lucan Purpose* (Nashville: Abingdon, 1966).

[52]See esp. Hans Conzelmann, *The Theology of St. Luke* (New York: Harper & Row, 1961).

[53]See, e.g., Ernst Haenchen, "The Book of Acts as Source Material for the History of Earliest Christianity," in *Studies in Luke-Acts*, pp. 258–278; I. Howard Marshall, *The Acts of the Apostles*, TNTC (Grand Rapids: Eerdmans, 1980), 20–21; idem, "Luke and His 'Gospel,'" 289–308; Fitzmyer, *Luke I–IX*, 9.

[54]See esp. the essay by W. C. van Unnik, "The 'Book of Acts' the Confirmation of the Gospel," *NovT* 4 (1960): 26–59.

view this intended reader as a former God-fearer, a Gentile, like Cornelius (Acts 10), who had been an active worshiper of the God of Israel without becoming a Jew.[55] Such a person would have wondered about the place of his new faith within the welter of religious and philosophical options available in the Greco-Roman world of his day. And he may particularly have wondered about the claims of Christians vis-à-vis Jews. Which movement—the Christian "way" or Judaism—could lay valid claim to be the heir of God's Old Testament people?[56] Luke seeks to secure the full belief and commitment of such a person by describing the historical foundation for Christian faith and by showing, through this historical survey, that the church of his, and Theophilus's day is the culmination of biblical history.[57] God's salvation was revealed in, and made available through, his Son, Jesus Christ. The message of that salvation was entrusted by Christ himself to his apostles, and through the empowering and directing of the Holy Spirit, they have now brought that message, and the salvation it mediates, to "the ends of the earth."[58] Only so broad a purpose is able to accommodate the richness of Luke-Acts. As part of this general purpose, of course, Luke pursues many subsidiary purposes—legitimation of the church in the eyes of Romans, vindication of Paul in the eyes of Jewish Christians, evangelism, and others.

SOURCES

The search for the sources of Luke's material in Acts is important for the light it might shed both on Luke's literary techniques as well as on the historical trustworthiness of his narrative.

The search for the sources of Luke's material in Acts is important for the light it might shed both on Luke's literary techniques as well as on the historical trustworthiness of his narrative. In the prologue to his gospel, Luke tells us that he has "carefully investigated everything from the beginning" (1:3) and mentions both written records (1:1) and oral transmission (1:2, "handed down"). Luke may be thinking here mainly of the gospel, but we can assume that he would have made the same careful investigation, and used all the sources he could lay his hands on, in writing his second volume. And in any case, the question of the extent to which written sources stand behind Acts naturally arises. The "we" passages that surface in Acts 16 and following, as well as the general shift from

---

[55]See Liefeld, "Luke," 8.802.

[56]These points are emphasized by Green, *Gospel of Luke,* 21–25 (see also Achtemeier/Green/Thompson, 266); Johnson, 218–19.

[57]See especially Walter T. Wilson, who argues convincingly that Luke, especially in Acts 10:1–11:18, adapts the "Greco-Roman foundation narrative" style to assure his Gentile readers that they were members of a secure community with historical foundations ("Urban Legends: Acts 10:1–11:18 and the Strategies of Greco-Roman Foundation Narratives," *JBL* 120 [2001]: 77–99).

[58]This theme is stressed by C. K. Barrett, *Luke the Historian in Recent Study* (London: Epworth, 1961), 56–61; Marshall, *Acts of the Apostles,* 20–21; Gasque, "Recent Study," 120–21: Luke wanted to scotch rumors to the effect that Paul was an apostate Jew.

a Palestinian to a wider Mediterranean setting that occurs at this point, makes it necessary to separate Acts 1–15 from Acts 16–28 in the investigation of the sources for Acts.

Acts 1–15

At the end of the nineteenth and beginning of the twentieth centuries, scholars working on Acts shared with their colleagues working on the Synoptic Gospels a preoccupation with written sources. Adolf von Harnack's source proposal for Acts 1–15 stands as a climax to this development. Harnack recognized, along with most scholars of his day and ours, that Luke has so uniformly imposed his own style on whatever sources he has used as to make it impossible to distinguish his sources through style and language.[59] Harnack appealed rather to geographic setting, to theological tendency, and, especially, to the presence of doublets to dissect Acts 1–15 into its component sources. Doublets are apparent duplicate narratives of the same story, and there are five of them, claimed Harnack, in Acts 1–5: two sermons of Peter (2:14–39; 3:12–26), two arrests of the apostles (4:3; 5:18), two appearances of the apostles before the Sanhedrin (4:8–20; 5:27–40), two estimates of the number of converts (2:41; 4:4), and two accounts of the sharing of material goods in the Jerusalem church (2:44–45; 4:32). Source critics often think that such doublets point to an amalgamation of two different sources, each with its own particular version of such incidents. Using these doublets in Acts 1–5 as his starting point, Harnack postulated the existence of three written sources in Acts 1–15: a "Jerusalem A" source, standing behind 3:1–5:16; 8:5–40; and 9:31–11:18; a "Jerusalem B" source, represented in 2:1–47 and 5:17–42; and an "Antiochene" source, which shows up in 6:1–8:4; 11:19–30; and 12:25–15:35.[60] Harnack's scheme has been very influential and has been adopted, sometimes with modifications, by a significant number of scholars.

Despite its popularity, Harnack's proposal is unlikely. Its foundation is shaky in that the evidence for doublets in Acts 1–5 is not strong. The narratives concerned are either so different from one another (e.g., the speeches of Peter), so integral to the progression of events (e.g., the two arrests and hearings of the apostles), or so integral to Luke's plan (e.g., the references to the community of goods and the numbers of the converted) that they are unlikely to be duplicates.[61] Beyond that, there is little basis for differentiating the material in Acts 1–15, beyond the obvious matter of setting, and this can be explained in any

---

[59]E.g., Henry J. Cadbury, *The Making of Luke-Acts* (New York: Macmillan, 1927), 65–70; Jacques Dupont, *The Sources of the Acts* (New York: Herder & Herder, 1964), 88; Haenchen, *Acts*, 81.

[60]Adolf von Harnack, *The Acts of the Apostles* (London: Williams & Norgate, 1909), 162–202.

[61]See Joachim Jeremias, "Untersuchungen zum Quellenproblem der Apostelgeschichte," *ZNW* 36 (1937): 205–21; Bruce, *Acts of the Apostles*, 23.

number of ways. We simply do not have enough data to identify written sources of this sort behind Acts 1–15.

A source proposal of a very different sort was advanced by C. C. Torrey, who argued from the presence of Semitisms that Acts 1:1–15:35 is the translation of a single Aramaic source.[62] Torrey's theory is now universally rejected. Although it is recognized that his proposal goes far beyond the available evidence, the discussion of the Semitic element in this first part of Acts and of its implications for Luke's sources continues. There is some reason to think that the distribution of Semitisms in these chapters points to the use, at places, of Aramaic sources,[63] but the evidence is not clear enough to justify firm conclusions or the identification of specific sources.

The sources behind Acts 1–15 cannot, then, be definitely pinpointed. It is likely that Luke depends on Aramaic sources for parts of these chapters, particularly for some of the speeches, and other written sources that we now have no means of isolating were perhaps used as well. But we should probably place as much if not more emphasis on oral reports as the basis for Luke's narrative.[64] Certainly Luke's two-year stay in Palestine during Paul's Caesarean imprisonment (his stay is a fair inference from the "we" passages) would have given him ample opportunity to interview people such as Philip, Mark, and Peter himself.[65] And if Luke was a native of Antioch, he could have had firsthand knowledge of the planting and growth of the church there, as well as of the labors of the missionaries Paul and Barnabas, sent out from that church.

Acts 16–28

Attention in these chapters is focused on the significance of the "we" passages. Dibelius thought that these passages indicated the existence of an "itinerary" source (perhaps a travel diary) that Luke used for much of this narrative.[66] We have argued above that the best explanation of the "we" in these texts is that Luke himself was with Paul on these occasions. His own eyewitness recollection (combined perhaps with notes he may have taken), along with close personal contact with Paul himself, fully accounts for the material in Acts 16–28.[67]

---

[62]Charles Cutler Torrey, *The Composition and Date of Acts*, HTS 1 (Cambridge: Harvard University Press, 1916), 3–41.

[63]See esp. Max Wilcox, *The Semitisms of Acts* (Oxford: Clarendon, 1965).

[64]Haenchen, *Acts*, 82.

[65]See Hemer, *Book of Acts*, 336–64.

[66]Martin Dibelius, "Style Criticism of the Book of Acts," in *Studies in the Acts of the Apostles,* ed. Heinrich Greeven (London: SCM, 1956), 4 (the original German essay was published in 1923); see also Kümmel, 184–85.

[67]Mention should at least be made of the very ambitious and very complicated textual/source scheme of M.-E. Boismard and A. Lamouille, *Le texte occidental des Actes des Apôtres: Reconstitution et rehabilitation,* 2 vols. (Paris: Editions Recherche sur les

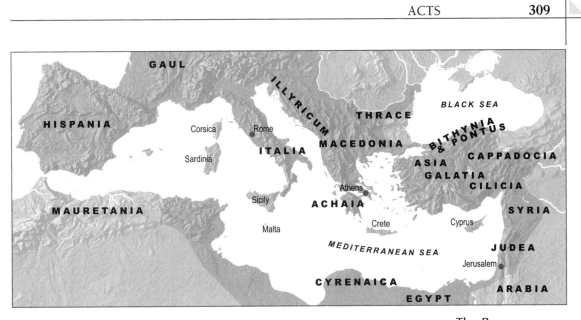

The Roman
Empire

TEXT

The text of Acts presents as interesting a problem as the text of any New Testament book. This is because the text has been preserved in two distinct forms: the form that is represented by the great uncials Sinaiticus (‫א‬) and Vaticanus (B), which is the basis for all modern Greek texts and English translations; and the form represented by the uncial Bezae Cantabrigiensis (D). The latter form of the text, often called Western because of its alleged geographic origin, is about 10 percent longer than the usually accepted text. These additions are of various kinds, extending from single words to whole sentences.

Some of these additions are very interesting. As we noted above, it is the Western text that identifies Luke as a native of Antioch by inserting in 11:28 the words, "And there was much rejoicing. And as *we* were gathered together. . . ." The Western text furnishes the wholly likely information that Paul used the rented quarters of Tyrannus in Ephesus "from 11 A.M. to 4 P.M.," that is, during the hot hours of the day when Tyrannus himself was not using the hall (19:9). An ethicizing tendency can be observed in the Western version of the apostolic decree (15:20, 29). In place of the shorter text's prohibition of food polluted by idols, sexual immorality, meat of strangled animals, and "blood"—a mixture of ritual and ethical points—Codex D and its allies list idolatry, sexual immorality, and "blood," and add after the list, "and not to do to others what they would not like to be done to themselves."

Scholars take three basic standpoints in their assessment of this Western text in Acts. A few have argued that it represents the original Lukan text, which

civilizations, 1984) (for a convenient summary in English, see J. Taylor, "The Making of Acts: A New Account," *RevBib* 97 [1990]: 504–24).

ℵ, B, and others have abbreviated.[68] Others have thought it might represent a completely separate recension that could have come from Luke himself.[69] The great majority, however, view the Western form of the text in Acts as a secondary modification of the generally accepted text.[70] This is almost certainly right. A comparison between the Western text and the text of ℵ and B shows generally that the Western text tends to smooth out grammatical difficulties, clarify ambiguous points, expand references to Christ, and add notes of historical detail and interest.[71] Accepted canons of textual criticism state that such features are typical of secondary texts. This is not, of course, to say that the Western text may not at points preserve the original reading. But the text, as a whole, must be considered a third- or fourth-century revision of the original, shorter text of Acts.[72]

ACTS IN RECENT STUDY

Survey of Research

Recent study of Acts must be understood against nineteenth- and early-twentieth-century background.[73] The assumption that Acts gives to us a straightforward historical narrative of the beginnings of the church was first seriously questioned at the beginning of the nineteenth century by the German critic W. M. L. de Wette.[74] He was followed by F. C. Baur and his disciples (the Tübingen School), who argued that Acts pursues a definite theological "tendency" (*Tendenz*; hence, *Tendenzkritik*). This tendency, formulated with the purpose of reconciling second-century church factions, determines what is contained in Acts. Luke does not, then, simply tell us about things "as they really happened."[75] Predictably, so new and radical a thesis stimulated a strong reac-

---

[68]Most notably, Clark, *Acts of the Apostles*.

[69]F. Blass, "Die Textüberlieferung in der Apostelgeschichte," *TSK* 67 (1894): 86–119; Zahn 3.8–41.

[70]E.g., James Hardy Ropes, *The Text of Acts*, vol. 3 of *Beginnings of Christianity*, ccxv–ccxlvi; Bruce, *Acts of the Apostles*, 40–47; Kümmel, 187–88.

[71]Eldon Jay Epp also discerns an anti-Jewish bias in Bezae (*The Theological Tendency of Codex Bezae Cantabrigiensis in Acts*, SNTSMS 3 [Cambridge: Cambridge University Press, 1966]).

[72]On the date of the text, see Kurt Aland and Barbara Aland, *The Text of the New Testament*, rev. ed. (Grand Rapids: Eerdmans, 1989), 69.

[73]This history is thoroughly surveyed in Gasque, *History*. See also Haenchen, *Acts*, 14–50; I. Howard Marshall, "Acts in Current Study," *ExpTim* 115 (2003): 49–52.

[74]See Gasque, *History*, 24–26.

[75]The fullest treatment of Acts from the Tübingen approach is that of Eduard Zeller, *The Contents and Origin of the Acts of the Apostles, Critically Investigated*, 2 vols. (London: Williams & Norgate, 1875–76); the German original was published in 1854.

tion, and numerous objections to the Tübingen approach from scholars of widely varying theological commitments appeared during the course of the nineteenth century. The turn of the century witnessed the work of two great Acts scholars, both of whom made a strong case for the essential historicity of Acts. In a series of books, the famous German historian and theologian Adolf von Harnack argued, among other things, that Acts was written at an early date by Luke the physician and must be considered a serious work of history.[76] William Ramsay went further. Ramsay, an archaeologist, started out as a skeptic but became firmly convinced of Luke's historical reliability as he discovered detail after detail in Acts that demonstrated firsthand acquaintance with conditions in the Roman Empire in the middle of the first century. Luke, Ramsay concluded, belongs in the first rank of ancient historians.[77]

At about the same time, scholars were showing considerable interest in the sources of Acts. Harnack himself, as we have seen above, was in the forefront of this development. As Ernst Haenchen puts it, scholarly attention had shifted from the question of what Luke was *willing* to say ("tendency criticism") to what he was *able* to say (source criticism).[78] Shortly after this, in the 1920s, the new discipline of form criticism began to be applied to Acts. The most prominent practitioner of form criticism in Acts was Martin Dibelius, who, in a series of articles, established influential methodological points and conclusions.[79] Dibelius argued that criticism of Acts must focus on the style of the narrative, since, in contrast to the gospels, one does not have written sources with which to make comparison. By analyzing the style of Acts, Dibelius believed we could isolate certain forms or narratives that Luke had used in his composition, from the rest of Acts, which was the product of Luke's own creativity. The speeches of Acts, Dibelius particularly emphasized, showed every sign of Luke's own creativity. The unique features of Acts rendered the shift from form-critical approaches to redaction-critical approaches to Acts less obvious than in the case of the Synoptic Gospels. Thus, the work of Hans Conzelmann and Ernst Haenchen builds directly on that of Dibelius, with perhaps slightly more interest in Luke's theology as a whole.[80] Both writers are quite skeptical about the historicity of Acts, arguing that Luke's desire to edify the church (Haenchen)

---

[76] Adolf von Harnack, *Luke the Physician* (New York: Putman, 1907), *The Acts of the Apostles,* and *Date of Acts.*

[77] See esp. Ramsay's *Bearing of Recent Discovery on the Trustworthiness of the New Testament,* reprint ed. (Grand Rapids: Baker, 1953), and *St. Paul: The Traveller and Roman Citizen.*

[78] Haenchen, *Acts,* 24.

[79] The relevant essays are collected in Dibelius, *Studies in the Acts of the Apostles.*

[80] See esp. Conzelmann, *Theology of St. Luke,* and also his commentary *Acts of the Apostles,* Hermeneia (Philadelphia: Fortress Press, 1987); Haenchen's major work is his commentary, *The Acts of the Apostles.*

or to explain the delay of the parousia (Conzelmann) has virtually erased any concern on his part with what really happened.

Recent Contributions

Recent study of the Acts has tended to focus on three areas: historicity, literary phenomena, and theological tendencies.

Historicity. Acts is the New Testament book that most nearly resembles historical narration, and it is the only source for most of what it narrates. Scholars have therefore long debated its historical accuracy, some doubting whether we can learn much at all of "what really happened" from Acts,[81] others insisting that Acts deserves to be considered as a serious and generally reliable historical source.[82] The same division of opinion is evident in contemporary scholarship. Gerd Lüdemann, while by no means dismissing Acts as a historical source, is generally skeptical.[83] He acknowledges the importance of the theological approach to Acts that has reigned supreme in recent studies but insists that the study of Acts as a historical source needs to be reopened. He attempts to distinguish Luke's redactional touches from the traditions he has inherited, and from this basis to assess the historical reliability of Acts.

But Lüdemann's generally negative conclusions are more than balanced by the contributions of two scholars who are much more positive toward the historical accuracy of Acts. Martin Hengel, while finding historical errors in Acts, is critical of the tendency in modern scholarship to dismiss Luke as a serious historian. "The radical 'redaction-critical' approach so popular today, which sees Luke above all as a freely inventive theologian, mistakes his real purpose, namely that as a Christian 'historian' he sets out to report the events of the past that provided the foundation for the faith and its extension. He does not set out primarily to present his own 'theology.'"[84] Hengel concludes that Luke deserves to be considered as trustworthy as any ancient historian.

Far more detailed than Hengel is Colin Hemer's *The Book of Acts in the Setting of Hellenistic History*, a magisterial and definitive defense of the historicity of Acts. Hemer compares Luke favorably with the highest standards of ancient historiography. He updates and expands the list of points at which Luke demon-

---

[81]E.g., the Tübingen School and many contemporary redactional approaches (e.g., Conzelmann, *Acts*).

[82]E.g., Harnack, Ramsay; and note also two of the classic treatments from this perspective: Eduard Meyer, *Ursprung und Anfänge des Christentums*, 3 vols. (Stuttgart: J. G. Cotta, 1921–23); and Alfred Wikenhauser, *Die Apostelgeschichte und ihr Geschichtswert*, NTAbh 8.3–5 (Münster: Aschendorff, 1921).

[83]Gerd Lüdemann, *Early Christianity According to the Traditions in Acts: A Commentary* (Philadelphia: Fortress Press, 1989).

[84]Hengel, *Acts and the History of Earliest Christianity*, 67–68.

strates his knowledge of, and accuracy about, first-century political, social, and geographic details. He also defends Luke at those points where he has been considered to be inaccurate and contests the scholars who think that Luke's theological concerns must have overridden his historical reliability. Hemer's work puts the defense of Luke's historical reliability on firmer ground than ever before. In addition to these works, mention should be made of the multivolume *The Book of Acts in its First Century Setting,* which situates Acts in its historical setting with respect to a wide variety of issues.

Literary Approaches. The last twenty years have witnessed an explosion of studies on literary aspects of the Bible. Scholars have been particularly interested in fitting the biblical books into ancient literary genres and in using contemporary literary techniques to open up new approaches to, and understandings of, the text of Scripture. Luke-Acts has been the focus of many such studies. The general tendency is to stress the unity of Luke and Acts and to use various literary methods, especially the study of narrative, to illuminate their relationship and the story that together they tell.[85] Charles H. Talbert may be taken as representative.[86] He emphasizes the parallels that Luke draws between the gospel on the one hand and Acts on the other, and between Acts 1–12 and Acts 13–28. Luke has selected and ordered events in such a way that the history of Jesus parallels the history of the church, while the "acts" of Peter parallel the "acts" of Paul. These patterns bind Luke's two works together and serve to emphasize the unity of the salvation-historical drama that is at the heart of Luke-Acts. Talbert also suggests that Luke-Acts may be compared with Diogenes Laertius's *Lives of Eminent Philosophers.*

Comparison of Acts with other ancient literature is not new, but in the past comparison was usually made with historical works. Recent scholarship has emphasized the dramatic and novelistic aspects of the book of Acts, with its travel narratives, stories of miracles, and accounts of dangers on the high seas. Richard Pervo takes these characteristics as indications that Luke was not intending to write history, but a historical novel.[87] While this is certainly going

> *Scholars have been interested in fitting the biblical books into ancient literary genres and using contemporary literary techniques to open up new understandings of the text of Scripture. Luke-Acts has been the focus of many such studies.*

---

[85]Emphasizing the unity are, for instance, Green, *The Theology of the Gospel of Luke,* 47–48; I. Howard Marshall, "Acts and the 'Former Treatise,'" in *The Book of Acts in Its First Century Setting,* 163–82; Robert C. Tannehill, *The Narrative Unity of Luke-Acts: A Literary Interpretation,* 2 vols. (Minneapolis: Fortress Press, 1990). See also the evaluation of David P. Moessner and David L. Tiede in the introduction to *Jesus and the Heritage of Israel: Luke's Narrative Claim upon Israel's Legacy* (Harrisburg: Trinity Press International, 2000), 1–3.

[86]Talbert, *Literary Patterns.*

[87]Richard Pervo, *Profit with Delight;* see also Vernon K. Robbins, "The We-Passages in Acts."

too far, the reminder from such scholars that Luke has written Acts in such a way that it makes for exciting reading is a salutary one.

Theological Themes.   In the middle 1960s, W. C. van Unnik noted that Luke-Acts had suddenly become a storm center in contemporary scholarship.[88] This was largely owing, he noted, to the new interest in Luke as a theologian, sparked by the application of redaction-critical techniques to the gospel. It was the proposal of Hans Conzelmann that led the way, and came to dominate, in the new theological approach to Luke.[89] Conzelmann argued that "Luke" (he did not think that Luke the physician was the author) wrote largely in order to explain to the church of his day the delay of the parousia. For some time after Jesus' death, the early church believed that Jesus would return in glory to bring an end to this earth in their own lifetimes. At some point, however, as time went by and Jesus did not return, the church came to realize that Jesus would not be coming back in the immediate future. So basic a shift in eschatological expectation demanded a massive reinterpretation of Christian theology. It is this reinterpretation that Luke provides. The heart of Luke's scheme is the replacement of the early Christian eschatological expectation with salvation history. In place of a church waiting for the Lord from heaven, Luke offers a historical outline of the course of saving events, divided into three periods: the period of Israel, the period of Jesus' ministry, and the period of the church. It is this segmentation of salvation history into its separate stages that the very structure of Luke's two-volume work provides. Luke writes to encourage Christians in his day to endure the pressures of living as believers in an indefinitely continuing world order. He thus tries to establish a role for the church. He stresses its authority by locating its establishment in apostles accredited by Jesus himself. He provides for its effective working by organizing it, with elders and bishops. This attention to the church, its authority and organization, has come to be called "early Catholicism" (*Frühkatholizismus*), because it is seen as leading on to the organized "universal" (catholic) church of the second century.

Reaction to Conzelmann's proposal has been vigorous and varied. Three points may be singled out as particularly important. First, as Oscar Cullmann and others have shown, "salvation history," in the sense of a series of stages through which God has brought his salvation to the world, is integral to the New Testament and to the message of Jesus himself.[90] It is not something invented by Luke. Second, it is questionable whether there was at any time in the early church a broadly held conviction that Jesus was *certain* to come back within a

---

[88]W. C. van Unnik, "Luke-Acts, a Storm Center in Contemporary Scholarship," in *Studies in Luke-Acts,* 15–32.

[89]Conzelmann, *The Theology of St. Luke.*

[90]Oscar Cullman, *Christ and Time: The Primitive Christian Conception of Time and History* (Philadelphia: Westminster, 1950).

few short years. Those sayings of Jesus in which he is thought to have said that he would return in glory within the lifetime of the first apostles (e.g., Matt. 10:23; Mark 9:1 par.; Mark 13:30 par.) probably do not mean that at all.[91] Moreover, several texts presuppose that the time of the parousia may be delayed (e.g., Luke 19:11–27; John 21:20–23). It can be demonstrated that the early Christians were strongly imbued with a sense of the Lord's *imminence* (that Jesus *could* return at any time) but not that they held to a notion of the *immediacy* of the Lord's return (that he definitely *would* return within a short period of time). The third important response to the scenario drawn by Conzelmann and others is to question the existence of "early Catholicism" in Luke. Luke has not, as these scholars claim, abandoned a doctrine of imminence: the church has not simply settled down into the world but exists in "the last days," eagerly awaiting the return of Jesus from heaven. Moreover, Luke displays little interest in the church as an institution or in the sacraments.[92]

While Luke's salvation history and "early Catholicism" continue to be debated, two other theological issues are attracting more attention and debate in contemporary scholarship. The first is Luke's social and political teaching. It is well known that Luke's gospel evinces a special interest in the problems of the poor and the outcasts and that Jesus has more to say about the economic aspects of discipleship in Luke's gospel than in any other. Stimulated by the agenda of liberation theology and by a new awareness of the materialistic preoccupations of Western society, scholars have devoted considerable attention to Luke's teaching on these matters. Many of the studies focus exclusively on the gospel, but several important ones bring Acts into the picture as well.[93]

Perhaps the most debated issue in Luke's theology in recent years has been his view of the Mosaic law and of the relationship between Israel and the church. The stimulus of the discussion has come above all from the writings of Jacob Jervell.[94] In opposition to those scholars who have seen in Luke-Acts the theme

---

[91]See, e.g., A. L. Moore, *The Parousia in the New Testament* (Leiden: Brill, 1966).

[92]See, e.g., Kümmel, 170–73, and on this and the subject of this paragraph, see esp. E. Earle Ellis, *Eschatology in Luke* (Philadelphia: Fortress Press, 1972); A. J. Mattill Jr., *Luke and the Last Things* (Dillsboro: Western North Carolina Press, 1979); I. Howard Marshall, *Luke: Historian and Theologian*, rev. ed. (Grand Rapids: Zondervan, 1989), esp. 77–88; Leon Morris, "Luke and Early Catholicism," in *Studying the New Testament Today*, vol. 1, ed. John H. Skilton (Nutley: Presbyterian & Reformed, 1974), 60–75.

[93]L. T. Johnson, *The Literary Function of Possessions in Luke-Acts*, SBLDS 39 (Missoula: SP, 1977); Richard J. Cassidy and Philip J. Scharper, eds., *Political Issues in Luke-Acts* (Maryknoll: Orbis, 1983); P. F. Esler, *Community and Gospel in Luke-Acts: The Social and Political Motivations of Lucan Theology* (Cambridge: Cambridge University Press, 1987).

[94]See particularly, Jacob Jervell, "The Divided People of God" and "The Law in Luke-Acts," in *Luke and the People of God* (Minneapolis: Augsburg, 1972), 41–74 and 133–51.

of the church as the new Israel—the new people of God that *replaces* Israel—Jervell insists that it is repentant Jews who constitute Israel in Luke-Acts and that Gentile Christians belong to this Israel as an "associate people." In keeping with this stress on the continuity of Israel, Jervell also argues that Luke has "the most conservative outlook within the New Testament" on the Mosaic law.[95] Jewish Christians are required to keep the law, while Gentile Christians must keep the part of the law that concerns them (see the apostolic decree). Jervell's thesis has met with considerable approval,[96] but also with some serious criticisms.[97] While Luke does not "transfer" the title "Israel" to the church, he certainly portrays the church as a new entity, made up of believing Jews and Gentiles.[98] Jervell's view of the Mosaic law is also vulnerable to criticism, several scholars showing that Luke-Acts takes a far more discontinuous view of the law than Jervell thinks.[99]

THE CONTRIBUTION OF ACTS

Historical

Without denying that Acts has as its main purpose the edification of believers and that its theological contributions are significant, we must not lose sight of the fact that Acts purports to narrate historical events. This narrative of historical events—the founding and growth of the church, with its particular emphasis on the career of Paul—is without parallel and therefore invaluable as a source for our knowledge of these events. Without Acts we would know nothing of the pouring out of the Spirit at Pentecost, the martyrdom of Stephen, the life of the early Jerusalem church, or the way in which the gospel first came to

---

[95]Jervell, "The Law in Luke-Acts," 141.

[96]See Robert L. Brawley, *Luke-Acts and the Jews: Conflict, Apology, and Conciliation,* SBLMS 33 (Atlanta: SP, 1987); Fitzmyer, *Luke I–IX,* 58–59.

[97]See particularly, Jack T. Sanders, "The Jewish People in Luke-Acts," in *Luke-Acts and the Jewish People: Eight Critical Perspectives,* ed. Joseph B. Tyson (Minneapolis: Augsburg, 1988), 51–75. Note also M. M. B. Turner, "The Sabbath, Sunday, and the Law in Luke/Acts," in *From Sabbath to Lord's Day,* ed. D. A. Carson (Grand Rapids: Zondervan, 1982), 99–157. See also the history of research on this question in Joseph B. Tyson, *Luke, Judaism, and the Scholars: Critical Approaches to Luke-Acts* (Columbia: University of South Carolina Press, 1999).

[98]See, e.g., I. Howard Marshall, "'Israel' and the Story of Salvation," in *Jesus and the Heritage of Israel,* 255–57.

[99]S. G. Wilson, *Luke and the Law,* SNTSMS 50 (Cambridge: Cambridge University Press, 1983); Craig L. Blomberg, "The Law in Luke-Acts," *JSNT* 22 (1984): 53–80; idem, "The Christian and the Law of Moses," in *Witness to the Gospel: The Theology of Acts,* ed. I. Howard Marshall and David Peterson (Grand Rapids: Eerdmans, 1998), 397–416; M. A. Seifrid, "Jesus and the Law in Acts," *JSNT* 30 (1987): 39–57.

Samaritans and Gentiles. We would have little knowledge of the life and missionary journeys of Paul against which to understand his letters and theology. But can we trust the information that Acts gives us on these matters? As we noted above, the historical reliability of Acts has been widely questioned. The doubts about Luke's accuracy concentrate on three main issues: Luke and ancient historical standards, the comparison of Acts with other sources of information, and the speeches of Acts.

Ancient Historical Standards. It is often suggested that we should not expect Luke to give us an accurate, true-to-life record of the facts because ancient historians were not careful to stick to the facts. They wrote to edify or to draw moral lessons and felt at liberty to play fast and loose with the way things really happened if it suited their purpose or if they did not have access to the facts. To insist on historical accuracy would be unfairly to impose modern standards of history on an ancient historian.

Standards for historical writing in the ancient world were certainly not as uniformly insistent on factual accuracy as those in our day. Many writers who claimed the name "historian" wrote more fiction than fact. But the best ancient historians were concerned with the facts and did not differ very much from the modern historian in this regard. Especially was this true for so-called "scientific" histories, with which Acts favorably compares.[100] Polybius, for instance, criticizes other historians for making up dramatic scenes in the interest of moral lessons or sensationalism and insists that the historian should "simply record what really happened and what really was said, however commonplace" (2.56.10).[101] A similar position is taken by Lucian in his essay "On Writing History." To be sure, the words of Thucydides are often quoted to substantiate a different position. Describing his procedure in writing his history of the Peloponnesian War, Thucydides says:

> As to the speeches that were made by different men, either when they were about to begin the war or when they were already engaged therein, it has been difficult to recall with strict accuracy the words actually spoken, both for me as regards that which I myself heard, and for those who from various

---

[100]See especially Loveday C. A. Alexander, "Acts and Ancient Intellectual Biography," in *The Book of Acts in Its Ancient Setting,* ed. Bruce W. Winter and Andrew D. Clarke, vol. 1 of *The Book of Acts in Its First Century Setting* (Grand Rapids: Eerdmans, 1993), 31–63.

[101]Quoted from the translation of W. R. Paton, *Polybius: The Histories,* vol. 1, LCL (Cambridge: Harvard University Press, 1922). On these points, see esp. A. W. Mosley, "Historical Reporting in the Ancient World," *NTS* 12 (1965–66): 10–26; Hemer, *Book of Acts,* 43–44, 75–79. See also W. C. van Unnik, "Luke's Second Book and the Rules of Hellenistic Historiography," in *Les Actes des Apôtres: Traditions, rédaction, théologie,* ed. J. Kremer, BETL 48 (Leuven: Leuven University Press, 1979), 37–60.

other sources have brought me reports. Therefore the speeches are given in the language which, as it seemed to me, the several speakers would express, on the subjects under consideration, the sentiments most befitting the occasion, though at the same time I have adhered as closely as possible to the general sense of what was actually said. (1.22)

While Thucydides, who is generally highly regarded as an ancient historian, admits that not all his speeches are verbatim reports, two things also need to be noted about this statement. First, he resorted to giving the general sense "befitting the occasion" only when he did not have firsthand data. Second, he did not make up rhetorical flights to match his own purposes but stuck to what was appropriate to the actual occasion.

We will come back to the issue of the speeches in Acts.[102] Here we want simply to point out that ancient authors testify to very high standards of historical reporting, standards that are not much different at all from those with which we are familiar. It is not fair, then, to conclude that a concern for the way things actually happened was foreign to ancient historians.

Comparison between Acts and Other Sources. Luke, then, had available to him standards of historiography almost as rigorous as those in our day. The question is whether he successfully met them or not. Only a careful comparison of Luke with other ancient sources for the same data can answer this question. Because of the lack of parallels to Acts, we do not have available to us a great deal of material for comparison. But we can test Luke at three points: his knowledge of first-century society, politics, and geography; his reporting of events recorded by other ancient historians; and his accuracy in depicting the history and theology of Paul.

William Ramsay,[103] A. N. Sherwin-White,[104] and Colin Hemer[105] have demonstrated the accuracy of Luke's knowledge about detail after detail of Roman provincial government, first-century geographic boundaries, social and religious customs, navigational procedures,[106] and the like. This accuracy shows not only that Luke knew the first-century Roman world but that he was intimately acquainted with the specific areas and regions in which his narrative is set.

Luke does not often record events that are also mentioned by other historians, and when he does, he does not usually give us enough detail to enable us to

---

[102]On Thucydides, see Hemer, *Book of Acts,* 421–26.

[103]Ramsay, *Bearing of Recent Discovery and St. Paul.*

[104]A. N. Sherwin-White, *Roman Society and Roman Law in the New Testament* (London: Oxford University Press, 1963).

[105]Hemer, *Book of Acts.*

[106]On the shipwreck voyage, see James Smith, *The Voyage and Shipwreck of St. Paul,* 4th ed. (London: Longman, Brown, Green & Longmans, 1880; reprint, Grand Rapids: Baker, 1978).

make comparisons. In the book of Acts, Luke's mention of the death of Herod Agrippa I (12:19–23), of a serious famine in the middle 40s (11:27–30), of the edict of Claudius expelling Jews from Rome (18:2), of the replacement of the Judean procurator Felix with Festus (24:27), and of an Egyptian terrorist active in the middle 50s (21:38) are all confirmed in secular historical sources. Only at two places has it been claimed that such a comparison finds Luke to be inaccurate. In 5:36–37, Luke has Gamaliel, the Jewish rabbi, mention the false messianic claims of a Theudas and, after him, of "Judas the Galilean." Josephus, however, also mentions a rebel named Theudas but places his activity in the years A.D. 44–46, about forty years after Judas and at least ten years after the setting of Acts 5 (*Ant.* 20.5.1). But Gamaliel may be referring to a different Theudas entirely; and in any case, as F. F. Bruce remarks, "where we have simply the one author's word against the other's, Luke is at least as likely to be right as Josephus."[107] The other problem is the Roman officer's reference to the "four thousand" men whom "the Egyptian" had led in revolt (Acts 21:38); Josephus, however, refers to thirty thousand (*Ant.* 20.8.6). But again, we should certainly prefer Luke to Josephus, especially since Josephus's numbers are often impossibly large.

The most serious challenge to Luke's accuracy involves a comparison between his story of Paul and the apostle's own accounts. We have examined some of the alleged discrepancies above and have concluded that there is no reason to drive a wedge between the Paul of Acts and the Paul of the epistles. The alleged historical contradictions almost all involve matters on which Paul's own evidence is incomplete or ambiguous. This is not surprising, for, granted the nature and purpose of Paul's letters, it is not to be expected that the apostle would have gone into the historical detail that we find in Acts.

Perhaps we should say something further here about one of the most famous problems in a comparison between Paul and Acts: the number of trips Paul made to Jerusalem after his conversion. Paul's own epistles mention only three such trips: three years after his conversion (Gal. 1:18); fourteen years after his conversion or, perhaps, after his first visit (Gal. 2:1); and a projected visit at the time of the writing of Romans (15:24). In Acts, however, we are told of five visits: the postconversion visit (9:26), the famine-relief visit (11:27–30), the visit for the apostolic council (chap 15), a visit between the second and third missionary journeys (18:22), and a visit at the end of the third missionary journey (21:17). Now, it is clear that the first visit in Acts corresponds to the one Paul mentions in Galatians 1:18, and the last to the one mentioned in Romans. But it is common to accuse Luke of fabricating one or more of the other visits, particularly because, it is usually argued, the visit in Galatians 2:1 must be the visit for the apostolic council (Acts 15), leaving no place for the famine relief visit of Acts 11:27–30.

[107]Bruce, *Acts of the Apostles,* 18.

But it is, in fact, more likely that Galatians 2:1 describes the famine-relief visit (see the introduction to Galatians, chap. 12 below). There would then be no contradiction between Paul and Acts, only a difference over the number of trips mentioned. But we have no reason to expect that Paul has told us of all his journeys to Jerusalem, so the problem disappears entirely. A similar situation prevails with respect to the other, less serious alleged discrepancies between the history of Paul in Acts and the details of his life furnished in his letters.

The Speeches of Acts. Many scholars think that Luke is most untrustworthy in the speeches of Acts. They point out that the speeches are all in the same general style, a style that is found in the narrative portions of Acts. And they claim that the theology of the speeches is distinctively Lukan, rather than Petrine, Pauline, or whatever. It is therefore concluded that Luke has followed the Thucydidean model (see the quotation above) and put on the lips of his speakers the sentiments that he felt were appropriate for the occasion.[108]

Several responses to this accusation are necessary. *First,* as we noted above, Thucydides claims that only when he did not have information available did he not report what was actually said. Some other ancient historians were far more free in inventing speeches, but there is no a priori reason to compare Luke with them instead of with those who did seek accuracy in recording speeches (e.g., Polybius; see 12.25b.1, 4). *Second,* uniformity of style in the speeches means only that Luke has not given us verbatim reports but has paraphrased in his own words. This is likely in any case, since many of the speeches were probably translated by Luke from Aramaic. It is also likely that almost all the speeches Luke reports were much longer than the summaries he has given us. But paraphrases and summaries of speeches can still accurately convey their contents. *Third,* it is alleged there are differences in the theology of the speeches. Peter's speeches in Acts 2 and 3, for instance, contain formulations of Christology (e.g., 2:36) and eschatology (e.g., 3:19–20) that fit very well the early days of the church and that differ from the formulations found in the speeches of Paul in Acts 13 and 17.[109] In no case can it be shown that the theology or sentiments expressed in the speeches are inappropriate for the occasion or impossible for the speaker. On the positive side, the fidelity of Luke to his sources in the gospel (Mark, Q) suggests that he has been equally faithful to his sources in Acts. This argument is

---

[108]See esp. Dibelius, "The Speeches of Acts and Ancient Historiography," in *Studies in the Acts of the Apostle,* 138–85; Cadbury, "The Speeches in Acts," in *The Beginnings of Christianity,* 5.405–27; Ulrich Wilckens, *Die Missionsreden der Apostelgeschichte,* WMANT 5 (Neukirchen-Vluyn: Neukirchener, 1961); Eduard Schweizer, "Concerning the Speeches in Acts," in *Studies in Luke-Acts,* 208–16.

[109]See, on Christology, C. F. D. Moule, "The Christology of Acts," in *Studies in Luke-Acts,* 159–85; and Richard N. Longenecker, *The Christology of Early Jewish Christianity* (London: SCM, 1970).

often contested. It is argued that Luke would have much greater respect for the words of Jesus than for the words of the apostles. But there is little to suggest that Luke would have made such a distinction. He claims to have the intention of instilling in his readers "the certainty of the things you have been taught" (Luke 1:4), and there is every reason to think that he has sought for accuracy in recording what people actually said, in Acts as much as in the gospel.[110]

Theological and Pastoral

As we argued above, Luke's primary purpose is to edify Christians by recounting how God's plan, coming to fulfillment in Jesus, had continued to unfold in the history of the early church. Perhaps Luke's most important contribution is precisely this careful linking of the apostolic proclamation of the Word of God with the word that Jesus both taught and fulfilled. The "Word of God" thus binds together Luke's two volumes,[111] as the salvation that the angel first announced on the night of Jesus' birth on a Judean hillside (Luke 2:10–12) is brought finally to the capital of the Roman Empire. Luke thus presents "the things that have been fulfilled among us" (Luke 1:1) as a continuation of the salvific history of the Old Testament, showing how this history reaches its culmination in Christ and flows from him through the Spirit-led apostles into a new phase, the church as the eschatological people of God.[112] By doing so, Luke gave to Theophilus, and continues to give to every Christian who reads his two volumes, an assurance that faith is solidly grounded in the acts of God in history and that the message we believe is the same message sent from God.

Luke in his two volumes gives us an assurance that faith is solidly grounded in the acts of God in history and that the message we believe is the same message sent from God.

While Luke makes clear the continuity in the message of salvation, he also reveals the progressive unfolding of new implications from that message. The historical veracity of Luke is seen in the way he makes clear the differences between the early Jerusalem community of believers and the later Gentile churches founded by Paul. The earliest Christians, Jews who believed that Jesus was the promised Messiah and that the messianic age had therefore dawned, continued to worship in the temple and were apparently loyal to the law and its institutions. Only by stages did the church move away from this Jewish outlook to a more universal orientation, as God made clear that he was doing a new work in which the law would no longer play a central role and in which Gentiles would share equally with the Jews in the blessings of God. A major contribution of Acts is the way the progress of this movement is portrayed, coming to a climax with Paul's announcement of judicial obduracy on the part of unbelieving Israel and the offer of salvation to the Gentiles (28:25–29).

---

[110]See, again, on the speeches, Hemer, *Book of Acts,* 415–26.

[111]Haenchen, *Acts,* 98; Longenecker, "Acts," 218.

[112]On this theme, see particularly Marshall, *Luke, Historian and Theologian;* idem, *Acts,* 20–21; Gasque, "Recent Study," 120–21.

Paul is the chief instrument through which this universalizing of the church takes place, and there is no doubt that he is Luke's hero.[113] Childs has suggested that Luke thus portrays a "canonical Paul," a figure who does not necessarily match the historical Paul but who can function as the representative apostle for a later age.[114] But it is questionable whether Luke presents Paul as a representative of the future. Rather, Luke suggests that Paul plays a decisive role in the foundation of a new period of salvation history, and in this sense, his significance is more for the past of the church than for its present or future. As we have already argued, there is little reason to think that the apostle portrayed in Acts is different from the apostle as he really was. Moreover, we must be careful not to give Paul too prominent a place in Luke's presentation. "When everything is interpreted so as to establish the authority and authenticity of Paul's ministry, Paul, rather than Jesus, becomes the key character in Luke-Acts."[115]

The basic theological/pastoral thrust of Acts may be fleshed out by looking more closely at six key themes.

The Plan of God. The outworking of God's plan acts as an overarching theme for Luke and Acts together (see chap. 5). The opening of the gospel announces the imminent fulfillment of God's promises to Israel (1:32–33, 54–55, 68–79), penultimately in the events of Jesus' ministry, death, and resurrection, but ultimately in the creation of the end-time people of God. Luke shows in Acts how the plan of God to bring salvation to the "ends of the earth" is fulfilled in the death of his servant-Messiah and in the ongoing witness of the church, which itself takes on the function of the servant (the phrase "the ends of the earth" is probably drawn from a servant passage, Isa. 49:6 [cf. 13:47]).[116] The specific mechanisms by which the plan of God is announced in the gospel are continued in the book of Acts: the note of divine necessity (1:16, 21; 3:12; 4:21; 9:16; 14:21; 17:3; 19:21; 23:11; 27:24); angelic intervention (5:19, 21; 12:7–11, 23; 27:23–24); visions (10:10–16; 16:9; 18:9; 22:17–21); the fulfillment of Scripture (1:20; 2:16–21, 25–28, 34–35; 3:22–23; 4:11, 25–26; 7:48–49; 8:31–35; 13:33–37, 40–41, 47; 15:15–18; 17:2–3; 26:22–23; 28:25–27).[117]

---

[113]E.g., Martin Hengel, *Between Jesus and Paul* (Philadelphia: Fortress Press, 1983), 2.

[114]Childs, 225–27.

[115]David Peterson, "Luke's Theological Enterprise: Integration and Intent," in *Witness to the Gospel,* 533.

[116]See on this esp. David W. Pao, *Acts and the Isaianic New Exodus,* WUNT 130 (Tübingen: Mohr-Siebeck, 2000), 91–93, passim.

[117]Luke's appeal to Scripture, of course, goes far beyond quotations. Along with other NT writers, he reveals *patterns* of saving events that predict the dawning of the age of salvation—cf. Darrell Bock, *Proclamation from Prophecy and Pattern: Lucan Old Testament Christology,* JSNTSup 12 (Sheffield: Sheffield Academic Press, 1987).

Luke is especially concerned to show that two critical events are rooted in the plan of God: Jesus' crucifixion (e.g., 2:23; 13:27) and the inclusion of Gentiles in the people of God (e.g., 10:1–16; 13:47; 15:15–18)—both of which were critical yet controversial components of the early Christians' interpretation of salvation history.

The Presence of the Future. Yet another key facet of early Christian self-understanding was the conviction that, with the coming of Christ and the Spirit, the "last days" had dawned. In the prophets, this phrase denotes that period of time when God would fulfill his promises by saving his people and judging their enemies. Luke clearly recognizes that a day of judgment and ultimate salvation lies in the future (cf. 3:21; 10:42), but he is particularly concerned to show that the early Christians were living in those "last days." This conviction emerges programmatically in Peter's claim that the phenomenon of speaking in tongues on the Day of Pentecost is just what Joel predicted would happen "in the last days" (2:16–17). But the notion suffuses the entire narrative, as the many Old Testament quotations reveal.

Salvation. As we noted in chapter 5, "salvation" is considered by most scholars to be the central theological theme in both Luke and Acts.[118] That Acts carries on the theme from the gospel is clear from a number of key passages:

"And everyone who calls on the name of the Lord will be saved." (2:21 [=Joel 2:32])

"And the Lord added to their number daily those who were being saved." (2:47b)

"Salvation is found in no one else, for there is no other name given under heaven by which we must be saved." (4:12)

"God exalted him to his own right hand as Prince and Savior that he might bring Israel to repentance and forgive their sins." (5:31)

"From this man's descendants God has brought to Israel the Savior Jesus, as he promised." (13:23)

"Brothers and sisters from the children of Abraham and you God-fearing Gentiles, it is to us that this message of salvation has been sent." (13:26)

"For this is what the Lord has commanded us: 'I have made you a light for the Gentiles, that you may bring salvation to the ends of the earth.'" (13:47 [=Isa. 49:6])

"They replied, 'Believe in the Lord Jesus, and you will be saved—you and your household.'" (16:31)

"Therefore I want you to know that God's salvation has been sent to the Gentiles, and they will listen!" (28:28)

---

[118]Joel Green argues that salvation is the integrating theme of Acts ("'Salvation to the Ends of Earth' [Acts 13:47]: God as Saviour in the Acts of the Apostles," in *Witness to the Gospel*, 83–106).

Salvation, the disciples initially expected, would mean the restoration of an earthly kingdom to Israel (1:6). Jesus does not clearly deny that this will be the case, but his emphasis on the witness of the apostles suggests that the saving power of God's kingdom is being realized in the forgiveness of sins offered in the gospel proclamation.

The Word of God. An easily overlooked yet vital theme in Acts is the power of the word of God.[119] Again and again, Luke attributes the growth and strength of the church to the dynamic activity of God's word. Preaching the word of God is what the apostles do wherever they go. "Received the word of God" is another way of saying "became a Christian" (11:1). Especially striking are those places where Luke, usually in transitional summaries, claims that the word of God "grew" or "spread" or "increased" (6:7; 12:24; 13:49; 19:20). For Luke the word of God is especially the message about God's gracious redemption through Jesus Christ. For all Luke's emphasis on the importance of apostolic preaching, therefore, he makes clear that it is only as they are faithful witnesses to the Word that spiritual transformation takes place. As C. K. Barrett notes, "Luke's stress on the proclamation of the Word . . . shows that the Word itself was the decisive factor," and that the church is an agency of salvation "only in so far as it provides the framework within which the preaching of the Word takes place."[120] Luke's stress on the power of the word reveals, suggests Talbert, that Luke is not an "early Catholic" but a "proto-Protestant" (using these designations in stereotypical fashion).[121]

The Holy Spirit. Attention to the work of the Spirit is another theme that binds together Luke and Acts. Indeed, many point to parallels at this point between the two: as Jesus is anointed by the Spirit at the commencement of his ministry, so the church is endued with the Spirit's power at the beginning of its ministry; as Jesus performs signs and wonders in the power of the Spirit, so the apostles heal people in the power of the Spirit; as the Spirit guides events in the gospels, so he guides events in Acts. Scholars often note that Luke in Acts concentrates especially on the prophetic activity of the Spirit: emboldening the early Christians for witness (e.g., 4:8, 31; 7:55; 13:9) and guiding the course of apostolic ministry (8:29, 39; 11:12; 13:2; 16:6, 7; 20:22).[122] Key here, of course, is

---

[119]See esp. Pao, *Acts and the Isaianic New Exodus,* 147–80; also Brian S. Rosner, "The Progress of the Word," in *Witness to the Gospel,* 215–33.

[120]Barrett, *Luke the Historian in Recent Study,* 72, 74.

[121]Charles H. Talbert, "The Redactional Critical Quest for Luke the Theologian," in *Jesus and Man's Hope,* vol. 1, ed. Donald G. Miller (Pittsburgh: Pittsburgh Theological Seminary, 1970), 220. He adds, "*Sola Scriptura* is a major plank in the Lucan theological platform."

[122]See, e.g., Max Turner, *Power from on High: The Spirit in Israel's Restoration and Witness in Luke-Acts,* JPTSS 9 (Sheffield: Sheffield Academic Press, 1996).

Peter's quotation of Joel 2:28: "I will pour out my Spirit on all people. Your sons and your daughters will prophesy . . ." (Acts 2:17). There is no doubt that this is an important function of the Spirit in Acts. But we should not ignore another important facet of the Spirit's work.[123] At key points in his narrative Luke introduces references to the Spirit "coming upon" or "filling" people: those who respond to Peter's Pentecost message (2:38); the Samaritans who are converted (8:15–17); Cornelius and his household (10:44). Possession of the Spirit, it becomes clear, is one of *the* indicators that a person belongs to the emerging people of God of the last days (see esp. 11:15–17; 15:8–9)—along with faith, repentance, and water baptism.[124]

The People of God. As we suggested above, perhaps Luke's most fundamental purpose in the Book of Acts is to help Christians answer the question "Who are we?" Two thousand years of church history sometimes prevent us from seeing just how basic that question was for the first believers. As long as Jews only were among the faithful, it could always be thought that this new group was just another sect of Jews who had some crazy notion about who the Messiah was. But as soon as Samaritans and Gentiles began entering the picture, identity within Judaism ceased to be an option. Something new had come into being—in continuity with the old, of course, but distinct from it as well. Luke, of course, leaves us in no doubt about whether the inclusion of Gentiles and the casting loose from temple and Torah were directed by God. And so a new name has to be coined to identify this new group: "Christians," followers of Christ (11:26).

BIBLIOGRAPHY

Kurt **Aland** and Barbara **Aland**, *The Text of the New Testament*, rev. ed. (Grand Rapids: Eerdmans, 1989) ▮Loveday C. A. **Alexander**, *The Preface to Luke's Gospel: Literary Convention and Social Context in Luke 1:1–4 and Acts 1:1*, SNTSMS 78 (Cambridge: Cambridge University Press, 1993) ▮idem, "Acts and Ancient Intellectual Biography," in *The Book of Acts in Its Ancient Setting*, ed. Bruce W. Winter and Andrew D. Clarke, vol. 1 of *The Book of Acts in Its First Century Setting* (Grand Rapids: Eerdmans, 1993), 31–63 ▮David E. **Aune**, *The New Testament in Its Literary Environment*, LEC 8 (Philadelphia: Westminster, 1987) ▮idem, *Studies in New Testament and Early Christian Literature* (Leiden: Brill, 1972) ▮C. K. **Barrett**, *A Critical and Exegetical Commentary on the Acts of the Apostles*, 2 vols., ICC (Edinburgh: T. & T. Clark, 1994, 1998) ▮idem, *Luke the Historian in Recent Study* (London: Epworth, 1961) ▮F. **Blass**, "Die

---

[123]See Green, *Theology*, 45–47.

[124]James D. G. Dunn argues that Acts presents these four as making up, together, "conversion-initiation" (*Baptism in the Holy Spirit*, SBT 15 [London: SCM, 1970])

Textüberlieferung in der Apostelgeschichte," *TSK* 67 (1894): 86–119 ▋Craig L. **Blomberg**, "The Christian and the Law of Moses," in *Witness to the Gospel: The Theology of Acts*, ed. I. Howard Marshall and David Peterson (Grand Rapids: Eerdmans, 1998), 397–416 ▋idem, "The Law in Luke-Acts," *JSNT* 22 (1984): 53–80 ▋Darrell **Bock**, *Luke, vol. 1: 1:1–9:50*, BECNT (Grand Rapids: Baker, 1994) ▋idem, *Proclamation from Prophecy and Pattern: Lucan Old Testament Christology*, JSNTSup 12 (Sheffield: Sheffield Academic Press, 1987) ▋M.-E. **Boismard** and A. **Lamouille**, *Le texte occidental des Actes des Apôtres: Reconstitution et rehabilitation*, 2 vols. (Paris: Editions Recherche sur les civilizations, 1984) ▋François **Bovon**, *Luke the Theologian: Thirty-three Years of Research (1950–1983)* (Allison Park: Pickwick, 1987) ▋Robert L. **Brawley**, *Luke-Acts and the Jews: Conflict, Apology, and Conciliation*, SBLMS 33 (Atlanta: SP, 1987) ▋F. F. **Bruce**, *The Acts of the Apostles: The Greek Text with Introduction and Commentary*, 2nd ed. (Grand Rapids: Eerdmans, 1952) ▋idem, "The Acts of the Apostles: Historical Record or Theological Reconstruction?" *ANRW* 25.3 (1985): 2569–2603 ▋idem, *The Book of Acts*, rev. ed., NICNT (Grand Rapids: Eerdmans, 1988) ▋idem, "Is the Paul of Acts the Real Paul?" *BJRL* 58 (1975–76): 282–305 ▋idem, *Paul: Apostle of the Heart Set Free* (Grand Rapids: Eerdmans, 1977) ▋F. C. **Burkitt**, *The Gospel History and Its Transmission*, 3rd ed. (Edinburgh: T. & T. Clark, 1911) ▋Henry J. **Cadbury**, *The Making of Luke-Acts* (New York: Macmillan, 1927) ▋idem, *The Style and Literary Method of St. Luke*, HTS 6 (Cambridge: Harvard University Press, 1919) ▋Richard **Cassidy** and Philip J. **Scharper**, eds., *Political Issues in Luke-Acts* (Maryknoll: Orbis, 1983) ▋Albert C. **Clark**, *The Acts of the Apostles: A Critical Edition, with Introduction and Notes on Selected Passages* (Oxford: Clarendon Press, 1933) ▋Hans **Conzelmann**, *Acts of the Apostles*, Hermeneia (Philadelphia: Fortress Press, 1987) ▋idem, *The Theology of St. Luke* (New York: Harper & Row, 1961) ▋Oscar **Cullmann**, *Christ and Time: The Primitive Christian Conception of Time and History* (Philadelphia: Westminster, 1950) ▋Martin **Dibelius**, *Studies in the Acts of the Apostles*, ed. Heinrich Greeven (London: SCM, 1956) ▋James D. G. **Dunn**, *Baptism in the Holy Spirit*, SBT 15 (London: SCM, 1970) ▋Jacques **Dupont**, *The Sources of the Acts* (New York: Herder & Herder, 1964) ▋E. Earle **Ellis**, "'The Ends of the Earth' (Acts 1:8)," *BBR* 1 (1991): 123–32 ▋idem, *Eschatology in Luke* (Philadelphia: Fortress Press, 1972) ▋Eldon Jay **Epp**, *The Theological Tendency of Codex Bezae Cantabrigiensis in Acts*, SNTSMS 3 (Cambridge: Cambridge University Press, 1966) ▋P. F. **Esler**, *Community and Gospel in Luke-Acts: The Social and Political Motivations of Lucan Theology* (Cambridge: Cambridge University Press, 1987) ▋Floyd V. **Filson**, "The Journey Motif in Luke-Acts," in *Apostolic History and the Gospel*, Fs. F. F. Bruce, ed. W. Ward Gasque and Ralph P. Martin (Grand Rapids: Eerdmans, 1970), 68–77 ▋idem, *Three Crucial Decades: Studies in the Book of Acts* (London: Epworth, 1964) ▋Joseph A. **Fitzmyer**, *The Acts of the Apostles: A New Translation with Introduction and Commentary*, AB 31 (New York: Doubleday, 1998) ▋idem, *The*

Gospel According to Luke I–IX, AB 28 (New York: Doubleday, 1982) ▮▮F. J. **Foakes Jackson** and Kirsopp **Lake**, eds., *The Beginnings of Christianity*, Part 1: *The Acts of the Apostles*, 5 vols. (London: Macmillan, 1920–33) ▮▮Bertil **Gärtner**, *The Areopagus Speech and Natural Revelation*, ASNU 21 (Uppsala: Gleerup, 1955) ▮▮W. Ward **Gasque**, "A Fruitful Field: Recent Study of the Acts of the Apostles," *Int* 42 (1988): 117–31 ▮▮idem, *A History of the Criticism of the Acts of the Apostles*, BGBE 17 (Tübingen: Mohr-Siebeck, 1975) ▮▮Beverly Roberts **Gaventa**, *The Acts of the Apostles*, ANTC (Nashville: Abingdon, 2003) ▮▮M. D. **Goulder**, *Type and History in Acts* (London: SPCK, 1964) ▮▮Joel **Green**, "'Salvation to the Ends of Earth' (Acts 13:47): God as Saviour in the Acts of the Apostles," in *Witness to the Gospel: The Theology of Acts*, ed. I. Howard Marshall and David Peterson (Grand Rapids: Eerdmans, 1998), 83–106 ▮▮idem, *The Theology of the Gospel of Luke* (Cambridge: Cambridge University Press, 1995) ▮▮Ernst **Haenchen**, *The Acts of the Apostles: A Commentary* (Philadelphia: Westminster, 1971) ▮▮idem, "The Book of Acts as Source Material for the History of Earliest Christianity," in *Studies in Luke-Acts*, ed. Leander E. Keck and J. Louis Martyn (Nashville: Abingdon, 1966), 258–78 ▮▮Adolf von **Harnack**, *The Acts of the Apostles* (London: Williams & Norgate, 1909) ▮▮idem, *The Date of Acts and of the Synoptic Gospels* (New York: Putman, 1911) ▮▮idem, *Luke the Physician* (New York: Putman, 1907) ▮▮Everett F. **Harrison**, *Interpreting Acts* (Grand Rapids: Zondervan, 1986) ▮▮Colin J. **Hemer**, *The Book of Acts in the Setting of Hellenistic History*, WUNT 49 (Tübingen: Mohr-Siebeck, 1989) ▮▮Martin **Hengel**, *Acts and the History of Earliest Christianity* (Philadelphia: Fortress Press, 1979) ▮▮idem, *Between Jesus and Paul: Studies in the Earliest History of Christianity* (Philadelphia: Fortress Press, 1983) ▮▮A. J. B. **Higgins**, "The Prologue to Luke and the Kerygma of Acts," in *Apostolic History and the Gospel*, 78–91 ▮▮W. K. **Hobart**, *The Medical Language of St. Luke* (Dublin: Hodges, Figgis, 1882) ▮▮Joachim **Jeremias**, "Untersuchungen zum Quellenproblem der Apostelgeschichte," *ZNW* 36 (1937): 205–21 ▮▮Jacob **Jervell**, *Luke and the People of God* (Minneapolis: Augsburg, 1972) ▮▮idem, *The Theology of the Acts of the Apostles* (Cambridge: Cambridge University Press, 1996) ▮▮idem, *Die Apostelgeschichte*, KEK (Göttingen: Vandenhoeck & Ruprecht, 1998) ▮▮L. T. **Johnson**, *The Literary Function of Possessions in Luke-Acts*, SBLDS 39 (Missoula: SP, 1977) ▮▮J. C. **Lentz**, *Luke's Portrait of Paul*, SNTSMS 77 (Cambridge: Cambridge University Press, 1993) ▮▮Walter L. **Liefeld**, "Luke," in *EBC* 8 ▮▮Richard N. **Longenecker**, "The Acts of the Apostles," in *EBC* 9 ▮▮idem, *The Christology of Early Jewish Christianity* (London: SCM, 1970) ▮▮idem, *Paul, Apostle of Liberty*, reprint ed. (Grand Rapids: Baker, 1976) ▮▮Gerd **Lüdemann**, *Early Christianity According to the Traditions in Acts: A Commentary* (Minneapolis: Fortress Press, 1989) ▮▮Robert **Maddox**, *Commentary on Acts* (Minneapolis: Fortress Press, 1989) ▮▮idem, *The Purpose of Luke-Acts*, FRLANT 126 (Göttingen: Vandenhoeck & Ruprecht, 1982) ▮▮I. Howard **Marshall**, "Acts and the 'Former Treatise,'" in *The Book of Acts in Its First Century Setting*, Vol. 1: *The Book in Its Ancient Literary*

Setting, ed. Bruce W. Winter and Andrew D. Clarke (Grand Rapids: Eerdmans, 1993), 163–82 ▦idem, *The Acts of the Apostles*, TNTC (Grand Rapids: Eerdmans, 1980) ▦idem, "'Israel' and the Story of Salvation," in *Jesus and the Heritage of Israel: Luke's Narrative Claim upon Israel's Legacy*, ed. David P. Moessner (Harrisburg: Trinity Press International, 2000), 255–57 ▦idem, *Luke: Historian and Theologian*, rev. ed. (Grand Rapids: Zondervan, 1989) ▦idem, "Luke and His 'Gospel,'" in *Das Evangelium und die Evangelien*, ed. Peter Stuhlmacher, WUNT 28 (Tübingen: Mohr-Siebeck, 1983), 289–308 ▦idem, "Acts in Current Study," *ExpTim* 115 (2003): 49–52 ▦I. Howard **Marshall** and David **Peterson**, eds., *Witness to the Gospel: The Theology of Acts* (Grand Rapids: Eerdmans, 1998) ▦A. J. **Mattill** Jr., "The Date and Purpose of Luke-Acts: Rackham Reconsidered," *CBQ* 40 (1978): 335–50 ▦idem, *Luke and the Last Things* (Dillsboro: Western North Carolina Press, 1979) ▦idem, "The Purpose of Acts: Schneckenburger Reconsidered," in *Apostolic History and the Gospel*, 108–22 ▦Eduard **Meyer**, *Ursprung und Anfänge des Christentums*, 3 vols. (Stuttgart: J. G. Cotta, 1921–23) ▦David P. **Moessner**, ed., *Jesus and the Heritage of Israel: Luke's Narrative Claim upon Israel's Legacy* (Harrisburg: Trinity Press International, 2000) ▦A. L. **Moore**, *The Parousia in the New Testament* (Leiden: Brill, 1966) ▦A. W. **Mosley**, "Historical Reporting in the Ancient World," *NTS* 12 (1965–66): 10–26 ▦C. F. D. **Moule**, "The Christology of Acts," in *Studies in Luke-Acts*, 159–85 ▦J. C. **O'Neill**, *The Theology of Acts in Its Historical Setting* (London: SPCK, 1961) ▦Darryl W. **Palmer**, "Acts and the Ancient Historical Monograph," in *The Book of Acts in its First Century Setting*, vol. 1 of *The Book in its Ancient Literary Setting*, ed. Bruce W. Winter and Andrew D. Clarke (Grand Rapids: Eerdmans, 1993), 1–29 ▦David W. **Pao**, *Acts and the Isaianic New Exodus*, WUNT 130 (Tübingen: Mohr-Siebeck, 2000) ▦Richard I. **Pervo**, *Profit with Delight: The Literary Genre of the Acts of the Apostles* (Philadelphia: Fortress Press, 1987) ▦Eduard **Plümacher**, *Lukas als hellenistischer Schriftsteller*, SUNT 9 (Göttingen: Vandenhoeck & Ruprecht, 1972) ▦Stanley E. **Porter**, *The Paul of Acts*, WUNT 115 (Tübingen: Mohr-Siebeck, 1999) ▦Richard Belward **Rackham**, *The Acts of the Apostles*, WC (London: Methuen, 1901) ▦William **Ramsay**, *The Bearing of Recent Discovery on the Trustworthiness of the New Testament*, reprint ed. (Grand Rapids: Baker, 1983) ▦idem, *St. Paul, the Traveller and the Roman Citizen* (London: Hodder & Stoughton, 1897) ▦Vernon K. **Robbins**, "The We-Passages in Acts and Ancient Sea Voyages," *BR* 20 (1975): 5–18 ▦J. A. T. **Robinson**, *Redating the New Testament* (Philadelphia: Westminster, 1976) ▦Brian S. **Rosner**, "The Progress of the Word," in *Witness to the Gospel: The Theology of Acts*, ed. I. Howard Marshall and David Peterson (Grand Rapids: Eerdmans, 1998), 215–33 ▦Gerhard **Schneider**, *Die Apostelgeschichte*, 2 vols., HTKNT (Freiburg: Herder, 1980–82) ▦Eduard **Schweizer**, "Concerning the Speeches in Acts," in *Studies in Luke-Acts*, 208–16 ▦M. A. **Seifrid**, "Jesus and the Law in Acts," *JSNT* 30 (1987): 39–57 ▦A. N. **Sherwin-White**, *Roman Society and Roman Law in the New Testament* (London: Oxford University Press, 1963) ▮James **Smith**, *The Voyage and Shipwreck of St. Paul,* 4th ed. (London: Longman, Brown, Green & Longmans, 1880; reprint, Baker, 1978) ▮Marion L. **Soards**, *The Speeches in Acts* (Louisville: Westminster/John Knox, 1994) ▮Charles H. **Talbert**, "The Redactional Critical Quest for Luke the Theologian," in *Jesus and Man's Hope,* vol. 1, ed. Donald G. Miller (Pittsburgh: Pittsburgh Theological Seminary, 1970) ▮idem, *Literary Patterns, Theological Themes, and the Genre of Luke-Acts,* SBLMS (Missoula: SP, 1974) ▮idem, *Luke and the Gnostics: An Examination of the Lucan Purpose* (Nashville: Abingdon, 1966) ▮Robert C. **Tannehill**, *The Narrative Unity of Luke-Acts: A Literary Interpretation,* 2 vols. (Minneapolis: Fortress Press, 1990) ▮J. **Taylor**, "The Making of Acts: A New Account," *RevBib* 97 (1990): 504–24 ▮Charles Cutler **Torrey**, *The Composition and Date of Acts,* HTS 1 (Cambridge: Harvard University Press, 1916) ▮C. M. **Tuckett**, ed., *Luke's Literary Achievement: Collected Essays,* JSNTSup 116 (Sheffield: Sheffield Academic Press, 1995) ▮C. H. **Turner**, "The Chronology of the New Testament," in *A Dictionary of the Bible,* ed. James Hastings, 5 vols. (Edinburgh: T. & T. Clark, 1898–1904), 1.403–25 ▮Max **Turner**, *Power from on High: The Spirit in Israel's Restoration and Witness in Luke-Acts,* JPTSS 9 (Sheffield: Sheffield Academic Press, 1996) ▮idem, "The Sabbath, Sunday, and the Law in Luke/Acts," in *From Sabbath to Lord's Day,* ed. D. A. Carson (Grand Rapids: Zondervan, 1982), 99–157 ▮Joseph B. **Tyson**, ed., *Luke-Acts and the Jewish People: Eight Critical Perspectives* (Minneapolis: Augsburg, 1988) ▮idem, *Luke, Judaism and the Scholars: Critical Approaches to Luke-Acts* (Columbia: University of South Carolina Press, 1999) ▮W. C. **van Unnik**, "The 'Book of Acts' the Confirmation of the Gospel," *NovT* 4 (1960): 26–59 ▮idem, "Luke-Acts, a Storm Center in Contemporary Scholarship," in *Studies in Luke-Acts,* 15–32 ▮idem, "Luke's Second Book and the Rules of Hellenistic Historiography," in *Les Actes des Apôtres: Traditions, rédaction, théologie,* ed. J. Kremer, BETL 48 (Louvain: Louvain University Press, 1979) ▮Philipp **Vielhauer**, "On the 'Paulinism' of Acts," in *Studies in Luke-Acts,* 33–50 ▮Paul W. **Walaskay**, *"And So We Came to Rome": The Political Perspective of St. Luke,* SNTSMS 49 (Cambridge: Cambridge University Press, 1983) ▮Johannes **Weiss**, *Absicht und literarischer Charakter der Apostelgeschichte* (Marburg: Vandenhoeck & Ruprecht, 1897) ▮John **Wenham**, *Redating Matthew, Mark, and Luke: A Fresh Assault on the Synoptic Problem* (Downers Grove: IVP, 1992) ▮Alfred **Wikenhauser**, *Die Apostelgeschichte und ihr Geschichtswert,* NTAbh 8.3–5 (Münster: Aschendorff, 1921) ▮Ulrich **Wilckens**, "Interpreting Luke-Acts in a Period of Existentialist Theology," in *Studies in Luke-Acts,* 60–83 ▮idem, *Die Missionsreden der Apostelgeschichte: Form- und Traditionsgeschichtliche Untersuchungen,* 2nd ed., WMANT 5 (Neukirchen-Vluyn: Neukirchener, 1961) ▮Max **Wilcox**, *The Semitisms of Acts* (Oxford: Clarendon Press, 1965) ▮David John **Williams**, *Acts* (San Francisco: Harper & Row, 1985) ▮S. G. **Wilson**, *Luke and the Law,* SNTSMS 50 (Cambridge: Cambridge University Press, 1983) ▮Walter T. **Wilson**, "Urban

Legends: Acts 10:1–11:18 and the Strategies of Greco-Roman Foundation Narratives," *JBL* 120 (2001): 77–99 ▥ Ben **Witherington** III, *The Acts of the Apostles: A Socio-Rhetorical Commentary* (Grand Rapids: Eerdmans, 1998) ▥ Eduard **Zeller**, *The Contents and Origin of the Acts of the Apostles Critically Investigated*, 2 vols. (London: Williams & Norgate, 1875–76).

CHAPTER EIGHT

NEW TESTAMENT LETTERS

Twenty-one of the twenty-six New Testament books are letters, comprising 35 percent of the New Testament text. Paul, with thirteen authentic epistles, is the most famous letter writer.[1] Why have Paul, James, Peter, John, Jude, and the unknown author of Hebrews chosen to communicate in this form? The question is particularly appropriate when we recognize that the letter was not a typical method of religious instruction among Jews.

The answer is probably twofold. *First,* the early Christian movement, with its fast growth and peripatetic missionaries, demanded a means of communication at a distance. The letter was the obvious solution. The abiding religious significance of the letters, in the sense of canonical, authoritative documents, was the product of later decision rather than intention at the time of writing. The early apostles, then, communicated their teaching in letters because it was convenient and necessary; they were not deliberately creating a new means of religious instruction. A *second* reason the letter may have been chosen by the apostles is its sense of personal immediacy. People in Paul's day saw the letter as a means of establishing personal presence from a distance,[2] and this perfectly served the needs of the apostles in pastoring their distant flocks.

In contemporary scholarship, although a lot of research has focused on the form and function of ancient letters, perhaps even more has been done on the extent to which letters in the first century were *pseudonymous,* that is, ostensibly written by a named person when in reality they were written by someone else. Inevitably that also requires that we evaluate the role of *amanuenses* (more-or-less

---

[1]For a brief but telling defense of this position, see Bo Reicke, *Re-examining Paul's Letters: The History of the Pauline Correspondence* (Harrisburg: Trinity Press International, 2001).

[2]E.g., Seneca, *Epist. Mor.* 75.1–2; and Robert W. Funk, "The Apostolic Parousia: Form and Significance," in *Christian History and Interpretation,* ed. W. R. Farmer, C. F. D. Moule, and R. R. Niebuhr (Cambridge: Cambridge University Press, 1966), 249–68.

scribes/secretaries) in the first century. In this chapter, then, we focus on various aspects of epistolography.

NEW TESTAMENT LETTERS AGAINST THEIR GRECO-ROMAN BACKGROUND

While letters were by no means unknown in the world of the ancient Near East (see, e.g., 2 Sam. 11:14–15; Ezra 4–5), it was in the Greco-Roman world that the letter became an established and popular method of communication. Scholars have therefore turned to the ancient theory and practice of letter writing to illuminate the New Testament letters.

The typical Greco-Roman letter was composed of an address and greeting, a body, and a conclusion.[3] The address and greeting were usually very short, typically taking the form, "A to B, greetings [χαίρειν, *chairein*]." This simple formula is found in the letter sent by the apostolic council to the churches (Acts 15:23) and in James 1:1. Some New Testament letters (Hebrews, 1 John) have no epistolary opening at all, raising questions about their genre. But most New Testament letters expand—sometimes considerably (see Rom. 1:1–7)—the address and change the simple greeting into a so-called grace-wish (e.g., all the Pauline letters, 1 and 2 Peter, and 2 John). This change is undoubtedly related to the purpose of the letters and was facilitated by the similarity between χαίρειν (*chairein*, "greeting") and χάρις (*charis*, "grace"). Ancient letters also often opened with a health-wish (see 3 John); perhaps the New Testament penchant for putting a thanksgiving (all the Pauline letters except Galatians, 2 Corinthians, 1 Timothy, and Titus) or blessing (2 Corinthians, Ephesians, 1 Peter) at the beginning of letters reflects this practice.

Several scholars have suggested that we can identify standardized formulas that were used to make the transition between the opening of the letter and its body.[4] These attempts have not commanded universal assent, however, and it is unlikely that any formula became standard enough to justify our drawing conclusions along these lines. Nor have attempts to identify a typical sequence in the body of the Greco-Roman letter been successful.[5] The varying purposes for which letters were written led, naturally enough, to many different kinds of letter bodies. However, many of the New Testament letters stand out from their contemporary secular models in length. Cicero wrote 776 letters, ranging in

---

[3]Examples of ancient letters have been collected by Stanley K. Stowers, *Letter Writing in Greco-Roman Antiquity* (Philadelphia: Westminster, 1986), 58–173. On the ancient theory of letter writing, see Abraham J. Malherbe, *Ancient Epistolary Theorists* (Atlanta: SP, 1988).

[4]E.g., John Lee White, *The Form and Function of the Body of the Greek Letter*, SBLDS 2, 2nd ed. (Missoula: SP, 1972).

[5]See Stowers, *Letter Writing*, 22.

length from 22 to 2,530 words; Seneca 124 letters, from 149 to 4,134 words in length; Paul averages 1,300 words in length, and Romans has 7,114. Ancient letters tended to close with greetings, and this is typical of New Testament letters also. In addition, New Testament letters usually add a doxology or benediction.

This brief survey reveals that New Testament letters resemble ancient letters but that the similarities are of a very general nature. Indeed, most of the widespread parallels involve elements that would need to be present in any letter. There are also differences between New Testament letters and other ancient letters, probably the product of Jewish influence,[6] and especially the special situation and purpose of their writing. These differences are perhaps most numerous in the letters of Paul. According to David Aune, "Paul in particular was both a creative and eclectic letter writer."[7]

Classifications of ancient letters have their beginning in Adolf Deissmann's famous distinction between "epistles" (carefully composed, public pieces of literature) and "letters" (unstudied, private communications). Deissmann put all the letters of Paul into the latter category, arguing that they bore the same signs of hasty composition and lack of literary pretensions as are found in the Greek papyri letters.[8] Deissmann's distinction was an artificial one, and it is now generally agreed that one cannot erect such rigid distinctions between a private letter and a public one. Greco-Roman letters are scattered across a spectrum that ranges from careful rhetorical masterpieces designed for wide dissemination to short, simple "send money" notes. The New Testament letters as a whole fall somewhere in the middle of this range, with some tending more toward the more literary end (e.g., Romans and Hebrews) and others more toward the common end (e.g., Philemon and 3 John). Many scholars have attempted more exact classification, often working from categories established through a study of Greco-Roman letters generally.[9] Such studies, however, have so far not led to solid conclusions.[10] Still other scholars have proposed that various letters of Paul

---

[6]Ibid., 25.

[7]David E. Aune, *The New Testament in Its Literary Environment* (Philadelphia: Westminster, 1987), 203.

[8]Adolf Deissmann, "Prolegomena to the Biblical Letters and Epistles," in *Bible Studies* (Edinburgh: T. & T. Clark, 1901), 1–59.

[9]See, e.g., Stowers, *Letter Writing*, 51–173.

[10]For instance, after establishing his categories in the Greco-Roman letters, Stowers observes no New Testament letter that exactly conforms to any of the categories; he finds, rather, parallels within the NT letters to various categories. Aune recognizes the difficulty in classifying the NT letters (*Literary Environment*, 203). See also Jerome Murphy-O'Connor, *Paul the Letter-Writer: His World, His Options, His Skills* (Collegeville: Liturgical Press, 1995), 95–98; Jeffrey T. Reed, "Using Ancient Rhetorical Categories to

follow rhetorical patterns established by the famous rhetorical schools of the Greco-Roman world.[11] But while Paul was undoubtedly influenced by rhetorical concepts—which were widespread in the Greco-Roman environment—attempts to classify his letters by reference to strict rhetorical models are failures.[12] We should probably content ourselves with identifying some of the particular aspects of each individual New Testament letter and draw parallels at specific points with other Greco-Roman letters.

THE USE OF AMANUENSES

A crucial and debated question is the degree of freedom that a letter writer might give to his or her scribe (amanuensis) in the choice of wording.

The value of papyrus and the low level of literacy meant that many ancient letters were dictated to trained scribes. The use of such scribes (or amanuenses) by New Testament authors is clearly indicated in Romans 16:22, where Tertius identifies himself as the one who "wrote down" the letter. It was typical, when an amanuensis had composed the letter, for the writer to add a final greeting in his own hand (see 2 Thess. 3:17 and Gal. 6:11). While we have no way of knowing for sure, it seems likely that most of the New Testament letters, including, of course, those of Paul, were produced in this way.[13]

A crucial and debated question is the degree of freedom that a letter writer might give to his or her scribe in the choice of wording.[14] A reasonable conclu-

Interpret Paul's Letters: A Question of Genre," in *Rhetoric and the New Testament: Essays from the1992 Heidelberg Conference,* ed. Stanley Porter and Thomas H. Olbricht, JSNTSup 90 (Sheffield: JSOT Press, 1993), 292–324.

[11]See, in general, Frank W. Hughes, "The Rhetoric of Letters," in *The Thessalonians Debate: Methodological Discord or Methodological Synthesis?* ed. Karl P. Donfried and Johannes Beutler (Grand Rapids: Eerdmans, 2000), 194–240. Perhaps the most famous attempt is that of Hans Dieter Betz, who argued in his commentary on Galatians that this letter fit the "apologetic" letter genre (*Galatians: A Commentary on Paul's Letter to the Churches in Galatia,* Hermeneia [Philadelphia: Fortress Press, 1979], 14–25).

[12]Expressing skepticism about the influence of the rhetorical schools on Paul and his letters are esp. R. Dean Anderson Jr., *Ancient Rhetorical Theory and Paul* (The Hague: Kok Pharos, 1996); Martin Hengel and Anna Maria Schwemer, *Paul between Damascus and Antioch: The Unknown Years* (Louisville: Westminster John Knox, 1997) 169–71; Jeffrey A. D. Weima, "The Function of 1 Thessalonians 2:1–12 and the Use of Rhetorical Criticism: A Response to Otto Merk," in *The Thessalonians Debate: Methodological Discord or Methodological Synthesis?* ed. Karl P. Donfried and Johannes Beutler (Grand Rapids: Eerdmans, 2000), 124–30; and, with respect to Galatians particularly, Phillip H. Kern, *Rhetoric and Galatians: Assessing an Approach to the Epistle,* SNTSMS 101 (Cambridge: Cambridge University Press, 1999).

[13]See esp. E. Randolph Richards, *The Secretary in the Letters of Paul,* WUNT 42 (Tübingen: Mohr-Siebeck, 1991); cf. also John White, *ANRW* 2.52.2, 1741.

[14]Otto Roller argued that amanuenses were almost always given a great deal of freedom (*Das Formular der paulinischer Briefe: Ein Beitrag zur Lehre vom antiken Briefe*

sion is that the freedom given to an amanuensis would have differed depending on the skill of the amanuensis and the nature of the relationship between the writer and the amanuensis.[15] It may be, for instance, that when Paul used a close and trusted companion for his amanuensis, he gave that person some degree of freedom to choose the exact wording of the letter—always, we can assume, checking the letter over and attesting to its accurate representation of his thoughts with his closing greeting. Many scholars think that the influence of various amanuenses may explain the differences in Greek style among the Pauline letters, rendering it difficult, if not impossible, to draw conclusions about authorship based on such criteria.[16]

THE COLLECTION OF PAUL'S LETTERS

Paul wrote his letters over a period of at least fifteen years, and to churches and individuals separated by thousands of miles. How and when were they gathered together into a single corpus, and what are the implications of that process for the canonical shape of the letters? Two basic theories about this process may be identified.

Theories of a Sudden Collection

Many scholars think that Paul's letters were neglected after they had been sent to their addressees and that it was only at some later time that someone took the initiative to gather them together. Since the first clear references to an actual corpus of the letters of Paul comes from Marcion, some suggest that he may have had something to do with the process. Marcion had a Pauline corpus of ten letters (he did not include the Pastorals). Later "orthodox" collection of the letters (e.g., the Muratorian Canon, at the end of the second century[17]) may have been a reaction to Marcion.

Another popular theory puts the time of the first collection about fifty years earlier. Goodspeed, followed by John Knox and C. L. Mitton, argues that Paul's letters were neglected by the church after they were written and that the publication of Acts (which he dates c. A.D. 90) led a devoted follower of Paul to initiate a collection. According to Goodspeed, this follower was none other than

---

[Stuttgart: Kohlhammer, 1933]), esp. 333); but his conclusions have been seriously questioned (e.g., Kümmel, 251).

[15]See again, especially, Richards, *The Secretary in the Letters of Paul;* and also Richard N. Longenecker, "On the Form, Function, and Authority of the New Testament Letters," in *Scripture and Truth*, ed. D. A. Carson and John D. Woodbridge (Grand Rapids: Zondervan, 1983), 101–14.

[16]E.g., Murphy-O'Connor, *Paul the Letter-Writer*, 34–35.

[17]On the date of the canon, see chap. 4, n. 7.

Onesimus (the runaway slave of Philemon), who wrote Ephesians as a covering letter for the collected corpus.[18]

Goodspeed's theory is open to objection at a number of points. Ephesians was probably written by Paul (see chap. 13 below); Acts was probably published much earlier than A.D. 90; and, most seriously, there is good reason to think that Paul's letters circulated among the churches long before the end of the century. Paul himself encouraged some of his letters to be read in other churches (see Col. 4:16), and it is certainly likely, granted the mobility of the early Christians, that exchanges of letters began at a fairly early date.[19] Another indication in the same direction is 2 Peter 3:16, which, while not necessarily speaking of a completed corpus of the letters of Paul, does refer to a number of Pauline letters. Despite the weight of scholarly opinion that dates 2 Peter in the beginning of the second century, there is good reason to date it as early as 64 or 65 (see chap. 22 below). It is possible, then, that another figure, earlier in the course of the church's history, was responsible for the collection. Guthrie, for instance, suggests that it may have been Timothy.[20]

Theories of a Gradual Growth

Any identification of an individual as responsible for the collection of Paul's letters remains completely speculative; it may be, rather, that no one person had a large role in the process. In fact, if Paul's letters began circulating shortly after they were written, it is perhaps more likely that the process was a gradual one. We simply do not have enough information to know. How soon this collection was complete is also impossible to know. Some scholars think that *1 Clement* (c. A.D. 96) assumes a completed collection; others just as emphatically think it does not. But Zahn has made a solid case for dating the collection sometime between the death of Paul and the end of the first century.[21] Whatever the date, the process we envisage here leaves little room for the extensive editorial work that some think went on as the Pauline letters were gathered. Instead of an editor or editors piecing letters of Paul together and generally rearranging the corpus, we should think rather of a simple process of collection and, eventually, copying.

---

[18]Goodspeed, 210–21; C. Leslie Mitton, *The Formation of the Pauline Corpus of Letters* (London: Epworth, 1955); John Knox, *Philemon Among the Letters of Paul* (London: Collins, 1960), 63–93.

[19]F. F. Bruce, "Paul the Apostle," in *ISBE* 3.706.

[20]Guthrie, 998–1000. C. F. D. Moule hypothesizes that Luke could have collected the letters of Paul and written the Pastoral Epistles to augment the collection (264–65).

[21]Theodor Zahn, *Geschichte des neutestamentlichen Kanons* (Erlangen: A. Deichert, 1888–92), 2.811–39.

PSEUDONYMITY AND PSEUDEPIGRAPHY[22]

Pseudonymity and pseudepigraphy denote the practice of ascribing written works to someone other than the author—that is, the works in question are falsely (*pseud-*) named (*onoma*, "name," hence "pseudonymity") or attributed (*epigraphos*, "superscription," hence "pseudepigraphy"). This must not be confused with anonymity, in which no formal claim is made (e.g., Matthew, John, and Hebrews are all formally anonymous). Similarly, one must distinguish between pseudepigraphical and apocryphal works. The word *apocrypha* is tied rather more to notions of canon than to notions of authenticity: certain wings of Christendom have argued that a collection of "apocryphal" works should be included in the canon. The matter of false attribution played little or no part in the identification of the fourteen or fifteen books or parts of books that constitute the Apocrypha (most of which Roman Catholics view as "deuterocanonical"). A book is either canonical or apocryphal (or deuterocanonical), regardless of whether or not it is pseudepigraphical.

Although "pseudonymity" and "pseudepigraphy" are today used almost synonymously, only the latter term has been traced back to antiquity (as early as an inscription from the second century B.C. found at Priene). Quite apart from the intrinsic interest of the subject—by what criteria do scholars decide that a document makes false claims regarding its authorship?—its bearing on New Testament interpretation arises from the fact that a majority of contemporary scholars hold that some of the New Testament books are pseudonymous. The list of ostensibly pseudonymous books varies considerably, but a broad consensus would label Ephesians and the Pastoral Epistles (attributed to Paul) pseudepigraphical, as well as 2 Peter (attributed to Peter). Some would add other books: Colossians, 2 Thessalonians, 1 Peter.

Extrabiblical Evidence

Preliminary Observations. Given the broadest definition, pseudonymity is a more extensive phenomenon than some have thought. It embraces every false claim of authorship, whether for good motive or ill, and whether advanced by the real author or by some later historical accident. It includes every instance of an author adopting, for whatever reason, a *nom de plume*—e.g., Mary Ann Evans writing under the name of George Eliot, or the three Brontë sisters (Charlotte, Emily, and Anne) publishing their poems under the title *Poems by Currer, Ellis, and Acton Bell*, or the English scholar Gervase Fen writing detective fiction under the name of Edmund Crispin. According to Galen (a learned physician from the second century A.D.), literary forgeries first circulated in large

---

[22]This section is an adaptation and expansion of an article originally prepared for *The Dictionary of New Testament Background*, ed. Craig A. Evans and Stanley E. Porter (Downers Grove: IVP, 2000), 856–64.

numbers when Alexandria and Pergamum began a race to outdo each other by increasing the number of volumes in their respective libraries: the Ptolemies of Egypt and King Eumenes of Pergamum offered large sums to acquire copies of the works of ancient authors. Among other things, Galen feels outraged and betrayed by the interpolations and corruptions introduced into the medical works he and Hippocrates had written.[23]

At this juncture it is vital to distinguish between pseudepigraphical works and literary forgeries.[24] A literary forgery is a work written or modified with the intent to deceive. All literary forgeries are pseudepigraphical, but not all pseudepigrapha are literary forgeries: there is a substantial class of writings which, in the course of their transmission, became associated with some figure or other— judgments made with the best will in the world, however fallacious. We do not know how the commentaries of Pelagius on Paul came to be associated with the name of Jerome (who violently opposed Pelagius), but that is what happened. Most hold that Lobon of Argos wrote the *Hymn to Poseidon* in the third century B.C., even though the hymn is widely attributed to Arion; but it is doubtful that Lobon himself had anything to do with the attribution. The reason this distinction is important is that debates over the authenticity of New Testament books are tied up with the motives of actual authors, since the texts are so early and so stable that the putative author's name is there from the beginning. For our purposes, it is sufficient to focus only on cases where demonstrable intent is involved and thus to exclude all pseudepigrapha that have become such owing to nothing more than the irretrievable accidents of history.

The motives of pseudepigraphers, ancient and modern, have been highly diverse and include the following:

(a) Sometimes literary forgeries have been crafted out of pure malice. According to Pausanius[25] and Josephus,[26] in the fourth century B.C. Anaximenes of Lampsacus destroyed the reputation of a contemporary historian, Theopompus of Chios, by writing, under the name of his rival, horrible invectives against three Greek cities (Athens, Sparta, and Thebes) and circulating them. Eusebius reports that in the fourth century A.D. the *Acts of Pilate* began to circulate (possibly written by the apostate Theotecnus), full of bitter slanders against the moral character of Jesus.[27] In modern times, czarist Russia produced the "Protocols of the Learned Elders of Zion."

(b) More commonly, as we have already seen, literary forgeries were prompted by promise of financial payment.

---

[23]In *Hipp. de nat. hominis* 1.42.

[24]See Bruce M. Metzger, "Literary Forgeries and Canonical Pseudepigrapha," *JBL* 91 (1972): 4.

[25]*History of Greece* 6.18.2ff.

[26]*Contra. Ap.* 1.24 (§221).

[27]*H.E.* 9.5.1.

(c) Sometimes the pseudepigrapher used an ancient name to gain credence for his writing *in order to support a position he knew to be false.* According to Strabo[28] in the sixth century B.C., either Solon or Pisistratus inserted a verse in Homer's *Iliad*[29] to support the Athenian claim to the island of Salamis. Herodotus says that Onomacritus was banished from Athens when it was shown he had interpolated a passage into the Oracles of Musaeus predicting that the islands off Lemnos would sink into the sea.[30] This third motive has some overtones of the first.

(d) Similarly, the pseudepigrapher sometimes used an ancient name to gain credence for his writing *in order to support a position he judged to be true.* This was especially the case in ancient "schools" in which the founder was highly venerated. Very few of the neo-Pythagoreans published their works under their own names. They attributed them to Pythagoras himself, even though he had been dead for centuries.[31] In the sixth century A.D. several works appeared claiming to be written by Dionysius the Areopagite (cf. Acts 17:34), though drawing on much later neoplatonic argumentation.

(e) A more idiosyncratic case of the same thing has occasionally occurred when an individual has ostensibly hidden his or her own name out of modesty, using the name of another. Perhaps the most famous instance is that of an encyclical that began to circulate about A.D. 440, ostensibly written by someone who identified himself as "Timothy, least of the servants of God." Bishop Salonius guessed the author was Salvian, a priest in Marseilles. Without admitting anything, Salvian responded to the bishop's sharp queries by saying that he thought that authors, out of humility and modesty, might be justified in using the name of another, so as not to seek glory for themselves.[32] One may perhaps be excused for thinking this is a trifle disingenuous. It is a strange modesty that thinks one's own writings are so good that they could and should be attributed to an ancient biblical hero. One easily imagines that this motive runs into another:

(f) A deep desire to get published and be widely read, for both personal and ideological reasons, doubtless characterizes more authors than the Brontë sisters, and may be the motive behind the motive of Salvian.

(g) More difficult to assign are the substantial numbers of pseudepigraphical writings that belong to specific genres. Doubtless more than one of the preceding motives were involved. But it is difficult to overlook what might almost be called a genre incentive. In the post-Aristotle period, the rise of the great Attic

---

[28]*Geog.* 9.1.10.

[29]Book B, line 258.

[30]*Hist.* 7.6.

[31]So Iamblichus, c. A.D. 250–325: *De vita Pythagorica* §198, following the 1937 Teubner edition by Ludwig Deubner.

[32]See Alfred E. Haefner, "A Unique Source for the Study of Ancient Pseudonymity," *ATR* 16 (1934): 8–15.

orators generated high interest in rhetoric and oratory. Students were taught to compose speeches based on models left by the ancient orators. The most skillful of these were doubtless difficult to distinguish from the originals. This drifted over into the reconstruction, by historians, of speeches that their subjects probably *would* have made (in the view of the historians). Some historians, of course, were more reflective about such practices than others.[33] Alexander has shown that from Isocrates on, one can distinguish between a more "scientific" historiography and a looser, more creative form—and Luke, at least (she insists), fits into the former category.[34] Furthermore, if complex motives were involved in the creation of pseudonymous speeches, the same can be said of letters. At least in the classical period, great leaders and thinkers were credited with important and voluminous correspondence. One hundred forty-eight letters are attributed to the sixth century B.C. tyrant Phalaris of Acragas (= Agrigentum), portraying him as a gentle and kind man and as a patron of the arts—though since the end of the seventeenth century scholars have known that these letters were almost certainly composed in the second century A.D., probably by a sophist.[35] The phenomenon is less common in Hellenistic times, but see below.

(h) Finally, there are several bodies of writings that are ascribed to some philosophical-religious-mythical figure, especially Orpheus, the Sibyl, and Hermes Trismegistus.[36]

Jewish Examples. Jewish literature evinces a fairly high occurrence of pseudepigraphical literature from about the middle of the third century B.C. to the third century A.D., much of it belonging to the genre of apocalyptic (broadly defined). One thinks of the *Psalms of Solomon, 1 Enoch, 2 Enoch, 3 Enoch*, the works of the Ezra cycle (e.g., *4 Ezra*), the *Treatise of Shem*, the *Apocalypse of Zephaniah*, the *Apocalypse of Abraham*, the *Apocalypse of Adam*, and many more. We may include here the various Testaments, most of which have apocalyptic sections (e.g., *Testaments of the Twelve Patriarchs, Testament of Job, Testament of Moses, Testament of Solomon*). Yet other genres are not unrepresented

---

[33]Cf. Thucydides, *Hist.* 1.22.

[34]Loveday Alexander, *The Preface to Luke's Gospel: Literary Convention and Social Context in Luke 1.1–4 and Acts 1.1*, SNTSMS 78 (Cambridge: Cambridge University Press, 1993).

[35]See the work of Richard Bentley, *Dissertations upon the Epistles of Phalaris . . .*, ed. with Introduction and Notes by Wilhelm Wagner (Berlin: S. Calvary, 1874 [first published 1697–99]).

[36]See especially Joseph A. Sint, *Pseudonymität im Altertum, ihre Formen und ihre Gründe* (Innsbruck: Universitätsverlag, 1960); W. Speyer, *Die literarische Fälschung im heidnischen und christlichen Altertum: Ein Versuch ihrer Deutung* (München: Beck, 1971); and some essays in Norbert Brox, ed., *Pseudepigraphie in der heidnischen und jüdisch-christlichen Antike*, WdF 484 (Darmstadt: Wissenschaftliche Buchgesellschaft, 1977).

(e.g., *Wisdom of Solomon*). Some works are of such mixed genre they are variously classified. The *Sibylline Oracles*, for example, appears to be made up of a strange mix of pagan oracles from various countries, Jewish writings from a wide spread of dates, and Christian moralizing interpolations—yet all the while the document maintains the claim that this conglomeration is the utterance of the Sibyl, an ancient prophetess, sometimes represented as the daughter-in-law of Noah. This arrangement, it must be said, is transparently designed to gain credence for the oracles as genuine prophecies.

The wide variety of "expansions" of Old Testament narratives are not normally pseudepigraphical, but some of the expansions that are also prayers must be placed in that category: e.g., *Prayer of Manasseh, Prayer of Joseph, Odes of Solomon*. Occasionally a later nonbiblical literary figure finds his name forged; today's scholars read not only Philo but Pseudo-Philo (first century A.D., like the real Philo).

Examples of pseudepigraphical letters from this milieu are harder to come by. The two cited by everyone are *Letter of Aristeas* and *Epistle of Jeremy*, neither of which is really a letter. The latter is a little sermon, and the former an account of the translation of the Old Testament into Greek. There is no epistle among the canonical writings of the Old Testament, so there was no authoritative precedent to follow. A false claim to writing a letter would probably be easier to detect than, say, a false claim to writing an apocalypse. Whatever the reason, pseudepigraphic letters among the Jews are extremely rare.

Extrabiblical Christian Examples. About the middle of the second century A.D., pseudonymous Christian works began to multiply, often associated with a great Christian leader. We are not here concerned with works that purport to tell us about esteemed Christian figures without making claims as to authorship, but only with those that are clearly pseudepigraphical. Some of these are apocalypses (e.g., the *Apocalypse of Peter*, the *Apocalypse of Paul*); some are gospels (e.g., *Gospel of Peter, Gospel of Thomas*, which is really no gospel at all, but mostly a collection of sayings attributed to Jesus). Several are letters claiming to be written by Paul: *3 Corinthians, Epistle to the Alexandrians, Epistle to the Laodiceans*. The latter was almost certainly written to provide the document mentioned in Colossians 4:16. It is a brief and rough compilation of Pauline phrases and passages (primarily from Philippians). The largest collection of pseudonymous epistles from the early period of the church's history is the set of fourteen letters of correspondence between the apostle Paul and Seneca. They are referred to by both Jerome (*De vir. ill.* 12) and Augustine (*Epist.* 153). The Muratorian Canon (c. A.D. 170–200) refers to the *Epistle to the Alexandrians* and the *Epistle to the Laodiceans* as "both forged in Paul's name" (*Mur. Can.* 64–65) and thus will not allow them to be included. This last observation leads to the next heading.

The Stance of the Church Fathers

All sides agree, then, that pseudepigraphy was common in the ancient world. Nevertheless, in Jewish and Christian circles it was not so common in epistles—and it is in the epistolary genre that the subject impinges on the New Testament documents. Does pseudonymity occur in the New Testament?

From a mere listing of pseudepigraphical sources, one might unthinkingly infer we should expect pseudonymous letters in the New Testament, since no one cared. But that is simply not the case, according to Donelson: "Both Greeks and Romans show great concern to maintain the authenticity of their collections of writings from the past, but the sheer number of the pseudepigrapha made the task difficult."[37] Similarly Duff: "It simply cannot be maintained that in the pagan culture surrounding the early Christians there was no sense of literary propriety, or no concern over authenticity."[38] Referring both to Christian and non-Christian sources, Donelson goes so far as to say, "No one ever seems to have accepted a document as religiously and philosophically prescriptive which was known to be forged. I do not know a single example."[39]

This is virulently the case in early Christian circles. We have already observed the stance of the Muratorian Canon and of Bishop Salonius. When Asian elders examined the author of an "Acts of Paul," which included the pseudonymous *3 Corinthians*, they condemned him for presuming to write in Paul's name—even though *3 Corinthians* had been highly esteemed in parts of the church and for a time was included in the canon of the Syrian and Armenian churches, apparently under the impression that Paul had written it. Nevertheless, its edifying content did not save it once its pseudonymous character was recognized. When, in about A.D. 200, Serapion, Bishop of Antioch, first read *Gospel of Peter,* he thought it might be genuine. When further investigation led him to conclude it was not, he rejected it, and provided a rationale for the church of Rhossus in Cilicia: "For we, brothers, receive both Peter and the other apostles as Christ. But pseudepigrapha in their name we reject, as men of experience, knowing that we did not receive such [from the tradition]."[40] Tertullian is blistering against the Asian elder who confesses that he wrote *Acts of Paul and Thecla*. All the elder's protestations that he had done so out of great love for the apostle did not prevent him from being

> It is in the epistolary genre that the subject of pseudepigraphy impinges on the New Testament documents. Does pseudonymity occur in the New Testament?

---

[37]Lewis R. Donelson, *Pseudepigraphy and Ethical Argument in the Pastoral Epistles,* HUT 22 (Tübingen: Mohr-Siebeck, 1986), 11.

[38]J. Duff, "A Critical Examination of Pseudepigraphy in First- and Second-Century Christianity and the Approaches to It of Twentieth-Century Scholars" (D.Phil. dissertation; University of Oxford, 1998).

[39]*Pseudepigraphy and Ethical Argument,* 11. Similarly, Philip Carrington, *The Early Christian Church* (Cambridge: Cambridge University Press, 1957), 1.259: "There seems to be no evidence at all that such missives [viz. letters] were freely composed in the names of contemporary persons who had recently died."

[40]Eusebius, *H.E.* 6.12.3; cf. 2.25.4–7—widely cited in the literature.

deposed from the ministry.[41] Similarly, when Cyril of Jerusalem provides a list of canonical books, he allows only four gospels, for the rest are "falsely written and hurtful" (*pseudepigrapha kai blabera*).[42]

We know of no exception to the evidence, which is far more extensive than this brief summary suggests. Ostensible exceptions turn out, under close inspection, to be unconvincing. For instance, Kiley rightly observes that the Muratorian Canon attaches to its list of New Testament books the *Wisdom of Solomon*, observing that it was written by the "friends of Solomon in his honor"—which surely, he suggests, demonstrates that "at least portions of the early church were able to detect the pseudepigraphical process."[43] But where it is clear that a "pseudepigraphical process" is observed by the Fathers, they universally condemn it. In this case, as Kiley himself observes in an extended footnote, the reference in the Muratorian Canon may not be to our *Wisdom of Solomon*, but to the book of Proverbs, which was at that time sometimes referred to as "the Wisdom of Solomon." But in that case pseudonymity is not an issue, since the book itself frankly distinguishes various collections of proverbs by different authors. Similarly, some have argued that Tertullian's words admit the legitimacy of at least some kinds of pseudonymity: "It is allowable that that which pupils publish should be regarded as their master's work."[44] But Guthrie has rightly shown that this is to misunderstand Tertullian. Tertullian is discussing how Peter stands behind Mark's gospel and how Paul informs Luke's writing. He does not suggest that the church received the second gospel as if it had been written by Peter when in fact it was written by Mark.[45]

The view that the New Testament includes some pseudepigrapha was not mooted until two centuries ago,[46] and became popular with the work of F. C. Baur. But so far as the evidence of the Fathers goes, when they explicitly evaluated a work for its authenticity, canonicity and pseudonymity proved mutually exclusive. Those who maintain that one or several of the New Testament epistles are pseudonymous should take a closer look at the evidence than they usually do. We do not say that it was impossible for New Testament Christians to use the pseudepigraphic method. We can easily imagine an early Christian feeling so sure he knew what Paul or Peter would have said in a given situation that he would write some piece, claiming the apostle's name for what he had himself composed. We should surely sympathize with the second-century presbyter who composed a "Pauline" writing "from love of Paul" and find little difficulty

---

[41]*De baptismo* 17.

[42]*Catech.* 4.36.

[43]Mark Kiley, *Colossians as Pseudepigraphy* (Sheffield: JSOT Press, 1986), 17–18.

[44]*Adv. Marc.* 4.5.

[45]Donald Guthrie, "Tertullian and Pseudonymity," *ExpTim* 67 (1955–56): 341–42.

[46]By E. Evanson, *The Dissonance of the Four Generally Received Evangelists* (Ipswich: G. Jermyn, 1792).

in imagining an earlier example of the same kind of thinking. The difficulty is not the idea of pseudonymity but the lack of *evidence* that the New Testament Christians gave any countenance to the idea.

Evidence Internal to New Testament Documents

All sides acknowledge that, however it is taken, the extrabiblical examples of pseudonymity cannot establish the ostensible pseudonymity of any New Testament document. Such material provides no more than a social world of plausibility (or implausibility!) for the acceptance of pseudepigrapha into the New Testament. Yet despite the consistent evidence from the early church outside the New Testament, many scholars assert, in the most confident terms, that writing letters in the name of another was common practice. Nowhere is evidence cited that any member of the New Testament church accepted the idea that a pious believer could write something in the name of an apostle and expect the writing to be welcomed. For example, in his standard textbook, P. N. Harrison says that the pseudo-Paul who wrote the Pastorals "was not conscious of misrepresenting the Apostle in any way; he was not consciously deceiving anybody; it is not, indeed, necessary to suppose that he did deceive anybody. It seems far more probable that those to whom, in the first instance, he showed the result of his efforts, must have been perfectly well aware of what he had done."[47] But Harrison produces no evidence for this alleged practice; he simply says that it was so. This is scarcely good enough. The onus is on those who uphold the idea that the writing of pseudonymous letters was an accepted practice among the early Christians to produce some evidence for their view. On the contrary, the evidence we have is that every time such a writing could be identified with any certainty, it was rejected.

Inevitably, this means that many scholars seek to establish the pseudepigraphical character of a particular document on purely *internal* grounds: anachronisms; a high percentage of words or phrases not found in the known writings of the author; a high number of words and phrases found in the ostensible author's agreed writings but now used in quite different ways; forms of thought and emphasis that seem at odds with the dominant strains of the agreed writings; and more of the same.

Although some scholars view such evidence as having no more weight than that which affects the balance of probabilities, many judge it to be so strong that there is no doubt in their minds that some New Testament books are pseudepigraphical.[48] In some cases, those who disagree with them are dismissed as

---

[47]P. N. Harrison, *The Problem of the Pastoral Epistles* (London: Oxford University Press, 1921), 12. For further examples, see below.

[48]E.g., Donelson, *Pseudepigraphy and Ethical Argument;* Metzger, "Literary Forgeries"; W. Speyer, *Die literarische Fälschung;* James H. Charlesworth, "Pseudonymity

beyond the pale—unworthy and perhaps incompetent opponents. But in fact, the issues are complex and interlocking. One might usefully gain insight into the nature of the debate at its best by reading the respective commentaries on Ephesians by Lincoln and O'Brien[49]—not only their introductions, but their exegeses wherever understanding of the text is affected by, or affects, the questions of authorship; or, with respect to the Pastoral Epistles, by reading the exchange between Porter and Wall;[50] or standard "Introductions."[51] The entire complex apparatus of technical scholarship and historical criticism, not to say theology and worldview, impinge on an interlocking web of judgments that bear on the question of whether or not there are pseudepigrapha among the New Testament documents. Scholars who answer "Yes" are inclined to argue that Ephesians, for example, has far too much realized eschatology for it to be Pauline; scholars who answer "No" highlight all the passages that retain futurist eschatology and argue that whatever differences remain are nothing more than different locations on the Pauline spectrum, variously applied by the apostle himself in different ways to meet certain pastoral needs. Scholars who answer "Yes" carefully list all the *hapax legomena* in Ephesians; scholars who answer "No" point out that Ephesians has no more *hapax legomena* than some undisputed Pauline letters. Such matters cannot be addressed here (many of them are briefly treated elsewhere in this volume), yet it is important to see that they impinge on our topic and that the evidence is "spun" by scholars in different ways and given very different weight.

There are three other bits of internal evidence that bear on the discussion: (1) The author of 2 Thessalonians is aware of forgeries made in his own name. He therefore warns his readers "not to become easily unsettled or alarmed by the teaching allegedly from us—whether by prophecy or by word of mouth or by letter" (2 Thess. 2:1–2)—and provides them with some signature or token to enable them to distinguish which letters purporting to come from him were authentic and which were not (3:17). If the author was not Paul (as many scholars think), then our pseudonymous author is in the odd position of condemning

---

and Pseudepigraphy," *ABD* 5.540–41; David G. Meade, *Pseudonymity and Canon: An Investigation into the Relationship of Authorship and Authority in Jewish and Early Christian Tradition*, WUNT 39 (Tübingen: Mohr-Siebeck, 1986).

[49]Andrew T. Lincoln, *Ephesians*, WBC 42 (Dallas: Word Books, 1990); Peter T. O'Brien, *The Letter to the Ephesians*, PNTC (Grand Rapids: Eerdmans, 1999).

[50]Stanley E. Porter, "Pauline Authorship and the Pastoral Epistles: Implications for Canon," *BBR* 5 (1995): 105–123; R. W. Wall, "Pauline Authorship and the Pastoral Epistles: A Response to S. E. Porter," *BBR* 5 (1995): 125–28; Stanley E. Porter, "Pauline Authorship and the Pastoral Epistles: A Response to R. W. Wall's Response," *BBR* 6 (1996): 133–38.

[51]E.g., Kümmel; Guthrie (see esp. the latter's "Appendix C: Epistolary Pseudepigraphy," 1011–28).

pseudonymous authors—a literary forgery that damns literary forgeries. If, on the other hand, the author was Paul, then the apostle himself makes it clear that he is aware of pseudonymity and condemns the practice (at least when people are using *his* name). (2) It is clear that Paul and perhaps other New Testament writers used amanuenses (e.g., Rom 16:22). There is a long and complex literature about how much freedom amanuenses enjoyed in the ancient world—much as one might, on the one hand, give one's secretary detailed dictation, or, on the other, simply ask him or her to write a letter along such and such a line, which becomes the "author's" once he or she has read it and signed it. These questions have a bearing on many critical debates and cannot be overlooked in discussions of authenticity. (3) The early Christians appear to have had no great urge to attach apostolic names to the writings they valued. More than half of the New Testament consists of books that do not bear the names of their authors (the four gospels, Acts, Hebrews, 1 John; even "the elder" of 2 and 3 John is not very explicit). Apparently, the truth in the documents and the evidence that the Holy Spirit was at work in the people who wrote them carried conviction, and the attachment of apostolic names *as the author* was not judged necessary—though some looser connection to an apostle obviously helped, such as Peter standing behind Mark's gospel (see chap. 4 above).[52] The onus is on upholders of theories of pseudonymous authorship to explain why this strong tradition of anonymity was discarded in favor, not of authors attaching their own names to what they wrote (as Paul did), but of other people's names.

> *The attachment of apostolic names as the author was not judged necessary—though some looser connection to an apostle obviously helped, such as Peter standing behind Mark's gospel.*

Some Contemporary Theories

1. Some are convinced that the New Testament contains many examples of literary forgeries and are unembarrassed by this conclusion. On this view, the pseudonymous author of 2 Peter (for instance) was clearly trying to deceive his readers into thinking that the apostle wrote the missive: he was a hypocrite.[53] Similarly Donelson on the Pastorals: the pseudonymous author, in "the interest of deception . . . fabricated all the personal notes, all the fine moments of deep piety, and all the careless but effective commonplaces in the letter. . . . [He] is quite self-consciously employing pseudonymity in order to deceive."[54] Meeks on Colossians is similar.[55]

---

[52]We must also recall that one of the reasons why Hebrews was eventually accepted into the canon in the West was that it *wrongly* came to be judged written by Paul (see chap. 19). Nevertheless, this was a later development; the person who penned Hebrews did not attempt the connection. Early Christians were more comfortable with anonymity than with pseudonymity.

[53]So Charlesworth, "Pseudonymity."

[54]*Pseudepigraphy and Ethical Argument*, 24.

[55]Wayne A. Meeks, "'To Walk Worthily of the Lord': Moral Formation in the Pauline School Exemplified by the Letter to the Colossians," in *Hermes and Athena:*

2. On the other side are those who similarly point out how often deception plays a role in pseudepigraphy, but recall how the church universally rejected any hint of such deception.[56] This is not to deny the complexity of motives that stand behind the various forms of pseudepigraphy lightly sketched above. It is to say that the letters of the New Testament, where pseudonymity is alleged to have taken place, are not educational exercises designed to ape the rhetorical styles of Attic orators. Nor are they writings that simply belong to a certain "school" of thought with a great but deceased head (whether Paul or Peter). The New Testament documents make concrete *claims* that the apostle is the author. Rather, the nature of the ostensibly pseudonymous claim is such that we must conclude that if the documents are in fact pseudonymous, the writers *intended* to deceive in a way that is morally reprehensible—and given the nature of the documents, this is simply not credible. Thus, in Ephesians the author refers to his earlier ministry, written and oral (3:3–4), his chains, his arrangement of the ministry of other of Paul's men (e.g., Tychicus, 6:21–22). He actually exhorts his readers to pray for his needs (6:19–20), when, on the assumptions of pseudonymity, the apostle was already dead! Yet he also exhorts his readers to put off falsehood and to speak truthfully (4:25; cf. also 4:15, 24; 5:9; 6:14). Similar things can be said about all the ostensibly pseudepigraphical works in the New Testament. It seems better to take the documents at face value, respect the opinion and care of the church fathers in this respect, and read the historical critical evidence for pseudonymity with historical critical discernment.

3. In recent years several mediating positions have been advanced. Aland and others have argued that the Holy Spirit breached the gap from ostensible author to real author.[57] Provided the Spirit inspired the text, what difference does it make who the human author was? But this solution is very awkward. It ignores the widespread recognition within earliest Christianity that there was such a thing as false prophecy. Worse, it overlooks that these "inspired" prophets were making *historical* claims that were either true or not true.

Meade argues that the most believable background to New Testament pseudepigraphy is neither the body of Greco-Roman parallels, nor the corpus of Second Temple Jewish pseudepigraphy, but the process within Jewish writing whereby an original deposit (oral or written) has been enlarged upon, with all

---

Biblical Exegesis and Philosophical Theology, ed. Eleonore Stump and Thomas P. Flint, University of Notre Dame Studies in the Philosophy of Religion 7 (Notre Dame: University of Notre Dame Press, 1993), 37–58.

[56]E.g., E. Earle Ellis, "Pseudonymity and Canonicity of New Testament Documents," in *Worship, Theology, and Ministry in the Early Church*, ed. Michael J. Wilkins and Terence Paige (Sheffield: JSOT Press, 1992), 212–24.

[57]Kurt Aland, "The Problem of Anonymity and Pseudonymity in Christian Literature of the First Two Centuries," in *The Authorship and Integrity of the New Testament*, by Kurt Aland et al.; Theological Collections 4 (London: SPCK, 1965), 1–13.

the later material being attributed to the earliest author.[58] This pattern, he argues, began within the Old Testament itself: Isaiah, the Solomonic corpus, Daniel. But in every case the ostensible parallels break down. On Meade's assumptions, the prophecy of Isaiah of Jerusalem was enlarged by contributions made more than a century later by others who followed in his train. But Ephesians or 2 Thessalonians or the Pastorals are not additions to a book, additions that seek to make contemporary the prophetic word of someone long dead. They are independent documents, written (even under Meade's assumptions) within a decade or so of the apostle's death. Nor is there anything like the personal claims and historical reminiscences of Ephesians or the Pastorals in Isaiah 40ff. True, there is evidence of a trajectory of developments in Second Temple Judaism and in the patristic era—but it is one thing to say that Jews and early Christians wrote pseudonymous apocalypses and acts, and quite another to say that they wrote letters purporting to come from one person but actually written by someone else. For that we need evidence, and Meade supplies none. Meade's theory sounds like an attempt to make the results work out after one has already bought into the dominant historical-critical assumptions.[59]

Marshall offers a third mediating position. He acknowledges the problem of pseudonymity,[60] but he suggests that other refinements are possible. We are already familiar with the debates over the role of an amanuensis. Furthermore, it is permissible for someone to edit and prepare for posthumous publication the work of an author recently deceased. In our world, that fact would be noted in the publication; in the ancient world, perhaps the closest analogy is found in the prologue to Ecclesiasticus. Marshall extrapolates: "It is not too great a step to a situation in which somebody close to a dead person continued to write as (they thought that) he would have done. An incomplete work can be completed by somebody else, but again in a modern situation this would be made quite explicit. [In a footnote, Marshall here adds, "The example of students attributing their works to the philosopher who taught them may belong here."] There is a rather fluid boundary between this and the previous possibility, depending on how far

---

[58]Meade, *Pseudonymity and Canon.*

[59]Meade has many statements such as this: "Attribution in the pseudonymous Pauline and Petrine epistles must be regarded primarily as an assertion of authoritative tradition, not of literary origin" (ibid., 193). But that is to be proved; strong assertion without evidence is not enough. Perhaps we should notice that Meade speaks of *1 Enoch* 91–103 as "The Epistle of Enoch" (p. 96), but there is nothing in that document like the epistolary forms with which we are familiar in the New Testament. It begins with, "Now, my son Methuselah, (please) summon all your brothers" and when they come, continues with, "Then he (Enoch) spoke to all of them" (*1 Enoch* 91:1, 3). Pseudonymous epistles are not as widespread as Meade would have us think.

[60]I. Howard Marshall, *A Critical and Exegetical Commentary on the Pastoral Epistles,* ICC (Edinburgh, T. & T. Clark, 1999), 79–83.

the actual words of the deceased are utilised."[61] But this suggestion appears to be the old argument for pseudonymity without the courage to call it that. We have already seen that the example of followers in the Pythagorean "school" constitutes no valid parallel. If all that Marshall is saying were that one of Paul's followers put finishing touches on a virtually completed manuscript very shortly after his death, that, doubtless, would be one thing; indeed, Marshall is close to suggesting that something like that took place in the preparation of 2 Timothy. But 1 Timothy and Titus, Marshall argues, though doubtless drawing from Paul's instruction and perhaps even some notes, were fresh compositions. If the theory is right, all it means is that at least 1 Timothy and Titus are properly pseudonymous, even if prepared in the name of Paul with the highest of motives, and the only reason they managed to be included in the canon is that the early church was snookered and failed to recognize their pseudonymity. This does not seem to be a very plausible reconstruction. Moreover, we are still left with the personal references to the apostle in place, making it extremely difficult to avoid all charges of deceit on the part of the ostensible pseudonymous writer.

The problem becomes all the more acute when we recall that all the Pastorals contain a warning about deceivers (1 Tim. 4:1; 2 Tim. 3:13; Titus 1:10); and in one passage the writer says that while in the past he had been a deceiver, that has all been changed now that he has been saved (Titus 3:3). Would a person who speaks of deceit like this put the name of Paul to a letter he himself had composed?[62] Would he say so firmly, "I am telling the truth, I am not lying" (1 Tim. 2:7)?[63]

The mediating position that is perhaps most widely followed today is some form of "school" theory.[64] Those who espouse it concur with the majority

---

[61]Ibid., 84, and also n. 106. Marshall rightly points out that others have offered variations of this theory before him, e.g., Harrison, *The Problem of the Pastoral Epistle*, 12.

[62]As Johnson points out, "The first generations of Christians . . . were very much concerned with the sources of spiritual teaching and with distinguishing between true and false teachers; they did not live in a charismatic fog (see only 1 Cor. 7:10–12; 14:29; 2 Cor. 11:13–15; 2 Thess. 2:2)" (p. 393). He agrees that pseudonymity was practiced in antiquity, but these words should give us pause when we are considering the practices of the early Christians.

[63]Even Meade agrees that this last passage "illustrates the difficulty of affirming the truth of Paul's authority and teaching by using a technique that involves deception" (*Pseudonymity and Canon*, 121). If the technique involves deception, what becomes of the assertion that pseudonymity was a transparent device in which readers recognized what was being done?

[64]E.g., James D. G. Dunn, "Pseudonymity," *DLNT*, 977–84; Denis Farkasfalvy, "The Ecclesial Setting of Pseudepigraphy in Second Peter and its Role in the Formation of the Canon," *The Second Century* 5 (1986): 3–29 (with an important response by William R. Farmer, 30–46); Richard Bauckham, *Jude, 2 Peter,* WBC (Waco: Word, 1986).

opinion that certain New Testament documents are pseudonymous, but they argue that no deception was involved because *within the "school"* of those churches or writers, everyone who needed to know understood that the writing was not really from the ostensible author. There was a kind of "living tradition" that allowed for its expansion in this way, and its adherents understood the process.

> *The mediating position on pseudepigraphy that is perhaps most widely followed today is some form of "school" theory, but it presents more problems than it resolves.*

If this position were genuinely sustainable, it would have its attractions. In reality, it presents more problems than it resolves. The "school" terminology suitable to the neo-Pythagoreans does not transfer very well to the church: the former constituted a closed, disciplined society. Moreover, even if the neo-Pythagoreans understood that some new publication was not penned by Pythagoras, doubtless some outsiders were duped. If the "school" mode of transmission was so ubiquitous and easily understood, why did none of the church fathers who addressed questions of authenticity view it as an appropriate model for their grasp of the New Testament documents? Moreover, the new treatises published by the neo-Pythagoreans did not include the kind of personal claims and allusions happily thrown in by the New Testament writers. Their "new truths" were tied up with new insights into numbers, not comments on Pythagoras's prison conditions or solicitations that the readers pray for him. One must not fly in the face of the evidence. Dunn, for instance, writes, "It is hard to believe that such a convention was not recognized, at least by most thoughtful readers, in the case of the Enoch corpus, the *Testaments of the Twelve Patriarchs* or the *Apocalypse of Adam,* all written probably between second century B.C. and second century A.D."[65] But the fact is that when "the most thoughtful readers" actually discuss the authenticity of various documents, where they become convinced that a document is pseudonymous it is invariably judged ineligible for inclusion in the canon.

In short, the search for parallels to justify the view that the intended readers of some New Testament documents would have understood them to be pseudonymous, so that no deception took place, has proved a failure. The hard evidence demands that we conclude either that some New Testament documents are pseudonymous and that the real authors intended to deceive their readers,[66] or that the real authors intended to speak the truth and that pseudonymity is not attested in the New Testament.[67]

---

[65]Dunn, "Pseudonymity," 978.

[66]On this point, see esp. Ellis, 17–29.

[67]"As with Colossians and Ephesians, there are only two real conclusions regarding authorship of the Pastoral Epistles: pseudonymous or authentic Pauline authorship" (McDonald/Porter, 497)

BIBLIOGRAPHY

K. **Aland**, "The Problem of Anonymity and Pseudonymity in Christian Literature of the First Two Centuries," *JTS* 12 (1961): 39–49, repr. in *The Authorship and Integrity of the New Testament*, by Kurt Aland et al., *Theological Collections* 4 (London: SPCK, 1965), 1–13 ▮▮Loveday **Alexander**, *The Preface to Luke's Gospel: Literary Convention and Social Context in Luke 1.1–4 and Acts 1.1*, SNTSMS 78 (Cambridge: Cambridge University Press, 1993) ▮▮R. Dean **Anderson** Jr., *Ancient Rhetorical Theory and Paul* (The Hague: Kok Pharos, 1996) ▮▮David E. **Aune**, *The New Testament in Its Literary Environment* (Philadelphia: Westminster, 1987) ▮▮Margaret **Barker**, "Pseudonymity," in *A Dictionary of Biblical Interpretation*, ed. R. J. C. Coggins and J. L. Houlden (Philadelphia: Trinity Press International, 1990), 568–71 ▮▮Richard **Bauckham**, *Jude, 2 Peter*, WBC (Waco: Word, 1986) ▮▮Richard **Bentley**, *Dissertations upon the Epistles of Phalaris . . .* , ed. with Introduction and Notes by Wilhelm Wagner (Berlin: S. Calvary, 1874 [first published 1697–99]) ▮▮Hans Dieter **Betz**, *Galatians: A Commentary on Paul's Letter to the Churches in Galatia*, Hermeneia (Philadelphia: Fortress Press, 1979) ▮▮Norbert **Brox**, *Pseudepigraphie in der heidnischen und jüdisch-christlichen Antike*, WdF 484 (Darmstadt: Wissenschaftliche Buchgesellschaft, 1977) ▮▮F. F. **Bruce**, "Paul the Apostle," in *ISBE* 3.706 ▮▮idem, *Tradition Old and New* (Grand Rapids: Zondervan, 1970) ▮▮P. **Carrington**, *The Early Christian Church*, 2 vols. (Cambridge: Cambridge University Press, 1957) ▮▮idem, "The Problem of the Pastoral Epistles: Dr. Harrison's Theory Reviewed," *ATR* 21 (1939): 32–39 ▮▮D. A. **Carson**, "Pseudonymity and Pseudepigraphy," in *The Dictionary of New Testament Background*, ed. Craig A. Evans and Stanley E. Porter (Downers Grove: IVP, 2000), 856–64 ▮▮James H. **Charlesworth**, "Pseudonymity and Pseudepigraphy," *ABD* 5.540–41 ▮▮Adolf **Deissmann**, "Prolegomena to the Biblical Letters and Epistles," in *Bible Studies* (Edinburgh: T. & T. Clark, 1901), 1–59 ▮▮Lewis R. **Donelson**, *Pseudepigraphy and Ethical Argument in the Pastoral Epistles*, HUT 22 (Tübingen: Mohr-Siebeck 1986) ▮▮J. **Duff**, "A Critical Examination of Pseudepigraphy in First- and Second-Century Christianity and the Approaches to It of Twentieth-Century Scholars" (D.Phil. dissertation; University of Oxford, 1998) ▮▮James D. G. **Dunn**, "Pseudonymity," *DLNT*, 977–84 ▮▮E. Earle **Ellis**, "Pseudonymity and Canonicity of New Testament Documents," in *Worship, Theology, and Ministry in the Early Church*, ed. Michael J. Wilkins and Terence Paige (Sheffield: JSOT Press, 1992), 212–24 ▮▮idem, "The Authorship of the Pastorals: A Résumé and Assessment," *EQ* 32 (1960): 151–61 ▮▮idem, *History and Interpretation in New Testament Perspective*, BIS 54 (Leiden: Brill, 2001) ▮▮E. **Evanson**, *The Dissonance of the Four Generally Received Evangelists* (Ipswich: G. Jermyn, 1792) ▮▮Denis **Farkasfalvy**, "The Ecclesial Setting of Pseudepigraphy in Second Peter and its Role in the Formation of the Canon," *The Second Century* 5 (1986): 3–29 (with an important response by William R. **Farmer**, 80–86) ▮▮Robert W. **Funk**, "The Apostolic Parousia: Form and Significance," in

Christian History and Interpretation, ed. W. R. Farmer, C. F. D. Moule, and R. R. Niebuhr (Cambridge: Cambridge University Press, 1966), 249–68 ▦ Conrad **Gempf,** "Pseudonymity and the New Testament," *Themelios* 17 (1992): 8–10 ▦ Donald **Guthrie,** "Tertullian and Pseudonymity," *ExpTim* 67 (1955–56): 341– 42 ▦ Alfred E. **Haefner,** "A Unique Source for the Study of Ancient Pseudonymity," *ATR* 16 (1934): 8–15 ▦ P. N. **Harrison,** "The Authorship of the Pastoral Epistles," *ExpTim* 67 (1955–56): 77–81 ▦ idem, *Paulines and Pastorals* (London: Villiers, 1964) ▦ idem, *The Problem of the Pastoral Epistles* (London: Oxford University Press, 1921) ▦ Martin **Hengel** and Anna Maria **Schwemer,** *Paul between Damascus and Antioch: The Unknown Years* (Louisville: Westminster John Knox, 1997) ▦ Frank W. **Hughes,** "The Rhetoric of Letters," in *The Thessalonians Debate: Methodological Discord or Methodological Synthesis?* ed. Karl P. Donfried and Johannes Beutler (Grand Rapids: Eerdmans, 2000), 194–240 ▦ M. R. **James,** *The Apocryphal New Testament* (Oxford: Clarendon, 1926) ▦ Phillip H. **Kern,** *Rhetoric and Galatians: Assessing an Approach to the Epistle,* SNTSMS 101 (Cambridge: Cambridge University Press, 1999) ▦ Mark **Kiley,** *Colossians as Pseudepigraphy* (Sheffield: JSOT Press, 1986) ▦ John **Knox,** *Philemon Among the Letters of Paul* (London: Collins, 1960) ▦ Andrew T. **Lincoln,** *Ephesians,* WBC 42 (Dallas: Word Books, 1990) ▦ Richard **Longenecker,** "On the Form, Function, and Authority of the New Testament Letters," in *Scripture and Truth,* ed. D. A. Carson and John D. Woodbridge (Grand Rapids: Zondervan, 1983), 101–14 ▦ idem, *Paul, Apostle of Liberty,* reprint ed. (Grand Rapids: Baker, 1976) ▦ Abraham J. **Malherbe,** *Ancient Epistolary Theorists* (Atlanta: SP, 1988) ▦ I. Howard **Marshall,** *A Critical and Exegetical Commentary on the Pastoral Epistles,* ICC (Edinburgh: T. & T. Clark, 1999) ▦ idem, "Recent Study of the Pastoral Epistles," *Themelios* 23/1 (1997): 3–29 ▦ David G. **Meade,** *Pseudonymity and Canon,* WUNT 39 (Tübingen: Mohr-Siebeck, 1986) ▦ Wayne A. **Meeks,** "'To Walk Worthily of the Lord': Moral Formation in the Pauline School Exemplified by the Letter to the Colossians," in *Hermes and Athena: Biblical Exegesis and Philosophical Theology,* ed. Eleonore Stump and Thomas P. Flint, University of Notre Dame Studies in the Philosophy of Religion 7 (Notre Dame: University of Notre Dame Press, 1993), 37–58 ▦ B. **Metzger,** "Literary Forgeries and Canonical Pseudepigrapha," *JBL* 91 (1972): 3– 24 ▦ idem, "A Reconsideration of Certain Arguments Against the Pauline Authorship of the Pastoral Epistles," *ExpTim* 70 (1958–59): 91–94 ▦ C. Leslie **Mitton,** *The Formation of the Pauline Corpus of Letters* (London: Epworth, 1955) ▦ Leon **Morris,** *Apocalyptic,* 2nd ed. (Grand Rapids: Eerdmans, 1973) ▦ Jerome **Murphy-O'Connor,** *Paul the Letter-Writer: His World, His Options, His Skills* (Collegeville: Liturgical Press, 1995) ▦ Peter T. **O'Brien,** *The Letter to the Ephesians,* PNTC (Grand Rapids: Eerdmans, 1999) ▦ Stanley E. **Porter,** "Pauline Authorship and the Pastoral Epistles," *BBR* 5 (1995): 105–123 ▦ idem, "Pauline Authorship and the Pastoral Epistles: A Response to R. W. Wall's Response," *BBR* 6 (1996): 133–38 ▦ Jeffrey T. **Reed,** "Using Ancient Rhetorical Categories to Interpret Paul's

Letters: A Question of Genre," in *Rhetoric and the New Testament: Essays from the 1992 Heidelberg Conference*, ed. Stanley Porter and Thomas H. Olbricht, *JSNTSup* 90 (Sheffield: JSOT Press, 1993), 292–324 ∎Bo **Reicke**, *Re-examining Paul's Letters: The History of the Pauline Correspondence* (Harrisburg: Trinity Press International, 2001) ∎E. Randolph **Richards**, *The Secretary in the Letters of Paul*, WUNT 42 (Tübingen: Mohr-Siebeck, 1991) ∎M. **Rist**, "Pseudepigraphy and the Early Christians," in *Studies in New Testament and Early Christian Literature*, ed. D. E. Aune (Leiden: Brill, 1972), 75–91 ∎Joseph A. **Sint**, *Pseudonymität im Altertum, ihre Formen und ihre Gründe* (Innsbruck: Universitätsverlag, 1960) ∎W. **Speyer**, *Die literarische Fälschung im heidnischen und christlichen Altertum: Ein Versuch ihrer Deutung* (München: Beck, 1971) ∎J. **Stevenson**, *A New Eusebius* (London: SPCK, 1963) ∎Stanley K. **Stowers**, *Letter Writing in Greco-Roman Antiquity* (Philadelphia: Westminster, 1986) ∎R. W. **Wall**, "Pauline Authorship and the Pastoral Epistles," A Response to S. E. Porter," *BBR* 5 (1995): 125–28 ∎Jeffrey A. D. **Weima**, "The Function of 1 Thessalonians 2:1–12 and the Use of Rhetorical Criticism: A Response to Otto Merk," in *The Thessalonians Debate: Methodological Discord or Methodological Synthesis?* ed. Karl P. Donfried and Johannes Beutler (Grand Rapids: Eerdmans, 2000), 114–31 ∎John Lee **White**, *The Form and Function of the Body of the Greek Letter*, SBLDS 2, 2nd ed. (Missoula: SP, 1972) ∎idem, *Light from Ancient Letters* (Philadelphia: Fortress Press, 1986) ∎Theodor **Zahn**, *Geschichte des neutestamentlichen Kanons*, 4 parts in 2 vols. (Erlangen: A. Deichert, 1888–92).

CHAPTER NINE

PAUL: APOSTLE AND THEOLOGIAN

Paul is so significant a figure in the New Testament and in the church's history that he has been called the second founder of Christianity. This, of course, is not true, for it ignores the continuity between Jesus and Paul and diminishes unfairly the contributions of men such as Peter, John, and Luke.[1] But there is no question that Paul played a vital role in the growth and establishment of the church and in the interpretation and application of God's grace in Christ. And Paul continues to minister to us today through the thirteen epistles of his that have become part of the canon of the New Testament. These epistles make up almost one-fourth of the New Testament, putting Paul just behind Luke in the percentage of the New Testament written by a single individual. And if one adds the sixteen chapters of Acts (13–28) that are almost entirely devoted to Paul, Paul figures in almost a third of the New Testament.

PAUL'S BACKGROUND

Who was this man Paul? Exploring his background will help us to understand him better and to interpret his words more accurately. Paul himself provides a rough outline of his background, but this material is scattered throughout his epistles. The basic historical details are conveniently grouped in the speeches Paul gave (as reported by Luke) to a hostile crowd of Jews on the steps of the temple (Acts 22:1–21) and to King Agrippa II and the Roman procurator Festus (Acts 26:2–23). (On the historical value of such material in Acts, see below on the chronology of Paul's missionary career, and chap. 7 above.)

---

[1]See especially the thorough study of David Wenham, *Paul: Follower of Jesus or Founder of Christianity?* (Grand Rapids: Eerdmans, 1995).

"Born in Tarsus of Cilicia" (Acts 22:3)

Tarsus was the major city in Cilicia, a region in the extreme southeastern part of Asia Minor.[2] In Paul's day the city was the capital of the Roman province Syria-Cilicia (see Gal. 1:21). It was prosperous, privileged (it was exempt from Roman taxation), and cultured, being famous for its schools.[3] Not only was Paul born in Tarsus, but he was also a citizen of this "no ordinary city" (Acts 21:39).

More important, however, was the fact that Paul was a citizen of Rome. The Romans did not confer citizenship on just anyone; only a small percentage of people who lived within the Roman Empire possessed this privilege. Paul's Roman citizenship was inherited from his family (Paul claims, "I was born a citizen" [Acts 22:28]), perhaps because of some deed of service performed by his father or grandfather for the Romans.[4] However achieved, Paul's Roman citizenship was an important and providential qualification for his role as missionary to the Roman Empire. It enabled him to escape detainment when his preaching brought disfavor (Acts 16:37–39), to avoid punishment (Acts 22:23–29), and to plead his case before the emperor's court in Rome (Acts 25:10–12).

As a Roman citizen, Paul had three names: a first name *(praenomen)*, family name *(nomen)*, and surname *(cognomen)*. Of these, we know only his *cognomen*, Παῦλος *(Paulos)*. Paul's native town may also have led him into his trade. A local product, *cilicium*, was used to make tents, and Luke tells us that Paul was himself a "tentmaker" (Acts 18:3).[5] This is presumably the trade that Paul pursued during his missionary work in order not to burden the churches with his support (e.g., 1 Thess. 2:9).

"Brought up in this city" (Acts 22:3)

This phrase in Paul's speech on the temple steps has given rise to a debate about whether Paul's early years were spent in Tarsus or Jerusalem. The issue has attracted so much attention because it figures in the debate about Paul's thought world: was he indebted more to the Greek world or to the Jewish world

---

[2]On Tarsus generally, see William M. Ramsay, *The Cities of St. Paul: Their Influence on His Life and Thought* (London: Hodder & Stoughton, 1907), 85–244; Colin J. Hemer, "Tarsus," in *ISBE* 4.734–36.

[3]Strabo, *Geog.* 14.5.14.

[4]F. F. Bruce, *Paul: Apostle of the Heart Set Free* (Grand Rapids: Eerdmans, 1977), 37–38. A few scholars have questioned whether Paul was really a Roman citizen (e.g., Calvin Roetzel, *Paul: The Man and the Myth* [Columbia: University of South Carolina Press, 1998], 19–22), but the tradition is solid (see Rainer Riesner, *Paul's Early Period: Chronology, Mission Strategy, Theology* [Grand Rapids: Eerdmans, 1998], 147–56).

[5]This is the meaning of the difficult word σκηνοποιός *(skēnopoios;* cf. Acts 18:3) has been given, although Ronald F. Hock and others argue that it means simply "leatherworker" (*The Social Context of Paul's Ministry* [Philadelphia: Fortress, Press, 1980]) and BDAG that it means "maker of stage properties" (928).

for his teaching? The contribution of this phrase to the debate depends on two issues. First, does "this city" refer to the city in which Paul is speaking (Jerusalem) or to the city he has just mentioned (Tarsus)? Nigel Turner has argued for the latter,[6] but the former is more likely, considering the setting of the speech. The second issue is the punctuation of the verse, the two possibilities being clearly represented in the TNIV and NRSV:

> TNIV: I am a Jew, born in Tarsus of Cilicia, but brought up in this city. I studied under Gamaliel and was thoroughly trained in the law of our ancestors. . . .

> NRSV: I am a Jew, born at Tarsus in Cilicia, but brought up in this city at the feet of Gamaliel, educated strictly according to our ancestral law. . . .

The TNIV, by putting a period after "this city," separates "brought up" from "under Gamaliel," and this suggests that "brought up" refers to Paul's parental nurturing as a young child. Paul would then be implying that, although born in Tarsus, he was raised in Jerusalem.[7] The NRSV rendering, on the other hand, by linking "brought up" with "at the feet of Gamaliel," requires that "brought up" refer to Paul's rabbinic education, a process that would have begun in his early teens. On this interpretation of the verse, Paul would perhaps be suggesting that he was brought up in Tarsus, moving to Jerusalem only when he went away to school.[8]

But the punctuation represented by the TNIV should probably be adopted. The three-stage sequence—born/brought up/educated—was a natural autobiographical pattern. Nevertheless, this does not solve the matter, nor is it the decisive point in the debate about Paul's background. On the one hand, Paul would have had ample opportunity to pick up Hellenistic ideas during his education in Jerusalem (Hellenism was by no means unknown in Jerusalem) or during his decade-long ministry in Tarsus after his conversion. On the other hand, even if Paul did spend the first ten or so years of his life in Tarsus, he need not have been imbued with Hellenistic ideas. Paul himself stresses that he was a "Hebrew of Hebrews" (Phil. 3:5), apparently meaning that both his parents and he himself were, linguistically and culturally, Jewish and Palestinian in their orientation (see 2 Cor. 11:22, and the contrast between Hebrew and Hellenist in Acts 6:1). The home in which he was raised, whether located in Tarsus or in

---

[6]Nigel Turner, *Grammatical Insights into the New Testament* (Edinburgh: T. & T. Clark, 1965), 83–84.

[7]See particularly W. C. van Unnik, *Tarsus or Jerusalem: The City of Paul's Youth* (London: Epworth, 1962).

[8]E.g., Richard N. Longenecker, *Paul, Apostle of Liberty* (Reprint: Grand Rapids: Baker, 1976), 25–27; Calvin J. Roetzel, *Paul: A Jew on the Margins* (Louisville: Westminster John Knox Press, 2003), 11–19.

Jerusalem, was one in which Aramaic was spoken and traditional Palestinian Jewish customs were preserved.[9] So to the extent that Paul's background influenced his theology, that influence was mainly Palestinian and Jewish. But having said this, we must also be careful not to erect rigid distinctions between "Hellenistic" and "Palestinian" or "Hellenistic" and "Jewish." There was a difference, as Paul's own claims imply. But the difference can be, and has at times, been exaggerated; Hellenistic ideas had penetrated Palestine and Judaism in the first century.[10] "In antiquity ideas did not flow in pipes,"[11] and Paul's world was one in which he was exposed to many different influences and combinations of influences.

"Thoroughly trained in the law of our ancestors . . . zealous for God" (Acts 22:3)

Not only was Paul by birth a "Hebrew of Hebrews," but, as he never tired of emphasizing (see also Acts 26:5; Gal. 1:14; Phil. 3:5–6), he was by conviction a serious and zealous follower of Judaism, a member of its "strictest sect" (Acts 26:5), the Pharisees. Although scholars disagree considerably over many aspects of first-century Pharisaism, several things are relatively clear. The Pharisees paid a great deal of attention to the "oral law," "the traditions of the elders" (Mark 7:3 par.), a body of regulations designed to interpret and supplement the written, Mosaic law. They had a number of fundamental disagreements with the Sadducees, stemming from the Pharisees' greater willingness to accept doctrines not clearly stated in the Pentateuch (e.g., the resurrection of the body; see Acts 23:6–8). They exercised great influence over the common people, who respected their zeal for their beliefs and their desire to sanctify all aspects of life.[12] Paul was trained under Gamaliel I (see Acts 26:3), a Pharisee of the school of Hillel. Hillel and his followers were generally known for their liberality, an attitude revealed in Gamaliel's advice to the Sanhedrin about the early church (Acts 5:34–39). Paul seems to have differed from his teacher at this point. By his own repeated admission, Paul's zeal for Judaism led him to persecute the early Christian movement (e.g., Acts 22:4a; 26:9–11; Gal. 1:13; Phil. 3:6). But Paul may

---

[9]Longenecker, *Paul, Apostle of Liberty,* 21–64; Bruce, *Paul: Apostle of the Heart Set Free,* 42.

[10]See esp. Martin Hengel, *Judaism and Hellenism* (Philadelphia: Fortress Press, 1974); cf. also Troels Engberg-Pedersen, ed., *Paul Beyond the Judaism/Hellenism Divide* (Louisville: Westminster John Knox Press, 2001).

[11]Leander E. Keck, *Paul and His Letters,* Proclamation Commentaries (Philadelphia: Fortress Press, 1979), 11.

[12]For a succinct orientation to the discussion, see Anthony J. Saldarini, "Pharisees," in *ABD* 5.289–303, and esp. Roland Deines, "The Pharisees between 'Judaisms' and 'Common Judaism,'" in *Justification and Variegated Nomism,* vol. 1: *The Complexities of Second Temple Judaism,* ed. D. A. Carson, Peter T. O'Brien, and Mark A. Seifrid, WUNT 140 (Tübingen: Mohr-Siebeck/Grand Rapids: Baker, 2001), 443–504.

not, after all, have differed much from his teacher. Gamaliel's advice as given before the Stephen incident revealed the extent to which at least some of the Christians were willing to do without the law and the temple. It may very well have been this development that turned Paul, and perhaps other Pharisees, against the fledgling Christian movement.[13]

"As I came near Damascus" (Acts 22:6)

The persecutor of Christians was turned into the foremost preacher of Christ by a sudden confrontation with the risen Jesus on the road to Damascus. Paul's Damascus-road experience is described once by Luke (Acts 9:3–6), twice by Paul in Acts (22:6–11 and 26:12–15) and once by Paul in his epistles (Gal. 1:15–16). In addition to these clear descriptions, other allusions to this event are probably to be found in many places in Paul.[14] Several scholars have suggested that the event and its implications played a basic role in the formation of much of Paul's theology.[15] Paul's encounter with Christ was no merely psychological experience, nor was it even a divinely given vision. Paul's companions saw the blaze of light, although they did not see Jesus himself (see Acts 9:7 with 22:9), and heard, but did not understand, the voice (cf. Acts 9:7 with 22:9).[16] Moreover, Paul makes clear that this appearance to him of the resurrected Jesus was fully on a par with the appearances to Peter and the others in the days between Jesus' resurrection and ascension (1 Cor. 15:5–8; see also 9:1).

The "revelation" (ἀποκάλυψις [apokalypsis]) of Christ to Paul came without any preparation. Paul gives no hint that before this point he was at all dissatisfied with his Jewish convictions or searching for a deeper experience of God. The texts that have sometimes been thought to indicate such a preparatory period are better interpreted otherwise. When Paul is warned by the heavenly voice that "it is hard for you to kick against the goads" (Acts 26:14), the meaning is not that Paul has been resisting the Spirit's wooing but that he should not

---

[13]See Longenecker, *Paul*, 33–37.

[14]Seyoon Kim, *The Origin of Paul's Gospel* (Tübingen: Mohr-Siebeck, 1981), 3–31.

[15]Esp. Kim, *Origin*, and Christian Dietzfelbinger, *Die Berufung des Paulus als Ursprung seiner Theologie*, WMANT 58 (Neukirchen-Vluyn: Neukirchener, 1985). See also the discussion in *The Road from Damascus: The Impact of Paul's Conversion on his Life, Thought, and Ministry*, ed. Richard N. Longenecker (Grand Rapids: Eerdmans, 1997).

[16]This difference is probably signaled by the shift from the genitive τῆς φωνῆς (*tēs phōnēs*, "the sound" [TNIV]) in Acts 9:7 to the accusative τὴν φωνήν (*tēn phōnēn*, "the voice" [TNIV]) in 22:9, although the significance of the change is debated (see Maximilian Zerwick, *Biblical Greek* [Rome: Pontifical Biblical Institute, 1963], §69; C. F. D. Moule, *An Idiom Book of New Testament Greek* [Cambridge: Cambridge University Press, 1971], 36).

now resist the will of God expressed in the revelation from heaven.[17] Neither does Romans 7:14–25 refer to a preconversion psychological struggle.[18] Rather, the descriptions of the experience in Acts, as well as Paul's allusions to it in Philippians 3:3–11, suggest a sudden and dramatic turn from zealous Jew and persecutor of the church to a follower of Jesus.

The Damascus-road encounter turned Paul into more than a follower of Jesus: it turned him into a preacher of Jesus. Although the relationship between the two is not stated the same way in all the accounts, each one makes clear that Paul's conversion was also a call to ministry (Acts 9:15; 22:15; 26:15–18 and Gal. 1:16). Indeed, some have gone so far as to argue that this revelation was properly a "call" experience and not a "conversion" experience at all.[19] But whatever the continuity between Judaism and Christianity, the New Testament makes clear that the two are distinct, that only within Christianity is salvation found. The change from one to the other is, then, appropriately called a conversion.[20] For Paul, however, conversion and call were bound up together. As Johannes Munck has emphasized, Paul viewed himself as a peculiar instrument in God's hands, one who, like the Old Testament prophets Isaiah and Jeremiah, would have an important role to play in salvation history.[21] It is significant in this light that, whereas ministry to Jews is certainly included in Paul's call (see Acts 9:15), Paul himself often emphasizes that his call was particularly a call to preach to Gentiles (Gal. 1:16; 1 Thess. 2:4; Rom. 1:1, 5; 15:15–16). The mission of carrying the gospel to the Gentiles was fundamental to Paul's call and to his being chosen as a vessel for God's use.

Whereas ministry to Jews is certainly included in Paul's call, Paul himself often emphasizes that his call was particularly a call to preach to Gentiles.

PAUL'S MISSIONARY CAREER AND ITS CHRONOLOGY

The Problem of Sources

While referring occasionally to his early life, past travels, and future plans, Paul's letters do not provide us with the kind of information necessary to

---

[17]See Johannes Munck, *Paul and the Salvation of Mankind* (London: SCM, 1959), 20–21. "Kicking against the goads" was a popular proverb meaning to resist the Deity (see Longenecker, *Paul,* 98–101).

[18]Paul is probably referring either to his experience as a regenerate person or to his experience as a Jew under the law, as typical of all Jews under the law.

[19]E.g., Krister Stendahl, *Paul Among Jews and Gentiles, and Other Essays* (Philadelphia: Fortress Press, 1976), 7–12.

[20]See also Alan Segal, who sees Paul's experience as typical of "conversions" in sectarian Judaism (*Paul the Convert* [New Haven: Yale University Press, 1990], 72–114). Cf. also Peter T. O'Brien, "Was Paul Converted?" in *Justification and Variegated Nomism,* vol. 2: *The Paradoxes of Paul,* ed. D. A. Carson, Peter T. O'Brien, and Mark A. Seifrid (Tübingen: Mohr-Siebeck/Grand Rapids: Baker, 2004), 361–91.

[21]Munck, *Paul,* 24–33.

reconstruct a "life of Paul." This is no more than what should be expected. Paul wrote his letters to deal with specific issues, and only where it was important to those issues, or where Paul was requesting prayer for a certain situation, does he mention his own history. Traditionally, then, an outline of Paul's missionary career has been built on the more detailed and sequential data provided by Acts, with Paul's letters fitted into the general scheme given by Luke. But several scholars contest the legitimacy of such an approach. They argue that the Pauline letters provide the primary data for reconstructing a life of Paul and that Acts, because its historical accuracy is questionable, should be used only in those specific places where its accuracy can be validated or where it corroborates data attained from a study of the letters.[22]

Outlines of Paul's career and its chronology constructed on the basis of these constraints look quite different from traditional models. There are two particular points at which most revisionist models disagree with the usual chronology developed on the basis of Acts. The first is the placement of the apostolic council. Luke places it before the second missionary journey, but the data of the Pauline Epistles, it is argued, suggest that the council followed the second journey. The second major area of difference is the number of visits Paul made to Jerusalem. The letters of Paul refer to only three: three years after Paul's conversion, the convening of the apostolic council, and the occasion when he delivered the collection money at the end of the third missionary journey. The two additional visits mentioned in Acts—the famine-relief visit of 11:27–30 and the visit between the second and third missionary journeys in 18:22—are therefore deemed to be unhistorical. Some revisionist schemes differ at many more points from the traditional outline of Paul's life based on the sequence of Acts.[23]

It is questionable, however, whether such revisions are helpful, let alone necessary. Paul's own writings are indeed the primary material for a study of his life. But since his own writings simply do not provide the necessary data for the piecing together of a chronology of his life, it is entirely legitimate to turn to other sources. Acts must be considered to be a reliable source of such data. It

---

[22]See esp. John Knox, *Chapters in a Life of Paul* (London: Adam & Charles Black, 1954), 13–43; Robert Jewett, *A Chronology of Paul's Life* (Philadelphia: Fortress Press, 1979), 7–24; Gerd Lüdemann, *Paul, Apostle to the Gentiles: Studies in Chronology* (Philadelphia: Fortress Press, 1984), 21–29.

[23]Lüdemann, for instance, relying a great deal on Paul's statements about the collection and the theology expressed in the letters, puts Paul's founding visit to the churches of Macedonia (e.g., Thessalonica) very early, in the early or middle 40s and has Paul returning to Jerusalem with the collection as early as A.D. 52 (see *Paul,* 262–63). On the issue of the Jerusalem visits and the apostolic council, see also Charles Buck and Greer Taylor, *Saint Paul: A Study of the Development of His Thought* (New York: Charles Scribner's Sons, 1969), 7–8. And for a detailed survey and thorough analysis of the various options, see esp. Riesner, *Paul's Early Period,* 3–227.

was written, as we have argued in chapter 7 above, by Luke, a companion of Paul, and we can expect his information about the apostle's movements to be quite good. Moreover, we have found good reason to respect Luke's historical accuracy. This does not mean that we should prefer Acts to Paul's letters when they differ. But many of the differences that have been found are the product of certain specific interpretations that are by no means the only ones possible. A careful comparison of Paul's statements about his movements with the movements of Paul recorded in Acts reveals an amazing degree of correspondence.[24] The relegation of Acts to a secondary status in the construction of a life of Paul is simply not legitimate. We will therefore use Acts as a key source in the following sketch of Paul's missionary career and its chronology. Having established a relative sequence of movements based on both Acts and the Epistles, we will then work toward an absolute chronology.

An Outline of Paul's Missionary Career

From Paul's Conversion to the First Missionary Journey. The decisive data in establishing a relative chronology for this earlier period come from Galatians 1:13–2:10. In this passage, Paul recounts his relationship with the Jerusalem apostles in order to demonstrate that his apostolic authority does not derive from them. He tells us that he first visited Jerusalem, as a Christian, three years after his conversion to "get acquainted with" Peter (1:18), and then he visited Jerusalem again "after fourteen years" (2:1) to set before the Jerusalem apostles the gospel that he was preaching among the Gentiles. This sequence raises two key issues: To which visits in Acts do the two visits Paul mentions here correspond? And how are we to understand the sequence of "after three years" and "after fourteen years"?

The first Jerusalem visit Paul mentions is clearly the same as the one Luke mentions in Acts 9:26–30. But is the visit of Galatians 2:1 to be identified with the famine-relief visit of Acts 11:27–30 or with the apostolic-council visit of Acts 15? Many scholars have argued for the latter equation. It is pointed out that Paul's characterization of this visit as involving questions about his gospel to the Gentiles fits the circumstances of the council of Acts 15. But there are details in Paul's description that do not correspond very well with the Acts 15 situation, and the circumstances of the letter to the Galatians suggest that it was written *before* the apostolic council (see chap. 12 below). This would require that Galatians 2:1 refer to the famine-relief visit of Acts 11:27–30.

Assuming these identifications, the specific temporal indicators Paul gives in this passage should be invaluable in constructing a relative chronology of

---

[24]See T. H. Campbell, "Paul's 'Missionary Journeys' as Reflected in His Letters," *JBL* 74 (1955): 80–87; Ben Witherington III, *The Paul Quest: The Renewed Search for the Jew of Tarsus* (Grand Rapids: Eerdmans, 1998), 327–31.

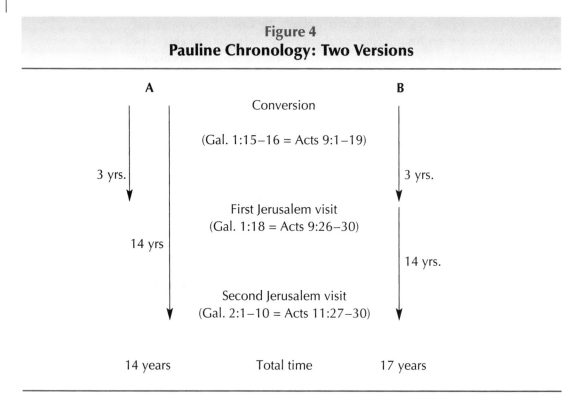

Figure 4
Pauline Chronology: Two Versions

A   B

Conversion

(Gal. 1:15–16 = Acts 9:1–19)

3 yrs.   3 yrs.

First Jerusalem visit
(Gal. 1:18 = Acts 9:26–30)

14 yrs

14 yrs.

Second Jerusalem visit
(Gal. 2:1–10 = Acts 11:27–30)

14 years   Total time   17 years

Paul's life. But these indicators are not as clear as might at first seem. It is generally agreed that the "three years" in Galatians 1:18 is the interval between Paul's conversion (1:15–16) and his first Jerusalem visit.[25] But do the "fourteen years" in 2:1 also begin with Paul's conversion, or do they begin with his first Jerusalem visit?[26] The former interpretation results in sequence A, the second in sequence B (see fig. 4).

For two reasons, sequence A should probably be preferred.[27] *First,* the prominence of Paul's conversion in Galatians 1 suggests that this event is the base for all his chronological notices in this context. *Second,* this sequence fits better with other chronological indications that we will note below.

---

[25]Lüdemann, however, takes the "three years" to refer back to what immediately precedes: Paul's return to Damascus (1:17) (*Paul,* 63).

[26]Here also, Lüdemann reckons the "fourteen years" from Paul's trip to Syria and Cilicia (1:21) (ibid.).

[27]J. Louis Martyn argues that a concurrent reading of the relevant time indicators in Galatians 1–2 fits with the intention of these passages (*Galatians: A New Translation with Introduction and Commentary,* AB 33A [New York: Doubleday, 1997], 180–82). For the opposite view, see Jerome Murphy-O'Connor, *Paul: A Critical Life* (Oxford: Clarendon Press, 1996), 6–8.

There is one more issue that must be decided: whether Paul is here counting years inclusively or exclusively. The exclusive method is the one with which we are familiar: the interval between event X and event Y is the interval *between* the years in which the events occur. If Paul's conversion was in A.D. 33, for instance, then his first Jerusalem visit "after three years" (Gal. 1:18) would be in 36. The inclusive method of reckoning an interval between event X and event Y includes the years in which both these events took place, as well as the years between. This would mean that the interval between Paul's conversion and his first Jerusalem visit could be as little as one and a third years (if, for instance, the conversion was late in 33 and the visit early in 35), and the interval between his conversion and his second Jerusalem visit as little as twelve and a third years. Although the point is debated, the inclusive method seems to have been more typical in the ancient world, so we may prefer it in interpreting Galatians 1–2.

Using the data from Galatians 1–2, supplemented by Acts 9–11, we can reconstruct the early years of Paul's missionary work. After his conversion, he stayed in Damascus a short time (Acts 9:19b) before leaving for "Arabia" (Gal. 1:17). Paul here refers not to the Arabian Peninsula but to the Nabataean Kingdom, northeast of the Dead Sea. Some think that Paul spent his time in Arabia meditating and hammering out his theology, and it is likely, considering the drastic change in perspective occasioned by his Damascus-road experience, that some of his time was so spent. But it is unlikely that this was simply a period of retreat. Paul's later difficulties with the king of the Nabataeans, Aretas, suggests strongly that he was engaged in active ministry during this time (2 Cor. 11:32).[28] After an indeterminate period, Paul returned again to Damascus (Gal. 1:17; Acts 9:20–22?), where his ministry was cut short by an attempt on the part of Jews and "the governor under King Aretas" to arrest or kill him (2 Cor. 11:32; Acts 9:23–24). Escaping in a basket lowered through a window in the city wall (2 Cor. 11:33; Acts 9:25), Paul then visited Jerusalem for the first time since his conversion, perhaps a little more than two full years after that event. While at first suspicious of this notorious persecutor of the church, the Jerusalem disciples were persuaded by Barnabas to receive Paul (Acts 9:26–27). Paul spent fifteen days getting acquainted with Peter without meeting any of the other apostles except James, the brother of the Lord (Gal. 1:18–19). Though accepted by his Christian brothers, Paul was rejected by his old associates: certain "Hellenistic Jews" tried to kill him, and he was forced to flee to Tarsus (Acts 9:28–30; see Gal. 1:21).

---

[28]See, e.g., Kirsopp Lake, "The Conversion of Paul," in *The Beginnings of Christianity*, Part 1: *The Acts of the Apostles*, ed. F. J. Foakes Jackson and Kirsopp Lake (London: Macmillan, 1920–33), 5.192–94; Martin Hengel and Anna Maria Schwemer, *Paul between Damascus and Antioch: The Unknown Years* (Louisville: Westminster John Knox, 1997), 106–77.

Some time after this, Barnabas, who had been sent from Jerusalem to investigate the reports of great numbers of Greeks becoming Christians in Antioch, invited Paul to leave Tarsus and join the work at Antioch (Acts 11:25–26a). Since Luke tells us that Barnabas and Paul spent a year with the church there (Acts 11:26b), and since during this year the famine-relief visit took place (Acts 11:27–30), Paul's arrival in Antioch must have been about twelve or thirteen years after his conversion. This means that Paul spent almost a decade in Tarsus, and it was perhaps during these years that some of the things took place that Paul mentions but that are not narrated in Acts (see 2 Cor. 11:22–27).[29]

From Paul's First Missionary Journey to His Death. Paul gives us no sequence of events or chronological indicators for the second stage of his missionary career—from the first missionary journey to the end of his life—comparable to what he provides for us in Galatians 1–2 for the first stage of his career. We are almost wholly dependent on Acts for this information. Unfortunately, while Luke provides us with a relatively straightforward account of this stage of Paul's life—and one that in no way contradicts Paul's own scattered autobiographical remarks—he is, with certain important exceptions, notoriously vague about chronology. Luke is fond of using phrases such as "a long time," "after some days," and "about this time," which provide little help is estimating elapsed time.

For instance, Luke introduces the first missionary journey in Acts 13:1–3 with no indication about its relationship in time to the other events he has been narrating. Nevertheless, we should probably view the narrative as a continuation of the Antiochian story that was begun in 11:19–30. If so, we can presume that the period of "a whole year" of ministry in Antioch mentioned in 11:26 is the time between Paul's joining of Barnabas and their setting out on the first missionary journey. This journey took Barnabas, Paul, and—for part of the way—John Mark to Barnabas's home, the island of Cyprus, and several cities in southern Galatia, namely, Pisidian Antioch, Iconium, Lystra, and Derbe (Acts 13:4–14:26). Estimates of the time necessary for this trip of about 1,400 miles[30] vary from one year to five years.[31] The best guess is about eighteen months,[32] but we simply have no way of knowing for sure.

---

[29]Bruce, *Paul, Apostle of the Heart Set Free,* 127–28.

[30]All the mileage estimates for Paul's journeys come from Barry J. Beitzel, *The Moody Atlas of Bible Lands* (Chicago: Moody, 1985), 177.

[31]See the discussion in Jewett, *Chronology,* 57–62. He opts for forty-six months. It is estimated that in Paul's day one could travel about one hundred miles a day by ship, and no more than fifteen or twenty by foot (Wayne A. Meeks, *The First Urban Christians: The Social World of the Apostle Paul* [New Haven: Yale University Press, 1983], 18).

[32]George Ogg, *The Odyssey of Paul* (Old Tappan: Fleming H. Revell, 1968), 65–71.

Following the first journey, Paul and Barnabas spent "a long time" in Antioch (Acts 14:28; cf. Gal. 2:11–14), before going to Jerusalem for the apostolic council (15:29). They then returned to Antioch for a period of time (15:30–33), where a dispute over John Mark's qualifications for continued missionary service led the two to go their separate ways (15:36–41). Paul's second missionary journey took him to southern Galatia, quickly through Asia Minor, and on to Macedonia—in particular, the cities of Philippi (see 1 Thess. 2:2), Thessalonica (see 1 Thess. 2:2; Phil. 4:15–16), and Berea (Acts 17:10–15)—and then Achaia, including Athens (see 1 Thess. 3:1) and Corinth (see 2 Cor. 11:7–9). Luke provides no specific time references until Paul comes to Corinth: he mentions that Paul stayed there for a period of eighteen months (Acts 18:11). This reference may indicate only the length of time spent in Corinth before the Gallio incident (18:12–17),[33] but probably indicates the total time spent in Corinth.[34] Once again, the total amount of time required for the second journey—about 2,800 miles—is hard to estimate, but the indications are that Paul did not spend much time in any place before Corinth, so two years may be about right.

After returning to Jerusalem (implied in Acts 18:22, with its reference to "the church"), Paul went to Antioch, where he spent "some time" (18:23). This stay, however, was probably not a long one, for Paul would have been anxious to return to Ephesus, where he had left Priscilla and Aquila (18:19). Nevertheless, he traveled "from place to place throughout the region of Galatia and Phrygia" (18:23; the reference is probably to the Phrygian part of Galatia) before arriving in Ephesus (19:1; see 1 Cor. 16:8). How long Paul spent here is not clear. In Acts 20:31, Paul tells the elders of the Ephesian church that he had spent "three years" with them. But this could be a rounding off (counting inclusively) of the period of two years and three months specified in Acts 19:8, 10. Luke, however, may not intend these two verses to summarize the entire stay in Ephesus. It is safest to conclude that Paul spent anywhere from two years and three months to three years in Ephesus. From Ephesus Paul moved north into Macedonia, where he met Titus returning from Corinth (Acts 20:1; cf. 2 Cor. 2:12–13). Some scholars speculate that it may have been at this time that Paul ministered in Illyricum (modern Albania and Yugoslavia; see Rom. 15:19), although neither Acts nor Paul's letters describe such a trip.[35] Paul probably wintered in Corinth (his three-month stay in Greece [Acts 20:2–3; cf. 2 Cor. 9:4]), before retracing his steps to Caesarea and Jerusalem (20:3–21:16). This journey, of approximately 2,700 miles, must have taken at least three and a half years, and probably four or five.

---

[33]Ogg, *Odyssey*, 114–15.

[34]Richard Longenecker, "Acts," in *EBC* 9.484; Riesner, *Paul's Early Period*, 208–9.

[35]Riesner (*Paul's Early Period*, 321) theorizes that Paul may also have spent a winter in Philippi before going on to Corinth.

Very shortly after his arrival in Jerusalem, Paul was imprisoned by the Roman authorities under suspicion that he had fomented a riot in the temple (Acts 21:27–36). Shortly thereafter he was transferred to Caesarea, where he spent two years (Acts 24:27). He was then sent on to Rome, on a voyage that began in the autumn (the "Fast" in 27:9 is almost certainly the Day of Atonement [see TNIV]) and ended in the spring, after three months shipwrecked on the island of Malta (28:11). Luke's account closes with Paul under house arrest for two years in Rome (28:30–31).

Many think that Paul's life ended at this point, but two considerations point decisively to a longer interval before his death. First, apparently reliable early church accounts associate Paul's death with Nero's persecution of Christians in A.D. 64–65. But it is unlikely that Paul's two-year stay in Rome brings us to this late a date (see below). Second, the evidence of the Pastoral Epistles points to a period of further ministry in the eastern Mediterranean after the Roman imprisonment of Acts 28:30–31 (see chap. 17 below). Almost certainly, then, Paul was released from this first Roman imprisonment for a period of further ministry. Whether this ministry took Paul to Spain, as he had originally planned (see Rom. 15:24), is uncertain.[36]

The Chronology of Paul's Missionary Career

Combining the evidence of Acts with indications in the letters of Paul enables us to establish a relative chronology of the life of Paul. But since neither Luke nor Paul furnishes us with any absolute dates in the career of Paul, the determination of absolute dates depends on the correlation of events mentioned in Acts and Paul with externally verifiable dates. The most important such event is Paul's appearance before the Roman proconsul of Achaia, Gallio, while he was in Corinth on the second missionary journey.[37] Inscriptions enable us to determine that Gallio was proconsul of Achaia from July of 51 to July of 52.[38] Luke suggests that Paul

---

[36]The key reference is in *1 Clement.* 5:1–7, where it is claimed that Paul reached "the limit of the West" (τὸ τέρμα τῆς δύσεως [*to terma tēs dyseōs*]). Many think that Clement, a Roman, can mean by this only regions west of Rome (see also the Muratorian Canon) and that Paul probably did preach in Spain (e.g., John J. Gunther, *Paul: Messenger and Exile* [Valley Forge: Judson, 1972], 141–50). Others, however, think that Clement might be referring to Rome itself, or otherwise doubt the reliability of the tradition, and question whether Paul ever reached Spain (Ogg, *Odyssey*, 188–92). The time required for ministry in the East in the Pastoral Epistles may make it unlikely that Paul reached Spain.

[37]Because he doubts the historicity of the incident, Lüdemann does not use the chronological implications of the Gallio incident in his reconstruction (*Paul*, 157–64).

[38]See, e.g., Jewett, *Chronology*, 38–40; Bruce, *Paul: Apostle of the Heart Set Free*, 253. There is a remote possibility that Gallio's tenure should be put a year later.

left Corinth rather quickly after the encounter with Gallio—"some time" (18:18) always denotes a rather short time in Acts (see also 9:23, 43; 27:7). This means that the extreme possibilities for Paul's eighteen-month stay in Corinth are spring 49 to autumn 51, and spring 50 to autumn 52. If, as many surmise, the Jews took advantage of a new proconsul to press their case against Paul, the former dates are slightly more likely. Either sequence of dates also fits Luke's reference to the edict of Claudius (18:2), which was probably issued in 49.[39]

This relatively secure date in the middle of Paul's missionary career is a fixed point from which we can work both backward and forward. Working backward first, an arrival of Paul in Corinth in the spring of A.D. 49 would place the beginning of the second missionary journey sometime in the summer or autumn of 48. The apostolic council must have been shortly before this, probably also in 48, with the first missionary journey in 46–47 or 47–48. This in turn puts Paul's famine-relief visit to Jerusalem in 45–47. This date fits Josephus's references to a severe famine in 45 or 46.[40] One problem with this date for the famine relief visit is that the death of Herod Agrippa I, narrated by Luke in the following chapter (12:19b–23), took place in 44. But there is every reason to think that Luke has arranged his material here topically and that the description of Agrippa's death is placed here simply because it is a natural sequel to the story of his persecution of believers (12:1–19a).

If the famine relief visit was in A.D. 45–47 and the "fourteen years" of Galatians 2:1 is to be reckoned inclusively and from the time of Paul's conversion (see above), then Paul's conversion could be dated anywhere from 32 to 35. Two other considerations impinge on the date for Paul's conversion. First, a certain amount of time, probably at least a year, must have elapsed between Jesus' crucifixion and Paul's conversion, to allow for the events of Acts 1–8.[41] If the

> *Luke's account closes with Paul under house arrest for two years in Rome. Many think that Paul's life ended at this point, but two considerations point decisively to a longer interval before his death.*

---

[39]The edict is mentioned by Suetonius in his *Life of Claudius* 25.4 but first dated in A.D. 49 by the historian Orosius (*Hist.* 7.6.15–16). Some dispute this date, favoring the date of 41 given by Dio Cassius, *Hist. Rom.* (40.6.6) (e.g., Lüdemann, *Paul*, 164–71), but Orosius is probably correct (see E. Mary Smallwood, *The Jews Under Roman Rule*, SJLA 20 [Leiden: Brill, 1976], 210–15; Riesner, *Paul's Early Period*, 157–201).

[40]Jos., *Ant.* 20.2.5. On the date, see Kirsopp Lake, "The Chronology of Acts," in *Beginnings of Christianity*, 5.452–55. Because there was no single, world-wide famine during these years, Luke's reference to a famine that affected "the entire Roman world" (ὅλην τὴν οἰκουμένην [*holēn tēn oikoumenēn*]) has been considered an exaggeration or an outright fabrication. But the several famines throughout the Roman world during these years justify Luke's generalization (K. S. Gapp, "The Universal Famine Under Claudius," *HTR* 28 [1935]: 258–65).

[41]An early Gnostic tradition held that Jesus' resurrection appearances—up to and including Paul's—lasted eighteen months (see Irenaeus, *Adv. Haer.* 1.30.14; *Ascension of Isaiah* 9:16), and some scholars are inclined to respect this tradition (e.g., Ogg, *Odyssey*, 24–30).

crucifixion is dated in A.D. 30, then the entire range of dates—32 to 35—is still open. But if Jesus was crucified in 33, then we are limited to the latter part of the range only. Second, Paul's reference to the involvement of King Aretas in seeking his arrest in Damascus (2 Cor. 11:32) may favor a date for this event after 37, since it is thought that only after this date would Aretas have had any influence over Damascus.[42] And Paul's escape from Damascus, as we have seen, must have taken place about two years or so after his conversion. Though there is considerable uncertainty about the date of Jesus' crucifixion, these two factors slightly favor the latter end of our range of dates for Paul's conversion—perhaps 34 or 35. The difficulties involved in interpreting Paul's reference to Aretas do not allow for any dogmatism,[43] so an earlier date for Paul's conversion cannot be excluded.

Working forward from the Gallio date, we find Paul ending the second missionary journey in the late summer or autumn of A.D. 51, and beginning the third probably relatively quickly, perhaps in the spring of 52. It is uncertain how long it would have taken Paul to reach Ephesus, but we can assume he was in that city from about mid or late 52 to mid or late 55. After leaving Ephesus, Paul may have spent considerable time in Macedonia or traveled to Illyricum;[44] at any rate, it is likely that he did not begin his return trip to Palestine until the spring of 57. This conclusion rests on the growing consensus among scholars that Festus must have replaced Felix as governor of Judea in 59.[45] Since we know

---

[42]See esp. Ogg, *Odyssey*, 16–23, and Jewett, *Chronology*, 30–33; W. P. Armstrong and J. Finegan, "Chronology of the New Testament," in *ISBE* 1.689–90.

[43]See esp. Riesner, *Paul's Early Period*, 75–89. Bruce offers the attractive suggestion that the "governor" who sought to arrest Paul was the head of the Jewish citizens of Damascus rather than a direct under-official of Aretas (*Paul: Apostle of the Heart Set Free*, 81–82).

[44]See, e.g., Colin J. Hemer, *The Book of Acts in the Setting of Hellenistic History*, WUNT 49 (Tübingen: Mohr-Siebeck, 1989), 258–61.

[45]See, e.g., Gunther, *Paul: Messenger and Exile*, 140–41; G. B. Caird, "Chronology of the New Testament," in *IDB*, 1.604–5; Jewett, *Chronology*, 40–44; Hemer, *Book of Acts*, 171; F. F. Bruce, *New Testament History*, 2nd ed. (Garden City: Doubleday, 1971), 345–46; Riesner, *Paul's Early Period*, 219–24. Some scholars argue for a much earlier date, 55 or 56, based on the fact that Pallas, a Roman official who was removed from office in 55 or 56, was instrumental in Felix's recall (see Lake, "Chronology," 464–67). But it is impossible to squeeze all that Josephus records as happening under Felix while Nero was emperor (A.D. 54 and later) into so short a time; and Pallas probably continued to exercise influence even after being removed from office. For these points, see Emil Schürer, *The History of the Jewish People in the Age of Jesus Christ (175 B.C.–A.D. 135)*, new ed., vol. 1, rev. and ed. by Geza Vermes and Fegus Millar (Edinburgh: T. & T. Clark, 1973), 465–66n. In contrast, Schürer argues that Felix was recalled in A.D. 60 (*History*, 465–66n) and Ogg in 61 (*Odyssey*, 146–70).

Table 6
Chronology of Paul's Missionary Career

Event	Probable date
Conversion	A.D. 34–35 (or earlier)
Ministry in Damascus and Arabia	35–37
First Jerusalem Visit	37
Ministry in Tarsus and Cilicia	37–45
Famine-Relief Visit	45, 46, or 47
First Missionary Journey	46–47 or 47–48
Apostolic Council	48 or 49
Second Missionary Journey	48 or 49–51
Third Missionary Journey	52–57
Caesarean Imprisonment	57–59
Voyage to Rome	59–60
Roman Imprisonment	60–62
Ministry in the East	62–64
Death	64–65

that Paul's two-year imprisonment in Caesarea ended shortly after Festus replaced Felix (Acts 25:1–12), then he must have returned to Palestine in the spring of 57. (We know that Paul's return to Jerusalem occurred in the spring because the Feast of Unleavened Bread took place during the trip [Acts 20:6] and because Paul was anxious to reach Jerusalem before Pentecost [20:16].)

If this reasoning is correct, Paul began his voyage to Rome in the autumn of 59 (Acts 27:9, stating that "sailing had already become dangerous because by now it was after the Day of Atonement," shows that it was autumn),[46] and he arrived in Rome in the spring of 60. On the assumption that Paul was released after the two-year period Luke mentions in Acts 28:30–31, he engaged in further ministry in the East (e.g., Ephesus [see 1 Timothy] and Crete [see Titus]) during the years 62–64. Paul was probably rearrested at the time of Nero's

---

[46]This reference may also corroborate the date of A.D. 59 for Paul's departure for Rome. W. P. Workman argued that the syntax of Acts 27:9 suggests that the date of the Day of Atonement in this year followed the date for the closing of sailing ("A New Date-Indication in Acts," *ExpTim* 11 [1899–1900]: 316–19). If, as is likely, September 24 was the traditional date for the end of safe navigation, then Paul must have sailed in a year when the Day of Atonement came later than September 24. This was true in the years 57, 59, and 62, and most scholars agree that 62 is too late, while 57 is too early. But Workman's date for the close of sailing may be too late; Vegetius (*De re Militari* 4.39) gives September 14 (Ogg, *Odyssey*, 174).

persecution and executed shortly thereafter (64 or 65). Table 6 summarizes our suggestions for the chronology of Paul's missionary career.

PAUL'S AUTHORITY AND THE SOURCES FOR HIS THOUGHT

Paul's Authority

Fundamental to Paul's ministry was his consciousness of being an apostle. Like the other apostles, he had seen the Lord (1 Cor. 9:1); and the Lord himself, not any human being, had called Paul to his apostleship (e.g., Gal. 1:1). Because Paul was an apostle by God's call, he could claim an authority equal to that of Peter, James, John, and the rest of the Twelve—those whom some of Paul's opponents had labeled "super-apostles" (2 Cor. 11:5). Paul writes from the consciousness of this apostolic authority in every one of his letters. True, Paul can sometimes distinguish between his teaching and the teaching of the Lord (e.g., 1 Cor. 7:6, 10, 12; 2 Cor. 11:17), and nowhere does Paul make it clear that he thought his letters to be inspired Scripture. Nevertheless, in differentiating his teaching from the Lord's, Paul does not suggest that his carries any less authority. Indeed, he can claim that what he writes is "the Lord's command" (1 Cor. 14:37). The distinction Paul makes is, then, between what he knows of the teaching of Jesus from his earthly ministry and what he now understands to be the Lord's demands of his people. And, while not perhaps conscious of writing inspired Scripture, Paul's apostolic stance enables him to interpret the Old Testament Scriptures with sovereign freedom and to make demands on his people that he considered to be as binding as anything in Scripture.

The Sources of Paul's Teaching

Revelation versus Tradition. Any discussion of the sources to which Paul is indebted for his teaching must reckon with Paul's claim that his gospel came "by revelation from Jesus Christ" (δι' ἀποκαλύψεως Ἰησοῦ Χριστοῦ [*di' apokalypseōs Iēsou Christou*], Gal. 1:12). This "revelation" refers to the appearance of Christ to Paul on the Damascus road (see 1:16). Paul makes clear that the gospel he had taught the Galatians came through this means, *not* through any human being. Paul's was a supernatural gospel, and we must never forget this claim. Without taking anything away from this point, however, we must recognize that Paul on other occasions indicates his indebtedness to Christians before him for his teaching. In 1 Corinthians 15:1–3, for instance, Paul asserts of the gospel that he preached to the Corinthians, "what I received [παρέλαβον (*parelabon*)] I passed on [παρέδωκα (*paredōka*)] to you." The word Paul uses here, παραλαμβάνω (*paralambanō*, "receive"), corresponds to language that the rabbis used to describe their transmission of traditions. What Paul seems to be asserting is that elements of his gospel teaching, such as the truth of Christ's death, burial, and resurrection (1 Cor. 15:3–5), were handed down to him by other people.

Some have found a contradiction in these claims of Paul, but a resolution is not hard to find. We need to distinguish between essence and form. The *essence* of the gospel, that Jesus of Nazareth was truly the Son of God, that he had been raised from the dead and that, therefore, he must have been crucified in accordance with God's plan and for God's own purposes, was, in principle, revealed to Paul in one life-changing moment on the Damascus road. And this truth carried far-reaching implications. For one thing, those Christians whom Paul had been persecuting must be right after all. For another, now that Messiah had come, the law could no longer be at the center of God's purposes. Especially was this true because the law itself pronounced a curse upon Jesus, since he had been "hung on a tree" (see Gal. 3:13 and Deut. 21:23). So Paul was led to conclude that the law could no longer be imposed as a condition of membership upon the people of God (see Galatians).[47] The *specifics* of the gospel, however, including many of the historical details, certain phraseology used to express the new truth, and early interpretations of the gospel events in light of Scripture, were passed on to Paul by those before him.[48]

Early Christian Traditions. We have no means of identifying just what early Christian traditions about Jesus were available to Paul, although we could certainly assume that many of the historical facts and theological emphases found in the speeches of Acts 1–8 were passed on to Paul by Peter and other believers during Paul's fifteen-day stay with him three years after his conversion (Gal. 1:18). First Corinthians 15:3ff., as we have seen, uses language that refers to the receiving and passing on of traditions.

Paul's letters themselves may, however, provide us with more information about the traditions he has used. Through stylistic and theological analysis, it is argued, we can identify within Paul's letters various early Christian creedal formulations, hymns, and traditional catechetical material. Unusual vocabulary, rhythmic and poetic patterns, and un-Pauline theological emphases are the criteria used to identify early Christian traditions that Paul may have quoted.[49] Philippians 2:6–11, to cite one of the most famous of these alleged quotations, has several unusual words, falls into lines of similar length that are capable of

> *We can't identify just what early Christian traditions about Jesus were available to Paul, although we could assume many were passed on to him by Peter and other believers during Paul's fifteen-day stay with him.*

---

[47]See Peter Stuhlmacher, "'The End of the Law': On the Origin and Beginnings of Pauline Theology," in *Reconciliation, Law, and Righteousness: Essays on Biblical Theology* (Philadelphia: Fortress Press, 1986), 134–54.

[48]See the discussion in, e.g., F. F. Bruce, *Tradition Old and New* (Grand Rapids: Zondervan, 1970); George Eldon Ladd, *A Theology of the New Testament*, rev. ed. Donald A. Hagner (Grand Rapids: Eerdmans, 1993), 386–94; Kim, *Origin*, 67–70.

[49]A good overview is found in Martin 2.248–75.

being arranged in a hymnic pattern, and introduces christological ideas not found in Paul elsewhere.[50]

Philippians 2:6–11 is probably, then, an early Christian hymn that Paul has quoted (though it is just possible that Paul himself is its author). It is also probable that there are other similar quotations in the Pauline letters. It would be quite natural for Paul, both to build common ground with his readers and to show his agreement with the early Christian teaching generally, to quote from such sources—just as a preacher today will quote from early Christian creeds, hymns, and the like. But we must register two cautions with respect to these sources. *First,* we must be careful not to overemphasize our ability to identify such passages. The line between quotation of a preexisting tradition and the use of traditional language in one's own composition is difficult, and often impossible, to draw. *Second,* we must be careful not to use inevitably speculative data about these traditions, such as the place of origin or theological tendency, to draw exegetical and theological conclusions. We simply do not know enough to justify such procedures.

The Earthly Jesus. Behind the early Christian tradition lay the teaching of Jesus himself. To what extent did the earthly Jesus constitute a source for Paul's teaching? Some have suggested that he contributed nothing at all. The most famous advocate of this view is Rudolf Bultmann, who interprets 2 Corinthians 5:16 to mean that Paul had no interest in the "Jesus of history."[51] Clearly this is not what the verse means. Rather, Paul is asserting that he no longer views Christ "from a worldly point of view." Still, the fact remains that Paul only rarely mentions an event (other than Jesus' death and resurrection) from Jesus' ministry and equally rarely quotes from Jesus' teaching. This does not mean, however, that Paul's teaching is not influenced by Jesus' teaching. A good case can be made, for instance, for thinking that Paul's eschatological teaching in 1 Thessalonians 4–5 and 2 Thessalonians 2 depends to some extent on the Olivet Discourse (Mark 13 par.).[52] It has long been recognized that the ethical teaching of

---

[50]The most comprehensive treatment in English is Ralph P. Martin, *Carmen Christi: Philippians 2:5–11 in Recent Interpretation and in the Setting of Early Christian Worship,* rev. ed. (Grand Rapids: Eerdmans, 1983). But see also the careful treatment in N. T. Wright, "ἁρπαγμός and the Meaning of Philippians 2:5–11," *JTS* 37 (1987): 321–52, and the doubts about the status of this text as pre-Pauline hymn by Gordon D. Fee, "Philippians 2:5–11: Hymn or Exalted Pauline Prose?" *BBR* 2 (1992): 29–46.

[51]Rudolf Bultmann, "The Significance of the Historical Jesus for the Theology of Paul," in *Faith and Understanding* (New York: Harper & Row, 1969), 241. See also, though in much less radical form, Graham Stanton, *Jesus of Nazareth in New Testament Preaching,* SNTSMS 27 (Cambridge: Cambridge University Press, 1974).

[52]See David Wenham, *The Rediscovery of Jesus' Eschatological Discourse,* in *GP* 4.372–73; idem, "Paul's Use of the Jesus Tradition: Three Samples," in *GP* 5:7–37.

Romans 12 has many similarities to the Sermon on the Mount.[53] Paul, then, certainly knew and used more of the teaching of Jesus than a mere count of his quotations suggests.[54] In fact, David Wenham's monograph-length study drew the conclusion (perhaps a bit over-stated) that "there is massive evidence of Pauline knowledge of Jesus traditions."[55] More important, essential aspects of Paul's theology, even if they cannot be demonstrated to be dependent on Jesus' teaching, are compatible with it.[56]

The Old Testament. Paul was deeply indebted to the Old Testament in the formulation of his teaching, as is revealed by the more than ninety quotations from the Old Testament in his letters.[57] Perhaps even more important, however, are the many allusions to the Old Testament—places where Paul uses Old Testament language without clearly quoting—and the inestimable degree to which the Old Testament has formed Paul's conceptual world. Paul, of course, uses the Old Testament selectively and interprets it in a definite context, reading it through the lens of Jesus' fulfillment of "the Law and the Prophets."

The Greek World. Nineteenth-century scholars frequently read Paul against the background of their own considerable knowledge of classical Greek literature and philosophy. Paul's indebtedness to the Greek world in which he grew up and in which he worked was assumed. Early in the twentieth century, the focus was narrowed, as the history-of-religions school stressed Paul's dependence on the Hellenistic mystery religions. These religions, which were very popular in Paul's day, stressed one's ability to be joined in a mystic relationship with a deity, secret mystery rites, and frequently a religious enthusiasm or ecstasy. Scholars such as Richard Reitzenstein, Wilhelm Bousset, and Rudolf Bultmann found many of these features in the letters of Paul and concluded that, to varying degrees, Paul had cast his teaching of Christ into the categories

---

[53]See esp. Michael Thompson, *Clothed with Christ: The Example and Teaching of Jesus in Romans 12.1–15.13*, JSNTSup 59 (Sheffield: Sheffield Academic Press, 1991).

[54]Arnold Resch counts 1,158 allusions to Jesus' teaching in Paul (*Der Paulinismus und die Logia Jesu*, TU 27 [Leipzig: Akademie, 1904]). The number is greatly exaggerated but helps put the matter in perspective.

[55]David Wenham, *Paul: Follower of Jesus or Founder of Christianity?* (Grand Rapids: Eerdmans, 1995), 381.

[56]See, e.g., F. F. Bruce, *Jesus and Paul* (Grand Rapids: Baker, 1974), 55–67.

[57]The exact number depends on how "quotation" is defined. E. Earle Ellis gives a figure of 93 (*Paul's Use of the Old Testament*, reprint ed. [Grand Rapids: Baker, 1981], 11); Christopher Stanley, 74 (not including the Pastorals and Ephesians) (*Paul and the Language of Scripture: Citation Technique in the Pauline Epistles and Contemporary Literature*, SNTSMS 69 [Cambridge: Cambridge University Press, 1992]).

provided by these religions.[58] In its most extreme form, Paul was thought to have drastically transformed the simple, ethically oriented message of Jesus into a speculative and mystical religion.

Wherever he was raised (see above), Paul must have known the Greek world well, and it is to be expected that he would use the language of that world to express the significance of Christ and even borrow its concepts where they could help illuminate aspects of the gospel.[59] But it is unlikely that we should consider the Greek world a source for Paul's teaching in the strict sense. It sometimes provided the clothing, but rarely, if ever, the body of teaching that was clothed. Particularly unlikely is the hypothesis that Paul borrowed from the mystery religions.[60] The parallels are simply not very close, and every one of the alleged cases of borrowing can be explained more satisfactorily in other terms.[61]

Judaism. In reaction against the tendency to interpret Paul against the Greek or Hellenistic world, many scholars have insisted that Paul's world was a Jewish one and that Judaism must have exerted the most influence on his teaching. C. G. Montefiore suggests that the Hellenistic Judaism of Paul's childhood in Tarsus was a key factor.[62] (Even if Paul was not raised in Tarsus, he spent most of his adult life in the Diaspora.) Albert Schweitzer thinks that apocalyptic Judaism is the key to Paul's teaching,[63] while W. D. Davies stresses rabbinic Judaism and Pharisaism.[64] Contemporary scholars are less willing than before to make clear-cut distinctions between, say, Palestinian Judaism and Hellenistic Judaism, or between apocalyptic Judaism and Pharisaic Judaism. Without justifying such distinctions when they are made absolute, we may say that it is now generally agreed that Paul's own thought world was decisively formed by

---

[58]The most famous name in this history-of-religions school is Richard Reitzenstein (*Hellenistic Mystery Religions: Their Basic Ideas and Significance* [ET Pittsburgh: Pickwick, 1978]; the final edition of the German original is dated 1927). See also Wilhelm Bousset, *Kyrios Christos*, reprint ed. (Nashville: Abingdon, 1970); Rudolf Bultmann (e.g., *Theology of the New Testament* [New York: Charles Scribner's Sons, 1951–55], 1.187–352).

[59]This point is strongly emphasized in T. Engberg-Pedersen, ed., *Paul in his Hellenistic Context* (Minneapolis: Fortress Press, 1995); see also Roetzel, *Paul: A Jew on the Marins*, 11–19.

[60]A classic on this point is J. Gresham Machen, *The Origin of Paul's Religion* (London: Hodder & Stoughton, 1921). See also H. A. A. Kennedy, *St. Paul and the Mystery Religions* (London: Hodder & Stoughton, 1913).

[61]To cite only one example, see the study of Romans 6 by Günter Wagner, *Pauline Baptism and the Pagan Mysteries* (Edinburgh: Oliver & Boyd, 1967).

[62]C. G. Montefiore, *Judaism and St. Paul* (London: Goschen, 1914).

[63]Albert Schweitzer, *The Mysticism of Paul the Apostle* (New York: H. Holt, 1931).

[64]W. D. Davies, *Paul and Rabbinic Judaism*, 4th ed. (Philadelphia: Fortress Press, 1980).

his Jewish upbringing. Paul's own claim to be a "Hebrew of the Hebrews" and a Pharisee must be allowed decisive weight on this matter. Paul's basic concepts are drawn, as we have seen, from the Old Testament, and he had learned the Old Testament in the context of the Judaism of his day. Paul's conversion, however, forced upon him a thoroughgoing reappraisal of his beliefs; the debt his teaching undoubtedly has to Judaism is the result of a deliberate choice and not of an unconscious carrying over of his Judaism into his new faith. But the complexity and significance of Paul's debt to his Jewish background require a separate discussion.

PAUL AND JUDAISM

First-century Judaism played a critical role in the development of Paul's theology. Not only, as we have seen, was Paul raised and educated in a strict Jewish environment, but also his theology was decisively shaped by his interaction with various Jewish and Jewish-Christian points of view. The Jewish matrix is most obvious in Galatians and Romans; but it is present in varying degrees in all the letters. Determining just what the Judaism of Paul's day looked like is therefore quite significant for any accurate interpretation of Paul and his teaching. Paul's theology might be compared to an ellipse that is traced around the two foci of Paul's own Christian convictions, acquired by revelation from God, and the Judaism within which and against which he worked out and applied that revelation. Change either of the foci, and the shape of the ellipse changes as well.

The "New Perspective"

The Protestant Reformers of the sixteenth century have decisively influenced the traditional understanding of the focal point of Paul's Judaism. Reacting to certain legalistic elements in the salvation teaching of the Roman Catholic Church of their day, Luther, Calvin, and others tended to find the same kind of legalism in the Judaism that Paul opposed in letters like Galatians. The Jews of Paul's day, the Reformers believed, held to a form of "works-righteousness": a person gained right standing with God by performing "the works of the law," meritorious deeds of obedience to the law that compelled God's favor and blessing. Against this legalism, Paul proclaimed that justification before God could be attained only by faith in the completed work of Christ, a faith that excluded, by its very nature, any deeds of obedience of any kind. Putting their Roman Catholic opponents in the guise of the Jews of Paul's day, the Reformers then took on the mantle of Paul, proclaiming that justification is *sola fide* and *sola gratia*.

This sketch of the Reformation situation is, of course, extremely simplified. There were, in fact, many different Roman Catholic perspectives, as there were many different nuances in the Reformers' viewpoints—especially when we

Against Jewish legalism, Paul proclaimed that justification before God could be attained only by faith in the completed work of Christ. The Reformers took on the mantle of Paul, proclaiming that justification is sola fide *and* sola gratia.

consider the so-called Radical Reformation. But the overview is sufficient for our purposes, because the general Reformation tendency to view the first-century Judaism which Jesus criticized and with which Paul interacted as legalistic became deeply embedded in New Testament scholarship of all varieties—including much traditional Roman Catholic scholarship.[65] Important and influential New Testament "background" books, such as the Strack-Billerbeck *Kommentar,* with its massive collection of Jewish material, lent a sense of legitimacy to this view of Jewish theology. Isolated voices of protest that Judaism was not being portrayed fairly were occasionally heard, but they were drowned out by the chorus of traditional scholarship.

But in 1977 a book was published that was destined to change the landscape dramatically. E. P. Sanders' *Paul and Palestinian Judaism* marks a watershed in interpretations of Judaism as a backdrop for Paul's theology.[66] What Sanders argued (at least in the main) was not new, but the time was apparently ripe for a sea change in the way New Testament scholars viewed first-century Judaism. Sanders' basic proposal found ready acceptance and has in many quarters, over the course of the last twenty-five years, attained the status of an assumed result of scholarship. Just what did Sanders argue?

Essentially, Sanders claims that the traditional view of first-century Judaism as a legalistic religion is wrong. After a study of Jewish sources likely to give us evidence about first-century Jewish beliefs, Sanders concludes that these sources almost unanimously portray a view of soteriology that he dubs "covenantal nomism." Foundational to the Jewish view of salvation is the covenant that God entered into with the people Israel. God has chosen Israel, and Jews in Paul's day believed that that original gracious choice was the basis for their salvation. Viewed from this perspective, Jews did not have to do the law to be saved; they were already saved. They obeyed the law, rather, to maintain their covenantal status. As Sanders put it, Jews did not do the law to "get in" (which would be legalism) but to "stay in" ("nomism").

What does this new view of Judaism have to do with Paul? Sanders' original study focused mainly on "Palestinian Judaism" but did have a section on Paul as well. Among other points, Sanders argued that Paul rejected covenantal nomism because of his "exclusivist soteriology": since salvation was, by definition, to be found in Christ alone, the law and its underlying covenant could not be a means of salvation. Most scholars, even those who agreed with Sanders' portrayal of first-century Judaism, were not satisfied with this response. They sought to discover in Paul theological reasons why Paul might have rejected the

---

[65]The tendency in modern scholarship to title this view "Lutheran Orthodoxy" is therefore singularly inapt.

[66]E. P. Sanders, *Paul and Palestinian Judaism: A Comparison of Patterns of Religion* (Philadelphia: Fortress Press, 1977).

covenantal nomism of his heritage. Various suggestions were offered. The most radical of these is that Paul did not reject his heritage at all. He still believed that Jews could find salvation through their covenant. It was only Gentiles who needed Christ for salvation. When Paul criticizes a Jewish viewpoint in his letters, he is not criticizing covenantal nomism at all, but only those Jews who opposed the offering of the gospel to the Gentiles.[67] But the most satisfying and certainly most popular suggestion was the one offered by James D. G. Dunn and followed up by a host of scholars.

Dunn was the first to use the language of "new perspective" to describe the impact of Sanders' view of Judaism on Pauline studies, and the name has stuck as a way of describing the movement as a whole.[68] What is attractive about Dunn's proposal is that it offers a comprehensive interpretation of Paul that fits neatly with the covenantal nomism that so many scholars are now persuaded was the actual Judaism with which Paul wrestled. Essentially, Dunn claims that what Paul opposes is the tendency of the Jews to confine salvation to their own nation.[69] It is ethnic exclusivism, not personal legalism, that Paul finds wrong with Judaism. The difference between Dunn's view and the traditional interpretation of Paul can perhaps be seen most clearly in their conflicting interpretations of texts such as Romans 3:20: "no one will be declared righteous in his sight by works of the law" (our own translation; cf. also Rom. 3:28 and Gal. 2:16; 3:2, 5, 10). The Reformers saw in this text an attack on Jewish works-righteousness: Jews were claiming that a person had to do "works" to be justified, and Paul was denying the possibility that this could ever happen. But according to Sanders' view of Judaism, no Jews argued such a position. So what is Paul opposing? Jewish ethnic exclusivism, responds Dunn. The phrase "works of the law" cannot be reduced to the simple "works," as the Reformers did. The "law" in the phrase is the Jewish Torah; and what Paul signifies by the phrase is Torah-faithfulness—and Torah-faithfulness understood as a means of setting Jews off from all other people. For the phrase has to be understood against the background of Jewish concern to preserve their God-given distinctiveness in the midst of Gentile dominance and even hostility. Faced with occupation by foreign

---

[67]Key exponents of this view are Lloyd Gaston ("Israel's Misstep in the Eyes of Paul," in *The Romans Debate*, ed. Karl P. Donfried, rev. ed. [Peabody: Hendrickson, 1991], 309–26) and John G. Gager, *Reinventing Paul* (New York: Oxford University Press, 2000). For a critique, see Frank Thielman, *From Plight to Solution: A Jewish Framework for Understanding Paul's View of the Law in Galatians and Romans*, NovT-Sup 61 (Leiden: Brill, 1989), 123–33.

[68]"The New Perspective on Paul," *BJRL* 65 (1983): 95–122; reprinted in *Jesus, Paul and the Law: Studies in Mark and Galatians* (Louisville: Westminster John Knox, 1990), 183–214.

[69]The best and one of the more recent places to find Dunn's argument is in his *The Theology of Paul the Apostle* (Grand Rapids: Eerdmans, 1998), esp. 334–89.

powers, the dispersion, and persecution, Jews in the centuries before Christ emphasized the practice of the law—and especially distinctive practices such as circumcision, Sabbath, and food laws—as a way of maintaining their unique identity and status as the people of God. (It is no accident, therefore, that these distinctive practices are just those singled out for debate in Galatians.) This context informs Paul's use of the phrase "works of the law" and his attacks on the law generally. The Jewish claim Paul opposes in Romans 3:20 and other such verses is not, then, that a person can be justified by what he or she does ("works"), but the typically Jewish claim that a person is justified by maintenance of covenant status through adherence to Torah.

What Dunn and the many others who have followed the general path he has laid out offer is, essentially, a new way of reading Paul—or at least some central elements of his theology. Of course, scholars who might generally be categorized as favoring the "new perspective" differ considerably on their interpretations of specific texts and theological issues. Generalization, while sometimes necessary, should be seen for what it is—an overview of tendencies that might not describe any particular scholar. Nevertheless, several tendencies mark the "new perspective on Paul."[70] *First,* Paul's theology is read against the background of the "story" of salvation history. Richard Hays and N. T. Wright are two of the foremost advocates of this new way of reading Paul.[71] The effect is to take many of the theological categories that have traditionally been interpreted in terms of individual experience and restrict them to the corporate experience of Israel and the people of God.[72] *Second,* and partly as a result of the first overarching approach, the foundational Reformation contrast between "faith" and "works" as two opposed means of being saved is reduced or, in some more radical proposals, eliminated. The central contrast Paul is dealing with is not anthropological—how a human being gets saved—but salvation-historical—

---

[70]Perhaps the most accessible treatment from a key figure in the movement is N. T. Wright, *What Saint Paul Really Said* (Grand Rapids: Eerdmans, 1997).

[71]See esp. Hays's monograph on Galatians (*The Faith of Jesus Christ: The Narrative Substructure of Galatians 3:1–4:11,* rev. ed. [Grand Rapids: Eerdmans, 2001]); several essays in Wright's *The Climax of the Covenant* (Minneapolis: Fortress Press, 1993); his more popular *What Saint Paul Really Said;* and, for a more programmatic look at his overall approach to New Testament theology, his Christian Origins and the Question of God series (*The New Testament and the People of God* [Minneapolis: Fortress Press, 1992]; *Jesus and the Victory of God* [Minneapolis: Fortress Press, 1996]). See also the series of essays evaluating Wright's approach in *Jesus and the Restoration of Israel,* ed. Carey C. Newman (Downers Grove: IVP, 1999).

[72]The move toward a more "corporate" reading of Paul's basic theological categories also reflects the famous criticism of Krister Stendahl to the effect that traditional readings of Paul imposed on him modern Western theories of individuality ("The Apostle Paul and the Introspective Conscience of the West," *HTR* 56 [1963]: 199–215).

how Gentiles in the new era of salvation can be added to the people of God. Third, in a related move, Paul's teaching on justification is shifted from a vertical focus—the human being *coram deo*, "before God"—to more of a horizontal one—Gentiles as equal partners with Jews within God's people. Some new perspectivists, therefore, noting the Old Testament background for "righteousness" language generally, insist that to be "justified" in Paul means to become a member of the people of God.[73] At the same time, justification is pushed out of the center of Paul's thought by the insistence that Paul only developed the doctrine in debate with Judaizers once he was well into his apostolic career.[74] In these ways, the "new perspective"—at least in certain of its manifestations—tends to offer a serious and potentially damaging challenge to a hallmark of Reformation theology: justification before God by faith alone, by grace alone.

Response to the New Perspective

As we have seen, covenantal nomism and the reinterpretation of Paul's theology that ensued have quickly become the dominant force in academic studies—so much so that observers speak of a "paradigm shift" in Pauline interpretation. Nevertheless, ever since the publication of Sanders' *Paul and Palestinian Judaism*, isolated voices have been raised in protest against one or more elements of the new paradigm. And in recent years, these voices have swelled to a chorus. As Charles H. Talbert has put it, "As many Pauline scholars celebrate the paradigm shift associated with Sanders' work, another shift of equal import seems to be occurring."[75] In the following sections, we want to explain why there might be reason to raise questions about the new perspective on Paul. Before detailing some of those questions, however, it is important to note the important contributions of the movement in general.

While we will note some criticisms of Sanders below, his interpretation did bring some necessary corrective to a skewed view of Judaism in traditional scholarship. For instance, the idea of a "treasury of merits"—merit accumulated by Jewish "super-saints" and available for other Jews to draw from—does not appear to have been a first-century teaching. Jews in Paul's day were certainly less legalistic than many traditional portrayals have suggested. For there is a tendency in these portrayals to miss what Sanders highlighted: the importance of the covenant as a foundation for Jewish life and thought. Jews thought of themselves as a special people because God had chosen them. Grace, the manner in which God first elected Israel, is therefore very much present in Judaism. Many Jews undoubtedly viewed their obedience to the law within this covenant context. They did not claim any special merit for their

> The "new perspective"—at least in some ways—tends to offer a serious and potentially damaging challenge to a hallmark of Reformation theology: justification before God by faith alone, by grace alone.

---

[73]A good overview of this approach is Richard B. Hays in *ABD* 3.1130–33.

[74]In this, the new perspective follows in the footsteps of Wrede and Schweitzer.

[75]Charles H. Talbert, "Paul, Judaism, and the Revisionists," *CBQ* 63 (2001): 4.

obedience and saw it, as Sanders has insisted, as a means of maintaining their status within God's people. At the same time, the general tendency of the new perspective as a whole to redirect our attention to the Jewish matrix of Paul's thought and teaching is a welcome one. Traditional studies of Paul—and this was certainly true of the Reformers—have sometimes neglected the degree to which he was focused on issues arising from the shift of ages that occurred with the coming of Christ. What status did Torah have in the new age? On what basis could Gentiles be admitted into the people of God? What did the enfranchisement of the Gentiles mean for God's promises to Israel? These were questions of absolutely basic importance in the first-century church, and Paul, as God's "point man" in bringing the gospel to Gentiles, was necessarily in the forefront of those who sought answers to these questions. There is no doubt but that traditional interpretations of Paul have focused on questions of anthropology at the expense of salvation-history. Nevertheless, Sanders' interpretation of Judaism and the "new perspective" is an over-reaction in the other direction. In the following paragraphs, we raise some questions with the new paradigm, beginning with covenant nomism and then moving on to the new perspective.

As a comprehensive explanation of first-century Judaism, Sanders' "covenantal nomism" requires qualification. *First,* the claim that covenantal nomism was the only soteriological paradigm within first-century Judaism must be questioned. Recent study is revealing the complexities of Second Temple Judaism and the divergent theological viewpoints and perspectives found in the material.[76] Sanders himself admitted that the late-first-century Jewish apocalyptic book *4 Ezra* did not fit the covenantal nomism paradigm; and it is likely that the book offers a viewpoint that existed in the time of Paul. Perhaps more serious is Sanders' methodology. He tends to claim that passages in Jewish literature that might appear to be legalistic are actually not because either (a) the larger structure of covenant and election must be assumed; or (b) the passages are homiletical in nature. But, to take the latter point first, homiletical passages often provide an important clue to how theology really is understood. To take a contemporary parallel: Which would provide a more accurate reading of the theology of a given pastor—his or her doctrinal statement or a transcript of one of his or her sermons? One could claim that the doctrinal statement, a carefully thought out document, should have precedence. But one could also argue that the sermon expresses more accurately what the preacher *really* believes. At any rate, it is not legitimate to exclude homiletical passages from consideration. Perhaps, however—turning now to the former point—Sanders thinks that homiletical passages should be excluded because they do not, by their very nature, specifically include the theology that lies behind the homily. The point is, in

---

[76]See especially *Justification and Variegated Nomism,* vol. 1.

general, well-taken. Certain theological truths can be so taken for granted that we feel no need to make reference to them. But if a homiletical passage assumes a theology that runs counter to the alleged informing theology, questions must be raised about whether that informing theology is, in practice, being honored. The rabbinic writings furnish a good example. Sanders notes many passages that may be taken, at face value, to teach that salvation is a matter of recompense: Jews earn salvation by doing the law. But he claims that these texts must be read in light of the all-embracing theory of election through the covenant. However, an important study of these texts now argues that, in fact, the two strands of soteriological teaching—salvation by election and salvation by "recompense"—run side by side in rabbinic literature as two alternative schemes.[77] And other scholars have argued that several Jewish writings from the New Testament period lack the undergirding covenantal structure that Sanders claims to be omnipresent.[78]

Another reason for thinking that, alongside covenant nomism, there existed in first-century Judaism a strand of legalism is the evidence from an important set of primary documents about first-century Judaism: the New Testament. As we have seen above, James Dunn and a number of other scholars have argued for reinterpretations of major Pauline letters such as Galatians and Romans that would remove any trace of accusation of Jewish legalism. Whether these attempts are successful is another matter. But even if the evidence from those books remains in doubt, almost all scholars admit that some of the New Testament books do teach or imply that some Jews based their salvation on the law. These books are often excluded from the process of reconstructing first-century Judaism because they are, in effect, propagandistic literature from an opposing viewpoint. And it must be granted that, as a general methodology, one should not determine the opinions of a group by looking at the way that group is portrayed by opponents. (Imagine the caricature that would result if we used Democratic campaign ads to reconstruct the Republican party platform!) But the New Testament writers are not exactly opponents of the Jews; as recent scholarship rightly emphasizes, New Testament writers and other first-century Jews carried on an extensive dialogue from within Judaism about just who had the right to carry the mantle of successors to the Old Testament faith. New

---

[77] Friedrich Avemarie, *Tora und Leben: Untersuchungen zur Heilsbedeutung der Tora in der frühenrabbinischen Literatur,* TSAJ 55 (Tübingen: Mohr-Siebeck, 1996); idem, "Erwählung und Vergeltung: Zur optionalen Struktur rabbinischer Soteriologie," *NTS* 45 (1999): 108–26. And see also, on a specific mishnaic text, Charles L. Quarles, "The Soteriology of R. Akiba and E. P. Sanders' *Paul and Palestinian Judaism,*" *NTS* 42 (1996): 185–95. Note also Graham N. Stanton, "The Law of Moses and the Law of Christ," in *Paul and the Mosaic Law,* ed. James D. G. Dunn (Grand Rapids: Eerdmans, 2000 [1996]), 105–6.

[78] E.g., Talbert, "Paul, Judaism and the Revisionists," 7–10.

Testament books must be considered when we seek to understand first-century Judaism—especially, of course, for those, like us, who place a high regard on the accuracy of the New Testament documents.

One final point along these lines might be made. All scholars acknowledge that first-century Judaism placed great emphasis on obedience to the law. Even if all our extant theological sources taught covenant nomism (which we question), one might still find significant pockets of legalism among the "Jews on the street." Any faith that emphasizes obedience, as Judaism undoubtedly did, is likely to produce some adherents who, perhaps through misunderstanding or lack of education, turn their obedience into a meritorious service which they think God must reward. Christianity, with considerable less emphasis on law, certainly produces such adherents; is it not likely that, as the New Testament suggests, first-century Judaism did also?

Our *second* general qualification of covenant nomism has to do with the first term in this description: the covenant. Sanders and those who have followed him base their interpretation of first-century Jewish soteriology on the assumption that God's covenant with Israel was the starting point for Jewish obedience to the law. This assumption runs into problems, however, when we begin to consider the many Jewish sectarian groups that flourished at this time. The Qumran covenanters, for instance, claimed to represent true Israel, and anathematized "mainline" Judaism. Clearly God's covenant with Israel—entered into, of course, with all of Israel—could not be the differentiating factor. Both the Qumran covenanters and, for instance, the Pharisees, started out at precisely the same point with respect to the covenant. What, then, led the Qumran covenanters to claim that they were "in" and the Pharisees were "out"? Adherence to the community through acceptance of its teaching and practices. In effect, therefore, for many Jewish groups in Paul's day, national election had been replaced by a form of individual election. And one's elect status was determined on the basis of adherence to the Torah as interpreted and practiced by the particular community. For such groups, "getting in" is not simply a matter of God's grace revealed in the covenant. More is involved, and at least some of that "more" appears to involve human works.[79] As I. Howard Marshall puts it, "For them and for other groups the problem was not one of 'staying in' the covenant people but of regaining entry by fulfilling the appropriate conditions laid down by the particular group."[80]

---

[79] Two of the key studies here are Mark Adam Elliott, *The Survivors of Israel: A Reconsideration of the Theology of Pre-Christian Judaism* (Grand Rapids: Eerdmans, 2000); and Ellen Juhl Christiansen, *The Covenant in Judaism and Paul,* AGJU 27 (Leiden: Brill, 1995).

[80] Marshall, "Salvation, Grace and Works in the Later Writings in the Pauline Corpus," *NTS* 42 (1996): 357 (he is referring especially to Mark Elliott's *Survivors of Israel*).

Third, and perhaps most important, is the increasingly widespread recognition that, on any reading of the data, first-century Judaism was synergistic.[81] Few scholars would deny that first-century Judaism believed that the grace of God was basic to salvation. But on Sanders' own showing, it also believed that, if one "got in" by grace, one "stayed in" by obedience. What mattered on the day of judgment, therefore—and what ultimately separated Jew from Jew—was the quality and consistency of obedience to the law. Particularly was this the case because the election through which grace was operative was, of course, a corporate election that took place a long time in the past. Israel as a nation was indeed chosen by God; but participation in that nation and its election were very much a matter of individual decision.[82] In practice, then, Jews were saved through both grace and works. And it is just this synergism that Paul seems to be attacking in a number of passages. As one of the conclusions in the most comprehensive review of covenantal nomism to date has it, "The category of covenantal nomism cannot itself accomplish what Sanders wants it to accomplish, viz. serve as an explanatory bulwark against all suggestions that some of this literature embraces works-righteousness and merit theology, precisely because covenantal nomism embraces the same phenomena."[83]

Assessments of first-century Judaism in the wake of Sanders will continue for some time. But after an initial period of almost universal acceptance, Sanders' covenantal nomism is entering a period of serious reassessment. Seyoon Kim accurately summarizes the situation:

> The pendulum which had swung too far toward the side of denying any element of works-righteousness in Second Temple Judaism has begun to swing back. When it eventually finds its equilibrium we may see that neither the traditional view of Judaism as a religion of pure works-righteousness nor the New Perspective that totally denies any element of works-righteousness in Judaism is right, but that Judaism was a covenantal nomism with an element of works-righteousness.[84]

---

[81]See, e.g., Robert H. Gundry, "Grace, Works, and Staying Saved: *Bib* 60 (1985): 19–20, 35–36; Stephen Westerholm, *Israel's Law and the Church's Faith* (Grand Rapids: Eerdmans, 1988), 143–50; Mark Seifrid, *Justification by Faith: The Origin and Development of a Central Pauline Theme,* NovTSup 68 (Leiden: Brill, 1992), 56–57, 71–81; Timo Laato, *Paulus und das Judentum: Anthropologische Erwägungen* (Åbo: Åbo Academy, 1991), 73–75, 195–211; Timo Eskola, *Theodicy and Predestination in Pauline Soteriology,* WUNT 100 (Tübingen: Mohr-Siebeck, 1998), 27–94; Lauri Thurén, *De-rhetorizing Paul: A Dynamic Perspective on Pauline Theology and the Law,* WUNT 124 (Tübingen: Mohr-Siebeck, 2000), 146–48.

[82]See Philip S. Alexander, "Torah and Salvation in Tannaitic Literature," in *Justification and Variegated Nomism,* 1:261–301.

[83]*Justification and Variegated Nomism,* 2:545.

[84]Seyoon Kim, *Paul and the New Perspective: Second Thoughts on the Origin of Paul's Gospel* (Grand Rapids: Eerdmans, 2002), 83–84.

The qualifications of Sanders' covenantal nomism that we have suggested remove one of the reasons for the "new perspective" on Paul. There were, we have suggested, Jews holding to a form of legalism, whose views Paul may well have been directly or indirectly criticizing in his letters. But, of course, removing one of the motivations for the new perspective does not invalidate it. Ultimately, the new perspective can only be supported or rejected on the basis of one issue: Does it offer a better interpretation of the key texts than competing schools of thought? This is a question that cannot even begin to be answered within the scope of a volume like this one. But we might respond briefly to two of the characteristic planks in the new perspective platform that we noted earlier.

First, the faith vs. "works of the law" antithesis. Considerable study has been devoted to the short phrase "works of the law," which appears only eight times in the Pauline letters and then only in Galatians and Romans, for interpretations of the phrase set the agenda for one's general direction of interpretation. As we have noted, Dunn and other advocates of the new perspective think the phrase functions as a shorthand for adherence to the law understood in its function of elevating Jews and separating Gentiles. Denying that a person can be justified through "works of the law," then, is denying that a person can be justified through the Jewish Torah covenant. Dunn then argues that this same general issue infuses virtually all of Paul's references to the law and to "works" in Galatians and Romans. But such an approach has the tail wagging the dog. Despite the citation of texts from the Dead Sea Scrolls, Dunn has not made out a case for giving the phrase this particular nuance. Rather than taking "works" in passages such as Romans 4, 9, and 11 to be an abbreviation for "works of the law," we should rather see "works of the law" as a subset of the more general "works." Paul makes reference to Jewish deeds in obedience to the Torah because it was especially claims about this form of "human works" that Paul had to deal with in the situations he addressed. But it is indicative of the larger issues he ultimately talks about in these texts that he moves in the same context to address the larger question of "faith vs. works" and "grace vs. merit" (see esp. Rom. 4:4–5; 11:5–7).[85] Moving in the

---

[85]Some recent treatments favoring the traditional view are Mark A. Seifrid, "Blind Alleys in the Controversy over the Paul of History," *TynB* 45 (1994): 77–85; Thomas R. Schreiner, "'Works of Law' in Paul," *NovT* 32 (1991): 217–44; Douglas J. Moo, *The Epistle to the Romans,* NICNT (Grand Rapids: Eerdmans, 1996), 206–10; idem, "'Law, "Works of the Law 'and Legalism in Paul," *WTJ* 45 (1983): 73–100; Stanton, "The Law of Moses," 183–85; Kim, *Paul and the New Perspective,* 57–75; J. C. de Roo, "The Concept of 'Works of the Law' in Jewish-Christian Literature," in *Christian-Jewish Relations through the Centuries,* ed. S. E. Porter and B. W. R. Pearson, JSNTSup 192 (Sheffield: Sheffield Academic Press, 2000), 116–47; R. Barry Matlock, "Sins of the Flesh and Suspicious Minds: Dunn's New Theology of Paul," *JSNT* 72 (1998): 79–80; Stephen Westerholm, *Perspectives Old and New on Paul: The "Lutheran" Paul and His Critics* (Grand Rapids: Eerdmans, 2004), esp. 297–340.

same direction is the treatment of "works" in the later Pauline epistles.[86] Ultimately, therefore, while the Reformers may have missed some of the salvation-historical nuances and implications of Paul's argument, they were right to discern in Paul a key antithesis between human doing and human believing as the means of accessing God's salvation.

Second, the attempt to redefine justification in terms of covenant identity and entrance into the people of God suffers from a similar problem: reversing what is primary and what is secondary. The need to interpret Paul's justification language against the background of the Old Testament and Judaism is clear. But the tendency in some modern scholarship is to restrict Paul's use of that language to the parameters established by that material. At the same time, modern scholarship has tended to downplay elements of Old Testament righteousness language that transcend the category of covenant.[87] Paul takes the language from the Old Testament, but he moves it in a different direction by universalizing the human condition. Jews themselves, in the light of God's revelation in Christ, can no longer claim to be "right" with God; they are "out" and need to get in, just as much as do Gentiles (see, e.g., Rom. 1:16–17; 3:22–24). With Christ, God is re-creating the people of God, identifying those who belong to his people on the basis of their faith. Justification language therefore alludes first of all to the human being before God. To be justified is primarily to be put in right relationship with God. The consequence of that justifying action is, of course, that the person enters into the people of God. But to make the latter primary is to miss the emphasis in Paul's own writings on the primacy of the question of the sinful human being faced with a wrathful God.[88] Luther's own experience led him to find in this issue the heart of Paul's gospel. And he was right to do so. Luther, of course, also made justification by faith the center of Pauline and New Testament theology. Here we may not agree with him; while justification by faith is a critical doctrine for Paul, guarding the grace and power of the gospel from any kind of legalistic or syncretistic modification, it probably cannot be elevated to the status of the central New Testament or even Pauline doctrine. But he was right to single out the doctrine as a critical one for Paul; and recent scholarship has tended to emphasize that, contrary to advocates of the new perspective, justification by faith was an important component of Paul's gospel from the beginning.[89]

---

[86]Marshall, "Salvation, Grace and Works," 339–58.

[87]See, e.g., Mark A. Seifrid, "Righteousness Language in the Hebrew Scriptures and Early Judaism," in *Justification and Variegated Nomism*, 1:415–42.

[88]See esp. Mark Seifrid, *Christ, Our Righteousness: Paul's Theology of Justification*, NSBT (Downers Grove: IVP, 2000).

[89]See, e.g., Martin Hengel and Anna Maria Schwemer, *Paul between Damascus and Antioch: The Unknown Years* (Louisville: Westminster/John Knox, 1997), 268–311; Kim, *Paul and the New Perspective*, 53–57, 85–100.

BIBLIOGRAPHY

Philip S. **Alexander**, "Torah and Salvation in Tannaitic Literature," in *Justification and Variegated Nomism*, vol. 1: *The Complexities of Second Temple Judaism*, ed. D. A. Carson, Peter T. O'Brien, and Mark A. Seifrid, WUNT 140 (Tübingen: Mohr-Siebeck/Grand Rapids: Baker, 2001), 261–301 ▪R. Dean **Anderson** Jr., *Ancient Rhetorical Theory and Paul* (The Hague: Kok Pharos, 1996) ▪W. P. **Armstrong** and J. **Finegan**, "Chronology of the New Testament," in *ISBE* 1.689–90 ▪Friedrich **Avemarie**, "Erwählung und Vergeltung: Zur optionalen Strucktur rabbinischer Soteriologie," *NTS* 45 (1999): 108–26 ▪idem, *Tora und Leben: Untersuchungen zur Heilsbedeutung der Tora in der frühenrabbinischen Literatur*, TSAJ 55 (Tübingen: Mohr-Siebeck, 1996) ▪Barry J. **Beitzel**, *The Moody Atlas of Bible Lands* (Chicago: Moody, 1985) ▪Wilhelm **Bousset**, *Kyrios Christos*, reprint ed. (Nashville: Abingdon, 1970) ▪F. F. **Bruce**, *Jesus and Paul* (Grand Rapids: Baker, 1974) ▪idem, *New Testament History*, 2nd ed. (Garden City: Doubleday, 1971) ▪idem, *Paul: Apostle of the Heart Set Free* (Grand Rapids: Eerdmans, 1977) ▪idem, "Paul the Apostle," in *ISBE* 3.706 ▪idem, *Tradition Old and New* (Grand Rapids: Zondervan, 1970) ▪Charles **Buck** and Greer **Taylor**, *Saint Paul: A Study of the Development of His Thought* (New York: Charles Scribner's Sons, 1969) ▪Rudolf **Bultmann**, "The Significance of the Historical Jesus for the Theology of Paul," in *Faith and Understanding* (New York: Harper & Row, 1969) ▪idem, *Theology of the New Testament*, 2 vols. (New York: Charles Scribner's Sons, 1951–55) ▪G. B. **Caird**, "Chronology of the New Testament," in *IDB* 1.604–5 ▪T. H. **Campbell**, "Paul's 'Missionary Journeys' as Reflected in His Letters," *JBL* 74 (1955): 80–87 ▪D. A. **Carson**, "Pseudonymity and Pseudepigraphy," in *Dictionary of New Testament Background*, ed. Craig A. Evans and Stanley E. Porter (Downers Grove: IVP, 2000), 856–65 ▪D. A. **Carson**, Peter T. **O'Brien**, and Mark A. **Seifrid**, eds., *Justification and Variegated Nomism*, vol. 1: *The Complexities of Second Temple Judaism*, WUNT 140 (Tübingen: Mohr-Siebeck/Grand Rapids: Baker, 2001); vol. 2: *The Paradoxes of Paul* (Tübingen: Mohr-Siebeck/Grand Rapids: Baker, 2004) ▪Ellen Juhl **Christiansen**, *The Covenant in Judaism and Paul*, AGJU 27 (Leiden: Brill, 1995) ▪Andrew **Das**, *Paul and the Jews* (Peabody: Hendrickson, 2003) ▪W. D. **Davies**, *Paul and Rabbinic Judaism*, 4th ed. (Philadelphia: Fortress Press, 1980) ▪Roland **Deines**, "The Pharisees between 'Judaisms' and 'Common Judaism,'" in *Justification and Variegated Nomism*, 1:443–504 ▪J. C. **de Roo**, "The Concept of 'Works of the Law' in Jewish-Christian Literature," in *Christian-Jewish Relations through the Centuries*, ed. S. E. Porter and B. W. R. Pearson, JSNTSup 192 (Sheffield: Sheffield Academic Press, 2000), 116–47 ▪Christian **Dietzfelbinger**, *Die Berufung des Paulus als Ursprung seiner Theologie*, WMANT 58 (Neukirchen-Vluyn: Neukirchener, 1985) ▪James D. G. **Dunn**, "The New Perspective on Paul," *BJRL* 65 (1983): 95–122; reprinted in *Jesus, Paul and the Law: Studies in Mark and Galatians* (Louisville: Westminster John Knox, 1990), 183–214

▥ idem, *The Theology of Paul the Apostle* (Grand Rapids: Eerdmans, 1998) ▥ Mark Adam **Elliott**, *The Survivors of Israel: A Reconsideration of the Theology of Pre-Christian Judaism* (Grand Rapids: Eerdmans, 2000) ▥ E. Earle **Ellis**, *Paul's Use of the Old Testament*, reprint ed. (Grand Rapids: Baker, 1981) ▥ T. **Engberg-Pedersen**, ed., *Paul in his Hellenistic Context* (Minneapolis: Fortress Press, 1995) ▥ idem, ed., *Paul Beyond the Judaism/Hellenism Divide* (Louisville: Westminster John Knox Press, 2001) ▥ Timo **Eskola**, *Theodicy and Predestination in Pauline Soteriology*, WUNT 100 (Tübingen: Mohr-Siebeck, 1998) ▥ Gordon D. **Fee**, "Philippians 2:5–11: Hymn or Exalted Pauline Prose?" *BBR* 2 (1992): 29–46 ▥ Robert W. **Funk**, "The Apostolic Parousia: Form and Significance," in *Christian History and Interpretation*, ed. W. R. Farmer, C. F. D. Moule, and R. R. Niebuhr (Cambridge: Cambridge University Press, 1966), 249–68 ▥ John G. **Gager**, *Reinventing Paul* (New York: Oxford University Press, 2000) ▥ K. S. **Gapp**, "The Universal Famine Under Claudius," *HTR* 28 (1935): 258–65 ▥ Lloyd **Gaston**, "Israel's Misstep in the Eyes of Paul," in *The Romans Debate*, ed. Karl P. Donfried, rev. ed. (Peabody: Hendrickson, 1991), 309–26 ▥ Robert H. **Gundry**, "Grace, Works, and Staying Saved," *Bib* 60 (1985): 1–38 ▥ John J. **Gunther**, *Paul: Messenger and Exile* (Valley Forge, Pa.: Judson, 1972) ▥ Richard **Hays**, *The Faith of Jesus Christ: The Narrative Substructure of Galatians 3:1–4:11*, rev. ed. (Grand Rapids: Eerdmans, 2001) ▥ Klaus **Hacker**, *The Theology of Paul's Letter to the Romans* (Cambridge: Cambridge University Press, 2003) ▥ Douglas **Harink**, *Paul Among the Postliberals: Pauline Theology Beyond Christendom and Modernity* (Grand Rapids: Brazos, 2003) ▥ Richard B. **Hays**, *The Faith of Jesus Christ: The Narrative Substructure of Galatians 3:1–4:11*, rev. ed. (Grand Rapids: Eerdmans, 2001) ▥ Colin J. **Hemer**, *The Book of Acts in the Setting of Hellenistic History*, WUNT 49 (Tübingen: Mohr-Siebeck, 1989) ▥ idem, "Tarsus," in *ISBE* 4.734–36 ▥ Martin **Hengel**, *Judaism and Hellenism*, 2 vols. (Philadelphia: Fortress Press, 1974) ▥ Martin **Hengel** and Anna Maria **Schwemer**, *Paul between Damascus and Antioch: The Unknown Years* (Louisville: Westminster John Knox, 1997) ▥ Ronald F. **Hock**, *The Social Context of Paul's Ministry* (Philadelphia: Fortress Press, 1980) ▥ A. M. **Hunter**, *Paul and His Predecessors*, rev. ed. (Philadelphia: Westminster, 1961) ▥ Robert **Jewett**, *A Chronology of Paul's Life* (Philadelphia: Fortress Press, 1979) ▥ Leander E. **Keck**, *Paul and His Letters*, Proclamation Commentaries (Philadelphia: Fortress Press, 1979) ▥ H. A. A. **Kennedy**, *St. Paul and the Mystery Religions* (London: Hodder & Stoughton, 1913) ▥ Seyoon **Kim**, *The Origin of Paul's Gospel* (Tübingen: Mohr-Siebeck, 1981) ▥ idem, *Paul and the New Perspective: Second Thoughts on the Origin of Paul's Gospel* (Grand Rapids: Eerdmans, 2002) ▥ John **Knox**, *Chapters in a Life of Paul* (London: Adam & Charles Black, 1954) ▥ Timo **Laato**, *Paulus und das Judentum: Anthropologische Erwägungen* (Åbo: Åbo Academy, 1991) ▥ George Eldon **Ladd**, *A Theology of the New Testament*, rev. ed. Donald A. Hagnar (Grand Rapids: Eerdmans, 1993) ▥ Kirsopp **Lake**, "The Chronology of Acts," in *The Beginnings of Christianity*, Part 1: *The Acts of the Apostles*, ed. F. J. Foakes Jackson and Kirsopp Lake, 5 vols. (London: Macmillan, 1920–33), 5.452–55 ▮idem, "The Conversion of Paul," in ibid., 192–94 ▮Richard **Longenecker**, "Acts," in *EBC* 9 ▮idem, *Paul, Apostle of Liberty*, reprint ed. (Grand Rapids: Baker, 1976) ▮idem, ed., *The Road from Damascus: The Impact of Paul's Conversion on his Life, Thought, and Ministry* (Grand Rapids: Eerdmans, 1997) ▮Gerd **Lüdemann**, *Paul, Apostle to the Gentiles: Studies in Chronology* (Philadelphia: Fortress Press, 1984) ▮J. Gresham **Machen**, *The Origin of Paul's Religion* (London: Hodder & Stoughton, 1921) ▮I. Howard **Marshall**, "Salvation, Grace and Works in the Later Writings in the Pauline Corpus," *NTS* 42 (1996): 339–58 ▮Ralph P. **Martin**, *Carmen Christi: Philippians 2:5–11 in Recent Interpretation and in the Setting of Early Christian Worship*, rev. ed. (Grand Rapids: Eerdmans, 1983) ▮J. Louis **Martyn**, *Galatians: A New Translation with Introduction and Commentary*, AB 33A (New York: Doubleday, 1997) ▮R. Barry **Matlock**, "Sins of the Flesh and Suspicious Minds: Dunn's New Theology of Paul," *JSNT* 72 (1998): 67–90 ▮Wayne A. **Meeks**, *The First Urban Christians: The Social World of the Apostle Paul* (New Haven: Yale University Press, 1983) ▮C. G. **Montefiore**, *Judaism and St. Paul* (London: Goschen, 1914) ▮Douglas J. **Moo**, *The Epistle to the Romans*, NICNT (Grand Rapids: Eerdmans, 1996) ▮idem, "'Law,' 'Works of the Law' and Legalism in Paul," *WTJ* 45 (1983): 73–100 ▮Johannes **Munck**, *Paul and the Salvation of Mankind* (London: SCM, 1959) ▮Jerome **Murphy-O'Connor**, *Paul: A Critical Life* (Oxford: Clarendon Press, 1996) ▮idem, *Paul the Letter-Writer: His World, His Options, His Skills* (Collegeville: Liturgical Press, 1995) ▮Carey C. **Newman**, ed., *Jesus and the Restoration of Israel* (Downers Grove: IVP, 1999) ▮Peter T. **O'Brien**, "Was Paul Converted?" in *Justification and Variegated Nomism*, vol. 2 ▮George **Ogg**, *The Odyssey of Paul* (Old Tappan: Revell, 1968) ▮John B. **Polhill**, *Paul and His Letters* (Nashville: Broadman & Holman, 1999) ▮Charles L. **Quarles**, "The Soteriology of R. Akiba and E. P. Sanders' *Paul and Palestinian Judaism*," *NTS* 42 (1996): 185–95 ▮William M. **Ramsay**, *The Cities of St. Paul: Their Influence on His Life and Thought* (London: Hodder & Stoughton, 1907) ▮idem, *Saint Paul, the Traveller and Roman Citizen* (London: Hodder & Stoughton, 1897) ▮Bo **Reicke**, *Re-examining Paul's Letters: The History of the Pauline Correspondence* (Harrisburg: Trinity Press International, 2001) ▮Richard **Reitzenstein**, *Hellenistic Mystery Religions: Their Basic Ideas and Significance* (Pittsburgh: Pickwick, 1978) ▮Arnold **Resch**, *Der Paulinismus und die Logia Jesu*, TU 27 (Leipzig: Akademie, 1904) ▮Herman **Ridderbos**, *Paul: An Outline of His Theology* (Grand Rapids: Eerdmans, 1975) ▮Rainer **Riesner**, *Paul's Early Period: Chronology, Mission Strategy, Theology* (Grand Rapids: Eerdmans, 1998) ▮idem, "The Pharisees between 'Judaisms' and 'Common Judaism,'" in *Justification and Variegated Nomism*, 1:443–504 ▮Calvin J. **Roetzel**, *Paul: The Man and the Myth* (Columbia: University of South Carolina Press, 1998) ▮idem, *Paul: A Jew on the Margins* (Louisville: Westminster John Knox Press, 2003) ▮Otto **Roller**, *Das Formular der paulinischer Briefe: Ein Beitrag zur Lehre vom antiken Briefe* (Stuttgart: Kohlhammer,

1933) ▮Anthony J. **Saldarini**, "Pharisees," *ABD* 5.289–303 ▮E. P. **Sanders**, *Paul and Palestinian Judaism: A Comparison of Patterns of Religion* (Philadelphia: Fortress Press, 1977) ▮Thomas R. **Schreiner**, "'Works of Law' in Paul," *NovT* 32 (1991): 217–44 ▮Emil **Schürer**, *The History of the Jewish People in the Age of Jesus Christ (175 B.C.–A.D. 135)*, new ed., vol. 1, rev. and ed. Geza Vermes and Fegus Millar (Edinburgh: T. & T. Clark, 1973) ▮Albert **Schweitzer**, *The Mysticism of Paul the Apostle* (New York: H. Holt, 1931) ▮Alan **Segal**, *Paul the Convert* (New Haven: Yale University Press, 1990) ▮Mark **Seifrid**, "Blind Alleys in the Controversy over the Paul of History," *TynB* 45 (1994): 73–95 ▮idem, *Christ, Our Righteousness: Paul's Theology of Justification*, NSBT (Downers Grove: IVP, 2000) ▮idem, *Justification by Faith: The Origin and Development of a Central Pauline Theme*, NovTSup 68 (Leiden: Brill, 1992) ▮E. Mary **Smallwood**, *The Jews Under Roman Rule*, SJLA 20 (Leiden: Brill, 1976) ▮Christopher **Stanley**, *Paul and the Language of Scripture: Citation Technique in the Pauline Epistles and Contemporary Literature*, SNTSMS 69 (Cambridge: Cambridge University Press, 1992) ▮Graham N. **Stanton**, "The Law of Moses and the Law of Christ," in *Paul and the Mosaic Law*, ed. James D. G. Dunn (Grand Rapids: Eerdmans, 2000 [1996]), 99–116 ▮idem, *Jesus of Nazareth in New Testament Preaching*, SNTSMS 27 (Cambridge: Cambridge University Press, 1974) ▮Krister **Stendahl**, "The Apostle Paul and the Introspective Conscience of the West," *HTR* 56 (1963): 199–215 ▮idem, *Paul Among Jews and Gentiles, and Other Essays* (Philadelphia: Fortress Press, 1976) ▮Peter **Stuhlmacher**, "'The End of the Law': On the Origin and Beginnings of Pauline Theology," in *Reconciliation, Law and Righteousness: Essays on Biblical Theology* (Philadelphia: Fortress Press, 1986), 134–54 ▮Charles H. **Talbert**, "Paul, Judaism, and the Revisionists," *CBQ* 63 (2001): 1–22 ▮Frank **Thielman**, *From Plight to Solution: A Jewish Framework for Understanding Paul's View of the Law in Galatians and Romans*, NovTSup 61 (Leiden: Brill, 1989) ▮Michael **Thompson**, *Clothed with Christ: The Example and Teaching of Jesus in Romans 12.1–15.13*, JSNTSup 59 (Sheffield: Sheffield Academic Press, 1991) ▮Lauri **Thurén**, *Derhetorizing Paul: A Dynamic Perspective on Pauline Theology and the Law*, WUNT 124 (Tübingen: Mohr-Siebeck, 2000) ▮W. C. **van Unnik**, *Tarsus or Jerusalem: The City of Paul's Youth* (London: Epworth, 1962) ▮Günter **Wagner**, *Pauline Baptism and the Pagan Mysteries* (Edinburgh: Oliver & Boyd, 1967) ▮David **Wenham**, *Paul: Follower of Jesus or Founder of Christianity?* (Grand Rapids: Eerdmans, 1995) ▮idem, "Paul's Use of the Jesus Tradition: Three Samples," in *GP* 5.7–37 ▮idem, *The Rediscovery of Jesus' Eschatological Discourse, GP* 4 ▮Stephen **Westerholm**, *Israel's Law and the Church's Faith* (Grand Rapids: Eerdmans, 1988) ▮idem, *Perspectives Old and New on Paul: The "Lutheran" Paul and His Critics* (Grand Rapids: Eerdmans, 2004) ▮Ben **Witherington** III, *The Paul Quest: The Renewed Search for the Jew of Tarsus* (Grand Rapids: Eerdmans, 1998) ▮W. P. **Workman**, "A New Date-Indication in Acts," *ExpTim* 11 (1899–1900): 316–19 ▮N. T. **Wright**, "ἁρπαγμός and the Meaning of Philippians 2:5–11," *JTS* 37

(1987): 321–52 ▥ idem, *The Climax of the Covenant* (Minneapolis: Fortress Press, 1993) ▥ idem, *Jesus and the Victory of God* (Minneapolis: Fortress Press, 1996) ▥ idem, *The New Testament and the People of God* (Minneapolis: Fortress Press, 1992) ▥ idem, *What Saint Paul Really Said* (Grand Rapids: Eerdmans, 1997) ▥ R. J. **Wyatt**, "Pharisees," in *ISBE* 3.822–29.

CHAPTER TEN

ROMANS

CONTENTS

Romans is the longest and most theologically significant of the letters of Paul, "the very purest gospel" (Luther). The letter takes the form of a theological treatise framed by an epistolary opening (1:1–17) and closing (15:14–16:27). The opening contains the usual prescript (1:1–7) and thanksgiving (1:8–15) and is concluded with a transitional statement of the theme of the letter: the gospel as the revelation of God's righteousness, a righteousness that can be experienced only by faith (1:16–17).

The gospel as the righteousness of God by faith (1:18–4:25). Righteousness of God by faith is the theme of the first major section of the letter. Paul paves the way for this theme by explaining why it was necessary for God to manifest his righteousness and why humans can experience this righteousness only by faith. Sin, Paul affirms, has gained a stranglehold on all people, and only an act of God, experienced as a free gift through faith, can break that stranglehold (1:18–3:20). God's wrath, the condemning outflow of his holy anger, stands over all sinners (1:18–19). And justly so. For God has made himself known to all people through creation; their turning from him to gods of their own making renders them "without excuse" (1:20–32). Even less excusable are Jews, for they have a clear and detailed statement of God's will in their law. Mere possession of that law or bearing the outward mark of God's covenant (circumcision) does not suffice to protect the Jews from God's wrath (2:1–3:8). So, Paul concludes, all people, both Jews and Gentiles, are helpless slaves of sin and cannot be brought into relationship with God by anything they might do (3:9–20).

Only God can change this tragic state of affairs, and this he has done by making available, through the sacrifice of his Son, a means of becoming righteous, or innocent, before God (3:21–26). This justification, Paul insists, can be gained only by faith (3:27–31), as is illustrated clearly in the case of Abraham (4:1–25).

The gospel as the power of God for salvation (5:1–8:39). Having shown how sinful human beings can be declared right before God through faith, Paul in the second major section of the letter draws out the significance of this act both for the future judgment and for the present earthly life. Being justified means "peace with God," or reconciliation to God, and especially a secure hope for vindication on the day of judgment (5:1–11). The ground for this hope is the believer's relationship to Christ, who, undoing the effects of Adam's sin, has won eternal life for all who belong to him (5:12–21). Nevertheless, although transferred into the new realm, where Christ, righteousness, grace, and life reign, the Christian still must battle the powers of this present realm: sin, the law, death, and the flesh. But we battle with confidence, knowing that Christ has set us free from the tyranny of these powers. Therefore sin can no longer dictate terms to us (6:1–14); God is now our master, which our lives must reflect (6:15–23). Likewise the law, which, because of sin, made the situation of people worse instead of better, no longer holds sway over the believer (7:1–25). Through the agency of God's Spirit, the Christian is assured of final victory over death and the power of the flesh (8:1–13). That same Spirit, making us God's children (8:14–17), provides additional assurance that the work God has begun in us will be brought to a triumphant conclusion: justification will assuredly lead to glorification (8:18–39).

The gospel and Israel (9:1–11:36). A key motif throughout Romans 1–8 is the question of the relationship between law and gospel, Jew and Gentile, God's old-covenant people and his new-covenant people. This is the theme of the third major section of the letter. Does the transfer of covenant privileges from Israel to the church mean that God has spurned his promises to Israel (9:1–6a)? Not at all, Paul answers. First, God's promises were never intended to guarantee salvation to every Israelite by birth (9:6b–29). Second, the people of Israel themselves are to blame for failing to embrace God's righteousness in Christ, despite God's clear word to them (9:30–10:21). Furthermore, some Israelites, like Paul, are being saved, and in them God's promises are being fulfilled (11:1–10). Finally, in the climax to his argument, Paul counters the arrogant boasting of some Gentile Christians by reminding them that it is only through Israel that salvation has come to them and that there awaits a day when God's promise to Israel will come to full realization and "all Israel will be saved" (11:12–36).

The gospel and the transformation of life (12:1–15:13). The last major section of Paul's theological treatise is devoted to the practical outworking of God's grace in the gospel. In an initial summary statement, Paul reminds his readers that this grace of God should stimulate sacrificial giving of themselves in service to God (12:1–2). This service can take various forms, as the manifold gifts God has given his people are exercised (12:3–8). The many detailed aspects of this service to God are to be permeated by love (12:9–21). Serving God does not mean, Paul cautions, that the Christian can ignore the legitimate claims that government makes on us (13:1–7). Nor, though free from the law, can Christians ignore the continuing validity of the commandment that summarizes the law: loving our neighbor as ourselves (13:8–10). The Christian is to serve God in this way, recognizing that the day of salvation is already casting the rays of its light on our path, and our lives must reflect that light (13:11–14). Finally, Paul tackles an issue that was apparently very divisive in the church at Rome and elsewhere, no doubt: the observance of certain dietary codes and rituals (14:1–15:13). Some of the Christians in Rome prided themselves on being strong in faith and looked down on others who were not convinced that their faith allowed them to eat any kind of food or to ignore set days of worship. They, in turn, condemned the so-called strong in faith as compromisers. Paul, while aligning himself with the strong, demands that each side respect the opinions of the other side and learn to live in mutual tolerance.

The epistolary conclusion (15:14–16:27) contains information about Paul's situation and travel plans (15:14–29), a request for prayer as he prepares to bring the collection to Christians in Jerusalem (15:30–33), a commendation of a sister in Christ and a long series of greetings (16:1–16), and a final warning about false teachers, followed by personal notes and a benediction (16:17–27 [vv. 25–27 are textually uncertain]).

AUTHOR

Romans claims to have been written by Paul (1:1), and there has been no serious challenge to this claim. Tertius, identified in 16:22, was probably Paul's amanuensis or scribe. While Paul may sometimes have given his amanuenses some freedom in choosing the wording of his letters, there is little evidence that this was the case in Romans. A few have wondered whether parts of Romans may have been written by someone else and incorporated into the letter by Paul, but none of these theories has proved convincing (see section "Integrity" below).

PROVENANCE AND DATE

There is little debate about whether Paul wrote Romans, nor about the general situation in which he wrote. According to 15:22–29, three localities figure in Paul's travel plans: Jerusalem, Rome, and Spain. Paul's immediate destination is Jerusalem. As his prayer in 15:30–33 reveals, Paul looks upon this trip to Jerusalem with considerable trepidation. He is bringing to the impoverished Jewish Christians in Jerusalem an offering gathered from the Gentile-Christian churches he has planted (15:25–27), and he is uncertain how the offering will be received. It is his hope that the offering will be acceptable to the Jewish believers and that this will help to cement relations between Jewish and Gentile Christians. But Paul is unsure about this and requests the Roman Christians to pray for this outcome.

The second stop Paul plans to make is in Rome, but only as a stopping-off point on his way to Spain (15:24, 28). This is not to minimize the strategic importance of Rome, but it reflects Paul's sense of calling to "preach the gospel where Christ [is] not known" (15:20). Paul's gaze is fixed on faraway Spain because the task of initial church planting in the eastern Mediterranean has been completed: "From Jerusalem all the way around to Illyricum, I have fully proclaimed the gospel of Christ" (15:19). As a result of his first three missionary journeys, thriving churches have been planted in major metropolitan centers throughout this region. These churches can carry on the task of evangelism in their respective areas while Paul pursues his calling in virgin territory.

When we compare these indications with the details of Paul's career from Acts, it is clear that Paul must be near the end of his third missionary journey as he writes Romans. It was then that Paul was preparing to return to Jerusalem, with Rome as his next destination (see Acts 19:21; 20:16). Corinth is the most likely place of writing. When Luke tells us that Paul spent three months in Greece (Acts 20:3), it was most likely Corinth where Paul stayed (see 2 Cor. 13:1, 10). Confirmation comes from Paul's commendation of a woman who lived in Cenchrea, a neighboring city to Corinth (16:1–2); and the Gaius who sends greetings in 16:23 may be the same Gaius whom Paul baptized in Corinth (1 Cor. 1:14). Some have also thought that the city treasurer Erastus (16:23) can be identified with the Erastus mentioned on an inscription found at Corinth.[1]

The date at which Paul wrote Romans will accordingly depend on the date of Paul's three-month stay in Greece; fixing this date depends, in turn, on the chronology of Paul's life and ministry as a whole. While we cannot be certain within a year or two, A.D. 57 is the best alternative (see table 6 in chap. 8).[2]

ADDRESSEES

Assuming that the text printed in our Greek and English Bibles is correct (for which see the next section), the letter is addressed to "all in Rome who are loved by God and called to be saints" (1:7; cf. also 1:15). We have no definite evidence about the origin of the church in Rome or about its composition at the time when

---

[1]See the discussion in David W. J. Gill, "Erastus the Aedile," *TynB* 40 (1989): 293–302.

[2]Most introductions and commentaries agree on this approximate date. Minimizing the historical value of Acts, Charles Buck and Greer Taylor date Romans in A.D. 47 (*Saint Paul: A Study of the Development of His Thought* [New York: Charles Scribner's Sons, 1969], 170–71); Gerd Lüdemann, in 51/52 or 54/55 (*Paul, Apostle to the Gentiles: Studies in Chronology* [Philadelphia: Fortress Press, 1984], 263). J. R. Richards puts it in 52–54 because he thinks on internal grounds that Romans must precede 1 Corinthians ("Romans and I Corinthians: Their Chronological Relationship and Comparative Dates," *NTS* 13 [1966–67]: 14–30).

Paul wrote to it. In about A.D. 180, Irenaeus identified Peter and Paul together as founders of the Roman church (*Adv. Haer.* 3.1.2), while later tradition names Peter as the founder and first bishop of the church (e.g., the *Catalogus Liberianus* [A.D. 354]). But neither tradition can be accepted. The letter itself makes clear that Paul was a stranger to the church in Rome (see 1:10, 13; 15:22), and it is unlikely that Paul would be planning the kind of visit described in 1:8–15 to a church founded by Peter. Nor is it likely that Peter went to Rome early enough to have established a church there.[3] Since no other apostle is associated with the founding of the church in Rome, we may agree with the assessment of the fourth-century "Ambrosiaster" that the Romans "have embraced the faith of Christ, albeit according to the Jewish rite, without seeing any sign of mighty works or any of the apostles."[4] If, then, we are to speculate, the most likely scenario is that Jews converted on the Day of Pentecost (see Acts 2:10) were the first to bring the gospel to the great capital.

"Ambrosiaster" is probably also correct in thinking that Christianity in Rome began among Jews ("according to the Jewish rite"). Jews made up a significant part of the citizenry of Rome by the end of the first century B.C.[5] Here, as Paul found, was the most fertile seedbed for the planting of the gospel—especially if returned pilgrims from Pentecost first planted the seed. That there were Jewish Christians in Rome by (probably) A.D. 49 is attested by the statement of Suetonius that Claudius the Roman emperor "expelled the Jews from Rome because they were constantly rioting at the instigation of Chrestus" (*Life of Claudius* 25.2). It is generally agreed that "Chrestus" is a corruption of the Greek Χριστός (*Christos*, "Christ") and that Suetonius's remark refers to violent debates within the Jewish community in Rome over the claims of Jesus to be the Christ. That this incident occurred in 49, as the fifth-century writer Orosius claims, is less certain, although the date receives indirect confirmation from Acts 18:2, where Luke says that Aquila and Priscilla had recently come to Corinth from Italy "because Claudius had ordered all the Jews to leave Rome."[6]

> We have no definite evidence about the origin of the church in Rome or its composition when Paul wrote to it. The most likely scenario is that Jews converted on the Day of Pentecost were the first to bring the gospel to the great capital.

---

[3]See the discussion in Oscar Cullmann, *Peter: Disciple, Apostle, Martyr* (Philadelphia: Westminster, 1962), 72–157.

[4]Ambrosiaster, *PL* 17, col. 46.

[5]See, e.g., Philo's *Embassy to Gaius;* and note the discussions in Harry J. Leon, *The Jews of Ancient Rome* (Philadelphia: Jewish Publication Society, 1960), 4–9; and Wolfgang Wiefel, "The Jewish Community in Ancient Rome and the Origins of Roman Christianity," in *The Romans Debate,* ed. Karl Donfried, rev. ed. (Peabody: Hendrickson, 1991), 85–96.

[6]See esp. E. Mary Smallwood, *The Jews Under Roman Rule,* SJLA 20 (Leiden: Brill, 1976), 210–16; and F. F. Bruce, "The Romans Debate—Continued," *BJRL* 64 (1982): 338–39. For a dissenting opinion, see Leon, *Jews,* 23–27. Some scholars argue, based on remarks in Dio Cassius, that the expulsion affected a relatively small number of Jews (Mark Nanos, *The Mystery of Romans: The Jewish Context of Paul's Letter* [Minneapolis:

Since the Romans at this point would not have distinguished Jews from Jewish Christians, both would have been affected by Claudius's expulsion. But as with similar expulsions on other occasions, the edict probably did not stay in force for long; and less than a decade later, we find the Jews Aquila and Priscilla back in Rome (Rom. 16:3). During its enforcement, however, the edict must have had a profound impact on the church in Rome. In the absence of Jewish Christians, those Gentiles who had been attracted to Christianity would have taken over the church, and Jewish Christians who then returned would probably be in a minority and perhaps be viewed with some condescension by the now-dominant Gentile wing.[7]

When Paul writes his letter, then, we may be certain that there were both Gentile and Jewish Christians in Rome, probably meeting in several house churches rather than in one large gathering.[8] Does Paul write to this mixed community as a whole? Or does he address himself to one segment of the community only? Only the evidence of the letter itself can answer these questions.

In turning to the letter, however, we are confronted with apparently conflicting data. On the one hand, there are indications that Paul had a Jewish-Christian audience in mind: (1) he greets the Jewish Christians Priscilla and Aquila and his "fellow Jews" Andronicus, Junia, and Herodion (16:3, 7, 11); (2) he addresses himself to a Jew in chapter 2 (e.g., v. 17); (3) he associates his readers with the Mosaic law: they are "not under law" (6:14, 15) because they have "died to the law" (7:4); and note 7:1: "I am speaking to those who know the law"; (4) Paul calls Abraham our "forefather" (4:1); and (5) much of the letter is devoted to issues that would be of particular interest to Jewish Christians: the sin of the Jews (2:1–3:8); the Mosaic law, seen in terms both of its inadequacy (3:19–20, 27–31; 4:12–15; 5:13–14, 20; 6:14; 7:1–8:4; 9:30–10:8) and of its establishment in Christ (3:31; 8:4; 13:8–10); the significance of Abraham, the fountainhead of Israel (chap. 4); and the place of Israel in salvation history (chaps. 9–11).

On the other hand, indications of a Gentile-Christian audience are equally evident: (1) in his address of the letter as a whole, Paul includes his readers among the Gentiles to whom he has been called to minister (1:5–6; cf. also 1:13 and 15:14–21); (2) he directly addresses "you Gentiles" in 11:13 (continued in

---

Augsburg/Fortress, 1996], 372–81; Achtemeier/Green/Thompson, 303–4). But there are solid reasons for thinking that the expulsion was quite general (Rainer Riesner, *Paul's Early Period: Chronology, Mission Strategy, Theology* [Grand Rapids: Eerdmans, 1998], 199–200).

[7]See esp. Wiefel, "Jewish Community," 96–101.

[8]It is noted, e.g., that the word *church* is absent from Romans; see F. F. Bruce, *Paul: Apostle of the Heart Set Free* (Grand Rapids: Eerdmans, 1977), 385–89. The Christian community may then have reflected the lack of centralization that characterized the Jewish community in Rome; see Romano Penna, "Les Juifs à Rome au temps de l'apôtre Paul," *NTS* 28 (1982): 327–28; Leon, *Jews*, 135–70.

the second person plural throughout 11:14–24); and (3) Paul's plea that the Christians in Rome "accept one another" (15:7) appears to be directed especially to Gentiles (see vv. 8–9).

We must consider several options in trying to reconcile these apparently conflicting indications of Paul's audience in the epistle to the Romans. First, we could downplay the evidence of a Gentile-Christian audience and conclude that the letter is addressed entirely or mainly to Jewish Christians.[9] It has been argued, for instance, that 1:6 simply designates the Roman Christians as being "among those who are called to belong to Jesus Christ" or that τοῖς ἔθνεσιν (tois ethnesin) in verse 5 means "nations" rather than "Gentiles" (see RSV). But neither alternative is convincing. In a context dealing with Paul's apostleship, ἔθνη (ethnē) almost certainly means "Gentiles," and the connection between verses 5 and 6 (ἐν οἷς ἐστε καὶ ὑμεῖς [en hois este kai hymeis], "among whom you *also*") is most naturally construed as numbering the readers of the letter among these Gentiles.[10]

In light of these verses, then, we might be inclined to the opposite conclusion: that Romans is directed only to Gentile Christians.[11] Indeed, there is more to be said for a Gentile-Christian audience than for a Jewish-Christian one. Not only is 1:5–6 very significant, coming in the address of the letter as a whole, but the evidence for a Jewish-Christian readership is not all that strong. The direct address to "a Jew" in chapter 2 is a literary device and implies nothing about the intended audience. Calling Abraham our father (4:1) would suggest a Jewish audience only if Paul was including all his readers in the designation. But this is not clear: he may be thinking only of himself and other Jewish Christians. Paul certainly suggests that his readers have had some experience with the Mosaic law (6:14; 7:4), but there is a sense in which even Gentiles, according to Paul, have been under the law. Moreover, many of the Gentiles in the Christian community in Rome were probably former God-fearers—worshipers of the God of Israel who had not been circumcised and thus had not been made members of the covenant community. As such, they would have learned much of the Mosaic

---

[9]This view was first made popular by F. C. Baur ("Über Zweck und Veranlassung des Römerbriefes und die damit zusammenhängenden Verhältnisse der römischen Gemeinde," in *Historisch-kritische Untersuchungen zum Neuen Testament* [Stuttgart: Friedrich Fromman, 1963], 1.147–266). See also Zahn 1.421–34.

[10]See Douglas J. Moo, *The Epistle to the Romans*, NICNT (Grand Rapids: Eerdmans, 1996), 53–54.

[11]See esp. Johannes Munck, *Paul and the Salvation of Mankind* (London: SCM, 1959), 200–209; Walter Schmithals, *Der Römerbrief als historisches Problem*, SNT 9 (Gütersloh: Gerd Mohn, 1975), 9–89; Jülicher, 112–15. While admitting that Jews were part of the congregation in Rome, Stowers nevertheless insists that Gentile-Christians are the "encoded" addressees (*A Rereading of Romans: Justice, Jews, and Gentiles* [New Haven: Yale University Press, 1994], 29–33).

law in the synagogue.[12] Finally, while much of Romans is indeed a debate with Judaism, it is not at all clear that such a debate would have been irrelevant to a Gentile audience. Quite the contrary. Gentiles as much as Jews needed to understand how the fulfillment of God's plan in Christ related to the Old Testament people of God and his promises to them, and to the historical continuation of that people in contemporary Judaism. In this regard, it is important to observe that Paul's teaching about the future of Israel in 11:12–24 is specifically directed to Gentiles.

While there is much to be said for confining Paul's audience to Gentile Christians, it is doubtful that we can exclude Jewish Christians entirely. Paul addresses himself to "*all* in Rome who are loved by God and called to be his holy people" (1:7), and it is certain that there were Jewish Christians in Rome. If, as we maintain (see below), chapter 16 is part of Paul's original letter to the Romans, at least those Jewish Christians mentioned there must be included within Paul's audience. Moreover, the "weak in faith" whom Paul addresses in 14:1–15:13 are quite possibly to be identified with a Jewish-Christian faction.

So it appears that Paul is addressing both Jewish and Gentile Christians in Romans. This might mean that Paul addresses Gentile Christians in some passages and Jewish Christians in others. The most detailed attempt to understand the letter in this way is that of Paul Minear. He discerns no fewer than five separate groups in the Christian community in Rome and thinks each section of Romans has one of these groups specifically in view.[13] But Paul does not say enough to make clear the existence of so many distinct groups. Nor, with the exception of one or two passages (e.g., 11:12–24), does this epistle hint at an audience restricted to only some of the Roman Christians. We must thus conclude that Paul addresses in Romans a mixed community of Jewish and Gentile Christians.[14] Almost certainly, however, Gentile Christians were in a majority large enough to justify Paul's including the Christian community in Rome within the sphere of those Gentiles to whom his apostleship was especially directed.

INTEGRITY, LITERARY HISTORY, AND TEXT

Thus far we have been discussing Romans on the supposition that the letter Paul sent to the Roman Christians was composed of the entire sixteen chapters

---

[12]Schmithals, *Römerbrief*, 69–82; J. D. G. Dunn, *Romans 1–8*, WBC 38A (Waco: Word, 1988), xlvii–xlviii.

[13]Paul Minear, *The Obedience of Faith: The Purposes of Paul in the Epistle to the Romans* (London: SCM, 1971).

[14]This is the conclusion of most introductions and commentaries; see, e.g., Kümmel, 309–11.

printed in our Bibles. But this supposition must now be examined, for a significant number of scholars doubt that this is the case. A few confine their argument to internal considerations. They claim that there are inconsistencies within the canonical Romans and that they can be explained only on the hypothesis that the letter is actually a combination of two or more original letters or that a redactor has inserted various interpolations into the text of Paul's original letter.[15] Not only are such theories bereft of any textual evidence, their proponents have manufactured inconsistencies in a letter that has been lauded through the centuries for its logical rigor and clarity of argument.[16]

There are, however, a number of other theories about the original form and literary history of Romans that deserve more serious consideration, for they arise from difficulties within the text of the letter. Central to these theories is the place of the doxology that is included at the very end of the letter in most modern texts and translations (16:25–27). It is omitted in some manuscripts and appears at different places in others. The following sequences are found in the Greek manuscript tradition:

1. 1:1–14:23; 15:1–16:23; 16:25–27   P[61] (?), B, C, D, 1739, et al.
2. 1:1–14:23; 16:25–27; 15:1–16:23;   A, P, 5, 33, 104
   16:25–27
3. 1:1–14:23; 16:25–27; 15:1–16:24   Y, the "majority" text, sy[h]
4. 1:1–14:23; 15:1–16:24   F, G, 629, [archetype of D?]
5. 1:1–15:33; 16:25–27; 16:1–23   P[46]

Since a doxology generally closes a letter, the presence of the doxology after chapter 14 or chapter 15 could indicate that the letter at one time ended at one or the other of these points. And this possibility is increased by other evidence.

1. Several manuscripts of the Latin Vulgate omit 15:1–16:23 entirely.

2. Another codex of the Vulgate (Amiatinus), while containing 15:1–16:24, omits the section summaries from this section.

3. Tertullian, Irenaeus, and Cyprian fail to refer to chapters 15 and 16 in places where they may have been expected to, if they had a sixteen-chapter form of the text.

---

[15]Schmithals posits a "Romans A" made up of chaps. 1–11 and 15:8–13 and a "Romans B" made up of 12:1–15:7; 15:14–32; 16:21–23 and 15:33, with various other minor interpolations and fragments (see his summary in *Römerbrief*, 180–211). J. Kinoshita also discerns two separate original letters in our Romans; significantly, however, he divides things very differently than does Schmithals ("Romans—Two Writings Combined," *NovT* 7 [1964]: 258–77). Another tack is taken by J. C. O'Neill, who identifies numerous editorial insertions in the text of Romans (*Paul's Letter to the Romans,* Penguin [Baltimore: Penguin, 1975]).

[16]See the review of O'Neill's commentary by Nigel M. Watson, "Simplifying the Righteousness of God: A Critique of J. C. O'Neill's *Romans*," *SJT* 30 (1977): 464–69.

These data suggest that a fourteen-chapter form of Romans was extant in the early church, which some scholars conclude was the original version. Noting that a few manuscripts (G and the OL g) omit reference to Rome in 1:7 and 1:15 (and Paul never mentions a particular destination elsewhere in chaps. 1–14), they argue that Paul first wrote chapters 1–14 as a general doctrinal treatise and later added chapters 15–16 when he sent this treatise to Rome.[17] This reconstruction is unlikely. The close connection between chapters 14 and 15 makes it impossible to think that 14 ever existed without at least the first part of 15.[18] How, then, did the fourteen-chapter recension of Romans come into existence? Lightfoot suggests that Paul himself may have abbreviated his letter to the Romans in order to universalize the epistle.[19] But this still fails to explain the abrupt break between chapters 14 and 15.[20] The same objection applies to Gamble's theory that the text was shortened after Paul's time in order to make the letter more universally applicable.[21] Perhaps the best explanation is also the earliest: that Marcion was responsible for cutting off the last two chapters of the letter.[22] Given his biases against the Old Testament, Marcion may have been unhappy with the Old Testament quotations in 15:3 and 15:9–12 and considered that 15:1 was the most convenient place to make the break.

In recent decades, however, some scholars have thought that Paul's letter to the Romans did not include chapter 16. The placement of the doxology after chapter 15 in the early and important manuscript P[46] suggests that some form of the letter may have ended there, and the contents of chapter 16, it is alleged, make it unlikely that it could have been addressed to the church in Rome. Nothing in chapters 1–15 has prepared us for the warning about false teachers in 16:17–20. But more important is the fact that Paul in chapter 16 greets twenty-five individuals by name, two families, one house church and an unspecified number of "brothers and sisters" and "saints." All this to a church he has never visited! Surely, it is argued, we must conclude that chapter 16 was originally an

---

[17]E.g., Kirsopp Lake, *The Earlier Epistles of St. Paul* (London: Rivingstons, 1919), 350–66.

[18]See, e.g., William Sanday and Arthur C. Headlam, *A Critical and Exegetical Commentary on the Epistle to the Romans*, ICC (Edinburgh: T. & T. Clark, 1902), xci; Harry Gamble Jr., *The Textual History of the Letter to the Romans: A Study in Textual and Literary Criticism* (Grand Rapids: Eerdmans, 1977), 84.

[19]J. B. Lightfoot, "The Structure and Destination of the Epistle to the Romans," in *Biblical Essays* (London: Macmillan, 1893), 287–320, 352–74; see also James Denney, "St. Paul's Epistle to the Romans," in *EGT* 2.576–82.

[20]See the criticisms of Lightfoot's view by Hort in *Biblical Essays*, 321–51.

[21]Gamble, *Textual History*, 115–24.

[22]See, e.g., Joseph A. Fitzmyer, *Romans: A New Translation with Introduction and Commentary*, AB 33 (New York: Doubleday, 1993), 55–65; Kümmel, 316; Guthrie, 421–22; Sanday and Headlam, *Romans*, lxvi.

independent letter—perhaps a commendatory letter for Phoebe[23]—or was tacked on when Paul sent his Romans letter to the church in Ephesus.[24]

This thesis rests on rather shaky ground. There is no direct textual evidence at all for a fifteen-chapter form of the letter. Warnings about false teachers are by no means out of keeping with passages such as 3:8, and Paul often includes such a last-minute reminder in his letters.[25] Nor are the number of greetings in chapter 16 incompatible with a Roman destination. Many of those greeted may have been, like Priscilla and Aquila, Jewish Christians who had been forced to flee Rome and who met Paul in the course of his travels. What more natural than that believers from Rome would have spent their enforced exile in the kind of Roman-influenced cities of the East in which Paul was busy establishing churches?

We have, then, good grounds for concluding that Paul's letter to the Roman Christians contained all sixteen chapters.[26] Whether the doxology should be included at the end of chapter 16 is another question. Although omitted entirely in only a few manuscripts, its varied placement suggests that it may have been added to round off one of the recensions of the letter in the early church.[27] Moreover, a concluding doxology is unparalleled in the letters of Paul, and the language of this one is said to be un-Pauline. But these arguments are not conclusive,[28] and we think it likely that 16:25–27 was Paul's own conclusion to this letter.

---

[23]E.g., Edgar J. Goodspeed, "Phoebe's Letter of Introduction," *HTR* 44 (1951): 55–57; Schmithals, *Römerbrief*, 125–51; Moffatt, 135–39; Jülicher, 109–12. J. I. H. McDonald has shown that so compact a letter of introduction is possible ("Was Romans XVI a Separate Letter?" *NTS* 16 [1969–70]: 369–72).

[24]This view is associated esp. with T. W. Manson; see his "Letter to the Romans— and Others," *BJRL* 31 (1948): 224–40. Some who adopt a similar view include G. Zuntz, *The Text of the Epistles: A Disquisition upon the Corpus Paulinum* (London: British Academy, 1953), 276–77; McNeile, 154–58; and Martin 2.194–96.

[25]Gamble, *Textual History*, 52. Ollrog, who thinks that chapter 16 belongs to the original letter, argues that 16:17–20a is a post-Pauline interpolation ("Die Abfassungsverhältnisse von Röm 16," in *Kirche, Fs.* Günther Bornkamm, ed. D. Lührmann and G. Strecker [Tübingen: Mohr-Siebeck, 1980], 221–44).

[26]In addition to other works cited in these notes, see Bruce N. Kaye, "'To the Romans and Others' Revisited," *NovT* 18 (1976): 37–77.

[27]See, e.g., Lake, *Earlier Epistles*, 343–46; Manson, "To the Romans and Others," 8.

[28]See Larry W. Hurtado, "The Doxology at the End of Romans," in *New Testament Textual Criticism: Its Significance for Exegesis, Fs.* Bruce M. Metzger, ed. E. J. Epp and G. D. Fee (Oxford: Clarendon Press, 1981), 185–99; I. Howard Marshall, "Romans 16:25–27—An Apt Conclusion," in *Romans and the People of God, Fs.* Gordon D. Fee, ed. Sven K. Soderlund and N. T. Wright (Grand Rapids: Eerdmans, 1999), 170–84.

NATURE AND GENRE

Romans has occasionally been viewed as a timeless treatise, a "compendium of Christian doctrine" (Melanchthon) that transcends time. However, while it certainly speaks to every generation of Christians, the message of Romans is embedded in a document written to a particular audience in a definite situation. To put it simply, Romans is a letter.

While Romans speaks to every generation of Christians, its message is embedded in a document written to a particular audience in a definite situation. To put it simply, Romans is a letter.

But what kind of letter? There were many types of letters in the ancient world, ranging from brief requests for money from children away from home to long essays intended to reach a wide audience (see chap. 8 above). Paul's letters generally fall somewhere between these extremes, but Romans is farther toward the latter end of the spectrum than any other of his letters (with the possible exception of Ephesians). To be sure, Romans is written within a set of definite circumstances that are enumerated in the epistolary opening and closing of the book (1:1–17; 15:14–16:27). But within this framework, Paul pursues an argument that develops according to the inner logic of the gospel. This stands in marked contrast to 1 Corinthians, for example, where Paul's agenda is set by the needs and questions of the Corinthians. The questions that occur in Romans (e.g., 3:1, 5, 27; 4:1; 6:1, 15) are literary devices by which Paul moves his own argument along.[29] Not once in chapters 1–13 does Paul allude to a specific circumstance or individual within the Roman Christian community. When he addresses his audience, he does so with terms that could be applied to any Christian group: "brothers and sisters" (7:4; 8:12; 10:1; 11:25); those "who know the law" (7:1); "you Gentiles" (11:13). Not even chapters 14–15 need have a specific situation at Rome in mind.[30]

We may, then, describe Romans as a tractate letter, one that has as its main component a theological argument or series of arguments.[31] Attempting a more definite genre identification is perilous. Bultmann and others have compared Romans to the diatribe, an argumentative genre popular with Cynic-Stoic philosophers.[32] Features of the diatribe found in Romans are the direct address of an opponent or interlocutor (see 2:1, 17), rhetorical questions, and the use of μὴ γένοιτο (mē genoito, "may it never be!") to reject the inference found in such questions (see 3:3–4, 5–6; 6:1–2, 15; 7:7, 13; 9:14; 11:1, 11). Bultmann viewed

---

[29]See esp. Günther Bornkamm, "The Letter to the Romans as Paul's Last Will and Testament," in *The Romans Debate*, 28.

[30]See Robert J. Karris, "Romans 14:1–15:13 and the Occasion of Romans," in *The Romans Debate*, 75–99.

[31]See Richard N. Longenecker, "On the Form, Function, and Authority of the New Testament Letters," in *Scripture and Truth*, ed. D. A. Carson and John D. Woodbridge (Grand Rapids: Zondervan, 1983), 104; Lightfoot, *Biblical Essays*, 315.

[32]Rudolf Bultmann, *Der Stil der paulinischen Predigt und die kynisch-stoische Diatribe*, FRLANT 13 (Göttingen: Vandenhoeck & Ruprecht, 1910).

the diatribe as polemical in orientation, but recent study has focused rather on its educative role and has raised the question whether the diatribe should be considered a genre at all.[33] In any case, while Paul clearly uses some of the devices of the diatribe, it was not so much a genre as a style that could be employed in many different genres.

Other attempts have been made to fit Romans into ancient literary categories: it has been labeled a memorandum,[34] an "epideictic" letter,[35] an ambassadorial letter,[36] a "protreptic" letter,[37] and a letter essay,[38] to name only a few. But Romans does not quite fit. To be sure, Romans has similarities to all of these genres. But this proves nothing more than that Paul has utilized various literary conventions of his day in getting his message across.[39]

PURPOSE

The treatise style of the letter to the Romans gives rise to one of the most debated questions about the letter: What was Paul's purpose in sending so heavy a theological exposition to the Christians in Rome? If we first turn to explicit statements of purpose in the letter itself, we find little to help answer this question. Paul writes about his reasons for visiting Rome, but not about his reason for writing to Rome. The only statement he makes on this latter point is too general to be of any real help: "I have written you quite boldly on some points to remind you of them again" (15:15).

The only remaining method of determining Paul's purpose is to fit the contents of the letter to its occasion. The general occasion of the letter is sketched above (see the section "Provenance and Date"). But it is the particular occasion, Paul's motivations in writing, that will lead to conclusions about purpose. Opinions on this question tend to move in two different directions: those that focus

---

[33]Stanley K. Stowers, *The Diatribe and Paul's Letter to the Romans*, SBLDS 57 (Chico: SP, 1981).

[34]Klaus Haacker, "Exegetische Probleme des Römerbriefs," *NovT* 20 (1978): 2–3.

[35]Wilhelm Wuellner, "Paul's Rhetoric of Argumentation in Romans: An Alternative to the Donfried-Karris Debate over Romans," in *The Romans Debate*, 128–46.

[36]Robert Jewett, "Romans as an Ambassadorial Letter," *Int* 36 (1982): 5–20.

[37]Stanley K. Stowers, *Letter Writing in Greco-Roman Antiquity* (Philadelphia: Westminster, 1986), 113–14; Anthony J. Guerra, *Romans and the Apologetic Tradition: The Purpose, Genre and Audience of Paul's Letter*, SNTSMS 81 (Cambridge: Cambridge University Press, 1995); Christopher Bryan, *A Preface to Romans: Notes on the Epistle in its Literary and Cultural Setting* (New York: Oxford University Press, 2000), 18–29.

[38]Martin Luther Stirewalt Jr., "Appendix: The Form and Function of the Greek Letter-Essay," in *The Romans Debate*, 147–71.

[39]According to James Dunn, "The distinctiveness of the letter far outweighs the significance of its conformity with current literary or rhetorical custom" (*Romans 1–8*, lix).

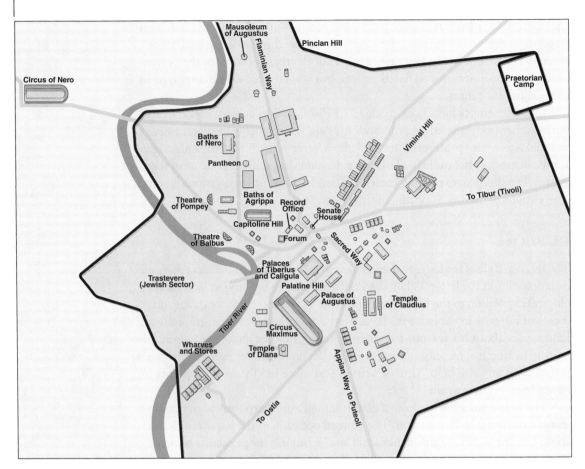

The City of Rome

on Paul's own circumstances and needs as the occasion for the letter, and those that stress the circumstances of the Christian community in Rome as its immediate occasion. Few solutions ignore one or the other of these factors entirely; the differences come in the importance accorded to each one.

We begin with those views that single out Paul's own circumstances as decisive. For the sake of convenience, these may be divided according to the location that is seen as central to Paul's concerns.

Spain. Paul's missionary-campaign plan is to travel to Spain in order to plant new churches in virgin territory (15:24–29). He is stopping in Rome on the way, and one of his undoubted purposes is to enlist the support of the church in Rome for his outreach there. Paul alludes to these hopes in 15:24 with the verb προπέμπω (*propempō*), which connotes "help on the way with material support." One of Paul's purposes in writing, then, may have been to introduce himself to the Roman Christians as a way of preparing for his visit and for his request for sponsorship. Indeed, some find this to be Paul's chief reason for writing.[40] They claim that the general theological tenor of the letter is due to Paul's desire to prove that he is orthodox and worthy of support.

Preparation for the mission in Spain was probably a major reason for the writing of Romans. But it cannot stand alone as a reason for the letter. Had this been Paul's overriding purpose, we would have expected mention of Spain long before chapter 15. Furthermore, the contents of Romans, while theological in nature, focus on a limited number of topics, treating these from a certain perspective: the salvation-historical disjunction of law and gospel, Jew and Greek. Something more definite than a desire to introduce himself is required to explain Paul's purpose in Romans.

Corinth/Galatia. Paul's concern with Jewish issues in Romans may be explained as stemming from his reflection on the struggle with the Judaizers that occupied him in Galatia and Corinth (see Galatians; 2 Cor. 3, 10–13). On this understanding of Romans, Paul's purpose in writing to Romans is to set forth his mature views on these issues as they have emerged from the rough-and-tumble of theological polemics. Paul's three-month stay in Corinth affords him the perfect opportunity to sum up these issues before he launches a new stage of missionary activity with its own problems and challenges. Lending support to this view is the relatively neutral stance that Paul takes in Romans on such issues as the law, circumcision, and Judaism.[41]

There is much to be said for this view, and probably it has captured part of the truth. But it leaves one crucial question unanswered: Why send this theological monograph to Rome?[42]

Jerusalem. This same objection applies to the view that Paul's letter to Rome embodies the speech he anticipates giving in Jerusalem when he arrives there with the collection.[43] That this upcoming visit and its consequences were on Paul's mind as he wrote Romans is clear (see 15:30–33). Moreover, this understanding of Paul's purpose would explain his preoccupation with issues

---

[40]E.g., Thorlief Boman, "Die dreifache Würde des Völke-apostels," *ST* 29 (1975): 63–69; Leon Morris, *The Epistle to the Romans* (Grand Rapids: Eerdmans, 1988), 7–17; Johnson, 343–44.

[41]For this approach, see particularly Bornkamm, "Last Will and Testament," 16–28; Munck, *Paul and the Salvation of Mankind,* 199; Kümmel, 312–13 (with some modifications); Manson, "To the Romans—and Others," 2; Kaye, "'To the Romans and Others' Revisited," 41–50.

[42]Bernhard Weiss suggested that it was the significance of Rome as the "capital of the world" that led Paul to send this tractate there (1.300–307), but nothing in Paul suggests this attitude toward Rome.

[43]See esp. Jacob Jervell, "The Letter to Jerusalem," in *The Romans Debate,* 53–64; note also Nils Alstrup Dahl, *Studies in Paul: Theology for the Early Christian Mission* (Minneapolis: Augsburg, 1977), 77.

pertaining to the relationship between Jews and Gentiles, since this was his underlying concern as he looked ahead to Jerusalem. But in addition to its failure to explain the Roman destination of the letter, this view shares with the previous one the problem of leaving the purpose of the letter separate from Paul's desire to visit Rome. His stress on this last point in both the introduction and the conclusion implies that the purpose for the letter must be related to the purpose for his visit.

At the beginning of the eighteenth century, F. C. Baur initiated a new way of looking at Romans. He rejected the then-popular "timeless treatise" approach to Romans and insisted that it be treated like any other letter of Paul's—one directed to issues arising from the church to which it was written.[44] Baur's general approach has enjoyed a resurgence in the last few decades. Unlike Baur, however, who thought Romans was a polemic against Jewish Christians, most modern scholars who share his approach think that other concerns are primary. Attention in this regard is directed particularly to the one text in Romans in which it appears that Paul has in mind a problem in the community at Rome: 14:1–15:13. This text rebukes two groups—the "weak in faith" and the "strong in faith"—for their intolerance of each other. It is likely that the weak are mainly Jewish Christians, and the strong are Gentile Christians. Here, it is argued, is the center of Romans. The treatise that precedes these chapters provides the necessary theological groundwork for this rebuke. And the rebuke, as the letter as a whole, focuses on the Gentile Christians, who are becoming arrogant toward the shrinking minority of Jewish Christians.[45]

To be sure, this interpretation has been rejected on the grounds that 14:1–15:13 is general parenesis, ethical guidance that has no basis in a specific circumstance.[46] But this is not convincing: the section is more naturally interpreted as arising from known divisions in the community in Rome.[47] One of Paul's purposes was to heal this division in the Christian community in Rome. But we doubt whether this was his primary purpose. Were this so, it is hard to understand why Paul would have waited until chapter 14 to make a practical application of his theology. Moreover, much of what Paul says in chapters 1–11 cannot serve as a basis for the exhortations in 14:1–15:13. Nor is it necessary that Romans be directed to the needs of the church addressed in just the same way that some of his other letters are. After all, Romans stands apart from all the

---

[44]Baur, "Zweck und Veranlassung des Römerbriefes," 153–60.

[45]Some important exponents of this general approach are Marxsen, 92–104; W. S. Campbell, "Why Did Paul Write Romans?" *ExpTim* 85 (1974): 264–69; Hans-Werner Bartsch, "The Historical Situation of Romans, with Notes by W. Gray," *Encounter: Creative Theological Scholarship* 33 (1972): 329–38; Karl P. Donfried, "A Short Note on Romans 16," in *The Romans Debate*, 48–49.

[46]Karris, "Occasion," 65–84.

[47]Donfried, "False Presuppositions," 107–11.

other letters Paul wrote to churches (except perhaps Colossians), as being the only one not written to a community that Paul had founded or been closely related to. Moreover, we have too few letters from Paul to justify any dogmatic judgments about the kinds of letters Paul could or could not have written. Finally, we must insist that even a theological treatise without specific reference to problems in Rome could still be directed to the needs of the church there— what church is without need of clear theological guidance?

Paul's purpose in Romans cannot be confined to any of these specific suggestions. It may be better to speak of Paul's several purposes in Romans.[48] Several intersecting factors come together to form what we might call Paul's missionary situation, and it is out of that situation that he writes to the Romans.[49] The past battles in Galatia and Corinth, the coming crisis in Jerusalem, the need to secure a missionary base for the work in Spain, the importance of unifying the divided Christian community in Rome around the gospel—these circumstances led Paul to write a letter in which he carefully set forth his understanding of the gospel, particularly as it related to the salvation-historical question of Jew and Gentile, law and gospel, continuity and discontinuity between the old and the new.[50]

We should note another factor that probably influenced Paul to focus on these questions: polemic against his theology as being anti-law, and perhaps anti-Jewish. Paul's need to combat Judaizers in Galatia and Corinth could very well have led to this false picture of the apostle to the Gentiles; and 3:8, where Paul mentions some who are slandering his teaching, suggests that Paul knew he had to defend himself against such accusations at Rome.[51]

ROMANS IN RECENT STUDY

Recent scholarship on Romans has focused on three issues: its nature/genre, its purpose, and its treatment of the Jews and the Mosaic law. We have considered

---

[48]See A. J. M. Wedderburn: *The Reasons for Romans* (Edinburgh: T. & T. Clark, 1989).

[49]So also L. Ann Jervis, *The Purpose of Romans: A Comparative Letter Structure Investigation,* JSNTSup 55 (Sheffield: JSOT, 1991).

[50]For this general approach, see Wikenhauser, 456–58; John Drane, "Why Did Paul Write Romans?" in *Pauline Studies, Fs. F. F. Bruce,* ed. D. A. Hagnar and M. J. Harris (Grand Rapids: Eerdmans, 1980), 212–23; A. J. M. Wedderburn, "The Purpose and Occasion of Romans Again," *ExpTim* 90 (1979): 137–41; C. E. B. Cranfield, *A Critical and Exegetical Commentary on the Epistle to the Romans,* ICC (Edinburgh: T. & T. Clark, 1975–79), 2.814; Dunn, *Romans 1–8,* lv–lviii.

[51]Jülicher, 115–18; Bruce, "Romans Debate," 334–35; Peter Stuhlmacher, "The Apostle Paul's View of Righteousness," in *Reconciliation, Law and Righteousness: Essays in Biblical Theology* (Philadelphia: Fortress Press, 1986), 76–77.

the first two in previous sections; and so important, complex, and significant for not only Romans but for Paul's theology is the third that we devoted a section in our chapter on Paul to this matter.

But closely related to this last matter have been a number of recent studies of Romans that have in common a distaste for the traditional interpretation of Romans. Three deserve mention here. Stanley Stowers takes to task generations of scholars for reading Romans in its Christian theological context rather than in its original historical and cultural context. He argues that the letter manifests a specific rhetorical strategy designed to convince Gentile Christians that the Jewish law is not the way to achieve the ancient goal of "self-mastery."[52] Second, Mark Nanos agrees with Stowers in identifying the audience as Gentile, but he thinks Paul's purpose is to convince Gentile Christians of the need to respect the historical and continuing theological importance of Israel as the people of God. He offers several fresh (and generally unconvincing) interpretations of key sections of Romans as he pursues this thesis.[53] Finally, Philip Esler, also criticizing a narrowly theological approach to Romans, focuses on the issues of social identity and ethnicity. Paul in Romans seeks to provide a new identity for the Christians in Rome, who are made up of both "Judeans" and "non-Judeans" (the terms he prefers, for historical reasons, over the usual "Jews" and "Gentiles").[54]

THEME AND CONTRIBUTION

Opinions about the theme of Romans have tended over time to move the center of attention from the beginning to the end of the letter. The Reformers, following the lead of Luther, singled out justification by faith, prominent especially in chapters 1–4, as the theme of the letter. At the beginning of the twentieth century, however, Albert Schweitzer argued that justification by faith was no more than a "battle" doctrine—a doctrine Paul used only to fight against Judaizers—and that the true theme of Romans is to be found in the teaching of Romans 6–8 about union with Christ and the work of God's Spirit.[55] Romans 9–11 was the next section to take center stage in the debate. Far from the excursus that some have found in these chapters, scholars such as Krister Stendahl think that the central theme of Romans is to be found here: the history of

---

[52]Stowers, *Rereading of Romans*.

[53]Nanos, *Mystery of Romans*.

[54]Philip F. Esler, *Conflict and Identity in Romans: The Social Setting of Paul's Letter* (Minneapolis: Fortress Press, 2003).

[55]Albert Schweitzer, *The Mysticism of Paul the Apostle* (London: A. & C. Black, 1931), the first draft of which was finished in 1904. For this general approach, see also W. Wrede, *Paul* (London: Philip Green, 1907).

salvation and of the two peoples, Jews and Gentiles, within this history.[56] Finally, it has been argued that the practical exhortation to unity in 14:1–15:13 is the true heart of the letter (see the previous section).

Each of these positions is alive in current scholarship, though sometimes in modified form. For example, the centrality of justification by faith is upheld by Ernst Käsemann—but only as one facet of the larger category "righteousness of God," interpreted to mean God's intervention in history to reclaim his creation for himself and to bring salvation to his people.[57] E. P. Sanders has followed Schweitzer in putting the stress on the "participationist" language of Romans 5–8.[58] A large number of scholars think that Romans is about the role of Israel in salvation history.[59] And other themes have also been singled out: God,[60] hope,[61] and salvation,[62] to name only a few.

It is possible that Romans does not have a single theme, that the most we can do is note recurring motifs within several distinct topics. But if we are to single out one theme, a good case can be made for "the gospel." This word and its cognate verb "to evangelize" are prominent in the introduction and in the conclusion of Romans, that is, in its epistolary frame, where we might expect to encounter any overarching topic. It is the word "gospel" that has pride of place in 1:16–17, which is so often (and probably rightly) taken to be the statement of the letter's theme. Moreover, as we have seen, Romans grows out of Paul's missionary situation, which makes natural a focus on that gospel with which Paul had been entrusted by his Lord. Romans, then, is Paul's statement of his gospel.[63]

> *It is possible that Romans does not have a single theme, only recurring motifs within several distinct topics. But if we are to single out one theme, a good case can be made for "the gospel."*

---

[56]See particularly Stendahl, "The Apostle Paul and the Introspective Conscience of the West," *HTR* 56 (1963): 199–215.

[57]See esp. Ernst Käsemann, "'The Righteousness of God' in Paul," in *New Testament Questions of Today* (Philadelphia: Fortress Press, 1969), 168–82, as well as idem, *Commentary on Romans* (Grand Rapids: Eerdmans, 1980).

[58]E. P. Sanders, *Paul and Palestinian Judaism* (Philadelphia: Fortress Press, 1977), 434–42.

[59]See, e.g., Hendrikus Boers, "The Problem of Jews and Gentiles in the Macro-Structure of Romans," *Neot* 15 (1981): 1–11; Jervell, "Letter to Jerusalem," 56; R. David Kaylor, *Paul's Covenant Community: Jew and Gentile in Romans* (Atlanta: John Knox, 1988), 18–19; Dunn, *Romans 1–8*, lxii–lxiii ("the integrating motif").

[60]Leon Morris, "The Theme of Romans," in *Apostolic History and the Gospel*, ed. W. Ward Gasque and Ralph P. Martin (Grand Rapids: Eerdmans, 1970), 249–63.

[61]John Paul Heil, *Romans: Paul's Letter of Hope*, AnBib 112 (Rome: BIP, 1987).

[62]J. Cambier, *L'évangile de Dieu selon l'épître aux Romains: Exégèse et théologie biblique*, vol. 1: *L'évangile de la justice et de la grace* (Brussels: Desclée de Brouwer, 1967), 34.

[63]For "gospel" as the central theme, see also Ulrich Wilckens, *Der Brief an die Römer*, EKKNT (Neukirchen-Vluyn: Neukirchener, 1978–82), 1.91.

This summary of the gospel in tractate form has rightly furnished theologians throughout the centuries with prime material for their work. While not a timeless summary of Paul's theology, Romans is nevertheless much less tied to specific first-century circumstances than almost any other book of the New Testament. Less translation from first-century culture to ours is needed than is usually the case. As James Denney says, "Is it not manifest that when we give [the conditions under which Paul wrote] all the historical definiteness of which they are capable, there is something in them which rises above the casualness of time and place, something which might easily give the epistle not an accidental or occasional character, but the character of an exposition of principles?"[64] On this point, Augustine, Luther, and Calvin have seen more clearly than their latter-day critics.[65]

Nevertheless, as we have seen, this statement of the gospel is made against a first-century background. The most important element in this background is also the most important issue that the early church had to face: the nature of the continuity between God's first "word" and his second, and between the people of that first word, Israel, and the people of that second word, the church. At this point in particular, Romans makes its contribution to the formulation of New Testament faith. For the way in which the relationship between the Old Testament and the New Testament, between law and gospel, Israel and church, is expressed—the degree of continuity and discontinuity—is fundamental to the construction of any *Christian* theology. Romans supplies the basic building blocks for the construction of that foundation.

As we have noted above and explained in more detail in chapter 9, recent scholarship on Romans emphasizes the "people" question in Romans: what the gospel means for the relationship of Jews and Gentiles in salvation history and in the church. And this emphasis is a needed corrective to the neglect of this issue in some traditional approaches. But as is so often the case in academia, the pendulum has swung too far. Paul's gospel has important implications for the relation of Jews and Gentiles. But Romans 1–8 makes clear that Paul's gospel is still basically targeted to the individual human being, locked up under sin and in need of the redemption available only in Jesus Christ. While justification by faith is not the theme of the letter, we should not forget that it is nevertheless a critical component of Paul's presentation of the gospel. To be "justified" is to be declared right with God. This verdict, Paul insists in Romans, is a manifestation of pure grace on God's part and therefore can be attained by sinful human beings only through faith. The contemporary theological climate offers challenges to this Reformation understanding of "justification by faith" at a num-

---

[64]Denney, "Romans," 570.

[65]See Stephen Westerholm, *Israel's Law and the Church's Faith* (Grand Rapids: Eerdmans, 1989), 222.

ber of points, but a careful reading of Romans reaffirms its truth and reminds us of its critical importance for the power of the gospel.

The tendency when explaining the significance of Romans is to dwell on theology as such. And the tendency is surely understandable, for no greater work of theology has ever been written. But it is worthwhile in conclusion to remind ourselves that, according to Romans, the gospel, while theological through and through, is at the same time practical through and through. As the phrase "the obedience of faith" suggests at the beginning of the letter (1:5 NRSV; cf. also 16:26), the gospel Paul presents in Romans is a life-transforming message. Faith in Christ must always be accompanied by obedience of him as Lord.[66] Chapters 12–15 are no afterthought or appendix to Romans; they are present precisely because the gospel is not truly understood or responded to unless it has changed the people it addresses. The lordship of Christ and the indwelling of the Spirit must inevitably change the way we "think" (12:2) and, thus, ultimately, the way we live.

BIBLIOGRAPHY

C. K. **Barrett**, *A Commentary on the Epistle to the Romans* (San Francisco: Harper & Row, 1957) ▥ Karl **Barth**, *The Epistle to the Romans* (London: Oxford University Press, 1933) ▥ Hans-Werner **Bartsch**, "The Historical Situation of Romans, with Notes by W. Gray," *Encounter: Creative Theological Scholarship* 33 (1972): 329–38 ▥ F. C. **Baur**, "Über Zweck und Veranlassung des Römerbriefes und die damit zusammenhängenden Verhältnisse der römischen Gemeinde," in *Historisch-kritische Untersuchungen zum Neuen Testament*, 2 vols. (Stuttgart: Friedrich Fromman, 1963), 1:147–266 ▥ Hendrikus **Boers**, "The Problem of Jews and Gentiles in the Macro-Structure of Romans," *Neot* 15 (1981): 1–11 ▥ Thorlief **Boman**, "Die dreifache Würde des Völkerapostels," *ST* 29 (1975): 63–69 ▥ Günther **Bornkamm**, "The Letter to the Romans as Paul's Last Will and Testament," in *The Romans Debate*, ed. Karl Donfried, rev. ed. (Peabody: Hendrickson, 1991), 16–28 ▥ F. F. **Bruce**, *Paul: Apostle of the Heart Set Free* (Grand Rapids: Eerdmans, 1977) ▥ idem, "The Romans Debate—Continued," *BJRL* 64 (1982): 334–59 ▥ Christopher **Bryan**, *A Preface to Romans: Notes on the Epistle in its Literary and Cultural Setting* (New York: Oxford University Press, 2000) ▥ Charles **Buck** and Greer **Taylor**, *Saint Paul: A Study of the Development of His Thought* (New York: Charles Scribner's Sons, 1969) ▥ Rudolf **Bultmann**, *Der Stil der paulinischen Predigt und die kynisch-stoische Diatribe*, FRLANT 13 (Göttingen: Vandenhoeck & Ruprecht, 1910) ▥ John **Calvin**, *Commentaries on the Epistle of Paul the Apostle to the Romans*, reprint ed. (Grand Rapids: Eerdmans, 1947) ▥ J. **Cambier**, *L'évangile de Dieu selon*

---

[66]On the meaning and significance of the debated phrase ὑπακοήν πίστεως (*hypakoēn pisteōs*), see Moo, *Epistle to the Romans*, 51–53.

l'épître aux Romains: Exégèse et théologie biblique, vol. 1: *L'évangile de la justice et de la grace* (Brussels: Desclée de Brouwer, 1967) ▮W. S. **Campbell**, "Why Did Paul Write Romans?" *ExpTim* 85 (1974): 264–69 ▮D. A. **Carson**, *Divine Sovereignty and Human Responsibility* (Atlanta: John Knox, 1981) ▮C. E. B. **Cranfield**, *A Critical and Exegetical Commentary on the Epistle to the Romans*, ICC, 2 vols. (Edinburgh: T. & T. Clark, 1975–79) ▮Oscar **Cullmann**, *Peter: Disciple, Apostle, Martyr* (Philadelphia: Westminster, 1962) ▮Nils Alstrup **Dahl**, *Studies in Paul: Theology for the Early Christian Mission* (Minneapolis: Augsburg, 1977) ▮James **Denney**, "St. Paul's Epistle to the Romans," in *EGT* 2 ▮Karl P. **Donfried**, "A Short Note on Romans 16," in *The Romans Debate*, 44–52 ▮John **Drane**, "Why Did Paul Write Romans?" in *Pauline Studies, Fs.* F. F. Bruce, ed. D. A. Hagnar and M. J. Harris (Grand Rapids: Eerdmans, 1980), 212–23 ▮James D. G. **Dunn**, "The New Perspective on Paul," *BJRL* 65 (1983): 95–122 ▮idem, *Romans 1–8, Romans 9–16*, WBC 38A/B (Waco: Word, 1988) ▮Philip F. **Esler**, *Conflict and Identity in Romans: The Social Setting of Paul's Letter* (Minneapolis: Fortress Press, 2003) ▮Joseph A. **Fitzmyer**, *Romans: A New Translation with Introduction and Commentary*, AB 33 (New York: Doubleday, 1993) ▮Harry **Gamble Jr.**, *The Textual History of the Letter to the Romans: A Study in Textual and Literary Criticism* (Grand Rapids: Eerdmans, 1977) ▮David W. J. **Gill**, "Erastus the Aedile," *TynB* 40 (1989): 293–302 ▮F. L. **Godet**, *Commentary on Romans*, reprint ed. (Grand Rapids: Kregel, 1977) ▮Edgar J. **Goodspeed**, "Phoebe's Letter of Introduction," *HTR* 44 (1951): 55–57 ▮R. H. **Gundry**, "Grace, Works, and Staying Saved in Paul," *Bib* 66 (1985): 1–38 ▮Klaus **Haacker**, "Exegetische Probleme des Römerbriefs," *NovT* 20 (1978): 1–21 ▮John Paul **Heil**, *Romans: Paul's Letter of Hope*, AnBib 112 (Rome: BIP, 1987) ▮Larry W. **Hurtado**, "The Doxology at the End of Romans," in *New Testament Textual Criticism: Its Significance for Exegesis, Fs.* Bruce M. Metzger, ed. E. J. Epp and G. D. Fee (Oxford: Clarendon Press, 1981), 185–99 ▮Jacob **Jervell**, "The Letter to Jerusalem," in *The Romans Debate*, 53–64 ▮Robert **Jewett**, "Romans as an Ambassadorial Letter," *Int* 36 (1982): 5–20 ▮Robert J. **Karris**, "Romans 14:1–15:13 and the Occasion of Romans," in *The Romans Debate*, 75–99 ▮Ernst **Käsemann**, *Commentary on Romans* (Grand Rapids: Eerdmans, 1980) ▮idem, "'The Righteousness of God' in Paul," in *New Testament Questions of Today* (Philadelphia: Fortress Press, 1969), 168–82 ▮Bruce N. **Kaye**, "'To the Romans and Others' Revisited," *NovT* 18 (1976): 37–77 ▮David **Kaylor**, *Paul's Covenant Community: Jew and Gentile in Romans* (Atlanta: John Knox, 1988) ▮J. **Kinoshita**, "Romans—Two Writings Combined," *NovT* 7 (1964): 258–77 ▮Otto **Kuss**, *Der Römerbrief*, 3 vols. (Regensburg: Pustet, 1963–78) ▮Kirsopp **Lake**, *The Earlier Epistles of St. Paul* (London: Rivingstons, 1919) ▮Harry J. **Leon**, *The Jews of Ancient Rome* (Philadelphia: Jewish Publication Society, 1960) ▮J. B. **Lightfoot**, "The Structure and Destination of the Epistle to the Romans," in *Biblical Essays* (London: Macmillan, 1893) ▮Richard N. **Longenecker**, "On the Form, Function, and Authority of the New Testament Letters," in *Scripture and Truth*, ed. D. A. Carson and John D. Woodbridge (Grand Rapids: Zondervan, 1983), 101–14 ▮idem, *Paul, Apostle of Liberty*, reprint ed. (Grand Rapids: Baker, 1976) ▮Gerd **Lüdemann**, *Paul, Apostle to the Gentiles: Studies in Chronology* (Philadelphia: Fortress Press, 1984) ▮J. I. H. **McDonald**, "Was Romans XVI a Separate Letter?" *NTS* 16 (1969–70): 369–72 ▮T. W. **Manson**, "Letter to the Romans—and Others," *BJRL* 31 (1948): 224–40 ▮I. Howard **Marshall**, "Romans 16:25–27—An Apt Conclusion," in *Romans and the People of God*, Fs. Gordon D. Fee, ed. Sven K. Soderlung and N. T. Wright (Grand Rapids: Eerdmans, 1999), 170–84 ▮Paul **Minear**, *The Obedience of Faith: The Purposes of Paul in the Epistle to the Romans* (London: SCM, 1971) ▮Douglas J. **Moo**, *The Epistle to the Romans*, NICNT (Grand Rapids: Eerdmans, 1996) ▮Leon **Morris**, *The Epistle to the Romans* (Grand Rapids: Eerdmans, 1988) ▮idem, "The Theme of Romans," in *Apostolic History and the Gospel*, ed. W. Ward Gasque and Ralph P. Martin (Grand Rapids: Eerdmans, 1970), 249–63 ▮Johannes **Munck**, *Paul and the Salvation of Mankind* (London: SCM, 1959) ▮John **Murray**, *The Epistle to the Romans*, 2 vols., NICNT (Grand Rapids: Eerdmans, 1959–65) ▮Mark **Nanos**, *The Mystery of Romans: The Jewish Context of Paul's Letter* (Minneapolis: Augsburg/Fortress, 1996) ▮W.-H. **Ollrog**, "Die Abfassungsverhältnisse von Röm 16," in *Kirche*, Fs. Günther Bornkamm, ed. D. Lührmann and G. Strecker (Tübingen: Mohr-Siebeck, 1980), 221–44 ▮J. C. **O'Neill**, *Paul's Letter to the Romans* (Baltimore: Penguin, 1975) ▮Romano **Penna**, "Les Juifs à Rome au temps de l'apôtre Paul," *NTS* 28 (1982): 321–47 ▮Heikki **Räisänen**, *Paul and the Law* (Tübingen: Mohr-Siebeck, 1983) ▮J. R. **Richards**, "Romans and I Corinthians: Their Chronological Relationship and Comparative Dates," *NTS* 13 (1966–67): 14–30 ▮William **Sanday** and Arthur C. **Headlam**, *A Critical and Exegetical Commentary on the Epistle to the Romans*, ICC (Edinburgh: T. & T. Clark, 1902) ▮E. P. **Sanders**, *Paul and Palestinian Judaism* (Philadelphia: Fortress Press, 1977) ▮idem, *Paul, the Law and the Jewish People* (Philadelphia: Fortress Press, 1983) ▮Walter **Schmithals**, *Der Römerbrief als historisches Problem*, SNT 9 (Gütersloh: Gerd Mohn, 1975) ▮Thomas R. **Schreiner**, *Romans*, BECNT (Grand Rapids: Baker, 1998) ▮Albert **Schweitzer**, *The Mysticism of Paul the Apostle* (London: A. & C. Black, 1931) ▮E. Mary **Smallwood**, *The Jews Under Roman Rule*, SJLA 20 (Leiden: Brill, 1976) ▮Sven K. **Soderlund** and N. T. **Wright**, eds., *Romans and the People of God*, Fs. Gordon D. Fee (Grand Rapids: Eerdmans, 1999) ▮Krister **Stendahl**, "The Apostle Paul and the Introspective Conscience of the West," *HTR* 56 (1963): 199–215 ▮Martin Luther **Stirewalt** Jr., "Appendix: The Form and Function of the Greek Letter-Essay," in *The Romans Debate*, 147–71 ▮Stanley K. **Stowers**, *The Diatribe and Paul's Letter to the Romans*, SBLDS 57 (Chico: SP, 1981) ▮idem, *Letter Writing in Greco-Roman Antiquity* (Philadelphia: Westminster, 1986) ▮idem, *A Rereading of Romans: Justice, Jews and Gentiles* (New Haven: Yale University Press, 1995) ▮Peter **Stuhlmacher**, "The Apostle Paul's View of Righteousness," in *Reconciliation, Law and Righteousness: Essays in Biblical Theology* (Philadelphia: Fortress

Press, 1986), 68–93 ▥ Francis **Watson,** *Paul, Judaism, and the Gentiles: A Sociological Approach,* SNTSMS 56 (Cambridge: Cambridge University Press, 1986) ▥ Nigel M. **Watson**, "Simplifying the Righteousness of God: A Critique of J. C. O'Neill's *Romans,*" *SJT* 30 (1977): 464–69 ▥ A. J. M. **Wedderburn**, "The Purpose and Occasion of Romans Again," *ExpTim* 90 (1979): 137–41 ▥ idem, *The Reasons for Romans* (Edinburgh: T. & T. Clark, 1989) ▥ Stephen **Westerholm**, *Israel's Law and the Church's Faith* (Grand Rapids: Eerdmans, 1989) ▥ Wolfgang **Wiefel**, "The Jewish Community in Ancient Rome and the Origins of Roman Christianity," in *The Romans Debate,* 85–101 ▥ Ulrich **Wilckens**, *Der Brief an die Römer,* 3 vols., EKKNT (Neukirchen-Vluyn: Neukirchener, 1978–82) ▥ W. **Wrede**, *Paul* (London: Philip Green, 1907) ▥ Wilhelm **Wuellner**, "Paul's Rhetoric of Argumentation in Romans: An Alternative to the Donfried-Karris Debate over Romans," in *The Romans Debate,* 152–74 ▥ G. **Zuntz**, *The Text of the Epistles: A Disquisition upon the Corpus Paulinum* (London: British Academy, 1953).

CHAPTER ELEVEN

1 AND 2 CORINTHIANS

CONTENTS

Both Corinthian epistles are occasional letters, that is, they are letters addressed to specific people and occasioned by concrete issues; the letter form is not a mere literary device by which the author shapes his views for general publication (sometimes called "tractate letters"). Questions have been raised about the cohesiveness and the authenticity of parts of these epistles, especially the second. These will be discussed below. As the texts stand, however, the letters fall into two books.

1 Corinthians

Following the proem, or salutation (1:1–3), and the thanksgiving for God's enriching work in the believers of the Corinthian church (1:4–9), Paul begins the first main division of the epistle (1:10–4:21), which deals with the church's profound internal divisions and fundamental misapprehensions as to the nature of Christian leadership. On the basis of reports brought to Paul by "some from Chloe's household" (1:11), Paul has learned of the party spirit by which various sectors of the church identified themselves with particular leaders, apparently boasting of the superior wisdom of their self-identification in each case (1:10–17). Paul despises such so-called wisdom: its categories are inimical to all that Paul holds dear—so much so that if its categories were to prevail, the gospel itself could be dismissed as God's folly (1:18–25), to become a Christian would mean to become a fool (1:26–31), and to preach the gospel without manipulative and self-promoting eloquence but with simple dependence on the truthfulness and power of the message of the crucified Messiah would be the essence of ignorance (2:1–5). Conversely, if God's folly is wiser than the world's wisdom, if Christians rejoice that God has chosen the "foolish" in order to shame the "wise" and to make it clear that Christ alone is our "wisdom from God," if Paul's priorities in preaching are foundational, then the Corinthians' pursuit of the world's wisdom implicitly contradicts their own Christian profession.

This does not mean that there is no sense in which the Christian gospel is wise. Far from it: God's wisdom is revealed not only in the cross of Christ in the public arena, but by the Spirit to individuals—for otherwise they would not understand it (2:6–16). Sadly, however, Paul could not address the Corinthian believers as if they were in fact spiritual, because they were not living up to their calling; they were still divided along party lines associated with well-known leaders (3:1–4) and were thus, at best, "infants." So Paul must clarify the nature of Christian leadership. In the rest of this chapter, he removes false impressions in this regard, first by two metaphors—one agricultural (3:5–9a) and one drawn from the construction industry (3:9b–15)—in order to stress the complementary nature of the leaders' work and their accountability to God for its quality. That leads to a warning against all who destroy the church (3:16–17).

Returning to the contrast between wisdom and folly, Paul directly assaults any remaining misconceptions about Christian leadership: the Corinthians are deceiving themselves if they think their partisan spirit is a mark of wisdom, when the Scriptures promote humility and when genuine Christian maturity recognizes that in Christ *all* Christian leaders—and everything else—have become part of the Christians' inheritance (3:18–23). Paul concludes by showing that Christian leaders and those who follow them must alike recognize that God alone is the One who makes the distinctions, and he alone rightly assesses performance (4:1–7). Indeed, the Corinthians should learn this lesson by the simple contrast between their own self-vaunting pretensions and the way the apostles are treated as the scum of the earth (4:8–13). They should learn to imitate the Christian conduct of their own father in Christ, the apostle Paul himself, and thus align themselves with what is normative in other churches (4:14–17). The prospect of Paul's impending visit constitutes both an intense final appeal and a scarcely veiled threat (4:18–21).

Whether the further reports that Paul deals with in chapters 5–6 also came from Chloe's people or from some other source—perhaps from Stephanas, Fortunatus, and Achaicus (16:17)—is unclear. Three issues dominate these chapters. The first is a case of incest (5:1–18), which leads Paul to clarify what he had meant in an earlier letter to the Corinthians (5:9–13); the second is a problem of litigation between believers (6:1–11); and the third has to do with some in the Corinthian congregation who so misunderstood their supposed spirituality that they thought they were free to engage in extramarital sexual unions, presumably on the ground that they involved merely the body (6:12–20).

In response to a written inquiry from the Corinthians (7:1), probably brought to Paul by Stephanas, Fortunatus, and Achaicus (16:17), Paul sets himself to address the topics they raise. The first has to do with marriage and related matters (7:1–40). The second, dealing with food sacrificed to idols (8:1–11:1), is sometimes alleged to include one or two excursuses, but the general line of argument is fairly clear. In 8:1–13, Paul insists that divisions of opinion as to whether it is proper to eat food that has been sacrificed to idols must be resolved on the basis of self-sacrificial love, not claims to superior knowledge. Chapter 9, cast in part as Paul's defense of his apostolicity, shows that Paul perceives the connection between this problem and the divisiveness he treated in chapters 1–4: in both cases a raw triumphalism prevails. Paul combats this evil and addresses both problems by pointing to his own commitment to self-denial as the very hallmark of his apostolicity: despite his many rights as an apostle, he voluntarily lays them aside so as to win as many as possible to Christ. This model of self-control and self-denial must characterize all Christians (9:24–27). The negative example of Israel thus becomes directly relevant: it is all too easy to begin well but not persevere, and thus to fall under God's judgment (10:1–13). If idolatry is to be avoided, Christians should not participate in worship in pagan temples (10:14–22).

The next three problems that Paul treats have to do with the public meetings of the Corinthian Christians. The first deals with the relationship between men and women, especially as it was surfacing in a dispute over the issue of head covering for women (11:2–16). The second addresses abuses at the Lord's Supper (11:17–34). And the third deals with the distribution and exercise of the Spirit's gifts (12:1–14:40), especially the relative value of prophecy and tongues (14:1–25). Here the apostle insists on the need for diversity in unity (chap. 12), the utter necessity and permanence of love, the "most excellent way" (chap. 13), the importance of intelligibility in the public meetings of the church (14:1–25), and the proper ordering of the church's corporate meetings so far as the exercise of the gifts is concerned (14:26–40). In the most distinctly theological chapter of the letter, Paul deals with the resurrection of believers (chap. 15), insisting that the proper prototype is the resurrection of Jesus Christ. He denies that any wedge can be driven between these two resurrections so far as their nature is concerned, thereby forcing his readers to direct their gaze and their aspirations to the triumph at the end. Paul brings his handling of the Corinthians' written agenda to a close by clearing up some questions on the collection (16:1–11) and on the coming of Apollos (16:12).

The epistle concludes with some final exhortations (16:13–18) and greetings (16:19–24).

2 Corinthians

Following the salutation (1:1–2), there is a lengthy thanksgiving (1:3–11). Such thanksgiving sections are characteristically placed after the salutation in many Hellenistic letters, including twelve of the thirteen letters in the Pauline corpus (the exception is Galatians); but this one is particularly long and emotional and focuses rather more on Paul's experiences (of "a deadly peril," 1:10) than is usually the case.

Paul plunges into a defense of his travel plans (1:12–2:13). He denies that he has acted in a worldly or fickle manner (1:12–14). After reviewing his plans

(1:15–22), he explains the reason why he changed them: he was reluctant to cause the Corinthians as much grief as he had on an earlier visit (1:23–2:4). This leads to instruction on how to forgive and comfort someone the congregation had properly punished, apparently for opposing Paul and thereby damaging the Corinthian believers (2:5–11). Paul then begins the recital of the events that have led to the writing of the present letter, including the failure of Titus to meet Paul in Troas with a report on the Corinthians, with the result that Paul sets out for Macedonia himself, apparently on the way to find out what was going on (2:12–13). The recital is broken up by an outburst of praise (2:14–17), followed by a long section that not only articulates probing perspectives on the nature of Christian ministry but ties this stance to a proper estimate of the tension between inaugurated and futurist eschatology (2:14–7:4).

Paul begins this long section by insisting that God himself has made the apostle competent for this ministry, which divides people around him as he serves as "the aroma of Christ among those who are being saved and those who are perishing" (2:14–3:6). This leads to a comparison and contrast between ministry under the old covenant and under the new (3:7–18). Since Paul has received this new-covenant ministry by the mercy of God, he is committed to integrity in the proclamation of the "gospel of the glory of Christ," regardless of how he himself is received (4:1–6). The treasure is Christ; the earthenware vessel in which the treasure is contained is Paul and his ministry (4:7–18). That does not mean this earthenware vessel will always be poor and perishing: the ultimate prospect is the transformation that comes when the "heavenly dwelling" swallows up Paul's mortality in life (5:1–10). With such a prospect before him, Paul's motives in life and ministry are to please Christ, not those to whom he ministers. Yet far from suggesting indifference toward his hearers, this gospel and this view of ministry ensure that it is nothing less than the love of Christ that compels him to serve as Christ's ambassador, proclaiming reconciliation and a new beginning on the basis of Christ's sacrifice for sins (5:16–21). Therefore Paul pleads with the Corinthians to have a heart open to God and to God's ambassador, so as not to receive God's grace in vain (6:1–13); for they must understand that proper response to God is exclusive (6:14–7:1). So Paul brings his appeal to a close (7:2–4).

At this point, Paul resumes his account of the return of Titus and the encouraging report he brought with him (7:5–16). Paul is almost euphoric with transparent relief that the Corinthians have responded with repentance and godly sorrow to the earlier rebukes by visit and letter. This means it is possible for Paul to bring up a matter of constant concern to him at this stage of his ministry, namely, the collection for the Christians in Jerusalem and the Corinthians' part in it (8:1–9:15). The Macedonians had set a high standard by their sacrificial giving (8:1–6); the Corinthians, who had been the first to respond, are now exhorted to bring the project to completion as fruitfully as they began it (8:7–15). Titus's mission is designed to further the cause (8:16–24) and to prepare the Corinthians for a visit by Paul himself, possibly accompanied by some Macedonians (9:1–5). Paul concludes by setting the collection within a theological framework that ties this ministry to the gospel and to the glory of God (9:6–15).

The nature of the relationship between chapters 1–9 and 10–13 is disputed (see the section "Occasion" below), but the latter chapters seem to depict Paul's response to a fresh outbreak of opposition at Corinth. Paul appeals for a faith that is obedient (10:1–6) and condemns the opposition for its ugly boasting and one-upmanship (10:7–18). In 11:1–15 he exposes the false apostles who have usurped authority in the church and denounces their false criteria. Then, answering fools according to their folly, Paul engages in a little boasting of his own—by inverting all the criteria of his opponents and boasting in things they would despise (11:16–33). In fact, Paul boasts in weakness, because he understands that his weakness is the condition under which the power of God powerfully operates through him (12:1–10). The Corinthians themselves are to blame for not taking decisive action against the opponents, who are channeling the church toward a cross-disowning triumphalism. Paul contrasts his own motives (12:11–21), begging the Corinthian believers to reconsider their course and warning them that if necessary, he will take strong action when he arrives on his third visit (13:1–10). The epistle ends with a final appeal, greetings, and the words of "the grace" (13:11–13 [vv. 11–14 in TNIV]).

AUTHOR

Paul is identified as the author in the opening verses of both epistles, and few have contested the claim. In the case of 2 Corinthians, various partition theories have been proposed (discussed below). In most such theories, the various sections are nevertheless ascribed to Paul. The most persistent exception is 2 Corinthians 6:14–7:1, which a number of scholars judge to be a later interpolation written, perhaps, by someone in the Pauline school. The theory can be tested only by jointly weighing the corresponding reconstructions of Paul's relationships with the Corinthian church and the literary evidence advanced to justify this partition. These matters will be treated shortly.

DESTINATION

Corinth was located on the isthmus that connects the Peloponnese with the rest of Greece. Not only was it ideally situated to control north-south trade, but because the port of Lechaeum lay a mile and a half to the north (on the Gulf of Corinth) and Cenchreae (Rom. 16:1) was just over seven miles to the east on the Saronic Gulf, it also provided an indispensable land link between east and west.

The wealthy and ancient city of Corinth was utterly destroyed by the Romans in 146 B.C., and its citizens were killed or sold into slavery. Roman

Paul is identified as the author in both epistles, and few have contested the claim. For 2 Corinthians, various partition theories have been proposed, but the various sections are usually ascribed to Paul.

might ensured that the prohibition against rebuilding it was respected. Nevertheless, a century later Julius Caesar founded the city afresh, this time as a Roman colony, and from 29 B.C. on, it served as the seat of a proconsul and the capital of the senatorial province of Achaia. The new city was populated by people from various parts of the empire, doubtless not a few of them retired soldiers. According to Strabo (*Geog.* 8.6.23c), many were freedmen from Rome, whose status was only a cut above slaves. Jews were certainly included in the new citizenry (a broken inscription of uncertain date, with the words "Synagogue of the Hebrews," has been discovered, confirming Acts 18:4). Some Greeks were also residents of the new Corinth, perhaps large numbers of them; but the Romans dominated the scene with their laws, culture, and religion. Much of the empire had been thoroughly Hellenized, however, so not only was the lingua franca Greek but doubtless many ties—religious, philosophical, and cultural—were quickly reestablished with the rest of the Greek peninsula. From Asia and Egypt came various mystery cults. Because there was no landed aristocracy in the new Corinth, there arose an aristocracy of wealth. Inevitably, the poor were correspondingly despised or ignored (see 1 Cor. 11:17–22).

It is important not to read the old city's character into the new city (as Pausanius 2.3.7 already makes clear). Old Corinth had such a notorious reputation that "to Corinthianize" could mean "to fornicate," and "Corinthian girl" was a way of referring to a whore. Clay votives of human genitals have come down to us from the old city. They were offered to Asclepius, the god of healing, in the hope that that part of the body, suffering from venereal disease, would be healed. Probably Strabo's description of the one thousand temple prostitutes of the old city's temple of Aphrodite was exaggerated,[1] but the reality must have been bad enough to win such an egregious reputation. Even so, it is far from clear that such associations were carried across to the new city; but traditions like that die hard; and as a great port city, Corinth likely did not establish a reputation for moral probity (see 1 Cor. 6:12ff.).

OCCASION

Historical Reconstruction

Paul first preached the gospel in Corinth during his second missionary journey (Acts 18). Supporting himself with his trade as a tentmaker or leatherworker, he lived with Aquila and Priscilla, who had recently moved to Corinth from Rome (Acts 18:1–3). As usual, Paul began his ministry by trying to convince all who attended the synagogue, Jews and Gentiles alike, that Jesus was

---

[1]H. Conzelmann, "Korinth und die Mädchen der Aphrodite: Zur Religionsgeschichte der Stadt Korinth," *NAG* 8 (1967–68): 247–61; Jerome Murphy-O'Connor, *St. Paul's Corinth: Texts and Archaeology* (Wilmington: Glazier, 1983), 55–57.

the promised Messiah (v. 4). Once Timothy and Silas rejoined him, Paul's ministry increased, possibly in part because they brought gifts from the Macedonian churches that freed him to devote more time to preaching (v. 5; cf. 17:14). As his ministry increased, so did the opposition. Paul was forced to move his ministry next door to the house of Titius Justus. So fruitful was his evangelism that not only many pagans but Crispus, the synagogue ruler, and his entire family believed in the Lord Jesus (vv. 7–8).

Only recently delivered from bruising punishment in Philippi (Acts 16), and having just barely escaped similar battering in Thessalonica and Berea (Acts 17), Paul approached Corinth "in weakness with great fear and trembling" (1 Cor. 2:3), but was encouraged by a dream in which the exalted Christ assured him of safety and much fruit (Acts 18:9–10). Paul stayed a year and a half, laying the only possible foundation, Jesus Christ himself (1 Cor. 3:10–11). After seeing the church well established, Paul left Corinth by ship (probably in the spring of A.D. 51; see discussion below in the section "Date"), crossing the Aegean Sea with Priscilla and Aquila, whom he left in Ephesus while he headed for Jerusalem—hoping, perhaps (if we follow the Western text of Acts 18:21), to arrive there before the Feast (Passover or Pentecost). He did not remain long in Jerusalem but soon returned to his home church in Antioch and shortly after returned to Ephesus. There he began an enormously fruitful ministry of two and a half years (probably the autumn of 52 to the spring of 55). During that period he wrote 1 Corinthians.

Meanwhile, others had come to build on the foundation that Paul had laid in Corinth. Apollos worked there (1 Cor. 3:6), and probably Peter as well.[2] There is no evidence that these or other leaders had fostered a party spirit, consciously attempting to form a coterie of personal devotees. Nevertheless, doubtless owing to factors still to be examined, the spiritually immature Corinthians formed partisan groupings that claimed to follow this or that leader (1 Cor. 1:11). The church as a whole was less than satisfied with Paul's leadership (1 Cor. 4:3, 15; 9:1–2), and the integrity of its life was marred by abuses at the Lord's Table (11:17–34), at least one notorious case of immorality (5:1–5; cf. 6:12–20), public litigation among members (6:1–8), uncertainties about the place of marriage (chap. 7) and the propriety of eating food that had been offered to idols (chap. 8), infatuation with the more spectacular of the charismatic gifts without any profound commitment to mutual love (chaps. 12–14), and a decidedly aberrant view of the resurrection (chap. 15).

How Paul first came to hear of some of these problems we cannot be sure, but apparently in response to a communication from them, he wrote them a

---

[2]See C. K. Barrett, "Cephas and Corinth," in *Abraham unser Vater: Juden und Christen im Gespräch über die Bibel, Fs. Otto Michel*, ed. O. Betz, M. Hengel, and P. Schmidt, AGSU 5 (Leiden: Brill, 1963), 1–12.

letter (referred to in 1 Cor. 5:9), most of whose contents are lost, but which forbade association with immoral people. This letter, sometimes referred to as "the previous letter," we may designate Corinthians A. Most scholars agree that it has not survived (though see discussion below). Perhaps the Corinthians had posed a question about church discipline, and Paul assumed this question as the context of his response, while in fact some of his readers took his response in the widest sense and thus misinterpreted him (1 Cor. 5:9–13).

At some point during his Ephesian ministry, Paul received reports from "some from Chloe's household" (1:11) about the ugly factionalism in Corinth. The three official delegates of the church—Stephanas, Fortunatus, and Achaicus (16:17)—brought not only the gift from the Corinthians but also the church's letter and their own verbal reports, which together established Paul's agenda as he wrote 1 Corinthians (which might be designated Corinthians B).

When Paul sent off 1 Corinthians, he fully intended to remain in Ephesus until Pentecost (probably A.D. 55), then cross the Aegean to Macedonia, visit the churches there, and travel south to Corinth, where he expected to remain "awhile, or even spend the winter" (16:5–8). Meanwhile, he sent Timothy, exhorting the Corinthians to receive him warmly and "send him on his way in peace" (1 Cor. 16:10–11; cf. Acts 19:22) so that he could return to Paul, presumably with a report. After sending the letter, Paul changed his plans a little: he now proposed to visit Corinth twice, once on the way to Macedonia and once on the way back, intending to sail from Corinth to Judea (2 Cor. 1:15–16). On this return leg he hoped to collect considerable money from Macedonia and Achaia (including Corinth) for the relief of the believers in Jerusalem, who were suffering from famine and persecution.

When he formulated these plans, Paul apparently felt no urgency to get to Corinth. After all, he was in no hurry to leave Ephesus, since "a great door for effective work" (1 Cor. 16:9) was still open for him there. But when Timothy arrived in Corinth, he found the situation beyond his ability to manage. Even 1 Corinthians, the apostle's letter, had not had the good effect Paul had envisaged. Whether Timothy himself returned with a grim report, or Paul found out about the dire situation some other way, the apostle abandoned any thought of further delay and immediately set out for Corinth. This turned into a distressing confrontation that Paul himself had warned the Corinthians they should avoid (1 Cor. 4:21)—a "painful visit," to use Paul's language (2 Cor. 2:1). We cannot determine whether or not Corinthians B (= 1 Corinthians) had helped the Corinthian believers resolve a number of matters, but it is quite clear that animus against Paul was still very strong and focused in one or two leaders whom the Corinthians either tacitly supported or refused to condemn. About the same time, and probably before the "painful visit," the church had been invaded by some self-designated Christian leaders. Probably they called themselves apostles (2 Cor. 11:13–15) and carried letters of recommendation with them (cf. 2 Cor. 3:1–3). They were not apostles in the way Paul was, a witness of the resurrection with a personal commission from Christ to evangelize where Christ was not known; they were probably apostles in the general sense that they were agents of others who had commissioned them. Possibly they were in some sense Judaizers,[3] that is, those who were trying to bring the church more into line with Jewish piety and practice (see 2 Cor. 11:16ff.)—though that point is disputed, as we shall see. It is far more likely that, despite any Jewish background they enjoyed (cf. 2 Cor. 11:21–22), they were deeply integrated into Greco-Roman life (see further discussion below in the section "The Character of Paul's Opponents").

From Paul's perspective at the time, the "painful visit" was a complete fiasco. At least one of the opponents had attacked him in deeply insulting ways (2 Cor. 2:5–8, 10; 7:12); worse, the work of the gospel was in serious jeopardy. Why Paul left at this point is uncertain. Perhaps he hoped time would heal some of the wounds and bring the Corinthians to their senses; perhaps he had other pressing engagements. In any case, he resolved not to return immediately. This opened him up to the charge of being fickle, willing to change his commitments at a whim, even though the fundamental reason why he did not return was to spare them the pain of another confrontation (2 Cor. 1:16ff.). But this did not mean Paul was prepared to let the situation slide. He sent them another letter, which we may designate Corinthians C. Written "out of great distress and anguish of heart and with many tears" (2 Cor. 2:4), this letter assured the Corinthians of Paul's love for them but also laid down the standards he expected in the churches in his charge and sought to determine if they would meet those standards (2:9). For this reason, Corinthians C is sometimes called the "tearful letter" or the "severe letter." Delivered by Titus (who may have been a more forceful person than Timothy), this letter demanded the punishment of the ringleader who had maligned and opposed Paul so maliciously (2:3–9; 7:8–12). In all probability this letter has also been lost.[4]

---

[3]The term "Judaizer" is problematic. In modern usage, a majority of scholars apply it to Jews who in some sense accept Jesus as the Messiah but who insist that Gentiles convert to Judaism before (or at least as part of) coming to faith in Jesus (see also chap. 12, on Galatians). But in the first century, "to Judaize" meant "to live like a Jew (even though one is not a Jew)," and in this sense a "Judaizer" would be a Gentile trying to live like a Jew. In deference to modern usage, however, we have retained the term in the contemporary sense. Those who think that the opponents are Judaizers include, from very different points in the theological spectrum, Paul Barnett, *The Second Epistle to the Corinthians*, NICNT (Grand Rapids: Eerdmans, 1997), esp. 33–40, and Michael D. Goulder, *Paul and the Competing Mission in Corinth* (Peabody: Hendrickson, 2001).

[4]This is much more likely than that the "severe letter" is in fact 1 Corinthians and that the person in question was the man guilty of incest (1 Cor. 5:1ff.), pace Philip E. Hughes, *Paul's Second Epistle to the Corinthians*, NICNT (Grand Rapids: Eerdmans,

Titus also had the responsibility to organize the collection for Jerusalem (2 Cor. 8:6). The fact that Paul could still expect the Corinthians to participate is evidence that he did not, despite the painful visit, regard the church as fundamentally apostate. He knew of their wealth and had boasted of their initial willingness not only to Titus (7:14) but also to the Macedonians (9:2). Probably he was afraid that some of the animus against him would degenerate into an unwillingness to cooperate in this financial assistance plan; probably he feared that the interlopers were by their strenuous demands for financial support (11:7, 12–20; 12:14) siphoning off funds that Paul felt should go to assist the poor believers in Jerusalem.

Meanwhile, Paul's ministry in Ephesus was providing another set of dangers and challenges, a "deadly peril" such that he "despaired of life itself," feeling upon himself "the sentence of death" (2 Cor. 1:8–10). We know nothing of the details. Shortly after the Demetrius riot (Acts 19:23–20:1), however, Paul left Ephesus for Troas (2 Cor. 2:12, 13—"Troas" might refer either to the port city or to the Troad region in which it lay), where he hoped not only to preach the gospel but to meet Titus returning with news of Corinth. Only the first of these hopes was happily realized. On the one hand, he "found that the Lord had opened a door" for him (2 Cor. 2:12); on the other, as he wrote, "I still had no peace of mind, because I did not find my brother Titus there" (2 Cor. 2:13). So Paul left Troas and headed for Macedonia (2:13); apparently, he had established a contingency plan to meet Titus there, should the meeting at Troas not take place. In Macedonia Paul pursued both his pastoral ministry (Acts 20:1–2) and his organizing of the collection for the Jerusalem believers (2 Cor. 8:1–4; 9:2). These churches were themselves facing "a very severe trial" and "extreme poverty" (8:2), owing not least to active persecution; but worse still, from Paul's perspective, was that Titus had not yet shown up, so he still had no idea how his severe letter had been received in Corinth. "When we came into Macedonia, this body of ours had no rest, but we were harassed at every turn—conflicts on the outside, fears within" (7:5).

Titus soon arrived, and Paul's distress rapidly changed to near euphoria (2 Cor. 7:6–7). Immediately after sending the severe letter, he had suffered second thoughts, fearing that he might hurt the Corinthians unduly; but with Titus's encouraging report, Paul's fear was displaced by joy. If his letter had wounded them, it was "only for a little while" (7:8). "Godly sorrow brings repentance that leads to salvation and leaves no regret," Paul observes, "but

---

1962), xxviii–xxx. The passages in 2 Corinthians referring to Paul's demand for the discipline of the ringleader betray no hint of sexual immorality in the individual concerned. The offense was against Paul, and the critical question revolved around whether or not the church would rally to the apostle (7:12). Moreover, 1 Corinthians does not sound intense enough to be the letter described in 2 Cor. 2:4. For the view that Corinthians C is in reality 2 Cor. 10–13, see discussion below in the section "The Integrity of 1 and 2 Corinthians."

worldly sorrow brings death" (7:10). Indeed, Paul's entire response, at least in 2 Corinthians 1–9, breathes an atmosphere of bruised relations that have recently eased. There is a noticeable sigh of relief that the worst is over.

That is what makes 2 Corinthians 10–13 so difficult to interpret: the tone in these chapters assumes that the situation in Corinth had become desperately dangerous yet again. Any further historical reconstruction is inextricably tied to questions about the integrity of the Corinthian epistles. But before exploring that issue, it is also essential to understand a little more of the life and social structure of first-century Corinth.

Reconstruction of the Social Setting

Until fairly recently, the dominant theory put forward to explain the Corinthian distortions was the wisdom speculation in Hellenistic Judaism.[5] Certainly many remarkable parallels can be found in the literature of Hellenistic Judaism to what is assumed to be the language of the Corinthians that calls forth these Pauline Epistles. What one must ask, however, at least of 1 Corinthians, is whether what is most convincing in these parallels is determined by Hellenistic Judaism or by Greek pagan thought more generally. It remains unlikely that Paul's intended readership was substantially Jewish (see 6:9–11; 8:7; 12:2, and discussion above). Moreover, as Fee points out,[6] Paul explicitly assigns "wisdom" to the Greek quest, while Jews demand "signs" (1:22). It is inadequate, with Davis, to dismiss the dichotomy on the grounds that it is merely an instance of Paul's rhetoric.[7] "Even as rhetoric, the statement is quite explicit, while the idea that the section reflects a Jewish midrashic homily against wisdom is speculative at best."[8] It appears that the most likely source of the spurious Corinthian approach to wisdom and spirituality is their own pagan past.

Attempts to become more specific about the *philosophical* roots of Corinthian paganism tend to go a little beyond the evidence. Winter has argued that one of the underlying problems of the Corinthian church was its reliance on the Sophist

What makes 2 Corinthians 10–13 so difficult to interpret is that the tone in these chapters assumes that the situation in Corinth had become desperately dangerous yet again.

---

[5]E.g., B. A. Pearson, *The* Pneumatikos-Psychikos *Terminology in 1 Corinthians: A Study in the Theology of the Corinthian Opponents of Paul and Its Relation to Gnosticism*, SBLDS 12 (Missoula: SP, 1973). R. A. Horsley, in a number of articles, has argued in favor of the personified wisdom found in Philo; see esp. his "Wisdom of Word and Words of Wisdom in Corinth," *CBQ* 39 (1977): 224–39; "Pneumatikos vs. Psychikos: Distinctions of Spiritual Status Among the Corinthians," *HTR* 69 (1976): 269–88. By contrast, J. A. Davis finds the closest parallels in the "Torah Wisdom" at Qumran and in Sirach. See his *Wisdom and Spirit: An Investigation of 1 Corinthians 1.18–3.20 Against the Background of Jewish Sapiential Traditions in the Greco-Roman Period* (Lanham: UPA, 1984).

[6]Gordon D. Fee, *The First Epistle to the Corinthians*, NICNT (Grand Rapids: Eerdmans, 1987), 13–14.

[7]Davis, *Wisdom and Spirit*, 189 n. 26.

[8]Fee, *First Corinthians*, 14.

movement.[9] By the first century A.D., he argues, the "second sophistic" had begun.[10] It was characterized by rhetors whose skill and training in oratory attracted public admiration, not to mention students to their schools. By this period, the particular philosophy held by rhetors was relatively incidental; it was their power to expatiate on it, to declaim in public assembly, to speak convincingly and according to strict conventions in legal, business, religious, and political contexts that won them their acclaim. Their influence in the Mediterranean world was enormous, not least in Corinth. They thought themselves wise, the purveyors of wisdom. Winter argues that, especially in 1 Corinthians 1–4, Paul self-consciously frames his argument to counter Sophist claims (not least in 2:1–5).

The evidence for so early a date of the second sophistic is not as convincing as some think.[11] Nevertheless, some of the features found in the movement (whatever the date) were certainly prevalent in Corinth, even if tied to larger social pressures. The last decade and a half has witnessed a flood of research that has, cumulatively, subtly changed and deepened perceptions of the primary thrusts and theological significance of these two letters. Much of this work has had to do with the social setting of first-century Corinth. It has sharpened our understanding of the problems Paul was confronting and correcting—and, as we shall see, some of these bear eerie resemblance to problems confronting many Christians today, especially Christians in the West.[12]

Because the refounded city of Corinth was initially made up of a nucleus of Roman settlers, in many ways this was a Roman city rather than a Greek city.[13] But its unique location controlling trade routes on the four points of the compass inevitably attracted traders, freed slaves, entrepreneurs, and sailors. Here was a city where one could make one's fortune, rise in power and wealth and honor.

---

[9]Bruce W. Winter, *Philo and Paul Among the Sophists*, SNTSMS 96 (Cambridge: Cambridge University Press, 1997).

[10]See esp. G. W. Bowersock, *Greek Sophists in the Roman Empire* (Oxford: Oxford University Press, 1969).

[11]See the review article by Jerome Murphy-O'Connor in *RevBib* 110 (2003): 423–33.

[12]See especially the introductions to the commentaries by Wolfgang Schrage, *Der erste Brief an die Korinther*, EKKNT, 4 vols. (Neukirchen-Vluyn: Neukirchener Verlag / Zürich: Benziger Verlag, 1991–2001); and Anthony C. Thiselton, *The First Epistle to the Corinthians*, NIGTC (Grand Rapids: Eerdmans, 2000). A few writers have offered sharp criticism of any analysis of the problems in Corinth that depends on analysis of the social structures of the city: see esp. J. J. Meggitt, *Paul, Poverty and Survival* (Edinburgh: T. & T. Clark, 1998). See the critique of Gerd Theissen, "Social Conflicts in the Corinthian Community: Further Remarks on J. J. Meggitt, *Paul, Poverty and Survival*," *JSNT* 25 (2003): 371–91.

[13]See David W. J. Gill, "Corinth: A Roman Colony in Achaea," *BZ* 37 (1993): 259–64. Cf. David E. Garland, *1 Corinthians*, BECNT (Grand Rapids: Baker, 2003), 3: "When Paul visited, the city was geographically in Greece but culturally in Rome."

The Roman patronage system provided a way to scramble up the ladder, but inevitably it was laced with corruption. Powerful patrons, benefactors, provided their clients with money, contacts, and inclusion; of course the recipients were expected to be loyal to their benefactors, promote their reputation for honor and generosity, and play the endless game of carefully calibrated self-promotion. The patronage system ran throughout the empire, but in a young and hungry trade-based city like Corinth, it attracted serious social climbers.[14] Corinth became a magnet "for the socially ambitious . . . [for] status-hungry people."[15]

A longstanding emphasis on rhetoric in both the Greek and the Roman worlds ensured that the lecture was not only a critical component of public and political communication but also an admirable art form. The best rhetoricians warned against corrupt motives: rhetoric that was merely audience-pleasing was debased.[16] Nevertheless, it was almost inevitable, in a fallen world, that gifted speakers were both admired and followed, not unlike movie stars today. Pogoloff and others have shown that at Corinth this inherent tendency in the rhetorical tradition mingled with the structure of social climbing and the love of status to turn favorite rhetors into heroes, and audiences into fans.[17]

These sorts of social pressures were still shaping immature Corinthian believers. The problem was not so much that they were relapsing into paganism, as that their Christian faith, however sincere, had not yet transformed the world-view they had adopted from the surrounding culture. They had not grasped how the theology of the cross not only constitutes the basis of our salvation but also and inevitably teaches us how to live and serve—and such teaching is in radical contradistinction to a world dominated by self-promotion and social climbing. Not only does the gospel seem like "foolishness" to the world (1 Cor. 1:18–25), but in the light of the cross, Paul insists that the party spirit and factionalism he finds so worrying (1:10–4:21) must be overthrown: "So then, no more boasting about human leaders!" (3:21). The scramble for one-upmanship not only generates factionalism, but it adopts prevailing attitudes about sexual matters

---

[14]On the nature of the benefactor/recipient system, especially in Corinth, see, inter alia, Ben Witherington III, *Conflict and Community in Corinth: A Socio-Rhetorical Commentary on 1 and 2 Corinthians* (Grand Rapids: Eerdmans, 1995); A. D. Clarke, *Secular and Christian Leadership in Corinth: A Socio-Historical and Exegetical Study of 1 Corinthians 1–6*, AGJU 18 (Leiden: Brill, 1993); J. K. Chow, *Patronage and Power: A Study of Social Networks in Corinth*, JSNTSup 75 (Sheffield: Sheffield Academic Press, 1992); Bruce W. Winter, *Seek the Welfare of the City* (Grand Rapids: Eerdmans, 1994).

[15]Witherington, *Conflict and Community*, 24.

[16]Quintilian, 2.2.9–12.

[17]Stephen M. Pogoloff, *Logos and Sophia: The Rhetorical Situation of 1 Corinthians*, SBLDS 134 (Atlanta: SP, 1992); cf. Duane Litfin, *St Paul's Theology of Proclamation: 1 Cor 1–4 and Greco-Roman Rhetoric*, SNTSMS 79 (Cambridge: Cambridge University Press, 1994).

(5:1–12; 6:12–20) and sanctions litigation between believers (6:1–11), even though Paul insists that in the light of the cross anyone with this attitude has "lost" already (6:7). In the actual outlook of the Corinthians, the theology of triumphalism trumps the theology of the cross: they think they are kings already, while the apostles who brought them the gospel eat everyone else's dirt at the end of the procession, condemned to die in the arena (4:8–13). Without the theology of the cross, Christians boast in their knowledge even while their attitudes destroy weaker Christians (8:1–11:1). Which charismatic gift they have becomes far more important than whether or not they love brothers and sisters in Christ (1 Cor. 12–13).[18] It becomes easy for such people, infatuated with those who are skilled in rhetoric, to become slightly contemptuous of an apostle who is much less interested in impressing people with his eloquence than in conveying the burning message of Christ crucified (1 Cor. 2:1–5; 2 Cor. 10:10; 11:6).[19]

A church full of people who are hungry to impress others and climb a little higher up the scales of social approval will not be a church characterized by deep spiritual unity. Small wonder Paul enlarges upon the "body" metaphor to explain how diversity and unity properly cohere.[20] The divisions of factionalism—"I follow Paul," "I follow Apollos," and so forth (1 Cor. 1:12)—mean that the apostle must invest time instructing the church as to how Christian leaders *should* be viewed: not as partisan heroes, but "as servants of Christ and as those entrusted with the mysteries God has revealed" (4:1). They are coworkers in God's field, they are co-builders of God's temple (1 Cor. 3). Even when Paul tells his readers to imitate him, he means them to do so insofar as he imitates Christ (11:1)—the Christ of the cross, the Christ whose death not only atones but establishes the fundamentals of self-denial and service to others.[21]

---

[18]On Paul's outworking of the theology of the cross in the Corinthian correspondence, see Alexander R. Brown, *The Cross and Human Transformation: Paul's Apocalyptic Word in 1 Corinthians* (Minneapolis: Fortress Press, 1995); Raymond Pickett, *The Cross in Corinth: The Social Significance of the Death of Jesus*, JSNTSup 143 (Sheffield: Sheffield Academic, 1997); D. A. Carson, *The Cross and Christian Ministry* (Grand Rapids: Baker, 2003).

[19]This does not mean, of course, that Paul uses no "rhetorical" devices in his appeals; any good communicator deploys such devices, inevitably borrowing, both consciously and unconsciously, from the patterns of the day. See Margaret M. Mitchell, *Paul and the Rhetoric of Reconciliation: An Exegetical Investigation of the Language and Composition of 1 Corinthians*, HUT 28 (Tübingen: Mohr-Siebeck, 1991).

[20]See Dale B. Martin, *The Corinthian Body* (New Haven: Yale University Press, 1995).

[21]So rightly Jeffrey A. Crafton, *The Agency of the Apostle*, JSNTSup 51 (Sheffield: Sheffield Academic Press, 1991); contra Elizabeth A. Castelli, *Imitating Paul: A Discourse of Power* (Louisville: Westminster John Knox, 1991), who thinks that Paul's demand that the Corinthians imitate him is a bid for power and intrinsically divisive.

Many of the individual questions that the apostle tries to sort out—whether complex matters regarding marriage and divorce (1 Cor. 7), appropriate stances regarding meat that has been offered up to pagan idols (1 Cor. 8–10),[22] appropriate head-gear for women who pray and prophesy (11:2–16), or divergent assessments of the charismatic gifts (12–14)—reflect a church with polarized opinions. In every case, the apostle must not only sort out the difficult matters, but try to do so in such a way that he brings some sort of reconciliation to the warring factions, while offering sometimes withering criticism of their immaturity and arrogance. Moreover, as Paul works through these matters, he is guided by more than personal preference. Even though he insists that Christians are not "under law" (i.e., not under the Mosaic law-covenant, 9:19–23), and even though Christ and his cross become the touchstone for fundamental attitudes, very substantial parts of Paul's ethical counsel are linked to his profound reading of the Old Testament Scriptures.[23]

Two further things must be said. *First,* the problems of factionalism and of immature expectations entertained by the Corinthians with respect to Paul and other leaders recur in 2 Corinthians,[24] where Paul still finds himself having to explain the theology of the cross: God's grace is perfected in weakness.[25] And *second,* the Corinthians' constant stress on what they already enjoy, what spiritual gifts they have already gained, how mature they already are, and the like, suggests that they have adopted a kind of over-realized eschatology that is far too confident in the blessings they think they already enjoy, and far too ignorant of, and too little anticipating, the blessings still to come.

The Integrity of 1 and 2 Corinthians

The historical and social reconstruction developed so far, though in its main outline enjoying widespread support, depends on the integrity of 1 Corinthians and of 2 Corinthians 1–9. If parts of these letters were written at different times,

---

[22]On which see especially Paul D. Gardner, *The Gifts of God and the Authentication of a Christian: An Exegetical Study of 1 Corinthians 8–11* (Lanham: UPA, 1994); Khiok-Khing Yeo, *Rhetorical Interaction in 1 Corinthians 8–10,* BIS 9 (Leiden: Brill, 1995).

[23]See especially Brian S. Rosner, *Paul, Scripture and Ethics: A Study of 1 Corinthians 5–7,* AGJU 12 (Leiden: Brill, 1994 / Grand Rapids: Baker, 1999); H. H. Drake Williams III, *The Wisdom of the Wise: The Presence and Function of Scripture Within 1 Cor. 1:18–3:23,* AGJU 49 (Leiden: Brill, 2001). Similar study easily extends these insights into later passages in 1 Corinthians, e.g., the appeals to Scripture in 1 Cor. 11:2–16.

[24]See the admirable summary of who the opponents are in Jan Lambrecht, *Second Corinthians,* SacPag 8 (Collegeville: Liturgical Press, 1999), 6–7.

[25]See especially Timothy B. Savage, *Power Through Weakness: Paul's Understanding of the Christian Ministry in 2 Corinthians,* SNTSMS 86 (Cambridge: Cambridge University Press, 1996).

perhaps by different authors, and somehow came together to constitute our present letters, then the reconstruction would have to be modified at various points. In the most skeptical interpretation, we would be left with too many unconnected fragments to make any widely believed reconstruction possible.[26] Some of the points of dispute will shortly be surveyed, but first the contribution of 2 Corinthians 10–13 must be assessed.

The Place of 2 Corinthians 10–13. There is equally widespread disagreement over the place of 2 Corinthians 10–13. Four principal theories address this issue.

1. Many argue that Paul, delighted by the news he received from Titus, immediately penned 2 Corinthians 1–9 (which thus becomes Corinthians D) and sent it off. They suggest that 2 Corinthians 10–13 is to be identified with Corinthians C, the severe and painful letter.[27]

The advantage of this theory is that it fully explains the remarkable difference in tone between 2 Corinthians 1–9 and 10–13. The former chapters transparently reflect the good news that Titus has brought with him. If Paul must still give some explanation of his movements (1:15–2:13) and outline again the nature of apostolic ministry (3:1–18), if he must still exhort the Corinthians to press on with the collection (chaps. 8–9), he does so with scarcely restrained joy and with restored confidence in the church's obedience and growing maturity. By contrast, the language and emphases in chapters 10–13 are alternately angry, broken, and scathingly ironic. Paul's joy has disappeared; his confidence in the maturity of the Corinthians has dissipated. No longer do we find Paul saying, "I am glad I can have complete confidence in you" (7:16); now he must say, "Examine yourselves to see whether you are in the faith; test yourselves. Do you not realize that Christ Jesus is in you—unless, of course, you fail the test?" (13:5). Moreover, proponents of this view argue that several passages in chapters 1–9 refer to statements *previously* made in chapters 10–13 (e.g., 1:23/13:2; 2:3/13:10; 2:9/10:6; 4:2/12:16; 7:2/12:17). And how, they ask, could Paul look forward to preaching the gospel "in the regions beyond you" (10:16) if he is already in Greece (more specifically, Macedonia) when he writes? Should he not

---

[26]For an admirable brief summary of the principal options, see Frank J. Matera, *II Corinthians: A Commentary,* NTL (Louisville: Westminster John Knox, 2003), 24–32.

[27]So, e.g., A. Plummer, *A Critical and Exegetical Commentary on the Second Epistle of St Paul to the Corinthians,* ICC (Edinburgh: T. & T. Clark, 1915), xxvii–xxxvi; R. H. Strachan, *The Second Epistle of Paul to the Corinthians,* MNTC (London: Hodder & Stoughton, 1935), xix; R. Bultmann, *The Second Letter to the Corinthians* (ET Minneapolis: Augsburg, 1985), 18; H. D. Wendland, *Die Briefe an die Korinther,* NTD 7 (Göttingen: Vandenhoeck & Ruprecht, 1965), 8; W. Schmithals, *Gnosticism in Corinth: An Investigation of the Letters to the Corinthians* (ET Nashville: Abingdon, 1971), 96.

have said "regions beyond *us*"? Surely it is easier to think he writes such words from Ephesus—which presupposes that they were written *before* chapters 1–9.

Nevertheless, the theory stumbles over several obstacles. First, no Greek manuscript of 2 Corinthians suggests that the epistle originally terminated at the end of chapter 9 or suggests that chapters 10–13 originally had a proem typical of the epistles Paul wrote to churches where he was known. This is not decisive, of course: one could argue that our 2 Corinthians was not published until the two parts had been fused together. But in that case one ought to be able to give convincing reasons why someone should have performed such fusion. Second, the expression "the regions beyond you" (τὰ ὑπερέκεινα ὑμῶν [*ta hyperekeina hymōn*]) does not demand that Paul not be writing from Greece. He may have thought of Achaia (where Corinth lay) as quite distinct from Macedonia; or he may have said "beyond you [Greeks]" in such a way as to refer to *their* land while excluding himself (as a Pole heading west might tell a German, on German soil, that he is going beyond "your country" on his way to France). Third, chapters 10–13 do not contain the one thing we are certain must have been in the severe letter, namely, the demand that a certain offender be punished (2:5–6; 7:12). Fourth, chapters 10–13 promise an imminent visit (12:14; 13:1), but Corinthians C, the severe letter, was sent *instead* of another painful visit (1:23; 2:1). Fifth, 12:18 clearly assumes that Titus had paid at least one visit to Corinth to assist in the collection; in other words, it presupposes either 8:6a or 8:16–19. Either way, it becomes hard to believe that chapters 1–9, where these two passages are embedded, were written *after* chapters 10–13, where 12:18 is located.

Still on the collection, if Paul was charged with using the funds himself (12:16), how could he later boast so freely to Titus (7:14) and to the Macedonians (9:2) about the Corinthians' generosity, without making some allusion to a patching up of misunderstanding on the point? It seems best to conclude that this first theory introduces more problems than it solves.

2. Some argue for the essential unity of 2 Corinthians: the entire book was written at one time.[28] Certainly this coheres with the textual evidence. If some reason must be given for the remarkable change in tone between chapters 1–9 and 10–13, there is no shortage of theories. Perhaps Paul had a sleepless night before composing the second part; perhaps the two parts of the book betray the

---

[28]E.g., E. B. Allo, *Saint Paul: Seconde Épître aux Corinthiens* (Paris: Gabalda, 1956), lii–liii; H. Lietzmann, supplemented by W. G. Kümmel, *An die Korinther I, II,* HNT 9 (Tübingen: Mohr-Siebeck, 1969), 139–40; R. V. G. Tasker, *The Second Epistle of Paul to the Corinthians,* TNTC (Grand Rapids: Eerdmans, 1958), 30–35; Hughes, *Second Corinthians,* xxiii–xxxv; Kümmel, 287–93; W. H. Bates, "The Integrity of II Corinthians," *NTS* 12 (1965–66): 56–59; Jan Lambrecht, *Second Corinthians,* 7–9; Paul Barnett, *The Second Epistle to the Corinthians,* esp. 17–23; David E. Garland, *2 Corinthians,* NAC (Nashville: Broadman & Holman, 2003), 33–44; James M. Scott, *2 Corinthians,* NIBC (Peabody: Hendrickson, 1998), 6–7.

ups and downs of a mercurial temperament; perhaps Paul finally exposes his deepest and hitherto repressed emotions on these matters. Better yet, Hughes argues that the difference in tone between the two parts of the book is greatly exaggerated: there is really no problem to solve. He draws comparisons between 1:13 and 10:11; 1:17 and 10:2; 2:1 and 12:14, 21 (see also 13:1–2); 2:17 and 12:19; 3:2 and 12:11; 6:13 and 11:2 (see also 12:14); 8:6, 8, 22 and 12:17–18.[29]

Similar lists of comparisons, however, could be drawn between 2 Corinthians 10–13 and 1 Corinthians, but no one would be brash enough to suggest they show that 2 Corinthians 10–13 once belonged to 1 Corinthians. Doubtless there is a difficult question of judgment involved: Are the two principal parts of our 2 Corinthians sufficiently different in tone to throw doubt on the assumption that they were written at the same time, under the same circumstances, in one letter? In our judgment, the differences in tone and emphasis are sufficiently strong that some account must be given of them, and the psychological solutions are not very satisfying. Was Paul's temperament so mercurial that it seriously affected his pastoral stance toward his converts, with no other cause than the day Paul happened to be writing? Is there any evidence that Paul was so emotionally immature and so full of repressed resentments that he was prone to losing control of himself? A more sympathetic reading is that Paul is constantly aware of what image he is projecting and takes it into account (see 1 Cor. 4:21). In 2 Corinthians 1–9, Paul is primarily engaged in building bridges toward the Corinthians, encouraging them, removing any obstacle in the way of their understanding; even the rebukes he administers are part of that design. By contrast, in chapters 10–13 Paul deploys sharp irony and dire threat, and whatever encouragement he offers is part of this pattern.

Harris offers a variation on this theory.[30] He suggests that when Paul received Titus's good report, he did not immediately write any part of 2 Corinthians. Instead, he continued his pastoral work in Macedonia and quite possibly engaged in pioneer evangelism along the Egnatian Way and right around to Illyricum (see Rom. 15:19–21). When he returned to Macedonia, he heard of fresh problems in Corinth and wrote the entire epistle. This has the effect of explaining the tone of 2 Corinthians 10–13, but the cost is high: it fails to explain why 2 Corinthians 1–9 is so positive, why there is such euphoria in Paul's words at the reception of Titus's good report (7:6–16). Like the other theories that argue for the essential unity of 2 Corinthians, this one does not adequately grapple with the differences in stance between chapters 1–9 and 10–13.

---

[29]Hughes, *Second Corinthians*, xxxi–xxxv.

[30]Murray J. Harris, "2 Corinthians," in *EBC* 10.305–6. In a more recent and technical commentary, however, Harris has changed his mind and followed much the same line adopted in this *Introduction*. See Harris, *The Second Epistle to the Corinthians*, NIGTC (Grand Rapids: Eerdmans, 2005), 29–51.

Other variations have been put forward. In chapters 1–7, Matera contends,[31] Paul is dealing with *two* issues. One has already been resolved (the one dealing with the "painful visit" and the Corinthian offender); the other, to do with the intruding false apostles, has *not yet* been resolved, so Paul takes up the latter crisis in chapters 10–13. But although this theory might account for the difference in the *substance* of the two sections, it does not readily account for the change of tone, unless the apostle manages to assume astonishingly bifurcated responses when the same people are involved in the two crises. The joy of chapter 7 is utterly unqualified, and so is the indignation of chapters 10–13. Barnett's explanation[32] is no more satisfying. He contends that ancient apologetic letters could move, rhetorically speaking, from seeking audience sympathy to strong attempts at emotional arousal—and that, he says, is what Paul is doing. But the emotional arousal sought in apologetic letters was indignation over the injustice of some case or other, not personal confrontation, rebuke, and even threat, which are the stuff of 2 Corinthians 10–13.

3. The most popular theory among recent commentators is that chapters 10–13 were written after 1–9. In this view, chapters 10–13 constitute the whole or part of another letter, Corinthians E. After Paul heard from Titus, he immediately wrote Corinthians D (= 2 Cor. 1–9) and sent it off. Shortly thereafter, however, he learned that the basically positive report brought by Titus was either premature or obsolete. The Corinthians had succumbed again to their carping criticism of Paul and had been wooed by the interlopers into a stance that was threatening the very integrity of the gospel—its ethical stance under the cross, if not its doctrinal formulations. Once more the Corinthians were failing to take decisive action against these leaders. They were succumbing to the blandishments of the intellectual and cultural arrogance typical of Sophists. Paul therefore responds with his fifth letter to the Corinthians, namely, 2 Corinthians 10–13.[33]

The primary advantage of this explanation—and it is very weighty—is that it fully accounts for the profound difference in stance between chapters 1–9 and 10–13. Correlatively, it explains why in 12:19–13:10 Paul envisages a third trip to Corinth, a visit that will be characterized by stern justice or (Paul hopes) happy reconciliation, but which is a visit unforeseen in, and inappropriate to, chapters 1–9. Some also argue that this theory best accounts for Paul's references to Titus's behavior in 12:17–18. There Paul, expecting a negative answer,

---

[31]Frank J. Matera, *II Corinthians*, 30–32.

[32]*The Second Epistle*, 17–18.

[33]So F. F. Bruce, *1 and 2 Corinthians* (London: Oliphants, 1971), 166–70; Victor Paul Furnish, *II Corinthians*, AB 32A (Garden City: Doubleday, 1984), 30–41; Ralph P. Martin, *2 Corinthians*, WBC 40 (Waco: Word, 1986), xl; Colin G. Kruse, *The Second Epistle of Paul to the Corinthians*, TNTC (Grand Rapids: Eerdmans, 1987), 29–35.

asks the Corinthians if Titus or any other of his emissaries had ever exploited them, presumably in connection with the collection. This, it is argued, presupposes that chapters 10–13 were written *after* 8:6, 16–24 and 9:3–5, where Paul tells his readers he is about to send Titus.

This last point is surely not very strong, since the first part of 8:6 demonstrates that Titus had been sent on an *earlier* visit to Corinth in connection with the collection, and 12:17–18 may refer to that earlier trip, thereby removing any need to postulate a time gap between 8:6, 16–24; 9:3–5; and 12:17–18. That no manuscript tradition supports the division of 2 Corinthians into two letters is important, though not decisive, since it might be argued that the two parts were published together: perhaps (it is suggested) they were copied onto the same scroll. If so, why should the conclusion of 2 Corinthians 1–9 be lost, along with the greetings, salutation, and thanksgiving of 2 Corinthians 10–13? In short, this theory is possible, and better than the other two, but it has to rely rather heavily on a stupid scribe early in the manuscript tradition.

4. Perhaps a minor modification to the third theory would improve it. If Paul was as eager to hear from Titus as 2 Corinthians 2:13 suggests, it is altogether natural to assume that, once he heard Titus' good report, he immediately set about communicating his relief to the Corinthians. He was grateful that his severe letter (= Corinthians C) had not done the damage he feared, delighted that the Corinthians had responded with repentance and obedience, and encouraged to learn that his most obstreperous and dangerous opponent had been disciplined. But even if he set to writing (or dictating) immediately, there is no reason to think he finished it promptly. This epistle is fairly long, and Paul was at this time extraordinarily pressed by his ministry in Macedonia. It is not unreasonable to suppose that the completion of the letter was delayed for weeks, or even longer: the phenomenon of unfinished letters is not entirely unknown today, and our letters are usually much shorter than 2 Corinthians! If during that time Paul received additional information about the situation in Corinth and learned that the church had once again plummeted into the disastrous state presupposed by 2 Corinthians 10–13, the abrupt change of tone that begins at 10:1 would be accounted for. In other words, one might reasonably postulate that after finishing chapters 1–9, but before completing the letter and sending it off, Paul received bad news from Corinth and changed his tack in the final chapters of his epistle.

Several objections have been raised against this reconstruction.

1. It has been argued that if Paul had received bad news from Corinth before chapters 1–9 had been sent, he would have torn them up and begun a new letter. But this overlooks how much of chapters 1–9 is valuable in its own right. Indeed, if Paul left some markers in chapters 10–13 that he *had* received fresh information about the disastrous turn the Corinthians were taking (see discussion below), then the Corinthian readers would become aware of the startling

contrast between Paul's joy at Titus' report and his broken indignation at their recent defection. This would have the effect of turning even the earlier chapters into an *implicit* rebuke, since the causes of Paul's joy—Corinthian repentance, obedience, and zeal—would no longer be operative.

2. The only serious difficulty with this theory is that nowhere in 2 Corinthians 10–13 does Paul explicitly state that he has received fresh information. It must be remembered (a point frequently forgotten) that this difficulty also attaches itself to the third theory, which meets it by positing that part of Corinthians E was lost when it was joined with Corinthians D to form 2 Corinthians. But it is possible to construct an alternative explanation as to why Paul makes no direct mention of the arrival of additional information. For instance, if some new report came to him which asserted that many Corinthian believers, influenced by the false apostles (2 Cor. 11:13–15), were accusing Paul of showing too much meekness and gentleness to be a true apostle, then his opening words in 2 Corinthians 10:1 would be sufficient to draw attention to his knowledge of the latest in their list of theological fads: "By the meekness and gentleness of Christ, I appeal to you. . . ." If charges were now widely circulating in Corinth that Paul's formal credentials left a great deal to be desired, in comparison with those of the interlopers (10:12–18), that he could not be much of a teacher because he refused to charge for his services (11:7–12; 12:13), that his apostolic status could not amount to much because he did not talk much about the supernatural visions of which others were eager to speak (12:1–10), then his responses in all these areas would be enough to alert his readers that these latest developments had reached his ears.

3. We have already seen that some think the movements of Titus can be explained only if we postulate a break between chapters 9 and 10 (cf. 8:6, 16–24; 9:3–5; and 12:17–18). But the pressure is eased if 12:17–18 refers to Titus's *earlier* trip to Corinth (8:6a).

4. Some find it unlikely that the Corinthian church could have tumbled so quickly into such disarray. A slightly cynical response might be that such critics have not witnessed very closely much contemporary church life. More important, neither 1 Corinthians nor 2 Corinthians 1–9 encourages us to think that this was a very stable church. The Corinthian believers seem to have been characterized by various forms of arrogance, prone to attach themselves to various leaders, rather overconfident of their own spiritual discernment, and badly compromised by the surrounding culture. Nor is this the end of the evidence. Forty years later, Clement of Rome finds it necessary to write to the Corinthian church and speak against their dissensions and anarchy.

In short, the evidence is not sufficient for giving a decisive account of 2 Corinthians 10–13. On the whole, however, the fourth theory seems marginally stronger than the third, which is considerably more believable than either of the other two.

We may well ask if Paul's Corinthian correspondence succeeded in turning the situation around, at least temporarily. Again, no decisive answer can be given. But there is some hope for an optimistic answer in the fact that, when the threatened third visit actually took place (2 Cor. 13:2–3), Paul found the time and tranquility to write his epistle to the Romans. That letter betrays some anxiety about the future (Rom. 15:30–31), but none about his present circumstances. It is unlikely that Paul would still be planning his trip to Spain (Rom. 15:24–28) if he thought his presence was still chronically necessary in Corinth (see 2 Cor. 10:15–16a). And the Corinthians did contribute to the collection for the poor believers in Jerusalem (Rom. 15:26–27), though how much this may reflect a healed relationship with Paul it is impossible to say.

> *Did Paul's Corinthian correspondence succeed in turning the situation around, at least temporarily? There is some hopefulness in that on his third visit there, Paul found the time and tranquility to write his epistle to the Romans.*

Other Alleged Interpolations in 2 Corinthians. It cannot be too strongly emphasized that "the literary and historical hypotheses stand or fall together."[34] In other words, those who find interpolations (a literary phenomenon) in 2 Corinthians usually provide a reconstructed history to account for the alleged interpolations—the more so if these interpolations include references to Paul's movements.[35] The principal theories of interpolation focus on three passages.

2 Corinthians 2:14–7:4. Some scholars argue that these chapters (usually without 6:14–7:1; see below) constitute the whole or a part of a separate letter. They note that excellent flow is achieved by reading 7:5 immediately after 2:13: the subject of Titus's itinerary and Paul's trip to Macedonia is continued. Some think that 2:14–7:4 once belonged with chapters 10–13 to constitute the severe letter (= Corinthians C);[36] others suggest that this is part of yet another letter, written before the severe letter, before the Corinthians had been taken over by Paul's opponents.[37]

But although 7:5 follows 2:13 rather nicely from a thematic point of view, other literary indications suggest there is a break. For instance, the words that begin 7:5 ("For when we came into Macedonia . . ."), although they pick up the theme of 2:13 ("So I said good-by to them and went on to Macedonia"), would be unduly repetitive if they followed on immediately. They sound much more as if Paul is *resuming* a theme, knowing he has digressed. Moreover, several linking

---

[34]C. K. Barrett, *A Commentary on the Second Epistle to the Corinthians,* BNTC/HNTC (London: Black, 1973), 17.

[35]See, for instance, most recently, Sze-kar Wan, *Power in Weakness: Conflict and Rhetoric in Paul's Second Letter to the Corinthians* (Harrisburg: Trinity Press International, 2000).

[36]So J. Weiss, *Earliest Christianity: A History of the Period A.D. 30–150* (New York: Harper & Row, 1959), 1:349; Bultmann, *Second Corinthians,* 18.

[37]Wendland, *Briefe an die Korinther,* 9; Schmithals, *Gnosticism in Corinth,* 98–100; G. Bornkamm, "The History of the So-called Second Letter to the Corinthians," *NTS* 8 (1961–62): 259–60.

words tie 7:4 with 7:5–7: παράκλησις (*paraklēsis*, "comfort"); χαρά/χαρῆναι (*chara/charēnai*, "joy"/"to be joyful"), θλῖψις/θλιβόμενοι (*thlipsis/thlibomenoi*, "troubles"/"being harassed"). David deSilva has convincingly defended the unity of chapters 1–9 on the grounds of rhetorical structure.[38] There are also thematic ties: for example, "I take great pride in you" (7:4) and "I am glad I can have complete confidence in you" (7:16). Moreover, any view that ties 2:14–7:4 to chapters 10–13 confronts all the problems discussed earlier that are associated with the entirely different pastoral stances reflected in the two sections.

To argue that 2:14–7:4 is an integral part of chapters 1–9 still leaves one with the responsibility of explaining why the line of thought from 2:13 to 7:5 is in some measure broken up. Many suggestions have been put forward. Some of them are convincing; most are not mutually exclusive but rather mutually supportive. Many have suggested that the mere mention of Titus's name (2:13) prompts Paul to make a conscious digression to express gratitude to God for the relief he felt when Titus did show up,[39] or to leap forward to a happy, theological articulation of the basis on which his restored relationship with the Corinthians must now rest. It has been argued that, just as 1:8–11 draws a contrast between human weakness and the power of God, so the same theme is repeated when Paul moves from the admission of his own weakness in 2:12–13 to the triumphant note of 2:14–17.[40] Others propose that Paul is concerned not to make the Corinthians feel guilty for the anxiety they caused him. Therefore, after so frankly admitting his anxiety (2:12–13), he quickly turns to emphasizing the victorious progress of the gospel everywhere (including Troas) and thus signals that he himself suffered no disastrous personal defeat for which they should feel responsible.[41] One writer thinks that the length of the interposing passage, 2:14–7:4, is occasioned by the fact that 2:14–16 is a second "traditional thanksgiving period" (all but one of the canonical Pauline Epistles contain at least one, normally right after the salutation; see 1:3–7). Typically, these thanksgiving periods anticipate the direction of Paul's argument, and in this way, 2:14–16 foreshadows the content of the following chapters.[42] Above all, one of the major themes of 2 Corinthians 1–9 is the assurance of God's comfort in our affliction, an idea found not only before and after this alleged interpolation (1:3–11; 7:5–7, 12–13)

---

[38]"Measuring Penultimate Against Ultimate Reality: An Investigation of the Integrity and Argumentation of 2 Corinthians," *JSNT* 52 (1993): 41–70.

[39]E.g., Plummer, *Second Corinthians*, 67; Kümmel, 291; Harris, "2 Corinthians," 303, 331; Allo, *Saint Paul*, 45.

[40]P. Bachmann, *Der zweite Brief des Paulus an die Korinther* (Leipzig: Deichert, 1922), 126–27.

[41]With various emphases, Zahn 3.343 n. 1; Hughes, *Second Corinthians*, 76–77.

[42]Margaret E. Thrall, "A Second Thanksgiving Period in II Corinthians," *JSNT* 16 (1982): 111–19.

but throughout it (e.g., 4:7–5:8; 6:1–10; 7:4).[43] In short, there do not appear to be adequate reasons for taking 2:14–7:4 as an interpolation, while there are sufficient reasons to explain the superficial hiatus.[44]

2 Corinthians 6:14–7:1. Within the larger section 2:14–7:4, these six verses are often taken to be a further interpolation,[45] and possibly non-Pauline.[46] The reasons most commonly advanced are as follows: (1) the passage constitutes a self-contained unit without any unambiguous references to the situation in Corinth; (2) it contains six hapax legomena (i.e., words or expressions that occur only here in the New Testament);[47] (3) the combination in 7:1, "body and spirit" (lit. "flesh and spirit," σάρξ [*sarx*] and πνεῦμα [*pneuma*]), is said to be un-Pauline, since Paul normally opposes the two; (4) the passage seems to interrupt the flow from 6:13 to 7:2, which make excellent sense if they are simply joined; (5) some hold that it betrays an exclusivism more characteristic of Pharisaism than of the apostle of liberty; and (6) some also hold that the apocalyptic dualism—righteousness/iniquity, Christ/Belial, light/darkness—is more typical of Qumran than of Paul.

The arguments that take the passage to be non-Pauline are not as strong as they first seem. It has often been noted that "Pauline outbursts containing a high percentage of *hapax legomena* are not uncommon (1 Cor 4:7–13 has six *hapaxes* and 2 Cor 6:3–10 [the verses preceding the passage under consideration] has four)."[48] Hughes observes that there are about fifty hapax legomena in 2 Corinthians alone.[49] Moreover, if (as Fee suggests) we query the significance of those unique words where elsewhere Paul uses a cognate term, only one remains, namely, "Belial," which is so common in Jewish writings that it is impossible to think Paul did not know the term.[50] Although Betz finds the exclusivism of this passage so remarkable[51] he judges it to be an *anti*-Pauline fragment, this is surely a strange judgment when one recalls such passages as

---

[43]Kruse, *Second Corinthians*, 37.

[44]See the summary of positions in Linda L. Belleville, *2 Corinthians*, IVPNTC (Downers Grove: IVP, 1996), 24–26.

[45]By the majority of contemporary scholars, including Wendland, *Briefe an die Korinther*, 212; and Schmithals, *Gnosticism in Corinth*, 94–95.

[46]By a minority of scholars, including Bultmann, *Second Corinthians*, 180 and n. 202; and J. Gnilka, "2 Cor 6:14–7:1 in Light of the Qumran Texts and the Testaments of the Twelve Patriarchs," in *Paul and Qumran*, ed. J. Murphy-O'Connor (London: Chapman, 1968), 48–68.

[47]Namely, ἑτεροζυγοῦντες (*heterozygountes*), μετοχή (*metoche*), συμφώνησις (*symphonesis*), Βελιάρ (*Beliar*), συγκατάθεσις (*sugkatathesis*), and μολυσμός (*molysmos*).

[48]Martin, 192.

[49]Hughes, *Second Corinthians*, 242.

[50]Gordon D. Fee, "II Corinthians vi.14–vii.1 and Food Offered to Idols," *NTS* 23 (1977): 144–45.

[51]H. D. Betz, "2 Cor.6:14–7:1: An Anti-Pauline Fragment?" *JBL* 92 (1973): 88–108.

Romans 8:9; 1 Corinthians 6:12–20; 10:14–22; Galatians 1:8–9. Qumran offers somewhat parallel formal dualism to the fourth gospel, but almost no one today suggests that John is made up of Qumran fragments; thus, there is simply insufficient evidence to support Fitzmyer's view[52] that this passage is an Essene composition reworked by some unknown Christian.[53] Moreover, although it is true that Paul regularly places "flesh" (σάρξ [*sarx*]) over against "spirit" where the spirit refers to the Holy Spirit (e.g., Gal. 6:16–25), here the entire expression "body and spirit" refers to the whole person. In short, the arguments in favor of the view that this is a non-Pauline fragment do not seem very convincing.

Still, the distinctiveness of the passage demands some explanation, and it is not entirely surprising that some have suggested that this is a Pauline excerpt from another letter, perhaps from the "previous" letter (= Corinthians A, referred to in 1 Cor. 5:9).[54] Quite apart from the difficulty of imagining why anyone (Paul or a later redactor) would interpolate such a passage here, there is another obvious hurdle: the "previous" letter forbade the believers from enjoying fellowship with *believers* who were behaving immorally; by contrast, this passage forbids believers from enjoying close fellowship with *unbelievers*, especially in the matter of idolatrous worship (see 1 Cor. 10:14–22).

A strong contingent of scholars insists on the authenticity and integrity of the passage,[55] though their explanations of the abruptness of its beginning and ending vary (most of which are not mutually exclusive). It has often been observed that 7:2 sounds more like a resumption of 6:13 than a mere continuation of it, which suggests that 6:14–7:1 is not an accidental digression. Some envisage a pause in dictation at 6:13;[56] Barrett suggests that Paul, aware of false apostles lurking in the background, opens his heart to urge restored relationships between the Corinthians and himself but warns them that this will entail a break with the world.[57] Dahl's view is similar (though he thinks the passage originated in a Qumran community and was reworked by Paul).[58] Hughes

---

[52]J. A. Fitzmyer, "Qumran and the Interpolated Paragraph in 2 Cor 6:14–7:1," in *Essays on the Semitic Background of the New Testament* (London: Chapman, 1971), 205–17.

[53]See Bruce, *1 and 2 Corinthians*, 214, who notes that such dualisms are not exclusive to Qumran.

[54]E.g., Wendland, *Briefe an die Korinther*, 212; Strachan, *Second Corinthians*, xv, 3–5; Schmithals, *Gnosticism in Corinth*, 94–95.

[55]E.g., Plummer, *Second Corinthians*, xxiii–xxvi, 208; Lietzmann, *An die Korinther*, 129; Allo, *Saint Paul*, liii, 193–94; Hughes, *Second Corinthians*, 241–44; Bruce, *1 and 2 Corinthians*, 214; Barrett, *Second Corinthians*, 194, Harris, "2 Corinthians," 303.

[56]Lietzmann, *An die Korinther*, 129; cautiously, Harris, "2 Corinthians," 303.

[57]Barrett, *Second Corinthians*, 194.

[58]N. A. Dahl, "A Fragment and Its Context: 2 Corinthians 6:14–7:1," in *Studies in Paul* (Minneapolis: Augsburg, 1972), 62–69.

suggests that, having rearticulated the nature of his spiritual authority in the previous chapters, Paul now uses it to warn against the ever-pressing threat of paganism, but in a spirit entirely free of censoriousness, as the surrounding verses attest.[59] Fee notes the many parallels with 1 Corinthians 10:14–22 and reconstructs a development to argue that this passage is still dealing with the question of food offered to idols.[60] Most convincing is the analysis of Beale, who argues that 2 Corinthians 5:14–7:7 constitutes a literary unit held together by the theme of reconciliation played out against the backdrop of new creation, this new creation itself understood to be the inaugurated fulfillment of the restoration promised in Isaiah 40–66.[61] If his analysis is right, the tightness of the conceptual argument and its background strongly discourage any analysis that breaks off a part of the text and declares it to be an independent fragment. In short, to accept the basic integrity of 2 Corinthians at this point seems considerably less problematic than the alternatives.[62]

2 Corinthians 8–9. Several scholars have argued that chapter 8 is an interpolation,[63] or that chapter 9 is,[64] or that each is a separate letter and that both have been interpolated into 2 Corinthians.[65] The issues are extraordinarily complex, and we review here the principal turning points.

1. It is argued that chapter 9 introduces the subject of the collection as if no mention has been made of it already. Chapter 9 must therefore follow chapter 7, and chapter 8 is an independent document with its conclusion lost (Weiss). This demands that Weiss reconstruct just when chapter 8 was written. He thinks chapter 8 commended Titus and two unnamed believers much earlier, before the arrival of Timothy with the bad news, indeed, before those from Chloe's house had arrived (1:11). It was the spontaneous enthusiasm of believers in Macedonia

[59]Hughes, *Second Corinthians*, 244.

[60]Fee, "II Corinthians vi.14–vii.1."

[61]G. K. Beale, "The Old Testament Background of Reconciliation in 2 Corinthians 5–7 and Its Bearing on the Literary Problem of 2 Corinthians 6.14–7.1," *NTS* 35 (1989): 550–81.

[62]The suggestion of J.-F. Collange, *Enigmes de la deuxième Épître de Paul aux Corinthiens*, SNTSMS 18 (Cambridge: Cambridge University Press, 1972), 282–84, 302–17, that Paul wrote two editions of a letter that began at 2:14, one ending with 6:13 (to the Corinthians) and the other running to 6:2 and then adding 6:14–7:4 (to other Christians in Achaia) is completely unverifiable and has not been adopted by anyone else.

[63]Esp. Weiss 1.353.

[64]So Bornkamm, 260; Schmithals, *Gnosticism in Corinth*, 97–98. Margaret E. Thrall, *II Corinthians*, ICC (Edinburgh: T. & T. Clark, 1994–2000), 1.3–49, argues for three separate items of correspondence assembled to form a single letter, the three being chaps. 1–8, 9, and 10–13, written in that order.

[65]Hans Dieter Betz, *2 Corinthians 8 and 9*, Hermeneia (Philadelphia: Fortress Press, 1985).

that "prompted [Paul] to press the matter with renewed zeal in Corinth. . . . [The Corinthians] had already a year ago, earlier than the Macedonians, made a beginning not only to 'will', but also to 'do' (viii.10). They should now carry out their program to completion (viii.11)."[66] But this is unlikely. Barrett has observed that 2 Corinthians 8:10 does not say that the Corinthians made a beginning not only to will but also to do, but the reverse: they made a beginning not only to do but also to will, reflecting the spontaneity of their initial response and the subsequent resolution that grew out of it.[67] Moreover, it is unlikely that there was any trip by Titus encouraging a collection before 1 Corinthians 16:1–4, not only because Titus is not mentioned there, but also because these verses presuppose that Paul's plans for the collection are still in the beginning stages.

2. The opening words of chapter 9, περὶ μὲν γάρ (*peri men gar,* "so now concerning," or the like), are often taken to be an introductory formula used to introduce new subjects, and therefore constitute evidence that chapter 8 (and perhaps chapter 9) is an interpolation. Certainly, Paul elsewhere uses a similar, though not identical formula to introduce new subjects (1 Cor. 7:1; 8:1; 12:1; 16:1, namely, περὶ δέ [*peri de*], "now concerning").

This argument, however, fails to take into account several important considerations. First, the two constructions are quite different, as Betz himself recognizes,[68] and the latter is in any case specifically introductory only because we are told that the apostle is taking up one topic after another *ad seriatim,* in response to the agenda established by a letter from the Corinthians (1 Cor. 7:1). Second, to label περὶ μὲν γάρ (*peri men gar*) an "introductory *formula*" already begs the issue, for it prompts the reader to take the expression *as a whole* (because it is a "formula"), rather than to consider the semantic contribution of each word. There is no evidence that this string of words constitutes a formula, introductory or otherwise, that would have been recognized as such in the first century. Third, this observation becomes important when Betz,[69] for instance, argues that γάρ (*gar,* "for"), which almost always connects its clause with something preceding, insists that that need not be the case here, since it is linked with the particle μέν (*men*), which points forward to the δέ (*de*) in verse 3 (overtranslating, this becomes "on the one hand . . . on the other hand" —that is, "On the one hand, I know you need no reminder . . . but just the same I am sending . . ."). That simply does not follow. The μὲν . . . δέ (*men . . . de*) construction makes its own semantic contribution; the preposition περί (*peri,* "concerning") brings up the subject (i.e., "this service to the saints"); and γάρ (*gar,* "for") connects this

---

[66]Weiss 1.353.

[67]Barrett, *Second Corinthians,* 20.

[68]Betz, *2 Corinthians 8 and 9,* 90.

[69]Ibid.; see also Hans Windisch, *Der zweite Korintherbrief,* KEK 6 (1924; reprint, Göttingen: Vandenhoeck & Ruprecht, 1970), 286ff.

clause with what precedes, either so as to say "I can make confident boasts about you, *for* . . ."[70] or, perhaps, so as to say "I have been speaking about the collectors, *for* it is unnecessary to speak about the collection itself."[71] In other words, there is no compelling evidence that περὶ μὲν γάρ (*peri men gar*) should be taken as an introductory formula. The expression reads much better as a resumptive, following the travel arrangements that take up 8:16–24, a resumptive that also, because of the μὲν . . . δέ (*men . . . de*) construction, prepares for the next step in the argument.

3. It is sometimes argued that Paul's appeal in 8:1–5 to the Macedonians to stir up the Corinthians, and his appeal in 9:1–2 to the Corinthians to stir up the Macedonians, are in conflict unless the respective chapters were once separate documents. This is too skeptical because it fails to recognize the various markers of sequence. In chapter 8, Paul tells of a *completed* work by the Macedonians, hoping to stir up the Corinthians to *complete* what they had already set out to do; in chapter 9, Paul tells how he had appealed to this *earlier readiness* of the Corinthians to stimulate the Macedonians to *undertake* the action they had now *completed*.

4. Some find that the different purposes for sending the envoys, articulated in the two chapters, constitute evidence that they were written at different times. In chapter 8, Paul says he is sending well-accredited envoys so as to avoid any suspicion of impropriety in the matter of the collection; in chapter 9 he says he is sending them to ensure that everything will be ready by the time he himself arrives. It is simpler to assume that Paul had complementary reasons for sending the envoys.

5. In support of the unity of chapters 8–9, it can be argued that the way "the brothers" are referred to in 9:3 rather presupposes that their credentials have already been introduced—which introduction is provided in chapter 8. Moreover, many commentators have sought to demonstrate that there is a logical progression of thought through these chapters as they now stand in 2 Corinthians.

In short, despite the various leaps in Paul's thought from time to time, a phenomenon for which he is noted, the evidence supports the basic integrity of 2 Corinthians 1–9.

The Integrity of 1 Corinthians. Relatively few voices question the Pauline origins of 1 Corinthians.[72] Some have argued that 14:33b–35 is a non-Pauline interpolation (see comments below in the section "Text"). Others have suggested the same for 1:2b, on the grounds that, since the letter was specifically written for the Corinthians, the words "together with all those everywhere who

---

[70]Barrett, *Second Corinthians*, 232.

[71]H. L. Goudge, *The Second Epistle to the Corinthians*, WC (London: Methuen, 1927), 86.

[72]See the summary of the situation provided by Raymond F. Collins, *First Corinthians*, SacPag 7 (Collegeville: Liturgical Press, 1999), 10–14.

call on the name of our Lord Jesus Christ—their Lord and ours," are utterly out of place.[73] This misreads Paul rather badly, on two grounds.

First, the Corinthian church was constantly tempted to think itself a cut above other churches, quite free to act without consideration of what other churches thought. Correspondingly, Paul repeatedly stresses that what he is teaching them "agrees with what I teach everywhere in every church" (4:17); this "is the rule I lay down in all the churches" (7:17)—so much so that if anyone "wants to be contentious" about what Paul is saying, he or she must face the brute fact that "we have no other practice—nor do the churches of God" (11:16; see also 14:33b). In this framework, Paul's firm linking in 1:2 of the Corinthian church to all believers everywhere has a great significance.

Second, there is evidence that Paul self-consciously writes with authority that transcends that of a pastor for a church he has planted, that at least on some occasions the content of his writing is nothing less than "the Lord's command" (1 Cor. 14:37).[74] There lies at least the potential for an authoritative reach that extends beyond the local congregation.

But some scholars who do not doubt the authenticity of the entire epistle nevertheless suggest that it is a pastiche of Pauline fragments. The impetus for this analysis largely derives from three bits of evidence: the reference to a previous letter in 5:9, the influence of various partition theories in 2 Corinthians, and the topical, not to say fragmented, nature of 1 Corinthians. Numerous competing theories have been advanced.[75]

Without detailing them at length, the following factors tell heavily against such theories.

1. The fragmented nature of 1 Corinthians is, as we have seen, best accounted for by the fact that Paul is responding to reports brought by those from Chloe's house, by Stephanas, Fortunatus, and Achaicus, and also to a letter sent from the Corinthian church that raised a number of questions. Paul's agenda was already set for him.

2. The partition theories on 1 Corinthians agree on so few points, and gain so few adherents, that it seems best to conclude that none of them has the cogency their individual proponents see in them.

3. The alleged contradictions between parts of 1 Corinthians, contradictions that give warrant to the partition theories, are in every case patient of convincing

---

[73]So, e.g., Schmithals, *Gnosticism in Corinth,* 258.

[74]See further D. A. Carson, *Showing the Spirit: A Theological Exposition of 1 Corinthians 12–14* (Grand Rapids: Baker, 1987), 131–34.

[75]See discussion in C. K. Barrett, *A Commentary on the First Epistle to the Corinthians,* BNTC/HNTC, 2nd ed. (London: Black, 1971); and Kümmel, 275–78. Perhaps the most widely discussed of the recent theories is that of J. C. Hurd, *The Origin of I Corinthians,* 2nd ed. (Macon: Mercer University Press, 1983).

exegetical resolutions. This is true, for instance, of the relation between 8:1–13 and 10:23–33, and between 11:2–16 and 14:33b–36.

4. Collins[76] and Fee[77] have shown that some of the unease about the smoothness of the flow of argumentation in this letter stems from the failure to recognize the frequency with which Paul makes use of an A-B-A pattern. That is, in the first A section Paul deals with the topic at hand within a broad theological framework; in the B section he partially digresses into some crucial explanation of an integral component of his argument; and in the second A section he returns to the topic but addresses it very specifically.[78]

The Character of Paul's Opponents in 1 and 2 Corinthians

The diversity of theories as to the nature of Paul's opponents in these two epistles makes it necessary to add some comments to what has already been written regarding the historical reconstruction (above). We begin by enumerating pitfalls to be avoided.

1. One must not read the situation of 2 Corinthians back into 1 Corinthians—at least, not without observing several distinctions. In particular, there is no evidence whatsoever that at the time of writing 1 Corinthians the apostle Paul was facing a church that had been taken over by leaders *from the outside*. By the time of 2 Corinthians 10–13, that has certainly happened.

2. Protestations to the contrary, there is no evidence that the root cause of the opposition behind 1 Corinthians was the influence of Judaizers (as defined above). Paul's insistence on his own Jewish credentials, in order to minimize their importance, does not take place until 2 Corinthians 11:16ff., and they are presented so as to confront the false apostles (2 Cor. 11:13–15), who, so far as we know, have not arrived on the scene at the time 1 Corinthians was written. More important, the argumentation in 1 Corinthians is not slanted to refute Jews—certainly not Jews from any conservative background. For instance, those who are wary of eating meat offered to idols (chaps. 8, 10) do not hesitate because of Jewish scruples, but because they were once idolaters themselves, and now they want to avoid what has been offered to idols (8:7; that is why they have a "weak conscience"). This means that before their conversion they were pagans, not religiously observant Jews. Those in 1 Corinthians 8 who feel perfectly free to eat such meat are also unlikely to be Jews. Both groups, in other words, spring from non-Jewish backgrounds. Again, as we shall see, the reasons why many

---

[76]John J. Collins, "Chiasmus, the 'ABA' Pattern, and the Text of Paul," in *Studiorum Paulinorum Congressus Internationalis Catholicus 1961*, AnBib 17–18 (Rome: BIP, 1963), 2.575–84.

[77]Gordon D. Fee, *The First Epistle to the Corinthians*, 16–17.

[78]E.g., (1) A: 8:1–13, B: 9:1–27, C: 10:1–22; (2) A: 1:10–2:5, B: 2:6–16, C: 3:1–23; (3) A: chap. 12, B: chap. 13, C: chap. 14.

Corinthians did not affirm the reality of the resurrection (1 Cor. 15) did not lie in, say, the theological commitments of (Jewish) Sadducees, but in a thought world indebted to certain forms of Greek philosophy.

3. Despite the strenuous arguments of Schmithals[79] and a few others,[80] there is no satisfactory evidence that the dominant problem confronting Paul was Gnosticism, in the sense usually understood of the full-blown movement that can be traced in the second and third centuries (see discussion in chap. 23, on the Johannine Epistles). Too much evidence has accumulated that forbids us from reading later sources back into the New Testament.[81] None of the essential features of mature Gnosticism are present in the Corinthian epistles, except some elements of the dualism between spirit and body, which can be accounted for on other grounds—in particular, the pervasive influence of Neoplatonism. Doubtless this was the sort of soil in which Gnosticism would later mushroom, but for the period in question, Hengel is surely right: "It is time to stop talking about Gnosticism in Corinth."[82]

More positively, we can state several things about Paul's opponents.

1. The opponents are simultaneously divided against each other and, in some measure, opposed to Paul. The former point is customarily stressed in the commentaries. The division within the community is apparent on the very surface of 1:10–4:21. If believers were taking each other to court (chap. 6), it is not hard to imagine that support for each side could be found within the church. If some were sexually promiscuous (6:12–20), others thought it best to be entirely celibate (chap. 7). Some thought they should not eat meat offered to idols; others thought it to be a matter of indifference—perhaps, even, a means of demonstrating their liberty. By the balanced way the arguments are put in 11:2–16, it appears that there were competing opinions in the church over the appropriateness of the head covering for women. Some differences were socioeconomic (11:18–19). Certainly there were differences of opinion over the relative status of various spiritual gifts (chaps. 12–14). These internal divisions go some way

---

[79]Schmithals, *Gnosticism in Corinth;* idem, *Paul and the Gnostics* (New York: Abingdon, 1972).

[80]E.g., U. Wilckens, *Weisheit und Torheit* (Tübingen: J. C. B. Mohr, 1959); R. Jewett, *Paul's Anthropological Terms: A Study of Their Use in Conflict Setting,* AGJU 10 (Leiden: Brill, 1971); Robert M. Grant, *Paul in the Roman World: The Conflict at Corinth* (Louisville: Westminster John Knox, 2001).

[81]E.g., R. M. Wilson, "How Gnostic Were the Corinthians?" *NTS* 19 (1972–73): 65–74; Pearson, *Terminology,* esp. 51–81; Edwin M. Yamauchi, *Pre-Christian Gnosticism: A Survey of the Proposed Evidences,* 2nd ed. (Grand Rapids: Baker, 1983); L. D. McCrary, "Paul's Opponents in Corinth: An Examination of Walter Schmithals' Thesis on Gnosticism in Corinth" (Ph.D. diss., Southwestern Baptist Theological Seminary, 1985).

[82]Martin Hengel, *Crucifixion* (ET London: SCM, 1977), 18 n. 10.

toward explaining what some have called the "yes, but" form of some of Paul's arguments (e.g., 7:1–2, 8–9; 8:1–6, 7; 14:5, 18–19).

In contrast, Fee minimizes the amount of internal division and stresses the opposition of virtually the entire church to Paul.[83] Certainly such opposition accounts, in part, for the defense of Paul's apostleship (chaps. 4, 9), for his insistence that they submit to his authority (14:37–38), and for his addressing himself, on issue after issue, to the *entire* church and its letter to him (7:1ff.). Fee's approach is a salutary correction and explains the continuing, festering relationship between Paul and the Corinthians alluded to in the "painful visit," the "severe letter," and especially in 2 Corinthians 10–13. The fact remains, however, that they have written to Paul and sought his opinion on a number of matters, and he feels free to instigate the collection among them (16:1–4): the breakdown between Paul and the Corinthians was far from total. More important, internal divisions and a fundamental misapprehension about Paul are not mutually exclusive faults, and it appears that Fee has minimized the latter.

2. The heart of the Corinthian opposition turns on several tightly held and intertwined positions. The Corinthians are convinced they are spiritual (see esp. chaps. 12–14), but their view of spirituality has less to do with the conduct and ethics than Paul insists on, and more to do with status. They appear to treat baptism and the Lord's Supper as almost magical rites guaranteeing life, regardless of conduct (10:1–5; 11:17–34). They are puffed up and arrogant (4:6, 18; 5:2). Their view of what is spiritual may be influenced by a neoplatonic depreciation of the material. That is probably what makes it possible for some of them to view sexual intercourse with a prostitute as morally indifferent (6:12–20); that is also why they take the stance they do regarding the resurrection. They do not deny that there is a future resurrection, as did the Sadducees; nor do they deny that Jesus rose from the dead. Rather, they think they have already been raised, that such "resurrection" pertains to their present spiritual existence, and what they will be at the end is nothing other than what they are now, minus their physical body. This unswerving confidence in their own spirituality is tied, as well, to a brand of "over-realized" eschatology that assumes that all or most of the blessings of the age to come are already being experienced in their fullness.[84] That accounts not only for Paul's scathing outburst in 1 Corinthians 4:8–13 but also for the kind of moral indifferentism and supercilious arrogance (4:6, 18; 5:2) that will not easily listen to the apostle (9:3; 14:37–38) precisely because he speaks so much of perseverance and self-denial in the context of a world order

---

[83]Fee, *First Corinthians*, esp. 5ff. In this he is largely returning to the stance of A. Robertson and A. Plummer, *A Critical and Exegetical Commentary on the First Epistle of St Paul to the Corinthians*, ICC (Edinburgh: T. & T. Clark, 1914).

[84]See esp. A. C. Thiselton, "Realized Eschatology at Corinth," *NTS* 24 (1977–78): 510–26.

that is still fallen and opposed to God and his gospel. Paul would not for a moment want to depreciate the presence and power of the Spirit in the believer's life and in the church in the present age. But for him this means the body is the Spirit's temple (6:19–20) and therefore must serve God wholly; and the resurrection is still to come.

3. As we have seen, by the time 2 Corinthians was complete, the Corinthian church had been invaded by outsiders. Although they were Jews (2 Cor. 11:21ff.), they were very familiar with the Hellenistic world (as Paul was), and they espoused many Greco-Roman values and rhetorical devices.[85] Inevitably, they gained instant credibility in a church like that in Corinth. But their values and their devices Paul eschewed, judging them inimical to the gospel itself (11:4). Thus 2 Corinthians 10–13 presents us with what might almost be called a new kind of Judaizing: a Hellenistic Jewish movement that opposed Paul but was less concerned (so far as we know) with circumcision and with detailed observance of the Mosaic law than with prestige and power in accord with the contemporary values of Corinthian society.[86] Paul's response (2 Cor. 10–13) is the most intense, revealing, and emotional of all his writings.

> *Paul's response to a Hellenitic Jewish movement in 2 Corinthians 10–13 is the most intense, revealing, and emotional of all his writings.*

DATE

Quite apart from constraints imposed on the dating of these epistles by the need to fit Paul's movements and writings together, there is one fixed point. There is an inscription recording a rescript of the Emperor Claudius to the people of Delphi that mentions Gallio as holding the office of proconsul in Achaia during the period of Claudius's twenty-sixth acclamation as *imperator*[87]—a period known from other inscriptions[88] to cover the first seven months of A.D. 52.[89] Proconsuls

---

[85]See E. A. Judge, "The Conflict of Aims in NT Thought," *JCE* 9 (1966): 32–45; idem, "Paul's Boasting in Relation to Contemporary Professional Practice," *AusBibRev* 16 (1968): 37–50; S. H. Travis, "Paul's Boasting in 2 Corinthians 10–12," *SE* 6.527–32; D. A. Carson, *From Triumphalism to Maturity: An Exposition of 2 Corinthians 10–13* (Grand Rapids: Baker, 1984), 16–27. Jerry L. Sumney, *Identifying Paul's Opponents: The Question of Method in 2 Corinthians*, JSNTSup 40 (Sheffield: Sheffield Academic Press, 1990), warns against extrapolating too far beyond the evidence. He himself thinks the intruders in 2 Cor. 10–13 were pneumatics rather than Judaizers or gnostics.

[86]Scott J. Hafemann, *2 Corinthians*, NIVAC (Grand Rapids: Zondervan, 2000), 33–34, suggests that the opponents offered fuller participation in the Spirit by means of *both* over-realized eschatology *and* being Jewish.

[87]See E. M. Smallwood, *Documents Illustrating the Principates of Gaius, Claudius, and Nero* (Cambridge: Cambridge University Press, 1967), p. 105 no. 376.

[88]*CIL* 3.476; 6.1256.

[89]For the bearing of this evidence on Pauline chronology generally, see chap. 7 above.

normally began their tour of duty on July 1, which means that Gallio probably ascended to the proconsulship on July 1, 51. However, it is possible that the rescript belongs to the very end of the seven-month period, in which case Gallio may have taken up his duties on July 1, 52. The latter date leaves only one month for the rescript, so the former date is perhaps marginally more likely.[90]

If the Jews made their united attack on Paul (Acts 18:12) fairly early during Gallio's proconsulship, then probably it was in the autumn of A.D. 51. After the case was dismissed, Paul stayed in Corinth for some time (Acts 18:18) and then sailed for Syria, probably in the spring of 52. Paul's two-and-a-half-year stint in Ephesus would have taken him to the autumn of 55. Paul wrote 1 Corinthians while he was in Ephesus, some time before Pentecost (16:8), probably during his last year—that is, early in 55, with 2 Corinthians being complete within the next year or so. By that time he was in Macedonia (2 Cor. 2:12–13; 7:5; 8:1–5; 9:2). Primarily because of the uncertainty over the beginning date of Gallio's proconsulship, all of these dates could be advanced by one year.

TEXT

The position with respect to the transmission of the text of both Corinthian epistles is inherently the same as in the rest of the Pauline Epistles. The Alexandrian text type is represented by the Chester Beatty papyrus P[46] (with some Western readings), by the uncials ℵ, B, and C, and by some minuscules. The Western text is represented by D, F, G, Old Latin, and Western church fathers; the Byzantine text by the overwhelming majority of (later) witnesses.

Although, as usual, there are many textual decisions to be made, the text of both epistles is in relatively good form. Some of the difficulties in 2 Corinthians stem from the fact that Paul, especially in chapters 10–13, is writing under enormous stress, which is reflected in his sometimes tortured Greek, certainly the most difficult Greek in the Pauline corpus.

In 1 Corinthians, the view that 14:33b–35 is a gloss was very much a minority position, until Fee defended it in his recent commentary.[91] Fee's stature as a textual critic has served to make this view more acceptable. The fact remains that although some witnesses place verses 34–35 after verse 40, not one omits it; and despite Fee, convincing reasons can be given not only as to why a minority of witnesses transposed this passage to the end of verse 40, but also as to how it should be understood within its context.[92]

---

[90]It is also possible that Gallio served a second year as proconsul, but this is unlikely.

[91]Fee, *First Corinthians*, 699–708.

[92]See D. A. Carson, "'Silent in the Churches': On the Role of Women in I Cor. 14:33b–36," in *Recovering Biblical Manhood and Womanhood,* ed. Wayne Grudem and John Piper (Westchester: Crossway, 1990), 140–153, 487–90.

ADOPTION INTO THE CANON

First Corinthians is already being cited in the last decade of the first century (by Clement of Rome: *1 Clem.* 37:5; 47:1–3; 49:5) and in the first decade of the second (by Ignatius: *Eph.* 16:1; 18:1; *Rom.* 5:1; *Phil.* 3:3). There was never any dispute about its admission to the canon.

The situation with 2 Corinthians is very different.[93] Although it is just possible that 1 Timothy 2:13–15 alludes to 2 Corinthians 11:1–3, and barely possible that 2 Corinthians finds an echo in Ignatius (*Eph.* 15:3 [2 Cor. 6:16]; *Trall.* 9:2 [2 Cor. 4:14]; *Phil.* 6:3 [2 Cor. 1:12; 11:9–10]), there is only disputed evidence of 2 Corinthians in *1 Clement*,[94] and no certain attestation of 2 Corinthians until Marcion's canon (c. A.D. 140). From about the middle of the second century there is undisputed evidence that 2 Corinthians was viewed as part of the Pauline corpus. The majority of scholars are surely right to insist that this by itself does not cast doubt on the authenticity of 2 Corinthians and that it should not be used to justify partition theories.[95] The puzzling question is why 2 Corinthians did not apparently circulate as widely and as rapidly as 1 Corinthians.

1 AND 2 CORINTHIANS IN RECENT STUDY

The greatest part of the scholarly energy expended on these epistles is tied up with the kinds of issues already explored (see section "Occasion" above), or with the exegesis of particular passages and attempts to delineate specific situations or backgrounds to such passages. Although the movement to establish a suitable Greco-Roman social analysis of 1 and 2 Corinthians stretches back a couple of decades,[96] much of the best of this work was done during the past ten or fifteen years, as we have seen. There is no need to canvass afresh this extensive literature. Three other areas, prominent in recent literature on the Corinthian epistles, may be briefly noted.

1. There is a wide-ranging debate over Paul's view of the law (see esp. chaps. 8, 9, 11 in this volume), and inevitably Paul's epistles to the Corinthians play a part in that debate. This owes something to a few passages that specifically

---

[93]See esp. Furnish, *II Corinthians*, 29–30.

[94]See *1 Clement*. 5:5–6 (2 Cor. 11:25); 38:2 (2 Cor. 9:12; but cf. 1 Cor. 16:17). See Donald A. Hagner, *The Use of the Old and New Testaments in Clement of Rome*, Nov TSup 34 (Leiden: Brill, 1973), esp. 212–13.

[95]Kümmel, 292, points out that even Galatians is unattested in Ignatius.

[96]E.g., Abraham Malherbe, *Social Aspects of Early Christianity* (Philadelphia: Fortress Press, 1983); Bruce J. Malina, *Christian Origins and Cultural Anthropology: Practical Models for Biblical Interpretation* (Atlanta: John Knox, 1986). Cf. Murphy-O'Connor, *St. Paul's Corinth*; Gerd Theissen, *The Social Setting of Pauline Christianity: Essays on Corinth* (ET Philadelphia: Fortress Press, 1982).

address the issue (notably 1 Cor. 9:19–23), but more to a perception that in these epistles Paul imposes some restraints, where in other passages he seems to see himself as free from law.[97]

2. Doubtless owing to the worldwide growth of the charismatic movement, numerous essays and books on 1 Corinthians 12–14 and related matters have attempted to break new ground on the nature of prophecy, the place of the χαρίσματα (*charismata,* "grace-gifts"), and the theology of the Spirit.[98]

3. Owing to the influence of the various feminist movements in the Western world, and assorted responses to them, a large body of literature has also grown up around 1 Corinthians 11:2–16 and 14:33b–36.[99]

THE CONTRIBUTION OF 1 AND 2 CORINTHIANS

Because so many of the topics treated in these epistles are occasional and closely related to particular cultural circumstances, 1 and 2 Corinthians offer potent opportunities to observe how the unchanging gospel, taught in the languages and cultures of the first century, was first applied to changing circumstances. For instance (to use the example of Childs, 275, 279–81), the particular form of the Corinthian denial of the resurrection may not be popular in the twentieth century (although, arguably, an adaptation of it is returning in some sectors of the New Age movement), but Paul's strenuous insistence on the historical reality of the resurrection of Jesus as part of the nonnegotiable "given" of the gospel may be applied in many circumstances. Also, 1 Corinthians 15 constitutes not only the earliest written list of the witnesses of Jesus' resurrection but the most important New Testament treatment of the nature of the resurrection.

No part of the Pauline corpus more clearly illuminates the character of Paul the man, Paul the Christian, Paul the pastor, and Paul the apostle than do these epistles. He thereby leaves us some substance in his invitation to imitate him, and thereby imitate Christ (1 Cor. 11:1).

Because in 1 and 2 Corinthians Paul passionately develops a theology of the cross that shapes Christian ethics, Christian priorities, and Christian attitudes, the apostle directly confronts all approaches to Christianity that happily seek to integrate a generally orthodox confession with pagan values of self-promotion.

---

[97]See John W. Drane, *Paul: Libertine or Legalist?* (London: SPCK, 1975).

[98]See the bibliographies in David E. Aune, *Prophecy in Early Christianity and the Ancient Mediterranean World* (Grand Rapids: Eerdmans, 1983); Wayne Grudem, *The Gift of Prophecy in the New Testament and Today,* 2nd ed. (Wheaton: Crossway, 2000); Carson, *Showing the Spirit;* Thomas W. Gillespie, *The First Theologians: A Study in Early Christian Prophecy* (Grand Rapids: Eerdmans, 1994).

[99]See bibliography in Antoinette Clark Wire, *The Corinthian Women Prophets: A Reconstruction Through Paul's Rhetoric* (Minneapolis: Fortress Press, 1991); Grudem and Piper, eds., *Recovering Biblical Manhood and Womanhood.*

The cross not only justifies, it teaches us how to live and die, how to lead and follow, how to love and serve. These two letters therefore speak volumes to contemporary Western Christianity, which often prides itself in its orthodoxy but is far more comfortable with twenty-first-century secularism than it has any right to be. Along the same lines, 1 Corinthians makes an enormous contribution to the doctrine of the church—its nature, unity, diversity, characteristics, conduct, interdependence, and discipline—even though there is very little in this epistle on church government (apart from inferences drawn from such passages as 5:1ff.).

These two epistles constitute the most telling condemnation of arrogance, self-promotion, boasting, and self-confidence in the Pauline corpus; conversely, they describe in practical terms the nature of Christian life and witness, emphasizing service, self-denial, purity, and weakness as the matrix in which God displays his strength. Perhaps the high-water mark is the emphasis on love as "the most excellent way" (1 Cor. 12:31–13:13) all Christians must pursue.

BIBLIOGRAPHY

E. B. **Allo**, *Saint Paul: Première Épître aux Corinthiens*, EBib (Paris: Gabalda, 1934) ▌idem, *Saint Paul: Seconde Épître aux Corinthiens*, EBib (Paris: Gabalda, 1956) ▌David E. **Aune**, *Prophecy in Early Christianity and the Ancient Mediterranean World* (Grand Rapids: Eerdmans, 1983) ▌P. **Bachmann**, *Der zweite Brief des Paulus an die Korinther* (Leipzig: Deichert, 1922) ▌Paul **Barnett**, *The Second Epistle to the Corinthians*, NICNT (Grand Rapids: Eerdmans, 1997) ▌C. K. **Barrett**, "Cephas and Corinth," in *Abraham unser Vater: Juden und Christen im Gespräch über die Bibel*, Fs. Otto Michel, ed. O. Betz, M. Hengel, and P. Schmidt, AGSU 5 (Leiden: Brill, 1963), 1–12 ▌idem, *A Commentary on the First Epistle to the Corinthians*, BNTC/HNTC, 2nd ed. (London: Black, 1971) ▌idem, *A Commentary on the Second Epistle to the Corinthians*, BNTC/HNTC (London: Black, 1973) ▌G. K. **Beale**, "The Old Testament Background of Reconciliation in 2 Corinthians 5–7 and Its Bearing on the Literary Problem of 2 Corinthians 6.14–7.1," *NTS* 35 (1989): 550–81 ▌Linda L. **Belleville**, *2 Corinthians*, IVPNTC (Downers Grove: IVP, 1996) ▌H. D. **Betz**, "2 Cor. 6:14–7:1: An Anti-Pauline Fragment?" *JBL* 92 (1973): 88–108 ▌idem, *2 Corinthians 8 and 9*, Hermeneia (Philadelphia: Fortress Press, 1985) ▌R. **Bieringer**, ed., *The Corinthian Correspondence*, BETL (Leuven: Leuven University Press, 1996) ▌Craig L. **Blomberg**, *1 Corinthians*, NIVAC (Grand Rapids: Zondervan, 1994) ▌G. **Bornkamm**, "The History of the Origin of the So-called Second Letter to the Corinthians," *NTS* 8 (1961–62): 258–64 ▌G. W. **Bowersock**, *Greek Sophists in the Roman Empire* (Oxford: Oxford University Press, 1969) ▌Alexander R. **Brown**, *The Cross and Human Transformation: Paul's Apocalyptic Word in 1 Corinthians* (Minneapolis: Fortress Press, 1995) ▌F. F. **Bruce**, *1 and 2 Corinthians* (London: Oliphants, 1971) ▌idem, *Paul: Apostle of the Heart Set*

Free (Grand Rapids: Eerdmans, 1977) ▥ R. **Bultmann**, *The Second Letter to the Corinthians* (ET Minneapolis: Augsburg, 1985) ▥ D. A. **Carson**, *From Triumphalism to Maturity: An Exposition of 2 Corinthians 10–13* (Grand Rapids: Baker, 1984) ▥ idem, *Showing the Spirit: A Theological Exposition of 1 Corinthians 12–14* (Grand Rapids: Baker, 1987) ▥ idem, *The Cross and Christian Ministry* (Grand Rapids: Baker, 2003 [1993]) ▥ idem, "'Silent in the Churches': On the Role of Women in I Cor. 14:33b–36," in *Recovering Biblical Manhood and Womanhood,* ed. Wayne Grudem and John Piper (Westchester: Crossway, 1990), 140–153, 487–90 ▥ Elizabeth A. **Castelli**, *Imitating Paul: A Discourse of Power* (Louisville: Westminster John Knox, 1991) ▥ Brevard S. **Childs**, *The New Testament as Canon: An Introduction* (London: SCM, 1984) ▥ J. K. **Chow**, *Patronage and Power: A Study of Social Networks in Corinth,* JSNTSup 75 (Sheffield: Sheffield Academic Press, 1992) ▥ A. D. **Clarke**, *Secular and Christian Leadership in Corinth: A Socio-Historical and Exegetical Study of 1 Corinthians 1–6,* AGJU 18 (Leiden: Brill, 1993) ▥ J.-F. **Collange**, *Enigmes de la deuxième Épître de Paul aux Corinthiens,* SNTSMS 18 (Cambridge: Cambridge University Press, 1972) ▥ John J. **Collins**, "Chiasmus, the 'ABA' Pattern and the Text of Paul," in *Studiorum Paulinorum Congressus Internationalis Catholicus 1961,* 2 vols., AnBib 17–18 (Rome: BIP, 1963) ▥ Raymond F. **Collins**, *First Corinthians,* SacPag 7 (Collegeville: Liturgical Press, 1999) ▥ H. **Conzelmann**, *1 Corinthians,* Hermeneia (Philadelphia: Fortress Press, 1975) ▥ idem, "Korinth und die Mädchen der Aphrodite: Zur Religionsgeschichte der Stadt Korinth," *NAG* 8 (1967–68): 247–61 ▥ Jeffrey A. **Crafton**, *The Agency of the Apostle,* JSNTSup 51 (Sheffield: Sheffield Academic Press, 1991) ▥ N. A. **Dahl**, "A Fragment and Its Context: 2 Corinthians 6:14–7:1," in *Studies in Paul* (Minneapolis: Augsburg, 1972), 62–69 ▥ J. A. **Davis**, *Wisdom and Spirit: An Investigation of 1 Corinthians 1.18–3.20 Against the Background of Jewish Sapiential Traditions in the Greco-Roman Period* (Lanham: UPA, 1984) ▥ David A. **deSilva**, "Measuring Penultimate Against Ultimate Reality: An Investigation of the Integrity and Argumentation of 2 Corinthians," *JSNT* 53 (1993): 41–70 ▥ John W. **Drane**, *Paul: Libertine or Legalist?* (London: SPCK, 1975) ▥ Gordon D. **Fee**, *The First Epistle to the Corinthians,* NICNT (Grand Rapids: Eerdmans, 1987) ▥ idem, "II Corinthians vi.14–vii.1 and Food Offered to Idols," *NTS* 23 (1977): 140–61 ▥ J. A. **Fitzmyer**, "Qumran and the Interpolated Paragraph in 2 Cor 6:14–7:1," in *Essays on the Semitic Background of the New Testament* (London: Chapman, 1971), 205–17 ▥ Victor Paul **Furnish**, *II Corinthians,* AB 32A (Garden City: Doubleday, 1984) ▥ Paul D. **Gardner**, *The Gifts of God and the Authentication of a Christian: An Exegetical Study of 1 Corinthians 8–11* (Lanham: UPA, 1994) ▥ David E. **Garland**, *2 Corinthians,* NAC (Nashville: Broadman & Holman, 2000) ▥ David W. J. **Gill**, "Corinth: A Roman Colony in Achaea," *BZ* 37 (1993): 259–64 ▥ Thomas W. **Gillespie**, *The First Theologians: A Study in Early Christian Prophecy* (Grand Rapids: Eerdmans, 1994) ▥ J. **Gnilka**, "2 Cor 6:14–7:1 in Light of the Qumran Texts and the Testaments of the Twelve Patriarchs," in *Paul and Qumran,* ed.

J. Murphy-O'Connor (London: Chapman, 1968), 48–68 ▦ H. L. **Goudge**, *The Second Epistle to the Corinthians*, WC (London: Methuen, 1927) ▦ Michael **Goulder**, *Paul and the Competing Mission in Corinth* (Peabody: Hendrickson, 2001) ▦ Robert M. **Grant**, *Paul in the Roman World: The Conflict at Corinth* (Louisville: Westminster John Knox, 2001) ▦ Wayne **Grudem**, *The Gift of Prophecy in the New Testament and Today*, 2nd ed. (Wheaton: Crossway, 2000) ▦ Wayne **Grudem** and John **Piper**, eds., *Recovering Biblical Manhood and Womanhood* (Westchester: Crossway, 1990) ▦ Scott J. **Hafemann**, *2 Corinthians*, NIVAC (Grand Rapids: Zondervan, 2000) ▦ Donald A. **Hagner**, *The Use of the Old and New Testaments in Clement of Rome*, NovTSup 34 (Leiden: Brill, 1973) ▦ Murray J. **Harris**, "2 Corinthians," in *EBC* 10 (Grand Rapids: Zondervan, 1976) ▦ idem, *The Second Epistle to the Corinthians*, NIGTC (Grand Rapids: Eerdmans, 2005), 29–51 ▦ Martin **Hengel**, *Crucifixion* (ET London: SCM, 1977) ▦ R. A. **Horsley**, "Pneumatikos vs. Psychikos: Distinctions of Spiritual Status Among the Corinthians," *HTR* 69 (1976): 269–88 ▦ idem, "Wisdom of Word and Words of Wisdom in Corinth," *CBQ* 39 (1977): 224–39 ▦ idem, *1 Corinthians*, ANTC (Nashville: Abingdon, 1998) ▦ Philip E. **Hughes**, *Paul's Second Epistle to the Corinthians*, NICNT (Grand Rapids: Eerdmans, 1962) ▦ R. **Jewett**, *Paul's Anthropological Terms: A Study of Their Use in Conflict Settings*, AGJU 10 (Leiden: Brill, 1971) ▦ E. A. **Judge**, "The Conflict of Aims in NT Thought," *JCE* 9 (1966): 32–45 ▦ idem, "Paul's Boasting in Relation to Contemporary Professional Practice," *AusBibRev* 16 (1968): 37–50 ▦ Simon J. **Kistemaker**, *1 Corinthians* (Grand Rapids: Baker, 1993) ▦ Colin **Kruse**, *2 Corinthians*, TNTC (Grand Rapids: Eerdmans, 1987) ▦ Jan **Lambrecht**, *Second Corinthians*, SacPag 8 (Collegeville: Liturgical Press, 1999) ▦ H. **Lietzmann**, supplemented by W. G. **Kümmel**, *An die Korinther I, II*, HNT 9 (Tübingen: Mohr-Siebeck, 1969) ▦ Duane **Litfin**, *St Paul's Theology of Proclamation: 1 Cor 1–4 and Greco-Roman Rhetoric*, SNTSMS 79 (Cambridge: Cambridge University Press, 1994) ▦ L. D. **McCrary**, "Paul's Opponents in Corinth: An Examination of Walter Schmithals' Thesis on Gnosticism in Corinth" (Ph.D. diss., Southwestern Baptist Theological Seminary, 1985) ▦ Abraham **Malherbe**, *Social Aspects of Early Christianity* (Philadelphia: Fortress Press, 1983) ▦ Bruce J. **Malina**, *Christian Origins and Cultural Anthropology: Practical Models for Biblical Interpretation* (Atlanta: John Knox, 1986) ▦ Peter **Marshall**, *Enmity in Corinth: Social Conventions in Paul's Relations with the Corinthians*, WUNT 23 (Tübingen: Mohr-Siebeck, 1987) ▦ Dale B. **Martin**, *The Corinthian Body* (New Haven: Yale University Press, 1995) ▦ Ralph P. **Martin**, *2 Corinthians*, WBC 40 (Waco: Word, 1986) ▦ Frank J. **Matera**, *II Corinthians: A Commentary*, NTL (Louisville: Westminster John Knox, 2003) ▦ J. J. **Meggitt**, *Paul, Poverty and Survival* (Edinburgh: T. & T. Clark, 1998) ▦ Margaret M. **Mitchell**, *Paul and the Rhetoric of Reconciliation: An Exegetical Investigation of the Language and Composition of 1 Corinthians*, HUT 28 (Tübingen: Mohr-Siebeck, 1991) ▦ Leon **Morris**, *The First Epistle of Paul to the Corinthians*, 2nd ed., TNTC (Leicester: IVP, 1985) ▦ Jerome **Murphy-O'Connor**, *St. Paul's*

Corinth: Texts and Archaeology (Wilmington: Glazier, 1983) ▥B. A. **Pearson**, *The Pneumatikos-Psychikos Terminology in 1 Corinthians: A Study in the Theology of the Corinthian Opponents of Paul and Its Relation to Gnosticism*, SBLDS 12 (Missoula: SP, 1973) ▥Raymond **Pickett**, *The Cross in Corinth: The Social Significance of the Death of Jesus*, JSNTSup 143 (Sheffield: Sheffield Academic Press, 1997) ▥A. **Plummer**, *A Critical and Exegetical Commentary on the Second Epistle of St Paul to the Corinthians*, ICC (Edinburgh: T. & T. Clark, 1915) ▥Stephen M. **Pogoloff**, *Logos and Sophia: The Rhetorical Situation of 1 Corinthians*, SBLDS 134 (Atlanta: SP, 1992) ▥A. **Robertson** and A. **Plummer**, *A Critical and Exegetical Commentary on the First Epistle of St Paul to the Corinthians*, ICC (Edinburgh: T. & T. Clark, 1914) ▥Brian S. **Rosner**, *Paul, Scripture and Ethics: A Study of 1 Corinthians 5–7*, AGJU 12 (Leiden: Brill, 1994 / Grand Rapids: Baker, 1999) ▥W. **Schmithals**, *Gnosticism in Corinth: An Investigation of the Letters to the Corinthians* (ET New York: Abingdon, 1971) ▥idem, *Paul and the Gnostics* (New York: Abingdon, 1972) ▥Wolfgang **Schrage**, *Der erste Brief an die Korinther*, EKKNT 7/1–4 (Neukirchen-Vluyn: Neukirchener Verlag/Zürich: Benziger Verlag, 1991–2001) ▥James M. **Scott**, *2 Corinthians*, NIBC (Peabody: Hendrickson, 1998) ▥V. George **Shillington**, *2 Corinthians*, BCBC (Scottdale/Waterloo: Herald, 1997) ▥E. M. **Smallwood**, *Documents Illustrating the Principates of Gaius, Claudius, and Nero* (Cambridge: Cambridge University Press, 1967) ▥Graydon F. **Snyder**, *First Corinthians: A Faith Community Commentary* (Macon: Mercer University, 1992) ▥R. H. **Strachan**, *The Second Epistle of Paul to the Corinthians*, MNTC (London: Hodder & Stoughton, 1935) ▥Jerry L. **Sumney**, *Identifying Paul's Opponents: The Question of Method in 2 Corinthians*, JSNTSup 40 (Sheffield: Sheffield Academic Press, 1990) ▥R. V. G. **Tasker**, *The Second Epistle of Paul to the Corinthians*, TNTC (Grand Rapids: Eerdmans, 1958) ▥Gerd **Theissen**, *The Social Setting of Pauline Christianity: Essays on Corinth* (ET Philadelphia: Fortress Press, 1982) ▥idem, "Social Conflicts in the Corinthian Community: Further Remarks on J. J. Meggitt, *Paul, Poverty and Survival*," *JSNT* 25 (2003): 371–91 ▥A. C. **Thiselton**, "Realized Eschatology at Corinth," *NTS* 24 (1977–78): 510–26 ▥Margaret E. **Thrall**, "A Second Thanksgiving Period in II Corinthians," *JSNT* 16 (1982): 101–24 ▥idem, *The Second Epistle to the Corinthians*, ICC, 2 vols. (Edinburgh: T. & T. Clark, 1994–2000) ▥S. H. **Travis**, "Paul's Boasting in 2 Corinthians 10–12," *SE* 6: 527–32 ▥Sze-kar **Wan**, *Power in Weakness: Conflict and Rhetoric in Paul's Second Letter to the Corinthians* (Harrisburg: Trinity Press International, 2000) ▥J. **Weiss**, *Earliest Christianity: A History of the Period A.D. 30–150*, 2 vols. (New York: Harper & Row, 1959) ▥H. D. **Wendland**, *Die Briefe an die Korinther*, NTD 7 (Göttingen: Vandenhoeck & Ruprecht, 1965) ▥U. **Wilckens**, *Weisheit und Torheit* (Tübingen: J. C. B. Mohr, 1959) ▥H. H. Drake **Williams III**, *The Wisdom of the Wise: The Presence and Function of Scripture Within 1 Cor. 1:18–3:23*, AGJU 49 (Leiden: Brill, 2001) ▥R. M. **Wilson**, "How Gnostic Were the Corinthians?" *NTS* 19 (1972–73): 65–74 ▥Hans **Windisch**, *Der zweite Korintherbrief*, KEK 6

(Göttingen: Vandenhoeck & Ruprecht, 1924; reprint, 1970 ▆B. W. **Winter**, *Philo and Paul Among the Sophists*, SNTSMS 96 (Cambridge: Cambridge University Press, 1997) ▆idem, *Seek the Welfare of the City* (Grand Rapids: Eerdmans, 1994) ▆Antoinette Clark **Wire**, *The Corinthian Women Prophets: A Reconstruction Through Paul's Rhetoric* (Minneapolis: Fortress Press, 1991) ▆Ben **Witherington III**, *Conflict and Community in Corinth: A Socio-Rhetorical Commentary on 1 and 2 Corinthians* (Grand Rapids: Eerdmans / Carlisle: Paternoster, 1995) ▆C. **Wolff**, *Der erste Brief des Paulus an die Korinther*, THNT 7 (Leipzig: Evangelische Verlagsanstalt, 1996) ▆Edwin M. **Yamauchi**, *Pre-Christian Gnosticism: A Survey of the Proposed Evidences*, 2nd ed. (Grand Rapids: Baker, 1983) ▆Khiok-khing, **Yeo**, *Rhetorical Interaction in 1 Corinthians 8–10*, BIS 9 (Leiden: Brill, 1995) ▆Günther **Zuntz**, *The Text of the Epistles: A Disquisition upon the Corpus Paulinum* (London: Oxford, 1953).

CHAPTER TWELVE

GALATIANS

CONTENT

Paul's opening greeting draws attention to his apostolic status—a foretaste of an emphasis that dominates the first chapter and a half of this epistle. Paul insists on his status as an apostle sent by God, and in his greeting reminds his readers that Christ gave himself to deliver us from "the present evil age" (1:1–5).

Without pausing for the customary thanksgiving, Paul expresses astonishment that the Galatians are deserting not only the gospel but God himself, "the one who called you by the grace of Christ" (1:6), for the gospel that was preached to the Galatians can be changed by neither apostles nor angels (1:6–10). He insists that his gospel was given him by revelation from Christ and relates his persecuting activities and his few contacts with the earlier apostles to show that his gospel could not have derived from mere reliance on what they said (1:11–2:5). And far from the Jerusalem leaders insisting that Gentiles become Jews, they agreed with Paul when he insisted that Titus, who had accompanied him to Jerusalem, should *not* be circumcised (2:1–5). Paul and the Jerusalem leaders agreed to a division of labor, with Peter at work as apostle to the Jews, while Paul was called as the apostle to the Gentiles, apparently with the implication that Gentiles would not be required to keep the Mosaic law (2:6–10). When later at Antioch Peter withdrew from table fellowship with Gentile Christians, perhaps under pressure from opponents in Jerusalem, Paul took issue with him and pointed out that even Jews were not saved by works of the law but by faith in Christ (2:11–14)—a fundamental perspective with which Peter himself would have agreed (cf. Acts 10:1–11:18). Sinners who are justified in Christ have died to the law and live "by faith in the Son of God" (Gal. 2:15–21). The apostle Paul is nervous about any theology that appears to rival Christ: he cannot abide the thought that "Christ died for nothing" (2:21).

In an emotional appeal, Paul reminds the Galatians that the Spirit was given to them, not on account of their observance of the law, but on account of their faith in Christ (3:1–5). Nor is this anomalous: even Abraham was justified by faith (3:6–9) and was given a promise that in his offspring *all* the nations of the earth would be blessed. The law of Moses functions differently: it brings a curse on sinners, the very curse that Christ bore on their behalf (3:10–14). In any case, the law cannot take precedence over or replace the covenant of promise that God made with Abraham 430 years earlier. Indeed, in several ways the law-covenant exercised several parenthetical functions until the coming of Christ (3:15–25)— functions that include turning sin into actual transgression and holding in custody the people of God until the coming of Christ to whom it pointed. The primacy of faith means that in our approach to God all human distinctions are removed; there is one great family of God (3:26–29). Christ's redeeming work has brought believers into their majority: they have grown up, as it were, reached adulthood, and can now function as sons rather than as minors still under the jurisdiction of household slaves. Indeed, the same privilege of sonship has been extended to Gentiles (4:1–7).

In their observance of the Sinaitic law, the Galatians were going back into the kind of slavery from which they had been rescued, and Paul pleads again that they not persist in rejecting his teaching (4:8–20). In complex and evocative typology, he reminds them from the Scriptures that Abraham had a son by Hagar (a slave woman) and another by Sarah (who was free). These, he insists, represent two covenants. By submitting to the law's requirements, the Galatians are going back to the old covenant, the covenant of slavery, though they are really children of the free woman (4:21–31). They should live in the freedom that Christ has won for them and not undergo the circumcision that means bondage (5:1–12). Paul contrasts life in the Spirit with that in the flesh (5:13–26), which leads to instruction about right living (6:1–10). Paul takes up the pen himself to close with an impassioned reminder that neither circumcision nor uncircumcision matters—but God's new creation does (6:11–18).

AUTHOR

The letter claims to have been written by Paul (1:1), and the claim rings true. It is the outpouring of a concerned evangelist and pastor over some tragic false teaching that had arisen among his converts. As Kümmel says, "That Galatians is a genuine, authentic Epistle is indisputable."[1] Far more disputed is the question of how Paul saw himself when he wrote—as a Jew (though a Christian Jew),

---

[1]Kümmel, 304. This does not mean that there have been no dissenters (Kümmel himself cites Bruno Bauer, "the radical Dutch critics," and R. Steck). See also J. C. O'Neill, who thinks that Paul wrote only about two-thirds of Galatians (*The Recovery of Paul's Letter to the Galatians* [London: SPCK, 1972]). But today most scholars would agree with Kümmel.

or as a convert to a new religion, and thus in some sense no longer a Jew. But we shall briefly explore that question below.

DESTINATION

During the third century B.C. some Gauls migrated to the inner plateau of Asia Minor and established a kingdom. Under Amyntas (first century B.C.) the kingdom extended to Pisidia, Lycaonia, and other places in the southern part of what is now Turkey, and most of the immigrants remained when, on the death of Amyntas (25 B.C.) the Romans took over and made it into the province of Galatia. The problem for us is whether the "Galatians" to which this epistle is addressed refers to ethnic Galatians in the north of the province or to the southerners of various races who were included in the Roman province. Toward the end of the third century, the southern area was detached, and the province was reduced to the northern sector. Traditionally, "Galatia" has thus been understood as the northern area. But was this the way Paul used the term? The apostle visited the southern area on his first missionary journey (Acts 13–14), but he is never explicitly said to have visited the northern area—though many think that this is what is meant in Acts 16:6 and 18:23.

In favor of South Galatia, note the following ten considerations:

1. We have information about people and places Paul knew and visited in the southern region, but none at all in the north (at best Acts 16:6 and 18:23 *may* indicate work in the north, but neither passage says that Paul founded churches there). This is in striking contrast to his work in other areas.[2] If Paul was writing to people in the north, we would expect some firm indication that he had been there at some time. It would be curious, to say the least, to have no information about churches to which such an important letter was sent.

2. The unusual expression "the region of Phrygia and Galatia" through which Paul traveled (Acts 16:6) is best understood as the area through which the apostle would go when he left Lystra and Iconium (Acts 16:2), that is, "the Phrygio-Galatic territory."[3] Those who hold the North Galatian theory take this to mean "Phrygia and the Galatian country": Ernst Haenchen argues that Φρυγία (*Phrygia*) is an adjective of two terminations and cannot qualify χώρα (*chōra*,

---

[2]J. B. Lightfoot, who, like other older commentators, favored the North Galatian theory, nevertheless comments: "It is strange that while we have more or less acquaintance with all the other important Churches of St Paul's founding, with Corinth and Ephesus, with Philippi and Thessalonica, not a single name of a person or place, scarcely a single incident of any kind, connected with the Apostle's preaching in Galatia, should be preserved in either the history or the epistle" (*Saint Paul's Epistle to the Galatians* [London: Macmillan, 1902], 21).

[3]τὴν Φρυγίαν καὶ Γαλατικὴν χώραν (*tēn Phrygian kai Galatikēn chōran*).

"land" or "region").[4] But C. J. Hemer has shown conclusively that it has three terminations and thus may well qualify the word.[5] F. F. Bruce's careful examination yields the conclusion that the expression can mean only "the territory through which Paul and his friends passed after leaving Lystra, the territory in which Iconium and Pisidian Antioch were situated."[6] The similar expression in Acts 18:23 seems to mean much the same.[7]

3. Paul normally (though not invariably) uses Roman imperial names for the provinces, and "Galatians" would be the way he would refer to people in Lycaonia and other districts. Against this are the facts that Paul's usage is not invariable, and in any case, "Galatians" would include the ethnic Gauls in the north.

4. "Galatians" was the only word available that embraced the people in all the cities of the first missionary journey: Antioch, Lystra, Iconium, and Derbe. Of course, this does not exclude the possibility that the term might be used of those in the north.

5. Paul speaks of "the Galatian churches" as included among the contributors to his collection for the believers in Jerusalem (1 Cor. 16:1), and in Acts 20:4 Luke lists a Berean, two Thessalonians, two South Galatians, and two Asians, who look suspiciously like the party bearing the gift. But Luke does not actually say so, and in any case there are no Corinthians in the list, so it may be incomplete.

6. The northern part of the country was not opened up like the southern area, through which a continual stream of commerce flowed. "Because of an illness" (Gal. 4:13), it is unlikely that Paul preached in this difficult mountainous country. A convalescent would look for a place much easier of access.

7. It is urged that it is unlikely that Paul's Jewish opponents would have pursued him into this difficult northern country and much more likely that they would have followed him to the southern cities. But how fanatical were they?

8. The words "you welcomed me as if I were an angel of God, as if I were Christ Jesus himself" (Gal. 4:14) are said to be an allusion to Paul's being welcomed as Hermes at Lystra (Acts 14:12). This is somewhat spoiled, however, by the fact that afterward the Lystrans stoned him (though this, too, is sometimes taken up into the argument with a reference in Gal. 6:17 to "the marks of Jesus" on Paul's body). The fact that he was welcomed as an angel is also sometimes used as an argument the opposite way: Paul could not have looked much like an angel when he came to the Galatians as a sick man!

---

[4]Ernst Haenchen, *The Acts of the Apostles* (Oxford: Blackwell, 1971), 483.

[5]C. J. Hemer, "The Adjective 'Phrygia,'" *JTS* 27 (1976): 122–26; idem, "Phrygia: A Further Note," *JTS* 28 (1977): 99–101.

[6]F. F. Bruce, "Galatian Problems. 2. North or South Galatians?" *BJRL* 52 (1970): 258.

[7]See also the detailed discussion of Rainer Riesner, *Paul's Early Period: Chronology, Mission Strategy, Theology* (Grand Rapids: Eerdmans, 1998), 281–88.

9. Ramsay, who did more than anybody to establish the southern theory, argued that the church developed along the great lines of communication, and these went through the southern parts of Galatia, not the north.[8]

10. Barnabas is mentioned three times (2:1, 9, 13), which seems to mean that he was known to the readers. But he accompanied Paul only on the journey when the South Galatian churches were established. It is objected that Barnabas is mentioned in 1 Corinthians 9:6, though we have no evidence that he was ever in Corinth. We should also bear in mind that Peter is mentioned (Gal. 2:7–8), though there is no evidence that he was ever in the north. The point carries little weight.[9]

Those who favor a reference to North Galatia have advanced at least eight reasons.

1. In the speech of the day, "Galatia" meant the place inhabited by the Gauls in the north. Against this, as we have seen, it was also used of the whole province.

2. In Acts, Antioch is called "Pisidian" (Acts 13:14), while Lystra and Derbe are cities of Lycaonia (Acts 14:6). Luke, it is said, uses such terms to denote geographic locations. Thus when he refers to "the region of Phrygia and Galatia" (Acts 16:6), we must understand him to mean geographic Phrygia and geographic Galatia—that is, North Galatia.

3. "Galatia" would not be used of Phrygians and the like because it would remind them of their subjection to Rome. This, however, is scarcely valid. Paul referred to himself as a Roman citizen. In any case, "Galatia" was the only term that covered all the cities mentioned. Some have pointed out that in modern times an audience of Welsh, Scots, and English people would be addressed as British, with none of them objecting—that is the only term that covers them all. So with ancient Galatia.

4. A similar objection is that "Paul could not possibly have addressed Lycaonians or Pisidians 'O foolish Galatians' (3:1), particularly since this linguistic usage is generally not attested."[10] But what usage is attested? As noticed in the previous section, "Galatians" was the only term available to cover all the inhabitants of the province of Galatia.

5. The fickle and superstitious character of the Galatians suits a Gallic

---

[8]W. M. Ramsay, *The Church in the Roman Empire* (London: Hodder & Stoughton, 1893), 10–11. Moffatt, however, cites Ramsay's question regarding Lystra: "How did the cosmopolitan Paul drift like a piece of timber borne by the current into this quiet backwater?" (99).

[9]This and other alignment factors are emphasized by T. H. Campbell, "Paul's 'Missionary Journeys' as Reflected in His Letter," *JBL* 74 (1955): 80–87; Ben Witherington III, *Grace in Galatia: A Commentary on Paul's Letter to the Galatians* (Grand Rapids: Eerdmans, 1998), 10–13.

[10]Kümmel, 298.

origin. But such a description scarcely applied only to Galatians: consider, for instance, the Corinthians.[11]

6. "The region of Phrygia and Galatia" (Acts 16:6; so also 18:23) is understood to mean "Phrygia and the Galatian region,"[12] which is taken to mean that Galatia was quite distinct from Phrygia (and presumably other districts such as Lycaonia). But as we have seen, the probable meaning is "the Phrygio-Galatic territory." It does not prove a distinction.

7. Paul writes, "Later I went to Syria and Cilicia" (Gal. 1:21 NIV; "then I went . . .: TNIV), on which Marxsen comments, "According to the South Galatian hypothesis he must have founded the Galatian churches at that time, but there is no mention of this."[13] But because Syria and Cilicia were not in the province of Galatia, this is irrelevant; it appears to refer to a trip different from that on which Paul founded the churches of southern Galatia (one made in the period subsequent to Acts 9:30).[14]

8. There is not the slightest hint in Galatians that Paul had experienced strong opposition when he preached in the Galatian cities. But Acts makes it clear that there was persecution in most of the cities the apostle visited.

From all this it appears that there is no final proof for either the North Galatian or the South Galatian theory. But it surely seems that, while the South Galatian theory comes short of complete demonstration, the arguments in its favor are considerably more compelling than those for North Galatia.[15]

While the South Galatian theory comes short of complete demonstration, the arguments in its favor are considerably more compelling than those for North Galatia.

DATE

If one adopts the North Galatian theory, then because Paul could not have spent enough time ministering in the north to plant churches until about halfway through his recorded missionary service, the date of Galatians, which of course

---

[11]F. F. Bruce points out that the argument reduces itself to this syllogism: "The Gauls were fickle and superstitious. Paul's Galatians were fickle and superstitious. Therefore: Paul's Galatians were Gauls." He adds that "the argument would be valid only if fickleness and superstition were not characteristic of other nations than the Gauls (and Galatians)" (*The Epistle to the Galatians* [Exeter: Paternoster; Grand Rapids: Eerdmans, 1982], 8).

[12]Moffatt holds that "διέρχεσθαι [*dierchesthai*] in 16[6], taken along with 18[23], implies preaching-activity, not simply travelling" (95). This would indicate that Paul evangelized North Galatia.

[13]Marxsen, 46.

[14]F. F. Bruce locates it in this period ("Galatian Problems. 1. Autobiographical Data," *BJRL* 51 [1969]: 301–2).

[15]Cf. F. F. Bruce's conclusion that the "the weight of the evidence . . . favours the South Galatian view" ("Galatian Problems. 2. North or South Galatians?" 266). Similarly J. A. T. Robinson, *Redating the New Testament* (Philadelphia: Westminster, 1976), 55; Riesner, *Paul's Early Period*, 281–91.

must have been written after the planting of the church, must be a little later—about the same time as Paul's letter to Rome. If the South Galatian theory is adopted, an early date is possible. An early date is supported by such considerations as the following:

1. In protesting that he had a divine commission and not one derived "from any human source" (1:12), Paul lists his contacts with the Jerusalem apostles. These include a visit to Peter (1:18), "then after fourteen years" a visit again "in response to a revelation" (2:1–2; "again" indicates a second visit). These correspond to the visits in Acts 9:26; 11:28–30. Paul's list must be complete, else his argument would be vitiated (see 1:20).

2. Paul does not mention the decree of the Council of Jerusalem (Acts 15), which would have been very suitable for his purpose. This suggests a visit before the council—though the point cannot be pressed unduly, as the apostle does not mention the decree in letters that are demonstrably later.

3. Peter's withdrawal from table fellowship with the Gentiles (2:12) is more likely to have been before rather than after the council.

4. The early date is not invalidated by Paul's words "I first [τὸ πρότερον (to proteron)] preached the gospel to you" (4:13), which some suggest means "on the first of my two visits" (NEB) and points to a date later than Paul's second missionary journey. In classical Greek the expression means on the former of two occasions, but in Hellenistic Greek it signifies "formerly, in the past" (as in John 6:62; 9:8; Heb. 4:6, etc.).[16] In any case, Paul visited his South Galatian churches twice during his first expedition (see Acts 14:21), so that even if the Greek expression is taken to mean "on the first of my two visits," the second visit may have been the return swing on the first missionary journey (Acts 14:21–26), rather than something later.

In contrast, a date during Paul's third missionary tour (c. 52–57) is favored by many.[17] The early date is excluded by those who hold the North Galatian theory, for on this view Paul had not been to Galatia (twice!) until this time.[18] A later date is supported by such arguments as these:

---

[16]On this passage BAGD remarks that "fr. a lexical point of view it is not poss[ible] to establish the thesis that Paul wished to differentiate betw[een] a later visit and an earlier one" (722). The later BDAG prefers the rendering "the first time," but acknowledges, "Naturally the transl. *once* is also prob., but from a linguistic point of view it is not poss. to establish the thesis that Paul wished to differentiate betw. a later visit and an earlier one" (889).

[17]E.g., Dieter Lührmann, *Galatians: A Continental Commentary* (Minneapolis: Fortress Press, 1992); Brown, 474–77; Ehrman, 331–33. Achtemeier/Green/Thompson, 372–75, remain undecided.

[18]On the other hand, it is possible to adopt a South Galatian theory and a late date, as Moisés Silva has done, in *Interpreting Galatians: Explorations in Exegetical Method*, 2nd ed. (Grand Rapids: Baker, 2001), 129–39.

1. The style and the thoughts expressed show an affinity with the Corinthian correspondence and with Romans, so the epistle to the Galatians accordingly should be dated close to them, say at Ephesus during Paul's third journey (Acts 19) or even on the subsequent journey through Greece.[19]

2. The visit to Jerusalem in Galatians 2 is so closely connected with the subject matter of the Council of Jerusalem of Acts 15 that the two must be regarded as independent accounts of the same visit (though some who favor the South Galatian theory see these as two different visits and simply hold that Paul wrote later than the council). Those who hold to the later date reason that Paul in his account in Galatians 1:18–2:2 did not include any mention of the famine visit of Acts 11:30 because on that occasion his business was with the elders, not the apostles. That reading is possible, but scarcely compelling. On the face of it, in Galatians 1–2 Paul purports to give a complete list of his trips to Jerusalem, and leaving out the one recorded in Acts 11:30 would leave him open to a charge of fudging the record. Moreover, one short verse, Acts 11:30, can scarcely be taken as a full account of all Paul did in Jerusalem on that occasion. Even if he went there primarily for the purpose of famine relief, it is scarcely conceivable that Paul would have kept himself away from the other apostles.[20] On the whole, then, it seems better to link the trip of Galatians 2:1–10 with Acts 11:25–30 than with Acts 15—and that of course means Galatians was most probably written before the Jerusalem Council of Acts 15.

3. It is argued that since Paul has already visited Galatia twice (4:13), the most likely visits are those of Acts 16:6 and 18:23. But we have already seen that the language does not necessarily mean two visits, and even if it does, the reference may be to the outbound and return visits of the first missionary journey (see comments on Gal. 4:13, above).

4. In 1 Corinthians there is little about persecution, but there is much in 2 Corinthians. Romans is calm; evidently the trouble is largely in the past. Galatians fits into this sequence between 2 Corinthians and Romans.[21]

---

[19]Lührmann, *Galatians*, 3, specifies that Galatians was written after the writing of 1 Corinthians. Somewhat anomalously, J. Louis Martyn, *Galatians*, AB 33A (New York: Doubleday, 1997), 20, specifies after the writing of 1 Thessalonians, but before the writing of either of the Corinthians epistles.

[20]Klijn finds "a striking parallel between Gal. 2,1–10 and Acts 11,25–30" (p. 94).

[21]Lightfoot argues this and finds support in the words "From now on, let no one cause me trouble, for I bear on my body the marks of Jesus" (6:17), which seem like "the language of one, who has lately passed through a fiery trial. . . . Does it not seem to follow naturally *after* the tumult of affliction, which bursts out in the Second Epistle to the Corinthians?" (*Galatians,* 51). Bruce very carefully examines the relationship between Galatians and other Pauline epistles and finds nothing inconsistent with the view that this is the earliest of Paul's letters (*Galatians,* 45–55).

The main point at issue is whether Paul is writing before or after the Council of Jerusalem (Acts 15). Those who advocate a late date say that he writes later, and some of them emphasize what they see as discrepancies between Acts and Paul's letters. They hold that Paul would never have accepted such an arrangement as the Council of Jerusalem reached according to the description in Acts; indeed, they find his recollection of what happened in Galatians 2. They point out that, though they are treated from different points of view, in both accounts the points at issue are circumcision and the relation of the Christian to the law. Others, who accept the North Galatian view, think that Acts and Galatians can be reconciled, but this entails the conclusion that Paul has omitted one of his visits to Jerusalem.

The Roman Provinces of Asia Minor

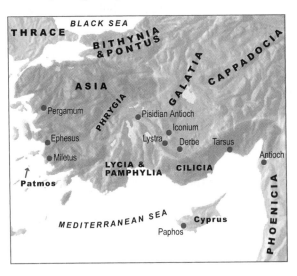

Certainly it is simpler and less arbitrary to accept both accounts. On balance, it seems best to hold that Paul's two visits to Jerusalem are those of Acts 9 and 11 (Gal. 2 will refer to private contacts on the famine visit on this view; it is hard to date Peter's vacillation after Acts 15), and that Paul wrote Galatians just prior to the Jerusalem Council.[22] If the council is rightly dated A.D. 48,[23] then this is the date of Galatians. That the letter precedes the Jerusalem Council seems indicated by the fact that Paul makes no mention of its verdict. Even if he did not make it his main argument,

---

[22] According to J. Knox, "If we could trust entirely the accuracy of the Acts account of Paul's visits to Jerusalem, the case for the early dating would be unassailable" ("Galatians, " in *IDB*, 2.342). That is not quite the case: some who hold to the reliability of Acts opt for the late date (see n. 18 above). To make the early dating "unassailable" one must simultaneously not only accept the reliability of Acts but also convincingly argue that the logic of Paul's account in Galatians identifies the trip of Galatians 2:1–10 with that of Acts 11:25–30. If instead, one judges that there are credible reasons for Paul not to mention the Acts 11 trip, then the late date is possible.

[23] This is the date given by George Ogg, *The Chronology of the Life of Paul* (London: Epworth, 1968), 200. It is also favored by Ronald Y. K. Fung; see his *Epistle to the Galatians* (Grand Rapids: Eerdmans, 1988), 28; John W. Drane, *Paul: Libertine or Legalist?* (London: SPCK, 1975), 140–43; see also chap. 9 above.

it is hard to see why he should omit all mention of such a significant support to his argument against accepting the whole Jewish Torah.

OCCASION[24]

From Acts 13–14 we learn that Paul and Barnabas evangelized the southern part of the province of Galatia by going first to the synagogues, where they preached to Jews and God-fearing Gentiles. But in each city Jews stirred up opposition, and the preachers turned to the Gentiles and made converts from among them. We need not doubt that, if the North Galatian theory is correct, the evangelization of the northern areas was brought about in much the same way. Throughout the region the church was predominantly Gentile.

But after Paul and Barnabas left the scene, apparently some Jewish Christians came into the area and taught that those who embrace the Christian salvation must submit to Jewish law, the Torah. So far as we know, local Jews did not teach this; they simply opposed the Christians.[25] Paul distinguishes the false teachers from the congregation (1:7; 4:17, etc.; perhaps they had a strong leader, 1:9; 5:10); indeed, he can imply that they were not Christians at all (1:6–7). Their emphasis on keeping the Mosaic law makes it almost certain they were Jews. Doubtless they thought of themselves as Jewish Christians; Paul is prepared to question the "Christian" component if they set up as necessary to salvation any rival to Jesus.

---

[24]There is an admirably succinct summary of the principal options in Timothy George, *Galatians*, NAC 30 (Nashville: Broadman & Holman, 1994), 50–60.

[25]We should mention here the theory of Mark D. Nanos, *The Irony of Galatians: Paul's Letter in First-Century Context* (Minneapolis: Fortress Press, 2002). Nanos disputes that the opponents were "Jewish Christians" (a label he judges to be anachronistic), and asserts that the problem has arisen because Jews from the local synagogues in Galatia have been influencing the fledgling Gentile Christ-believers, telling them that, even though they had withdrawn from the civic and imperial cults, if they became Jewish they would be safe from danger and would enjoy all the privileges of being under an established *religio licta* (a legally permitted religion). But there does not seem to be any textual evidence for a Roman persecution of Galatian Christians at this time. Indeed, a case can be made that around this time there was an outbreak of Jewish persecution of Christians in Jerusalem (see Markus Bockmuehl, "1 Thessalonians 2:14–16 and the Church in Jerusalem," *TynB* 52 [2001]: 1–31), and this may account, at least in part, for the passion of the agitators, and perhaps for the conflict between Paul and Peter (2:11–14). Moreover, in countless details, Nanos's position, though vigorously advanced, remains unconvincing (e.g., his insistence that the singular εὐαγγέλιον [*euangelion*, "gospel"] does not mean "gospel" at all but refers to "glad tidings" in some broader sense). Nor is it at all clear that Paul supported a two-covenant theology, one for Jews and one for Gentiles, however attractive such a position is in post-holocaust theology.

From Galatians we gather that *Paul's authority* was undermined by the argument that he was inferior to the earlier apostles. Paul seems to have this in mind from first to last: "sent not with a human commission nor by human authority, but by Jesus Christ and God the Father" (1:1); "let no one cause me trouble, for I bear on my body the marks of Jesus" (6:17).

Circumcision was insisted on: they "are trying to compel you to be circumcised" (6:12; see also 5:2–6). Paul points out that the acceptance of circumcision means the acceptance of the obligation to carry out the whole law of which it is a part (5:3), whatever the false teachers may have said. The keeping of the law was apparently insisted on, for he also writes, "You are observing special days and months and seasons and years!" (4:10).[26] He also speaks of his converts as wanting "to be under the law" (4:21) and as "trying to be justified by law" (5:4). Putting all this together, it seems that the false teachers saw Christianity as a modified Judaism; they were teaching that to be in covenant relationship to God means to submit to the requirements of the law. Therefore, they were persuading the Galatians to submit to the way of the law instead of enjoying freedom in Christ.

In recent years some have argued that all or at least most of the laws that these interlopers were pressing on the Galatians were the legislative pieces that established "boundary markers"—the practices that differentiated Jews from other people, in particular circumcision, food laws, and Sabbath. Paul wants those things dropped because he wants to build a unified church composed of Jew and Gentile alike, and the boundary markers inevitably provoke division.[27] Certainly Paul is constantly at pains to unite Jewish Christians and Gentile Christians. Nevertheless, this "new perspective" on Paul is too narrow. Paul casts the function of the law in more sweeping terms than boundary markers (esp. chap. 3), not least its capacity to establish transgression (3:19), and he ties the heart of his debate to the exclusive sufficiency of the cross of Christ to see a person declared "just" before God.[28] This debate has generated a correlative dis-

---

[26]This may refer to "planetary powers or astrological signs of the zodiac" (Martin, 2.153). The στοιχεῖα (*stoicheia*, "basic principles") to which both Jews (4:3) and Gentiles (4:9) had been subjected are best understood in terms of "legalism as a principle of life" (Bruce, *Galatians*, 203).

[27]See especially James D. G. Dunn, *The Epistle to the Galatians*, BNTC (Peabody: Hendrickson, 1993). This is especially tied to Dunn's earlier view that the expression "the works of the law" refers to such boundary markers. More recently he has preferred a slightly more nuanced approach, something like "observance of the whole law with a view to maintaining exclusive Jewish claims." In addition to the commentary, see also his *The Theology of Paul's Letter to the Galatians*, NTT (Cambridge: Cambridge University Press, 1993), 84–87 and passim.

[28]See especially chap. 9 in this *Introduction*. Cf. D. A. Carson, Peter T. O'Brien, and Mark A. Seifrid, eds., *Justification and Variegated Nomism* (Tübingen: Mohr-Siebeck/

cussion about the extent to which Paul sees himself to be a Jew, and his movement as a kind of sect within the fold of Judaism, or, conversely, sees himself as belonging to what is in effect a new religion.[29]

Whether or not they were Christians in Paul's eyes, *the false teachers* evidently sprang from the Jewish-Christian camp. Christians had opposed Peter (Acts 11:2–3), and at a later time James could speak of "many thousands of Jews" who believed, "and all of them are zealous for the law" (Acts 21:20). Clearly there was a strong group of these people, and at least on occasion they could be active propagandists, as when they went from Judea to Antioch and taught the new converts, "Unless you are circumcised, according to the custom taught by Moses, you cannot be saved" (Acts 15:1). If they followed Paul to Antioch, it is not unlikely that they followed him to Galatia. They may not have been many in number, for Paul writes, "A little yeast works through the whole batch of dough" (Gal. 5:9). Sometimes it is contended that Paul's opponents were Gentiles who had accepted circumcision and wanted others to do the same. But this supposition scarcely outweighs the evidence that there were zealous Jewish Christians, anxious to insist on the law. G. Howard thinks that they may not have been opponents in the strict sense but that they claimed that Paul was really teaching what they taught.[30] The vehemence with which Paul opposes them makes this unlikely.

Libertinism is sometimes detected in 5:13ff. with such exhortations as "do not use your freedom to indulge the sinful nature" (5:13), and "walk by the Spirit, and you will not gratify the desires of the sinful nature" (5:16). But it is better to see this as a perversion of Paul's teaching that in Christ believers are free. In every age it has been easy to deduce that if we are saved by grace, it does not matter how we live. One suspects that the agitators were decrying Paul's teaching as inadequately safeguarding moral probity. But if their solution to this perennial challenge was a return to the Mosaic law-covenant, the price was too high: it betrayed an inability to grasp how the law properly functioned across the sweep of redemptive history.

Criticisms of Paul seem to have been made. "If I am still preaching circumcision" (5:11) appears to mean that Paul had been accused of preaching

---

Grand Rapids: Baker, 2001–2004), esp. vol. 2, *The Paradoxes of Paul;* and Stephen Westerholm, *Perspectives Old and New on Paul: The "Lutheran" Paul and His Critics* (Grand Rapids: Eerdmans, 2004).

[29]See esp. Peter T. O'Brien, "Was Paul Converted?" in *Justification and Variegated Nomism,* vol. 2.

[30]Thus Howard says, "The agitators at Galatia were Jewish Christians, Judaizers from Jerusalem who were forcing the Galatians to be circumcised and to keep the law. They did not themselves oppose Paul but insisted that he like them taught circumcision" (*Paul: Crisis in Galatia* [Cambridge: Cambridge University Press, 1979], 19). On the use of the term "Judaizer," see n. 3 in chap. 11, above.

circumcision when it suited him (see his circumcision of Timothy [Acts 16:3])—and this despite the fact that he insisted that Titus *not* be circumcised (2:1–5). "Am I *now* trying to win human approval, or God's approval? Or am I trying to please people?" (1:10, emphasis added) indicates that some were saying that the apostle was simply interested in human approval. In the life of a man who became "all things to all people," including becoming like a Jew in order to win Jews (1 Cor. 9:20–22), there could not lack incidents that gave opponents the opening to charge him with inconsistency.[31]

The gospel was seriously compromised by this new teaching. Paul complains that his correspondents were "turning to a different gospel," immediately adding, "which is really no gospel at all" (1:6–7). What the Galatians were in danger of doing was not adding some interesting new insights into the meaning of Christianity but of returning to the law-covenant in such a way that the climactic triumph of the gospel was implicitly called into question.

The epistle to the Galatians is the result of news of these happenings reaching Paul. He immediately recognized that what his converts were doing meant that they were renouncing the heart of the Christian way, and he wrote straightaway to correct the situation. He did not observe all the niceties of correct letter writing but sent off an impassioned appeal to the Galatians to return to the faith in which they had been saved. This lively letter has become a classic expression of the meaning of justification by faith in Christ alone.

Paul sent off an impassioned appeal to the Galatians to return to the faith in which they had been saved. The lively letter has become a classic expression of the meaning of justification by faith in Christ alone.

TEXT

Galatians contains a number of minor variants, but on the whole there are no serious doubts about the text of this letter. There is some confusion between the Aramaic name Cephas and the Greek name Peter in 1:18; 2:9, 11, 14; but in each case this seems to be nothing more than the substitution of the better-known Greek name for the unfamiliar Aramaic form. It is not certain whether we should add "of Christ" after "grace" in 1:6 or whether the subject "God" should be read before the verb "was pleased" in 1:15, but the sense is not greatly affected by these and similar variants. We have this letter substantially as Paul wrote it.

---

[31]To circumcise Timothy and to refuse to circumcise Titus, for instance, was certainly inconsistent at the level of mere performance. But from Paul's perspective, both actions were deeply principled. He refused to permit Titus to be circumcised in a Christian context where circumcision would have signaled that Titus (and Paul, too) agreed that one needed to be a proper Jew to accept the Jewish Messiah—and that would have jeopardized the exclusive sufficiency of Christ. In the context of a Jewish synagogue, however, where Paul was resolutely trying to win people to Christ and no one was reading in any Christological implications, the circumcision of Timothy was merely part and parcel of his willingness to "become all things to all people so that by all possible means [he] might save some" (1 Cor. 9:22).

ADOPTION INTO THE CANON

Galatians was accepted from very early days. There seem to be reminiscences of expressions from this letter in Barnabas, *1 Clement*, Polycarp, Justin Martyr, and other writers from the end of the first century and from the second. No dispute about its genuineness seems to have arisen in early times. Burton's verdict, "There is no other letter which has any better claim to be regarded as [Paul's] work than Galatians,"[32] is to be endorsed. That it appears first in some lists of the Pauline Epistles (such as Marcion's), points to a recognition of its importance as well as its authenticity.

GALATIANS IN RECENT STUDY

We may omit further reference to perennial debates over the date of this letter and the location of its first readers (see above).

Discussion continues as to the identity of the teachers Paul is opposing, and some recent writers are suspicious of the term "Judaizers." A few have suggested that they were not Jewish but may even have been some of Paul's own converts,[33] their further studies in the Old Testament Scriptures to which Paul had introduced them having led them to think that keeping of the law was indispensable. All this raises the question whether there is more than one group that Paul is opposing or whether he is engaging in a unified argument. Despite the contentions of some who hold to multiple groups of opponents, there is no real evidence in Galatians that Paul is fighting on two fronts; his enemies appear to have been one determined group. Most likely, the false teachers were Jews or Jewish Christians who came in from outside and advocated some form of Judaism.[34]

Rising interest in rhetorical criticism has raised questions about the literary genre of this epistle. Thus H. D. Betz sees Galatians as "an example of the 'apologetic letter' genre." He says that in antiquity rhetoric "has little in common with the truth, but it is the exercise of those skills which make people believe something to be true." It is not easy to see this as a fair description of what Paul is doing. His deep concern for truth is evident on every page. Even less acceptable is Betz's contention that Galatians is a "magical letter." Paul speaks of a curse on false preachers (1:9) and a blessing on "all who follow this rule" (6:16). Betz sees this as meaning that the letter itself bears the blessing and

---

[32]E. de Witt Burton, *A Critical and Exegetical Commentary on the Epistle to the Galatians*, ICC (Edinburgh: T. & T. Clark, 1921), lxv.

[33]Notably J. Munck, *Paul and the Salvation of Mankind* (Richmond: John Knox, 1959), 87ff.

[34]E. P. Sanders sees it as "likely that they were 'right wing' Jewish Christians" who would emphasize such passages as Gen. 17:9–14 (*Paul, the Law, and the Jewish People* [Philadelphia: Fortress Press, 1985], 18).

the curse.[35] But there is some doubt as to whether antiquity did in fact recognize the category of "magical letter," and there is even more doubt that, if it did, Paul would have used it. It is hard to think of anyone more opposed to magic than Paul was.[36] The argument advanced by Pheme Perkins that Paul's rhetoric is overheated and was the prime cause of the division between Jew and Christian owes less to a sympathetic understanding of how Paul reads the Old Testament and rather more to a contemporary commitment to pluralism.[37]

A good deal of recent discussion centers on the arguments put forward by E. P. Sanders[38] and those who have been influenced by him. Sanders rejects the idea that the Jews of the day saw the keeping of the law as the means whereby they merited salvation. Palestinian Jews, Sanders avers, universally adhered to "covenantal nomism"; that is, the Jews were saved by grace because of their membership in the people with whom God had made a covenant, and adherence to the law was their means of "staying in." This has served as a salutary corrective of some harsh and anachronistic views about Jewish beliefs in the first century, but it stands in serious need of qualification. Specifically, it has been objected that Sanders does not take seriously enough Jewish teaching about the rewards of righteousness and the punishment of sin;[39] nor is his exegesis of Paul above criticism.[40] Sanders has given a useful corrective to some earlier views, but he cannot be said to have come up with a universally acceptable solution to the problem.[41]

Sanders thinks that the fundamental distinction between Paul and Judaism turns, not on justification, but on Christology. Christians accepted Jesus as Messiah; most Jews did not. Sanders rejects the commonly held view that Paul taught (or assumed) that people cannot keep the law. "The whole thrust of the argument is that righteousness was never, in God's plan, intended to be by

---

[35]H. D. Betz, *Galatians,* Hermeneia (Philadelphia: Fortress Press, 1979), 14, 24, 25.

[36]According to Childs, "Betz's argument is here very weak. Not only is the category of 'magical letter' in itself highly suspect, but its application to Galatians is tenuous in the extreme" (p. 302). On the broader problems associated with Betz's uncontrolled reliance on Greco-Roman parallels, see esp. Philip H. Kern, *Rhetoric and Galatians: Assessing an Approach to Paul's Epistle,* SNTSMS 101 (Cambridge: Cambridge University Press, 1998).

[37]Pheme Perkins, *Abraham's Divided Children: Galatians and the Politics of Faith* (Harrisburg: Trinity Press International, 2001).

[38]See esp. E. P. Sanders, *Paul and Palestinian Judaism* (Philadelphia: Fortress Press, 1977); idem, *Paul, the Law, and the Jewish People.*

[39]See especially *Justification and Variegated Nomism,* vol. 1.

[40]E.g., see R. H. Gundry, "Grace, Works, and Staying Saved in Paul," *Bib* 66 (1985): 1–38; Westerholm, *Perspectives Old and New;* and *Justification and Variegated Nomism,* vol. 2.

[41]See further chap. 9 of this volume.

law. . . . [T]he problem with the law is not that it cannot be fulfilled. Paul has a view of God's intention which excludes righteousness by the law." Jews generally insisted that those who would become members of the people of God must become full proselytes, with the consequent acceptance of the law of Moses. But for Paul, those who are "of the works of the law" are under a curse (Gal. 3:10 KJV).[42]

Sanders's views have been popularized and expounded at many levels. Essayists question "the Protestant understanding of Galatians," that is, "the clear, deliberate expression of the Pauline gospel of justification by faith, as opposed to works."[43] Gordon prefers to put the emphasis on the opposition of the Torah to faith in Christ and asks, "Shall the people of God be identified by Torah or by Christ?"[44] In this he is undoubtedly drawing attention to an important truth, but it must not be forgotten that Galatians does speak significantly often of being justified by faith (2:16 [2x]; 3:8, 11, 24) or "justified in Christ" (2:17), not by works of law (2:16 [3x]; 3:11). In correcting a view that overlooks the contrast between Christ and Torah and simply opposes faith to works, we must not overlook the truth that justification by faith in Christ is by its very nature opposed to any view of justification by works, those of the Torah or any other.

Whether or not his work is accepted without criticism, Sanders has so set the agenda of recent Pauline studies that a substantial part of current work largely presupposes his findings and proceeds to build on them. For instance, in his recent monograph, Barclay thoughtfully examines Paul's ethics as expressed in Galatians.[45] At the level of his exegesis of large parts of Galatians 5 and 6, Barclay's work is careful and stimulating; how he relates it to the rest of the epistle, however, turns in large part on adopting, rather uncritically, large parts of Sanders's structure. By contrast, Thielman[46] argues against Sanders at a pressing point. Sanders thinks the fundamental difference between (unconverted) Jew and Christian in Paul is Christology. Therefore, on matters such as sin and grace and forgiveness, Paul is really arguing "from solution to plight": that is, Paul knows the solution, namely Jesus, and then argues back to the plight. Thielman argues that when Paul in Galatians and Romans professedly sets out the plight (i.e., sin, or rebellion against God and his law) and then turns to the

---

[42]According to Sanders, "God sent Christ; he did so in order to offer righteousness; this would have been pointless if righteousness were already available by the law (2:21); the law was not given to bring righteousness" (*Paul, the Law, and the Jewish People*, 27).

[43]E.g., T. David Gordon, "The Problem at Galatia," *Int* 41 (1987): 32.

[44]Ibid., 40.

[45]John M. G. Barclay, *Obeying the Truth: A Study of Paul's Ethics in Galatians* (Edinburgh: T. & T. Clark, 1988).

[46]Frank Thielman, *From Plight to Solution: A Jewish Framework for Understanding Paul's View of the Law in Galatians and Romans*, NovTSup 61 (Leiden: Brill, 1989).

solution, he is not resorting to a pedagogical device but is borrowing from a standard pattern in both the Old Testament and in the Judaism of his day.

The influence of Sanders should not lead us to overlook other topics of debate over the epistle to the Galatians.[47] Mention should be made of a number of stances that have been eclipsed by more recent debates. For instance, Paul begins the letter by asserting his apostleship and its importance. W. Schmithals has given a good deal of attention to the nature of the apostolate and has strongly argued that there were gnostic apostles ranged in opposition to Paul.[48] The difficulty with his position is that there is no evidence for developed Gnosticism during Paul's lifetime. That Paul valued his apostleship highly is clear, and that he faced opposition is not in doubt. But that Gnosticism is involved is highly improbable on the basis of the facts available to us.[49]

Again, Cosgrove has argued that the question Paul is addressing in this epistle is explicitly articulated in Galatians 3:5 (our translation): "Does the one who supplies you with the Spirit and works wonders among you do so because of works of the law or because you heard [the gospel] and believed?" In others words, Paul and his readers share a charismatic background, and the question that now exercises the Galatians is the *ground* of Christian life in the Spirit.[50] Although Cosgrove attempts to justify his choice of Galatians 3:5 as the pivotal articulation of the epistle's theme, his methodological rationale is far from convincing. Moreover, it is hard to believe that the Galatians are concerned about the law (including such initiatory matters as circumcision), not with respect to conversion, but exclusively with respect to progress in the life of the Spirit. Nevertheless, there is an eschatological awareness in Cosgrove's work that is salutary.[51]

Three more foci of discussion may be briefly mentioned.

First, regardless of the position one adopts on many of these matters in Galatians, they are inevitably tied to a pair of related questions: How does Galatians relate to Romans? And to what extent does Paul in Galatians uphold any continuity between the law and the gospel that he preaches? There is still no

---

[47]See esp. the range of topics treated in Mark D. Nanos, ed., *The Galatians Debate: Contemporary Issues in Rhetorical and Historical Interpretation* (Peabody: Hendrickson, 2002).

[48]W. Schmithals, *The Office of Apostle in the Early Church* (Nashville: Abingdon, 1969).

[49]John W. Drane remarks that "the whole of Schmithals' argument here (and, indeed, throughout the whole of his work) is based on the assumption that Gnosticism as a system was of pre-Christian origin." He goes on to say that this belief "simply cannot be substantiated on the basis of any known evidence" (*Paul: Libertine or Legalist?* 17).

[50]Charles H. Cosgrove, *The Cross and the Spirit: A Study in the Argument and Theology of Galatians* (Macon: Mercer University Press, 1989).

[51]Somewhat similarly, see Walter Bo Russell III, *The Flesh/Spirit Conflict in Galatians* (Lanham: UPA, 1997).

broad consensus.[52] *Second,* Richard B. Hays has advanced the most comprehensive defense of the view that expressions such as πίστις Χριστοῦ (*pistis Christou*) and parallels should be understood to be reflecting a subjective genitive, "the faith of [Jesus] Christ," rather than an objective genitive, "faith in [Jesus] Christ."[53] Despite the prevalence of this view, sober linguistic theory and careful investigation of ostensible parallels strongly favor the objective genitive.[54] The issue, of course, is not narrowly linguistic. One's conclusion on this matter turns in part on whether one thinks that "the story of Jesus Christ" in each context where the expression occurs primarily aims at presenting Jesus' faithfulness, or at making Jesus the object of the faith of others. And *third,* the glorious annihilation of categories in Galatians 3:26–29, when people close with Christ, has inevitably generated a plethora of essays and books adopting various stances toward feminism.[55]

THE CONTRIBUTION OF GALATIANS

This short letter has an importance out of all proportion to its size. There is always a tendency for people to think that their salvation (however it is understood) is something that is to be brought about by their own achievement. How they understand salvation may vary, and the kind of achievement they see as necessary may correspondingly vary. But that their eternal destiny rests in their own hands seems a truism so obvious that it scarcely needs stating. Christianity has often been understood as nothing more than a system of morality, as the careful observance of a sacramental system, as conformity to standards, as a linking up with others in the church, and so on. There is always a need for Paul's forthright setting out of the truth that justification comes only through faith in

> *This short letter has an importance out of all proportion to its size. There is always a need for Paul's forthright setting out of the truth that justification comes only through faith in Christ, not by works.*

[52]Among the more useful works are Vincent M. Smiles, *The Gospel and the Law in Galatia: Paul's Response to Jewish-Christian Separatism and the Threat of Galatian Apostasy* (Collegeville: Liturgical Press, 1998); idem, "The Concept of 'Zeal' in Second-Temple Judaism and Paul's Critique of It in Romans 10:2," *CBQ* 64 (2002): 282–99.

[53]R. B. Hays, *The Faith of Jesus Christ: The Narrative Substructure of Galatians 3:1–4:11,* 2nd ed. (Grand Rapids: Eerdmans, 2002). Many anticipated him: e.g., Richard N. Longenecker, *Galatians,* WBC 41 (Dallas: Word Books, 1990), 87–88.

[54]See esp. R. Barry Matlock, "Detheologizing the πίστις Χριστοῦ Debate: Cautionary Remarks from a Lexical Semantic Perspective," *NovT* 42 (2000): 1–23; idem, "Πίστις in Galatians 3.26: Neglected Evidence for 'Faith in Christ'?" *NTS* 49 (2003): 433–39; and especially Moisés Silva, "Faith Versus Works of the Law," in *Justification and Variegated Nomism,* 2.217–48.

[55]See esp. Richard Hove, *Equality in Christ? Galatians 3:28 and the Gender Dispute* (Wheaton: Crossway Books, 1999); Troy W. Martin, "The Covenant of Circumcision (Genesis 17:9–14) and the Situational Antitheses in Galatians 3:28," *JBL* 122 (2003): 111–25.

Christ. This must be said over against those who stress the importance of works done in accordance with the Torah or of any other achievement.

The Christian way stresses what God has done in Christ rather than what sinners do. There can be no improvement on the divine action by any human achievement, either by way of ritual observance or moral improvement. The cross is the one way of salvation, and no part of Scripture makes this clearer than does Galatians.[56]

We should not miss the importance of Paul's appeal to Abraham (3:6–29). This takes the reader back to a time when the law had not been given; the covenant established with Abraham takes precedence over the law (3:17). The law cannot annul the promise of God. Those who were forsaking simple reliance on the promise of God were turning from the divinely appointed way and mistaking the real purpose of the law (3:19). If Paul's Galatian friends would give proper consideration to the example of Abraham, they would see the serious error into which they were falling when they began to rely on the Torah.[57] If we read the account of Abraham and his faith in its proper sequence in the unfolding history of redemption instead of anachronistically assuming, with many Jews, that Abraham must have kept the law, it becomes clear that God's way has always been the way of promise and faith. In short, this little book contributes to how Christians ought to be putting their Bibles together. Moreover, Paul insists that Christ came at the appointed time to redeem enslaved sinners (4:4–5), and he further specifies that Christ did this work of redemption "by becoming a curse for us" (3:13). This is a significant contribution to our understanding of the atonement.

Along with the emphasis on justification by faith in Christ is an emphasis on Christian freedom: "It is for freedom that Christ has set us free" (5:1); believers are literally to "walk by the Spirit" (5:16). Even those who are justified by faith in Christ sometimes find it easy to subject themselves to the slavery of a system. Paul's words remain the classic expression of the liberty that is the heritage of everyone who is in Christ.

Galatians is a constant reminder of how important it is to understand what the Christian faith implies for Christian living. Even Peter and Barnabas could

---

[56]Cf. Johnson's questions: "Is God ultimately a passive bookkeeper who, after shaping the world, lets it alone, concerned only to tally the relative merits of his creatures? Or is God one who is at every moment creating anew, redeeming, sanctifying, the source of all that is, and the goal toward which all things tend? Does God act in strange and unexpected ways, or is God locked into his own past?" (305).

[57]"By grounding his argument in the faith of Abraham, Paul removes the debate from the sphere of merely contingent history. The Galatians have just not made a human misjudgment, but committed themselves to an alternative which severed their continuity with the father of the faith" (Childs, 308).

go astray. Paul does not complain of their theology, but of their practice when "those who belonged to the circumcision group" induced them to withdraw from table fellowship with Gentiles (2:11–14). No letter makes clearer than this one the importance of living out all the implications of salvation through the cross.

BIBLIOGRAPHY

John M. G. **Barclay**, *Obeying the Truth: A Study of Paul's Ethics in Galatians* (Edinburgh: T. & T. Clark, 1988) ▐Markus **Barth**, "The Kerygma of Galatians," *Int* 21 (1967): 131–46 ▐H. D. **Betz**, *Galatians*, Hermeneia (Philadelphia: Fortress Press, 1979) ▐idem, "The Literary Composition and Function of Paul's Letter to the Galatians," *NTS* 21 (1974–75): 353–79 ▐A. C. M. **Blommerde**, "Is There an Ellipsis Between Gal. 2,3 and 2,4?" *Bib* 56 (1975): 100–102 ▐Markus **Bockmuehl**, "1 Thessalonians 2:14–16 and the Church in Jerusalem," *TynB* 52 (2001): 1–31 ▐P. **Borgen**, "Paul Preaches Circumcision and Pleases Men," in *Paul and Paulinism, Fs.* C. K. Barrett, ed. M. D. Hooker and S. G. Wilson (London: SPCK, 1982), 37–46 ▐Udo **Borse**, *Der Brief an die Galater*, RNT (Regensburg: Friedrich Pustet, 1984) ▐F. F. **Bruce**, "'Abraham Had Two Sons': A Study in Pauline Hermeneutics," in *New Testament Studies, Fs.* Ray Summers, ed. H. L. Drumwright and C. Vaughan (Waco: Word, 1975), 71–84 ▐idem, *Commentary on Galatians*, NIGTC (Grand Rapids: Eerdmans, 1982) ▐idem, "The Conference in Jerusalem—Galatians 2:1–10," in *God Who Is Rich in Mercy, Fs.* D. B. Knox, ed. P. T. O'Brien and D. G. Peterson (Homebush West, NSW: Anzea, 1986), 195–212 ▐idem, "The Curse of the Law," in *Paul and Paulinism, Fs.* C. K. Barrett, ed. M. D. Hooker and S. G. Wilson (London: SPCK, 1982), 27–36 ▐idem, "Galatian Problems," *BJRL* 51 (1968–69): 292–309; 52 (1969–70): 243–66; 53 (1970–71): 253–71; 54 (1971–72): 250–67; 55 (1972–73): 264–82 ▐idem, "Paul and the Law of Moses," *BJRL* 57 (1974–75): 259–79 ▐E. de Witt **Burton**, *A Critical and Exegetical Commentary on the Epistle to the Galatians*, ICC (Edinburgh: T. & T. Clark, 1921) ▐T. H. **Campbell**, "Paul's 'Missionary Journeys' as Reflected in His Letter," *JBL* 74 (1955): 80–87 ▐D. A. **Carson**, "Pauline Inconsistency: Reflections on I Corinthians 9.19–23 and Galatians 2.11–14," *Churchman* 100 (1986): 6–45 ▐D. A. **Carson**, Peter T. **O'Brien**, and Mark A. **Seifrid**, eds., *Justification and Variegated Nomism*, vol. 1: *The Complexities of Second Temple Judaism* (Tübingen: Mohr-Siebeck/Grand Rapids: Baker, 2001) ▐vol. 2: *The Paradoxes of Paul* (Tübingen: Mohr-Siebeck/Grand Rapids: Baker, 2004) ▐Charles H. **Cosgrove**, *The Cross and the Spirit: A Study in the Argument and Theology of Galatians* (Macon: Mercer University Press, 1989) ▐idem, "The Law Has Given Sarah No Children (Gal. 4:21–30)," *NovT* 29 (1987): 219–35 ▐Charles B. **Cousar**, *Galatians*, Interpretation (Atlanta: John Knox, 1982) ▐John W. **Drane**, *Paul: Libertine or Legalist?* (London: SPCK, 1975) ▐J. D. G. **Dunn**, *The Epistle to the Galatians*, BNTC (Peabody:

Hendrickson, 1993) ▮idem, *The Theology of Paul's Letter to the Galatians*, NTT (Cambridge: Cambridge University Press, 1993) ▮idem, "Once More—Gal 1 18: ἱστορῆσαι Κηφᾶν: In Reply to Otfried Hofius," *ZNW* 76 (1985): 138–39 ▮idem, "The Relationship Between Paul and Jerusalem According to Galatians 1 and 2," *NTS* 28 (1981–82): 461–78 ▮idem, "Works of the Law and Curse of the Law," *NTS* 31 (1984–85): 523–42 ▮Gerhard **Ebeling**, *The Truth of the Gospel: An Exposition of Galatians*, trans. David Green (Philadelphia: Fortress Press, 1985) ▮Philip F. **Esler**, *Galatians* (London: Routledge, 1998) ▮W. **Foester**, "Die Δοκοῦντες in Gal. 2," *ZNW* 36 (1937): 286–92 ▮Ronald Y. K. **Fung**, *The Epistle to the Galatians* (Grand Rapids: Eerdmans, 1988) ▮idem, "Justification, Sonship, and the Gift of the Spirit: Their Mutual Relationships as Seen in Galatians 3–4," *CGSTJ* 3 (1987): 73–104 ▮Timothy **George**, *Galatians*, NAC (Nashville: Broadman & Holman, 1994) ▮T. David **Gordon**, "The Problem at Galatia," *Int* 41 (1987): 32–43 ▮R. H. **Gundry**, "Grace, Works, and Staying Saved in Paul," *Bib* 66 (1985): 1–38 ▮Ernst **Haenchen**, *The Acts of the Apostles* (Oxford: Blackwell, 1971) ▮G. Walter **Hansen**, *Galatians*, IVPNTC (Downers Grove: IVP, 1994) ▮Richard B. **Hays**, "Christology and Ethics in Galatians: The Law of Christ," *CBQ* 49 (1987): 268–90 ▮idem, *The Faith of Jesus Christ: The Narrative Substructure of Galatians 3:1–4:11*, 2nd ed. (Grand Rapids: Eerdmans, 2002) ▮C. J. **Hemer**, "The Adjective 'Phrygia,'" *JTS* 27 (1976): 122–26 ▮idem, "Phrygia: A Further Note," *JTS* 28 (1978): 99–101 ▮J. D. **Hester**, "The Rhetorical Structure of Galatians 1:11–2:14," *JBL* 103 (1984): 223–33 ▮D. **Hill**, "Salvation Proclaimed: IV. Galatians 3:10–14," *ExpTim* 93 (1981–82): 196–200 ▮O. **Hofius**, "Gal 1:18: ἱστορῆσαι Κηφᾶν," *ZNW* 75 (1984): 73–85 ▮M. D. **Hooker**, "Paul and 'Covenantal Nomism,'" in *Paul and Paulinism*, 47–56 ▮Richard **Hove**, *Equality in Christ? Galatians 3:28 and the Gender Dispute* (Wheaton: Crossway Books, 1999) ▮G. **Howard**, *Paul: Crisis in Galatia* (Cambridge: Cambridge University Press, 1979) ▮J. J. **Hughes**, "Hebrews ix 15ff. and Galatians iii 15ff.: A Study in Covenant Practice and Procedure," *NovT* 21 (1979): 27–96 ▮L. Ann **Jervis**, *Galatians*, NIBC (Peabody: Hendrickson, 1999) ▮R. **Jewett**, "The Agitators and the Galatian Congregation," *NTS* 17 (1970–71): 198–212 ▮Philip H. **Kern**, *Rhetoric and Galatians: Assessing an Approach to Paul's Epistle*, SNTSMS 101 (Cambridge: Cambridge University Press, 1998) ▮G. D. **Kilpatrick**, "Peter, Jerusalem, and Galatians 1:13–2:14," *NovT* 25 (1983): 318–26 ▮J. B. **Lightfoot**, *Saint Paul's Epistle to the Galatians* (London: Macmillan, 1902) ▮Andrew T. **Lincoln**, *Paradise Now and Not Yet*, SNTSMS 43 (Cambridge: Cambridge University Press, 1981) ▮Bruce W. **Longenecker**, *The Triumph of Abraham's God: The Transformation of Identity in Galatians* (Edinburgh: T. & T. Clark, 1998) ▮Richard N. **Longenecker**, *Galatians*, WBC 41 (Dallas: Word, 1990) ▮Dieter **Lührmann**, *Galatians: A Continental Commentary* (Minneapolis: Fortress Press, 1992) ▮D. J. **Lull**, "'The Law Was Our Pedagogue': A Study in Galatians 3:19–25," *JBL* 105 (1986): 481–98 ▮Troy W. **Martin**, "The Covenant of Circumcision (Genesis 17:9–14) and the Situational Antitheses in Galatians 3:28," *JBL*

122 (2003): 111–25 ▯ J. Louis **Martyn**, *Galatians: A New Translation with Intro-duction and Commentary*, AB 33A (New York: Doubleday, 1997) ▯ Frank J. **Matera**, *Galatians*, SacPag 9 (Collegeville: Liturgical Press, 92) ▯ R. Barry **Matlock**, "Detheologizing the πίστις Χριστοῦ Debate: Cautionary Remarks from a Lexical Semantic Perspective," *NovT* 42 (2000): 1–23 ▯ idem, "Πίστις in Galatians 3.26: Neglected Evidence for 'Faith in Christ'?" *NTS* 49 (2003): 433–39 ▯ Scot **McKnight**, *Galatians*, NIVAC (Grand Rapids: Zondervan, 1995) ▯ D. J. **Moo**, "'Law,' 'Works of the Law,' and Legalism in Paul," *WTJ* 45 (1983): 73–100 ▯ J. **Munck**, *Paul and the Salvation of Mankind* (Richmond: John Knox, 1959) ▯ Mark D. **Nanos**, *The Irony of Galatians: Paul's Letter in First-Century Context* (Minneapolis: Fortress Press, 2002) ▯ idem, ed., *the Galatians Debate: Contemporary Issues in Rhetorical and Historical Interpretation* (Peabody: Hendrickson, 2002) ▯ Peter T. **O'Brien** "Was Paul Converted?" in D. A. Carson, Peter T. O'Brien and Mark A. Seifried, *Justification and Variegated Nomism*, 2.361–91 ▯ George **Ogg**, *The Chronology of the Life of Paul* (London: Epworth, 1968) ▯ J. C. **O'Neill**, *The Recovery of Paul's Letter to the Galatians* (London: SPCK, 1972) ▯ Pheme **Perkins**, *Abraham's Divided Children: Galatians and the Politics of Faith* (Harrisburg: Trinity Press International, 2001) ▯ W. M. **Ramsay**, *The Church in the Roman Empire* (London: Hodder & Stoughton, 1893) ▯ P. **Richardson**, "Pauline Inconsistency: I Corinthians 9:19–23 and Galatians 2:11–14," *NTS* 26 (1979–80): 347–62 ▯ Rainer **Riesner**, *Paul's Early Period: Chronology, Mission Strategy, Theology* (Grand Rapids: Eerdmans, 1998) ▯ J. A. T. **Robinson**, *Redating the New Testament* (Philadelphia: Westminster, 1976) ▯ Walter Bo **Russell III**, *The Flesh/Spirit Conflict in Galatians* (Lanham: UPA, 1997) ▯ E. P. **Sanders**, "On the Question of Fulfilling the Law in Paul and Rabbinic Judaism," in *Donum Gentilicium*, Fs. D. Daube, ed. E. Bammel, C. K. Barrett, and W. D. Davies (Oxford: Oxford University Press, 1980), 103–26 ▯ idem, *Paul and Palestinian Judaism* (Philadelphia: Fortress Press, 1977) ▯ idem, *Paul, the Law, and the Jewish People* (Philadelphia: Fortress Press, 1985) ▯ T. R. **Schreiner**, "Is Perfect Obedience to the Law Possible? A Re-examination of Galatians 3:10," *JETS* 27 (1984): 151–60 ▯ idem, "Paul and Perfect Obedience to the Law: An Evaluation of the View of E. P. Sanders," *WTJ* 47 (1985): 245–78 ▯ Moisés **Silva**, *Interpreting Galatians: Explorations in Exegetical Method*, 2nd ed. (Grand Rapids: Baker, 2001) ▯ idem, "Faith Versus Works of the Law," in *Justification and Variegated Nomism*, 2.217–48 ▯ Vincent M. **Smiles**, *The Gospel and the Law in Galatia: Paul's Response to Jewish-Christian Separatism and the Threat of Galatian Apostasy* (Collegeville: Liturgical Press, 1998) ▯ idem, "The Concept of 'Zeal' in Second-Temple Judaism and Paul's Critique of It in Romans 10:2," *CBQ* 64 (2002): 282–99 ▯ G. M. **Taylor**, "The Function of πίστις Χριστοῦ in Galatians," *JBL* 85 (1966): 58–76 ▯ Frank **Thielman**, *From Plight to Solution: A Jewish Framework for Understanding Paul's View of the Law in Galatians and Romans*, NovTSup 61 (Leiden: Brill, 1989) ▯ P. **Vielhauer**, "Gottesdienst und Stoicheiadienst im Galaterbrief," in *Rechtfertigung*, Fs. E. Käsemann, ed.

J. Friedrich, W. Pöhlmann, and P. Stuhlmacher (Tübingen: Mohr-Siebeck, 1976), 543–55 ▪Stephen **Westerholm**, *Perspectives Old and New on Paul: The "Lutheran" Paul and His Critics* (Grand Rapids: Eerdmans, 2004) ▪M. **Wilcox**, "The Promise of the 'Seed' in the New Testament and the Targums," *JSNT* 5 (1979): 2–20 ▪Sam K. **Williams**, *Galatians*, ANTC (Nashville: Abingdon, 1994) ▪idem, "Justification and the Spirit in Galatians," *JSNT* 29 (1987): 91–100 ▪R. M. **Wilson**, "Gnostics—in Galatia?" *SE* 4: 358–67 ▪Ben **Witherington III**, *Grace in Galatia: A Commentary on Paul's Letter to the Galatians* (Grand Rapids: Eerdmans, 1998) ▪N. H. **Young**, "Paidagogos: The Social Setting of a Pauline Metaphor," *NovT* 29 (1987): 150–76.

CHAPTER THIRTEEN

EPHESIANS

CONTENTS

After the opening greeting (1:1–2) Paul expresses praise to God for his predestining and redeeming activity in Christ (1:3–14)—all to the praise of God's glorious grace. The Father has blessed "us" with every spiritual blessing, having chosen us in Christ before the foundation of the world, and having predestined us in love (1:3–5). All the blessings he has given us have come to us "in Christ," "the One he loves" (1:3, 6), the Son who is already seated in the heavenly realms. And among these blessings is the fact that we have been marked with a "seal"—none other than the promised Holy Spirit (1:13). Small wonder Paul turns to thanksgiving and prayer for the letter's recipients (1:15–23).

Chapter 2 reminds them of their sinfulness and of their salvation by grace to do good works (2:1–10), then addresses the peace and the unity Christ brings between Jew and Gentile as God constructs one new humanity (2:11–22). Paul speaks of "the mystery of Christ" with the Gentiles being brought into membership of the one body with God's ancient people Israel (3:1–6) and of the way God's eternal purpose was worked out in Christ (3:7–13). This leads into prayer for the readers, especially to the end that Christ will dwell in their hearts through faith, and that they will have the power to grasp more of the limitless dimensions of God's love for them in Christ. The prayer ends in a doxology (3:14–21).

The importance of keeping "the unity of the Spirit" is stressed (4:1–6), as are the gifts of God to the church, enabling growth in love (4:7–16). The readers are exhorted to live as children of light (4:17–5:21). These exhortations include the highest theological incentives. For instance, the readers are encouraged to follow "God's example" (5:1) precisely because as children they are morally bound to reflect the character of their Father; they are urged to follow "the way of love, just as Christ loved us and gave himself up for us" (5:2). Directions for family life follow, with exhortations to wives and husbands—including a powerful typological connection between, on the one hand, husband and wife, and, on the other, Christ and the church (5:22–33)—to children and parents (6:1–4), and to slaves and masters (6:5–9). Paul urges his readers to put on the armor God provides (6:10–18), and concludes with a request that they use the weapon of prayer on his behalf (6:19–20). The letter closes with final greetings (6:21–24).

AUTHOR

That Ephesians is an authentic Pauline letter is the traditional view, but in modern times this has been widely denied. The view that Paul wrote it is supported by such arguments as the following:[1]

1. The letter claims to have been written by Paul, not only in its opening (1:1) but also in the body of the letter (3:1). Any letter coming down from antiquity should be held to be by the author it mentions unless there is strong evidence to the contrary. There are many personal notes: the writer has heard of the readers' faith and love (1:15), and he gives thanks and prays for them (1:16); he calls himself "the prisoner of Christ Jesus" (3:1; 4:1); he asks for the readers' prayers (6:19–20). The comment in 6:21 is virtually incoherent if the author is not Paul. This sort of thing is not proof, but it indicates that the man who claims to be Paul was known to the readers and was confident that his claim would not be overthrown.

2. From early days the letter was in wide circulation, and its authenticity does not seem to have been doubted. It was accepted by Marcion (as the letter to the Laodiceans); it is in the Muratorian Canon and was used by heretics as well as the orthodox. It was apparently viewed as a Pauline letter by Ignatius, Polycarp, Clement of Rome, Hermas, and others of the apostolic fathers. No one seems to have queried Pauline authorship until the modern period.[2]

3. Pauline features abound. The structure is like that of the undisputed epistles, and there is a good deal of Pauline language, including words that occur in this letter and the undisputed writings of Paul but nowhere else in the New Testament.[3] H. J. Cadbury has asked an interesting question: "Which is more likely—that an imitator of Paul in the first century composed a writing ninety

> *From early days the letter was in wide circulation, and its authenticity does not seem to have been doubted. No one seems to have queried Pauline authorship of Ephesians until the modern period.*

---

[1]In addition to the standard commentaries and introductions, see A. van Roon, *The Authenticity of Ephesians*, NovTSup 39 (Leiden: Brill, 1974); the thoughtful review by A. T. Lincoln, *WTJ* 40 (1977–78): 172–75 (though Lincoln subsequently changed his mind, viz. *Ephesians*, WBC 42 [Dallas: Word Books, 1990]); and the essay by Clinton E. Arnold, "Introducing Ephesians: Establishing Believers in Christ," *SWJT* 39 (1966): 4–13; idem, "Ephesians, Letter to the," *DPL*, 238–46.

[2]See Harold W. Hoehner, *Ephesians: An Exegetical Commentary* (Grand Rapids: Baker, 2002), 2–20. His detailed work demonstrates that Brown's assertion (p. 629) that 70–80 percent of scholars have adopted the view that this letter was not written by Paul is impressively mistaken.

[3]"It is difficult to believe that an imitator could have produced a work so like the writings of Paul and yet so splendid and original: difficult to believe some other spiritual

or ninety-five per cent in accordance with Paul's style or that Paul himself wrote a letter diverging five or ten per cent from his usual style?"[4] Robert M. Grant noticed this question and posed one of his own: "'Which is more likely,' we might well ask—'that we can determine the authenticity of a letter written ninety or ninety-five per cent in accordance with Paul's style, and his outlook, or that we cannot?' *This* question, it would appear, can be answered. We are not in a position to judge, and since the authenticity of the letter cannot be disproved it should be regarded as genuine."[5]

4. The relationship to Colossians may be argued in more ways than one. Those who reject Pauline authorship hold that it would not be possible for one person to write two letters with such resemblances (e.g., the words about Tychicus; see Eph. 6:21–22 and Col. 4:7–8), but also with such significant differences (e.g., the "mystery" is the unity of Jews and Gentiles in Christ in Eph. 3:3–6, whereas it is Christ in Col. 2:2). But those who see Paul as the author "are equally emphatic that two minds could not have produced two such works with so much subtle interdependence blended with independence."[6] Ephesians is not so much a copy of parts of Colossians as a development of it. There may be similar vocabulary, but there are also curious differences. It is not unreasonable to think of Paul as producing Colossians with a specific situation in mind, and not long after, as writing Ephesians with broader purposes. It is also possible that he made use of an amanuensis and allowed him some freedom in one or other of the letters. But against this is the fact that the other Pauline letters give no evidence of secretarial latitude, or at least of such secretarial latitude as this theory requires. Why should Paul treat this letter differently from the others?[7]

5. Paul is not mentioned in Revelation, which was addressed to the church at Ephesus among others (see Rev. 2:1; cf. 2 Pet. 3:15). The question may be asked: Why should an author, writing pseudonymously, select the name of Paul in writing to an area where, granted the failure of Revelation to mention Paul, there is no evidence that the apostle was still highly revered?[8] In any case, the

---

genius was to be found in the Church at this time whose mind was so like Paul's and whose thought was so sublime" (Clogg, 96).

[4] H. J. Cadbury, "The Dilemma of Ephesians," *NTS* 5 (1958–59): 101.

[5] Grant, 202.

[6] Guthrie, 511.

[7] Johnson finds two major weaknesses in the argument that an imitator of Colossians produced this letter: "If Colossians was followed so assiduously, why does the usage even of the shared vocabulary differ in such interesting ways? And if the forger had available to him other genuine letters, why weren't they used in a more effective and convincing way?" (369).

[8] Most of those who argue for the pseudonymity of Ephesians date the epistle as late as c. A.D. 90, almost thirty years after Paul's death and not long removed from the most likely date for the composition of the Apocalypse.

custom of writing letters in the name of someone else does not seem to have been as widely practiced in the early church as some claim. (See the section "Pseudonymity" in chap. 8.)

6. Many of the themes of Ephesians have the closest parallels in the undisputed Pauline epistles—for example, justification by faith, the place of grace, the dominance of flesh in the unredeemed, the work of Christ as reconciliation, the place of the Jews and of the law. Those who oppose Pauline authorship argue that this results from imitation, but that is to be proved. There is undoubtedly Pauline teaching in this letter.

7. Paul was a prisoner when he wrote the letter (3:1; 4:1), which accords well with this claim. There is development from the earlier letters, but this is natural enough as the apostle gets closer to the end of his life. The letter is very naturally understood as Paul's words to a church he sees as needing further instruction on some important aspects of the faith. Such an understanding seems to many scholars a better way of seeing the letter than the alternatives that are suggested. No suggested pseudepigraphical situation has anything like the aptness of the view that Paul is writing from his final imprisonment.

But many modern scholars are not persuaded by such considerations. They hold that the evidence points to someone other than Paul as the writer.

1. The theology of Ephesians is said to be such that we cannot ascribe the writing to Paul. There are Pauline features, such as the clear statement of justification by faith (2:5–8), but some emphases dominate here that are at best weakly attested in the undisputed letters of Paul—including the cosmic function of the church (3:10) and an emphasis on realized eschatology. Moreover, here the writer asserts that the Ephesian believers are "built on the foundation of the apostles and prophets" (2:20), whereas Paul in the undisputed letters understands Christ to be the one foundation (1 Cor. 3:11).

Undoubtedly some developments have taken place. Nevertheless, it is another matter to show that these developments represent a stage beyond what Paul could have reached in his own lifetime, or that the themes here stressed are not the sort of thing that the apostle could reasonably be expected to emphasize, granted the particular setting that calls this letter forth. For instance, Arnold has argued rather convincingly that the cosmic functions of Christ and the heightened emphasis on realized eschatology are prompted by the author's transparent desire to strengthen his readers in their ongoing struggle against the "principalities and powers"[9] (on which more below). Lincoln has demonstrated how much futurist eschatology surfaces in Ephesians.[10] Moreover, even in this

---

[9]Clinton E. Arnold, *Ephesians: Power and Magic. The Concept of Power in Ephesians in Light of Its Historical Setting*, SNTSMS 63 (Cambridge: Cambridge University Press, 1989).

[10]Lincoln, *Ephesians*, lxxxix–xc.

letter Christ is "the chief cornerstone" (2:20), which surely accords rather well with the passage in 1 Corinthians.

Others argue that in Ephesians ἐκκλησία (*ekklēsia*) always refers to the universal church, while Paul normally uses the word for the local congregation. Yet insofar as it is true that Paul's usage of the word in this letter extends beyond the local congregation, that reality becomes less surprising if this is a general letter written to circulate around a number of churches in the Roman province of Asia (see discussion below). Some note that although Paul refers to the parousia in all his undisputed letters, it is absent from Ephesians (but is this fair to 1:14; 4:30; 5:6; 6:8?). This letter pictures Paul as commissioned to bring about the unity of Jews and Gentiles in the church (3:2–6), whereas the historical Paul, it is argued, saw himself as the apostle of the Gentiles. Once again, a critic of the critics cannot help wondering if distinctions are being forced out of the texts: after all, in Romans 11:17–24 Paul has both Jews and Gentiles in the one olive tree. Ephesians uses marriage as a picture of the union between Christ and the church (5:23–33), which is sometimes said to be quite impossible for the author of 1 Corinthians 7, who, it is argued, does not seem to value marriage highly enough to warrant this sort of lofty typological connection. But surely it is no more impossible than that in the Old Testament some texts portray Israel as the bride of Yahweh, and others lay down legislation on sexual matters. After all, even in 1 Corinthians 7, where celibacy can be called a χάρισμα (*charisma*, "grace gift"), marriage can also be called a χάρισμα (1 Cor. 7:7). Clearly, a fair bit of this sort of criticism fails to acknowledge that in neither passage does the writer undertake to say *everything* he thinks about marriage—and it is far from clear that the two passages are mutually exclusive in outlook. What appears to some as impossible for one mind is for others an obvious possibility for such a wide-ranging and inventive mind as Paul's.[11]

2. The language of Ephesians includes words not found elsewhere in Paul, e.g., ἀσωτί (*asōtia*, "wantonness"; but cf. Titus 1:6), πολιτεία (*politeia*, "citizenship," "commonwealth").[12] This argument is somewhat spoiled by Harrison's examination of the hapax legomena (words that occur in no other writing in the New Testament). He finds that in Ephesians there are an average of 4.6 such words to the page, which is in line with the figures for other letters (5.6 in 2 Corinthians, and 6.2 in Philippians).[13] It is also pointed out that in this letter

---

[11]F. W. Danker, under the heading "Theology," begins, "Beyond question this Epistle fits within boundaries largely familiar in other Pauline letters"; he demonstrates this with references to Paul's letters ("Ephesians," in *ISBE* 2.113–14).

[12]By contrast, some think that Ephesians is *too* Pauline: it contains reminiscences of too many Pauline letters (see G. Johnston, "Ephesians," in *IDB* 2.110–11).

[13]P. N. Harrison, *The Problem of the Pastoral Epistles* (London: Oxford University Press, 1921), 20.

different expressions are used for the same thing. For example, whereas in other writings Paul uses οἱ οὐρανοί (*hoi ouranoi*) for "heaven," in Ephesians we have ἐν τοῖς ἐπουρανίοις (*en tois epouraniois*) as well. So also in this letter we find Christ called ὁ ἠγαπημένος (*ho ēgapēmenos,* "the One [God] loves," Eph. 1:6) and the verb χαριτόω (*charitoō,* lit. "to endue with grace"; cf. Eph. 1:6) where Paul normally has χάριν δίδωμι (*charin didōmi,* lit. "I give grace"). Paul usually refers to Satan, but in this letter we find "the devil." Such differences are interesting, but they come far short of proof, especially with a writer as versatile as Paul.[14] Perhaps there is marginally more to be said for the fact that some of these words are used by the apostolic fathers, which might be taken as evidence for a late date for this letter. But most scholars acknowledge that the Epistle to the Ephesians was known and quoted by the early church fathers, including quite possibly Clement of Rome, and certainly Ignatius, so that "the possibility that the vocabulary of Ephesians influenced these writers needs to be considered more seriously."[15]

3. More significant is the style of this letter. The length of the sentences is specially noteworthy.[16] In modern translations these long sentences tend to be broken up, with the result that the reader does not realize the length. But 1:3–14 is one sentence, 1:15–23 is another, as is 3:1–7 (see KJV). The style is often labeled *pleonastic,* that is, there is a fullness to it, the sentences abounding in prepositional phrases, relative clauses, participles, and multiplying synonyms (e.g., in 1:19 four words are used to denote power). Schnackenburg asserts that "there is scarcely anything comparable in Paul."[17] Once again, however, the difference is somewhat exaggerated. The pleonastic style dominates only the first half of the letter; the style of the second half falls within customary Pauline range. Unless one postulates two authors for the two halves (and this is not seriously entertained), we might be wiser to seek an explanation of the peculiar style of the first half in its substance: the style accords with the lofty doxologies, prayers, and sweeping theological themes. When Paul tackles similar themes in his undisputed letters, his style can become similarly florid (cf. Rom. 8:28–39; 11:33–36).

4. Ephesians is taken by many to be an "early Catholic" writing. It is suggested that the author looks back on the apostles as a closed group (2:20; 3:5) and that there is an un-Pauline interest in various orders of ministry (4:11; but should we not bear in mind 1 Cor. 12:28–30?). But to describe the apostles and prophets as "holy" (ἅγιοι, *hagioi,* 3:5) is scarcely anomalous, when Paul typi-

---

[14]L. Cerfaux asks how an imitator can "avoid betraying himself by awkward phrases, wordiness, or allusions which correspond to his own interests. The forgers or plagiarists of antiquity have not accustomed us to such skill. As an example of their lack of it, let anyone read the so-called *Letter to the Laodiceans!*" (Robert/Feuillet, 503).

[15]Arnold, "Introducing Ephesians," 5.

[16]E.g., see Achtemeier/Green/Thompson, 381.

[17]Rudolf Schnackenburg, *The Epistle to the Ephesians* (Edinburgh: T. & T. Clark, 1991), 26.

cally uses the same term for all Christians. True, the apostles and prophets are said to be the foundation of God's household (2:20), but the writer says nothing about them having passed off the scene—and this foundational role in no way threatens the exclusive authority of Christ, since after all he is the one who gives them to the church (4:11–12). Even in an undisputed letter, Paul on occasion leaves little doubt of his awareness of his apostolic authority (e.g., 1 Cor. 14:37).

5. The relationship to Colossians is considered such that the same writer could not have produced the two.[18] The twin reasons commonly advanced, however, tend to cancel each other out.

First, Colossians is usually held to be a genuine Pauline letter, and Ephesians is thought to be the work of an imitator who used Colossians for some of his thoughts and language. Why would an author send so similar a letter to the same region so soon after the first? Surely it makes more sense to suppose that Ephesians was written two or three decades later, and by someone else. Yet it must be said that the degree of dependence has been exaggerated. One pair of passages (Eph. 6:21–22 and Col. 4:7–8), regarding the commendation of Tychicus, boasts twenty-nine consecutive words in common. Apart from this pair, there are only three pairs where seven words are exact parallels, and two more where five words are exactly paralleled. True, there are numerous common themes and some common vocabulary. Nevertheless, if there is such direct dependence as some think, one marvels at what is *not* copied. For instance, Reicke reasonably asks, "[I]f Ephesians had been copied from Colossians, why would the author have omitted Timothy's name when he is mentioned in the latter as Paul's coauthor (Col. 1:1)? And why are all the other names in Colossians missing in Ephesians except that of Tychicus, who is described similarly in both letters as Paul's delegate to the recipients (Col. 4:7–8; Eph. 6:21–22)? No theory of imitation offers a suitable explanation of this incongruity."[19] Still, we must allow any writer some flexibility, and the best explanation to many seems to be that the same man wrote Colossians and then Ephesians a little later, with many of the same thoughts running through his head and with a more general application of the ideas he had so recently expressed.

Second, granted that Colossians is genuinely Pauline, some doubt that Ephesians is authentic because it does not follow Colossians closely enough. For instance, on occasion the same word is used with different meaning, or at least a different referent (e.g., μυστήριον [*mystērion*]; cf. Eph. 3:2–13 and Col. 1:25–2:3). But when one observes the range of things referred to by "mystery" in the undisputed Paulines (cf., for instance, Rom. 11:25–26 and 1 Cor. 2:7), one marvels that this objection could be taken seriously. Moreover, these doubts about

---

[18]This argument is especially important to C. L. Mitton, *Ephesians* (London: Oliphants, 1976), 11–13, and to Lincoln, *Ephesians*, xlvii–lvi.

[19]Bo Reicke, *Re-examining Paul's Letters: The History of the Pauline Correspondence* (Harrisburg: Trinity Press International, 2001), 79.

the authenticity of Ephesians are predicated on the assumption that Ephesians was written after Colossians and is at least in some measure dependent on it. But even this stance is not unquestioned: a few have argued that the dependence runs the other way, and one major study postulates a lost common source.[20]

It is also possible to regard both Colossians and Ephesians as inauthentic. Some have taken that route. But in that case the author of Colossians appears merely to use Philemon to lead people to think of Colossians as a genuine Pauline product, and Ephesians looks like another work by the same pseudepigrapher. This time, however, he does not bother to use personal references, and he also introduces some curious stylistic differences. All in all, such a procedure seems improbable.

In short, the relationship between Ephesians and Colossians does not appear to be determinative of very much in the domain of authenticity.[21]

Markus Barth recognizes four schools of thought today: those who accept Paul as the author, those who see Paul as responsible for an original script that has been augmented by an editor,[22] those who reject Pauline authorship, and those who think that there is not enough evidence to decide.[23] While he recognizes the strength of the other views, he produces an argument "which more than others favors the authenticity of Ephesians and encourages the reader to understand the letter on the basis of its Pauline origin."[24]

PROVENANCE

This letter seems to have been written from the same place as Colossians, and its provenance is discussed under that for Colossians.

DATE

The letter speaks of Paul as in prison (3:1; 4:1). This is usually taken to refer to his imprisonment in Rome toward the end of his life, which would mean a date

---

[20]van Roon, *The Authenticity of Ephesians,* 426.

[21]On the complicated issues stemming from the ostensible relationship between Ephesians and Colossians, see esp. Ernest Best, *A Critical and Exegetical Commentary on Ephesians,* ICC (Edinburgh: T. & T. Clark, 1998), 20–25, and the literature there cited; also Peter T. O'Brien, *The Letter to the Ephesians,* PNTC (Grand Rapids: Eerdmans, 1999), 8–21.

[22]Cf. Martin's view that "it was Luke who published this letter under the apostle's aegis" (2.224). Cf. also John Muddiman, *The Epistle to the Ephesians,* BNTC (London: Continuum, 2001), 20–24, who sees Ephesians as the expansion of some earlier writing of Paul but does not venture to identify the final writer.

[23]Markus Barth, *Ephesians,* AB 34–34A (New York: Doubleday, 1974), 38.

[24]Ibid., 41.

in the early 60s. Those who reject Pauline authorship usually date Ephesians in the years 70–90, the period during which the Pauline letters are thought to have been collected. If it was not written by Paul, it must belong to the immediate post-apostolic period, but there are no criteria for locating it with precision. It cannot be much later than about 90, for it seems to be referred to by Clement of Rome, who is usually thought to have written his own letter c. A.D. 96.

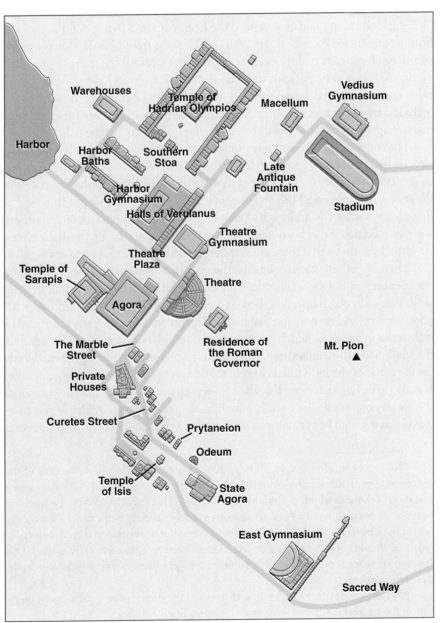

The City of Ephesus

DESTINATION

There is a problem posed by the fact that "in Ephesus" is absent from 1:1 in some of the best manuscripts (P[46], ℵ, B, 424[c], 1739), in Basil and Origen, apparently also in Marcion (who called the letter "the epistle to the Laodiceans"), and in Tertullian. The tone of the letter is impersonal, and some parts of it seem to indicate that the writer did not know the readers—for example, "ever since I heard about your faith in the Lord Jesus" (1:15) and "surely you have heard . . ." (3:2; 4:21). But Paul had evangelized the Ephesians and had spent quite a long time among them (Acts 19:8, 10; 20:31). The warmth of his affection for them and theirs for him is plainly evident in their last farewell (Acts 20:17–38, esp. vv. 36–37). It is very difficult to imagine that Paul would have written such a calm and impersonal letter to such dear friends. The words, however, are included by almost all manuscripts and by all the ancient versions; even the manuscripts that lack the words have "To the Ephesians" in the title.[25]

The suggestion is accordingly put forward that this was originally meant as a circular letter, probably conveyed by Tychicus, who would supplement it with his own comments (Eph. 6:21). It happens that the copy meant for the Ephesians is the ancestor of almost all the manuscripts that survive. A variant of this view is that a letter without an address was kept by the church at Ephesus, and in time it was assumed that it had been sent to that church. It would accord with the circular-letter hypothesis that there are no references to specific problems or disputes.

There is nothing decisive against the view that one letter was sent to a number of churches, but some objections are urged. An important one is that a circular letter with no name attached is very feasible in an age familiar with photocopiers (and even in one that had to depend on carbon paper), but it makes little sense in an age in which every copy had to be laboriously made by hand. If the whole had to be handwritten, there seems no reason for omitting the two words for the name of the individual church.[26] The saving in time would be miniscule. It is also to be borne in mind that the copies with the omission lack "in" as well as the place name: surely "in" would remain in each copy of the circular. It is further urged that it would be very curious if no copy of a circular survived other than that

---

[25]Kümmel confidently says, "The superscription comes first from the time of the collecting of the Pauline letters, and therefore merely passes on an early Christian interpretation of those to whom it was addressed" (353). This may conceivably be true, but how can we possibly know? We have no copies of MSS as early as the time of the collection of the Epistles, so we have no information about superscriptions then or before. In any case, should not some respect be accorded a Christian opinion as early as this? This is not to argue for accepting the assignation to the Ephesians, but simply for care in the use of the evidence.

[26]"[The] supposition of a letter with a gap in the prescript or a subsequent insertion of the address is without any parallel in antiquity" (Kümmel, 355).

to one particular church: even those manuscripts that lack "in Ephesus" do not have another name inserted. Furthermore, some critics hold that a circular for churches in the general area of Ephesus might be expected to convey some greetings of a general character. At the same time, attention is also drawn to personal touches in Ephesians. Would Paul write to *every* church, "I ask you, therefore, not to be discouraged because of my sufferings for you, which are your glory" (3:13)?[27]

Perhaps the best form of the circular-letter theory is that which sees Paul as having sent such a letter with Tychicus when he sent Colossians and that the letter was copied and circulated from Ephesus. Since it was a circular, there would be a blank instead of the name of the recipients, but the letter would be known to be associated with Ephesus, and in time that name was attached to it.[28]

Another suggestion is that this letter was really meant for the Laodiceans, as Marcion thought. If it is held that it is the Laodicean copy of a circular letter, it is open to all the objections noted; furthermore, whereas there are many copies existent with the address to Ephesus, not one survives addressing Laodicea. And if it is held that it is the letter referred to in Colossians 4:16, there is the further problem that Ephesians and Colossians are so like one another that one wonders why the churches should go through the process of exchanging them. In any case, most scholars hold that Ephesians is later than Colossians; and if this judgment is correct, then Colossians 4:16 refers to another writing.

E. J. Goodspeed has suggested that the letter was written as an introduction to the whole Pauline corpus. The thought is that when some loyal Paulinist first made a collection of the Pauline Epistles, he wrote this letter in the style of his beloved master as a way of introducing readers to some of Paul's thinking. Possibly the collection was first made at Ephesus, which would explain why so many manuscripts bear this address.[29]

There are difficulties in the way of this hypothesis. One is that we have no record of Ephesians ever standing first in a collection of the Pauline letters. There is variation in the order of Paul's epistles, but no order has Ephesians standing in the position of an introduction to the whole. There is also the resemblance to Colossians. These two letters resemble each other more than any other two in the Pauline corpus. If someone was writing an introduction, why should this one epistle receive so much attention? And why should the words about Tychicus (6:21–22) be included? They fit quite well in a letter to an individual church or in a circular letter to be carried by Tychicus, but it is not easy to see

---

[27]Francis Lyall adduces an argument from the legal allusions he finds in Ephesians. He points out that Ephesus was a main seat of government, a place where Roman law was known, and notes that "the Epistle to the Colossians, addressed to a smaller church outside Ephesus, does not contain the same measure of legal allusions as Ephesians" (*Slaves, Citizens, Sons* [Grand Rapids: Zondervan, 1984], 232).

[28]Wikenhauser makes this suggestion (426).

[29]Harrison discusses this view, noting some cogent objections (337–39).

why they should be included in an introduction. In most forms of this hypothesis it is held that the Pauline letters fell into neglect and that the appearance of Acts stirred up interest in the great apostle. But there is no real evidence of the supposed neglect, or that the publication of Acts would have had such an immediate influence throughout the church that a collection of Pauline writings would be made. It cannot be said that the theory has compelling force.

In the end we must probably conclude that we do not know for sure for whom the letter was originally intended. The evidence of the great mass of the manuscripts and the improbabilities of all the other views may drive us back to the view that it was meant for the church at Ephesus. If we feel that the absence of characteristic Pauline expressions of warmth (that would be expected in a letter to a church where he had spent as much time as he did at Ephesus) and of references to concrete situations are significant, then we will probably think of some form of a circular letter. But we are left with difficulties whatever view we adopt.[30]

> *Most of Paul's letters are occasional, written for a specific purpose on a specific occasion, but it is not easy to see any particular occasion that called forth this letter to the Ephesians.*

PURPOSE

There is no unanimity in understanding the letter's aim. Clearly it is meant to give instruction to the readers, but the instruction is not given in the way with which we are familiar from the Pauline writings generally. Most of Paul's letters are occasional, written for a specific purpose on a specific occasion, but it is not easy to see any particular occasion that called forth this letter.[31] Indeed, some question whether it should be called a letter at all.[32] N. A. Dahl rejects such views: "It belongs to a type of Greek letters—genuine and spurious—which substitute for a public speech rather than for private conversation."[33]

But what is the occasion of this public speech? Some point to a possible tension between Jewish and Gentile Christians and think Paul is trying to secure

---

[30]One should perhaps observe that the decision about the authenticity of the phrase ἐν Ἐφέσῳ (*en Phesō*, "in Ephesus") does not determine absolutely whether or not one judges this letter to have become a circular in the western parts of Asia Minor. O'Brien, *Ephesians*, 47–49, thinks the phrase is not original; Arnold, *DPL*, 244–45, thinks it is authentic; and both think the letter quickly served as a circular.

[31]Some scholars classify an epistle such as Romans as a "tractate letter": see Richard N. Longenecker, "On the Form, Function, and Authority of the New Testament Letters," in *Scripture and Truth*, ed. D. A. Carson and John D. Woodbridge (Grand Rapids: Zondervan, 1983), 101–14.

[32]"Presumably the author has no particular church in mind. He is meditating, and developing certain thoughts—and clothes them in the form of a letter"; "it is not really a letter, but a treatise or a 'wisdom address'" (Marxsen, 192).

[33]N. A. Dahl, "Ephesians," in *IDBSup*, 268. He also says, "Ephesians has been seen as the mature fruit of Paul's thought, as the beginning of its distortion, or an inspired re-interpretation" (ibid.).

unity. Others suggest that the letter is meant to instruct Gentile converts in important aspects of their new faith. Some who date the writing later than Paul propose that it was written to further the ecclesiastical interests of early Catholicism. Others have suggested that it is an attempt to set out some of the greatest truths for which the early Christians stood. Faced with such diversity, some scholars give up altogether the attempt to find a single aim and think there are several purposes behind the letter.

All this means that there is a solemnity about the letter and an absence of specifics that show that it is devoted to a general articulation of what is profitable for believers. We must not specify a concrete situation or a concrete problem and say that the letter is addressed exclusively to this. By contrast, we may discern a heresy that is being countered by the epistle to the Colossians, but there is no specific false teaching against which Ephesians is aimed. Among the various theories that have been advanced, certain points of convergence are worth noting: Gentile believers are primarily in view; although there is no concrete crisis that calls forth this epistle, apparently Paul thought his readers needed to be exhorted to pursue unity and a distinctively Christian ethic; there is an emphasis (begun in Colossians) on cosmic reconciliation in Christ (cf. 1:9–10, 20–23; 2:10–22; 3:6);[34] in general there is an effort to give Paul's readers a distinctively Christian identity. We can say that it is an important statement of the gospel that may well have been greatly needed in more than one first-century situation.

TEXT

As we have already noted, there is the practically insoluble question of whether to include "in Ephesus" in 1:1. But apart from that one passage, the text is reasonably straightforward. There is a handful of very uncertain readings, such as πάντας (*pantas*, "everyone") in 3:9, and ἰδίαις (*idiais*, "own") in 4:28, but such variations are minor. Apart from the destination in the opening sentence, we can say that we are not in real doubt about anything substantial in the letter.[35]

ADOPTION INTO THE CANON

We have no record of anyone in the early church raising a question about the canonicity of Ephesians. There were disputes about its destination, Marcion

---

[34]On this point, see Max Turner, "Ephesians," in *New Bible Commentary*, ed. D. A. Carson, R. T. France, J. A. Motyer, and G. J. Wenham (Downers Grove: IVP, 1994), 1223; O'Brien, *Ephesians*, 56–57.

[35]T. K. Abbott offers a series of notes "on some readings peculiar to one or two MSS" in which he looks at the most important readings in a selected group of important MSS (*A Critical and Exegetical Commentary on the Epistles to the Ephesians and to the Colossians*, ICC [Edinburgh: T. & T. Clark, 1897], xl–xlv).

claiming that it was written to the Laodiceans, and Basil later saying that in ancient copies it was addressed, not to the Ephesians, but to the saints who are also faithful in Christ Jesus. Clement of Rome probably refers to it, though without mentioning the author. Ignatius quotes from it, as do Polycarp and others. It appears in Marcion's canon (where, as we have seen, it is said to be addressed to the Laodiceans) and in the Muratorian Canon.[36] No serious doubt about its authenticity has come down to us from the Fathers.

EPHESIANS IN RECENT STUDIES

A generation ago there was a tendency on the part of some scholars to find elements of Gnosticism behind most of the New Testament writings, so it is not surprising that some have found it here. Thus, Bultmann finds "the Gnostic Redeemer-myth" and specifically "the descent and re-ascent of the Redeemer" in 4:8–10. In the quotation from Psalm 68:19 he finds "the idea that he conquered the inimical spirit-powers by his journey to heaven" (with the idea of victory over the cosmic powers also in Col. 2:15).[37] It is "Gnostic language" when the writer refers to "the ruler of the kingdom of the air" (2:2; so also 1:21; 3:10) and to the "spiritual forces of evil in the heavenly realms" (6:12).[38] However, terms such as πλήρωμα (*plērōma*, "fullness," 1:23, etc.) are frequently found in gnostic literature. That the author has on occasion used language that also occurs in the later gnostics can scarcely be denied, but that he is either indebted to Gnosticism or writing in opposition to it has not been demonstrated. It is not along such lines that a fruitful understanding of this letter is to be sought,[39] not least because full-blown Gnosticism is a post-Christian development that belongs to the second century.

A good deal of attention has been paid to the question of authorship in recent studies. The relation to Colossians has been scrutinized closely, and new considerations, such as the parallels between Ephesians and some of the Qumran writings, have been produced. This points to traditions shared by some parts of Judaism and by some early Christians,[40] and many recent scholars detect

---

[36]The best brief summary is that of Hoehner, *Ephesians,* 2–6.

[37]Rudolf Bultmann, *Theology of the New Testament* (London: SCM, 1952–55), 1.175.

[38]Ibid., 1.173.

[39]"There has emerged a growing consensus shared even by its defenders that the interpretation of the traditions underlying Ephesians cannot be restricted to Gnostic influence" (Childs, 318).

[40]Markus Barth points to passages in Ephesians reflecting traditions in the Old Testament, in intertestamental Judaism, in Jewish worship, in Qumran, in the worship of the early Christians, in early Christian hymns and parenetic traditions, in traditions of a Gentile origin and character, etc. ("Traditions in Ephesians," *NTS* 30 [1984]: 3–25). Clearly,

common tradition underlying both Colossians and Ephesians. This means that similarities are not necessarily to be explained by direct borrowing; there may well be independent use of the common stock of tradition. This will not account for all the similarities, and in the end there must be some more direct relationship, but it puts the problem in different perspective.

The letter's emphasis on the church is unmistakable; Ephesians clearly tells us more about the church than do other writings in the Pauline corpus. This has generated a great deal of discussion. For many, this focus on the church is a natural and acceptable development, but for Käsemann (among others) it is a distortion of the real Christian message. In Ephesians, he writes, "the gospel is domesticated." The world "may be its sphere. But it is so only as the frame into which the picture of the church fits." He goes on to complain that here "Christology is integrated with the doctrine of the church. . . . Christ is the mark towards which Christianity is growing, and no longer in the strict sense its judge."[41] Yet in some ways this is too narrow a perspective. The massive vision of a new humanity, a new household of God, rising together to reconcile warring human beings to each other and to God (chap. 2)—and all of this the product of God's predestining love (1:3–14) and unqualified grace (2:8–10)—is entirely in line with Pauline emphases on God's sweeping sovereignty in constituting his people (Rom. 9–11) and giving them the ministry of reconciliation (2 Cor. 5).[42]

More theologically telling are those studies that recognize distinctive emphases in Ephesians but relate such emphases to central themes in the Pauline corpus. For example, Lincoln examines what it means to be seated with Christ in the heavenly realms (Eph. 2:6) and concludes that it is a kind of spatial equivalent of inaugurated eschatology.[43] Caragounis[44] and Bockmuehl[45] have examined

---

many traditions are reflected in the letter. Peter T. O'Brien finds that much of the language of the prayers in Ephesians can be paralleled in the Qumran literature ("Ephesians 1: An Unusual Introduction to a New Testament Letter," *NTS* 25 [1978–79]: 515).

[41]Ernst Käsemann, *Jesus Means Freedom* (Philadelphia: Fortress Press, 1972), 89.

[42]Contra Margaret Y. MacDonald, *Colossians and Ephesians*, SacPag 17 (Collegeville: Liturgical Press, 2000), who argues, largely on social-scientific grounds, that both Colossians and Ephesians expand Paul's ideas in cosmic and universalistic directions. There is indeed a gentle shift in emphasis, but all of the principal theological themes in these letters are already found *in nuce* in the undisputed letters of Paul.

[43]Andrew T. Lincoln, *Paradise Now and Not Yet: Studies in the Role of the Heavenly Dimension in Paul's Thought, with Special Reference to His Eschatology*, SNTSMS 43 (Cambridge: Cambridge University Press, 1981).

[44]Chrys C. Caragounis, *The Ephesian Μυστήριον: Meaning and Content* (Lund: Gleerup, 1977).

[45]Markus N. A. Bockmuehl, *Revelation and Mystery in Ancient Judaism and Pauline Christianity*, WUNT 36 (Tübingen: Mohr-Siebeck, 1990).

the "mystery" language in the Pauline corpus that is especially rich in Ephesians. The latter's work, cast against the backdrop of first-century understanding of the nature of revelation, is especially suggestive. Moreover, the cosmic conflict against "principalities and powers," for which only the whole armor of God is adequate, depicts a world of dangerous opponents, sweeping from pure abstractions through demonology to literary personifications. The breadth of the vision invests the nature of the Christian struggle with breathtaking significance, while offering assurance that God and his gospel provide the only solace and hope.[46]

THE CONTRIBUTION OF EPHESIANS

The letter begins with a section putting strong emphasis on the divine action in bringing salvation. Paul refers to the spiritual blessings in Christ that believers enjoy and goes on to speak of God as having chosen these believers before the creation of the world (1:4; see also v. 11). Their salvation did not take place because they earned it but because God planned it, a truth that is otherwise expressed in terms of predestination that is linked with God's will and pleasure (1:5) and again with his plan (1:11). This opening also includes references to sonship through Christ, redemption through his blood, and sealing with the Holy Spirit (1:5, 7, 13). This massive emphasis on the place of the divine is expanded with continuing references to grace.[47]

Christ's saving work is stressed in the opening, a work that has significant implications for Christology. This emphasis persists throughout the letter; it is plain everywhere that who Christ is and what he does is at the heart of the Christian way. It is he who brings about the reconciliation of Jew and Gentile in the church in the notable section on the breaking down of hostility and the making of peace between them (2:11–22). Christ "himself is our peace" (2:14). This is more than the overcoming of human hostility. Part of Christ's work is "to bring unity to all things in heaven and on earth under Christ" (1:10). The powers in the heavenly realms are to know "the manifold wisdom of God" through the church (3:10). There is an importance in Christ's saving work that we cannot

---

[46]In addition to Arnold, *Ephesians: Power and Magic*, see especially Chris Forbes, "Pauline Demonology and/or Cosmology? Principalities, Powers and the Elements of the World in Their Hellenistic Context," *JSNT* 85 (2002): 51–73; and Peter T. O'Brien, "Principalities and Powers: Opponents of the Church," in *Biblical Interpretation and the Church: An International Study*, ed. D. A. Carson (Exeter: Paternoster, 1984), 110–50.

[47]The Greek word χάρις (*charis*, "grace") occurs twelve times in Ephesians, a total exceeded in the New Testament only in Acts, Romans, and 2 Corinthians, all of which are considerably longer.

fathom, and there is an importance in the very existence of the church that we are not able fully to comprehend.[48]

Ephesians emphasizes the importance of the Christian's growth in knowledge. This is expressed in a variety of ways. Sometimes it comes out in simple statements about knowledge, as when Paul says that God "made known to us the mystery" (1:9; cf. "the mystery of the gospel," 6:19). "Mystery" (μυστήριον [mystērion]) does not mean something difficult to work out (as in our use of the term) but something impossible to work out until God discloses it. What we could never work out for ourselves God has now made known (cf. 3:3 and the making known of God's "manifold wisdom" [3:10]). It is significant, accordingly, that the word mystērion occurs more often in Ephesians than in any other book of the New Testament; this book emphasizes the divine disclosure. The same basic idea may be conveyed with the concept of enlightenment: "I pray that the eyes of your heart may be enlightened in order that you may know . . ." (1:18), which is to be seen against the background of the darkness of the Gentiles (4:18). The readers are "light in the Lord" and they are to live as "children of light" and "find out what pleases the Lord" (5:8–10); they are to "understand what the Lord's will is" (5:17). No one who has grappled with the thought of this letter can doubt the importance of growing in knowledge.

One of the important things that the readers must know is expressed in the prayer that they may be "rooted and established in love" and be able "to grasp how wide and long and high and deep is the love of Christ, and to know this love that surpasses knowledge" (3:17–19). The word ἀγάπη (agapē, "love") occurs more often in this book than in any other in the New Testament except 1 Corinthians and 1 John. The reader sees the wonderful thing that Christian love is and the importance of living in love in a world that knows so little of it.

The church is "a holy temple in the Lord," a building in which Christ is "the chief cornerstone" and in which "God lives by his Spirit" (2:20–22). From another point of view, church members are both "fellow citizens with God's people and also members of his household" (2:19; cf. 1:5), a household that derives its name from the Father and that has members in heaven as well as on earth (3:14–15). The bringing of Gentiles as well as Jews into membership of the one body is explained as a mystery (3:4–6), a deep and hidden truth that none of us could have worked out but that has now been revealed by God.[49]

---

[48]Clogg sees this as very relevant to our modern situation. We feel ourselves "in the grip of a vast mechanism and of inexorable laws of physics and the like, and human freedom seems to have no meaning in the face of cosmic forces. We learn from this epistle to believe that all these but subserve a spiritual purpose, and that spiritual purpose is summed up in Christ" (101).

[49]Nevertheless, there is a sense in which this disclosure is linked to fresh insight in the Scriptures themselves (as in Rom. 16:25–27): cf. Thorsten Moritz, A Profound Mystery: The Use of the Old Testament in Ephesians, NovTSup 85 (Leiden: Brill, 1996).

There is a unity that believers should strive to preserve (4:3); indeed, Paul draws attention to a whole series of unities, including one Spirit, one Lord, one God and Father, one body and one hope, one faith, one baptism (4:4–6), even though there are diverse gifts of apostles, prophets, and others in the church (4:11–13). Clearly, the writer wants his readers to catch the splendid vision of one church, thoroughly united in the Lord, though it contains members of various races and is equipped by God to render significant service in this world.

A considerable section of the letter is given over to an emphasis on the importance of lives lived in conformity with the salvation that God has given believers. The kind of life the Gentiles live is contrasted with the new life believers live (4:17–5:21); the darkness of the old way is set over against the light there is in the Lord (5:8). This has important entailments for specific groups—wives and husbands, children and parents, slaves and masters (5:22–6:9). While wives are to be subject to their husbands, Paul has much more to say about the obligations marriage lays on husbands: they are to love their wives just as Christ loved the church—which, at the least, must mean self-sacrificially and for their good. Such a love prevails over other ties, such as those that previously bound a man to his parents. This kind of love leads Paul to speak of "a profound mystery—but I am talking about Christ and the church" (5:32). The section on the Christian's armor is a further incentive to wholehearted Christian service as well, as a reminder that there is full provision made for those who engage in Christian service (6:10–18).

In this letter we cannot miss the supreme place of God, who brings salvation despite the unworthiness of sinners. Nor can we overlook the greatness of Christ or the fact that the church, his body, occupies an important place in God's working out of his great purpose.

BIBLIOGRAPHY

T. K. **Abbott**, *A Critical and Exegetical Commentary on the Epistles to the Ephesians and to Colossians,* ICC (Edinburgh: T. & T. Clark, 1897) ▥Clinton E. **Arnold**, *Ephesians: Power and Magic: The Concept of Power in Ephesians in Light of Its Historical Setting,* SNTSMS 63 (Cambridge: Cambridge University Press, 1989) ▥idem, "Ephesians, Letter to the," *DPL*, 238–46 ▥idem, "Introducing Ephesians: Establishing Believers in Christ," *SWJT* 39 (1996): 4–13 ▥Markus **Barth**, *Ephesians,* AB 34–34A (Garden City: Doubleday, 1974) ▥idem, "Traditions in Ephesians," *NTS* 30 (1984): 3–25 ▥P. **Benoit**, *Les épîtres de saint Paul aux Philippiens, à Philémon, aux Colossiens, aux Ephésiens,* 2nd ed. (Paris: Cerf, 1953) ▥E. **Best**, *A Critical and Exegetical Commentary on Ephesians,* ICC (Edinburgh: T. & T. Clark, 1998) ▥idem, "Ephesians 1:1 Again," *in Paul and Paulinism,* ed. M. D. Hooker and S. G. Wilson (London: SPCK, 1982), 273–79 ▥Rudolf **Bultmann**, *Theology of the New Testament,* 2 vols. (London: SCM, 1952–55) ▥H. J. **Cadbury**,

"The Dilemma of Ephesians," *NTS* 5 (1958–59): 91–102 ▮D. A. **Carson**, ed., *The Church in the Bible and the World* (Grand Rapids: Baker, 1987) ▮H. **Conzelmann**, *Der Brief an die Epheser*, NTD (Göttingen: Vandenhoeck & Ruprecht, 1965) ▮F. L. **Cross**, ed., *Studies in Ephesians* (London: Mowbray, 1956) ▮Chris **Forbes**, "Pauline Demonology and/or Cosmology? Principalities, Powers and the Elements of the World in their Hellenistic Context," *JSNT* 85 (2002): 51–73 ▮E. J. **Goodspeed**, *The Key to Ephesians* (Chicago: University of Chicago Press, 1956) ▮idem, *The Meaning of Ephesians* (Chicago: University of Chicago Press, 1933) ▮P. N. **Harrison**, *The Problem of the Pastoral Epistles* (London: Oxford University Press, 1921) ▮E. **Käsemann**, *Jesus Means Freedom* (Philadelphia: Fortress Press, 1972) ▮Walter L. **Liefeld**, *Ephesians*, IVPNTC (Downers Grove: IVP, 1997) ▮A. T. **Lincoln**, *Ephesians*, WBC 42 (Dallas: Word Books, 1990) ▮idem, review of *The Authenticity of Ephesians*, by A. van Roon, *WTJ* 40 (1977–78): 172–75 ▮A. **Lindemann**, "Bemerkungen zu den Adressaten und zum Anlass des Epheserbriefes," *ZNW* 67 (1976): 235–51 ▮Richard N. **Longenecker**, "On the Form, Function, and Authority of the New Testament Letters," in *Scripture and Truth*, ed. D. A. Carson and John D. Woodbridge (Grand Rapids: Zondervan, 1983), 101–14 ▮Francis **Lyall**, *Slaves, Citizens, Sons* (Grand Rapids: Zondervan, 1984) ▮Margaret Y. **MacDonald**, *Colossians and Ephesians*, SacPag 17 (Collegeville: Liturgical Press, 2000) ▮Ralph **Martin**, *Ephesians, Colossians, and Philemon*, Interpretation (Atlanta: John Knox, 1991) ▮C. Leslie **Mitton**, *The Epistle to the Ephesians* (Oxford: Clarendon Press, 1951) ▮Thorsten **Moritz**, *A Profound Mystery: The Use of the Old Testament in Ephesians*, NovTSup 85 (Leiden: Brill, 1996) ▮P. T. **O'Brien**, *The Letter to the Ephesians*, PNTC (Grand Rapids: Eerdmans, 1999) ▮idem, "Ephesians 1: An Unusual Introduction to a New Testament Letter," *NTS* 25 (1978–79): 504–16 ▮idem, "Principalities and Powers: Opponents of the Church," in *Biblical Interpretation and the Church: An International Study*, ed. D. A. Carson (Exeter: Paternoster, 1984), 110–50 ▮Arthur G. **Patzia**, *Colossians, Philemon, Ephesians*, GNC (San Francisco: Harper & Row, 1984) ▮Pheme **Perkins**, *Ephesians*, ANTC (Nashville: Abingdon, 1997) ▮J. Armitage **Robinson**, *St. Paul's Epistle to the Ephesians*, 2nd ed. (London: Clark, 1922) ▮M. **Santer**, "The Text of Ephesians 1:1," *NTS* 15 (1968–69): 247–48 ▮R. **Schnackenburg**, *Ephesians: A Commentary* (Edinburgh: T. & T. Clark, 1991) ▮E. F. **Scott**, *The Epistles of Paul to the Colossians, to Philemon, and to the Ephesians*, MNTC (New York: Harper, 1930) ▮Klyne **Snodgrass**, *Ephesians*, NIVAC (Grand Rapids: Zondervan, 1996) ▮Max **Turner**, "Ephesians," *New Bible Commentary*, ed. D. A. Carson, R. T. France, J. A. Motyer, and G. J. Wenham (Downers Grove: IVP, 1994), 1222–44 ▮A. **van Roon**, *The Authenticity of Ephesians*, NovTSup 39 (Leiden: Brill, 1974) ▮B. F. **Westcott**, *St. Paul's Epistle to the Ephesians* (London: Macmillan, 1906).

CHAPTER FOURTEEN

PHILIPPIANS

CONTENTS

After the normal opening greetings (1:1–2) Paul thanks God for the Philippians and prays for them (1:3–11). He goes on to point out that his imprisonment has advanced the gospel (1:12–18), and he looks forward to being set free in response to their prayers (1:19–26). He urges them to live as Christians should, even though this means suffering (1:27–30)—indeed, Christians have been called to suffering. In a magnificent passage (which most take to be a hymn), Paul urges his readers to be humble and to follow the example of Christ, who, although (or is it "because"?) he was "in very nature God," became a man and underwent death on a cross. God therefore exalted him to the highest place (2:1–11). This leads to a further confident exhortation to his readers to serve God faithfully (2:12–18).

Paul expresses his hope to send Timothy (whom he praises warmly) to them soon—and indeed, to come himself (2:19–24). He also speaks of sending Epaphroditus, who had been very near to death but had apparently recovered from his illness (2:25–30). The apostle warns against people who were evidently advocating circumcision; he himself had had every reason for confidence in his life as a Jew, but he now sees all that as "loss for the sake of Christ"; to know Christ is much more important (3:1–11). Paul makes it clear that he has not reached perfection: he is still pressing on toward the goal. He invites the Philippians, as they anticipate the return of the Lord Jesus, to join with him and not to follow the example of people he castigates as "enemies of the cross of Christ" (3:12–4:1).

With the main part of the letter over, there come greetings to people who have worked with the apostle (4:2–3), a call to rejoice in the Lord, and encouragement to pray without anxiety but with the assurance that God's peace will guard them (4:4–7). They should practice Christian virtues wholeheartedly (4:8–9). Paul goes on to thank the Philippians for sending him help in his troubles, the only church to have done so (4:10–20). This leads into final greetings and the grace (4:21–23).

AUTHOR

The letter claims to have been written by Paul, and no serious doubt is raised against this claim. The style is Pauline, and while it is difficult to assign the letter to a specific point in the life of Paul, the situation presupposed rings true.

But although the letter as a whole is almost universally recognized to come from Paul, there is widespread debate over the origin of the "hymn"[1] in Philippians 2:5–11. Some of the vocabulary is unusual—μορφή (*morphē*, "form," vv. 6, 7), ἁρπαγμός (*harpagmos*, "something to be grasped," NIV; "something to be used to his own advantage," TNIV v. 6); ὑπερυψόω (*hyperypsoō*, "to exalt [him] to the highest place," v. 9); and other words are not found elsewhere in Paul—and the rhythmic style is not common in Paul, though it is the kind of thing we find in religious Hebrew poetry. Both the language and the rhythm would perhaps fit if the passage were a Greek translation of a Hebrew or Aramaic composition.[2] The passage speaks of Christ as "a servant" (v. 7), and Vincent Taylor sees this as "the strongest argument" that the passage is pre-Pauline.[3] Both before and after the hymn, Paul exhorts the Philippians to right conduct, and it is argued that the apostle would not stop in his exhortations to compose such an exquisite song and then go right back to them. Nor would he have omitted such characteristic themes as redemption through the cross, the resurrection, and the place of the church.

---

[1]We shall continue to attach the term "hymn" to this passage, even though some have doubted the accuracy of this label. For a defense of this category and its outworking in the passage, see Peter T. O'Brien, *The Epistle to the Philippians: A Commentary on the Greek Text*, NIGTC (Grand Rapids: Eerdmans, 1991), 186–202. For the view that this is not a hymn, see Gordon D. Fee, "Philippians 2:5–11: Hymn or Exalted Pauline Prose?" *BBR* 2 (1992): 29–46; idem, *Paul's Letter to the Philippians*, NICNT (Grand Rapids: Eerdmans, 1995), 40–43.

[2]R. P. Martin has made a detailed study of the passage, and he cites E. Lohmeyer for the view that "the poet's mother-tongue was Semitic"; "Lohmeyer contrived to show that the Greek text must be based on an underlying Semitic original" (*Carmen Christi*, SNTSMS 4 [Cambridge: Cambridge University Press, 1967], 46). In his first remarks on authorship Martin finds the arguments "finely balanced" (45), but after a detailed exegesis he decides that Paul has made use of an earlier hymn. He thinks of the passage as "a missionary manifesto of some Christian or Christian group whose outlook reaches forth to the world beyond the confines of Jewish Christianity and sees that the cosmic Christ, the universal Lord, is the one true answer to the religious quests of the Graeco-Roman world" (298–99).

[3]Vincent Taylor, *The Person of Christ in New Testament Teaching* (London: Macmillan, 1959), 63. Elsewhere, Taylor speaks of Paul's "comparative neglect of the Servant-conception of Isaiah lii.13–liii" (*The Atonement in New Testament Teaching* [London: Epworth, 1945], 65).

This reasoning leads some scholars to the view that the hymn is a pre-Pauline composition, perhaps coming from the early Palestinian church. It is fairly countered that there are passages that are undoubtedly Pauline that have as many unusual words in a comparable space and that there are Pauline passages with a rhythmic style (e.g., 1 Cor. 1:26–31; 2 Cor. 11:21–29). As for the early Palestinian flavor, Paul's mother tongue was Aramaic (Acts 22:2; 2 Cor. 11:22), so this does not preclude his authorship. The contention that the passage uses a servant theology, whereas Paul does not, is countered by the fact that the passage has a very Pauline reference to "death on a cross" (v. 8—this is a characteristic Pauline expression; indeed, those who deny Pauline authorship of the whole often see it as a Pauline insertion). It is not easy to take seriously the view that the interruption of the hortatory sequence rules out Paul as author. Paul's letters sometimes take unexpected turns, and it is not legitimate to expect that a letter will always follow a given line without deviation. Moreover, this view does not reckon with the possibility that Paul had composed the hymn at an earlier time and simply inserted it at this point in the argument. The absence of characteristic Pauline themes is surely not very significant. There is no place where Paul mentions them all; his selection is always shaped by the needs of the moment, and perhaps at this point he chooses not to use themes he found significant elsewhere.

When we turn to the structure and central argument of this passage, similar debate rages. In an earlier day this was often taken as a solemn doctrinal pronouncement of the apostle and made the basis for kenotic theories of the incarnation. In more recent times close attention has been given to its form, and it is now widely agreed that we should see it both as poetry and as liturgy—in short, as a hymn.[4] But there is wide disagreement as to whether there are three strophes or four or five or six, or whether we should think of six couplets. Each view tends to be supported by treating words and phrases as secondary additions, probably made by Paul when he adapted the original to his argument.[5] It is difficult to resist the conclusion that many modern scholars have insisted far too strongly that a first-century Christian hymn must conform to modern standards of versification.

Paul places this passage into his argument urging the Philippians to be Christlike, specifically to live in humility. It is pointed out that the hymn as com-

---

[4]But cf. n. 1 above.

[5]Not much more than that it is a hymn is agreed on. "It quickly becomes apparent . . . that although much has been written on these verses there is little that can be agreed upon, whether the topic discussed is the precise form of this section, its authorship, its place and purpose in the letter, the sources used in its composition, and so on" (Gerald F. Hawthorne, *Philippians*, WBC [Waco: Word, 1983], 76). Hawthorne is so impressed by the lack of agreement on insertions and the like that he treats it all as part of the original hymn.

monly understood is the earliest example known to us of a division of Christ's life into his preexistence, his life on earth, and his exaltation to heaven. This analysis, however, has been disputed by some. G. S. Duncan, for example, points to the Peshitta (the Bible in Syriac, from the early fifth century) to justify understanding verse 6 as "'He was in the image of God' (i.e., truly man; Gen. 1:26)."[6] So understood, the passage contrasts Jesus, who deliberately took the lowly way, with Adam (or perhaps with fallen angels), who pursued the path of self-aggrandizement, which led to disaster. But other study has convincingly shown that Philippians 2:6 must be understood to mean that Christ's "equality with God" was not something he *exploited;* that is, such equality was intrinsically his, but so great was his humility and subservience to the will of his Father that he chose not to exploit it but took the path of humiliation, incarnation, and death on a cross.[7]

That Paul made use of an existing hymn is usually accepted, and while some students hold that Paul wrote it, the more common opinion is that Paul has taken someone else's composition and adapted it to his purpose. Inevitably this leads to speculation as to how Paul "adapted" it. For instance, H. Koester holds that the background for the Christology of the hymn "was provided by a version of the Suffering Servant theme which developed in the speculative wisdom of Judaism." Paul has taken up what was originally written about wisdom and used it of Christ. This has meant some reshaping of the hymn with the insertion of a number of prose phrases, which means that "it is no longer possible to reconstruct the original poetic form."[8] One recalls with relief the sage counsel of Morna Hooker.[9]

Largely building on the work of E. Käsemann,[10] Ralph Martin rejects the commonly accepted view that the hymn is used as a lesson in humility. The introduction should be understood, he thinks, not as in the KJV ("Let this mind be in you which was also in Christ Jesus"), but rather to say, "Act as befits those who are in Christ Jesus." The controlling motive in Paul's ethics "is not imitation, but death and resurrection." Besides, the end of the hymn, with Christ in glory and honor, is a curious way of inculcating humility. Martin sees the hymn

---

[6]G. S. Duncan, "Philippians," in *IDB*, 3.791. Similarly, James D. G. Dunn relies on such Adam-Christology to justify his conclusion that the preexistence of Christ is not taught in this passage (*Christology in the Making* [London: SCM, 1980], 114–21).

[7]See Roy W. Hoover, "The Harpagmos Enigma: A Philological Solution," *HTR* 64 (1971): 95–119; and esp. N. T. Wright, "ἁρπαγμός and the Meaning of Philippians 2:5–11," *JTS* 37 (1986): 321–52. Christ "did not regard being equal with God as . . . something to use for his own advantage" (Hoover, "Harpagmos Enigma," 118).

[8]H. Koester, "Philippians," in *IDBSup*, 666.

[9]See n. 16 below.

[10]E. Käsemann, "A Critical Analysis of Philippians 2:5–11," in *God and Christ: Existence and Province*, ed. Robert W. Funk, *JTC* 5 (New York: Harper & Row, 1968), 45–88. (Käsemann originally wrote this article in 1950, in German.)

as meaning, rather, "Become in your conduct and church relationships the type of persons who, by that *kenosis,* death and exaltation of the Lord of glory, have a place in His body, the Church."[11] But against this C. F. D. Moule can say, "I see the whole passage as an exhortation to follow the example of Christ";[12] similarly, J. L. Houlden heads his discussion of the passage: "Christ the Model of Humility."[13] It cannot be said that there is unanimity on the point, but recent study has rather convincingly exposed the weaknesses of the strand of interpretation set in motion by Käsemann.[14] In any case, what cannot easily be gainsaid is that Paul is urging the importance of humility.

Oakes criticizes the Käsemann-Martin line (on this we think he is right), but then overstates the evidence in another direction by insisting that the Christhymn is the thematic center of this letter[15] and that the material is cast so as to constitute a contrast between Christ and the imperial cult. The evidence for the latter is at most suggestive. The fact remains that Christians everywhere have rejoiced in the Christology of the hymn—which is both humbling and triumphant—whether or not they contrasted this Christ with any imperial rival.

The arguments as to whether Paul wrote the passage himself or took over this piece from something well known in certain early churches are thus fairly evenly balanced. The passage is doubtless too short for us to be able to offer convincing reasons one way or the other. But what must be said with some firmness is that if the passage was not written by Paul, we have no idea who did write it (the suggestions are legion and are pure speculation). Moreover, on the assumption that Paul quoted it, he surely did so because as *he* was using it the

---

[11]Martin, *Carmen Christi,* 288, 291. Martin thinks that the hymn may have been used in a baptismal context. He also holds that it portrays "a soteriological drama." These verses "are not a piece of Christological speculation which answers our question who Christ was, but the record of a series of events of saving significance which declare what He did" (295). See also discussion of this hymn in Martin's *Philippians,* NCB (Greenwood: Attic, 1976). This, of course, does not mean that we may not draw some conclusions about the nature of the person who could accomplish all this.

[12]C. F. D. Moule, "Further Reflexions on Philippians 2, 5–11" in *Apostolic History and the Gospel,* ed. W. Ward Gasque and Ralph P. Martin (Grand Rapids: Eerdmans, 1970), 269.

[13]J. L. Houlden, *Paul's Letters from Prison* (London: SCM, 1977), 67.

[14]See esp. Wright, "ἁρπαγμός."

[15]Peter Oakes, *Philippians: From People to Letter,* SNTSMS 110 (Cambridge: Cambridge University Press, 2001). On this point Oakes is following Peter Wick, *Der Philipperbrief: Der formale Aufbau des Briefs als Schlüssel zum Verständnis seines Inhalts,* BWANT 135 (Stuttgart: Kohlhammer, 1994), 58–81. This point is severely criticized by Jeffrey T. Reed, *A Discourse Analysis of Philippians: Method and Rhetoric in the Debate over Literary Integrity,* JSNTSup 136 (Sheffield: Sheffield Academic Press, 1997), 362–64.

passage was saying the sort of thing he himself would say—which means we must interpret it within its Pauline framework.[16]

PROVENANCE

When Paul wrote this letter, he was a prisoner (1:7, 13, 17). He recognizes that death might be the outcome of his predicament (1:20; 2:17), but on the whole, he anticipates a speedy release and looks forward to rejoining his Philippian friends (1:25–26; 2:23–24). These facts are interesting, but they tell us nothing of the location of the prison.

We read of Paul's being held at Caesarea for two years (Acts 23:33; 24:27) as well as at Rome (Acts 28:16). The apostle himself says that he had been in prison "more frequently" than others (2 Cor. 11:23), which makes it clear that he had undergone more imprisonments than those mentioned in Acts (Clement of Rome says that Paul was in jail seven times [1 Clem. 5:6]). There are thus three possibilities: the imprisonment at Caesarea, that at Rome, and an incarceration on one of the other occasions, of which no record has survived.

Traditionally it has been held that this imprisonment was at Rome. There is a reference to "the Praetorium" (1:13, JB; "palace guard," TNIV), understood to refer to the praetorian guard centered at Rome. There Paul lived in his rented house with a soldier to guard him (Acts 28:16, 30–31). This would fit the situation in Philippians, as would the reference to "those who belong to Caesar's household" who send greetings through Paul (4:22). From the letter we gather that Paul was in a position to organize his coworkers—for example, he could send Timothy and Epaphroditus to Philippi (2:19, 25)—and this accords with the situation at Rome. So does the fact that a good number of "the brothers and sisters" had been encouraged by Paul's chains to preach the gospel (1:14), which seems to mean that there was a well-established church there. The Marcionite prologue is usually cited as early evidence that Rome was the place of origin of the letter. Another line of argument is that in Philippians the apostle is faced with death or release (1:20), but elsewhere than in the capital city he could appeal to Caesar against an adverse verdict.

All this makes a strong case for Rome, and it is not surprising that Rome has very often been judged to be the place from which the letter was written. But

When Paul wrote this letter, he was a prisoner, but doesn't say where. There are three possibilities: the imprisonment at Caesarea, that at Rome, and an incarceration on another occasion, of which no record has survived.

---

[16]Cf. Morna D. Hooker, "Philippians 2:6–11," in *Jesus und Paulus, Fs.* Werner Georg Kümmel, ed. E. Earle Ellis and Erich Grässer, 2nd ed. (Göttingen: Vandenhoeck & Ruprecht, 1978), 152: "If the passage is pre-Pauline, then we have no guide lines to help us in understanding its meaning. Commentators may speculate about the background—but we know very little about pre-Pauline Christianity, and nothing at all about the context in which the passage originated. It may therefore be more profitable to look first at the function of these verses in the present context and to enquire about possible parallels within Paul's own writings." Hooker is quoted approvingly by Fee, *Paul's Letter to the Philippians*, 46.

a problem arises from the journeys mentioned or implied in the letter. One jour-ney is necessary for whoever brought the Philippians the news of Paul's impris-onment, a second for Epaphroditus as he brought their gift to Paul (2:25), a third for the news of Epaphroditus's illness to get to Philippi, and a fourth for the con-cern of the Philippians to have been reported to the sufferer (2:26). Paul envis-ages three more journeys, apparently all to be accomplished in the near future: those of Timothy to Philippi and back with news (2:19) and that of Epaphrodi-tus (2:25). Philippi is a long way from Rome (about 1,200 miles), and such jour-neys would take months, so it is likely that the place of imprisonment was much closer to Philippi than was Rome.

The list may possibly be shortened a little by contending that we need not assume that the Philippians had heard that Paul was in prison: they may have heard of Paul's appeal to Caesar and dispatched Epaphroditus to Rome to await him. There was plenty of time, for Paul was delayed by being shipwrecked and spending the winter in Malta. This possibility may be conceded, but it is con-jecture, and some judge the argument from the journeys to be a weighty one. It must be admitted, however, that some weigh the evidence from geography rather differently. Thus Moisés Silva, observing that not more than three com-munications have taken place at the time of writing (one of which may have occurred even before Paul reached Rome) allows two months per trip—a gen-erous estimate—and concludes that not more than four to six months are required. Silva contends that the argument from geography should be dropped[17] (nor is he alone in this argument).

A further objection arises from Paul's stated intention of going to Philippi if he is released (2:24). When he wrote to the Roman church, he said that he intended going on to Spain after he had been with them (Rom. 15:24, 28). He may have changed his mind, but if so, we would expect some reference to a change of plan. We should also notice the comment that the Philippians had had no opportunity to send a gift to him until the one for which he gives them thanks (4:10). If Paul is writing from Rome toward the end of his life, this is very curious.[18]

The objections to Rome as the place of origin are weighty enough to cause a number of scholars to look at the evidence for some other place, and two sites have been put forward: Caesarea and Ephesus. Caesarea is favored by the fact that we know that Paul was imprisoned there for two years (Acts 24:27).[19] The

---

[17]*Philippians,* WEC (Chicago: Moody, 1988), 5–8.

[18]"If he is writing from Rome, it is ten years or so since they sent to him: and it seems strange they had had no opportunity to send to him in so long a time. And during that time he had passed through Philippi twice (Acts xx.1, 3, 6)" (Clogg, 77).

[19]L. Johnson at one time argued that the captivity letters were written during this period ("The Pauline Letters from Caesarea," *ExpTim* 68 [1956–57]: 24–26), but more recently has left the site of the imprisonment open (Johnson, 369).

praetorium may well have been Herod's praetorium (see Acts 23:35), where Paul was placed when he was taken to that city. It is further urged that the polemic against false teachers is similar to that against Judaizers[20] in earlier letters and that Philippians must accordingly be seen as early. (There is no such polemic in Romans, and it is likely that the Judaizers were not active by the time Paul got to Rome.) Against Caesarea is its distance from Philippi; we are up against much the same problem in fitting in the journeys as in the Roman hypothesis. The argument that the church in the center from which Paul wrote must have been of some size is a difficulty, for we have no reason for thinking of a strong church at Caesarea. Moreover, the contention about the Judaizers loses force when we reflect that the imprisonment at Caesarea immediately preceded that in Rome; there was no considerable interval for a change in the false teachers being opposed. There seems no convincing reason for holding that Caesarea was the place of origin.[21]

There have been strong advocates of Ephesus. We have no explicit statement that Paul was ever imprisoned in that city, but the apostle's words about his many imprisonments (2 Cor. 11:23) allows for periods of imprisonment other than the ones explicitly described—and certainly Paul was at one time in very serious trouble there (1 Cor. 15:32; see also 2 Cor. 1:8–11), which may well have meant time in prison, among other hardships. Ephesus was not far from Philippi (about one hundred miles), and the journeys mentioned in the letter would not have been difficult; indeed, one of them may be mentioned in Acts, for Paul sent Timothy to Macedonia from Ephesus (Acts 19:22; as far as we know, Timothy was not with Paul in Rome). He himself went to Macedonia from Ephesus (Acts 20:1—which might well be the fulfillment of his confident hope, mentioned in Phil. 2:24). The literary affinities of Philippians are usually held to be with Galatians, Corinthians, and Romans rather than with the later letters, Ephesians and Colossians,[22] though this may not mean much. A similar comment could be made about the suggestion that the Judaizing controversy is behind this letter and that this suits the earlier period better than the time Paul was in Rome, for we actually know little about what the Judaizers were doing at

---

[20]On the ambiguity surrounding this term, see chap. 11 n. 3 above.

[21]Gerald F. Hawthorne does not find that the evidence points conclusively to any city but argues that "it seems best for the sake of the understanding and explanation of Philippians to make a decision about where it was written and to exegete the text in the light of that decision. Hence, the assumption made in this commentary is that Philippians was written by Paul from prison in Caesarea" (*Philippians,* xliii). By contrast, Childs remarks, "Caesarea has been virtually eliminated as a possibility" (331).

[22]This argument is especially strong in the presentation of Frank S. Thielman, "Ephesus and the Literary Setting of Philippians," in *New Testament Greek and Exegesis, Fs.* Gerald F. Hawthorne; ed. Amy M. Donaldson and Timothy B. Sailors (Grand Rapids: Eerdmans, 2003), 205–23.

that later time. Attention is drawn to inscriptions showing that a section of the praetorian guard was stationed at Ephesus, which means that the reference to the praetorium would suit that city. Representatives of the emperor at Ephesus might well be those Paul has in mind when he refers to the saints of Caesar's household (4:22). Some scholars hold that certain parts of Philippians show that Paul had not been back to that city since he founded the church there (1:30; 4:15–16; see also 1:26; 2:12, 22), which would not be true at the time of the Roman imprisonment (cf. Acts 20:1–6). Others, probably correctly, do not think that Philippians proves so much. Another factor that is variously evaluated is the failure of Philippians to mention Luke, who certainly spent time with Paul in Rome (2 Tim. 4:11). The silence may be linked with the fact that Paul's Ephesian ministry is not in one of the "we" sections in Acts.[23]

This represents a strong but far from conclusive case for Ephesus as the place of Paul's imprisonment. It is objected that at the time Paul was in Ephesus he was giving a good deal of emphasis to the collection for the poor saints in Jerusalem. He mentions it in every letter known to have been written during that period, but there is no reference to it in Philippians. Furthermore, Paul speaks of the church in the city from which he wrote as divided, some supporting him and some being very opposed to him (Phil. 1:15–17), but the church at Ephesus, a church of Paul's own founding, seems at that period to have strongly supported him (see Acts 20:36–38). Most of the evidence can be interpreted in more than one way, and there seems no *decisive* reason for holding that this or any other city is proven. The traditional view has many supporters,[24] but this is also the case for Ephesus. Perhaps there is a little more to be said for Ephesus than for Rome, but we can say no more than this (and many would hold that we are not entitled to say even this).[25]

DATE

Dating this epistle depends, of course, on identifying the imprisonment during which Paul wrote it. If it was written during his time under guard in Rome, we must date it about 61–62. If it came from Caesarea, then its date will be a little

---

[23]G. S. Duncan argued the case strongly in his *St. Paul's Ephesian Ministry* (New York: Scribner's, 1929); he reiterated his view with minor modifications in "Were Paul's Imprisonment Epistles Written from Ephesus?" *ExpTim* 67 (1955–56): 163–66.

[24]One of the ablest defenses of this position is found in Markus Bockmuehl, *The Epistle to the Philippians*, BNTC (Peabody: Hendrickson, 1998), 25–32.

[25]Guthrie, who favors Rome as the site, says of Ephesus: "The cumulative effect of this evidence is undoubtedly strong but it falls short of proof. If the Roman hypothesis were proved untenable the Ephesian would probably be unchallenged as an alternative theory" (555). Kümmel, however, says that "the probability of the Ephesian hypothesis is the slightest" (235).

earlier, perhaps 59–60. If we could be sure that Paul wrote it at Ephesus or at Corinth, it would be a few years earlier still. In view of our uncertainties, we can scarcely do better than say that it was written during the period from the mid–50s to the early 60s.

OCCASION

We can discern a number of personal factors that may have prompted Paul to write this letter. *First* is the matter of Epaphroditus. This man had been sent to Paul by the Philippian church "to take care of [Paul's] needs" (Phil. 2:25). He apparently had discharged his task but had fallen ill, so ill indeed that he nearly died. The Philippians had heard of the illness, and Epaphroditus was upset about this (2:26–27). The Philippians perhaps had not realized just how serious Epaphroditus's illness had been, or perhaps some were critical of the time he had stayed with Paul. So Paul tells them to honor people like this man (2:29). It is also possible that there had been some criticism of Paul for keeping Epaphroditus with him instead of sending him back earlier. Whatever the exact circumstances, Paul writes to make clear to the Philippians that their messenger had done his task well and that he had undergone great danger in discharging it. Paul is sending him back with a warm commendation.

Second, the Philippian church had sent a gift to Paul (4:14–18; cf. 2:25). Since he does not mention this until quite late in the letter, it is probable that this is not the first time Paul has expressed his thanks. But it is plain that he greatly appreciated the help that this church had given him; he writes warmly about their generosity. A genuine appreciation of all that the Philippians had done for him is certainly part of the reason Paul picked up his pen.[26]

Third, Paul gives the Philippians news about his own circumstances (1:12ff.). The Philippians had been praying for him (1:19), and Paul recognizes them as partners with him in the gospel (1:5). Accordingly, he acquaints them with enough of his circumstances for them to see the way the gospel had been advanced by what was happening to him.

A further reason for writing may have been to commend Timothy to them and possibly to prepare the way for a visit he himself would pay (2:19–24). His commendation of Timothy suggests that the Philippians did not know him well. Paul wants to ensure that his young colleague will receive a warm welcome when he comes to Philippi.[27]

---

[26]On similarities and distinctions between Christian giving and receiving and the Greco-Roman benefaction system, see G. W. Peterman, *Paul's Gift from Philippi: Conventions of Gift-Exchange and Christian Giving,* SNTSMS 92 (Cambridge: Cambridge University Press, 1997).

[27]Small wonder, then, that Loveday C. A. Alexander, "Hellenistic Letter-Forms and the Structure of Philippians," *JSNT* 38 (1989): 87–110, suggests that Paul is

Apart from these personal motives, however, inevitably there were broader pastoral concerns. Although the Philippian church appears to be, in general, a spiritually thriving Christian community, there were some problems. The believers there faced at least some challenges from outsiders (1:28–30), and Paul recognizes their need for unity (2:1–4) and specifically pleads with two women to be at peace with each other (4:2). His exhortation to wholehearted service (1:27–2:18) may be connected with a recognition that all is not well. Paul offers warnings against false teachers (3:2–4), people who are "enemies of the cross of Christ" (3:18). But we go beyond the evidence when we make any one of these concerns the driving theme that controls the rest of the letter.[28]

TEXT

"The epistle presents no textual questions of importance," wrote Marvin R. Vincent almost a century ago.[29] At one level, nothing that has happened since then disturbs this verdict. Text-critical study, however, has become far more sophisticated since Vincent's day, so that even variants judged relatively minor when taken in isolation begin to assume importance as part of an exegetical and textual tradition as soon as they are placed within the *pattern* of variations of a MS or a text type. Recent study has carefully classified the 112 variants (not itself an exhaustive list) reported in NA26.[30]

ADOPTION INTO THE CANON

This is one of the letters about whose canonicity there appears to have been no dispute. Echoes of the epistle have been discerned in *1 Clement* and Ignatius, while Polycarp speaks of Paul as having written letters to the Philippian church (*Phil.* 3:2). It is included in Marcion's canon, and there is no evidence that anyone entertained doubts about its being part of the Pauline corpus.

---

writing a letter of cordial affection to cement the bonds between him and the Philippians that already exist. Bockmuehl, *The Epistle to the Philippians* (33) takes a similar view.

[28]E.g., Paul A. Holloway, *Consolation in Philippians: Philosophical Sources and Rhetorical Strategy*, SNTSMS 112 (Cambridge: Cambridge University Press, 2001), who argues that "consolation" is what Paul is offering as he writes from prison to Christians who are themselves suffering in various ways. That there is some suffering, and, correspondingly, some consolation, cannot be denied; that this constitutes Paul's controlling theme is far from evident.

[29]Marvin R. Vincent, *A Critical and Exegetical Commentary on the Epistles to the Philippians and to Philemon*, ICC (Edinburgh: T. & T. Clark, 1897), xxxvii.

[30]So Silva, *Philippians*, 22–27.

PHILIPPIANS IN RECENT STUDY

Apart from the regular plethora of articles dealing with details and the perennial discussion on the "Christ hymn" of Philippians 2 (discussed above under "Author"), three main areas have featured in recent study of this epistle: questions about the location of Paul's imprisonment at the time he wrote the letter, the unity of the letter, and the identification of Paul's opponents. There is nothing approaching unanimity on any of these subjects. We will ignore the location of Paul's imprisonment since we have said enough on that point and briefly probe the other two, ending this section with two or three specialist studies of peculiar interest.

The Unity of the Letter

Until comparatively recent times there has not been much discussion of the unity of Philippians. Some awkward sequences have been noticed, but these have been accepted as what we can expect in a dictated letter from a man like Paul. But in the last half-century there has been a tendency to find two or even three letters in what had been taken as a unity (Childs dates this tendency from 1950). A number of considerations are urged in support of the hypothesis.

1. In some places the break in sense is quite marked, notably at 3:1 and 4:9. Thus 3:1 appears to be leading into the end of a letter, but 3:2 goes off on a warning against false teachers; is it perhaps part of another Pauline letter? The transition from 4:9 to 4:10 also seems to many to require an explanation.

2. Epaphroditus is reported as very ill in 2:25–30, but there is no indication of this when the same man is referred to in 4:18. It is argued that there has been a change in his health, and that change presupposes a lapse of time.

3. Paul's opponents are not the same throughout the letter. There is a sharp, even merciless attack on false teachers in 3:2–4, but nothing in the preceding part of the letter prepares us for anything like this. The conclusion is drawn that fragments from more than one letter have been combined.[31]

4. Some scholars discern fragments in 4:1–9, 20–23. Both of these could be construed as appropriate ends of original letters.

5. Polycarp speaks of Paul as having written "epistles" to the Philippians (*Phil.* 3.2). This is evidence that more than one such letter was written, and it therefore opens the way for the hypothesis that some have been combined in our present Philippians.

Evidence of this sort leads a number of scholars to the conclusion that parts of two or perhaps three letters were put together by an unknown hand.[32] It is

---

[31]T. E. Pollard, however, compares chapter 3 with the rest of the letter and concludes that there are "marked verbal agreements between chapter iii as a whole and the rest of the letter" ("The Integrity of Philippians," *NTS* 13 [1966–67]: 66).

[32]"The composition breaks abruptly at 2,19; 3,2; 4:2,10. It is possible—but cannot be proved—that Phil. is a conflation of various writings which Paul composed and sent

not uncommon to see the first letter as 4:10–20 (thanks for the Philippians' gift), a second as 1:1–3:1; 4:4–7, 21–23 (warning against division), and a third as 3:2–4:3, 8–9 (attack on false teachers).

But the evidence is far from compelling.[33] Sudden breaks in sense are not altogether unknown in Paul (note the several breaks in Rom. 16:16–27), and those in Philippians are no greater than we might expect in a letter put together by this writer. The argument demands much more consistency in following a theme than Paul (or for that matter anyone else) always shows. It is better to see Philippians as one letter with the abrupt changes of subject that we all tend to introduce from time to time. The references to Epaphroditus are quite in order; there is no reason why the man's illness should be brought up every time he is mentioned. That a number of things in chapter 4 might be suitably used toward the end of a letter does not mean that any of them was deliberately intended to be so used. And the letters of which Polycarp speaks were not necessarily combined. We need suppose no more than that only one of them survives. (Most of Paul's correspondence has surely been lost; we cannot think that a man who could write so powerfully wrote no more than thirteen letters throughout the whole of his ministry.)[34]

More recently, Jeffrey Reed has subjected Philippians to a minute discourse analysis in hopes of sorting out the literary integrity of the epistle once and for all. His carefully understated conclusions about what can and cannot be demonstrated, and with what degree of plausibility, provide salutary warnings for those with more fertile imaginations.[35]

Paul's Opponents

Paul writes of opponents who "preach Christ out of envy and rivalry" (Phil. 1:15) and who try to stir up trouble for him (1:17). This makes it seem as though they are church members, but a little later he refers to them as opposing the church and goes on to speak of his readers as suffering for Christ (1:28–29). In 3:2 the

---

to Philippi at various times" (Wikenhauser, 437). He adds, "At any rate, the entire Epistle bears the stamp of Paul's language and style."

[33]See David E. Garland, "The Composition and Unity of Philippians: Some Neglected Literary Factors," *NovT* 27 (1985): 141–73.

[34]B. S. Mackay has a strong refutation of the idea that Philippians is made up of three letters ("Further Thoughts on Philippians," *NTS* 7 [1960–61]: 161–70).

[35]Jeffrey T. Reed, *A Discourse Analysis of Philippians*. Several essays anticipating Reed appealed to rhetoric or to textlinguistics (= discourse analysis) to discuss the unity of the book: e.g., Duane F. Watson, "A Rhetorical Analysis of Philippians and Its Implications for the Unity Question," *NovT* 30 (1988): 57–88; V. Koperski, "Textlinguistics and the Integrity of Philippians: A Critique of Wolfgang Schenk's Arguments for a Compilation Hypothesis," *EphThLov* 68 (1992): 331–67; David Alan Black, "The Discourse Structure of Philippians: A Study in Textlinguistics," *NovT* 37 (1995): 16–49.

opponents are "dogs," and the subsequent references to circumcision and to Paul's fleshly qualifications in Judaism indicate that they are Judaizers of some sort. Paul goes on to say that he has not attained perfection (3:12); thus, it is at least possible that the false teachers claimed that they did, although that is a far cry from being a necessary inference. Later he writes of "enemies of the cross of Christ" and insists that "their god is their stomach, and their glory is in their shame" (3:18–19).

It is possible that all this refers to one group of people. Klijn refuses to see a variety of opponents: "The most acceptable solution for the problem is to assume that the persons referred to are Jews."[36] This view has not won wide acceptance, and it certainly seems more likely that Paul is confronted by people who are in some sense Christians.[37] How else would they be preaching the gospel, however maliciously (1:15)? (Klijn does not bring this verse into his argument.) The references to libertarianism ("their god is their stomach") and to perfectionism point some critics to a form of Gnosticism or to some kind of pre-gnostic teaching. The latter is a possibility, as long as one does not smuggle in the full-blown Gnosticism of the second century; evidence of its existence in Paul's day is lacking. Another view is that the opponents were Judaizers and that "their god is their stomach" refers to Jewish food laws. We can say only that in the present confused discussion, several possibilities are regularly canvassed in the literature. One of the most promising approaches carefully analyzes the nature of Paul's rhetorical argument to try to gain clarity regarding the opponents he is confronting.[38]

It is likely that Paul envisages opponents of more than one kind. He seems to be fighting on two fronts, being opposed within the church by some who did not agree with his preaching, and outside it by some who made the whole church suffer. The references to Jewish practices make it clear that either Jewish opponents or Judaizers were involved, who may well have held to some opinions that were later taken up into the great gnostic systems.[39]

THE CONTRIBUTION OF PHILIPPIANS

Many of Paul's letters were called forth by the need to set things right in a given church, to oppose false teaching, or to correct lax practice. But Philippians is

---

[36]Klijn, 110. He concludes his discussion of the point by noting, "The opponents, therefore, are Jews who will not tolerate Paul in their own missionary territory."

[37]H. Koester argues that the people opposed in chapter 3 are "Christian missionaries of Jewish origin and background" ("The Purpose of the Polemic of a Pauline Fragment," *NTS* 8 [1961–62]: 331).

[38]E.g., David A. deSilva, "No Confidence in the Flesh: The Meaning and Function of Philippians 3:2–21," *TrinJ* 15 (1994): 27–54.

[39]Johnson thinks that they may not have been Paul's opponents at all and that he refers to them as a counterexample to show his correspondents what they must not do (346).

Many of Paul's letters were called forth by serious problems in churches. But Philippians is that comparative rarity: a letter to a church of Paul's own foundation with which he is, on the whole, well pleased.

that comparative rarity: a letter to a church of Paul's own foundation with which he is, on the whole, well pleased. There is something wholesome and edifying in the quiet thanksgiving Paul sends to the church in Philippi as he recalls their support of him and his ministry, something gently probing about his instructions on giving and receiving—not least how he reflects, or dissents from, the expectations of his surrounding culture. This letter reveals something of the apostle's satisfaction when his converts made progress in the faith. He does oppose false teaching here as elsewhere, but the main thrust of the letter lies elsewhere. As he is writing, he makes some comments on the opponents he and the Philippian church faced, but for the most part he is taken up with more enjoyable things.

Outstanding, of course, is the hymn in 2:6–11. Although controversy surrounds it, this passage brings readers a clear message about the greatness of Christ and his condescension in taking a lowly place to bring salvation. Paul thought of Christ as one who was "in very nature God," who took the lowest place and died on the cross to bring salvation. Now he is exalted to the highest possible place, and Paul looks forward to the time when every knee will bow to him and every tongue confess him as Lord. As Christ was vindicated, so also shall his people be, and that constitutes powerful incentive to press on (2:12–13). Moreover, on any reading this hymn is early—at least as early as Philippians, and maybe earlier—so it constitutes powerful evidence for the confession of a high Christology at a very early date in the church's life.

The letter is also an encouragement to Christians who find others preaching the gospel in ways they do not like. It is of permanent value to us all to have it laid down so firmly that what matters is that the gospel be preached (1:12–18). Paul rejoices in this, and indeed the note of joy is sounded throughout this letter (the noun χαρά [*chara*, "joy"] occurs five times, and the verb χαίρειν [*chairein*, "to rejoice"] nine times in this short letter; only Luke with twelve has more occurrences of the verb). That Christians are a rejoicing people is important.

Also significant is what Paul calls "partnership in the gospel" (1:5). Throughout the letter there is a harmony between writer and readers and a series of glimpses of what it is to work together in the cause of Christ. Paul encourages his friends, assures them of his affection for them, teaches them lessons from his own circumstances, and adds to their knowledge of the Christian way. He prays for them, warns them about false teaching, exhorts them to steadfastness in the Christian life, and sends Timothy to them. In the nature of the case, we do not learn as much of what the Philippians contributed to the relationship, but it is clear that they had a concern and affection for Paul, that they sent one of their number to look after him when he was in trouble, that they sent him gifts at a time when no other church helped him, and that they obeyed his directions. It is a beautiful picture of Christian harmony.

The epistle has a notable section in which Paul emphasizes the importance of concentrating on the essentials over against "confidence in the flesh" (3:4). He stresses the place of the cross and the resurrection in Christian salvation. The suffering of the Christian fits in with this. Paul draws attention to the way the gospel is advanced through his own sufferings (1:14–18; cf. 2:16–17), and he sees the sufferings of the Philippians (as they experience the same struggle as he), as God's gift to them (1:29–30).[40] The important thing is the service of Christ. Then at the end of the letter, he records his magnificent assurance that "my God will meet all your needs according to the riches of his glory in Christ Jesus" (4:19).

BIBLIOGRAPHY

Loveday A. **Alexander**, "Hellenistic Letter-Forms and the Structure of Philippians," *JSNT* 37 (1989): 87–110 ▓F. W. **Beare**, *The Epistle to the Philippians*, HNTC (New York: Harper & Bros., 1959) ▓David Alan **Black**, "The Discourse Structure of Philippians: A Study in Textlinguistics," *NovT* 37 (1995): 16–49 ▓L. Gregory **Bloomquist**, *The Function of Suffering in Philippians*, JSNTSup 78 (Sheffield: JSOT Press, 1993) ▓Markus **Bockmuehl**, *The Epistle to the Philippians*, BNTC (Peabody: Hendrickson, 1998) ▓P. **Bonnard**, *L'épître de saint Paul aux Philippiens et l'épître aux Colossiens*, CNT (Neuchâtel: Delachaux & Niestlé, 1950) ▓F. F. **Bruce**, *Philippians*, GNC (San Francisco: Harper & Row, 1983) ▓idem, "St. Paul in Macedonia: 3. The Philippian Correspondence," *BJRL* 63 (1981): 260–84 ▓C. O. **Buchanan**, "Epaphroditus' Sickness and the Letter to the Philippians," *EQ* 36 (1964): 157–66 ▓G. B. **Caird**, *Paul's Letters from Prison* (Oxford: Oxford University Press, 1976) ▓D. A. **Carson**, *Basics for Believers: An Exposition of Philippians* (Grand Rapids: Baker Book House, 1996) ▓W. J. **Dalton**, "The Integrity of Philippians," *Bib* 60 (1979): 97–102 ▓David A. **deSilva**, "No Confidence in the Flesh: The Meaning and Function of Philippians 3:2–21," *TrinJ* 15 (1994): 27–54 ▓S. **Dockx**, "Lieu et date de l'épître aux Philippiens," *RevBib* 80 (1973): 230–46 ▓G. S. **Duncan**, *St. Paul's Ephesian Ministry* (New York: Scribner's, 1929) ▓idem, "Were Paul's Imprisonment Epistles Written from Ephesus?" *ExpTim* 67 (1955–56): 163–66 ▓James D. G. **Dunn**, *Christology in the Making* (London: SCM, 1980) ▓Gordon D. **Fee**, *Paul's Letter to the Philippians*, NICNT (Grand Rapids: Eerdmans, 1995) ▓G. **Friedrich**, *Der Brief an die Philipper*, NTD (Göttingen: Vandenhoeck & Ruprecht, 1962) ▓David E. **Garland**, "The Composition and Unity of Philippians: Some Neglected Literary Factors," *NovT* 27 (1985): 141–73 ▓Joachim **Gnilka**, *Der Philipperbrief*, HTKNT (Freiburg: Herder, 1976) ▓Gerald F. **Hawthorne**, *Philippians*, WBC (Waco: Word, 1983) ▓Paul A.

---

[40]See L. Gregory Bloomquist, *The Function of Suffering in Philippians*, JSNTSup 78 (Sheffield: JSOT Press, 1993).

Holloway, *Consolation in Philippians: Philosophical Sources and Rhetorical Strategy*, SNTSMS 112 (Cambridge: Cambridge University Press, 2001) ▪Morna D. **Hooker**, "Philippians 2:6–11," in *Jesus und Paulus, Fs.* Werner Georg Kümmel, ed. E. Earle Ellis and Erich Grässer, 2nd ed. (Göttingen: Vandenhoeck & Ruprecht, 1978), 151–64 ▪Roy W. **Hoover**, "The Harpagmos Enigma: A Philological Solution," *HTR* 64 (1971): 95–119 ▪J. L. **Houlden**, *Paul's Letters from Prison* (London: SCM, 1977) ▪R. **Jewett**, "Conflicting Movements in the Early Church as Reflected in Philippians," *NovT* 12 (1970): 362–90 ▪L. **Johnson**, "The Pauline Letters from Caesarea," *ExpTim* 68 (1956–57): 24–26 ▪E. **Käsemann**, "A Critical Analysis of Philippians 2:5–11," in *God and Christ: Existence and Province*, ed. Robert W. Funk, *JTC* 5 (New York: Harper & Row, 1968), 45–88 ▪H. **Koester**, "The Purpose of the Polemic of a Pauline Fragment" *NTS* 8 (1961–62): 317–32 ▪V. **Koperski**, "Textlinguistics and the Integrity of Philippians: A Critique of Wolfgang Schenk's Arguments for a Compilation Hypothesis," *EphThLov* 68 (1992): 331–67 ▪J. B. **Lightfoot**, *St. Paul's Epistle to the Philippians* (1868; reprint, Grand Rapids: Zondervan, 1965) ▪B. S. **Mackay**, "Further Thoughts on Philippians," *NTS* 7 (1960–61): 161–70 ▪A. J. **Malherbe**, "The Beasts at Ephesus," *JBL* 87 (1968): 71–80 ▪Ralph P. **Martin**, *Carmen Christi*, SNTSMS 4 (Cambridge: Cambridge University Press, 1967) ▪idem, *Philippians*, NCB (Greenwood, S.C.: Attic, 1976) ▪Richard R. **Melick** Jr., *Philippians, Colossians, Philemon*, NAC (Nashville: Broadman, 1991) ▪C. F. D. **Moule**, "Further Reflections on Philippians 2, 5–11," in *Apostolic History and the Gospel*, ed. W. Ward Gasque and Ralph P. Martin (Grand Rapids: Eerdmans, 1970), 264–76 ▪Peter **Oakes**, *Philippians: From People to Letter*, SNTSMS 110 (Cambridge: Cambridge University Press, 2001) ▪Peter T. **O'Brien**, *The Epistle to the Philippians: A Commentary on the Greek Text*, NIGTC (Grand Rapids: Eerdmans, 1991) ▪Carolyn **Osiek**, *Philippians, Philemon*, ANTC (Nashville: Abingdon, 2000) ▪G. W. **Peterman**, *Paul's Gift from Philippi: Conventions of Gift-Exchange and Christian Giving*, SNTSMS 92 (Cambridge: Cambridge University Press, 1997) ▪T. E. **Pollard**, "The Integrity of Philippians," *NTS* 13 (1966–67): 57–66 ▪B. D. **Rahtjen**, "The Three Letters of Paul to the Philippians," *NTS* 6 (1959–60): 167–73 ▪Jeffrey T. **Reed**, *A Discourse Analysis of Philippians: Method and Rhetoric in the Debate over Literary Integrity*, JSNTSup 136 (Sheffield: Sheffield Academic Press, 1997) ▪Wolfgang **Schenk**, *Die Philipperbrief des Paulus: Kommentar* (Stuttgart: Kohlhammer, 1984) ▪Moisés **Silva**, *Philippians*, WEC (Chicago: Moody, 1988) ▪Vincent **Taylor**, *The Atonement in New Testament Teaching* (London: Epworth, 1945) ▪idem, *The Person of Christ in New Testament Teaching* (London: Macmillan, 1959) ▪Frank S. **Thielman**, "Ephesus and the Literary Setting of Philippians," in *New Testament Greek and Exegesis, Fs.* Gerald F. Hawthorne, ed. Amy M. Donaldson and Timothy B. Sailors (Grand Rapids: Eerdmans, 2003), 205–223 ▪Marvin R. **Vincent**, *Critical and Exegetical Commentary on the Epistles to the Philippians and to Philemon*, ICC (Edinburgh: T. & T. Clark, 1897) ▪Duane F. **Watson**, "A Rhetorical

Analysis of Philippians and Its Implications for the Unity Question," *NovT* 30 (1988): 57–88 ▥Peter **Wick**, *Der Philipperbrief: Der formale Aufbau des Briefes als Schlüssel zum Verständnis seines Inhalts,* BWANT 135 (Stuttgart: Kohlhammer, 1994) ▥N. T. **Wright**, "ἁρπαγμός and the Meaning of Philippians 2:5–11," *JTS* 37 (1986): 321–52.

CHAPTER FIFTEEN

COLOSSIANS

CONTENTS

The opening greeting (1:1–2) is followed by thanksgiving for the faith and the love of the Colossian Christians (1:3–13). Paul then launches into a magnificent section on the greatness of Christ (1:15–20) in which he brings out the truth that he is "the image of the invisible God," that he was active in the creation of all things—indeed, we are also told (uniquely in the New Testament) that all things were made *for* him—and that he is the head of the church. The apostle goes on to Christ's reconciling work (1:21–23) and relates something of his own sufferings as he works for Christ, of his struggling for believers such as those in Colosse and Laodicea whom he has not met (1:24–2:5).

Paul exhorts his readers to live in Christ and warns them against being taken captive by a "hollow and deceptive philosophy" (2:6–8). He comes back to the greatness of Christ, in whom "all the fullness of the Deity lives in bodily form," and reminds them of the salvation Christ has brought about (2:9–15). In the light of this they should not submit to people's ideas about food laws and religious festivals (2:16–23). This leads to the truth that believers have been "raised with Christ"; they should live in accordance with this great fact. Paul goes into some detail about the things they should avoid and the things they should do (3:1–17); he gives directions about the way people should live in Christian households, speaking of wives, husbands, children, fathers, slaves, and masters (3:18–4:1). He rounds off this section with injunctions to pray and to be wise in their behavior toward outsiders (4:2–6).

Tychicus, he says, will bring the Colossians news of him, as will Onesimus. This leads to greetings from a number of Paul's companions to the Colossian Christians (4:7–15). There is an injunction to circulate this letter and to exchange it with one to the Laodiceans, a command for Archippus (4:16–17), and a short form of the usual Pauline ending to a letter (4:18).

AUTHOR

The authorship of this letter has been the subject of considerable discussion. Until the nineteenth century no serious question about Pauline authorship seems to have been raised. Even then questions were raised only by a minority of scholars. In the period between the two wars in the last century, Bultmann and others began to speak of Colossians as "deutero-Pauline," and that tendency has grown since 1945. It is plain enough that there is a connection with Paul, but many recent scholars think that a follower of Paul rather than the apostle himself actually penned the book. No new evidence has been adduced; the considerations urged against the traditional view have simply come to be seen as more weighty. Some, including Kümmel, Moule, Bruce, O'Brien, and Garland,[1] still argue for Paul as the author; others think "deutero-Pauline" is a better description.[2]

The letter claims to have been written by Paul in the opening (1:1), in the "I, Paul" of 1:23, and in "I, Paul, write this greeting in my own hand" (4:18; cf., this is "the distinguishing mark in all my letters" [2 Thess. 3:17]). This claim has usually been accepted through the centuries, but in modern times it has been disputed on three main grounds: language, theology, and the relation to Ephesians.[3]

---

[1]Kümmel, 340–46; C. F. D. Moule, *The Epistles of Paul the Apostle to the Colossians and to Philemon* (Cambridge: Cambridge University Press, 1962); F. F. Bruce, *The Epistles to the Colossians, to Philemon, and to the Ephesians,* NICNT (Grand Rapids: Eerdmans, 1984); Peter T. O'Brien, *Colossians, Philemon,* WBC (Waco, Tex.: Word, 1982); David E. Garland, *Colossians/Philemon,* NIVAC (Grand Rapids: Zondervan, 1998).

[2]E.g., Charles Masson, *L'épître aux Colossiens,* CNT (Paris: Delachaux & Niestlé, 1950); E. Lohse, *Colossians and Philemon,* Hermeneia (Philadelphia: Fortress Press, 1971); E. Schweizer, *The Letter to the Colossians: A Commentary* (Minneapolis: Augsburg, 1982; German original, EKKNT, 1976); Joachim Gnilka, *Der Kolosserbrief,* HTKNT (Freiburg: Herder, 1980); Marxsen, 176–86; Perrin/Duling, 207–18; cautiously, Brown, 610–17.

[3]Also advanced are one or two fairly idiosyncratic reasons for denying the authenticity of this epistle. For instance, Marxsen finds "the most serious doubts as regards the Pauline authorship" arising from the link between 1:21–23 and the statements about Epaphras: "the authority of Paul is claimed for the authorization of other men." Marxsen speaks of the letter's "emphasis upon the apostolate—tantamount in effect to the doctrine of 'apostolic succession'" (180). This is more than curious. The only use of "apostle" is in 1:1, and the only references to Epaphras are in 1:7 (where we learn that he is a "dear fellow servant" and "a faithful minister of Christ on our behalf," and that he brought news) and in 4:12 (he is "one of you" and "a servant of Christ Jesus," and he sends greetings). This is a very slender basis on which to erect such a far-reaching doctrine as apostolic succession. It surely presents no serious obstacle to seeing Paul as the author. Although E. Lohse does not argue for Pauline authorship, he points out that in Colossians "teaching is described as a charge of the entire church" and thus not of successors of the apostles; "the church is not bound to a definite order of office and of offices" ("Pauline Theology in the Letter to the Colossians," *NTS* 15 [1968–69]: 216).

Language and Style

Colossians has quite a number of hapax legomena, but this is not a strong argument against the authenticity of this epistle, for the same is true of all of Paul's letters. Harrison has shown that in this respect Colossians falls well within the normal Pauline range.[4] Synonyms such as "wisdom and understanding" (1:9) and "teach and admonish" (3:16) are joined together, a phenomenon alleged to be un-Pauline, as is the verbose style. The latter judgment is somewhat subjective; indeed, it is precarious to lay down how far Paul can differ from the style we find in the generally accepted letters. All the more is this the case, in that Colossians contains a number of stylistic features found elsewhere in the New Testament only in Paul.[5] Differences in vocabulary may be accounted for in part at least by his use of words needed to oppose a new heresy, and in style because he makes use of poetic forms. Furthermore, most scholars hold that there is a good deal of traditional matter in this letter, and this will account for some unusual vocabulary and style.

Theology

This objection comes in two forms: the absence of important Pauline concepts, and the presence of concepts of which Paul makes no use elsewhere. Under the first head is the absence of such characteristic Pauline terms as justification, law, and salvation. But this proves little, because a similar observation may be made about some of Paul's other epistles. There was no need (and no place) for the use of every Pauline concept or term in every letter. Actually, this argument may be used in favor of Pauline authorship. Although Paul himself did in fact omit some of his characteristic doctrines in each of his letters, it is very difficult to think of someone professing to write in Paul's name who would omit all the Pauline topics that are absent from this letter. Surely it would be an elementary precaution to use the apostle's most characteristic doctrines.

Under the second head, this letter refers to cosmic aspects of Christ's person (1:16–20; also 2:9–10) and to his headship over the church, viewed as his body (1:18; 2:19). It is also suggested that 1:15–20 is the adaptation of a pre-Christian hymn. This latter is no real objection, for if a pre-Christian writing has been adapted or incorporated, this could just as easily have been done by Paul as by an imitator.

> Colossians has quite a number of hapax legomena, but this is not a strong argument against the authenticity of this epistle, for the same is true of all of Paul's letters.

---

[4]P. N. Harrison, *The Problem of the Pastoral Epistles* (London: Oxford University Press, 1921), 20–22.

[5]Kümmel lists such features as pleonastic καί (*kai,* "and") after διὰ τοῦτο (*dia touto,* lit. "on account of which," 1:9), οἱ ἅγιοι αὐτοῦ (*hoi hagioi autou,* "his saints," 1:26), ἐν μέρει (*en merei,* here with the rare meaning "concerning" or "with regard to," 2:16) and others. He concludes by saying, "The language and style of Colossians, therefore, give no cause to doubt the Pauline origin of the Epistle" (241).

As for the cosmic Christ, while what is said in Colossians is an advance on what we see in the undisputed Pauline letters, we surely have the beginnings of the concept in such expressions as "one Lord, Jesus Christ, through whom all things came and through whom we live" (1 Cor. 8:6), and "at the name of Jesus every knee should bow, in heaven and on earth and under the earth" (Phil. 2:10; cf. also the στοιχεῖα [*stoicheia*, perhaps "basic principles"] from whom Christ set believers free [Gal. 4:3, 9]). The development in Colossians is real, but it is not divorced from its roots in earlier Pauline writings. Furthermore, Paul has the idea of the church as a body in a number of writings (Rom. 12:4–5; cf. Gal. 3:28; the concept is developed in 1 Cor. 12). It is but a step from this to the idea that Christ is the head of the body.[6] We cannot judge such objections as these decisive.

Perhaps the theological argument that has garnered most support for inauthenticity has to do with eschatology. On the basis of 2:12–13; 3:1 ("having been buried with him in baptism, in which you were also raised with him through your faith in the working of God . . . God made you alive with Christ. . . . Since, then, you have been raised with Christ"), many have argued that Colossians betrays a form of realized eschatology that destroys the tension between the "already" and the "not yet" that is characteristic of the authentic Paul.[7] The rebuttal of Luke Timothy Johnson is precisely right:

> Apart from the issue of how much latitude an author has before he reaches self-inconsistency, and apart from the rather obvious shifts in eschatological emphasis in the undisputed letters, this charge simply misreads these sections of Colossians. It is clear from 2:20 and 3:1–4 that the "death" to sin in baptism leads to a "resurrection life" not of glory but of faith, which requires of the Colossians a conversion of their behavior. Their "life" indeed is "hid with God in Christ"; only at the end, "when Christ our life appears," will they themselves be in a state of "glory" (3:4). The language is slightly different, but the thought is virtually identical to that found in Rom. 6:1–14. And though the language underscores the transformation of human character that has occurred through faith and baptism—one has died to the old and been raised to new life—it should not be taken as a statement on eschatology as such.[8]

---

[6]It is, nevertheless, a distinct step to move from picturing the church as a body whose members are the members of the church and that is animated by the Spirit, to picturing the church as a body of which Christ is the head. See the useful essay by Edmund P. Clowney, "Interpreting the Biblical Models of the Church: A Hermeneutical Deepening of Ecclesiology," in *Biblical Interpretation and the Church*, ed. D. A. Carson (Exeter: Paternoster, 1984), 64–109.

[7]So, for instance, Petr Pokorný, *Colossians: A Commentary* (Peabody: Hendrickson, 1991), 126–35.

[8]Johnson, 394–95.

A few authors have suggested that Timothy, who is named in the first verse, functioned as Paul's amanuensis, and was given considerable freedom,[9] even though Paul himself authenticated the final product with his own hand (4:18). This is possible, but the freedom assigned to an (ostensible) amanuensis must in this case be limited, considering the number of first-person references the apostle himself makes in the letter (1:23–25; 1:29–2:5; 4:3–18).[10] Certainly this theory is preferable to the one that judges the present "shell" to be non-Pauline, while affirming that there are recoverable "authentic fragments"[11]—a theory which masterfully combines the uncertainties of predominantly subjective judgments regarding authenticity with the subjective judgments of many forms of source criticism.

Relation to Ephesians

Doubtless Ephesians and Colossians stand in close relationship. Some scholars argue that one person would never produce two such similar writings, that the resemblances mean that the author of one of these letters has written in imitation of the other. This is a very subjective argument. It may be countered by saying that the two epistles are best understood as the expressions of the one writer, more or less repeating some of the same thoughts on two occasions not very far removed from one another and for somewhat different audiences. In any case, it is a curious argument that we should reject a writing as Pauline because of its resemblances to another writing in the Pauline corpus.

It seems, then, that the arguments against Pauline authorship are not decisive. They do not reckon sufficiently with the fact that a mind like Paul's was capable of adaptation to new situations and to the adoption of new vocabulary and new concepts where older ones do not meet the need.[12] They also fail to give a reason for addressing the letter to the unimportant town of Colosse.[13] Surely an imitator would have selected a city of some importance, such as Laodicea or

---

[9]E.g., Schweizer, *The Letter to the Colossians,* 23–24; James D. G. Dunn, *The Epistles to the Colossians and Philemon,* NIGTC (Grand Rapids: Eerdmans, 1996), 35–39.

[10]So, rightly, Pokorný, *Colossians: A Commentary,* 18 (though Pokorný himself opts for pseudonymity).

[11]So Markus Barth and Helmut Blanke, *Colossians,* AB 34B (Garden City: Doubleday, 1994), 125–26.

[12]L. Cerfaux has commented: "It is not wise to attempt a priori to set limits on the potentialities of a thought as original and powerful as that of St. Paul, which changes very rapidly and rises to new syntheses. It is plausible that the reaction against the syncretism of Colossae was a powerful stimulant to Paul's thought" (Robert/Feuillet, 490).

[13]Many (e.g., Arthur G. Patzia, *Ephesians, Colossians, Philemon,* NIBC 10 [Peabody: Hendrickson, 1990], 3) have pointed out that the city of Colosse declined in importance during the Hellenistic and Roman periods, and in Paul's day was certainly the least important city in the area, entirely eclipsed by Laodicea (ten miles to the west)

Hierapolis. In view of the letter's claim and of the many undoubtedly Pauline features it manifests, we should accept it as an authentic Pauline writing.

This is supported by a number of links with Philemon, which almost all scholars take to be a genuine letter of the apostle. In both epistles, greetings are sent from Aristarchus, Mark, Epaphras, Luke, and Demas, who plainly were with Paul when he wrote (Col. 4:10–14; Philem. 23–24). Onesimus, the slave at the center of the letter to Philemon, is sent with Tychicus and referred to as "one of you" (Col. 4:9). Archippus, "our fellow soldier" (Philem. 2), is given a message to "complete the work" he has received in the Lord (Col. 4:17). In light of such references it is difficult to argue that Colossians was not written by Paul.[14]

PROVENANCE

When he wrote this letter, Paul was in prison (Col. 4:3, 10, 18). For the general possibilities of Rome, Caesarea and Ephesus, see the discussion above on Philippians (chap. 14, under "Provenance"). It is probable that Ephesians, Colossians, and Philemon were written from the same place. The personal links mentioned in the previous paragraph are clear evidence that Colossians and Philemon were written at much the same time, while the case for Ephesians rests on the general similarities to Colossians. But there are no such personal links or general resemblances in Philippians, and that letter may have been written from a different place.[15]

Paul's request for a guest room to be prepared (Philem. 22) favors Ephesus as the place of origin of Colossians and Philemon, for Colosse was not far from that city, while preparations for a guest room might be premature if Paul was in Rome. Against this is the fact that Luke and Mark are mentioned as being with Paul when he wrote, but Acts does not include the Ephesian ministry among the "we" sections, and Mark was not with Paul on the second missionary journey (Acts 15:36–41). The runaway slave Onesimus had come to know Paul in his prison, and he would find it easier to get to Ephesus from Colosse than to Rome. He may have preferred, however, to go farther away and lose himself in the anonymity of populous Rome. If Ephesians was written in the same general

---

and Hierapolis (sixteen miles to the northwest). Indeed, Colosse was devastated by an earthquake in A.D. 61, and never rebuilt.

[14]Indeed, some have argued that the most compelling reason for accepting the authenticity of Colossians is its artless links with Philemon: e.g., Murray J. Harris, *Colossians and Philemon,* EGGNT (Grand Rapids: Eerdmans, 1991), 3–4.

[15]Bo Reicke argues that Philippians was written from Rome and the other three from Caesarea ("Caesarea, Rome, and the Captivity Epistles," in *Apostolic History and the Gospel, Fs.* F. F. Bruce, ed. W. Ward Gasque and Ralph P. Martin [Exeter: Paternoster, 1970], 277–86).

period as Colossians, it is unlikely that Paul would write to the Ephesian church while he was in jail in that very city. But this can be countered by arguing that Ephesians was originally a circular and could have been written anywhere. The arguments for and against Ephesus seem to cancel each other out.[16]

Caesarea is a possibility, but it is hard to envisage a reason that Onesimus would choose that city to flee to. Furthermore, we do not know that Paul there enjoyed the same kind of liberty to engage in evangelism that he enjoyed in Rome (Acts 28:30–31; but cf. Acts 24:23). Again, Paul's request for accommodation is not likely from Caesarea, for when he wrote Colossians, he was hoping for speedy release; while he was in Caesarea, however, his only hope of release lay in an appeal to Caesar. Moreover, if Paul were writing from Caesarea, we might have expected him to include Philip among those Jews who "have proved a comfort to me" (Col. 4:11 cf. Acts 21:8).

Objections to these other centers leave us with Rome. Some object that Paul's plan was to go to Spain, not Colosse, after Rome. Nevertheless, he may well have abandoned that plan, and, if one holds that the best interpretation of the Pastoral Epistles is that they were written by the apostle after his *first* Roman imprisonment before his final and fatal Roman imprisonment, the Pastoral Epistles themselves provide evidence that Paul circulated again in Asia Minor.[17] Moreover, Luke was with Paul in Rome (Acts 28:14; 2 Tim. 4:11) and apparently Aristarchus was also (Acts 27:2; cf. Col. 4:10). We cannot say that any center is conclusively favored by the evidence, but more can be said for Rome than for anywhere else.

DATE

There is not much evidence for the date, and clearly a good deal depends on our conclusion about the place of imprisonment. If we think that Rome was the place, we will have a date in the early 60s, probably 61, since after that Colosse was so devastated by earthquake that it is inconceivable that the destruction would not have been mentioned by any informed and compassionate writer.[18] If Paul wrote from a city other than Rome, the date of composition could be backed up into the late 50s.

---

[16]Martin, however, favors an imprisonment near Ephesus (2.216–22).

[17]See the discussion in chap. 17 of this volume.

[18]Indeed, Bo Reicke, *Re-examining Paul's Letters: The History of the Pauline Correspondence* (Harrisburg: Trinity Press International, 2001), 76, writes, "All attempts to make Colossians a deutero-Pauline composition of the period A.D. 70–100 are rendered null and void by documents that demonstrate that Colosse lost its cultural importance through an earthquake in 61."

OCCASION

The church at Colosse was not of Paul's foundation (2:1). Epaphras had apparently been the preacher who brought the Christian gospel to that city (1:7). Paul describes him as "a faithful minister of Christ on our behalf" (1:7), which seems to mean that Paul had sent him to Colosse. Paul could not preach in every place, and it made sense to send trusted fellow workers to proclaim the gospel in places where he could not go himself. If so, he would retain an interest in the progress of such a church, and this letter may well have arisen out of such an interest. The apostle had heard that some false teachers had come to Colosse, so he wrote to refute their errors, lest the fledgling church be harmed.

The precise nature of the false teaching is not clear (as is always the case when we have none of the teaching itself, but only what is written to refute it), but some things are fairly plain. Paul puts emphasis on the supremacy of Christ (1:15–19), so it seems that the false teachers detracted in some way from a high Christology. Evidently they thought that Christ was no more than a beginning; to go on to spiritual maturity, it was necessary to follow their rules and practices. They may well have spoken of Christ in warm terms, but in the last resort they saw him as a created being and therefore as less than God. In the face of such teachings, Paul insists that Christ is "the image of the invisible God" and the Father's agent in bringing creation about (1:15–16). Every created thing owes its existence to him, even the angelic powers that these teachers invited people to worship. All God's "fullness" dwells in Christ (1:19; 2:9). He is supreme over all, and there is no way of going on to some higher spirituality by deserting him.

Paul also speaks of "hollow and deceptive philosophy" (2:8). Unfortunately for us, he does not explain what this means—the Colossians knew quite well, so why should he?

It seems that the false teaching had a Hellenistic aspect: "wisdom and knowledge" (2:3) may point to Greek roots, as perhaps do asceticism ("harsh treatment of the body" [2:23]) and "fullness" (πλήρωμα [plērōma], 1:19). There are puzzling references in 2:8, 20 to what TNIV calls "elemental spiritual forces" (τὰ στοιχεία τοῦ κόσμου [ta stoicheia tou kosmou]), an expression that some take to mean "elemental spirits" (RSV) and some, "elementary teaching" (KJV "rudiments"; cf. Heb. 5:12).[19] "Elemental spirits" would mean that the false teaching found a place

---

[19]τὸ στοιχεῖον (to stoicheion) originally meant "one of a row" and was used of such things as the alphabet (letters placed in a row), which leads to elementary teaching in general (the ABCs of the subject). Again, letters are the elements of which words are made up, and the word came to be used of the elements of which the universe is composed ("the elements" of 2 Pet. 3:10, 12). The word occurs again in Gal. 4:3, 9. Bruce holds that in both Galatians and here we should think that "in the divine providence there was a time when the stoicheia fulfilled a supervisory role in the lives of the people of God, as a slave-attendant looked after a freeborn child till he came of age. The coming of age of the people

for the worship of spirits, "elementary teaching" that the Colossians had failed to progress in the faith and were still taken up with elementary things.

But we must not see the error as simply a Greek aberration, for the references to circumcision (Col. 2:11; 3:11) show that there were Jewish elements in it as well.[20] "Human tradition" (2:8) may also point to Jewish teaching, perhaps the tradition of the elders. The Jews did not worship angels, but they had quite an interest in them; "the worship of angels" (2:18) may refer to some development of Jewish speculation about these celestial beings. Sabbath observance (2:16) was plainly Jewish, and the religious festivals and new-moon celebrations with which it is linked may also be Jewish in origin. The food regulations (2:16, 21) may be Jewish, but many religions had such regulations, so we cannot insist on it.

Our best understanding of the false teaching, then, is that it was a blend of Jewish and Hellenistic teachings.[21] Such syncretism was a feature of the ancient world, and it need not surprise us that when it appeared, it constituted an attraction for new and imperfectly instructed Christians: it was the sort of teaching that attracted first-century people.[22] Indeed, it is precisely because of the prevalence of such syncretism that Morna D. Hooker can question whether there was any Colossian heresy. She points out that if we find a modern Christian pastor telling people that Christ is greater than any astrological forces and that if Christians read their horoscopes in the newspaper they are succumbing to the pressures of contemporary society, we do not think of an invasion of the church by

> *Our best understanding of the false teaching in Colosse is that it was a blend of Jewish and Hellenistic teachings. Such syncretism was a feature of the ancient world, the sort of teaching that attracted first-century people.*

---

of God coincided with the advent of faith in Christ: to remain under the control of the *stoicheia* after that was a sign of spiritual immaturity" (*The Epistles to the Colossians, to Philemon, and to the Ephesians*, 100). There is an excellent treatment of the term in Peter T. O'Brien, *Colossians, Philemon*, 129–32.

[20]G. Bornkamm finds several strands: "It originates in a gnosticized Judaism, in which Jewish and Iranian-Persian elements, and surely also influence of Chaldean astrology, have peculiarly alloyed themselves and have united with Christianity" ("The Heresy of Colossians," in *Conflict at Colossae*, ed. Fred O. Francis and Wayne A. Meeks [Missoula: SP, 1975], 135). This leads Andrew J. Bandstra to ask, "Is not the syncretistic nature of the religion Bornkamm and others have pictured so unusual that one may legitimately ask whether such a religion ever actually existed?" ("Did the Colossian Errorists Need a Mediator?" in *New Dimensions in New Testament Study*, ed. Richard N. Longenecker and Merrill C. Tenney [Grand Rapids: Zondervan, 1974], 330).

[21]There are useful summaries of opinions on the so-called Colossian heresy in O'Brien, *Colossians, Philemon*, xxx–xli, and in the annotated bibliography of David M. Hay, *Colossians*, ANTC (Nashville: Abingdon, 2000), 173–77. See also the major study of Clinton E. Arnold, *The Colossian Syncretism*, WUNT 77 (Tübingen: Mohr-Siebeck, 1995), who rightly throws into the syncretistic mix a good deal of local "magic."

[22]Thus, Martin Dibelius holds that "the church was threatened with danger from a syncretistic movement, one of the numerous eclectic cults of Asia Minor which flourished at that critical moment in the history of religion" (*A Fresh Approach to the New Testament and Early Christian Literature* [London: Ivor Nicholson & Watson, 1936], 167).

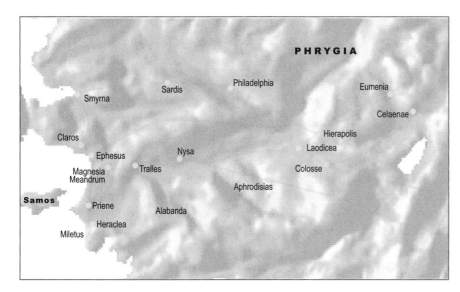

The Region around
Colosse

false teachers.[23] She thinks the situation in Colosse may have been something like that. Paul is concerned enough about it to spend time pointing the Colossians to right practices and right thinking, but he evidently does not think that the church is in a parlous state. His general satisfaction with the Colossian believers shines through the letter (see 1:3–5; 2:5; 3:7). But whether or not Hooker is right, we may be reasonably sure that Paul judges the believers in Colosse to be in danger of popular syncretism and writes in part to protect them from the threat.

TEXT

There is no reason to doubt that we have the text of the letter substantially as Paul wrote it. There are a few places where it is impossible to be sure of the right reading, but they do not affect the sense as a whole. As an example, in 3:6 after "the wrath of God is coming," quite a few manuscripts add "upon those who are disobedient." It is not easy to decide whether the additional words were added by scribes who remembered Ephesians 5:6, or whether they were accidentally dropped by a copying mistake. But whatever reading we adopt, the

---

[23]Morna D. Hooker, "Were There False Teachers in Colossae?" in *Christ and Spirit in the New Testament, Fs.* C. F. D. Moule, ed. B. Lindars and S. S. Smalley (Cambridge: Cambridge University Press, 1973), 315–31. Kirsopp and Silva Lake said some time ago, "There is room for doubt as to whether Paul is arguing against Gentile Christians— in other words, against heresy—or against Gentiles who are endeavouring to convert Christians to their way of thinking. This point has, perhaps, not met with sufficient attention, and writers have spoken too lightly of the Colossian 'heresy'" (Lake, 151).

sense is much the same. There are problems with 2:18, 23, but these appear to center on the meanings of unusual vocabulary rather than uncertainty about the text. So with other disputed readings.[24]

ADOPTION INTO THE CANON

There may be a reference to Colossians in the *Epistle of Barnabas,* but otherwise we must come down to Justin Martyr in the middle of the second century for references to this letter. But it is accepted by Marcion, included in the Muratorian Canon, found in the Syriac and Old Latin versions, and cited by authors such as Irenaeus, Clement of Alexandria, and Tertullian. No real doubt as to its canonicity appears to have been raised in antiquity, and the church seems to have had no difficulties in recognizing it as Scripture.

COLOSSIANS IN RECENT STUDY

It is strongly urged by some that the actual authorship of the letter does not matter. It is agreed that there is a Pauline connection; at the very least the author must have come from the devoted followers of Paul, and he has given a Pauline viewpoint in this letter. Such scholars tend to give most attention to the way the letter adapts the Pauline position to the situation in which the author finds himself.

As Childs emphasizes, "The letter to the Colossians is firmly anchored to the apostle Paul, both to his person and to the gospel which he proclaimed."[25] He is not arguing that Paul necessarily wrote the letter, but that whether he did so or not, there is a strong connection between the apostle and the writing. Neither Timothy nor Epaphras can be thought of as the author, he maintains, and the letter identifies with Paul in the opening and closing and in the body as well (1:23–2:5). He points to the way the Colossians are told to remain in the tradition that Paul represents and that was delivered to them. Childs holds that conservatives have been too ready to insist on Pauline authorship. Much more important, he thinks, is the fact that "in Colossians a false teaching called forth a specific apostolic response which used the heresy as a transparency through which to unfold a new and positive witness to the truth of the gospel."[26]

---

[24]It is difficult to understand why Enslin says that "the text of the letter is in a very bad state of preservation" (292). He cites only 2:18–19 (which he says is "completely unintelligible") to support his view. O'Brien recognizes differences of opinion about details here but says "the general drift of Paul's thought is reasonably clear" (*Colossians, Philemon,* 141). Ralph P. Martin agrees: "These verses abound with difficulties both linguistic and conceptual. Mercifully the drift of Paul's thought is clear" (*Colossians and Philemon,* NCB [London: Oliphants, 1974], 92).

[25]Childs, 344.

[26]Ibid., 346.

There has been a good deal of interest in the false teaching at Colosse. The problem is how to work up all that Paul says about the errors into a coherent system. A generation ago it was common to see the Colossians as opposed by some form of Gnosticism—all the more so, since Gnosticism was syncretistic, gathering in from many sources. Indeed, Kümmel says, "Today there are hardly any differences in basic opinion. Paul, with obvious correctness, sees in the heretical teaching Gnosticism, secret wisdom of a syncretistic sort (2:8, 18), which combines ascetic, ritualistic worship of the elements with Jewish ritualism and Jewish speculation about angels."[27] But this is too sweeping. Full-blown Gnosticism is nowadays widely recognized to be a second-century development; and in any case, syncretism did not have to wait for its arrival.[28]

Mature Gnosticism is a series of systems propagated in the second century by great teachers such as Valentinus and Basilides. It featured a great number of heavenly intermediaries, or aeons, emanations from deity bridging the gap from the high good God to this material creation. Typically there was a contrast between spirit (which was good) and matter (which was evil). Gnosticism was eclectic, gathering teachings from a variety of sources, and we need not doubt that some of those teachings were to be found in the first century. But its characteristic teachings, such as those just mentioned, were not.[29] Behind Colossians there certainly lie some teachings that were later found in some of the forms of Gnosticism, but that does not mean that Gnosticism as such was the problem in this city. Childs is more correct in saying, "Although there is a wide agreement that some form of Jewish syncretism is represented, there remains a continuing disagreement on the precise nature of the opposition."[30] Moreover, the Jewish aspects of what Paul is confronting cannot be overlooked. As if to establish yet another pole, N. T. Wright argues that "all the elements of Paul's polemic in Colossians make sense as a warning against Judaism."[31]

The problem is that we do not know of any teachers who combined all the features Paul is opposing. A given scholar may select certain features and say that they give us the essentials, but others will not agree with the selection. The

---

[27]Kümmel, 239.

[28]See especially Arnold, *The Colossian Syncretism*.

[29]See discussion in chap. 23 below.

[30]Childs, 343.

[31]N. T. Wright, *The Epistles of Paul to the Colossians and to Philemon*, TNTC (Grand Rapids: Eerdmans, 1986), 27. Wright holds that Paul wrote to ex-pagans to warn them against the dangers of Judaism. But while this accounts for the Jewish elements, the treatment of the more Hellenistic and even magical elements seems somewhat forced. Still focusing almost exclusively on the Jewish side of things, Thomas J. Sappington, *Revelation and Redemption at Colossae*, JSNTSup 53 (Sheffield: Sheffield Academic Press, 1991) argues that Paul is confronting an ascetic-mystical piety rooted in Jewish apocalypticism.

Colossians were new Christians. They had not long left paganism (or Judaism, especially if some of them had been God-fearers), and it was all too easy for them to revert to practices and ways of thinking to which they had been accustomed in their pre-Christian days, which they still encountered and whose attractiveness they found impossible to deny.

A further feature of recent discussion has been an interest in what is seen as traditional and liturgical material that the author has taken up and used to advance his argument. There has been a concentration on 1:15–20, which is widely seen as a hymn adapted by the author to set forward important teaching about Christ and his functions.[32]

THE CONTRIBUTION OF COLOSSIANS[33]

The false teachers interposed a barrier between God and God's people. They thought of elemental spirits that stood in the way and permitted access to God only by the path of asceticism. In the face of all such claims, Paul stresses the supremacy of Christ, who is "the image of the invisible God," the one who brought creation about and holds it together, supreme over creation, preeminent in everything. And together with all this, he is "the head of the body, the church," the one who made peace by the blood he shed on the cross (1:15–20). This combination of the greatness of Christ and of his saving work for believers runs through the epistle. It makes nonsense of any claim that other powers are involved in bringing people to God or that meritorious practices like asceticism pave the way.

Christ has reconciled believers (1:22); he is in them, "the hope of glory" (1:27). There is an unusual way of looking at the atonement when Paul says that God forgave us our sins, "having canceled the charge of our legal indebtedness, which stood against us and condemned us; he has taken it away, nailing it to the cross" (2:14)—yet even here the thought is not far removed from Paul's treatment of the law in Galatians 3. Again, in Christ are "all the treasures of wisdom and knowledge" (2:3); "all the fullness of the Deity lives" in him "in bodily form" (2:9) and believers "have been brought to fullness" in Christ (2:10). When they were dead in sins, God made them alive with Christ (2:13). They died with Christ "elemental spiritual forces of this world" (2:20), and they have been raised with him (3:1). Christ "is all, and is in all" (3:11), and they are "God's chosen people" (3:12). They give thanks to God the Father through Christ

---

[32]Contra J. C. O'Neill, "The Source of the Christology in Colossians," *NTS* 26 (1979–80): 87–100, who argues that this is not a hymn, but a borrowing of non-hymnic traditional materials.

[33]See John M. G. Barclay, *Colossians and Philemon*, NTG (Sheffield: Sheffield Academic Press, 2001), 75–96.

(3:17). The great themes of Christ's outstanding excellence and the completeness of the salvation that he brought about in dying for his people on the cross run through this letter. They are not put in quite this way elsewhere, and Colossians accordingly has something to say that is distinctive.

Paul insists on the supremacy of Christ over all the supernatural forces the Colossians were treating with such respect. Some of us may miss part of the relevance of what he is saying because we do not believe in those forces in the way the Colossians did. But with rising occultism in the West, our skepticism is being mocked; and in any case, it has often been pointed out that in modern times there is a widespread belief that we are the creatures of our heredity and our environment and that in the grip of such powers we can never be really free. It is part of the message of Colossians that in Christ we can overcome anything. The cross means a disarming of all the powers opposed to God's purpose (2:15), and this remains an important part of the Christian way.

Because Paul had never been to Colosse and had not met members of the church there (2:1), the love and the tender concern for them that comes through in every line of the letter are all the more significant. This letter brings out, as does perhaps no other New Testament writing, the truth that all believers form one church. Paul is emphatic that in the church there is "no Gentile or Jew, circumcised or uncircumcised, barbarian, Scythian, slave or free, but Christ is all, and is in all" (3:11). We who are members of the body of Christ belong together, and we cannot be indifferent to the concerns and the interests of other members. The letter makes clear for all of us the importance of concern for the whole church and not only for that little segment in which we live.

But along with that emphasis on the oneness of the church, we should heed the teaching of the letter that there are differences that distinguish believers. Paul gives directions to wives and husbands, children and fathers, slaves and masters (3:18–4:1). All are servants of Christ and must live as such, but that does not obliterate relationships in society. Our positions differ, and while a common obligation to live out the faith rests on all of us, the precise form that takes differs according to our circumstances.

In every generation Christians are tempted to go along with the philosophy of the times. It is never a comfortable thing to be out of step with what our community holds to be the best thinking of the day. But that thinking may be out of step with God, who made us all. Paul's warning about "hollow and deceptive philosophy, which depends on human tradition and the elemental spiritual forces of this world" (2:8) is never out of season. At the same time, we should listen to the warnings about distracting religious practices, the observance of religious festivals that detract from what is central (2:16), and the habit of making rules the essence of religion (2:20–21). Such practices generate a false humility and really promote unspirituality (2:18). Nothing can make up for losing connection with the head (2:19).

> *The great themes of Christ's outstanding excellence and the completeness of the salvation that he brought about in dying for his people on the cross run through this letter in a distinctive way not found elsewhere.*

BIBLIOGRAPHY

T. K. **Abbott**, *The Epistles to the Ephesians and to the Colossians*, ICC (Edinburgh: T. & T. Clark, 1897) ▪Clinton E. **Arnold**, *The Colossian Syncretism: The Interface Between Christianity and Folk Belief at Colosse*, WUNT 77 (Tübingen: Mohr-Siebeck, 1995) ▪E. **Bammel**, "Versuch zu Col 1:15–20," *ZNW* 52 (1961): 88–95 ▪Andrew J. **Bandstra**, "Did the Colossian Errorists Need a Mediator?" in *New Dimensions in New Testament Study*, ed. Richard N. Longenecker and Merrill C. Tenney (Grand Rapids: Zondervan 1974), 329–43 ▪John M. G. **Barclay**, *Colossians and Philemon*, NTG (Sheffield: Sheffield Academic Press, 1997) ▪Markus **Barth** and Helmut **Blanke**, *Colossians*, AB 34B (Garden City: Doubleday, 1994) ▪G. **Bornkamm**, "The Heresy of Colossians," in *Conflict at Colossae*, ed. Fred O. Francis and Wayne A. Meeks (Missoula: SP, 1975), 123–45 ▪F. F. **Bruce**, *The Epistles to the Colossians, to Philemon, and to the Ephesians*, NICNT (Grand Rapids: Eerdmans, 1984) ▪G. B. **Caird**, *Paul's Letters from Prison* (Oxford: Oxford University Press, 1976) ▪C. C. **Caragounis**, *The Ephesian Mysterion: Meaning and Content* (Lund: Gleerup, 1977) ▪W. **Carr**, "Two Notes on Colossians," *JTS* 24 (1973): 492–500 ▪Edmund P. **Clowney**, "Interpreting the Biblical Models of the Church: A Hermeneutical Deepening of Ecclesiology," in *Biblical Interpretation and the Church: Text and Context*, ed. D. A. Carson (Exeter: Paternoster, 1984), 64–109 ▪Martin **Dibelius**, *A Fresh Approach to the New Testament and Early Christian Literature* (London: Ivor Nicholson & Watson, 1936) ▪James D. G. **Dunn**, *The Epistle to the Colossians and Philemon*, NIGTC (Grand Rapids: Eerdmans, 1996) ▪J. **Ernst**, *Pleroma und Pleroma Christi: Geschichte und Deutung eines Begriffs der paulinischen Antilegomena*, BU 5 (Regensburg: Pustet, 1970) ▪Fred O. **Francis** and Wayne A. **Meeks**, eds., *Conflict at Colossae* (Missoula: SP, 1975) ▪David E. **Garland**, *Colossians/Philemon*, NIVAC (Grand Rapids: Zondervan, 1998) ▪Joachim **Gnilka**, *Der Kolosserbrief*, HTKNT (Freiburg: Herder, 1980) ▪Murray J. **Harris**, *Colossians and Philemon*, EGGNT (Grand Rapids: Eerdmans, 1991) ▪P. N. **Harrison**, *The Problem of the Pastoral Epistles* (London: Oxford University Press, 1921) ▪Morna D. **Hooker**, "Were There False Teachers in Colossae?" in *Christ and Spirit in the New Testament*, Fs. C. F. D. Moule, ed. Barnabas Lindars and Stephen S. Smalley (Cambridge: Cambridge University Press, 1973), 315–31 ▪S. E. **Johnson**, "Unsolved Questions About Early Christianity in Anatolia," in *Studies in New Testament and Early Christian Literature*, Fs. Allen P. Wikgren, ed. D. E. Aune, NovTSup 33 (Leiden: Brill, 1972), 181–93 ▪E. **Käsemann**, *Essays on New Testament Themes* (London: SCM, 1964), 149–68 ▪J. B. **Lightfoot**, *Saint Paul's Epistles to the Colossians and to Philemon*, 9th ed. (London: Macmillan, 1890) ▪Eduard **Lohse**, *Colossians and Philemon*, Hermeneia (Philadelphia: Fortress Press, 1971) ▪idem, "Pauline Theology in the Letter to the Colossians," *NTS* 15 (1968–69): 211–20 ▪Margaret Y. **MacDonald**, *Colossians and Ephesians*, SacPag 17 (Collegeville: Liturgical Press, 2000) ▪G. H. C. **Macgregor**, "Principalities and Powers: The Cosmic Background of St Paul's Thought," *NTS* 1 (1954–55): 17–28 ▥Ralph P. **Martin**, *Colossians and Philemon*, NCB (London: Oliphants, 1974) ▥Charles **Masson**, *L'épître aux Colossiens*, CNT (Paris: Delachaux & Niestlé, 1950) ▥C. F. D. **Moule**, *The Epistles of Paul the Apostle to the Colossians and to Philemon* (Cambridge: Cambridge University Press, 1962) ▥Peter T. **O'Brien**, *Colossians, Philemon*, WBC (Waco: Word, 1982) ▥J. C. **O'Neill**, "The Source of the Christology in Colossians," *NTS* 26 (1979–80): 87–100 ▥Arthur G. **Patzia**, *Ephesians, Colossians, Philemon*, NIBC (Peabody: Hendrickson, 1990) ▥Petr **Pokorný**, *Colossians: A Commentary* (Peabody: Hendrickson, 1991) ▥T. E. **Pollard**, "Colossians 1:12–20: A Reconsideration," *NTS* 27 (1980–81): 572–75 ▥Bo **Reicke**, "Caesarea, Rome, and the Captivity Epistles," in *Apostolic History and the Gospel, Fs. F. F. Bruce*, ed. W. Ward Gasque and Ralph P. Martin (Exeter: Paternoster, 1970), 277–86 ▥Thomas E. **Sappington**, *Revelation and Redemption at Colossae*, JSNTSup 53 (Sheffield: Sheffield Academic Press, 1991) ▥Eduard **Schweizer**, *The Letter to the Colossians: A Commentary* (Minneapolis: Augsburg, 1982; German orig., EKKNT, 1976) ▥Robert W. **Wall**, *Colossians and Philemon*, IVPNTC (Downers Grove: IVP, 1993) ▥H. **Weiss**, "The Law in the Epistle to the Colossians," *CBQ* 34 (1972): 294–314 ▥N. T. **Wright**, *The Epistles of Paul to the Colossians and to Philemon*, TNTC (Grand Rapids: Eerdmans, 1986).

CHAPTER SIXTEEN

1 AND 2 THESSALONIANS

CONTENTS

Both of these letters were sent to a newly founded church in the important Macedonian city of Thessalonica (modern Salonika). Situated on one of the best natural harbors in the northern Aegean and the meeting place of four major roads, Thessalonica was in Paul's day a bustling commercial city of around 100,000 people. The geographer Strabo calls it the "metropolis of Macedonia."[1] Paul visited the city on his so-called second missionary journey, after being released from custody in Philippi (Acts 17:1–9), probably in A.D. 48 or 49. Paul's stay in Thessalonica was tumultuous. He and Silas, who was ministering with him, had preached in the synagogue for three Sabbaths when some of the Jews fomented a riot against the Christian preachers. Paul, Silas, and Jason, a Thessalonian with whom the apostles were staying, were hauled before the city authorities and released after posting bail. But the situation was serious enough that Paul and Silas had to be sent away.

Comparison of Paul's references to the Thessalonian visit in his letters with Luke's account has led some scholars to call into question the historicity of Luke's narrative. Especially problematic, it is thought, are Luke's inclusion of Jews among the new converts and the suggestion that Paul and Silas spent only about three or four weeks in the city. Paul, it is alleged, would not have described former Jews or God-fearers as people who had "turned to God from idols" (1 Thess. 1:9). And several details of his stay in Thessalonica do not square with a brief three- or four-week stay—for instance, Paul's claim to have worked long enough to set an example (1 Thess. 2:9) and his praise of the Philippians for sending him money twice while he was in Thessalonica (Phil. 4:15–16).[2] But such criticism is unfounded.

---

[1] A concise description of the city is found in Rainer Riesner, *Paul's Early Period: Chronology, Mission Strategy, Theology* (Grand Rapids: Eerdmans, 1998), 337–41.

[2] For these criticisms, see, e.g., Charles A. Wanamaker, *The Epistles to the Thessalonians*, NIGTC (Grand Rapids: Eerdmans, 1990), 6–7.

As Riesner has recently pointed out, the God-fearers who apparently made up the bulk of the converts were still, in Jewish eyes, Gentiles. Embracing the Christian faith would indeed have been a turn from idols to the true God.[3] As far as the length of Paul's stay, two points must be made. First, Luke is, in fact, very vague about the length of stay. He claims that Paul and Silas preached for three Sabbaths in the synagogue and that some time after that certain Jews instigated a riot. But how long after, he does not say. A stay of two to four months is not at all unlikely.[4] Second, it is possible that all the activity mentioned by Paul in the Thessalonian letters could be accommodated within a period of about a month.[5] Luke's account, while no doubt abbreviated, has every claim to represent accurately the basic facts of Paul's brief and interrupted stay in Thessalonica.

There is general agreement about the basic structure of both the letters to the Thessalonians. Various refinements of the basic scheme have been offered, especially by those who think that Greco-Roman rhetorical categories might help explain the movement of the letters.[6] But Paul's letters have not proven themselves very amenable to such rhetorical analysis (see chap. 8).

1 Thessalonians

The letter begins with the typical salutation (1:1–3), which mentions Paul, Silas, and Timothy as the senders of the letter. Paul then gives thanks for the Thessalonians and for their wholehearted commitment to the message the apostles preached to them (1:4–10). The body of the letter falls into two obvious sections, with the former, 2:1–3:13, focusing on Paul's interactions with the Thessalonians and the second, 4:1–5:11, on Paul's exhortations to the Thessalonians. Paul begins by rehearsing the circumstances of his ministry in Thessalonica (2:1–12). He then turns from the way he preached the gospel to the way the Thessalonians received it, giving thanks again for their reception of the word and reminding them that their very suffering is proof of their commitment and

---

[3]Riesner, *Paul's Early Period*, 348–49.

[4]William M. Ramsay, *Saint Paul, the Traveller and Roman Citizen* (London: Hodder & Stoughton, 1897), 227–28; Riesner, *Paul's Early Period*, 363–64; Wikenhauser, 363.

[5]The syntax of Phil. 4:15–16 makes it possible that only one of the Philippians' gifts was sent to Thessalonica (Peter T. O'Brien, *The Epistle to the Philippians: A Commentary on the Greek Text*, NIGTC [Grand Rapids: Eerdmans, 1991], 535–36). See also I. Howard Marshall, *1 & 2 Thessalonians*, NCB (Grand Rapids: Eerdmans, 1983), 5; Leon Morris, *The First and Second Epistles to the Thessalonians*, rev. ed., NICNT (Grand Rapids: Eerdmans, 1991), 3–4.

[6]See, e.g., F. W. Hughes, "The Rhetoric of 1 Thessalonians," in *The Thessalonian Correspondence*, ed. Raymond F. Collins, BETL 87 (Leuven: Leuven University Press, 1990), 94–116. He is followed by Karl Donfried, "The Theology of 1 Thessalonians," in *The Theology of the Shorter Pauline Letters* (Cambridge: University Press, 1993), 3–7.

divine approval (2:14–16). This same persecution forced Paul to cut short his stay in the city and aroused his fears about the Thessalonians' fortitude (2:17–3:5). But Timothy has arrived to report that all is well (3:6–13).

Paul begins his exhortations by reminding the Thessalonians of three critical ways they need "to live in order to please God" (4:1): by avoiding sexual immorality, by loving each other, and by working hard with their own hands (4:3–12). He then turns to an issue that was causing great distress among the Thessalonians: the death of some of their number. He emphasizes the advantages that the dead in Christ will have when the Lord returns (4:13–18) and encourages them to lead exemplary lives in light of the coming day of the Lord (5:1–11). The letter closes in a typical way, with final brief exhortations, a wish-prayer, a request for prayer, and greetings (5:12–28).

2 Thessalonians

Paul again associates Silas and Timothy with him in the salutation of the second letter (1:1–2). The thanksgiving section (1:3–12) quickly moves into encouragement in the face of persecution, again a critical problem for the Thessalonians. It is probably this persecution that had led the Thessalonians into erroneous ideas about the presence of the day of the Lord, which Paul corrects in 2:1–12. Paul then exhorts the Thessalonians to stand firm in their faith and prays for their encouragement (2:13–17). This leads Paul to request prayer for himself, Silas, and Timothy, that they also might be faithful in their ministry and kept safe from the persecutors (3:1–5). The problem of idleness, mentioned by Paul in 1 Thessalonians 4:11–12, has apparently worsened, so Paul launches an extended exhortation on the subject (3:6–15). The letter ends with a brief wish-prayer, an authentication in Paul's own hand, and a grace wish (3:16–18).

AUTHOR

Three separate but related matters must be tackled: (1) the co-authorship of the letters; (2) alleged interpolations in 1 Thessalonians; and (3) the Pauline authorship of 2 Thessalonians.[7]

The Co-Authorship of the Letters

As we have seen, both letters name Paul, Silas, and Timothy as the authors of the letters. Yet the letters are traditionally ascribed to Paul alone. Is this fair?

---

[7]A few scholars (e.g., Walter Schmithals, *Paul and the Gnostics* [Nashville: Abingdon, 1972], 123–181; Earl J. Richards, *1 and 2 Thessalonians*, SacPag 13 [Collegeville: Liturgical Press, 1995], 11–19) have advanced compilation theories, according to which our 1 Thessalonians is a composite of two or more original letters and fragments. But the theories are wildly speculative.

Many scholars answer no. They note the way the first-person plural dominates both letters, even in the thanksgiving section, which does not happen in most of the other Pauline letters, including three of them that name someone else in the salutation (1 Corinthians, Philippians, Philemon).[8] The inclusion of more than one person in the salutation of a letter was most unusual in antiquity; readers would probably have read the plural "we" as a genuine indication of authorship.[9] However, there is reason to pause before drawing this conclusion. First person singular references do pop up in both letters (1 Thess. 2:18; 3:5; 5:27; 2 Thess. 2:5; 3:17). These would be most unusual if the letters had been genuinely co-authored. The first person plural may, then, be no more than a literary device, an "authorial plural" appropriate to the parenetic form of the letters.[10] Perhaps, however, a mediating solution is the best. Paul's mention of Silas and Timothy, because of their close associations with the Thessalonians, must be taken seriously. But Paul is the primary author. It is his voice that we hear in the letters, and their ascription to the apostle is not, therefore, unjustified.

Interpolations in 1 Thessalonians

Although the Tübingen School rejected the Pauline authorship of 1 Thessalonians, few scholars have followed in their footsteps. 1 Thessalonians is one of the seven letters ascribed to Paul that is included in the critical canon of authentic Pauline letters. But scholars do argue for interpolations—sections of the letter that are alleged to be additions to the original—in 1 Thessalonians. Various scholars have singled out sections, including 2:1–10 and 5:1–11; but the only alleged interpolation that has drawn significant support is 2:13–16. These verses, it is claimed, must have been written after the fall of Jerusalem in A.D. 70 because the claim that "the wrath of God has come upon them [i.e., the Jews] at last" must reflect that event. Moreover, the apparently altogether negative evaluation of the Jews' final salvation conflicts with Paul's hope for the salvation of "all Israel" (Rom. 11:26).[11] The difficulty of these verses, both in terms of their harshness and of their potential conflict with Romans 11, should not be minimized. Yet we possess no textual evidence that these verses were ever absent from 1 Thessalonians. The idea that early Christians could easily have inserted passages into the letters of Paul they collected has no historical justification and

> *Paul's mention of Silas and Timothy, because of their close associations with the Thessalonians, must be taken seriously. But Paul is the primary author. It is his voice that we hear in the letters.*

---

[8]F. F. Bruce, *1 & 2 Thessalonians*, WBC (Waco: Word, 1982), xxxii–xxxiii.

[9]See Jerome Murphy-O'Connor, *Paul the Letter-Writer: His World, His Options, His Skills* (Collegeville: Liturgical Press, 1995), 16–19.

[10]Abraham J. Malherbe, *The Letters to the Thessalonians: A New Translation with Introduction and Commentary*, AB (New York: Doubleday, 2000), 86–89.

[11]For these arguments and others, see esp. B. A. Pearson, "1 Thessalonians 2:13–16: A Deutero-Pauline Interpolation," *HTR* 64 (1971): 79–94.

runs into almost insuperable difficulties when the actual logistics of the procedure are considered.[12]

Moreover, the verses make good sense in their context. Paul's commendation for the way the Thessalonians received God's word and his encouragement to them about the persecution they are experiencing fit the theme of 2:1–12 very nicely. And the claim that God's wrath has now "at last" fallen on the Jews matches other New Testament assertions that widespread Jewish rejection of Jesus Messiah brings to a climax Israel's sin and refusal to listen to God (Matt. 23:32; Acts 7:51–53).

The Pauline Authorship of 2 Thessalonians

A far more significant problem confronts us when we turn to 2 Thessalonians, which claims to have been written by Paul, Silas, and Timothy. Moreover, Paul attests his personal involvement at the end of the letter: "I, Paul, write this greeting in my own hand, which is the distinguishing mark in all my letters. This is how I write" (3:17). No responsible early church authority ever questioned Paul's authorship of 2 Thessalonians. It is included as a Pauline letter in Marcion's canon (c. A.D. 140) and in the Muratorian Canon (c. 180–200?[13]). Very early fathers, such as Polycarp, Ignatius, and Justin, seem to have known the letter. Irenaeus quotes it by name. Despite this strong tradition, a significant number of contemporary scholars deny that Paul wrote the letter.

Questions about Pauline authorship were first raised at the beginning of the nineteenth century, although they were not taken seriously until championed by F. C. Baur in the middle of the century. Still, Baur's general radicalism tended to blunt the force of his arguments against 2 Thessalonians, and all but a few scholars continued to favor Pauline authorship. But the arguments of C. Masson in 1957 and, especially, Wolfgang Trilling in 1972 have turned the tide of critical scholarship against the Pauline authorship of the letter.[14] As a result, 2 Thessalonians is generally not included among the seven-letter Pauline canon-within-a-canon accepted by modern critical orthodoxy.

Several arguments against the Pauline authorship of 2 Thessalonians have been advanced over the years. It has been claimed that the vocabulary and style

---

[12]See, e.g., Bo Reicke, *Re-examining Paul's Letters: The History of the Pauline Correspondence*, ed. David P. Moessner (Harrisburg: Trinity Press International, 2001), 30–34. And for a cogent argument against an interpolation in 1 Thess. 2:13–16, see Wanamaker, *The Epistles to the Thessalonians*, 30–33. See also Carol J. Schlueter, *Filling Up the Measure: Polemical Hyperbole in 1 Thessalonians 2.14–16*, JSNTSup 98 (Sheffield: JSOT, 1994).

[13]For the date of the Muratorian fragment, see chap. 4, n. 7.

[14]Charles Masson, *Les deux épîtres de Saint Paul aux Thessaloniciens*, CNT (Neuchâtel: Delachaux & Niestlé, 1957); Wolfgang Trilling, *Untersuchungen zum zweiten Thessalonicherbrief* (Leipzig: St. Benno, 1972).

of 2 Thessalonians are distinctive when compared to the assured Pauline letters.[15] But the wide variety of conclusions that scholars have reached using such analyses, combined with the need to reckon with the possible influence that Paul's co-authors or an amanuensis might have had on the Greek of the letter, have tended to diminish the number and effectiveness of such arguments. Another argument against authenticity focuses on alleged details in the letter that are claimed to reflect a post-Pauline period. The focus on "traditions" (παραδόσεις [*paradoseis*]) passed on to the Thessalonians (2:15), for instance, resembles the emphasis on "sound teaching" in the Pastorals, also alleged to be post-Pauline. The eschatology of 2 Thessalonians, it is alleged, bears close resemblance to the eschatology of the Revelation, a late-first-century book.[16] The portrayal of the "man of lawlessness" in 2:1–11 is said to reflect the "Nero *redivivus*" myth, an "urban legend" that circulated widely in the years after the death of the Emperor Nero in A.D. 68. And some have even suggested that the combination of "realized eschatology" (2:1ff.) and laziness (3:6–14) reflects late-first-century Gnosticism.[17] But these arguments are not given much weight in current scholarship. Contemporary analysis of apocalyptic tends to downplay the kind of historical reference implied in identifying Paul's "man of lawlessness" with Nero. The eschatological teaching of 2 Thessalonians contains nothing that could not have been current in the Judeo-Christian world of the middle of the first century. The craze to find gnostics behind every New Testament false teaching tree has—justly—passed. And the reference to the "traditions" in 2 Thessalonians 2:16 is no different than the reference to "the teaching" in the universally acknowledged Pauline Romans 6:17.

The contemporary argument against the authenticity of 2 Thessalonians focuses rather on two points that are at first sight paradoxical: 2 Thessalonians is too similar to 1 Thessalonians to have been written by Paul; and 2 Thessalonians is too unlike 1 Thessalonians to have been written by Paul. We will unpack each argument before assessing it.

Similarities to 1 Thessalonians. The basic argument here is that no author would duplicate material from one letter in another written so soon after to the same audience as would be the case if Paul had written both 1 and 2 Thessalonians. Some of the agreements between the letters are shown in Table 7.

Some of these agreements, of course, are rather trivial; others are more substantial. The opening salutations of 1 Thessalonians and 2 Thessalonians, for instance, are closer in wording than any other two in the Pauline letters. But perhaps even more important than the verbal parallels are the structural parallels.

---

[15]E.g., A. Q. Morton and James McLeman, *Christianity and the Computer* (London: Hodder & Stoughton, 1964).

[16]See, for these last two points, Brown, 594.

[17]Marxsen, 37–44.

Table 7
Verbal Similarities between 1 and 2 Thessalonians

1 Thessalonians	2 Thessalonians
1:1a "Paul, Silas and Timothy, To the church of the Thessalonians in God the Father and the Lord Jesus Christ"	1:1a "Paul, Silas and Timothy, To the church of the Thessalonians in God our Father and the Lord Jesus Christ"
1:3 "Your work produced by faith [τοῦ ἔργου τῆς πίστεως; *tou ergou tēs pisteōs*]"	1:11 "every deed prompted by your faith [ἔργον πίστεως; *ergon pisteōs*]"
1:3 "faith . . . love . . . endurance [ὑπομονή; *hypomonē*]"	1:3–4 "faith . . . love . . . perseverance [ὑπομονή; *hypomonē*]"
1:4 "brothers and sisters loved by God"	2:13 "brothers and sisters loved by the Lord"
2:9 "Surely you remember, brothers and sisters, our toil and hardship; we worked night and day in order not to be a burden to anyone while we preached the gospel of God to you"	3:8 "We worked night and day, laboring and toiling so that we would not be a burden to any of you"
4:1 "As for other matters"	3:1 "As for other matters"
4:5 "who do not know God"	1:8 "who do not know God"
5:28 "The grace of our Lord Jesus Christ be with you"	3:18 "The grace of our Lord Jesus Christ be with you all"

Every major paragraph in 1 Thessalonians, it is claimed, has a counterpart in 2 Thessalonians. Both letters feature an unusual Pauline double thanksgiving (1 Thess. 1:2 and 2:13; 2 Thess. 1:3 and 2:13), and a transitional benediction (1 Thess 3:11–13; 2 Thess. 2:16–17). As Ernest Best puts the argument, "The structure of 2 Th. is so similar to that of I Th. and so dissimilar from that of the remaining Pauline letters that it could only have been devised by someone deliberately using I Th. as a model."[18]

Differences from 1 Thessalonians. For all their similarities, there are also striking differences between 1 and 2 Thessalonians. A few scholars have noted verbal inconsistencies,[19] and others argue that 2 Thessalonians is more "formal" in

---

[18]Ernest Best, *A Commentary on the First and Second Letter to the Thessalonians*, HNTC (New York: Harper & Row, 1972), 50 (Best, however, is ultimately unconvinced by the argument; he opts for the Pauline authorship of 2 Thessalonians). See also, e.g., Brown, 592.

[19]D. D. Schmidt concludes that the style of 2 Thessalonians is closer to that of Ephesians and Colossians (which he considers to be non-Pauline) than to 1 Thessalonians

tone than 1 Thessalonians. But attention focuses mainly on the eschatological teaching in the two letters. In 1 Thessalonians, Paul displays the strong sense of imminence so typical, it is alleged, of the very early church. He assumes that he will be alive at the time of the parousia (4:17—"*we* who are still alive," emphasis added) and cautions his readers not to try to calculate the "times and dates" (5:1–4). The parousia appears to be just around the corner and quite impossible to predict. In 2 Thessalonians, however, the author warns his readers about thinking the parousia is imminent. Indeed, he lists events—the "rebellion" and the revelation of the "man of lawlessness"—that must take place before the Lord can return (2:1–4). If 1 Thessalonians reflects Paul's eschatology, it is argued, 2 Thessalonians must reflect that of someone else.

For those who find this pattern of similarity and dissimilarity sufficient reason to deny that the same author is responsible for both letters, several options are open. Harnack tried to rescue Pauline authorship of both letters by positing that 1 Thessalonians was directed to Gentiles in the church and 2 Thessalonians to Jews.[20] E. Earle Ellis suggested that the first letter was written to the entire church but that 2 Thessalonians was written to Paul's coworkers ("the brothers" of 2 Thess. 1:3).[21] But insufficient evidence for such a change in audience exists, and Harnack and Ellis have had few followers. Others suggest that one of Paul's associates may have been the dominant voice in 2 Thessalonians, Timothy usually being singled out as the likely candidate.[22] Childs thinks that 2 Thessalonians might have been written much later than 1 Thessalonians by a person under Paul's direction and signed by him to authenticate the letter.[23] But Childs offers no convincing explanation for the situation that would have called forth the letter at such a later period. Most scholars who are convinced that Paul could not have written both letters opt for pseudonymity. They suggest that a follower of Paul's wrote 2 Thessalonians in his name sometime late in the first century.[24] Such a procedure, it is argued, was quite acceptable in the ancient

("The Syntactical Style of 2 Thessalonians: How Pauline Is It?" in *The Thessalonian Correspondence*, 383–93).

[20]Adolf von Harnack, "Der Problem des zweiten Thessalonicherbriefes," in *Sitzungesberichte der königlichen preussischen Akademie des Wissenschaften zu Berlin* 31 (1910): 560–78. Harnack's suggestion was taken up by Kirsopp Lake (cf. *The Earlier Epistles of St. Paul: Their Motive and Origin* [London: Rivingstons, 1911], 83–85).

[21]E. Earle Ellis, "Paul and His Co-Workers," *NTS* 17 (1970–71): 449–51.

[22]E.g., Donfried, "The Theology of 2 Thessalonians," in *The Theology of the Shorter Pauline Letters*, 86–87.

[23]Childs, 370.

[24]See, e.g., Masson, *Les deux épîtres de Saint Paul aux Thessaloniciens*; Trilling, *Untersuchungen zum zweiten Thessalonicherbrief*; J. A. Bailey, "Who Wrote II Thessalonians?" *NTS* 25 (1979): 131–45; G. Holland, "'A Letter Supposedly from Us': A Contribution to the Discussion about the Authorship of 2 Thessalonians," in *The Thessalonian*

world as a way of carrying on the authority and influence of a great teacher from the past.

Despite these arguments, a significant number of scholars—and by no means all of them evangelical—continue to maintain the Pauline authorship of 2 Thessalonians.[25] They are unconvinced that the relationship of the letters requires different authors and unpersuaded by the alternative accounts of the origin of 2 Thessalonians. We agree; and we will build the case for Pauline authorship, first, by responding to the objections noted above, and second, by bringing up what seem to us to be insuperable problems in the way of the pseudonymous theory.

Similarities between 1 Thessalonians and 2 Thessalonians certainly exist. But these have been overdrawn. Exact verbal parallels are few and are found mainly in the opening and closing parts of the letters—sections in which we might expect the repetition of formulaic language. The same is true of the allegedly close parallels in structure. Even a cursory reading of the two letters reveals significant differences. For example, the second letter has nothing even remotely resembling the long section on Paul's interactions with and ministry to the Thessalonians found in the first letter (2:1–3:13). More to the point is the issue of how best to explain the parallels that exist. Which is more likely? That an unknown follower of Paul chose a few passages and structural elements to duplicate? Or that Paul himself, writing two letters to the same church with the same associates within several months used some of the same language and forms in both? The latter scenario seems to us at least as probable as the former.

A different issue arises when we consider the differences between the letters. For as we have seen, the main point of difference lies in theology—and here we face the possibility of a later "Paulinist" deliberately altering the apostle's original eschatology to suit the needs of a new time. But this possibility only becomes likely if we conclude that Paul could not have held the eschatological views propounded in the two letters at about the same time. But we have no good reason to deny this. As we have seen, the main problem is that 1 Thessalonians appears to teach that the end is both imminent and its time incalculable, whereas 2 Thessalonians warns against imminence and claims that certain "signs" will precede the end. But many Jewish apocalypses contain the same mixture of imminence and warning signs. More to the point, we find this same mixture in the eschatology of the gospels. Compare, for instance, Matthew 24:33—"When you see all

Correspondence, 394–402; Richards, *1 and 2 Thessalonians,* 19–24; Frank W. Hughes, *Early Christian Rhetoric and 2 Thessalonians,* JSNTSup 30 (Sheffield: JSOT, 1989).

[25]Especially solid arguments are found in Best, *The First and Second Epistles to the Thessalonians,* 37–59; Morris, *The First and Second Epistles to the Thessalonians,* 17–23; Wanamaker, *The Epistles to the Thessalonians,* 17–28; Malherbe, *The Letters to the Thessalonians,* 364–74; Robert Jewett, *The Thessalonian Correspondence: Pauline Rhetoric and Millenarian Piety* (Philadelphia: Fortress Press, 1986), 3–18.

these things, you know that it is near, right at the door"—with Matthew 24:44b—"The Son of Man will come at an hour when you do not expect him." Paul's focus on imminence in 1 Thessalonians and on preliminary events in 2 Thessalonians arises because of the different pastoral situations he is addressing. There is no good reason to deny that he could have held the two views at the same time as part of his overall eschatology. The different problems being addressed in the two letters require Paul to stress different sides of his stable eschatological teaching.[26]

To be sure, another factor comes into play. Many critics are sure that Paul could not have taught the eschatology of 2 Thessalonians because it would interfere with the popular scenario according to which Paul and other early Christians held to a strong doctrine of immediacy—Christ would come back within a few years—while only in the second generation did that hope wane, bringing with it the "early Catholic" notion of indefinite postponement of the parousia. But without pursuing the matter here, there are very good reasons to question this neat developmental scenario. Critics have simultaneously overemphasized the idea of "immediacy" in Jesus and the early church and downplayed the importance of imminence in later Christian writings. We find no reason why Paul could not have taught the eschatology of 2 Thessalonians 2, dependent as it seems to be on Daniel and the teaching of Jesus, in about A.D. 50. Moreover, Nicholl has recently put forward a plausible scenario in which both letters are replying to two stages of the same eschatological crisis.[27] If he is right, the similarities and dissimilarities between the two epistles both make sense, and even the brevity of time during which they were both composed.

If the reasons why scholars reject the Pauline authorship of 2 Thessalonians are not persuasive, even less persuasive are their explanations for an alternative origin of the letter. Scholars routinely claim that writing letters in someone else's name was a recognized and acceptable practice in the ancient world. But the evidence does not support the claim. Pseudonymous writings were, of course, quite common, especially in the apocalyptic genre of the Jewish world. But the evidence for pseudonymous *epistles* is meager at best (see chap. 8 above). So the

---

[26]See, e.g., Johnson, 287–88.

[27]Colin R. Nicholl, *From Hope to Despair in Thessalonica: Situating 1 and 2 Thessalonians*, SNTSMS 126 (Cambridge: Cambridge University Press, 2004). Nicholl argues that Paul addresses in 1 Thessalonians a Christian church believing that the parousia is imminent, but which instead of being filled with joy at the prospect, are filled with fear because they think that the unexpected deaths of some of their number makes them wonder how many of the remainder are among the non-elect. In the second letter, Paul finds the situation still more dire: some false word of prophecy or some letter purporting to come from Paul has convinced the church that the parousia is already behind them, engendering community-wide despair. Whether one thinks this analysis is the most plausible is probably not as important as recognizing that the problems addressed by the two letters are simultaneously similar and distinguishable.

general notion that a follower of Paul's might have quite innocently and without any intent to deceive written in his name faces serious difficulties. But the difficulties multiply exponentially when we consider 2 Thessalonians 3:17: "I, Paul, write this greeting in my own hand, which is the distinguishing mark in all my letters. This is how I write." Brown suggests that the theory of pseudonymity can be rescued if "the writer is symbolically insisting on the genuineness of the message, not of the penmanship,"[28] but he provides no evidence that this kind of wording at the end of a letter would be taken in this way. Malherbe's judgment is on target: a pseudonymous writer who inserts such a claim, along with references to earlier oral and written teaching by Paul (2:2, 15), "would have been audacious to a degree beyond belief."[29]

> Since the reasons for rejected Pauline authorship are not compelling and the pseudonymous alternative lacks credibility, 2 Thessalonians should be accepted as a genuine letter of the apostle Paul.

Since the reasons for rejected Pauline authorship are not compelling and the pseudonymous alternative lacks credibility, 2 Thessalonians should be accepted as a genuine letter of the apostle Paul.

SITUATION, SEQUENCE OF LETTERS, AND DATE

Paul's concern to let the Thessalonians know just how much he regrets being separated from them leads him to go into some detail about his movements after he left Thessalonica (1 Thess. 2:17–3:13). Having been "separated" from them after a "short time" (2:17), Paul was anxious to return and comfort the Thessalonians in the midst of the persecution that had arisen. But "Satan blocked our way" (2:18). Paul then mentions being left alone in Athens (3:1), from where he sent Timothy to Thessalonica to discover how the church there was faring (3:2). It is Timothy's return with good news about the state of the church that occasions the letter (3:6). Scholars who treat the historicity of the book of Acts with skepticism seek to situate the letter in Paul's ministry on the basis of this information alone. Using a revisionist Pauline chronology drawn from the letters, some of these scholars conclude that Paul might have written 1 Thessalonians in the early 40s.[30] Another approach, more respectful of Acts, places 1 Thessalonians in the middle 50s on Paul's third missionary journey.[31]

But there is no reason to reject the accuracy of Luke's report of Paul's activities (see chap. 7); and the vast majority of scholars conclude that the informa-

---

[28]Brown, 593.

[29]Malherbe, *The Letters to the Thessalonians*, 373; cf. also McNeile, 117. Robert Jewett concludes, "While the likelihood of definitely proving Pauline authorship of 2 Thessalonians remains at a modest level, the improbability of forgery is extremely high" (*Thessalonian Correspondence*, 17–18; cf. 3–18).

[30]See, e.g., Richards, *1 and 2 Thessalonians*, 7–8; Donfried, "The Theology of 1 Thessalonians," 9–12.

[31]Schmithals, *Paul and the Gnostics*, 181–91; this date is left open as a serious possibility in Achtemeier/Green/Thompson, 438–39.

tion Paul provides in 1 Thessalonians meshes very well with what Luke tells us of Paul's ministry in Macedonia and Achaia in Acts 17 and 18. Luke describes the sudden but serious persecution that forced Paul and Silas to leave Thessalonica suddenly for Berea (17:5–9, 10). When Jews from Thessalonica arrive to pursue charges against Paul and Silas, Paul is sent away by himself by night to Athens, while Silas and Timothy (who has joined them) stay in Berea (17:13–14). Paul waits for Silas and Timothy in Athens, where he is provoked by widespread idolatry to preach in the marketplace. His preaching leads to a request to present his teaching to the Areopagus. After an indeterminate time, Paul then moves on to Corinth (18:1), where Silas and Timothy eventually rejoin him (18:5). The fit between these details and Paul's sketchier version of events in 1 Thessalonians is very close. Some traditions put Paul's writing of 1 Thessalonians in Athens,[32] but Acts 18:5, combined with Paul's mention of Achaia in 1 Thessalonians 1:8, are conclusive reasons to situate the writing of 1 Thessalonians in Corinth. According to the most likely general Pauline chronology, then, 1 Thessalonians will have been written in A.D. 50, early in Paul's stay in Corinth and perhaps four to six months after his ministry in Thessalonica.[33]

Before we move on to 2 Thessalonians, however, an important preliminary matter needs to be settled: Is 2 Thessalonians really an accurate title for the letter? We must remember that the titles of the New Testament books were added when the letters were collected; they are not part of the original text. The early Christians who called one letter 1 Thessalonians and the other 2 Thessalonians were probably making a judgment about their chronological relationship—it is unlikely that the enumeration reflects only the canonical order, based perhaps on relative length. But is that judgment correct? At least some scholars think it was not. The idea that 2 Thessalonians was written before 1 Thessalonians has had occasional advocates through the years,[34] and it has been advanced recently in the major commentary of Charles Wanamaker. Wanamaker cites several reasons for reversing the order, but the most important are: (1) in 2 Thessalonians, persecution is treated as a present reality (2 Thess. 1:4–7), while in 1 Thessalonians it is past (1 Thess. 2:14); (2) the authenticating signature of 2 Thessalonians 3:17 makes best sense if 2 Thessalonians were the first letter Paul wrote to the church; (3) 2 Thessalonians corresponds remarkably well with Paul's remarks in 1 Thessalonians 3:1–5 about Timothy's mission to Thessalonica; and (4) Paul's claim in 1 Thessalonians 5:1 that he has no need to instruct the Thessalonians about the time of the end makes best sense if he had already written 2 Thessalonians 2:1–12.[35]

---

[32]The tradition is found in the Marcionite Prologues and in the superscriptions in some MSS (cf. Malherbe, *The Letters to the Thessalonians,* 71–72).

[33]On the chronology, see especially Riesner, *Paul's Early Period,* 364–66.

[34]See esp. T. W. Manson, "St. Paul in Greece: The Letters to the Thessalonians," *BJRL* 35 (1952–53): 428–47.

[35]Wanamaker, *Epistles to the Thessalonians,* 37–45.

Since the usual order of the letters is based on nothing more than tradition and historical/literary reasoning, a reversal of the order meets with no theological problems. Nevertheless, there are solid reasons for retaining the usual sequence. First, the arguments in favor of a reversal of sequence are by no means conclusive. 1 Thessalonians 2:14 need not indicate that the persecution was past when Paul wrote; he is simply referring to the persecution he had *heard about* in the past. The authenticating signature in 2 Thessalonians is probably added because of the apparent existence of Pauline forgeries (2:2). 1 Thessalonians 3:1–5 could describe the content of 2 Thessalonians, but the description is quite vague, and, had Paul sent Timothy with a letter, we might have expected him to mention it (cf. 1 Cor. 5:9). And finally, 1 Thessalonians 5:1–2 could as easily refer to Paul's oral teaching when he was at Thessalonica as to 2 Thessalonians. Second, at least two strong arguments in favor of the usual sequence of letters can be marshaled. Second Thessalonians 2:15 seems to presume that Paul had already written a letter to the Thessalonians. Granted the short period of time involved, this would almost have to be 1 Thessalonians. And the familial tone of 1 Thessalonians suggests an initial letter to a group of very recent converts.[36]

If, then, we maintain the usual sequence of the letters, the close relationships between 1 and 2 Thessalonians that we noted above strongly suggest that it was written very shortly after 1 Thessalonians—either late in A.D. 50 or early in A.D. 51.

OPPONENTS AND PURPOSE

The content of 1 Thessalonians reveals that Paul had three basic purposes in writing: to clear up any misconceptions about his own motives in light of his hasty departure from Thessalonica (chaps. 1–3); to remind the Thessalonians of some key ethical implications of their new faith (4:1–12); and to comfort the Thessalonians over the death of some of their fellow Christians (4:13–5:11). Further discussion of the first and third of these purposes is required.

Paul's defensive posture about his motives and methods in preaching the gospel to the Thessalonians in 2:1–12 has occasioned lively debate. On one side are those who find in this passage evidence that Paul was combating definite opponents, usually thought to be Jews (cf. Acts 17:5)[37] but also identified as spiritual enthusiasts[38] or gnostics.[39] On the other side are those who think that Paul refers to his own example out of a purely parenetic concern. Abraham

---

[36]For these points and others, see esp. Jewett, *The Thessalonian Correspondence,* 26–30; Malherbe, *The Letters to the Thessalonians,* 361–64.

[37]E.g., James Everett Frame, *A Critical and Exegetical Commentary on the Epistles of St. Paul to the Thessalonians,* ICC (Edinburgh: T. & T. Clark, 1912), 9–20.

[38]Jewett, *The Thessalonian Correspondence,* 149–70.

[39]Schmithals, *Paul and the Gnostics,* 136–55.

Malherbe is the chief exponent of this latter view. In a series of articles and now in his commentary, he notes the similarities between Paul's description of his own motive and methods and those of ancient philosopher/teachers such as Dio Chrysostom (a younger contemporary of Paul's). Paul, Malherbe argues, is following the pattern of Dio and other teachers who use an antithetical style to make positive claims about their purity of motives. No opponents of any kind need be posited.[40] However, if Malherbe is quite right to protest that there is no good evidence for definite opponents in 1 Thessalonians, he has gone too far in denying any apologetic motive in 2 Thessalonians 2:1–12. As Malherbe and others have pointed out, the claims to purity of motive, especially with regard to the taking money, that are found in the ancient philosophers arise precisely because they needed to distance themselves from immoral and unscrupulous wandering teachers such as the sophists.[41] Paul would be well aware that some in Thessalonica, especially those who opposed the gospel, would jump at the chance of discrediting his message by accusing him of being no better than one of these sophists—especially when he left at the first sign of persecution. Paul's extensive defense of his ministry in 2:1–12, therefore, while not directed against any specific opponents, is probably directed against this general criticism that he must have known was circulating in the city.[42]

Paul's eschatological teaching in 4:13–5:11 is designed to comfort the Thessalonians over the death of some of their fellow-Christians (4:13, 18; 5:11). The focus on chronology in 4:13–18 strongly suggests that the Thessalonians must have thought that their dead brothers and sisters would be at a disadvantage compared to living believers at the time of Christ's return in glory. But there is lively debate over just what their misunderstanding might have been. Some think that in these early days of Paul's ministry he was so convinced of the near return of Christ that he did not bother to teach about the resurrection of believers.[43] But as we have noted above, the emphasis on imminence in the early church has been

---

[40]See esp. Malherbe, "Gentle as a Nurse: The Cynic Background to 1 Thess. 2," *NovT* 12 (1970): 203–17 (republished in *Paul and the Popular Philosophers* [Minneapolis: Fortress Press, 1989], 35–48); idem, *Paul and Thessalonians: The Philosophical Tradition of Pastoral Care* (Philadelphia: Fortress Press, 1987); idem, *The Letters to the Thessalonians*, 81–86, 153–56.

[41]See, for instance, Bruce W. Winter, "The Entries and Ethics of Orators and Paul (1 Thessalonians 2:1–12)," *TynB* 44 (1993): 54–74.

[42]See esp. Winter, "Entries and Ethics"; Riesner, *Paul's Early Period*, 368–70; Jeffrey A. D. Weima, "The Function of 1 Thessalonians 2:1–12 and the Use of Rhetorical Criticism: A Response to Otto Merk," in *The Thessalonians Debate: Methodological Discord or Methodological Synthesis?* ed. Karl P. Donfried and Johannes Beutler (Grand Rapids: Eerdmans, 2000), 114–31; Traugott Holtz, "On the Background of 1 Thessalonians 2:1–12," in *The Thessalonians Debate*, 69–80.

[43]See, e.g., Gerd Luedemann, *Paul: Apostle to the Gentiles: Studies in Chronology* (Philadelphia: Fortress Press, 1984), 212–38.

overdrawn. And in any case, it is unlikely that Paul would have omitted so basic a Christian teaching as the resurrection in his preaching. Nevertheless, Paul's stay in Thessalonica was abruptly cut short because of the persecution. Perhaps Paul had not yet mentioned, or at least not yet developed, his teaching about the resurrection of Christians before he had to leave the city.[44] However, the passage does not read as if Paul were teaching about the resurrection of believers for the first time; the emphasis falls on the chronological relationship between living and dead believers at the time of the parousia. Probably, then, the Thessalonians knew about both the resurrection of dead Christians and the rapture of living ones but did not know how to relate these to each other. They were distressed over the prospect that dead believers, although eventually raised, might miss out on the joyful reunion with the Lord at the time of his return.[45]

In 1 Thessalonians, therefore, Paul seeks to strengthen the faith of new converts. He does so by reminding them that they have been transformed by a powerful and reliable word from God, by encouraging them to hold fast to basic Christian ethical standards, and by comforting them about their brothers and sisters who have died. In 2 Thessalonians, Paul pursues the same basic purpose, with his focus especially on the problems occasioned by a fresh outbreak of persecution. He puts the Thessalonian persecution into eschatological perspective (chap. 1) and deals with two issues that both probably arose because of the Thessalonians' suffering: their erroneous notion that the day of the Lord had arrived (2:1–12), and their tendency to idleness (3:6–15).

1 AND 2 THESSALONIANS IN RECENT STUDY

Scholars continue to investigate the traditional areas of study that we have surveyed above: authorship, situation, theology. But three foci that typify recent trends in New Testament study generally have particularly occupied scholars' time: sociological investigation, literary analysis, and developmental theological proposals.

Contemporary scholarship insists that we root the New Testament documents in their social settings if we ever hope to understand them. In keeping with this concern, several scholars have analyzed factors in first-century society that help us understand Paul's original mission in Thessalonica and his letters to the church there.[46] Wayne A. Meeks, followed by Malherbe, for instance,

---

[44]See Marshall, *1 & 2 Thessalonians*, 120–22; Riesner, *Paul's Early Period*, 384–86.

[45]So, essentially, Best, *The First and Second Epistles to the Thessalonians*, 180–84; Wanamaker, *The Epistles to the Thessalonians*, 165–66; Malherbe, *The Letters to the Thessalonians*, 283–85.

[46]See, for instance, the lengthy discussion in Gene L. Green, *The Letters to the Thessalonians*, PNTC (Grand Rapids: Eerdmans, 2002), 1–47. Todd D. Still suggests that the social context might shed light on the nature of the conflict that Paul and the

has drawn attention to the importance of the *insula*, the row of shops facing the street in Roman cities like Thessalonica, as a setting for Paul's preaching.[47] Paul makes clear that he occupied himself in his trade of tent-making while he preached to the Thessalonians (1 Thess. 2:9). We can imagine the apostle taking advantage of the open-front shop where he worked to share the good news with passers-by.

More controversial is the suggestion that the socioreligious situation addressed in the Thessalonian correspondence might have comparable modern situations to which the letters are particularly apposite. Robert Jewett, for instance, posits a "Millenarian model" behind the Thessalonian letters.[48] There are, of course, similarities between the audiences and problems addressed in New Testament letters and modern audiences and problems. But sociological analysis across so many centuries must proceed extremely cautiously; there are simply too many variables and unknowns.

The literary turn in New Testament studies has thrown 1 Thessalonians into the scholarly spotlight. Since most scholars regard 1 Thessalonians as the first of Paul's letters, its form and genre have become the subject of intense scrutiny. Paul Schubert initiated this approach as long ago as 1939,[49] but it has taken off in the last decade. Attention is focused especially on the possible parallels between the components of 1 Thessalonians and standard Greco-Roman rhetorical categories. Other scholars debate the general rhetorical category to which the letter belongs, the most popular options being the "consolatory letter"[50] and the "friendship letter."[51] And the general category of rhetoric operative in the letter is debated, some thinking the praise and blame emphasis of

> *Since most scholars regard 1 Thessalonians as the first of Paul's letters, its form and genre have become the subject of intense scrutiny.*

Thessalonians experienced (*Conflict at Thessalonica: A Pauline Church and Its Neighbours*, JSNTSup 183 [Sheffield: Sheffield Academic Press, 1999]); while J. R. Harrison argues that the eschatology of 1 Thessalonians may be crafted in response to the cosmic and soteriological claims being made for the Roman Emperor ("Paul and the Imperial Cult at Thessaloniki," *JSNT* 25 [2002]: 71–96).

[47]Wayne A. Meeks, *The First Urban Christians* (New Haven: Yale University Press, 1983); Malherbe, *The Letter to the Thessalonians*, 64–67.

[48]See Jewett, *The Thessalonian Correspondence*.

[49]Paul Schubert, *Form and Function of the Pauline Thanksgiving* (Berlin: Töpelmann, 1939).

[50]See, e.g., Abraham Smith, *Comfort One Another: Reconstructing the Rhetoric and Audience of 1 Thessalonians* (Louisville: Westminster John Knox, 1995), 42–60; Donfried, "The Theology of 1 Thessalonians," 38–41. J. Chapa thinks the letter cannot formally be classified as a letter of consolation, although it contains some similarities to these letters ("Is First Thessalonians a Letter of Consolation?" *NTS* 40 [1994]: 150–60).

[51]E.g., Johannes Schoon-Janssen, "On the Use of Elements of Ancient Epistolography in 1 Thessalonians," in *The Thessalonians Debate*, 179–90; Malherbe, *Paul and the Thessalonians*, 68–78.

the letter puts in the category of epideictic (that is, designed for rhetorical effect),[52] while others emphasize parenesis (exhortation).[53] Analysis of the literary features of the letter and comparison with existing Greco-Roman categories can shed light on the way the argument of the letter proceeds, but it must be said that the benefits of most of the comparative studies appear to be minimal.[54]

The early date of the Thessalonian letters has also made them a focus of a different kind of study: comparison of their theological content with the later Pauline letters. Such comparison often, it is claimed, reveals the primitive nature of the theology found in the Thessalonian letters and at the same time reveals just how much Paul developed key elements of what would typify his later theology only at a comparatively late date. Particularly singled out in this regard is the doctrine of justification by faith, which is said to be absent from the Thessalonian letters. But two important recent books mount a serious challenge to this developmental hypothesis. In *Paul Between Damascus and Antioch,* Martin Hengel and Anna Maria Schwemer demonstrate that key Pauline doctrines—such as justification and the significance of the cross—are indeed present in 1 Thessalonians, albeit in a more muted form than elsewhere.[55] And Riesner, in his *Paul's Early Years,* reminds us that Paul has been preaching the gospel for at least fifteen years when 1 Thessalonians was written; he was no novice preacher. It is not development but situation that dictates what Paul includes in 1 Thessalonians. "Paul's theology as evident in 1 Thessalonians, compared with that of his later letters, cannot simply be characterized as a theology in the early stages of development; rather, it is situationally determined, and only those specific themes move to the foreground which the apostle's pastoral concerns consider necessary."[56] Paul had left Thessalonica only a few months before writing; he had no need in 1 Thessalonians to rehearse all the theological points he had taught when he was there.

---

[52]Steve Walton, "What has Aristotle to do with Paul? Rhetorical Criticism and 1 Thessalonians," *TynB* 46 (1995): 229–50.

[53]Wanamaker, *The Epistles to the Thessalonians,* 60–61; Malherbe, *The Letters to the Thessalonians,* 81–86.

[54]See A. Vanhoye, "La Composition de 1 Thessaloniciens," *The Thessalonian Correspondence,* 73–86; B. C. Johanson, *To All the Brethren: A Text-Linguistic and Rhetorical Approach to 1 Thessalonians,* ConBNT 16 (Stockholm: Almquist & Wiksells, 1987), 187–88.

[55]Martin Hengel and Anna Maria Schwemer, *Paul Between Damascus and Antioch: The Unknown Years* (Louisville: Westminster/John Knox, 1997), 302–7.

[56]Riesner, *Paul's Early Years,* 394–403 (quotation on 403).

THE CONTRIBUTION OF THE THESSALONIAN EPISTLES

When one thinks of the distinctive contribution of the Thessalonian letters, one thinks immediately of eschatology. And to be sure, the letters are a basic source for the eschatological teaching of Paul and the New Testament in general. Although eschatological teaching is concentrated in 1 Thessalonians 4:13–5:11 and 2 Thessalonians 2:1–12, Paul implies its importance for the letters generally by identifying Jesus early in 1 Thessalonians as the one "who rescues us from the coming wrath" (1:10). In 1 Thessalonians 4:13–18, as a way of comforting the Thessalonians in light of their misunderstanding of the relationship between dead and living believers at the parousia, Paul goes into more detail than anywhere else on the precise sequence of events. At the parousia, God will regather all the saints with Jesus. But they will be regathered in a particular order: "the dead in Christ will rise first" (4:16), and only then will those believers who are still alive be "caught up together with them in the clouds to meet the Lord in the air" (4:17).

In addition to confirming the New Testament teaching about the resurrection of dead Christians, this text also pins down its time—at the parousia—and teaches the doctrine of the "rapture": the "snatching up" of living Christians to meet Christ when he returns. Many scholars also find in this text an important confirmation of the idea that Paul and other early Christians believed in an imminent parousia. The accuracy of this conclusion depends on what we mean by "imminent." As we noted above, Paul's use of "we" to refer to those who will be alive when the Lord returns does not necessarily mean that he was certain he would be alive at the parousia; and if this is what is meant by "imminency," we must question whether Paul teaches it. But he clearly reckons fully and even hopefully with the possibility that he might be alive when Christ returns. And if, therefore, we mean by "imminency" the keen expectation that the parousia could occur within a very short period of time, then 1 Thessalonians can, indeed, be said to teach imminency.

The following paragraph (5:1–11) emphasizes this idea of imminence further by comparing the parousia to the coming of a thief in the night (v. 2). Nevertheless, here it is the unbeliever, Paul claims, who will be caught by surprise when the Lord returns. Believers, knowing that the day of Christ's return is coming, will prepare themselves for it by living appropriately for the day that has already dawned (vv. 7–8). The juxtaposition of the presence of the "Day" with its future coming reflects and contributes to the characteristic New Testament inaugurated eschatology.

In 2 Thessalonians, Paul confronts quite a different situation and thus focuses on a different side of his eschatology. Two important points emerge. First, Paul makes clear the reality of future judgment for those who are now tormenting the Thessalonians (1:6–10). Second, the day of the Lord, the time when

God through Jesus intervenes to save his people and judge their enemies, will only occur after other preliminary events: the "rebellion" and the revelation of the man of lawlessness (2:3). A few expositors think Paul might be referring to the destruction of Jerusalem in A.D. 70, but it is more likely that his focus is on events that will immediately precede the parousia. Paul's language probably points to an outbreak of general religious apostasy, focused especially on a last great "antichrist" figure. Quite debated is another aspect of the passage, Paul's reference to a "restrainer" that is now holding back the outbreak of final evil (vv. 7–8). Dozens of suggestions for the identity of this "restrainer" have been offered, the most common—and most likely—being civil government and the Holy Spirit.

But it would be a mistake to think that the Thessalonian letters contribute only to our understanding of eschatology. Two other themes should especially be noted. First, 1 Thessalonians exhibits a striking emphasis on the word of God. Paul refers to the word, or the message of the gospel, using a variety of formulations, nine times in chapters 1–2. And sometimes lost in the discussions of Paul's description of his own motives and methods in preaching in chapters 1–2 is the centrality of the word (1:5, 6, 8; 2:2, 4, 8, 9, 13) and the faith that is the natural and appropriate response to that word. Paul's purpose in these chapters is essentially to show the Thessalonians how he tried his best to get out of the way of the word of God—to let it loose so that it would have its full impact on their lives. It is not Paul the preacher who is important, but the message that he proclaimed. Paul identifies that message with the "word of God," and is thankful that the Thessalonians accepted it "not as a human word, but as it actually is, the word of God, which is indeed at work in you who believe" (2:13). These verses remind us of the active and powerful nature of God's word, the message of the gospel. As Hengel and Schwemer put it, we find in 1 Thessalonians especially a strong "Word of God theology."[57]

A final significant contribution of 1 Thessalonians stems especially from its overall purpose: to strengthen the faith of new converts. Paul writes to nurture a young Christian community in the midst of a hostile and pluralistic environment—a situation not far off from the situation the church in our day faces.[58] 1 Thessalonians deals with many of the problems faced by new converts, such as alienation from family and friends and the cooling of one's initial spiritual ardor. The persecution that so quickly arose was an immediate and painful sign of the alienation that they were experiencing. Paul reminds the church that such persecution is the norm to be expected (2:14–16; cf. 2 Thess. 1:5) and that it is their rootedness in the word of God that will keep them steadfast (1:6; 2:13).

---

[57]Hengel and Schwemer, *Paul Between Damascus and Antioch,* 304; cf. also Donfried, "The Theology of 1 Thessalonians," 55.

[58]See Donfried, "The Theology of 1 Thessalonians."

Paul therefore uses many familial images to remind the Christians that their faith in Christ has introduced them into a new spiritual and eternal family. Paul himself acted as both father (2:11) and mother (2:7) to the fledging congregation. The Christians themselves are, of course, "brothers and sisters" (2:1, 14, 17; 3:7; 4:1, 6, 10, 13; 5:1, 4, 12, 14, 25); and they need to exhibit the "love for one another" that should typify family (4:9–10).[59]

BIBLIOGRAPHY

J. A. **Bailey**, "Who Wrote II Thessalonians?" *NTS* 25 (1978–79): 131–45 ▥G. K. **Beale**, *1–2 Thessalonians*, IVPNTC (Downers Grove: IVP, 2003) ▥E. **Best**, *A Commentary on the First and Second Epistles to the Thessalonians*, HNTC (London: Adam & Charles Black, 1977) ▥H. **Boers**, "The Form-Critical Study of Paul's Letters: 1 Thessalonians as a Case Study," *NTS* 22 (1975–76): 140–58 ▥F. F. **Bruce**, *1 & 2 Thessalonians*, WBC 45 (Waco: Word, 1982) ▥idem, "St. Paul in Macedonia: 2. The Thessalonian Correspondence," *BJRL* 62 (1980): 328–45 ▥J. **Chapa**, "Is First Thessalonians a Letter of Consolation?" *NTS* 40 (1994): 150–60 ▥Raymond F. **Collins**, "Apropos the Integrity of I Thes.," *EphThLov* 55 (1979): 67–106 ▥L.-M. **Dewailly**, *La jeune église de Thessalonique: Les deux premières épîtres de Saint Paul* (Paris: Cerf, 1963) ▥Martin **Dibelius**, *A Fresh Approach to the New Testament and Early Christian Literature* (London: Ivor Nicholson & Watson, 1936) ▥Karl Paul **Donfried**, "The Cults of Thessalonica and the Thessalonian Correspondence," *NTS* 31 (1985): 336–56 ▥idem, "The Theology of 1 Thessalonians," in *The Theology of the Shorter Pauline Letters* (Cambridge: Cambridge University Press, 1993) ▥K. G. **Eckart**, "Der zweite echte Brief des Apostels Paulus an die Thessalonicher," *ZTK* 58 (1961): 30–44 ▥E. Earle **Ellis**, "Paul and His Co-Workers," *NTS* 17 (1970–71): 437–52 ▥J. E. **Frame**, *A Critical and Exegetical Commentary on the Epistles of St. Paul to the Thessalonians*, ICC (Edinburgh: T. & T. Clark, 1912) ▥Charles H. **Giblin**, *The Threat to Faith: An Exegetical and Theological Re-examination of 2 Thessalonians 2*, AnBib 31 (Rome: Pontifical Biblical Institute, 1967) ▥Gene L. **Green**, *The Letters to the Thessalonians*, PNTC (Grand Rapids: Eerdmans, 2002) ▥Adolf von **Harnack**, "Der Problem des zweiten Thessalonicherbriefes," in *Sitzungsberichte der königlichen preussischen Akademie des Wissenschaften zu Berlin* 31 (1910): 560–78 ▥J. R. **Harrison**, "Paul and the Imperial Cult at Thessaloniki," *JSNT* 25 (2002): 71–96 ▥Martin **Hengel** and Anna Maria **Schwemer**, *Paul Between Damascus and Antioch: The Unknown Years* (Louisville: Westminster John Knox, 1997) ▥W. **Hendriksen**, *Exposition of I and II Thessalonians* (Grand Rapids: Baker, 1955) ▥R. F. **Hock**, "The Workshop as a Social Setting for Paul's Missionary Preaching," *CBQ* 41 (1979): 438–50 ▥G. **Holland**, "'A Letter Supposedly from Us': A Contribution to the Discussion about the

---

[59]See Riesner, *Paul's Early Period*, 371–72.

Authorship of 2 Thessalonians," in *The Thessalonian Correspondence*, ed. Raymond F. Collins, BETL 87 (Leuven: Leuven University Press, 1990), 394–402 ▥Traugott **Holtz**, "On the Background of 1 Thessalonians 2:1–12," in *The Thessalonians Debate: Methodological Discord or Methodological Synthesis?* ed. Karl P. Donfried and Johannes Beutler (Grand Rapids: Eerdmans, 2000), 69–80 ▥Frank W. **Hughes**, *Early Christian Rhetoric and 2 Thessalonians*, JSNTSup 30 (Sheffield: JSOT Press, 1989) ▥idem, "The Rhetoric of 1 Thessalonians," in *The Thessalonian Correspondence*, ed. Raymond F. Collins, BETL 87 (Leuven: Leuven University Press, 1990) ▥Jacob **Jervell**, *Die Apostelgeschichte*, KEK (Göttingen: Vandenhoeck & Ruprecht, 1998) ▥Robert **Jewett**, *The Thessalonian Correspondence: Pauline Rhetoric and Millenarian Piety* (Philadelphia: Fortress Press, 1986) ▥B. C. **Johanson**, *To All the Brethren: A Text-Linguistic and Rhetorical Approach to 1 Thessalonians*, ConBNT 16 (Stockholm: Almqvist & Wiksell, 1987) ▥Edwin A. **Judge**, "The Decrees of Caesar at Thessalonica," *RTR* 30 (1975): 1–7 ▥Bruce N. **Kaye**, "Eschatology and Ethics in 1 and 2 Thessalonians," *NovT* 17 (1975): 47–57 ▥Kirsopp **Lake**, *The Earlier Epistles of St. Paul: Their Motive and Origin* (London: Rivingstons, 1911) ▥A. **Lindemann**, "Zum Abfassunszweck des Zweiten Thessalonicherbriefes," *ZNW* 68 (1977): 35–47 ▥R. N. **Longenecker**, "The Nature of Paul's Early Eschatology," *NTS* 31 (1985): 85–95 ▥idem, "On the Form, Function, and Authority of the New Testament Letters," in *Scripture and Truth*, ed. D. A. Carson and John D. Woodbridge (Grand Rapids: Zondervan, 1983), 101–14 ▥Gerd **Luedemann**, *Paul: Apostle to the Gentiles. Studies in Chronology* (Philadelphia: Fortress Press, 1984) ▥A. **Malherbe**, "Gentle as a Nurse: The Cynic Background to 1 Thess. 2," *NovT* 12 (1970): 203–17 (republished in *Paul and the Popular Philosophers* [Minneapolis: Fortress Press, 1989], 35–48) ▥idem, *The Letters to the Thessalonians: A New Translation with Introduction and Commentary*, AB (New York: Doubleday, 2000) ▥idem, *Paul and the Thessalonian: The Philosophical Tradition of Pastoral Care* (Philadelphia: Fortress Press, 1987) ▥T. W. **Manson**, "St. Paul in Greece: The Letters to the Thessalonians," *BJRL* 35 (1952–53): 428–47 ▥I. Howard **Marshall**, *1 and 2 Thessalonians*, NCB (Grand Rapids: Eerdmans, 1983) ▥Charles **Masson**, *Les deux épîtres de Saint Paul aux Thessaloniciens*, CNT (Neuchâtel: Delachaux & Niestlé, 1957) ▥C. L. **Mearns**, "Early Eschatological Development in Paul: The Evidence of I and II Thessalonians," *NTS* 27 (1980–81): 137–57 ▥Wayne **Meeks**, *The First Urban Christians* (New Haven: Yale University Press, 1983) ▥Leon **Morris**, *The First and Second Epistles to the Thessalonians*, rev. ed., NICNT (Grand Rapids: Eerdmans, 1991) ▥A. Q. **Morton** and James **McLeman**, *Christianity and the Computer* (London: Hodder & Stoughton, 1964) ▥Jerome **Murphy-O'Connor,** *Paul the Letter-Writer: His World, His Options, His Skills* (Collegeville: Liturgical Press, 1995) ▥Colin R. **Nicholl**, *From Hope to Despair in Thessalonica: Situating 1 and 2 Thessalonians*, SNTSMS 126 (Cambridge: Cambridge University Press, 2004) ▥B. A. **Pearson**, "1 Thessalonians 2:13–16: A Deutero-Pauline Interpolation," *HTR* 64 (1971): 79–94 ▥William

M. **Ramsay**, *Saint Paul, the Traveller and Roman Citizen* (London: Hodder & Stoughton, 1897) ▥Bo **Reicke**, *Re-examining Paul's Letters: The History of the Pauline Correspondence*, ed. David P. Moessner (Harrisburg: Trinity Press International, 2001) ▥Earl J. **Richards**, *1 and 2 Thessalonians*, SacPag 11 (Collegeville: Liturgical, 1995) ▥Earl **Richards**, Edgar **Krentz**, Robert **Jewett**, and Jouette M. **Bassler**, "The Theology of the Thessalonian Correspondence," in *Pauline Theology*, vol. 1, *Thessalonians, Philippians, Galatians, Philemon*, ed. Jouette M. Bassler (Minneapolis: Fortress Press, 1991), 37–85 ▥Rainer **Riesner**, *Paul's Early Period: Chronology, Mission Strategy, Theology* (Grand Rapids: Eerdmans, 1998) ▥B. **Rigaux**, *Les épîtres aux Thessaloniciens* (Paris: Gabalda, 1956) ▥Carol J. **Schlueter**, *Filling Up the Measure: Polemical Hyperbole in 1 Thessalonians 2.14–16*, JSNTSup 98 (Sheffield: JSOT Press, 1994) ▥D. D. **Schmidt**, "The Syntactical Style of 2 Thessalonians: How Pauline Is It?" in *The Thessalonian Correspondence*, ed. Raymond F. Collins, BETL 87 (Leuven: Leuven University Press, 1990) ▥W. **Schmithals**, "Die Thessalonicherbriefe als Briefkompositionen," in *Zeit und Geschichte, Fs. R. Bultmann*, ed. E. Dinkler (Tübingen: Mohr-Siebeck, 1964), 295–315 ▥idem, *Paul and the Gnostics* (Nashville: Abingdon, 1972) ▥Johannes **Schoon-Janssen**, "On the Use of Elements of Ancient Epistolography in 1 Thessalonians," in *The Thessalonians Debate: Methodological Discord or Methodological Synthesis?* ed. Karl P. Donfried and Johannes Beutler (Grand Rapids: Eerdmans, 2000), 179–90 ▥P. **Schubert**, *Form and Function of the Pauline Thanksgiving* (Berlin: Töpelmann, 1939) ▥Abraham **Smith**, *Comfort One Another: Reconstructing the Rhetoric and Audience of 1 Thessalonians* (Louisville: Westminster John Knox, 1995) ▥Todd D. **Still**, *Conflict at Thessalonica: A Pauline Church and its Neighbours*, JSNTSup 183 (Sheffield: Sheffield Academic Press, 1999) ▥Wolfgang **Trilling**, *Untersuchungen zum zweiten Thessalonicherbrief* (Leipzig: St. Benno, 1972) ▥A. **Vanhoye**, "La Composition de 1 Thessaloniciens," in *The Thessalonian Correspondence*, ed. Raymond F. Collins, BETL 87 (Leuven: Leuven University Press, 1990), 73–86 ▥Steve **Walton**, "What has Aristotle to do with Paul?—Rhetorical Criticism and 1 Thessalonians," *TynB* 46 (1995): 229–50 ▥Charles A. **Wanamaker**, *The Epistles to the Thessalonians*, NIGTC (Grand Rapids: Eerdmans, 1990) ▥Jeffrey A. D. **Weima**, "The Function of 1 Thessalonians 2:1–12 and the Use of Rhetorical Criticism: A Response to Otto Merk," in *The Thessalonians Debate: Methodological Discord or Methodological Synthesis?* Karl P. Donfried and Johannes Beutler (Grand Rapids: Eerdmans, 2000), 114–31 ▥Jeffrey A. D. **Weima** and Stanley **Porter**, *An Annotated Bibliography of 1 and 2* Thessalonians (Leiden: Brill, 1998) ▥Bruce W. **Winter**, "The Entries and Ethics of Orators and Paul (1 Thessalonians 2:1–12)," *TynB* 44 (1993): 54–74.

CHAPTER SEVENTEEN

THE PASTORAL EPISTLES

THEIR RELATIONSHIP TO OTHER PAULINE EPISTLES

The two epistles to Timothy and that to Titus are usually classed together under the title "Pastoral Epistles," a title that was apparently given to them by D. N. Berdot in 1703 and followed by Paul Anton in 1726.[1] The term is almost universally used in modern discussions. It is objected that the title is not completely appropriate because the letters are not taken up with pastoral duties. However, since they are directed to people with pastoral responsibility and with the task of appointing pastors, the expression is unobjectionable. The three letters form a unit in that they are the only New Testament letters addressed to individuals with such responsibilities (Philemon is addressed to an individual, but not one in a position like that of Timothy or Titus).

Despite a number of similarities that link these three letters, nothing conclusively demonstrates that they were written at the same time or from the same place, or that the author intended them to be studied together. They are almost routinely treated as a group in modern studies, and it is necessary to consider the three together if we are to follow modern writing. But there are differences among them that may be important. For example, while 1 Timothy has quite a lot to say about the ministry of the church, 2 Timothy has practically nothing and Titus very little to say on this subject. False teaching is being opposed in all three letters, and it is usual to treat this teaching as though it were the same in all cases,[2]

---

[1]So Donald Guthrie, *The Pastoral Epistles and the Minds of Paul* (London: Tyndale, 1957), 11.

[2]This view is part of a sustained effort in some recent scholarship to construct a definite and believable background to all three Pastoral Epistles, taken together. It is forcefully presented (though from very different perspectives) by, among others, David C. Verner, *The Household of God: The Social World of the Pastoral Epistles*, SBLDS 71 (Chico: SP, 1983); Gordon D. Fee, *1 and 2 Timothy, Titus*, GNC (San Francisco: Harper

but we need to ask if it really is. From another angle, Johnson points out that the Thessalonian correspondence might well look different if we decided to isolate these letters from all the other Pauline writings and treat them as a group on their own. He puts the other side of the coin in this way: "[I]f Titus is read with other travel letters, or 2 Timothy with other captivity letters, their strangeness is greatly diminished."[3] In discussing problems that arise from these three writings, we should bear in mind that things would look a lot different if we studied each one by itself or in a different grouping.

Contemporary critical orthodoxy insists that the Pastorals were all written by someone other than Paul and at a time considerably later than that of the apostle. Considerations of style, vocabulary, attention to church order, and attitude to orthodoxy and to heretical teachings are some of the things that lead most scholars to hold that the letters are pseudonymous and that they do not fit into Paul's world. Despite all their differences, there are many links with Paul's teaching, so it is generally held that they come from a convinced Paulinist. The writer, it is argued, addresses the problems of his own day as one who has drunk deeply from the Pauline well. He is trying to say to the people of his own day what he thought Paul would have said, had he been confronted by the situation of that day. The following considerations are important.

Vocabulary and Syntax

A strong argument is produced from the vocabulary differences between the three Pastoral epistles and the other ten epistles usually attributed to Paul. P. N. Harrison, building on the work of previous scholars, compiled some impressive statistics.[4] He pointed out that the three Pastorals make use of 902 words, of which 54 are proper names. Of the remaining 848 words, 306 (more than a third of the total) do not occur in the other ten Pauline letters. Of these 306, at least 175 occur nowhere else in the New Testament. The argument is then developed in two ways.

First, it is pointed out that this leaves 542 words shared by the Pauline letters and the Pastorals, of which no more than 50 are characteristic Pauline words in the sense that they are not used by other writers in the New Testament. Of the 492 words that are found in all three bodies—the Pastorals, the rest of Paul, and the rest of the New Testament—there are, of course, the basic words without

---

& Row, 1984); and Philip Towner, *The Goal of Our Instruction: The Structure of Theology and Ethics in the Pastoral Epistles,* JSNTSup 34 (Sheffield: Sheffield Academic Press, 1989). By contrast, others, as we shall see, as adamantly refuse to permit many generalizations that cover all three letters.

[3]Johnson, 424.

[4]P. N. Harrison, *The Problem of the Pastoral Epistles* (London: Oxford University Press, 1921), 20ff.

which it would be impossible to write at all, and words that every Christian writer would necessarily use (e.g., "brother," "love," "faith"). Again, some words have different meanings from book to book. Paul, for example, uses ἀν-τέχομαι *(antechomai)* with the sense "to support," "to aid" (1 Thess. 5:14); the Pastorals, with the meaning "to hold fast" (Titus 1:9); κοινός *(koinos)* means "Levitically unclean" in Paul (Rom. 14:14) and "common" (as in "the common faith") in the Pastorals (Titus 1:4).

Second, it is argued that many of the words in question are found in the apostolic fathers and the apologists of the early second century. Of the 306 words in the Pastorals that are not in the Pauline Epistles, 211 are found in these sec-ond-century writings.[5] This kind of reasoning leads many to the conclusion that the author of the Pastorals was not Paul but probably a writer living at the end of the first century or toward the beginning of the second century. It is held to be unreasonable to think that in his old age Paul would suddenly produce a wealth of new words—moreover, words that are found in a later period.

Third, scholars point out that of the 214 Greek particles found in the ten Pauline letters, 112 do not occur in the Pastoral Epistles. From this many infer that there is a comparative poverty of style in the latter: the connective tissue of the Pastoral Epistles is apparently very different from that of the Pauline ten.

The arguments sound impressive, but they are not as convincing as they seem to be at first sight. Those who put them forward do not always notice, for example, that most of the words shared by the Pastorals and the second-century writers are also found in other writings prior to A.D. 50.[6] It cannot be argued that Paul would not have known them, nor can it be argued that Paul's total vocabulary is the number of words in the ten letters (2,177 words). It is not nec-essary to argue that Paul produced hundreds of new words in his old age, for if he could use 2,177 words, there is no reason for supposing that he could not use another 306 words, most of which are known to have been current in his day. That some of the words are used with different meanings signifies no more than that the contexts are different. Paul also uses words with different meanings in different contexts in the ten letters.

It is misleading simply to say that the Pastorals have 306 words that do not occur in the ten Paulines. On Harrison's own figures, of the 306 there are 127 that occur in 1 Timothy alone, 81 in 2 Timothy alone, and 45 in Titus alone.[7]

---

[5]Ibid., 70.

[6]So Donald Guthrie (*The Pastoral Epistles and the Mind of Paul* [London: Tyndale, 1956], 9), citing among others F. R. M. Hitchcock, "Tests for the Pastorals," *JTS* 30 (1928–29): 272–79; idem, "Philo and the Pastorals," *Hermatheua* 56 (1940): 113–35.

[7]Harrison, *Problem*, 137–39. There are 75 words used in 1 Timothy that are not found elsewhere in the New Testament, plus 52 in 1 Timothy that are also in the non-Pauline New Testament books. For 2 Timothy the figures are 48 + 33 and for Titus 30 + 15.

This means that the vast majority are found in only one of the Pastorals and that the three differ from one another as much as (or more than) they differ from Paul. Are we to say that there were three pseudonymous writers? The statistics constitute no impressive argument for a single author. Or to put the argument in a different way, if the figures show that the three Pastorals were written by one author, they also show that that author may well have been Paul.

True, Harrison makes a good deal of the fact that 112 particles, prepositions, and pronouns appear in the ten but not in the three.[8] He sees it as unlikely that "within a very few years we should find the same writer producing three epistles without once happening to use a single word in all that list—*one or other of which has hitherto appeared on the average nine times to every page that Paul ever wrote.*"[9] Once again he has produced what seems to be a very cogent argument. But Guthrie points out that he has not taken into consideration all the evidence. There are another 93 particles, prepositions, and pronouns, all but 1 appearing in the Pastorals, and all but 7 in Paul. He adds these to Harrison's list and points out that of the 205 there are 92 occurrences in the Pastorals, which compares favorably with the 131 occurrences in Romans, 113 in 2 Corinthians, 86 in Philippians, and so forth. He concludes that "Dr. Harrison's deductions from the connective tissue would seem to be invalid."[10]

This is to be borne in mind when related arguments are put forward. For example, it is pointed out that there are no more than half a dozen references to the Holy Spirit in the Pastorals, whereas Paul refers to him ninety times. This raises the question whether there are places in these letters where Paul must speak of the Spirit. He refers to him on those six occasions when it was appropriate, and we are not in a position to say that the Paul of the ten letters would have referred to him more often. Nor are the references to the Holy Spirit within the ten letters evenly distributed. We must be on our guard against taking up a position of omniscience about what went on in Paul's mind.

The arguments from the vocabulary of the Pastoral Epistles have become more sophisticated during recent decades. Grayston and Herdan began the move toward sophisticated statistical counts,[11] seeking to bolster Harrison's conclusions. Others have fastened on syntactical structures: the length of sentences,

---

[8]Harrison, *Problem*, 36–37.

[9]Ibid., 35 (Harrison's italics).

[10]Guthrie, *The Pastoral Epistles and the Mind of Paul*, 13.

[11]K. Grayston and G. Herdan, "The Authorship of the Pastoral Epistles in the Light of Statistical Linguistics," *NTS* 6 (1959–60): 1–15. A little more recently, A. Q. Morton and some of his colleagues have deployed statistical analyses of such features as the closing word in Pauline sentences, the length of sentences, the spread of different types of conjunction, and the like. See especially his *Literary Detection* (Bath: Bowker, 1978). This work is admirably assessed by Anthony Kenny, *A Stylometric Study of the New Testament* (Oxford: Clarendon, 1986).

word order, the relative frequency of various parts of speech, the positioning of particles, and the like.[12] But here, too, the arguments have proved weak. Statisticians object to the brevity of the Epistles and to the lack of statistical controls. And even where there are observable differences, the statistics themselves cannot tell us *why* the differences exist.[13] Is it because of different authors, or because of different topics, or because these epistles were written to individuals with certain challenges and not to churches with quite a different set of challenges, or because of different amanuenses?[14]

Rhetorical Style

The argument from style embraces both the kinds of arguments advanced by the letters and the manner of composition. One writer concludes, "One notes also that the dramatic vivacity of Pauline argumentation, with its emotional outbursts, its dialogue form of thought, its introduction of real or imaginary opponents and objections, and the use of metaphor and image, is replaced by a certain heaviness and repetitiousness of style."[15] The kinds of differences commonly noted include the fact that there is no opening thanksgiving in 1 Timothy and Titus (though there is one in 2 Timothy, and there isn't one in Galatians), the relative lack of personal material in 1 Timothy and Titus, and the particular patterns of the arguments in the Pastorals—including such little touches as the repeated "Here is a trustworthy saying that deserves full acceptance"[16] (found nowhere outside the Pastoral Epistles).

> Undoubtedly there are differences of style in the Pastoral Epistles. The question is how to account for them.

---

[12]E.g., D. L. Mealand, "Computers in New Testament Research: An Interim Report," *JSNT* 33 (1988): 97–115; idem, "Positional Stylometry Reassessed: Testing a Seven Epistle Theory of Pauline Authorship," *NTS* 35 (1989): 266–86; idem, "The Extent of the Pauline Corpus: A Multivariate Approach," *JSNT* 59 (1995): 61–92; K. Neumann, *The Authenticity of the Pauline Epistles in the Light of Stylo-statistical Analysis* (Atlanta: SP, 1990).

[13]See inter alios, A. E. Bird, "The Authorship of the Pastoral Epistles—Quantifying Literary Style," *RTR* 56 (1997): 118–37; J. J. O'Rourke, "Some Considerations About Attempts at Statistical Analysis of the Pauline Corpus," *CBQ* 35 (1973): 483–90; T. A. Robinson, "Grayston and Herdan's 'C' Quantity Formula and the Authorship of the Pastoral Epistles," *NTS* 30 (1984): 282–88; Kenny, *Stylometric Study*.

[14]For instance, George K. Barr, "Two Styles in the New Testament Epistles," *LLC* 18 (2003): 235–48, argues on the basis of scalometric analysis that the differences between the first four Pauline Epistles and the Pastoral Epistles point, not to different authors, but to differences in style that may be found within the works of one author.

[15]J. C. Beker, "Pastoral Letters" in *IDB*, 3.670.

[16]See especially L. R. Donelson, *Pseudepigraphy and Ethical Argument in the Pastoral Epistles*, HUT 22 (Tübingen: Mohr-Siebeck, 1986); B. Fiore, *The Function of Personal Example in the Socratic and Pastoral Epistles*, AnBib 105 (Rome: Pontifical Biblical Institute, 1986).

Undoubtedly there are differences. The question is how to account for them. If one opts for a pseudonymous author, the differences are explained, but a new set of difficulties has been introduced (as we shall see). Alternatively, one must ask if the differences can be accounted for without appealing to a pseudonymous writer. There are very few convincing control studies to probe the range of expression found in one author writing letters across a span of almost a quarter of a century to persons and groups as diverse as those represented by the Pauline corpus. One wonders whether the difference in style between the Pastorals and the ten Pauline letters is greater than the difference that might legitimately be expected between private letters to trusted fellow workers and public letters to churches, letters usually addressing specific difficulties. And if it is difficult to be certain what inferences should be drawn from the acknowledged differences, it is equally difficult to be certain what inferences should be drawn from incidental similarities.[17]

The uncertainties are compounded if we reflect on the possible influence of an amanuensis. Noting that many of the non-Pauline terms in the Pastorals are found in Luke, C. F. D. Moule suggested that Luke might well have been Paul's amanuensis (and Luke is certainly with Paul, at least in 2 Tim. 4:11).[18] The argument has been developed by Stephen G. Wilson—though he thinks that the Luke in question, the author of the Gospel and Acts, wrote the Pastorals toward the end of the first century and that he was someone other than the Luke who was Paul's companion.[19] Since most of the arguments are the same for both the historical Luke who was the companion of Paul and for the hypothetical Luke

---

[17]E.g., Thomas D. Lea and Hayne P. Griffin Jr., *1, 2 Timothy, Titus*, NAC 34 (Nashville: Broadman Press, 1992), 40, note that the Paul of the Pastorals can quote a minor Greek poet (Epimenides) in Titus 1:12, and the Paul depicted in Acts 17:28 can also quote minor pagan sources (Menander). The Paul of the Pastorals sometimes attaches an individual's profession to his name (e.g., "Alexander the metalworker," 2 Tim. 4:14; "Zenas the lawyer," Tit. 3:13); so also the Paul of the rest of the Pauline corpus (e.g., "Erastus, who is the city's director of public works," Rom. 16:23; "our dear friend Luke, the doctor," Col. 4:14).

[18]"The Problem of the Pastoral Epistles: A Reappraisal," *BJRL* 47 (1965): 430–52 (reprinted in C. F. D. Moule, *Essays in New Testament Interpretation* [Cambridge: Cambridge University Press, 1982], 113–32).

[19]Stephen G. Wilson, *Luke and the Pastoral Epistles* (London: SPCK, 1979). Indeed, Wilson goes so far as to suggest that the Pastoral Epistles constituted Luke's third volume. See also Jerome D. Quinn, "The Last Volume of Luke: The Relation of Luke-Acts and the PE," in *Perspectives on Luke-Acts*, ed. C. Talbert (Macon: Mercer University Press, 1978), 62–75. Quinn appears a little more cautious in his *The Letter to Titus*, AB 35 (New York: Doubleday, 1990), 19, repeated in Jerome D. Quinn and William C. Wacker, *The First and Second Letters to Timothy*, ECC (Grand Rapids: Eerdmans, 2000), 20.

writing at the end of the first century, several recent commentators have leaned toward the view that the historical Luke was Paul's amanuensis.[20] This solution is doubtless possible, but against it is the fact that the ten Pauline letters, all or most of which were written by the hand of an amanuensis, do not come out sounding exactly like the Pastorals, so at the least one would have to infer that in the case of the Pastorals his procedure must have been somewhat different for the two corpora, perhaps because he gave Luke more liberty than he gave earlier amanuenses. Yet even this counter-argument can be tempered, in that it probably presupposes too great a uniformity among the ten. Indeed, on other grounds, Michael Prior stands the amanuensis theory on its head: he recognizes that the Pastoral Epistles are somewhat different from the ten Paulines, but suggests that the reason is not because they are pseudonymous but because they "are private letters in a double sense"—not only were they written to individuals, but they were written by Paul himself *without* an amanuensis. For most of the ten, and perhaps for all of them, Paul used an amanuensis; for six of the ten, Timothy is listed as the coauthor. But in the case of the Pastorals, Prior suggests, Paul wrote everything himself—and this accounts for the differences.[21] This solution is no more transparent than others that have been put forward. Nevertheless, the fact that it can be defended testifies to how much we do not know, and it prompts us to tread cautiously before we adopt too readily the explanation provided by pseudonymity.

If we extend discussion of style to matters of literary genre, there is a little more to be said. Johnson and others have argued that 1 Timothy and Titus fit comfortably into the genre of the mandate letter, and 2 Timothy into the genre of the testament. Both fit Paul's situation admirably and were common enough to have been known by him, but they would have been somewhat alien to someone writing in his name several decades later. Thus, careful reflection on the literary genre supports apostolic authorship.[22] The mandate letter in particular, in which a senior official instructs a junior in his responsibilities as a delegate, alternates instruction about the delegate's duties with passages that focus on the character of the delegate. When the letter was read to the people to whom the delegate was sent, the will of the chief administrator would be clear, and the standards expected of the delegate would simultaneously encourage

---

[20]Gordon D. Fee, *1 and 2 Timothy, Titus*, NIBC (Peabody: Hendrickson, 1988), 26; George W. Knight, *The Pastoral Epistles: A Commentary on the Greek Text*, NIGTC (Grand Rapids: Eerdmans, 1992), 50–52. See also E. Earle Ellis, *Pauline Theology: Ministry and Society* (Grand Rapids: Eerdmans, 1989), 104–11.

[21]Michael Prior, *Paul the Letter-Writer and the Second Letter to Timothy*, JSNTSup 23 (Sheffield: JSOT Press, 1989), 37–59.

[22]So Luke Timothy Johnson, *Letters to Paul's Delegates: 1 Timothy, 2 Timothy, Titus*, The New Testament in Context (Valley Forge: Trinity Press International, 1996), 106–8, passim.

the delegate to faithfulness and provide some written security for the readers against whimsical authority usurped by the delegate, giving them fair grounds on which to complain. Some of this explanation is overwrought, and letters reflecting Egyptian officialdom cannot be applied without certain care and hesitation to a letter from the apostle Paul to a Timothy or Titus. In other words, mandate letters do not constitute a knock-down argument in defense of authenticity.[23] Nevertheless, they provide one plausible parallel to the authority structure and delegation implicit in 1 Timothy and Titus when the documents are read as the personal pieces they purport to be. But that is as much as can be said.

Historical Problems

Many scholars draw attention to the difficulty of fitting the situations envisaged in the Pastorals into what we learn of the life of Paul from Acts and the Pauline letters.[24] It is argued that this is quite impossible, and it is therefore suggested that the author of these letters has manufactured allusions that would give the impression of an historical setting. For example, Paul's only known contact with Crete was his brief stop there en route to Rome as a prisoner (Acts 27:7–13), and this does not easily square with Titus 1:5 ("The reason I left you in Crete. . . ."). We do not have any source to confirm Paul's wintering at Nicopolis (Titus 3:12). Similarly, the personalia in the Timothys do not easily square with what we know of Paul's ministry. Of course, some scholars make room for these events by suggesting they took place *after* Paul's imprisonment in Rome recorded in Acts 28, under the assumption that Paul was released and served for two or three more years before finally being martyred in Rome. After all, *1 Clement* 5:7 reports that Paul journeyed "to the outer limits of the West" (Spain?), which could only have happened after Acts 28. But the critics remain unconvinced that *1 Clement* has got this right,[25] not least because both *1 Clement* and Acts "agree that the goal [of mission to the ends of the earth] is achieved *before* (or in Acts precisely *during*) the one and only imprisonment of Paul"[26]—and so it is best to believe that "the outer limits of the West" refers to Rome itself, and that Paul died in Rome on his first and only visit there.

To these objections one may reply in two possible ways. Several scholars have undertaken to show that the historical data reflected in the Pastorals *could*

---

[23]See the important cautions of Margaret M. Mitchell, "PTebt 703 and the Genre of 1 Timothy: The Curious Career of a Ptolemaic Papyrus in Pauline Scholarship," *NovT* 44 (2002): 344–70.

[24]E.g., Kümmel, 377–78.

[25]Ibid.

[26]Martin Dibelius and Hans Conzelmann, *The Pastoral Epistles*, Hermeneia (Philadelphia: Fortress Press, 1972), 3 (emphasis theirs).

fit within the confines of Paul's known ministry. After all, we know fairly little of what Paul did during those years, and there are huge gaps when other events could be squeezed in. When did he undergo his frequent imprisonments, his five beatings at the hands of the Jews, his three shipwrecks, and the other sufferings that he mentions once only (2 Cor. 11:23–27)? One may say, "I cannot see how to fit the incidents mentioned in the Pastorals into Paul's earlier life," but one may not say, "Those incidents *cannot* be fitted into Paul's earlier life." For example, we know from Acts 20:31 that Paul spent three years in Ephesus. Acts records none of Paul's trips during those years, even though we know from 2 Corinthians 1:23–2:1 that the apostle visited Corinth during this time. What other journeys might he have made during the same period, journeys not reported in Acts? We simply do not have enough information. Especially if we do not take the Pastorals as a unit but consider the letters individually, historical data pose no insuperable difficulty to Pauline authorship.[27]

The other possibility, of course, is that there were two Roman imprisonments, only the first of which is recorded in Acts. One must recall that although Acts finishes with Paul in prison in Rome, the apostle has reasonable prospects of being released. Festus thought that Paul "had done nothing deserving of death" (Acts 25:25), while Agrippa held that there was no case against him and that, had he not appealed to Caesar, he could have been freed (Acts 26:32). Even when he was in Rome, "Paul was allowed to live by himself, with a soldier to guard him" (Acts 28:16); he "stayed there in his own rented house and welcomed all who came to see him" (Acts 28:30); he was free enough to be able to summon Jewish leaders and hold a meeting with them. This does not look like the preliminary to an execution. There is nothing improbable about Paul being set at liberty and engaging in further activities of the sort envisaged in the Pastorals. Moreover, the reference in *1 Clement* to "the outer limits of the West" reads far more naturally, in the Roman Empire, as a reference to Spain than to Rome. Finally, numerous other patristic sources stipulate that Paul was released from his imprisonment in Rome and ministered once again in the East.[28] Indeed, some scholars have worked out detailed post-incarceration itineraries for the

---

[27]For some suggestions as to how the information in the Pastorals can be fitted into what we know of Paul's movements from other sources, see inter alios J. A. T. Robinson, *Redating the New Testament* (Philadelphia: Westminster, 1976), 67–85, and the literature there cited; C. Spicq, *Les épîtres Pastorales,* 4th ed., 2 vols. (Paris: Gabalda, 1969); S. de Lestapis, *L'énigme des Pastorales de Saint Paul* (Paris: Gabalda, 1976); Philip H. Towner, *1 and 2 Timothy, Titus,* IVPNTC (Downers Grove: IVP, 1994); Bo Reicke, *Re-examining Paul's Letters: The History of the Pauline Correspondence* (Harrisburg: Trinity Press International, 2001), 51–59, 68–73, 85–91.

[28]Viz., the Muratorian Canon, Eusebius, Athanasius, Epiphanius, Jerome, Theodore of Mopsuestia, Pelagius, and Theodoret. See Knight, *The Pastoral Epistles,* 17–19.

apostle.[29] One cannot prove such theories, of course, for there is insufficient evidence. But even Marshall, who defends a variation of the pseudonymity theory, concludes, "It follows that there is no insuperable obstacle to the historical possibility of the scenario described [i.e., Paul being released from prison and ministering in the East for several years, before re-arrest, imprisonment, and martyrdom], whether as part of an authentic letter of Paul or as fragments of an authentic letter."[30]

It is no less important to put the shoe on the other foot and squarely face the difficulties of fitting the personal reminiscences in the Pastorals into the framework envisaged by those who see the letters as pseudonymous. Why then should we read of Paul's cloak and his scrolls (2 Tim. 4:13)? Or of his leaving Timothy in Ephesus when he went to Macedonia (1 Tim. 1:3)? Of his hope to come to Timothy soon but with no certainty that he would not be delayed (1 Tim. 3:14–15)? What is the point of saying that Onesiphorus searched for Paul in Rome and found him (2 Tim. 1:16–17)? Or of his instruction to Titus to help Zenas the lawyer and Apollos (Titus 3:13)? It is not easy to see what to make of these and other such references on the theory that the letters come from the end of the first century or the beginning of the second, and from an author who did not know Paul's situation. Surely any such writer would fit his reminiscences into what is known of Paul's life. No convincing reason has been suggested for the manufacture of hypothetical situations of this nature. Moreover, all such references in all three of these letters bear the stamp of historical particularity. There is nothing like the legendary touches that are such a feature of, say, the second-century *Acts of Paul*. The Pastorals are much more akin to the accepted letters of Paul than they are to the known pseudonymous documents that circulated in the early church.

The False Teachers

It is usually assumed that the same false teaching is opposed in all three letters. This may or may not be the case, but some of it, at any rate, certainly included a strong Jewish element. There are references to "teachers of the law" (1 Tim. 1:7), "the circumcision group" (Titus 1:10), "Jewish myths" (Titus 1:14), and "arguments and quarrels about the law" (Titus 3:9).

There is also a warning against "what is falsely called knowledge" (1 Tim. 6:20), which, along with references to "myths and endless genealogies" (1 Tim. 1:4; cf. 4:7; Titus 3:9), is often taken to refer to gnostic systems. This is supported by passages mentioning ascetic practices (e.g., 1 Tim. 4:3). But full-blown

---

[29]For two quite different itineraries, see W. Metzger, *Die letzte Reise des Apostels Paulus* (Stuttgart: Calwer, 1976); and Jerome Murphy-O'Connor, *Paul: A Critical Life* (Oxford: Clarendon, 1996). They are nicely summarized in I. Howard Marshall, *A Critical and Exegetical Commentary on the Pastoral Epistles,* ICC (Edinburgh: T. & T. Clark, 1999), 68–71.

[30]Marshall, *Pastoral Epistles,* 71.

Gnosticism belongs to a time well into the second century, and these letters do not belong there. There is nothing in the way of false teaching as described in these letters that does not fit into what is known during the time of Paul's ministry (e.g., Colossians).[31]

The Ecclesiastical Organization

Many scholars believe that the understanding of church life that is presupposed in these letters could not have appeared during Paul's lifetime. Specifically, they see a strongly organized church with an ordained ministry.

We should first notice that Paul seems to have had some interest in the ministry, for even on the first missionary journey he and Barnabas appointed elders in the churches they had so recently founded (Acts 14:23). The salutation at the head of the epistle to the Philippians finds Paul addressing the overseers (bishops) and deacons at Philippi as well as the saints there (Phil. 1:1).

Second, to find an interest in the ministry in the Pastorals we must exclude 2 Timothy, for in that letter there is nothing about an ordained ministry or any form of church organization. Paul does speak of God's χάρισμα *(charisma)* that is in Timothy through the laying on of his hands (2 Tim. 1:6), but this may well be the equivalent of a later confirmation rather than of ordination (it leads on to thoughts of "power, of love and of self-discipline," which are just as relevant to the Christian life as to the Christian ministry). In Titus there is a direction to "appoint elders in every town" (Titus 1:5) and an indication of the kind of people who should be made elder or bishop (the two terms appear to denote the same office). It is in 1 Timothy that we get considerable teaching about the ministry. Here we find mention of the qualities that are to be sought in overseers and deacons (chap. 3) and an indication that elders are honored persons, to be treated with respect and to be paid for their work (5:17–20). The elder seems clearly to be equated with the overseer (bishop) in Titus 1:5–7, and there is nothing in the other two letters to indicate any other system. Despite the inferences drawn by some, there is really nothing in any of the Pastorals that demands any more organization than the "overseers and deacons" of Philippians 1:1. There is also a "list of widows" (1 Tim. 5:9), but it is not clear what this means (in any case, widows seem to have had a special place from the beginning [Acts 6:1]). Clearly, none of this amounts to much in the way of organization, certainly to nothing more than can have appeared in the church in comparatively early days.

Theology

Many contend that these three letters contain quite a number of Hellenistic terms for the salvation event, terms that Paul would not have used. Thus, we

---

[31]Even Kümmel says that the heresy opposed in these letters is "quite conceivable in the lifetime of Paul" (267).

read of "the appearing of our Savior, Jesus Christ, who has destroyed death and has brought life and immortality to light through the gospel" (2 Tim. 1:10); there is "one mediator between God and human beings" (1 Tim. 2:5); "the grace of God has appeared that offers salvation to all people" (Titus 2:11). These and other such expressions, however, often incorporate Pauline terms—perhaps used in a different way, but still Pauline. And there are many terms used as Paul uses them, such as Christ's coming to save sinners (1 Tim. 1:15); salvation because of divine mercy, not our works (Titus 3:5); the importance of faith in Christ (1 Tim. 3:13), of election (Titus 1:1), and of grace (2 Tim. 1:9). The discussion along these lines is inconclusive. Those who think of an author other than Paul are impressed by the number of new terms and the new uses of old ones; those who think Paul wrote the letters stress the number of common terms and see the new ones and new uses as no more than the legitimate variation in use that characterizes anyone writing in a variety of situations.

The problem may be illustrated by considering these words: "We know that the law is good if one uses it properly. We also know that the law is made not for the righteous but for lawbreakers and rebels" (1 Tim. 1:8–9). On this passage Moule comments, "It is astonishing that anyone could seriously attribute to Paul at any stage of his life the definition there offered of wherein the goodness of the law lies,"[32] while Zahn cites the same passage in support of Pauline authorship and goes on to speak of "the bold statement (1 Tim. i.9) that for the just man, and consequently for the sinner who has been made righteous by the mercy of the Saviour (1 Tim. i.13–16), there is no law."[33] When such diverse pronouncements can be made on the same passage, clearly it does not tell conclusively against Pauline authorship. The same may be said at many points. While some statements are confidently urged by objectors as proving that Paul could not have been the author, they are all accepted by others as things that Paul would have said.

But it is not only a matter of terminology. Many suggest that the entire piety of the Pastorals is different. There is a demand for "godliness" (εὐσέβεια [*eusebeia*], 1 Tim. 2:2 etc.), correct teaching (1 Tim. 6:3), and, above all, "sound doctrine" (2 Tim. 4:3). Kümmel speaks of "this rational, ethicized description of the Christian life and the Christian demand" and cites M. Dibelius, who "called this Christianity which is settling down in the world and which speaks a strongly Hellenistic language a 'bourgeois' Christianity," and Bultmann for the view that it is "a somewhat faded Paulinism."[34] There is no denying that there is a

---

[32]Moule, "Problem," 432.

[33]Zahn 2.121. "Nowhere in these Epistles do we find sentences that sound so 'un-Pauline' as 1 Cor. vii.19, and which can be so readily mistaken as a fusion of genuine Pauline teaching with its opposite, as Gal. v.6" (ibid.).

[34]Kümmel, 270. This unimaginative view of the contents has been drawn into an argument for the authenticity of these letters. Would someone imaginative enough to produce pseudonymous letters produce this kind of writing?

difference of emphasis in these letters, but the question is whether such writers as these are exaggerating. Granted that there is something of a change of pace, can it be seriously denied that Paul looked for such things as godliness (2 Cor. 1:12), correct teaching (Rom. 6:17), and sound doctrine (see his emphasis on knowledge, his repeated "I would not have you ignorant," and his fierce denunciations of false doctrine, e.g., Gal. 1:8–9)? Moreover, even an undisputed Pauline letter sometimes boasts forms of ethical argument found in no other Pauline writing (e.g., Paul's formidable "as if not" argument in 1 Corinthians 7). How many novel arguments or words are permitted before someone cries that we must be dealing with a pseudonymous author? Again we reach an impasse. To some the general tone of the Pastorals seems quite incompatible with that of the ten Pauline letters; to others it is no more than a development, appropriate enough in different circumstances.[35]

Parts of these letters are almost universally recognized to be very Pauline, and some scholars suggest that the author has made use of authentic fragments originally written by Paul. P. N. Harrison, for example, finds five such fragments,[36] but he has not won universal support for the hypothesis. No one seems to have been able to give a convincing reason for the fragments being preserved. (What happened to the letters of which they were parts? How did only parts survive?) Nor is it clear why the author should have inserted the fragments in the scattered places suggested. There is the further difficulty that the main reason for the identification of the fragments is that they fit in with what we know about some part of the life of Paul—but is that a sufficient criterion? Is there any reason why the particular epistle in which they occur should not have been written as a whole at that time? Or that the fragments should not fit into another part of Paul's life? Moreover, although the alleged fragments can be shown to be Pauline in substance, Cook has demonstrated that in style and vocabulary they cannot be distinguished from the rest of the material in the Pastoral Epistles.[37] It cannot be said that the hypothesis has a great deal to commend it.

There is a problem about the view that these letters are pseudonymous that is rarely faced. According to Childs, "The purpose served by the Pastorals is strongly biased by its initial literary classification as pseudepigraphical. Its

---

[35]This raises the whole question of "early Catholicism," for which see chap. 5, above, the section "Luke in Recent Study." See also Moisés Silva, "The Place of Historical Reconstruction in New Testament Criticism," in *Hermeneutics, Authority, and Canon,* ed. D. A. Carson and John D. Woodbridge (Grand Rapids: Zondervan, 1986), 105–33, 383–88.

[36]Harrison, *Problem,* 115–27. Harrison later modified his theory to include only three fragments. Others have looked for genuine pieces of Pauline writing embedded in the letters. But none of them seems to agree with any of the others, which makes the whole endeavor seem suspect and subjective.

[37]D. Cook, "The Pastoral Fragments Reconsidered," *JTS* 35 (1984): 120–31.

meaning cannot be obtained from the verbal sense of the text, but must be derived from a reconstruction of the author's 'real' intentions which have been purposely concealed. . . . The kerygmatic witness of the text is, thereby, rendered mute, and its interpretation is made dependent on other external forces which are set in a causal relationship."[38] There is no agreement on the exact situation of the pseudonymous author, no certainty about the problems he faced or the time he faced them or the ecclesiastical situation out of which he faced them. How then can we discover the real meaning of what he says?[39]

Amongst recent writers, one of the arguments pressed most strongly against Pauline authorship of the Pastorals is that the picture of Paul reflected here could not have come from his pen. Here "Paul" puts himself forward as not only an apostle but a saint and the sole authority for the gospel, the example to be followed, the prototype of the Christian convert. But this argument is far from convincing. After all, when writing to the Corinthians, Paul urges his readers to imitate him (1 Cor. 11:1). Elsewhere he clearly presents himself as in some ways a model to be followed (e.g., Phil. 3), and his envoys are to remind his readers not only of his doctrine but of his way of life in Christ. Moreover, once again this argument can be stood on its head, for some of what is said in the Pastorals seems unlikely from the pen of a later admirer of Paul. Would such a person refer to Paul

---

[38]Childs, 382–83. It should be added that Childs is very sympathetic toward a pseudonymous understanding of these letters.

[39]This goes beyond the normal run of uncertainty connected with some *anonymous* New Testament documents such as Hebrews, for in such cases there is no intrinsic attempt to write in the name of another, which inevitably has the effect of *masking* reality. The point is frankly faced by Brown (668–70), who, though defending the pseudonymous position, nevertheless acknowledges, "If one accepts pseudepigraphical authorship, virtually every issue pertinent to the letters has to be rethought." By this he includes the Pastorals' authority, whether they were composed as a group, the historicity of the travels they report and of the geographical addressees, and so forth. For once we enter the domain of the fictive, it becomes very difficult to know where to draw the line. As an example, one might reflect on the work of Jouette M. Bassler, *1 Timothy 2 Timothy Titus,* ANTC (Nashville: Abingdon, 1996), 30, who draws attention to the late-second-century pseudonymous *Acts of Paul,* which describes the apostle as advocating celibacy, converting a prominent young woman and severing her connections with her own family. Bassler suggests that the opponents Paul confronts in the Pastorals may have defended their positions by appealing to similar legends about Paul. "If so," writes Bassler, "the author of the Pastoral Letters responds with the device of pseudonymity, countering legends about Paul with letters purportedly from him" (p. 30); similarly Dennis R. MacDonald, *The Legend and the Apostle: The Battle for Paul in Story and Canon* (Philadelphia: Westminster, 1983). Thus, false teaching wrongly but honestly believed to come from the apostle is being overturned by false letters written with the intent to deceive in the direction of orthodoxy. The genius of this reconstruction is exceeded only by its implausibility.

as the chief of sinners (1 Tim. 1:15)? Would he dredge up, many years after Paul's death, the fact that he had been "a persecutor and a violent man" (1 Tim. 1:13)? And we may wonder whether such a person would remind people that at a critical hour there was nobody who stood by the great apostle (2 Tim. 4:16). All the historical references in these letters ring true as statements coming from the life of Paul, but the same cannot be said of a date quite a long time after he had died.[40]

> *All the historical references in these letters ring true as statements coming from the life of Paul, but the same cannot be said of a date quite a long time after he had died.*

It is assumed by those who deny the Pauline authorship of the Pastoral Epistles that pseudonymous epistles were accepted as quite natural among the early Christian communities. This view has been aided by the fact that pseudonymous writings of other sorts (e.g., apocalypses) were certainly widely accepted in the first century, and pseudonymous gospels and "acts" were widely accepted in the second. But by "widely accepted" we do not mean to suggest that they were accepted by those responsible for compiling normative lists of books. There is no example of the Fathers knowingly accepting into the canon a pseudonymous book of *any* genre. And beyond this, the historical place of pseudonymous letters is murky at best. In any case, the subject is not simple, and that is why we dealt with it more extensively in chapter 8 of this book.

THE PASTORAL EPISTLES IN RECENT STUDY

Because issues relating to authorship, provenance, date, and the like can be tackled from so many perspectives, it is not surprising that a considerable percentage of recent essays and books on the Pastoral Epistles treat such matters. But we have said enough on these topics, and so mention here a handful of other areas that have drawn attention.[41]

Some debates regarding the alleged institutionalization of the church primarily address the question of date, and thus indirectly the question of authorship. But several works provide rather disparate theories of the relationships among the offices mentioned. Young, arguing that elders and bishops are not identical, holds that the former are senior people who maintain and teach the

---

[40]From another point of view, Johnson comments, "Even those who like myself are not absolutely convinced that they come directly from Paul, think some of the reasons given for assigning their composition to a pseudepigrapher unconvincing" (423). Johnson also points to the differences between the letters as a problem. "Why would three such letters be produced, each of which was directed to a situation that was internally consistent yet very difficult to make consistent with the situations the other two were directed to? Here we would have a forger able subtly to create the verisimilitude of an established church (in Ephesus) and a new church (in Crete), together with the appropriate sort of directions to each, and yet not able to imitate more convincingly the Pauline samples available to him" (430).

[41]See especially the helpful essay by I. Howard Marshall, "Recent Study of the Pastoral Epistles," *Themelios* 23/1 (1997): 3–29.

tradition and who constitute a sort of governing council that, among other things, appoints and advises the bishop.[42] This is not the most obvious way of reading Titus 1:5–9, and her assertions about elders appointing bishops seem little more than fanciful. The most detailed recent study in this area, by Robert Campbell, argues that the term "elders" refers to senior people in a community and is never the title to an office. Campbell asserts that in the early church each elder was the senior head (and thus the "overseer") of the individual house church, and that these elders met together to govern the house churches in the area. What we find in the Pastorals, Campbell says, is the need to legitimate a single "overseer" (ἐπίσκοπος, *episkopos,* "bishop") in a local area as leader of the elders/overseers of the individual house churches.[43] On this view, Titus is charged with appointing a single overseer/bishop in each city, and the Pastoral Epistles reflect what might be called *monoepiscopacy.* Campbell asserts that confusion in terminology persisted until the time of Ignatius, who as bishop tried to curb the power of the elders still trying to maintain their independence. Once again, however, this is not the obvious way to read Titus 1:5–9, and it cannot easily be squared with the terminology of 1 Peter 5:1–5 (which of course would be irrelevant to this discussion only if a purely local trend were in view in the Pastorals).

Approaches to the structure of these epistles have been highly varied. Some commentators argue that there is no overall structure, and it is best to identify, label, and explain each paragraph without trying too hard (and, they would say, artificially) to show how each paragraph is related to all the others.[44] Others detect parallels between the individual Pastoral Epistles and the conventions of various kinds of letter-writing in the ancient world. Still others have deployed the tools of discourse analysis to try to explain a little more closely how each of the documents hangs together and constitutes an argument, a thought-through presentation.[45] We concur that careful rereading of these letters confirms that they are "orderly compositions."[46]

Perhaps the most penetrating study of the theology of the Pastoral Epistles as a group is that of Philip Towner.[47] Towner convincingly shows that the

---

[42]Frances Young, "On EPISKOPOS and PRESBUTEROS," *JTS* 45 (1994): 124–48.

[43]Robert Alastair Campbell, *The Elders: Seniority within Earliest Christianity,* SNTW (Edinburgh: T. & T. Clark, 1994).

[44]So Fee, *1 and 2 Timothy, Titus;* A. T. Hanson, *The Pastoral Epistles,* NCB (Grand Rapids: Eerdmans, 1982).

[45]E.g., J. Banker, *A Semantic Structure Analysis of Titus,* ed. J. Callow (Dallas: SIL, 1987); R. C. Blight, *A Literary-Semantic Analysis of Paul's First Discourse to Timothy,* ed. J. Beekman (Dallas: SIL, 1997).

[46]The expression is that of Marshall, "Recent Study," 18.

[47]Towner, *The Goal of Our Instruction.*

distinctive ethics of these documents are grounded in their Christology, soteriology, and eschatology.[48] All of these areas have been probed repeatedly. To comment on but one of them: Many commentators note that the Pastoral Epistles repeatedly and distinctively designate God as Savior (e.g., 1 Tim. 1:1; 2:3; Tit. 1:3). Far from depreciating Christ, however, he is not only presented as the exclusive mediator (1 Tim. 2:5–6) but is linked with God in final judgment (2 Tim. 4:1) and is also himself designated Savior (e.g., 2 Tim. 1:10), with an emphasis on his "appearing" (ἐπιφανεία, *epiphaneia*);[49] indeed, in one passage he is designated "our great God and Savior" (Tit. 2:13; cf. 3:4).

Finally, although in some ways the Pastoral Epistles reflect the more-or-less common New Testament "household codes" of conduct, in several ways they draw applications within the church that are not elsewhere worked out so explicitly. Most controversial of all the passages is 1 Timothy 2:9–15, regarding women and what Paul will and will not permit them to do. The extraordinary volume of literature that has sprung up around these verses may be usefully divided into three groups. The first seeks to domesticate or limit possible application today by finding evidence for a peculiar situation in the first-century culture or heresy within church that the author was addressing—a situation that no longer exists today.[50] The second focuses on detailed matters of exegesis and concludes that as a matter of theological principle Paul insists on role distinctions between men and women, arguing that there are no unambiguous first-century cultural features that justify ignoring the relevance of such texts today.[51] The third group agrees with the second in its main contention, that Paul draws distinctions between the roles of men and women, but concludes that in this regard the apostle is morally blinded by his own times, so that his restrictions should not only be ignored but should be actively overturned by those who are more enlightened today.[52] The debate continues.

---

[48]See the useful summary of Walter L. Liefeld, *1 and 2 Timothy, Titus*, NIVAC (Grand Rapids: Zondervan, 1999), 29–38.

[49]See esp. Andrew Y. Lau, *Manifest in Flesh: The Epiphany Christology of the Pastoral Epistles*, WUNT 86 (Tübingen: Mohr-Siebeck, 1996).

[50]E.g., Fee, *1 and 2 Timothy, Titus*, 35–38; Liefeld, *1 and 2 Timothy, Titus*, 97–114; and esp. Linda L. Belleville, *Women Leaders and the Church: Three Crucial Questions* (Grand Rapids: Baker, 2000), 162–80.

[51]E.g., Knight, *Pastoral Epistles*; and esp. Andreas J. Köstenberger, Thomas R. Schreiner, and H. Scott Baldwin, *Women in the Church: A Fresh Analysis of 1 Timothy 2:9–15* (Grand Rapids: Baker, 1995).

[52]E.g., U. Wagener, *Die Ordnung des "Hauses Gottes": Der Ort von Frauen in der Ekklesiologie und Ethik der Pastoralbriefe*, WUNT 65 (Tübingen: Mohr-Siebeck, 1994).

1 TIMOTHY

Contents

The salutation (1:1–2) is followed by a warning against false teachers of the law who promote controversies rather than set forward God's work (1:3–11). Paul expresses thanks for the way God's mercy and grace have been at work in him (1:12–17). This epistle is designed to aid Timothy as he fights the good fight (1:18–20). Paul urges that prayer be offered for all, especially those in authority, so that they may promote conditions in which people will come to salvation (2:1–7). From the further thought of prayer in the right spirit, Paul moves to the way women should dress and live (2:8–15). Then he discusses the qualifications to be sought in bishops (3:1–7) and deacons (3:8–10, 12–13), with a short section on either deacons' wives or female deacons (3:11). He explains his concern for God's household and cites a little poem about the incarnation (3:14–16). There is a further warning about false teachers (4:1–5), followed by some exhortations to Timothy to be a good servant of Christ and not to neglect the gift he was given when hands were laid on him (4:6–16). Paul offers advice about how to treat older and younger men, older and younger women, and widows (5:1–16) and gives special instructions regarding elders (5:17–20), Timothy's own behavior (5:21–25), and slaves (6:1–2). Once again, Paul warns against false teachers and the danger of the love of money (6:3–10); he urges Timothy to flee from all such conduct, charging him to live uprightly (6:11–16). Timothy should order rich people to do good and thus lay up treasure where it matters (6:17–19). The letter ends with another exhortation to Paul's young friend to be firm in the faith (6:20–21a). Finally, Paul appends the grace wish (6:21b).

Provenance

Not enough is known to identify the place of origin with certainty. The best suggestion is that the letter was written from Macedonia. Paul does not explicitly say that he was in that province when he wrote, but he does say, "As I urged you when I went into Macedonia, stay there in Ephesus" (1:3). This appears to mean that he had been with Timothy in Ephesus, from which point he went on to Macedonia, leaving his young assistant behind. Now in Macedonia, Paul writes reiterating the instruction he had given Timothy at the point of departure.

Date

If Paul was released from his imprisonment in Rome and wrote this letter during the course of his subsequent missionary activities, we should date it during the 60s, probably the early 60s. It has traditionally been held that the apostle was martyred under Nero (who died in 68). The chronology of his life is not absolutely certain, but it is usually thought that he arrived in Rome, as narrated in Acts, in 59 or 60. Allowing for the couple of years of his imprisonment there

(Acts 28:30), he would have been released in 62. His letter to the Romans shows that he wanted to go to Spain, and he may have done this immediately on release and gone to Macedonia later. Or he may have gone immediately to the East and left a trip to Spain until a later time. Many modern scholars think that we should place his death at the height of the Neronian persecution, say in 64, in which case 1 Timothy will be a year or two earlier. Eusebius says Paul died in 67; if this is correct, we could put the writing of the letter at 65 or even 66.

Another suggestion is that we should take the reference to Paul's departure for Macedonia (1:3) to be that mentioned in Acts 20:1, after the riot in Ephesus. Timothy was with Paul again in Acts 20:4, but evidently Acts 20:2 covers quite an interval of time, and there could have been a letter between Acts 20:1 and 20:4. J. A. T. Robinson thinks 1 Timothy may contain the gist of the charge Paul gave when he gathered the disciples and exhorted them (Acts 20:1). He dates the letter in the autumn of A.D. 55, when Timothy was quite a young man (cf. 1 Cor. 16:10–11, which Robinson thinks was written in the same year) and in need of the kind of directions Paul gives in this letter.[53] Not many have been convinced by this argument (the date seems to most students to be far too early), but it must remain a possibility.

Those who take the letter to be pseudonymous generally locate it at the end of the first century or even some time during the second century. Kümmel thinks of a time "just after the turn of the second century," for a later date is opposed by the strong Pauline teaching and what he sees as "the rudimentary character of the Gnosticism which is resisted."[54] Marxsen, however, makes it somewhat later. He dates all three Pastorals at "a time well into the second century."[55] If we remove this letter from the lifetime of Paul, there is clearly nothing very definite on which to fix our date. Everything then depends on our subjective estimate of the situation presupposed in the letter, and various second-century dates are suggested.

On the whole, it seems that there is most to be said for the first suggestion, that the letter was written somewhere in the middle 60s. We should at least bear in mind the possibility of Robinson's suggestion: if we judge it was written during Paul's earlier ministry, the mid–50s is as good a suggestion as any.

Destination

As it stands, the letter is a private communication to Timothy, written by his mentor to give him the guidance he needed for his work as a superintendent of churches. Those who see the letter as pseudonymous think of it rather as a general instruction to anyone in a place of authority and perhaps also as a letter to

---

[53]Robinson, *Redating*, 82–83.
[54]Kümmel, 272.
[55]Marxsen, 215.

give guidance about the Christian way that would be suitable for the general Christian public. "Grace be with you" (6:21) is plural, and some have therefore argued that the letter was meant for others than Timothy. It is countered that Timothy would be expected to pass on to his congregations the counsel that this letter contains and that Paul is simply sending this little prayer for them all. It is not easy to think that the letter as a whole is meant for a wide public. In such a case, what are we to make of words such as "Timothy, my son" (1:18); "I hope to come to you soon" (3:14); "don't let anyone look down on you because you are young" (4:12); "stop drinking only water" (5:23)? This letter is surely a personal letter to an individual, whatever public use he might have been expected to make of the teaching given throughout it.

> *First Timothy is surely a personal letter to an individual, whatever public use he might have been expected to make of the teaching given throughout it.*

Text

The most detailed text-critical study of the Pastorals (including 1 Timothy) is that of Elliott.[56] There is nothing else that approaches the comprehensiveness of this study. At the level of one detail, a certain amount of controversy has been generated by the claim of O'Callaghan and others to the effect that a fragment from Qumran, 7Q4, contains a part of 1 Timothy.[57] But the fragment boasts only 21 letters, three of them illegible, two or three uncertain, and assumptions have to be made about textual variants. Virtually no one today thinks the identification holds up.[58]

There are variant readings in 1 Timothy, of course, but for the most part the text is in reasonable shape. The best-known problem is whether to read ὅς (hos, "who") or θεός (theos, "God") in 3:16, but it is generally agreed that the former is correct. Another interesting variant is found twice, namely at 1:15 and 3:1, where most editors read πιστός (pistos, "faithful"), but where some witnesses have ἀνθρώπινος (anthrōpinos, "human"). The witnesses supporting the variant are mostly in Latin, though in 3:1 D lends its support. In favor of "human" is the consideration that in a number of places elsewhere in the Pastorals there are references to "faithful" sayings, and scribes may have been tempted to make this one conform. But this is not held to outweigh the solid textual support for πιστός (pistos). All told, Metzger discusses seventeen passages, which is not unduly large for a book of this length.[59]

---

[56]J. K. Elliott, *The Greek Text of the Epistles to Timothy and Titus*, SD 36 (Salt Lake City: University of Utah Press, 1968).

[57]Of his various essays, see especially J. O'Callaghan, "Les papyrus de la grotte 7 de Qumrân," *NRT* 95 (1973): 188–95. O'Callaghan views the identification as certain; Carsten P. Thiede, *the Earliest Gospel Manuscript? The Qumran Fragment 7Q5 and Its Significance for New Testament Studies* (Carlisle: Paternoster, 1993), as merely possible.

[58]See the summary provided by Marshall, *Pastoral Epistles*, 10–11.

[59]Metzger, 639–44.

Adoption into the Canon

This letter is quoted by Polycarp, Athenagoras, and later writers. Clearly, it was widely regarded as written by Paul and accepted as canonical. It seems to have been rejected by Tatian (second half of the second century), but he had a very individualistic viewpoint and cannot be regarded as representative of any widely held opinion. Marcion also rejected it along with the other Pastorals (perhaps because of the respect it affords the Old Testament).[60] But he rejected so many books accepted by others that we cannot take his omission as significant of wide hesitation in the church of his day. Apart from these idiosyncratic individuals, 1 Timothy seems to have been accepted universally as part of the correspondence of the apostle Paul. In modern times there have been serious doubts raised as to the authenticity of this and the other Pastoral Epistles, but this does not correspond to any widely held opinion in antiquity.[61]

The Contribution of 1 Timothy

This is a very personal letter. From elsewhere in the New Testament we know that Paul was very fond of Timothy; he speaks of his love for the younger man and of his conviction that he was faithful (1 Cor. 4:17). Paul says further that Timothy could remind the Corinthians of Paul's way of life, which indicates a certain intimacy and shows that Paul trusted him. It accords with this that he likens Timothy's relationship to him to that of a son to his father (Phil. 2:22), and with a cheerful disregard for consistency speaks of him as a brother (and fellow worker, 1 Thess. 3:2). He links Timothy with himself in the opening greetings in six of his epistles (2 Cor. 1:1; Phil. 1:1; Col. 1:1; 1 Thess. 1:1; 2 Thess. 1:1; Phile.1), which argues that he was a trusted colleague. Paul asks the Corinthians to ensure that Timothy "has nothing to fear" if he should visit them (1 Cor. 16:10), which seems to indicate a certain diffidence about the young man. He sent him to the Thessalonians, he assures them, "to strengthen and encourage you in your faith" (1 Thess. 3:2), and he plans to send him to the Philippians, explaining, "I have no one else like him, who will show genuine concern for your welfare" (Phil. 2:20).

All this gives point to Paul's greeting, "To Timothy my true son in the faith" (1 Tim. 1:2). The letter is written to a younger man for whom the apostle had a deep affection and with whom he had for years entrusted important missions. What Paul now says brings out the truth that Christians are linked in the service of the Lord and that there is significant help they can and should give to one another.

---

[60]Tertullian, *Adv. Marc.* 5.21.

[61]The information is nicely set out by Marshall, *Pastoral Epistles,* 2–8.

The letter is important also for the light it sheds on the ministry of the Christian church.[62] Throughout all the years of its history, the ministry has been of great importance. It has taken a variety of shapes—some very authoritarian, some egalitarian. It has been strongly hierarchical in some of its forms, while in others the very idea of a hierarchy has been rejected. However it has been understood, it has been seen as at the heart of ecclesiastical organization. It comes as something of a surprise to realize that, apart from the Pastoral Epistles, the New Testament has very little to say about it (and when it does, it speaks of forms like the apostle or the prophet, which, at least in their narrowest definitions, have ceased to exist). It is accordingly important that 1 Timothy has so much to say about ministers—more, indeed, than has any other New Testament writing.

Paul says nothing about ordination in this letter, unless he has it in mind when he refers to "the prophecies once made about you" (1:18) or to the gift given when the elders "laid their hands on you" (4:14). In either case this is possible, but the point is that in neither case does Paul mention ordination, and both passages may be otherwise explained. However we understand these passages, clearly what matters to Paul is that those in the ministry should be upright people, leaders whose character is beyond reproach. So he gives instructions about the bishop (ἐπίσκοπος [episkopos], 3:1–7). The TNIV appropriately renders the Greek "overseer," for there is no reason for holding that in New Testament times the office discharged anything like the functions it came to have in the church and that arise in our minds when the word "bishop" is used today. But TNIV obscures the fact that it was this office and no other that very shortly evolved into the monarchical bishop. One of our problems about the early history of the ministry is that we do not know precisely what functions the New Testament "bishop" discharged, but it appears to be an alternative title for "elder" or "pastor" (see Titus 1:5–7). Paul is much more interested in his character than in his ecclesiastical activities. The church has all too often reversed this priority, and 1 Timothy is of permanent value in pointing to the truth that the quality of Christian life, though not the only mandated characteristic, is of paramount importance in discerning who is fit for office in the Christian church.

Although it is usually agreed that the elder and the bishop were identical in the church of this period, Paul does not explicitly equate them in this letter as he does in Titus 1:5–7. Still, he does not differentiate them either, and there is no reason for taking 5:17–19 as referring to anyone other than the bishops of chapter 3. The elders, we learn, are active in directing the affairs of the church, though what form their direction took is not stated. Evidently some had administrative duties, and others were concerned with preaching and teaching, these

---

[62]J. B. Lightfoot's classic dissertation on "The Christian Ministry" still merits careful attention and has much to say about the teaching in the Pastorals (*Saint Paul's Epistle to the Philippians* [London: Macmillan, 1885], 181–259).

latter being singled out as worthy of special honor. Paul combines an Old Testament passage with a saying of Jesus to bring out the truth that the elders are to be paid for their work (5:18; cf. Deut. 25:4; Luke 10:7). And he makes it clear that the elder is not to be accused lightly (5:19).

Paul also has something to say about deacons, and once again the emphasis is on character (3:8–10), with some emphasis on the importance of family life (3:12). Between these two references there is another that may refer to the wives of deacons or may tell us something about female deacons (3:11). Paul does not stipulate of deacons, as he does of overseer/elders, that they must be "able to teach" (3:2). In both cases, however, the emphasis is on character and conduct.

The church has all too often neglected this emphasis. There have been battles as some have tried to exercise wide-ranging authority, and others have resisted this strenuously. There have been discussions as to whether the ministers in one church can recognize those in another; the validity of orders has been a matter of prime concern. Indeed, in the modern ecumenical movement the recognition of ministries has been a matter of profound interest. The strong emphasis on character in this letter is of the greatest importance, coupled as it is with a total bypassing of all that is implied in the term "the validity of orders." This does not mean that we can neglect proper arrangements in recognizing ministries. But Paul is teaching the whole church that there are more important considerations than the proper arrangements for a service of ordination.

While he thus has a good deal to say about the way those who are called into the ministry should live, he is not silent either about the conduct of others in the church. Paul insists on the importance of prayer (2:8) and on the way believers should behave, including women (2:9–15), believers generally (3:14–15), older and younger people (5:1–2), widows (5:3–16), slaves (6:1–2), and the rich (6:17–19). There are different duties for people in different stations, but all who profess to be Christians must be careful that their lives reflect their doctrines. The letter keeps reminding readers of the importance of upright Christian living.

First Timothy is also a protest against needless controversies. There are warnings against those who "devote themselves to myths and endless genealogies" (1:4; "godless myths," 4:7). Those who forbid marriage and introduce food laws are also condemned (4:3), and Timothy is warned against "an unhealthy interest in controversies and quarrels . . . that result in envy" (6:4). Perhaps some in the modern church should give heed to the warning against people who "think that godliness is a means to financial gain" (6:5), while the modern community is almost a classic illustration of the saying, "The love of money is a root of all kinds of evil" (6:10).

An interesting and permanently valuable part of this letter is the way Paul refers to the past in such a way as to afford guidance for the future. Thus, he looks back to the time when he was with Timothy and to the teaching he then gave him; he exhorts him to continue in the course then urged (1:3–11). It is the same elsewhere: the instructions Paul has given in the past will enable Timothy to act in the future (3:14–15). Sometimes those who deny the Pauline authorship of this letter cavil at the insistence on sound doctrine: it sounds too narrow. But in Paul's mind this sound doctrine is grounded in the essentials of the gospel. Paul writes of "the sound doctrine that conforms to the gospel concerning the glory of the blessed God" (1:10–11). He refers to Jesus as the "one mediator between God and human beings" and goes on to say that he "gave himself as a ransom for all people." It was to spread this message that Paul "was appointed a herald and an apostle . . . and a true and faithful teacher of the Gentiles" (2:5–7). The writer is clear that the events that constitute the gospel form the basis of the whole Christian message. Whatever the circumstances in which Timothy finds himself, the gospel is to form the message he proclaims, the gospel that Paul preached and that is central to the life of the whole Christian church.

Even many who see the letter as pseudonymous make the point that the writer is still appealing to Paul. The letter stands as a reminder that there are some truths that persist from age to age. The meaning of the gospel of Christ is not to be modified in the interests of Christians living in circumstances very different from those of Paul.

2 TIMOTHY

Contents

This is a letter written at a time when Paul was contemplating his own death (4:6–8), so it has the character of a testamentary charge. There is a special solemnity about a letter written in such circumstances. It begins with a normal form of greeting (1:1–2) and moves to thanksgiving and encouragement (1:3–7). This leads to an exhortation to Timothy not to be ashamed of Paul, because Paul is not ashamed of the gospel (1:8–14). After some historical reminiscences (1:15–18), Timothy is urged to be strong in Christ's grace (2:1–7) and is reminded of the essentials of the gospel (2:8–13). He is to be a workman who does not need to be ashamed but who teaches faithfully. With this is linked a warning about the false teachers and exhortations to upright living (2:14–26). Paul prophesies of troubles "in the last days," when all manner of evil flourishes (3:1–9). He gratefully confesses that the Lord has protected him in his troubles (3:10–13) and exhorts Timothy to continue in the teaching he has had from infancy, specifically the teaching from the Scriptures, which are God-breathed and valuable (3:14–17). This leads to a charge to Timothy to preach the word steadfastly (4:1–5). Paul speaks of his impending death and preparedness for it (4:6–8). There follow a series of remarks about individuals (4:9–15) and the information that Paul had been forsaken at his first defense (4:16–18). The letter closes with greetings and the grace (4:19–22).

Provenance

Paul writes in the consciousness that his life is nearly over (4:6). His word for "defense" (ἀπολογία [*apologia*], 4:16) is often used of a defense in a law court. It seems, then, that we are to think of Paul as in prison faced with the prospect of speedy execution. He says that Onesiphorus searched for him and found him in Rome (1:16–17), which makes it likely that that was the place of his current imprisonment. Paul asks Timothy to come to him and pick up Mark on the way (4:11), so we know that this imprisonment in Rome is not that related in Acts (Timothy was with him when he wrote Colossians, as was Mark [Col. 1:1; 4:10; Philem. 24], two letters generally held to have been written from Rome). Paul appears to have been in Asia Minor not long before he wrote, for he speaks of having left a cloak at Troas (4:13), of Erastus having stayed in Corinth, and of his having left Trophimus sick in Miletus (4:20). We learn from Acts that Paul had been in prison in Caesarea for two years (Acts 24:27) prior to being sent to Rome and that his journey there was via Crete and Malta. He had thus not been in Asia Minor for quite some time. It is unlikely that he is writing from his imprisonment in Caesarea (which would fit the references to Asia Minor), for Trophimus was with him in Jerusalem when he was arrested (Acts 21:29) and probably Timothy also (Acts 20:4).[63] It seems much more likely that Paul was released from the imprisonment mentioned in Acts and engaged in missionary activities for a period before being imprisoned again. The probabilities are that 2 Timothy was written during this second imprisonment in Rome.

Date

The evidence bearing on the dating of the letter has largely been canvassed in the section on "Provenance," where we saw that the letter probably was written from Rome during an imprisonment later than the one described in Acts. In that case, the letter was written in the early or middle 60s. If we follow Eusebius in dating the martyrdom of Paul in 67, then that or the preceding year will be the date of 2 Timothy. But most modern scholars think that Paul was executed in 64 or 65, so a date in those years is more likely.

Those who deny the Pauline authorship of the letter class it with the other Pastorals and usually date it some time toward the end of the first or in the second century. The three are normally discussed together, so the arguments are the same as those for 1 Timothy (see above).

---

[63]Robinson maintains that the letter was written from Caesarea (*Redating*, 67–82). But he has to argue that Luke has confused Tychicus with Trophimus (76), for which there is no evidence.

Destination

The letter purports to have been written to Timothy (1:1–2), and the contents bear this out. Personal touches such as the references to Lois and Eunice (1:5) are very natural in such a letter and hard to explain otherwise. So with Timothy's tears (1:4) and Paul's laying hands on him (1:6) and with the references to Paul's being deserted (1:15; 4:10). The prayers for Onesiphorus, together with the information that he made a hard but successful search for Paul and the reference to his previous activities in Ephesus (1:16–18) are the kind of thing we might expect in a private letter. The same is true of personal admonitions to Timothy (2:1–2, 22–26; 3:14; 4:2, 5) and the little chatty section at the end when Paul gives news of friends and some information about himself (4:9–22). The letter is throughout so personal that it is probably the hardest of the three Pastorals to claim as pseudonymous.

Those who deny that it was a letter written to Timothy point to the plural in the grace at the end (4:22). But this surely means no more than that Paul extends his greetings to the Christians who were with Timothy at the time he wrote. There does not seem anything else on which to base a theory of other recipients than Timothy, unless we go along with the whole theory of pseudonymity, in which case we must say that we do not know to whom the letter was written.

Second Timothy is throughout so personal that it is probably the hardest of the three Pastoral Epistles to claim as pseudonymous.

Text

See the corresponding section on 1 Timothy above for important work on all the Pastorals. The text of this letter seems fairly well preserved. There are no great problems, and it is perhaps significant that the longest discussion in Metzger is that over the form of the grace in 4:22. All told, he discusses fifteen passages, but none of the variants gives us a significant difference of meaning. Westcott and Hort think that ὧν (*hōn*, "which") in 1:13 is a primitive corruption,[64] but the sense is not greatly changed if we accept their alteration to give the meaning "hold as a pattern the word (= teaching) which you heard from me."

Adoption into the Canon

There may be echoes of this letter in *1 Clement* (end of the first century) and in the letters of Ignatius (beginning of the second), though these are disputed. It seems clear, however, that Polycarp quoted some passages. There is not the slightest doubt that Irenaeus refers to the letter, citing it as written by Paul to Timothy. Clement of Alexandria does the same, and from these early days on, the letter was almost universally accepted. Tatian seems to have rejected it along with 1 Timothy, while Marcion did not have any of the Pastorals in his canon— but he rejected so much of the New Testament that this is not surprising. He

---

[64]WH, 135.

probably did not like the high regard for the Old Testament that the letter reveals. None of the Pastorals is found in the Chester Beatty Papyrus P[46], which is dated c. A.D. 200, but the codex is incomplete and may originally have contained the letters. If it did not, it is worth noticing that it also omits Philemon, so that the reason may be that the codex contained only letters to churches. All three are included in the Muratorian Canon. The church in general seems to have had little hesitation over accepting 2 Timothy.

The Contribution of 2 Timothy

The deep conviction of the writer that he was about to be put to death for holding the Christian faith (4:6–8) is to be kept in mind in all discussions of this letter. Paul does not envisage writing anything further to Timothy, nor perhaps to anyone else. He hopes that Timothy will be able to reach him before the end (4:9), and his request for his cloak and his scrolls (4:13) shows that he anticipated an interval before his execution. Nevertheless, the letter is written in the shadow of the scaffold and is to be seen as what Paul considered to be important in his last communication to a trusted subordinate. Not the least of the letter's values is that it shows us the way a Christian martyr should face death. Those who live comfortably in secure communities should not belittle this contribution, for in many lands with anti-Christian governments, people still die for their faith. Indeed, there have been more Christian martyrs during the past century and a half than in the previous eighteen centuries combined. Certainly martyrdom for the faith is much more common than most Western Christians realize, and accordingly it is well that we appreciate Paul's attitude to dying for Christ—his calm contemplation of what lay ahead and the quiet faith that undergirded all he was doing and his going about his necessary business. There is no fanaticism here, nor any attempt at grandstanding. The apostle writes from a lowly posture and sets the example of the way Christians should die for their faith. He writes also of how they should live for it, even if this means suffering along the way (e.g., 1:8).

Paul also brings out something of the importance of their heritage. He speaks of "the good deposit that was entrusted to you" (1:14; the same word "deposit" is used in v. 12, with possibly much the same meaning, so the RSV). In line with this, Paul has much to say about what God has done, such as his reference to the gospel, followed by the power of God, salvation, the call to a holy life, grace given in Christ "before the beginning of time" and now revealed in our Savior, the destruction of death, and the gift of life and immortality (1:8–10)—an enormous freight to be carried within three verses. It is of abiding importance that believers are not given a list of instructions as to what constitutes the path of the service of God and then left to themselves as they try to work it all out. The foundation of all Christian life is what God has already done, and Paul makes it clear that all that Christians are asked to do is to live out the consequences of

God's saving act. This they can do without timidity, for God has given them "power, love and self-discipline" (1:7). In line with this, the apostle exhorts Timothy to pass the teaching on "to reliable people who will also be qualified to teach others" (2:2). There is a "given" about the Christian faith; it is something inherited from the very beginning of God's action for our salvation, and it is to be passed on as long as this world lasts. Paul is not arguing that believers should be insensitive to currents of thought and action in the world about them, nor is he saying that the Christian is a kind of antiquarian, interested in antiquity for its own sake. He is saying that there is that about the essence of the Christian faith that is not open to negotiation. God has said and done certain things, and Christians must stand by those things whatever the cost. We should bear in mind his notable statement about Scripture (3:16–17); God has spoken, and we neglect what he has said to our peril.

Paul is clear that the cost of discipleship may be great. He speaks of suffering, both his own and that of other believers (1:8, 12; 2:9, 12; 3:11–12). He likens Christian service to that of a soldier, an athlete, and a hardworking farmer (2:3–6). He leaves Timothy in no doubt that, while our salvation is a free gift from God, it is also demanding. In living out its implications, the believer is going to run into difficulties and will find that the God who sent his Son to die on the cross is always served at cost. Paul uses the illustration of the variety of articles in a large house—some costly, some cheap, some for noble purposes, and some for ignoble; the believer is to aim at being fit for noble purposes (2:20–21). Cleansing is costly.

The Christian will meet with opposition, sometimes from people who profess to be Christians themselves. Part of the value of this letter to us is its warning against those who wander from the truth (2:14–18). Especially is this true because we, like Paul, are in "the last days," when there will be people who have a form of godliness but deny its power (3:1–5). In accord with this, Paul insists on the importance of "sound teaching" (1:13), which some people will reject, gathering teachers "to say what their itching ears want to hear" (4:3). Paul is not contending for adherence to some dead orthodoxy; rather, he insists that God has laid a "solid foundation" that stands firm (2:19).

TITUS

Contents

The opening greeting (1:1–4) is longer than Paul's usual greeting and contains a reminder that God has promised eternal life and brought it to pass in due course. Paul has left Titus in Crete to set things in order in the church, and he now urges him to appoint elders in every town, giving directions about the kind of person required for this office (1:5–9). There is a contrast with the "many rebellious people" to be found in Crete; Paul warns Titus against them (1:10–16). He goes on to detail what must be taught to older men (2:2), older women, who will teach younger women (2:3–5), young men (2:6–8), and slaves (2:9–10). All believers are to live uprightly, awaiting "the appearing of the glory of our great God and Savior, Jesus Christ" (2:11–15). People in authority are to be obeyed (3:1–2). There is a contrast between the way people lived before they became Christians and the good lives that follow Christ's saving work in them (3:3–8). They should avoid foolish divisions (3:9–11). The letter is rounded off with some instructions about various individuals and then closing greetings (3:12–15).

Provenance

Paul, as we have just seen, reminds Titus why he left him in Crete (1:5). The only other references to Crete in the New Testament are in the account of Paul's voyage to Rome in Acts 27, a time when the apostle was briefly in the harbor of Fair Havens (Acts 27:8), but it is impossible to think of him as doing significant evangelism on the island at that time. But from 1:5 we learn that he had left Titus to complete what had to be done, which seems to imply that he had done work there himself and had left Titus to complete it. Unfortunately we have no information as to when this took place. At the time of writing, Paul was in or on the way to Nicopolis, where he planned to spend the winter (3:12), but we do not know when he was there either. There are considerable gaps in the story Acts tells of Paul's missionary journeys, but it is plausibly argued that had he done such a work in Crete as this letter presupposes, it could scarcely have been omitted in its entirety. While certainty is unattainable, it seems probable that, as in the case of 1 and 2 Timothy, we should think that Paul was released after the Roman imprisonment narrated in Acts and that he engaged in a further period of missionary activity. Whereas 2 Timothy presupposes a further arrest of Paul, Titus comes from the period of active missionary service.

Date

Those who think that Paul was executed during his first (and thus only) Roman imprisonment, but who are nevertheless convinced that Paul wrote this epistle, must suggest an alternative reconstruction for the movements of Titus, for these affect the date. These scholars remind us that when Romans was written, Titus was in Corinth, busy about the collection (2 Cor. 8; 12:17–18), and that he was probably not with the apostle at that time, since he is not mentioned in the greetings of Romans 16:21–23, as Timothy is. Paul was finishing off the collection himself (Rom. 15:28), so that after Titus's service in Corinth, Paul may have sent him to Crete and left him there while he himself set off for Jerusalem. The letter to Titus, Robinson thinks, may have been written while Paul was on the way to Jerusalem, which gives a date of A.D. 57.[65] If we date

---

[65]Robinson, *Redating*, 81–82.

this letter during Paul's ministry as described in Acts, this is as good a suggestion as any. It is perhaps supported by the fact that the church in Crete was a very young church, lacking even elders (Titus 1:5).

But to most scholars such a date seems very improbable. Acts puts Paul neither in Crete nor in Nicopolis, so it seems better to think of this letter, like the other Pastorals, as coming from a time after Paul's release from a first Roman imprisonment. In that case, it was written before 2 Timothy, and somewhere around the same period as 1 Timothy—that is, not later than the middle 60s.

Those who see the letter as pseudonymous usually date it at the end of the first or the beginning of the second century (see above on 1 Timothy).

Destination

Little needs to be added to what was said under the other two Pastorals. The letter is addressed to Titus, and there is nothing in it inconsistent with his being the recipient. There are not as many personal references as in the letters to Timothy, but the remarks at the end (3:12–15) ring true. Titus was evidently a trusted helper, and Paul looks to him to act responsibly.

Adoption into the Canon

There may well be an echo of Titus 3:1 in Clement of Rome, and certainly some second-century writers quote Titus, including Tertullian and Irenaeus. Oddly enough, although Tatian rejects both letters to Timothy, he accepts this letter to Titus. Like the other Pastorals, Titus is absent from Marcion's canon (probably for the same reasons) and present in the Muratorian Canon. From the end of the second century it was universally recognized. For its absence from P[46], see the comment on 2 Timothy.

The Contribution of Titus

This letter brings out something of what we might call the civilizing function of Christianity. Titus was clearly in charge of a very young church in a very unpromising situation. Elders had not yet been appointed, and Titus was to appoint them. (By contrast, the church that Timothy served was well established, and there a bishop was not to be "a recent convert" [1 Tim. 3:6].) In Crete, where Titus found himself, there was the possibility that a candidate for the eldership might have unconverted children or children who were "wild and disobedient" (1:6). The elder himself must be "not overbearing, not quick-tempered, not given to drunkenness, not violent, not pursuing dishonest gain" (1:7). He is to function in a community of which one of their own people said, "Cretans are always liars, evil brutes, lazy gluttons" (1:12), a testimony with which Paul evidently agrees. In that situation it would seem that neither Paul nor Titus had a moment's hesitation about establishing the church. The letter is clear evidence that the Christian church is not intended to function only in cozy, respectable, middle-class environments. The gospel is for the most unpromising of people.

This is seen also in the instructions to those who have been converted. The older women are not to be addicted to wine (2:3), the younger, to love their husbands and children (2:4); slaves are not to steal from their masters (2:10); people are to respect authority, do what is good, and not to engage in slander (3:1–2). All this is surprising in directions to a group of Christians. It shows both that these Cretans were unpromising material and that Paul expected them nevertheless to produce qualities of Christian character.

> *The letter to Titus is clear evidence that the Christian church is not intended to function only in cozy, respectable, middle-class environments. The gospel is for the most unpromising of people.*

Moreover, the gospel is to be taken to such people, despite the strong opposition of rival teachers. Some of these are successful, for they are "disrupting whole households," even though they aim only at their own dishonest gain (1:11). Apparently there was quite a Jewish flavor to the false teaching: its adherents belong to "the circumcision group" (1:10), they teach "Jewish myths" (1:14); they "claim to know God," even though their actions show this to be a lie (1:16); and they argue about the law and engage in foolish controversies (3:9). But this letter makes it clear that the strength and the nature of the opposition make no difference: Christian teachers are to press on with their task of evangelism and of leading the converts into a lifestyle that brings glory to God.

Paul takes no position of superiority but makes it plain that he owes everything to "the kindness and love of God our Savior" and specifically to what God has done in Christ (3:3–7). He puts the highest standard before the Cretans, for "the grace of God has appeared that offers salvation to all people" (2:11). The letter makes it plain that the Christian way is an urging of people not to pull themselves up by their bootstraps, but rather to rely on the grace of God. This grace "teaches" (2:12); it educates people like the Cretans—and any other group.

We should not miss Paul's reference to the parousia, as he waits for "the blessed hope—the appearing of the glory of our great God and Savior, Jesus Christ" (2:13; note here the way he speaks of Christ). The letter emphasizes what God has done to bring salvation and the certainty of its culmination when Christ comes back.

BIBLIOGRAPHY

H. R. **Balz**, "Anonymität und Pseudepigraphie im Urchristentum," *ZTK* 66 (1969): 403–436 ▌J. **Banker**, *A Semantic Structure Analysis of Titus*, ed. J. Callow (Dallas: SIL, 1987) ▌George K. **Barr**, "Two Styles in the New Testament Epistles," *LLC* 18 (2003): 235–48 ▌C. K. **Barrett**, *The Pastoral Epistles*, NClarB (Oxford: Clarendon, 1963) ▌Jouette M. **Bassler**, *1 Timothy 2 Timothy Titus*, ANTC (Nashville: Abingdon, 1996) ▌Linda L. **Belleville**, *Women Leaders and the Church: Three Crucial Questions* (Grand Rapids: Baker, 2000) ▌J. H. **Bernard**, *The*

Pastoral Epistles (Cambridge: Cambridge University Press, 1899) ▮A. E. **Bird**, "The Authorship of the Pastoral Epistles—Quantifying Literary Style," *RTR* 56 (1997): 118–37 ▮R. C. **Blight**, *A Literary-Semantic Analysis of Paul's First Discourse to Timothy*, ed. J. Beekman (Dallas: SIL, 1997) ▮M. M. **Bourke**, "Reflections on Church Order in the New Testament," *CBQ* 30 (1968): 493–511 ▮L. H. **Brockington**, "The Problem of Pseudonymity," *JTS* 4 (1953): 15–22 ▮Norbert **Brox**, *Die Pastoralbriefe*, RNT, 4th ed. (Regensburg: Pustet, 1969) ▮Rudolf **Bultmann**, *Theology of the New Testament*, 2 vols. (London: SCM, 1952–55), 2:95–118 ▮Robert Alastair **Campbell**, *The Elders: Seniority within Earliest Christianity*, SNTW (Edinburgh: T. & T. Clark, 1994) ▮P. **Carrington**, "The Problem of the Pastoral Epistles: Dr. Harrison's Theory Reviewed," *ATR* 21 (1939): 32–39 ▮Raymond F. **Collins**, *1 & 2 Timothy and Titus*, NTL (Louisville: Westminster John Knox, 2002) ▮S. **de Lestapis**, *L'énigme des Pastorales de Saint Paul* (Paris: Gabalda, 1976) ▮M. **Dibelius** and H. **Conzelmann**, *The Pastoral Epistles*, Hermeneia (Philadelphia: Fortress, 1972) ▮Lewis R. **Donelson**, *Pseudepigraphy and Ethical Argument in the Pastoral Epistles*, HUT 22 (Tübingen: Mohr-Siebeck 1986) ▮E. Earle **Ellis**, *Pauline Theology: Ministry and Society* (Grand Rapids: Eerdmans, 1989) ▮Gordon D. **Fee**, *1 and 2 Timothy, Titus*, GNC (San Francisco: Harper & Row, 1984) ▮B. **Fiore**, *The Function of Personal Example in the Socratic and Pastoral Epistles*, AnBib 105 (Rome: Pontifical biblical Institute, 1986) ▮K. **Grayston** and G. **Herndon**, "The Authorship of the Pastorals in the Light of Statistical Linguistics," *NTS* 6 (1959–60): 1–15 ▮Donald **Guthrie**, "Pastoral Epistles," in *ISBE* 3:679–87 ▮idem, *The Pastoral Epistles* (Grand Rapids: Eerdmans, 1957) ▮idem, *The Pastoral Epistles and the Mind of Paul* (London: Tyndale, 1956) ▮A. T. **Hanson**, "The Domestication of Paul: A Study in the Development of Early Christian Theology," *BJRL* 63 (1981): 402–18 ▮idem, *The Pastoral Epistles*, NCB (Grand Rapids: Eerdmans, 1982) ▮idem, *Studies in the Pastoral Epistles* (London: SPCK, 1968) ▮P. N. **Harrison**, "The Authorship of the Pastoral Epistles," *ExpTim* 67 (1955–56): 77–81 ▮idem, *Paulines and Pastorals* (London: Villiers, 1964) ▮idem, *The Problem of the Pastoral Epistles* (London: Oxford University Press, 1921) ▮F. R. M. **Hitchcock**, "The Pastorals and a Second Trial of Paul," *ExpTim* 41 (1929–30): 20–23 ▮idem, "Philo and the Pastorals," *Hermatheua* 56 (1940): 113–35 ▮idem, "Tests for the Pastorals," *JTS* 30 (1928–29): 272–79 ▮J. L. **Houlden**, *The Pastoral Epistles: I and II Timothy, Titus*, PNTC (London: Penguin, 1976) ▮M. R. **James**, *The Apocryphal New Testament* (Oxford: Clarendon, 1926) ▮Luke Timothy **Johnson**, *The First and Second Letters to Timothy: A New Translation with Introduction and Commentary*, AB 35A (New York: Doubleday, 2001) ▮R. J. **Karris**, "The Background and Significance of the Polemic of the Pastoral Epistles," *JBL* 92 (1973): 549–64 ▮J. N. D. **Kelly**, *A Commentary on the Pastoral Epistles*, HNTC (New York: Harper, 1963) ▮Anthony **Kenny**, *A Stylometric Study of the New Testament* (Oxford: Clarendon, 1986) ▮Andreas J. **Köstenberger**, Thomas R. **Schreiner**, and H. Scott **Baldwin**, *Women in the Church: A Fresh Analysis of*

1 Timothy 2:9–15 (Grand Rapids: Baker, 1995) ▥Andrew Y. **Lau**, *Manifest in Flesh: The Epiphany Christology of the Pastoral Epistles,* WUNT 86 (Tübingen: Mohr-Siebeck, 1996) ▥Thomas D. **Lea** and Hayne P. **Griffin Jr.**, *1, 2 Timothy Titus,* NAC 34 (Nashville: Broadman Press, 1992) ▥Walter L. **Liefeld**, *1 and 2 Timothy, Titus,* NIVAC (Grand Rapids: Zondervan, 1999) ▥J. B. **Lightfoot**, "The Date of the Pastoral Epistles," in *Biblical Essays* (London: Macmillan, 1904), 397–410 ▥idem, *Saint Paul's Epistle to the Philippians* (London: Macmillan, 1885) ▥W. **Lock**, *A Critical and Exegetical Commentary on The Pastoral Epistles,* ICC (Edinburgh: T. & T. Clark, 1924) ▥Dennis R. **MacDonald**, *The Legend and the Apostle: The Battle for Paul in Story and Canon* (Philadelphia: Westminster, 1983) ▥I. Howard **Marshall**, *A Critical and Exegetical Commentary on the Pastoral Epistles,* ICC (Edinburgh: T. & T. Clark, 1999) ▥idem, "Recent Study of the Pastoral Epistles," *Themelios* 23/1 (1997): 3–29 ▥D. L. **Mealand**, "Computers in New Testament Research: An Interim Report," *JSNT* 33 (1988): 97–115 ▥idem, "Positional Stylometry Reassessed: Testing a Seven Epistle Theory of Pauline Authorship," *NTS* 35 (1989): 266–86 ▥idem, "The Extent of the Pauline Corpus: A Multivariate Approach," *JSNT* 59 (1995): 61–92 ▥Wayne A. **Meeks**, "'To Walk Worthily of the Lord': Moral Formation in the Pauline School Exemplified by the Letter to the Colossians," in *Hermes and Athena: Biblical Exegesis and Philosophical Theology,* ed. Eleonore Stump and Thomas P. Flint, University of Notre Dame Studies in the Philosophy of Religion 7 (Notre Dame: University of Notre Dame Press, 1993), 37–58 ▥W. **Metzger**, *Die letzte Reise des Apostels Paulus* (Stuttgart: Calwer Verlag, 1976) ▥Margaret **Mitchell**, "PTebt 703 and the Genre of 1 Timothy: The Curious Career of a Ptolemaic Papyrus in Pauline Scholarship," *NovT* 44 (2002): 344–70 ▥A. Q. **Morton**, *Literary Detection* (Bath: Bowker, 1978) ▥C. F. D. **Moule**, "The Problem of the Pastoral Epistles: A Reappraisal," *BJRL* 47 (1965): 430–52 ▥Jerome **Murphy-O'Connor**, *Paul: A Critical Life* (Oxford: Clarendon Press, 1996) ▥K. **Neumann**, *The Authenticity of the Pauline Epistles in the Light of Stylo-statistical Analysis* (Atlanta: Scholars Press, 1990) ▥J. **O'Callaghan**, "Les papyrus de la grotte 7 de Qumrân," *NRT* 95 (1973): 188–95 ▥J. J. **O'Rourke**, "Some Considerations About Attempts at Statistical Analysis of the Pauline Corpus," *CBQ* 35 (1973): 483–90 ▥Michael **Prior**, *Paul the Letter-Writer and the Second Letter to Timothy,* JSNTSup 23 (Sheffield: JSOT Press, 1989) ▥Jerome D. **Quinn**, *The Letter to Titus,* AB 35 (New York: Doubleday, 1990) ▥idem, "The Last Volume of Luke: The Relation of Luke-Acts to the Pastoral Epistles," in *Perspectives on Luke-Acts,* ed. C. Talbert (Macon: Mercer University Press, 1978), 62–75 ▥Jerome D. **Quinn** and William C. **Wacker**, *The First and Second Letters to Timothy: A New Translation with Notes and Commentary,* ECC (Grand Rapids: Eerdmans, 2000) ▥W. M. **Ramsey**, "Historical Commentary on the First Epistle to Timothy," *Exp* 7 (1909): 481–94; 8 (1910): 1–21, 167–85, 264–82, 339–57, 399–416, 557–68; 9 (1910): 172–87, 319–33, 433–40 ▥Bo **Reicke**, *Re-examining Paul's Letters: The History of the Pauline Correspondence* (Harrisburg: Trinity Press International, 2001) ▌▌M. **Rist**, "Pseudepigraphy and the Early Christians," in *Studies in New Testament and Early Christian Literature,* ed. D. E. Aune (Leiden: Brill, 1972), 75–91 ▌▌J. A. T. **Robinson**, *Redating the New Testament* (Philadelphia: Westminster, 1976) ▌▌T. A. **Robinson**, "Grayston and Herdan's 'C' Quantity Formula and the Authorship of the Pastoral Epistles," *NTS* 30 (1984): 282–88 ▌▌E. F. **Scott**, *The Pastoral Epistles,* MNTC (London: Hodder & Stoughton, 1936) ▌▌Moisés **Silva**, "The Place of Historical Reconstruction in New Testament Criticism," in *Hermeneutics, Authority, and Canon,* ed. D. A. Carson and John D. Woodbridge (Grand Rapids: Zondervan, 1986), 105–33, 383–88 ▌▌C. Spicq, *Epîtres Pastorales,* 4th ed., 2 vols. (Paris: Gabalda, 1969) ▌▌J. **Stevenson**, *A New Eusebius* (London: SPCK, 1963) ▌▌Carsten P. **Thiede**, *The Earliest Gospel Manuscript? The Qumran Fragment 7Q5 and Its Significance for New Testament Studies* (Carlisle: Paternoster, 1993) ▌▌Philip H. **Towner**, *1–2 Timothy & Titus,* IVPNTC (Downers Grove: IVP, 1994) ▌▌idem, *The Goal of Our Instruction: The Structure of Theology and Ethics in the Pastoral Epistles,* JSNTSup 34 (Sheffield: Sheffield Academic Press, 1989) ▌▌David C. **Verner**, *The Household of God: The Social World of the Pastoral Epistles,* SBLDS 71 (Chico, Calif.: SP, 1983) ▌▌U. **Wagener**, *Die Ordnung des "Hauses Gottes": Der Ort von Frauen in der Ekklesiologie und Ethik der Pastoralbriefe,* WUNT 65 (Tübingen: Mohr-Siebeck, 1994) ▌▌S. G. **Wilson**, *Luke and the Pastoral Epistles* (London: SPCK, 1979) ▌▌Michael **Wolter**, "Die anonymen Schriften des Neuen Testaments: Annäherungsversuch an ein literarisches Phänomen," *ZNW* 79 (1988): 1–16 ▌▌Frances **Young**, "On EPISKOPOS and PRESBUTEROS," *JTS* 45 (1994): 124–48.

CHAPTER EIGHTEEN

PHILEMON

CONTENTS

Philemon is the shortest (335 words in the Greek text) and the most personal of all the letters of Paul. Paul writes to his "dear friend" (v. 1) Philemon about a sensitive matter. A slave of Philemon's, Onesimus, has encountered Paul, who is under Roman arrest, and has been converted (v. 10). Paul, in conformity with Roman law, is sending Onesimus back to his master, Philemon. Paul writes to explain these circumstances, to encourage Philemon to accept Onesimus back as a "brother" (v. 16), and to delicately suggest yet a further favor from Philemon—that he send Onesimus back to Paul and perhaps set him free (v. 21). Nevertheless, while intensely personal—one might almost say private—the letter is more than just a personal note. Paul does not write by himself, but is joined by Timothy (v. 1); and the letter is addressed not only to Philemon but to Apphia and Archippus as well (v. 2). The letter to Philemon therefore falls somewhere between the simple private letter and public letter intended for a broad audience.[1]

The letter to Philemon follows the usual Pauline letter structure, with an opening (vv. 1–3), a thanksgiving (vv. 4–7), a body (vv. 8–20 [or 22]), and a closing (vv. 21 [or 23]–25). The opening identifies Paul, "a prisoner of Christ Jesus," as the sender, along with Timothy, "our brother." The letter is addressed to Philemon, along with Apphia, who may be Philemon's wife, and Archippus. A few scholars speculate that Archippus may be the son of Philemon and Apphia, but we really have no way of knowing. The opening concludes with Paul's usual grace and peace wish-prayer (v. 3). Paul's thanksgiving focuses on Philemon's exemplary Christian character (vv. 4–5, 7); he also prays that Philemon might be active in sharing his faith (v. 6). The end of verse 7 reveals the way Paul has carefully crafted the letter to present the strongest possible appeal to Philemon. He com-

---

[1]See esp. Markus Barth and Helmut Blanke, *The Letter to Philemon: A New Translation with Notes and Commentary*, ECC (Grand Rapids: Eerdmans, 2000), 112–15.

mends him because he has "refreshed the hearts of the saints"; in verse 20, Paul asks that Philemon "refresh my heart" also.

The body of the letter falls into four sections. In the first (vv. 8–11), Paul introduces the central topic of the letter: he appeals to Philemon for "my son Onesimus" (v. 10). Onesimus, Paul says, "became my son while I was in chains," almost certainly meaning that Paul has been the instrument through which Onesimus has come to Christ. These verses continue the tone of delicate appeal that characterizes the entire letter. Paul could have "ordered" Philemon to do what he wants, but he prefers that Philemon not feel constrained so that he can act out of love (vv. 8–9). Verse 11 features another word-play. The name Onesimus means "useful"; Paul claims that Onesimus, who formerly did not live up to his name, may now do so because of his conversion.[2] Second (vv. 12–16), Paul explains that he is sending Onesimus back to Philemon and hints quite plainly at what he wants Philemon to do: allow Onesimus to return and join in ministry with Paul (v. 13). But Paul again refrains from issuing a command; he wants Philemon to act by his own free will (v. 14). But he also wants Philemon to be reconciled with Onesimus—indeed, to go further and treat him, befitting his new status, as a brother and no longer as a slave (v. 16). In the third section of the body, Paul repeats his request that Philemon welcome Onesimus as a fellow believer (v. 17) and adds that he himself will repay Philemon for any losses Philemon has incurred because of Onesimus (v. 18–19). Paul undergirds his appeal with a reminder that Philemon owes to Paul his "very self," implying that Paul was involved in Philemon's conversion. Paul ends the body of the letter with a final appeal (v. 20), which, as we have seen, picks up language from verse 7.

Some commentators think that verses 21–22 are the final part of the body, but they are better seen as the beginning of the closing. Having made his appeal in the body of the letter, Paul now expresses confidence that Philemon will do what he asks (vv. 20–21). Indeed, Paul says, he is sure that Philemon will do "more than I ask"—perhaps a hint that Paul would like Philemon not only to send Onesimus back to Paul but also give him his freedom. The letter ends with typical closing elements: a reference to travel plans (v. 22), conveyance of greetings from ministry associates and friends (vv. 23–24), and a grace wish (v. 25).

AUTHOR

We need say very little here. Only the radical critics of the Tübingen School ever denied the Pauline authorship of Philemon. Contemporary scholars unanimously view Paul as the author.

---

[2]The name Onesimus, for obvious reasons, was often given to slaves; but the name is attested for non-slaves as well (*NewDocs* 4.96).

OCCASION

The traditional explanation surrounding Onesimus suffers from one key difficulty: How was it that he just happened to run into a man in prison who knew his own master?

The traditional explanation of the situation presumed in Philemon runs as follows. The slave Onesimus has run away from his master, Philemon, perhaps compounding his crime by robbing his master (cf. v. 18, "if he has done you any wrong or owes you anything"). In his flight, he somehow encounters Paul, who is under judicial constraint—whether in prison or under house arrest. Paul brings Onesimus to Christ and now faces a dilemma. Even though Onesimus has been a godsend to Paul in his difficult straits and he would like to keep him with him, Roman law requires Paul to send Onesimus back to his master. So Paul obeys the law, sending Onesimus back to Philemon, but asking Philemon, whom Paul knows and has, indeed, been instrumental in converting, to send Onesimus back to Paul and perhaps even set him free.

This traditional explanation suffers from one key difficulty: How was it that Onesimus just happened to run into a man in prison who knew his own master? Such a coincidence seems more in keeping with a Dickens novel than with sober history. To explain this curious encounter and to answer some other alleged difficulties with the usual scenario, several alternative reconstructions of the circumstances have been proposed. One of the earliest of these schemes, and surely the most elaborate, was proposed by John Knox in 1935.[3] In what C. F. D. Moule calls "a fascinating detective story,"[4] Knox, building on some of the ideas of his own teacher, E. J. Goodspeed, argues that the letter we call Philemon was actually written to Archippus. Archippus was the owner of Onesimus, and he had sent Onesimus to Paul. Paul was now returning Onesimus, via Philemon, the overseer of the Lycus Valley churches. But he was also requesting that Onesimus be released for Christian service. This is the "ministry" (*diakonia;* TNIV "work") that Archippus is to complete, according to Colossians 4:17. The letter, therefore, though ultimately directed to Archippus, was sent to Laodicea, where Philemon was located. The letter to Philemon is therefore the mysterious letter to Laodicea that Paul mentions in Colossians 4:16. Again, following Goodspeed, Knox further proposes that Philemon was included in the canon because Onesimus eventually became the influential bishop of Ephesus (Ignatius mentions this "Onesimus") and wanted to include his own "charter of liberty" in the New Testament.

Despite its ingenuity and its ability to explain some puzzling features of Philemon, Knox's proposal has not met with much acceptance. While many scholars are open to the possibility that the Onesimus of Philemon and the

---

[3]*Philemon Among the Letters of Paul;* a second edition appeared in 1959 (New York: Abingdon).

[4]*The Epistles of Paul the Apostle to the Colossians and to Philemon,* CGTC (Cambridge: Cambridge University Press, 1968), 14.

Onesimus of Ignatius might be one and the same,[5] they have also pointed out insuperable problems with Knox's general reconstruction. The "ministry" of Colossians 4:17, considering Paul's normal use of this word, cannot be simply the release of a slave. The delicacy Paul shows in writing Philemon is incompatible with public reading of the letter such as Paul asks for the letter to Laodicea in Colossians 4:17. And the natural antecedent of the second person singular pronouns throughout Philemon is not Archippus, as Knox thinks, but Philemon. It is his house in which the church meets (v. 2) and him to whom Paul appeals throughout the letter.[6]

A far more modest modification of the usual scenario builds on the provision in Roman law that a home could be considered a place of sanctuary. Onesimus had heard of Paul from his master Philemon; and, in danger of his life because of his runaway status, he flees to Paul's home (where he is under house-arrest) for protection.[7] But the option that has gained the most support holds that Onesimus was not, in legal terms, a "fugitive" (*fugitivus*), or runaway slave, but a slave who, having put himself in the wrong with his master (perhaps through misappropriation of funds; cf. v. 18), was seeking mediation through Paul, a "friend of the master" (*amicus domini*).[8] This hypothesis avoids the serious difficulty of how a fugitive slave would ever have encountered Paul and explains well the focus on reconciliation in the letter. The one difficulty with the proposal is that if, as we think likely, Paul was in Rome when he wrote Philemon (see below), it is unlikely that Onesimus would have gone as far as Rome to find a mediator.

A decision between this last scenario and the traditional one is therefore not easy. But perhaps the difficulty of thinking that Onesimus would have gone as far as Rome to seek mediation is greater than the difficulty of explaining the

---

[5]E.g., Moule, *Colossians and Philemon,* 21; Peter T. O'Brien, *Colossians, Philemon,* WBC (Waco: Word, 1982), 268.

[6]For these points and others, see esp. Moule, *Colossians and Philemon,* 16–18.

[7]E. R. Goodenough, "Paul and Onesimus," *HTR* 22 (1929): 181–83; F. F. Bruce, *Paul, Apostle of the Heart Set Free* (Grand Rapids: Eerdmans, 1977), 397–98. A more radical suggestion is that someone, probably Archippus, had sent Onesimus to Paul and that Paul writes to the church to ask that Onesimus be set free so he could continue to minister with Paul (Sara C. Winter, "Paul's Letter to Philemon," *NTS* 33 [1987]: 1–15). But the hypothesis faces insuperable difficulties (see, inter alia, James D. G. Dunn, *The Epistles to the Colossians and to Philemon,* NIGTC [Grand Rapids: Eerdmans, 1996], 301).

[8]See esp. P. Lampe, "Keine 'Sklavenflucht' des Onesimus," *ZNW* 76 (1988): 135–37; Brian M. Rapske, "The Prisoner Paul in the Eyes of Onesimus," *NTS* 37 (1991): 187–203; cf. also Dunn, *Colossians and Philemon,* 304–5; Joseph A. Fitzmyer, *The Letter to Philemon: A New Translation with Introduction and Commentary,* AB 34C (New York: Doubleday, 2000), 16–23.

encounter between Paul and Onesimus. We can envisage many possibilities; for example, Onesimus, having successfully fled as far as Rome, might have had second thoughts about his escape and sought out Paul for refuge and assistance.

PROVENANCE AND DATE

Decisions about the provenance and date of Philemon are bound up with those of Colossians, to which Philemon is closely related. Both letters include Timothy as the co-sender; both refer to Epaphras (Col. 1:7; Philem. 23) and Archippus (Col. 4:17; Philem. 2); both include Mark, Aristarchus, Demas, and Luke among Paul's companions (Col. 4:10, 14; Philem. 24); and Colossians refers to Onesimus (4:9). And since Onesimus is a resident of Colosse (Col. 4:9), we are safe in assuming that Philemon was also. Both letters were therefore almost certainly written at the same time and place and sent together to Colosse. Paul was in prison when he wrote both letters. As we noted in chapter 15, scholars debate about whether this imprisonment was in Ephesus (A.D. 55 or 56?), Caesarea (A.D. 57–59; cf. Acts 23:23–26:32), or Rome (A.D. 60–62; cf. Acts 28:14–31). Scholars today generally dismiss Caesarea from consideration, with the trend favoring Ephesus.[9] And two references in Philemon are said to favor an Ephesian provenance: Onesimus is more likely to have fled to the nearest metropolitan center rather than to the distant capital; and Paul's request that Philemon make ready a guest room for him (Philem. 22) makes sense only if Paul is in reasonable traveling distance.

Neither argument, however, is compelling. Onesimus may well have wanted to get as far away from Colosse as possible, and the teeming cosmopolitan population of Rome offered obvious advantages to a person trying to hide from the authorities. The argument from Paul's request for lodging is a stronger one. Still, Paul could have been in Colosse in about five weeks if released from confinement in Rome; and his reference to a possible imminent arrival is probably calculated to put a bit of extra pressure on Philemon to accede to Paul's wishes. There is therefore no reason to deny that Philemon might have been written in Rome; and we have seen reasons to place the writing of Colossians (and Ephesians) in Rome in the early 60s (see chaps. 13 and 15).[10]

---

[9]See, e.g., Brown, 507–8; Eduard Lohse, *Colossians and Philemon*, Hermeneia (Philadelphia: Fortress Press, 1971), 188; N. T. Wright, *The Epistles of Paul to the Colossians and to Philemon: An Introduction and Commentary*, TNTC (Grand Rapids: Eerdmans, 1986), 165; Fitzmyer, *Philemon*, 9–11.

[10]Favoring a Roman provenance for Philemon are McDonald/Porter, 480; F. F. Bruce, *The Epistles to the Colossians, to Philemon, and to the Ephesians*, NICNT (Grand Rapids: Eerdmans, 1984), 193–96; O'Brien, *Colossians, Philemon*, xlix–liii, 269; and Barth/Blanke, *The Letter to Philemon*, 121–26.

PHILEMON IN RECENT STUDY

The renewed concern with social setting and the significance of social relationships is manifest in Norman R. Peterson's analysis of Philemon, *Rediscovering Paul: Philemon and the Sociology of Paul's Narrative World*.[11] But two issues have dominated recent study of Philemon: the historical and social circumstances that lie behind the letter, and the nature of the letter's contribution to the Christian canon. We have treated the former above; the latter we take up below.

THE CONTRIBUTION OF PHILEMON

The short length and personal focus of Philemon raise an obvious question: Why is it in the canon? Goodspeed and Knox, followed by a number of other scholars, have suggested that personal circumstances account for its presence: Onesimus, having become bishop of Ephesus, uses his influence to insure its inclusion. But even if there is some truth in the proposal, we are surely to seek other reasons more nearly related to the overall purpose of Scripture (1 Tim. 3:16). In this light, we may note two particularly significant contributions of Philemon.

First, the letter gives us a beautiful picture of the mutual love and respect that is to characterize the body of Christ at work. By refusing to exercise his apostolic authority, Paul puts himself in the role of a Christian appealing to a fellow Christian. He wants Philemon to act out of love and not because he demands it—as, Paul makes clear, was his right (v. 8). To be sure, we must not be naïve and ignore the several subtle ways that Paul brings pressure on Philemon to do what he wants. Still, Philemon is left with his options open; the decision is his. Even as Philemon is to act out of love, so Paul has already set an example of selflessness. Onesimus, as Paul makes movingly clear (v. 12), has become very dear to him. The decision to send him back to Philemon and to allow Philemon to make the final decision about his fate is a hard one, compelled not only by demands of legality (about which Paul says nothing) but, more importantly, by the mutual love and respect that is to govern the relations among believers. And, finally, we should not forget that Onesimus must also do what might be very difficult for him: return to his master and face the music. Each of the three key characters in the book therefore must sacrifice his own self-interest in the interests of fellow believers—thereby living out Paul's own exhortation: "in humility value others above yourselves, not looking to your own interests but each of you to the interests of the others" (Phil. 2:3–4).

Second, Philemon contributes to our understanding of the Christian approach to social issues such as slavery. Exactly what Philemon has to teach us on this matter is debated. Paul, of course, does not attack the institution of slavery, either here or elsewhere in his letters—probably because the institution

> *The letter to Philemon gives us a beautiful picture of the mutual love and respect that is to characterize the body of Christ at work.*

---

[11]Philadelphia: Fortress Press, 1985.

was so deeply rooted in the culture as to make any such attack both inconceivable and futile.[12] But he does make clear that the conversion of Onesimus has put him into an entirely new relationship to his owner, Philemon, who is to welcome him "no longer as a slave, but better than a slave, as a dear brother" (v. 16). It is not clear whether Paul is here saying "Onesimus, though still your slave, is to be treated as a brother" or "Onesimus, as a brother, can no longer be considered a slave at all." But the nature of slavery—the ownership of one human being by another—would appear to be incompatible with the equality that is to mark Christian fellowship. So Paul probably intends the latter. As Marshall therefore concludes, "the fuller implication of Paul's teaching here is that the Christian faith is incompatible with the ownership of slaves."[13] While not attacking the institution of slavery as such, therefore, the letter does "bring us into an atmosphere in which the institution of slavery could only wilt and die."[14] That it took so long for this to happen is a sad chapter in Christian blindness to the implications of the gospel.

BIBLIOGRAPHY

John M. G. **Barclay**, "Paul, Philemon and the Dilemma of Christian Slave-Ownership," *NTS* 37 (1991): 161–86 ▥idem, *Colossians and Ephesians*, NTG (Sheffield: Sheffield Academic Press, 2001) ▥S. Scott **Bartchy**, "Slavery (New Testament)," *ABD* 6.65–73 ▥Markus **Barth** and Helmut **Blanke**, *The Letter to Philemon: A New Translation with Notes and Commentary*, ECC (Grand Rapids: Eerdmans, 2000) ▥F. F. **Bruce**, *The Epistles to the Colossians, to Philemon, and to the Ephesians*, NICNT (Grand Rapids: Eerdmans, 1984) ▥idem, *Paul: Apostle of the Heart Set Free* (Grand Rapids: Eerdmans, 1977) ▥J. Duncan M. **Derrett**, "The Functions of the Epistle to Philemon," *ZNW* 79 (1988): 63–91 ▥James D. G. **Dunn**, *The Epistles to the Colossians and to Philemon*, NIGTC (Grand Rapids: Eerdmans, 1996) ▥Joseph A. **Fitzmyer**, *The Letter to Philemon: A New Translation with Introduction and Commentary*, AB 34C (New York: Doubleday, 2000) ▥E. R. **Goodenough**, "Paul and Onesimus," *HTR* 22 (1929): 181–83 ▥H. **Greeven**, "Prüfung der Thesen von J. Knox zum Philemonbrief," *TLZ* 79 (1954): 373–78 ▥John **Knox**, *Philemon Among the Letters of Paul* (London: Collins, 1960) ▥P. **Lampe**, "Keine 'Sklavenflucht' des Onesimus," *ZNW* 76 (1988): 135–37 ▥J. B. **Lightfoot**, *St*

---

[12]See John M. G. Barclay, "Paul, Philemon and the Dilemma of Christian Slave-Ownership," *NTS* 37 (1991): 161–86. Barclay distances himself from this conclusion in a later publication; see idem, *Colossians and Philemon*, NTG (Sheffield: Sheffield Academic Press, 2001), 119–26.

[13]See I. Howard Marshall, "The Theology of Philemon," in *The Theology of the Shorter Pauline Letters* (Cambridge: University Press, 1993), 188–90 (190).

[14]Bruce, *Paul*, 401.

Paul's Epistles to the Colossians and to Philemon (London: Macmillan, 1876)
▐Eduard **Lohse**, *Colossians and Philemon*, Hermeneia (Philadelphia: Fortress Press,
1971) ▐F. **Lyall**, "Roman Law in the Writings of Paul: The Slave and the Freed-
man," *NTS* 17 (1970–71): 73–79 ▐Ralph P. **Martin**, *Colossians and Philemon*,
NCB (London: Marshall, Morgan & Scott, 1974) ▐I. Howard **Marshall**, "The
Theology of Philemon," in *The Theology of the Shorter Pauline Letters* (Cambridge:
University Press, 1993) ▐C. F. D. **Moule**, *The Epistles of Paul the Apostle to the
Colossians and to Philemon* (Cambridge: Cambridge University Press, 1968) ▐Peter
T. **O'Brien**, *Colossians, Philemon*, WBC (Waco: Word: 1982) ▐Norman R. **Peter-
son**, *Rediscovering Paul: Philemon and the Sociology of Paul's Narrative World*
(Philadelphia: Fortress Press, 1985) ▐Brian M. **Rapske**, "The Prisoner Paul in the
Eyes of Onesimus," *NTS* 37 (1991): 187–203 ▐William J. **Richardson**, "Princi-
ple and Context in the Ethics of the Epistle to Philemon," *Int* 22 (1968): 301–16
▐W. **Schenk**, "Der Brief des Paulus an Philemon in der neueren Forschung (1945–
87)," *ANRW* 2.25.4 (1987), 3439–95 ▐Peter **Stuhlmacher**, *Der Brief an Philemon*,
EKKNT (Zürich: Benziger ▐Neukirchen-Vluyn: Neukirchner, 1975) ▐W. L.
Westermann, *The Slave Systems of Greek and Roman Antiquity* (Philadelphia:
American Philosophical Society, 1955) ▐Sara C. **Winter**, "Paul's Letter to Philemon," *NTS* 33 (1987): 1–15 ▐N. T. **Wright**, *The Epistles of Paul to the Colossians
and to Philemon: An Introduction and Commentary*, TNTC (Grand Rapids: Eerdmans, 1986).

CHAPTER NINETEEN

HEBREWS

CONTENTS

The book begins without the salutation and the naming of writer and addressees that characterize all New Testament epistles except 1 John and that are common in epistles of the Greco-Roman period. Yet it concludes in a typically epistolary way, with a benediction, some personal remarks, and a final farewell (13:20–25). Moreover, judging by the specificity of the warnings and moral exhortations that punctuate the document, the writer has specific readers in mind (see 5:12; 6:10; 10:32). The natural way to take 13:22 is that the writer is referring to the entire book (though he does not actually call it an "epistle" or "letter").[1] It seems justifiable to designate this book an epistle,[2] not least because that is how it has been classified throughout most of its history in the church.

"Epistle" or "letter" in the New Testament period was an extremely broad category, however (see chap. 8 above). The wealth of rhetorical devices in Hebrews has suggested to many (probably rightly) that this work was originally a homily or series of homilies that have been turned into the published form of a somewhat anomalous letter.[3] This seems considerably more likely than the suggestion that the opening lines were somehow lost or that the present conclusion was added later—suggestions for which there is no textual evidence. In any case, it has been shown that Hebrews 13 is integral to the work as a whole.[4]

---

[1] This despite the NIV "I have written you only a short letter"; cf. TNIV "I have written to you quite briefly."

[2] See esp. C. Spicq, *L'épître aux Hébreux,* 2 vols., EBib (Paris: Gabalda, 1952–53), 1.19–20.

[3] F. F. Bruce calls Hebrews "a homily in written form, with some personal remarks added at the end" (*The Epistle to the Hebrews,* NICNT, rev. ed. [Grand Rapids: Eerdmans, 1990], 389).

[4] Harold W. Attridge, *The Epistle to the Hebrews,* Hermeneia (Philadelphia: Fortress Press, 1989), 13–21.

The general theme of Hebrews—the unqualified supremacy of God's Son, Jesus Christ, a supremacy that brooks no challenge, whether from angelic or human beings—is not in dispute. Correlatively, the covenant he has inaugurated is superior to any covenant that has preceded it; his priesthood is better than Levi's; the sacrifice he has offered is superior to those offered under the Mosaic code; and in fact, the very purpose of antecedent revelation was to anticipate him and point to him and to all the blessings he has brought with him. This theme of the supremacy of Christ is not the stuff of an abstract essay; its purpose is repeatedly disclosed by the parenetic passages (2:1–4; 3:7–4:11; 4:14–16; 5:11–6:12; 10:19–39; 12:1–13:17) designed to warn the readers not to turn back from the Christian faith to the forms of piety they once knew.

It is also widely agreed that this book has been carefully constructed. What is not agreed is the shape of that structure. Some have focused on large thematic movements, concluding that the argument for the superiority of Jesus and of the Christian faith extends from 1:1 to 10:18, after which exhortations take over (10:19–13:25).[5] Most find this suggestion too undiscriminating: exhortations abound in the earlier section, and the argument continues in the latter. By drawing attention to catchwords, literary inclusions, and the like, some have argued that the body of the book is nestled between an introduction (1:1–4) and a conclusion (13:20–21), to which have been added the glosses of an accompanying letter (13:19, 22–25), and that this body is made up of five chiastically arranged divisions (i.e., 1:5–2:18, the name higher than the angels; 3:1–5:10, Jesus the merciful high priest; 5:11–10:39, Jesus the high priest in the order of Melchizedek; 11:1–12:13, faith and endurance; 12:14–13:19, the peaceful fruit of righteousness).[6] This has been shown to be a bit contrived;[7] nor does it explain the book's intensity, its passion. Others believe there is a lengthy prologue (1:1–4:13) and a lengthy epilogue (10:19–13:25), between which are two expositions of Jesus as high priest (4:14–6:20; 7:1–10:18).[8] Still others appeal to rhetorical devices to justify assorted outlines that vary enormously.[9] Some of them, at least, are not very convincing, such as the view that the book's structure is controlled by the parenetic passages that stand in parallel forms at the beginning and end of each large division (in Kümmel's scheme, 1:1–4:13; 4:14–10:31; 10:32–13:17, followed by

---

[5]E.g., Guthrie, 717–21; idem, *The Letter to the Hebrews,* TNTC (Grand Rapids: Eerdmans, 1983), 58–59.

[6]So A. Vanhoye, *La structure littéraire de l'épître aux Hébreux*, SN 1 (Paris: Desclée de Brouwer, 1963); Hugh Montefiore, *A Commentary on the Epistle to the Hebrews,* HNTC (San Francisco: Harper, 1964).

[7]See Attridge, *Hebrews,* 15–16.

[8]E.g., Hans Windisch, *Der Hebräerbrief,* HNT 14, 2nd ed. (Tübingen: Mohr-Siebeck, 1931).

[9]E.g., Barnabas Lindars, "The Rhetorical Structure of Hebrews," *NTS* 35 (1989): 382–406.

an epistolary conclusion). But it is far from clear that the parenetic passages should be divided up (e.g., do 10:26–31 and 10:32–39 belong in separate divisions?), and some parenetic passages are thereby largely ignored (e.g., 2:1–4).

Attridge rightly observes that most of the smaller units are well marked and that there is little dispute over them.[10] The question is how to tie these units into the larger structure of the book. His own attempt seeks a balance between the "static organizational principles of the discourse" and its "dynamic, developmental features," that is, the movement of thought; but the result diminishes the concrete contrasts the epistle repeatedly draws.[11] For example, Attridge says that 1:5–2:18 presents Christ the eternal Son as the high priest whose perfected or exalted status was achieved through suffering; the comparison between Christ and the angels is merely a "superficial rubric" used to develop this theme.

Perhaps the most detailed and consistent outline is that of Guthrie.[12] After surveying many other proposals, he deploys the tools of discourse analysis (= text-linguistics) to draw attention to the complex interplay of exposition and exhortation that runs through this document. His monograph is nuanced and allows for subtleties such as overlaps. In a later commentary he works out his proposal in practical and believable terms.[13] Occasionally one wonders if the structure is a trifle rigid, and his work needs to be supplemented by an appreciation of the rhetoric of Hebrews.[14]

In light of continuing debates on the structure, the following summary surveys the flow of thought with as few judgments as possible on the best way to form a hierarchy of the individual units.

The exordium (1:1–4) stresses the superiority and finality of the divine revelation that appeared in God's Son, Jesus Christ. Verse 4 is transitional, preparing the way for the first sustained argument of the superiority of the Son: he is superior to angelic beings (1:5–14). The first warning or admonition section immediately follows: if this revelation is superior, it is desperately important not to drift away from the gospel it brings, especially when we bear in mind the terrible judgments that befell those who ignored even the earlier, lesser revelation (2:1–4). Chapter 2 briefly continues the contrast between Jesus and the angels (2:5, 9), but only to remind the readers that human destiny transcends that of the angels and that in order to bring humanity to that destiny, Jesus has

---

[10]Attridge, *Hebrews*, 14.

[11]Ibid., 17–21.

[12]George H. Guthrie, *The Structure of Hebrews: A Text-Linguistic Analysis*, NovTSup 73 (Leiden: Brill, 1994).

[13]George H. Guthrie, *Hebrews*, NIVAC (Grand Rapids: Zondervan, 1998).

[14]See especially David A. deSilva, *Perseverance and Gratitude: A Socio-Rhetorical Commentary on the Epistle "to the Hebrews"* (Grand Rapids: Eerdmans, 2000); and Andrew H. Trotter Jr., *Interpreting the Epistle to the Hebrews* (Grand Rapids: Baker, 1997).

identified himself with mortal, fallen human beings (2:5–18). In short, he has become their "merciful and faithful high priest in service to God" (2:17).

Before turning to the theme of high priest, however, the author shows in what way Jesus is faithful, and thereby introduces another contrast. Both Moses and Jesus were faithful in their service, but Jesus was the son of the household (3:1–6). Mention of Moses' service in God's household leads to a stern warning not to fall away into unbelief as many of Moses' generation did (3:7–19). But this is cast in terms of an exposition of Psalm 95:7–11 (Heb. 3:7–11) and of the relations among the rest to which the psalm's readers are invited, the rest intrinsic to entering the land of Canaan, and even the rest God enjoys from the time of the completion of his initial creative work (3:7–4:11). Joshua led his generation into the Promised Land, but the fact that later Scripture writers promise more rest proves that possession of the land cannot be the ultimate "rest." The rest Jesus provides is superior to that of Joshua's day and is of a piece with the "rest" of God himself. Any thought of escaping the perceptive authority of this revelation is therefore utter folly (4:12–13).

The author returns to the theme of Jesus as high priest, stressing the encouragement Christians enjoy in coming to One who is so able to sympathize with their weaknesses (4:14–16). The same qualifications that applied to the high priests of the old covenant (5:1–4) are superlatively found in Christ (5:5–10) for our encouragement. The section ends by referring to Jesus as the "high priest in the order of Melchizedek," but before the significance of this title is explored, the author again intrudes into the discussion a stern warning (5:11–6:20): he condemns spiritual immaturity (5:11–6:3), warns that apostates cannot be recovered (6:5–8), and encourages his readers to persevere (6:9–12) in light of the certainty of God's promise (6:13–20).

The writer then again picks up the theme of the Melchizedekian priesthood (7:1–28), linking Genesis 14:18–20 and Psalm 110 so as to demonstrate the superiority of the priesthood of Melchizedek above that of Levi, and to show that Jesus belongs to the former. The crucial point to which the argument leads is the permanent efficacy of Jesus' sacrifice. Unlike the sacrifices of the old covenant, which made nothing perfect (7:19), the sacrifice of Jesus is able "to save completely those who come to God through him" (7:25). Indeed, perfection in this epistle is essentially a matter of completion—in particular, the completion of God's plan of salvation.[15] In that light, the Levitical high priest and the old sanctuary are but shadows of the new covenant and the new high priest that the Old Testament prophets themselves foresaw (Heb. 8:1–13; Jer. 31:31–34). Indeed, the announcement of the new covenant had already in principle made the Mosaic

---

[15]See esp. David Peterson, *Hebrews and Perfection: An Examination of the Concept of Perfection in the "Epistle to the Hebrews,"* SNTSMS 47 (Cambridge: Cambridge University Press, 1982).

covenant obsolete (8:13). That truth leads to an exposition of the ritual of the tabernacle, especially the Day of Atonement (9:1–10), in order to show that Christ's sacrifice achieves a permanent effect that the old sacrifices never aspired to (9:11–28). In fact, the old order was designed to be a shadow of the reality that has been introduced by the new (10:1–10). Even the enthronement of the new high priest attests the finality and permanent efficacy of his sacrificial work.

Once again there is a lengthy parenetic section (10:19–11:39) designed to encourage the readers to press on with their Christian profession. To turn aside is profoundly dangerous in light of the exclusive sufficiency of the new covenant. What is required is persevering faith; and this too has been modeled by the Scriptures (11:1–40). The readers must look to Jesus, the pioneer (not "author") and perfecter of our faith (12:1–3)—the one who has both opened up the way to God and completed (or perfected) all that was necessary. In that light, any trials they face are to be borne as discipline from the loving hand of God (12:4–11); to fall away from want of persistence is to align oneself with Esau (12:12–17). Eager to draw further contrasts between the old covenant and the new in order to foster perseverance, the author sets off the heavenly Zion, to which Christians come, with the earthly Sinai of the old covenant (12:18–29), thus tightly merging biblical exposition and parenesis.

The concluding exhortations (13:1–17) are shaped to counter particular ways in which the readers' incipient backsliding is in danger of manifesting itself. There are ethical injunctions to obey (13:1–6). The readers will do well both to follow the example of those who first brought them the gospel (13:7–8) and to submit to their current leaders (13:17). Intertwined with this practical encouragement is the exhortation to offer the "sacrifice of praise," a sacrifice contrasted with the sacrifices of the old covenant, since they are fulfilled in the sacrifice of Jesus "outside the camp" (13:9–16). If this entails sharing his disgrace, so be it: the implication is that it is infinitely better to share his disgrace than to defect from his grace.

The author concludes with a request for prayer (13:18–19), his own prayer and doxology (13:20–21), some personal notes (13:22–23), and final greetings and a benediction (13:24–25).

AUTHOR

In the earliest text of Hebrews that has come down to us—P[46] (early third century)—this epistle is placed in the Pauline corpus, right after Romans.[16] This undoubtedly reflects the conviction of the Eastern church, itself dependent on the more cautious assessment of several notable Alexandrian scholars, whose opinions are largely preserved by Eusebius. In particular, both Clement of

---

[16]For the diversity of placement in the manuscripts, see Metzger, 661–62.

Alexandria (c. A.D. 150–215) and Origen (185–253) preserve the tradition that Paul is the author of Hebrews, even though they recognize the difficulties attached to the view. The Greek of Hebrews is more polished than that of Paul, and the consistent quality of the rhetoric is quite remarkable. Doubtless because of similarities between the Greek of Hebrews and the Greek of Luke-Acts, Clement supposes that Paul wrote to the Hebrews in Hebrew and suggests that our Greek text is Luke's translation (*H.E.* 6.14.2). Clement explains the lack of a Pauline superscription by saying that Paul was writing for Hebrews who had formed strong biases against him, and therefore he prudently left his name off. Although Origen insists that the content of Hebrews is not inferior to what is found in Paul's acknowledged letters (*H.E.* 6.25.12), he suggests that one of Paul's disciples took notes of what the apostle said and wrote the material up for him (*H.E.* 6.14.13). He is aware that some think this unnamed party is Luke, and others Clement of Rome, but Origen himself refuses to speculate: "But who wrote the epistle, in truth God knows" (*H.E.* 6.25.14).

In the Western church, Pauline authorship was resisted until the latter half of the fourth century. The Muratorian Canon, Irenaeus, and Hippolytus of Rome all agree that Paul was not the author. But the only alternative suggestion is that of Tertullian (in the second century), who insists that Hebrews has more authority than the *Shepherd of Hermas*, owing to the eminence of its author, whom he identifies as Barnabas, as if he is making an ascription that is commonly agreed in his circles (*On Modesty* 20). When Eusebius wrote (c. 325), many in Rome still did not consider Hebrews to be Pauline.

It was the combined opinion of Jerome and Augustine that shifted opinion in the West. Here it was not so much the weight of literary criticism that persuaded them as the fact that admission of a book to the canon was greatly helped by recognition of apostolic authorship. Both Jerome (*Epistle* 129.3) and Augustine (*Forgiveness of Sins* 1.50) refer to the prestigious opinion of the Eastern churches. The former acknowledges that many in the West still had doubts and says that it does not matter who the author really was, since the work is "honored daily by being read in the churches." Despite such weighty support for Pauline authorship, Western synods initially preserved some distinction between Hebrews and the generally recognized Paulines. Both the Synod of Hippo (A.D. 393) and the Third Synod of Carthage (397) enumerate, "Of Paul the apostle, thirteen epistles; of the same to the Hebrews, one." By the Sixth Synod of Carthage (419), fourteen epistles are ascribed to Paul. By and large, Pauline authorship is thereafter affirmed in the West, although even so, the most learned commentators raise caveats. Thus, Thomas Aquinas affirms that Luke translated the epistle into excellent Greek.[17]

---

[17]Thomas Aquinas, *Preface to the Epistle to the Hebrews*, quoted by Spicq, *Hébreux* 1.198 n. 1.

Not until the Reformation questioned countless ancient traditions was this one submitted to forceful reexamination. Calvin (on 13:23) argued for Clement of Rome or Luke as the author; Luther proposed (for the first time, so far as we know) Apollos. The (Roman Catholic) Council of Trent responded by insisting there are fourteen Pauline epistles—though few Catholic scholars would espouse that view today.

The last major defense of the Pauline authorship of Hebrews was written more than half a century ago.[18] Today virtually no one would repeat the effort.[19] Quite apart from the differences in vocabulary, Greek style, and rhetoric, which cannot of themselves disprove Pauline authorship but make it a less plausible alternative, the absence of a self-identifying salutation at the beginning of the document—Paul's normal practice—makes it hard to believe that Paul wrote it. Moreover, numerous common Pauline themes are missing, and, conversely, the high priesthood of Christ, so central to Hebrews, does not figure largely in the acknowledged Pauline epistles. Above all, it is almost impossible to believe that Paul would identify himself as one of those who heard the gospel, not from the Lord, but from "those who heard him" (2:3; cf. Gal. 1:11–12).

Neither Luke nor Clement of Rome draws many votes today. The points of connection between Luke and Hebrews are too slight to support a theory of common authorship. Clement of Rome must be dismissed as a likely candidate, not only because he appears to quote Hebrews in several places (though doubtless one could argue that he is quoting his own work!), but especially because his treatment of several themes is so widely removed from the approach of Hebrews. For example, he chooses to buttress his arguments about the nature of the church's ministry by appealing to the ceremonial laws of the Old Testament—a stance utterly at variance with the arguments of Hebrews.

At least in the case of Paul, Luke, and Clement of Rome, there are some extant writings that can be compared with the epistle to the Hebrews. Evidence

---

[18]William Leonard, *The Authorship of the Epistle to the Hebrews: Critical Problem and Use of the Old Testament* (Rome: Vatican Polyglot Press, 1939). The work to which this one is greatly indebted is Charles Forster, *The Apostolical Authority of the Epistle to the Hebrews: An Inquiry, in Which the Received Title of the Greek Epistle Is Vindicated, Against the Cavils of Objectors, Ancient and Modern, from Origen to Sir J. D. Michaëlis, Chiefly upon Grounds of Internal Evidence Hitherto Unnoticed: Comprizing a Comparative Analysis of the Style and Structure of This Epistle, and of the Undisputed Epistles of St. Paul, Tending to Throw Light upon Their Interpretation* (London: James Duncan, 1838).

[19]The two exceptions are Eta Linnemann, "Wiederaufnahme-Prozess in Sachen des Hebräerbriefes," *Fundamentum* 21 (2000): 101–12; 22 (2001): 52–65, 88–110 (and nicely refuted by Rainer Riesner, "Der Hebräer-Brief nach altkirchlichen Zeugnissen," *EuroJTh* 11/1 [2002]: 15–29); and David Alan Black, "On the Pauline Authorship of Hebrews," *Faith & Mission* 16/2 (1999): 32–51; 16/3 (1999): 78–86.

in support of other writers is entirely circumstantial, since no undisputed document from their pens has come down to us. There are four principal options.

1. Those who suggest Barnabas is the author point out that he was a Levite from Cyprus (Acts 4:36) and therefore a member of the Hellenist party in the Jerusalem church.[20] On this ground, it is suggested he may have shared the anti-temple perspectives of Stephen (Acts 7:48–50). For a time he was a close collaborator of Paul (Acts 9:27; 11:30; 13:1–14:28), and since he was called υἱὸς παρακλήσεως (huios paraklēseōs, "Son of Encouragement," Acts 4:36), it is entirely appropriate that he should write τὸν λόγον τῆς παρακλήσεως (ton logon tēs paraklēseōs, a "word of exhortation," Heb. 13:22).

But παράκλησις (paraklēsis, "encouragement" or "exhortation") is sufficiently common in the New Testament that it cannot be restricted to an association with only one person. The epistle to the Hebrews is not so much anti-temple as interested in demonstrating the obsolescence in principle of the *biblical* cultus (which of course was first connected with the tabernacle, not the temple). That Barnabas was a Hellenistic Jew makes him at least potentially qualified to write a Christian book so deeply interacting with the LXX but hardly identifies him as the author.

2. Luther's suggestion of Apollos has gathered a fair bit of support.[21] He is described as ἀνὴρ λόγιος (anēr logios, "a learned man"—more probably, "an eloquent man") with "a thorough knowledge of the Scriptures" (Acts 18:24). He was a native of Alexandria, and many writers have found numerous connections between the epistle to the Hebrews and the writings of Philo of Alexandria. Judging by the Corinthian correspondence (esp. 1 Cor. 1–4), he had some sort of connection with the Pauline mission.

But although Luther's suggestion is a brilliant guess, there is insufficient evidence to make it testable. Moreover, many have pointed out that although Hebrews shares some important vocabulary with Philo, the basic elements of his thought are far removed from the Neoplatonism and Stoicism that undergird so much of Philo.[22] Of course, Apollos may have transformed the categories

---

[20]See the extended bibliography in Spicq, *Hébreux* 1.199 n. 8, to which may be added J. A. T. Robinson, *Redating the New Testament* (Philadelphia: Westminster, 1976), 200–220. On this question, one of the best treatments remains that of Brooke Foss Westcott, *The Epistle to the Hebrews*, 3rd ed. (London: Macmillan, 1909), lxxx–lxxxiv.

[21]See bibliography in Attridge, *Hebrews*, 4; to which may be added Paul Ellingworth, *The Epistle to the Hebrews: A Commentary on the Greek Text*, NIGTC (Grand Rapids: Eerdmans, 1993), 3–21 (the name of Apollos "is perhaps the least unlikely of the conjectures which have been put forward" [p. 21]).

[22]See esp. Ronald Williamson, *Philo and the Epistle to the Hebrews*, ALGHJ 4 (Leiden: Brill, 1970).

in which he was trained as he improved his knowledge of the Christian way. But this is to pile speculation on speculation.

3. From the time of Harnack, a number of scholars have suggested that Priscilla is the author, perhaps in conjunction with her husband Aquila in the minor role.[23] That might account for the interchange between "we" and "I" in the book (the former is more common). They were sufficiently informed that they undertook the teaching of Apollos (Acts 18:26), and they must have known Timothy (see Heb. 13:23), since, like them, he worked with Paul in Corinth and Ephesus (Acts 18:5; 19:22; 1 Cor. 16:10, 19). The disappearance of the author's name might then be accounted for by appealing to antifeminist tendencies in the church. Once again, however, there is too little evidence to support the thesis. Above all, this theory seems to be ruled out by the self-reference in the masculine singular in 11:32.

4. Similar objections can be raised against theories that advance Silas, Timothy, Epaphras, the deacon Philip, or Mary the mother of Jesus as the author of this book.

It is far better to admit our ignorance. We do not know who wrote it; almost certainly the first readers did. In all likelihood the author was a Hellenistic Jew who had become a Christian, a second-generation believer (Heb. 2:3). He was steeped in the LXX (none of his numerous quotations from the Old Testament depend on the Hebrew) and, judging by his excellent vocabulary and Greek style, had enjoyed a good education.

PROVENANCE

If we are uncertain who the author of the epistle to the Hebrews was, we are still less certain about the book's geographic provenance. The only explicit clue is found in 13:24: "Those from Italy send you their greetings." Unfortunately, the expression is unclear. It may refer to a group of Italian believers who left their native land and were sending their greetings home (in which case the epistle was sent "to" Italy, but we cannot specify the place from which it was sent),[24] or it may refer to believers *in* Italy (in which case we cannot identify the destination, but the author is writing *from* Italy).[25] Because we cannot be certain which is meant, the ambiguity in the NEB rendering is attractive: "Greetings to you from our Italian friends."

---

[23]Adolph von Harnack, "Probabilia über die Addresse und den Verfasser des Hebräerbriefes," *ZNW* 1 (1900): 16–41; Ruth Hoppin, *Priscilla: Author of the Epistle to the Hebrews* (New York: Exposition, 1969).

[24]See RSV: "those who come from Italy."

[25]Alexander Nairne translates, "Those who are in Italy and send their greetings with mine from Italy" (*The Epistle of Priesthood* [Edinburgh: T. & T. Clark, 1913], 433).

Even if we could be reasonably certain who wrote the book, that would not necessarily establish its geographic provenance, since the writer may have moved around quite a bit (as Paul did). As for the book's conceptual provenance, in a work as clearly polemical and parenetic as this one, it is important to recognize that much of the argument may be shaped less by the author's personal interests than by his perception of his readers' critical needs. In that case, analysis of the book's conceptual categories may reveal more about the work's intended readers than about the author.

Analysis of the book's conceptual categories may reveal more about the work's intended readers than about the author.

DATE

It is difficult to be certain about the date of Hebrews. The principal points in the debate are these:

1. That the addressees and apparently the author himself belong to the second generation of Christians (2:3) does not yield much concrete information, since "second generation" must be understood not chronologically but genealogically. Probably one should infer that the epistle was not written before A.D. 50; most would insist not before 60.

2. Although some of the quotations of Hebrews in *1 Clement* are disputed, it is exceedingly difficult to dismiss the repeated references to Hebrews 1 in *1 Clement* 36:1–6.[26] The majority of scholars date *1 Clement* to A.D. 96. If accepted, this would put a terminus ad quem on the date of Hebrews. It must be admitted, however, that the primary reason for dating *1 Clement* so precisely is that some words from the first chapter—"the sudden and repeated misfortunes and calamities which have befallen us"—refer to persecution of Christians under the Emperor Domitian. Evidence for such persecution is slight (see discussion under "Date" in chap. 24 below). If it is discounted, the range of possible dates for *1 Clement* is opened up from about 70[27] to about 140,[28] with several mediating positions. The very late dates are unlikely, since *1 Clement* is cited as an authoritative source by Clement of Alexandria, and the 96 date still seems most plausible; but it is important to recognize the limits of our knowledge.

3. If, as seems likely, the Timothy mentioned in Hebrews 13:23 is the younger companion of Paul, then the epistle to the Hebrews must have been written within his lifetime. Paul co-opted him into missionary service c. A.D.

---

[26]See esp. Donald A. Hagner, *The Use of the Old and New Testaments in Clement of Rome*, NovTSup 34 (Leiden: Brill, 1973), 179–95; Paul Ellingworth, "Hebrews and 1 Clement: Literary Dependence or Common Tradition," *BZ* 23 (1979): 437–40; Herbert Braun, *An die Hebräer*, HNT (Tübingen: Mohr-Siebeck, 1984), 3, 32.

[27]So Robinson, *Redating*, 327–34, largely dependent on G. Edmundson, *The Church in Rome in the First Century*, BL (Oxford: Oxford University Press, 1913), 188–202.

[28]So Elmer T. Merrill, *Essays on Early Christian History* (London: Macmillan, 1924), 217–41; Laurance L. Welborn, "On the Date of 1 Clement," *BR* 29 (1984): 35–54.

49, but we do not know how old he was at the time. Still, this probably establishes the upper limit for Hebrews to be about 100, very close to the upper limit imposed by the traditional dating of *1 Clement*.

4. Many have attempted to tie the words of Hebrews 12:4 ("In your struggle against sin, you have not yet resisted to the point of shedding your blood") to the particular period of persecution leading up to the persecution under Nero. If the language is figurative, signaling nothing more than strenuous opposition to sin, the passage has no bearing on the date of the book. But even if the passage is understood, somewhat more naturally, to refer to the deaths of martyrs, it is exceedingly difficult to draw undisputed inferences. For example, one might conclude that this rules out the church in Rome during or immediately after Nero's persecution, because Christians at that time did lose their lives. That might suggest a date *earlier* than Nero's persecution (A.D. 64). Alternatively, one might suppose this was written to believers elsewhere in the empire who had heard what their fellow believers had *already* suffered under Nero but who had not themselves faced opposition that had gone so far. In that case, the book was written *after* Nero. Similar arguments have been mooted with respect to the reign of Domitian. Above all, opposition from the synagogue sporadically broke out here and there in every decade of the first century after A.D. 30, making it rather hazardous to use Hebrews 12:4 to isolate a particular date.

5. One of the most commonly presented arguments turns on the occurrence of present-tense verbs in connection with the ritual (7:8; 9:6–7, 9, 13; 13:10). In English translation, they read as if the ceremonies are continuing at the time the author is writing. There are two flaws in this argument. First, the present tense in Greek, even in the indicative, does not necessarily refer to present time. Even traditional approaches to Greek grammar observe the frequency of the so-called historic present in Greek; a more linguistically informed approach, appealing to aspect theory, doubts that the (morphological) "present tense" has any immediate bearing on time.[29] Second, Clement of Rome, writing after the destruction of the temple, uses the present tense to describe similar ritual (*1 Clem.* 41); similarly, Josephus alternates between present and past tense in his discussion of the tabernacle and its furnishings (*Ant.* 4.102–50) and of the vestments of the priests (*Ant.* 4.151–87). Some also point out that the epistle to the Hebrews never specifically mentions the temple; its focus is the biblical tabernacle. This suggests (they argue) that the destruction of the second temple would not have been of great interest to the author; therefore, silence as to its destruction is no evidence of an early date.

But although the linguistic argument is not decisive, another form of this argument is far stronger. When Josephus, for instance, describes the tabernacle, furnishings, and priestly vestments, he is not engaged in a theological argument

---

[29]See Stanley E. Porter, *Verbal Aspect in the Greek of the New Testament*, SBG 1 (Bern: Peter Lang, 1989).

about their obsolescence, about their utter replacement by the corresponding realities of the new covenant, the idea that lies at the very heart of the argument in Hebrews. When the author of Hebrews cites Jeremiah's prophecy of a new covenant (Jer. 31:31–34; Heb. 8:7–12), he concludes that by calling this covenant new, God through Jeremiah "made the first one obsolete; and what is obsolete and outdated will soon disappear" (8:13). The law-covenant "can never, by the same sacrifices repeated endlessly year after year, make perfect those who draw near to worship. Otherwise, would they not have stopped being offered?" (10:1–2). It is difficult not to conclude that the sacrifices were still being offered when the author wrote such lines as these. Although he does not directly refer to the temple, he could not have spoken in such terms if he did not see the sacrifices at the temple in fundamental continuity with those established for the tabernacle. By the same token, if the sacrifices of the temple had ended (as they did in A.D. 70),[30] it is hard to imagine how he could have resisted pointing this out. As Lindars indicates, the thrust of his rhetoric is to establish the exclusive finality of Christ's sacrifice[31] and to prevent his readers from returning to the sacrificial system from which they had been weaned when they first became Christians. Had the temple sacrifices already ceased, his argument would have had to be cast in a different guise. True, this is an argument from silence; but it is a powerful argument from silence because, given the nature of the author's polemic, we expect noise: it is hard to imagine how the author could maintain such silence if he were writing after the destruction of the temple. Although not conclusive, this constitutes strong support for a date before 70 for Hebrews.[32]

6. The strongest argument for a late date turns on the attempt to plot where this book should lie on the trajectory of the development of early Christianity. For instance, it is often argued that the Christology of Hebrews (esp. 1:1–3) reflects the same sort of high Christology found in, say, Luke-Acts, 1 Peter, or the Pastorals, all of them frequently dated to 75–90. But not only is the dating of these documents also disputed, with many scholars insisting on a date before 70 for one or more of these books, but also, and more importantly, the Christology of Hebrews 1:1–3 is certainly no "higher" than that found in such passages as

---

[30]The attempt of Kenneth W. Clark in "Worship in the Jerusalem Temple After A.D. 70," *NTS* 6 (1959–60): 269–80, to prove what his title announces is entirely unconvincing; similarly Otto Michel, *Der Brief an die Hebräer,* KEK, 12th ed. (Göttingen: Vandenhoeck & Ruprecht, 1966), 56–58. Cf. Robinson, *Redating,* 202–3.

[31]Lindars, "Rhetorical Structure."

[32]Modern supporters of a date before A.D. 70 include Bruce, *Hebrews,* 20–22; George Wesley Buchanan, *To the Hebrews,* AB 36 (Garden City: Doubleday, 1972), 261; August Strobel, *Der Brief an die Hebräer,* NTD (Göttingen: Vandenhoeck & Ruprecht, 1975), 83; Philip Edgcumbe Hughes, *A Commentary on the Epistle to the Hebrews* (Grand Rapids: Eerdmans, 1977), 30–32; Donald A. Hagner, *Hebrews,* GNC (San Francisco: Harper, 1983), xviii–xix; and George H. Guthrie, *Hebrews* (1998), 19–23.

1 Corinthians 8:6, Philippians 2:6–11, or Colossians 1:15–20. Yet the overwhelming majority of scholars recognize these passages to be pre–70, and many of them think they represent *pre*-Pauline thought.

Thus, although one cannot decisively rule out any date between about A.D. 60 and 100,[33] the preponderance of evidence favors a date before 70.[34]

DESTINATION

Because the author refers to experiences in the lives of his readers (e.g., 10:32–34), we are right to assume that he has a specific group in mind as he writes. Many ancient commentators, and some moderns, think the addressees lived in Palestine, perhaps even in Jerusalem.[35] The strength of this view turns on the repeated references to the cultus. The complete silence on the temple (as opposed to the tabernacle), however, slightly weakens this theory. The epistle is written in polished Greek, and none of the Old Testament quotations and allusions unambiguously depend on Hebrew or Aramaic: from this we must conclude either that the author knew no Semitic tongue or that his readers, if in Jerusalem, were all expatriates, Greek speakers choosing to live in Jerusalem or the surrounding area. In any case, judging by the large numbers of Jews from around the empire that visited Jerusalem at the high feasts, especially Passover, there were countless Jews who did not live in Palestine but who nevertheless looked to the cultus in Jerusalem for cleansing and for a secure relationship with God. If that is so, it is hard to see what evidence in the book supports Jerusalem or Palestine as the destination, above many other places in the empire.

Although many other candidates for destination have been advanced, including Alexandria, Antioch, Bithynia and Pontus, Caesarea, Colosse, Corinth, Cyprus, Ephesus, and Samaria, the only other suggestion that has garnered a fair measure of support is Rome.[36] In the literature that has come down

---

[33]So many commentators: e.g., Craig R. Koester, *Hebrews: A New Translation with Introduction and Commentary,* AB 36 (New York: Doubleday, 2001), 50–54.

[34]William L. Lane, *Hebrews,* WBC 47A-B (Dallas: Word Books, 1991), lxvi, assigns a tentative date for the composition of this epistle "to the insecure interval between the aftermath of the great fire of Rome (A.D. 64) and Nero's suicide in June, A.D. 68."

[35]E.g., Buchanan, *Hebrews,* 255–56; Hughes, *Commentary,* 19. Sir William Ramsay suggested that Hebrews was written to the Jerusalem church from Caesarea while Paul was imprisoned there (c. A.D. 57–59), penned by one of Paul's companions, possibly Philip the evangelist (*Luke the Physician* [London: Hodder & Stoughton: 1908], 301ff.).

[36]Interpreters support Rome with varying degrees of confidence; see Bruce, *Hebrews,* 10–14; Robinson, *Redating,* 205–13; Simon J. Kistemaker, *Exposition of the Epistle to the Hebrews,* NTC (Grand Rapids: Baker, 1984), 17–18; Raymond E. Brown and John P. Meier, *Antioch and Rome* (New York: Paulist, 1983), 139–58; Lane, *Hebrews,* liii-lx; see also the next two notes.

to us, this is the first place the epistle was known (in the writings of Clement of Rome; see the section "Provenance" above). The fact that the Roman church, and the West in general, took so long to ascribe it to Paul may argue that they enjoyed positive information that it was *not* written by the apostle. As we have seen, this view entails taking "those from Italy" (Heb. 13:24) to refer to some Italians who left Italy and at the time of writing were living elsewhere (like Priscilla and Aquila), and the Greek certainly allows that interpretation. Both Harnack[37] and Manson[38] attempted to tie this theory into the early history of Christianity at Rome, Harnack envisaging that the addressees were in a house church in Rome, and Manson envisaging a conservative Jewish-Christian faction there—and their theories have been taken up and developed by numerous recent commentators.

Doubtless Rome is as good a guess as any, but it is not much more than a guess. Fortunately, few exegetical issues depend on determining the geographic location of the addressees. The situation that calls forth this epistle is far more important.

PURPOSE

Any assessment of the purpose of Hebrews is inextricably tied to one's understanding of who the addressees were: one cannot discuss the purpose without presupposing some things about the addressees, and vice versa. In the earliest form of the text that has come down to us, P[46], this book had the title Πρὸς Ἑβραίους (*Pros Hebraious,* "To [the] Hebrews"). Apparently Clement of Alexandria, writing c. A.D. 180, knew the book under this title, since he speaks of it as having been written Ἑβραίοις (*Hebraiois,* "for Hebrews"; *H.E.* 6.14.3–4). Most scholars assume that this is a later editorial label attached to the work for convenient reference and therefore should not influence our efforts to establish the identity of the addressees. This may be too skeptical (cf. comments in chap. 3 above on the author of Matthew). In any case, it is the content of the book that must finally determine the direction of the discussion, not least because, even if the title is original, it has some ambiguity (e.g., it could refer to Jewish Christians whose mother tongue is Hebrew/Aramaic [Acts 6:1] or to Christians who are Jewish by birth, irrespective of their mother tongue [Phil. 3:5]).[39]

All agree that the book is written for Christians, who are urged to maintain their confession (e.g., 3:6, 14; 4:14; 10:23). Their ethnic background is more disputed. Although the book is steeped in Old Testament allusions and Levitical

---

[37]Harnack, "Probabilia."

[38]William Manson, *The Epistle to the Hebrews: An Historical and Theological Reconsideration* (London: Hodder & Stoughton, 1951).

[39]See Zahn 2.296.

ritual, it does not necessarily follow that either the author or the readers are Jewish Christians; doubtless some Gentile believers immersed themselves in the Greek Old Testament. It is often pointed out that the author's knowledge of Jewish ritual, like the knowledge that he presupposes of his readers, is a literary knowledge: it is drawn from the Old Testament and perhaps from other Jewish texts, not (so far as the epistle shows) from any close observation of or participation in the temple ritual in Jerusalem. A number of scholars take this line.[40] Some argue that the warnings against turning "away from the living God" (3:12) better suit former pagans in danger of apostasy than Jews who, if they relapsed into Judaism, would still be serving the living God of their fathers. Others suggest that these are Gentile Christians in danger of abandoning the exclusive claims of Christ and seeking a deeper way in Judaism, a variation on the "Judaizing" controversy. Some think Hebrews attempts to adapt Jewish apocalyptic to a Jewish environment, or tries to dissipate misplaced sacramental piety.

These lines of reasoning have not proved convincing to all scholars. When the author warns against turning "away from the living God" (3:12), he adduces the example of the Israelites under Moses' leadership who turned away from God. If such language applies to ancient Israelites, it is hard to imagine a reason why it could not be applied to first-century Jews. The "elementary teachings" of 6:1 presuppose a background in Judaism, and the author's driving insistence that the old covenant has been eclipsed by the new makes sense only if the readers are still trying to live under it, or if they imagine that, having passed beyond it, they may legitimately revert to it. Moreover, as Bruce points out,[41] nothing in this epistle suggests that the problem the author confronts is Judaizing propaganda.[42] In particular, the nonmention of circumcision makes sense if the epistle is directed to a Jewish-Christian community but would be quite surprising if the readers are Gentile believers in danger of being seduced by the so-called Judaizers.

Furthermore, the author cites the Greek Old Testament as if he assumes that his readers will recognize its authority. That would be true of Hellenistic Jews who had converted to Christianity. Even if they were tempted to modify

---

[40]E.g., Marcus Dods, "The Epistle to the Hebrews," in *EGT*; J. Moffatt, *A Critical and Exegetical Commentary on the Epistle to the Hebrews*, ICC (Edinburgh: T. & T. Clark, 1924); Windisch, *Hebräerbrief*; E. F. Scott, *The Epistle to the Hebrews* (Edinburgh: T. & T. Clark, 1922); G. Vos, *The Teaching of the Epistle to the Hebrews* (Grand Rapids: Eerdmans, 1956); Ernst Käsemann, *The Wandering People of God: An Investigation of the Letter to the Hebrews* (ET Minneapolis: Augsburg, 1984 [from 2nd ed., 1957]); Gerd Theissen, *Untersuchungen zum Hebräerbrief*, SNT 2 (Gütersloh: Mohn, 1969); deSilva, *Perseverance and Gratitude* (2000); Craig R. Koester, *Hebrews* (2001).

[41]Bruce, *Hebrews*, 6 n. 13.

[42]On the difficulties surrounding the terms "Judaizing" and "Judaizers," see chap. 11 n. 3.

some elements of their Christian belief and return in some measure to their erstwhile commitment to Judaism, their confidence in what we call the Old Testament would not be shaken. Pagans who had converted to Christianity, should they be tempted to return to their paganism, would surely also be tempted to abandon their submission to the Scriptures that had contributed to their becoming Christians. Moreover, not a few of the author's arguments for the superiority of Jesus turn on challenging the assumption that the cultic regulations of the Sinai code were final (e.g., 7:11). Christians converted from paganism and currently in danger of reverting to paganism would scarcely need that kind of argument; Christians in danger of reverting to Judaism certainly would.

Among those who believe the intended readers are Jewish Christians, many have attempted to identify a particular subset of Jews. Bornhäuser infers from 5:12 (the author's insistence that by this point his readers should be teachers) that they were not ordinary Jewish-Christians but some of the "large number of priests" who "became obedient to the faith" (Acts 6:7).[43] Spicq at first defended this theory[44] and then modified it by suggesting that they were "Esseno-Christians," including former members of the Qumran community.[45] Several scholars have urged variations on this theme.[46] But the most that can reasonably be said is that the Jewish background of the readers was probably not so much in the conservative rabbinic traditions of Palestine as in Hellenistic Judaism influenced by various nonconformist Jewish sects, of which the Essenes are but one example.[47]

Others think that the readers have been attracted, not to a form of Jewish faith and practice independent of Christianity, but to a form of Jewish Christianity more conservative than what the author himself approves.[48] There is a sense in which this appears to be correct, and another in which it seems quite false. It is probably correct in that there is no conclusive evidence that the readers thought of themselves as apostates. They probably did not set out to abandon the Christian gospel and return to Judaism. In that sense the readers are turning to a form of "Jewish Christianity" more conservative than what the

---

[43]Karl B. Bornhäuser, *Empfänger und Verfasser des Briefes an die Hebräer*, BFCT 35/3 (Gütersloh: Bertelsmann, 1932).

[44]Spicq, *Hébreux* 1.226ff.

[45]C. Spicq, "L'épître aux Hébreux: Apollos, Jean-Baptiste, les héllenistes, et Qumrân," *RevQ* 1 (1958–59): 365–90, esp. 390.

[46]E.g., Hans Kosmala, *Hebräer-Essener-Christen*, SPB 1 (Leiden: Brill, 1959); Hughes, *Commentary*, 10–15.

[47]See F. F. Bruce, "'To the Hebrews' or 'To the Essenes'?" *NTS* 9 (1962–63): 217–32. See the excellent discussion of conceptual backgrounds in R. M. Wilson, *Hebrews*, NCB (Grand Rapids: Eerdmans, 1987), 18–27.

[48]So J. V. Dahms, "The First Readers of Hebrews," *JETS* 20 (1977): 365–75; Brown and Meier, *Antioch and Rome*, 151–58.

author himself approves. But the author's point is that what the readers are in danger of adopting is *in fact* no Christianity at all. It is nothing less than apostasy; hence the strong parenetic passages. The lengthy expositions intertwined with the parenesis provide the grounds for this judgment. To return to reliance on the cultic structures of the old covenant is not only to fail to appreciate the way they pointed to Christ across the years of redemptive history, but it is implicitly to assign to them a redemptive effectiveness that they never possessed and simultaneously to depreciate the exclusive significance of Christ's sacrifice.

The reasons the readers have for reverting to some form of Judaism (overlaid, perhaps, with continuing protestations of faithfulness to Christianity) are not spelled out in detail; they are simply hinted at. For instance, it appears that they were tired of bearing the shame of living outside the mainstream of their cultural heritage (13:13). They were in danger of focusing on novel teachings (13:9) at the expense of the apostolic gospel (13:7–8). It is also possible that fear was a contributing motivation. The religion of the Jews was recognized by the Romans; Christianity was not. To return to the fold of Judaism might alleviate the threat of persecution by the state authorities. In any case, the discipline of the Christians was apparently fading as they withdrew from regular meetings (10:25; this *may* signal that the readers belonged to a house church that was no longer meeting with the rest of the church). But whatever their reasons, it is not so much the *reasons* that interest the author as the *outcome:* Christ, his sacrifice, and his priestly work are so relativized that they are effectively denied, and apostasy is only a whisker away. It is to prevent just such a calamity that the author writes this epistle.

TEXT

The major witnesses are nicely set out by Attridge[49] and Weiss.[50] The manuscript tradition is not unlike that of the Pauline corpus, though somewhat idiosyncratic by comparison. The most important witnesses are overwhelmingly Alexandrian.[51] The Byzantine tradition is represented by the uncials K and L (both ninth century) and many later minuscules; the Western text type is represented by D (Codex Claromontanus, sixth century) and the Old Latin. On the whole, the text of Hebrews is well preserved, though difficult decisions are called for in several passages (e.g., 1:8; 11:17, 37; 12:3, 7).

---

[49]Attridge, *Hebrews,* 31–32.

[50]Hans-Friedrich Weiss, *Der Brief an die Hebräer,* KEK (Göttingen: Vandenhoeck & Ruprecht, 1991), 127–32.

[51]See Frank W. Beare, "The Text of the Epistle to the Hebrews in P46," *JBL* 63 (1944): 379–96; and esp. Spicq, *Hébreux* 1.412–32.

ADOPTION INTO THE CANON

In the Western church, as we have seen above under "Author," although the epistle to the Hebrews was widely known and quoted, it was not at first received as canonical. In addition to the evidence from Clement of Rome, a number of other early Western fathers allude to it or cite it (e.g., Ignatius, *Phil.* 9:1; *Shepherd of Hermas* 2.3.2; Justin Martyr, *Dial.* 116.1), but none treats it as apostolic or canonical. The Muratorian Canon (c. A.D. 170–80) excludes Hebrews.

Doubtless when it was incorporated into the Pauline corpus—probably in Alexandria, in the second century—it was being acknowledged to have canonical status. Indeed, its canonicity was never (so far as we know) doubted in Alexandria or in the Eastern church, whatever doubts may have been entertained about its authorship (by Origen and others, as we have seen). Eusebius (*H.E.* 3.3.5) includes Hebrews among the "acknowledged" books, though he is aware of doubts in the West. The Syrian fathers never dispute its canonical status. And eventually, as we have seen, the convictions of the Eastern church won out in the West, owing to the influence of Jerome and Augustine.[52]

HEBREWS IN RECENT STUDY

In addition to studies that continue to probe the setting and circumstances that called forth this epistle, we may mention the considerable and ongoing interest in the following areas:

1. The peculiar christological emphases of Hebrews capture the attention of many scholars.[53] There are clear links with John and Paul (e.g., in the "Son" language and in the high Christology of Heb. 1:1–3), but the exposition of the priestly work of Christ, both on earth and in heaven, is much fuller here than anywhere else in the New Testament. Hebrews also displays firm interest in the historical Jesus.[54]

2. In particular, considerable attention has been devoted to what this epistle says about Melchizedek and to comparison of this treatment with other Jewish traditions about him, not least in the Dead Sea Scrolls.[55]

---

[52]For a brief overview of Reformation responses, see Hughes, *Commentary*, 23–24; Bruce, *Hebrews*, 24–25.

[53]See the bibliography in Attridge, *Hebrews*, 25 n. 197; and esp. William R. G. Loader, *Sohn und Hoherpriester: Eine traditionsgeschichtliche Untersuchung zur Christologie des Hebräerbriefes*, WMANT 53 (Neukirchen-Vluyn: Neukirchener, 1981).

[54]See Bertram L. Melbourne, "An Examination of the Historical-Jesus Motif in the Epistle to the Hebrews," *AUSS* 26 (1988): 281–97.

[55]E.g., Fred L. Horton, *The Melchizedek Tradition: A Critical Examination of the Sources to the Fifth Century A.D. and in the Epistle to the Hebrews*, SNTSMS 30 (Cambridge: Cambridge University Press, 1976); Paul J. Kobelski, *Melchizedek and*

3. The epistle's interest in Melchizedek is part and parcel of its detailed appeal to many Old Testament texts. Only Matthew in the New Testament rivals this book for the range and hermeneutical complexity of the Old Testament texts it cites. Inevitably, this phenomenon has drawn much scholarly attention.[56]

4. Käsemann introduced us to the pilgrim theme in Hebrews in *The Wandering People of God,* which in turn fed assessments of the readers. Ongoing attempts at delineating the profile of the readers are today sometimes tinged with the premises of sociological analysis.[57] The most comprehensive and nuanced treatment is still that of Hurst.[58]

5. Several themes in Hebrews attract continual attention, either because they are more prominent in Hebrews than elsewhere in the New Testament or because the treatment of them is distinctively nuanced. They include perfection,[59] (Sabbath-) rest (Heb. 4),[60] faith (Heb. 11),[61] and the theme of the new covenant.[62] On the latter, the ground-breaking work of John Hughes should be

> *The epistle greatly enriches New Testament Christology, especially with respect to Jesus' priestly work, the finality of his sacrifice, the nature of his sonship, the importance of the incarnation, and his role as "pioneer."*

Melchireša', CBQMS 10 (Washington, D.C.: Catholic Biblical Association, 1981); Marie E. Isaacs, *Sacred Space: An Approach to the Theology of the Epistle to the Hebrews,* JSNTSup 73 (Sheffield: JSOT Press, 1992).

[56]E.g., Simon J. Kistemaker, *The Psalm Citations in the Epistle to the Hebrews* (Amsterdam: Soest, 1961); Friedrich Schröger, *Der Verfasser des Hebräerbriefes als Schriftausleger,* BU 4 (Regensburg: Pustet, 1968); Dale F. Leschert, *Hermeneutical Foundations of Hebrews: A Study in the Validity of the Epistle's Interpretation of Some Core Citations from the Psalms,* NABPRDS 10 (Lewiston: Edwin Mellen Press, 1994). See the fine survey of George H. Guthrie, "Hebrews' Use of the Old Testament: Recent Trends in Research," *Currents in Biblical Research* 1 (2003): 271–94.

[57]E.g., Richard W. Johnson, *Going Outside the Camp: The Sociological Function of the Levitical Critique in the Epistle to the Hebrews,* JSNTSup 209 (Sheffield: Sheffield Academic Press, 2001).

[58]Lincoln D. Hurst, *The Epistle to the Hebrews: Its Background and Thought,* SNTSMS 65 (Cambridge: Cambridge University Press, 1990).

[59]E.g., Peterson, *Hebrews and Perfection.*

[60]E.g., Otfried Hofius, *Katapausis: Die Vorstellung vom endzeitlichen Ruheort im Hebräerbrief,* WUNT 11 (Tübingen: Mohr-Siebeck, 1970); A. T. Lincoln, "Sabbath, Rest, and Eschatology in the New Testament," in *From Sabbath to Lord's Day: A Biblical, Historical, and Theological Investigation,* ed. D. A. Carson (Grand Rapids: Zondervan, 1982), 197–220; Jon Laansma, *"I Will Give You Rest": The Rest Motif in the New Testament with Special Reference to Mt 11 and Heb 3–4,* WUNT 98 (Tübingen: Mohr-Siebeck, 1997).

[61]E.g., Erich Grässer, *Der Glaube im Hebräerbrief* (Marburg: Elwert, 1965).

[62]E.g., Susanne Lehne, *The New Covenant in Hebrews,* JSNTSup 44 (Sheffield: JSOT Press, 1990); John Dunnill, *Covenant and Sacrifice in the Letter to the Hebrews,* SNTSMS 75 (Cambridge: Cambridge University Press, 1992); Knut Backhaus, *Der Neue Bund und das Werden der Kirche: Die Diatheke-Deutung des Hebräerbriefs im Rahmen der frühchristlichen Theologiegeschichte,* NTAbh 29 (Münster: Aschendorff, 1996).

noted: he has convincingly demonstrated that, rightly understood, the term διαθήκη (*diathēkē*) should not be taken to mean "testament" but should be understood as "covenant" throughout Hebrews 9.[63]

THE CONTRIBUTION OF HEBREWS

Much of the canonical contribution peculiar to Hebrews lies in the distinctive emphases of the book that also draw scholarly attention as just outlined. The epistle to the Hebrews greatly enriches New Testament Christology, especially with respect to Jesus' priestly work, the finality of his sacrifice, the nature of his sonship, the importance of the incarnation (see esp. chap. 2), and his role as "pioneer" (ἀρχηγός [*archēgos*]).

Similarly, because of its extensive use of Old Testament texts, this epistle enables us to explore the hermeneutical assumptions of first-century Christians so as better to learn how to read the Old Testament. The nature of typology, the understanding of prophecy that goes far beyond merely verbal prediction, and the interplay between exegesis of specific texts and the constraints of redemptive history are all exemplified in Hebrews. It thus also provides many of the working elements for developing biblical theology.

The epistle joins other New Testament books (e.g., Acts and Galatians) in providing an independent slant on the difficult movement from an understanding of Israel as the locus of the people of God, constrained by the law-covenant of Sinai, to the church as the people of God, constrained by the covenant sealed by Jesus' death and resurrection. Finally, Hebrews links with some other New Testament books (e.g., 1 John) that are vitally interested in the problem of the perseverance of Christians and the nature and danger of apostasy. It continues to speak volumes to those whose hope pursues the comfort provided by religious externalism instead of pursuing "the city with foundations, whose architect and builder is God" (Heb. 11:10).

BIBLIOGRAPHY

Harold W. **Attridge**, *The Epistle to the Hebrews*, Hermeneia (Philadelphia: Fortress Press, 1989) ▮Knut **Backhaus**, *Der Neue Bund und das Werden der Kirche: Die Diatheke-Deutung des Hebräerbriefs im Rahmen der frühchristlichen Theologiegeschichte*, NTAbh 29 (Münster: Aschendorff, 1996) ▮Frank W. **Beare**, "The Text of the Epistle to the Hebrews in p[46]," *JBL* 63 (1944): 379–96 ▮Samuel **Bénétreau**, *L'Épître aux Hébreux*, CEB, 2 vols. (Vaux-sur-Seine: Édifac, 1989–

---

[63]John J. Hughes, "Hebrews ix 15ff. and Galatians iii 15ff.: A Study in Covenant Practice and Procedure," *NovT* 21 (1979): 27–96. He has been followed by, inter alios, Lane, *Hebrews*, 226–52.

90) ▥David Alan **Black**, "On the Pauline Authorship of Hebrews," *Faith & Mission* 16/2 (1999): 32–51; 16/3 (1999): 78–86 ▥Karl B. **Bornhäuser**, *Empfänger und Verfasser des Briefes an die Hebräer*, BFCT 35/3 (Gütersloh: Bertelsmann, 1932) ▥Herbert **Braun**, *An die Hebräer*, HNT 14 (Tübingen: Mohr-Siebeck, 1984) ▥Raymond E. **Brown** and John P. **Meier**, *Antioch and Rome* (New York: Paulist, 1983) ▥F. F. **Bruce**, *The Epistle to the Hebrews*, NICNT, rev. ed. (Grand Rapids: Eerdmans, 1990) ▥idem, "'To the Hebrews' or 'To the Essenes'?" *NTS* 9 (1962–63): 217–32 ▥George Wesley **Buchanan**, *To the Hebrews*, AB 36 (Garden City: Doubleday, 1972) ▥Kenneth W. **Clark**, "Worship in the Jerusalem Temple After A.D. 70," *NTS* 6 (1959–60): 269–80 ▥J. V. **Dahms**, "The First Readers of Hebrews," *JETS* 20 (1977): 365–75 ▥Franz **Delitzsch**, *Commentary on the Epistle to the Hebrews*, 2 vols. (Edinburgh: T. & T. Clark, 1871; reprint, Minneapolis: Klock & Klock, 1978) ▥David A. **deSilva**, *Perseverance in Gratitude: A Socio-Rhetorical Commentary on the Epistle "to the Hebrews"* (Grand Rapids: Eerdmans, 2000) ▥Marcus **Dods**, "The Epistle to the Hebrews," in *EGT* vol. 4 ▥John **Dunnill**, *Covenant and Sacrifice in the Letter to the Hebrews*, SNTSMS 75 (Cambridge: Cambridge University Press, 1992) ▥G. **Edmundson**, *The Church in Rome in the First Century*, BL (Oxford: Oxford University Press, 1913) ▥Paul **Ellingworth**, *The Epistle to the Hebrews: A Commentary on the Greek Text*, NIGTC (Grand Rapids: Eerdmans, 1993) ▥idem, "Hebrews and 1 Clement: Literary Dependence or Common Tradition," *BZ* 23 (1979): 437–40 ▥Charles **Forster**, *The Apostolical Authority of the Epistle to the Hebrews* (London: James Duncan, 1838) ▥David **Gooding**, *An Unshakeable Kingdom: The Letter to the Hebrews for Today* (Grand Rapids: Eerdmans, 1989) ▥Robert **Gordon**, *Hebrews, Readings* (Sheffield: Sheffield Academic Press, 2000) ▥Erich **Grässer**, *Der Glaube im Hebräerbrief* (Marburg: Elwert, 1965) ▥idem, "Der Hebräerbrief, 1938–1963," *ThR* 30 (1964): 138–226 ▥Rowan A. **Grier**, *The Captain of Our Salvation* (Tübingen: Mohr-Siebeck, 1973) ▥Donald **Guthrie**, *The Letter to the Hebrews*, TNTC (Grand Rapids: Eerdmans, 1983) ▥George H. **Guthrie**, *The Structure of Hebrews: A Text-Linguistic Analysis*, NovTSup 73 (Leiden: Brill, 1994) ▥idem, *Hebrews*, NIVAC (Grand Rapids: Zondervan, 1998) ▥idem, "Hebrews' Use of the Old Testament: Recent Trends in Research," *Currents in Biblical Research* 1 (2003): 271–94 ▥Donald A. **Hagner**, *Hebrews*, GNC (San Francisco: Harper, 1983) ▥idem, *The Use of the Old and New Testaments in Clement of Rome*, NovTSup 34 (Leiden: Brill, 1973) ▥idem, *Encountering the Book of Hebrews: An Exposition* (Grand Rapids: Baker, 2002) ▥Adolph von **Harnack**, "Probabilia über die Addresse und den Verfasser des Hebräerbriefes," *ZNW* 1 (1900): 16–41 ▥Jean **Héring**, *The Epistle to the Hebrews* (London: Epworth, 1970) ▥Otfried **Hofius**, *Katapausis: Die Vorstellung vom endzeitlichen Ruheort im Hebräerbrief*, WUNT 11 (Tübingen: Mohr, 1970) ▥Ruth **Hoppin**, *Priscilla: Author of the Epistle to the Hebrews* (New York: Exposition, 1969) ▥Fred L. **Horton**, *The Melchizedek Tradition: A Critical Examination of the Sources to the Fifth Century A.D. and in the Epistle to the Hebrews*, SNTSMS 30 (Cambridge:

Cambridge University Press, 1976) ▥ Graham **Hughes**, *Hebrews and Hermeneu-tics: The Epistle to the Hebrews as a New Testament Example of Biblical Interpreta-tion*, SNTSMS 36 (Cambridge: Cambridge University Press, 1979) ▥ John J. **Hughes**, "Hebrews ix 15ff. and Galatians iii 15ff.: A Study in Covenant Practice and Procedure," *NovT* 21 (1979): 27–96 ▥ Philip Edgcumbe **Hughes**, *A Commen-tary on the Epistle to the Hebrews* (Grand Rapids: Eerdmans, 1977) ▥ Lincoln D. **Hurst**, *The Epistle to the Hebrews: Its Background and Thought*, SNTSMS 65 (Cambridge: Cambridge University Press, 1990) ▥ Marie E. **Isaacs**, *Sacred Space: An Approach to the Theology of the Epistle to the Hebrews*, JSNTSup 73 (Sheffield: JSOT Press, 1992) ▥ Richard W. **Johnson**, *Going Outside the Camp: The Sociolog-ical Function of the Levitical Critique in the Epistle to the Hebrews*, JSNTSup 209 (Sheffield: Sheffield Academic Press, 2001) ▥ Ernst **Käsemann**, *The Wandering People of God: An Investigation of the Letter to the Hebrews* (ET Minneapolis: Augs-burg, 1984 [from 2nd ed., 1957]) ▥ Simon J. **Kistemaker**, *Exposition of the Epistle to the Hebrews*, NTC (Grand Rapids: Baker, 1984) ▥ idem, *The Psalm Citations in the Epistle to the Hebrews* (Amsterdam: Soest, 1961) ▥ Paul J. **Kobelski**, *Melchizedek and Melchireša'*, CBQMS 10 (Washington, D.C.: Catholic Biblical Association, 1981) ▥ Craig R. **Koester**, *Hebrews: A New Translation with Introduction and Com-mentary*, AB 36 (New York: Doubleday, 2001) ▥ Hans **Kosmala**, *Hebräer-Essener-Christen*, SPB 1 (Leiden: Brill, 1959) ▥ Jon **Laansma**, *"I Will Give You Rest": The Rest Motif in the New Testament with Special Reference to Mt 11 and Heb 3–4*, WUNT 98 (Tübingen: Mohr-Siebeck, 1997) ▥ William L. **Lane**, *Hebrews*, WBC 47A-B, 2 vols. (Dallas: Word Books, 1991) ▥ Susanne **Lehne**, *The New Covenant in Hebrews*, JSNTSup 44 (Sheffield: JSOT Press, 1990) ▥ William **Leonard**, *The Authorship of the Epistle to the Hebrews: Critical Problem and Use of the Old Testa-ment* (Rome: Vatican Polyglot Press, 1939) ▥ Dale F. **Leschert**, *Hermeneutical Foundations of Hebrews: A Study in the Validity of the Epistle's Interpretation of Some Core Citations from the Psalms*, NABPRDS 10 (Lewiston: Edwin Mellen Press, 1994) ▥ A. T. **Lincoln**, "Sabbath, Rest, and Eschatology in the New Testa-ment," in *From Sabbath to Lord's Day: A Biblical, Historical, and Theological Inves-tigation*, ed. D. A. Carson (Grand Rapids: Zondervan, 1982), 197–220 ▥ Barnabas **Lindars**, "The Rhetorical Structure of Hebrews," *NTS* 35 (1989): 382–406 ▥ Eta **Linnemann**, "Wiederaufnahme-Prozess in Sachen des Hebräerbriefes," *Funda-mentum* 21 (2000): 102–112; 22 (2001): 52–65, 88–110 ▥ William R. G. **Loader**, *Sohn und Hoherpriester: Eine traditionsgeschichtliche Untersuchung zur Christologie des Hebräerbriefes*, WMANT 53 (Neukirchen-Vluyn: Neukirchener, 1981) ▥ William **Manson**, *The Epistle to the Hebrews: An Historical and Theological Recon-sideration* (London: Hodder & Stoughton, 1951) ▥ Elmer T. **Merrill**, *Essays on Early Christian History* (London: Macmillan, 1924) ▥ Otto **Michel**, *Der Brief an die Hebräer*, KEK, 12th ed. (Göttingen: Vandenhoeck & Ruprecht, 1966) ▥ J. **Moffatt**, *A Critical and Exegetical Commentary on the Epistle to the Hebrews*, ICC (Edin-burgh: T. & T. Clark, 1924) ▥ Hugh **Montefiore**, *A Commentary on the Epistle to* *the Hebrews,* HNTC (San Francisco: Harper, 1964) ▥Alexander **Nairne**, *The Epistle of Priesthood* (Edinburgh: T. & T. Clark, 1913) ▥David **Peterson**, *Hebrews and Perfection: An Examination of the Concept of Perfection in the "Epistle to the Hebrews,"* SNTSMS 47 (Cambridge: Cambridge University Press, 1982) ▥Victor C. **Pfitzner**, *Hebrews,* ANTC (Nashville: Abingdon Press, 1997) ▥William **Ramsay**, *Luke the Physician* (London: Hodder & Stoughton: 1908) ▥Rainer **Riesner**, "Der Hebräer-Brief nach altkirchlichen Zeugnissen," *EuroJTh* 11/1 (2002): 15–29 ▥J. A. T. **Robinson**, *Redating the New Testament* (Philadelphia: Westminster, 1976) ▥Friedrich **Schröger**, *Der Verfasser des Hebräerbriefes als Schriftausleger,* BU 4 (Regensburg: Pustet, 1968) ▥E. F. **Scott**, *The Epistle to the Hebrews* (Edinburgh: T. & T. Clark, 1922) ▥C. **Spicq**, *L'épître aux Hébreux,* 2 vols., EBib (Paris: Gabalda, 1952–53) ▥idem, "L'épître aux Hébreux: Apollos, Jean-Baptiste, les héllenistes, et Qumrân," *RevQ* 1 (1958–59): 365–90 ▥Ray C. **Stedman**, *Hebrews,* IVPNTC (Downers Grove: IVP, 1992) ▥August **Strobel**, *Der Brief an die Hebräer,* NTD (Göttingen: Vandenhoeck & Ruprecht, 1975) ▥James **Swetnam**, *Jesus and Isaac: A Study of the Epistle to the Hebrews in the Light of the Aqedah,* AnBib 94 (Rome: Pontifical Biblical Institute, 1981) ▥R. V. G. **Tasker**, *The Gospel in the Epistle to the Hebrews* (London: Tyndale, 1950) ▥Gerd **Theissen**, *Untersuchungen zum Hebräerbrief,* SNT 2 (Gütersloh: Mohn, 1969) ▥Andrew H. **Trotter Jr.**, *Interpreting the Epistle to the Hebrews* (Grand Rapids: Baker, 1997) ▥A. **Vanhoye**, *La structure littéraire de l'épître aux Hébreux,* SN 1 (Paris: Desclée de Brouwer, 1963) ▥G. **Vos**, *The Teaching of the Epistle to the Hebrews* (Grand Rapids: Eerdmans, 1956) ▥Hans-Friedrich **Weiss**, *Der Brief an die Hebräer,* KEK (Göttingen: Vandenhoeck & Ruprecht, 1991) ▥Laurance L. **Welborn**, "On the Date of 1 Clement," *BR* 29 (1984): 35–54 ▥Brooke Foss **Westcott**, *The Epistle to the Hebrews,* 3rd ed. (London: Macmillan, 1909) ▥Ronald **Williamson**, *Philo and the Epistle to the Hebrews,* ALGHJ 4 (Leiden: Brill, 1970) ▥R. M. **Wilson**, *Hebrews,* NCB (Grand Rapids: Eerdmans, 1987) ▥Hans **Windisch**, *Der Hebräerbrief,* HNT 14, 2nd ed. (Tübingen: Mohr-Siebeck, 1931).

CHAPTER TWENTY

JAMES

CONTENTS

As early as the fourth century, the seven letters that follow Hebrews in the canon were known as the Catholic (i.e., "universal") Epistles (see Eusebius, *H.E.* 2.23.25). The name was given to these letters because, unlike the Pauline Epistles, they appeared to be addressed to the church in general rather than to a single congregation. Modern scholars generally question this assumption, arguing that each of these letters was written, if not to a single congregation, at least to a specific and delimited area.

The letter of James is no exception. While addressed generally to "the twelve tribes scattered among the nations" (1:1), it is probably intended for a limited number of Christian congregations to the north and east of Palestine (see below on addressees). But the category of "catholic" or "general" epistle still fits James in a certain sense. The letter lacks any reference to specific local issues or persons and is made up of a series of loosely related homilies. Partly for this reason, the letter resists clear structural demarcation. Indeed, Luther, not the kindest critic of James, accused the author of "throwing things together . . . chaotically."[1] This judgment was substantially endorsed by the form critics, who treated James as a collection of loosely strung together parenetic components.[2] However, several scholars have recently argued for a tighter structure for the letter. Adapting the epistolary structure identified by F. O. Francis,[3] Davids finds in James a careful literary structure: a "double opening statement" (1:2–27); a body (2:1–5:6); and a conclusion (5:7–20). He further argues that each section repeats the three basic

---

[1]Luther, "Preface to the New Testament" (1522), in *LW* 33.397.

[2]See esp. Martin Dibelius, *Commentary on the Epistle of James,* rev. by H. Greeven, Hermeneia (Philadelphia: Fortress Press, 1976), 1–7.

[3]"The Form and Function of the Opening and Closing Paragraphs of James and I John," *ZNW* 61 (1970): 110–26.

themes of the letter: testing, wisdom/pure speech, and poverty/wealth.[4] H. Frankemölle uses a rhetorical analysis, identifying 1:2–18 as the opening (the *exordium*) and 5:7–20 as the closing (the *peroratio*). These texts display similar wording and themes, acting as the frame around the body of the letter. The opening section announces the key themes of the letter; therefore, structurally, each of the topics that James takes up can be attached to one of the brief exhortations found in 1:2–18.[5]

If Luther and Dibelius are to be faulted for not finding enough structure in the letter, however, Davids and Frankemölle are probably to be criticized for finding more than is actually there.[6] It seems best to recognize several key motifs that are central to James' concern but to acknowledge that they are often mixed together with other themes in paragraphs that cannot be labeled as neatly as we might like. For instance, "testing" figures prominently in both the opening (1:2–4, 12) and closing (5:7–11) sections of the letter. While not the topic of the letter as a whole, the experience of testing, James suggests, is the context in which it must be read. This testing, though taking many forms (1:2) is particularly manifest in the poverty and oppression that so many of the readers of the letter are suffering (2:6–7; 5:4–6).

The letter exhibits the three parts typical of the Greek letter: opening (1:1), body (1:2–5:11), and closing (5:12–20). The body of the letter falls into four general sections.

Trials and Christian maturity (1:1–18). After the address and salutation (1:1), James opens with a section in which he attacks several issues, among which Christian suffering ("trials") is the most prominent (1:2–18). He encourages his readers to find meaning and purpose in their suffering (1:2–4), to pray in faith for wisdom (1:5–8), and to apply a Christian worldview to poverty and wealth (1:9–11). After coming back to the subject of trials (1:12), he moves into the issue of temptation (1:13–15), a transition eased by the fact that the words πειράζω (*peirazō*) and πειρασμός (*peirasmos*) can connote either "trials" or "temptations." The section concludes with a reminder of God's goodness in giving (1:16–18).

---

[4]Peter Davids, *The Epistle of James,* NIGTC (Grand Rapids: Eerdmans, 1982), 22–29.

[5]H. Frankemölle, "Das semantische Netz des Jakobusbriefes: Zur Einheit eines unstrittenen Briefes," *BZ* 34 (1990), esp. 190–93 (and cf. the chart on p. 193). See also W. H. Wuellner, "Der Jakobusbrief im Licht der Rhetorik und Textpragmatic," *Linguistica Biblica* 44 (1978–79): 5–66; J. H. Elliott, "The Epistle of James in Rhetorical and Social Scientific Perspective: Holiness-Wholeness and Patterns of Replication," *BTB* 23 (1993): 71–81.

[6]Lack of neat rhetorical organization is no drawback if such organization does not meet the needs of the situation (Richard Bauckham, *James: Wisdom of James, Disciple of Jesus the Sage* [London: Routledge, 1999], 62–63).

True Christianity seen in its works (1:19–2:26). The second section of the letter is marked out by a focus on three related words: "word [of God]" (esp. 1:19–27), "law" (esp. 2:1–13), and "works" (esp. 2:14–26). After a warning about loose speech and anger (1:19–20), James encourages his readers to "accept the word planted in you" (1:21) and then expands this exhortation by showing that true receiving of God's word involves *doing* it (1:22–27). As an important instance of "doing the word," James cites the need for Christians to be impartial in their treatment of others. Only so will they fulfill the "royal law" and escape judgment (2:1–13). The significance of Christians' actions in avoiding judgment sparks James's famous discussion of faith and works (2:14–26). James insists that true faith is always marked by obedience and that only such faith evidenced in works will bring salvation.

Dissensions within the community (3:1–4:12). No obvious breaks distinguish the third section of the letter. But we may view James's warnings about improper speech (3:1–12; 4:11–12) as indicative of an inclusio in which James focuses generally on the problem of dissensions among Christians and its roots in envy. Harking back to a topic touched on earlier (1:19–20, 26), James uses a series of vivid and memorable images to warn Christians about the power and danger of the tongue (3:1–12). He then tackles the problem of dissensions head on, tracing such external unrest to the wrong kind of wisdom (3:13–18) and to frustrated desires (4:1–3). The passage 4:4–10 issues a stern warning about a compromising kind of Christianity and summons the readers to repentance. The section ends with a final exhortation about speech (4:11–12).

Implications of a Christian worldview (4:13–5:11). This section is the least obvious, but we suggest that its major general theme has to do with a Christian worldview. One implication is the need to take God into account in all the plans we make (4:13–17). Another is the recognition that God will judge the wicked rich (5:1–6) and reward the righteous (5:7–11) at the time of the Lord's return.

Concluding exhortations (5:12–20). The letter's closing lacks many of the features often found in these sections (e.g., travel plans, greetings, personal prayer requests), suggesting that James is a more formal letter. James focuses rather on exhortation: prohibiting oaths (5:12), urging prayer, especially for physical healing (5:13–18), and calling all believers to look after one another's spiritual health (5:19–20).

AUTHOR

The letter claims to have been written by "James, a servant of God and of the Lord Jesus Christ" (1:1). The lack of elaboration points to a well-known James, and it is natural to think first of those men by this name who are mentioned in the New Testament. There are at least four: (1) James the son of Zebedee, brother of John, one of the Twelve (see, e.g., Mark 1:19; 5:37; 9:2; 10:35; 14:33);

(2) James the son of Alphaeus, also one of the Twelve (see Mark 3:18, perhaps the same as "James the younger" in Mark 15:40); (3) James the father of Judas (Luke 6:16; Acts 1:13);[7] (4) James, "the Lord's brother" (Gal. 1:19), who plays a leading role in the early Jerusalem church (see Acts 12:17; 15:13; 21:18).

Of these four, the last is by far the most obvious candidate for the authorship of this letter.[8] James the father of Judas is too obscure to be seriously considered; the same is true, to a lesser degree, of James the son of Alphaeus. James the son of Zebedee, on the other hand, is given a prominent role among the Twelve, but the date of his martyrdom—c. A.D. 44 (see Acts 12:2)—is probably too early to allow us to associate him with the letter. We are left, then, with James the brother of the Lord, who is certainly the most prominent James in the early church.

Corroborating this decision are the striking similarities between the Greek of the Epistle of James and that of the speech attributed to James in Acts 15:13–21.[9] Also in keeping with this identification are the frequent allusions to the teaching of Jesus within the letter, the Jewish atmosphere of the book, and the authority assumed by the author in addressing "the twelve tribes scattered among the nations." Early Christian testimony is not unanimous on the point but tends to favor the same identification. Origen identifies "James the apostle" as the author,[10] but only the sometimes unreliable Latin translation of Origen by Rufinus explicitly mentions the brother of the Lord. Eusebius claims that the letter was generally attributed to James the Lord's brother but that there were some dissenters (*H.E.* 3.25.3; 2.23.25).[11]

The case for identifying the letter with James the brother of the Lord is, then, quite strong. Despite this, alternative theories of authorship have been propounded, and these must now be considered.[12]

> *Of the four candidates for authorship of this letter—James the son of Zebedee, James the son of Alphaeus, James the father of Judas, and James "the Lord's brother"—the last is by far the most obvious.*

---

[7]In the expression Ἰούδαν Ἰακώβου (*Ioudan Iakōbou*, lit. "Judas of James," Luke 6:16), the genitive Ἰακώβου (*Iakōbou*) probably indicates "son of" ("Judas son of James") but could mean "brother of."

[8]However, some Spanish writers, from the seventh century on, claimed that their patron, James the son of Zebedee, was the author; and Calvin (p. 277) suggests that James the son of Alphaeus may have written the letter.

[9]For these parallels and discussion, see particularly J. B. Mayor, *The Epistle of St. James* (London: Macmillan, 1913), iii–iv. J. Painter (*Just James: The Brother of Jesus in History and Tradition* [Columbia: University of South Carolina Press, 1997], 234–48) uses these similarities and several other factors to argue that Luke was the editor of the letter that we now have in the New Testament.

[10]Origen, *Comm. on John,* frag. 126.

[11]Guthrie, 723–26.

[12]Two other theories may be mentioned. R. Eisenman identified the author with the Teacher of Righteousness known from the Qumran literature ("Eschatological 'Rain' Imagery in the War Scroll from Qumran and in the Letter of James," *JNES* 49

1. A few scholars have attributed the letter to an unknown James.[13] But while this is possible and would conflict with nothing in the letter itself, the simplicity of the author's identification points to a well-known individual—and such a person is likely mentioned in the New Testament.

2. The most important alternative is that the letter is pseudonymous—that it was written by an unknown early Christian in the name of James.[14] Advocates of this view agree that the "James" in the salutation points to James the brother of the Lord but are convinced that this James could not have written this letter. They base this conclusion on four main arguments:

First, it is thought to be inconceivable that a brother of the Lord would have written such a letter without alluding to his special relationship to Christ or to his confrontation with the resurrected Christ (cf. 1 Cor. 15:7). This objection presupposes that blood relationship to Christ was highly valued in the early church. But this is doubtful, particularly in the case of James, who derived no spiritual benefit from his earthly relationship to Christ (see John 7:1–5). It is noteworthy in this respect that the author of Acts never calls James "the brother of the Lord." In fact, the importance of physical ties to Christ emerged only later in the history of the church; the reticence of the letter in this respect favors an early date.[15]

A second reason for denying the letter to James the brother of the Lord is the language and cultural background of the letter. It is written in fairly good Hellenistic Greek and evidences certain literary touches in its choice of vocabulary and style (e.g., the incomplete hexameter in 1:17). Moreover, the author alludes

---

[1990]: 173–84); for a brief response, see Painter, *Just James*, 230–34, 277–88. And, in what now must be regarded as little more than a curiosity of scholarship, two nineteenth-century scholars suggested that an original Jewish document had been "Christianized" with a couple of superficial references to Jesus (1:1; 2:1) (L. Massebieau, "L'épître de Jacques—est-elle l'oeuvre d'un Chrétien?" *Revue de l'Histoire des Religions* 32 [1895]: 249–83; F. Spitta, "Der Brief des Jakobus," *Zur Geschichte und Literatur des Urchristentums* [Göttingen: Vandenhoeck & Ruprecht, 1896], 2:1–239). A. Meyer (*Der Rätsel des Jacobusbriefes* [Berlin: Töpelmann, 1930]) suggested that this original Jewish document was based on the "testament" of Jacob to his twelve sons (Genesis 49).

[13]E.g., Erasmus; Luther; Hunter, 168–69 (though cautiously); J. Moffatt, *The General Epistles: James, Peter, and Judas* (London: Hodder & Stoughton, 1928), 2.

[14]Some of the more important presentations of this view are Kümmel, 411–14; James Hardy Ropes, *A Critical and Exegetical Commentary on the Epistle of St. James*, ICC (Edinburgh: T. & T. Clark, 1916), 43–52; Dibelius, *Commentary on the Epistle of James*, 11–21; Sophie Laws, *A Commentary on the Epistle of James*, HNTC (San Francisco: Harper & Row, 1980), 38–42.

[15]See the important article of Gerhard Kittel, "Der geschichtliche Ort des Jakobusbriefes," *ZNW* 41 (1942): 73–75; and also R. Bauckham, *Jude and the Relatives of Jesus in the Early Church* (Edinburgh: T & T Clark, 1990), 125–30.

to concepts derived from Greek philosophy and religion (e.g., the phrase ὁ τροχὸς τῆς γενέσεως [ho trochos tēs geneseōs; "the whole course of one's life"] in 3:6). Could a Galilean Jew with the reputation of being a conservative Jewish Christian and who, as far as we know, never left Palestine, write such Greek with such sophisticated allusions? Many answer no.

But this answer is not so obviously the right one, for three reasons. First, while the Greek of the letter is undoubtedly well polished, its quality should not be exaggerated. Ropes concludes that "there is nothing to suggest acquaintance with the higher styles of Greek literature."[16] James's style is not that of a literary Atticist but that found in other Hellenistic-Jewish works of his day, such as *Testaments of the Twelve Patriarchs* and Sirach. Second, we must not underestimate the extent to which Palestinian Jews in the first century were conversant with Greek. Recent discoveries suggest that Greek was a language widely used in Palestine and that someone like James would have had ample opportunity to become fluent in the language.[17] Indeed, J. N. Sevenster used James as a test case for his investigation into Greek influence in Palestine and concluded that the brother of the Lord could very well have written the letter.[18] Third, the religious and philosophical concepts alluded to in James are of the sort that would have been fairly widespread among the general population.[19] We conclude, then, that the language of the letter is no obstacle to identifying the brother of the Lord as its author.

A third, more theological reason for thinking that James the brother of the Lord could not have written this epistle has to do with the way the Old Testament law and Judaism generally are treated.[20] In both Galatians (2:12) and Acts (21:17–25), it is argued, James appears to be a spokesman for a conservative Jewish-Christian position on these matters. Later legend magnifies this characteristic, seeing James as zealous for the law and respected by most of his Jewish contemporaries.[21] Yet the letter takes a somewhat liberal view of the law, ignoring its ritual demands and calling it "the perfect law that gives freedom" (1:25; 2:12).

---

[16]Ropes, *James*, 25. Zahn minimizes the quality of the Greek even more (1.112).

[17]See esp. J. N. Sevenster, *Do You Know Greek? How Much Greek Could the First Jewish Christians Have Known?* (Leiden: Brill, 1968).

[18]Ibid., 191; see also J. H. Moulton, W. F. Howard, and Nigel Turner, *A Grammar of New Testament Greek* (Edinburgh: T. & T. Clark, 1908–76), 4:114.

[19]Martin Hengel has demonstrated the degree to which first-century Palestine was permeated with Hellenistic concepts (*Judaism and Hellenism* [Philadelphia: Fortress Press, 1974]). With respect to James, see also Hengel's article, "Der Jakobusbrief als antipaulinische Polemik," in *Tradition and Interpretation in the New Testament*, Fs. E. Earle Ellis, ed. G. F. Hawthorne and Otto Betz (Grand Rapids: Eerdmans, 1987), 252.

[20]Dibelius labels this the decisive argument against the traditional position (*James*, 17–18).

[21]We are dependent on Hegesippus's account of James's death as recorded in Eusebius (*H.E.* 2.23) for much of this information.

A response to this argument would be to note that both sides of the polarity just sketched are exaggerated. On the one hand, the legends that picture James as a hidebound Jewish traditionalist are probably tendentious.[22] Nor is the New Testament evidence about James's theological position clear. Galatians 2:12 tells us only that the Judaizers in Antioch *claimed* to come from James, and Acts 21:17–25 betrays no extreme Jewish viewpoint. On the other hand, James's rather liberal pronouncement on the question of the law and circumcision in Acts 15 paints a very different picture. Moreover, the letter of James, while not encouraging obedience to the ritual law, does not prohibit it—and we can surmise that this may have been a non-issue for James and his readers. Nor does the view of the law in the letter conflict in any way with what we can assume to have been James's position.

The final reason for thinking that James must be pseudonymous turns on the relationship between Paul and the letter of James concerning the doctrine of justification. As is well known, James (esp. 2:20–26) takes an approach to this issue that many find to be at variance with Paul's view. Yet it is also generally thought that what James says fails to meet Paul's position directly—that he is arguing with a garbled or misunderstood form of Paul's teaching on this matter. These circumstances, it is argued, can be accounted for only by presuming that the letter of James was written considerably later than Paul. Kümmel succinctly summarizes the point: "The debate in 2:14ff. with a misunderstood secondary stage of Pauline theology not only presupposes a considerable chronological distance from Paul—whereas James died in the year 62—but also betrays a complete ignorance of the polemical intent of Pauline theology, which lapse can scarcely be attributed to James, who as late as 55/56 met with Paul in Jerusalem (Acts 21:18ff.)."[23]

The relationship between James 2:14–26 and Paul's teaching is the most vexing theological issue in the letter, and we consider this later (see "The Contribution of James"). But assuming that the relationship between James 2 and Paul is as described above (that it responds to a misunderstood form of Paul's teaching), there is an alternative explanation for the situation. Could not the letter of James have been written at a time during which Paul's teaching was beginning to have an impact on the church, yet *before* Paul had had the chance to discuss with James just what his teaching on justification truly meant?[24] Such a circumstance would explain the fact that James seems to have Paul's distinctive emphasis on justification by faith in mind, yet does not fairly grapple with Paul's

---

[22]See J. B. Lightfoot, *The Epistle of St. Paul to the Galatians* (London: Macmillan, 1890), 366; R. B. Ward, "James of Jerusalem in the First Two Centuries," *ANRW* 2.26.1 (1992), 799–810.

[23]Kümmel, 413.

[24]For this argument, see particularly Kittel, "Der geschichtliche Ort," 96–97; see also Walter Wessel, "Letter of James," in *ISBE* 2.965.

real point with the doctrine. In other words, James's contact with Paul's doctrine would be only indirect, coming from those who have misunderstood Paul's teaching and taken the idea of justification by faith alone as an excuse for moral laxity. It is to this garbled form of Paul's teaching that James responds because he is writing before he had the opportunity to learn from Paul himself just what Paul means by the doctrine. If this situation is possible (and it makes more sense of James 2 than to suppose that someone with Paul's letters in hand would so seriously misunderstand him), then the teaching of James 2 offers no difficulty to thinking that the Lord's brother could have written it.

3. A third general position on the authorship of James admits the force of both the evidence for identifying the writer of the letter with the brother of the Lord *and* of the objections brought against that identification. A mediating position is therefore adopted, according to which James's teaching lies at the base of the letter but has undergone a later editing that has put it in the form we now have it.[25] The main objection to this view is that it is unnecessary. We have seen that the arguments against the ascription of the letter to James the brother of the Lord do not hold water. It is far simpler, then, to view James as the author of the letter in the form that we now have it than to hypothesize levels of redaction for which there is no textual or solid historical evidence.

We conclude, then, that James the brother of the Lord is the author of the letter. This is the natural implication of the letter's own claims, it is corroborated by New Testament and early Christian evidence, and it has no decisive argument against it.[26] Moreover, the chief alternative theory—that the letter is pseudonymous—faces quite serious general objections having to do with the acceptability of pseudonymous letters in the ancient world.[27]

PROVENANCE

If the author of the letter is unknown, then almost any provenance is possible for it. For instance, Laws, noting resemblances between James and several works

---

[25]See esp. Davids, *The Epistle of James,* 12–13; Ralph P. Martin, *James,* WBC (Waco: Word, 1988), lxix–lxxviii; Wiard Popkes, *Adressaten, Situation, und Form des Jakobusbriefe,* SBS 125/126 (Stuttgart: Katholisches Bibelwerk, 1986), 184–88.

[26]Among recent scholars, Luke T. Johnson, *The Letter of James,* AB37A (Garden City: Doubleday, 1995) concludes that the letter could well have been written by James of Jerusalem (see 121). See also T. C. Penner, *The Epistle of James and Eschatology: Re-Reading an Ancient Christian Letter* (Sheffield: Sheffield Academic Press, 1996), 35–103; Hengel, "Der Jakobusbrief als antipaulinische Polemik," 252; Bauckham, *James,* 11–25.

[27]See esp. L. R. Donelson, *Pseudepigraphy and Ethical Argument in the Pastoral Epistles,* HUT 22 (Tübingen: Mohr-Siebeck, 1986); S. E. Porter, "Pauline Authorship and the Pastoral Epistles: Implications for Canon," *BBR* 5 (1995): 105–23; and the treatment of pseudonymity and pseudepigraphy in chap. 8 of this book.

of Roman origin—1 Peter, *1 Clement*, Hermas—thinks the letter may have been written in Rome.[28] If, as we think, James the brother of the Lord is the author of this letter, then it was probably written from Jerusalem during his tenure as leader of the Christian church in Jerusalem (tradition makes James the first bishop of Jerusalem). While it may say as much about the readers as the author, the social and economic backdrop assumed in the letter also fits a Palestinian provenance: merchants ranging far and wide in search of profits (4:13–17), absentee landlords taking advantage of an increasingly poor and landless labor force (2:5–7; 5:1–6), and heated religious controversy (4:1–3).

DATE

The explanation offered above for the relationship between the teaching of James 2:14–26 and Paul requires that James be dated sometime after Paul's teaching had begun to have an influence and before James and Paul met at the Jerusalem Council (Acts 15). Paul was engaged in a ministry of teaching and preaching from the time of his conversion (c. A.D. 33), and the Jerusalem Council is probably to be dated in 48 or 49. If, then, we allow some time for Paul's teaching of justification by faith to develop and become known, the most likely date for the letter of James is sometime in the early or middle 40s.[29] Such a date fits the circumstances and emphases of the letter very well. There is no hint of conflict between Jewish and Gentile Christians (such as we would have expected if the letter was written after the Jerusalem Council), the theology of the letter is relatively undeveloped,[30] and such a date fits well with the way James uses Jesus traditions.[31]

There are two main alternatives to this dating. Some scholars who identify James the brother of the Lord as the author date the letter toward the close of his life (he was martyred in A.D. 62). Alleged in favor of this date are (1) the need to have Paul's letters sufficiently well known that James could be responding to Paul's teaching, and (2) the typical second-generation problem of worldliness that James confronts in the letter.[32] Yet worldliness hardly needs a period of time to develop, and, as we have argued, James 2:14–26 makes better sense if James

---

[28]Laws, *James*, 25–26.

[29]For this dating, see, inter alia, Zahn 1.125–28; Guthrie, 749–53; Mayor, *James*, cxliv–clxxvi; Wessel, "James," 965; and esp. Kittel, "Der geschichtliche Ort," 71–102.

[30]Although James is far from being "untheological"; see, e.g., Luke Timothy Johnson, *Brother of Jesus, Friend of God: Studies in the Letter of James* (Grand Rapids: Eerdmans, 2004), 245–48.

[31]Penner, *The Epistle of James and Eschatology*, 264–77; P. J. Hartin, *James and the Q Sayings of Jesus*, JSNTSup 47 (Sheffield: JSOT Press, 1991), 148–64.

[32]F. J. A. Hort, *The Epistle of St. James* (London: Macmillan, 1909), xxv; R. V. G. Tasker, *The General Epistle of James*, TNTC (Grand Rapids: Eerdmans, 1956), 31–33; Hengel, "Jakobusbrief," 252.

has never heard Paul or read any of his letters. The second alternative, a date sometime toward the end of the first century, is generally adopted by those who think the letter is pseudonymous.[33]

DESTINATION/ADDRESSEES

James has been included among the so-called General Epistles because it does not address a specific church. Yet the letter was almost certainly intended for a specific audience. Several features of the letter make it clear that the addressees were Jewish Christians:[34] the unself-conscious way in which the Old Testament law is mentioned (1:25; 2:8–13), the reference to their meeting place as a synagogue (2:2), and the widespread use of Old Testament and Jewish metaphors. Furthermore, passages such as 5:1–6 suggest that most of the readers were poor—although a good case can be made that 1:9–11; 2:1–4; and 4:13–17 presume the presence of some wealthier Christians among the readers.

The letter's address gives more detailed information: "To the twelve tribes scattered among the nations" (1:1). But this designation is so general as to be of little help in identifying the addressees. "Twelve tribes" need not even indicate a Jewish-Christian audience, since the phrase may have been one of many drawn from the Old Testament to designate the church as the new covenant people of God.[35] The word translated "scattered among the nations"—διασπορά (*diaspora,* "Diaspora")—was used to denote Jews living outside of Palestine (see John 7:35) and, by extension, the place in which they lived. But the word also had a metaphorical sense, characterizing Christians generally as those who live away from their true heavenly home (1 Peter 1:1). The early date and Jewishness of James favors the more literal meaning.[36] Like other Jewish authors before him, James sends consolation and exhortation to the dispersed covenant people of God.[37]

---

[33]E.g., Kümmel, 414.

[34]To be sure, a few scholars think that the address of the letter must include all Christians (e.g., M. Klein, *"Ein vollkommens Werk": Vollkommenheit, Gesetz und Gericht als theologische Themen des Jakobusbriefes* [Stuttgart: Kohlhammer, 1995], 185–90; F. Vouga, *L'épître de S. Jacques* [Geneva: Labor et Fides, 1984], 24–26; E. Baasland, "Literarische Form, Thematik und geschichtliche Einordnung des Jakobusbriefes," *ANRW* 2.25.5 [1988], 3676–77).

[35]After the exile, the twelve tribes no longer existed physically, but the phrase became a way of denoting the regathered people of God of the last days (see Ezek. 47:13; Matt. 19:28; Rev. 7:4–8; 21:12).

[36]See, e.g., Achtemeier/Green/Thompson, 497–98; Mayor, *The Epistle of St. James,* 30–31; F. J. A. Hort, *The Epistle of St. James* (London: Macmillan, 1909), xxiii–xxiv; J. B. Adamson, *The Epistle of James,* NICNT (Grand Rapids: Eerdmans, 1976), 49–50.

[37]D. J. Verseput, "Wisdom, 4Q185, and the Epistle of James," *JBL* 117 (1998): 700–3; Bauckham, *James,* 14–16.

The word *diaspora* might have an even more specific force. Acts tells us of Christians from Jerusalem who were "scattered" (from the verb διασπείρω [*diaspeirō*], a word cognate to "Diaspora" in James 1:1) because of persecution and "traveled as far as Phoenicia, Cyprus and Antioch, spreading the word only among Jews" (Acts 11:19).[38] Identifying James's readers with these early Jewish Christians would fit the date of the letter and would furnish an explanation of the circumstances that called it forth: James, the leader of the Jerusalem church, must minister to his scattered flock by mail. While tentative, this suggestion is better than most in explaining the circumstances of the letter.

NATURE/GENRE

While the letter of James has a typical epistolary introduction, it lacks the usual epistolary postscript. Moreover, it does not contain any personal touches such as greetings, travel plans, or prayer requests. All this suggests that James is best viewed as what we might call a literary letter.[39] Probably it was intended for those several communities in which James's scattered parishioners had settled. More precise identification of the genre of James demands that we give attention to four further features of the letter.

The first is the flavor of pastoral admonition that pervades the letter. Imperative verbs occur with greater frequency in James than in any other New Testament book. James rebukes and exhorts his readers, and any theology that is taught comes only in conjunction with this overriding purpose.

A second feature that must be considered is its looseness of structure. We have suggested a division of the letter into four main parts. Yet these divisions are by no means well defined, as is clear from the diversity of suggested outlines for the letter. The difficulty arises from the fact that James moves rapidly from topic to topic, sometimes spending a paragraph or so on a given topic (e.g., 2:1–13, 14–26; 3:1–12), but more often changing subjects after only a few verses.

James's extensive and very effective use of metaphors and figures of speech is a third noteworthy feature of his letter. The images James uses to make his points—the billowing sea, the withered flower, the brushfire—are universal in their appeal and go a long way toward accounting for the popularity of the letter.

A fourth feature of the letter is the degree to which James shares words and ideas with other teachings and works of literature of his day. The most important of these sources is the teaching of Jesus. The degree to which James is permeated by parallels to Jesus' teaching can only be accounted for if James so

---

[38]Tasker draws attention to this parallel (*James*, 39).

[39]Peter H. Davids, "The Epistle of James in Modern Discussion," *ANRW* 2.25.5 (1988), 3628–29.

thoroughly knew that teaching—probably in oral form—that it had molded his own views and attitudes.[40] But James also shares vocabulary and concepts with early Jewish works, especially the *Testaments of the Twelve Patriarchs*, Sirach, and, to a lesser extent, Philo and Wisdom of Solomon. The nature of these parallels does not suggest direct borrowing; rather, they appear to result from James's sharing of a similar background with the authors of these works.

Do these features enable us to define the genre of James more definitely? Ropes suggests *diatribe*, a popular format used for instruction and debate among some Greek authors.[41] More popular is the identification of James as *parenesis*. Dibelius, who is the best-known advocate of this identification, notes four features of this genre, all of which he finds in James: eclecticism (borrowing from traditional material), the unstructured stringing together of moral admonitions, repetition, and general applicability.[42] That these features are evident in James is clear, but it must be questioned whether they need be confined to a specific genre or style. Taking the place of parenesis is *wisdom* as probably the most popular genre identification for James.[43] Indeed, many contemporary scholars insist that parenesis should be seen as one component of wisdom literature.[44] But the issue of wisdom is not at all central to the book as a whole; most of the letter, in fact, does not consist of the brief "proverbs" familiar from wisdom books. Much depends on how broadly we understand wisdom. Contemporary scholarship has a tendency to subsume a great deal under that rubric. Suffice it to say here that only a very broad definition of wisdom would enable us to categorize James as a whole as wisdom, and we are not convinced that so broad a definition is justified. Perhaps a better way of viewing James is to see it as a *homily,* or series of homilies, put into a letter in order to address Christians at a distance from their "pastor."[45]

---

[40]A list of the parallels between James and the teaching of Jesus can be found in Davids, *James,* 47–48.

[41]Ropes, *James,* 10–16.

[42]Dibelius, *James,* 5–11. See also L. G. Perdue, "Paraenesis and the Epistle of James," *ZNW* 72 (1981): 241–56.

[43]With varying emphases and in different degrees, see, e.g., Brown, 740; H. Frankemölle, *Der Brief des Jakobus* (Gütersloh: Gütersloher, 1994), 80–88; W. R. Baker, *Personal Speech-Ethics in the Epistle of James,* WUNT 68 (Tübingen: Mohr-Siebeck, 1995), 7–12; Ben Witherington III, *Jesus the Sage: The Pilgrimage of Wisdom* (Minneapolis: Fortress, 1994), 238–47.

[44]J. G. Gammie, "Paraenetic Literature: Toward the Morphology of a Secondary Genre," *Semeia* 50 (1990): 43–51; Hartin, *James and the Q Sayings of Jesus,* 21–80.

[45]See G. H. Rendall, *The Epistle of St. James and Judaistic Christianity* (Cambridge: Cambridge University Press, 1927), 33; Davids, *James,* 23; and esp. Wessel, "James," 962 (who is summarizing the results of his doctoral dissertation).

ADOPTION INTO THE CANON

The letter of James appears to have influenced several late-first-century works, among them the *Shepherd of Hermas* and *1 Clement*.[46] Clement of Alexandria is said to have written a commentary on James, but no such work has survived.[47] Origen is the first to cite James as Scripture, and other third-century works show acquaintance with the letter. Eusebius cites James frequently and accords it canonical status. But by classifying it among the "disputed books" (see *H.E.* 3.25.3), he also serves notice that some in his day questioned its status. He may be referring to some in the Syrian church who were slow to accept as canonical all the General Epistles. But James is included in the Syriac translation, the Peshitta, and is quoted approvingly by Chrysostom (d. 407) and Theodoret (d. 458). The Western part of the early church witnesses to a similar situation, although acceptance of James came a bit later. James is not found in either the Muratorian Canon or the Mommsen catalogue (reflecting the African canon c. 360).[48] The earliest clear references to James date from the fourth century (Hilary of Poitiers and Ambrosiaster). Decisive for the acceptance of James in the Western church was Jerome's full acceptance of the book.

James thus came to be recognized as canonical in all parts of the ancient church, and while there were hesitations on the part of some, no one rejected the book outright. Should these hesitations give us pause about the status of James? No. They were probably the product of a combination of uncertainty about the identity of the author (which James?) and the relative neglect of the book. Being practical and Jewish in its flavor, James was not the sort of book that would have been widely used in the doctrinal controversies of the early church.

James came in for its most severe criticism at the hands of Luther. His passionate embracing of Paul's teaching on justification by faith alone as the heart of Scripture made it difficult for him to accept James. He therefore relegated it to a secondary status in the New Testament, along with Jude, Hebrews, and Revelation. Nevertheless, Luther did not exclude James from the canon, and despite his criticisms, he quoted James approvingly many times.[49] Compared with those

---

[46]See the discussion in Mayor, *James*, lxix–lxxi, lxxxviii–cix. He discerns allusions to James in many more New Testament and early Christian writings, but most of these are probably indirect.

[47]See B. F. Westcott, *A General Survey of the History of the Canon of the New Testament* (London: Macmillan, 1889), 357–58.

[48]Some think, however, that the omission of James from the Muratorian Canon is accidental, since the text of the canon is damaged (Westcott, *History of the Canon*, 219–20). See, for the contrary opinion, Franz Mussner, *Der Jakobusbrief*, HTKNT (Freiburg: Herder, 1981), 41.

[49]D. Stoutenberg, "Martin Luther's Exegetical Use of the Epistle of St. James" (M.A. thesis, Trinity Evangelical Divinity School, 1982), 51.

"chief books" that clearly taught justification by faith, James appeared to Luther to be an "epistle of straw" (i.e., one made of straw; his allusion is to 1 Cor. 3:12). But he can also say, "I would not prevent anyone from including or extolling him as he pleases, for there are otherwise many good sayings in him."[50] We do not wish to minimize Luther's criticism of James: he clearly had difficulties with it. But his difficulties arose from a somewhat imbalanced perspective induced by his polemical context. Considered in a more balanced way, James can be seen to be making an important contribution to our understanding of Christian theology and practice, one that in no way conflicts with Paul or any other biblical author (see "Contribution" below). On both historical and theological grounds, James fully deserves the canonical status that the church has accorded it.

JAMES IN RECENT STUDY

The general turn to literary approaches in contemporary New Testament scholarship is manifested in the attempts to classify and analyze James in accordance with ancient rhetorical categories.[51] James's very strong condemnation of the rich (esp. 5:1–6) has naturally made his letter a favorite of those who are propounding various forms of liberation theology.[52] Perhaps the most interesting development, however, has been the attention given to the social setting of the letter. In keeping with a renewed interest in this matter in New Testament studies generally, scholars have sought to identify the historical and social setting of the letter and then to use this reconstruction as a hermeneutical key in their interpretation. One such reconstruction views James as directed to oppressed and impoverished Jewish Christians who are attracted by the revolutionary philosophy that eventually led to the Zealot movement. James champions their cause (e.g., 5:1–6) and the rights of oppressed poor people at the same time that he cautions them about using violent means to ease their situation (4:1–3).[53] Such reconstructions can be illuminating, but we must be careful not to be more definite than the text allows us to be, lest we force the letter into a single mold that it was not meant to fill.[54]

---

[50]*LW* 35:397.

[51]See above and see also Wesley Hiram Wachob, *The Voice of Jesus in the Social Rhetoric of James,* SNTSMS 106 (Cambridge: Cambridge University Press, 2000).

[52]E.g., P. V. Maynard-Reid, *Poverty and Wealth in James* (Maryknoll: Orbis, 1987); E. Tamez, *The Scandalous Message of James: Faith without Works Is Dead* (New York: Crossroad, 1990).

[53]Martin, *James,* lxii–lxix.

[54]The subjectivity involved in such reconstructions is evident from the fact that another recent attempt to identify James's setting comes to very different conclusions: James's readers were members of a Hellenistic, Pauline-influenced missions church (Popkes, *Adressaten, Situation, und Form des Jakobusbriefes,* 71).

THE CONTRIBUTION OF JAMES

Chief among James's contributions is his insistence that genuine Christian faith must become evident in works. He resolutely opposes the tendency all too common among Christians to rest content with a halfhearted, compromising faith that seeks to have the best of both this world and the next. Double-mindedness is the basic sin for James (see 1:8; 4:8), and he insists that Christians repent of it and get back on the road to the whole and perfect character that God desires.

The very strength of James's assertions on this point raises questions about the theological standpoint of the letter, particularly when James pursues his point to the extent that he ties justification to works (2:14–26). For at this point, he appears to contradict Paul's insistence that justification comes by faith alone (see Rom. 3:28). Many are content to find here an indication of the deep diversity within the New Testament, thinking that Paul and James say different *and conflicting* things about how a person is justified before God.[55] But so damaging an admission in unnecessary. Prior to chapter 2, James has already made clear that salvation is a matter of God's initiative.[56] And James's teaching in chapter 2 may be harmonized with Paul in at least two different ways. The first, and more popular of the two, argues that James is using the verb "justify" (δικαιόω [*dikaioō*]) in the sense of "vindicate before people" (the verb is used this way in, e.g., Luke 7:29). Paul and James, then, are talking about different things: Paul of the declaration of our righteousness, and James of the demonstration of our righteousness. Another possibility is to take "justify" in James to mean "vindicate at the last judgment," a force the word often has in Judaism (see Matt. 12:37). On this view, both Paul and James are referring to the sinner's righteousness before God, but Paul is focusing on the initial reception of that status and James on the way that status is vindicated before God in the judgment.[57]

Such theological harmonization is, we think, absolutely necessary, but it should not lead us to ignore the important contribution made either by Paul or by James. When faced with legalism, with the attempt to base salvation on human works, Paul needs to be heard—as he was so powerfully at the time of the Reformation. But when faced with quietism, with the attitude that dismisses works as unnecessary for Christians, James needs to be heard—as he was equally powerfully in the time of the Wesleys.

---

[55]E.g., James G. D. Dunn, *Unity and Diversity in the New Testament* (Philadelphia: Westminster, 1977), 251–52.

[56]See Douglas J. Moo, *The Letter of James,* PNTC (Grand Rapids: Eerdmans, 2000), 44–48, 108–16; Timo Laato, "Justification according to James: A Comparison with Paul," *TrinJ* 18 (1997): 47–61.

[57]For elaboration, see esp. Moo, *James*, 37–43.

BIBLIOGRAPHY

J. B. **Adamson**, *The Epistle of James*, NICNT (Grand Rapids: Eerdmans, 1976) ∎E. **Baasland**, "Literarische Form, Thematik und geschichtliche Einordnung des Jakobusbriefes," *ANRW* 2.25.5 (1988), 3676–77 ∎W. R. **Baker**, *Personal Speech-Ethics in the Epistle of James*, WUNT 68 (Tübingen: Mohr-Siebeck, 1995) ∎Richard **Bauckham**, *James: Wisdom of James, Disciple of Jesus the Sage* (London: Routledge, 1999) ∎idem, *Jude and the Relatives of Jesus in the Early Church* (Edinburgh: T. & T. Clark, 1990) ∎Christoph **Burchard**, *Der Jakobusbrief*, HNT 15/1 (Tübingen: Mohr-Siebeck, 2000) ∎John **Calvin**, *Commentaries on the Catholic Epistles*, reprint ed. (Grand Rapids: Eerdmans, 1948) ∎J. **Cantinat**, *Les épîtres de Saint Jacques et de Saint Jude* (Paris: Gabalda, 1973) ∎Bruce **Chilton** and Jacob **Neusner**, eds., *the Brother of Jesus: James the Just and His Mission* (Louisville: Westminster John Knox, 2001) ∎Peter **Davids**, *The Epistle of James*, NIGTC (Grand Rapids: Eerdmans, 1982) ∎idem, "The Epistle of James in Modern Discussion," *ANRW* 2.25.5 (1988) 3628–29 ∎Martin **Dibelius**, *Commentary on the Epistle of James*, rev. by H. Greeven, Hermeneia (Philadelphia: Fortress Press, 1976) ∎L. R. **Donelson**, *Pseudepigraphy and Ethical Argument in the Pastoral Epistles*, HUT 22 (Tübingen: Mohr-Siebeck, 1986) ∎James G. D. **Dunn**, *Unity and Diversity in the New Testament* (Philadelphia: Westminster, 1977) ∎David Hutchinson **Edgar**, *Has God Not Chosen the Poor? The Social Setting of the Epistle of James*, JSNTSup 206 (Sheffield: Sheffield Academic Press, 2001) ∎R. **Eisenman**, "Eschatological 'Rain' Imagery in the War Scroll from Qumran and in the Letter of James," *JNES* 49 (1990): 173–84 ∎J. H. **Elliott**, "The Epistle of James in Rhetorical and Social Scientific Perspective: Holiness-Wholeness and Patterns of Replication," *BTB* 23 (1993): 71–81 ∎F. O. **Francis**, "The Form and Function of the Opening and Closing Paragraphs of James and 1 John," *ZNW* 61 (1970): 110–26 ∎H. **Frankemölle**, *Der Brief des Jakobus* (Gütersloh: Gütersloher, 1994) ∎idem, "Das semantische Netz des Jakobusbriefes: Zur Einheit eines unstrittenen Briefes," *BZ* 34 (1990): 161–97 ∎J. G. **Gammie**, "Paraenetic Literature: Toward the Morphology of a Secondary Genre," *Semeia* 50 (1990): 43–51 ∎P. J. **Hartin**, *James and the Q Sayings of Jesus*, JSNTSup 47 (Sheffield: JSOT Press, 1991) ∎Martin **Hengel**, "Der Jakobusbrief als antipaulinische Polemik," in *Tradition and Interpretation in the New Testament*, Fs. E. Earle Ellis, ed. G. F. Hawthorne and Otto Betz (Grand Rapids: Eerdmans, 1987), 248–78 ∎idem, *Judaism and Hellenism*, 2 vols. (Philadelphia: Fortress Press, 1974) ∎F. J. A. **Hort**, *The Epistle of St. James* (London: Macmillan, 1909) ∎Luke Timothy **Johnson**, *The Letter of James*, AB 37A (Garden City: Doubleday, 1995) ∎idem, *Brother of Jesus, Friend of God: Studies in the Letter of James* (Grand Rapids: Eerdmans, 2004) ∎Gerhard **Kittel**, "Der geschichtliche Ort des Jakobusbriefes," *ZNW* 41 (1942): 71–105 ∎M. **Klein**, *"Ein vollkommens Werk": Vollkommenheit, Gesetz und Gericht als theologische Themen des Jakobusbriefes* (Stuttgart: Kohlhammer, 1995) ∎R. J. **Knowling**, *The Epistle of*

St. James, 2nd ed. (London: Methuen, 1910) ▮Timo **Laato,** "Justification according to James: A Comparison with Paul," *TrinJ* 18 (1997): 47–61 ▮idem, *Rechtfertigung bei Jakobus: Ein Vergleich mit Paulus* (Saarijärvi: Gummerus Kirjapaino Oy, 2003) ▮Sophie **Laws,** *A Commentary on the Epistle of James,* HNTC (San Francisco: Harper & Row, 1980) ▮Ralph P. **Martin,** *James,* WBC (Waco: Word, 1988) ▮L. **Massebieau,** "L'épître de Jacques—est-elle l'oeuvre d'un Chrétien?" *Revue de l'Histoire des Religions* 32 (1895): 249–83 ▮P. V. **Maynard-Reid,** *Poverty and Wealth in James* (Maryknoll: Orbis, 1987) ▮J. B. **Mayor,** *The Epistle of St. James* (London: Macmillan, 1913) ▮A. **Meyer,** *Der Rätsel des Jakobusbriefes* (Berlin: Töpelmann, 1930) ▮C. L. **Mitton,** *The Epistle of St. James* (Grand Rapids: Eerdmans, 1966) ▮J. **Moffatt,** *The General Epistles: James, Peter, and Judas* (London: Hodder & Stoughton, 1928) ▮Douglas J. **Moo,** *The Letter of James,* TNTC (Grand Rapids: Eerdmans, 1985) ▮idem, *The Letter of James,* PNTC (Grand Rapids: Eerdmans, 2000) ▮J. H. **Moulton,** W. F. **Howard,** and Nigel **Turner,** *A Grammar of New Testament Greek,* 4 vols. (Edinburgh: T. & T. Clark, 1908–76) ▮Franz **Mussner,** *Der Jakobusbrief,* HTKNT (Freiburg: Herder, 1981) ▮J. **Painter,** *Just James: The Brother of Jesus in History and Tradition* (Columbia: University of South Carolina Press, 1997) ▮T. C. **Penner,** *The Epistle of James and Eschatology: Re-Reading an Ancient Christian Letter* (Sheffield: Sheffield Academic Press, 1996) ▮L. G. **Perdue,** "Paraenesis and the Epistle of James," *ZNW* 72 (1981): 241–56 ▮Wiard **Popkes,** *Adressaten, Situation, und Form des Jakobusbriefe,* SBS 125/126 (Stuttgart: Katholisches, 1986) ▮idem, *Der Brief des Jakobus,* THNT (Leipzig: Evangelische Verlagsanstalt, 2001) ▮S. E. **Porter,** "Pauline Authorship and the Pastoral Epistles: Implications for Canon," *BBR* 5 (1995): 105–23 ▮G. H. **Rendall,** *The Epistle of St. James and Judaistic Christianity* (Cambridge: Cambridge University Press, 1927) ▮James Hardy **Ropes,** *A Critical and Exegetical Commentary on the Epistle of St. James,* ICC (Edinburgh: T. & T. Clark, 1916) ▮J. N. **Sevenster,** *Do You Know Greek? How Much Greek Could the First Jewish Christians Have Known?* (Leiden: Brill, 1968) ▮F. **Spitta,** "Der Brief des Jakobus," *Zur Geschichte und Literatur des Urchristentums,* vol. 2 (Göttingen: Vandenhoeck & Ruprecht, 1896), 1–239 ▮E. **Tamez,** *The Scandalous Message of James: Faith without Works is Dead* (New York: Crossroad, 1990) ▮R. V. G. **Tasker,** *The General Epistle of James,* TNTC (Grand Rapids: Eerdmans, 1956) ▮D. J. **Verseput,** "Wisdom, 4Q185, and the Epistle of James," *JBL* 117 (1998): 691–707 ▮F. **Vouga,** *L'épître de S. Jacques* (Geneva: Labor et Fides, 1984) ▮Wesley Hiram **Wachob,** *The Voice of Jesus in the Social Rhetoric of James,* SNTSMS 106 (Cambridge: Cambridge University Press, 2000) ▮R. B. **Ward,** "James of Jerusalem in the First Two Centuries," *ANRW* 2.26.1 (1992), 799–810 ▮Walter **Wessel,** "James, Letter of," in *ISBE* 2:959–65 ▮B. F. **Westcott,** *A General Survey of the History of the Canon of the New Testament* (London: Macmillan, 1889) ▮Ben **Witherington** III, *Jesus the Sage: The Pilgrimage of Wisdom* (Minneapolis: Fortress, 1994) ▮W. H. **Wuellner,** "Der Jakobusbrief im Licht der Rhetorik und Textpragmatic," *Linguistica Biblica* 44 (1978–79): 5–66.

CHAPTER TWENTY-ONE

1 PETER

CONTENTS

In his first letter, Peter writes to Christians in Asia Minor who are suffering for their faith. He comforts them with reminders of the solid hope for salvation they enjoy because of Christ's death and resurrection and challenges them to maintain the highest standards of holy living as a witness to their persecutors. Unlike Paul, who often develops a theological point before applying it, Peter mixes imperative and indicative almost from the beginning of the letter. Indeed, apart from the thanksgiving section in 1:3–9 and the "stone" passage in 2:4–10, every paragraph of 1 Peter opens with a command, with theology brought in along the way to ground the command.

The usual letter opening (1:1–2) is distinguished by the way Peter's twofold address of his readers introduces the key motifs of the letter. These Christians are, on the one hand, "God's elect." God has chosen them to be his people, indeed, to represent him and mediate his presence as "priests" (2:5, 9–10). As such, they are to follow the central demand of God's people from the Old Testament to "Be holy as I [God] am holy" (1:15–16), embodying the "way of life" (ἀναστροφή [anastrophē], a key word in the letter; cf. 1:15, 18; 2:12, 3:1, 2, 16; the cognate verb occurs in 1:17) appropriate for the elect. But on the other hand, these Christians are also "strangers in the world" (1:1). Precisely because they are chosen by God and to the extent that they live as God's elect, they incur surprise (4:4) and hostility (4:4; 1:6; 3:13–17) from the unbelievers among whom they live. Such suffering should not surprise them (4:12), for the lot of God's people, following their Savior and example Jesus Christ, is to suffer for the sake of righteousness, and in so doing, testify to God's glory and goodness (2:19–25; 3:9, 15–16). In a phrase, Peter calls on his readers to exhibit "piety under pressure" as a means of glorifying God and of witnessing to a hostile but watchful world.

After the letter opening (1:1–2), the body of 1 Peter (1:3–5:11) falls into three sections, marked out by Peter's address "dear friends" (ἀγαπητοί [agapētoi], "beloved") in 2:11 and 4:12. The first section (1:3–2:10) focuses on the privileges and responsibilities of being God's people. Peter uses the typical epistolary thanksgiving (1:3–9) to encourage his readers by reminding them that their new birth has provided for them a secure hope and inheritance—future salvation. In a brief digression (1:10–12), Peter accentuates the importance of this salvation by mentioning that the prophets predicted it and angels themselves long to understand it. The responsibilities of God's people become dominant in 1:13–2:3, as Peter calls on his readers to exhibit a holy way of life rooted in their new birth and stimulated by God's act of redeeming them in Christ. While provided for them through the work of Christ, the salvation for which they hope is also something that, by their behavior, they need to "grow up in" (2:2). In the conclusion to this section (2:4–10), Peter plays on the metaphor of Christ as "stone" to remind his readers of their new status: God's people, destined to declare his praises.

In a juxtaposition that duplicates the original address in 1:1, the reminder that the readers are God's chosen people (2:9–10) is followed immediately in the beginning of the next major section (2:11–4:11) by the warning that they are also "aliens and strangers in the world." Dominating this section is the demand that the readers take this designation seriously by exhibiting a lifestyle different from, yet attractive to, the hostile world in which they live (2:11–12). They should do so, first, by their "submission"—the key idea in 2:13–3:7. Peter begins generally, with the demand that they submit to "every human authority" (2:13), then specifies some of these "authorities": the government (for all believers) (2:14–17), masters (for slaves) (2:18–25), and husbands (for wives) (3:1–7). Peter here adapts the form of the Hellenistic "household code" to remind his readers that their conversion has not exempted them from the duties appropriate to this world. But these duties are transformed by the example of Christ (2:21–25) and by the purpose of those duties: to testify to God's power and goodness (3:1).

The "finally" in 3:8 marks the last stage in the section on submission, as Peter reminds all believers of the responsibility they have to live in harmony with both believers and, as far as possible, unbelievers (3:8–12). The underlying issue of suffering surfaces directly in 3:13–17. Peter's focus is on the need for believers to respond to the hostility they are experiencing with bold witness and attractive conduct. Attached to this demand for right conduct, as is typically the case in 1 Peter, is another christological passage (3:18–22). The interpretation of these verses is hotly disputed, some scholars thinking that Peter here describes a "descent" of Christ into Hades between his death and resurrection to preach to the dead,[1] while others think Peter depicts the pre-incarnate Christ preaching

---

[1] This view became popular in the early centuries of the church.

the gospel through Noah.[2] But the view that has gained something of a consensus among scholars is that Peter uses certain Old Testament (Gen. 6) and Jewish (esp. *1 Enoch*) traditions to proclaim Christ as the one who has won and declared his victory over evil powers.[3] Such an interpretation fits the context well, for Peter grounds his call on believers not to be afraid of their persecutors (3:14) with the reminder that even evil spiritual beings have been conquered by Christ. The second major section concludes with a further call to a distinctive lifestyle (4:1–6) and a series of general exhortations grounded in the nearness of the end (4:7–11).

The third major section begins somewhat abruptly with a final exhortation about the right response to suffering (4:12–19). The final verse of the paragraph reprises Peter's key demands: Christians should suffer "according to God's will"; they should commit themselves to "their faithful Creator"; and they should "continue to do good." In 5:1–5, Peter exhorts the leaders of the communities to exercise their responsibilities with the right motives and calls on the others in the community (e.g., the "young men") to submit to that leadership. The body of the letter concludes with a final exhortation to the readers to be strong in the face of opposition and to commit themselves fully to God (5:7–11).

The letter's closing (5:12–14) mentions two of Peter's companions, Silvanus (or Silas), who helped with the letter, and Mark, and mentions that "She who is in Babylon" sends greetings: probably the church in Rome.

OCCASION

As our survey of the contents has made clear, the situation that occasioned 1 Peter is suffering. But just what is the nature of the suffering? While the problem lies beneath virtually every verse of the letter, Peter refers directly to the suffering of his readers in three texts. In 1:6, he refers simply to "all kinds of trials." We learn much more from 3:13–17, which mentions suffering in general (vv. 14, 17) but also refers specifically to people who "speak maliciously" against the believers (v. 16; cf. also 4:5). Finally, in 4:12–19, Peter labels the suffering his readers are undergoing a "fiery ordeal" (v. 12), speaks of their sharing in the sufferings of Christ (v. 13), and suggests that they are suffering because they bear the name "Christian" (vv. 14 and 16). These references strongly suggest that the suffering these believers were experiencing was not the trials of ordi-

---

[2]See esp. Wayne A. Grudem, *The First Epistle of Peter,* TNTC (Grand Rapids: Eerdmans, 1988), 203–39; also John S. Feinberg, "1 Peter 3:18–20: Ancient Mythology and the Intermediate State," *WTJ* 48 (1986): 303–36.

[3]See, for instance, the latest two major commentaries in English, with full bibliographies: Paul J. Achtemeier, *1 Peter,* Hermeneia (Philadelphia: Fortress, 1996), 252–62; John H. Elliott, *1 Peter: A New Translation with Introduction and Commentary,* AB 37B (New York: Doubleday, 2000), 637–710.

nary life (illness, poverty, death) but some kind of persecution. If we could identify this persecution more precisely, we would be in a better position to understand the letter and to situate it in its specific historical setting.

Following Achtemeier's lead, we can set out the possibilities under three basic headings: a general official persecution, a local official persecution, or a local unofficial persecution.[4] Peter's reference to "fellow believers throughout the world" who are undergoing the same suffering as his readers (5:9) has inclined many scholars in the past to the first option. But the three relevant possibilities for such a general and official persecution—under Nero in 64–65, under Domitian in 90–95, and under Trajan in 97–117—must all be rejected for lack of compelling evidence that the persecutions attained any kind of empire-wide status. More attractive, at least initially, is the possibility that Peter's readers were suffering from the persecution mentioned in the correspondence between Pliny the Younger and the Emperor Trajan that took place c. 110. Pliny had been sent to Bithynia (one of the provinces included in the address of 1 Peter) to clean up an administrative mess. In his letter Pliny refers to the persecution of Christians and asks the emperor's advice about general policy and specific guidelines for his own procedure. However, in addition to the problem of this persecution being far too late for the apostle Peter to respond to, the evidence from 1 Peter itself does not point to an official persecution. What is implied, rather, is the hostility Christians were known to have faced from the general Roman population. By refusing to engage in the quasi-religious customs surrounding the official Roman governmental structures, by resolutely setting themselves against some of the immoral practices prevalent at the time, and by meeting so often on their own to celebrate the Lord's Supper, Christians were regarded with suspicion and hostility. The readers of 1 Peter were probably being criticized, mocked, discriminated against, and perhaps even brought into court on trumped-up charges. This situation fully explains the references to suffering in 1 Peter—including 5:10, since Christians throughout the empire were indeed suffering this same kind of treatment, and 4:14, 16, since the readers were indeed suffering because they followed Christ and bore his name. With very few dissenting voices, most recent scholars on 1 Peter agree that this is the kind of suffering the readers of the letter were experiencing.[5] If so, however, we are given no real help in pinning down the specific historical occasion of the epistle.

---

[4]Achtemeier, *1 Peter,* 28–36.

[5]E.g., J. N. D. Kelly, *A Commentary on the Epistles of Peter and of Jude,* HNTC (New York: Harper & Row, 1969), 5–11; Brown, 713–14; Achtemeier, *1 Peter,* 28–36; Elliott, *1 Peter,* 97–103. However, F. W. Beare (*The First Epistle of Peter,* 2nd ed. [Oxford: Blackwell, 1958], 29–34) insists that only an official, state-sponsored persecution can explain the data in 1 Peter.

SOURCES AND COMPOSITION

Probably no other letter in the New Testament is said to rely so much on traditional material as is 1 Peter. Some sources are obvious and undebated. For instance, 1 Peter quotes the Old Testament eight times (1:24–25a=Isa. 40:6–8; 2:6=Isa. 28:16; 2:7=Ps. 118:22; 2:8=Isa. 8:14; 2:22=Isa. 53:9; 3:10–12=Psa. 34:12–16; 4:18=Prov. 11:31; 5:5=Prov. 3:34), alludes to it much more often, and is suffused with Old Testament concepts and vocabulary. Scholars estimate that no other book in the New Testament, with the exception of Hebrews and Revelation, depends so heavily on the Old Testament. That Peter relies on various early Christian traditions is also clear, though the specifics are debated. Some scholars think Peter shows clear dependence on the words of Jesus; others are not so sure.[6] It was virtually a consensus forty years ago that 1 Peter knew and used certain Pauline epistles, especially Romans and Ephesians.[7] But most modern scholars now insist, rightly, that the similarities are due not to literary dependence but to common use of early Christian tradition.[8]

More ambitious, but also now out of favor, are those theories that find behind 1 Peter specific liturgical or catechetical documents. The liturgical hypothesis was first suggested by R. Perdelwitz, who argued that 1:3–4:11 was a baptismal sermon that Peter had taken over.[9] H. Preisker took this theory a step further, suggesting that 1:3–4:11 incorporated specifically the baptismal liturgy of the Roman church, with 4:12–5:11 being the general sermon to the whole community.[10] The ultimate form of this theory is found in F. L. Cross, who, noting the frequency of references to πάσχω (*paschō*, "suffer"), suggested

---

[6]See Robert H. Gundry, "'*Verba Christi*' in 1 Peter," *NTS* 13 (1966–67): 336–50; idem, "Further *Verba* on *Verba Christi*," *Bib* 55 (1974): 211–32; Ernest Best, "I Peter and the Gospel Tradition," *NTS* 16 (1969–70): 95–113.

[7]See, e.g., Beare, *The First Epistle of Peter*, 9. Ernest Best thinks that 1 Peter knows Romans indirectly but Ephesians more directly (*1 Peter*, NCB [Grand Rapids: Eerdmans, 1982], 32–36); J. Ramsay Michaels, on the other hand, thinks that the only NT book that 1 Peter may depend upon is Romans (*1 Peter*, WBC [Waco: Word, 1988], xliii–xliv).

[8]A significant essay shifting the focus was Eduard Lohse, "Paranesis and Kerygma in 1 Peter." The essay (in German) was first published in 1957 and can now be found (translated) in *Perspectives on First Peter*, ed. Charles Talbert (Macon: Mercer University Press, 1986), 37–59.

[9]R. Perdelwitz, *Die Mysterienreligion und das Problem des I Petrusbriefes* (Giessen: Töpelmann, 1911).

[10]Appendix by H. Preisker in H. Windisch and H. Preisker, *Die katholischen Briefe*, HNT, rev. ed. (Tübingen: Mohr, 1951), 152–62. See also Beare, *The First Epistle of Peter*, 6–8, who thinks that 1:1–4:11 is a baptismal discourse and 4:12–5:11 a genuine epistle (to which 1:1–2 and 5:12–14 belong). See also M.-E. Boismard, *Quatre hymnes baptismales dans la première épître de Pierre* (Paris: Cerf, 1961).

that 1:3–4:11 was the celebrant's part of the baptismal rite of Easter.[11] Much less ambitious, and therefore more likely, is C. F. D. Moule's argument that 1:1–4:11 and 5:12–14 is a letter to Christians only threatened with persecution, while 1:1–2:10 and 4:12–5:14 is a letter to those already suffering.[12]

As might be suspected, driving these theories is the perception of an important break in the letter at 4:12. Before then, it is argued, Peter deals with suffering as a possibility (see esp. 3:14); but with 4:12, the "fiery ordeal" has arrived. Some kind of partition theory has been thought necessary to explain this abrupt shift. But in fact, as most contemporary scholars agree, the break at 4:12 is more perceived than real. Suffering is a reality that the readers are dealing with throughout the letter (see 1:6; 2:18–25; 3:13–17; 4:5). No textual evidence supports any partition theory. The liturgical hypotheses are especially open to criticism. Baptism is mentioned only once in the epistle (3:21), while claims that the rite is referred to in various metaphors throughout are simply not justified. Nor is it at all clear how the readers of Peter's letter would benefit from hearing the liturgy of the Roman church. As Ernest Best puts it, "It is impossible to envisage the situation in Asia Minor which would have called out the need for the liturgy, nor the circumstances in Rome which would have led to its communication."[13] Modern scholarship is virtually unanimous in maintaining the literary integrity of 1 Peter.

AUTHOR

The letter that the early church entitled "The First [Epistle] of Peter" (*Petrou A'*) is aptly named. "Peter, an apostle of Jesus Christ" is named as the author (1:1) and 2 Peter is identified as "my second letter to you" (2 Pet. 3:1)—probably a reference to what we call 1 Peter. Early testimony to the letter and to Peter's authorship is strong. Some scholars think that *1 Clement*, written from Rome in A.D. 96, quotes from 1 Peter, but this is unlikely. What is generally agreed is that the letter of Polycarp to the Philippians, written in about 135, reveals acquaintance with 1 Peter. Irenaeus, toward the end of the second century, is the first patristic writer to mention 1 Peter by name. Of all the General Epistles, it is only 1 Peter that Eusebius classifies among the "undisputed" New Testament books (*H.E.* 3.3.25). To be sure, the letter is missing from the Muratorian Canon; but the document is mutilated, and 1 Peter may have originally been included. All in all, as Michaels concludes, "Aside from the four Gospels and the letters of Paul, the external attestation for 1 Peter is as strong, or stronger, than that for any other NT book."[14]

---

[11]F. L. Cross, *I Peter, A Paschal Liturgy* (London: Mowbray, 1954).

[12]C. F. D. Moule, "The Nature and Purpose of I Peter," *NTS* 3 (1956–57): 1–11.

[13]Ernest Best, *1 Peter*, NCB (Grand Rapids: Eerdmans, 1982), 22.

[14]Michaels, *1 Peter*, xxxiv.

Despite this strongly attested claim of authorship, a significant number—perhaps even a majority—of contemporary scholars deny that Peter was the author of the letter. Various reasons for this conclusion have been advanced in the history of scholarship. Two that were quite popular in the past are now generally discounted: that the letter reflects a world-wide, government-sponsored persecution that could only have taken place after Peter's death, and that the letter depends on Pauline epistles that Peter would not have come to know in his lifetime. As we have seen, most scholars now doubt the premises of both of these arguments. But other reasons are still thought to be sufficient to make the case against Petrine authorship.

1. If Peter wrote the letter, and "Babylon" in 5:13 refers to Rome as the place of writing, then he must have written shortly before his death in A.D. 64–65. Yet Paul was present and active in the church at Rome at about this same time; Paul's failure to mention Peter in his letter to Rome (c. A.D. 57) or in his letters written from Rome (Ephesians, Colossians, Philemon, Philippians [?], A.D. 60–62) makes it difficult to think Peter was present in Rome during this time.

2. The letter is addressed to mainly Gentile Christians in five provinces in Asia Minor. Yet when Peter and Paul met in Jerusalem in the late 40s, it was agreed that Paul would evangelize Gentiles while Peter, with James and John, would concentrate on Jews (Gal. 2:1–10). And Paul himself evangelized in at least two of the provinces mentioned in 1 Peter 1:1 (Galatia and Asia; cf. Galatians and Acts 19). It is therefore hard to imagine the historical Peter involved with Christians that the New Testament places in the province of Paul.

3. The church order presupposed in 1 Peter 5:1–5 reflects a time after his death. Christ is pictured as the "Chief Shepherd," with pastors being his undershepherds; and elders, because Peter must warn them about greed, have paid positions.

4. If Peter had written the letter, we would have expected reminiscences based on his close association with Jesus during his earthly life.

5. 1 Peter is said to be too "Pauline" in its theology to have been written by Peter, who famously disputed theological points with Paul (Gal. 2:11–14).

6. The quotations from the Old Testament in the letter follow the LXX closely. It is thought to be unlikely that Peter, granted his background, would have used a Greek Old Testament text.

7. The Greek of the letter is smooth and competent, with rhetorical flourishes. Indeed, along with Hebrews and Luke-Acts, it is some of the best Greek in the New Testament. An older generation of scholarship tended to insist that Peter, a fisherman from Galilee labeled "unschooled" (ἀγράμματος [agrammatos]) in Acts 4:13, would hardly have known Greek at all. But recent research on languages in first-century Palestine has revealed that Greek was widely used (see pp. 240, 624). Peter probably grew up using Greek to converse with buyers of his fish. But contemporary scholars, well aware of Peter's likely knowledge

of Greek, still insist that it is unlikely that Peter ever would have attained the ease and facility in the language that the letter demonstrates. Achtemeier states the case clearly:

> The type of Greek found in 1 Peter reveals that whether or not the author was born a Greek, he had enjoyed some level of formal education: if not an "advanced" education in rhetoric or philosophy, at least a "middle" education that would have included, along with geometry, arithmetic, and music, a reading of such classical authors as Homer. While one may surely presume some facility in Greek even among Palestinian fishermen in the first century who lacked formal education, the kind of Greek found in this epistle was probably beyond such a person.[15]

Most contemporary scholars conclude that these arguments are sufficient to render Peter's authorship of the letter improbable. They therefore claim that 1 Peter is pseudonymous, written perhaps by someone in a "Petrine school" after his death.[16]

Nevertheless, a careful consideration of these objections to Petrine authorship reveals that most are without foundation and none is conclusive.

1. The most likely reconstruction of Paul's life is that he left Rome after his imprisonment there in A.D. 60–62 for a time of ministry in the eastern Mediterranean (see the Pastoral Epistles, chap. 17). Paul would therefore have been absent from Rome for at least a year or so, giving Peter ample time to come to the city and write the letter attributed to him. Scholars have even suggested that the resemblances between 1 Peter and Romans might be due to Peter's acquaintance with that letter during his stay in Rome—although this is uncertain. In any case, we must posit some scenario that gets both Paul and Peter in Rome together by A.D. 64–65—when reliable tradition has them perishing under Nero.

2. The agreement to divide up the mission field along ethnic lines was apparently never intended to be exclusive or permanent. Paul continued to evangelize Jews in every city he visited; and 1 Corinthians 1 implies that Peter had spent enough time in Corinth to attract a following among the mainly Gentile Christians there. There is debate about just what geographic area is intended by the list of provinces in 1:1 (see below); but it is quite possible that the reference is to the north-central part of Asia Minor, an area that Paul never visited.

---

[15]See Achtemeier, *1 Peter*, 4–5.

[16]A representative recent statement of this hypothesis is found in Elliott, *1 Peter*, 118–30. See also, e.g., Best, *1 Peter*, 49–63; Achtemeier, *1 Peter*, 1–43; R. P. Martin, "The Theology of James, 1 Peter, and 2 Peter," in *The Theology of the Letters of James, Peter and Jude* (Cambridge: Cambridge University Press, 1994), 91–92; M. L. Soards, "1 Peter, 2 Peter, and Jude as Evidence for a Petrine School," *ANRW* 2.25.5 (1988), 3827–49; Brown, 718–19; McDonald/Porter, 535–37.

3. Nothing in 1 Peter 5:1–4 reflects a church order that was not in place by the early 60s. Moreover, the argument cuts both ways, because the omission of any reference to "orders" of ministry (deacons as well as elders, for instance) might indicate an early date.[17]

4. While the letter never explicitly refers to Peter's association with Jesus during his earthly ministry, a number of scholars have discerned allusions to that association (see esp. 5:1 [cp. 1:8] and also 2:23).[18] However, the evidence is ambiguous at best ("witness" in 5:1 could well have the sense "one who testifies to"). A more cogent point is whether Peter would certainly have referred to his earthly connection with Jesus in any letter that he wrote. That he could do so, where it suited his purposes, is clear from 2 Peter 1:16–18. But there is no reason to expect that he would make such an allusion if the argument did not call for it. Moreover, critics sometimes at this point argue out of both sides of their mouth: 1 Peter could not have been written by Peter because it contains no historical Jesus allusions; 2 Peter could not have been written by Peter because it contains such allusions.

5. While the argument was popular in an earlier period, the claim that 1 Peter is Pauline in its theology is now considerably more nuanced. Peter shares many key ideas and expressions with Paul—as their dependence on common Christian tradition would make overwhelmingly probable. (The degree of theological disagreement between Peter and Paul has been grossly exaggerated.[19]) But Peter uses these ideas and expressions in ways quite distinct from Paul.

6. and 7. These arguments, both relating to the Greek of the letter, can be taken together. And they are probably the key to the argument over authorship. As even critics of Petrine authorship acknowledge, most if not all of these first five arguments are inconclusive.[20] The reliance of 1 Peter on the LXX and the clear and literate Greek of the letter cannot be doubted. The question is whether these are sufficient to exclude Peter as the author of the letter. A common response among defenders of Petrine authorship is to appeal to the involvement of an amanuensis, who may have been responsible for the Greek style. Silvanus, who is named in 5:12 as the one "through whom" Peter wrote the letter, is usually identified as that amanuensis. This Silvanus is also named "Silas" (hence the TNIV text), and was an important coworker of Paul's (cf. Acts 15:22–24, 40; 16:19, 25, 29; 17:14–15; 18:15; 2 Cor. 1:19), even named as the co-author of 1 and 2 Thessalonians (1 Thess. 1:1; 2 Thess. 1:1). Silvanus may, then, not only

---

[17]See, e.g., Achtemeier, *1 Peter*, 37.

[18]E.g., E. G. Selwyn, *The First Epistle of St. Peter* (London: Macmillan, 1949), 28; Grudem, *The First Epistle of Peter*, 21.

[19]N. Brox, *Der erste Petrusbrief*, EKKNT, 2nd ed. (Zürich: Benziger Verlag, 1986), 51.

[20]See esp. the reasoned and sober assessment of Achtemeier, *1 Peter*, 2–43.

be responsible for the good Greek of the letter but also for some of its "Paulinisms."[21] However, criticism of this hypothesis has come from both defenders and critics of Pauline authorship. The issue is whether the language of 1 Peter 5:12, διὰ Σιλουανοῦ ... ἔγραψα (*dia Silouanou ... egrapsa;* "through Silvanus ... I have written") can refer to the involvement of an amanuensis or whether it must refer to the person who carried the letter.[22] While there appears to be at least one instance of this terminology referring to a writer of a letter,[23] the preponderance of occurrences seems to indicate the carrier of a letter.[24] Nevertheless, this evidence in no way obviates the hypothesis that the Greek of 1 Peter is to some extent the work of an amanuensis. We know that most first-century letter-writers employed an amanuensis, giving to them various degrees of freedom of expression (see pp. 334–35). So Peter is likely to have used an amanuensis, whether or not he is named in the letter.[25] And that amanuensis could have been Silvanus, for to conclude that 5:12 refers to him as the carrier of the letter does not mean that he could not have been the composer of the letter as well. The possibility that an amanuensis was responsible for the good Greek of 1 Peter must, therefore, remain a live possibility.

But apart from the amanuensis hypothesis, we might also question whether it is quite so clear that Peter himself could not have written the Greek of this letter. To be sure, it is unlikely that Peter ever received any formal education. But would formal education really be necessary to attain the fluency in Greek represented in the letter? The example of erudite writers in many languages who came from humble origins and had little formal schooling seems to call into question this assumption. The fact is that we simply do not know how good Peter's Greek might have gotten in the thirty years between Jesus' death and resurrection and the probable date for 1 Peter, if Peter were the author.

The case against Petrine authorship is therefore not at all a strong one. We agree with I. Howard Marshall that "if there ever was a weak case for pseudonymity, surely it is in respect to this letter."[26] Only the issue of language stands

The case against Petrine authorship is not at all a strong one. Only the issue of language stands in the way of authenticity, and that problem is far outweighed by the notion of pseudonymity.

---

[21]See C. A. Bigg, *A Critical and Exegetical Commentary on the Epistles of St. Peter and St. Jude,* 2nd ed. (Edinburgh: T. & T. Clark, 1902), 5; Wikenhauser, 505–6; Selwyn, *The First Epistle of St. Peter,* 10–17 (Selwyn even appeals to parallels between 1 Peter and 1 and 2 Thessalonians).

[22]Arguing the second alternative are, e.g., Grudem, *The First Epistle of Peter,* 23–24 (a defender of Petrine authorship) and Achtemeier, *1 Peter,* 7–9 (a critic of Petrine authorship).

[23]Eusebius, *H.E.* 4.23.11, referring to Clement as the author of *1 Clement.*

[24]See the evidence laid out in Elliott, *1 Peter,* 872–73.

[25]See Peter H. Davids, *The First Epistle of Peter,* NICNT (Grand Rapids: Eerdmans, 1990), 6–7.

[26]I. Howard Marshall, *1 Peter* (Leicester: IVP, 1991), 21.

in the way of authenticity; and this problem is far outweighed by the problem of thinking that a pseudonymous letter would have been written and accepted in the early church.[27]

PROVENANCE

The greetings Peter transmits from "She who is in Babylon" (5:13) suggest that the letter was written in the place Peter calls Babylon. Since the historical city of Babylon in Mesopotamia, often mentioned in the pages of the Old Testament, had no Jewish population in Peter's day (see Josephus, *Ant.* 18.371–79) and was almost deserted in A.D. 115 when the Emperor Trajan visited, almost no one thinks Peter wrote his letter from there. Another, very small Roman military colony in Egypt called "Babylon" existed in Peter's day, but this too is a very unlikely provenance for 1 Peter.[28] Contemporary scholars are virtually unanimous in viewing "Babylon" as a symbol for worldly power drawn from Babylon's role vis-à-vis Israel in the Old Testament. A few have suggested that the referent is a way simply of referring to God's people in exile,[29] but most agree that, in keeping with the application of Babylon in Revelation, Peter refers to Rome, the center of worldly influence in his day. "She who is in Babylon" will then be the church (ἐκκλησία [*ekklēsia*], a feminine word) in Rome.

DATE

Scholars who think that 1 Peter is pseudepigraphical will occasionally date the letter as late as the early second century, often because they are convinced that the correspondence between Pliny and Trajan holds the clue to the letter's occasion.[30] But the tendency among contemporary scholars, who generally attribute the letter to a Petrine school, is to put the letter sometime between 70 and 100.[31] On the assumption that Peter is the author (which we have argued above), the letter almost surely was written in A.D. 62–63. An earlier date is unlikely because Peter probably only arrived in Rome in the 60s, Paul was probably not in Rome when Peter wrote, and because the letter seems to reflect a "settled sit-

---

[27]In his otherwise very careful and balanced assessment, Achtemeier betrays the inherent problem in the pseudepigraphical hypothesis by his very weak attempt to justify the procedure via appeal to the authority of a teacher and the "therapeutic lie" (*1 Peter,* 39–41).

[28]On NT Babylon, see Duane F. Watson in *ABD* 1.565–66.

[29]E.g., Martin, "The Theology of James, 1 Peter, and 2 Peter," 93.

[30]E.g., Beare, *The First Epistle of Peter,* 11–19; F. Gerald Downing, "Pliny's Prosecutions of Christians: Revelation and 1 Peter," *JSNT* 34 (1988): 105–23.

[31]E.g., Best, *1 Peter,* 63–64; Achtemeier, *1 Peter,* 43–50; Elliott, *1 Peter,* 134–38; Brown, 721–22.

uation" with regard both to theology and church life.[32] A date after A.D. 63 is unlikely because we need to leave time before Peter's martyrdom for 2 Peter.[33]

AUDIENCE AND DESTINATION

Peter's focus on the Jewish mission (cf. Gal. 2:7) and the many Old Testament quotations and allusions in the letter have led some interpreters, particularly in the early church, to think that the audience of the letter is mainly Jewish.[34] But Peter refers to his readers in ways that strongly suggest they were Gentile in background. Especially telling are 1:18—"the empty way of life handed down to you from your ancestors"; 2:10—"Once you were not a people"; and 4:3—"For you have spent enough time in the past doing what pagans choose to do—living in debauchery, lust, drunkenness, orgies, carousing and detestable idolatry." The first could conceivably describe Jews who lived an empty life apart from the fulfillment of God's promises in Christ. But the language "not my people" points to Gentiles (cf. Rom. 9:24–25; Eph. 2:11–12), as do the sins enumerated in 4:3. Faced with these conflicting data, and recognizing that the area to which 1 Peter is directed had a significant Jewish population, many scholars conclude that the letter is directed to a mixed Jewish/Gentile audience.[35] But the explicit references we have mentioned suggest that, whatever the population of the churches may have been, Peter's intended audience is mainly, if not exclusively, Gentile.[36]

These Christians lived in five regions of Asia Minor (occupied today by the nation of Turkey): Pontus, Galatia, Cappadocia, Asia, and Bithynia. These names could designate geographic areas, which some favor because it would tend to exclude territory that Paul had evangelized.[37] But reference to Roman provinces is more likely. And this conclusion need not mean that Peter was "infringing" on Pauline territory. Peter need not be referring to every locality

---

[32]For this latter point, see Selwyn, *The First Epistle of St. Peter*, 40–41.

[33]See especially Grudem, *The First Epistle of Peter*, 35–37. If, contrary to the consensus tradition, Peter was not martyred at the same time as Paul, other options open up. Davids, for instance, suggests that Silvanus might have begun working with Peter after Paul's death, helping him compose the letter in the years 64–68 (*The First Epistle of Peter*, 10–11). Michaels, similarly, thinks Peter might have survived the Neronian persecution and written the letter sometime in the 70s (*1 Peter*, lvii–lxvii).

[34]According to Selwyn (*The First Epistle of St. Peter*, 42), most of the Greek fathers took this view.

[35]E.g., Selwyn, *The First Epistle of St. Peter*, 42–44; Grudem, *The First Epistle of Peter*, 37–38.

[36]For Gentile predominance, see Kelly, *A Commentary on the Epistles of Peter and of Jude*, 4; Davids, *The First Epistle of Peter*, 8; Achtemeier, *1 Peter*, 50–51.

[37]Guthrie, 783.

within these provinces; probably he has in mind only the northern part of Galatia and Cappadocia and the northeastern part of Asia. A difficulty for the provincial interpretation, however, is the separation of the names of Pontus and Bithynia, which were joined as one province in Peter's time. However, they may have been separated, because Peter lists the provinces in the order in which the emissary carrying the letter would have traveled through them.[38] Peter's reference to "those who have preached the gospel to you" (1:12) suggests that he did not personally evangelize these Christians.

1 PETER IN RECENT STUDY

Three trends in modern New Testament scholarship generally show up in recent study of 1 Peter. The first is the tendency to posit the existence of apostolic "schools," devotees of influential teachers who carried on the spirit of their teachers after their death and who may have been responsible for some of the books traditionally attributed to these apostles. A Johannine school has received most attention, but a Pauline school, and, more recently, as we have noted above, a Petrine school have been posited. That the impressive personality and work of the apostles left a strong mark on their followers cannot be doubted. But we have virtually no evidence from the first century for such schools. And in any case, advocates of the school hypothesis have not yet overcome the objection that the pseudepigraphical letter was simply not recognized as a valid literary convention in the first century—no matter how close the pseudepigrapher to the teacher in whose name he claims to write.

A second trend that has surfaced in connection with 1 Peter is the careful analysis of the way New Testament books communicate. W. L. Schutter argues, for instance, that the density of Old Testament material in 1 Peter qualifies the letter as a "homiletical midrash," a pastoral document using the Old Testament to encourage and instruct.[39] First Peter is indeed, as we noted above, permeated with Old Testament allusions and language. But we doubt that Peter focuses on Old Testament exposition as such to the extent necessary to characterize the letter as a midrash. Another work paying close attention to the letter's method of communication is the dissertation of Barth L. Campbell, which analyzes the letter in accordance with ancient rhetorical standards and the emphasis in Greco-Roman culture on honor and shame.[40] Falling generally into this category also

---

[38]See esp. Colin Hemer, "The Address of 1 Peter," *ExpTim* 89 (1977–78): 239–43. Hemer is refining an earlier similar suggestion of F. J. A. Hort.

[39]W. L. Schutter, *Hermeneutics and Composition in First Peter*, WUNT 30 (Tübingen: Mohr, 1989).

[40]Barth L. Campbell, *Honor, Shame and the Rhetoric of 1 Peter*, SBLDS 160 (Atlanta: SP, 1998).

is the work of David Balch, who studies the function and purpose of the "household codes" (2:18–3:6) in the letter. Balch claims that these codes are apologetic devices intended to squelch rumors that Christians, because of the "liberated ethic," encouraged social anarchy. Peter therefore uses these codes to counsel assimilation to reigning cultural practices.[41] However, while an over-enthusiastic reading of Christian "liberation" was a problem in the early church (see 1 Corinthians), the material Balch treats in 1 Peter has strong roots in biblical teaching. It cannot be considered simple accommodation to the culture. Nor does the letter as a whole suggest such an assimilationist approach.[42]

A third way in which recent study of 1 Peter follows the wider field of study is found in the interest in the readers' social status. In this respect, the work of John H. Elliott on 1 Peter contributed not only to the study of the letter but to the developing methodology of social science research. In his 1981 monograph, *A Home for the Homeless,* Elliott argued that some key terminology that Peter uses to characterize his readers is to be understood not theologically but sociologically. Elliott focuses on the terms πάροικος/παροικία (*paroikos/paroikia*), "aliens"/"sojourn" (2:11; 1:17) and παρεπίδημος (*parepidēmos*), "strangers" (1:1; 2:11). In each case, he argues that the terms do not indicate the readers' spiritual status, acquired as a result of conversion to Christ, but their social status before conversion. Peter's readers were not strangers in this world because their true home had become heaven; they were literally aliens and exiles, estranged from the society around them because of their legal and social status.[43] Peter therefore encourages the readers by reminding them that they have a true "home" (οἰκία [*oikia*]) in the Christian community. While bringing a valuable reminder of the need to situate New Testament letters in the real first-century world, Elliott's thesis has not met with much acceptance. Most damaging to his thesis is the fact that the key combination of words πάροικος/παροικία and παρεπίδημος are never found in secular Greek but are found in the LXX. This background strongly points to a theological rather than legal or social significance for the language.[44]

---

[41]D. L. Balch, *Let Wives Be Submissive: The Domestic Code in 1 Peter,* SBLMS 26 (Chico: SP, 1981); see also, idem, "Hellenization/Acculturation in 1 Peter," in *Perspectives on 1 Peter,* 79–102.

[42]See esp. John H. Elliott, "1 Peter, its Situation and Strategy: A Conversation with David Balch," in *Perspectives on 1 Peter,* 61–78; Bruce W. Winter, *Seek the Welfare of the City: Christians as Benefactors and Citizens* (Grand Rapids: Eerdmans, 1994), 13–17.

[43]John H. Elliott, *A Home for the Homeless: A Sociological Exegesis of 1 Peter, Its Situation and Strategy* (Philadelphia: Fortress, 1981). See also his commentary, *1 Peter,* 94, 101–2.

[44]See Moses Chin, "A Heavenly Home for the Homeless: Aliens and Strangers in 1 Peter, "*TynB* 42 (1991): 96–112; Achtemeier, *1 Peter,* 71; Steven Richard Bechtler, *Following in His Steps: Suffering, Community, and Christology in 1 Peter,* SBLDS 162 (Atlanta: SP, 1998), 64–83.

THE CONTRIBUTION OF 1 PETER

The contribution of 1 Peter to the theology of the New Testament tends to be overlooked because the letter stands in the shadows of the much more considerable contribution of the Pauline letters. And even when attention is given to 1 Peter itself, the letter is often viewed, as we have noted, as a late and prosaic distillation of Paul's theology. To be sure, Peter's heavy reliance on common early Christian teaching means that his original contributions are few. Moreover, his theology is inseparably bound up with his ethical appeal. But three of Peter's theological/ethical emphases deserve mention.

First, appropriately enough in a letter to suffering Christians, Peter emphasizes hope.[45] His opening praise of God turns immediately to the "living hope" that results from the new birth (1:3), and Peter expounds this hope via the concepts of "inheritance" (v. 4) and salvation (vv. 5, 9). Salvation in 1 Peter, while sharing the typical "now/not yet" New Testament eschatological tension (see 3:21), is future-oriented: it is "ready to be revealed in the last time" (1:5; cf. also v. 9 and 2:2). Similarly, grace, while enjoyed by believers already (4:10), also has a future focus: it will be "brought to you when Jesus Christ is revealed" (1:13). Christians need to respond to their suffering with a gentle witness and a firm adherence to what is good so that we might "be overjoyed when his [Christ's] glory is revealed" (4:13; see also 5:1 and 5:4). Our suffering, Peter reminds us, will be only for a "little while" (1:6; 5:10); this world itself is transitory and destined soon to fade away (4:7). A commitment to maintain Christian conduct in the face of societal pressure can be strengthened by the reminder of the place on the eschatological timeline that Christians in this world occupy.

A second distinctive contribution of Peter lies in his repeated insistence that Christians belong to the ancestral people of God. Few documents in the New Testament so resolutely apply Old Testament language of Israel to Christians.[46] The "inheritance," a term redolent of God's promises to Israel, belongs securely to believers (1:4). Christians are those who are promised God's final salvation and glory (see above). This very salvation, Peter reminds us, was promised by the Old Testament prophets (1:10–12). As God's people, believers are to follow the code of "conduct" (ἀναστροφή [*anastrophē*]) demanded of God's covenant partner—a code that has at its heart the demand that they be holy as God is holy (1:15–16). It is God's word, about which Isaiah speaks, that has been preached to us and has led to our new birth (1:23–25). Christian wives are to imitate Sarah and the "holy women of the past" (3:5–6). Christians now make

---

[45]On "hope" in 1 Peter, see esp. Martin, "The Theology of James, 1 Peter, and 2 Peter," 88–89.

[46]See esp. Victor Paul Furnish, "Elect Sojourners in Christ: An Approach to the Theology of I Peter," *Perkins School of Theology Journal* 28 (1975): 1–11; Michaels, *1 Peter,* xliv–lv; Achtemeier, *1 Peter,* 69–72.

up "the household [οἰκία, *oikia*] of God" (4:17, our translation). But the pinnacle of this theme comes in 2:4–10, where Peter describes Christians as the new temple—a "spiritual house" (v. 5)—the new priesthood (vv. 5 and 9), and the new "chosen people," a "holy nation" called out to declare God's wondrous works. This language is all the more remarkable when we remember that Peter's readers are, at least mainly, Gentiles. For all his emphasis on this point, however, it must be said that it is probably not fair to Peter to speak of a "transfer" of privileges and titles from Israel to the church. For Peter says nothing about the condition of the nation of Israel; his emphasis is entirely on the inclusion of these mainly Gentile believers in the historic people of God. By repeatedly insisting on this point, Peter brings comfort to suffering Christians. Though aliens and strangers in this world, we have a secure and unassailable home in the household of God.

Finally, 1 Peter contains a very extensive Christology. This Christology is not taught in one passage but is taught by means of repeated references, and it is a Christology of action. Jesus' death, resurrection, ascension, and return run like a leitmotif throughout the letter. Again and again Peter traces the blessings that believers now enjoy or hope to enjoy to Christ's death and/or resurrection (1:3, 18–21; 2:24–25; 3:18; 4:1). Jesus' victory over evil spiritual beings, proclaimed at his ascension, means that Christians need not fear their power (3:14, 19–22). And it is Jesus' return in glory that will usher in the time of salvation and blessing for the people of God (1:7, 13; 5:4). While Jesus' acts provide the basis on which Christians can experience God's grace now and in the future, they also stand as a model for Christians to imitate. As he suffered and entered into glory (1:11), so must those who belong to him (4:13; cf. 5:1). When suffering, Peter stresses, Christians should imitate their Savior, who did not revile his persecutors but entrusted himself to God (2:21–23).

Ultimately, of course, the three key theological foci are intertwined: Peter encourages suffering Christians by reminding them of their present identity as God's people and their secure hope of ultimate blessing—both rooted in the death, resurrection, and victory of Christ.

BIBLIOGRAPHY

Paul J. **Achtemeier**, *1 Peter*, Hermeneia (Philadelphia: Fortress Press, 1996) ▥D. L. **Balch**, *Let Wives Be Submissive: The Domestic Code in 1 Peter*, SBLMS 26 (Chico: SP, 1981) ▥idem, "Hellenization/Acculturation in 1 Peter," in *Perspectives on First Peter*, ed. Charles Talbert (Macon: Mercer University Press, 1986), 79–102 ▥F. W. **Beare**, *The First Epistle of Peter*, 2nd ed. (Oxford: Blackwell, 1958) ▥Steven Richard **Bechtler**, *Following in His Steps: Suffering, Community, and Christology in 1 Peter*, SBLDS 162 (Atlanta: SP, 1998) ▥Ernest **Best**, *1 Peter*, NCB (Grand Rapids: Eerdmans, 1982) ▥idem, "I Peter and the Gospel Tradition," *NTS*

16 (1969–70): 95–113 ∎C. A. **Bigg**, *A Critical and Exegetical Commentary on the Epistles of St. Peter and St. Jude,* 2nd ed. (Edinburgh: T. & T. Clark, 1902) ∎M.-E. **Boismard**, *Quartre hymnes baptismales dans la première épître de Pierre* (Paris: Cerf, 1961) ∎N. **Brox**, *Der erste Petrusbrief,* EKKNT, 2nd ed. (Zürich: Benziger Verlag, 1986) ∎Barth L. **Campbell**, *Honor, Shame and the Rhetoric of 1 Peter,* SBLDS 160 (Atlanta: SP, 1998) ∎A. **Casurella**, *A Bibliography of Literature on First Peter,* New Testament Tools and Studies 16 (Leiden: Brill, 1996) ∎Moses **Chin**, "A Heavenly Home for the Homeless: Aliens and Strangers in 1 Peter," *TynB* 42 (1991): 96–112 ∎H. J. B. **Combrink**, "The Structure of 1 Peter," *Neot* 9 (1975): 34–63 ∎F. L. **Cross**, *1 Peter: A Paschal Liturgy* (London: Mowbrays, 1954) ∎W. J. **Dalton**, *Christ's Proclamation to the Spirit: A Study of 1 Peter 3:18–4:6,* AnBib 23, rev. ed. (Rome: Pontifical Biblical Institute, 1989) ∎Peter H. **Davids**, *The First Epistle of Peter,* NICNT (Grand Rapids: Eerdmans, 1990) ∎J. H. L. **Dijkman**, "1 Peter: A Later Pastoral Stratum?" *NTS* 33 (1987): 265–71 ∎F. Gerald **Downing**, "Pliny's Prosecutions of Christians: Revelation and 1 Peter," *JSNT* 34 (1988): 105–23 ∎John H. **Elliott**, *1 Peter: A New Translation with Introduction and Commentary,* AB 37B (New York: Doubleday, 2000) ∎idem, "1 Peter, its Situation and Strategy: A Conversation with David Balch," in *Perspectives on First Peter,* ed. Charles Talbert (Macon: Mercer University Press, 1986), 61–78 ∎idem, *The Elect and the Holy: An Exegetical Examination of 1 Peter 2:4–10 and the Phrase* βασιλείαν ἱεράτευμα, NovTSup 12 (Leiden: Brill, 1966) ∎idem, *A Home for the Homeless: A Sociological Exegesis of 1 Peter, Its Situation and Strategy* (Philadelphia: Fortress Press, 1981) ∎idem, "The Rehabilitation of an Exegetical Step-Child: 1 Peter in Recent Research," *JBL* 95 (1976): 243–54 ∎John S. **Feinberg**, "1 Peter 3:18–20: Ancient Mythology and the Intermediate State," *WTJ* 48 (1986): 303–36 ∎Victor Paul **Furnish**, "Elect Sojourners in Christ: An Approach to the Theology of I Peter," *Perkins School of Theology Journal* 28 (1975): 1–11 ∎L. **Goppelt**, *Der erste Petrusbrief,* KEK (Göttingen: Vandenhoeck & Ruprecht, 1978) ∎Wayne A. **Grudem**, *The First Epistle of Peter,* TNTC (Grand Rapids: Eerdmans, 1988) ∎R. H. **Gundry**, "Further *Verba* on *Verba Christi,*" *Bib* 55 (1974): 211–32 ∎idem, "Verba Christi in 1 Peter," *NTS* 13 (1966–67): 336–50 ∎C. J. **Hemer**, "The Address of 1 Peter," *ExpTim* 89 (1977–78): 239–43 ∎F. J. A. **Hort**, *The First Epistle of St Peter I.1–II.17* (London: Macmillan, 1898) ∎J. N. D. **Kelly**, *A Commentary on the Epistles of Peter and of Jude,* HNTC (New York: Harper & Row, 1969) ∎Eduard **Lohse**, "Paranesis and Kerygma in 1 Peter, in *Perspectives on First Peter,* ed. Charles Talbert (Macon: Mercer University Press, 1986), 37–51 ∎I. Howard **Marshall**, *1 Peter* (Leicester: IVP, 1991) ∎R. P. **Martin**, "The Theology of James, 1 Peter, and 2 Peter," in *The Theology of the Letters of James, Peter and Jude* (Cambridge: Cambridge University Press, 1994) ∎J. Ramsey **Michaels**, *1 Peter,* WBC 49 (Waco: Word, 1988) ∎Leon **Morris**, *The Cross in the New Testament* (Grand Rapids: Eerdmans, 1965) ∎C. F. D. **Moule**, "The Nature and Purpose of 1 Peter," *NTS* 3 (1956–57): 1–11 ∎W. **Munro**, *Authority in Peter and Paul,* SNTSMS 45 (Cam-

bridge: Cambridge University Press, 1983) ▮F. **Neugebauer**, "Zur Deutung und Bedeutung des 1. Petrusbriefes," *NTS* 26 (1979–80): 61–86 ▮R. **Perdelwitz**, *Die Mysterienreligionen und das Problem des I. Petrusbriefes*, RVV 11.3 (Giessen: Töpelmann, 1911) ▮K. H. **Schelkle**, *Die Petrusbrief, der Judasbrief*, HTKNT, 5th ed. (Freiburg: Herder, 1980) ▮W. L. **Schutter**, *Hermeneutics and Composition in First Peter*, WUNT 30 (Tübingen: Mohr-Siebeck, 1989) ▮E. G. **Selwyn**, *The First Epistle of St. Peter* (London: Macmillan, 1949) ▮M. L. **Soards**, "1 Peter, 2 Peter, and Jude as Evidence for a Petrine School," *ANRW* 2.25.5 (1988), 3827–49 ▮Alan M. **Stibbs** and Andrew F. **Walls**, *The First Epistle General of Peter* (London: Tyndale, 1959) ▮C. H. **Talbert**, ed., *Perspectives on First Peter* (Macon: Mercer University Press, 1986) ▮H. **Windisch** and H. **Preisker**, *Die katholischen Briefe*, HNT, 3rd ed. (Tübingen: Mohr-Siebeck, 1951) ▮Bruce W. **Winter**, *Seek the Welfare of the City: Christians as Benefactors and Citizens* (Grand Rapids: Eerdmans, 1994).

CHAPTER TWENTY-TWO

2 PETER

CONTENTS

Peter frames his second letter with references to grace and knowledge:

> 1:2: "Grace and peace be yours in abundance through the knowledge of God and of Jesus our Lord" (cf. also references to "knowledge" in vv. 3, 5, and 8).
>
> 3:18a: "But grow in the grace and knowledge of our Lord and Savior Jesus Christ."

His purpose, as 3:18 makes clear, is to encourage his readers to become mature in their understanding and practice of the grace of God in Christ. And for this to happen, they need to come to "know" Christ better. The contents of the letter reveal that they need to grow in their knowledge of Christ because they are threatened by teaching that might cut off that growth. And because of this, while Peter's overall purpose is the positive one of encouraging spiritual growth, the letter is dominated by negative descriptions of, and warnings about, false teachers. The overall structure of the letter falls into a chiastic arrangement. In 1:1–15 and 3:14–18, Peter exhorts the readers positively to "make every effort" (1:5 and 3:14; a form of σπουδή [spoudē] in both verses) to advance in their spiritual pilgrimage. In 1:16–21 and 3:1–13, he emphasizes that his readers need to hold fast to the conviction that Christ will return to judge the world—a belief that the false teachers mocked. And in the center of the letter (chap. 2), we find a long description and denunciation, using Old Testament illustrations and imagery, of the false teachers.

The five sections we have isolated above can also be seen in the light of typical Greek epistolary style, with 1:1–15 the letter opening; 3:14–18 its closing; and 1:16–3:13 the body, which falls in turn into three sections. The salutation (1:1–2) identifies "Simon Peter, a servant and apostle of Jesus Christ" as the author, gives only a theological description of the readers, and concludes with a grace wish. In place of the thanksgiving that is typical at this point in New Testament letters, an opening exhortation, based on God's gifts and promises to his people, follows (1:3–11). Then comes a paragraph that effects the transition from the opening to the body (1:12–15). Peter writes, as it were, on his deathbed, reminding his readers for a last time of the truth that they need to embrace. The opening paragraph of the body focuses on the parousia of Christ (1:16–21). In the face of skeptics (not clearly mentioned at this point), Peter insists that Christians can have absolute confidence that Jesus will come again. In the transfiguration of Christ, Peter and the other apostles with him have already seen, proleptically, the coming Christ in all his glory. And the prophets—utterly reliable because the Spirit speaks through them—confirm the same truth.

Peter's denunciation of the false teachers in chapter 2 can be divided into four sections. In the first (2:1–3a), the false teachers are introduced and a basic description of them is given. In 2:3b–10a, Peter condemns the false teachers but at the same time comforts his readers about their fate in the end, using a series of examples from the Old Testament, all introduced with "if" (vv. 4, 5, 6, 7, 9). A further description of the false teachers follows, focused on their arrogance and sensuality (2:10b–16). Peter concludes his denunciation of the false teachers with a final description and condemnation (2:17–22).

In the third section of the body, Peter turns directly to his readers again, reminding them that this is the second letter he has written to them and encouraging them to "remember" (a key concept in the letter) the teaching of the Lord and the prophets, who clearly predicted the parousia and day of judgment (3:1–13). Peter criticizes the skepticism of the false teachers by citing the creation and the flood as signal examples of God's direct intervention. So will he intervene again on the day of judgment.

Peter concludes with a final exhortation (3:14–18), buttressed by an appeal to the letters of Paul, and a doxology.

LITERARY AFFINITIES

As a preliminary to our discussion of other matters, and as a topic of interest in its own right, we need first to analyze the relationship of 2 Peter to other New Testament writings. Particularly important is the relationship of 2 Peter to Jude. Both letters devote much of their space to denouncing false teachers, and in very similar language. Note the parallels between the two:

Jude		2 Peter
4	the false teachers' "condemnation" from the past	2:3
4	[they] "deny" the "Sovereign [and] Lord"	2:1
6	angels confined for judgment (note the rare word ζόφος [*zophos*, "darkness"])	2:4
7	Sodom and Gomorrah as examples of judgment of gross evil	2:6

8	[they] "reject [Jude]/despise [2 Pet.] authority"	2:10
9	"the archangel Michael . . . did not . . . condemn him for slander [Jude]/"angels . . . do not heap abuse" [2 Pet.]	2:11
12	[the false teachers are] "blemishes"	2:13
12	"clouds without rain, blown along by the wind" [Jude]/ "springs without water and mists driven by a storm" [2 Pet.]	2:17
18	ungodly [Jude] desires/"scoffers" following their own evil [2 Pet.]	3:3

None of these parallels is especially long, but taken together they are nevertheless striking: many involve words and expressions not found elsewhere in the Bible, and as can be seen in the outline above, they occur in the same order in both letters.

The similarity in order and the rarity of language elsewhere in the Bible make it probable that some kind of literary relationship exists between the two letters. Four main explanations have been offered for that relationship. First, a few scholars have argued that the same author had a hand in writing both letters. One attractive hypothesis, for instance, has Jude as the scribe (or amanuensis) that Peter used when writing his letter. Jude then added his own note to Peter's warnings.[1] But no evidence for Jude's relationship to 2 Peter exists, and it is difficult, on this hypothesis, to explain why Jude would have written his letter at all. Most scholars therefore think that Peter and Jude borrowed from one another when they wrote their letters. This could have happened in three different ways: (1) Peter could have borrowed from the letter of Jude; (2) Jude could have used the letter of 2 Peter; or (3) both Peter and Jude could have used another document that we no longer have.

The last suggestion, though well argued by Michael Green,[2] is unlikely. Nothing really seems gained by the proposal, so the simpler solutions should be preferred. The church fathers generally held that Jude borrowed from 2 Peter, but the apostolic stature of Peter rather than any solid tradition seems to have been the reason for their conclusion. Most modern scholars, on the other hand, think that Peter has used Jude. They argue generally that it makes perfect sense to think that Peter would have wanted to expand on Jude, whereas it is hard to imagine why there would have been a need for Jude if 2 Peter already existed. Advocates of Peter's use of Jude make three other specific points: (1) Peter's failure to include the references to noncanonical books found in Jude suggests that

---

[1]J. A. T. Robinson, *Redating the New Testament* (London: SCM, 1976), 193–99; and R. Riesner, "Der Zweite Petrus-Brief und die Eschatologie," in *Zukunftserwartung in Biblischer Sicht. Beiträge zur Eschatologie,* ed. G. Maier (Giessen: Brunnen, 1984), 130–31.

[2]See esp. Michael Green, *The Second Epistle General of Peter and the General Epistle of Jude,* TNTC (Grand Rapids: Eerdmans, 1968), 50–55.

it was written later, when the church has a stronger "canon consciousness"; (2) Jude's tight structure makes it likely that it was freely composed rather than based on another document; and (3) the false teaching combated in 2 Peter is probably later than that combated in Jude.[3] Not all of these arguments are convincing. The shorter book need not always be the earlier; one can easily imagine a situation in which an author may want to extract points from another book that are particularly relevant to his or her situation. Arguments about the false teachers are very slippery because we have a great deal of trouble identifying just who they were. And it is quite unlikely that either letter was written late enough to make the development of "canon consciousness" a factor in the situation. On the other hand, the argument from structure does carry some weight.[4]

Nevertheless, though somewhat out of favor in current scholarship, the hypothesis that Jude used 2 Peter should also be seriously considered.[5] On this reading of the situation, Peter, having written a letter castigating false teachers in a specific community, shared its contents with Jude. Jude then borrowed freely those portions of 2 Peter that were relevant to a similar false teaching that he was dealing with in his community. Some support for this direction of borrowing might be found in a comparison of 2 Peter 3:3 and Jude 17–18:

> 2 Peter 3:3: "Above all, you must understand that in the last days scoffers will come, scoffing and following their own evil desires."

> Jude 17–18: "But, dear friends, remember what the apostles of our Lord Jesus Christ foretold. They said to you, 'In the last times there will be scoffers who will follow their own ungodly desires.'"

The text from Jude reads very much like a quotation of 2 Peter 3:3. The balance of evidence between the two main borrowing hypotheses is therefore a fine one. The soundest conclusion is agnosticism about the direction of borrowing between the two letters.

OCCASION

Peter's main reason for writing is the appearance of false teachers in the community (2:1–3). Identifying these false teachers would help us to pin down the

---

[3]For these arguments, see esp. Kümmel, 430–31; Richard J. Bauckham, *Jude, 2 Peter*, WBC (Waco: Word, 1983), 141–43.

[4]See the detailed comparison and discussion in Duane F. Watson, *Invention, Arrangement, and Style: Rhetorical Criticism of Jude and 2 Peter*, SBLDS 104 (Atlanta: SP, 1988), 163–87.

[5]See, e.g., Zahn, 2.238–55; Charles Bigg, *A Critical and Exegetical Commentary on the Epistles of St. Peter and St. Jude*, ICC (Edinburgh: T. & T. Clark, 1902), 216–24; Guthrie, 924.

date and circumstances of the letter. However, this is not easy, since Peter is more interested in condemning the false teaching than in describing it. The only clear doctrinal problem that surfaces is eschatological skepticism (2 Pet. 3:3–4, in conjunction with 1:16–21). Beyond that, Peter focuses most of his attention on the sinful lifestyle of the false teachers: they used God's grace as an excuse for a libertine lifestyle (2 Pet. 2:19–20), resisted any kind of authority (perhaps especially spiritual authorities, like angels; 2 Pet. 2:10–11), and engaged in all manner of "sins of the flesh" (illicit sex, perhaps including homosexuality; excessive drinking and eating; greed for money—2 Pet. 2:13–16, 18–20).

> *Peter's main reason for writing is the appearance of false teachers in the community, but identifying these false teachers is not easy, since Peter is more interested in condemning the false teaching than in describing it.*

The most popular suggestion is that these false teachers are to be identified with gnostics. But quite apart from the very late date of Gnosticism per se, the lack of some of the characteristic gnostic doctrines—such as dualism—renders this hypothesis unlikely.[6] A number of recent interpreters therefore suggest that the problem may have been "incipient gnosticism."[7] This suggestion may be on target, although it is so vague in its outlines that it really furnishes no help in pinning down the specific circumstances of the letter. Similarly vague is the suggestion of Jerome Neyrey that the popular Greco-Roman philosophy of Epicureanism may have influenced the false teachers. The Epicureans were known especially for their denial of providence, the afterlife, or any kind of divine judgment—just the view that seems to be taken by the false teachers according to chapter 3. And although the licentious lifestyle often held to be synonymous with Epicureanism is a popular caricature, their denial of providence and the activity of the gods in daily life could easily lead to such a lifestyle.[8]

These conflicting proposals suggest that we do not have enough evidence to identify the false teachers that lie behind 2 Peter. Indeed, our very quest to identify them with a particular group may be misguided. People in the ancient world, as in our day, were bombarded by viewpoints and ideas from many different perspectives. They could probably not have themselves always distinguished the exact religious or philosophical sources for their ultimate beliefs and habits of life. The false teachers, in other words, may have been influenced both by the

---

[6]See, e.g., Michel Desjardins, "The Portrayal of the Dissidents in 2 Peter and Jude: Does It Tell Us More About the 'Godly' than the 'Ungodly'?" *JSNT* 30 (1987): 92–95; Bauckham, *Jude, 2 Peter,* 156–57.

[7]Cf. J. N. D. Kelly, *A Commentary on the Epistles of Peter and of Jude,* HNTC (New York: Harper, 1969), 227–31.

[8]Jerome H. Neyrey, *2 Peter, Jude: A New Translation with Introduction and Commentary,* AB 37C (New York: Doubleday, 1993), 122–28. Neyrey cites the Roman moralist Lactantius: "If any chieftain or pirates or leaders of robbers were exhorting his men to acts of violence, what other language could he employ than to say the same things which Epicurus says: that the gods take no notice; that they are not affected with anger or kind feeling; that the punishment of a future state is not to be dreaded, because the souls die after death, and there is no future state of punishment at all" (*Inst.* 3.17).

broad philosophical climate of Epicureanism and by incipient gnosticism—and by other movements as well.

AUTHOR

Despite the claim in the first verse that the letter was written by "Simon Peter, a servant and apostle of Jesus Christ"—a claim bolstered by personal reminiscence (1:13–14 and 1:15–16)—most modern scholars do not think that the apostle Peter wrote this letter. Indeed, for no other letter in the New Testament is there a greater consensus that the person who is named as the author could not, in fact, be the author. Scholars cite six main arguments.[9]

    1. The Greek of the letter could not have been written by the apostle Peter. The vocabulary and style are quite distinct from that of 1 Peter. And even if the Greek of 1 Peter is not the apostle's—because of the use of an amanuensis or because it is pseudonymous—the Greek of 2 Peter could not be attributed to Peter. The vocabulary is different from anything found elsewhere in the New Testament: fifty-seven words are not found elsewhere in the New Testament, thirty-two of which are not in the LXX either. Some of these words seem to be taken from Greco-Roman religion and philosophy. The style is repetitive and somewhat cumbersome, "pretentiously elaborate," as Kelly puts it.[10] Most scholars are therefore convinced that the author of 2 Peter must have had a Greco-Roman formal education and that Peter, the fisherman from Galilee, could therefore not have written the Greek of the letter.

    2. The false teaching combated in the letter is second-century Gnosticism.

    3. In 2 Peter 3:15–16, the author implies that the letters of Paul belong to the category "the Scriptures" (αἳ γραφαί [*hai graphai*]). Some scholars think that the text implies a full collection of the Pauline epistles, and such a collection could not, of course, have existed during Peter's lifetime. But the text implies nothing about a collection, referring only to an undetermined number of letters. Nevertheless, a problem for Petrine authorship still exists in that it is argued that New Testament letters were not regarded as canonical until after the time of the apostle Peter.

    4. References to the death of "our fathers" (interpreted as the earliest Christian generation), the importance of apostolic tradition (cf. 3:2, 16), and the teaching that the parousia might be delayed for a long time (3:8) betray a late date, when the hope for an imminent parousia had faded and a fixed ecclesiastical

---

[9]For these points, see especially Kümmel, 430–33; Joseph B. Mayor, *The Epistle of St. Jude and the Second Epistle of St. Peter: Greek Text with Introduction, Notes and Comments* (Grand Rapids: Baker, 1979 [=1907]), cxv–cxlv; Bauckham, *Jude, 2 Peter,* 158–62; Ernst Käsemann, "An Apologia for Primitive Christian Eschatology," in *Essays on New Testament Themes* (Philadelphia: Fortress Press, 1982), 169–77.

[10]Kelly, *A Commentary on the Epistles of Peter and of Jude,* 228.

authority had arisen. These two factors are but two of the characteristics of a movement some scholars have dubbed "early Catholicism." The fading of the early church's expectation—based on Jesus' own teaching (e.g., Mark 9:1; 13:30)—that their Lord would return in the very near future led to a series of theological and practical adjustments. Church order and the passing on of apostolic teaching suddenly became important means to secure the health of the church for a long period in history. Ethical demands became less radical and more "accommodating" to the culture. Scholars discern these tendencies in a number of New Testament books, which they then relegate to the post-apostolic period. Prominent among these is 2 Peter.[11]

5. The letter is not strongly attested in the early church. Kelly claims that "no NT document had a longer or tougher struggle to win acceptance than 2 Peter."[12] It is claimed that no church father before Origen quotes from the letter; it is missing in the Muratorian Canon (c. 180–200[13]); Eusebius expressed doubts about its authenticity, classifying it among the "disputed" books (*H.E.* 3.3.1); and Jerome, likewise, notes that Peter "wrote two epistles which are called Catholic, the second of which, on account of its difference from the first in style, is considered by many not to be by him" (*De vir. ill.* i).

6. The reference to Peter's imminent death and the focus on remembrance of Peter's teaching (1:12–15) reveal that the letter takes the form of a "testament." This form, modeled on Jacob's final words of advice to his twelve sons in Genesis 49, became popular in the period of Second Temple Judaism (the best-known book is *The Testaments of the Twelve Patriarchs*). But these "testaments" were invariably pseudonymous.

Scholars who are convinced by these arguments conclude that 2 Peter is pseudonymous, perhaps the work of a "Petrine school."[14] The most attractive form of this proposal holds that the author of 2 Peter would simply have been using a well-known literary device—the "testament"—that was not intended to deceive anyone and would not, in fact, have deceived anyone.[15]

---

[11]On early Catholicism and 2 Peter, see esp. Käsemann, "Apologia," 169–95.

[12]Kelly, *A Commentary on the Epistles of Peter and of Jude*, 224.

[13]On the date of this canon, see chap. 4, n. 7.

[14]On the "Petrine school" hypothesis, see especially M. L. Soards, "1 Peter, 2 Peter, and Jude as Evidence for a Petrine School," *ANRW* 2.25.5 (1988), 3827–49.

[15]See esp. Bauckham, *Jude, 2 Peter*, 131–35, 158–62; also H. Paulsen, *Der zweite Petrusbrief und der Judasbrief* (Göttingen: Vandenhoeck & Ruprecht, 1992), 93–95; Achtemeier/Green/Thompson, 527–29. David Meade takes a similar view, arguing that references to people like Peter at the beginning of many books was not intended to be a claim to authorship but was only a claim that the book carried on the tradition associated with that name (David G. Meade, *Pseudonymity and Canon: An Investigation Into the Relationship of Authorship and Authority in Jewish and Earliest Christian Tradition*, WUNT 39 [Tübingen: Mohr-Siebeck, 1986]; cf. 179–86 on 2 Peter).

Nevertheless, while they are decidedly in the minority, some scholars continue to maintain that Peter wrote this letter. They respond to the six points above as follows.

1. While certainly distinctive, the Greek of 2 Peter is not as distinctive as many scholars have suggested. Several scholars note that the author may be consciously imitating the so-called "Asiatic" style, a form of rhetorical speech that was becoming popular at the time.[16] Could not Peter, seeking to create as much common ground as possible with his readers, have adopted just such a style? The claim that a Galilean fisherman could not have written the Greek of the letter cannot stand without knowing much more than we do about how that Galilean fisherman spent the thirty or more years between abandoning his nets and the date of this letter. Ministry in Asia Minor, Greece, and Rome might very well have furnished Peter with a training in Greek, and even a rhetorical style, similar or even superior to that to be had in the classroom.

2. As we have noted above, it is very improbable that the false teachers were gnostics. Since we cannot identify the particular heresy being taught, we cannot assign a date to the letter on this basis. Certainly there is nothing that the false teachers are propagating that could not fit the period of Peter's life.

3. How early were New Testament books considered to be canonical? We cannot be sure. But we do know that the apostles considered their own words to carry an authority tantamount to Scripture (e.g., 1 Cor. 5:3; 2 Cor. 10:11; 2 Thess. 2:15; 3:14). They thought of themselves as inspired by the same Spirit who inspired the prophets (1 Pet. 1:10–12). They expected their letters to be read in church along with the Old Testament (cf. Col. 4:16).[17] Moreover, Paul can cite a word of Jesus as "Scripture" (1 Tim. 5:18—although, of course, many scholars consider this also to be a late work). Therefore, while somewhat unexpected, the description of Paul's letters as "Scripture," especially since the reference is allusive, is possible by the end of Peter's life.

4. While 2 Peter has sometimes been singled out as a showcase for "early Catholicism," the epistle in fact fits the model badly. The letter does not emphasize the church as an institution or refer to traditional forms of teaching as the basis for its response to heresy. As Bauckham concludes, "the label 'early Catholic' is no help in understanding 2 Peter."[18] The more important question is whether the specific elements of the letter often singled out as indicative of a late date must in fact be so taken. "Our fathers" in 3:4 (NIV) could refer to an earlier Christian generation; but it could equally well refer—as it often does in the New Testament—to the "ancestors" of the Jewish nation, and especially to

---

[16]E.g., Green, *The Second Epistle of Peter*, 18; Bo Reicke, *The Epistles of James, Peter, and Jude*, AB 37 (New York: Doubleday, 1964), 146–47; Watson, *Invention, Arrangement, and Style*, 144–46.

[17]See Green, *Second Epistle of Peter*, 29–30, for these points.

[18]Bauckham, *Jude, 2 Peter*, 153.

the patriarchs, Abraham, Isaac, and Jacob. For, as vv. 5–7 make clear, the "scoffers" were apparently citing the unchangeableness of the world since creation as evidence for their skepticism about the parousia. Peter's appeal to the "command" of Jesus Christ (3:2) and to the letters of Paul (3:15–16) does not imply the existence of a fixed tradition. And Peter's teaching about the parousia is quite in keeping with the thrust of the New Testament in general: its coming cannot be dated (3:8, 10), so believers need to be prepared for that day to arrive at any time (3:9, 11–12).

5. The problem with the attestation of 2 Peter has been exaggerated. A number of second-century writers may show influence from it, while *The Apocalypse of Peter* (110–40) almost certainly does.[19] The omission of the book from the Muratorian Canon (along with 1 Peter, it should be noted) may be due to the fragmentary state of the text. And Eusebius, while noting the doubts of some of his contemporaries, himself affirmed the authenticity of the letter. Therefore, while, as Green puts it, "no book of the Canon is so poorly attested among the Fathers," at the same time "no excluded book has nearly such weight of backing as 2 Peter."[20] More important, there is a good explanation for the neglect of 2 Peter. So many Petrine forgeries were in existence that the Fathers moved very cautiously in separating out 2 Peter from these other spurious books.[21]

6. Similarities between 2 Peter and the Jewish "testament" form are clear. But we must not forget that the overarching genre category to which 2 Peter belongs is the letter. And all the evidence we possess suggests that pseudepigraphical letters were not common in the first or second centuries and that the few we know about were rejected as forgeries. L. R. Donelson concludes, after a thorough study of the evidence from the early Christian centuries: "No one ever seems to have accepted a document as religiously and philosophically prescriptive which was known to be forged. I do not know of a single example."[22]

---

[19]Robert E. Picirilli, "Allusions to 2 Peter in the Apostolic Fathers," *JSNT* 33 (1988): 57–83; Bauckham, *Jude, 2 Peter,* 162; Riesner, "Der Zweite Petrus-Brief und die Eschatologie," 127.

[20]Green, *The Second Epistle of Peter,* 13. Granted the strength of the early evidence, Michael J. Kruger concludes that the burden of proof must fall on those who deny the letter's authenticity. We should ask, he claims, "What reasons are there to put 2 Peter out of the canon considering its authentication by the consensus of the 4th-century church?" ("The Authenticity of 2 Peter," *JETS* 42 [1999]: 651).

[21]See esp. Green, *The Second Epistle of Peter,* 14–15.

[22]L. R. Donelson, *Pseudepigraphy and Ethical Argument in the Pastoral Epistles,* HUT 22 (Tübingen: Mohr-Siebeck, 1986), 11. We have good reason to think that the early Christians also condemned *any* kind of book that was pseudonymous; Green notes the strong reaction against *The Gospel of Peter* and *The Acts of Paul and Thecla* (*The Second Epistle of Peter,* 32). See the extended discussion on pseudonymity in chap. 8 of this volume.

The very fact that 2 Peter was accepted as a canonical book, then, presumes that the early Christians who made this decision were sure that Peter wrote it.[23] The appeal to the "testament" form as a way of preserving both the letter's pseudonymity and its acceptability must therefore be rejected.

We are therefore left with the choice of accepting the letter's *prima facie* claim to have been written by the apostle Peter or viewing it as a forgery hardly deserving of canonical status. Since the usual arguments against Petrine authorship are not finally conclusive,[24] we prefer the former option.

DATE AND PROVENANCE

Scholars who consider 2 Peter pseudonymous generally date the epistle in the early second century, claiming that it must postdate the apostolic generation and the collection of Paul's letters.[25] If, however, Peter wrote the letter, it must be dated before about A.D. 65, when reliable early tradition records Peter's death as a martyr at the time of the Emperor Nero's persecution of Christians in Rome. A few interpreters date 2 Peter before 1 Peter.[26] But the letter itself suggests that Peter wrote very shortly before his death. In 1:13–14, referring to the Lord's prophecy about his death in John 21:18–19, he says the time of his "departure" from this life is near (1:13–14). Peter is almost certainly, then, writing from Rome,[27] and perhaps with Nero's persecution already underway. The apostle senses that the time for the fulfillment of the Lord's prophecy about his martyrdom had come, and he writes a final note of advice and caution before his end.

DESTINATION AND AUDIENCE

Peter addresses his letter to "those who through the righteousness of our God and Savior Jesus Christ have received a faith as precious as ours" (1:1). The lack

---

[23]The connection between authorship and canonicity is the burden of the article by Stanley E. Porter, "Pauline Authorship and the Pastoral Epistles: Implications for Canon," *BBR* 5 (1995): 105–23.

[24]Michael J. Gilmour concludes that the usual historical arguments about the authorship of 2 Peter are inconclusive ("Reflections on the Authorship of 2 Peter," *EQ* 73 [2001]: 291–309).

[25]See, e.g., Brown, 767; Kümmel, 305; H. Balz and W. Schrage, *Die "katolischen" Briefe: Die Briefe des Jakobus, Petrus, Johannes, und Judas,* NTD, 12th ed. (Göttingen: Vandenhoeck & Ruprecht, 1980), 122–28. Bauckham, however, prefers a much earlier date: A.D. 80–90 (*Jude, 2 Peter,* 157–58).

[26]E.g., Zahn, 2.209–10; Riesner, "Der Zweite Petrus-Brief und die Eschatologie," 129, 133–35.

[27]Peter wrote 1 Peter from Rome (= "Babylon" in 5:12) shortly before this; and we know that he was martyred in Rome.

of specifics led Christians in the past to classify 2 Peter as a "general" or "catholic" letter, it being thought that it was addressed generally to the church worldwide. But the letter suggests a definite and restricted destination. The Christians to whom he writes are being threatened by a specific false teaching, and they have apparently received, or are aware of, at least two letters of Paul (3:15). Perhaps a group of churches in the same area is addressed.[28] We could be more precise about the destination if we were sure that 2 Peter 3:1—"this is now my second letter to you"—alludes to 1 Peter. For 1 Peter is explicitly addressed to Christians in the north-central part of Asia Minor. A few scholars question whether 1 Peter is in view here,[29] but it seems likely.[30] And if this is so, then we can also conclude that the readers of 2 Peter, like those of 1 Peter, were mainly Gentiles. Some internal evidence from 2 Peter supports this conclusion. When Peter compares the readers' faith to "ours" in 1:1, the "ours" probably refers to Jewish Christians. And Peter's warning about escaping "the corruption in the world caused by evil desires" (1:4) fits Christians from a Gentile background better than Jewish Christians. To be sure, some scholars have argued for a Jewish audience because of the many allusions in chapter 2 to Old Testament and Jewish traditions.[31] But we know that Gentile converts to Christianity early became acquainted with the Old Testament, and each of the allusions Peter makes would have made good sense to those who had this kind of knowledge. The language of the letter points in the same direction. As we have seen, many scholars find it difficult to believe that Peter could have used some of the philosophical and religious terminology that we find in 2 Peter. But we should see this as evidence that Peter has adapted his message to his audience. By using religious language that his readers would have been familiar with, he contextualizes the gospel to meet their needs.

> *Many scholars don't believe that Peter could have used some of the philosophical and religious terminology we find in 2 Peter, but we should see this as evidence that Peter has adapted his message to his audience.*

2 PETER IN RECENT STUDY

As we have seen, 2 Peter is not mentioned often by the fathers of the church—probably because it is short and so focused on false teaching that it makes little significant theological contribution. These same factors, coupled with the "early Catholic" label that some have put on the letter, undoubtedly explain the relative paucity of academic work on 2 Peter. In fact, Robert Wall decries the relative neglect of 2 Peter in biblical-theological formulations, arguing that the letter

---

[28]Bauckham, *Jude, 2 Peter*, 165–66.

[29]E.g., Green, *The Second Epistle of Peter*, 123–24.

[30]G. H. Boobyer identifies a number of similarities between the letters, including some parallels between 2 Peter 3:1–4 and 1 Peter ("The Indebtedness of 2 Peter to 1 Peter," in *New Testament Essays: Studies in Memory of T. W. Manson*, ed. A. J. B. Higgins [Manchester: University of Manchester Press, 1959], 34–53).

[31]Zahn, 2.194–209.

provides an important complement to the theology of 1 Peter.[32] However, while not nearly as numerous as the studies on most other New Testament books, several recent books and articles devoted to 2 Peter have taken up some of the typical emphases of recent New Testament academic work. Rhetorical criticism is applied to 2 Peter (and Jude) by Duane F. Watson in his monograph *Invention, Arrangement, and Style: Rhetorical Criticism of Jude and 2 Peter.* Note also the attempt to explain the polemic in 2 Peter according to modern understandings of rhetoric by du Toit.[33] The contemporary interest in locating New Testament books within their social context is exemplified in the commentary of Jerome Neyrey. He ignores some of the usual questions of New Testament introduction, such as author, date, provenance, and destination, and focuses on the way the letter communicates within its social context. Toward this end, Neyrey isolates key first-century cultural-social concerns—honor/shame, patron/client relationships, purity/pollution—and couples these with insights from modern sociology (e.g., the relationship between the physical body and the social body) to offer a new approach to the letter. The reminder that the New Testament documents must be read in their social context is a salutary one, and Neyrey offers some valuable insights into the letter. Nevertheless, social science criticism should be seen as a complement to, and not a replacement of, traditional historical-critical approaches.

THE CONTRIBUTION OF 2 PETER

Peter's second letter contributes to our understanding of the faith in three ways in particular.

First, his extended polemic against the false teachers reminds us of the seriousness of deviating from the faith either in theology or in morals. The particular false teachers against whom Peter writes strayed theologically by casting doubt on the parousia and coming judgment (1:16–21; 3:3–4). Their immoral lifestyle, so picturesquely condemned by Peter in chapter 2, was probably an offshoot of their theological error. Why worry about morality if there is no day of reckoning? Second Peter implies that theological error quickly translates into moral error. At the same time, Peter's strong pronouncements of condemnation (2:4, 9, 12, 13, 17, 20–21) remind us that both theological and moral error are serious matters.

Second, Peter enhances our understanding of biblical eschatology through his positive teaching about the day of the Lord in 3:7–13. The text abounds with textual, exegetical, and theological difficulties, but Peter's main point seems to

---

[32]Robert W. Wall, "The Canonical Function of 2 Peter," *BI* 9 (2001): 64–81.

[33]A. du Toit, "Vilification as a Pragmatic Device in Early Christian Epistolography," *Bib* 75 (1994): 403–12.

be clear: this world is destined to be "destroyed" by fire and to be replaced by a "new heaven and a new earth" (v. 13). The promise of a "new heaven and new earth" comes from Isaiah 65:17 and 66:22, and the image is taken up also, of course, in Revelation 21:1. More controversial is Peter's claim of a final great conflagration. Many scholars think that the idea has been taken from Stoicism. But the Stoics taught that the world would be destroyed and re-created many times—an idea far distant from Peter's portrayal of a single and decisive event. More likely is that Peter has drawn the idea from Old Testament imagery that associates fire with the day of the Lord (Isa. 30:30; 66:15–16; Nah. 1:6; Zeph. 1:18; 3:8), imagery that was taken even further in Jewish apocalypses. To be sure, some think that Peter uses destruction by fire in this passage as a metaphor for the judgment of human beings. But the focus on the physical world in verses 5–7 and the reference to "heavens and earth" seems deliberately chosen to refer to the physical universe (see v. 5).

Only the book of Revelation in the New Testament speaks so directly about the cosmic effects of the day of the Lord. Just how Peter envisages the transfer from this world to the "new heavens and new earth" is not clear. Does he think that the new will replace the old? or that the old will be transformed into the new? The language of "destruction" in verses 10–12 might point to the former. But other biblical texts seem to point toward a transformation (Matt. 19:28; Acts 3:21; Rom. 8:19–22). And the language of "destroy" in the Bible can refer simply to judgment without implying annihilation—as it almost certainly does in verse 7, where Peter refers to the "destruction of the ungodly." Peter's language does not allow us to resolve the issue certainly. Probably there is continuity as well as discontinuity in the shift from the present heavens and earth to the new heavens and earth.[34]

Peter's third signal contribution is to highlight the importance of "memory" in the Christian life. Peter claims that he wrote both his letters "as reminders to stimulate you to wholesome thinking" (3:1); and the concept of memory and its negative correlate, "forgetting," play a key role in the letter, especially in the transition from introduction to body (1:12, 13, 15) and in the concluding part of the letter (3:5, 8). Peter's use of the "testament" form undoubtedly has something to do with this emphasis. In his last words to his spiritual charges, Peter does not focus on new teaching but on encouraging believers to remember the teaching they have already received. This "remembering," of course, is no mere intellectual act; it is an act of the will, an imprinting of God's truth on the heart and the mind in a way that cannot help but lead to practical consequences. In place of the novelty propagated by the false teachers, Peter reasserts the old truth of the apostolic teaching.

---

[34]See on this, e.g., Murray Harris, *Raised Immortal: Resurrection and Immortality in the New Testament* (Grand Rapids: Eerdmans, 1983), 168–70.

BIBLIOGRAPHY

Richard J. **Bauckham**, *Jude, 2 Peter,* WBC 50 (Waco: Word, 1983) ▮▮H. **Balz** and W. **Schrage**, *Die "katolischen" Briefe: Die Briefe des Jakobus, Petrus, Johannes, und Judas,* NTD, 12th ed. (Göttingen: Vandenhoeck & Ruprecht, 1980) ▮▮Charles **Bigg**, *A Critical and Exegetical Commentary on the Epistles of St. Peter and St. Jude,* ICC (Edinburgh: T. & T. Clark, 1902) ▮▮G. H. **Boobyer**, "The Indebtedness of 2 Peter to 1 Peter," in *New Testament Essays: Studies in Memory of T. W. Manson,* ed. A. J. B. Higgins (Manchester: University of Manchester Press, 1959), 34–53 ▮▮J. D. **Charles**, *Virtue Amidst Vice: The Catalog of Virtues in 2 Peter 1,* JSNTSup 150 (Sheffield: Sheffield Academic Press, 1997) ▮▮Michel **Desjardins**, "The Portrayal of the Dissidents in 2 Peter and Jude: Does It Tell Us More About the 'Godly' than the 'Ungodly'?" *JSNT* 30 (1987): 89–102 ▮▮L. R. **Donelson**, *Pseudepigraphy and Ethical Argument in the Pastoral Epistles,* HUT 22 (Tübingen: Mohr-Siebeck, 1986) ▮▮Anders **Gerdmar**, *Rethinking the Judaism-Hellenism Dichotomy: A Historiographical Case Study of Second Peter and Jude,* ConBNT 36 (Stockholm: Almqvist & Wiksell, 2001) ▮▮Michael J. **Gilmour**, "Reflections on the Authorship of 2 Peter," *EQ* 73 (2001): 291–309 ▮▮idem, "Second Peter in Recent Research: A Bibliography," *JETS* 42 (1999): 673–78 ▮▮Michael **Green**, *The Second Epistle General of Peter and the General Epistle of Jude,* 2nd ed. (Grand Rapids: Eerdmans, 1987) ▮▮idem, *2 Peter Reconsidered* (London: Tyndale, 1961) ▮▮E. **Käsemann**, "An Apologia for Primitive Christian Eschatology," in *Essays on New Testament Themes* (Philadelphia: Fortress Press, 1982), 169–95 ▮▮J. N. D. **Kelly**, *A Commentary on the Epistles of Peter and of Jude,* HNTC (New York: Harper, 1969) ▮▮R. **Knopf**, *Die Briefe Petri und Judä,* KEK, 7th ed. (Göttingen: Vandenhoeck & Ruprecht, 1912) ▮▮Steven J. **Kraftchick**, *Jude, 2 Peter,* ANTC (Nashville: Abingdon, 2002) ▮▮Michael J. **Kruger**, "The Authenticity of 2 Peter," *JETS* 42 (1999): 645–71 ▮▮Richard N. **Longenecker**, "On the Form, Function, and Authority of the New Testament Letters," in *Scripture and Truth,* ed. D. A. Carson and John D. Woodbridge (Grand Rapids: Zondervan, 1983), 101–14 ▮▮Joseph B. **Mayor**, *The Epistle of St. Jude and the Second Epistle of St. Peter: Greek Text with Introduction, Notes and Comments* (Grand Rapids: Baker, 1979 [=1907]) ▮▮David G. **Meade**, *Pseudonymity and Canon: An Investigation Into the Relationship of Authorship and Authority in Jewish and Earliest Christian Tradition,* WUNT 39 (Tübingen: Mohr-Siebeck, 1986) ▮▮Douglas J. **Moo**, *2 Peter and Jude,* NIVAC (Grand Rapids: Zondervan, 1996) ▮▮Jerome H. **Neyrey**, *2 Peter, Jude: A New Translation with Introduction and Commentary,* AB 37C (New York: Doubleday, 1993) ▮▮idem, "The Apologetic Use of the Transfiguration in 2 Peter 1:16–21," *CBQ* 42 (1980): 504–19 ▮▮idem, "The Form and Background of the Polemic in 2 Peter," *JBL* 99 (1980): 407–31 ▮▮H. **Paulsen**, *Der zweite Petrusbrief und der Judasbrief* (Göttingen: Vandenhoeck & Ruprecht, 1992) ▮▮Robert E. **Picirilli**, "Allusions to the 2 Peter in the Apostolic Fathers," *JSNT* 33 (1988): 57–83 ▮▮Stanley E. **Porter**, "Pauline Authorship and the

Pastoral Epistles: Implications for Canon," *BBR* 5 (1995): 105–23 ▮Bo **Reicke**, *The Epistles of James, Peter, and Jude*, AB 37 (New York: Doubleday, 1964) ▮R. **Riesner**, "Der Zweite Petrus-Brief und die Eschatologie," in *Zukunftserwartung in Biblischer Sicht: Beiträge Zur Eschatologie*, ed. G. Maier (Giessen: Brunnen, 1984) ▮K. H. **Schelkle**, *Die Petrusbriefe, der Judasbrief*, HTKNT (Freiburg: Herder, 1961) ▮E. M. **Sidebottom**, *James, Jude, and 2 Peter*, NCB (London: Thomas Nelson, 1967) ▮M. L. **Soards**, "1 Peter, 2 Peter, and Jude as Evidence for a Petrine School," *ANRW* 2.25.5 (1988), 3827–49 ▮A. **Vögtle**, "Die Schriftwerdung der apostolischen Paradosis nach 2 Petr. 1,12–15," in *Neues Testament und Geschichte*, *Fs.* O. Cullmann, ed. H. Baltensweiler et al. (Zürich: TVZ; Tübingen: Mohr-Siebeck, 1972), 297–306 ▮Robert W. **Wall**, "the Canonical function of 2 Peter," *BI* 9 (2001): 64–81 ▮Duane F. **Watson**, *Invention, Arrangement, and Style: Rhetorical Criticism of Jude and 2 Peter*, SBLDS 104 (Atlanta: SP, 1988).

CHAPTER TWENTY-THREE

1, 2, 3 JOHN

CONTENT AND STRUCTURE

1 John

Like the Epistle to the Hebrews, 1 John does not exhibit any of the formal characteristics that are normally associated with the openings of letters written in Greek in the first century. Nevertheless, the personal references, the common ties the author shares with his readers, and the explicit historical referents (e.g., 2:19) make it clear that this writing was not intended to be an abstract paper, a mere brochure,[1] or a tractate for all Christians everywhere.[2] It was meant to be read as a pastoral letter to a congregation or to a number of congregations. There is something to be said for the view that its atypical form is a reflection of its author's intention to send it to several congregations along with an accompanying note personalizing each delivery: 2 John could be one such note and may be the only one that has come down to us (3 John does not qualify nearly so well).

The structure of 1 John is disputed, largely because John takes up a number of themes and keeps returning to them in slightly different connections. One of the best surveys of structure is by Marshall,[3] though his own proposal—that no structure is believable because John probably connects his various sections by virtue of mere associations of ideas—sounds more haphazard than the flow of the epistle will allow. Although most see between the prologue (1:1–4) and the conclusion (5:14–21) two large sections (1:5–2:29; 3:1–5:13) broken down in various ways, Schnackenburg's suggestion of three divisions has much to

---

[1]Stephen S. Smalley, *1, 2, 3 John*, WBC (Waco: Word, 1984), xxxiii. For a survey of the discussion on 1 John's literary genre, see R. E. Brown, *The Epistles of John*, AB 30 (Garden City: Doubleday, 1982), 86–92.

[2]Contra Kümmel, 437.

[3]I. Howard Marshall, *The Epistles of John*, NICNT (Grand Rapids: Eerdmans, 1978), 22–27.

commend it: the first treats fellowship with God as walking in the light (1:5–2:17), the second deals directly with the present situation of the church or churches to which John addresses himself (2:18–3:24), and the third divides those who belong to God from the "world" by the tests laid out in the epistle (4:1–5:12).[4] Virtually all sides agree that John lays down three tests: (1) true believers must believe that Jesus truly is the Christ come in the flesh, and this belief must work itself out in (2) righteousness and (3) love.

2 and 3 John

It is widely agreed that these two short epistles bear the form of letters. Ostensibly written to "the lady chosen by God and to her children," 2 John is directed to another congregation—whether to a house church within the same city or to the church of another city is unclear—to warn against the dangers inherent in traveling preachers, some of whom are "deceivers, who do not acknowledge Jesus Christ as coming in the flesh" (7). But even here, John insists that true believers walk not only in the truth but in transparent love for one another, in line with the command "you have heard from the beginning" (6). This message occupies the central section (4–11) between the introduction (1–3) and the conclusion (12–13).

By contrast with 2 John, which mentions no one by name except Jesus Christ, 3 John is addressed to Gaius about the activities of Diotrephes, who not only "loves to be first" (9) but has become so powerful that he is even refusing the emissaries of the writer, ejecting from the church those who take a softer line. John encourages Gaius (who may have belonged to the church where Diotrephes held court) to follow instead the example of Demetrius and warns that he is coming to expose Diotrephes.

AUTHOR

The external evidence is consistent and can be briefly stated. Possible allusions are found in many of the documents from the end of the first century and the first half of the second century. The most likely are the following: (1) Clement of Rome describes God's elect people as being "perfected in love" (*1 Clem.* 49:5; 50:3, c. A.D. 96; cf. 1 John 2:5; 4:12, 17–18); (2) the *Didache* (estimated date ranges from 90 to 120) has something similar (10:5), a parallel made more impressive in this case by the mention in the next verse of the world passing away (10:6; cf. 1 John 2:17); (3) the *Epistle of Barnabas* (c. 130) speaks of Jesus as "the Son of God come in the flesh" (5:9–11; 12:10; cf. 1 John 4:2; 2 John 7); (4) Polycarp warns against deceiving false brothers in these terms: "For every-

---

[4]R. Schnackenburg, *The Johannine Epistles: A Commentary* (New York: Crossroad, 1992), 11–13. His subdivisions are less insightful.

one who does not confess Jesus Christ to have come in the flesh is Antichrist" (*Phil.* 7:1, c. 135), surely dependent on 2 John 7 and 1 John 4:2–3; cf. 1 John 2:22. Numerous other allusions are proposed, most of them less plausible than these.[5]

However, the first author to refer specifically to a Johannine epistle as the work of John is Papias of Hierapolis in the middle of the second century, who, according to Eusebius (*H.E.* 3.39.17), "used testimonies drawn from the former Epistle of John." It is important to note that "former" is Eusebius's word, not Papias's; one cannot deduce from it that Papias knew of more than one Johannine epistle. By the time of Irenaeus (c. A.D. 180), at least the first and second epistles are explicitly attributed to John, the disciple of the Lord and the author of the fourth gospel (*Adv. Haer.* 3.16.18). Writing at about the same time, Clement of Alexandria knows of more than one Johannine epistle, since he refers to "the greater epistle" and ascribes it to the apostle John (see *Strom.* 2.15.66; cf. 3.4.32; 3.5.42; 4.16.100). Thereafter the evidence becomes plentiful.[6]

The external evidence for 2 and 3 John is not as strong as for 1 John, partly owing to the fact that they are so brief and somewhat less theologically focused and thus unlikely to be quoted so often. We have already noted that 2 John is linked with 1 John by Irenaeus and that Clement knows of more than one Johannine epistle. So far as our records go, it is Origen (d. A.D. 253) who first mentions all three epistles, but according to Eusebius (*H.E.* 6.25.10), he does so in part to acknowledge that not everyone accepted the authenticity of 2 and 3 John. Origen's pupil Dionysius of Alexandria (d. 265) insisted that John the apostle wrote the fourth gospel and 1 John (but not Revelation) and knew about 2 and 3 John (see further the section "Adoption into the Canon" below). Never is any of the three Johannine epistles attributed to anyone other than John the son of Zebedee.

As for the internal evidence, nothing in any of the Johannine Epistles points unambiguously to a specific author. All the arguments finally turn on the relation of these epistles to the fourth gospel. Methodologically, it is easiest first to deal with the relation of 1 John to the gospel, and then to consider the relation of 2 John and 3 John to 1 John.

A superficial reading of the fourth gospel and 1 John reveals many striking similarities in theme, vocabulary, and syntax.[7] The same stark polarities prevail:

> *The external evidence for 2 and 3 John is not as strong as for 1 John, but never is any of the three Johannine epistles attributed to anyone other than John the son of Zebedee.*

---

[5]The evidence is conveniently set out in A. E. Brooke, *A Critical and Exegetical Commentary on the Johannine Epistles,* ICC (Edinburgh: T. & T. Clark, 1912), liiff. See Brown, *Epistles of John,* 6ff., for a slightly more skeptical view of the evidence.

[6]This evidence is nicely summarized in Colin G. Kruse, *The Letters of John,* PNTC (Grand Rapids: Eerdmans, 2000), 11–14.

[7]The most comprehensive lists of linguistic similarities and dissimilarities are still found in Brooke, *Johannine Epistles,* i–xix, 235–42, and in Robert Law, *The Tests of Life* (1914; reprint, Grand Rapids: Baker, 1979), 341–63.

light and darkness, life and death, truth and falsehood, love and hate—with no third alternative. The same relatively simple syntax is found in both, combined with a marked penchant for parallelism. Poythress has shown that the prevalence of asyndeton and the relative infrequency of intersentence conjunctions in both documents argue for the same author.[8] Stott has demonstrated that the same "scheme of salvation" pervades both 1 John and the fourth gospel.[9] To offer but a few examples: In our unredeemed state we are "of the devil," who has sinned and lied and murdered "from the beginning" (1 John 3:8/John 8:44); we are "from the world" (2:16; 4:5/8:23; 15:19); therefore, we "sin" (3:4/8:34) and "have" sin (1:8/9:41), "walk in the darkness" (1:6; 2:11/8:12; 12:35), and are "dead" (3:14/5:25). God loved us and sent his Son to be "the Savior of the world" (4:14/4:42) so that "we might live" (4:9/3:16). Believing in him or in his "name" (5:13/1:12), we pass from death to life (3:14/5:24). We "have life" (5:11, 12/3:15, 36; 20:31), for life is in the Son of God (5:11–12/1:4; 14:6). This is what it means to be "born of God" (2:29; 3:9; 5:4, 18/1:13). There is much more of the same.

Those who argue for a different author for the two documents usually appeal to three kinds of phenomena.[10]

1. There are subtle but significant differences between John and 1 John in both doctrine and wording, even when they are formally parallel. For instance, it is commonly argued that only in John is the λόγος (*logos*, "Word") personal (see John 1:1, 14); in 1 John 1:1–4, the "word" is the "word of life," and it is the life that is personal. In the fourth gospel, the Holy Spirit is the παράκλητος (*paraklētos*, "Paraclete" or "Counselor," John 14–16); in 1 John 2:1, it is Jesus himself. John affirms that "God is Spirit"; 1 John says, rather, that he is light (1:5) and love (4:8, 16). In the fourth gospel, the death of Jesus is presented as his being "lifted up" and "glorified"; in the epistle, the purpose of Jesus' death is propitiatory (2:2; 4:10). It is often argued that in the fourth gospel the eschatology is profoundly "realized" (i.e., people enjoy eternal life already), while in 1 John much more place is given to Jesus' future, personal coming (2:28; 3:2; 4:17).

On close examination, these and similar objections carry little weight. It is true that the prologue to the fourth gospel uses λόγος *(logos)* to refer to the preincarnate Son of God, but it uses the same word numerous times throughout the

---

[8]Vern Poythress, "The Use of the Intersentence Conjunctions *De, Oun, Kai,* and Asyndeton in the Gospel of John," *NovT* 26 (1984): 312–34; idem, "Testing for Johannine Authorship by Examining the Use of Conjunctions," *WTJ* 46 (1984): 350–69. Cf. discussion in chap. 6 on the fourth gospel.

[9]John R. W. Stott, *The Letters of John,* TNTC (Grand Rapids: Eerdmans, 1988), 21–23.

[10]See esp. C. H. Dodd, *The Johannine Epistles,* MNTC (London: Hodder & Stoughton, 1946), esp. xlviiff.; Georg Strecker, *The Johannine Letters,* Hermeneia (Minneapolis: Fortress Press, 1996), xxxv–xlii; or, at a more popular level, D. Moody Smith, *First, Second, and Third John,* Interpretation (Louisville: John Knox Press, 1991), 11–15.

gospel with its more common meaning of "message" (e.g., 8:31), and some scholars think that even in 1 John the personal usage has not disappeared (i.e., they understand the text to say that it is the "word of life," not the "life," that has appeared). That Jesus should be called the παράκλητος *(paraklētos)* in 1 John is scarcely surprising, for Jesus in John insists he is sending *another* Paraclete (John 14:16): one could surely argue common authorship from this, rather than disparate authorship. The suggestion that the one who wrote that God is spirit is unlikely to have written that he is light and love is almost silly on the face of it. If the fourth gospel looks at Jesus' death as a "lifting up" and a "glorification," it is partly because it is focusing on the historical Jesus and partly because it is intent on showing that the cross was not the defeat that some Jews thought it was. If 1 John casts Jesus' death in terms of its propitiatory significance, that owes much to his polemical purpose: he is concerned to show that sin has serious effects, and the only way to remove those effects is by the provision that God himself has made. In any case, the presentation of Jesus' death in the fourth gospel is not univocal: other themes intrude there and overlap with those of 1 John (see John 1:29; 3:14–16, 36; 6:51; 10:11, 15; 11:49–52; etc.). We should speak of complementarity of vision and thought, of differentiation in application, not of mutual contradiction. Finally, although the eschatological emphases of the two books are not identical, the complementary truth is also found in both books: the fourth gospel reserves space for futurist eschatology (5:28–29; 6:39–40, 44, 54; 11:24–26; 12:48; 14:3), while 1 John insists that those who believe may have confidence that they experience eternal life as a present possession.

2. There are words and expressions in John's gospel not found in 1 John, and vice versa (see Brooke's commentary for the lists). Today most scholars acknowledge that nothing decisive can be based on these lists. The divergent vocabularies enjoy greater similarity than those of, say, Luke and Acts, known to come from the same pen, or of Ephesians and Colossians, or of 1 Timothy and Titus. "The variations in phrase suggest common authorship rather than servile, or even intelligent, copying."[11]

3. Those who are persuaded that a "Johannine School" accounts for the Johannine corpus of the New Testament are inclined to see different members of the "school" writing different parts of the corpus (i.e., the Gospel of John, the Johannine Epistles, and Revelation).[12] Indeed, the "we" who apparently attest the reliability of the author of the fourth gospel (at least on one reading of John 21:24) might be the same "we" that stands behind 1 John (e.g., 1 John 1:1–5).[13]

---

[11]Brooke, *Johannine Epistles,* xvi.

[12]E.g., John Painter, *1, 2, 3 John,* SacPag 18 (Collegeville: Liturgical Press, 2002), 44–51; R. Alan Culpepper, *The Gospel and Letters of John,* IBT (Nashville: Abingdon, 1998), esp. chap. 3, "The Gospel and Letters as the Literature of a Community."

[13]So Painter, *1, 2, 3 John,* 45–46.

But a great deal is being made to ride on a "Johannine School" whose existence is not more certain than a number of questionable inferences (on which see below) and on the term "we," which experience in reading the New Testament shows can turn up in highly diverse contexts and with even more diverse referents.

Although a few scholars have argued that 2 John and 3 John were written by a person other than the one who wrote 1 John, not many have been persuaded by them. The links of both vocabulary and theme are too many (granted the brevity of the second and third epistles) to justify such skepticism (e.g., "Jesus Christ has come in the flesh" [2 John 7/1 John 4:2]; "deceiver" and "antichrist" [2 John 7/1 John 2:22]; those who love and do good show that they are "from God" [3 John 11/1 John 3:10; 4:4, 7]).

More difficult to explain, on the traditional view, is why the author of 2 John and 3 John should refer to himself as ὁ πρεσβύτερος (*ho presbyteros*, "the elder"). This certainly does not give justification to the position of Eusebius, and of many modern scholars who have followed him, who argue that the fourth gospel and the Johannine Epistles were written, not by John the apostle, but by John the elder (see discussion in the section "Author" in chap. 6). Note, however, that there is nothing anomalous about an apostle designating himself as an elder (1 Pet. 5:1; cf. Papias, in the discussion just reported). Furthermore, the term "elder" can refer to an old man (see Philem. 9, using the cognate term πρεσβύ-'της [*presbytēs*]).[14] If the author is John the son of Zebedee, the last of the apostles, it is not inappropriate for him to make a dual allusion. This interpretation may be strengthened by observing the article: John refers to himself as "*the* elder." He could scarcely refer to himself as "the apostle": that would surely sound a trifle pompous, even if he was the last of the Twelve to survive. He was simply *an* apostle (note the usage of Paul in Rom. 1:1, and of Peter in 1 Peter 1:1). But he could be *the* elder in the Ephesus region, precisely because he was not just an ordinary elder.

Two other factors argue for apostolic authorship.[15]

1. Although in most of the "we" passages in the Johannine Epistles the pronoun includes the Christian readers and is set over against the "they" of the "world" (i.e., non-Christians, including heretics—e.g., 2:3; 3:2, 11; 4:19), in a few passages the most reasonable exegesis suggests that the "we" refers to the author and his fellow eyewitnesses in contrast to the "you" of the Christian readers. This is particularly true in 1:1, 3; 4:14; 5:6–7. Despite vigorous protests to the contrary, in these passages the author distinguishes himself as writer from his

---

[14]Indeed some, as we shall see below, argue that even πρεσβύτερος (*presbyteros*) primarily refers to an old man.

[15]These points are argued in detail by such commentators as B. F. Westcott (*The Epistles of St John* [1892; reprint, Appleford: Marcham Manor, 1966]; Marshall (*Epistles of John*), and Stott (*Letters of John*). See also the forthcoming NIGTC commentary on the Johannine Epistles by D. A. Carson.

readers, as eyewitness from second-generation believers, and as authoritative teacher from those who are being taught.

2. The latter distinction (between authoritative teacher and those being taught) deserves expansion. It is not simply the sweep and tone of the writer's authority that is at issue, though that is impressive (e.g., 2:1–2, 8, 15, 17, 23, 28; 3:6, 9; 4:1, 8, 16; 5:21), not least when he brands certain people as liars, deceivers, and antichrists (cf. Gal. 1:8, 9). Rather, it is that he does so *across congregations* (2 and 3 John). Indeed, it is this fact that prompts Käsemann to argue that the author of the Johannine Epistles was not the apostle John but the first of what became monarchical bishops, leading directly to the stance of Ignatius that the church exists where the bishop is.[16] That means, of course, that it is Diotrephes who is trying to preserve the more primitive pattern of local church autonomy. Few have agreed with Käsemann; the more obvious motive for Diotrephes' power play is simply that he loved to be first (3 John 9)—a problem not unknown in either the ancient church (see 2 Cor. 10–13) or the modern. But that means that the most obvious explanation for this cross-congregational authority is that the author of these epistles was an apostle, since elders per se did not, so far as we know, enjoy such authority.

Almost inevitably, the most fundamental reasons advanced today for rejecting Johannine authorship of these epistles turn, not on the hard evidence or on source theories[17] that have almost universally been abandoned, but on reconstructions of the development of the Johannine "circle" or "community" or "school." This reconstruction exercises such controlling power in contemporary discussion that the possibility of apostolic authorship is prematurely ruled out in favor of a document refracting the light from community beliefs. These matters are treated at some length in chapter 6 above on the fourth gospel, and they also have a bearing on our understanding of the purpose of these epistles (see the section "Purpose" below).

PROVENANCE

Whether one thinks in terms of apostolic authorship or of a Johannine school, the most likely provenance is Ephesus. The evidence that John the son of Zebedee (and for that matter Philip the evangelist and his daughters) moved to Ephesus at the time of the Jewish War (A.D. 66–70) and ultimately died there is not overwhelming, but it is consistent. It depends in large part on the witness of Polycrates, bishop of Ephesus, writing to Victor, bishop of Rome, c. 190 (so

---

[16]E. Käsemann, "Ketzer und Zeuge," *ZTK* 48 (1951): 292–311.

[17]In particular, J. C. O'Neill, *The Puzzle of 1 John* (London: SPCK, 1966); Rudolf Bultmann, *The Johannine Epistles*, ET Hermeneia (Philadelphia: Fortress Press, 1973); W. Nauck, *Die Tradition und der Charakter des ersten Johannesbriefes*, WUNT 3 (Tübingen: Mohr-Siebeck, 1957). Cf. Marshall, *Epistles of John*, 27–30.

Eusebius, *H.E.* 3.31.3; 5.24.2), and the witness of Irenaeus (*Adv. Haer.* 3.1.1), who knew both Papias and Polycarp. Several witnesses could also point to the tombs of Philip and his daughters and of the beloved disciple (see discussion in chaps. 6 and 24).

Those who judge the external evidence to be late and unreliable deny any connection with Ephesus and postulate other centers, largely on the basis of conceptual links with literature thought to come from those centers. Thus, on the grounds that the Johannine Epistles are tied in some way to the fourth gospel and that the gospel shares some conceptual links with *Odes of Solomon,* thought to have originated in Syria, Kümmel cautiously postulates Syria.[18] Methodologically, this approach appears to be far too cavalier with specific historical witnesses and far too trusting of our ability to establish the closest conceptual links (not to mention our utter ignorance of how far a document such as the *Odes of Solomon* circulated toward the end of the first century).

DATE

The date of the Johannine Epistles is entirely bound up with the date of the fourth gospel and their relationship to it. As we have seen, although a few date the Gospel of John before A.D. 70, and a majority assign it to the last decade of the first century, we have cautiously suggested 80–85. The question to be posed, then, is whether the epistles were written before or after the gospel.

Certainty is impossible; the decision depends, finally, on one's understanding of the respective purposes of the fourth gospel and of the Johannine Epistles. We will argue that the epistles, unlike the gospel, were written in part to establish and encourage the faith of Christians in the wake of rising controversy over proto-Gnosticism (see the section "Purpose" below). Since this movement was on the ascendancy at the end of the first century (though it did not reach full flowering until well into the second century), it seems best to date the epistles *after* the fourth gospel. This judgment is confirmed by the evidence that suggests that at least some of the gnostic heretics were using the fourth gospel for their own purposes: certainly John was a favorite of gnostics in the second century (though John 1:14, "the Word became flesh," was ultimately destructive of their beliefs). Probably, therefore, some time elapsed between the publication of the fourth gospel and that of the epistles, enough at least to allow what John perceives to be the improper use of his earlier work to gain enough steam to cause schism in the church (see 1 John 2:19). Constrained at the other end by apparent allusions to 1 John in some of the subapostolic fathers, it appears best to date the Johannine epistles to the early 90s.

---

[18]Kümmel, 246–47, 445.

One recent commentator argues that 2 and 3 John were written around A.D. 100, and possibly as late as 130, with 1 John and the Gospel of John coming not later than the middle of the second century.[19] Quite apart from the highly conjectural reconstructions in which he engages, he must question the dating of P^{52}, which contains a portion of John 18 and is usually dated to 125: he assigns this and other early evidence "to the realm of the creation of pious legends,"[20] assigning them to A.D. 200 or even later. The patristic evidence is handled with similar aplomb. Although one wants to admire independent judgment, it is difficult to be quite so positive about technically sophisticated scholarship that discounts so much of the evidence.

DESTINATION

First John mentions no addressee and preserves no specific greetings, formal thanksgiving, or any of the other formal touches that normally characterize a first-century letter. The second epistle is addressed to "the lady chosen by God and to her children," almost certainly not a respected Christian matron and her family but a local congregation. It can scarcely be thought that this epistle is directed to the universal church, since it reports greetings from "the children of your sister, who is chosen by God" (2 John 13), which must be understood to be salutations from another congregation: the universal church has no sister. Even so, it is just possible that the author chose this form of address not only for its symbolic connections but also because it was flexible enough to be used with respect to *several* congregations.[21] The third epistle is addressed to an individual, Gaius by name, not to be associated with Gaius of Corinth (1 Cor. 1:14; Rom. 16:23) or Gaius of Macedonia (Acts 19:29), and probably not Gaius of Derbe (Acts 20:4)—though a fourth-century document, the *Apostolic Constitutions* (7.46.9), makes this latter connection. The document is late, and "Gaius" was an exceedingly common name in the Roman Empire.

The geographic destination cannot be more than an inference from what is reconstructed of the documents' provenance. Probably, therefore, these epistles were sent to churches (and an individual) somewhere in the Ephesus area, including, perhaps, the territory spanned by the seven churches of Revelation 2–3.

Probably these epistles were sent to churches (and an individual) somewhere in the Ephesus area, including, perhaps, the territory spanned by the seven churches of Revelation 2–3.

PURPOSE

A few scholars have argued that 1 John is pastoral and not polemical, that there is no need to reconstruct a group of heretics or secessionists. The first epistle

---

[19]So Strecker, *The Johannine Letters,* xxxv–xlii.

[20]Ibid., xli n. 78.

[21]See Judith M. Lieu, *The Second and Third Epistles of John* (Edinburgh: T. & T. Clark, 1986), 64–68.

was written to foster Christian assurance and to ward off possible developments in the community's theology that could have ultimately led to schism;[22] or, if there was trouble, it was caused by nothing more than the undisciplined exercise of prophetic gifts.[23]

Although John does intend to edify his readers, most scholars rightly reject this view as an inadequate explanation of the evidence. Some believers have already seceded (1 John 2:18–19), and John is writing to warn his readers about false teachers who are actively trying to deceive them (2:26). Paul's prophecy to the Ephesian elders (Acts 20:29–30), renewed to Timothy (2 Tim. 3:1–7; 4:3–4), was coming true: "savage wolves" were rending the flock, and John labels them "false prophets" (1 John 4:1), "deceivers" (2 John 7), and "antichrists" (1 John 2:18; 4:3; 2 John 7). Probably their secession owed much to their failure to convert more of the congregation(s) to which they once belonged (1 John 2:18–19): many Christians by their adherence to the truth had "overcome them" (1 John 4:4). Still, John finds he must reassure the faithful and explain in straightforward terms the differences between the two groups and thereby give them grounds for their own assurance and confidence before God (1 John 5:13) at a time when they were being made to feel inferior and spiritually threatened.

The differences between John's readers and John's opponents are substantial. The secessionists denied that Jesus was the Christ (2:22)—not apparently meaning that they disbelieved that Jesus was the Messiah of Old Testament expectation, but that the human Jesus really was the Christ, the Son (2:23; 4:15; 2 John 9). They denied that Christ had come in the flesh (4:2; 2 John 7). Judging by 1 John 1:6–10, they also denied that they were in any sense dominated by or even subject to sin: it did not inhere in their nature, display itself in their behavior, or hinder their fellowship with God. Meanwhile their own conduct was so haughty, loveless, and schismatic that they denied the very gospel they claimed that only they understood, prompting some of the more hesitant amongst those left behind to wonder at times if they had the Spirit at all (see 2:26–27).

What, then, could account for this matrix of errors? Probably the majority of contemporary commentators still hold that the external evidence demands that we postulate one of three movements:

Gnosticism. This theosophical potpourri was anchored in neoplatonic dualism, which fostered a dichotomy between matter (evil) and spirit (good). In the classic gnostic myth that comes down to us from third-century sources,[24] there is an ultimate Father from whom a variety of spiritual beings emanate. One of

---

[22]So Judith M. Lieu, "'Authority to Become Children of God': A Study of 1 John," *NovT* 23 (1981): 210–28.

[23]So F. Büchsel, *Die Johannesbriefe,* THNT (Leipzig: Deichert, 1933), 4–5; cf. G. M. Burge, *The Anointed Community: The Holy Spirit in the Johannine Tradition* (Grand Rapids: Eerdmans, 1987).

[24]See *DBI,* 264–66.

these, Wisdom, tries to act independently from another, Thought, and unintentionally produces a misshapen being, Wisdom's son Ialdabaoth, who steals enough of her power to become the creator of the spiritual powers who rule this world and with whose help the physical universe, including Adam and Eve, comes into being. The biblical stories are then retold to accommodate the changes. The fall narrative (Gen. 3), for instance, becomes an attempt to impart true knowledge (*gnosis*) to those imprisoned in evil matter by the action of their evil creator. Adam ultimately begets Seth, who receives some pure spirit. This sets up a dichotomy in the human race: some have their origins in this spirit-life; others are nothing but matter. Later versions of the myth tell of a gnostic redeemer who explains their origins to the "elect" (i.e., not to those who are sovereignly chosen by God, but to those who are chosen by virtue of their possession of spirit-life and who therefore have the capacity to receive this "knowledge," thereby liberating them). The structure of gnostic myths varies considerably.[25] Valentinus, in the second century, taught that the Godhead is made up of thirty "aeons," regarded as male and female pairs. Among them, Intellect and Truth produced Word and Life, who in turn produced Man and Church. Whatever the precise structure, some scholars argue that the heretics presupposed by 1 and 2 John have been influenced by Gnosticism and are concerned with deliverance from the flesh by the acquisition of knowledge.

Docetism. More particularly, a branch of Gnosticism known as Docetism (from δοκέω [*dokeō*], "it seems") applied the same reasoning so as to reject the incarnation. Docetism asked, How can a spirit-being, "Christ" or the "Son of God," good by definition, actually become flesh, which is evil by definition? Although such a spirit-being may temporarily *assume* it, it could never *become* it. Docetists so misconceived the true locus of evil that they fell into sin and puffed themselves up with gnostic pride.

The heresy of Cerinthus. No less commonly, appeal is made to Cerinthus, about whom we learn chiefly from Irenaeus and Eusebius. Eusebius, for instance, preserves Polycarp's report that John the apostle fled the bathhouse in Ephesus when he found that Cerinthus was in it, on the ground that God could at any time reach down and destroy this "enemy of the truth" (*H.E.* 3.3.4; cf. 3.28.6; 4.14.6). Irenaeus gives an account of Cerinthus's heretical views (*Adv. Haer.* 1.16.1; 3.2.1, 7, 8), which severed the man Jesus from the divine Christ (or from the Spirit, according to Epiphanius's report of the heresy [*Haer.* 28.1]). The Christ (or the Spirit) came upon Jesus at his baptism and left him to suffer alone on the cross (since the Christ/Spirit himself is impassible).

---

[25]See esp. the many important sources brought together by James M. Robinson, ed., *The Nag Hammadi Library*, rev. ed. (San Francisco: HarperSanFrancisco, 1990), beginning, perhaps, with *The Apocryphon of John* (104–23) and *Eugnostos the Blessed*, set out in parallel with *The Sophia of Jesus Christ* (220–43).

The explanatory power of these proposed backgrounds is considerable, but caution must be exercised. For example, Marshall points out that some of what we know about Cerinthus (e.g., his belief that Jesus was the son of an inferior creator-god) is not reflected in the Johannine Epistles, while some of what the epistles oppose (e.g., the claim to sinlessness) is not known to have been associated with Cerinthus.[26] Schnackenburg, who favors a background in Docetism of the kind opposed by Ignatius a mere decade or two later (e.g., *Smyr.*1–3; *Magn.* 11; *Trall.* 9–10), nevertheless acknowledges that there are critical differences: for example, the Docetists opposed by Ignatius are tied to Jewish rites and beliefs, of which there are no traces in the Johannine Epistles.[27]

Above all, the dates of Gnosticism itself are disputed. Full-blown Gnosticism is almost certainly an amalgam of Jewish, Christian, and pagan deviations, an amorphous movement whose flowering is not only later than the New Testament but is also so diverse in its manifestations that very few generalizations can be made. The most plausible conclusion is that the movement was gaining strength when John wrote his epistles, and some of the contours of the particular form it took in this case can be hesitantly delineated from these letters. Doubtless this form cannot be precisely identified with any of the manifestations that have come down to us independently. The point is that rather few have been preserved for us, and the most we can say is that so far as the epistles of John go, the discernible errors and abysmal practices that are being opposed have much in common with the Docetism and Cerinthianism of which we know all too little.

Some contemporary scholars, however, pay little attention to this external evidence and go down one of two other tracks. Some think that the explanation of 1 John lies in its rhetoric, which, rightly understood, does not demand that we invest too much time seeking opponents: the rhetoric is self-justifying, not polemical.[28] (We briefly assess some of this work below under "Recent Study.") Others seek to trace out divergent streams of "Johannine Christianity," largely by establishing trajectories from the fourth gospel (or from perceived distinguishable traditions in the fourth gospel) to a complex situation that can be retrieved from the Johannine Epistles.[29] Virtually all of these scholars exhibit far more sympathy for John's opponents than John did, and sometimes more for the opponents than for John himself.

---

[26]Marshall, *Epistles of John*, 18.

[27]Schnackenburg, *The Johannine Epistles*, 17–24.

[28]E.g., John Painter, *1, 2, and 3 John*, passim; Ruth B. Edwards, *The Johannine Epistles*, NTG (Sheffield: Sheffield Academic Press, 1996); Judith Lieu, *The Theology of the Johannine Epistles* (Cambridge: Cambridge University Press, 1991).

[29]E.g., Brown, *Epistles of John*; Smalley, *1, 2, 3 John*; Kenneth Grayston, *The Johannine Epistles*, NCB (Grand Rapids: Eerdmans, 1984); J. L. Houlden, *The Johannine Epistles*, BNTC (London: Black, 1973); Pierre Bonnard, *Les épîtres johanniques*, CNT (Geneva: Labor & Fides, 1983); Georg Strecker, *The Johannine Letters*.

Smalley, who at least is sympathetic to the epistles, nevertheless insists that distinctions between heresy and orthodoxy have not yet been made at this period in the church's life—an extraordinary judgment when Paul was making them almost half a century earlier (see Gal. 1:8–9; 2 Cor. 11:4; see further John 14:6; Acts 4:12). Houlden thinks the fourth gospel is adventurous and speculative and judges that the "dissidents" simply wanted to go a little farther in the same direction, while the epistles are a conservative "rearguard action" to reassert traditional doctrine. Smalley postulates three groups—one that denies Jesus' humanity, another that denies Jesus' deity, and a group of seceders (who may have overlapped with the others)—all quite apart from the traditionalists.

Brown engages in considerable speculation and uncontrolled inferences to tease out the contours of two groups, divided, not in their acceptance of the authority of the fourth gospel, but in its interpretation. One group seceded; the other group produced at least 1 John and 2 John; and the two groups disagreed fundamentally, especially in the areas of Christology, ethics, eschatology, and pneumatology (with his commentary primarily focusing on the first two). Brown does not think it is possible for the historian to judge which group understood the fourth gospel correctly. Because of this stance, he argues, for instance, that the secessionists did not deny the humanity of Jesus (since they held John 1:14 to be authoritative) but denied that the humanity of Jesus was significant for revelation or salvation. Perhaps—but the texts do not say so, and a great deal is made to rest on the postulate that both sides adopted the fourth gospel. Brown thinks that in the aftermath of the struggle the "secessionists" (he cannot think of them as heretics) drifted off into the later "heretical" movements (Cerinthianism, Montanism, Docetism, etc.), while those remaining "were swallowed up by the 'Great Church.'"[30]

Detailed evaluation is not possible in short compass. Methodologically, the heart of the problem is the heaping up of merely possible inferences (see discussion in chap. 6 and below in "The Johannine Epistles in Recent Study") and the too-ready distancing from the external sources. It still seems best to conclude that John is combating proto-Gnosticism, an embryonic Docetism or Cerinthianism that has already divided Christians. Over against the emphases of his opponents—emphases that he frankly aligns with all that is non-Christian—John stresses the truth that Jesus is Christ come in the flesh and that genuine belief in this Jesus works itself out in obedience to the commands of God and in love for God's people.

If this is approximately correct, the purpose of 2 John is primarily to warn a congregation or house church against admitting traveling teachers who espouse such false teaching. Although many have attempted to find similar heresy behind 3 John (whether in Diotrephes or in the writer!), the epistle itself betrays no such

---

[30]Brown, *Epistles of John,* 103.

aberrations and is perhaps nothing other than an apostolic warning against someone who is attempting to appropriate all local authority. Even so, we would have
to conclude that this was taking place against the background established by the
other two epistles. We might therefore speculate that Diotrephes was using the
danger of heresy to build his own power base. But it is hard to imagine that he
himself is a heretic, or John would surely have denounced him for it.

TEXT

The detailed work of Richards,[31] supplemented marginally by the work of
Amphoux,[32] has shown that in all probability the text of the Johannine Epistles
is supported by three text types—Alexandrian (with three subgroups), Byzantine (seven subgroups), and Mixed (three subgroups)—not two or four, as some
have argued.

Only a few passages contain variants of substantial exegetical significance,
the most notorious being the addition of the "Trinitarian witnesses" at 1 John 5:7–
8a: "For there are three that bear record in heaven, the Father, the Word, and the
Holy Ghost: and these three are one. And there are three that bear witness in
earth" (KJV). This is certainly a gloss. It is found in no Greek manuscript before
the fourteenth century, except for one eleventh- and one twelfth-century manuscript, where the words have been added in the margin by a much later hand. None
of the early Greek fathers quotes the words, and it is quite certain that had they
known of them, they would have used them in the ancient Trinitarian debates.
None of the ancient versions supports the gloss, including the early editions of the
(Latin) Vulgate. The words first appear in a fourth-century Latin treatise (not a
biblical manuscript), after which some Latin fathers start to use them.

ADOPTION INTO THE CANON

The earliest witnesses to the Johannine Epistles have already been surveyed.[33]
The first mention of all three epistles is in a context that reports at least some
hesitation as to the suitability of 2 and 3 John for inclusion in the canon: Origen
(c. A.D. 231) writes that John "left an epistle of a very few lines and, it may be,
a second and a third, for not all say that these [i.e., the second and the third] are
genuine" (quoted by Eusebius, *H.E.* 6.25.10). Eusebius (c. 325) includes 1 John
among the *homologoumena*, or acknowledged books, but places 2 and 3 John

---

[31]W. L. Richards, *The Classification of the Greek Manuscripts of the Johannine Epistles*, SBLDS 35 (Missoula: SP, 1977).

[32]B. Amphoux, "Note sur le classement des manuscrits grecs de 1 Jean," *RHPR* 61
(1981): 125–35.

[33]See Lieu, *Second and Third Epistles*, 5–36.

among the *antilegomena*, the disputed books (*H.E.* 3.25.2–3)—though he says they are "well known and acknowledged by most," whether they were written by John the apostle or by "another of the same name" (certainly referring to the "John the elder" theory, which depends at least in part on his misreading of Papias; see the section "Author" in chap. 6). He himself is persuaded that all three Johannine Epistles were written by John the apostle (*H.E.* 6.25.10). The Muratorian Canon refers to two epistles by John, but probably 1 and 2 John are in mind, not 2 and 3 John.

First John belongs to a group of New Testament epistles often called catholic, or general, because they are not addressed to a specific community or individual. Origen applies the term "catholic" to 1 John (*Comm. on Matt.* 17.19) and his disciple Dionysius, bishop of Alexandria, speaks of 1 John as John's "catholic epistle," possibly in contrast to 2 and 3 John (*H.E.* 7.25.7, 10). A little later, 2 and 3 John were reckoned among the seven catholic epistles (James, 1–2 Peter, 1–3 John, Jude—so Eusebius, *H.E.* 2.23.25), where "catholic" has come to mean almost "canonical"—that is, canonical in addition to the canonical epistles of Paul. All three Johannine Epistles are included in Athanasius's list of twenty-seven New Testament books (A.D. 367) and in the lists approved by the Councils of Hippo (393) and of Carthage (397). The Peshitta included 1 John but not 2 and 3 John. Not until the next century, with the publication of the Philoxenian version (508), were the two shorter epistles (along with 2 Peter, Jude, and Revelation, which had also been omitted) included in a Syriac New Testament. In Reformation times, debates over the authorship of 2 and 3 John were again raised, both on the Roman Catholic side (Cajetan) and in the humanist tradition represented by Erasmus, but not over their canonicity.

1, 2, AND 3 JOHN IN RECENT STUDY

With few exceptions (though they are notable),[34] the driving force behind many studies of the Johannine Epistles until about a decade ago was the attempt to delineate the contours—more, the trajectories of the changing contours—of the Johannine community.[35] We have already argued that this is a mistake.[36] It is not that nothing profitable can be said about the communities to which the

---

[34]E.g., Richards, *Classification;* Lieu, *Second and Third Epistles;* Edward Malatesta, *Interiority and Covenant: A Study of* εῖναι ἐν *and* μένειν ἐν *in the First Letter of Saint John,* AnBib 69 (Rome: BIP, 1978).

[35]E.g., the commentaries by Brown, Smalley, and Strecker, and such books as John Bogaert, *Orthodox and Heretical Perfectionism,* SBLDS 33 (Missoula: SP, 1977); D. Bruce Woll, *Johannine Christianity in Conflict,* SBLDS 60 (Chico: SP, 1981); Rodney A. Whitacre, *Johannine Polemic: The Role of Tradition and Theology,* SBLDS 67 (Chico: SP, 1982).

[36]See esp. chap. 6 above.

epistles were sent; rather, it is that merely possible inferences regarding those communities must not be allowed to control the exegesis. Many of the criticisms Brevard Childs levels against Brown could rightly be applied to a number of modern commentaries.[37] According to Childs, Brown's exegesis of the Johannine Epistles is made to rest so entirely on his detailed reconstructions of his opponents, including not only their theology but their motives, that the edifice becomes precariously speculative. Since Brown argues that the competing perspectives of the epistles and of the secessionists turn on different interpretations of the fourth gospel, at every point he attempts to reconstruct the origin of each doctrinal stance and the riposte; but "what purports to be an historical investigation is actually an exercise in creative imagination with very few historical controls."[38] Every clause in the text of 1 John is historicized—not simply passages that call for it (e.g., 2:19). The result is a flattening of exegesis in which virtually every passage serves exclusively as polemic, and entire ranges of exegetical options are foreclosed; the necessary circularity in all historical reconstructions is in danger of becoming vicious. For instance, the sin unto death (5:16–17) is simply identified with the sin of the secessionists. There is a continuing need for treatments of the Johannine Epistles that are less speculative in their handling of historical reconstructions and more profound in their reflection on theological, canonical connections.

While this focus on the history and profile of the Johannine community shows no sign of abating, the last decade or so has nevertheless witnessed a broadening of research foci. The current interest in the literary and rhetorical character of New Testament texts has found its exponents in the study of the Johannine Epistles.[39] We noted above that some of this emphasis on rhetoric leads some scholars to attempt a reading of 1 John that is depolemicized (see n. 27). Although Griffith does not put quite so much emphasis on the function of rhetoric, his conclusions are similar: he argues that 1 John is not in the least a polemical book, but simply a hortative treatise: John is not fighting anyone, but is exhorting people to persevere in the gospel, largely against the kind of Jewish inroads (he argues) that stand behind debates in Galatians.[40] That someone can

---

[37]Childs, 482–85.

[38]Ibid., 483.

[39]E.g., Hans-Josef Klauck, "Zur rhetorischen Analyse der Johannesbriefe," *ZNW* 81 (1990): 205–24; Duane F. Watson, "1 John 2:12–14 as *Distributio, Conduplictio*, and *Expolitio*: A Rhetorical Understanding," *JSNT* (1989): 97–110; idem, "A Rhetorical Analysis of 2 John According to Greco-Roman Conventions," *NTS* 35 (1989): 104–30; idem, "A Rhetorical Analysis of 3 John: A Study in Epistolary Rhetoric," *CBQ* 51 (1989): 479–501; idem, "Amplification Techniques in 1 John: The Interaction of Rhetorical Style and Invention," *JSNT* 51 (1993): 99–123.

[40]Terry Griffith, *Keep Yourselves from Idols: A New Look at 1 John*, JSNTSup 233 (Sheffield: Sheffield Academic Press, 2002).

seriously argue such a case reminds us how many of our reconstructions are built on disputable inferences, and it demands that we check the foundations again. In this instance, however, it is difficult to deny a polemical thrust to this first epistle, in the light of 2:18–19, and its implications for the surrounding verses. And the view that the danger against which John is warning is a return to Judaism, rather than the threat of proto-Gnosticism, strikes us as historically odd: it probes very little into the texture of the Greco-Roman world, and it does not explain why 1 John is in substance and emphasis so very different from books like Galatians and Hebrews, where something rather more akin to the dangers Griffith sees are actually being confronted. Other slightly "maverick" positions are worth weighing. In chapter 17 (on the Pastoral Epistles), we noted the contribution of R. Alastair Campbell, whose provocative work on "elders" is equally applicable (and disputable) with reference to 2 John and 3 John.

THE CONTRIBUTION OF THE JOHANNINE EPISTLES

Taken together, the Epistles of John stand poised as a demonstration of the critical importance of testing all attempts to rearticulate the gospel by the immutables of the gospel revelation. Doubtless John's opponents saw themselves as being on the leading edge of Christian reflection (2 John 9). By contrast, John reverts to what was "from the beginning," to the testimony of the first eyewitnesses, to incontrovertible christological givens, to the perennial newness of the "old" command to love one another, to the irrefragable connection between genuine faith and obedience. This stance has a bearing on what teachings a church will listen to (2 John). At the practical level, whether heresy stands behind 3 John or not, this holistic vision insists that there is no place for petty gurus in the church who will not bow to apostolic admonition and authority.

The Johannine Epistles make an important contribution to the doctrine of assurance (see 1 John 5:13). If other New Testament writings make it clear that the objective grounds of our confidence before God are in Christ and his death and resurrection on our behalf, such that Christian assurance is not much more than a concomitant of genuine faith, these epistles insist that a distinction must be made between genuine and spurious faith. Spurious faith does not have the right to assurance before God; genuine faith can be authenticated not only by the validity of its object (in this case, the belief that Jesus is Christ come in the flesh) but also by the transformation it effects in the individual: genuine Christians learn to love one another and obey the truth. Christian assurance is not, for John, an abstract good; it is intimately tied to a continuing and transforming relationship with the covenant God, who has revealed himself in Jesus Christ.

The Johannine Epistles open an unrivaled window onto at least one part of the New Testament church toward the end of the apostolic age. Though their treatment of certain subjects is distinctive, here there is measured but emphatic

Taken together, the Epistles of John stand poised as a demonstration of the critical importance of testing all attempts to rearticulate the gospel by the immutables of the gospel revelation.

emphasis on eternal life that was with the Father and has been mediated by the Son (1 John 1:2); on the Son's atonement (2:1–2; 3:8; 4:10; 5:6); and on the Holy Spirit (2:20–27; 3:24–4:6). These documents afford us the opportunity to draw some lines, however hesitantly, between the church as reflected in the earliest writings of the New Testament and the church at the end of the first century, and constitute the sinews that stretch out toward the subapostolic fathers and the patristic era.

BIBLIOGRAPHY

Chr. B. **Amphoux**, "Note sur le classement des manuscrits grecs de 1 Jean," *RHPR* 61 (1981): 125–35 ▥John **Bogaert**, *Orthodox and Heretical Perfectionism*, SBLDS 33 (Missoula: SP, 1977) ▥Pierre **Bonnard**, *Les épîtres johanniques*, CNT (Geneva: Labor & Fides, 1983) ▥A. E. **Brooke**, *A Critical and Exegetical Commentary on the Johannine Epistles*, ICC (Edinburgh: T. & T. Clark, 1912) ▥Raymond E. **Brown**, *The Epistles of John*, AB 30 (Garden City: Doubleday, 1982) ▥F. **Büchsel**, *Die Johannesbriefe*, THNT (Leipzig: Deichert, 1933) ▥Rudolf **Bultmann**, *The Johannine Epistles*, ET Hermeneia (Philadelphia: Fortress Press, 1973) ▥G. M. **Burge**, *The Anointed Community: The Holy Spirit in the Johannine Tradition* (Grand Rapids: Eerdmans, 1987) ▥R. Alan **Culpepper**, *The Gospel and Letters of John*, IBT (Nashville: Abingdon Press, 1998) ▥C. H. **Dodd**, *The Johannine Epistles*, MNTC (London: Hodder & Stoughton, 1946) ▥Ruth B. **Edwards**, *The Johannine Epistles*, NTG (Sheffield: Sheffield Academic Press, 1996) ▥Kenneth **Grayston**, *The Johannine Epistles*, NCB (Grand Rapids: Eerdmans, 1984) ▥Terry **Griffith**, *Keep Yourselves from Idols: A New Look at 1 John*, JSNTSup 233 (Sheffield: Sheffield Academic Press, 2002) ▥Martin **Hengel**, *The Johannine Question* (London: SCM, 1989) ▥J. L. **Houlden**, *The Johannine Epistles*, HNTC (San Francisco: Harper, 1973) ▥E. **Käsemann**, "Ketzer und Zeuge," *ZTK* 48 (1951): 292–311 ▥Hans-Josef **Klauck**, *Der erste Johannesbrief*, EKKNT 23/1 (Zürich: Benziger / Neukirchen-Vluyn: Neukirchener Verlag, 1991) ▥idem, *Der zweite und dritte Johannesbrief*, EKKNT 23/2 (Zürich: Benziger / Neukirchen-Vluyn: Neukirchener Verlag, 1992) ▥idem, "Zur rhetorischen Analyse der Johannesbriefe," *ZNW* 81 (1990): 205–24 ▥Colin G. **Kruse**, *The Letters of John*, PNTC (Grand Rapids: Eerdmans, 2000) ▥Robert **Law**, *The Tests of Life* (1914; reprint, Grand Rapids: Baker, 1979) ▥Judith M. **Lieu**, "'Authority to Become Children of God': A Study of 1 John," *NovT* 23 (1981): 210–28 ▥idem, *The Second and Third Epistles of John* (Edinburgh: T. & T. Clark, 1986) ▥idem, *The Theology of the Johannine Epistles* (Cambridge: Cambridge University Press, 1991) ▥Edward **Malatesta**, *Interiority and Covenant: A Study of* εἶναι ἐν *and* μένειν ἐν *in the First Letter of Saint John*, AnBib 69 (Rome: BIP, 1978) ▥I. Howard **Marshall**, *The Epistles of John*, NICNT (Grand Rapids: Eerdmans, 1978) ▥W. **Nauck**, *Die Tradition und der Charakter des ersten Johannesbriefes*, WUNT 3 (Tübingen: Mohr-Siebeck, 1957) ▥J. C. **O'Neill**, *The Puzzle of 1 John*

(London: SPCK, 1966) ▥John **Painter**, *1, 2, and 3 John*, SacPag 18 (Collegeville: Liturgical Press, 2002) ▥Vern **Poythress**, "Testing for Johannine Authorship by Examining the Use of Conjunctions," *WTJ* 46 (1984): 350–69 ▥idem, "The Use of the Intersentence Conjunctions *De, Oun, Kai,* and Asyndeton in the Gospel of John," *NovT* 26 (1984): 312–34 ▥David **Rensberger**, *1 John 2 John 3 John*, ANTC (Nashville: Abingdon Press, 1997) ▥W. L. **Richards**, *The Classification of the Greek Manuscripts of the Johannine Epistles*, SBLDS 35 (Missoula, Mont.: SP, 1977) ▥James M. **Robinson**, ed., *The Nag Hammadi Library*, rev. ed. (San Francisco: HarperSanFrancisco, 1990) ▥Rudolf **Schnackenburg**, *The Johannine Epistles: A Commentary*, 3 vols. (New York: Crossroad, 1992) ▥Stephen S. **Smalley**, *1, 2, 3 John*, WBC 51 (Waco: Word, 1984) ▥D. Moody **Smith**, *First, Second, and Third John*, Interpretation (Louisville: John Knox Press, 1991) ▥John R. W. **Stott**, *The Letters of John*, TNTC (Grand Rapids: Eerdmans, 1988) ▥Georg **Strecker**, *The Johannine Letters*, Hermeneia (Minneapolis: Fortress Press, 1996 [German orig. 1989]) ▥Duane F. **Watson**, "1 John 2:12–14 as *Distributio, Conduplictio,* and *Expolitio:* A Rhetorical Understanding," *JSNT* (1989): 97–110 ▥idem, "A Rhetorical Analysis of 2 John According to Greco-Roman Conventions," *NTS* 35 (1989): 104–30 ▥idem, "A Rhetorical Analysis of 3 John: A Study in Epistolary Rhetoric," *CBQ* 51 (1989): 479–501 ▥idem, "Amplification Techniques in 1 John: The Interaction of Rhetorical Style and Invention," *JSNT* 51 (1993): 99–123 ▥B. F. **Westcott**, *The Epistles of St John* (1892; reprint, Appleford: Marcham Manor, 1966) ▥Rodney A. **Whitacre**, *Johannine Polemic: The Role of Tradition and Theology*, SBLDS 67 (Chico: SP, 1982) ▥D. Bruce **Woll**, *Johannine Christianity in Conflict*, SBLDS 60 (Chico: SP, 1981).

CHAPTER TWENTY-FOUR

JUDE

CONTENTS

The letter of Jude is brief yet dense. The author's prose is spare and pointed, without much elaboration, and he is therefore able to pack a lot of material into a short space. Moreover, the letter follows a careful and obviously deliberate structure. The opening (vv. 1–4) contains the usual identification of author—"Jude, a servant of Jesus Christ and a brother of James"—and addressees. Similar to 2 Peter, another "general" epistle, Jude addresses his readers in terms of their theological identity rather than their geographical locale: "To those who have been called, who are loved in God the Father and kept for Jesus Christ" (v. 1). After this salutation, Jude makes the transition into the letter body in the last two verses of the opening. He indicates his original desire to write a positive note of encouragement but then introduces the reason why he has written this particular letter: false teachers have invaded the church (v. 4).

The largest part of the body of the letter is given to the false teachers (vv. 5–16). Jude proceeds in three stages (vv. 5–10, vv. 11–13, vv. 14–16). And these stages exhibit certain parallels: each uses illustrations or quotations from the Old Testament and Jewish writers to describe or pronounce condemnation on the false teachers (three of them in both stages one and two), and each applies the traditional material to the false teachers with the word "these" (οὗτοι [*houtoi*]). In the first stage, Jude cites three examples of God's judgment from the Pentateuch (the wilderness generation, the angels who sinned [cf. Gen. 6:1–3], and the people of Sodom and Gomorrah) and then puts the false teachers into the same category (vv. 8–10). In the second stage, Jude pronounces a "woe" on the false teachers and then associates them with three notorious Old Testament sinners— Cain, Balaam, and Korah (cf. Num. 16:1–35), each of whom in one way or another rebelled against the Lord. In a rapid-fire sequence, he then portrays the sinful behavior and character of the false teachers (vv. 12–13; note "these" in v. 12). The third stage of the section on false teachers again begins with a traditional reference—but this time it is not to the Old Testament but to a Jewish writing from the Old Testament Pseudepigrapha. In verses 14–15, Jude quotes *1 Enoch* 1:9 (with allusion to 60:8 and 93:3) as a way of announcing the false teachers' condemnation. He concludes with another brief description of "these" sinful people (v. 16).

Verses 17–19 effect the transition from condemnation and description of false teachers to direct encouragement of the saints. Signaling a shift in focus with the address "dear friends" (ἀγαπητοί [*agapētoi*]), Jude once again quotes tradition—but in this case the predictions of "the apostles" and the "Lord Jesus Christ" about scoffers who would arise. "These" false teachers are none other than those scoffers. Two exhortations to believers follow in verses 20–21, the second of which—"keep yourselves in God's love"—echoes the salutation—"those who . . . are . . . kept for Jesus Christ."[1] Verses 22–23 are very difficult textually, but most modern translations (such as TNIV) decide for the text containing three exhortations to the believers to reach out to those affected by the false teaching.[2]

The conclusion of the letter eschews the typical greetings, references to coworkers, travel plans, and requests for prayer in favor of a justly famous doxology (vv. 24–25).

OCCASION

Jude makes quite clear the occasion of his letter: false teachers "have secretly slipped in among" the believers to whom he writes. Jude's description of them is dominated by condemnation of their licentious lifestyle. They are boastful (v. 16), selfish (v. 12), scornful of authority (vv. 8–10), greedy (v. 12), and sexually immoral (vv. 4, 8). Claiming to be leaders of the community, they have nothing of substance to offer in their teaching (vv. 12–13). These false teachers resemble very closely the false teachers who are described and condemned in 2 Peter. For all their similarities, however, one significant difference is also to be noted: Jude makes no direct reference to the eschatological skepticism that apparently lay at the heart of the agenda of the false teachers who are condemned in 2 Peter. Some scholars therefore warn against lumping together the false

[1]Carroll D. Osburn has shown that Jude exhibits something of an inclusio in its structure ("Discourse Analysis and Jewish Apocalyptic in the Epistle of Jude," in *Linguistics and New Testament Interpretation,* ed. David Alan Black [Nashville: Broadman, 1992], 288–89).

[2]A good defense of the three-exhortation text is Sakae Kubo, "Jude 22–23: Two Division Form or Three?" in *New Testament Criticism: Its Significance for Exegesis, Fs. Bruce M. Metzger,* ed. E. J. Epp and Gordon D. Fee (Oxford: Clarendon Press, 1981), 239–53.

teachers in 2 Peter and in Jude.[3] However, while Jude never explicitly mentions eschatological skepticism, his claim that the false teachers fulfill the predictions of Jesus and the apostles about "scoffers" might point to this theological error. Probably, then, Jude and 2 Peter are writing about the same general "movement" of false teaching, with some possible difference in emphasis between the two factions they deal with.

When we try to determine just what this movement was, however, we face the same problem we confronted in 2 Peter: the descriptions of the false teachers are so vague as to make a precise identification impossible. Scholars again single out gnostics or "proto-gnostics,"[4] but none of the truly distinctive gnostic doctrines is mentioned in Jude. The data from Jude suggest rather some kind of antinomian group,[5] perhaps influenced by an "over-realized" eschatology.[6] No greater precision is possible. As with most issues connected with Jude, therefore, the specific occasion of the letter must remain uncertain.

AUTHOR

The name "Jude" in most English versions (v. 1) translates the same Greek word ('Ιουδάς [*Ioudas*]), also translated as "Judah" and "Judas." In addition to the Old Testament patriarch (and the territory named after him), five men with the name *Ioudas* are mentioned in the New Testament: "Judas Iscariot," Jesus' betrayer; "Judas the Galilean," an infamous revolutionary (Acts 5:37); "Judas son of James," one of the Twelve (Luke 6:16; Acts 1:13); "Judas, also called Barsabbas," an early Christian prophet (Acts 15:22, 27, 32); and a brother of Jesus named "Judas" (Mark 6:3; Matt. 13:55). Any of the last three men could have been intended as the referent in verse 1. But the Jude of verse 1 is also described as "a servant of Jesus Christ and a brother of James" (v. 1). This James is almost certainly the man who became a prominent leader in the early church (see Acts 15:13–21; 21:18; Gal. 2:9) and who wrote the letter we now have in the New Testament. And this James was a "brother of the Lord" (Gal. 1:19; see also

---

[3]See esp. Richard Bauckham, *Jude, 2 Peter*, WBC (Waco: Word, 1983), 154–57.

[4]E.g., H. Balz and W. Schrage, *Die "katolischen" Briefe: Die Briefe des Jakobus, Petrus, Johannes, und Judas*, NTD, 12th ed. (Göttingen: Vandenhoeck & Ruprecht, 1980), 224–25; H. Paulsen, *Der zweite Petrusbrief und der Judasbrief* (Göttingen: Vandenhoeck & Ruprecht, 1992), 46–49 (?).

[5]See, e.g., G. Sellin, "Die Häretiker des Judasbriefes," *ZNW* 76–77 (1985–86): 207–25. A few scholars theorize that the group may have been radical Paulinists (E. Earle Ellis, "Prophecy and Hermeneutic in Jude," in *Prophecy and Hermeneutic in Early Christianity*, WUNT 18 [Tübingen: Mohr-Siebeck/Grand Rapids: Eerdmans, 1978], 230–32; Bauckham, *Jude, 2 Peter*, 163–68).

[6]See Jerome H. Neyrey, *2 Peter, Jude*, AB 37C (New York: Doubleday, 1993), 31–32.

Mark 6:3/Matt. 13:55; John 7:5). So the Jude of verse 1 is the brother of the Lord mentioned in the gospels.

This conclusion is confirmed by the witness of the early church. The Muratorian Canon (A.D. 180–200?[7]) includes the letter, and Tertullian and Clement of Alexandria consider it to be canonical. To be sure, Eusebius (H.E. 2.23.25; 3.25.3) lists Jude among the "contested" writings, but the doubts that existed were probably due to the references to noncanonical writings in the letter rather than to a contrary tradition. Nevertheless, a good many contemporary scholars claim that Jude, the brother of the Lord, could not have written the letter. A few scholars have suggested that it might have been written by a Jude not mentioned elsewhere in the New Testament,[8] but this is most unlikely. Most scholars who think that Jude the brother of the Lord could not have written it conclude that the letter is pseudonymous.[9] Since we know so little about Jude and have no other writings from his hand, many of the usual arguments against authenticity are not relevant. But three reasons for thinking that Jude could not have written the letter are usually given.[10] First, it is argued that the Greek is too good to have been written by a Jew from Galilee. However, as we have noted many times in this volume, gauging the degree of felicity in a language about someone of whom we know nothing is impossible. Galilean origins simply cannot be taken to preclude a person from becoming a very effective Greek stylist.[11] Second, the letter's references to the teaching of the apostles (v. 17) and to "the faith that was once for all entrusted to the saints" (v. 4 NIV) are held to reflect a late, "early Catholic" context, when apostolic tradition had been enshrined as the touchstone for orthodoxy. But verse 17 does not refer to a body of traditional teaching but to predictions of both apostles and Jesus. That Jude is not himself an apostle is suggested by the reference, but nothing about a fixed tradition is suggested either. Nor does the text require that the apostles are in the past. "It is not the apostles themselves, but their missionary activity in founding these particular churches, which belongs to the past."[12] And the use of "faith" in the sense of "that which is to be believed" (*fides quae creditur*) rather than "the faith that believes" (*fides qua creditur*) is no indication of a late date. The usage is well

---

[7]On the date of the Canon, see chap. 4, n. 7.

[8]E.g., a Bishop Jude mentioned in an ancient list of Jerusalem bishops or an unknown Jude (see A. R. C. Leaney, *The Letters of Peter and Jude* [Cambridge: Cambridge University Press, 1967], 83, for this last option; and Kümmel, 427–28, mentions, but does not support, the other).

[9]E.g., J. N. D. Kelly, *The Epistles of Peter and of Jude* (New York: Harper & Row, 1969), 232–34.

[10]A succinct summary of these points is provided by Kelly, *The Epistles of Peter and of Jude*, 233–34.

[11]See Bauckham, *Jude, 2 Peter,* 15–16.

[12]Ibid., 13.

established in early New Testament books (e.g., Gal. 1:23; 1 Cor. 16:13). Third, the failure of Jude to mention the fact that he was a brother of Jesus is said to stand against his authorship. But this argument cuts both ways. Richard Bauckham has shown that the brothers of Jesus gained prominence in the Palestinian Christian community;[13] surely a later writer seeking to lend authority to his writing by referring to Jude would have broadcast the relationship. We may surmise that James was a significant figure in the life of the churches to whom Jude is writing, and Jude refers to him for this reason. But for the purposes of this letter, as Clement of Alexandria pointed out long ago, it was more important for Jude to identify himself as a "servant" of Jesus Christ, a title that lent authority to his writing, than as a "brother" of the Lord.[14]

Since the arguments against Jude's authorship are so weak, there is no reason not to take the claim of the letter at face value and to conclude that the author was indeed Jude the brother of the Lord.[15]

DATE, PROVENANCE, DESTINATION, AND AUDIENCE

Those who think that Jude is pseudonymous usually date it around A.D. 100.[16] However, if, as we have argued, Jude the brother of the Lord is indeed the author, then the letter cannot be dated after about A.D. 90, the latest we can realistically expect even a younger brother of Jesus to have lived. At the other extreme, how early might the letter be? Richard Bauckham has made a strong case for a date in the 50s, citing the Jewish, apocalyptic-flavored atmosphere of the letter.[17] So early a date presupposes that the literary relationship between 2 Peter and Jude is to be explained by Jude's precedence, and as we have seen, this is the prevailing scholarly opinion (see chap. 21). But it is quite possible that the reverse is true, and that Jude has used 2 Peter. If so, then we must date Jude after 2 Peter, which was probably written in A.D. 64–65. In either case, the similar descriptions of the false teaching in the letters suggests that they were written at about the same time.[18] We should probably date Jude also in the middle-to-late 60s.

---

[13]Richard Bauckham, *Jude and the Relatives of Jesus in the Early Church* (Edinburgh: T. & T. Clark, 1990), 45–133.

[14]Bigg, *A Critical and Exegetical Commentary on the Epistles of St. Peter and St. Jude,* ICC (Edinburgh: T. & T. Clark, 1901), 318.

[15]See also Bauckham, *Jude, 2 Peter,* 14–16; Michael Green, *The Second Epistle General of Peter and the General Epistle of Jude,* TNTC (Grand Rapids: Eerdmans, 1968), 42–46; Achtemeier/Green/Thompson, 533; Guthrie, 902–5; McDonald/Porter, 542.

[16]E.g., Leaney, *The Letters of Peter and Jude,* 82; Kelly, *The Epistles of Peter and of Jude,* 233–34; Balz/Schrage, *Die "katholischen" Briefe,* 226; Paulsen, *Der zweite Petrusbrief und der Judasbrief,* 44–45; Kümmel, 429; Brown, 757–58.

[17]*Jude, 2 Peter,* 13–14.

[18]Bigg, *The Epistles of St. Peter and St. Jude,* 316.

Nothing certain can be determined about the letter's provenance or destination. Despite its traditional categorization as a "general" letter, Jude was certainly written to a definite church or group of churches. And, although we might infer that Jude, as a brother of Jesus, and like his other brother, James, remained in Palestine, Paul's references to the "brothers of the Lord" in 1 Corinthians 9:5 suggests that at least some of Jesus' brothers traveled extensively. Guesses (and they are little more than that) about the location of these churches that Jude addresses include Egypt,[19] Asia Minor,[20] and Antioch.[21] More important is the profile of the readers that one can deduce from the letter. A few scholars have argued that the antinomianism of the false teachers suggests a Gentile audience. But antinomianism is not confined to Gentiles; and the degree to which the author assumes that his readers are familiar not only with the Old Testament but also with Jewish traditions points to a Jewish-Christian audience—perhaps set in the midst of a Gentile culture.[22]

> *Despite its traditional categorization as a "general" letter, Jude was certainly written to a definite church or group of churches.*

JUDE IN RECENT STUDY

Jude has been called "the most neglected book in the New Testament."[23] Though this may still be true, scholars are beginning to pay more attention to the work. In keeping with a trend evident in scholarship on many New Testament books, attention has been given recently to the rhetorical nature of Jude. Duane F. Watson has argued that the letter employs a traditional rhetorical structure, with *exordium* (the case to be argued—v. 3), *narratio* (the concerns that move the rhetor to address the matter—v. 4), *probatio* (illustrations and arguments to support the case—vv. 5–16), and *peroratio* (summary and appeal to the emotions—vv. 17–22).[24] These labels describe the argument of the letter rather accurately, though whether Jude is consciously adopting an ancient rhetorical model or simply reflecting styles of argument current in his culture is impossible to say. Adopting a modern approach to interpreting rhetoric, coupled with the recognition that texts sometimes need to be "deconstructed," Lauri Thurén warns that much of Jude's language about the false teachers, because it is stereotypical, may

---

[19]Kelly, *The Epistles of Peter and of Jude,* 237; J. J. Gunther, "The Alexandrian Epistle of Jude," *NTS* 30 (1984): 549–62.

[20]Ellis, "Prophecy and Hermeneutic in Jude," 235–36; Bauckham, *Jude, 2 Peter,* 16 (as a "strong possibility").

[21]Green, *The Second Epistle of Peter and the Epistle of Jude,* 48; Guthrie, 914.

[22]Bauckham, *Jude, 2 Peter,* 16; Guthrie, 914.

[23]The title of the 1975 article on Jude by Douglas J. Rowston (*NTS* 21 [1975]: 554–63).

[24]Duane F. Watson, *Invention, Arrangement, and Style: Rhetorical Criticism of Jude and 2 Peter,* SBLDS 104 (Atlanta: SP, 1988), 29–79; cf. also Stephan J. Joubert, "Persuasion in the Letter of Jude," *JSNT* 58 (1995): 75–87.

not actually tell us much about them.[25] J. Daryl Charles has summarized his work on Jude in a monograph that contributes valuable insights into the structure and sequence of argument in the letter.[26]

THE CONTRIBUTION OF JUDE

People do not like to dwell on the negative. That may be one reason why Jude is such a neglected letter. But we need to hear the negative: we need to understand that false teachers exist, that their teaching can be both attractive and dangerous, and that their condemnation is certain. All these points Jude makes abundantly clear. Jude's strategy in making these points is particularly effective: by associating the false teachers with sinners, rebels, and heretics in the Old Testament and Jewish tradition, Jude effectively reminds us that defections from true revelation and sound morals are to be expected in every generation. The atmosphere of postmodernism in which the church now lives requires us to guard vigilantly against the temptation to welcome heresy in the name of "tolerance."

What contribution do Jude's references to noncanonical traditions make to our understanding of the canon? Two such references (not mentioning several possible allusions) are found in the letter: the story of Michael's dispute with the devil over Moses' body in verse 9 (according to Clement of Alexandria and Origen, found in *The Assumption of Moses*); and the quotation from *1 Enoch* in verses 14–15. Jude's inclusion of this material in the midst of his references to the Old Testament has led many scholars to conclude that the Old Testament canon was not fixed in Jude's day. Yet there are indications in other New Testament books that the Old Testament canon was closed by this period of time. How then are we to explain these references in Jude? Does he hold to a wider canon than others at his time? We cannot answer these questions definitively, but two points should be made. First, Jude cites neither of these books as "Scripture"—γραφή *(graphē)* does not occur—nor does Jude use traditional formulas to introduce either text. To be sure, Jude does claim that Enoch "prophesied" (v. 14). However, this does not necessarily mean that he regards Enoch as a prophet, but only that, in the book he is using, Enoch is portrayed as prophesying. Second, Jude's reference to these texts implies nothing about his view of the books in which they are found. He may very well believe that the story about Moses' body and Enoch's prophecy are "true"; but this does not mean that he regards everything in either of the books concerned as true. And it is even pos-

---

[25]Lauri Thurén, "Hey Jude! Asking for the Original Situation and Message of a Catholic Epistle," *JSNT* 43 (1997): 451–65.

[26]J. Daryl Charles, *Literary Strategy in the Epistle of Jude* (Scranton: University of Scranton Press, 1993).

sible that Jude simply cites this material because it is well known to his audience without himself making any commitment to its truthfulness.[27]

BIBLIOGRAPHY

H. **Balz** and W. **Schrage**, *Die "katolischen" Briefe: Die Briefe des Jakobus, Petrus, Johannes, und Judas,* NTD, 12th ed. (Göttingen: Vandenhoeck & Ruprecht, 1980) ▥Richard J. **Bauckham**, *Jude and the Relatives of Jesus in the Early Church* (Edinburgh: T. & T. Clark, 1990) ▥idem, *Jude, 2 Peter,* WBC (Waco: Word, 1983) ▥idem, "The Letter of Jude: An Account of Research," *ANRW* 2.25.5 (1988), 3791–3826 ▥C. **Bigg**, *A Critical and Exegetical Commentary on the Epistles of St. Peter and St. Jude,* ICC (Edinburgh: T. & T. Clark, 1901) ▥J. Daryl **Charles**, *Literary Strategy in the Epistle of Jude* (Scranton: University of Scranton Press, 1993) ▥M. **Desjardins**, "Portrayal of the Dissidents in 2 Peter and Jude: Does It Tell Us More About the 'Godly' Than the 'Ungodly'?" *JSNT* 30 (1987): 89–102 ▥E. Earle **Ellis**, "Prophecy and Hermeneutic in Jude," in *Prophecy and Hermeneutic in Early Christianity: New Testament Essays,* WUNT 18 (Tübingen: Mohr-Siebeck/Grand Rapids: Eerdmans, 1978), 221–36 ▥I. H. **Eybers**, "Aspects of the Background of the Letter of Jude," *Neot* 9 (1975): 113–23 ▥Michael **Green**, *The Second Epistle General of Peter and the General Epistle of Jude,* TNTC, 2nd ed. (Grand Rapids: Eerdmans, 1987) ▥J. J. **Gunther**, "The Alexandrian Epistle of Jude," *NTS* 30 (1984): 549–62 ▥R. **Heiligenthal**, "Der Judasbrief: Aspekte der Forschung in den letzten Jahrzehnten," *ThR* 51 (1986): 117–29 ▥idem, *Zwischen Henoch und Paulus: Studien zum theologiegeschichtlichen Ort des Judasbriefes* (Tübingen: Franke, 1992) ▥Stephan J. **Joubert**, "Persuasion in the Letter of Jude," *JSNT* 58 (1995): 75–87 ▥J. N. D. **Kelly**, *A Commentary on the Epistles of Peter and Jude,* HNTC (New York: Harper & Row, 1969) ▥Steven J. **Kraftchick**, *Jude, 2 Peter,* ANTC (Nashville: Abingdon, 2002) ▥Sakae **Kubo**, "Jude 22–23: Two Division Form or Three?" in *New Testament Criticism: Its Significance for Exegesis. Essays in Honour of Bruce M. Metzger,* ed. E. J. Epp and Gordon D. Fee (Oxford: Clarendon Press, 1981), 239–53 ▥A. R. C. **Leaney,** *The Letters of Peter and Jude* (Cambridge: Cambridge University Press, 1967) ▥J. B. **Mayor**, *The Epistle of St. Jude and the Second Epistle of Peter* (London: Macmillan, 1907) ▥Douglas J. **Moo**, *2 Peter and Jude,* NIVAC (Grand Rapids: Zondervan, 1996) ▥Jerome H. **Neyrey**, *2 Peter, Jude,* AB 37C (New York: Doubleday, 1993) ▥Carroll D. **Osburn**, "Discourse Analysis and Jewish Apocalyptic in the Epistle of Jude," in *Linguistics and New Testament Interpretation,* ed. David Alan Black (Nashville: Broadman, 1992), 287–319 ▥H. **Paulsen**, *Der zweite Petrusbrief und der Judasbrief* (Göttingen: Vandenhoeck &

---

[27]As Charles points out, Jude's readers were apparently "into" apocalyptic, so he is probably choosing material that will communicate to them (*Literary Strategy in the Epistle of Jude,* 160–61).

Ruprecht, 1992) ▥Ruth Anne **Reese**, *Writing Jude: The Reader, the Text, and the Author in Constructs of Power and Desire*, BIS 51 (Leiden: Brill, 2000) ▥Bo **Reicke**, *The Epistles of James, Peter, and Jude*, AB 37 (New York: Doubleday, 1964) ▥Douglas J. **Rowston**, "The Most Neglected Book in the New Testament," *NTS* 21 (1974–75): 554–63 ▥K. H. **Schelkle**, *Die Petrusbriefe, der Judasbrief*, HTKNT (Freiburg: Herder, 1961) ▥G. **Sellin**, "Die Häretiker des Judasbriefes," *ZNW* 76–77 (1985–86): 207–25 ▥Lauri **Thurén**, "Hey Jude! Asking for the Original Situation and Message of a Catholic Epistle," *JSNT* 43 (1997): 451–65 ▥Duane F. **Watson**, *Invention, Arrangement, and Style: Rhetorical Criticism of Jude and 2 Peter*, SBLDS 104 (Atlanta: Scholars, 1988) ▥F. **Wisse**, "The Epistle of Jude in the History of Heresiology," in *Essays on the Nag Hammadi Texts, Fs.* Alexander Böhlig, ed. M. Krause (Leiden: Brill, 1972), 133–43.

CHAPTER TWENTY-FIVE

REVELATION

CONTENTS

The structure of Revelation is hotly debated, mainly because conclusions on this matter radically affect one's understanding of the historical referents and eschatology of the book. Major divisions in the book are often based on significant repeated phrases. References to "what must come to pass," or something like it, occur in 1:1, 1:19, 4:1, and 22:6. Another such formula is John's reference to being "in the Spirit" (1:10, 4:2, 17:3, 21:10).[1] These literary markers suggest that 1:1–20 (or 1:1–8) and 22:[6]10–21 are, respectively, the prologue and epilogue, and that the letters to the seven churches in chapters 2–3 form a separate unit. There seems to be some basis for this division in 1:19, where it is plausible to think that "what you have seen" refers to the vision in chapter 1, "what is now" to the letters in chapters 2–3, and "what will take place later" to chapters 4 and following.[2]

The material from 4:1 to 22:5 has been structured in many different ways. The simplest is to note the places where an interruption in the visionary mode occurs and where the seer is invited to "come and see." This results in a threefold division, 4:1–16:21; 17:1–21:8; and 21:9–22:5. Others think that the section

---

[1]See, e.g., Richard Bauckham, *The Climax of Prophecy: Studies on the Book of Revelation* (Edinburgh: T. & T. Clark, 1993), 4–5; Christopher R. Smith, "The Structure of the Book of Revelation in Light of Apocalyptic Literary Conventions," *NovT* 36 (1994): 373–93.

[2]It is possible, however, that "what you saw" refers to all the visions of Revelation, which contain both "what is" and "what will follow" (see esp. G. K. Beale, *The Book of Revelation: A Commentary on the Greek Text*, NIGTC [Grand Rapids: Eerdmans, 1999], 152–70), or that there is no relationship between the phrases and the parts of the book (Jan Lambrecht, "A Structuration of Revelation 4,1–22,5," in *L'Apocalypse johannique et l'apocalyptique dans le Nouveau Testament*, ed. J. Lambrecht, BETL 53 [Louvain: Louvain University Press, 1980], 79–80).

divides in half, chapters 12–22 repeating the material of chapters 1–11.³ The book of Revelation has been likened to a seven-act play, with seven scenes in each act.⁴ Others find a chiastic structure.⁵ More often, the three series of sevens—seals (6:1–17; 8:1), trumpets (8:2–9:21; 11:15–19), and bowls (15:1–16:21)—are used as the basis of the structure. Chapters 4–5 (or chap. 4 alone) are then viewed as an inaugural vision that sets the tone for what follows, with 17:1–22:5 giving the details of the eschatological denouement. Interrupting the sequence of events—that is, between the sixth and seventh seals (chap. 7), the sixth and seventh trumpet (10:1–11:14), and the seventh trumpet and the bowls (12:1–14:20)—are further visions that give the reader perspective on the unfolding of the septets of judgment. This last concept seems to provide the best approach to the structure, and we follow it in the outline of contents below.⁶

Prologue (1:1–20). The book opens with a brief introduction (1:1–3), address and salutation (1:4–8), and vision of the glorified Christ (1:9–20). (Some take this vision, with chaps. 2–3, as an introduction to the letters to the seven churches.)

Messages to seven churches (2:1–3:22). John is commanded by the risen Christ to address messages to seven churches in seven cities within the Roman province of Asia: Ephesus (2:1–7), Smyrna (2:8–11), Pergamum (2:12–17), Thyatira (2:18–29), Sardis (3:1–6), Philadelphia (3:7–13), and Laodicea (3:14–22). Each letter contains (1) a greeting to the ἄγγελος (*angelos*, "angel" or "messenger") of the church; (2) a description of the risen Christ, drawn from the vision in 1:9–20; (3) praise for the church (except in the letter to Laodicea); (4) criticism of the church (except in the letters to Smyrna and Philadelphia); (5) a warning; (6) an exhortation, beginning, "Whoever has ears . . ."; and (7) a promise.

A vision of heaven (4:1–5:14). John is taken up to heaven "in the Spirit," where he sees the sovereign God seated on the throne and receiving worship. The transcendence of God depicted in this vision sets the stage for the drama that unfolds: John sees a sealed scroll in God's hand, and only a "Lamb, looking as if it had been slain," is accounted worthy to break the seven seals and open the scroll (5:1–14).

The seven seals (6:1–8:5). John describes what he sees as each seal is opened by the Lamb: conquest (6:1–2), slaughter (6:3–4), famine (6:5–6), death (6:7–8), martyrs crying out for justice (6:9–11), and natural disasters, signifying the

---

³Henry Barclay Swete, *The Apocalypse of St. John,* 3rd ed. (London: Macmillan, 1911), xxxvii–xliv.

⁴John Wick Bowman, "Book of Revelation," in *IDB* 4.64–65.

⁵Elisabeth Schüssler Fiorenza, *The Book of Revelation: Justice and Judgment* (Philadelphia: Fortress Press, 1985), 174–77.

⁶For this outline, with minor modifications, see Leon Morris, *The Revelation of St. John,* TNTC, rev. ed. (Grand Rapids: Eerdmans, 1987), 43–44.

"wrath of the Lamb" (6:12–17). Then, before the seventh seal is described, John sees two visions, each of them depicting a great mass of people: 144,000 from the tribes of Israel who had been sealed by God (7:1–8) and an innumerable multitude who had "come out of the great tribulation" (7:9–17). The opening of the seventh seal brings silence in heaven and the introduction of the seven trumpets (8:1–5).

The seven trumpets (8:6–11:19). In his vision, John now observes the disasters that come upon the earth as angels blow each of the trumpets: hail and fire from heaven (8:7), a mountain thrown into the sea (8:8–9), a great star falling from the sky (8:10–11), astronomical changes (8:12–13), destructive locusts (9:1–12), and a huge conquering army (9:13–21). As was the case with the seals, John interjects two visions before he narrates the events connected with the seventh trumpet. John sees an angel with a little scroll that he is instructed to eat (10:1–11) and two witnesses, who prophesy, are killed, and are raised again (11:1–14). The seventh trumpet contains no specific event but inaugurates hymns that praise God for his triumph and judgments (11:15–19).

Seven significant signs (12:1–14:20). John interrupts his numbered septets to give a series of visions. But the number seven, so obviously basic to Revelation, is not abandoned, since the events narrated in these visions are seven in number: a woman who gives birth to a son (12:1–6); a war in heaven between Michael and his angels and a dragon, identified with Satan, who is cast out of heaven (12:7–12); a war on earth between Satan and the woman and her child (12:13–13:1a); the worldwide worship of a beast who comes out of the sea (13:1b–10); the worldwide domination of a beast who comes out of the earth (13:11–18); the praise of the Lamb from the 144,000 (14:1–5); and the harvesting of the earth, done by "one like a son of man" and angels (14:14–20). As with the first two septets (seals and trumpets), there is a vision inserted between the sixth and the seventh in this series (see 14:6–13).

The seven bowls (15:1–16:21). John now sees "in heaven another great and marvelous sign: seven angels with the seven last plagues" (15:1). Those who had triumphed over the beast sing praises to God (15:2–4) as the angels come out of the temple with the plagues (15:5–8). These plagues are then described with the imagery of bowls that the angels pour out on the earth (16:1). The pouring out of the bowls brings, successively, painful sores "on the people who had the mark of the beast and worshiped his image" (16:2), a turning of the sea into blood (16:3), a turning of the rivers and springs of water into blood (16:3–7), scorching heat from the sun (16:8–9), destruction of the beast's dominion (16:10–11), the drying up of the Euphrates River and the coming of evil spirits in preparation for "the battle on the great day of God Almighty" at "Armageddon" (16:12–16), and, climactically, the "it is done" of utter earthly destruction (16:17–21).

The triumph of Almighty God (17:1–21:8). These visions describe and celebrate the triumph of God in the world, as his sovereignty, seen by John in heaven in chapter 4, is now manifested in the world—and the world to come. John depicts both the judgment of the wicked and the reward of the righteous. His first vision reveals the evil and destiny of "the great prostitute," "the great city that rules over the kings of the earth" (17:1–18). This great city, named Babylon to suggest an ungodly suppressor of God's people, is now condemned and destroyed, as those who profited from her mourn her (18:1–19:5). In the midst of judgment, however, is salvation, as John hears the praise of a great multitude who had been invited to share in the wedding supper of the Lamb (19:6–10). John next portrays the victory over the beasts and the assembled nations won by the rider on a white horse (19:11–21). There follows John's famous description of the "thousand years" (hence the "millennium"), during which Satan is bound, and which separates the "first" resurrection from the second (20:1–6). John then depicts the final rebellion and destruction of Satan (20:7–10) and God's judgment of all the dead before the great white throne (20:11–15). The passing of the first earth leads to John's vision of "a new heaven and a new earth." Here God resides with his people (21:2–5), and the righteous are separated from the wicked (21:6–8).

The new Jerusalem (21:9–22:9). This section has many parallels with the angelic vision in 17:1–19:10.[7] In his vision, John sees the "bride, the wife of the Lamb," in the image of a new Jerusalem, whose features and dimensions are described in considerable detail (21:9–21). There will be no need for temple or sun or moon in this city, for God and the Lamb are there, and there will be no wickedness (21:22–22:5). In a transitional section, John climaxes his prophecy with the quotation of Jesus promising to come again soon and a final reference to his own visionary experience (22:6–9).

Epilogue (22:10–21). John is promised that the message contained in the visions he has seen is "trustworthy and reliable" and that there will be reward for those who are faithful and true. This reward is brought by Jesus himself, who is "coming quickly."

AUTHOR

Early Christian Testimony

As early as the middle of the second century, Revelation was ascribed to John, "one of the apostles of Christ" (Justin, *Dial.* 81). Other second-century works and writers make the same claim: a lost commentary on Revelation by Melito, bishop of Sardis (c. A.D. 165; see Eusebius, *H.E.* 4.26.2); Irenaeus (c. 180; *Adv. Haer.* 3.11.1, 4.20.11, 4.35.2); and the Muratorian Canon (A.D. 180–200?). Whether Papias, an even earlier witness than these (d. c. 130), can be added to this list is disputed, but a good case can be made that he both knew

---

[7]See esp. David E. Aune, *Revelation 1–5*, WBC 52A (Dallas: Word, 1997), xcv–xcvii.

Revelation and attributed it to John.[8] The evidence of these writers is particularly strong in that two of them (three, if Papias is included) could well be reporting firsthand evidence. Sardis, where Melito was bishop, was one of the churches addressed in Revelation (1:11; 3:1–6). Irenaeus was from Smyrna, also a church addressed in Revelation (1:11; 2:8–11), and claims to have heard Polycarp, who had talked with John the apostle himself. Papias knew John the apostle personally. The early tradition is confirmed by the third-century fathers Tertullian, Hippolytus, and Origen. Not only do these authors ascribe Revelation to John the apostle, but they do so without any hint of there being a contrary claim. No New Testament book, concludes Gerhard Maier, has a stronger or earlier tradition about its authorship than does Revelation.[9]

Nevertheless, the association of John the apostle with Revelation, while early and widespread, is not unanimous. Marcion rejected the book (but then he rejected most of the New Testament, including the Gospel of John). The second-century group called the "Alogoi" also rejected the apostolic origin of Revelation, suggesting that it was written by Cerinthus. But particularly clear and strong in his dissent from the tradition of apostolic authorship was Dionysius, a third-century bishop of Alexandria. As recorded by Eusebius (*H.E.* 7.25.7–27), Dionysius claimed on three grounds that John the apostle could not have written Revelation: (1) the author of Revelation makes no claim to be an apostle or eyewitness and does not describe himself, as does the author of the Gospel of John, as "the beloved disciple"; (2) the conceptions and arrangement of Revelation are completely different from those of the fourth gospel and 1 John; and (3) the Greek of Revelation differs drastically from the Greek of the fourth gospel and 1 John. If then (as Dionysius thought), John the apostle wrote the gospel and 1 John, he could not have written Revelation. Revelation must have been written by some other person named John; in fact, Dionysius had heard it said that there were two tombs of significant Christians named John in Ephesus.

Dionysius' views are shared by most contemporary scholars, and we will examine the arguments below. For the moment, we want to estimate the value of his witness as an ancient authority. This value is not great. Dionysius makes no claim to be passing on tradition; his rejection of apostolic authorship is based entirely on arguments from the content of Revelation. Moreover, his arguments themselves are motivated by theological bias. Several early Fathers (e.g., Justin, Irenaeus, Tertullian) interpreted Revelation 20:1–6 as teaching what was called *chiliasm,* the doctrine that Christ would establish a thousand-year reign on earth (usually called premillennialism today). Other church fathers, however, found this doctrine abhorrent because of its alleged Jewish roots and materialism. Dionysius was one of these, and his rejection of apostolic authorship of

---

[8]See esp. Gerhard Maier, *Die Johannesoffenbarung und die Kirche,* WUNT 25 (Tübingen: Mohr-Siebeck, 1981), 1–69.

[9]Ibid., 107.

Revelation has as its purpose the discrediting of its alleged chiliastic teaching.[10] This does not mean that Dionysius was wrong or that his arguments are therefore without force. But it does mean that his opinion, being independent of any tradition and motivated by polemical concerns, will be only as valuable as the arguments he uses to support it.

Contemporary Discussion

Dionysius of Alexandria rejected apostolic authorship of Revelation for the purpose of discrediting its alleged chiliastic teaching.

1. Internal Evidence. Revelation claims to be written by "John" (1:1, 4, 9; 22:8). Addressing himself to his readers, he calls himself "your brother and companion in the suffering and kingdom and patient endurance that are ours in Jesus" (1:9). The author, however, never makes any other claims about himself, and this suggests that he was someone well known to his readers. Which John would have been better known to the churches of Asia Minor in the late first century than John the apostle, whom reliable early church tradition places in Ephesus at the end of his life (see below)? The author's claim to be mediating prophetic words that are authoritative for the readers (e.g., 22:9, 18–19) has also been seen to be indicative of apostolic authorship.[11] While there is something to this argument, it must be admitted that people other than apostles were gifted with prophecy in the early church; that authority, even scriptural authority, does not depend on apostolic status (e.g., Mark, Luke, the author to the Hebrews); and that the authority of Revelation comes more from the One who revealed the visions than from the author himself. Nevertheless, the author's assumption that what he relates will be accepted by the readers simply on the basis of his name alone points more naturally to an apostle than to someone else.

2. Arguments against Apostolic Authorship. Despite this internal evidence, the majority of contemporary scholars deny that John the apostle wrote Revelation. Their reasons for doing so are essentially the same as those of Dionysius.

Lack of apostolic claims. First, it is claimed that the author cannot be an apostle. He never claims to be such, never alludes to gospel events, and never claims a special relationship with Christ. Furthermore, passages such as 18:20 and 21:14, with their allusions to the significant role of the apostles, show that the author was not numbered among the Twelve.[12]

This argument carries little weight. The author's failure to mention his apostolic status may well be because he is so well known to those to whom he writes that such an identification is not needed. Reference to the events of Jesus'

---

[10]See ibid., 96–107, and esp. 107, where Maier notes that Dionysius's judgment was motivated by church politics and dogmatics. See also Ned B. Stonehouse, *The Apocalypse in the Ancient Church* (Goes: Oosterbaan & Le Cointre, 1929).

[11]Guthrie, 936.

[12]So, e.g., R. H. Charles, *A Critical and Exegetical Commentary on the Revelation of St. John*, ICC (Edinburgh: T. & T. Clark, 1920), 1.xliii–xliv; Aune, *Revelation 1–5*, li.

life or to any personal relationship between the author and Jesus would be out of place in a book like Revelation. And the significance accorded to the apostles is no greater than that found in passages such as Ephesians 2:20 (and see Matt. 16:17–19).

Theological differences. Both other key arguments against John the apostle as the author of Revelation depend for their validity on the assumption that the apostle wrote the fourth gospel and the Epistles of John. These arguments will therefore not be convincing to the many contemporary critics who deny that John the apostle wrote the fourth gospel or the Johannine Epistles. But we have argued in this book that John the apostle did write these books, and we must, then, reckon with the problems that confront any attempt to establish unity of authorship for all the Johannine books.

The first of the problems is that the theology of Revelation appears to be quite distinct from that of the fourth gospel and of 1 John. This emerges particularly in three doctrines: theology proper, Christology, and eschatology. The God of Revelation, it is argued, is a God of majesty and judgment, whereas the God of the gospel and the epistles is a God of love. A similar contrast is found in Christology: while the fourth gospel focuses on Christ as revealer and redeemer, Revelation pictures Christ as conquering warrior and ruler. The fourth gospel is frequently said to exhibit "realized eschatology," a view of history and eternity in which "the last things" are viewed as completely realized in the incarnation, death, and resurrection of Christ. Revelation, on the other hand, focuses almost exclusively on a coming of Christ at the end of history. The same author, it is then concluded, cannot be responsible for both books; the theological perspective is too different.[13]

But the contrasts are both overdrawn and incapable of proving much. Both the fourth gospel and Revelation teach that God is *both* loving and judging, that Christ is *both* redeemer and sovereign Lord, and that "the last things" have *both* been realized in Jesus' death and resurrection (at least in principle) and await the end of history for their consummation. Differences between John's gospel and Revelation on these points have been magnified by a narrow and one-sided interpretation of the fourth gospel. That the theological emphases of the fourth gospel and of Revelation are different, no one can deny. But the different settings and purposes for the two books adequately explain these differences in emphasis. There is no reason on such grounds to think the same person could not have written both. Indeed, there is much evidence suggesting commonality of authorship: the description in both books of Jesus as "Word" (John 1:1; Rev. 19:13), "lamb" (John 1:29; Rev. 5:6 and elsewhere—although different Greek words are used) and "shepherd"; a "replacement of the temple" theme

---

[13]E.g., Kümmel, 472.

(John 4:21; Rev. 21:22); a love of antithesis (darkness-light, truth-falsehood); and many others.[14]

Stylistic differences. Dionysius's third argument against unity of authorship between the fourth gospel and Revelation is the most telling: the differences in the Greek. The Greek of Revelation, as R. H. Charles has commented, is "unlike any Greek that was ever penned by mortal man."[15] Particularly striking are the many grammatical solecisms, or irregularities. One example is the neglect of the proper case after a preposition, as in 1:4: ἀπὸ ὁ ὢν καὶ ὁ ἦν καὶ ὁ ἐρχόμενος (*apo ho ōn kai ho ēn kai ho erchomenos*: "from him who is, and who was, and who is to come," TNIV). Charles concluded that it was the Greek of one who was thinking in Hebrew while writing in Greek.[16] Stephen Thompson has shown further that it was biblical rather than postbiblical Hebrew or Aramaic that influenced the author and that Revelation is almost certainly not a translation of an original Hebrew or Aramaic work.[17] In contrast, the Greek of the fourth gospel, while simple and having its share of Semitisms,[18] is accurate and clear.[19] Most contemporary scholars agree with Dionysius: the same person could not have written both books.[20]

Nevertheless, many scholars have attempted to explain the differences in a way that would be compatible with common authorship. Hort and Westcott suggested that a great amount of time intervened between the two books, John having written Revelation in the late 60s and the fourth gospel in the 90s.[21] But it is doubtful that the books can be dated so far apart; nor does the passage of

---

[14]See esp. F. Godet, *Commentary on the Gospel of St. John,* 3 vols. (Edinburgh: T. & T. Clark, 1899–1900), 1.182–90. In a major study, André Heinze finds many similarities between Revelation and the other Johannine books as well as some significant differences (*Johannesapokalypse und johanneische Schriften: forschungs- und traditionsgeschichtliche Untersuchungen,* BWANT 142 [Stuttgart: Kohlhammer, 1998]).

[15]Charles, *Revelation* 1.xliv. For an exhaustive examination of the Greek of the book, see Aune, *Revelation 1–5,* clx–ccxi.

[16]See Charles's extensive discussion in *Revelation* 1.cxvii–clix. Note also Swete, *Apocalypse,* cxx–cxxx.

[17]Stephen Thompson, *The Apocalypse and Semitic Syntax,* SNTSMS 52 (Cambridge: Cambridge University Press, 1985). Thompson, however, has been criticized for overplaying the evidence; see Stanley E. Porter, *Verbal Aspect in the Greek of the New Testament, with Reference to Tense and Mood,* SBG 1 (Berne: Peter Lang, 1989), 111–56 and the literature there cited.

[18]Or more commonly, Semitic enhancements. See n. 14 in chap. 2 above.

[19]Charles outlines the differences clearly (*Revelation* 1.xxix–xxxii).

[20]E.g., ibid. 1.xxix and G. R. Beasley-Murray, *The Book of Revelation,* NCB (London: Marshall, Morgan & Scott, 1974), 35–36.

[21]F. J. A. Hort, *The Apocalypse of St. John I–III* (London: Macmillan, 1908), xii; B. F. Westcott, *The Gospel According to St. John* (reprint, Grand Rapids: Eerdmans, 1971), lxxxvi.

time in itself explain the differences. Others argue that the differences are due to the fact that John, exiled in Patmos, is writing without the aid of an amanuensis that he was able to use for the gospel and the epistles.[22] There may be some truth to this, but it is doubtful that the Greek of Revelation can be set down to inadequate knowledge of the language, for the author is not at all consistent in his breaking of grammatical rules. In the example cited above, for instance, the author goes on in the very same verse to use the correct case after the same preposition (ἀπὸ τῶν ἑπτὰ πνευμάτων [apo tōn hepta pneumatōn]: "from the seven spirits," TNIV). As Charles made clear in his magisterial treatment of the grammar of Revelation, the author follows certain rules of his own, and his solecisms appear to be deliberate. Many scholars therefore think that the author deliberately chose to write Greek as he did perhaps because of the immediacy of the visionary experience,[23] or as a protest against the upper classes.[24] Another factor to keep in mind is the genre difference between the gospel and Revelation. Whatever genre we finally assign to Revelation, its striking difference in form from the gospel is quite clear, and this likely had an impact (perhaps a serious impact) on the Greek style. Whatever his reason, if the author of Revelation has written as he has deliberately, then it is not clear that the person who wrote the fourth gospel could not also have written Revelation. As G. B. Caird says, "Because a man writes in Hebraic Greek, it does not inevitably follow that this is the only Greek he is capable of writing."[25] And, before leaving this matter of the language, we must point out that, as in the case of the theology of the two books, the Greek style of the two shows many similarities.[26]

Conclusion

While the difference in Greek style is a problem, we are not convinced that the arguments of Dionysius or his latter-day followers make it impossible for the same person to have written both the fourth gospel and Revelation. We are thus inclined to accept the testimony of those who were in a position to know about these matters, and we attribute both books to John the apostle, "the beloved disciple."[27]

---

[22]George Eldon Ladd, *A Commentary on the Revelation of John* (Grand Rapids: Eerdmans, 1972), 7–8; Morris, *Revelation*, 39.

[23]Zahn 3.432–33; Ibson T. Beckwith, *The Apocalypse of John: Studies in Introduction* (New York: Macmillan, 1919), 355.

[24]Adela Yarbro Collins, *Crisis and Catharsis: The Power of the Apocalypse* (Philadelphia: Westminster, 1984), 47.

[25]G. B. Caird, *A Commentary on the Revelation of St. John the Divine* (New York: Harper & Row, 1966), 5.

[26]See Charles, *Revelation* 1.xxix–xxxvii, for a list.

[27]Apostolic authorship is hesitantly accepted by, among others, Guthrie, 932–48; Robert H. Mounce, *The Book of Revelation*, NICNT (Grand Rapids: Eerdmans, 1977),

If this identification is rejected, then there are four other possibilities. First, Revelation could have been written by another well-known John in the ancient church. Dionysius, after suggesting (and properly rejecting) John Mark,[28] mentions a second John (in addition to the apostle John) buried in Ephesus. This second John is often identified with an "elder John" whom Papias mentions (see Eusebius, *H.E.* 3.39.4–5), and this "elder John" is thought by some to have written Revelation.[29] But it is doubtful whether Papias refers to two different men named John at all (see the section "Author" in chap. 6); the whole thesis is most improbable. Another well-known John in the early church was John the Baptist, and J. Massyngberde Ford has suggested that he could be responsible for much of Revelation.[30] But her theory is too far-fetched to command assent (see "Composition and Genre" below).

A second possibility is that Revelation, like Jewish apocalypses, is pseudonymous—written by an unknown person in John's name. But Charles has shown this hypothesis to be unlikely,[31] and it is rarely argued.

Much more popular of late has been a third option: that Revelation, like the other Johannine books, was written by an anonymous member of a Johannine "school" or "circle." Such a hypothesis seems to offer an attractive solution to the problem of explaining both the similarities and differences among these books.[32] Yet, as A. Y. Collins says, the hypothesis "is clearly not the result of careful historical-critical research, but a prior assumption that shapes the result of the research."[33] We have elsewhere argued that the "school" or "circle" hypothesis is untenable (see esp. chap. 6, the section "Stylistic Unity and the Johannine 'Community'").

We are left, then, as the only real alternative to John the apostle's authorship, authorship by an unknown John, and this is the explanation held by most who demur from the traditional identification.[34] Yet we might question whether

---

25–31; John F. Walvoord, *The Revelation of Jesus Christ* (Chicago: Moody, 1966), 11–14. Beale (*The Book of Revelation*, 34–36) thinks it is possible.

[28] J. N. Sanders, however, appears to defend the idea ("St. John on Patmos," *NTS* 9 [1962–63]: 75–85).

[29] The solution was quite popular at the turn of the century but has lately fallen out of favor. See, however, John J. Gunther, "The Elder John, Author of Revelation," *JSNT* 11 (1981): 3–20; Martin Hengel, *The Johannine Question* (Philadelphia: Trinity Press International, 1989), 127 (as one possibility).

[30] J. Massyngberde Ford, *Revelation*, AB 38 (Garden City: Doubleday, 1975), 3–37.

[31] Charles, *Revelation* 1.xxxviii–xxxix.

[32] An early advocate of the idea was Johannes Weiss, *Offenbarung des Johannes*, FRLANT 3 (Göttingen: Vandenhoeck & Ruprecht, 1904), 146–64.

[33] Collins, *Crisis and Catharsis*, 33; see also Fiorenza, *Book of Revelation*, 85–113.

[34] E.g., Kümmel, 469–72; Wikenhauser, 648–53; Collins, *Crisis and Catharsis*, 33. Charles called him "John the Prophet" (*Revelation* 1.xxxviii–l); Aune, *Revelation 1–5*, xlviii–lvi.

a John who is never mentioned in the abundant sources for first-century Asian church life would have had sufficient stature to write a book of this sort, so different from anything else in the New Testament, simply under his own name. Particularly does this seem unlikely when we recall that there *was* a John who was well known in this area at just this period. Guthrie's question is to the point: "Was the Asiatic church overrun with brilliant Christians by the name of John, who would only need to announce their name for the Christians to know which was meant?"[35]

PROVENANCE

John writes from Patmos, a rocky and rugged island about six miles wide and ten miles long, some forty miles southwest of Ephesus in the Aegean Sea. The island was used by Roman authorities as a place of exile (see Pliny, *Nat. Hist.* 4.23), and John indicates that this was his reason for being there: "because of the word of God and the testimony of Jesus" (1:9).[36] Early tradition (e.g., Origen) says that the emperor himself condemned John to exile in Patmos, but it is more likely, considering John's extensive ministry in Asia Minor, that it was a local Roman official from this region who sent John to Patmos is order to get him out of the way.[37]

DATE

Early Christian Testimony

Early Christian writers date Revelation in the reign of one of four different Roman emperors (see Table 8).

Contemporary Discussion

As can be seen from Table 8, a date for Revelation in the reign of Domitian, and probably toward the end of that reign (c. 95–96), receives the most support from the early church fathers. Irenaeus, a key source for this tradition, was in the position, as we noted above, to have direct information about the matter. Most scholars have been inclined to follow Irenaeus in his dating of Revelation at the close of the reign of Domitian. Dates in the reign of Claudius or Trajan are, respectively, too early and too late, and have attracted virtually no adherents. A date shortly after the reign of Nero (68–69), however, has considerable support

---

[35]Guthrie, 946.

[36]Although a few scholars think John might mean only that he was there on a missionary visit.

[37]See Sanders, "St. John on Patmos," 76.

Table 8
Early Christian Writings and the Date of the Revelation

Emperor	Ruled	Sources dating Revelation by emperor
Claudius	41–54	Epiphanius, *Haer.* 51.12
Nero	54–68	Syriac versions of Revelation
Domitian	81–96	Irenaeus (*Adv. Haer.* 5.30.3) ("toward the end of the reign of Domitian"); Victorinus, *Apoc.* 10.11; Eusebius, *H.E.* 3.18; Clement of Alexandria (*Quis div.* 42) and Origen (*Matt.* 16.6) both locate Revelation in the reign of "the tyrant," probably referring to Domitian
Trajan	98–117	A synopsis of the life and death of the prophets attributed to Dorotheus; Theophylact on Matt. 20:22

and is the main alternative to the Domitianic date.[38] There are six key areas of evidence to consider in coming to a decision.

The persecution of Christians. The degree to which the Christians to whom John writes were being persecuted is debated. While many have thought that the book presupposes a widespread, intense, officially promulgated persecution, most recent scholars are more cautious. An extreme view is that virtually no persecution was occurring; it was only John's hostility toward Roman society that led him to speak as if persecution were occurring.[39] But the emerging consensus seems to be that many Christians were indeed being persecuted, that this persecution came from both Jews and the general populace, that the government may have been behind some of the persecution, and that John expected the persecution to worsen in the very near future.[40] Advocates of the Domitianic date have generally appealed to the early Christian tradition that pictured the years 95–96 as a period of intense persecution. Advocates of the earlier date, for their part,

---

[38]The most important advocates of the early date are Hort, *Apocalypse I–III*, xii–xxxiii, and J. A. T. Robinson, *Redating the New Testament* (Philadelphia: Westminster, 1976), 221–53. See also Albert A. Bell Jr., "The Date of John's Apocalypse: The Evidence of Some Roman Historians Reconsidered," *NTS* 25 (1979): 93–102; Kenneth L. Gentry Jr., *Before Jerusalem Fell: Dating the Book of Revelation* (Tyler: ICE, 1989); Christopher Rowland, *The Open Heaven* (New York: Crossroad, 1982), 403–13; J. C. Wilson, "The Problem of the Domitianic Date of Revelation," *NTS* 39 (1995): 587–605; P. E. Hughes, *The Book of Revelation*, PNTC (Grand Rapids: Eerdmans, 1990), 10.

[39]E.g., Collins, *Crisis and Catharsis*, 69–73; Leonard L. Thompson, *The Book of Revelation: Apocalypse and Empire* (Oxford: Oxford University Press, 1990).

[40]See especially the thorough review of the evidence in Beale, *The Book of Revelation*, 12–15.

point out that the evidence for this persecution is quite slim. The clearest evidence comes from later writers (Orosius, Eusebius, Sulpicius Severus); whereas those more contemporary to Domitian's time, both Christian and pagan, say nothing about a systematic persecution of Christians.[41] In contrast, evidence for a persecution of Christians under Nero is clear and irrefutable. Although we have no evidence that Nero's persecution extended beyond Rome, if we are looking for a period when Christians in Asia Minor were likely to be persecuted, a time during which Christians were being persecuted elsewhere is more likely than a time when we are not sure that they were being persecuted at all.

Advocates of an early date have a point: many scholars have exaggerated the evidence for a persecution of Christians under Domitian. The evidence suggests rather that Domitian in the last years of his reign instituted a purge of Roman aristocrats who might challenge his power. The wife of one of those purged, Domitilla, whose husband, Flavius Clemens, was executed, was probably a Christian, although it is not clear that either she or her husband were singled out because of her faith.[42] There is little evidence, however, that the Neronian persecution of Christians in Rome had lasting effects or spread to the provinces. Advocates of neither date can thus appeal to solid evidence for persecution in Asia Minor. We are confined to assumptions, and the assumption of persecution of Christians in Asia Minor under Nero has no more to be said for it than a similar persecution under Domitian (see the next point).

Worship of the emperor. The conclusion just reached must be modified in light of another consideration: the assumption within Revelation that worship of the emperor had become an issue for Christians (see 13:4, 15–16; 14:9–11; 15:2; 16:2; 19:20; 20:4).[43] We have no solid evidence for the date at which the emperors made worship of their own person a requirement, but there is clear evidence that Domitian stressed his deity, ordering that he be addressed as *dominus et deus* ("lord and god").[44] Domitian apparently made this confession a test of loyalty. It is indeed possible that some Christians tried to avoid the predicament this placed them in by taking refuge in the synagogue, where some of the traditional legal exceptions granted Jews in this regard still applied. This may help explain the tensions between Jews and Christians evident in the letters to

---

[41]See, e.g., S. R. F. Price, *Rituals and Power: The Roman Imperial Cult in Asia Minor* (Cambridge: Cambridge University Press, 1984).

[42]See Dio Cassius, *Hist. Rom.* 68.14. Note the survey of the situation in M. R. Charlesworth, "The Flavian Dynasty," *CAH* 11 (1936): 41–42.

[43]We should mention that we are not here presuming a so-called preterist interpretation of Revelation, in which everything in the book applies only to John's day. Some of these texts could be genuinely prophetic, envisaging a situation that did not prevail in the first century. Nevertheless, some of the texts suggest that the problem was real for John's readers (cf. Mounce, *Revelation*, 33).

[44]Cf. Suetonius, *Domitian* 13; Charlesworth, "Flavian Dynasty," 41–42.

the seven churches.[45] In response to this reasoning, advocates of the earlier date appeal to the fact that emperors since Augustus (d. A.D. 14) had made claims to deity and that, granted Nero's character, it is quite possible that he could have stressed such claims. But the fact remains that our hard evidence points to the last years of Domitian as being the time when Christians would most likely have collided with the claims of the emperor cult.

The conditions of the churches. Several elements in the letters to the seven churches are said to be much more compatible with a date in the 90s than one in the 60s: the spiritual stagnation in several of the churches; the wealth of the Laodicean church (the city was destroyed by an earthquake in A.D. 60–61); the existence of the church at Smyrna (the church may not have existed until 60–64); the lack of any mention of Paul, who had labored in Ephesus for so long, and perhaps as late at 64. Not all these points are equally persuasive,[46] but Colin Hemer, after an exhaustive study of the local settings of the churches, claims that his findings generally confirm the Domitianic date.[47]

The existence of a Nero myth. Popular hatred and fear of Nero led to stories circulating after his death to the effect that he would return to Rome leading a Parthian army. Passages in Revelation that speak of the beast recovering from a mortal wound (e.g., 13:3–4), it is argued, allude to a Nero-redivivus myth, and it must have taken time for the myth to circulate and become known. However, the Nero myth is not really very close to what is actually said of the beast in the Revelation, so the argument carries little weight. Moreover, many of those who argue that the number 666 in 13:18 is a cryptic reference to Nero hold that this link is entirely independent of such a myth.

The existence of the Jerusalem temple. Revelation 11:1–2, it is argued, presumes that the temple in Jerusalem was still standing at the time Revelation was written.[48] This argument is not without force, but it is mitigated by two considerations: the possibility that John is using a source; and, more important, the possibility that John refers to a rebuilt or metaphoric temple rather than to the temple of Jesus' day.

Revelation 17:9–11. This passage enumerates seven kings, who are apparently to be taken as emperors of Rome (the allusion to the seven hills in v. 9 is unmistakably a reference to Rome). "Five," says John, "have fallen, one is, the other has not yet come; but when he does come, he must remain for a little while. The beast who once was, and now is not, is an eighth king. He belongs to the seven and is going to his destruction." The assumption of the text is that the

---

[45]Colin J. Hemer, *The Letters to the Seven Churches of Asia in Their Local Setting,* JSNTSup 11 (Sheffield: JSOT Press, 1986), 7–12.

[46]See Robinson, *Redating,* 229–31 for a rebuttal.

[47]Hemer, *Letters to the Seven Churches,* 2–11.

[48]E.g., Robinson, *Redating,* 238–42.

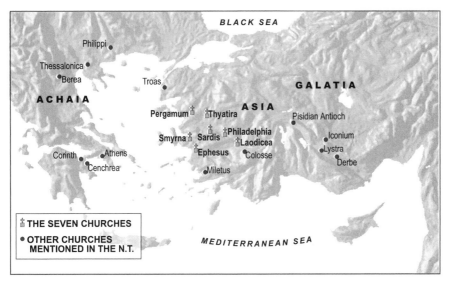

sixth king in the sequence is now in power. Taking these data, and beginning with the first of the Roman emperors, Augustus, brings us to Galba, who reigned only a short time after the death of Nero. Here, then, is what appears to be a relatively objective indication that Revelation was written in A.D. 68–69.[49]

This argument carries some weight, but it is not decisive because the text is not entirely clear. Is it referring to emperors in John's day or to future kings? Should we start counting the emperors from Augustus; or from Julius Caesar, who first claimed imperial rights; or perhaps from Caligula, the first persecuting emperor?[50] Should we include the three minor emperors who reigned for only very brief periods in 68–69? None of these questions can be answered certainly.[51]

Conclusion

Various other minor points are disputed,[52] but these cover the main arguments. The last two factors appear to favor a date shortly after Nero, but the conditions generally presumed in Revelation are more likely to have existed in

---

[49]E.g., Hort, *Apocalypse I–III,* xxvi; Robinson, *Redating,* 242–48.

[50]For the last alternative, see A. Strobel, "Abfassung und Geschichtstheologie des Apokalypse nach Kp. 17, 9–12," *NTS* 10 (1963–64): 433–45.

[51]See the discussion in Collins, *Crisis and Catharsis,* 58–64.

[52]E.g., Charles (*Revelation* 1.xlvi–l) and others have argued that early traditions indicate that John was martyred between A.D. 64 and 70. But this tradition is very much inferior to the one that has John ministering in Ephesus to a ripe old age (Leon Morris, *Studies in the Fourth Gospel* [Grand Rapids: Eerdmans, 1969], 280–83; Beckwith, *Apocalypse,* 362–93).

the reign of Domitian than earlier (the second and third points). We are inclined, then, to follow the oldest tradition on this point and date Revelation in the last years of Domitian.

DESTINATION

John directs the record of his visions to seven churches in the Roman province of Asia, which incorporated approximately the western third of Asia Minor. These churches were probably personally known to John from years of ministry in the area. His reason for selecting these seven churches, as well as the order in which they are listed, probably has to do with geography and communications. As Ramsay pointed out long ago, the cities in which the churches are located are all centers of communication; a messenger bearing Revelation to the cities would arrive from Patmos in Ephesus, travel by secondary road north to Smyrna and Pergamum, and then go east on the Roman road to Thyatira, Sardis, Philadelphia, and Laodicea.[53]

COMPOSITION AND GENRE

Sources and Theories of Composition

Revelation borrows more extensively from the Old Testament than any other New Testament book.[54] Most of the references come not in explicit quotations but in allusions and conceptual borrowings. John also makes use of Jewish apocalyspses, though to a lesser degree than is sometimes thought. Some have thought that John also betrays a knowledge of several New Testament books: Charles lists Matthew, Luke, 1 Thessalonians, 1 and 2 Corinthians, Colossians, and Ephesians.[55] But this is not so clear, since almost all the similarities could have arisen from John's knowledge of the oral tradition of Jesus' life and teaching and of general early Christian teachings. Still, since it is likely that John had read at least Mark and Luke by this date (on their dates, see "Date" in chaps. 4 and 5 above), we must allow the possibility of direct borrowing.

During the heyday of source analysis of the Scriptures in the late nineteenth and early twentieth centuries, a number of scholars found evidence of sources behind the canonical book of Revelation. Charles, for instance, thinks one-fifth

---

[53]William Ramsay, *The Letters to the Seven Churches of Asia* (London: Hodder & Stoughton, 1904), 171–96. See also Hemer, *Letters to the Seven Churches*, 14–15; Barry J. Beitzel, *The Moody Atlas of Bible Lands* (Chicago: Moody, 1985), 185.

[54]See the lists of parallels in Charles, *Revelation* 1.lxviii–lxxxiii; Swete, *Apocalypse*, cxxxix–clii; and esp. G. K. Beale, *John's Use of the Old Testament in Revelation*, JSNTSup 166 (Sheffield: Sheffield Academic Press, 1998).

[55]Charles, *Revelation* 1: lxxxiii–lxxxvi.

of the book is dependent on written sources, Greek and Hebrew in language and Jewish and Christian in origin.[56] He also argues that the author of most of the book died before finishing it and that "a faithful but unintelligent disciple" pasted together the material in 20:4–22:21, but in an order radically different from what the author intended.[57] But Charles's rearrangement of the material causes more problems than it solves. Neither has his identification of sources much to be said for it. Revelation demonstrates a consistency in style that prevents any inferences about sources on the basis of linguistic considerations. Moreover, the book is so thoroughly permeated with traditional language and conceptions that it is impossible to identify sources through these means either. Evidence for sources is often found in the existence of doublets, or passages that appear to be roughly parallel. But repetition of material is part of the nature of Revelation.

Undeterred by these hindrances, a number of scholars have gone even further, arguing that the book of Revelation is made up of two or more large blocks of material. Boismard thinks that two parallel apocalypses have been combined.[58] J. Massyngberde Ford argues that chapters 4–11 stem from John the Baptist, and 12–22 from a disciple of John, with 1–3; 22:16a, 20b; 21 being added by a Jewish-Christian disciple.[59] Neither theory has much positive evidence in its favor, but both rest (particularly in Ford's case) on imaginative and implausible connections and inferences. More recently, David Aune has presented a detailed case for a two-stage composition process. He thinks that a "first edition" of the book, containing 1:7–12a and 4:1–22:5 and strongly apocalyptic in flavor, was produced around A.D. 70. A "second edition," adding the remaining sections and redacting the whole toward a more prophetic and parenetic model, was then completed in the early year's of the reign of Trajan.[60] But we doubt whether the data require a two-stage process, which, in any case, seems to fly in the face of John's claims to have received the visions of the book at a single point in time while on Patmos.

Genre

As Beasley-Murray notes, the opening verses of Revelation appear to suggest three different genre identifications: apocalypse (1:1), prophecy (1:3), and epistle (1:4).[61] Each has its defenders, and each plays a role in the complex literary phenomenon of Revelation.

---

[56]Ibid., lxii–lxv.

[57]Ibid., l–lv.

[58]M. E. Boismard, "The Apocalypse," in Robert/Feuillet, 701–7.

[59]Ford, *Revelation*, 3–37. A useful survey of source and compilation hypotheses can be found in Fiorenza, *Book of Revelation*, 159–80.

[60]Aune, *Revelation 1–5*, cv–xxxiv.

[61]Beasley-Murray, *Revelation*, 12.

Identification with the genre "apocalypse" or "apocalyptic" is complicated by continuing debate over just what apocalyptic is: Is it a type of eschatology, or is it a literary genre, or both? Current researchers generally answer that it embraces both but that we should distinguish the two, "apocalyptic" being used to describe a certain kind of eschatology, and "apocalypse" to denote a literary genre.

The literary genre apocalypse began to appear in the second century B.C. as a response to persecution and oppression. The authors of apocalypses claim to be passing on heavenly mysteries revealed to them by an angel or some other spiritual being.[62] Apocalypses are typically pseudonymous, written in the name of a great figure in Israel's past (e.g., Adam, Moses, Enoch). By so projecting themselves into the past, the authors of apocalypses can put historical surveys of God's dealings with his people and with the world in the form of prophecy. These historical surveys, which are found in many, though not all, apocalypses, culminate with the breaking in of God's kingdom, which is expected in the very near future.

The writers of apocalypses usually use extensive symbolism in their historical reviews. The kind of eschatology found in these books (though not confined to them) is then called apocalyptic. It is characterized by a dualistic conception of history: the present world, with its sin, rebellion against God, and persecution of God's people, is sharply contrasted with the world to come, when God will intervene to establish his kingdom.[63] Just at this point "apocalyptic" is often contrasted with "prophecy," which, it is argued, looks for God's salvation to be manifested through the processes of this world rather than through a breaking in of a new world. The prophet is also sometimes contrasted with the apocalypticist in his claim to speak directly from the Lord.

It takes only a casual acquaintance with Revelation to see that it possesses many of the features just described. Its message comes through visions given by angels. It is communicated through extensive use of symbols, strongly contrasts

---

[62]Christopher Rowland judges this to be the key to apocalyptic (*The Open Heaven* [London: SPCK, 1982], 14, 21, 356–57).

[63]A collection of apocalypses in English translation can be found in J. H. Charlesworth, ed., *The Old Testament Pseudepigrapha*, vol. 1 (Garden City: Doubleday, 1983). Some of the key treatments of apocalyptic include H. H. Rowley, *The Relevance of Apocalyptic*, 2nd ed. (London: Lutterworth, 1947); D. S. Russell, *The Method and Message of Jewish Apocalyptic* (London: SCM, 1964); Klaus Koch, *The Rediscovery of Apocalyptic* (London: SCM, 1972); Paul D. Hanson, *The Dawn of Apocalyptic*, 2nd ed. (Philadelphia: Fortress Press, 1979); and Leon Morris, *Apocalyptic* (London: Tyndale, 1973). Three collections of important essays are *Semeia* 14 (1979); Paul D. Hanson, ed., *Visionaries and Their Apocalypses* (Philadelphia: Fortress Press, 1983); and D. Helmbold, ed., *Apocalypticism in the Mediterranean World and the Near East* (Tübingen: Mohr-Siebeck, 1983).

this world with the world to come, and looks for deliverance in the near future. Considering these similarities to Jewish apocalyptic and the apparent claim in 1:1 (the first three words in Greek are Ἀποκάλυψις Ἰησοῦ Χριστοῦ [*Apokalypsis Iēsou Christou*], "the revelation from Jesus Christ," TNIV), it is no wonder that many scholars are convinced that Revelation belongs in the literary genre apocalypse. Yet there are problems with this identification. The most notable one is the fact that Revelation, unlike Jewish apocalypses, is not pseudonymous. John speaks in his own name. If, then, pseudonymity is considered essential to the genre apocalypse, Revelation clearly cannot be an apocalypse.[64] Others respond, however, by insisting that pseudonymity is not necessary to the genre and that Revelation is an apocalypse "with a difference." And of course there is another difference: Jewish apocalypticists ground their hope in a future event, while John in the Revelation grounds his hope in the past sacrifice of Jesus Christ, the "Lamb that has been slain."[65] This does not necessarily mean that the Revelation is not an apocalyptic book, since modifications to the basic apocalyptic scheme could well be introduced without abandoning the apocalyptic perspective per se. But these issues at least suggest that other genre identifications should be considered.

It is difficult, however, to find another genre to which Revelation belongs. John certainly suggests that he stands in a prophetic role, and there is a tendency in current scholarship to view Revelation as a prophecy. But a better suggestion is to find elements of both prophecy and apocalyptic in Revelation.[66] Despite the impression given by some scholars, no rigid distinction between these two is possible. They are combined in many Old Testament books (e.g., Daniel, Isaiah, Zechariah) and in Jesus' Olivet Discourse.[67] In his consciousness of inspiration and of the authority that he assumes, John is truly a prophet. But his prophecy makes use of the forms current in Jewish apocalypses.

Yet another genre to be considered is epistle. This may seem odd at first, but epistle was a very broad genre (see discussion in chap. 8 above), and Revelation, with its opening address and salutation (1:4–5, 9–11), presents itself as a circular letter to seven churches in Asia Minor. Nevertheless, the contents of Revelation as a whole do not fit altogether naturally the category of epistle. The complicated character of Revelation therefore suggests that we should not place

---

[64]See, e.g., Bruce W. Jones, "More About the Apocalypse as Apocalyptic," *JBL* 87 (1968): 325–27. Also doubting the appropriateness of the apocalyptic classification is James Kallas, "The Apocalypse: An Apocalyptic Book?" *JBL* 86 (1967): 69–80.

[65]Kümmel claims that Revelation represents "a total recasting of the apocalyptic view of history out of the Jewish into the Christian mold" (461).

[66]See, e.g., John J. Collins, "Pseudonymity, Historical Reviews, and the Genre of the Revelation of John," *CBQ* 39 (1977): 329–43; Fiorenza, *Book of Revelation*, 133–58; Aune, *Revelation 1–5*, lxx–xc.

[67]See esp. George Eldon Ladd, "Why Not Prophetic-Apocalyptic?" *JBL* 76 (1957): 192–200.

it neatly into one genre category. Elements of prophecy, apocalypse, and letter are combined in a way that has no close parallel in other literature.[68]

TEXT

Kurt and Barbara Aland claim, "In the book of Revelation the textual scene and its history differs greatly from the rest of the New Testament."[69] This is due to two factors. First, Revelation has far fewer Greek manuscript witnesses than any other New Testament book. It originally circulated independently of the rest of the New Testament, and the nature of the book, combined with suspicions about it in the East, where the bulk of Greek manuscripts were produced, cut down the number of copies made. Extant are only five papyrus manuscripts, the longest containing eight chapters (P[47], from the third century), and eleven uncials, only six of which contain any substantial portion of text, and only three of which contain the whole book (Sinaiticus [‏א‎], from the fourth century; Alexandrinus [A], from the fifth century; and 046, from the tenth century). The textual critic, then, has much less evidence on which to base decisions. At least the contemporary critic has more to go by than did Erasmus, who, in his first edition, for lack of *any* Greek manuscript evidence for some verses in the Revelation, translated the Latin Vulgate back into Greek![70]

A second factor that makes the text of Revelation unique is the value of the witnesses that are available. While in most of the New Testament, Sinaiticus (‏א‎) is considered to have a text superior to that found in Alexandrinus (A), the situation is reversed in Revelation: Alexandrinus, in combination with Ephraemi (C) (where it is extant), is considered the best text available.[71] Dependence on these uncials is all the more important because one of the most respected uncials for the New Testament text, Vaticanus (B), does not include Revelation. The combination of few witnesses and variant text types requires that textual decisions in Revelation be based on methods appropriate to its own peculiar text situation.[72]

> The complicated character of Revelation suggests that we should not place it neatly into one genre category. Elements of prophecy, apocalypse, and letter are combined in a way that has no close parallel in other literature.

---

[68]The trend of scholarship is toward such a "mixture" of genres; see, Fiorenza, *Book of Revelation*, 164–70; Richard Bauckham, *The Theology of the Book of Revelation* (Cambridge: Cambridge University Press, 1993), 1–17; J. Ramsey Michaels, *Interpreting the Book of Revelation* (Grand Rapids: Baker, 1992), 29–33; Wilfrid J. Harrington, *Revelation*, SacPag 16 (Collegeville: Liturgical, 1993), 1–8; Jürgen Roloff, *The Revelation of John* (Minneapolis: Fortress Press, 1993), 5–8; Beale, *The Book of Revelation*, 37–43.

[69]Kurt Aland and Barbara Aland, *The Text of the New Testament*, 2nd ed. (Grand Rapids: Eerdmans, 1989), 246.

[70]See Bruce M. Metzger, *The Text of the New Testament: Its Transmission, Corruption, and Restoration*, 2nd ed. (New York: Oxford University Press, 1968), 99–100.

[71]Charles, *Revelation* 1.clx–clxvi; Aland and Aland, *Text*, 247.

[72]J. Delobel, "Le text de l'Apocalypse: Problèmes de méthode," in *L'Apocalypse johannique*, 151–66. The two major studies of the text of Revelation are H. C. Hoskier,

ADOPTION INTO THE CANON

Revelation may be alluded to by Ignatius (A.D. 110–117) and Barnabas (before 135) and is probably used by the author of the *Shepherd of Hermas* (c. 150).[73] As we noted above under "Author," Revelation is quoted as authoritative by (perhaps) Papias (d. 130), Justin (middle of the second century), and Irenaeus (180), and is found in the Muratorian Canon (180–200?). Marcion rejected Revelation from his canon (see Tertullian, *Adv. Marc.* 4.5), but this is not surprising, since he rejected any New Testament book that smacked of the Old Testament or Judaism—and Revelation is filled with Old Testament allusions. Eusebius also mentions that Revelation was rejected by a Gaius, a church official in Rome at the beginning of the second century (*H.E.* 3.27.1–2). His reason was probably the use to which the Montanists, a Christian sect that stressed prophecy and the nearness of the eschaton, were putting Revelation. By denying canonical status to one of their most important books, Gaius could hope to discredit the movement.[74] The same reason probably lies behind the rejection of Revelation on the part of the group known as the "Alogoi." In any case, these scattered rejections of Revelation in the Western church did not affect its canonicity, and from this point forward there is no hint of doubt about Revelation's full canonical status in the West.

The situation in the East was quite different. The authority accorded to Revelation by Papias and Justin was seconded by third-century scholars such as Clement of Alexandria and Origen. But the Egyptian bishop Dionysius disagreed. As we have seen, he questioned the apostolic authorship of the book in an effort to minimize its authority. His questions led other churchmen in the East to question its canonicity, among them Eusebius, who says that many in his day questioned its status (*H.E.* 3.25.1–4). The Council of Laodicea (360) did not recognize it as canonical, and it is omitted from the earliest editions of the Syriac Peshitta.

At first sight, these doubts about Revelation seem somewhat disturbing. But on closer examination, they can be seen to be somewhat extraneous to the issue of canonicity. As Maier has shown in great detail, the doubts about Revelation stemmed from no considered argument or historical knowledge but were the result of distaste for the eschatology of the book.[75] Revelation seemed to teach, and was interpreted by many in the early church to teach, a doctrine of the last things that was too earthly focused, too materialistic for many of the Eastern

---

Concerning the Text of the Apocalypse, 2 vols. (London: Bernard Quaritch, 1929), and Josef Schmid, *Studien zur Geschichte des griechischen Apokalypsetextes,* 3 vols. (Munich: Kaiser, 1955–56).

[73]Guthrie, 929–30.

[74]See the discussion in the section "Author" in chap. 6 above, and in Maier, *Johannesoffenbarung,* 79–85.

[75]Maier, *Johannesoffenbarung,* passim.

fathers. We should not, then, be much influenced by them in our assessment of the canonicity of the book. A similar point must be made about latter-day critics of the Revelation. Luther, for instance, relegated it to a secondary status in his New Testament, saying, "My spirit cannot accommodate itself to this book. There is one sufficient reason for the small esteem in which I hold it—that Christ is neither taught nor recognized."[76] One might wonder at this point whether Luther was reading the same book that we have in our Bibles, the book that makes "the Lamb that was slain" the linchpin in God's plan for history and the end of history. At any rate, such theological prejudice should not be allowed to affect our judgments about the book's rightful place in the canon.

REVELATION IN RECENT STUDY

Scholarship on Revelation, in keeping with New Testament scholarship generally, has moved away from a concern with sources and historical background to a concern with the final literary product and its setting.[77] Attention has been given to the genre of Revelation (see above) and to the genre of the letters to the seven churches,[78] as well as to the structure and literary techniques of the book.[79] The social-theological setting out of which the book arose has also been investigated, one of the more interesting theories being that the Revelation is the product of a Christian "prophetic circle."[80] Collins has used sociological theories to argue that John was writing to help his readers find a new identity and to learn to cope with their sense of having failed to meet their own expectations.[81] Several other studies combine a focus on the social context of Revelation, with particular perspectives on language and rhetoric.[82] These tend to distinguish between the actual

---

[76]From the preface to Luther's 1522 Bible.

[77]See Fiorenza, *Book of Revelation,* 20–21. Her essay "Research Perspectives on the Book of Revelation" (pp. 12–32) gives a helpful overview of the terrain. See also U. Vanni, "L'Apocalypse johannique: Etat de la question," in *L'Apocalypse johannique,* 21–46, and Jon Paulien, "Recent Developments in the Study of the Book of Revelation," *AUSS* 26 (1988): 159–70.

[78]John T. Kirby, "The Rhetorical Situations of Revelation 1–3," *NTS* 34 (1988): 197–207; D. E. Aune, "The Form and Function of the Proclamations to the Seven Churches (Revelation 2–3)," *NTS* 36 (1990): 182–204.

[79]E.g., Fiorenza, *Book of Revelation,* 159–80; Lambrecht, "Structuration," 77–104.

[80]See David E. Aune, "The Social Matrix of the Apocalypse of John," *BR* 26 (1981): 16–32; idem, "The Prophetic Circle of John of Patmos and the Exegesis of Revelation 22:16," *JSNT* 37 (1989): 103–16; Fiorenza, *Book of Revelation,* 133–56.

[81]Collins, *Crisis and Catharsis.*

[82]See, e.g., Thompson, *The Book of Revelation;* Stephen D. O'Leary, *Arguing the Apocalypse: A Theory of Millennial Rhetoric* (New York: Oxford University Press, 1994); E. S. Fiorenza, *Revelation: Vision of a Just World* (Minneapolis: Fortress Press, 1991) (a "critical feminist-political" interpretation).

world in which John lived, and the world that he perceived and created in the Revelation. The book is "deconstructed," stripped of the particular biases that John brought to the interpretations of his visions. Study of the Revelation continues to be affected also by continuing research into apocalyptic, which is now focusing on the wider dimensions of the movement and on its social matrix.[83]

Other studies, more traditional in their orientation, have also appeared. John's Greek continues to be the subject of interest, with two recent monographs on the subject.[84] Alan James Beagley, in a monograph on the enemies of the church in Revelation, concludes that Jewish-Christian antipathy plays a key role in the book.[85] Two studies stand out in particular. The first is Colin J. Hemer's study of the setting of the seven churches of the Revelation, in which the student of Revelation is provided with a cornucopia of background data that sheds new light on the text.[86] The second in the magisterial study by Gerhard Maier of the interpretation of, and attitude toward, Revelation in the history of the church.[87] His work puts to rest many of the theories about Revelation that tend to undercut its apostolic origin or canonical status.

THE CONTRIBUTION OF REVELATION

Methods of Interpretation

Any estimate of the contribution of Revelation to our understanding of Christ and the gospel demands some decision about the basic intent and subject matter of the book. What do John's visions refer to? What are we to learn from them? The church has never come to anything close to unanimity on this point. As Gerhard Maier says after his survey of interpretations, Revelation has been "the exercise field of hermeneutics par excellence."[88] We may categorize the majority of interpretations under the usual four headings.[89]

The preterist approach. This approach, also known as the "contemporary-historical" *(zeitgeschichtlich),* is the most common today. It insists that the visions of John grow out of and describe events in John's own day. The symbols

---

[83]See, e.g., Helmbold, *Apocalypticism.*

[84]G. Mussies, *The Morphology of Koine Greek as Used in the Apocalypse of John,* NovTSup 27 (Leiden: Brill, 1971); Thompson, *Semitic Syntax.*

[85]Alan James Beagley, *The "Sitz im Leben" of the Apocalypse, with Particular Reference to the Role of the Church's Enemies,* BZNW 50 (Berlin: de Gruyter, 1987).

[86]Hemer, *Letters to the Seven Churches.*

[87]Maier, *Johannesoffenbarung.*

[88]Ibid., 622.

[89]See, e.g., Merrill Tenney, *Interpreting Revelation* (Grand Rapids: Eerdmans, 1957), 135–46. R. H. Charles has a fine history of interpretation up to the early twentieth century in his *Studies in the Apocalypse,* 2nd ed. (Edinburgh: T. & T. Clark, 1915), 7–78.

in the visions all refer to people, countries, and events in the world of that day; and John's purpose is to exhort his readers to remain faithful to Christ as they wait for God to deliver them into his eternal kingdom.

The historical approach. Several movements in the Middle Ages grew up in the conviction that the millennium was about to dawn. To buttress their beliefs, they found in the Revelation a sketch of history from the time of Christ to their own day. This approach (the *kirchengeschichtlich*) was popular with the Reformers also, enabling them to identify the beast in the Revelation with the papacy.

The futurist approach. A consistently futurist (or *endgeschichtlich*) approach holds that everything in the Revelation from chapter 4 to the end finds its fulfillment in the very last days of human history. The view is also held in a more moderate form, according to which some of the events in these chapters—particularly the earlier ones—take place in history before the end.

The idealist approach. Some scholars are convinced that we are on the wrong track altogether in trying to identify the events portrayed in John's visions. The symbolism is designed, they argue, to help us understand God's person and ways with the world in a general way, not to enable us to map out a course of events. Revelation, then, teaches us "the action of great principles and not special incidents."[90]

Along with several recent commentators,[91] we find some truth in all four of these views. Yet it is the futurist approach that comes closest to doing justice to the nature and purposes of Revelation. As we have seen, Revelation adapts and modifies the apocalyptic perspective. Jewish apocalyptic writers projected themselves back into time so that they could describe the imminent breaking into history of God's eternal kingdom as the culmination of history. By writing in his own name, John discards the historical survey and confronts his readers with an elaborate vision of the establishment of Christ's reign in history. Revelation is about eschatology, not history.[92]

Nevertheless, the peculiar eschatological stance of the early church demands that we not ignore the degree to which John pictures this eschatological climax against the backdrop of events in his own day. It is likely, for instance, that John's depiction of the "great prostitute," "Babylon," that is doomed to fall (18:1–4), has some reference to the Roman Empire of his own day, and that the terrible persecution described in Revelation would remind John's readers of their own oppression. To some extent, then, John, while describing the end, describes it against the background of his first-century situation. But this is typical of bib-

---

[90]William Milligan, *The Revelation of St. John*, 2nd ed. (London: Macmillan, 1887), 153.

[91]E.g., Morris, *Revelation*, 15–22; Mounce, *Revelation*, 41–45; Tenney, *Interpreting Revelation*, 145–46.

[92]Fiorenza, *Book of Revelation*, 46.

lical prophecy in both Old and New Testaments. While revealing his plan for history, God has not often revealed its timing; and biblical prophets have always pictured "the day of the Lord," the eschaton, in terms of their own time. Moreover, it is clear that history itself contains many prefigurements of that end; John himself reminds us that, while "the antichrist is coming, even now many antichrists have come" (1 John 2:18).[93]

The Contribution of Revelation

Revelation makes significant contributions to a number of areas of New Testament theology. It conveys a sense of the sovereignty of God that no other New Testament book approaches. The vision of God on his throne and of the worship he receives helps us to see beyond our earthly circumstances to the Lord of earth and heaven and reminds us that only God is ultimately worthy of our devotion and praise. As Richard Bauckham puts it, "The effect of John's visions, one might say, is to expand his readers' world, both spatially (into Heaven) and temporally (into the eschatological future), is, to put it another way, to open their world to divine transcendence."[94]

Revelation offers a high Christology, in that Jesus is constantly portrayed in terms appropriate only to God. It is significant in this regard, as Beasley-Murray points out, that the opening vision of the book is not of God the Father but of Jesus Christ (1:12–20) and that both God the Father and Jesus Christ are called "the Alpha and the Omega" (1:8; 22:13).[95] In these ways and in many others, John makes clear that the sovereign God is accomplishing his purposes on earth through the Son, very God himself.

But while the Revelation focuses on Christ's glory, power, and role in judgment, the cross is never out of sight. The powerful rider on the white horse, we are constantly reminded, is none other than the "lamb that was slain." Without dwelling on the crucifixion of Christ, John makes it clear that all that Christ does to wrap up human history is rooted in his sacrificial death. John has restructured the typical Jewish apocalyptic perspective with his christological focus.[96]

If, as we have argued, Revelation focuses on the end of history, then it is in the area of eschatology that it makes its most important contribution. Nowhere are we given a more detailed description of the events of the end; and while many interpreters have been guilty of finding far more specifics in John's visions than his symbolism allows and of unwisely insisting that only their own circumstances fit those specifics, we should not go to the other extreme and ignore those details that John does make relatively clear.

The book of Revelation conveys a sense of the sovereignty of God that no other New Testament book approaches.

---

[93]See particularly Ladd, *Revelation,* 10–14, for this approach.
[94]*The Theology of the Book of Revelation,* 7.
[95]Beasley-Murray, *Revelation,* 24.
[96]See Childs, 311–12.

But it is shortsighted to think of eschatology simply in the sense of what will happen in the end times. For the End, in biblical thought, shapes and informs the past and the present. Knowing how history ends helps us understand how we are to fit into it now. Particularly is this so because the New Testament makes clear that even now we are in "the last days." Thus, Revelation reminds us of the reality and severity of evil, and of the demonic forces that are active in history. Beasley-Murray's comment is insightful: "It is ironical that the century which has witnessed the death of the Devil and the Antichrist in theology has experienced the most appalling manifestations of demonic statecraft, the most terrible desolation of war, and the most widespread oppression of the Christian faith in all history."[97] At the same time, the degree to which Revelation exhorts believers should not be neglected. As the letters to the seven churches in chapters 2–3 reveal, not all the Christians to whom John writes were faithful. There is a conflict in Revelation not only between the church and the world but also within the church.[98]

John's visions also place in clear relief the reality of God's judgment. A day will come when his wrath will be poured out, when sins will have to be accounted for, when the fate of every individual will depend on whether or not his or her name is "written in the Lamb's book of life." Equally clear, of course, is the reward that God has in store for those who "keep the word of endurance" and resolutely stand against the devil and his earthly minions, even at the cost of life itself. John's visions are a source of comfort for suffering and persecuted believers in all ages.

BIBLIOGRAPHY

Kurt **Aland** and Barbara **Aland**, *The Text of the New Testament*, 2nd ed. (Grand Rapids: Eerdmans, 1989) ▥ D. E. **Aune**, "The Form and Function of the Proclamations to the Seven Churches (Revelation 2–3)," *NTS* 36 (1990): 182–204 ▥ idem, *Revelation 1–5*, WBC 52A (Dallas: Word, 1997) ▥ idem, *Revelation 6–16*, WBC 52B (Dallas: Word, 1998) ▥ idem, *Revelation 17–22*, WBC (Dallas: Word, 1998) ▥ idem, "The Social Matrix of the Apocalypse of John," *BR* 26 (1981): 16–32 ▥ idem, "The Prophetic Circle of John of Patmos and the Exegesis of Revelation 22:16," *JSNT* 37 (1989): 103–16 ▥ Margaret **Barker**, *The Revelation of Jesus Christ* (Edinburgh: T. & T. Clark, 2000) ▥ Richard **Bauckham**, *The Climax of Prophecy: Studies on the Book of Revelation* (Edinburgh: T. & T. Clark, 1993) ▥ idem, *The Theology of the Book of Revelation* (Cambridge: Cambridge University Press, 1993) ▥ Alan James **Beagley**, *The "Sitz im Leben" of the Apocalypse, with Particular Ref-

---

[97]Beasley-Murray, *Revelation*, 43.

[98]See, e.g., Michaels, *Interpreting Revelation*, 40–41; Beale, *The Book of Revelation*, 28–33.

erence to the Role of the Church's Enemies, BZNW 50 (Berlin: de Gruyter, 1987) ▥ G. K. **Beale**, *The Book of Revelation: A Commentary on the Greek Text*, NIGTC (Grand Rapids: Eerdmans, 1999) ▥ idem, *John's Use of the Old Testament in Revelation*, JSNTSup 166 (Sheffield: Sheffield Academic Press, 1998) ▥ G. R. **Beasley-Murray**, *The Book of Revelation*, NCB (London: Marshall, Morgan & Scott, 1974) ▥ Ibson T. **Beckwith**, *The Apocalypse of John: Studies in Introduction* (New York: Macmillan, 1919) ▥ Barry J. **Beitzel**, *The Moody Atlas of Bible Lands* (Chicago: Moody, 1985) ▥ Albert A. **Bell** Jr., "The Date of John's Apocalypse: The Evidence of Some Roman Historians Reconsidered," *NTS* 25 (1979): 93–102 ▥ Wilhelm **Bousset**, *Die Offenbarung Johannis*, rev. ed. (Göttingen: Vandenhoeck & Ruprecht, 1906) ▥ John Wick **Bowman**, "Book of Revelation," in *IDB*, 4.58–71: G. B. **Caird**, *A Commentary on the Revelation of St. John the Divine*, HNTC (New York: Harper & Row, 1966) ▥ R. H. **Charles**, *A Critical and Exegetical Commentary on the Revelation of St. John*, 2 vols., ICC (Edinburgh: T. & T. Clark, 1920) ▥ idem, *Studies in the Apocalypse*, 2nd ed. (Edinburgh: T. & T. Clark, 1915) ▥ J. H. **Charlesworth**, ed., *The Old Testament Pseudepigrapha*, vol. 1 (Garden City: Doubleday, 1983) ▥ M. R. **Charlesworth**, "The Flavian Dynasty," *CAH* 11 (1936): 41–42 ▥ Adela Yarbro **Collins**, *Crisis and Catharsis: The Power of the Apocalypse* (Philadelphia: Westminster, 1984) ▥ John J. **Collins**, "Pseudonymity, Historical Reviews, and the Genre of the Revelation of John," *CBQ* 39 (1977): 329–43 ▥ J. **Delobel**, "Le text de l'Apocalypse: Problèmes de méthode," in *L'Apocalypse johannique et l'apocalyptique dans le Nouveau Testament*, ed. J. Lambrecht, BETL 53 (Louvain: Louvain University Press, 1980), 151–66 ▥ A. **Feuillet**, *The Apocalypse* (Staten Island: Alba House, 1965) ▥ Elisabeth Schüssler **Fiorenza**, *The Book of Revelation: Justice and Judgment* (Philadelphia: Fortress Press, 1985) ▥ idem, *Revelation: Vision of a Just World* (Minneapolis: Fortress Press, 1991) ▥ J. Massyngberde **Ford**, *Revelation*, AB 38 (Garden City: Doubleday, 1975) ▥ Kenneth L. **Gentry Jr.**, *Before Jerusalem Fell: Dating the Book of Revelation* (Tyler: ICE, 1989) ▥ John J. **Gunther**, "The Elder John, Author of Revelation," *JSNT* 11 (1981): 3–20 ▥ Paul D. **Hanson**, *The Dawn of Apocalyptic*, 2nd ed. (Philadelphia: Fortress Press, 1979) ▥ idem, ed., *Visionaries and Their Apocalypses* (Philadelphia: Fortress Press, 1983) ▥ Wilfrid J. **Harrington**, *Revelation*, SacPag 16 (Collegeville: Liturgical Press, 1993) ▥ André **Heinze**, *Johannesapokalypse und johanneische Schriften: Forschungs- und traditionsgeschichtliche Untersuchungen*, BWANT 142 (Stuttgart: Kohlhammer, 1998) ▥ D. **Helmbold**, ed., *Apocalypticism in the Mediterranean World and the Near East* (Tübingen: Mohr-Siebeck, 1983) ▥ Colin J. **Hemer**, *The Letters to the Seven Churches of Asia in Their Local Setting*, JSNTSup 11 (Sheffield: JSOT Press, 1986) ▥ William **Hendriksen**, *More than Conquerors: An Interpretation of the Book of Revelation*, 6th ed. (Grand Rapids: Baker, 1952) ▥ F. J. A. **Hort**, *The Apocalypse of St. John I–III* (London: Macmillan, 1908) ▥ H. C. **Hoskier**, *Concerning the Text of the Apocalypse*, 2 vols. (London: Bernard Quaritch, 1929) ▥ Philip Edgcumbe **Hughes**, *The Book of Revelation: A Commentary*, PNTC (Grand Rapids: Eerdmans, 1990)

▓Dennis E. **Johnson**, *Triumph of the Lamb: A Commentary on Revelation* (Phillipsburg: Presbyterian and Reformed, 2001) ▓Bruce W. **Jones**, "More About the Apocalypse as Apocalyptic," *JBL* 87 (1968): 325–27 ▓James **Kallas**, "The Apocalypse: An Apocalyptic Book," *JBL* 86 (1967): 69–80 ▓Craig S. **Keener**, *Revelation*, NIVAC (Grand Rapids: Zondervan, 2000) ▓John T. **Kirby**, "The Rhetorical Situations of Revelation 1–3," *NTS* 34 (1988): 197–207 ▓Simon J. **Kistemaker**, *Exposition of the Book of Revelation*, NTC (Grand Rapids: Baker, 2001) ▓Klaus **Koch**, *The Rediscovery of Apocalyptic* (London: SCM, 1972) ▓Judith L. **Kovacs** and Christopher **Rowland**, *Revelation: The Apocalypse of Jesus Christ* (Oxford: Blackwell, 2003) ▓George Eldon **Ladd**, *A Commentary on the Revelation of John* (Grand Rapids: Eerdmans, 1972) ▓idem, "Why Not Prophetic-Apocalyptic?" *JBL* 76 (1957): 192–200 ▓Jan **Lambrecht**, "A Structuration of Revelation 4,1–22,5," in *L'Apocalypse johannique*, 77–104 ▓Gerhard **Maier**, *Die Johannesoffenbarung und die Kirche*, WUNT 25 (Tübingen: Mohr-Siebeck, 1981) ▓Bruce J. **Malina** and John J. **Pilch**, *Social-Science Commentary on the Revelation* (Minneapolis: Fortress Press, 2000) ▓Bruce M. **Metzger**, *The Text of the New Testament: Its Transmission, Corruption, and Restoration,* 2nd ed. (New York: Oxford University Press, 1968) ▓J. Ramsey **Michaels**, *Interpreting the Book of Revelation* (Grand Rapids: Baker, 1992) ▓William **Milligan**, *The Revelation of St. John,* 2nd ed. (London: Macmillan, 1887) ▓Paul S. **Minear**, *I Saw a New Earth* (Washington, D.C.: Corpus, 1968) ▓Leon **Morris**, *Apocalyptic* (London: Tyndale, 1973) ▓idem, *The Revelation of St. John*, TNTC, rev. ed. (Grand Rapids: Eerdmans, 1987) ▓Robert H. **Mounce**, *The Book of Revelation*, NICNT (Grand Rapids: Eerdmans, 1977) ▓G. **Mussies**, *The Morphology of Koine Greek as Used in the Apocalypse of John*, NovTSup 27 (Leiden: Brill, 1971) ▓Stephen D. **O'Leary**, *Arguing the Apocalypse: A Theory of Millennial Rhetoric* (New York: Oxford University Press, 1994) ▓Grant R. **Osborne**, *Revelation*, BECNT (Grand Rapids: Baker, 2002) ▓Jon **Paulien**, "Recent Developments in the Study of the Book of Revelation," *AUSS* 26 (1988): 159–70 ▓Stanley E. **Porter**, *Verbal Aspect in the Greek of the New Testament, with Reference to Tense and Mood*, SBG 1 (Berne: Peter Lang, 1989) ▓Vern **Poythress**, *The Returning King: A Guide to the Book of Revelation* (Phillipsburg: Presbyterian and Reformed, 2000) ▓S. R. F. **Price**, *Rituals and Power: The Roman Imperial Cult in Asia Minor* (Cambridge: University Press, 1984) ▓William **Ramsay**, *The Letters to the Seven Churches of Asia* (London: Hodder & Stoughton, 1904) ▓Matthias **Rissi**, *Time and History: A Study of the Revelation* (Richmond: John Knox, 1966) ▓J. A. T. **Robinson**, *Redating the New Testament* (Philadelphia: Westminster, 1976) ▓Jürgen **Roloff**, *The Revelation of John* (Minneapolis: Fortress Press, 1993) ▓Christopher **Rowland**, *The Open Heaven* (New York: Crossroad, 1982) ▓H. H. **Rowley**, *The Relevance of Apocalyptic,* 2nd ed. (London: Lutterworth, 1947) ▓D. S. **Russell**, *The Method and Message of Jewish Apocalyptic* (London: SCM, 1964) ▓J. N. **Sanders**, "St. John on Patmos," *NTS* 9 (1962–63): 75–85 ▓Josef **Schmid**, *Studien zur Geschichte des griechischen Apokalypsetextes*, 3 vols. (Munich: Kaiser,

1955–56) ▥Christopher R. **Smith**, "The Structure of the Book of Revelation in Light of Apocalyptic Literary Conventions," *NovT* 36 (1994): 373–93 ▥Ned B. **Stonehouse**, *The Apocalypse in the Ancient Church* (Goes: Oosterbaan & Le Cointre, 1929) ▥A. **Strobel**, "Abfassung und Geschichtstheologie des Apokalypse nach Kp. 17, 9–12," *NTS* 10 (1963–64): 433–45 ▥Henry Barclay **Swete**, *The Apocalypse of St. John*, 3rd ed. (London: Macmillan, 1911) ▥Merrill **Tenney**, *Interpreting Revelation* (Grand Rapids: Eerdmans, 1957) ▥Leonard L. **Thompson**, *The Book of Revelation: Apocalypse and Empire* (Oxford: Oxford University Press, 1990) ▥Stephen **Thompson**, *The Apocalypse and Semitic Syntax*, SNTSMS 52 (Cambridge: Cambridge University Press, 1985) ▥U. **Vanni**, "L'Apocalypse johannique: Etat de la question," in *L'Apocalypse johannique*, 21–46 ▥John F. **Walvoord**, *The Revelation of Jesus Christ* (Chicago: Moody, 1966) ▥Johannes **Weiss**, *Offenbarung des Johannes*, FRLANT 3 (Göttingen: Vandenhoeck & Ruprecht, 1904) ▥J. C. **Wilson**, "The Problem of the Domitianic Date of Revelation," *NTS* 39 (1995): 587–605 ▥Ben **Witherington** III, *Revelation*, NCBC (Cambridge: Cambridge University Press, 2003).

CHAPTER TWENTY-SIX

THE NEW TESTAMENT CANON

INTRODUCTION

Etymologically, κανών (*kanōn*, "canon") is a Semitic loanword that originally meant "reed" but came to mean "measuring reed" and hence "rule" or "standard" or "norm." In the course of time, it came to have the purely formal sense of "list" or "table." In ecclesiastical usage during the first three centuries, it referred to the normative doctrinal and ethical content of Christian faith. By the fourth century, it came to refer to the list of books that constitute the Old and New Testaments.[1] It is this latter sense that predominates today: the "canon" has come to refer to the closed collection of documents that constitute authoritative Scripture.

The first Christians, of course, possessed no New Testament canon; they relied on the gospel that was being preached by the apostles and others, and on the books in what we now call the Old Testament canon. The *historical* question of the New Testament canon, then, is how the twenty-seven books that make up our New Testament came to be recognized as authoritative and distinctive from other literature. The answer depends on careful reading of the Fathers. This was done in a piecemeal way in the previous chapters, as the account of how each New Testament book was adopted into the canon was briefly related; major studies put this material together and treat it in some detail.[2]

---

[1]See H. W. Beyer, "κανών," in *TDNT* 3.596–602.

[2]See esp. Theodor Zahn, *Geschichte des neutestamentlichen Kanons*, 4 vols. (Erlangen: A. Deichert'sche Verlagsbuchhandlung, 1888–92); Brooke Foss Westcott, *A General Survey of the History of the Canon of the New Testament*, 7th ed. (London: Macmillan, 1896); Bruce M. Metzger, *The Canon of the New Testament: Its Origin, Development, and Significance* (Oxford: Clarendon Press, 1987); and, more briefly, David G. Dunbar, "The Biblical Canon," in *Hermeneutic, Authority, and Canon*, ed. D. A. Carson and John D. Woodbridge (Grand Rapids: Zondervan: 1986), 297–360, 424–46; R. P. Meye, "Canon of the NT," in *ISBE* 1.601–606; Eckhard Schnabel, "History, Theology and the Biblical Canon: An Introduction to Basic Issues," *Themelios* 20/2 (1995):

But the *theological* questions relating to the canon are in many ways more important—and certainly more disputed. What is the relation between canon and authority? Which comes first, a book's canonical status or its functional authority? What is the relationship between the authority of the text and the authority of the ecclesiastical body that recognizes (some would say "confers") its canonical status? Are the reasons (as opposed to the conclusions) adopted by the early church regarding the contours of the canon binding on us today? If not, are the conclusions themselves in jeopardy? In what follows there is no attempt at rigorous treatment of any of the subjects introduced. We present only the briefest survey of some of the most important points in the contemporary debate and some indication of the directions in which the evidence takes us.

THE RELEVANCE OF THE OLD TESTAMENT CANON

A New Testament introduction is not the place to review the complex questions about the development of the Old Testament canon. But one point of dispute must be raised since it bears on how we conceive of the formation of the New Testament canon: Was there already a "closed" Old Testament canon that could serve as a model for the formation of the New Testament canon?

Until recently, the critical consensus of the past two centuries was that the Old Testament came to be canonically recognized in three separate steps, corresponding to the three divisions of the Hebrew canon. The Torah (here understood to mean the Pentateuch) achieved canonical status toward the end of the fifth century B.C.; the Prophets achieved similar status about 200 B.C., and the Writings only toward the end of the first century A.D. at the Council of Jamnia (or Jabne).

This critical consensus is now breaking up. Among the more important turning points in the discussion are these:

1. The role—even the existence—of the Council of Jamnia is increasingly being questioned. Probably Lightstone goes too far when he dismisses the Jamnian picture of a college of rabbis in the last decade of the first century as nothing more than the imaginative product of third- and fourth-century traditions,[3]

16–24; Arthur G. Patzia, *The Making of the New Testament: Origin, Collection, Text and Canon* (Leicester: IVP, 1995). For the fullest display of the range of current debate, see the large volume edited by Lee Martin McDonald and James A. Sanders, *The Canon Debate* (Peabody: Hendrickson, 2002).

[3]Jack N. Lightstone, "The Formation of the Biblical Canon in Judaism of Late Antiquity: Prolegomenon to a General Reassessment," *SR* 8 (1979): 141–42. See also Jack P. Lewis, "What Do We Mean by Jabneh?" *JBR* 32 (1964): 125–32; Robert C. Newman, "The Council of Jamnia and the Old Testament Canon," *WTJ* 38 (1976): 319–49; David E. Aune, "On the Origins of the 'Council of Javneh' Myth," *JBL* 110 (1991): 491–93; and cf. the literature cited by Gerhard Hasel, "Proposals for a Canonical Biblical Theology," *AUSS* 34 (1996): 23–33.

but it is now widely accepted that, assuming there was an academy of rabbis at Jamnia, it did not constitute an authoritative council that decisively ruled on a number of issues but was both a college and, to a lesser extent, a legislative body. For instance, Leiman argues that although Jamnia discussed whether Ecclesiastes and perhaps Canticles made the hands unclean (i.e., whether or not they were inspired), it was more by way of theological probing than binding decision, for the same topics were being discussed a century later.[4] Indeed, one might argue that the fact that these books were so discussed in the first century demonstrates that they were already widely assumed to have some sort of canonical status; otherwise there would have been little to question. One thinks of Luther's later questioning of the status of James: his historical and theological probing was predicated on the virtually unanimous assumption of James's canonical status. So far as our sources go, there is no evidence whatsoever that Jamnia assigned canonical status to any book not previously recognized or rejected any book previously accepted.

2. Although there is evidence from Josephus (*Contra Ap.* 1.37–42), Philo (*De Vita Contemp.* 3.25), and other sources that the tripartite division of the Hebrew canon was a commonplace in the first century A.D., evidence for the hypothesis that the canonical process followed these three divisions sequentially is much harder to come by. It is altogether reasonable that the Pentateuch was viewed as a closed canon first, not to be added to; as for the rest of the process, there is far too little evidence of consistent groupings of the biblical books to allow much more than speculation.

3. One of the most frequently cited arguments in support of the view that the Pentateuch was recognized by about 400 B.C. and the Prophets not until about 200 B.C. lies in the fact that the Samaritans accepted only the Pentateuch as canonical, and the Samaritan schism is customarily dated to the close of the fourth century B.C. But this assumes, without evidence, that before the schism Jewish and Samaritan views of the canon were identical. Moreover, many would agree with Coggins that the decisive period for the theological development of Samaritanism was from the third to the first century A.D.[5]

4. One of the most entrenched arguments for the late dating of the Writings is the assumed Maccabean date of Daniel and the fact that Daniel is placed among the Writings, not among the Prophets. But quite apart from the fact that many conservative scholars still argue for a sixth-century date for Daniel, John

---

[4]Sid Z. Leiman, *The Canonization of the Hebrew Scriptures: The Talmudic and Midrashic Evidence* (Hamden: Archon, 1976), 121–24. See also Roger Beckwith, *The Old Testament Canon of the New Testament Church and Its Background in Early Judaism* (Grand Rapids: Eerdmans, 1985), 276–77.

[5]R. J. Coggins, *Samaritans and Jews: The Origins of Samaritanism Reconsidered* (Oxford: Blackwell, 1975), 164.

Barton has recently argued, rather convincingly, that apart from the Penta-teuch,[6] there were no recognized sequences of Old Testament books. The fact that these books were in separate scrolls meant that ordered sequences were impossible. The various classifications that have come down to us reflect the organization of material on thematic grounds, not on the grounds of a corpus of books judged as a group to be canonical; and the Jewish grouping that excluded Daniel from the Prophets has to do with the fact that Jews preferred to see the prophets as *"tradents,* those who stand in a line of historical succession and hand on tradition from one generation to the next"[7]—which is why the so-called his-torical books were also listed with the prophets.

5. Nevertheless, there is ample evidence that in some contexts, both Jewish and Christian, Daniel was viewed as a prophet (as David could be viewed as a prophet, even though the Psalms ascribed to him constitute part of the Writ-ings).[8] The simplest explanation is that "prophecy" and "prophets" could be viewed from several different angles: in terms of predictive content, access to divine mysteries, calling people back to the given revelation, and so forth.

6. But doubtless it goes too far to conclude that although the Prophets and the Writings were viewed in the first century as Scripture and therefore author-itative, they were not viewed as canonical, since "canonical" assumes a closed list. Only the Torah (it is argued) was viewed as canon: no one could add to the books of the Law.

Certainly the notion of a fixed list of canonical books assumes that the pro-duction of authoritative books has ceased, or is in abeyance. Arguably, however, that was part of the common belief in the first century. Josephus, in the passage already cited, is a strong witness to a *closed* canon in first-century Judaism, over against surrounding religions with multiplied holy books. That biblical books circulated in individual scrolls implies no definite sequence; it does not rule out the perception that the production of such books had ceased, that is, that the canon was closed.

7. Indeed, there is considerable cumulative evidence that pre-Christian Judaism held that classical prophecy had ceased. First Maccabees 9:23–27

---

[6]Even this exception may be conceding too much. The ancient Hebrew-Aramaic list of the books of the Old Testament preserved in MS 54 of the library of the Greek patriarchate in Jerusalem (see J.-P. Audet, "A Hebrew-Aramaic List of Books of the Old Testament in Greek Transcription," *JTS* 1 [1950]: 135–54) preserves the follow-ing order: Genesis, Exodus, Leviticus, Joshua, Deuteronomy, Numbers, Ruth, Job, Judges. . . . Paul E. Kahle thinks this "is possibly the oldest list available to us" (*The Cairo Geniza* [Oxford: Blackwell, 1959], 218). See also Leon Morris, *Ruth,* TOTC (London: Tyndale, 1968), 231.

[7]John Barton, *Oracles of God: Perception of Ancient Prophecy in Israel After the Exile* (London: DLT, 1986), 15.

[8]See esp. ibid., 35–37.

(c. 100 B.C.) bemoans this cessation; Josephus ties the closing of the canon to the fact that the line of prophets had failed. The fact that the Qumran covenanters wrote commentaries only on biblical books suggests that they viewed them as a category apart. Josephus and others do refer to some individuals *after* the closing of the canon as prophets, as Aune points out;[9] but Aune himself admits that "canonical and eschatological prophecy had a special status that distinguished them from prophetic activity in the intervening period."[10] In other words, "prophet" and "prophecy" were not technical terms that always had precisely the same force, and there is ample evidence that, as used to refer to the phenomenon that had produced the Hebrew canon, "prophecy" was viewed in the first century as an activity that had ceased and that would not return until the time of eschatological promise. Opinions vary considerably over the date of the closing of the Old Testament canon, from about 500 B.C. (for Law and Prophets) to about A.D. 200.[11] Increasingly, however, it is recognized that any date later than the first century B.C. must fly in the face of too much evidence.

8. Some have argued that the LXX, which as it has come down to us in manuscripts from the fourth and fifth centuries A.D. includes most of the apocryphal books,[12] constitutes evidence that Diaspora Judaism, or at least Alexandrian Judaism, had a different canon; and since most early Christians used Greek versions of the Old Testament (the LXX or something very much like it), it is therefore futile to look to Semitic sources for the delineation of the canon. But this argument is sharply questioned by Sundberg and others.[13] They point out that our evidence for the LXX is late (fourth and fifth centuries A.D. and later), certainly influenced by Christian scribes, and not supported by any independent attestation of the beliefs of Alexandrian or Diaspora Jews. Furthermore, the most natural reading of two Alexandrian Christian fathers, Origen and Athanasius, suggests that they held to a Jewish canon that differed but little from the traditional Jewish (and Semitic) reckoning.[14] Sundberg himself denies that the Writings were canonical (i.e., a *closed* corpus of Scripture) in

---

[9]David E. Aune, *Prophecy in Early Christianity and in the Ancient Mediterranean World* (Grand Rapids: Eerdmans, 1983), 103–52.

[10]Ibid., 368 n. 2.

[11]The extremes are represented by David Noel Freedman and A. C. Sundberg respectively. For discussion, see Barton, *Oracles*, 27–29.

[12]B (Codex Vaticanus, fourth century) includes all of the Apocrypha except 1 and 2 Maccabees; א (Codex Sinaiticus, fourth century) includes Tobit, Judith, 1 and 2 Maccabees, Wisdom, and Ecclesiasticus; A (Codex Alexandrinus, fifth century) includes all of the Apocrypha, plus 3 and 4 Maccabees and the *Psalms of Solomon*.

[13]Albert C. Sundberg Jr., *The Old Testament of the Early Church* (Cambridge: Harvard University Press, 1964).

[14]Respectively, *H.E.* 4.26 (Origen as cited by Eusebius), and *Ep. List.* 39 (= NPNF2 4:552).

either Hebrew or Greek sources in the first century; whether or not scholars have followed him in this particular, most have been persuaded by his demolition of the theory of the Alexandrian canon.[15]

9. There is ample evidence that the New Testament writers cited most of the books that constitute the Old Testament as Scripture, but there is no unequivocal evidence that the New Testament writers viewed the Old Testament Scriptures as a closed canon. Of course, that does not mean they did *not* so view it: arguments from silence can be tricky. And there are several lines of evidence in the New Testament that at least suggest that they recognized a closed canon.

First, the quotation patterns of the New Testament largely line up with predominant Jewish evidence for the shape of the canon. New Testament writers quote every book in the Pentateuch (in its Jewish, not Samaritan, form) and many of the other canonical books, from both the Prophets (Kings, Isaiah, Jeremiah, Ezekiel, and the Minor Prophets) and the Writings (Psalms, Job, Proverbs, Daniel, Chronicles). Even some Old Testament books not certainly quoted in the New may be alluded to (e.g., Josh. 1:5 in Heb. 13:5; Judges in Heb. 11:32).

Second, when literature outside the corpus of what is now recognized to be the Old Testament canon is cited (e.g., Cleanthes in Acts 17:28; Menander in 1 Cor. 15:33; Epimenides in Titus 1:12; *1 Enoch* in Jude 14–15), it is not referred to as Scripture (γραφή [*graphē*]) or assigned to the Holy Spirit or to God as the ultimate author.

Third, there is no hint that the New Testament writers want to jettison any of the canonical Old Testament as being incompatible with their developing Christian faith. Paul goes so far as to insist that the reason "the Scriptures" were written was for the instruction and encouragement of Christians (Rom. 15:3–6; see also 1 Cor. 10:11; 2 Tim. 3:14–17; 1 Pet. 1:10–12; Heb. 11:39–40).

Fourth, many New Testament passages, although cast as refutation or correction of traditional Jewish theology, nevertheless appeal to what both sides have in common, namely, agreed Scriptures (e.g., Mark 7:6–7, 10–13; 11:17; 12:10–11, 24; Luke 4:16–21; John 6:45; 10:34–35; 15:25; Acts 17:2–3, 11; 18:24, 28; 24:14–15; 26:22; Rom. 3:1–2; Gal. 3).

Fifth, it is probable, though not certain, that Jesus' reference to all the blood from that of Abel to that of Zechariah son of Berekiah (Matt. 23:35) runs from

---

[15]An exception is the stimulating book by Martin Hengel, *The Septuagint as Christian Scripture: Its Prehistory and the Problem of Its Canon* (Edinburgh: T. and T. Clark, 2002). But the price Hengel pays for his argument is his rigorous denial that prophecy in any sense did cease (*pace* Josephus), and his ultimate plea for a maximalist "canon" that would include not only the Apocrypha and Pseudepigrapha, but Josephus and Philo as well (126–27). His view of canon is akin to that of Harold Bloom when he talks about *The Western Canon.* See the divergent but penetrating reviews of Andrew Shead (*Themelios* 28/3 [2003]: 59–61) and James A. Sanders (*BBR* 13 [2003]: 271–74).

the first man to be killed to the last one in the Hebrew canon to be killed (Zechariah son of Jehoiada, in 2 Chron. 24:20, 22). Zechariah was certainly not the last to be killed on any chronological scale: within the period of time represented by the Old Testament, the last chronologically was probably Uriah son of Shemaiah (Jer. 26:20–23). If the identification with the Zechariah of 2 Chronicles 24:20, 22 is correct, he was chosen because of his place *in the recognized canon.*

It appears, then, that there is adequate evidence to support the view that there was a (closed) canon of Scripture to serve as a model in the formation of the New Testament canon. Even if this point is disputed, there is entirely convincing evidence that the Torah and the Prophets were viewed as closed collections by the first century A.D.

> *There is adequate evidence to support the view that there was a (closed) canon of Old Testament Scripture to serve as a model in the formation of the New Testament canon.*

THE FORMATION OF THE NEW TESTAMENT CANON

If we think of the New Testament canon as a "closed" list of recognized books, the principal turning points are well known and not largely in dispute. The first such closed list to come down to us is that of Marcion. Heavily influenced by Syrian dualism, Marcion rejected the entire Old Testament and accepted only one gospel—a highly edited edition of Luke—plus his edition of ten letters of Paul, excluding the Pastorals. But although Marcion's list is the first, it is going too far to say that the very idea of a Christian Bible is the work of Marcion.[16] Paul's letters were already circulating in collected form, and probably the four canonical gospels were as well. More important, the idea of New Testament Scripture, certainly well established in the first part of the second century, presupposes some sort of canonical limit sooner or later.

Undoubtedly the work of Marcion and of other heretics spurred the church to publish more comprehensive and less idiosyncratic lists. In the same vein, the Montanist movement, which sought to elevate the voice of prophecy to a level of supreme authority in the church—a level it did not enjoy even in Paul's day (1 Cor. 14:37–38)—also served to force the church to make public decisions as to the standard of orthodoxy. By the end of the second century, the Muratorian list, though virtually valueless as a guide to the *origin* of the New Testament books to which it refers, reflects the view of the great church in recognizing a New Testament canon not very different from our own. The list is fragmentary, so that Matthew and Mark do not appear; but doubtless they are presupposed,

---

[16]So, rightly, F. F. Bruce, "New Light on the Origins of the New Testament Canon," in *New Dimensions in New Testament Study,* ed. Richard N. Longenecker and Merrill C. Tenney (Grand Rapids: Zondervan, 1974), 12, against the magisterial work of H. von Campenhausen, *The Formation of the Christian Bible* (Philadelphia: Fortress Press, 1972), 148.

since Luke is referred to as the third gospel, and John as the fourth. Luke is also recognized to be the author of "the acts of all the apostles." Thirteen letters are recognized as authentically Pauline. The list includes an *Epistle to the Laodiceans* and another to the Alexandrians (which some take to be Hebrews). Two Johannine epistles and Jude are accepted. The apocalypses ascribed to John and to Peter are both accepted, but the list admits that there was some opposition to the public reading of the latter work. The *Shepherd of Hermas* is accepted for private but not for public reading, on the grounds of its being such a recent composition. Gnostic, Marcionite, and Montanist writings are all rejected; a rather odd passage recognizes the Wisdom of Solomon to be canonical.

The pattern by which this or that Father cites the various New Testament books as Scripture has been lightly surveyed throughout this *Introduction,* but such a pattern does not itself establish when the New Testament canon as a closed list of books was recognized. Discussion of such a "closed list" demands further reflection. In a seminal book, Barton has attempted to look at issues surrounding the canon from an array of fresh perspectives.[17] One of the points he makes is that the word *canon* has a frequently unrecognized ambiguity connected with it (see n. 15, above). It might refer to books supportive of the "rule of faith" and thus be a fairly broad category that could include more books, or it might refer to a "fixed list" that is inherently exclusionary. Barton surveys some of the arguments advanced for different dates for the New Testament canon, arguments advanced by Zahn (first century), Harnack (second century), and Sundberg (fourth century), and argues that these four positions are not as far apart as it might first appear because they mean slightly different things by "canon."

Moreover, Barton also points out that many of the arguments used to determine what books were viewed as belonging in the New Testament canon turn on the way those books are quoted by the Fathers or whether they are found on this or that list. But two important bits of evidence have often been overlooked. *First,* drawing on the work of Stuhlhofer,[18] Barton counts the number of times the New Testament (and other) books are actually cited by the Fathers in proportion to each book's length. He discovers there are three clear groups: those New Testament books that are quoted frequently (viz., the four gospels and the major Pauline letters), those quoted less frequently (the rest of the New Testament), and books that are scarcely quoted at all (viz., those that were excluded from the canon). In other words, there is a sharp demarcation in actual frequency of usage between the New Testament books and all other claimants: actual usage was

---

[17]John Barton, *Holy Writings, Sacred Text: The Canon in Early Christianity* (Louisville: Westminster John Knox, 1997).

[18]F. Stuhlhofer, *Der Gebrauch der Bibel von Jesus bis Euseb: eine statistische Untersuchung zur Kanongeschichte* (Wuppertal: Brockhaus, 1988).

establishing the canon. *Second,* Christians early adopted the codex (i.e., books bound more or less as ours are, glued or sewn down one edge) over the scroll. As a result they could put many New Testament books together—and, despite some exceptions, there is early and widespread attestation of our twenty-seven New Testament documents being bound together in various configurations.[19]

It remains important, nonetheless, to understand what the Fathers said about these matters. For information as to the lists they espoused, the most important source is probably Eusebius of Caesarea (c. 260–340), whose views were largely indebted to the Alexandrian fathers Clement and Origen. In discussing the New Testament canon, Eusebius deploys a tripartite classification: the recognized books (*homologoumena*), the disputed books *(antilegomena),* and the books put forward by heretics in the name of the apostles but rejected by those Eusebius regards as orthodox. In the first category, Eusebius includes the four gospels, Acts, fourteen Pauline epistles (Eusebius includes Hebrews, though he is aware that the church in Rome did not hold Hebrews to be Pauline), 1 Peter, 1 John, and, apparently (though with some reservation) the Apocalypse. Eusebius subdivides the disputed books into those generally accepted (James, Jude, 2 Peter, and 2 and 3 John) and those that are not genuine (*Acts of Paul, Shepherd of Hermas, Apocalypse of Peter, Epistle of Barnabas,* the *Didache,* and, perhaps, the Apocalypse).[20] The third category, embracing clearly heretical writings, includes gospels such as those of Peter and Thomas, acts of Andrew and John, and similar writings (*H.E.* 3.25).

In other words, the Gospels, Acts, the thirteen Paulines, 1 Peter, and 1 John are universally accepted very early; most of the remaining contours of the New Testament canon are already established by the time of Eusebius. The Cheltenham manuscript, thought to represent North African views c. A.D. 360, includes all the New Testament books except Hebrews, James, and Jude. The first list that includes all and only the twenty-seven books of our New Testament is that of the Easter Letter by Athanasius in 367—clearly prescriptive rather than

---

[19]See further J. K. Elliott, "Manuscripts, the Codex and the Canon," *JSNT* 63 (1996): 105–23. Although Elliott in a later review criticizes him, David Trobisch, *The First Edition of the New Testament* (New York: Oxford University Press, 2000), marshals similar arguments, and others not quite so convincing, to reason for a mid-second-century New Testament canon.

[20]Uncertainty about where Eusebius places the Apocalypse turns on his own confused way of expressing himself. Although the Apocalypse was almost universally recognized as Scripture in the second century, it fell under suspicion in the Eastern church. Eusebius's stance seems to vary from initial acceptance of the Apocalypse as the work of the apostle John, to rejecting it completely as a forgery by the heretic Cerinthus, to accepting the canonical status of the book while denying its apostolic authorship. See the discussion of Robert M. Grant, *Eusebius as Church Historian* (Oxford: Clarendon Press, 1980), 126–37.

descriptive for the Alexandrian church. The sixtieth canon of the Council of Laodicea (c. 363) includes all twenty-seven books except the Apocalypse, but the manuscript evidence suggests this canon may have been a later addition (though in all probability still fourth century).[21] The Third Council of Carthage (397), attended by Augustine, recognized the twenty-seven New Testament books, and thereafter in the West there was little deviation from that stance.

The Eastern church, at least as represented by the Syriac (Peshitta), omitted 2 Peter, 2 and 3 John, Jude, and the Apocalypse, a pattern followed by the native (as opposed to the Greek-speaking) Syrian church today. Still, it is important to recognize that not a few Fathers from the Eastern church recognized exactly those twenty-seven books that constitute our canon today.[22] At the other extreme, the Ethiopian church recognizes not only the standard twenty-seven books but adds eight others, mostly dealing with church order.[23] Nevertheless, Dunbar is right to conclude:

> Yet it is fair to say that wherever Christians in particular localities have been concerned to know the extent of the New Testament and have searched for this knowledge in a spirit of open communication with the larger church, unanimity of opinion has generally been the result. So it is significant that the reopening of the questions of canon by the leaders of the Protestant Reformation led to a narrowing of the Old Testament canon over against Roman Catholic usage but effected no similar change in the extent of the New Testament canon.[24]

Indeed, it is important to observe that, although there was no ecclesiastical machinery like the medieval papacy to enforce decisions, nevertheless the worldwide church almost universally came to accept the same twenty-seven books. It was not so much that the church selected the canon as that the canon selected itself. This point has frequently been made, and deserves repeating:

---

[21]See Metzger, *Canon*, 210.

[22]See Westcott, *History of the Canon*, 445–48.

[23]See R. W. Cowley, "The Biblical Canon of the Ethiopian Orthodox Church Today," *ÖstK* 23 (1974): 318–23.

[24]Dunbar, "Biblical Canon," 317–18. In a footnote, Dunbar points out that this is true even with Martin Luther, who raised the strongest questions about the *antilegomena* (p. 432 n. 117). It is often pointed out that the table of contents of Luther's translation of the Bible separates Hebrews, James, Jude, and Revelation from the rest of the books and discontinues counting them (e.g., Meye, "Canon," 605); it is not always pointed out that this configuration was in the 1522 edition but was dropped in subsequent editions, along with the most strident of his negative judgments on these books (expressed in his prefaces). Only his negative judgment on James continued to the end of his life. See Paul Althaus, *Theology of Martin Luther* (ET Philadelphia: Fortress Press, 1966), 83–85.

The fact that substantially the whole church came to recognize the same twenty-seven books as canonical is remarkable when it is remembered that the result was not contrived. All that the several churches throughout the Empire could do was to witness to their own experience with the documents and share whatever knowledge they might have about their origin and character. When consideration is given to the diversity in cultural backgrounds and in orientation to the essentials of the Christian faith within the churches, their common agreement about which books belonged to the New Testament serves to suggest that this final decision did not originate solely at the human level.[25]

Whatever the pressures that encouraged the church to issue canonical lists—including persecution, distance from the historical Jesus, the pressure of Montanism, the rise of Gnosticism and other movements with scriptures to be rejected—the *criteria* used by the church in discussions as to what books were canonical were primarily three:[26]

1. One basic requirement for canonicity was conformity to the "rule of faith" (ὁ κανὼν τῆς πίστεως [*ho kanōn tēs pisteōs*]; in Latin, *regula fidei*), conformity between the document and orthodoxy, that is, Christian truth recognized as normative in the churches. Although many scholars have denied that any clear distinction was made between "orthodoxy" and "heresy" in subapostolic times, let alone in the New Testament, it is hard not to detect the roots of the distinction in passages such as Galatians 1:8–9; Colossians 2:8ff.; 1 Timothy 6:3ff.; and 1 and 2 John. And already in Ignatius there is considerable concern to distinguish the true from the false. This concern rapidly increased with time.

2. Perhaps the most commonly mentioned criterion in the Fathers is apostolicity, which as a criterion came to include those who were in immediate contact with the apostles. Thus, Mark's gospel was understood to be tied to Peter; Luke's to Paul. When the Muratorian Fragment rejects the *Shepherd of Hermas* for public reading, it does so on the ground that it was too recent and therefore cannot find a place "among the prophets, whose number is complete, or among the apostles" ("the prophets" here refers to the Old Testament books, and "the apostles" to the New). For the same reason, wherever the Fathers suspect pseudonymity, they reject the work.

Thus, as we have seen (chap. 8), the New Testament itself voices principled rejection of pseudonymous letters (esp. 2 Thess. 2:2; 3:17); now we observe that the Fathers universally reject pseudonymity as an acceptable literary category for documents bearing the authority of Scripture. This leaves very little space for the common modern assertion that pseudonymity was a widely acceptable practice in the ancient world. That pseudonymous apocalypses were widespread

---

[25]Barker/Lane/Michaels, 29.
[26]See Metzger, *Canon*, 251–54.

is demonstrable; that pseudonymous letters were widespread is entirely unsupported by evidence; that *any* pseudonymity was knowingly accepted into the New Testament canon is denied by the evidence.[27]

3. Scarcely less important a criterion is a document's widespread and continuous acceptance and usage by churches everywhere. Thus, Jerome insists it does not matter who wrote Hebrews, for in any case it is the work of a "church-writer" (*ecclesiastici viri*, by which he probably means someone writing in conformity with the truth taught in the churches, a variation of the first criterion) and is in any case constantly read in the churches (*Epist.* 129). If the Latin churches were slow to accept Hebrews and the Greek churches were slow to accept the Apocalypse, Jerome accepts both, in part because many ancient writers had accepted both of them as canonical.[28]

THE SIGNIFICANCE OF THE NEW TESTAMENT CANON

It must be admitted that this more or less traditional approach to the canon is in danger of giving a false impression, namely, that the church took inordinately long to recognize the *authority* of the documents that constitute the New Testament. This is entirely false. Discussion of the canon is discussion of a *closed* list of authoritative books. The books themselves were necessarily circulating much earlier, most of them recognized as authoritative throughout the church, and all of them recognized in large swaths of the church.[29]

There was an authoritative message from the beginning. Already in his early preaching Jesus set himself up as an authority on a par with, and in some sense fulfilling, Old Testament Scriptures (Matt. 5:17–48, esp. vv. 21ff.). The revelation of the good news, the gospel of God's dear Son, was so bound up with the life, ministry, death, and resurrection of Jesus that accounts of this "good news" came to be called gospels. This good news was passed on by apostles: in Acts 2, Luke insists that the believers who constituted the first church devoted themselves to the apostles' teaching. Already in 2 Corinthians 3:14, Paul writes of Jews reading the Scriptures of the *old* covenant.[30] By implication, a *new* covenant

> *It is a false impression that the church took inordinately long to recognize the authority of the documents that constitute the New Testament. Rather, discussion of the canon is discussion of a closed list of authoritative books.*

---

[27]See further the discussion on "Pseudonymity and Pseudepigraphy" in chap. 8 above.

[28]Perhaps it should be mentioned that the Fathers do not recognize a work as canonical on the grounds that it is inspired, since they freely apply "inspiration" and related expressions to noncanonical books as well (see Metzger, *Canon*, 254–57). "Inspiration" in modern theological discussion is a theological construct drawing from a number of important historical and theological structures and is commonly more tightly defined than in the rather flexible usage of the first centuries.

[29]Theo Donner, "Some Thoughts on the History of the New Testament Canon," *Themelios* 7/3 (1983): 23–27.

[30]The reference is probably to the Torah, not to the entire Old Testament; see v. 15.

has dawned, the new covenant foretold by Jeremiah (esp. 31:31–34; cf. Heb. 8) and announced by Jesus in the words of institution on the night he was betrayed ("This cup is the new[31] covenant in my blood"). Implicitly, new covenant *Scriptures* are not far away. The epistle to the Hebrews begins by contrasting the former period of revelation with what has taken place "in these last days" in which God has revealed himself in his Son (Heb. 1:1–3). The locus and source of all authoritative new-covenant revelation rests, finally, in the Son. The apostles, in the narrower sense of that term,[32] were viewed as those who mediated such revelation to the rest of the church; but precisely because that revelation was tied to the Jesus who appeared in real history, an implicit closure was built into the claim. There could not be an unending stream of "revelations" about Jesus if those revelations were detaching themselves from the Jesus who presented himself in real history and who was confessed by the first eyewitnesses and apostles.

Thus, there was both extraordinary authority and implicit closure from the very beginning. Extracanonical recognition of this pair comes as early as Ignatius. When he is challenged by some men (presumably Jews) who refuse to believe anything in the gospel that is not to be found in "our ancient records" (the Old Testament?), Ignatius responds, "But for my part, my records are Jesus Christ, for me the sacred records are his cross and death and resurrection and the faith that comes through him" (*Phil.* 8:2). Arguably, the genesis of the New Testament canon lies in the appeal to "gospel" and "apostle,"[33] with Jesus Christ himself ultimately standing behind both.

If, then, we pursue the question as to when and how the various New Testament books were read as authoritative witnesses to the gospel, instead of the question as to when and how the canon was *closed,* we are forced back, not to the closed lists prepared by Fathers who tend to be later, but to the use of the New Testament books (as compared with other sources) in the early Fathers. Then we discover that even most of the *antilegomena* are widely cited. Hebrews, for instance, is quoted extensively in *1 Clement* (probably A.D. 90–110); James is attested in *1 Clement* and *Shepherd of Hermas* (mid-second century). Indeed, even within the New Testament, an Old Testament passage and a gospel quotation can lie adjacent to each other and be introduced by the phrase "Scripture says" (1 Tim. 5:18). Even if this quotation is not from a written gospel, the passage is at least evidence that a teaching of the Lord Jesus enjoys the same authority status as Old Testament Scripture. In 2 Peter 3:16 the epistles of Paul are recognized as Scriptures.

---

[31]"New" is retained in Luke and Paul (1 Cor. 11:23–26), omitted by Matthew and Mark.

[32]See D. A. Carson, *Showing the Spirit* (Grand Rapids: Baker, 1987), 88–91.

[33]See Donald Robinson, *Faith's Framework: The Structure of New Testament Theology* (Sutherland, NSW: Albatross, 1985).

Three other strands of evidence are important:

1. In the earliest stages of transmission, before efforts were made to provide written records (see Luke 1:1–4), the "tradition" was passed on orally. As has often been recognized,[34] "tradition" (παράδοσις [*paradosis*]) has no necessary negative overtones in the New Testament. For instance, in Paul traditions have bad overtones when they are simply human or are utterly divorced from the gospel (Gal. 1:14; Col. 2:8); they are to be cherished and tightly held when they *are* the gospel, as passed on by an accredited messenger (1 Cor. 11:2; 2 Thess. 2:15; 3:6).

2. But this does not mean that oral tradition was widely viewed as intrinsically superior to the written documents that soon began to circulate. The one passage that everyone cites to justify the perception that the oral tradition was more highly cherished is a statement of Papias reported by Eusebius (*H.E.* 3.39.4), which in Campenhausen's translation reads, "That which comes from books seems to me not to be of such service as that which begins as living speech and remains so."[35] It has been convincingly argued that Papias magnifies the importance of oral tradition for his *commentary* on the words of the Lord, not for the actual content of those words.[36] The slighting reference to books probably refers to the writings of heretics who at this point were doing what Papias was: commenting on the received words of the Lord, but from their own theological perspective. Papias's response, in effect, is that he prefers to retain the traditional (oral) interpretations of the Lord's words. After all, elsewhere Papias rushes to deny that there is any error in Mark's gospel, even though that gospel is not a chronological presentation: surely this would be a strange maneuver if Papias disparaged *all* written records.

3. If we ask when and how the first collections of at least some of the New Testament books were made, the brief answer is that we do not know. We do know that by the middle of the second century at the latest, the four canonical gospels were being circulated together as the fourfold gospel "according to Matthew," "according to Mark," and so forth. Probably earlier still, the Pauline Epistles were in wide circulation. The process of circulating such materials was doubtless aided by the wide use that Christians made of the codex form of books. Until that time, valuable writings were normally published in scrolls. The

---

[34]See esp. F. F. Bruce, "Scripture in Relation to Tradition and Reason," in *Scripture, Tradition, and Reason: A Study in the Criteria of Christian Doctrine, Fs.* Richard P. C. Hanson, ed. Richard Bauckham and Benjamin Drewery (Edinburgh: T. & T. Clark, 1988), 35–64.

[35]See Campenhausen's discussion in *Formation*, 130ff. Similarly, see Bruce, "Scripture," 37–38.

[36]This line of interpretation appears to have originated with J. B. Lightfoot, *Essays on the Work Entitled Supernatural Religion* (London: Macmillan, 1893), 156ff.

adoption of the codex (more or less like modern books, with individual leaves sewn or glued on one edge) not only made the books more "user-friendly" but made it easier to publish several different books together in one volume.[37]

That Paul wrote other letters that have not come down to us is certain (see 1 Cor. 5:9; Col. 4:16), but the principles of selection, and the party or parties that put together the collection, have not been identified in any of our sources. Nevertheless, on the basis of a number of carefully drawn inferences, it is entirely plausible to suppose that the collection was put together by Paul's associates, such as Timothy, shortly after Paul's martyrdom.[38]

Finally, four contemporary approaches to the significance of the canon should be briefly noted.

1. Some (e.g., H. Koester) have argued that the notion of a canon should be abolished. There is no qualitative difference between the New Testament books and other early Christian literature, they say; whatever sources shed light on the early Christian movement should be treated the same way, so that James, for example, should not be treated with more respect or as having more authority than, say, Clement of Rome.

Clearly, this view becomes plausible only if one rejects not only the notion of canon as a closed list of authoritative books but also the notion of Scripture. The view is also helped along by an easy willingness to abandon rather quickly the established heritage of the church, and especially by critical views that read several of the canonical books as late, pseudonymous writings, completed *after* a number of other early Christian sources that have come down to us.

2. There is at present a complex debate about the possibility of a "canon within the canon." All of us tend to lean rather more heavily on some parts of the canon than on others—just as Luther and Calvin made much more of Romans and Galatians than of 1 Peter, for example, or the Apocalypse. Why not therefore make a virtue of necessity and recognize that different groups have the freedom, perhaps even the obligation, to define certain parts of the canon as being definitive for them? A more attenuated form of this theory suggests that we should think of the canon as a spiral, with the outermost elements (James, 2 Peter) gradually giving way to the inner core, the very heart of genuine Christianity (John, Romans).[39]

But surely the notions of Scripture and canon forbid such approaches. True, preachers may more greatly stress one part than another, judging them to be

---

[37]See Moule, 239–41.

[38]See Guthrie, 986–1000.

[39]So C. K. Barrett, "The Centre of the New Testament and the Canon," in *Die Mitte des Neuen Testaments: Einheit und Vielfalt neutestamentlicher Theologie, Fs. Eduard Schweizer,* ed. Ulrich Luz and Hans Weder (Göttingen: Vandenhoeck & Ruprecht, 1983), 5–21.

more immediately relevant to their contexts than other parts. Some parts of the New Testament may continually wield greater influence because they are longer and more comprehensive. But to raise pragmatic pastoral choices and the accidents of composition to the obligation to relativize the canon is to deny that there is a canon that must stand as the test of our pastoral choices.

3. Traditional Roman Catholic theology has sometimes spoken of the church's role in *forming*, or *establishing*, the canon, and this in turn gives rise to a view of the church's authority rather different from that in Protestantism, which locates the deposit of the gospel in Scripture; whereas conservative Catholicism locates the deposit of the faith in the church, Scriptures being one component of that deposit.

Some of the resulting debates are dissipating today because both Protestantism and Roman Catholicism are in a state of enormous flux. But some of the problems associated with the Protestant position are largely alleviated if the distinction advocated here between Scripture and canon is carefully maintained. The church's role is not to *establish* what books constitute Scripture. Rather, the scriptural books make their own way by widespread usage and authority, and the church's role is to *recognize* that only certain books command the church's allegiance and obedience, and not others—and this has the effect of constituting a canon, a closed list of authoritative Scripture.

4. There has been considerable interest in the rise of so-called canon criticism. Although this branch of study has many forms,[40] the heart of its assumption is that, whatever sources and pressures have gone into making Scripture as we know it, the text as it stands represents the church's handling of its own traditions, including the peculiar interpretations established by inner-biblical connections, and these must be accepted as normative for the church.

There is much that is healthy about this movement. It represents a determined effort to read the Bible as a whole and to read biblical books as finished products. In practice, however, some exponents of canon criticism tend to espouse abstract truths that can be inferred from the text as a whole but reject numerous biblical claims that have historical referents. This inconsistency conjures up the specter of a certain kind of raw fideism: adhere to the canon where it cannot be tested, and reserve judgment where it can. This form of fideism makes canon criticism as frequently practiced (at least in some circles) intrinsically unstable.

In short, that God is a self-disclosing, speaking, covenant-keeping God who has supremely revealed himself in a historical figure, Jesus the Messiah, establishes the necessity of the canon and, implicitly, its closure. The notion of canon forbids all self-conscious attempts to select only part of the canon as the

---

[40]E.g., Childs; James A. Sanders, *From Sacred Story to Sacred Text* (Philadelphia: Fortress Press, 1987).

governing standard of the Christian church: that would be to de-canonize canon, a contradiction in terms. Because the canon is made up of books whose authority ultimately springs from God's gracious self-revelation, it is better to speak of recognizing the canon than of establishing it. And canonical theology cannot rightly be divorced from hard questions that tie God's revelation to real history.

BIBLIOGRAPHY

Paul **Althaus**, *Theology of Martin Luther* (ET Philadelphia: Fortress Press, 1966) ▥J.-P. **Audet**, "A Hebrew-Aramaic List of Books of the Old Testament in Greek Transcriptions," *JTS* 1 (1950): 135–54 ▥David E. **Aune**, *Prophecy in Early Christianity and in the Ancient Mediterranean World* (Grand Rapids: Eerdmans, 1983) ▥idem, "On the Origins of the 'Council of Javneh' Myth," *JBL* 110 (1991): 491–93 ▥C. K. **Barrett**, "The Centre of the New Testament and the Canon," in *Die Mitte des Neuen Testaments: Einheit und Vielfalt neutestamentlicher Theologie, Fs.* Eduard Schweizer, ed. Ulrich Luz and Hans Weder (Göttingen: Vandenhoeck & Ruprecht, 1983), 5–21 ▥John **Barton**, *Oracles of God: Perception of Ancient Prophecy in Israel After the Exile* (London: DLT, 1986) ▥idem, *Holy Writings, Sacred Text: The Canon in Early Christianity* (Louisville: Westminster John Knox, 1997) ▥Richard **Bauckham**, "Tradition in Relation to Scripture and Reason," in *Scripture, Tradition, and Reason: A Study in the Criteria of Christian Doctrine, Fs.* Richard P. C. Hanson, ed. Richard Bauckham and Benjamin Drewery (Edinburgh: T. & T. Clark, 1988), 117–45 ▥Roger **Beckwith**, *The Old Testament Canon of the New Testament Church and Its Background in Early Judaism* (Grand Rapids: Eerdmans, 1985) ▥F. F. **Bruce**, "New Light on the Origins of the New Testament Canon," in *New Dimensions in New Testament Study,* ed. Richard N. Longenecker and Merrill C. Tenney (Grand Rapids: Zondervan, 1974), 3–18 ▥idem, "Scripture in Relation to Tradition and Reason," in *Scripture, Tradition, and Reason,* 35–64 ▥H. von **Campenhausen**, *The Formation of the Christian Bible* (Philadelphia: Fortress Press, 1972) ▥R. J. **Coggins**, *Samaritans and Jews: The Origins of Samaritanism Reconsidered* (Oxford: Blackwell, 1975) ▥Theo **Donner**, "Some Thoughts on the History of the New Testament Canon," *Themelios* 7/3 (April 1983): 23–27 ▥David G. **Dunbar**, "The Biblical Canon," in *Hermeneutics, Authority, and Canon,* ed. D. A. Carson and John D. Woodbridge (Grand Rapids: Zondervan: 1986), 297–360, 424–46 ▥J. K. **Elliott**, "Manuscripts, the Codex and the Canon," *JSNT* 63 (1996): 105–23 ▥Robert M. **Grant**, *Eusebius as Church Historian* (Oxford: Clarendon Press, 1980) ▥F. W. **Grosheide**, *Some Early Lists of the Books of the New Testament* (Leiden: Brill, 1948) ▥Gerhard F. **Hasel**, "Proposals for a Canonical Biblical Theology," *AUSS* 34 (1996): 23–33 ▥Martin **Hengel**, *The Septuagint as Christian Scripture: Its Prehistory and the Problem of Its Canon* (Edinburgh: T. & T. Clark, 2002) ▥Paul E. **Kahle**, *The Cairo Geniza* (Oxford: Blackwell, 1959) ▥Sid Z. **Leiman**, *The Canonization of the Hebrew Scriptures: The Talmudic and Midrashic*

Evidence (Hamden: Archon, 1976) ▮Jack P. **Lewis**, "What Do We Mean by Jabneh?" *JBR* 32 (1964): 125–32 ▮J. B. **Lightfoot**, *Essays on the Work Entitled Supernatural Religion* (London: Macmillan, 1893) ▮Jack N. **Lightstone**, "The Formation of the Biblical Canon in Judaism of Late Antiquity: Prolegomenon to a General Reassessment," *SR* 8 (1979): 135–42 ▮Lee Martin **McDonald** and James A. **Sanders**, ed., *The Canon Debate* (Peabody: Hendrickson, 2002) ▮Bruce M. **Metzger**, *The Canon of the New Testament: Its Origin, Development, and Significance* (Oxford: Clarendon Press, 1987) ▮Leon **Morris**, *Ruth,* TOTC (London: Tyndale, 1968) ▮Robert C. **Newman**, "The Council of Jamnia and the Old Testament Canon," *WTJ* 38 (1976): 319–49 ▮Arthur G. **Patzia**, *The Making of the New Testament: Origin, Collection, Text & Canon* (Leicester: IVP, 1995) ▮Donald **Robinson**, *Faith's Framework: The Structure of New Testament Theology* (Sutherland, NSW: Albatross, 1985) ▮James A. **Sanders**, *From Sacred Story to Sacred Text* (Philadelphia: Fortress Press, 1987) ▮Eckhard **Schnabel**, "History, Theology and the Biblical Canon: An Introduction to Basic Issues," *Themelios* 20/2 (1995): 16–24 ▮F. **Stuhlhofer**, *Der Gebrauch der Bibel von Jesus bis Euseb: Eine statistische Untersuchung zur Kanongeschichte* (Wuppertal: Brockhaus, 1988) ▮Albert C. **Sundberg** Jr., *The Old Testament of the Early Church* (Cambridge: Harvard University Press, 1964) ▮David **Trobisch**, *The First Edition of the New Testament* (New York: Oxford University Press, 2000) ▮Brooke Foss **Westcott**, *A General Survey of the History of the Canon of the New Testament,* 7th ed. (London: Macmillan, 1896) ▮Theodor **Zahn**, *Geschichte des neutestamentlichen Kanons,* 4 vols. (Erlangen: A. Deichert'sche Verlagsbuchhandlung, 1888–92).

SCRIPTURE INDEX

NAME INDEX

Biblical names are listed in the Subject Index.

SUBJECT INDEX

We want to hear from you. Please send your comments about this
book to us in care of zreview@zondervan.com. Thank you.

GRAND RAPIDS, MICHIGAN 49530 USA

WWW.ZONDERVAN.COM